EUROPEAN FAMILY LAW IN ACTION

EUROPEAN FAMILY LAW SERIES

EUROPEAN FAMILY LAW IN ACTION

Volume V: Informal Relationships

Edited by
Katharina BOELE-WOELKI
Charlotte MOL
Emma VAN GELDER

intersentia
Cambridge – Antwerp – Portland

Intersentia Ltd
Sheraton House | Castle Park
Cambridge | CB3 0AX | United Kingdom
Tel.: +44 1223 370 170 | Email: mail@intersentia.co.uk

Distribution for the UK:
NBN International
Airport Business Centre, 10 Thornbury Road
Plymouth, PL6 7 PP
United Kingdom
Tel.: +44 1752 202 301 | Fax: +44 1752 202 331
Email: orders@nbninternational.com

Distribution for the USA and Canada:
International Specialized Book Services
920 NE 58th Ave. Suite 300
Portland, OR 97213
USA
Tel.: +1 800 944 6190 (toll free)
Email: info@isbs.com

Distribution for Germany and Switzerland::
Stämpfli Verlag AG
Wölflistrasse 1
Postfach 5662
3001 Bern
Switzerland
Tel.: +41 31 300 66 77
Email: verlag@staempfli.com

Distribution for other countries:
Intersentia Publishing nv
Groenstraat 31
2640 Mortsel
Belgium
Tel.: +32 3 680 15 50
Email: mail@intersentia.be

European Family Law in Action. Volume V: Informal Relationships
Katharina Boele-Woelki, Charlotte Mol and Emma van Gelder (eds.)

ISBN 978-1-78068-323-2
D/2015/7849/127
NUR 822

British Library Cataloguing in Publication Data. A catalogue record for this book is available from the British Library.

PREFACE

The fifth volume of the European Family Law in Action publications contains detailed information concerning the law on informal relations in twenty-eight European jurisdictions. It has been compiled under the auspices of the Commission on European Family Law (CEFL). The CEFL is an independent academic commission. It aims to contribute to the further harmonisation of family law in Europe through drafting Principles which are based on extensive comparative research.

The previous four volumes entitled European Family Law in Action, which were published in 2003, 2005 and 2007, include national reports on the grounds for divorce, maintenance between former spouses, parental responsibilities and property relations between spouses (Nos. 2, 3 9 and 24 of this series). Upon the basis of this comparative material the Commission on European Family Law has formulated the *Principles of European Family Law regarding Divorce, Maintenance between Former Spouses, Parental Responsibilities and Property Relations between Spouses,* which were published in December 2004 as No. 7, in March 2007 as No. 16 and in July 2013 as No. 33 in this series. To date, the CEFL Principles have been used as a source of inspiration during several national legislative procedures, for example in Croatia, the Czech Republic, the Netherlands and Portugal, but court decisions have also referred to the CEFL Principles.

In order to prepare the fifth set of *Principles of European Family Law on Informal Relationships* the national experts of the CEFL (see pp. xvii-xx) have drafted comprehensive reports on the basis of a detailed questionnaire (see p. 1-9). According to CEFL's working definition, an informal relationship refers to a relationship between a couple, that is not formalised as a marriage or as a registered partnership/civil union. Informal relationships are, in other words, strictly between couples who usually (but not necessarily) live together and share a household: relationships between siblings, between parents and children (whether adults or not), between friends, etc. do not fall within the definition.

The national reports, together with the relevant legal provisions, are available on CEFL's website (www.ceflonline.net) whereas this book integrates all the given answers in order to provide a straightforward simultaneous comparison of the different solutions chosen within the national systems. The comparative perspective reveals that within Europe only a few countries have legislated on informal relationships (Croatia, Finland, Hungary, Ireland, Portugal, Scotland, Slovenia, certain Autonomous Communities in Spain (such as Catalonia), and Sweden), whereas in the majority of jurisdictions the general law of obligations is applied.

This book is the first compilation on the legal aspects of informal relationships in Europe that contains reliable and inclusive comparative material covering twenty-eight jurisdictions. It enables an explicit and systematic comparison which will eventually lead to a new set of CEFL Principles. Given the huge amount of comparative information, however, this may take some time.

Emma van Gelder and Charlotte Mol, two Legal Research Masters students at Utrecht's School of Law, have undertaken the editing of the national reports and this volume. They have done an excellent job!

Katharina Boele-Woelki
Chair of the CEFL
Utrecht, June 2015

CONTENTS

AUTHORS

AUSTRIA	*Prof. dr. Marianne Roth* University of Salzburg
	Dr. Claudia Reith University of Salzburg
BELGIUM	*Prof. Frederik Swennen* University of Antwerp
	Prof. Dimitri Mortelmans University of Antwerp
BULGARIA	*Dr. Velina Todorova* Plovdiv University, Sofia
CROATIA	*Dr. Branka Rešestar* University of Osijek
	Nataša Lucić University of Osijek
CZECH REPUBLIC	*Prof. Milana Hrusaková* Palacký University, Olomouc
DENMARK	*Prof. Ingrid Lund-Andersen* University of Copenhagen
ENGLAND AND WALES	*Prof. Anne Barlow* University of Exeter
	Prof. Nigel Lowe Cardiff University

ESTONIA	*Dr. Triin Uusen-Nacke* Tartu County Court
	Sille Vahaste-Pruul University of Tartu
FINLAND	*Dr. Salla Silvola* Ministry of Justice, Helsinki
FRANCE	*Prof. Frédérique Ferrand* University Jean Moulin Lyon 3
	Laurence Francoz-Terminal University Jean Moulin Lyon 3
GERMANY	*Prof. Nina Dethloff* University of Bonn
	Prof. em. Dieter Martiny European University Viadrina
	Mirjam Zschoche University of Bonn
GREECE	*Prof. Achilles G. Koutsouradis* University of Thessaloniki
	Dr. Anna-Maria Konsta University of Thessaloniki
HUNGARY	*Dr. Orsolya Szeibert* Eötvös Loránd University
REPUBLIC OF IRELAND	*Prof. Geoffrey Shannon* Law Society of Ireland
ITALY	*Prof. Maria Donata Panforti* University of Modena and Reggio Emilia
LATVIA	*Dr. Inese Libina-Egner* Vice-president Latvian Parliament, Riga

LITHUANIA	*Inga Kudinavičiūtė-Michailovienė* Mykolas Romeris University, Vilnius
LUXEMBOURG	*Dr. Françoise Hilger* University of Luxemburg
THE NETHERLANDS	*Prof. Wendy Schrama* University of Groningen
NORWAY	*Prof. Tone Sverdrup* University of Oslo
PORTUGAL	*Prof. Guilherme de Oliveira* University of Coimbra
	Rosa Martins University of Coimbra
	Paula Vitor University of Coimbra
RUSSIA	*Prof. Masha Antokolskaia* VU University Amsterdam
SCOTLAND	*Prof. Jane Mair* University of Glasgow
SLOVAKIA	*Dr. Róbert Dobrovodský* Ministry of Justice, Trnava
SLOVENIA	*Prof. Barbara Novak* University of Ljubljana
SPAIN	*Prof. Cristina González Beilfuss* University of Barcelona
	Dr. Monica Navarro-Michel University of Barcelona
SWEDEN	*Prof. Margareta Brattström* Uppsala University

Prof. Maarit Jänterä-Jareborg
Uppsala University

LisaMarie Eriksson
Uppsala University

SWITZERLAND

Prof. Ingeborg Schwenzer
University of Basel

Tomie Keller
University of Basel

QUESTIONNAIRE

Drafted by the Organising Committee

July 2014

A. GENERAL

1. What kinds of formal relationships between a couple (e.g. different/same-sex marriage, different/same-sex registered partnership, etc.) are regulated by legislation? Briefly indicate the current legislation.

2. To what extent, if at all, are informal relationships between a couple regulated by specific legislative provisions? Where applicable, briefly indicate the current specific legislation. Are there circumstances (e.g. the existence of a marriage or registered partnership with another person, a partner's minority) which disqualify the couple?

3. In the absence of specific legislative provisions, are there circumstances (e.g. through the application of the law of obligations or the law of property) under which informal relationships between a couple are given legal effect (e.g. through the application of the law of obligations or the law of property)? Where applicable briefly indicate the leading cases.

4. How are informal relationships between a couple defined by either legislation and/or case law? Do these definitions vary according to the context?

5. Where informal relationships between a couple have legal effect:
   a. When does the relevant relationship begin?
   b. When does the relevant relationship end?

6. To what extent, if at all, has the national constitutional position been relevant to the legal position of informal relationships between a couple?

7. To what extent, if at all, have international instruments (such as the European Convention on Human Rights) and European legislation (treaties, regulations, and directives) been relevant in your jurisdiction to the legal position of informal relationships between a couple?

8. Give a brief history of the main developments and the most recent reforms of the rules regarding informal relationships between a couple. Briefly indicate the purpose behind the law reforms and, where relevant, the main reasons for not adopting a proposal.

9. Are there any recent proposals (e.g. by Parliament, law commissions or similar bodies) for reform in this area?

B. STATISTICS AND ESTIMATIONS

10. How many marriages and, if permissible, other formalised relationships (such as registered partnerships and civil unions) have been concluded per annum? How do these figures relate to the size of the population and the age profile? Where relevant and available, please provide information on the gender of the couple.

11. How many couples are living in an informal relationship in your jurisdiction? Where possible, indicate trends.

12. What percentage of the persons living in an informal relationship are:
    a. Under 25 years of age?
    b. Between 26-40 years of age?
    c. Between 41-50 years of age?
    d. Between 51-65 years of age?
    e. Older?

13. How many couples living in an informal relationship enter into a formal relationship with each other:
    a. Where there is a common child?
    b. Where there is no common child?

14. How many informal relationships are terminated:
    a. Through separation of the partners?
    b. Through the death of one of the partners?

15. What is the average duration of an informal relationship before its termination? How does this compare with the average duration of formalised relationships?

16. What percentage of children are born outside a formal relationship? Of these children, what percentage are born in an informal relationship? Where possible, indicate trends.

17. What is the proportion of children living within an informal relationship who are not the couple's common children (excluding foster children)?

18. How many children are adopted within an informal relationship:
    a. By one partner only?
    b. Jointly by the couple?
    c. Where one partner adopted the child of the other?

19. How many partners in an informal relationship have been in a formal or an informal relationship previously?

C. DURING THE RELATIONSHIP

20. Are partners in an informal relationship under a duty to support each other, financially or otherwise:
    a. Where there are no children in the household?
    b. Where there are common children in the household?
    c. Where there are other children in the household?

21. Are partners in an informal relationship under a general duty to contribute to the costs and expenses of their household?

22. Does a partner in an informal relationship have a right to remain in the home against the will of the partner who is the owner or the tenant of the home?

23. Are there specific rules on a partner's rights of occupancy of the home:
    a. In cases of domestic violence?
    b. In cases where the partner owning or renting the home is absent?

24. Are there specific rules on transactions (e.g. disposal, mortgaging, subletting) concerning the home of partners in an informal relationship:
    a. Where the home is jointly owned by the partners?
    b. Where the home is owned by one of the partners?
    c. Where the home is jointly rented by the partners?
    d. Where the home is rented by one of the partners?

25. Under what circumstances and to what extent can one partner act as an agent for the other?

26. Under what circumstances can partners in an informal relationship become joint owners of assets?

27. To what extent, if at all, are there specific rules governing acquisitions and/or transactions in respect of household goods? In answering this question briefly explain what is meant by household goods.

28. Are there circumstances under which partners in an informal relationship can be regarded as joint owners, even if the title belongs to one partner only?

29. How is the ownership of assets proved as between partners in an informal relationship? Are there rebuttable presumptions?

30. How is the ownership of assets proved as regards third parties? Are there rebuttable presumptions?

31. Under what circumstances, if any, can partners in an informal relationship become jointly liable for debts?

32. On which assets can creditors recover joint debts?

33. Are there specific rules governing the administration of assets jointly owned by the partners in an informal relationship? If there are no specific rules, briefly outline the generally applicable rules.

D. SEPARATION

34. When partners in an informal relationship separate does the law grant maintenance to a former partner? If so, what are the requirements?

35. What relevance, if any, upon the amount of maintenance is given to the following factors/circumstances:
    a. The creditor's needs and the debtor's ability to pay maintenance?
    b. The creditor's contributions during the relationship (such as the raising of children)?
    c. The standard of living during the relationship?
    d. Other factors/circumstances (such as giving up his/her career)?

36. What modes of calculation (e.g. percentages, guidelines), if any, apply to the determination of the amount of maintenance?

37. Where the law provides for maintenance, to what extent, if at all, is it limited to a specific period of time?

38. What relevance, if any, do changed circumstances have on the right to continued maintenance or the amount due?

39. Is the maintenance claim extinguished upon the claimant entering:
    a. Into a formal relationship with another person?
    b. Into an informal relationship with another person?

40. How does the creditor's maintenance claim rank in relation to:
    a. The debtor's current spouse, registered partner, or partner in an informal relationship?
    b. The debtor's previous spouse, registered partner, or partner in an informal relationship?
    c. The debtor's children?
    d. The debtor's other relatives?

41. When partners in an informal relationship separate, are specific rules applicable to the determination of the ownership of the partners' assets? If there are no specific rules, which general rules are applicable?

42. When partners in an informal relationship separate, are specific rules applicable subjecting all or certain property (e.g. the home or

household goods) to property division? If there are no specific rules, which general rules are applicable?

43. Do the partners have preferential rights regarding their home and/or the household goods? If so, what factors are taken into account when granting these rights (e.g. the formal ownership of the property, the duration of the relationship, the needs of each partner, the care of children)?

44. How are the joint debts of the partners settled?

45. What date is decisive for the determination and the valuation of:
    a. The assets?
    b. The debts?

46. On what grounds, if any, and to what extent may a partner upon separation claim compensation upon the basis of contributions made or disadvantages suffered during the relationship?

E. DEATH

47. Does the surviving partner have rights of inheritance in the case of intestate succession? If yes, how does this right compare to that of a surviving spouse or a registered partner, in a marriage or registered partnership?

48. Does the surviving partner have any other rights or claims on the estate (e.g. any claim based on dependency, compensation, or maintenance) in the case of intestate succession?

49. Are there specific rules dealing with the home and/or household goods?

50. Can a partner dispose of property by will in favour of the surviving partner:
    a. In general?
    b. If the testator is married to or is the registered partner of another person?
    c. If the testator has children?

51. Can partners make a joint will disposing of property in favour of the surviving partner:
    a. In general?
    b. If either testator is married to or is the registered partner of another person?
    c. If either testator has children?

52. Can partners make other dispositions of property upon death (e.g. agreements as to succession or gifts upon death) in favour of the surviving partner:
    a. In general?
    b. If either partner is married to or is the registered partner of another person?
    c. If either partner has children?

53. Is the surviving partner entitled to a reserved share[1] or to any other rights or claims on the estate (e.g. any claim based on dependency, compensation, or maintenance) in the case of a disposition of property upon death (e.g. by will, joint will, or inheritance agreement) in favour of another person?

54. Are there any statistics or estimations on how often a relationship is terminated by the death of one of the partners?

55. Are there any statistics or estimations on how common it is that partners in an informal relationship make a will in favour of the other partner?

56. Are there any statistics or estimations on how common it is that a partner in an informal relationship is the beneficiary to the other partner's life insurance?

F. AGREEMENTS

57. Are there specific rules concerning agreements between partners in an informal relationship? Where relevant, please indicate these specific rules. If not, which general rules apply?

---

1 See Regulation no. 650/2012 of the European Parliament and of the Council of 4 July 2012 on jurisdiction, applicable law, recognition and enforcement of decisions and acceptance and enforcement of authentic instruments in matters of succession [2012] OJ L 201/107.

58. Are partners in an informal relationship permitted to agree on the following issues:
    a. The division of tasks as between the partners?
    b. The contributions to the costs and expenses of the household?
    c. Their property relationship?
    d. Maintenance?
    e. The duration of the agreement?

59. Are partners in an informal relationship permitted to agree on the legal consequences of their separation?

60. Are the agreements binding:
    a. Between the partners?
    b. In relation to third parties?

61. If agreements are not binding, what effect, if any, do they have?

62. If specific legislative provisions regulate informal relationships, are the partners permitted to opt in or to opt out of this specific regulation?

63. When can the agreement be made (before, during, or after the relationship)?

64. What formal requirements, if any, govern the validity of agreements:
    a. As between the partners?
    b. In relation to a third party?

65. Is independent legal advice required?

66. Are there any statistics or estimations on the frequency of agreements made between partners in an informal relationship?

67. Are there any statistics or estimations regarding the content of agreements made between partners in an informal relationship?

G. DISPUTES

68. Which authority is competent to decide disputes between partners in an informal relationship?

69. Is that the same authority as for spousal disputes?

70. Can the competent authority scrutinise an agreement made by the partners in an informal relationship? If yes, what is the scope of the scrutiny?

71. Can the competent authority override or modify the agreement on account of fairness towards a partner, the rights of a third party, or on any other ground (e.g. a change of circumstances)?

72. What alternative dispute-solving mechanisms (e.g. mediation or counselling), if any, are offered or required with regard to disputes arising out of informal relationships?

73. What are the procedural effects of an agreement on ADR between partners in an informal relationship? Can any partner seize the competent authority in breach of the ADR clause?

74. Are there any statistics or estimations on how common it is that partners in an informal relationship include an ADR clause in their agreement?

PART A
GENERAL

QUESTION 1

What kinds of formal relationships between a couple (e.g. different/same-sex marriage, different/same-sex registered partnership, etc.) are regulated by legislation? Briefly indicate the current legislation.

AUSTRIA

In Austria, one has to differentiate between marriage and registered partnerships: The former is regulated by the Austrian Marriage Act, which entered into force in 1938 and was last amended in 2013.[1] The latter was recently introduced by the Austrian Registered Partnership Act, which entered into force in 2010 and enables same-sex couples to register their partnership at the competent district authority.[2] Hence, two different kinds of formal relationships exist in Austria: on the one hand, marriage, which is open to different-sex couples, and, on the other hand, the registered partnership of same-sex couples.

BELGIUM

Two kinds of formal relationships between a couple are regulated in Belgian law.

A marriage can be entered into by two unmarried persons of the opposite or same- sex (Art. 143 Belgian Civil Code) who are not too closely related (Art. 161-164 Belgian Civil Code) and have reached the age of majority. A court dispensation as to the marriageable age is possible (Art. 144, 145 and 148 Belgian Civil Code). During a marriage, general personal and property rights and obligations apply irrespective of the single matrimonial property regime (Art. 212 et seq. Belgian Civil Code). The default regime is a community of accrued gains, but spouses can opt for

---

1 For an overview see M. HINTEREGGER, *Familienrecht*, Verlag Österreich, Vienna, 2013, at p. 23 et seq.

2 See e.g. H. JESSER-HUß, 'Die eingetragene Partnerschaft', *JAP*, 2010/2011/13, at p. 111; K. GRÖGER, 'Das Eingetragene Partnerschafts-Gesetz (EPG)', *ÖJZ*, 2010/23, at p. 197.

any other (mixed) regime (Art. 1387 et seq. Belgian Civil Code). A divorce can only be obtained through court proceedings, either on the basis of mutual consent or upon a separate or joint request on the basis of the irretrievable breakdown of the marriage (Art. 229-230 Belgian Civil Code). In the latter case, post-divorce support is due to the ex-spouse in need, for a maximum period of the duration of the marriage (Art. 301 Belgian Civil Code). In the case of the dissolution of the marriage by death, the surviving spouse is entitled to at least the usufruct or lease of the main residence and the household goods or to half of the deceased's estate under forced heirship rules (Arts. 745*bis* and 915*bis* Belgian Civil Code). In case of an annulment of the marriage, the aforementioned consequences of marriage apply in favour of the *bona fides* spouse(s) and the children of the marriage (Art. 201-202 Belgian Civil Code).

Legal cohabitation *(wettelijke samenwoning/cohabitation légale)* can be entered into by two unmarried and not legally cohabiting persons of the opposite or the same-sex who have reached the age of majority (Art. 1475 Belgian Civil Code). The impediments to marriage based on kinship do not apply. A dispensation as to the age of majority is not possible. The Belgian Supreme Court found that legal cohabitation did not concern the status of persons at the time of its introduction.[3] Due to subsequent legal amendments, legal cohabitation *anno* 2015 has however become a formal relationship. During cohabitation, a primary regime of only property rights and obligations exists (Art. 1477 Belgian Civil Code). The default property regime between the cohabitants is separation of property, but they can opt for a joint ownership regime (Art. 1478 Belgian Civil Code). The cohabitation can be dissolved by a joint or unilateral declaration before the civil registrar. There is no maintenance obligation. Legal cohabitation is automatically dissolved by death or by marriage. The surviving cohabitant is a default heir of the usufruct or lease of the main residence and the household goods, but can be disinherited (Art. 745*octies* Belgian Civil Code). Specific rules apply when the surviving cohabitant is an heir on the basis of kinship (Art. 745*octies* and 1478 Belgian Civil Code). In either case of the dissolution of the cohabitation, the Family Court can issue an interim order (e.g. on household expenses) that will apply for a maximum of one year (Art. 1479 Belgian Civil Code). In the case of an annulment of the cohabitation, the benefit of putative cohabitation applies in favour of the *bona fides* cohabitant(s) (Art. 1476 *quinquies*, § 2 Belgian Civil Code).

[3] Cass. 17 January 2013, *RW* 2013-2014, 903, with note SWENNEN.

BULGARIA

Bulgarian legislation regulates only different-sex marriage as a kind of formal relationship. Despite the fact that the Bulgarian Family Code (2009), as the main source of family law, grants protection to any type of family, legal consequences for partners only arise from a marriage:

> 'Right to enter into a marriage and to have a family
> Article. 3. Any person shall have the right to contract a marriage and to have a family under the conditions provided for by this code.
> Civil marriage
> Article. 4. (1) Only a civil marriage, concluded in the form prescribed by this Code, shall give rise to the consequences which the law prescribes for marriage.
> (2) A religious ceremony is not a legal act.'

CROATIA

Two kinds of formal relationships between a couple are regulated by the Croatian legislation:

- Different-sex marriage and
- Same-sex registered partnership

Marriage is regulated by the Croatian Family Act (Official Gazette no. 75/14, 83/14). The Croatian Family Act defines marriage as a 'legally regulated union of a man and a woman' (Art. 12). It governs the personal and property relations of spouses, their maintenance rights and the legal relations between spouses and children during and after the marriage. The legal effects of marriage in other areas of the law (e.g. inheritance law, tax law, social security law, pensions law, labour law etc.) are foreseen by the respective legislation.

Same-sex registered partnerships are subject to the Croatian Partnership Act (Official Gazette no. 92/14). The Croatian Partnership Act denotes a life partnership as a 'union of family life of two persons of the same sex concluded before the competent authority in accordance with the provisions of this Act' (Art. 2). It envisages both the legal effects of a registered same-sex partnership from the point of view of family law and its legal effects with respect to other areas of the law. The Croatian Partnership Act extends almost all the legal effects of a marriage to a registered same-sex partnership. The only difference between a marriage and a registered same-sex partnership can be found in the legal regulation of relations with children.

CZECH REPUBLIC

In the Czech Republic there are only two forms of formal relationships regulated by the law, marriage (according to the Czech Civil Code, Act n. 89/2012 Col.), and registered partnership (according to the Act No. 115/2006 Sb., on Registered Partnership amending certain related acts).

Marriage is a traditional institution for opposite-sex couples. Marriage is a permanent union of a man and a woman formed in a manner provided by the Czech Civil Code. The primary purpose of marriage is the foundation of a family, proper upbringing of children and mutual support and assistance (S. 655 Czech Civil Code).

There are five legal impediments to marriage that prevent certain people from entering a marriage (S. 672–676 Czech Civil Code). Marriage may not be entered into by a minor lacking full legal capacity (S. 672(1) Czech Civil Code). A person whose legal capacity to enter into marriage has been limited may not enter into marriage (S. 673 Civil Code). Marriage may not be entered into by a person who has previously entered into marriage or a person who has previously entered into a registered partnership or another similar union abroad while this marriage, registered partnership or other similar union entered into abroad still lasts (S. 674 Czech Civil Code). Marriage may not be entered into between ancestors and descendants or between siblings; the same applies to individuals whose family relationship was created by adoption. (S. 675 Czech Civil Code). Finally, marriage may not be entered into between a tutor and his or her pupil, between a child and the person to whose care the child has been entrusted, or between a foster parent and the child placed in foster care. (S. 676 Czech Civil Code). If a marriage has been entered into despite the existence of a legal impediment, the court must declare the marriage invalid on the application of anyone having a legal interest therein, unless the marriage was impeded by limited legal capacity.

The current legislation aims to provide both husband and wife with equal rights and duties, which is being reflected in matrimonial property law and child care. According to S. 687(1), spouses have equal rights and duties.

Spouses also have a duty to maintain and support each other to such an extent that, in principle, ensures the same material and cultural standards for both of them. The duty to maintain and support between spouses takes precedence over the children's or parents' duty to maintain and support (S. 697(1) Czech Civil Code).

In marriage there is a specific property law (matrimonial property law according to S. 708 et seq. Czech Civil Code). What belongs to spouses, has property value and is not excluded from the legal relations forms part of the community property of the spouses (hereinafter 'community property'). This does not apply if community property is extinguished by means of a statute during the marriage (S. 708(1) Czech Civil Code).

Marriage can be terminated only by divorce (S. 755 et seq. Czech Civil Code), declaring an individual dead (S. 71 Czech Civil Code), by one spouse's death or by a sex change (S. 29(2) Czech Civil Code: sex change does not affect the personal status of an individual or his personal and property situation; however, marriage or registered partnership are terminated by it). The rights and duties of a man and woman whose marriage has terminated to their common child and their property rights and duties in the period following the termination of marriage are governed, by analogy, by the provisions on the rights and duties of divorced spouses to their common child and on their property rights and duties in the period following divorce; a court is to decide, of its own motion, on the care each of the parents will take of their common child thereafter.

The only formal relationship legally regulated for same-sex couples in the Czech Republic is civil union (registered partnership). This is quite a new institution in the Czech jurisdiction, since the Act allowing gay and lesbian couples to get registered was adopted in 2006. Although it has many supporters, same-sex couples who enter a civil union still are not granted the same rights as couples that get married. For instance, a registered couple is not allowed to adopt a child and there is no specific property law. According to S. 1(1) Czech Act on Registered Partnership: registered partnership is a permanent association of two individuals of the same sex established in the manner provided by the Act No. 115/2006 Sb., on Registered Partnership and amending certain related acts. Partners have a duty to maintain and support each other according to S. 10 Czech Act on Registered Partnership just as in marriage.

DENMARK

In 1989 Denmark was the first country in the world to introduce a Registered Partnership Act for same-sex couples.[4] The effects of a registered partnership were almost the same as the effects of a marriage, apart from in relation to children. These exceptions in relation to children have since been repealed.

In June 2012, as the fourth of the Nordic countries to do so, Denmark introduced same-sex marriages and they have the same legal status as marriages between couples of the opposite sex, with a few exceptions.[5] Provisions in Danish legislation containing gender-specific rules for one of the parties in a marriage do not apply to a marriage between two persons of the same sex. The same applies to provisions in international treaties, unless there are special agreements on this. A previously registered partnership may be converted into a marriage. A registered partnership that is not converted still remains in force, although the Danish Registered Partnership Act of 1989 was repealed at the same time as same-sex couples were allowed to marry.

As regards the status as a co-mother to a child, in 2014 an amendment to the Danish Child Act was enacted. According to the Act it is possible to become a co-mother if a woman gives birth to a child and she is married to or in a registered partnership with another woman.[6]

Persons of the same sex have the right to be married in church. However, it is up to the individual minister in question to decide whether or not he or she wants to conduct or to bless a marriage between two persons of the same sex.[7]

Couples of a different sex have never had a right to register their partnerships.

---

4 Act No. 372 of 7 June 1989, with effect from 1 October 1989. The Act is described by I. LUND-ANDERSEN, 'The Danish Registered Partnership Act', in K. BOELE-WOELKI & A. FUCHS, *Legal Recognition of Same-Sex Couples in Europe*, Intersentia, Antwerp, 2003, pp. 13-23; and by I. LUND-ANDERSEN, 'The Nordic Countries: Same Direction – Different Speeds', in K. BOELE-WOELKI & A. FUCHS (eds.), *Legal Recognition of Same-Sex Relationships in Europe*, Intersentia, Antwerp, 2012, pp. 3-17.

5 Act No. 532 of 6 June 2012 with effect from 15 June 2012.

6 Consolidating Act No. 18 of 10 January 2014 with effect from 1 December 2013.

7 Act No. 531 of 6 June 2012 with effect from 15 June 2012.

ENGLAND AND WALES

In England and Wales, the following formal couple relationships are recognised and their formation is governed by legislation which sets out the formalities and requirements for:

- Heterosexual marriage - English Marriage Act 1949
- Same-sex marriage - English Marriage (Same-Sex Couples) Act 2013 which further amends English Marriage Act 1949
- Registered and exclusively same-sex Civil Partnership - English Civil Partnership Act 2004
- Divorce and nullity of all marriages is governed by the English Matrimonial Causes Act 1973 Part I.
- Dissolution and nullity of civil partnerships is governed by Chapter 2 of the English Civil Partnership Act 2004.[8]

ESTONIA

The legal regulation of marriage is implied in the Estonian Family Law Act (entered into force 01.07.2010).[9] As compared to the former Family Law, adopted in 1995 and being mainly based on the Marriage and Family Code of the Estonian SSR, the legal regulation of entering into a marriage and divorcing in the new Estonian Family Law Act did not bring along any principal changes. As for legal norms, the new law included provisions with regard to the general legal consequences of marriage and also marital property rights were drastically changed.[10] The procedure for entering into a marriage and divorcing is regulated in the Estonian Vital Statistics Registration Act.[11] The Estonian Family Law Act § 1 specifies the prerequisites for contracting a marriage. According

---

8 The only possible formal heterosexual relationship recognised is marriage. Different-sex civil partnerships are not permitted and were explicitly ruled out by the Coalition Government in 2013 (although in December 2014, it was announced that this is to be subject to challenge by way of judicial review in *R v Royal Borough of Kensington and Chelsea ex parte Steinfeld and Keiden* - see further www.theguardian.com/lifeandstyle/2014/dec/02/couple-challenge-ban-heterosexual-civil-partnerships and is already subject to a challenge as part of an application to the European Court of Human Rights in *Ferguson & Others v UK*, File No. 8254/11, lodged on 2 February 2011).

9 Perekonnaseadus (adopted on 18 November 2009). - RT I 2009, 60, 395; RT I, 29.06.2014, 104 available in English at: www.riigiteataja.ee/en/eli/ee/Riigikogu/act/522082014005/consolide.

10 See K. KULLERKUPP, 'Statutory Marital Property Law *de lege lata* and *de lege ferenda*', *Juridica International*, 2001, pp. 78-88.

11 Perekonnaseisutoimingute seadus (adopted on 20 May 2009, entered into force on 1 July 2010). - RT I 2009, 30, 177; RT I, 29.06.2014, 6, available in English at: www.riigiteataja.ee/en/eli/ee/Riigikogu/act/509072014015/consolide.

to § 1(1) of the Estonian Family Law Act, a marriage is contracted between a man and a woman. Only adults may marry. A court may extend the active legal capacity of a person who has attained at least 15 years of age pursuant to the provisions concerning an extension of the active legal capacity of minors for the performance of acts required for entering into a marriage and for the exercise of the rights and performance of the obligations related to a marriage (§ 1 Estonian Family Law Act (2,3)). A marriage has to be contracted in the presence of a vital statistics official. Vital statistics officials include notaries and ministers of religion who are entitled to perform vital statistics procedures pursuant to the Estonian Vital Statistics Registration Act. A marriage is void if it has been contracted between persons of the same sex (§ 10(1) Estonian Family Law Act). A court may annul a marriage if the spouses are of the same sex due to sex reassignment during the marriage (§ 9(1) item 7). The regulation of transactions in the General Part of the Estonian Civil Code Act[12] shall not be applied to the contracting of marriages.[13]

On 9 October 2014 the Estonian Parliament adopted the Estonian Registered Partnership Act (in English also called the Cohabitation Bill).[14] The Estonian Registered Partnership Act regulation is gender-neutral, covering legal relations between persons who have entered into a registered partnership agreement and legal relations with third persons.[15] According to § 26 of the Estonian Registered Partnership Act, January 1, 2016 has been established as the date when the Estonian Registered Partnership Act and its implementing legislation will enter into force. The Estonian Registered Partnership Act provides regulations on proprietary relationships, maintenance obligations and other mutual rights and obligations for all cohabiting couples, including the rights and obligations that concern the children from such unions. According to § 1(1) of the Estonian Registered Partnership Act, a registered partnership agreement may be entered into between two natural persons of whom at least one has his or her residence in Estonia. Only adults with active legal capacity may enter into a registered partnership agreement and - different from contracting a marriage - minors cannot enter into a registered partnership agreement even if a court has extended their

---

12 Tsiviilseadustiku üldosa seadus (adopted on 27 March 2002, entered into force on 1 July 2002). - RT I 2002, 35, 216; RT I, 13.03.2014, 103, available in English at: www.riigiteataja.ee/en/eli/ee/Riigikogu/act/528032014002/consolide.

13 T. GÖTTIG and T. UUSEN-NACKE, 'Perekonnaõiguse seosed teiste tsiviilõiguse valdkondadega', *Juridica*, 2010, No. 2, pp. 86-101.

14 Kooseluseadus. - RT I, 16.10.2014, 1 (in Estonian), available in English at: www.riigiteataja.ee/en/eli/ee/Riigikogu/act/527112014001/consolide.

15 riigikogu.ee/?op=ems&page=eelnou&eid=ea84e71c-291a-4c91-88b0-bd64af650d21&.

active legal capacity.[16] An adult with restricted active legal capacity may only enter into a registered partnership agreement if he or she sufficiently understands the legal consequences of a registered partnership agreement. If a guardian has been appointed to look after a person's interests, it is presumed that the person in question is unable to understand the legal consequences of a registered partnership agreement unless otherwise provided in the ruling concerning the appointment of a guardian (§ 1(3) Estonian Registered Partnership Act). A registered partnership agreement cannot be entered into between persons of whom at least one is married or has already entered into a valid registered partnership agreement at the time of the proposed registered partnership contract. A registered partnership agreement must be notarially authenticated (§ 3(1) Estonian Registered Partnership Act). A notary shall examine the prerequisites for entering into a registered partnership agreement. A notary shall not authenticate the act if there is a reason to presume that grounds for the annulment or nullity of the registered partnership agreement exist. The details of a registered partnership agreement shall be entered in the population register pursuant to the procedure provided for in the Estonian Vital Statistics Registration Act and the selection of the proprietary relationship of the parties shall be entered in the proprietary relationship register pursuant to the procedure provided for in the Estonian Proprietary Relationship Register Act (§ 3(4) Estonian Registered Partnership Act). At this point in time the implementing regulations for the Estonian Registered Partnership Act are still being drafted, so it is impossible to analyse the amendments to other legal acts as a result of adopting the Estonian Registered Partnership Act, and the situation is also further complicated by the fact that a proprietary relationship register does not currently exist, only a marital property register. According to § 1(1) of the Estonian Marital Property Register Act,[17] the marital property register is a state register for the registration of proprietary rights provided for in spouses' marital property contracts and, in the cases provided by law, other proprietary rights.

16 According to § 9(1) General Part of the Estonian Civil Code Act a court may extend the restricted active legal capacity of a minor of at least 15 years of age if this is in the interest of the minor and the minor's level of development permits this.

17 Abieluvararegistri seadus (adopted on 9 November 1995, entered into force on 1 September 1996). – RT I 1995, 87, 1540; RT I, 21.06.2014, 14 (in Estonian), available in English at: www.riigiteataja.ee/en/eli/520012014005/consolide.

FINLAND

According to Finnish law, there are two kinds of formal relationships: a marriage and a registered partnership.

According to the Finnish Marriage Act currently in force, a marriage can only be concluded between a man and a woman (S. 1). In December 2014, Parliament accepted an amendment to the Finnish Marriage Act, according to which also two persons of the same sex may, in the future, enter into a marriage. The amendment will enter into force on 1 March 2017.

According to the Finnish Act on Registered Partnerships (950/2001), two persons of the same sex can register their partnership (S. 1). The legal effects of the registration are almost identical to marriage. However, the provisions of the Finnish Paternity Act (700/1975)[18] on the establishment of paternity on the basis of marriage (the *pater est* provisions) do not apply to registered partnerships, nor do the provisions of the Finnish Adoption Act (22/2012) on joint adoption or the provisions of the Finnish Names Act (694/1985) on the family name based on marriage. With regard to property consequences, the legal effects are identical to a marriage.

FRANCE

French law regulates opposite and same-sex marriages as well as opposite and same-sex registered partnerships (*pacte civil de solidarité*, PACS). According to Art. 143 French Civil Code, a marriage is possible between two persons of the opposite or of the same sex (*'deux personnes de sexe différent ou de même sexe'*). Same-sex marriage was recently introduced in French law by Law Act no. 2013-404 of 17 May 2013.[19] The French Constitutional Council has held that the new statute is compatible with the Constitution.[20]

---

[18] The new Finnish Paternity Act (11/2015) was accepted by Parliament on 15.12.2014. However, it will not enter into force until 1.1.2016. The *pater est* provisions remain essentially the same.

[19] *Loi no 2013-404 du 17 mai 2013 ouvrant le mariage aux couples de personnes de même sexe, Journal Officiel* (JORF) no 114, 18 May 2013, at p. 8253. See also *Circulaire* of 29 May 2013 *de présentation de la loi ouvrant le mariage aux couples de personnes de même sexe (dispositions du Code civil).*

[20] CC, 17 May 2013, no. 2013-669, at para. 22. *'Considérant, en troisième lieu, qu'en ouvrant l'accès à l'institution du mariage aux couples de personnes de même sexe, le législateur a estimé que la différence entre les couples formés d'un homme et d'une femme et les couples de personnes de même sexe ne justifiait plus que ces derniers ne puissent accéder au statut et à la protection*

After several drafts[21] which were presented between 1993 and 1998 and finally rejected, the registered partnership was created by Law Act no. 99-944 of 15 November 1999 *relative au pacte civil de solidarité*,[22] which introduced a new Title (now Title XIII) in Book 1 of the French Civil Code (Art. 515-1 to 515-8). From the very beginning, the registered partnership called *pacte civil de solidarité* was defined as 'a contract between two natural persons having reached the age of majority, of the opposite or same sex, in order to organise their living together'.[23] The Constitutional Council[24] held that the new statutes were compatible with the French Constitution, but it however formulated several interpretation guidelines to be followed by the courts (*réserves d'interprétation*). Three decrees followed to specify the conditions for the application of the new statute.[25] Law Act no. 99-944 of 15 November 1999 aimed to put an end to discrimination between same-sex and opposite-sex partners in the case law of the *Cour de cassation*[26] (the highest civil and criminal court) and to adapt the law to social reality. It was then extensively amended by a new Law Act no. 2006-728 of 23 June 2006,[27] which extended the legal effects of the PACS and therefore brought it more into line with a marriage.

Law Act no. 99-944 of 15 November 1999 also introduced in the French Civil Code a definition of 'informal relationships' (*concubinage*). According to Art. 515-8, it is '*une union de fait, caractérisée par une vie commune présentant un caractère de stabilité et de continuité, entre deux personnes, de sexe différent ou de même sexe, qui vivent en couple*' (a factual union, characterised by a common life with the character of stability and continuity, between two persons of the opposite or same sex, living as a

juridique attachés au mariage; qu'il n'appartient pas au Conseil constitutionnel de substituer son appréciation à celle du législateur sur la prise en compte, en matière de mariage, de cette différence de situation'.

21 *Contrat d'union civile, contrat d'union civile et sociale, contrat d'union sociale, pacte d'intérêt commun* were contemplated, see *J. Classeur Civil*, Art. 515-1 to 515-7-1, by F. GRANET-LAMBRECHTS, 2013, no. 3.

22 *JORF* no. 265, 16 November 1999, p. 16959.

23 Art. 515-1 of the French Civil Code: '*Un pacte civil de solidarité est un contrat conclu par deux personnes physiques majeures, de sexe différent ou de même sexe, pour organiser leur vie commune*'.

24 CC, 9 November 1999, no. 99-419 DC, *JORF* 16 Nov. 1999.

25 Décret no. 99-1089 of 21 December 1999 (for the application of Art. 515-1 et seq. of the French Civil Code), Décret no. 99-1090 of 21 December 1999 and Décret no. 99-1091 of 21 December 1999 (relating to the treatment of data and their retention), see *JORF* 24 December 1999, at pp. 19216 et seq.

26 See e.g. Cass. Soc., 11 July 1989, 2 decisions, *JCP G* 1990, II, 21 553 with note MEUNIER; Cass. Civ. III, 17 December 1997, no. 95-20779, *Dr. Famille* 1998, comm. 36 with note LÉCUYER. See also B. BEIGNIER, 'A propos du concubinage homosexuel', *D.*, 1998. at p. 215.

27 *JORF* 24 June 2006, at p. 9513.

couple). The law does not specify any duration to be taken into account in order to consider whether the stability and continuity of the relationship are established. The main change entailed by Art. 515-8 of the French Civil Code is to admit that '*concubinage*' can exist between same-sex partners, whereas the case law of the *Cour de cassation* restricted the possible legal effects of *concubinage* to opposite-sex partners.

GERMANY

Under German law marriage exists between a man and a woman, §§ 1303 et seq. German Civil Code (*Bürgerliches Gesetzbuch*; BGB). The Civil Code does not expressly state that a spouse must be of the opposite sex to their spouse. However, this requirement is accepted generally.[28]

There is no same-sex marriage in Germany; it is only possible to enter a registered partnership. The legal basis for registered homosexual unions is the German Act on Registered Life Partnerships (*Lebenspartnerschafts-gesetz*; LPartG) of 16 February 2001 as amended.[29] After an unsuccessful attempt by representatives of gay and lesbian groups to enter into a marriage under existing law, the Federal Constitutional Court declared that the legislature was nevertheless free to enact some kind of law in this regard.[30] The intention of the legislature was to abolish discrimination against same-sex relationships, for which the alternative of marriage was not available – that right being reserved for heterosexuals. This was also in line with developments in Community law, which does not allow discrimination based on 'sexual orientation' (now Art. 19 TFEU, former Art. 13 EC Treaty).[31] The German registered partner model closely followed the pattern of the Nordic partnership laws.

However, since there was a constitutional challenge to the Act, the legislature reserved marriage for partners of the opposite sex and avoided endowing partnership with the same meaning as marriage. Later

[28] N. DETHLOFF, *Familienrecht*, Beck, Munich, 2012, at § 3 No. 13.

[29] Act on Registered Life Partnerships introduced by Art. 3 § 25 of the Act to end discrimination of same-sex unions (*Gesetz zur Beendigung der Diskriminierung gleichgeschlechtlicher Gemeinschaften*) of 16 February 2001, Official Gazette (BGBl.) 2001 I, p. 266 (English translation in K. BOELE-WOELKI and A. FUCHS (eds.), *Legal Recognition of Same-Sex Couples in Europe*, Intersentia, Antwerp, 2003, at p. 256 et seq.).

[30] BVerfG, 4.10.1993, *Neue Juristische Wochenschrift (NJW)*, 1993, 3058. Cf. A. RÖTHEL, 'Eingetragene Lebenspartnerschaft', in: R. HAUSMANN and G. HOHLOCH (eds.), *Das Recht der nichtehelichen Lebensgemeinschaft – Handbuch*, E. Schmidt, Berlin, 2004, at p. 137 and 147 et seq.

[31] See N. WITZLEB, 'The German 'Registered Life Partnership' – A Marriage That Dares Not Speak Its Name?', *Australian Journal of Family Law (Austr. J. Fam. L.)*, 2002, at p. 227 et seq.

the Federal Constitutional Court (*Bundesverfassungsgericht*; BVerfG) upheld the German Act on Registered Life Partnerships,[32] and after a later reform,[33] the civil law provisions on registered partnerships are in most respects nearly identical to marriage.[34]

Matrimonial law does not apply to informal relationships. A general application of matrimonial law by way of analogy is also not accepted (see Question 2).[35]

GREECE

There is an explicit and detailed provision in Greek law only for marriage (between heterosexual partners), to be found in Art. 1350 et seq., 1372 et seq. and 1386 et seq. of the Greek Civil Code, for engagements, as an option preliminary to marriage, in Art. 1346-1349 of the Greek Civil Code, and for cohabitation between two heterosexual partners on the basis of a formal (notarized) cohabitation pact, as envisaged in the specific legislation (Law 3719/2008).[36] What the legislator describes as a

---

32 BVerfG, 17.7.2002, *Entscheidungen des Bundsverfassungsgerichts (BVerfGE)*, 105, 313 = *NJW*, 2002, 2543, 2548 = *Zeitschrift für das gesamte Familienrecht (FamRZ)*, 2002, 1169, 1172 - 1173. See more in detail A. SANDERS, 'Marriage, Same-Sex Partnership, and the German Constitution', *German Law Journal*, 2012, at p. 911, 913 and 925 et seq.

33 Laws of 15.12.2004, BGBl. 2004 I, p. 3396 and 6.2.2005, BGBl. 2005 I, p. 203.

34 However, there are still problems in social security law, see Case C-147/08, *Jürgen Römer v. Freie und Hansestadt Hamburg* [2011] ECR I-3591 = *Europäische Zeitschrift für Wirtschaftsrecht (EuZW)*, 2011, 432; BVerfG, 7.7.2009, *NJW*, 2010, 1439 = *FamRZ*, 2009, 1977.

35 N. DETHLOFF, *Familienrecht*, Beck, Munich, 2012, at § 8 No. 5.

36 A. KOTZAMBASSI (ed.), *Cohabitation pact and family law amendments*, Sakkoulas, Athens/Thessaloniki, 2009 [in Greek]; Th. PAPACHRISTOU, N. KOUMOUTZIS and Chr. TSOUCA, *Cohabitation Pact*, Sakkoulas, Athens, 2009 [in Greek]; I SPYRIDAKIS, *The cohabitation pact according to Law 3719/2008*, Ant. Sakkoulas, Athens, 2009 [in Greek]; P. AGALLOPOULOU, 'Greek law 3719/2008 on cohabitation between persons of opposite sex', *International Family Law*, 2009, pp. 85 et seq.; P. AGALLOPOULOU, 'Financial consequences of cohabitation between persons of the opposite sex according to Greek law', in: B. VERSCHRAEGEN (ed.) *Family Finances*, Jan Sramek Verlag, Vienna, 2009, pp. 293-304; E. MOUSTAIRA, 'Matrimonios del mismo sexo: Un estudio comparativo de la realidad jurídica en varios países', in: C. LASARTE (ed.), *Familia, matrimonio y divorcio en los álbores del siglo XXI*, UNED and EL DERECHO, Madrid, 2006, pp. 59-69; A.G. KOUTSOURADIS, 'Law 3719/2008: audietur et altera pars et cetera!', *EfAD*, 2009, pp. 56 et seq. [in Greek]; E. VASSILAKAKIS, 'Aspects de droit international privé de couples homosexuels', *RHDI* 2006, pp. 145, 146; Th. PAPACHRISTOS, 'Critical comments on Law 3719/2008', *EfAD*, 2008, pp. 1018 et seq. [in Greek]; E. KOUNOUGERI-MANOLEDAKI, 'The new Law 3719/2008: a first assessment', *EfAD*, 2008, pp. 1016 et seq. [in Greek]; C. STAMBELOU, 'Cohabitation pact and equality', *Chronika Idiotikou Dikaiou*, 2009, pp. 189 et seq. [in Greek]; G.S.P. KATROUNGALOS, '3+1 views on 'same-sex marriage'', no. 3, manesis.blogspot.com (10 February 2010; in Greek). A. VARKA, 'Cohabitation pact - a contractual form of family', *Elliniki Dikeossini*, 2009, pp. 401 et seq. [in Greek]; T. PAPAZISSI, 'Same-sex marriage: valid, null or inexistent? (opinion)',

'free union',[37] which also relates to heterosexual couples, but is not given a legal definition anywhere in the Greek Civil Code, is only taken into consideration for the purposes of the imposition of a quasi-penalty, e.g. in Art. 1444(2) of the Greek Civil Code, where, if the divorced spouse is living with another partner in a state of free union, she loses her rights to maintenance, or in the context of assisted reproduction procedures, where the legislator, for the sake of the children to be born, in a way assimilates the partners of a free union to a married couple.[38]

The law on protection in cases of intra-family violence (Law 3500/2006) also protects the members of a family living, as persons of different gender, in a free union, i.e. it protects one partner against the other and the children, whether they are the children of both partners or only one (Art. 1(3)).

In very recent legislation there is also Art. 15 of Law 4272/2014, which, in cases where a woman wishes to donate a fertilised egg to be implanted in

---

Chronika Idiotikou Dikaiou, 2009, pp. 851 et seq. [in Greek]; V. SOTIROPOULOS, 'The right to marriage: the judicial pursuit of a non-existent prohibition', *Nomiko Vima*, 2009, pp. 2002 et seq., at pp. 2005-2007 [in Greek]; T. VIDALIS, 'Same-sex marriage', manesis.blogspot.com (10 February 2010; in Greek); S. MITAS, 'The (sexual) "lives of others." Right to marriage and sexual freedom', manesis.blogspot.com [in Greek]; L. PAPADOPOULOU, 'Same-sex marriage in light of gender equality', manesis.blogspot.com [in Greek]; L. PAPADOPOULOU, 'Same-sex marriage?', *Dikeomata tou Anthropou*, 2008, pp. 405 et seq. [in Greek]; K. CHRISTODOULOU, 'Cohabitation pact. Issues of substantive and procedural law', *Dikeomata tou Anthropou*, 2009, pp. 346 et seq. [in Greek].

[37] For a discussion on the new forms of family see P. AGALLOPOULOU, 'Les différents types de famille contemporaines selon le droit hellénique', *Revue hellénique de droit international*, 2002, pp. 22 et seq., and P. AGALLOPOULOU, 'Free unions', in: M. STATHOPOULOS, K. BEYS, Ph. DORIS and I. KARAKOSTAS (eds.), *Studies in honour of Apostolos G. Georgiadis*, Athens/Komotini, 2006, at p. 3 and 7 [in Greek]; P. GALLOPOULOU, 'Modifications du droit de la famille hellénique dues aux changements socio-familiaux', *Revue hellénique de droit international, 1997*, pp. 621 et seq.; E. MOUSTAIRA, 'Grèce: Régimes Matrimoniaux, successions, et libéralités dans les relations internationales et internes', in: *Livre Bleu du Notariat Latin*, 3ème éd., Brussels 2003, v. II, pp. 1319-1410; C. DELIYIANNI-DIMITRAKOU, 'Le droit social de l'Union européenne façe aux nouvelles formes de famille', in: I. SCHÖMANN (ed.), *Mélanges à l'honneur de Yota Kravaritou: a trilingual tribute*, European Trade Union Instituts, Brussels, 2011, pp. 49 et seq.; E. MOUSTAIRA, '"Grèce", Étude sur les régimes matrimoniaux des couple mariés et sur le patrimoine des couples non mariés dans le droit international privé et le droit interne des États membres de l' Union Européenne', effectuée à la demande de la Commission Européenne, Direction générale Justice et Affaires intérieures, Unité A3 Coopération judiciaire en matière civile, 2003, available at: ec.europa.eu/civiljustice/publications/docs/regimes/report_regimes_030703_fr.pdf.

[38] See, for example, Art. 1456(1) of the Greek Civil Code (written notarized consent of two partners to assisted reproduction), Art. 1457 Greek Civil Code (post-mortem fertilization of a woman with the sperm of the deceased partner).

another woman, requires that the donor's partner gives his written consent.

HUNGARY

There are two kinds of formal relationships in Hungarian law, marriage and a registered partnership.[39] Spouses are one man and one woman who have entered into a marriage before a registrar. Registered partners are two men or two women who declare their intention to enter into this partnership also before the registrar. Marriage is regulated in the Fourth Book (Family Law Book) of the Hungarian Civil Code[40] which entered into force in March 2014. The earlier legislation which had provided rules on marriage for the last sixty years was the Hungarian Family Act.[41] Registered partnerships have a relatively short legal history in Hungary. The Act on registered partnership[42] of 2009 entered into force in July 2009. As a main rule the Act determines that in questions not regulated by this Act the rules concerning marriage are to be applied analogously. Although a registered partnership results in the consequences of a marriage as a main rule, there are some exceptions primarily concerning children. The Hungarian Civil Code does not mention anything about registered partners but according to the mentioned imperative rule the regulations of the Hungarian Civil Code on marriage and spouses are generally to be applied to registered partnerships and registered partners. While marriage is also protected by the Hungarian Basic Law[43] as Article L states that 'Hungary shall protect the institution of marriage, the conjugal union of a man and a woman based on voluntary and mutual consent', a registered partnership is not mentioned in the Hungarian Basic Law.

---

39 According to a literal translation, this institution is called 'registered cohabitation', but it corresponds (in terms of its content) with the institution of a registered partnership as this terminology is used in this context in Europe. (Registered partnership would be *bejegyzett partnerkapcsolat* in Hungarian but the Act uses the phrase *bejegyzett élettársi kapcsolat*, that is to say registered cohabitation.) O. SZEIBERT-ERDŐS, 'Same-sex partners in Hungary. Cohabitation and registered partnership', *Utrecht Law Review*, 2008, pp. 212-221.

40 Act No. V. 2013 on the Civil Code.

41 Act No. IV. 1952 on Marriage, Family and Guardianship.

42 Act No. XXIX 2009 on Registered Partnership, Modification of Legal Rules in Connection with Registered Partnership and Facilitation of Proof of Cohabitation.

43 The Hungarian Basic Law was adopted in 2011 and entered into force in January 2012.

REPUBLIC OF IRELAND

In Ireland a person can be married, a civil partner in the case of a same-sex relationship only or, if in an informal relationship, a 'cohabitant' and in some cases a 'qualified cohabitant'. Marriage is not available for same-sex couples nor is civil partnership/civil union available for opposite sex couples.

Heterosexual marriage is governed by the Irish Marriage Act 1972. The Act has been modified by the Irish Age of Majority Act 1985, the Irish Family Law Act 1995 and the Irish Civil Registration Act 2004 (as amended). In *Zappone and Gilligan v Revenue Commissioners* [2006] IEHC 404, the High Court held that the right to marry under the Constitution was confined to the union of a man and a woman.

Same-sex civil partnerships were not recognised in law until the Irish Civil Partnership and Certain Rights and Obligations of Cohabitants Act 2010. This Act provides for a scheme of civil registration of same-sex partnerships together with a range of rights and responsibilities for registered civil partners.

Cohabitants were similarly afforded no recognition in Irish law prior to the introduction of the Irish Civil Partnership and Certain Rights and Obligations of Cohabitants Act 2010. Under this Act, 'cohabitants' may enter into valid agreements regarding their financial affairs during the course of their relationship or when their relationship ends and 'qualified cohabitants' can seek redress orders from the court in certain circumstances.

The Irish Children and Family Relationships Bill contains provisions which will affect civil partners and cohabitants if the Act is passed by the Irish parliament. Notably, the Irish Children and Family Relationships Bill 2015 will enable an eligible adult to apply to court for a guardianship order. An eligible adult is a person who is in a marriage or civil partnership with a child's parent, or has cohabited with them for three years, and has shared responsibility for the child's care for a 2 year period. This will enable step-parents to seek guardianship and is an important reform, in that it enables step-parents to acquire parental responsibility without having to resort to adoption. These proposed amendments alter significantly existing legislation which precludes a person who is married to, in a civil partnership with or cohabiting with a child's parent from making such an application to become a guardian. Moreover, a person may be eligible to apply for guardianship where they have cared for the child for one year, and no other parent or guardian is able to or will fulfil the rights and duties of the role. For example, this provision will allow foster parents to be appointed as guardians after a 12 month period.

ITALY

The only kind of formal relationship currently regulated by Italian legislation is marriage between a man and a woman. All other kinds of relations are therefore informal.

Marriage is regulated by Art. 29 of the Italian Constitution and Art. 79 to 230*bis* of the Italian Civil Code.

LATVIA

Latvian national laws and other legislative acts only regulate the legal order of marriage.

Article 110 of the Constitution of the Republic of Latvia stipulates that the State protects and supports marriage - a union between a man and a woman - the family, the rights of parents and the rights of the child.[44]

Part One of the Civil Law on Family Law Chapter 1 on Marriage[45] contains the detailed legal order of marriage including engagement, entering into and termination of marriage, personal rights of spouses, as well as the property rights of spouses.

LITHUANIA

Two kinds of formal relationships between couples are regulated by legislation: Marriage between different-sex couples and registered partnerships (cohabitation) between different-sex couples.

- Marriage between different-sex couples
  The Civil Code of the Republic of Lithuania (Official gazette. 2000, No. 74-2262, hereafter Lithuanian Civil Code) defines marriage as the main legal form for the creation of family relations. According to Art.

---

[44] Constitution of the Republic of Latvia: Law of the Republic of Latvia. Latvijas Vēstnesis, 1 July 1993, no.43.

[45] Civil Law. First part. Family rights. Law of the Republic of Latvia. "Ziņotājs", 10 June 1993, no.22.

3.7 of the Lithuanian Civil Code, a marriage is a voluntary agreement between a man and a woman to create legal family relations and which is entered into by means of the procedure provided for by law.

Article 38 of the Constitution of the Republic of Lithuania provides that a marriage shall be entered into upon the free consent of man and woman. The State shall also recognise marriages registered in a church. Marriages formed according to the procedure established by the Church (confessions) shall be entered in the official records in accordance with Article 3.304 of the Lithuanian Civil Code. The formation of a marriage in accordance with the procedures established by the Church (confessions) shall entail the same legal consequences as that emanate from the formation of a marriage at a Register Office provided that: 1) the conditions laid down in Articles 3.12 to 3.17 of the Lithuanian Civil Code have been satisfied; 2) the marriage has been formed according to the procedures established by the canons of a religious organisation registered in and recognised by the Republic of Lithuania; 3) the formation of a marriage in the procedure established by the Church (confessions) has been recorded at the Register Office in the procedure provided for herein.

Book III of the Lithuanian Civil Code regulates the personal and property relations of spouses and their maintenance rights as well as the legal relations between parents and children. Book V of the Lithuanian Civil Code regulates the law of succession. The legal effects of a marriage in other areas of the law (for example, tax law, social security law, pension law, labour law etc.) are prescribed by relevant legislation.

- Registered partnership (cohabitation) between a different-sex couple
  Registered partnerships (cohabitation) are regulated in the Lithuanian Civil Code, Book III 'Family Law', Part 6 'Rights and duties of other members of the family', chapter 15 'Persons living together outside of legal marriage (cohabitation)'. Articles 3.229-3.235 regulate the property relations of a man and a woman who, after registering their partnership in the procedure laid down by the law, have been cohabiting for at least one year with the aim of creating family relations without having registered their union as a marriage (cohabitees). Although the Lithuanian Civil Code has been in force for more than 13 years (from 2001 onwards) norms regulating relations between cohabitants are still lacking, because no special law has been

adopted since.[46] Such inconsistency and the lack of legal clarity obviously influence legal disputes within society and the different approaches within the case law. The above-mentioned provisions of the Lithuanian Civil Code (Arts. 3.229-3.235) have not been applied in practice; however they have not been abolished either, so they are referred to in the answers to some of the questions.

LUXEMBOURG

There are three forms of formal relationships in Luxembourg law:

- Different-sex marriage, Art. 144 et seq. of the Luxembourg Civil Code;
- Same-sex marriage introduced by the recent law of 4.7.2014;
- Same/different-sex registered partnership introduced by the law of 9.7.2004.

THE NETHERLANDS

Marriage (both for opposite and same-sex couples) and registered partnerships (both for opposite and same-sex couples) are regulated as formal relationships, implying state intervention and a formal act to start and to end the relationship. The entering into, the legal effects and the ending of a marriage are regulated in Book 1 of the Dutch Civil Code.[47] For both types of formal relationships the same rules apply.[48]

Informal relationships are also regulated by legislation, but in a rather haphazard way. Since these relationships are not of a formal nature, the specific legislation has to define one or more conditions in order to define which relationships qualify and which do not. In most areas of the law in which formal relationships are relevant, the informal relationships of cohabitating couples (opposite and same-sex) are regulated as well.[49] Non-marital cohabitation has legal effects in, for instance, maintenance

46 Article 28 of the Lithuanian Civil Code provides that the norms of Chapter XV (Cohabitation between persons without a marriage registration) of the Lithuanian Civil Code, 'shall come into force from the moment of the adoption of the Law on partnership registration.' According to Art. 50 of the Lithuanian Civil Code, such a Law was to be drafted by 1 January 2002.

47 W.M. SCHRAMA, 'Marriage and alternative status relationships in the Netherlands', in: J. EEKELAAR and R. GEORGE (eds.), *Routlegde Handbook of Family Law and Policy*, Routledge, London, 2014, pp. 14-25.

48 With two exceptions.

49 W.M. SCHRAMA, *De niet-huwelijkse samenleving in het Nederlandse en Duitse recht*, Kluwer, Deventer, 2004, at p. 123-166.

law, rent law, inheritance law, criminal law, taxation law, pensions law and social security law. However, in Book 1 of the Dutch Civil Code on family law, there is no *lex specialis*, no set of legal rules regulating the entering into, the legal effects and the ending of such informal relationship.

NORWAY

Marriage is regulated by the Norwegian Marriage Act 1991. In 2008, an amendment to the Act gave same-sex couples the right to enter into marriage on the same basis as different-sex couples. Before this legislation came into force on 1 January 2009, two people of the same sex were allowed to register their partnership and thus obtain the same rights as married couples throughout the legal system with very few exceptions. However, this opportunity to register partnerships is no longer available – the Registered Partnership Act 1993 was repealed as of 1 January 2009 when the Marriage Act was amended to include same-sex couples. Existing partnerships will still remain in force, and registered partners can have their partnerships converted into marriage, if they agree.[50]

PORTUGAL

The traditional different-sex Catholic marriage was the only kind of formal relationship between a couple regulated by Portuguese law up to 1910, with exceptions where a civil marriage seemed to be allowed. Following Portuguese Decree Law No. 1 of 25 December, a different-sex civil marriage was the only one permitted up to 1940. Since the signing of the Treaty between Portugal and the Holy See (1940) and the Portuguese Decree Law No. 30615, of 25 July, both different-sex Catholic marriages and different-sex civil marriages were allowed, although they were ruled by different laws and were subjected to different types of courts. Law No. 16/2001, of June 22 (religious freedom), introduced the right to celebrate marriage according to any religion provided it is 'rooted' in Portugal, thereby having civil effects. Law No. 9/2010, of 31 May, recognised a same-sex civil marriage.

There is no registered partnership according to Portuguese law.

---

50 The Norwegian Marriage Act, S. 95.

RUSSIA

Russian law currently regulates only one kind of formal relationship – a different-sex marriage. Article 1(2) of the Russian Family Code states that the recognition of only a formally registered marriage is one of the leading principles in Russian Family Law.[51] Marriage is regulated by parts II and III of the Russian Family Code of the Russian Federation.[52] Chapter 3 governs the formation of marriage; Chapter 4 governs the termination of marriage; Chapter 5 governs the annulment of marriage; Chapter 6 governs the personal rights and duties of spouses; Chapter 7 governs the statutory regime of matrimonial property; Chapter 8 governs the contractual regime of matrimonial property; and Chapter 9 governs the liability of spouses.

SCOTLAND

Scots law recognises two types of formal relationships between a couple: marriage and civil partnership. The formation of marriage is regulated primarily by the Marriage (Scotland) Act 1977 and civil partnership by the Civil Partnership Act 2004. Both Acts have recently been significantly amended by the Marriage and Civil Partnership (Scotland) Act 2014 which changed the meaning of marriage to include both different- and same-sex couples.[53]

Civil partnership was introduced in 2004[54] as a legal relationship for same-sex couples. With very minor differences, it was designed to be the legal equivalent of marriage. Between the introduction of civil partnership in 2004 and the coming into force of the Marriage and Civil Partnership (Scotland) Act in December 2014, Scots law had two formal relationships regulated by law in very similar terms: marriage which was open only to different-sex couples and civil partnership which was open only to same-sex couples. The effect of the reforms introduced by the 2014 Act is that marriage now includes either same-sex or different-sex

---

51 Н.С. Румянцева, 'Имущественные права супругов в гражданском браке', *Семейное и жилищное право*, 2009, at p. 22.

52 Further referred to as the Russian Family Code. *Семейный кодекс Российской Федерации*, adopted on 8 December 1995, in force since 1 March 1996. *Собрание законодательства Российской Федерации*, 1996, No. 1, item 15. For an English translation, see W. Butler and J. Henderson, *Russian Legal Texts. The Foundation of a Rule-of-Law State and a Market Economy*, Simmons and Hill Publishing Ltd, The Hague, 1998, at p. 517- 593.

53 Marriage (Scotland) Act 1977, S. 26(2).

54 Civil Partnership Act 2004.

couples[55] while civil partnership remains restricted to same-sex couples.[56] The Scottish government has indicated that it plans to consult in the future on possible reform of civil partnership.

The contemporary legal regulation of both marriage and civil partnership focuses on formation and dissolution. There are detailed legal rules concerning formation of the relationships,[57] grounds for divorce (marriage)[58] and dissolution (civil partnership)[59] and statutory principles for property sharing and financial provision on divorce or dissolution[60] but there is very little legal regulation of the intervening relationship itself. Scots law operates a system of strict separation of property during marriage or civil partnership by means of a provision to the effect that neither relationship will affect the property or legal capacity of the parties.[61] The only significant exception to this absence of legal regulation of the relationship is the obligation of aliment, or maintenance, which applies between spouses and civil partners.[62] Although highlighted as a significant legal consequence of marriage or civil partnership, and one which distinguishes these formal relationships from informal relationships, in practice parties rarely seek to enforce their right to aliment except in the context of relationship breakdown. The relative absence of legal regulation of the relations between spouses and civil partners is important to bear in mind when considering the treatment of informal relationships.

It should also be noted that Scots law to a very great extent respects the autonomy of spouses, and now civil partners, to regulate the consequences of their relationships. Marriage contracts, ante-nuptial, post-nuptial and separation agreements have a long and well-established history in Scots law and, in the context of separation at least, are commonly used in contemporary families.[63] They are legally enforceable, do not require judicial scrutiny or approval and are open only to very

[55] Marriage is now defined as meaning 'marriage between persons of different sexes and marriage between persons of the same-sex', Marriage (Scotland) Act 1977, S. 26(2).
[56] Civil Partnership Act 2004, S. 1.
[57] Marriage (Scotland) Act 1977; Civil Partnership Act 2004, S. 85-100.
[58] Divorce (Scotland) Act 1976.
[59] Civil Partnership Act 2004, S. 117-122.
[60] Family Law (Scotland) Act 1985, S. 8-16.
[61] Family Law (Scotland) Act 1985, S. 24.
[62] Family Law (Scotland) Act 1985, S. 1-7.
[63] For recent research into the use of separation agreements in Scots family law, see J. MAIR, F. WASOFF and K. MACKAY, *All Settled? A study of legally binding separation agreements and private ordering in Scotland* (unpublished report), University of Glasgow, 2013, available at: eprints.gla.ac.uk/85810, at chapter 2.

limited challenge. While there is little research evidence in respect of agreements between unmarried couples, and they have rarely come before the courts, it is widely assumed that cohabitation agreements would be equally respected by Scots law.[64]

SLOVAKIA

The Slovak Family Act regulates that a relationship between spouses is created by the free decision of a man and a woman made in the form stipulated by statute. The Slovak Family Act regulates in detail the prerequisites and conditions of the formation and termination of marriage. It also deals with void and apparent marriage. The rights and duties of spouses of a personal nature are only generally regulated by the Slovak Family Act. The rights and duties of spouses with a property nature (coverage of family needs, mutual duty of maintenance and property relationships arising from common property) are regulated by both the Slovak Family Act and the Slovak Civil Code.

Marriage is defined in Art. 1 of the fundamental principles of the Slovak Family Act as a union between a man and a woman. Family law doctrine defines marriage as a permanent union of (one) man and (one) woman established by free decision, the formation and termination of which is regulated by statute. Under the Slovak Family Act, the purpose of marriage is to create a harmonious and permanent social union guaranteeing a due upbringing of children. Slovak law does not permit same-sex marriages or other alternative unions of same-sex couples (e.g. registered partnerships).

The supremacy of marriage was also recently manifested by the National Council (Parliament) of Slovakia. On 4 June 2014, the Council adopted a Constitutional Law (no. 490/2014) amending the 1992 Constitution, which entered into force on 1 September 2014. Article 41 of the law defines marriage as 'a unique union between a man and a woman'. The explanatory memorandum that accompanies the law explicitly states that same-sex couples will not have the possibility to enter into a marriage. Of the 123 members of Slovakia's Parliament who voted on the measure, only 18 voted against adopting the amendment. The amendment specifically denies same-sex couples the legal protection associated with

64 F. WASOFF, J. MILES and E. MORDAUNT, *Legal Practitioners' Perspectives on the Cohabitation Provisions of the Family Law (Scotland) Act 2006* (unpublished report), University of Cambridge, Nuffield Foundation, 2010, available at: crfr.ac.uk/assets/Cohabitation-final-report.pdf, at pp. 77-84.

marriage by specifying that 'it will be impossible for the rights and duties associated with marriage to be conferred in any way other than a legally recognised union between a man and a woman.'

SLOVENIA

Slovene family law regulates three forms of life union: marriage, an extramarital union and a (registered) same-sex partnership union. The first two forms of life union are intended only for partners of a different sex and are regulated by the Marriage and Family Relations Act (hereinafter the Slovenian Marriage Act),[65] while a registered same-sex partnership is regulated by a special law, separately from the system of the other two heterosexual life partnerships. It is regulated by the Registration of Same-Sex Civil Partnership Act (hereinafter the Slovenian Partnership Act).[66]

Marriage is a legally regulated life union between a man and a woman. A marriage is concluded before the competent state body since a civil marriage is compulsory. An administrative unit has jurisdiction for concluding a marriage but it may delegate its competence to a municipality. A marriage is concluded in the presence of a registrar and two witnesses with contractual capacity. A marriage is validly concluded at the moment when the couple express their agreement to its conclusion. Concluding a marriage creates legal consequences both between the spouses (for example, it creates common assets between the spouses and there is a duty to maintain or support each other) and in relation to children, whereby a marriage bears the presumption that the mother's husband is the father of the children.

A same-sex partnership union creates legal consequences if it is registered before an official of an administrative unit by means of a signature attesting to a declaration on registration.[67] The legal consequences for the partners in the areas of maintenance, assets and housing are for the most part the same as for a married couple. A partner, for instance, has the possibility after the cessation of the union to continue

---

65 Uradni list RS (Official Journal) No. 69/2004 (consolidated text), 101/2007, 122/2007, 90/2011, 84/2012.

66 Uradni list RS (Official Journal) Nos 65/2005, 55/2009. The Registration of Same-Sex Civil Partnership Act entered into force in July 2005 but only began to be applied a year later, when the executive act for its implementation was also adopted (Regulation on the registration of same-sex civil partnerships, Uradni list RS (Official Journal) No. 55/2006).

67 Para. 3 of Art. 6 of the Slovenian Partnership Act.

leasing relations. However, they are entirely different in the regulation of rights in the event of the illness of the other partner.[68] In the case of the illness of the other partner, a registered partner has an unlimited right to be informed about the illness of his or her partner, while under the general arrangement, family members may only be informed if the person who is ill did not explicitly prohibit communicating his or her health data, the right to visit the partner in hospital and the right to decide on the treatment of the partner if the partner cannot herself or himself decide thereon. Married partners do not have such rights - for an adult person who does not have the capacity to consent, the right of consent is given under the general arrangement to a guardian. Under the legislation, registered partners do not have other rights than those enumerated in the Slovenian Partnership Act, e.g., in the tax and social spheres; an exception is the regulation of inheritance (a partner inherits under the general arrangement of the Slovenian Inheritance Act).[69] The law also does not regulate the relations of same-sex partners concerning children, such as the duty to care for the children of their partner, the possibility of adoption, or fertilisation with biomedical assistance.[70]

SPAIN

According to Art. 44 of the Spanish Civil Code both men and women can enter into marriage. In 2005 this provision was amended in order to add a second paragraph establishing that the conditions and effects of marriage do not vary depending on whether the intended spouses are of the same or the opposite sex.[71] Marriage was thereby opened up to same-sex couples. Article 44 applies throughout Spain, since marriage falls under the legislative competence of the Spanish Central State in accordance with Art. 149.1.8 of the Spanish Constitution.

Registered partnership regimes have been developed in some of the Spanish legal systems. This is so in the case of Basque law.[72] According

[68] Art. 21 and 22 of the Slovenian Partnership Act.

[69] Uradni list SRS (Official Journal) Nos 23/1978, RS 17/1991-I; Uradni list RS (Official Journal) Nos 13/1994, 40/1994, 82/1994, 117/2000, 67/2001, 83/2001, 73/2004.

[70] Because implementing regulations for the registration procedure were only adopted in the summer of 2006 and because same-sex couples believe that the law is discriminatory in a number of provisions in comparison to the legal regulation of the life unions of different-sex couples, there are currently only a small number of partnership unions registered in Slovenia.

[71] Ley 13/2005, de 1 de julio, por la que se modifica el Código civil en material de derecho a contraer el matrimonio (BOE núm. 157, de 2 de julio de 2005).

[72] Ley 2/2003, de 7 de mayo, reguladora de las parejas de hecho (BOE núm. 283, de 25 de noviembre de 2011).

to Art. 3.1 of a special statute on *de facto* couples (the terminology is misleading), couples have to register in order to be governed by the special regime on *de facto* couples. Registration is a constitutive requirement and both same-sex and opposite-sex couples may register. The law of Galicia [73] and that of the Balearic Islands [74] contains analogous provisions.

Other Spanish laws, however, follow a so-called double track model: special partnership regimes apply to couples that formally constitute their relationship (very often by notarial deed and without registration) and to couples that have cohabited for a certain time period or fulfil certain factual conditions. Catalan law furnishes an example of this model. According to Art. 234-1 of the Catalan Civil Code two people who cohabit in a manner analogous to marriage qualify as a so-called stable couple in three circumstances:

- if cohabitation lasts for more than two years without interruption; or
- if the couple have a common child; or
- if the couple formalises their relationship by notarial deed.

Couples qualifying as a stable couple are governed by special provisions of the Catalan Civil Code that do not apply to other informal relationships.

The Catalan model is followed by the law of Aragon[75] and Navarre.[76] This report will focus on the Catalan Civil Code (as an example of a Spanish legal system that does have specific provisions on informal relationships) and the Spanish Civil Code (as an example of a Spanish legal system that does not have specific provisions on informal relationships).

Since terminology may be misleading to those unfamiliar with the Spanish Constitution, it is important to mention that the Spanish Civil

[73] Ley 2/2006, de 14 de junio, de derecho civil de Galicia, as amended by Ley 10/2007, de 28 de junio, de reforma de la disposición adicional tercera de la Ley 2/2006, de 14 de junio, de derecho civil de Galicia (BOE núm. 226, de 20 de septiembre de 2007).

[74] Ley 18/2001, de 19 de diciembre, de Parejas Estables (BOE num. 14, de 16 de enero de 2002).

[75] Decreto Legislativo 1/2011, de 22 de marzo, del Gobierno de Aragón, por el que se aprueba, con el título de 'Código del Derecho Foral de Aragón', el Texto Refundido de las Leyes civiles aragonesas (BOA núm. 67, de 29 de marzo de 2011).

[76] Ley foral 6/2000, de 3 de julio, para la igualdad jurídica de las parejas estables (BOE núm. 214 de 6 de septiembre de 2000).

Code does not apply, as regards this subject matter, throughout the country, but coexists with other legal systems in those Autonomous Communities with jurisdiction to legislate in matters of civil law (Balearic Islands, Catalonia, Aragon, Navarre, Basque Country and Galicia). This issue and the conflict of law matters connected to it will not be dealt with in this report. The special statutes on unmarried couples of Autonomous Communities that have no jurisdiction to legislate in matters of private law will not be taken into account either, since they do not contain provisions falling within the scope of this report.[77]

SWEDEN

Swedish law recognises two types of formal relationships. The first and traditional one is marriage which, following law reform carried out in 2009, applies to spouses irrespective of their sex, i.e., irrespective of whether they are of the same sex or of opposite sexes. The legislation regarding marriage is found in the Swedish Marriage Code (in Swedish, *Äktenskapsbalk 1987:230*), which regulates, for example, marriage conclusion and divorce, and the rights and duties of the spouses during marriage and upon its termination by divorce.

The second formal relationship between couples, recognised by Swedish law, is the institution of registered partnership which was introduced into legislation in 1994 through the Registered Partnership Act (in Swedish, *Lag 1994:1117 om registrerat partnerskap*) and aimed solely at couples of the same sex. This enactment, which was formally abolished in 2009 as redundant following the introduction of a gender neutral marriage concept (see above), still continues to apply to same-sex couples who have registered their partnership according to this legislation without later converting it into a marriage. The essence of the Registered Partnership Act, with successive amendments until its abolition in 2009, was to place registered partners on the same legal footing as married couples. Since 1 May 2009, when the revised Marriage Code with the gender-neutral marriage concept entered into force, it is no longer possible to enter into a registered partnership in Sweden. A characteristic of Swedish law is that marriage and the existing registered partnerships concluded in Sweden have the same legal effects. The difference was access to the one or the other, depending on the sex of the individuals concerned. Once marriage became an available option for same-sex

77 If they contain such provisions they would be unconstitutional. See Decision by the Constitutional Court on the law on unmarried couples of the Autonomous Community of Madrid (STC 81/2013).

couples, there was no need for the Swedish model of registered partnership.

SWITZERLAND

In Switzerland two kinds of formal relationships between a couple are known: marriage and a registered partnership.

Marriage is only open to persons of a different sex. It is commonly defined as the mutual consent of a man and a woman of full age to form an exclusive, long-lasting and officially recognised and formalised partnership. Matrimonial law is governed by Art. 90 et seq. Swiss Civil Code[78] (first division of the Swiss family law).

In 2007 the Swiss law on Registered Partnership[79] entered into force. This kind of formal relationship is only open to same-sex couples. The statute on registered partnerships largely mirrors the matrimonial law. Substantive differences can be found as far as financial regulations during ongoing partnerships and upon their dissolution are concerned. Furthermore, same-sex couples are not allowed to adopt children[80] or to gain access to medically assisted procreation.

78 Schweizerisches Zivilgesetzbuch, SR 210.

79 Partnerschaftsgesetz, SR 211.231. For details see I. SCHWENZER and A. BOCK, 'New Statutory Rules on Registered Partnerships and Protection Against Domestic Violence', in: B. ATKIN, *The International Survey of Family Law,* Jordan Publishing, Bristol, 2008, at p. 445 et seq.

80 At the time of writing, a draft allowing step-parent adoption in same-sex relationships is pending.

QUESTION 2

To what extent, if at all, are informal relationships between a couple regulated by specific legislative provisions? Where applicable, briefly indicate the current specific legislation. Are there circumstances (e.g. the existence of a marriage or registered partnership with another person, a partner's minority) which disqualify the couple?

AUSTRIA

A comprehensive legal framework regulating informal relationships is currently lacking in Austria.[1] Generally, one has to distinguish between the internal (the relations between the partners) and external (the relations between a partner in an informal relationship and third persons) dimension of informal relationships.[2] Where the Austrian legislator has introduced specific rules for informal relationships, they mainly concern the latter. These provisions equate partners in an informal relationship with spouses and they are aimed at avoiding outcomes that would be contrary to the principle of equality:[3]

- Section 14 Austrian Tenancy Act stipulates that after the death of one partner the other partner is entitled to step into the tenancy agreement

1 Austrian Supreme Court, Legal Proposition RS0109605, Judgement of 01.04.1998, 9 Ob 96/98b.

2 F. LINDER, in: E. GITSCHTHALER and J. HÖLLWERTH (eds.), *Kommentar zum Ehe- und Partnerschaftsrecht*, Springer, Vienna, 2011, at p. 1085.

3 The following list is not exhaustive, but includes the most important provisions commonly referred to in the legal literature. For further examples see e.g. M. NEUMAYR, 'Neue Regeln für nichteheliche Lebensgemeinschaften? Von den öffentlich-rechtlichen Folgen einer Lebensgemeinschaft im Außenverhältnis bis zum "Zivilpakt"', in: Österreichischer Juristentag (ed.), *Zivilrecht - Neue Regelungen für nichteheliche Lebensgemeinschaften*, Manzsche Verlags- und Universitätsbuchhandlung, Vienna, 2013, pp. 119-136, at p. 121 et seq.

and become the contracting party of the agreement, if the informal relationship has existed for at least 3 years.[4]

- Section 5 para. 1 Austrian Condominium Act allows two natural persons to jointly purchase a condominium. Before the amendment of the Austrian Condominium Act in 2002 this possibility was restricted to spouses.
- Section 55 Austrian Copyright Act determines that a partner in an informal relationship may - after the death of the other partner - take single photographs of portraits that were created upon order. Section 77 Austrian Copyright Act contains the so-called 'protection of the letter' *(Briefschutz)* according to which letters, personal diaries and similar confidential notes must not be disclosed to the public, if after the death of the author the legitimate interests of close relatives would be violated by such disclosure. Pursuant to S. 77 para. 2 the term 'close relatives' includes partners in an informal relationship.
- According to S. 382b, c and d Austrian Enforcement Act a violent partner may be ordered to leave the common home. Before 1997 this option was only available to spouses.
- Section 72 para. 2 Austrian Criminal Code stipulates that partners in an informal relationship should be treated like relatives pursuant to S. 72 para. 1 Austrian Criminal Code. Hence, if the Austrian Criminal Code provides for particular consequences for relatives, these provisions equally apply to partners in an informal relationship.[5] As an example reference can be made to the grounds for exemption from punishment, e.g. if vehicles have been used without permission (S. 136 para. 4 Austrian Criminal Code).
- The Austrian Code of Criminal Procedure also contains rules for partners in an informal relationship by referring to the term relatives contained in S. 72 Austrian Criminal Code, which includes partners in an informal relationship. Partners in an informal relationship are, for example, exempted from the duty to testify or may refuse to testify against the other partner.[6]
- Section 20 Austrian Jurisdiction Act regulates the grounds for excluding a judge from particular proceedings and explicitly refers to

---

[4] F. LINDER, in: E. GITSCHTHALER and J. HÖLLWERTH (eds.), *Kommentar zum Ehe- und Partnerschaftsrecht,* Springer, Vienna, 2011, at p. 1099.

[5] For further provisions contained in the Austrian Criminal Code see F. LINDER, in: E. GITSCHTHALER and J. HÖLLWERTH (eds.), *Kommentar zum Ehe- und Partnerschaftsrecht,* Springer, Vienna, 2011, at p. 1102 et seq.

[6] Sections 156 para. 1 No. 1, 157 para. 1 No. 1 Austrian Code of Criminal Procedure; for further provisions contained in the Austrian Code of Criminal Procedure see F. LINDER, in: E. GITSCHTHALER and J. HÖLLWERTH (eds.), *Kommentar zum Ehe- und Partnerschaftsrecht,* Springer, Vienna, 2011, at p. 1103 et seq.

partners in an informal relationship. Hence, a judge is excluded in matters concerning his/her partner.[7]

- Section 321 para. 1 No. 2 Austrian Code of Civil Procedure allows a witness to refuse to testify if the answer to the question concerns his/her partner.
- Pursuant to S. 32 Austrian Insolvency Code close relatives are *inter alia* persons who live with the debtor in an extramarital partnership. In this case the partner has to prove that he/she neither knew nor must have been aware of the intent of the debtor to disadvantage the creditor.[8]
- Section 106 para. 3 Austrian Income Tax Act states that a partner is a person with whom the taxpayer is married or is living together in an informal relationship with at least one child. Hence, also some provisions of tax law refer to informal relationships.[9]
- Also social law contains provisions with regard to informal relationships,[10] e.g. the health insurance of an insured person may also cover his/her partner in an informal relationship provided that they are not relatives, that they have been living in a joint household for at least 10 months and that the partner is responsible for the household without being paid for his/her work.[11]
- Section 2 Austrian Law on Reproductive Medicine states that medically-assisted reproduction is only allowed in a marriage or an informal relationship, including same-sex couples. Apart from some very limited exceptions, the egg cells and the sperm of the spouses/partners must be used for the medically-assisted reproduction.
- Further, the Austrian Supreme Court has included partners in an informal relationship under the term relatives pursuant to S. 67

---

7 F. LINDER, in: E. GITSCHTHALER and J. HÖLLWERTH (eds.), *Kommentar zum Ehe- und Partnerschaftsrecht*, Springer, Vienna, 2011, at p. 1105.

8 Cf. A. DEIXLER-HÜBNER, *Scheidung, Ehe- und Lebensgemeinschaft*, LexisNexis ARD ORAC, Vienna, 2013, at marg. No. 234.

9 See e.g. section 33 para. 4 No. 1 Austrian Income Tax Act.

10 S. FERRARI, 'Rechtsregeln für nichteheliches Zusammenleben in Österreich', in: I. KROPPENBERG et al. (eds.), *Rechtsregeln für nichteheliches Zusammenleben*, Gieseking Verlag, Vienna, 2009, pp. 167-206, at p. 174.

11 Section 123 para. 7a General Austrian Social Security Act; for further provisions contained in the General Austrian Social Security Act see F. LINDER, in: E. GITSCHTHALER and J. HÖLLWERTH (eds.), *Kommentar zum Ehe- und Partnerschaftsrecht*, Springer, Vienna, 2011, at p. 1103 et seq.; M. NEUMAYR, 'Neue Regeln für nichteheliche Lebensgemeinschaften? Von den öffentlich-rechtlichen Folgen einer Lebensgemeinschaft im Außenverhältnis bis zum "Zivilpakt"', in: Österreichischer Juristentag (ed.), *Zivilrecht – Neue Regelungen für nichteheliche Lebensgemeinschaften*, Manzsche Verlags- und Universitätsbuchhandlung, Vienna, 2013, pp. 119-136, at p. 124 et seq.; A. DEIXLER-HÜBNER, *Scheidung, Ehe und Lebensgemeinschaft*, LexisNexis ARD ORAC, Vienna, 2013, at marg. No. 241c.

para. 2 Austrian Insurance Contract Act. Hence, the insurer cannot have recourse against the injuring party if this party is the partner of the injured person and the harm was not caused by gross negligence.[12]

- According to the Austrian Hospitalization Act, which regulates the removal of mentally ill persons to mental hospitals, partners in an informal relationship are entitled to appeal against the reception order.[13]
- Also labour law recognises informal relationships: An employee is entitled to payment, even if he/she is not able to work due to the sickness or the death of his/her partner.[14]

The provisions above clearly indicate the increasing tendency of the Austrian legislator to consider informal relationships and to treat them equally to marriages.[15] In this regard it should be noted that even if explicit provisions are lacking, the Austrian Supreme Court has decided that partners in an informal relationship can be included under the term 'close relatives'.[16]

As to the second question the Austrian Supreme Court has held that an informal relationship can exist, even if one of the partners is married.[17] In the decided case the informal partners had lived together for 17 years and had five joint children. They were not married for the only reason that the married partner feared the costs of the divorce. Despite the existing marriage the Austrian Supreme Court has recognised the informal relationship.[18] In contrast, in another decision the Austrian

12 S. FERRARI, 'Rechtsregeln für nichteheliches Zusammenleben in Österreich', in: I. KROPPENBERG et al. (eds.), *Rechtsregeln für nichteheliches Zusammenleben*, Gieseking Verlag, Vienna, 2009, pp. 167-206, at p. 175.

13 Section 28 para. 1 Austrian Hospitalization Act.

14 For further examples regarding labour law see M. NEUMAYR, 'Neue Regeln für nichteheliche Lebensgemeinschaften? Von den öffentlich-rechtlichen Folgen einer Lebensgemeinschaft im Außenverhältnis bis zum "Zivilpakt"', in: Österreichischer Juristentag (ed.), *Zivilrecht – Neue Regelungen für nichteheliche Lebensgemeinschaften*, Manzsche Verlags- und Universitätsbuchhandlung, Vienna, 2013, pp. 119-136, at p. 119 et seq.

15 M. NEUMAYR, 'Neue Regeln für nichteheliche Lebensgemeinschaften? Von den öffentlich-rechtlichen Folgen einer Lebensgemeinschaft im Außenverhältnis bis zum "Zivilpakt"', in: Österreichischer Juristentag (ed.), *Zivilrecht – Neue Regelungen für nichteheliche Lebensgemeinschaften*, Manzsche Verlags- und Universitätsbuchhandlung, Vienna, 2013, pp. 119-136, at p. 129.

16 Austrian Supreme Court, Judgement of 29.08.2002, 8 Ob 127/02p.

17 Austrian Supreme Court, Judgement of 16.06.1983, 7 Ob 595/83.

18 See also S. FERRARI, 'Rechtsregeln für nichteheliches Zusammenleben in Österreich', in: I. KROPPENBERG et al. (eds.), *Rechtsregeln für nichteheliches Zusammenleben*, Gieseking Verlag, Vienna, 2009, pp. 167-206, at p. 170.

Supreme Court in an obiter dictum stated that an informal relationship requires 'to some extent the absence of a spouse'.[19]

BELGIUM

Belgian family law does not contain a default legal definition of informal relationships and does not, as such, regulate their formation, content and dissolution.

BULGARIA

In family law as well as in other areas of law specific legislative provisions regulate some aspects of an informal relationship. Where regulated, the informal relationship between a heterosexual couple is equated with a marriage, as a consequence of living together. These consequences are grouped on the basis of the interest protected.

Regulation in favour of the partners/couple: The family legislation regulates a few legal consequences of an informal relationship:

- Consequences affecting the common children – parents, irrespective of the type of their relationship (marriage or informal), acquire parental rights and duties (joint parental responsibilities) and exercise them together or based on mutual consent (Art. 122 paras 1-2 and 123 of the Bulgarian Family Code).
- If the couple separate the law provides for a mechanism to rearrange the exercise of parental rights and duties by agreement or by a court decision if parents are not able to reach an agreement (Art. 127 of the Bulgarian Family Code).
- Each partner is entitled to protection against domestic violence: The Bulgarian Protection against Domestic Violence Act (2006, last amended in 2011) provides for protection (equivalent to that which is available to spouses) against domestic violence (Art. 2 and 3).

Other areas of law also regulate some consequences of an informal relationship:

- An (informal) couple have access to artificial reproductive treatment (ART). The Bulgarian Health Act (2004, last amended in 2014) does

19 Austrian Supreme Court, Judgement of 29.08.2002, 8 Ob 127/02p.

not make access to ART conditional upon the matrimonial status of the couple[20] (Art. 129 and 130, para. 1 of the Bulgarian Health Act).

- An opportunity to donate organs or tissue to a partner based on additional prerequisites - permission from the Commission on Ethics in Transplantation and the duration of the cohabitation (Art. 26 of the Bulgarian Transplantation of Organs, Tissue and Cells Act of 2004, last amended in 2011).
- The (informal) couple have access to mutual insurance (Art. 232 of the Bulgarian Insurance Code of 2006, last amended in 2013). The Code specifies the consequences upon the termination of the cohabitation (separation/no longer living together).
- Transferring the rights to financial compensation for victims of crime - if the victim has died as a result of the crime, the person with whom the victim lived in an informal relationship will receive the compensation which is due (Art. 3, para. 2 of the Bulgarian Support and Financial Redress to Crime Victims Act (2007, last amended in 2010).
- A partner in an informal relationship has the right to refuse to testify against the other partner in civil and criminal procedures (Art. 166, para. 1/2 of the Bulgarian Civil Procedure Code of 2008, last amended in 2014 and Art. 119 and 121 of the Bulgarian Penal Procedure Code of 2005, last amended in 2014).
- The informal partner of an EU citizen has a privileged status in relation to the right to enter, reside in and leave Bulgarian territory (Act of 2006 on the Rights of EU Citizens and Members of their Family to Enter, Reside in and Leave the Republic of Bulgaria, last amended in 2011). The partner in an informal relationship is considered to be a family member (para. 1 of the Additional Provision to the Act).
- The Bulgarian Taxes and Securities Procedure Code (2006, last amended in 2014) provides for equal legal consequences for both formal and informal families. Under para. 1, p. 2 of the Additional Provision to the Code: 'The "household" includes spouses, persons living in factual cohabitation as well as their children and relatives living together with them.' The income of the two partners is calculated, together with their expenses, for the purpose of establishing the basis for taxation (Art. 123, para. 1). Otherwise the basis for the taxation of persons is always individual income (this is equal to married persons).

[20] More in: S. STAVRY, 'Factual cohabitation - A Quasi Marriage or a Fact of Normative Steroids?', 20.05.2012, available at: challengingthelaw.com/semeino-i-nasledstveno-pravo/faktichesko-sajitelstvo/.

Regulation in favour of the interests of the public:

- Social assistance benefits are granted to the household with the income of each partner in an informal relationship being included in the calculation: Art. 2, para. 3 of the Bulgarian Social Assistance Act (1998, last amended in 2014) in conjunction with Art. 9, para. 3 of the Bulgarian Implementing Regulation concerning the Social Assistance Act (1998, last amended in 2014). This means that an informal couple receive social assistance (benefits) as a (formal) family (para. 1, p. 2 of the Additional Provision to the Bulgarian Implementing Regulation concerning the Social Assistance Act).
- An informal relationship (equal to a formal family) is a ground to establish a conflict of interests thus giving rise to the obligation to legally declare this relationship (Bulgarian Civil Servants Act, Bulgarian Judicial Power Act, Bulgarian Mediation Act, Bulgarian Public Notaries and Notarial Deeds Act, Bulgarian Civil Procedure Code and many others).
- The Bulgarian Forfeiture of Illegally Acquired Property Act (of 2012, last amended in 2014) defines partners in the informal relationship as members of the family for the purpose of investigating acquisitions (Art. 1, para. 3 of the Additional Provision).

There are no circumstances prescribed by law which disqualify the couple.

CROATIA

Two kinds of informal relationships between a couple are regulated by specific legislative provisions:

- Different-sex cohabitation
- Same-sex informal partnership

Cohabitation is an informal relationship between a heterosexual couple regulated by the Croatian Family Act. It is almost a legal equivalent of marriage. According to Art. 11 paragraph 2 of the Croatian Family Act, cohabitation and marriage imply, in the light of family law, the same personal, property and other legal effects. Except in family law, cohabitation and marriage are legally equal in many other areas of law, e.g. inheritance law, social security law, pensions law etc.

According to Art. 11 paragraph 1 of the Croatian Family Act, cohabitation is a life union between an unmarried man and an unmarried woman. There are no other circumstances which disqualify the couple pursuant to the Croatian Family Act. Nevertheless, legal practice shows that only those couples who meet the requirements for the conclusion of a valid marriage are encompassed by the institution of cohabitation. These requirements are as follows: having reached the age of majority, possessing reasoning ability, the absence of consanguinity in the direct line and the lateral line to the fourth degree, and a free marital and partnership status (Art. 25-28 of the Croatian Family Act).[21]

A same-sex informal partnership is an informal relationship between a homosexual couple regulated by the Croatian Partnership Act. Informal same-sex partnerships are almost legally equal to same-sex registered partnerships. According to Art. 3 paragraph 1 of the Croatian Partnership Act, a same-sex informal partnership is a union of family life between two persons of the same sex who, despite the fact that they meet the criteria for the conclusion of a valid same-sex registered partnership, have not entered into one. The requirements for the conclusion of a valid same-sex registered partnership include the following: having reached the age of majority, possessing reasoning ability, the absence of consanguinity in the direct line and the lateral line to the fourth degree, and a free marital and partnership status (Art. 8-11 of the Croatian Partnership Act).

CZECH REPUBLIC

The position of partners in an informal relationship is not regulated nor is the term 'informal relationship' defined in Czech legislation, but according to books and articles an informal relationship is defined as a living arrangement in which an unmarried couple lives together in a long-term relationship that resembles a marriage.[22] The Czech Civil Code uses the term 'close person' and says that people related by affinity and people permanently living together are also presumed to be close persons (S. 22(1) Czech Civil Code). This definition could also cover partners in an informal relationship; thus all the cases cited below could equally apply to partners in an informal relationship.

---

21 Judgment of 9 October 2011, Municipal Court of Zagreb, CXLIII-P2-633/08-34; Judgment of 8 July 2009, County Court of Koprivnica, Gž 1752/2008-2; Judgment of 21 October 2008, County Court of Varaždin, Gž. 1168/08-2.

22 M. Hrušáková, Z. Králíčková, L. Westphalová et al., *Rodinné právo*, C.H. Beck, Prague, 2015, at p. 114.

In the Czech Civil Code there is a specific maintenance obligation when the partner (man) in an informal relationship is obliged to provide the payment of certain costs for an unmarried mother, by way of maintenance and support. In accordance with S. 920 Czech Civil Code: if the child's mother is not married to the child's father, the child's father must provide her with maintenance for two years from the birth of the child and provide her with a reasonable contribution to cover the costs associated with pregnancy and childbirth. The man whose paternity is presumed has the duty to reimburse the costs associated with pregnancy and childbirth even if the child is not born alive. A court may, on the application of a pregnant woman, order the man whose paternity is presumed to provide an amount needed for maintenance and a contribution to cover the costs associated with pregnancy and childbirth in advance. A court may, on the application of a pregnant woman, also order the man whose paternity is presumed to provide in advance an amount needed to provide for the maintenance of the child for a period for which the woman would be entitled to maternity leave as an employee under another legal regulation.

As for protection against domestic violence, the substantive regulation in S. 751-753 of the Czech Civil Code (special provisions against domestic violence) is, in accordance with S. 3021 Czech Civil Code, also applicable to partners in an informal relationship (S. 3021 Czech Civil Code: the provisions of S. 751-753 on domestic violence also apply to cohabitation of persons other than spouses).

For the law of succession to apply (S. 1475 et seq. Czech Civil Code), the partners to an informal relationship have to live together in the common household for at least one year before the death of one of the partners. If this condition is fulfilled, the living partner can inherit from his position in the second class of heirs or in the third class of heirs (S. 1636(1) and S. 1637(1) Czech Civil Code).

As for the lease of an apartment and the lease of a building, there is a special provision regarding the death of one of the partners in an informal relationship who is the lessee. If one of the partners who is the lessee dies and there is no joint lease of the apartment, the lease passes to a member of the lessee's household who was living in the apartment on the day of the lessee's death and has no apartment of his own. If such a person is someone other than the lessee's spouse, partner, parent, sibling, son-in-law, daughter-in-law, child or grandchild, the lease passes to such a person only if the lessor consents to the passage of the lease to that person (S. 2279(1) Czech Civil Code). It means that in case of the death of one partner, the other has a right to stay in the apartment without the permission of the lessor. A lease of an apartment in such cases is to end no later than two years from the date of the passage of the lease (S. 2279(2) Czech Civil Code).

For the purposes of the criminal law (see Czech Criminal Code, Act No. 40/2009 Coll.) where the term 'close person' is used as well, the condition of a long period of living together in a common household is not necessary, but it is only possible to use this term if the injury suffered by one of the partners is considered by the other partner as his own injury (S. 125 Czech Criminal Code). As for S. 100 of Act No. 141/1961 Coll., Czech Code of Criminal Procedure, concerning the right to refuse to testify, a witness is entitled to refuse to testify if the testimony would incriminate himself, his relative in the direct line of descent, his siblings, adoptive parent, adoptive spouse, partner or mate, or other persons in a family or similar, or if it would conflict with the law by which the partner considered the injury as his own injury (S. 100(2) Czech Code of Criminal Procedure).

There are no circumstances in an informal relationship which can disqualify the couple as in marriage where the existence of another marriage or registered partnership causes an invalidity of marriage (legal impediment according to S. 674 Czech Civil Code).

DENMARK

In most cases if a person is in an existing marriage or registered partnership this will disqualify them from being regulated by specific provisions concerning informal relationships.

An informal relationship between a couple is regulated by several laws. The following are some of the most important rules:

- The legal relation between parents and children:
  - The Danish Children's Act and the Danish Parental Responsibility Act: The legal situation of children born within an informal relationship and within a formal relationship is nearly the same.
  - The Danish Adoption Act: Cohabitants can adopt subject to the same conditions as married couples.
- Relations between partners in an informal relationship:

- During the relationship:
  - According to the Danish Act on Names cohabitants can have the same surname;
  - Danish Social Security Acts: When a couple is presumed to be cohabitants, a number of social benefits fall by the wayside.
- On separation:
  - According to the Danish Act on Rent a court can substitute the tenant with his or her cohabiting partner if there are special grounds for doing so.
- On death:
  - According to the Danish Act on Rent a surviving cohabitant is entitled to extend the lease;
  - According to the Danish Inheritance Tax Act a surviving cohabitant is only required to pay a low rate of inheritance tax;
  - The Danish Inheritance Act regulates extended cohabitants' wills and extends the testamentary powers of cohabitants;
  - The Danish Administration of Estates Act has a rule on a surviving cohabitant's right to take possession of the former joint dwelling and household goods;
  - The Danish Insurance Contracts Act allows a cohabitant to be a beneficiary under the heading of 'next of kin';
  - The Danish Liability and Compensation Act states that a surviving partner will be compensated for the loss of the breadwinner.

ENGLAND AND WALES

Informal cohabiting relationships between both different and same-sex couples are recognised in a number of legal contexts but on a piecemeal basis, with different definitions of who will be recognised as cohabiting applying in different situations and to different degrees in England and Wales. Providing the couple are each over 16 years of age (the age of consent to sexual intercourse), they will normally be able to access remedies available to cohabitants unless there is a more general reason for not permitting this (e.g. the minimum age for making an adoption application is 21). However a partner who is under 18 may need leave (permission) of the court, or may need an adult to take the legal action on their behalf. In some contexts, cohabitants are treated as identical to married couples and civil partners. In others, they are considered similar but have inferior rights and remedies. In yet other contexts, cohabitants are treated as completely separate and unrelated individuals. This situation causes confusion for those affected, who often falsely believe that cohabitants are treated as married in all contexts. This is sometimes referred to as the 'common law marriage' myth.[23]

The contexts where there is recognition are listed below:

- Means-tested social security benefits and tax credits
  All means-tested social security benefits and tax credits treat cohabiting couples as if they were married or civil partnered (the so-called 'cohabitation rule'), assessing their financial eligibility and need together as a couple, even though there is no legal obligation between cohabitants to financially support each other.

  The main benefits and tax credits with governing legislation are:

  - Income Support, Housing Benefit & Council Tax Reduction – English Social Security Contributions and Benefits Act 1992;
  - Income-related Employment and Support Allowance – English Welfare Reform Act 2007;
  - Income-based Jobseeker's Allowance – English Jobseekers Act 1995;
  - Pension Credit – English State Pension Credit Act 2002;
  - Child Tax Credit & Working Tax Credit – English Tax Credits Act 2002;
  - Universal Credit – English Welfare Reform Act 2012.

  The legislation which governs each of these benefits takes a partner's income into account when assessing eligibility as if they were married or civil partnered. There are different but similar definitions of 'living together' for different benefits. The old terminology of 'living together as husband and wife in the same household' was developed in social security law (*Crake and Butterworth v SBC* 1980 (reported as SB/38)) which indicated that the fact that a man and a woman lived in the same household might raise the question as to whether they were living together as husband and wife but ruled that, in each case, it was necessary to find out why they lived in the same household. If there was an explanation which indicated that they were not there because they were living together as man and wife, they could not be so

[23] See further, A. Barlow and G. James, 'Regulating Marriage and Cohabitation in 21st Century Britain', *Modern Law Review*, Vol. 67, No. 2, 2004, pp. 143-176; A. Barlow, S. Duncan, G. James and A. Park, *Cohabitation, Marriage and the Law: Social Change and Legal Reform in the 21st Century*, Hart Publishing, Oxford, 2005; N. Lowe and G. Douglas, *Bromley's Family Law*, Oxford University Press, Oxford, 2015, at chapter 24.

described for supplementary benefits purposes (paragraph 7). The phrase was extended to 'living together as civil partners in the same household' following the English Civil Partnership Act 2004 and the test now refers more generally to 'living together as a couple in the same household'.

This approach has also been adopted in the Tax Credit legislation without further definitions or guidance. A 'couple' is defined as follows in S. 3(3) English Tax Credits Act 2002 which states that a claim for a tax credit may be made:

> '(a) jointly by the members of a couple both of whom are aged at least sixteen and are in the United Kingdom ...'

The Act then goes on, in Section 3(5), to define a 'couple' as:

> '(a) a man and woman who are married to each other and are neither –
> i. separated under a court order, nor
> ii. separated in circumstances in which the separation is likely to be permanent,
> (b) a man and woman who are not married to each other but are living together as husband and wife,
> (c) two people of the same sex who are civil partners of each other and are neither
> i. separated under a court order, nor
> ii. separated in circumstances in which the separation is likely to be permanent, or
> (d) two people of the same sex who are not civil partners of each other but are living together as if they were civil partners.'

The tax authority (HMRC) state in their manuals[24] that they will use the criteria adopted by the Department for Work and Pensions (DWP) which administers social security for the purpose of deciding if a couple are living as husband and wife or as civil partners which include looking for the presence of one or more of the following:

- Living in the same household;
- Stability of relationship;
- Financial support;

---

24 HMRC have four manuals which provide online guidance on the legislation. See for example, HMRC Tax Credits Claimant Compliance Manual, Section CCM15040, 'Undisclosed Partners: Couples who are Unmarried and not Civil Partners', available at www.hmrc.gov.uk/manuals/ccmmanual/CCM15040.htm.

- Dependent children;
- Public acknowledgement of the couple relationship;
- Sexual relationship.

- Domestic violence
  In this context, cohabiting couples are treated the same as married couples and civil partners in terms of personal protection, but legislation provides them with an inferior remedy in terms of regulation of occupation rights in the family home, unless the applicant is considered an 'entitled applicant' because they own, or jointly own, the family home or are a renting tenant or joint renting tenant of the home.

  The English Family Law Act 1996 Part IV extends domestic violence remedies of non-molestation orders and occupation orders to 'Associated Persons'. Section 62(3) Family Law Act 1996 defines this concept to include cohabitants:

  > 'For the purposes of this Part, a person is associated with another person if
  > ...
  > b) they are cohabitants or former cohabitants.'

  Cohabitants are defined in S. 62(1) as follows:

  > '(a) "cohabitants" are two persons who are neither married to each other nor civil partners of each other but are living together as husband and wife or as if they were civil partners;
  > (b) "cohabit" and "former cohabitants" are to be read accordingly, but the latter expression does not include cohabitants who have subsequently married each other or become civil partners of each other.'

  In the domestic violence context, children (including those between 16 and 18 years of age who may be a cohabiting partner) can apply for non-molestation or occupation orders only with leave of the court (S. 43 English Family Law Act 1996). The court has power to deal with the matter as a child protection issue within such family proceedings.

- Statutory wrongful death suits
  Here remedies for a bereaved cohabiting partner are available and may be the same as for married couples as in the English Pneumoconiosis (Workers' Compensation) Act 1979. This requires eligible claimants to be 'a reputed spouse who was residing with the deceased' (S. 3(c)).

There is no minimum duration of that relationship specified.

However, S. 1(3) English Fatal Accidents Act 1976, as amended, which provides for compensation for negligent deaths, requires an eligible cohabitant partner to show that they – 'lived in the same household with the deceased for a period of at least two years immediately before the death as the husband or wife (or as the civil partner) of the deceased'.

A specified minimum duration of the cohabitation relationship of two years is applied here. Furthermore, unlike married and civil partner couples, cohabiting couples are excluded from the bereavement damages aspect of the claim (which provides compensation for loss of companionship with their deceased partner). Cohabitants therefore have an inferior remedy.

- Succession to rented tenancies of the family home
  Here the rights and remedies vary according to the category of rented tenancy which applies to the family home. Broadly, tenancies granted in the private housing sector are governed by different legislation to those granted by local authorities in the public sector. Much social housing is now provided in the independent sector with different rules again. The rules governing a cohabiting partner's eligibility to succeed to their deceased partner's tenancy therefore depends on which category of tenancy the family home falls into and whether a minimum duration of the cohabitation is required to have taken place in the home prior to the tenant's death.[25]

  English Private Rent Act tenancies (of which there are now very few remaining) are governed by Schedule 1 to the English Rent Act 1977 as amended and private/independent sector 'assured' or 'assured shorthold' tenancies are governed by the English Housing Act 1988.

  Here, in both cases, cohabitants are given identical rights to married and civil partner couples irrespective of the duration of the relationship.

[25] For further detail on different-sex cohabitants, see A. BARLOW, *Cohabitants and the Law*, Butterworths, London, 2001, at chapter 3; More generally, see A. ARDEN, A. DYMOND and C. HUNTER, *Manual of Housing Law*, Sweet & Maxwell, London, 2012.

A cohabitant is included within words 'spouse' and 'civil partner' which consequently entitles them to succeed to a statutory tenancy under Schedule 1 to the English Rent Act 1977:

> '2(1). The surviving spouse or surviving civil partner (if any) of the original tenant, if residing in the dwelling-house immediately before the death of the original tenant, shall, after the death, be the statutory tenant if and so long as he or she occupies the dwelling-house as his or her residence.
> 2(2). For the purpose of this paragraph,
> (a) a person who was living with the original tenant as his or her wife or husband shall be treated as the spouse of the original tenant, and
> (b) a person who was living with the original tenant as if they were civil partners shall be treated as the civil partner of the original tenant.'

Cohabitants are similarly able to succeed to a private or independent sector 'assured periodic' tenancy (or in principle also to a short fixed term 'assured shorthold' tenancy which has little security of tenure) governed by S. 17 English Housing Act 1988 as amended, regardless of the duration of the relationship:

> 'For the purposes of this section—
> (a) a person who was living with the tenant as his or her wife or husband shall be treated as the tenant's spouse, and
> (b) a person who was living with the tenant as if they were civil partners shall be treated as the tenant's civil partner.'

In the case of a secure tenancy granted by a local authority and governed by S. 87 English Housing Act 1985 however, the surviving cohabitant partner is required to have - lived together 'as husband and wife' or 'as civil partners' for a period of 12 months in the property with the deceased as their only or principal home to be eligible to succeed to the tenancy. There is no time qualification period for spouses or civil partners to succeed. These same rules apply to succession to local authority or independent sector Introductory Tenancies under S. 131 & 140(1) English Housing Act 1996.

- Homelessness legislation
  The homelessness legislation in the English Housing Act 1996 Part VII, as amended, places a statutory duty on local authorities to find accommodation for those not intentionally homeless and their families where appropriate. This defines a member of the family (S. 178(3)) to include spouses and civil partners and those who 'live

together as husband and wife or as if they were civil partners' and provides identical rights to those who are formally married or civil partnered. It imposes no minimum duration qualification period for the relationship.

- Inheritance
  Under the English Inheritance (Provision for Family and Dependants) Act 1975, as amended, cohabitants are eligible to apply for reasonable financial provision (limited to what is reasonable for their maintenance) from the estate of a deceased cohabiting partner whether different-sex or same-sex provided they lived for a period of two years prior to the date of the partner's death in the same household as the deceased as their husband or wife or as their civil partner (S. 1A & 1B). This remedy is inferior to that of spouses and civil partners whose claim is not limited to what is reasonable for their maintenance and is likely to be more generous where assets are available under the estate and is generally in line with the financial provision which would be provided on divorce or dissolution of the formal relationship.

- Adoption
  Different and same-sex cohabiting couples are eligible to adopt a child in England and Wales provided they are over 21 (except where one of them is the parent of the child, in which case that partner need only be 18).

  Section 144(4)(b) English Adoption and Children Act 2002 defines a couple as:

  > 'two people (whether of different sexes or the same sex) living as partners in an enduring family relationship.'

  There is no requirement that the couple should be living in the same household and so the provision extends beyond cohabitants and could for example include couples Living Apart Together. There is also no statutory definition of 'enduring family relationship' but the adoption agency will be concerned to ensure that there is a stable relationship which has been in existence for some time and is likely to last.[26] In *Re T and M (Adoption)* [2010] EWHC (Fam) 964, [2011] 1 FLR

[26] The Suitability of Adopters Regulations 2005 (SI 2005/1712) state that in the case of any couple, the adoption agency must have regard to the need for stability and permanence

1487, a case concerning the application by a lesbian partner to adopt her partner's child with whom (for reasons relating to issues around the child's unusual health issues) she was not residing, Mr Justice Hedley indicated in his judgment that what was required to fall within the definition was firstly, an unambiguous intention to create and maintain a family life and secondly, a factual matrix consistent with that intention.

In none of these situations where the law recognises the informal cohabiting relationship does legislation specifically exclude a cohabitant who remains married or civil partnered to a former partner from the definition of cohabitant. However, this fact may in some circumstances influence the court which may, in the exercise of its discretion, decide to deny them the remedy applied for.

Living Apart Together couple relationships where there is no cohabitation within a joint household are not recognised as an informal family relationship as such in England and Wales. Such couples are not regulated in any specific way. They are generally treated as two separate, unrelated individuals. However, domestic violence personal protection remedies, such as the non-molestation order in S. 42 English Family Law Act 1996 may extend to them if they are 'associated' under S. 62 English Family Law Act 1996, as this includes couples who 'have or have had an intimate personal relationship with each other which is or was of significant duration'.

If there is financial dependency of one partner on the other and this can be proved, the dependant partner may be an eligible applicant who is then able to make a claim for financial provision (limited to maintenance) on the death of the other partner from the deceased partner's estate under the English Inheritance (Provision for Family and Dependants) Act 1975.

If they are judged to be living as partners in 'an enduring family relationship', they may also be eligible to adopt as a couple under the English Adoption and Children Act 2002.

---

in their relationship. See further LOWE and DOUGLAS, *Bromley's Family Law*, Oxford University Press, Oxford, 2015, at p. 705-6.

ESTONIA

There is no special law in Estonian legislation that would regulate informal relationships. Up until the adoption of the Estonian Registered Partnership Act in 2014, Estonian laws lacked alternative opportunities to acknowledge family relationships other than a marriage. An exceptional legislative reference to an informal relationship was made in Decree no. 82 of the Government of the Republic in 1999, now already repealed, clause 39.15 of which read 'Approval of the roll-call questionnaire, forms of roll-call sheets and the roll-call rules for the roll-call of people and their dwellings in the year 2000',[27] according to which a person who was not in a legal marriage, but rather in a self-determined marital relationship with his/her cohabitant and had a common place of residence with his/her cohabitant was considered as being in cohabitation.

In its decision on 3 December 2014, the Supreme Court of the Republic of Estonia emphasised that extramarital relationships do not entail similar obligations as those resulting from a marriage, including the fact that the parties are not subject to mutual support and arrangements concerning the common household, in contrast to the situation of spouses according to Estonian Family Law Act § 15.[28]

If we first look at the Constitution of the Republic of Estonia,[29] the family as a fundamental aspect in the preservation and growth of the nation, and being the foundation of society, enjoys the protection of the government. The protection referred to in subsection 1 § 27 of the Estonian Constitution extends to the citizens of Estonia and to the citizens of a foreign state who are currently residing in Estonia, as well as to stateless persons (Estonian Consitution § 9).[30] Neither the Estonian Constitution nor any other legal acts of Estonia have defined the term 'family'. The family as referred to in the Estonian Constitution undoubtedly comprises the relations between a man and a woman in an official marriage. The Administrative Law Chamber of the Supreme Court stated in its decision of June 19, 2000,[31] that subsection 1 of § 27 of the Estonian Constitution also protects a family cohabitation between a man and a woman, which is not that which is prescribed under the law,

---

27 RT I 1999, 32, 431 (in Estonian), repealed by RT I 2006, 38, 289.

28 Decision of the Civil Chamber of the Supreme Court 3-2-1-109-14, at para. 14.

29 Eesti Vabariigi Põhiseadus (adopted on 28 June 1992, entered into force on 3 July 1992). - RT 1992, 26, 349; RT I, 27.04.2011, 2 (in Estonian), available in English at: www.riigiteataja.ee/en/eli/530102013003/consolide.

30 Decision of the Supreme Court 3-4-1-9-04, at para. 13.

31 Decision of the Administrative Law Chamber of the Supreme Court 3-3-1-16-00, at para. 1.

from groundless interventions by the state. The Estonian Consitution's § 7(5) obliges the family to provide for those family members who are in need. In its decision of January 21, 2004, the Supreme Court[32] stated that the Estonian Social Welfare Act[33] extends the meaning of a family member to persons jointly spending one or more sources of revenue or sharing a common household, but the Court did not deal more closely with the effect of this act for maintenance obligations.

In clauses 40-41 of its decision of May 5, 2014,[34] the Constitutional Review Chamber of the Supreme Court found that the second sentence of section 2 of § 22 of the Estonian Social Welfare Act provides a definition of the family for the purpose of granting subsistence benefits. According to this definition, persons who are married or living in the same household in a conjugal relationship, their children and their parents who are in need of assistance or other persons jointly using one or more sources of income or with a shared household are deemed to be family members. Two conditions must be met for determining that the income is considered to be family income pursuant to the second sentence of the Estonian Social Welfare Act § 22(2). Firstly, persons must live in the same dwelling and, secondly, they must use the source of income jointly or they must have a shared household. Thus, the right to receive a subsistence benefit pursuant to sections 1 and 2 of § 22 of the Estonian Social Welfare Act very much depends on the actual facts. If disputes over these facts arise that would exclude the right to receive a subsistence benefit, the burden of proof must in general rest with the administrative authority. Thus, no legal prerequisite can be derived from § 22(2) of the Estonian Social Welfare Act that people who live together automatically provide maintenance to each other, and the Estonian Social Welfare Act certainly does not oblige them to do so.

At the same time, this provision only regulates subsistence benefits and cannot be extended to other cases. It was stressed in the analysis concerning the obligations of the family with regard to family members in need of assistance, compiled by the Ministry of Justice and the Ministry of Social Affairs, that although the Estonian Constitution allows for the establishment of an obligation to assist family members who find it difficult to cope, this does not mean that a family member has,

[32] Decision of the Supreme Court 3-4-1-7-03, at para. 18.
[33] Sotsiaalhoolekande seadus (adopted on 8 February 1995, entered into force on 1 April 1995). – RT I 1995, 21, 323; RT I, 13.12.2014, 44 (in Estonian), available in English at: www.riigiteataja.ee/en/eli/ee/Riigikogu/act/509072014019/consolide.
[34] Decision of the Supreme Court 3-4-1-67-13.

pursuant to this provision, a legal commitment to assist family members who are in need of assistance. For a legal commitment to arise, the legislature must establish this commitment in another law.[35] This analysis refers to the fact that a legal commitment to pay for social services lies only with those family members who have the obligation to assist the member of the family who is in need of assistance under the Estonian Family Law Act. This means that only spouses and direct blood relatives can be required to pay for social services. The pertinent legal acts have not imposed such an obligation on the cohabitant of the person needing assistance and so the cohabitant is not legally obliged to pay for the necessary social services of his or her partner.

However, direct references to informal relationships can nevertheless be found in different legal acts. These are mainly legal acts of a public law nature, primarily norms of procedural law. The norms which apply to the partners in the named informal relationship do not directly regulate the non-marital cohabitation as such, but are mainly intended to avoid a conflict of interests: the partners in an informal relationship are considered to be persons who are close to the person performing certain acts.[36] Not much attention has been paid to informal relationships in the legal literature[37] and a more profound research, before the analysis of the Ministry of Justice in 2009,[38] dates back to the year 2002.[39] Back then the authors were of the opinion that there was no direct need for the possible supplementary regulation of informal relationships or the inclusion of an informal relationship as an independent status in the pertinent legislation. The authors reached the conclusion that in 2002 cohabitation was not an entirely extrajudicial or unregulated phenomenon in Estonian civil law, but in reaching this conclusion they still took account of the possibilities of the cohabiting couple to regulate mutual relations in transactions. In the opinion of the authors, considering the different types of informal relationships which existed, a large degree of flexibility

---

[35] A. HENBERG, K. MULLER and A. ALEKAND, 'Perekonna kohustused abi vajavate pereliikmete ees', Justiitsministeerium /Sotsiaalministeerium, 2012, available at: digar.nlib.ee/digar/show/?id=120309.

[36] A. OLM, 'Mitteabieluline kooselu ja selle õiguslik regulatsioon', Justiitsministeerium, Õiguspoliitika osakond, Eraõiguse talitus, Tallinn, 2009, at para. 3.4. It can be understood from the position of A. Olm that the Estonian legislator also still refers to an informal relationship, but a direct reference in the legislation is lacking.

[37] A. OLM, 'Non-married Cohabiting Couples and Their Constitutional', *Juridica International*, 2013, No. 1, pp. 104-111.

[38] A. OLM, 'Mitteabieluline kooselu ja selle õiguslik regulatsioon', Justiitsministeerium, Õiguspoliitika osakond, Eraõiguse talitus, Tallinn, 2009, at para. 3.4.

[39] K. KAMA and K. KULLERKUP, 'Vabaabielu versus abielu: varalised suhted muutuvate kooseluvormide kontekstis', *Juridica*, 2002, No. 6, pp. 359-368.

should possibly be maintained in the case of a separate regulation concerning different forms of cohabitation. This could be attained by the application of the general provisions of civil law, under which it is always possible to assess the nature of a specific relationship. The Estonian Family Law Act does not prescribe a special regulation in the case of an informal relationship, and also after the adoption of the Estonian Registered Partnership Act the legal relations between couples living in an informal relationship, who do not want to confirm their partnership by concluding a registered partnerhip agreement and entering it in the register, have not changed. The legal literature and judicial practice are in agreement that the principles of marital proprietary rights cannot be directly extended to informal relationships, and according to the valid legal regulation there can be no analogous extension of the proprietary rights emanating from a marriage to an informal relationship.

Also, the Ministry of Social Affairs published the results of a research project in 2008 which concerned couples living in an informal relationship,[40] but this was mostly a socio-political analysis.

FINLAND

There are over 70 statutes across all administrative sectors which include references to cohabiting couples, but whose focus is not on the legal effects of cohabitation *per se*. However, in 2011 Parliament accepted an Act that concentrates particularly on the rights and obligations of cohabiting partners. The Finnish Act on the Dissolution of the Household of Cohabiting Partners (later referred to as the Finnish Cohabitation Act) came into force on 1 April 2011. Due to the large number of specific provisions and the extent of variations across specific areas of the law, the following comments are restricted to the Finnish Cohabitation Act. Further comments concerning the definitions involved in the various areas of the law are made under Question 4.

The Finnish Cohabitation Act regulates issues of property law and procedure related to the separation of a cohabiting couple. It applies both to situations where the dissolution is based on separation as well as the death of the spouse. The Finnish Cohabitation Act contains a specific definition of cohabitation to be applied in the context of the Act. It is

---

[40] L. JÄRVISTE, K. KASEARU and A. REINOMÄGI, 'Abielu ja vaba kooselu: trendid, regulatsioonid, hoiakud, Poliitikauuringute Keskus Praxis', Sotsiaalministeerium, Tallinn, 2008, available (in Estonian) at: digar.nlib.ee/digar/show/?id=31418.

recognised in the rationale of the Act that other definitions do and may exist. The Finnish Cohabitation Act is non-mandatory in nature, i.e. derogations from almost all of the provisions of the Act are allowed, if this has been agreed upon by the partners.

According to the Finnish Cohabitation Act, the concept of cohabiting partners refers to partners who live in a relationship (a cohabiting partnership) in a shared household and who have lived in a shared household for at least five years or who have, or have had, a common child or joint parental responsibility for a child. A person who is married or in a registered partnership cannot, however, be deemed to be a cohabiting partner. Cohabiting partners can be either of a different sex or the same sex. Not having attained the age of majority does not disqualify the couple from the application of the Act. However, as is stated in the rationale for the Act, a cohabiting partner who has not attained the age of majority and wishes to enter into legally valid agreements on the property consequences related to the partnership may require a legal guardian for doing so according to the Finnish Guardianship Services Act (442/1999).

FRANCE

Informal relationships as '*concubinage*' are only defined in Art. 515-8 of the French Civil Code (see under Question 1). '*Concubinage*' is also mentioned in different kinds of statutes such as the French Civil Code, the French Judicial Code, the French Social Security Code, the French Labour Code or the French Social Welfare and Family Code. Numerous rights are recognised for partners living together, especially in social security law.

Some examples can be provided:

- The 'recognised partner' (*concubin notoire*) can request the benefit of the transfer of a residential lease if the other partner dies or leaves the dwelling, subject to the condition that they had lived together for at least one year (Art. 14 of Law Act no. 89-462 of 6 July 1989).[41] In

[41] Comp. ECtHR, *Kozak v. Poland*, No. 13102/02, 2.3.2010: In deciding the applicant's claim to be entitled to succeed to a tenancy, the domestic courts had concentrated almost exclusively on the homosexual nature of his relationship with his partner, concluding that, since Polish law did not recognise same-sex marriages, a *de facto* marital relationship could only exist between a man and a woman. In its choice of means to protect traditional families, the State had to take into account developments and changes in society, including the fact that there was not just one way or one choice in the sphere of leading and living one's family and private life. Given the State's narrow margin of appreciation in cases of a difference in treatment on the basis of sexual orientation, a blanket exclusion of persons living in a homosexual relationship from succession to a tenancy could not be considered acceptable.

contrast to spouses, partners in an informal relationship are not *ex lege* joint holders of the lease.

- According to Art. 828 of the French Code of Civil Procedure, in proceedings before the first-instance civil courts *juridiction de proximité* and *tribunal d'instance*,[42] a party can be represented or assisted by several persons, in particular their '*concubin*' (partner) or the person with whom they have entered into a PACS. These changes were introduced by Law Act no. 2007-1787 of 20 December 2007.
- In the field of social security benefits, the partner (*concubin)* is treated in the same way as a spouse. According to Art. L. 161-14 of the French Social Security Code,[43] for example, the partner who lives together with a person covered by social security, and is effectively maintained by this person, can benefit from this social insurance.[44] With regard to child benefit (*allocations familiales*), partners living together also have the same rights as married parents.
- With regard to the death of a partner after an industrial accident, Art. L. 434-8 of the French Social Security Code states that the surviving spouse, partner (*concubin)* or PACS partner is entitled to a life pension (*rente viagère).*[45] However, in the case of a new marriage, a PACS or an informal relationship (*concubinage)* of the entitled partner, the life pension ceases (Art. L. 434-9).[46] Although some exceptions are provided when certain conditions apply if there are common children).
- Since Law Act no. 2011-814 of 7 July 2011 (Art. L. 1231-1 of the French Social Welfare and Family Code), it is now possible for a person who has lived together with the recipient for at least two years to donate an organ for his or her benefit. The same applies to any person who can prove the existence of a close and stable relationship with the recipient for at least two years.
- Assisted reproduction is not only available for spouses, but also for a man and a woman bound by a PACS or living together as *concubins*[47] (see Art. 311-20 of the French Civil Code and Art. L. 2141-1 et seq.

[42] The same applies before the Labour court (Art. R. 1453-2 of the French Labour Code) and the court for rural leases (Art. 884 French Code of Civil Procedure) etc. Before all these courts, the proceedings are oral and the parties are not under a duty to be represented by a lawyer. Before the Commercial court, the parties can be assisted or represented by 'any person of their choice' (Art. 853 French Code of Civil Procedure).

[43] Law Act no. 93-121 of 27 January 1993.

[44] This applies for health insurance as well as for maternity benefit.

[45] Law Act no. 2011-1906 of 21 December 2011.

[46] The right to a life pension can be reactivated under some conditions if the new marriage, PACS or *concubinage* comes to an end.

[47] Before Law Act no. 2011-814 of 7 July 2011, the *concubins* had to establish that they had been living together for at least two years. This requirement has now been deleted.

Social Welfare and French Family Code).[48] *Concubins,* however, cannot adopt a child jointly.

By contrast, a widow(er)'s allowance (in the form of a retirement pension) is only paid to the surviving *spouse*[49] (see Art. L. 353-1 of the French Social Security Code and Art. 48 *Code des pensions civiles et militaires* (French Code of civil and military pensions for civil servants and persons in military service)).[50] Recently, the Court of cassation[51] has confirmed that the protection of marriage is an important and legitimate reason which can justify different treatment between married and non-married couples. The couple can choose freely to enter into a marriage or a registered partnership (*libre choix des intéressés*). By limiting the possibility to claim a widow(er)'s allowance to a spouse, Art. L. 353-1 of the French Social Security Code simply applies the consequences of a civil status specifically characterised by the legislator, so that the different treatment between married and non–married persons in respect of social rights is based on an '*objective criterion*'. According to the Court of cassation, this legal solution does not violate Art. 1 of the First Protocol to the ECHR nor Art. 14 ECHR.

In tax law, partners have to complete separate income tax returns; a common child has to be mentioned in the tax return of only one partner (if they have several common children, the partners can agree that one child will be declared by partner A and the other child by partner B. This may have interesting consequences since the parent including a child in his or her tax return receives some fiscal reductions). Property tax (*taxe foncière)* must be paid by the partner who is the owner of the property. If the partners have bought a property together, they are joint debtors of the property tax. The local residence tax (*taxe d'habitation*) has to be paid by the partner who is the leaseholder. By contrast, Art. 885 E of the French Tax Code states that in the case of a recognised *concubinage*, the tax base for the wealth tax (*impôt de solidarité sur la fortune*) takes all the property of both partners and their minor children into account.

---

48 According to the Constitutional council (CC, 17 May 2013, no. 2013-669), the principle of equality does not require in this respect that same-sex partners should be treated in the same way.

49 Cass. Civ. II, 23 January 2014, no. 13-11362, *RTD civ.* 2014, p. 342.

50 The surviving spouse or ex-spouse entitled to the widow(er)'s pension loses this right upon his or her remarriage or '*concubinage notoire*' (recognised cohabitation), Art. 49 of the French Code of civil and military pensions.

51 Cass. Civ. II, 23 January 2014, no. 13-11362, *Bull. Civ.* II, no. 23.

GERMANY

Despite growing social acceptance of unmarried cohabitation, there are no statutory rules in family law dealing with the effect of non-marital cohabitation between two parties.

The law gives only partial recognition to cohabitation in specified areas of the law (for example, a right to succeed to a tenancy upon the death of the tenant, § 563 para. 2 s. 4 of the German Civil Code). According to a special provision there can be a restriction or refusal of maintenance after divorce for gross inequity (§ 1579 German Civil Code). A maintenance claim is to be refused, reduced or restricted in time where the person entitled lives in a stable long-term relationship (*verfestigte Lebensgemeinschaft;* § 1579 No. 2 German Civil Code).

In social security law in general, a cohabitant does not hold the same position as a spouse. However, in the case of means-tested, family-based social security benefits, the resources of a cohabitant may be taken into account. The purpose of these provisions is mainly to equate an informal relationship and marriage within the framework of social security benefits. An unmarried applicant must not be in a better position than a married person.[52] This is especially the case if one of the cohabitants makes a social assistance claim. § 20 German Social Security Law (*Sozialgesetzbuch*) XII concerns a 'community similar to marriage' (*eheähnliche Gemeinschaft*).[53] In § 39 German Social Security Law XII there is a presumption that where the applicant lives together with another person, he or she will get benefits for his or her support according to the income and means of this person.

Since 2006 there has been a general definition in § 7 para. 3 No. 3c German Social Security Law II in the framework of a 'community of needs' (*Bedarfsgemeinschaft*). This refers to a situation where the cohabitants live together in a common household in such a way that it can be reasonably assumed that there is a reciprocal will to be responsible for each other and to support the partner (*Verantwortungs- und Einstehensgemeinschaft*). This definition makes the application of the law easier for the social security authorities.[54]

---

52 P. UDSCHING, 'Sozialrecht', in: R. HAUSMANN and G. HOHLOCH (eds.), *Das Recht der nichtehelichen Lebensgemeinschaft*, E. Schmidt, Berlin, 2004, at p. 639, No. 1 et seq.

53 Former §§ 16, 122 Federal Social Assistance Act (Bundessozialhilfegesetz; BSHG).

54 See M. LÖHNIG, 'Anh. zu §§ 1297 et seq.', in: J. VON STAUDINGER, *Kommentar zum Bürgerlichen Gesetzbuch,* Sellier-de-Gruyter, Berlin, 2012, at No. 14, p. 269.

As regards housing benefits, the household members (*Haushaltsmitglieder*) of the applicant are specifically defined. These include spouses and registered partners as well as persons who live together with the applicant such that it can be reasonably assumed that there is a reciprocal will to be responsible for and support each other, § 5 para. 1 No. 3 German Housing Benefits Law (*Wohngeldgesetz*).[55] Such a reciprocal commitment is presumed if at least one of the four requirements of § 7 para. 3 No. 3c German Social Security Law is met (§ 5 para. 2 German Housing Benefits Law).

There is no statutory provision clarifying whether an informal relationship or a *de facto* community exists where one of the involved partners is married to another person or is a registered partner of another person. Some authors argue that such a *de facto* community may also exist under these circumstances.[56] There is case law supporting this view; however, it originates from the field of social assistance where the income of a married partner has been taken into account for the receipt of social security benefits.[57] In these situations only the factual circumstances which affect the income are relevant.

In tax law, especially in income tax law, a cohabitant is in principle not recognised as a family member. However, particularly in cases of modest means, maintenance for the partner is recognised as an exceptional cost (*außergewöhnliche Belastung*) in the sense of § 33a German Income Tax Law (*Einkommensteuergesetz*; EStG).[58]

GREECE

Informal relationships of cohabitation involving persons of the same or different gender, who do not opt to crystallise their relationship in one of the legal forms (engagement, marriage, agreement on cohabitation between heterosexual partners) available in Greek law, are not subject to any particular legal provision. In fact, such a provision does not exist. According to the country's Supreme Court (Areios Pagos), these

---

55 Housing Benefits Law (Wohngeldgesetz) of 24.9.2008, BGBl. I, p. 1856, as amended.

56 G. BRUDERMÜLLER, 'Einl. vor § 1297', in: O. PALANDT, *Bürgerliches Gesetzbuch*, Beck, Munich, 2015, at No. 11; M. WELLENHOFER, 'Anh. zu § 1302', in: *Münchener Kommentar zum Bürgerlichen Gesetzbuch*, Beck, Munich, 2013, at No. 4.

57 See for § 122 BSHG Administrative Court (Verwaltungsgerichtshof; VGH) Mannheim, 28.4.1993 *NJW*, 1993, 2886; Higher Administrative Court (Oberverwaltungsgericht; OVG) Hamburg, 23.8.1995, *NJW*, 1996, 1225.

58 Federal Fiscal Court (Bundesfinanzhof; BFH), 17.12.2009, *FamRZ*, 2010, 902 = *NJW*, 2010, 1838.

relationships, which the Court has described as atypical or irregular, are located on the margins of legal life.

Of course the parallel existence (even if inactive) of another formal relationship with a third party, such as a marriage, may be socially acceptable but will have adverse consequences: there will be grounds for divorce or a reasonable suspension of conjugal cohabitation.

The Greek Supreme Court has consistently ruled that in the event of a tort against one of the partners, resulting in his or her death, there can be no claim by the surviving partner for damages for emotional distress, pursuant to Art. 932 para. 1 of the Greek Civil Code, the view being taken that a family whose members would be entitled to such compensation under the law does not, in this case, exist.[59] It is significant that Art. 5 of Law 3500/2006 on protection against domestic violence does grant a victim who is not married, but is a member of a free union, a claim for damages, under Art. 932 para. 1 of the Greek Civil Code, for an amount of at least 1,000 Euro.

HUNGARY

There is one informal relationship between a couple in Hungarian law, this is cohabitation. Cohabitation is regulated in the Hungarian Civil Code within the framework of two Books. The general rules on cohabitation are included in the Sixth Book (Book on the Law of Obligations) and the so-called family law consequences are regulated in the Family Law Book.

The Sixth Book regulates cohabitation as a special contract. The Third Part of this Book is on special contracts and cohabitation is included under the last title, namely Title XXV. Cohabitation can be found between civil law companies (Title XXIV) and the Fourth Part on torts, in Art 6:514-517. These provisions contain the definition of cohabitation including a reference to the fact that cohabitation is a factual relationship, and if the conceptual elements of the definition are present then cohabitation exists, while if the community of life terminates the cohabitation then ceases.[60] Cohabitants may enter into a cohabitants' property agreement[61] but also a default property regime is regulated.[62] The essential rules on a property agreement resemble those of the

59 See Supreme Court - Areios Pagos, judgment Nos. 21/2000, 486/2011, 775/2011.
60 Art. 6:514(1)-(2) Hungarian Civil Code.
61 Art. 6:515(1)-(4) Hungarian Civil Code.
62 Art. 6:516(1)-(4) Hungarian Civil Code.

matrimonial property agreement regulated in the Family Law Book but the default property regime distinctly differs from the default matrimonial property regime. The last issue to be regulated in the Book on the Law of Obligations concerning cohabitation concerns the partners' agreement on the use of the common dwelling after the termination of the cohabitation.[63] These Articles cover all relationships which exist as cohabitation.

The provisions concerning cohabitants in the Family Law Book may only be invoked in special circumstances. Following the detailed rules on marriage in the Second Part of the Family Law Book, the Third Part provides some regulations on the so-called family law consequences of cohabitation. It consists of two titles, the first is on the maintenance of cohabitants which concerns the maintenance obligation of the former cohabitant[64] and the second is on the judicial arrangement of the use of the common dwelling after the termination of the cohabitation.[65] The right to maintenance depends upon the duration of the cohabitation and it must have lasted for at least one year and having a common child; the regulations resemble those which are applicable to the maintenance of a former spouse. The same requirements, namely cohabitation for at least a year and a common child play a role if one cohabitant intends to request a judicial arrangement on the use of the common dwelling. These rules are also mainly based upon the model for the use of the matrimonial home after divorce.

Concerning the effective rules it has to be emphasised that the old regime for cohabitation is also being applied by the judiciary during the transitional period. The Act on Transitory Regulations in Connection with the Hungarian Civil Code[66] provides that the rules which were effective before March 2014 are to be applied to obligations which already existed when the (new) Civil Code entered into force. Henceforth, the old rules have to be applied in the case of cohabitation which came into existence before March 2014.

Cohabitation was regulated in the Civil Code of 1959 in a somewhat laconic way before March 2014.[67] One provision provided a definition of

63 Art. 6:517(1)-(3) Hungarian Civil Code.
64 Art. 4:86-91 Hungarian Civil Code.
65 Art. 4:92-95 Hungarian Civil Code.
66 Act No. CLXXVII. 2013.
67 O. SZEIBERT-ERDŐS, 'Unmarried Partnerships in Hungary', in: K. BOELE-WOELKI (ed.), *Common Core and Better Law in European Family Law*, Intersentia, Antwerp, 2005, at pp. 313-333.

cohabitation while another prescribed the default property regime for cohabitants which differed from that of today.

Cohabitation may exist (also legally) if one partner is married to or is the registered partner of a third party or if both of them have a valid marriage or a registered partnership with third and fourth parties. Nevertheless, two communities of life cannot co-exist in a legally recognised way. The existence of a mere matrimonial bond without a matrimonial community of life on either cohabitant's side[68] does not exclude their qualification as cohabitants but if there is also a matrimonial community of life or a community of life with a registered partner no cohabitation exists. Both in the case of marriage and a registered partnership the community of life is presumed *ex officio*.

REPUBLIC OF IRELAND

Cohabitants were not recognised in Irish law in any way prior to the introduction of the Irish Civil Partnership and Certain Rights and Obligations of Cohabitants Act 2010. Part 15 of this Act covers situations where one cohabitant wishes to claim in the courts against the other, upon the termination of their relationship, for 'redress' either in the form of a compensatory maintenance order, a property adjustment order, a pension adjustment order or for an order for provision from the estate of the other cohabitant. In addition, S. 202 of the Act gives legal validity to agreements entered into by cohabitants to provide for financial matters during the relationship or when the relationship ends through death or otherwise.

Prior to the commencement of the Act, disputes following cohabitant relationship breakdown were not dealt with by family law legislation and couples who cohabited acquired no rights against each other. In particular, in the case of a property dispute between cohabiting couples, the parties were required, on failing to reach a compromise, to bring a claim in the civil courts by way of equitable proceedings under the Irish Partition Acts 1868-1876. Now, applications under the redress scheme for those who come within the definition of 'qualified cohabitants' are dealt with *in camera* in the family courts. It is worth noting, however, that the redress scheme merely provides a right to apply to court for relief and

[68] The same is true if the registered partnership exists as a mere bond without a community of life.

not an automatic entitlement to have one or more of the abovementioned orders made in the applicant's favour.

Disqualifying circumstances are oriented towards preventing certain couples from having access to the courts.

Those who do not come within the definition of 'cohabitants' include people who are already married to someone else (S. 172 (6) of the Irish 2010 Act), underage partners (i.e. persons under 18), people in incestuous relationships, and those who would be prohibited from marrying in the State (S. 172 (4) of the Irish 2010 Act).

ITALY

The Italian legal system does not provide for a comprehensive and consistent regulation of couples' relationships outside marriage. However, many specific legislative provisions refer expressly to informal relations, in most cases applying the same rules to partners in such relationships, as are applied to spouses. The principal provisions among these, with reference to the ones enacted most recently, may be listed as follows:[69]

- protection orders against family abuse (Art. 330, 333, 342 *bis* and 342 *ter* Italian Civil Code as modified or introduced by the law of 28 March 2001, n. 149 and the law of 5 April 2001, n. 154);
- measures for the protection of partially or entirely dependent persons (*amministrazione di sostegno*) (Art. 408, 410, 411 and 426 Italian Civil Code, as amended by the law of 9 January 2004, n. 6);
- access to medically assisted procreation (Art. 5 of the law of 19 February 2004, n. 40);
- rules on child custody in the case of the separation of their parents (Art. 4 of the law of 8 February 2006, n. 54);
- adoption. Adoption is only available to spouses who have been married for at least three years, but it is also possible for spouses who have been cohabiting for three years before marriage (text of Art. 6 of the law of 4 May 1983, n. 184 as substituted by the law of 29 March 2001, n. 149). In this case the relevance of the cohabitation is subject to the two partners ultimately marrying. In addition, the legal institution of 'adoption in particular cases' (Art. 44 of the same law) also

69 See G. OBERTO, *I diritti dei conviventi. Realtà e prospettive tra Italia ed Europa*, Cedam, Padua, 2012, at p. 26 et seq.; R. BASSETTI, *Contratti di convivenza e di unione civile*, Giappichelli, Turin, 2014, at p. 4 et seq.

explicitly allows persons who are not married to adopt. Cases which are considered to be 'particular' include: that of a child who is orphaned and the adopter is a relative within the sixth degree or is connected to the minor by a stable and lasting relationship which pre-existed the parent's death; that of an adoptee who is a disabled child and an orphan; that of a child for whom pre-adoptive foster care has proved to be impossible;
- parental leave (law of 8 March 2000, n. 53; Italian Legislative Decree 26 March 2001, n. 151);
- organ donation (law of 1 April 1999, n. 91);
- under Art. 1 of the law of 29 July 1975, n. 405 family counselling is available for those who require it, including '*de facto* couples';
- abortion (Art. 5 of the law of 22 May 1978, n. 194);
- civil responsibility for motorized vehicles (RCA) (Italian Legislative Decree 7 September 2005, n. 209);
- public housing schemes (*edilizia residenziale pubblica*) (law of 17 February 1992, n. 179);
- civil registry (*anagrafe*): regarding registration at the registry, a family is defined as 'a group of persons who are bound by marriage, kinship, affinity, adoption, guardianship, or affective bonds, who usually cohabit or dwell in the same municipality' (Art. 4, para. 1, Decree of the President of the Italian Republic 30 May 1989, n. 223);
- measures in favour of the victims of terrorism and organised crime (law of 20 October 1990, n. 302);
- criminal law rules dealing with family abuse (Art. 572 of the Italian Penal Code), the more general rules dealing with cases where the crime is aggravated by being committed within the family (Art. 61 n. 11 a) of the Italian Penal Code);
- criminal law concerning sexual violence (law of 15 February 1996, n. 66);
- rules in penal procedural law, especially Art. 199, para. 3 (a) of the Italian Code of Penal Procedure allowing the informal partner to avoid testifying as a witness);
- prison regulations (*ordinamento penitenziario*) (Art. 3, law of 26 July 1975, n. 354) allowing an inmate to be entitled to prison leave (*permesso di uscita*) in order to visit a relative or a cohabitant who is seriously ill;
- rules in tax law (Art. 37 para. 3 Decree of the President of the Italian Republic 29 September 1973 n. 600).

Several municipalities have introduced Registers of civil unions for *de facto* couples, both heterosexual and homosexual.[70] Such registers are aimed at proving the existence of cohabitation and at allowing the partners to have access to the benefits and assistance offered by the same municipality to married couples.

The existence of a marriage, the situation of being separated[71] or the minority status of a partner do not disqualify the couple.

LATVIA

Latvian national laws and other legislative acts do not contain a general legal order of informal relationship.

However, there are some separate legislative acts in which the legislature has regulated the legal status of two persons living together. For example, since 2009 the Latvian Criminal Procedure Law has contained the term 'immediate family' (*tuvinieki*) – a person with whom the relevant natural person is living together and with whom he or she has a common (joint) household.[72] This was proposed in 2008 by the Ministry of Justice, indicating that, in criminal procedure, a person with whom the relevant natural person is living together and has a common household can be considered as 'immediate family' (*tuvinieki*). For example, a family living in a cohabitation that has common children, but which has not registered their relationship according to the procedure prescribed by law for marriage, can be regarded as 'immediate family'. Therefore, it was stated that these people must have the same rights in criminal procedure as people living in a legal marriage.[73] Then, since 29 October 2014 the Latvian Criminal Law has stipulated that not only the betrothed, spouse, parents, children, brothers and sisters, grandparents and grandchildren of a person who has committed a crime (i.e. the accused), but also the person with whom the accused is living and with whom he or she has a common (joint) household, are not liable for previous unpromised

70 For instance, the municipality of Empoli (Florence) was the first to pass rules on this Register in 1993; Milan introduced this Register on 26 July 2012.

71 L. BALESTRA, 'La famiglia di fatto', in: G. FERRANDO (ed.), *Il nuovo diritto di famiglia*, Zanichelli, Bologna, 2008, at p. 1039.

72 Criminal Procedure Law: Law of the Republic of Latvia. Latvijas Vēstnesis, 11 May 2005., no. 74, at S. 12, Part 5.

73 Ministry of Justice letter No. 1-7.2/3609 of 13 August 2008 to Legal Affairs Committee of Saeima. Available at: titania.saeima.lv/LIVS/SaeimaLIVS.nsf/0/38b91523a30b8184c22574b00036ac5b/$FILE/2972-Jur.pdf.

concealment or failure to inform.[74] Likewise, the person with whom the accused is living and with whom he or she has a joint (single) household is not held liable for refusal to testify.[75]

Similarly, the Latvian Administrative Violations Code stipulates that a witness has the right to refuse to testify against the person with whom the relevant natural person is living and with whom he or she has a joint (single) household.[76] Also, more severe punishment is likely if intentional minor bodily injury is inflicted upon the person with whom the offender is in the first or second degree of kinship, or upon the spouse or former spouse, or upon the person with whom the offender is or has been in an unregistered spousal relationship (*nereģistrētas laulāto attiecības*), or upon the person with whom the offender has a joint (single) household.[77]

Also, since 31 March 2013 in the Latvian Civil Procedure Law there has been in force the principle of provisional protection against domestic violence which provides that an application for provisional protection against domestic violence may be brought not only by spouses, but also by people who are living or have lived in a common household; people who have or are expecting a common child regardless of whether these people have ever been married or lived together; and people between whom there are or have been close personal or intimate relationships.[78]

LITHUANIA

Articles 3.229-3.235 of the Lithuanian Civil Code regulate property relations between cohabitants who live together in a registered partnership without being legally married. Partnership conditions laid down by the Lithuanian Civil Code are comparable to those for a marriage: having reached the age of majority, possessing full legal capacity, being of a different sex, absence of a marriage or a blood relationship, and registration. In addition, just as in the case of marriage, partners entering into cohabitation should be unified by a common goal to build a family-type relationship. There are also certain restrictions: a

---

74 The Criminal Law. Law of the Republic of Latvia. Latvijas Vēstnesis, 8 July 1998, no.199/200, at S. 22, Part two.

75 S. 303 Latvian Criminal Law.

76 Latvian Administrative Violations Code: Law of the Republic of Latvia. "Ziņotājs", 20 December 1984, no.51, at Para. 3 S. 264.

77 S. 167.2 Part 2 Latvian Administrative Violations Code.

78 Civil Procedure Law: Law of the Republic of Latvia. Latvijas Vēstnesis, 3 November 1998, no. 326/330, at S. 450.44.

partnership is only allowed between adults, so the courts shall not permit the registration of a partnership between minors; a partnership is subject to the verification criterion, i.e. the partners must have lived together for at least one year; in the case of a partnership, the legal regulation covers only some of the property relations between partners but does not cover personal non-property relations between them.[79]

LUXEMBOURG

Informal relationships between a couple are not regulated by any specific legislative provisions in Luxembourg; the specific nature of the informal relationship is not regulated. The existence of a marriage or a registered partnership with another person may have a consequence for the stability of the relationship; indeed, the term 'stability' may be important for judges when informal relationships have legal consequences.

THE NETHERLANDS

In almost all fields of law in which marriage and registered partnership are legally relevant, (some types of) informal relationships are also legally relevant. This does not imply that informal relationships always have the same rights and duties, although in most legal areas they do.

Each specific regulation defines the types of informal relationships which qualify under that act. It is impossible to give a general definition.[80] Only one element is common to all definitions: they apply to couples of the opposite sex and same sex alike.[81] Sometimes a specific cohabitation period is required, in other acts a notarial cohabitation contract or being registered at the same address is necessary, etc. In some legislative provisions, some types of family relations are included, but mostly specific provisions only apply to non-relatives. A minimum age of 18 years for the partners is in many areas of the law not explicitly required or not relevant.[82] For instance, in relation to rent law, there appears to be no problem if a 17-year-old partner wishes to qualify as a co-tenant on

---

79 V. MIKELĖNAS, *Šeimos teisė (*Family law*)*, Justitia, Vilnius, 2009, at p. 209.

80 W.M. SCHRAMA, *De niet-huwelijkse samenleving in het Nederlandse en Duitse recht*, Kluwer, Deventer, 2004, at p. 200-205.

81 In no statute or act is this explicitly included in the definitions; apparently it is clear within the Dutch legal system that it includes all types of couples.

82 For instance on the basis of the *Participatiewet* only persons of at least 18 years are allowed to apply for social benefits.

the basis of cohabitation with the tenant.[83] In practice, this will not often occur, however.

In the field of private law non-marital cohabitation is relevant for a number of topics:[84]

- Maintenance: In 1971 a new provision (Art. 1:160 Dutch Civil Code) entered into force with the first legal recognition of non-marital cohabitation (back then called concubinage). This did not have a positive effect for the couple, since living together as if they were married (later completed with 'or had registered their partnership') implied the direct and irreparable loss of the right to maintenance towards an ex spouse. This provision generated a great deal of case law and was discussed in Parliament in 2005. Despite the debate, it remained unchanged.[85]
- The protection of vulnerable adults: Since 1982 informal relationships play a role in the regulation of the protection of vulnerable adults in Book 1 of the Dutch Civil Code. The 'other[86] life partner' ('*andere levensgezel*') has the right to apply to the court for an order to place the property of the partner under administration.[87] Moreover, the life companion is one of the persons who is preferably appointed as the administrator of the property by the court.[88] The term life partner refers to relationships which are similar to those of married couples.[89] A joint household is not a prerequisite for the application of the provision. The same provisions are applicable regarding the appointment of a curator and the judicial protection of vulnerable adults.[90]
- Landlord and tenant law: Since 1979 the legal position of a partner living together with a tenant has been regulated in order to protect informal cohabitants. The person having a joint stable household with a tenant for a minimum of two years is entitled to certain rights in relation to the tenant and the landlord. The tenant and his/her co-resident may request the landlord to qualify him/her as a co-tenant. If the landlord refuses, the tenant and co-resident may

83 Art. 7:267 Dutch Civil Code.
84 W.M. SCHRAMA, 'The Dutch approach to informal lifestyles: Family function over family form?', *International Journal of Law, Policy and the Family*, 2008, pp. 311-332.
85 *Kamerstukken* II, 2002-2003, 28 600 VI, no. 104.
86 The word 'other' referring to other than a married or registered partner.
87 Art. 1:432 para. 1 Dutch Civil Code.
88 Art. 1:435 para. 4 Dutch Civil Code.
89 *Kamerstukken* II, 1979-1980, 15 350, no. 8, p. 3.
90 Art. 1:379 and 383 para. 3 Dutch Civil Code, respectively Art. 1:451 para. 1 and 452 para. 3 Dutch Civil Code.

apply to the courts (Art. 7:267 Dutch Civil Code). The status of co-tenant is important, since the co-tenant may take over the rental contract if the tenant wants to terminate his/her contract. Even more important is that in the case of separation the co-tenant may request the courts to determine which partner is most entitled to the dwelling.
- Inheritance law: In Book 4 of the Dutch Civil Code regulating inheritance law, since 2003 a surviving informal partner may qualify for a very limited set of rights if he/she had a durable joint household with the deceased partner[91] or the other life partner had a joint household and if they had a notarial cohabitation contract with a duty to support each other.[92]

The reception of new non-traditional lifestyles in public law started in 1981.[93]

- Inheritance tax law: Even in 1981 public policy shifted to include non-marital cohabitation in inheritance tax law. In the course of time new definitions have been introduced and redefined (*Successiewet* 1956). As a result, a rather complicated set of definitions and criteria applies.[94] The incentive for the government has been to erase the differences between married and unmarried couples. When a surviving partner qualifies under the Act,[95] the same exemption and tax rate will apply as to married and registered couples.[96]
- Income tax law: The *Algemene wet rijksbelastingen* describes what types of informal relationships qualify for taxation purposes.[97] However, in the Dutch Income Tax Act 2001 a number of other situations are qualified as partner situations as well.[98] The same tax provisions for formal and informal couples apply.[99]

---

91 Art. 4:28 para. 2 Dutch Civil Code.

92 Art. 4:82 Dutch Civil Code.

93 W.M. SCHRAMA, 'The Dutch approach to informal lifestyles: Family function over family form?', *International Journal of Law, Policy and the Family*, 2008, pp. 311-332.

94 N.C.G. GUBBELS, 'Gehuwden en ongehuwd samenwonenden in de inkomstenbelasting en de schenk- en erfbelasting', *FJR*, 2013, 3; C.J.M. MARTENS, 'Successiewet 1956/ Overdrachtsbelasting', in: A. AUTAR, W. KOLKMAN and W. SCHRAMA (eds.), *Compendium samenwonen*, SDU, The Hague, 2013, at p. 96-97.

95 Art. 1a Dutch Inheritance Tax Act 1956 and Art. 5a para. 1 sub. b *Algemene Wet Rijksbelastingen*: unmarried, adult, notarial cohabitation contract, registered at the same address.

96 Art. 24 para. 2, sub. a Dutch Inheritance Tax Act 1956.

97 Art. 5a para. 1 sub. b *Algemene Wet Rijksbelastingen*: unmarried, adult, notarial cohabitation contract, registered at the same address.

98 Art. 1.2 Dutch Income Tax Act 2001. For instance if the two persons have a child together or are registered as partners in relation to a pension scheme. See: N.C.G. GUBBELS, 'Gehuwden en ongehuwd samenwonenden in de inkomstenbelasting

- Social security and social benefits: In social security law cohabiting couples qualify as married couples if they share a joint household. A joint household is defined as the situation in which two people live in the same house and take care of each other, by means of sharing costs or otherwise. In a number of cases couples qualify, regardless of their intention, as a joint household on the basis of certain facts. If a cohabiting couple have a child, they are qualified as a joint household (Art. 3 para. 4b *Participatiewet*). When cohabiting partners have concluded a cohabitation contract with a duty to take care of each other (*zorgverplichting*), they are considered to be a qualifying couple, regardless of their own wishes.
- Criminal law and criminal procedural law: In criminal law and criminal procedural law the reception of non-marital cohabitation has encountered difficulties. In general, non-marital cohabitation has no legal effects in these areas of the law.[100] For instance, the right not to testify against a spouse or registered partner (Art. 217 para. 3 Dutch Code of Criminal Procedure) is not applicable to non-marital partners,[101] a difference which is allowed according to the ECHR. It has ruled that states are entitled to set limits on the scope of testimonial privilege and to draw the line at marriage, given its special status and its social, personal and legal consequences.[102]

An exception to the policy of ignoring informal couples in the Dutch Criminal Code has recently been made: in case a person physically abuses his/her life partner, the same provision applies as for spouses and registered partners, resulting in a possibility to increase the sentence by one third.[103]

---

en de schenk- en erfbelasting', *FJR*, 2013, 3 and C.J.M. MARTENS, 'Inkomstenbelasting', in: A. AUTAR, W. KOLKMAN and W. SCHRAMA (eds.), *Compendium samenwonen*, SDU, The Hague, 2013, at p. 64-66.

99 With one exception.

100 W.M. SCHRAMA, 'Familierelaties terecht (niet) in het strafrecht?', *Delikt en Delinkwent*, 2009, pp. 353-375.

101 The prior Supreme Court decision (HR 31 May 2005, ECLI:NL:HR:2005:AS2748) has been criticised: W.M. SCHRAMA, 'Waarom moet een verdachte naar het stadhuis gaan?', *NJB*, 2006, at p. 257-260.

102 Critical: W.M. SCHRAMA, 'Het EHRM slaat geen nieuwe piketpaaltjes in het relatierecht: Geen schending Art. 8 EVRM door beperking van het verschoningsrecht tot formele relaties', *AA*, 2013, at p. 281-285.

103 Art. 304 para. 1 Dutch Criminal Code.

NORWAY

Informal relationships remain largely unregulated by statute. Most striking in this respect is the fact that there are no specific legislative provisions for regulating the financial consequences of the termination of cohabitation. The Norwegian Household Community Act 1991[104] applies to cohabitants and other people who live together in a household. However, this act only provides a limited opportunity for a household member to purchase what was previously the common residence and household goods at market value upon the termination of the household.

The Norwegian Household Community Act applies to two or more unmarried adults who have lived together in a household, and includes cohabitants, siblings, students and others who live together. Thus, a marriage or a registered partnership will disqualify the couple.

In 2008 Parliament enacted a law which gave unmarried cohabitants who have children together[105] a right to either inherit approximately 40,000 Euros or to postpone the settlement and keep part of the deceased's estate undivided.[106] In this law, cohabitation is defined as two people above the age of eighteen living together in a marriage-like relationship as long as they are not married, registered partners or cohabiting with others.[107] Same-sex couples are included in this definition. The two people must permanently reside together, but it is expressly stated that shorter periods of separation due to education, work, illness and the like are no disqualification. Two people who are so closely related that they cannot marry are excluded from the definition.[108]

PORTUGAL

Law No. 7/2001, of 11 May, as amended by Law No. 23/2010, of 30 August, brings together the main protective effects afforded to *de facto* unions. It deals with the requisites for recognition, evidence, equivalence

---

104 The Norwegian Act relating to the right to the joint residence and household goods when a household community ceases to exist 1991 (The Norwegian Household Community Act).

105 This implies that they have, have had or expect a child together.

106 The Norwegian Inheritance Act, S. 28(b) and 28(c). The law came into force on 1 July 2009.

107 See the Norwegian Inheritance Act, Chapter III A and J. ASLAND and P. HAMBRO, 'New Developments and Expansion of Relationships Covered by Norwegian Law', in: B. ATKIN (ed.), *The International Survey of Family Law*, Jordan Publishing Limited, Bristol, 2009, pp. 378-384.

108 The Norwegian Inheritance Act, S. 28(a).

to marriage in labour, tax and pensions law, permanence in the household in the event of death or a breakdown, adoption and the requisites of a formal dissolution whenever any of the members intend to receive any benefits derived from the union.

Article 496 of the Portuguese Civil Code, as amended by Law No. 23/2010, gives the surviving member the right to be compensated for the moral damages derived from the death of the partner against anyone who caused that death.

Article 2010 of the Portuguese Civil Code, as amended by Law No. 23/2010, gives the surviving member a right to maintenance over the patrimony received by the deceased member's successors.

Some circumstances inhibit the legal protection of *de facto* unions, according to Art. 2 of Law No. 7/2001: a) aged below 18, b) both legal or *de facto* incompetence, c) an already existing ongoing marriage of any of the members, unless a formal separation has been declared, d) a blood relationship or affinity in the direct line, or a collateral blood relationship in the second degree, e) a criminal conviction by one of the members for homicide or attempted homicide against the other member's spouse.

Additionally, there are several legal provisions that may be found in different Acts that refer directly to the *de facto* union. For example, Art. 3(3) of the Portuguese Nationality Act (Act 37/81, October 3rd, as amended by Act 43/2013, July 3rd); Art. 6(1) of the Assisted Reproduction Act (Act 32/2006, July 26th).

RUSSIA

At present, Russian law contains no specific provisions governing informal relationships.

SCOTLAND

Informal relationships between couples are regulated by Scots law where they fall within the definition of 'cohabitation'. Within the context of family law, cohabitants have some protection in respect of occupancy of the family home,[109] there are statutory presumptions of joint owner-

[109] Matrimonial Homes (Family Protection) (Scotland) Act 1981.

ship[110] and, where the relationship comes to an end by death[111] or otherwise,[112] a cohabitant may apply to the court for a discretionary payment.

Informal relationships are legally recognised and given some protection by the Matrimonial Homes (Family Protection) (Scotland) Act 1981 in respect of occupancy of the family home. The 1981 Act was designed to provide greater security to a spouse or cohabitant who has no legal title to the family home, according to general property law, by granting them occupancy rights. It also introduced a framework of orders which can be used by the court to regulate occupancy of the home in the context of domestic violence. While non-entitled spouses have automatic occupancy rights,[113] a non-entitled cohabitant must apply to the court for grant of occupancy rights,[114] with any grant of occupancy rights being subject to a maximum period of six months.[115]

More recently, new rights for cohabitants in respect of financial provision and property were introduced by the Family Law (Scotland) Act 2006.[116] The 2006 Act introduced presumptions of equal ownership concerning ownership of household goods[117] and rights in money and moveable property derived from a household allowance.[118] It also provided cohabitants with a right to apply to the court for a discretionary payment where cohabitation ends otherwise than by death[119] and where their cohabitant dies intestate.[120]

Although the detailed definition in each Act is slightly different,[121] the broad basis of cohabitation is the same: it involves living together as if husband and wife. Originally cohabitation was defined for different-sex couples by reference to marriage and for same-sex couples by reference to civil partnership but, since the introduction in 2014 of same-sex marriage, cohabitants are now all defined by reference to marriage. Two

---

110 Family Law (Scotland) Act 2006, S. 26 and 27.
111 Family Law (Scotland) Act 2006, S. 29.
112 Family Law (Scotland) Act 2006, S. 28.
113 Matrimonial Homes (Family Protection) (Scotland) Act 1981, S. 1.
114 Matrimonial Homes (Family Protection) (Scotland) Act 1981, S. 18.
115 Matrimonial Homes (Family Protection) (Scotland) Act 1981, S. 18(1): this six month period may be extended for subsequent period or periods, in each case not exceeding six months.
116 Matrimonial Homes (Family Protection) (Scotland) Act 1981, S. 25-29A.
117 Family Law (Scotland) Act 2006, S. 26.
118 Family Law (Scotland) Act 2006, S. 27.
119 Family Law (Scotland) Act 2006, S. 28.
120 Family Law (Scotland) Act 2006, S. 29.
121 Matrimonial Homes (Family Protection) (Scotland) Act 1981, S. 18(1) and (2); Family Law (Scotland) Act 2006, S.25.

people are cohabiting where they are or were not married or in a civil partnership with each other but are or were living together as if married to each other.[122] Although the test is based on the concept of living together 'as if they were married', there is nothing to indicate any intention to limit cohabitation to those who possess legal capacity to marry. In fact, the absence of such capacity has sometimes been highlighted as part of the justification for introducing legal protection to couples who were not able to benefit from formalised relationships.[123]

Beyond the scope of family law, there is also some statutory recognition of cohabitants in terms of social security entitlement,[124] housing,[125] compensation for negligent death[126] or personal injury[127] of a cohabitant and application for temporary relief from creditors in respect of the family home.[128]

SLOVAKIA

Unlike German, Swiss, Austrian, Turkish, or Greek family law, Slovak family law does not regulate the legal institution of engagement (a promise to marry). The formation of a marriage is preceded by a factual engagement, but the act of engagement itself has no legal effects. Therefore in answer to the question: to what extent is the informal relationship between a couple regulated by specific Slovak legislative provisions, it could be stated that the Family Act partly provides legal recognition to a man and a woman entering into a marriage (the future spouses – a fiancé and a fiancée, *snúbenec*). There are a few provisions in the Family Act (e.g. § 1, 2, 4) on future spouses' pre-marriage obligations. For example, they must file a marriage application with the competent civil registry office, the application needs to include personal details relating to the spouses, declarations by the spouses concerning their surname and the surname of their common children in marriage, and declarations by the spouses that they are not aware of any marriage

---

122 Interpreted in accordance with the Marriage and Civil Partnership (Scotland) Act 2014, S. 4(2) and (3).

123 See e.g. Scottish Law Commission, Paper No 86, *The Effects of Cohabitation in Private Law*, 1990 at para. 6.8 where the possibility of a surviving spouse and a surviving cohabitant was acknowledged.

124 Social Security Contributions and Benefits Act 1992, S. 137(1); Social Security Administration Act 1992, S. 78.

125 Housing (Scotland) Act 2001.

126 Damages (Scotland) Act 2011.

127 Administration of Justice (Scotland) Act 1982.

128 Mortgage Rights (Scotland) Act 2001, S. 1.

impediments and that they are aware of each other's health situation. The documents enumerated in the Slovak Act on Civil Registries must be enclosed with the application.

SLOVENIA

For the creation of an extramarital union, a formal confirmation of the union is not required. It suffices for its recognition that a man and a woman live together for an extended period and that no reasons exist which would result in a marriage being invalid, such as the relationship between the partners being within the prohibited degrees of consanguinity, an already concluded marriage with another partner, or a permanent unsoundness of mind by a partner because of a serious mental illness. Since the law has also regulated same-sex partnership unions, it must also apply[129] that nobody may conclude a marriage or plan an extramarital union while still being in a registered same-sex union. This requirement derives not only from the principle of monogamy within marriage or an extramarital union but also from the principle of monogamy within a same-sex partnership, with which an already existing marriage is an impediment to the registration of a same-sex partnership union.[130]

The legal consequences of an extramarital union appear on the basis of the law alone (without a court decision) and irrespective of whether the partners who have been living together for an extended period even really desire this. The legal consequences of an extramarital union are the same in a relationship between extramarital partners as in a marriage: from the moment when they start to live together, common property of the partners is created (which is normally divided in half at the time of the cessation of the union); and an unsupported partner has the right to demand maintenance from the other partner. An extramarital union does not have legal consequences in the relation of the extramarital partners with the children. There is no presumption of fatherhood, so in this case fatherhood must be recognised or legally established.[131]

---

129 The Slovenian Marriage Act does not determine this, because after the adoption of the Partnership Act it still remained unchanged.

130 Indent 2 para. 1 Art. 3 of the Slovenian Partnership Act.

131 K. ZUPANČIČ, 'Report on Slovenian Family Law Regulation', in: A. BERGMANN and M. FERID, *Internationales Ehe- und Kindschaftsrecht,* Verlag für Standesamtswesen, Frankfurt am Main, 1997, at p. 32.

An extramarital union only creates the same legal consequences between the partners as a marriage in relation to rights that the Slovenian Marriage Act recognises, i.e., the partners primarily obtain the right to share common property and the right to maintenance. In other legal spheres that the Slovenian Marriage Act does not regulate, an extramarital union has legal consequences only if legislation in this sphere so determines. Legal consequences are determined by, e.g., the inheritance, housing, pension and invalidity legislation.

If a dispute exists between the partners about the existence of an extramarital union, the existence of the extramarital union can only be decided as a prior question which is important for resolving a main question, for example, the question of whether inheritance rights exist after the death of a partner, whether the right to maintenance exists, or whether common property has been created that should be shared. The resolution of the prior question on the existence of the extramarital union only has effect for the case in which the question was resolved.

Although family legislation on extramarital unions is not intended for couples of the same sex and although regulations in the field of family law and other legal fields create the impression that same-sex partners living together do not exist at all, let alone that the law would regulate relations between them, this is not entirely the case. Same-sex partners from an actual life union enjoy certain rights with the aid of interpretation of applicable provisions in the light of the constitutional principle of the prohibition of discrimination (Art. 14 of the Slovenian Constitution).[132] Under family regulations, same-sex partners living together have the right to the unilateral adoption of children (interpretation of Art. 135 of the Slovenian Marriage Act)[133] and the right as former or current partners to have contact with the children of their present or former partner from a *de facto* life partnership if the child has a family connection with them and they are personally connected to the child and this is to the child's benefit (a child's contact with other persons, para. 1 Art. 106a of the Slovenian Marriage Act). Regulations outside family law recognise the status of a narrower family member for a partner from a *de facto* life partnership in the sphere of medicine (interpretation of point 15 at Art. 2 of the Slovenian Patients' Rights

[132] Uradni list RS (Official Journal) Nos 33/1991-I, 42/1997, 66/2000, 24/2003, 69/2004, 68/2006, 47/2013.

[133] Decision of the Ministry of Labour, Family and Social Affairs, no. 12030-7/2011/4 of 14 July 2011 (unpublished), and decision of Domžale Social Work Centre, no. 12037-1/2011-2 of 27 December 2011 (unpublished).

Act).[134] The Slovenian Patients' Rights Act, for example, recognises for narrower family members the right of consent in the use and other processing of medical and other personal data on a deceased patient (under para. 4 Art. 44 of the Slovenian Patients' Rights Act[135]), the right to information on the state of health of the patient (under para. 5 Art. 45 of the Slovenian Patients' Rights Act), the right to demand 'the initiation of a procedure for the protection of a patient's rights (under para. 3 Art. 48 of the Slovenian Patients' Rights Act). On the basis of the decision of the Constitutional Court RS, No. U-I-212/10-15 of 14 March 2013,[136] the right of non-registered same-sex partners living together to inherit to the same extent as extramarital partners of a different sex is explicitly recognised.

SPAIN

The Spanish Civil Code does not contain a special legal regime governing informal relationships even though these relationships are dealt with by that Code and special statutes at random, in connection with certain matters. In 1987, for example, a reform of adoption law equated partners and spouses in connection with joint adoption[137] and in 1994 the Spanish Law on leasehold[138] granted legal rights to partners in an informal relationship. This Law requires partners to have had two years of cohabitation or to have a common child in order to qualify as a *de facto* couple, but does not specify circumstances that disqualify a couple.

Catalan law has developed a new institution called the 'stable couple', with rules contained in the second Book of the Catalan Civil Code (On persons and the family), in a special Chapter in the Title devoted to the family (Chapter IV of Title III). A same-sex or opposite-sex couple qualifies as a stable couple under Catalan law if the partners cohabit in a manner analogous to marriage and fulfil one of the two following conditions: (a) continuous cohabitation for more than two years; or (b) having a common child. However, certain personal circumstances will disqualify the couple. Article 234.2 of the Code establishes that non-

---

134 B. NOVAK, D. KOROŠEC, B. IVANC, T. BALAŽIC, in: D. KOROŠEC (ed.), *Zakon o pacientovih pravicah s komentarjem* (Patients' Rights Act with commentary), GV Založba, Ljubljana, 2009, at p. 38.

135 Uradni list RS (Official Journal) No'. 15/2008.

136 Uradni list RS (Official Journal) No. 31/2013.

137 Ley 21/1987, de 11 de noviembre, por la que se modifican determinados articulas del Código Civil y de la Ley de Enjuiciamiento Civil en materia de adopción (BOE núm. 275 de 17 de noviembre de 1987).

138 Ley de Arrendamientos Urbanos (BOE núm 282 de 25 de Noviembre de 1994).

empancipated minors or relatives in the first degree of the descending line (children and parents) or up to the second degree of the collateral line (siblings and first degree cousins) cannot constitute a stable couple. In addition, a stable couple cannot be constituted if one of the partners cohabits with a third person or if one or both partners are married and have not separated from their spouse (legal separation is not required, *de facto* separation suffices). It is worthwhile mentioning that this last requirement has been modified by the legislature. Originally, when legislation on stable couples was enacted in 1998,[139] a 'stable couple' as therein defined, could not be constituted by married persons. In 2010 this requirement was removed and married individuals who have factually separated from their spouse qualify. The legislature justified the change in the Preamble to the 2010 Statute that enacted Book II of the Catalan Civil Code. Since the overall purpose of the rules on stable couples is to solve problems related to the break-up of the relationship, an unequal treatment based on the circumstance that one or both partners in an informal relationship are married to another person, is unjustified. The second reason is that the requirement that none of the partners continued to be married disqualified an estimated 30% of the cohabiting hetero-sexual couples. Problems related to the break-up of couples not qualifying as stable couples were left to case law, which created legal uncertainty. This is precisely what the special rules on stable couples sought to avoid.

SWEDEN

Since 1 January 1974, Swedish law has contained specific enactments focusing on informal relationships between couples living habitually together and sharing a household. The current special body of regulation is found in the Swedish Cohabitation Act (in Swedish, *Sambolag 2003:376)* focusing on two people who habitually live together as a couple sharing a joint household (§ 1). Swedish law calls the parties to such a relationship 'cohabitees', or 'cohabitants', or 'the cohabiting couple' (in Swedish: *sambor, det sammanboende paret*); this terminology will also be largely used in the Swedish national report. Both opposite-sex and same-sex couples are covered by this legislation. It should be noted that the material scope of application of the Swedish Cohabitation Act is limited to the regulation of how the couple's joint home and household goods, if they qualify as so-called cohabitation property (in Swedish:

---

[139] Ley 10/1998, de 15 de julio, de uniones estables de pareja (BOE núm. 198, de 19 de agosto de 1998).

samboegendom), are to be distributed upon the termination of the relationship, in addition to protecting one cohabitee's interests in this property against unilateral actions taken by the other cohabitee. The Act also includes a mandatory regulation on the so-called 'take-over right' of the couple's joint dwelling upon termination of the relationship, regulates the partners' freedom of contract regarding the 'cohabitation property' and includes procedural provisions.

If one (or both) of the parties to the informal relationship is in a legally existing formal relationship (marriage or registered partnership) with another person, the Swedish Cohabitation Act is explicitly, according to § 1 para. 3-4, not applicable. The *travaux préparatoires* to the enactment indicate furthermore that a person cannot be in an informal relationship, subject to this enactment, with more than one person at a time.[140] Even if there is some support in the legal literature for the position that people who, according to the Swedish Marriage Code, are forbidden to marry each other because of close kinship, are to be excluded from the scope of the Swedish Cohabitation Act,[141] there is no case law on this issue.

Interestingly enough, the Swedish Cohabitation Act can cover situations where one or two people under the age of majority (i.e., 18 years) live together in a joint household. This is made explicit through § 9, para. 2, authorising a cohabitee or a prospective cohabitee under the age of 18 to sign an agreement concerning (future) division of the 'cohabitation property'. The *travaux préparatoires*, likewise, state that the Act covers relationships between persons of at least 15 years of age, if the other criteria for the Act's application are met.[142] An underage person must, nevertheless, have the consent of his or her custodial parents to live in and share a joint household with another person, since a child's residence falls within the scope of parental responsibilities.[143]

Apart from the specific regulation in the Swedish Cohabitation Act, special provisions addressing couples living with each other in informal relationships can be found in other Swedish enactments. An example is the Swedish Social Insurance Code (in Swedish: *Socialförsäkringsbalk 2010:110*) as regards the right to a so-called adjustment pension (in Swedish: *omställningspension*) following the death of the other partner to

140 Government Bill, Prop. 1986/87:1, p. 369.

141 F. GRAUERS, *Ekonomisk familjerätt*, Thomson Förlag, Stockholm, 2008, at p. 231.

142 Bet. 2002/03:LU19 p. 11.

143 Swedish Children and Parents Code (in Swedish, *Föräldrabalken 1949:381)*, Chapter 6, § 2 and 11.

the informal relationship. Under certain conditions (which require more than the fulfilment of the criteria set out in the Swedish Cohabitation Act, § 1), the surviving partner may qualify for this pension as if he or she had been married to the deceased, Chapter 80, § 4. Another example is to be found in the Swedish Code of Land Law (in Swedish: *Jordabalk 1970:994*) explicitly placing partners to an informal relationship on the same footing as spouses regarding the right to take over the lease of the joint dwelling, Chapter 12, § 33. Certain provisions in Swedish legislation, in particular within the area of social welfare, are drafted in a neutral manner covering 'households with children', without regard to other legal 'etiquette'.

SWITZERLAND

There is no comprehensive regulation of informal relationships under Swiss law. Statutory rules on informal relationships have repeatedly been rejected by the Swiss legislature. Until the 1990s unmarried cohabitation was even a criminal offence in some Swiss cantons.

In a few more recent Swiss laws the term factual relationship (*faktische Lebensgemeinschaft*) is expressly mentioned.[144] They mostly concern procedural rights, such as grounds for recusal or the right to refuse cooperation or to testify.[145]

With regard to the Swiss adult protection law, a partner in an informal relationship may be entitled to represent his or her partner in relation to medical procedures. According to Art. 378 para. 1 No. 4 Swiss Civil Code, representation may be assigned to any person (and thus in particular including the partner in an informal relationship) who cohabits with the person lacking capacity of judgement and regularly and personally provides him or her with support. The partner in an informal relationship is, however, only entitled to represent the other partner if that partner has not assigned another person to represent him or her, if there is no deputy (*Beistand*) with a right to act as a representative or if there is no spouse/registered partner who cohabits with the person concerned or who regularly and personally provides him or her with

[144] E.g. Art. 42^{quinquies}(b) Disability Insurance Act, Invalidenversicherungsgesetz, SR 831.20; Art. 420 Swiss Civil Code (*faktische/r Lebenspartner/in*), see also the next footnote.

[145] E.g. Art. 47 para. 1(c) and Art. 165 para. 1(a) Swiss Civil Procedure Code, Schweizerische Zivilprozessordnung, SR 272; Art. 56(c) and Art. 168 para. 1(a) Swiss Criminal Procedure Code, Schweizerisches Strafprozessrecht, SR 312.0.

support.[146] Moreover, if the partner in an informal relationship has been appointed as the deputy of his or her partner, the adult protection authority may wholly or partly absolve him or her alike other family members from certain duties (Art. 420 Swiss Civil Code).

Outside Swiss family law, a specific legislative provision on informal relationships can be found with regard to occupational pensions. According to Art. 20a para. 1(a) of the Swiss Law on an occupational pension for old age, survivors and invalids,[147] a pension fund has the possibility to include the partner in an informal relationship as a beneficiary in its regulation. Thus, a partner in an informal relationship may have the right to survivors' benefits if the respective pension fund has opted for this possibility and, further, if at the time of the death of the partner the relationship (*Lebensgemeinschaft*) had lasted for more than five years without interruption.[148] Alternatively, any person (and therefore including the partner in an informal relationship) who has been supported to a considerable extent by the insured person or has to support common children may also be entitled to such benefits.[149] It is up to the pension fund to regulate whether or not a partner is entitled to such benefits in cases where the insured partner was still married or in a registered partnership with another person.[150]

In cases of the death of the partner in an informal relationship, the surviving partner may be entitled to damages under tort law. According to Art. 45 para. 3 Swiss Code of Obligations,[151] compensation must be granted if a person is deprived of his or her means of support as a result of homicide (*Versorgerschaden*). It is not necessary that such support is statutorily granted. Rather, the Swiss Federal Supreme Court has held that the partner in an informal relationship is entitled to such damages if he or she has actually been supported by the deceased and would most probably also have been supported by him or her in the future.[152]

---

146 Art. 378 para. 1 Swiss Civil Code (order of persons entitled to represent).

147 Bundesgesetz über die berufliche Alters-, Hinterlassenen- und Invalidenvorsorge, SR 831.40. For details see L. GLANZMANN-TARNUTZER, 'Die Lebenspartnerrente gemäss Art. 20a Abs. 1 lit. a BVG', *Aktuelle Juristische Praxis*, 2014, at p. 1145 et seq.

148 The pension fund may stipulate further requirements, see Swiss Federal Supreme Court, BGE 137 V 383 E.3.2 (substantive requirements); BGE 136 V 127 (formal requirements).

149 Art. 20a para. 1 (a) Swiss Law on an occupational pension for old age, survivors and invalids.

150 L. GLANZMANN-TARNUTZER, 'Die Lebenspartnerrente gemäss Art. 20a Abs. 1 lit. a BVG', *Aktuelle Juristische Praxis*, 2014, at p. 1145, 1154.

151 Schweizerisches Obligationenrecht, SR 220.

152 Swiss Federal Supreme Court, BGE 114 II 144 E.2.

Furthermore, the surviving partner may be entitled to an appropriate sum for pain and suffering (*Genugtuung*). Pursuant to Art. 47 Swiss Code of Obligations the court may grant the dependants of the deceased such (additional) compensation in cases of homicide. Recently, such compensation was granted to a partner in an informal relationship in a case where the deceased was still married and the surviving spouse was also entitled to an appropriate sum for pain and suffering.[153]

[153] Swiss Federal Supreme Court, BGE 138 III 157.

QUESTION 3

In the absence of specific legislative provisions, are there circumstances (e.g. through the application of the law of obligations or the law of property) under which informal relationships between a couple are given legal effect (e.g. through the application of the law of obligations or the law of property)? Where applicable briefly indicate the leading cases.

AUSTRIA

Initially, it should be noted that the rules on marriage and engagement cannot by applied by analogy to informal relationships.[1] However, due to the lack of a specific statutory regime for informal relationships certain legal consequences especially regarding the dissolution of an informal relationship arise from the application of the general rules of the law of obligations and property law.[2] In particular rules regulating (i) civil law associations *(Gesellschaft bürgerlichen Rechts)*, (ii) donations, (iii) unjust enrichment, and (iv) service contracts are applied with regard to informal relationships.

If a partner in an informal relationship works in the company of the other partner[3] or the partners have built a house together,[4] it was often assumed that the partners had impliedly concluded a civil law association pursuant to S. 1175 General Austrian Civil Code.[5] According

---

1 F. MEISSEL and M. PRESLMAYR, 'Leistungsabgeltung in der Lebensgemeinschaft', in: F. HARRER and R. ZITTA (eds.), *Familie und Recht*, Verlag Orac, Vienna, 1992, pp. 515-544, at p. 517 et seq.

2 E. MÖSCHL, *Die nichteheliche Lebensgemeinschaft*, LexisNexis ARD ORAC, Vienna, 2007, at marg. No. 75.

3 Austrian Supreme Court, Judgement of 17.03.1993, 3 Ob 515/92.

4 Austrian Supreme Court, Judgement of 07.10.1987, 3 Ob 545/87.

5 M. WITTMANN-TIWALD, 'section 1175 General Austrian Civil Code', in: A. KLETEČKA and M. SCHAUER, *ABGB-ON 1.02*, Manz Verlag, Vienna, 2014, at marg. No. 32; U. AICHHORN, *Das Recht der Lebenspartnerschaften, Ehe und Lebensgemeinschaft*, Springer, Vienna, 2003, at p. 407 et seq.

to the prevailing case law an impliedly concluded civil law association requires that effort, capital and other material assets are put together for an economic purpose, the association is at least loosely organised and grants participation rights to both partners.[6] Despite the fact that the Austrian Supreme Court does not apply strict criteria when it comes to the question whether partners in an informal relationship have concluded a civil law association,[7] the Court decided that a mere accumulation of property is not sufficient for establishing a civil law association.[8]

If, for some reason, a civil law association cannot be assumed, and one partner made a contribution without expecting something in return, the contribution can be qualified as a donation.[9] The question whether a contribution is deemed to be a donation is evaluated by having regard to the overall conduct of the person who made the contribution.[10] But even if the contribution was made upon a donation contract, the contract can be challenged due to an error (also an error in motivation) or the donation can be revoked upon gross ingratitude.[11]

If, however, the contribution cannot be considered as a donation, because it was rendered with regard to a particular purpose, the rules on unjust enrichment come into play, especially S. 1435 General Austrian Civil Code.[12] If someone renders a service, including providing money, goods and services in terms of a certain purpose, the contribution may be reclaimed, provided that the particular purpose was obvious to the beneficiary and could not finally be achieved.[13] In terms of an informal relationship the particular purpose could be the further existence of the informal relationship or entering into a marriage; achieving the purpose must not be impossible *ex ante*. Only permanent investments excluding favours or expenses caused by everyday life can, however, be reclaimed,

6 M. WITTMANN-TIWALD, 'section 1175 General Austrian Civil Code', in: A. KLETEČKA and M. SCHAUER, *ABGB-ON 1.02*, Manz Verlag, Vienna, 2014, at marg. No. 33; H. KLAAR, 'Rechtsfragen nichtehelicher Lebensgemeinschaft', *AnwBl*, 1989, at p. 18.

7 Austrian Supreme Court, Judgement of 15.10.1998, 2 Ob 200/98w.

8 Austrian Supreme Court, Judgement of 20.04.2010, 1 Ob 23/10d.

9 Section 938 General Austrian Civil Code; E. MÖSCHL, *Die nichteheliche Lebensgemeinschaft*, LexisNexis ARD ORAC, Vienna, 2007, at marg. No. 78.

10 Austrian Supreme Court, Judgement of 18.04.2002, 6 Ob 44/02t.

11 U. AICHHORN, *Das Recht der Lebenspartnerschaften, Ehe und Lebensgemeinschaft*, Springer, Vienna, 2003, at p. 401 et seq.

12 E. MÖSCHL, *Die nichteheliche Lebensgemeinschaft*, LexisNexis ARD ORAC, Vienna, 2007, at marg. No. 83.

13 E. MÖSCHL, *Die nichteheliche Lebensgemeinschaft*, LexisNexis ARD ORAC, Vienna, 2007, at marg. No. 83.

because otherwise the other partner would no longer be enriched.[14] Although, generally, services can be reclaimed under S. 1435 General Austrian Civil Code, the Austrian Supreme Court is reluctant to apply this provision to housekeeping activities; rather the Court in this regard refers to S. 1152 General Austrian Civil Code, which regulates service contracts. Section 1152 General Austrian Civil Code stipulates that in the absence of an agreement reasonable compensation is deemed to have been agreed. However, the Austrian Supreme Court has taken the opposite view and has stated that performances rendered within an informal relationship are considered to be complimentary.[15] Only in exceptional circumstances is the person rendering the performance entitled to payment, e.g. if it was rendered in expectation of a subsequent counter-performance.[16]

Finally, the Austrian Supreme Court has decided that the rules on the so-called 'relative surety' *(Angehörigenbürgschaft)* apply equally to partners in an informal relationship.[17] Hence a surety is infringing public morals and is therefore void if the undertaken liability is contrary to the guarantor's economic capacity and his/her free will was - at the time of assuming the surety - somehow diluted *(verdünnte Willensfreiheit)* and the creditor was aware of both facts.

BELGIUM

In the absence of specific legal provisions and of (implicit) agreements (part F. hereinafter), the general law of obligations and property law regulate the internal and external dimensions of informal relationships, both during the relationship and upon its termination. We think that it is important to stress that legal recognition is and should not be limited to a couple, but may also concern households beyond the couple.[18]

---

14 Austrian Supreme Court, Judgement of 13.07.2000, 6 Ob 30/00f; cf. A. DEIXLER-HÜBNER, *Scheidung, Ehe und Lebensgemeinschaft*, LexisNexis ARD ORAC, Vienna, 2013, at marg. No. 254.

15 Austrian Supreme Court, Judgement of 17.03.1999, 9 Ob 31/99w.

16 Austrian Supreme Court, Judgement of 19.12.2001, 9 Ob 291/01m; Austrian Supreme Court, Judgement of 27.01.1983, 6 Ob 817/82; H. KLAAR, 'Rechtsfragen nichtehelicher Lebensgemeinschaft', *AnwBl*, 1989, at p. 18.

17 Austrian Supreme Court, Judgement of 30.06.1988, 1 Ob 87/98w; F. LINDER, in: E. GITSCHTHALER and J. HÖLLWERTH (eds.), *Kommentar zum Ehe- und Partnerschaftsrecht*, Springer, Vienna, 2011, at p. 1099.

18 F. SWENNEN, *Het personen- en familierecht. Identiteit en verwantschap vanuit juridisch perspectief*, Intersentia, Antwerp, 2015, at n° 50.

For the internal dimension, both the law of obligations and property law are relevant to redress the situation between informal partners (1) during their relationship and (2) upon separation. (1) The possible contractual basis of transfers of money (or other resources) during the informal relationship is often disputed, particularly whether such transfers are loans or donations. *Actori incumbit probatio*: the existence of a particular contract must be proven according to the common law on evidence,[19] which requires written proof (Art. 1341 Belgian Civil Code). The moral impossibility to provide oneself with written proof (Art. 1348 Belgian Civil Code) during an informal relationship is only rarely accepted.[20] In the absence of a proven contractual basis, informal partners may try to rely on quasi-contracts and on property law. Firstly, the theory on natural obligations applies. A natural obligation exists when (a) a person subjectively considers he has a moral duty to perform, (b) in circumstances that are also considered to give rise to a moral duty by society at large and (c) performance cannot be enforced under civil law prior to the voluntary commencement of performance or promise to perform. Under Belgian law a moral duty exists to contribute to household expenses during an informal relationship.[21] Secondly, informal partners may seek compensation on the basis of *negotio gestorum*, but all conditions of this theory would rarely be fulfilled between informal partners.[22] Thirdly, investments by one partner in movable or immovable property can be balanced on the basis of property law. Firstly, joint owners must equally share in the rights and the charges of the joint property (Art. 577-2, § 3, 5 and 7 Belgian Civil Code). The sole owner is furthermore under an obligation both to compensate the accessories he wants to maintain on the basis of accession (Art. 555 and 566 Belgian Civil Code) and to reimburse the necessary and useful costs which the other partner has incurred.[23] Only insofar as, or to the extent that, transfers between informal partners cannot be based on the aforementioned bases, can the parties rely on undue payment and unjust

---

19 Cass. 26 October 2006, *RW* 2009-2010, 615.

20 For example, in Antwerp 14 March 2000, *AJT* 2000-2001, 835, with note WILMS but for example not in the District Court of Nivelles 25 October 2012, *Le Pli Juridique* 2013, N° 25, at p. 7, with note JASSOGNE.

21 K. WILLEMS, *De natuurlijke verbintenis*, die Keure, Bruges, 2011, at p. 255-258.

22 Ghent 20 November 2008, *TBBR* 2011, 44, with note BOULY and S. EGGERMONT, *De juridische bescherming van private relaties*, PhD, University of Antwerp, Antwerp, 2015, at n° 388.

23 For example, District Court of Oudenaarde 19 September 2005, *RABG* 2006, 774. Also see C. DECLERCK and V. ALLAERTS, 'Grondslag en waardering van vergoedingsrechten en schuldvorderingen tussen partners. Ontwikkelingen 2011-2013', in: P. SENAEVE (ed.), *Personen- en familierecht*, die Keure, Bruges, 2014, at p. 65-79.

enrichment.[24] This is particularly useful when a partner has excessively contributed to the household expenses.[25] (2) Upon the dissolution of the informal relationship, the ex- or surviving partner may firstly rely on a natural obligation to claim a contribution to the former household's expenses during a 'term of notice' and, to a lesser extent, to provide maintenance.[26] In the case of separation, tort law applies. Whereas the termination of an informal relationship is not a fault as such, the circumstances in which the relationship is terminated may give rise to tortious liability.[27] Damages then constitute a functional equivalent of the contribution to the household expenses or maintenance.

For the external dimension, vis-à-vis third parties, both the concept of legitimate expectation – e.g. that informal partners were actually married or legally cohabiting[28] – and the theory on apparent agency[29] are relevant.

BULGARIA

It is consistent court practice (case law) to acknowledge a compensation claim/right of each informal partner to damages after the death of the other partner. Such a principle is based on the understanding that informal relationships between heterosexual partners are similar to spousal relationships. In its leading Decision No. 5 of 1969 (issued in order to amend point 2 of Supreme Court Decision No. 4 of 1961 listing the circle of persons entitled to damages) the Supreme Court stated that:

> 'The circle of persons entitled to damages is justified by the court and it encompasses close relatives as well as the spouse. ... the informal partner who had cohabited with the deceased is also entitled, provided that the cohabitation neither constituted a crime nor was contrary to public morals ...'

The above reasoning was confirmed in 1984 (Supreme Court Decision No. 5 of 1984/civil case 2/84). In a recent case, the Supreme Court of

24 District Court of Ghent 28 June 2005, *T.Not.* 2005, 464.

25 V. DEHALLEUX, 'La répétition de la contribution excessive aux charges du ménage: proposition d'une nouvelle issue aux conflits entre cohabitants de fait', *TBBR* 2009, at p. 144.

26 K. WILLEMS, *De natuurlijke verbintenis*, die Keure, Bruges, 2011, at p. 290-301.

27 K. WILLEMS, *De natuurlijke verbintenis*, die Keure, Bruges, 2011, at p. 301-303.

28 G. COPS and K. SABBE, 'Niet getrouwd, wel gescheiden. Juridische aspecten van de beëindiging van de samenwoning', *NFM* 2002, at p. 10.

29 B. TILLEMAN, *Lastgeving*, Story-Scientia, Deurne, 1997, at n° 164.

Cassation has again validated the compensation right of partners in an informal relationship, providing the following reasoning:

> '... the factual cohabitation between the petitioner and the deceased was of sufficient duration (around 12 years) to lead to the conclusion that a sustainable close relationship had been established, similar to the one between spouses ...'

Irrespective of the ambiguous legal definition of beneficiaries, the courts recognise that an equivalent legal effect should be given to a marriage and a factual relationship with regard to access to family benefits for children. According to para. 1, p. 1 of the Additional Provision to the Bulgarian Family Benefits for Children Act (of 2002, last amended in 2013) 'The 'family' involves the spouses and the underage children ...'. In its Decision No. 11053 of 2013, case No. 4005/2013, the Supreme Administrative Court considered that:

> 'The legislature does not make a difference between children looked after in families (based on a marriage) and children looked after by parents who have not entered into a marriage. Children of unmarried parents or of parents not living together or cohabiting cannot be placed in an unprivileged position ...'

The official interpretation of this legal provision is that in cases of an informal relationship, the meaning of 'family' would involve the parent plus the child/children.[30] In this way, a somewhat strange legal construction has been created with the aim of providing a privileged status for children from an informal relationship. It is assumed that in the majority of cases the children of informal couples would live without one parent. In order to compensate for such a disadvantaged status the definition in question allows the access to benefits to be calculated on the basis of one parent's income. However, the available statistics do not support such an assumption (the majority of children born within informal families do in fact live with both of their parents). Therefore the definition should be questioned because it supports outcomes which are contrary to the public interest.

In its Decision No. 14060 of 2012, case No. 2482/12, the Supreme Administrative Court (3rd Division) confirmed the equal legal standing of formal and informal spousal relationships in relation to tenancy

---

30 See: Letter No. 91-01-224 of 26.08.2002 from the National Insurance Institution to the Ministry of Labour and Social Policy in relation to the application of the Family Benefits for Children Act and its Implementing Regulation (cited in the decision of the Supreme Administrative Court).

contracts. According to the facts of the case, a contract to rent a municipal apartment was signed by a mother with two children to provide her and her children with a family home. The municipality terminated the contract and sought to evict the woman based on a claim for a breach of contract because the contracting party had commenced a common relationship with a man. The municipality came to this interpretation based on a prohibition in the contract on re-renting the home to a third person. The Court considered that interpretation to be contrary to the national legislation which recognised and allowed for extramarital cohabitation especially where children have been born and are being looked after. According to this interpretation a man together with whom the contractor lives should not be considered as a third person but rather as a partner within an informal relationship that gives both partners the right to benefit equally from the contract. In its reasoning the Court also invoked Art. 7 and 9 of the EU Charter of Fundamental Rights that are directly applicable.

CROATIA

Informal relationships between a couple (of a different or same sex) are regulated by specific legislative provisions in Croatia.

Cohabitations are regulated by the Croatian Family Act. Same-sex informal partnerships are regulated by the Croatian Partnership Act.

CZECH REPUBLIC

The position of partners in an informal relationship is not regulated by the Czech Act on Registered Partnership nor is the term 'informal relationship' defined in Czech legislation. The Czech Civil Code uses the term 'close person' and says that persons related by affinity and persons permanently living together are also presumed to be close persons (S. 22(1) Czech Civil Code). This definition could also cover the partners in an informal relationship; that is why all the sections of the Czech Civil Code mentioned below could also be used while speaking about partners in an informal relationship.

There is no specific property law concerning an informal relationship. If partners to an informal relationship own something together, they are co-owners according to S. 1115 et seq. Czech Civil Code.

When the law of succession is applied, in some cases the partner can inherit from his or her partner who has died. This occurs when none of the deceased's descendants inherit; then those who lived with the deceased in the common household for at least one year before his death and, as a result, cared for the common household, inherit along with the deceased's parents or siblings (S. 1636(1) Czech Civil Code and S. 1637(1) Czech Civil Code). On the other hand these circumstances do not always apply strictly to informal relationships.

As for the lease of an apartment and the lease of a building, there is a special provision concerning the death of one of the partners in an informal relationship who is the lessee. If one of the partners who is the lessee dies and there is no joint lease of the apartment, the lease passes to a member of the lessee's household who was living in the apartment on the day of the lessee's death and has no apartment of his own. If such a person is someone other than the lessee's spouse, partner, parent, sibling, son-in-law, daughter-in-law, child or grandchild, the lease passes to such a person only if the lessor consents to the passage of the lease to that person (S. 2279(1) Czech Civil Code). It means that in case of the death of one partner, the other has a right to stay in the apartment without the permission of the lessor. A lease of an apartment in such cases is to end no later than two years from the date of the passage of the lease (S. 2279(2) Czech Civil Code).

For the purposes of the criminal law (see Czech Criminal Code, Act No. 40/2009 Coll.) where the term 'close person' is used as well, the condition of a long period of living together in a common household is not necessary, but it is only possible to use this term if the injury suffered by one of the partners is considered by the other partner as his own injury (S. 125 Czech Criminal Code). As for S. 100 of Act No. 141/1961 Coll., Czech Code of Criminal Procedure, concerning the right to refuse to testify, a witness is entitled to refuse to testify if the testimony would incriminate himself, his relative in the direct line of descent, his siblings, adoptive parent, adoptive, spouse, partner or mate, or other persons in a family or similar, or if it would conflict with the law by which the partner considered the injury as his own injury (S. 100(2) Czech Code of Criminal Procedure).

DENMARK

In Denmark the division of the cohabitants' property is based on case law and the principles of property law.[31] The first case came before the Supreme Court in 1980.[32] The Court concluded that joint ownership cannot be established in cohabitation beyond the general rules on joint ownership. To protect the financially weaker party the Court ruled that the weaker party can claim compensation if the stronger party has obtained unjust enrichment. This includes both a property law assessment and a family law assessment. According to a later decision by the Supreme Court the cohabitation must have been for at least two years and nine months.[33] In a decision in 1984 the Supreme Court ruled that if a cohabitant has exclusively worked in the home raising the children of the relationship, compensation will only be paid in extraordinary circumstances.[34]

In a 1985 decision, the Supreme Court synthesised its view on how to assess these cases in an informal rule:

> 'Based on Supreme Court decisions in similar cases, especially those quoted in *Ugeskrift for Retsvæsen* (Weekly Law Journal) 1980, p. 480 and 1982, p. 93, it must be considered as established law that when a long-lasting cohabitation is dissolved, a partner who, by contributing to the partners' shared expenses – or in other ways – has, to a considerable degree, made it possible for the other partner to create or maintain a not inconsiderable fortune, may be granted a certain amount, the size of which will be based on an assessment taking into consideration the length of the cohabitation, the partners' financial conditions etc.'[35]

In some cases a principle of reasonable expectations can support such an assessment.[36] The case law will also be relevant for homosexual couples who have neither married nor registered their partnership.

---

31 See J. ASLAND et al., *Nordisk Samboerrett*, Gyldendal Norsk Forlag, Oslo, 2014, at p. 131-135; I. LUND-ANDERSEN and I. NØRGAARD, *Familieret*, Jurist- og Økonomforbundets Forlag, Copenhagen, 2012, at p. 327-332; I. LUND-ANDERSEN, *Familieøkonomien*, Jurist- og Økonomforbundets Forlag, Copenhagen, 2011, at p. 361-425; and H.V. GODSK PEDERSEN and I. LUND-ANDERSEN, *Family Law in Denmark*, Kluwer Law International, Alphen aan den Rijn, 2011, at p. 80.

32 See *Ugeskrift for Retsvæsen* (Weekly Law Journal) 1980, at p. 480.

33 See *Ugeskrift for Retsvæsen* (Weekly Law Journal) 1982, at p. 93.

34 See *Ugeskrift for Retsvæsen* (Weekly Law Journal) 1984, at p. 166.

35 See *Ugeskrift for Retsvæsen* (Weekly Law Journal) 1985, at p. 607.

36 See *Ugeskrift for Retsvæsen* (Weekly Law Journal) 1984, at p. 166.

Apart from making this special family law claim for compensation, the financially weaker party can make a claim on the basis of general property law on e.g. loans, gifts and unjust enrichment.[37] A claim for unjust enrichment may be possible if the claimant has made payments that are significantly different from the parties' allocation of their obligations, for example if one of them has repaid a large loan taken out by the other. The amount will be allocated by a discretionary calculation. At most it will be equal to the enrichment and it may not exceed the loss of the person making the payment.

ENGLAND AND WALES

Although previously the English Law of Tort (obligations) had been used by informal, former cohabiting couples to obtain injunctions against their ex-partner for assault or harassment, the current domestic violence legislation (English Family Law Act 1996 Part IV) now covers this situation. In addition, the criminal and civil protection provided by the English Protection from Harassment Act 1997 which does not require proof of any relationship between the parties has also made this redundant and provides for restraining orders as well as criminal sanctions.

However, in the absence of any family law remedies governing family property on separation from cohabitation, property law is still applied and the law of trusts in particular has been actively used to fill the gap in family law. It is now most commonly used in family home disputes between cohabiting partners on relationship breakdown. Where there are no children of the family, this is the only possibility where the non-owner cohabitant wishes to try and establish that they are entitled to a share of the equity (or of the beneficial as opposed to the formal legal ownership) in the family home owned by their partner.

Property law in England and Wales separates legal ownership from so-called 'beneficial' or 'equitable' ownership and it is the latter which will dictate how the property is owned and how ultimately the proceeds of sale from the property will be distributed between the owners. Usually, legal and beneficial ownership will coincide but will not do so if that presumption can be displaced by evidence of a different common

---

[37] See J. ASLAND et. al., *Nordisk Samboerrett*, Gyldendal Norsk Forlag, Oslo, 2014, at p. 135-136; I. LUND-ANDERSEN and I. NØRGAARD, *Familieret*, Jurist- og Økonomforbundets Forlag, Copenhagen, 2012, at p. 325-327; and I. LUND-ANDERSEN, *Familieøkonomien*, Jurist- og Økonomforbundets Forlag, Copenhagen, 2011, at p. 285-321.

intention which has been relied upon by the non-legal owner. The court has power to determine whether a cohabitant has a beneficial share in a property (typically the family home although it can be used in respect of any property) which is formally legally owned by their partner/former partner, and to declare the respective shares of each partner in the property. If shared beneficial ownership is established, then the formal legal owner holds the home on trust for themselves and their partner in the shares determined by the court.

Applications can be made under S. 14 of the English Trusts of Land and Appointment of Trustees Act 1996 for declarations as to the beneficial ownership of the family home (or indeed other property). This statutory provision and the criteria for determining applications in S. 15 are considered by the court alongside the law developed by the courts around common intention 'constructive trusts' and previously, and perhaps still where there is a mixed family and commercial investment involved, 'resulting trusts'.

Resulting trusts are relatively straightforward. The common intention to share beneficial ownership is evidenced solely by each partner's direct financial contributions to the purchase or acquisition of the property. Their respective shares in the property will then reflect the proportion of each partner's financial contribution. So if a couple are found to have contributed £80,000 and £20,000 respectively to their home which cost £100,000 and was purchased in the name of the larger contributor and legal owner, they will beneficially jointly own the home. The legal owner holds the home on trust for them both in respective shares of 80% to 20% of its current value.

Constructive trusts most typically arise where just one partner is the legal owner of the property and the non-owner wishes to get a declaration of joint beneficial ownership from the court. However, where the home is legally owned in joint names but no declaration has been made as to the beneficial shares of ownership, the court can make a declaration as to how the property is held beneficially under a constructive trust. The starting point with joint ownership situations is that it is owned in equal shares but this presumption can be rebutted.

The statutory criteria in S. 15(1) English Trusts of Land and Appointment of Trustees Act 1996 for set out the matters to which the court must have regard when exercising its S. 14 powers and include:

- the intentions of the person(s) who created the trust;
- the purpose for which the trust is held;
- the welfare of any minor who occupies or might reasonably occupy the trust property as his home and the interests of any secured creditor or any beneficiary.

The leading cases are:

- *Gissing v Gissing* [1971] AC 886 in which the House of Lords originally confirmed that beneficial interests could be founded under common intention resulting or constructive trusts;
- *Lloyds Bank plc v Rossett* [1991] 1 AC 107 in which the House of Lords categorised two types of common intention constructive trust. First, (known as *Rossett 1*) where it is shown there is an agreement or understanding between the parties to share the property despite the legal ownership being solely in one partner's name. This requires the non-owner partner to provide evidence that they have then relied on this agreement to their detriment. It covers situations where the owner partner has misrepresented the reason for putting the property in their sole name (e.g. the young age of the partner (*Eves v Eves* [1975] 3 All ER 768, CA; or complications for a divorce from an ex-spouse as in *Grant v Edwards* [1986] Ch 638 CA), as well as where a promise such as 'Don't worry about the future because [the house] is half yours and I will always look after you' has been made by the legal owner (*Hammond v Mitchell* [1991] 2 All ER 109). However, there must be detrimental reliance referable to the promise or understanding such as significant expenditure or work on the property by the non-legal owner for a constructive trust to be found to exist.
- *Rossett 2* is where the common intention and the detrimental reliance is evidenced by the conduct of the parties and may typically comprise direct contributions to the purchase price or mortgage or significant work on the property. A small direct contribution may be sufficient as in *Midland Bank v Cooke* [1995] 4 All ER 562, CA, where the half share of a cash wedding present which became part of small deposit paid for the home was enough. Facilitating the payment of the mortgage was enough in *Le Foe v Le Foe and Woolwich plc* [2001] 2 FLR 970.
- *Stack v Dowden* [2007] UKHL 17; [2007] 2 AC 432 indicated that in joint ownership cases at least, resulting trusts were not appropriate to determine family home beneficial ownership. Rather, constructive trusts were the appropriate route. The case confirmed the starting point was a presumption that joint ownership meant a common intention to share ownership equally, but that this could be displaced

in exceptional cases. The House of Lords urged that a wider view of what could amount to a contribution to the acquisition of the home should be taken and 'the whole course of dealing' between the partners looked at in order to quantify their respective shares. Yet it was stated that unlike in the divorce context, the overall aim was not to achieve fairness between the parties. It also remains the case that the acts must be referable to the purchase, so facilitating the mortgage payments will count but child care alone, for example, is unlikely to sufficient.

- *Jones v Kernott* [2011] UKSC 53; [2012] 1 AC 776 was another joint ownership case which sought to rebut the equal share presumption and did so successfully. Here, one partner had left the home and taken their share of the endowment life assurance policy proceeds, had left the other partner to pay the mortgage but had not formally transferred the home into her sole name or declared unequal shares. The Supreme Court here indicated that in quantifying the shares, the court's role was to determine a fair outcome and could infer what was intended in such a joint ownership case. Two Supreme Court Justices went as far as to indicate they could impute what the intentions of reasonable and just people would have been, had they thought about it at the time. Future cases may clarify the situation in time.

Another possibility although it overlaps with constructive trusts and is far less used is the doctrine of proprietary estoppel. In order to establish this, a claimant must show a representation made by one partner which is relied upon by the claimant who suffers detriment as a consequence.

In *Wayling v Jones* (1995) 69 P & CR 170; [1995] 2 FLR 1029, a gay couple ran a hotel together which was owned by one of them. The deceased owner had left this hotel to his partner in his will. Shortly before his death, the deceased had sold his hotel business and purchased another hotel where they both lived and which was run by the deceased's partner for little remuneration, to his detriment. Thus although the will left the original hotel which the deceased no longer owned to the partner, the court found that the estate was 'estopped' (prevented) from denying the gift to the surviving partner of the new hotel.

The steps to establishing proprietary estoppel set out above were summarised in *Thorner v Majors* [2009] UKHL 18; [2009] FLR 405.

ESTONIA

In relations governed by private law, the main circle of legal relations is formed by the mutual proprietary relations of the partners in an informal relationship.[38] The provisions of the Estonian Law of Obligations Act[39] can be applied when the parties have not otherwise regulated their mutual proprietary relations, primarily the provisions of the Estonian Law of Obligations Act which regulate the a partnership contract. Before the Estonian Law of Obligations Act entered into force on July 1, 2002, the provisions on the joint operation contract, § 438 et seq. of the Civil Code of the Estonian SSR,[40] could be applied to the proprietary relations in an informal relationship. In the judgement of the Supreme Court of December 20, 2005, in the civil case 3-2-1-142-05, the Supreme Court found that, in the opinion of the chamber, the partners in an informal relationship can purchase property with common ownership on the basis of a joint operation contract.[41]

In a partnership contract under the Estonian Law of Obligations Act (§ 580 et seq. Estonian Law of Obligations Act), two or more persons (partners) undertake to act in order to achieve a mutual objective and to help the objective to be achieved in the manner established by the contract, above all by making contributions. The contribution made by a partner may be any form of promoting a mutual objective, including the transfer of assets to the partnership, grant the use of assets to the partnership or the provision of services to the partnership (§ 581(1) Estonian Law of Obligations Act).

According to section 1 of § 77 of the General Part of the Estonian Civil Code Act and section 1 of § 11 of the Estonian Law of Obligations Act, a partnership contract can also be concluded orally. According to the first sentence of section 1 of § 230 of the Estonian Code of Civil Procedure, the party who bases his or her actions on a partnership contract must provide evidence of this partnership contract.

---

38 A. OLM, 'Mitteabieluline kooselu ja selle õiguslik regulatsioon', Justiitsministeerium, Õiguspoliitika osakond, Eraõiguse talitus, Tallinn, 2009, at para. 4.1.

39 Võlaõigusseadus (adopted on 26 September 2001, entered into force on 1 July 2002). – RT I 2001, 81, 487; RT I, 29.06.2014, 109 (in Estonian), available in English at: www.riigiteataja.ee/en/eli/ee/Riigikogu/act/516092014001/consolide.

40 Eesti NSV tsiviilkoodeks (Civil Code of the Estonian SSR). – ENSV Ülemnõukogu Teataja 1964, 25 (234) lisa (in Estonian).

41 Decision of the Civil Chamber of the Supreme Court 3-2-1-142-05, at para. 13.

The legal information department of the Supreme Court has undertaken a profound analysis of the application of partnership contracts[42] and one part of this analysis deals with the application of the provisions of partnership contracts to the different forms of informal partnerships. According to this analysis, the courts have considered, for example, the renovation of a shared residence and jointly raising children to amount to a joint objective. Thus, the Court has stated that shared family life is the objective of the partnership: the contributions of one party in a shared family life were monetary transfers and the contribution of the other party was the organisation of the subsistence of the family.[43]

The courts have considered it possible to apply the provisions of a partnership contract to the relations between the parties when one of the parties has worked to increase the property belonging to the other party without receiving extra compensation. According to the courts, the prerequisite in applying the partnership regulation to the proprietary relations of the partners in an informal partnership does not have to be the partnership contract, concluded with direct declarations of intent, but it is sufficient if the factual behaviour of the parties refers to the conclusion of the contract. The partnership can be assumed if the partners have a common household and a common objective can be discerned from their behaviour, which may amount to making common efforts to enable the use of a shared place of residence.

This broad interpretation by the courts, which does not really fit within the objective of the regulation of the partnership contract under the Estonian Law of Obligations Act, in regulating the proprietary relations in an informal relationship after the end of cohabitation must presumably change in the future.

Namely, the Civil Chamber of the Supreme Court found in its decision of December 3, 2014, that the informal partnership (a free marriage) between a man and a woman with a shared permanent household cannot be automatically regarded as a partnership and thus the provisions of the Estonian Law of Obligations Act[44] cannot be applied. In the opinion of the chamber, an informal partnership between persons does not meet the criteria of a partnership. The provisions on the partnership contract should be applied to the proprietary relations of cohabiting parties if one

42 Seltsinguleping, Kohtupraktika analüüs. Riigikohtu õigusteabe osakond, 2014, available at: www.riigikohus.ee/vfs/1673/Seltsinguleping_Piho_Moller.pdf (in Estonian).

43 Decision 2-11-33881 of the Tartu County Court of 15 December 2011.

44 Decision of the Civil Chamber of the Supreme Court 3-2-1-109-14, at para. 13.

of the parties has worked to preserve or increase the value of the property belonging to the other party, without receiving extra compensation for this, e.g. building or constructing a shared place of residence. At the same time the partnership contract presumes the conclusion of a contract via a direct or indirect declaration of intent: thus, if the parties have not concluded a partnership contract, their behaviour should be intepreted in order to discover whether a parnership contract in fact exists. Identifying a common objective on the basis of the behaviour of cohabiting parties generally presumes the existence of a shared household; however, the references in the legal literature clearly state that cohabitation in isolation is insufficient to apply the provisions of the partnership contract to the informal partnership relationship.[45] In the decision of December 20, 2005, the Supreme Court found[46] that the contract of joint operation for purchasing an apartment with common ownership must be authenticated by a notary. Therefore, if such a contract has not been concluded by the partners in an informal partnership, it is impossible to proceed from the fact that the common objective of the parties was the purchase of an apartment with common ownership. In addition, the Supreme Court noted that the contract of joint operation could have been concluded also for other objectives than for purchasing a shared object. If the parties did not regulate their proprietary relations with a contract in acquiring, improving or managing an apartement, the party who has incurred expenses in this respect may file a claim for unjustified enrichment against the other party. The liquidation provisions of the partnership can be applied to the distribution of specific items of higher value (e.g. immovable property) acquired during the informal partnership with a shared household if: both parties have made noticeable and comparable financial contributions (evaluated on a monetary basis) to acquire or improve the item and when acquiring or improving the item the parties had at least a common intention with regard to the lasting establishment of an economically common material value (joint property).[47]

According to the General Part of the Estonian Civil Code Act § 5, civil rights and obligations arise from transactions, events provided by law, other acts which create civil rights and obligations as prescribed by law, and from unlawful acts.

---

45 P. Varul, I. Kull, V. Kõve and M. Käerdi, *Võlaõigusseadus II. Kommenteeritud väljaanne* (Law of Obligations II. Commented Edition), Juura, Tallinn, 2007, at p. 641 (in Estonian).

46 Decision of the Civil Chamber of the Supreme Court 3-2-1-142-05, at para. 14.

47 Decision of the Civil Chamber of the Supreme Court 3-2-1-109-14, at para. 19.

So, as referred to in this provision, the civil rights and liabilities of the partners in an informal partnership are incurred in relation to third parties as well as towards each other on the basis of transactions or the law. Thus, legal relations between the partners in an informal partnership may be incurred on the basis of *negotiorum gestio*, a gratuitous contract or unjustified enrichment.

The regulation of a lease contract under the Estonian Law of Obligations Act regulation deserves attention. According to § 289 of the Estonian Law of Obligations Act, the lessee of a dwelling has the right to house in that dwelling his or her spouse, minor children and parents who are incapacitated for work without the consent of the lessor unless it is agreed in the lease contract that the lessee may do so only with the consent of the lessor. The partner in an informal partnership is not included in this list. At the same time, § 289 has been entitled 'Accommodation of the family members of the lessee of a dwelling' and the partner in an informal partnership should be included in the term 'family member'. The legal literature is rather unclear as to whether the housing of unlisted persons in such a dwelling is a breach of contract – the right of the lessee to house other persons may be derived from the wording of the lease contract.[48] According to § 391(1) of the Estonian Law of Obligations Act, upon the death of a lessee of a dwelling, the spouse who lived in the dwelling together with the lessee has the right to take the place of the lessee in the lease contract. If the lessee did not have a spouse who has this right or who does not wish to take the place of the lessee in the lease contract, other family members who lived in the dwelling together with the lessee have the right to take the place of the lessee in the lease contract pursuant to an agreement between them.

§ 129 of the Estonian Law of Obligations Act regulates the compensation for patrimonial damage upon death. According to § 129(6) of the Estonian Law of Obligations Act, if a person who has died has maintained, on a continuous basis up to his or her death, another person with whom the deceased lived together as a family or whom the deceased person maintained on the basis of a moral obligation, the person who has caused the death and who is therefore obliged to compensate for the damage

48 P. VARUL, I. KULL, V. KÕVE and M. KÄERDI, *Võlaõigusseadus II. Kommenteeritud väljaanne* (Law of Obligations II. Commented Edition), Juura, Tallinn, 2007, at p. 187 (in Estonian); at the same time there is an opinion that § 289 of the Estonian Law of Obligations Act exhaustively list persons who have the right to use the thing together with the lessee (A. OLM, 'Mitteabieluline kooselu ja selle õiguslik regulatsioon', Justiitsministeerium, Õiguspoliitika osakond, Eraõiguse talitus, Tallinn, 2009, at para. 4.4).

shall pay compensation to that person if: the person needs maintenance, and he or she cannot receive maintenance in any other manner, and the person who has died would presumably have continued to maintain the person in the future. The legal literature has also acknowledged that a cohabiting partner should be considered as a person with whom the deceased person lived 'together as in a family' and that he or she therefore has a right to rely on section 6, § 129 of the Estonian Law of Obligations Act, which considers the factual maintenance relationship between the deceased and the surviving person in question.[49] Third-party liability towards the partner in an informal partnership is also a possibility.

According to the Estonian Law of Obligations Act § 767(1), if a healthcare service is provided to an unconscious or incapable patient, the immediate family of the patient must be informed of his or her state of health. The immediate family here means the spouse, parents, children, and siblings of the patient. Other persons who are close to the patient may also be deemed to be immediate family members if this can be concluded from the patient's way of life (§ 767(2) of the Estonian Law of Obligations Act).

An informal partnership in itself does not change aspects of ownership. Each person shall remain the owner of his/her possessions. Things purchased during the relationship are acquired according to the general rules of property law, i.e. either subject to the sole ownership of one party or common ownership.[50] According to § 90(1) of the Estonian Law of Property Act,[51] a possessor of movable property and any earlier possessor shall be deemed the owner of the thing during the possessor's possession until the contrary is proved. The presumption of ownership concerning the possessor of the movable property, under § 90, generally involves also the presumption of the co-possessor's common ownership, which provides certain protection to the (non-owner) spouse as well as to other cohabiting partners. In the case of immovable property, this presumption is not valid, as it concerns primarily the household and the consumer goods used in daily life.[52]

---

49 K. KAMA and K. KULLERKUPP, 'Vabaabielu versus abielu: varalised suhted muutuvate kooseluvormide kontekstis', *Juridica*, 2002, No. 6, pp. 359-368.

50 Decision of the Civil Chamber of the Supreme Court 3-2-1-109-14, at para. 17.

51 Asjaõigusseadus (adopted on 9 June 1993, entered into force on 1 December 1993). – RT I 1993, 39, 590; RT I, 08.07.2014, 7 (in Estonian), available in English at: www.riigiteataja.ee/en/eli/ee/Riigikogu/act/510072014007/consolide.

52 K. KAMA and K. KULLERKUPP, 'Vabaabielu versus abielu: varalised suhted muutuvate kooseluvormide kontekstis', *Juridica*, 2002, No. 6, pp. 359-368.

Persons in an informal partnership have been referred to by the Estonian legislation in several different legal areas. As for social security law, the Estonian Social Welfare Act[53] should be noted, § 22(2) of which stipulates that the granting of a subsistence benefit is based on the income of the benefit applicant and his or her family members. Upon the granting of a subsistence benefit, persons who are married or living in the same dwelling in a conjugal relationship, their children and parents in need of assistance or other persons using one or more sources of income jointly or with a shared household are deemed to be family members.

§ 117 of the Estonian Bankruptcy Act[54] stipulates that the persons in question are deemed to be connected with a debtor who is a natural person. According to § 117(1) of the Estonian Bankruptcy Act, the spouse of the debtor is deemed to be connected with a debtor even if the marriage was contracted after the conclusion of the transaction which is subject to recovery, and the former spouse of the debtor if the marriage was terminated within one year before the conclusion of the transaction and persons who live in a shared household with the debtor or who lived in a shared household with the debtor during the year preceding the conclusion of the transaction which is subject to recovery. In its decision of May 21, 2012,[55] the Supreme Court found that the following indicated that the person in question is connected to the debtor: a common child of the debtor and the defendant as well as when, during the legal proceedings, the debtor has recognised cohabitation with the defendant. The specification of the persons connected to the debtor on the basis of the Estonian Bankruptcy Act is important in enforcement proceedings. According to the Estonian Code of Enforcement Procedure[56] § 188, a court shall declare invalid a transaction which has been entered into by a debtor within three years before an action by a claimant for a declaration of invalidity relating to the transaction has been filed in order to knowingly damage the interests of the claimant if the counterparty knew or should have known thereof at the time of entering into the transaction.

---

53 Sotsiaalhoolekande seadus (adopted on 8 February 1995, entered into force on 1 April 1995). - RT I 1995, 21, 323; RT I, 13.12.2014, 44 available in English at: www.riigiteataja.ee/en/eli/ee/Riigikogu/act/509072014019/consolide.

54 Pankrotiseadus (adopted on 22 January 2003, entered into force on 1 January 2004). - RT I 2003, 17, 95; RT I, 21.06.2014, 20, available in English at: www.riigiteataja.ee/en/eli/ee/Riigikogu/act/511072014018/consolide.

55 Decision of the Civil Chamber of the Supreme Court 3-2-1-62-12, at para. 9.

56 Täitemenetluse seadustik (adopted on 20 April 2005, entered into force on 1 January 2006). - RT I 2005, 27, 198; RT I, 31.12.2014, 14, available in English at: www.riigiteataja.ee/en/eli/ee/Riigikogu/act/521012015001/consolide.

It is presumed that a counterparty knew or should have known that a transaction damages the interests of another party if the counterparty is a person connected with a debtor or the transaction was entered into six months before the commencement of enforcement proceedings or the seizure of the assets of the debtor. Persons connected with a debtor shall be determined according to § 117 of the Estonian Bankruptcy Act.

The provisions regarding the impartiality of a judge under Estonian civil procedural law state that if the partners in an informal partnership are participants in the proceedings, this is a fact which may give rise to doubts as to the impartiality of the judge. According to § 23 item 2 of the Estonian Code of Civil Procedure,[57] a judge shall not adjudicate a civil matter and shall remove himself or herself in a matter involving his or her spouse or cohabitee. The Estonian Code of Administrative Court Procedure[58] refers to the regulation of the Estonian Code of Civil Procedure with regard to the removal of a judge.

According to § 49(1) item 4 of the Estonian Code of Criminal Procedure,[59] a judge is required to remove himself or herself from a criminal proceeding if he or she is or has been a person who is/was close to the accused, victim or civil defendant. The circle of close persons shall be determined on the basis of § 71(1) Estonian Code of Criminal Procedure and it includes the spouse, the person in a permanent cohabitation and his/her parent, including after the end of a marriage or permanent cohabitation (§ 71(1) item 5).

The Estonian Code of Misdemeanour Procedure[60] does not directly refer to the partner in an informal partnership, but according to § 25(1) item 3, an official of a body conducting extrajudicial proceedings or a judge is required to remove himself or herself if he or she cannot remain impartial.

---

57 Tsiviilkohtumenetluse seadustik (adopted on 20 April 2005, entered into force on 1 January 2006). - RT I 2005, 26, 197; RT I, 31.12.2014, 5 (in Estonian), available in English at: www.riigiteataja.ee/en/eli/ee/Riigikogu/act/504092014001/consolide.

58 Halduskohtumenetluse seadustik (adopted on 27 January 2011, entered into force on 1 January 2012). - RT I, 23.02.2011, 3; RT I, 31.12.2014, 9 (in Estonian), available in English at: www.riigiteataja.ee/en/eli/508072014005/consolide.

59 Kriminaalmenetluse seadustik (adopted on 12 February 2003, entered into force on 1 July 2004). - RT I 2003, 27, 166; RT I, 30.12.2014, 9 (in Estonian), available in English at: www.riigiteataja.ee/en/eli/520012015017/consolide.

60 Väärteomenetluse seadustik (adopted on 22 May 2002, entered into force on 1 September 2002). - RT I 2002, 50, 313; RT I, 12.07.2014, 12 (in Estonian), available in English at: www.riigiteataja.ee/en/eli/521082014006/consolide.

According to § 9(1) item 5 Estonian Code of Enforcement Procedure, a bailiff shall not conduct enforcement proceedings and shall remove himself or herself by a decision if he or she is a spouse of a debtor or a claimant, or a person permanently living together with a debtor or a claimant, even if the marriage or permanent cohabitation has ended. There are numerous examples of recognising unregistered cohabitation in Estonian laws with regard to avoiding corruption. For example, according to § 120 (1 and 2) of the Estonian Public Procurement Act,[61] a member of the Review Committee will not review a request and will remove him/herself from reviewing the request in the event of the occurrence of a fact that gives reason to cast doubts as to his or her impartiality. The occurrence of this fact will be presumed if a member of the Review Committee reviewing a request is the spouse, cohabitee, or also the sibling or any other direct blood relative of the spouse or cohabitee, including after the termination of the marriage or permanent cohabitation with a party to the proceedings or to the legal representative of the party to the proceedings.

The Estonian Taxation Act[62] also includes procedural public law provisions, according to § 49(1) item 2 of which an official of a tax authority shall not conduct proceedings in a matter if he or she is a relative (parent, child, adoptive parent, adopted child, brother, sister, grandparent or grandchild), a relative by marriage (the spouse's parent, child, adoptive parent, adopted child, brother, sister, grandparent or grandchild) or a family member of a participant in the proceedings or of a representative of a participant in the proceedings. The partner in an informal partnership should be treated as a family member. According to § 6(2) item 3 of the Estonian Victim Support Act,[63] a victim support volunteer cannot be a person who is a grandparent, parent, brother, sister, child or grandchild, spouse or cohabitee of an official of the Social Insurance Board who provides victim support services and supervises him or her, or a parent, brother, sister or child of the spouse or cohabitee.

---

61 Riigihangete seadus (adopted on 24 January 2007, entered into force on 1 May 2007). – RT I 2007, 15, 76; RT I, 12.07.2014, 123 (in Estonian), available in English at: www.riigiteataja.ee/en/eli/509072014009/consolide.

62 Maksukorralduse seadus (adopted on 20 February 2002). – RT I 2002, 26, 150; RT I, 23.12.2014, 20 (in Estonian), available in English at: www.riigiteataja.ee/en/eli/523012015008/consolide.

63 Ohvriabi seadus (adopted on 17 December 2003). – RT I 2004, 2, 3; RT I, 15.03.2014, 24 (in Estonian), available in English at: www.riigiteataja.ee/en/eli/517062014014/consolide.

§ 84(2) of the Estonian Credit Institutions Act[64] lists persons with equivalent economic interests to the persons related to a credit institution. These persons include the spouse or cohabitee, children, parents, sisters and brothers of a manager of a credit institution, of the head of an internal audit unit or of the chairman of an audit committee.

Several laws restrict official relationships of subordination and they also directly refer to partners in an informal partnership. The Estonian Military Service Act[65] § 92(3) item 4 allows a serviceman/woman to be appointed to a civilian post, as long as that person is not a spouse of an immediate superior or a person in a relationship with an immediate superior which is similar to a marriage (hereinafter an unmarried partner) or a grandparent of an active serviceman, a parent or descendant of a parent of the immediate commander or his or her spouse or his or her unmarried partner, including a child or grandchild. According to the Estonian Civil Service Act[66] § 15(4), a person may not be employed in a government post if he or she is a spouse or a partner in a marriage-like relationship (an unmarried partner) or a grandparent or parent of an official who has direct control over the corresponding post, or a parent or a descendant of the parent, including a child and grandchild, of a spouse or an unmarried partner. According to § 15(2) item 4 of the Estonian Prosecutor's Office Act,[67] a person shall not be appointed as a prosecutor if he or she is a spouse, cohabitant or grandparent of the person who exercises direct control over the position of a prosecutor, or who is a parent or a relative in the descending line of the person exercising direct control over the position of a prosecutor or their spouse or cohabitant, including a child and grandchild.

Several laws recognise the right of the partner in an informal partnership not to testify, in order to avoid being in a situation of conflict in judicial proceedings. According to § 257(1) item 5 of the Estonian Code of Civil Procedure, the spouse of or a person permanently living together with

---

64 Krediidiasutuste seadus (adopted on 9 February 1999). – RT I 1999, 23, 349; RT I, 23.12.2014, 28 (in Estonian), available in English at: www.riigiteataja.ee/en/eli/517062014001/consolide.

65 Kaitseväeteenistuse seadus (adopted on 13 June 2012, entered into force on 1 April 2013). – RT I, 10.07.2012, 1; RT I, 22.12.2014, 3 (in Estonian), available in English at: www.riigiteataja.ee/en/eli/519092014003/consolide.

66 Avaliku teenistuse seadus (adopted on 13 June 2012). – RT I, 06.07.2012, 1; RT I, 18.02.2014, 4 (in Estonian), available in English at: www.riigiteataja.ee/en/eli/509072014003/consolide.

67 Prokuratuuriseadus (adopted on 22 April 1998). – RT I 1998, 41, 625; RT I, 21.12.2012, 16 (in Estonian), available in English at: www.riigiteataja.ee/en/eli/ee/Riigikogu/act/513112013015/consolide.

the plaintiff or defendant has the right to refuse to testify as a witnesses, even if the marriage or permanent cohabitation has come to an end. According to § 71(1) item 5 of the Estonian Code of Criminal Procedure, the spouse of or a person permanently living together with the suspect or accused, and the parents of the spouse or person, even if the marriage or permanent cohabitation has come to an end, have the right to refuse to testify as witnesses. The presentation, taking and examination of evidence in administrative matters is subject to the provisions of the Estonian Code of Civil Procedure, thus, also the right of witnesses to refuse to testify during an administrative court procedure. The Estonian Taxation Act does not prescribe the right to refuse to give evidence to the partner in an informal partnership.

FINLAND

Not applicable. Cohabitation is given legal effect under written law.

FRANCE

The law of obligations and the law of property can also be used by partners in an informal relationship. Especially in the case of the breakup of the relationship, legal instruments such as unjust enrichment, *de facto* partnership (*société créée de fait),* and tort law are sometimes used to compensate one of the partners. See under Question 41 et seq. If they buy property together (joint ownership, *indivision),* the partners can agree on an accretion clause (*tontine, clause d'accroissement).* Indeed, at the time of the joint acquisition it is possible to insert in the contract a clause according to which each party will be reputed to have been the exclusive owner of the asset since its acquisition, provided the other party dies first.[68] At the time of the death of one of the co-contracting parties, the other becomes retroactively the sole owner of the asset.[69] This avoids the payment of inheritance taxes, which are very high if the partners are neither married nor registered partners (60%).[70] However, the French Tax Code lays down specific conditions which have to be fulfilled (the

---

68 The legality of such a clause has been established for a long time in French contract law. See Cass. Civ 1, 3 February 1959, D. 1960, at p. 592 note De LA MARNIERRE.

69 However, the Court of cassation held that such a clause was not valid and that the contract must be considered to be a bequest if the deceased partner was much older than her partner, was very ill and had solely paid the price of the property in full (Cass. Civ. I, 10 May 2007, no. 05-21011, *RJPF* 2007-9/31, with note VALORY.

70 For more details, see under Question 52.

low amount of the transaction; the property purchased must be the partners' common and principal home, etc.).

Cohabitants can also make the choice to acquire real estate under a real estate non-commercial company scheme (*Société civile immobilière*). According to this scheme the real estate is owned by the company and each of the cohabitants owes a percentage of the shares therein. Shares can be easily transferred from the one to the other according to general principles of company law.

GERMANY

Existing informal relationships between a couple are given legal effect in landlord and tenant law. A leading case of the Federal Constitutional Court paved the way by allowing the application of the precursor to § 563 German Civil Code in the 'Unmarried civil partner as tenant case'[71] (see Question 4).

Legal effects are mainly recognised after termination of the relationship. Under certain circumstances a former cohabitant's claims for compensation may be admitted. This is done with the help of the law of obligations. The leading case was a decision of the Federal Supreme Court of 1 April 1965.[72] In that case the cohabitants built a house together. Despite the fact that the house was registered to only one of the cohabitants, upon that cohabitant's death the non-registered cohabitant was able to file a claim for compensation against the registered cohabitant's heir. The legal basis for the claim was the law of civil partnerships (§§ 705 et seq. German Civil Code; see Question 46).

Proprietary aspects are assessed by application of the law of property (see Question 28).

A leading case in public law decided that the income of a cohabitant was to be taken into account for recipients of unemployment benefits[73] (see Question 5).

---

71 For the former § 569a German Civil Code BVerfG, 3.4.1990, *BVerfGE*, 82, 6 = *NJW*, 1990, 1593. English translation in Federal Constitutional Court (ed.), *Decisions of the Bundesverfassungsgericht*, vol. 5, Family-related decisions 1957 - 2010, Nomos, Baden-Baden, 2013, p. 311.

72 Federal Supreme Court (Bundesgerichtshof; BGH), 1.4.1965, *FamRZ*, 1965, 368.

73 BVerfG, 17.11.1992, *BVerfGE*, 87, 234 = *NJW*, 1993, S.643 = *FamRZ*, 1993, 164.

GREECE

Informal relationships are subject in general to the provisions of the law of obligations and of property law. The Athens Court of Appeal has ruled that straightforward informal cohabitation is a *de facto* relationship without any legal consequences.[74]

The Supreme Court has classed informal cohabitations among those atypical or, from the legal perspective, irregular situations which lie on the margins of legal life. It is also accepted that not even the provisions on unjust enrichment are applicable, given that the benefits accruing to one partner from the other are not without legal cause, but are granted *causa donandi*, in the context of the relationship of mutual confidence between the partners. Extra-marital cohabitation, and the tacit agreement, within the relationship of mutual confidence thereby created, on the performing of services or the provision of material support between the cohabitants is a reason for protecting the material benefits for one partner or the other within the relationship, which precludes any claim of unjust enrichment.[75]

It has moreover been claimed by another court (Kozani Single-Member Court of First Instance)[76] that not even the provisions on a silent partnership agreement are applicable to informal cohabitation. However, in one of its rulings,[77] the Supreme Court took a more tempered view: 'There is no scope for the application, *mutatis mutandis*, of the provisions on silent partners to free unions, since there is no similarity between the two relationships. It will, however, be possible to apply directly the aforesaid provisions, as well as those on unjust enrichment, if in a specific case of free cohabitation there exist other conditions for the application of the said provisions'.[78]

HUNGARY

As the Hungarian Civil Code of 1959 was modernised in 1977, the regulation on cohabitation was introduced at that time. Therefore, there is no need to apply the law of obligations or the law of property. On the other hand, there are some judicial cases where the relationship between the couple has not been qualified as cohabitation although it originally

---

74 Athens Court of Appeal, judgment No. 5530/2009.
75 See Supreme Court - Areios Pagos, judgment Nos. 874/2008 and 206/2011.
76 Kozani Single-Member Court of First Instance, judgment No. 204/2009.
77 Supreme Court - Areios Pagos, judgment No. 874/2008.
78 As translated by the authors of the Greek report.

seemed to be cohabitation, but one partner contested this later on. If some elements which are required for cohabitation are lacking and the court decides that there is in fact no cohabitation, there is sometimes a need to refer to the law of obligations or the law of property. However, although the judgments do not exclude other legal solutions, whenever a legal proposal to apply unjust enrichment has emerged in order to solve property relations, it has been rejected.

REPUBLIC OF IRELAND

This can be seen in property law - as properties can be owned by a couple in an informal relationship under a joint tenancy or under a tenancy in common. Where property is held in a joint tenancy, each tenant has an equal undivided share of the property that will pass automatically to the surviving joint tenant(s) upon the death of one joint tenant. Under a tenancy in common, the co-owners each hold a distinct, independent but undivided share of the property, not necessarily equal, which will pass upon the death of one tenant to whomever he stipulates under a will or alternatively, on intestacy. Relevant and instructive cases include the following:

- Joint tenancy: Irwin v Deasy [2011] IESC 15.
- Tenancy in common: MC v BS [2008] IEHC 463.

Section 36 of the Irish Family Law Act 1995 governs property disputes between married couples. While this provision does not apply to disputes between couples in an informal relationship, S. 44 of the Irish Family Law (Divorce) Act 1996 provides that it operates in respect of couples who had previously been engaged. Where an agreement to marry is terminated, S. 36 of the 1995 Act applies as if the parties to the agreement were married, to any dispute between them, or any claim by one of them, in relation to property in which either or both of them had a beneficial interest while the agreement was in force.

Guardianship, access and custody disputes concerning the children of couples in an informal relationship, whether they have cohabited or not, are conducted through applying to the District Family or Circuit Family Courts for orders under the Irish Guardianship of Infants Act 1964. For maintenance of children, applications are made to the family courts under the Irish Family Law (Maintenance of Spouses and Children) Act 1976.

The Irish Domestic Violence Act 1996 (as amended) provides protection to persons in informal relationships. A person can apply for a barring order against a cohabitant where the applicant and the respondent have lived together in an intimate and committed relationship for six months in aggregate out of the previous nine months. As a barring order effectively removes the respondent from his or her home, cohabitants can only apply for same where they have an equal or greater interest in the property in question than the respondent. The remedy of a safety order is more widely accessible to those in informal relationships. A person can seek a safety order where they are neither the respondent's spouse or civil partner nor related to them within the prohibited degrees of relationship, but have lived with the respondent in an intimate and committed relationship prior to the application for a safety order. In addition, a parent of a child can always apply for a safety order against the other parent of their child, without any cohabitation requirement whatsoever.

The Irish Children and Family Relationships Bill 2015 makes extensive provision for informal relationships and, when enacted, will bring about fundamental change to the law in this area. This new legislation will enable an eligible adult to apply to court for a guardianship order as detailed in Question 1.

ITALY

Given the absence of a comprehensive regulation of informal relationships provided for by the law, informal relationships are sometimes given legal effect by the courts through an effective, though patchy, set of rules.

In the case of the death of a partner in an informal relationship and when this death has been caused by an unlawful act by a third party, the courts have determined that the surviving partner has the right to compensation against the wrongdoer (Art. 2043 Italian Civil Code). This rule has been acknowledged in more recent case law, while older decisions used to hold the view that no right to compensation accrued in the case of cohabitation, as the cohabitant had no 'right' to maintenance from the deceased partner.[79] The current case law, on the contrary, has also

[79] Cass. 21 September 1981 n. 8209, in *Dir. Prat. Assic.* 716; compare G. FERRANDO, *Diritto di famiglia*, Zanichelli, Bologna, 2013, at p. 152.

extended compensation to interested parties, such as, indeed, cohabitants who only have expectations vis-à-vis the victim but no rights.[80]

LATVIA

The Senate of the Supreme Court of the Republic of Latvia, Department of Administrative Cases, in a judgment[81] of 28 February 2008, has analysed the meaning of the word 'family' within the social sphere. The case was about assistance in solving a housing issue. The Court pointed out that, in social rights, the solution to many questions and the provision of assistance applies to the concept of 'the family'. In this judgment the Court referred to the European Court of Human Rights (for example, see judgement of the European Court of Human Rights in the case Keegan v. Ireland) where, according to Art. 8 of the European Convention on Human Rights, it has been recognised that the concept of 'the family' is not limited to relationships based on marriage; it can contain other *de facto* family ties when people live together without entering into marriage.

Then on 27 July 2010, in a later judgment[82] in the same case the Department of Administrative Cases of the Senate of the Supreme Court pointed out that, since it had ascertained that the people concerned actually created a common family, refusal of assistance to one of the people in a family for an obviously formal reason was impermissible (including the reason that people have not formally registered their marriage). In assessing whether there actually was a family, the Court heard the explanations of the applicant and third parties regarding the existence of extended cohabitation, that within this cohabitation two sons had been born, that the family had common expenses (family budget), and that all the members of the family shared psychological and emotional links. Accordingly, the Court concluded that, for an extended period, there had been a *de facto* family life, without a marriage. In this

80 See extensively L. BARDARO, 'Il convivente della vittima', in: P. CENDON (ed.), *Trattato dei nuovi danni*, Cedam, Padua, 2011, at p. 215 et seq.; Cass. 10 March 1994, n. 2322, in *Giur. It.*, 1995, I, 1, 1370; Cass. 24 March 1994 n. 2988, in *Giust. Civ.*, 1994, p. 1849. Compare also G. OBERTO, *I diritti dei conviventi. Realtà e prospettive tra Italia ed Europa*, Cedam, Padua, 2012, at p. 204 et seq.; R. TOMMASINI, 'La famiglia di fatto', in: M. BESSONE (ed.), *Trattato di diritto privato*, Giappichelli, Turin, 1999, at p. 412.

81 Senate of the Supreme Court of the Republic of Latvia Department of Administrative cases judgement of 28 February 2008 No. SKA-53/2008. Available at: tiesas.lv/nolemumi.

82 Senate of the Supreme Court of the Republic of Latvia, Department of Administrative Cases, judgment of 27 July 2010 No. SKA-307/2010. Available at: tiesas.lv/nolemumi.

case the Court viewed the concept of the family in a broader sense and context, detecting the existence of a joint family and its right to qualify for assistance regarding housing issues.

On 25 January 2011 a State Police Officer (AZ) died while on duty, arresting a group of criminals for committing armed robbery. According to the Latvian Law on Remuneration of Officials and Employees of State and Self-Government Authorities, if the official (employee) has died in an accident due to injuries, his forced heirs receive a lump sum benefit. According to the Latvian Civil Law the forced heirs are the spouse and descendants, but if there are no descendants, then ascendants of the nearest degree of kinship. In this particular case the person had no forced heirs, but an application was received from DV in which she stated that she was cohabiting with the deceased police officer. The judgment of the District Court of Jēkabpils in case No. C16073311[83] on 4 August 2011 recognised the fact that DV had cohabited with the deceased for more than one and a half years and that they had a common household.

The Court, however, pointed out that currently Latvian laws and other legislative acts do not regulate the beginning, amendment or termination of any legal relationship that is based on living together and having a common household outside a formal marriage. But simultaneously the Court indicated that, without actually deciding on this question, in essence there was no reason to restrict the realisation of the rights of DV. In the judgment the Court stated that there was enough evidence in the case proving that DV and the deceased police officer were living together and had a common household. All the witnesses told of circumstances proving that between DV and the deceased police officer there was a personal, close and long-term relationship.

This was also confirmed by the photos taken over an extended period of time that were submitted with the case. They were accepted by the Court. Furthermore, the Court ascertained that DV and AZ had given a mutual promise to get married. This was confirmed by witnesses and by DV's testimony. Though the legislature had not prescribed rules that would provide assistance for the deceased person's relatives who were not his forced heirs, but between whom there had been close, continuous, family-like ties, in this specific case the Cabinet of Ministers issued an order to pay a lump sum benefit to DV. The annotation of the Cabinet of

[83] District Court of Jēkabpils judgment on 4 August 2011 in case No. C16073311 (not published).

Ministers order[84] contains a reference to the Constitutional Court's judgment where it recognises that the formal application of the law, ignoring the actual conditions that substantially differentiate this case from other typical cases, is unacceptable. Therefore in atypical cases the authority has the right to depart from the legal consequences prescribed by law. In this specific case during the life time of AZ there had been established a personal, close and long-term relationship with a person, DV, who was not his forced heir.

As a turning point in the solution of this issue in the practice of the court, can be regarded the 1 February 2012 judgment No. SKC-4/2012[85] of the Senate of the Supreme Court of the Republic of Latvia, Department of Civil Cases. In this case the Court had to assess whether the cohabiting partner was a member of the tenant's family according to the first part of S. 9 of the Latvian Law on Residential Tenancy. This part of the Section provides that a tenant has the right to accommodate his or her spouse, parents (adopters), brothers and sisters incapable of work and adult children who do not have their own family in the residential space which the tenant is renting. The court established that, according to the stated section of the Law, other persons cannot be recognised as a tenant's family members. The Senate pointed to the legislature's decision for the time being to regulate the legal status of two people living together only in certain legislative acts, and not to equate partnerships to the concept of marriage.

The Senate considered that the legislature must make a clear decision on the issue of whether an actual cohabitation of two people has the same legal consequences as a registered marriage. Taking into account that the periodically updated discussions on this issue in the public domain and in Parliamentary commissions had not led to a shared opinion, the Senate concluded that amendments to Latvian national laws and other legislative acts, or the creation of a new legislative act or laws was being considered but had not yet been made. That in turn meant that neither the Senate, nor the other court authorities which hear civil cases, in essence has the jurisdiction so far as advancing the development of the law is concerned, to equate the actual cohabitation of two people to

[84] The annotation of the Cabinet of Ministers order. Available at: tap.mk.gov.lv/lv/mk/tap/?pid=40219042&mode=mk&date=2012-12-18.

[85] Senate of the Supreme Court of the Republic of Latvia, Department of Civil Cases, judgment of 1 February 2012 No,SKC-4/2012. Available at: at.gov.lv/lv/judikatura/judikaturas-nolemumu-arhivs/senata-civillietu-departaments/hronologiska-seciba_1/2012-hronologiska-seciba/.

registered marriage or to give the cohabiting partner the same rights as a spouse. This derives from the principle of the division of power which separates the legislature from the judiciary and legitimises the creation of new law only in cases when it does not interfere with the legislative powers. The Senate emphasised that within the courts' authority lie rights and laws, but not decisions on political questions.

Soon after this judgment came into force the City of Riga Latgale Urban District Court on 4 November 2014 refused the application of IV to recognise the fact that IV was sharing a common household as a spouse with ER who died fulfilling his duties at the State Fire and Rescue Service of Latvia.[86] The Court did not question that IV and ER had lived together, had a personal and close relationship, a common budget and hence a common household. But the Court objected to the applicant's request to recognise the fact that they led the common household as spouses. And the reason for claiming this was to receive a lump sum benefit. Consequently, though the actual conditions of this case were very similar to those in the judgment of the District Court of Jēkabpils in 2011, the judgment in the earlier case reached a completely opposite conclusion.

In the City of Riga case, the Court referred to the Senate of the Supreme Court of the Republic of Latvia, Department of Civil Cases' judgment of 1 February 2012 No. SKC-4/2012, stating that unlike marriage which is based on a legal agreement about cohabitation, actual cohabitation in a partnership has no legal basis. And that is exactly why the legal consequences of a marriage agreement in the field of personal rights and property relations cannot be applied to partnership. Thus, from the perspective of law, one can talk about partnership only as a fact in itself that does not create any legal relationship. Also, since the Senate had pointed out that the legislature must make a clear decision on the issue of whether an actual cohabitation by two people has the same legal consequences as a registered marriage, in this specific case the Court's opinion was that the finding as a legal fact that IV shared a common household with ER would not create any legal consequences, namely that the finding of such a fact did not include IV in the circle of people who have a right to the lump sum benefit.

Therefore, after 2012 when the Senate of the Supreme Court of the Republic of Latvia, Department of Civil Cases, made the judgment in

86 City of Riga Latgale Urban District Court judgment of 4 November 2014 in case No. C 29 5802 14 (not published).

case No. SKC-4/2012, the courts have stated very clearly that, in the absence of a legal order, they do not have the authority in the field of law advancement to equate the actual cohabitation of two people to registered marriage or to give the cohabiting partner the same rights as a spouse. Therefore, it is most likely that it cannot be expected, without the necessary legal order, that the courts would grant any legal consequences to existing informal relationships. The Cabinet of Ministers of the Republic of Latvia in the response letter to the Ombudsmen of the Republic of Latvia pointed out that it agrees with the judgment of the Senate of the Supreme Court of the Republic of Latvia, Department of Civil Cases, of 1 February 2012 in case No. SKC-4/2012 that the issue of whether an actual cohabitation of two people has the same legal consequences as a registered marriage, must be resolved by the legislature instead of being left up to the decision of the court.[87]

LITHUANIA

Bearing in mind that Art. 3.229-3.235 of the Lithuanian Civil Code are not applied in practice, the courts usually rely on general provisions while considering material disputes between non-married individuals, such as the provisions of Book IV, 'Material Law', of the Lithuanian Civil Code on the division of joint-partial property between co-owners as well as the provisions of Book VI, 'Law of Obligations', of the Lithuanian Civil Code regarding an agreement on joint activities (a partnership) in creating joint-partial property.

When dealing with cases regarding the division of property between a man and a woman living together outside of marriage, the Supreme Court of the Republic of Lithuania (hereafter Lithuanian Supreme Court) follows certain key criteria, such as: 1) cohabitation is still recognised as only an union between a man and a woman; 2) the principle of monogamy must be complied with; 3) cohabitation entails more than one year of having lived together.[88] This requirement is established in order to ensure that only partners with stable relations are guaranteed legal protection; 4) an overall economy (even under the circumstances when there exists a distribution of work between the couple, i.e. when one person takes care of the household and the other earns the main income,

[87] Cabinet of Ministers of the Republic of Latvia letter No. 18/TA-219/5175 of 3 May 2012. Available at: tiesibsargs.lv/par-mums/konsultativas-padomes/par-partnerattiecibu-tiesisko-regulejumu/.

[88] Ruling of the Lithuanian Supreme Court of 15 September 2009, civil case No. 3K-3-389/2005; Ruling of the SCL of 13 June 2006, civil case No. 3K-7-332/2006.

there might be an agreement on joint activity by creating common partial property).[89] An overall economy means the distribution of roles within the household, a total budget, etc.; 5) this union is considered to be a family. This attribute can be proved by witnesses. It should be noted that judicial practice does not provide an exhaustive list of cohabitation features, since in every case the courts decide with regard to concrete circumstances and the evidence provided. Important features might be the same as those which are specific to a marriage, for example both cohabitees share a dwelling and raise and educate their common children. Persons who meet the requirements of the characteristic features of cohabitees established by court practice might have a claim to part of the common property when their cohabitation comes to an end, provided that the parties have decided on joint activity by creating common partial property.

The Supreme Court of Lithuania has issued a clarifying ruling that the existence of an agreement on joint activities (a partnership) in creating joint-partial property shall be recognised in cases when non-married individuals live together (especially when cohabitation is persistent rather than being of a casual nature), jointly manage property, and contribute to the creation of common property with their personal financing and joint work.[90] According to Art. 6.969 and 6.970 of the Lithuanian Civil Code, partners (cohabitees) may conclude an agreement on joint activities according to which property could be acquired under joint-partial ownership. In dealing with cases concerning the division of joint-partial property acquired during cohabitation, the prevailing presumption is that the partners' contributions shall be deemed to be equal.[91] The contributions by the parties to an agreement are deemed equal unless the agreement provides otherwise, and then a corresponding share of the property is assigned to each partner according to their contributions in monetary terms, property, and personal input and with consideration being given to joint property management. In addition, the share of the personal property is determined for each individual taking into consideration his/her contribution to the joint property management in terms of money, property, personal input as well as labour.[92]

89 Ruling of the Lithuanian Supreme Court 5 April, 2011, civil case No. 3K-3-152/2011; Ruling of the Lithuanian Supreme Court of 21 February, civil case No 3K-5-51/2014.
90 Ruling of the Lithuanian Supreme Court of 28 March 2011, civil case No. 3K-3-134/2011.
91 Ruling of the SCL of 30 November 2010, civil case No. 3K-3-482/2010.
92 Ruling of the SCL of 8 April 2008, civil case No. 3K-3-235/2008.

LUXEMBOURG

Case law gives legal effects to *concubinage* (an informal relationship) if it is durable and stable.

THE NETHERLANDS

Except for specific legal provisions, informal relationships as such do not have legal effects under the law of property or the law of obligations. In the internal relationship between the partners, general property law and the law of obligations determine if and what legal effects might arise. It is not the cohabitation itself, but rather the actual behaviour of the partners during the relationship which might give rise to legal effects. When partners have not concluded an explicit cohabitation contract, it is often unclear what the legal position of the partners is. During the relationship this is not problematic, since problems seldom arise. After the separation of the informal partners, this might alter. Problems might arise in relation to unravelling the financial and property relations between the partners. In this respect, it is important to realise that the party autonomy is substantial according to Dutch law. When partners reach a separation agreement, in which they deal with the legal consequences of the breakdown, the lack of a *lex specialis* is in this respect not relevant. However, when partners do not come to terms, the question arises what their respective legal position is. The law on obligations and property law offers an extensive domain for conflicts. Many issues might result in a conflict and in advance it is difficult to predict whether a court will find the claim and/or its ground acceptable. It is the qualification of the legal relation between the partners that causes most problems. Whether money or assets can be redistributed depends on whether parties have concluded an implicit contract (Art. 3:37 Dutch Civil Code) and what its content would be (repayment, no repayment, netting, no netting, a gift (Art. 7:175 Dutch Civil Code)) or outside contract law, whether the legal relationship resulted in unjust enrichment (Art. 6:212 Dutch Civil Code) or undue payment (Art. 6:203 Dutch Civil Code) or constitutes a natural (unenforceable) obligation.[93] The basic problem is that anything is

[93] C. FORDER, *Het informele huwelijk: de verbondenheid tussen mens, goed en schuld*, Kluwer, Deventer, 2000; C. FORDER, 'Vermogensrechtelijke perikelen in het huwelijk onder de bezem', *NJB*, 2006, at p. 17-18; A. HEIDA, 'Geschillen na het einde van een samenlevingsrelatie', *Tijdschrift voor scheidingsrecht*, 2013; W.M. SCHRAMA, 'Verbintenisrechtelijke afwikkeling', in: M.L.C.C. DE BRUIJN-LÜCKERS et al. (eds.), *Relatierecht, SDUCommentaar*, SDU, The Hague, 2014, pp. 2041-2060; W.M. SCHRAMA, 'Groot vermogensrechtelijk nadeel als gevolg van een liefdesrelatie', *Tijdschrift voor Familie- en Jeugdrecht*, 2009, pp. 92-98; W.M. SCHRAMA, 'Vermogensverschuivingen na scheiding van ongehuwde samenlevers: contractuele grondslagen (deel 1)', *Tijdschrift Relatierecht*

possible: there are no clear underlying legal norms which determine how to qualify what has happened. In particular in separation situations, where both partners will argue on the basis of diametrically opposed views, both in regard to the facts and the legal norms, what is the judge supposed to do? Case law at the lower level shows a wide variety of claims and judgements, partially to be attributed to different facts, but also to strongly differing opinions among legal professionals.[94]

Leading cases of the Supreme Court demonstrate that there is substantial room for the acceptance of implicit contracts between partners. On the basis of the facts, there might be grounds to deduce an implicit consensus between the partners as to some contested right.[95] It might be a contract holding a title for joint ownership, or a duty to redistribute money or assets after a relationship breakdown. Even though the Supreme Court case law lays down legal norms concerning implicit contracts,[96] the legal unpredictability is still considerable.

NORWAY

In cohabitation, non-statutory legal precedent for acquiring co-ownership emerged through Supreme Court practice in the 1970s and 1980s.[97] As long as the cohabitants have not agreed who is to be deemed the owner of particular items of property, co-ownership may be established based on the cohabitants' indirect contribution in the form of domestic work and/or payment of the family's expenses. This method of acquisition departs sharply from the traditional methods of acquiring co-ownership, and is only recognised in cohabitation and in marriage.[98] The rule covers

en Praktijk, 2014, pp. 25-28 and W.M. SCHRAMA, 'deel II', *Tijdschrift Relatierecht en Praktijk*, 2014, at p. 38-42.

94 W.M. SCHRAMA, 'Verbintenisrechtelijke afwikkeling', in: M.L.C.C. DE BRUIJN-LÜCKERS et al. (eds.), *Relatierecht, SDUCommentaar*, SDU, The Hague, 2014, pp. 2041-2060. Two illustrative examples: Rb. Rotterdam 27 January 2010, LJN BM7429 decided that on the basis of an implicit contract one partner had to pay € 350,000 to the other partner, after a relationship of 22 years, as opposed to Hof Den Haag 2 November 2010 (to be found in: HR 8 June 2012, ECLI:NL:HR:2012:BV9539) which ruled that the woman, who had stopped working after the second child's birth, had to pay almost € 50,000 after the breakdown of the relationship for the costs of the household that her partner had paid during the relationship as she did not have any income.

95 HR 16 January 1987, NJ 1987, 912; HR 26 May 1989, NJ 1990, 23; HR 17 December 2004, LJN AR3636; HR 22 September 2006, LJN AX1571; HR 8 June 2012, LJN BV9539.

96 The Supreme Court is not allowed to rule on facts, so it leaves plenty of room for debate. Moreover, the facts of cases tend to differ as well.

97 Rt. 1978 p. 1352 and Rt. 1984 p. 497. P. LØDRUP and T. SVERDRUP, *Familieretten*, 2011, at Chapter 7.

98 For marriage, this rule is codified in the Norwegian Marriage Act, S. 31 third paragraph.

not only the common residence, but also other items of property for common personal use, e.g. a second home, a car or a boat.

In order to establish co-ownership, two conditions must be met: both parties must have contributed - directly or indirectly - to the acquisition, and the acquisition must constitute a joint project. Co-ownership is determined on the basis of a discretionary assessment of the size and nature of the contributions and the joint project. In practice, a homemaker's indirect contributions in the form of care for small children are sufficient in the majority of cases to make her/him an equal co-owner of an item bought by the breadwinner with income earned during the same period of time. If the children are of compulsory school age and the homemaker still works full-time at home, her/his work will normally constitute a lesser contribution.

In practice, co-ownership limits the exclusive right of the cohabitants to dispose of an item, and the creditors must respect this co-ownership as well. However, the greatest overall financial significance of such co-ownership occurs when the cohabitants separate. Upon dissolution, each cohabitant retains his or her property and his or her debts.

Compensation to avert unjust enrichment may also be granted on termination of the relationship. These non-statutory rules developed through Supreme Court practice in the 1980s, see Norwegian Supreme Court Reports in Rt. 1984 p. 497, Rt. 2000 p. 1089 and Rt. 2011 p. 1168. The cohabitant must have provided the other party with a significant financial benefit in order to receive any compensation. In addition, the granting of compensation must be reasonable. Compensation is only to be granted in exceptional cases. These case-law rules have proved to be ill-suited to correct imbalances in settlements after relationship breakdown. In contrast to the precisely phrased laws with predictable outcomes found in other areas of family law, they contain a degree of ambiguity, leading to an increased level of litigation. The weaker party will often find it too costly to enforce her/his rights through the legal system, especially since compensation is rarely granted. Furthermore, general impressions seem to suggest that a whole range of details are given legal relevance in practice. An unlimited number of facts and incidents are subject to dispute and the rules seem to create conflicts.

PORTUGAL

The most widespread opinion in family law strongly suggests that cohabitants may regulate some aspects of their common life through an ordinary contract, under the general principle of autonomy in private matters – a 'cohabitation contract'. The same opinion also suggests that cohabitants are liable in solidarity for ordinary debts which may arise in meeting the normal costs of common life, in the same way as married couples are. None of the suggestions have been subject to court decisions, however.

It seems obvious that rules on the indivision of the joint ownership regime are applicable to property in a *de facto* union.

The case law has also followed the general regime of unjust enrichment in order to solve problems related to the distribution of the property of cohabitants upon the termination of the relationship (e.g. Decisions of the Supreme Court of 29.03.2004, 31.03.2009, 29.09.2009, 31.05.2011).

RUSSIA

The Russian Supreme Court has consistently denied the possibility of applying provisions of the Russian Family Code to informal relationships by way of analogy.[99] Russian law considers informal partners to be strangers to one another.

Property relationships between informal partners are governed by the general rules of civil law and not by the rules of family law. There are two situations in which the property of informal partners may be governed by the rules of the Civil Code of the Russian Federation[100] governing joint ownership (Art. 244-255):

- when informal partners jointly acquire property in the names of both of them;

---

99 Постановление Пленума Верховного Суда РСФСР от 21 февраля 1973 года № 3, Бюллетень Верховного Суда РСФСР, 1973, № 5; Постановление Пленума Верховного Суда РФ от 25 апреля 1995 года № 6, Бюллетень Верховного Суда РФ. 1995, № 7.

100 Further referred to as the Russian Civil Code. *Гражданской кодекс Российской Федерации*. Adopted on 21 October 1994, in force since 1 January 1995. *Собрание законодательства Российской Федерации* 1994, No. 32, item 3301. For an English translation, see: 21 *Review of Central and Eastern European Law*, 1995, No. 3/4, at p. 245-430.

- when informal partners enter into an agreement stating that all or part of any property acquired by them during their relationship will become their joint property.

Informal partners may enter into an agreement to regulate their relationship, even though Russian law does not provide for any specific agreements for regulating such relationships. As a general principle of Russian civil law is that any agreement which does not violate the law is valid, an agreement between informal partners can also be valid. In the absence of any specific regulation, the legal nature, form and other requirements of such agreements are subject to discussion. Some authors consider a cohabitation agreement to be an agreement *sui generis,* while others consider it to be a kind of joint entrepreneurship agreement.[101]

SCOTLAND

The starting point for Scots family law is that marriage, and equally civil partnership, do not affect the property rights or legal capacity of either party to the relationship[102] and it is well established that in questions of property or obligations it is the general rules which apply regardless of the personal relationship which exists between the parties.[103] It is therefore not surprising that a similar approach would be taken to informal relationships.

It is possible that the law of unjustified enrichment might be used to compensate an unmarried cohabitant where he or she has contributed to the improvement of property owned solely by the other cohabitant. In practice, however, this remedy has been very little used. *Shilliday v Smith*[104] is the leading case and here the woman was successful in recovering money which she had spent on improving and repairing her partner's home while they were cohabiting. Despite occasional interest in unjustified enrichment, particularly where, as in this case, contribution has been made in the expectation of a forthcoming marriage which does

101 С.Ю. ФИЛИППОВА, 'Гражданско-правовые средства достижения цели построения семьи путем фактических брачных отношений', *Семейное и жилищное право*, 2010, at p. 7.

102 Family Law (Scotland) Act 1985, S. 24(1).

103 This approach is clearly seen in *MacLure v MacLure* 1911 SC 200 and *Millar v Millar* 1940 SC 56.

104 *Shilliday v Smith* 1998 SC 725.

not subsequently take place, there is relatively little evidence of its use in practice.[105]

SLOVAKIA

§ 115 of the Slovak Civil Code defines the household (*domácnosť*). It consists of natural persons who live permanently together and share their living costs. There are many other references to the legal term 'household' in other provisions of the Slovak Civil Code. According to Slovak doctrine and the case law of the Supreme Court of Czechoslovakia it is not sufficient if the persons in question simply live together even if they equally share the costs for electricity, gas or other costs relating to the premises where they live.[106] The household is a common society. If both of the spouses live in a matrimonial household, the possibility of establishing that household with another person is *de facto* excluded. The intention of natural persons to live permanently together in a household needs to be expressed by the way in which they live together.

§ 116 of the Slovak Civil Code defines a close person (*blízka osoba*) as a relative in the direct line, a sibling and a spouse; other persons in a family or similar relationship shall be considered to be persons who are close to each other if an injury suffered by one of them is reasonably felt by the other person as an injury suffered by him or her.

For the sake of this questionnaire merely the second half of the definition is relevant: other persons in a family or similar relationship shall be considered to be persons who are close to each other if an injury suffered by one of them is reasonably felt by the other person as an injury suffered by him or her.

In many of its provisions the Slovak Civil Code refers to the household or a close person. One of the relevant examples is the legal reference in the provisions on the law of inheritance.[107]

---

105 See e.g. *Satchwell v McIntosh* 2006 SLT (Sh Ct) 117; *McKenzie v Nutter* 2007 SLT (Sh Ct) 17; *Thomson v Mooney* 2014 Fam LR 15. For further discussion, see G. JUNOR, 'Unjustified enrichment in the family context', *Family Law Bulletin*, 2012, pp. 2-4.

106 See Decision of the Supreme Court of Czechoslovakia No. 34/1960.

107 See Question 47.

SLOVENIA

The Slovenian Marriage Act contains general provisions by which an extramarital union between partners has the same legal consequences as a marriage in relation to rights that the Marriage Act recognises.

The decision of the Constitutional Court RS No. U-I-212/10-15 of 14 March 2013 on the inheritance of same-sex partners living together is important for the legal recognition of a life union of unregistered same-sex partners, because in it the Constitutional Court used the definition of an extramarital union under Art. 12 of the Slovenian Marriage Act for a judgement on whether a life union of same-sex partners is proven. By this decision, the Constitutional Court made it necessary for the legislator also in regulating family relations to consider the legal recognition of *de facto* life unions of same-sex partners.[108]

SPAIN

The Spanish Civil Code does not have specific legal provisions on informal relationships. Case law solves the legal issues related to these relationships in an ad hoc manner leading to inconsistencies and uncertainty. Many decisions stem from the assumption that these relationships cannot be equated to marriage, with the consequence that rules on married couples cannot be applied by analogy. There are, however, cases that have applied the rules of *pensión compensatoria* (Art. 97 Spanish Civil Code), a provision for financial relief in cases of marriage breakdown, if the factual situation fulfilled the conditions required by statute (e.g. STS 5-7-01, 16-7-02). This trend seems to be gaining ground in more recent decisions. There are, however, other decisions based on the law of property (e.g. STC 18-5-92, 29-10-97, 4-6-98), resorting to company law (STS 18-2-93), applying general principles such as those of abuse of rights and good faith (STS 11-12-92 and 23-11-04), tort law (STS 16-12-96) or the doctrine of unjust enrichment (STS 11-12-92; 17-6-03). The legal status of unmarried couples is therefore uncertain unless partners resort to self-regulation. Agreements entered into by the partners on the basis of the general principle of party autonomy (Art. 1255 Spanish Civil Code) are always given precedence. They are, however, not very common in practice.

[108] B. NOVAK, 'Aktuelle Entwicklungen im slowenischen Recht', *FamRZ*, No. 18, 2013, at p. 1464.

SWEDEN

General principles on the law of obligations and the law of property are applicable to a couple living together in an informal relationship. It follows that the two cohabitants can enter into legal transactions with each other or, for example, acquire property jointly and become co-owners, just like any other people.

In some cases, according to case law, cohabitees as well as spouses may be deemed to have acquired joint ownership rights to property in circumstances where such an outcome does not self-evidently follow from a more strict application of general principles of the law of obligations or property law. The reason for this more flexible approach lies in the taking account of the realities of family life, whether in marriage or in unmarried cohabitation, calling for a less formal approach to issues of acquisition of title.[109] When it comes to property acquired for joint use, case law provides that one presumption applies for primarily household goods acquired for joint use, and another for other types of property; both presumptions often result in co-ownership for cohabitants. An example of the first kind of situation is the Court of Appeal judgment RH 1986:25: the cohabiting man and woman were considered to be joint owners of the furniture bought by the man for their joint use. The Swedish Supreme Court decisions NJA 1980 p. 705, NJA 1981 p. 693, NJA 1982 p. 589 and NJA 2013 p. 242 illustrate the second type of presumption, which has resulted in joint ownership of assets such as real estate property, condominiums, holiday cottages, horses, boats, etc. The construction of joint ownership is often called 'caveat ownership' or 'concealed co-ownership'.[110] It applies to couples in marriage or in an informal cohabitation relationship, when certain criteria specified by case law are met (see below, under Questions 27-29). According to the Supreme Court in NJA 2008 p. 826, it is to be seen as a rule of presumption of joint ownership, belonging to the field of family law and aimed at providing financial protection to the partner who financially

[109] See the preparatory works in NJA II 1921 p. 89 to the Swedish Marriage Code of 1921, the Swedish Supreme Court decision *NJA 2002 p. 142* and M. BRATTSTRÖM, 'Egendomsförhållanden undet bestående samboende', in: J. ASLAND et al., *Nordisk samboerrett*, Gyldendal, Oslo, 2014, at p. 71 et seq. (see Chapter 2.2, in the English version of the book, to be published by Intersentia in 2015).

[110] See M. BRATTSTRÖM, 'The Protection of a Vulnerable Party when a Cohabitee Relationship Ends – An Evaluation of the Swedish Cohabitees Act', in B. VERSCHRAEGEN (ed.), *Family Finances*, Jan Sramet Verlag, Vienna, 2008, at p. 350. See also M. JÄNTERÄ-JAREBORG, 'Rechtsregeln für nichteheliches Zusammenleben in Schweden' (in English), in: I. KROPPENBERG et al. (eds.), *Rechtsregeln für nichteheliches Zusammenleben*, Gieseking Verlag, Vienna, 2009, pp. 207-226, at p. 222 et seq.

contributed to an acquisition made by the other partner, solely in the latter's name.

SWITZERLAND

Couples in an informal relationship may enter into an agreement regulating their relationship, especially concerning questions of property. However, they rarely make use of this possibility. Furthermore, it is not clear to what extent such agreements are legally allowed.

Where a couple have not regulated their relationship, general legal rules may apply, such as the law of obligations (e.g. the law of simple partnership, tenancy law, employment law) or the law of property. With regard to matrimonial law, the Swiss Federal Supreme Court has refused to apply matrimonial property law directly or by analogy to informal relationships.[111]

Informal relationships were first given a certain degree of legal recognition with regard to the termination of spousal support. Already under the old Swiss divorce law (before the reform of the Swiss divorce law in 2000), the Swiss Federal Supreme Court held in 1978 that spousal support ceases to exist in cases where the entitled person is living with another person in a 'qualified informal relationship'.[112] Such a qualified informal relationship was regularly assumed by the courts if the relationship had lasted for more than five years,[113] irrespective of the actual capacity of being supported by the new partner.[114] This legal practice was in principle confirmed under the reformed divorce law.[115] Nowadays, spousal support (during a marriage or after divorce) may be suspended, reduced, revoked or denied if the entitled person lives with another person in a qualified informal relationship.[116]

---

111 Swiss Federal Supreme Court, BGE 108 II 204 E.3.

112 Swiss Federal Supreme Court, BGE 104 II 154. For details see A. BÜCHLER and H. STEGMANN, 'Der Einfluss der nichtehelichen Lebensgemeinschaft auf den nachehelichen Unterhaltsanspruch', *Die Praxis des Familienrechts*, 2004, at p. 229 et seq.

113 E.g. Swiss Federal Supreme Court, BGE 118 II 235; BGE 109 II 188.

114 Swiss Federal Supreme Court, BGE 116 II 394 E.3.

115 Under the application of Art. 129 Swiss Civil Code. See Swiss Federal Court, BGer 5P.135/2005 (22.7.2005). Under the reformed divorce law the suspension of spousal support has in some cases already been granted after three years, see Swiss Federal Supreme Court, BGer 5C.296/2001 (12.3.2002); BGer 5A_81/2008 (11.6.2008).

116 For details see D. DIEZI, *Nachlebensgemeinschaftlicher Unterhalt*, Stämpfli, Bern, 2014, at p. 126 et seq.

Also with regard to spousal support, an informal relationship may - under very restricted conditions - have a promotive influence on the assessment of spousal support after divorce. When determining whether and to what extent spousal support has to be ensured, the duration of the marriage is one of the factors which must be considered in particular (Art. 125 para. 2 No. 2 Swiss Civil Code). According to the Swiss Federal Supreme Court, a (long-lasting) informal relationship preceding a (short) marriage may have an influence on the assessment of spousal support if this relationship already had a lasting influence on the lives of the couple (*Lebensprägung*) which justifies its consideration.[117]

In 1982 the Swiss Federal Supreme Court held that in particular upon dissolution some legal protection for informal relationships has to be ensured.[118] Under certain circumstances, financial problems upon the dissolution of informal relationships have since then been addressed by the Swiss Federal Supreme Court by applying principles of the Swiss Code of Obligations relating to simple partnerships (Art. 530 et seq. Swiss Code of Obligations).[119] The simple partnership is a contractual relationship in which two or more persons agree to combine their efforts or resources in order to achieve a common goal. Thus, if unmarried partners have formed an economic unit with joint finances to which both have contributed either financially or through work and labour, compensation may be sought upon the dissolution of the informal relationship.[120] These cases extensively depend on the court's interpretation of the parties' intention to enter into a legally binding relationship and of the common partnership goal pursued by the partners. However, up to now, only financial contributions[121] or contributions in the form of work and labour in the joint or the other partner's business[122] have given rise to compensation. Taking care of the household and caring

117 Swiss Federal Supreme Court, BGE 135 III 59 E.4.4. See also Swiss Federal Supreme Court, BGE 132 III 598 E.9.2 (less strict conditions).

118 Swiss Federal Supreme Court, BGE 108 II 204 E.3.a).

119 For details see M. COTTIER and C. CREVOSIER, 'Die nichteheliche Lebensgemeinschaft als einfache Gesellschaft', *Aktuelle Juristische Praxis*, 2012, at p. 33 et seq.

120 Swiss Federal Supreme Court, BGE 108 II 204 E.4. a). The rules of simple partnership cannot automatically be applied to all financial questions relating to an informal relationship. Rather, the court has to decide individually regarding the relevant circumstances of every case, see also Swiss Federal Supreme Court, BGer 4A_383/2007 (19.12.2007).

121 E.g. Swiss Federal Supreme Court, BGer 4A_383/2007 (19.12.2007).

122 E.g. Swiss Federal Supreme Court, BGer 4C.195/2006 (12.10.2007); BGE 109 II 228.

for the children does not amount to a contribution as required in a simple partnership.[123]

Furthermore, informal relationships are given legal effect outside private law. There is a tendency to give legal effect to informal partnerships in connection with the exclusion or limitation of social benefits or social insurance benefits.[124] With regard to social benefits the Swiss Federal Supreme Court has considered both of the salaries of a cohabiting couple when determining social benefits,[125] even though there is no legal duty to support each other in an informal relationship. A similar decision was made regarding a social insurance case, where the calculation for the reduction for health insurance was based on the income of both partners in an informal relationship.[126]

In cases of debt enforcement (*Schuldbetreibung*) an informal relationship is similarly treated as a marriage when assessing the minimum living wage (*Existenzminimum*) of the debtor. The Swiss Federal Supreme Court generally assumes that not only the accommodation costs but also the basic living expenses (so-called *Grundbetrag*) will be shared equally amongst the partners. These (assumed) savings are reflected by the fact that the basic living expenses of a debtor in an informal relationship are reduced[127] from that of a single person to as much as a half of the basic living expenses of a married couple.[128] However, different from a married debtor, any financial support by the debtor to his or her informal partner will not be considered in the assessment of the minimum living wage. Such support will only be respected if there are common children (and thus, with regard to debt enforcement, families are treated in the same way irrespective of the parents' marital status).[129]

---

123 Compensation was denied in Swiss Federal Supreme Court, BGer 4A_441/2007 (17.01.2008), where a woman in an informal relationship had taken care of the common child for 16 years.

124 D. DIEZI, *Nachlebensgemeinschaftlicher Unterhalt*, Stämpfli, Bern, 2014, at p. 131 et seq.

125 Swiss Federal Supreme Court, BGE 129 I 1; BGer 1P.184/2003 (19.8.2003).

126 Swiss Federal Supreme Court, BGE 134 I 313.

127 The guidelines for debt enforcement and insolvency propose a *Grundbetrag* for a single person of CHF 1200 and for a married couple of CHF 1700. In the case of an informal relationship, the amount for basic living expenses would be reduced from CHF 1200 to as much as CHF 850.- (= half of CHF 1700).

128 Swiss Federal Supreme Court, BGE 130 III 765 E.2.4; BGE 132 III 483 E.4.2.

129 Swiss Federal Supreme Court, BGE 106 III 11 E.3.

Finally, with regard to aliens law, an informal relationship of a certain duration may under certain circumstances lead to permission for residence.[130]

[130] Swiss Federal Supreme Court, BGer 2C_702/2011 (23.2.2012); BGer 2C_97/2010 (4.11.2010).

QUESTION 4

How are informal relationships between a couple defined by either legislation and/or case law? Do these definitions vary according to the context?

AUSTRIA

In Austria, no general definition of the term informal relationship *(nichteheliche Lebensgemeinschaft)* exists.[1] According to the case law an informal relationship exists if three requirements are cumulatively fulfilled, although in the individual case one of the criteria may be less marked or even completely non-existent:[2]

- Similarity to marriage
- Residential, economic and sexual community *(Wohn-, Wirtschafts-, Geschlechtsgemeinschaft)*
- Long-term relationship.[3]

An informal relationship is defined as a relationship similar to marriage and which prima facie appears to be equivalent to marriage.[4] A residential community means that the partners are living together in a joint home with the intention that this place is their centre of life.[5] Another criterion for an informal relationship constitutes the sexual community: the partners have a sexual relationship, except where they

1 C. FISCHER-CZERMAK, 'Wann liegt eine nichteheliche Lebensgemeinschaft vor?', in: E. WAGNER and W. BERGTHALER (eds.), *Interdisziplinäre Rechtswissenschaft – Schutzansprüche und Schutzaufgaben im Recht, Festschrift für Ferdinand Kerschner*, Verlag Österreich, Vienna, 2013, pp. 337-352, at p. 338.

2 Austrian Supreme Court, Judgement of 27.05.1988, 3 Ob 61/88; Austrian Supreme Court, Judgement of 31.01.1990, 2 Ob 503/90; Austrian Supreme Court, Judgement of 16.03.2007, 6 Ob 28/07x.

3 J. STABENTHEINER, 'Die nichteheliche Lebensgemeinschaft – ein Überblick', *NZ*, 1995, at p. 49.

4 Austrian Supreme Court, Judgement of 20.06.2000, 3 Ob 209/99b.

5 See C. FISCHER-CZERMAK, 'Wann liegt eine nichteheliche Lebensgemeinschaft vor?', in: E. WAGNER and W. BERGTHALER (eds.), *Interdisziplinäre Rechtswissenschaft – Schutzansprüche und Schutzaufgaben im Recht, Festschrift für Ferdinand Kerschner*, Verlag Österreich, Vienna, 2013, pp. 337-352, at p. 340.

are physically not able to have a sexual relationship or have reached an advanced age.[6] A mere sexual relationship with some overnight stays and joint journeys is, however, not sufficient to establish an informal relationship.[7] The economic community obliges the partners to contribute financially to the common household, to share his/her goods with the partner and to support the other partner. Further, it is of crucial importance that the relationship is of a long-term nature.[8] A further distinctive feature - particularly in comparison to a marriage - is that an informal relationship can be unilaterally terminated at any time.[9] When determining whether an informal relationship exists, the circumstances of the individual case have to be duly taken into account.

BELGIUM

There are a plethora of legal provisions in which informal relationships, mostly based on cohabitation, are taken into account for the regulation of a variety of subjects. The difficulty in finding a broadly applicable definition is one of the reasons why informal cohabitation is not yet institutionalised in law.[10]

Only some provisions concern the law of persons and family law, and more broadly private law:

- the Family Court may terminate post-divorce support when the debtor cohabits with another person as if they were married (Art. 301, § 10 Belgian Civil Code);
- joint and second parent adoption is possible in case the (two) adopter(s) have continuously and effectively cohabited since at least three years, and no impediment to marriage based on kinship exists (Art. 343, § 1, b) Belgian Civil Code);

---

6 Austrian Supreme Court, Legal Proposition RS0047017, Judgement of 21.05.2014, 3 Ob 31/14a; C. FISCHER-CZERMAK, 'Wann liegt eine nichteheliche Lebensgemeinschaft vor?', in: E. WAGNER and W. BERGTHALER (eds.), *Interdisziplinäre Rechtswissenschaft – Schutzansprüche und Schutzaufgaben im Recht, Festschrift für Ferdinand Kerschner*, Verlag Österreich, Vienna, 2013, pp. 337-352, at p. 345.

7 Austrian Supreme Court, Judgement of 21.05.1996, 5 Ob 2104/96i.

8 Austrian Supreme Court, Judgement of 05.10.1999, 2 Ob 314/98k.

9 Austrian Supreme Court, Judgement of 18.12.2007, 10 ObS 121/07b; C. FISCHER-CZERMAK, 'Wann liegt eine nichteheliche Lebensgemeinschaft vor?', in: E. WAGNER and W. BERGTHALER (eds.), *Interdisziplinäre Rechtswissenschaft – Schutzansprüche und Schutzaufgaben im Recht, Festschrift für Ferdinand Kerschner*, Verlag Österreich, Vienna, 2013, pp. 337-352, at p. 346.

10 F. SWENNEN, *Het personen- en familierecht. Identiteit en verwantschap vanuit juridisch perspectief*, Intersentia, Antwerp, 2015, at. n° 681.

- besides the spouse and the legal cohabitant, the person with whom one constitutes a *de facto* family unit is preferably appointed as a guardian (Art. 496/3, para. 2 Belgian Civil Code and also see Art. 14 Patient Rights Act and Art. 909 Belgian Civil Code on a conflict of interests vis-à-vis gifts);
- other provisions assimilate the person with whom one cohabits *de facto* with a spouse or legal cohabitant (e.g. with regard to a conflict of interests as a guardian, Art. 398 Belgian Civil Code);
- mediation is allowed with regard to disputes arising from a *de facto* cohabitation (Art. 1724, para. 1, 4° Belgian Code of Civil Proceedings).

Most provisions concern 'public family law' in that they attach consequences to informal relationships in branches of public law, particularly criminal law, immigration law, social (security) law and tax law. We will provide one example for each branch of the law:

- Article 410 Belgian Criminal Code includes in its definition of domestic violence as an aggravating circumstance, besides the spouse, any person with whom the offender lives or has lived together and has or has had a durable affective and sexual relationship;
- Article 47/1, 1° Belgian Aliens Act considers as family members of the Union citizen: the persons with whom he has a durable relationship, duly attested with all means, and taking into account its intensity, duration and stability (Art. 47/3, para. 1 Belgian Aliens Act);
- a dependant in social security law can be the person with whom the person entitled cohabits, except in case he also has a dependent spouse or cohabits with a non-dependent spouse (Art. 123 Royal Decree of 3 July 1996);
- Article 1.1.0.0.2, par. 5, 4°, c) Flemish Taxation Code defines a partner *inter alia* as the persons (plural!) who continuously cohabited for at least one year in a joint household, with a view to applying the same tax rates as between spouses in the context of donations and successions. The registration in the population register constitutes a rebuttable presumption of partnership.

Interestingly, most of those provisions do not disqualify an informal couple on the basis of the co-existence of a formal relationship or of minority. The current piecemeal approach, however, is fairly inconsistent and unstructured.

BULGARIA

In Bulgaria there is no common legal definition of informal relationships between a couple. Some statutes that provide for the legal effect of cohabitation do define an informal relationship, but others do not. To some extent legal definitions depend on the context. There is a common feature among all the definitions: the fact that the couple are sharing a common living space.

Registration (of a common address):
Definitions related to the public interest tend to be stricter. For instance, the Bulgarian Social Assistance Act defines an 'informal relationship between a couple' as: 'living together in one home ... registered at one address' (para. 1, point 2 of the Additional Provision). This definition is the only one which is explicit with regard to the need for formal proof for the existence of an informal relationship. The meaning of 'address' is not specified. Since the Bulgarian Civil Registration Act (of 1999, last amended in 2013) allows for two types of addresses - permanent (Art. 93) and current (Art. 94) it could be either of them.[11]

Similar is the definition in the Bulgarian Taxes and Securities Procedure Code, the central aspect of which is again common living. The statutory term here is 'household': 'The "household" includes spouses, persons living in factual cohabitation as well as their children and relatives living together with them' (para. 1, p. 2 of the Additional Provision). If proof is needed it could be either the official registered address or a witness statement to that effect. The Supreme Administrative Court has accepted a witness statement as proof of the informal relationship between a couple (Decision No. 7383 of 2013, case No. 2461/13, related to the status of civil servants).

Duration:
Different is the approach adopted by the Bulgarian Transplantation of Organs, Tissue and Cells Act: 2 years of living together that can be sufficiently proved is the core of its definition (Art. 26, para. 2, p. 2 of the Act).

The case law reveals a strong correlation between the duration of the informal relationship and its legal effect:

11 A common address is accepted by the Courts as proof of an informal relationship between a couple in order to establish an entitlement to protection against domestic violence. Decision of the V. District Court N 1720/31.3.2014 case № 1843/2014.

> '... the de-facto family spousal relationship has been durable and sustainable and children have possibly been born within it ...'[12]

Informal relationships between couples are:

> 'Sustainably established close relationships that are not duly formalised.'[13]

The more recent case law supports that view. A court has stated that an intimate relationship which had only lasted for one month did not qualify the applicant to be protected under the Bulgarian Protection against Domestic Violence Act.[14]

The existence of children is not a specific requirement for informal relationships to have legal effect.

To sum up: the legislation does share a common concept of informal relationships between a couple and it simply amounts to 'living together'. This is reflected in the definitions interpreted above. Living together seems to demonstrate all other relationships between a couple - mutual support, common duties (towards the household and the children), protection, emotional and other relationships. Some statutes require more certainty as to the stability of the relationship which is proved by its duration (e.g. in cases of donorship).

The Bulgarian Family Code does not define informal relationships. The legal effect on parenthood stems from the established parenthood.

CROATIA

Article 11 paragraph 1 of the Croatian Family Act defines cohabitation as 'a relationship between an unmarried woman and an unmarried man, which lasts for at least three years or less if the partners have a common child or if the relationship has been succeeded by marriage.'

The definitions of cohabitation provided by legislation and case law do not vary according to the family law context.

However, the definitions of cohabitation do vary considerably across the laws. Cohabitation is not only defined by the Croatian Family Act but

---

12 Supreme Court Decision No. 5 of 1969.
13 Supreme Court Decision No. 5 of 1984/civil case 2/84.
14 Order of 10.01.12 of the B. District Court, case No. 42/2012.

also by many other laws in which cohabitation entails legal effects. It is the consequence of the fact that the definition of cohabitants in the Croatian legal system is not always the same. Depending on the type of cohabitants' rights and/or obligations, there are different answers to the question of who is to be recognised as a cohabitant in the Croatian legal system. In other words, due to differences in the definition across the laws, we are faced with inconsistent legislation, which sometimes creates legal uncertainty.

For example, the Inheritance Act (Official Gazette no. 48/03, 163/03, 35/05, 127/13) defines cohabitation as a union which lasts for a longer period of time subject to the condition that all the requirements for the conclusion of a valid marriage have been fulfilled (Art. 8 paragraph 2); the Pension Insurance Act (Official Gazette no. 157/13, 151/14) binds the existence of cohabitation to joint life in the same household for at least three years and lays down that the status of the cohabitation shall be determined in non-contentious proceedings (Art. 22 paragraph 3); the Act on Medically Assisted Reproduction (Official Gazette no. 86/12) sees cohabitation as a union of unmarried people who are not members of any other extramarital or same-sex union and who meet the criteria for the conclusion of a valid marriage and stipulates that the existence of a cohabitation shall be demonstrated by a declaration certified by a notary public (Art. 11).

Article 3 paragraph 1 of the Croatian Partnership Act defines a same-sex informal partnership as follows: 'A union of family life of two persons of the same sex who have not registered their life partnership with the competent authority shall be regarded as a same-sex informal partnership if the union lasts for at least three years and if it has met the prescribed requirements for the validity of life partnership since its beginning.'

The uniformity of the definitions of a same-sex informal partnership in the legislation and case law cannot be compared since relevant legal practice has not yet been developed.

CZECH REPUBLIC

Informal relationship is defined neither by legislation, nor by case law, therefore we can only present a definition used in law-related books or articles that refer to informal relationships as 'a living arrangement in which an unmarried couple lives together in a long-term relationship that resembles a marriage'.[15]

The position of partners in an informal relationship is not regulated by the Czech Act on Registered Partnership nor is the term 'informal relationship' defined in Czech legislation. The Czech Civil Code uses the term 'close person' and says that persons related by affinity and persons permanently living together are also presumed to be close persons (S. 22(1) Czech Civil Code). This definition could also cover the partners in an informal relationship and then could be applied in S. 1636(1), S. 1637(1), S. 2279(1), S. 3021 et seq. Czech Civil Code.

DENMARK

The definitions vary according to the context, e.g.:

- Danish Social Security Acts: The couple live in a marriage-like relationship and the new partner contributes to the shared household.
- The Danish Inheritance Act, The Danish Inheritance Tax Act, The Danish Administration of Estates Act, and the Danish Insurance Contracts Act: 1) Cohabitants who have lived together in a marriage-like relationship for the last two years prior to death, or 2) cohabitants who have, have had or are expecting children together.

ENGLAND AND WALES

Each statute defines cohabiting relationships differently, although there are common elements. In all cases, (except most recently for adoption which refers to a couple living 'as partners in an enduring family relationship' under S. 144(4)(b) English Adoption and Children Act 2002), it is required that the couple is living 'as husband and wife' or 'as civil partners'. In some contexts, living in a common household is also required (e.g. tenancy succession under the English Rent Act 1977 and the English Housing Act 1988) and in others, a minimum duration of the relationship is additionally required (as in secure tenancy succession under the Housing Act 1985 or the right to apply for financial provision on death as in the English Inheritance (Provision for Family and Dependants) Act 1975). The omission of a specified minimum duration in the adoption context in S. 144(4)(b) English Adoption and Children Act

15 M. HRUŠÁKOVÁ, Z. KRÁLÍČKOVÁ, L. WESTPHALOVÁ et al., *Rodinné právo*, C. H. Beck, Prague, 2015, at p. 114.

2002 seems to have introduced a more flexible stability test for the informal relationship in this context.

ESTONIA

Estonian legislation uses several definitions to define an informal relationship. The current author uses the English translations that are available on the official page of Riigi Teataja ('State Gazette'; www.riigiteataja.ee/en/). The references to 'marriage' and 'cohabitation' mainly exist side by side in the laws. For example, the Estonian Social Welfare Act § 22(2) item 1 states as follows: 'persons who are married or in a relationship similar to marriage'. The Estonian Code of Civil Procedure 'in a matter of his or her spouse or cohabitee' (§ 23 item 2) or 'the spouse of or a person permanently living together' (§ 257(1) item 5). The same definition is used in § 71(1) item 5 of the Estonian Code of Criminal Procedure and § 9(1) item 5 of the Estonian Code of Enforcement Procedure. § 117(1) item 2 of the Estonian Bankruptcy Act refers to 'persons who live in a shared household with the debtor'. § 6(2) item 3 of the Estonian Victim Support Act uses the word 'cohabitee', as does § 84(2) of the Estonian Credit Institutions Act. The Estonian Military Service Act[16] § 92(3) item 4 defines a cohabiting partner as 'a person in a relationship similar to marriage (hereinafter unmarried partner)'. The Estonian Civil Service Act[17] § 15 item 4 uses the definition: 'a partner in the marriage-like relationship (unmarried partner)'. Before adopting the Estonian Registered Partnership Act, a proposal was made in the legal literature to use 'cohabitation' as a general term, covering all possible forms of cohabitation, including marriage and an informal relationship.[18]

In § 129(6) of the Estonian Law of Obligations Act regulating a claim for the compensation of damage we can find the following: 'the person with whom the deceased lived together as a family or whom the deceased person maintained on the basis of a moral obligation'.

---

16 Kaitseväeteenistuse seadus (adopted on 13 June 2012, entered into force on 1 April 2013). – RT I, 10.07.2012, 1; RT I, 29.06.2014, 101 (in Estonian), available in English at: www.riigiteataja.ee/en/eli/519092014003/consolide.

17 Avaliku teenistuse seadus (adopted on 13 June 2012). – RT I, 06.07.2012, 1; RT I, 18.02.2014, 4 (in Estonian), available in English at: www.riigiteataja.ee/en/eli/509072014003/consolide.

18 A. OLM, 'Non-married Cohabiting Couples and Their Constitutional', *Juridica International*, 2013, pp. 104-111.

FINLAND

There are over 70 statutes across all administrative sectors which include references to cohabiting couples. The definition of cohabitation varies according to the context and the statute in question.

The most common specific reference to cohabitation in the social sector concerns 'a man and a woman who cohabit in circumstances akin to marriage'. The legal effect of such a relationship is equated with that of married couples.[19] Statutes of this type do not specify the minimum length of time required for the cohabitation, but presume that the partners live in a common household and that the cohabitation is continuous.[20]

The requirement that the cohabiting partners are of the opposite sex is almost exclusively confined to statutes concerning social benefits and social insurance.[21] Even the provisions that do not specifically refer to the requirement of being 'a man and a woman', but refer, in a gender-neutral fashion, to 'persons cohabiting in circumstances akin to marriage' may be interpreted as only applying to a couple of the opposite sex. This is due to the fact that, at present, a marital bond can only be concluded between a man and a woman and 'circumstances akin to marriage' are therefore only possible between a man and a woman. Such an interpretation has specifically been provided in the rationale of statutes such as the Finnish Employment Accidents Act (608/1948) and the Finnish Entrepreneurs' Pensions Act (1271/2006).

---

19 For example, S. 3 of the Finnish Act on Social Assistance (1412/1997) and S. 7a of the Finnish Act on Customer Payments in Social and Health Care (734/1992).

20 The Social Insurance Institution (*Kansaneläkelaitos/Folkpensionsanstalten*), which administers the social insurance and social benefits scheme in Finland, has issued a number of guidelines related to the various schemes. According to the guidelines, the interpretation of a cohabitee relationship may vary according to the scheme in question. According to the national benefit schemes such as the housing benefit scheme and the widow(er)'s pension scheme, the cohabitation relationship is automatically presumed to exist without a waiting period if a man and a woman live together at the same address without being married and they are not closely related to each other. Evidence to the contrary is considered on a case by case basis. According to some other schemes, such as entitlement to the Finnish social insurance scheme or the study grant scheme, having lived together for at least six months is required in order to qualify as constant cohabitation (www.kela.fi/kelan-etuusohjeet).

21 For example, the Finnish National Pensions Act (568/2007), the Finnish Health Insurance Act (1224/2004), the Finnish Act on the Protection of the Livelyhood of Unemployed Persons (1290/2002), the Finnish Act on Social Assistance (1412/1997) and the Finnish Act on a General Housing Allowance (938/2014).

On the other hand, an interpretation according to which circumstances akin to marriage can only materialise in opposite-sex relationships has been expressly rejected in legislation outside the fields of social benefits and social insurance. For example, in the rationale of the Finnish Administrative Procedure Act (434/2003) and the Finnish Criminal Investigation Act (805/2011), the provisions relating to 'persons living in circumstances akin to marriage' have been stated to include also cohabiting couples of the same sex.

Hence, if the statute itself does not specify whether the condition of 'circumstances akin to marriage' refers to a couple of the opposite sex, its interpretation remains somewhat unclear and there is room for interpretation in individual cases. In order to eliminate this ambiguity, there has been a growing tendency to replace the notion of 'circumstances akin to marriage' with the notion of 'persons living in circumstances akin to marriage or other partnership'[22] or with the notion of 'a cohabiting partner'.[23]

Although the great majority of references relating to cohabiting couples do not state a minimum duration for the cohabitation in order to have legal effect, there are a number of provisions that do so. The required minimum period of time varies according to the subject matter from one[24] or two[25] years up to five years.[26]

Some definitions even require that the cohabiting couple have a common child or common custody of a child. The requirement of a child can exist either as an independent criterion for cohabitation to have legal effect[27] or, more commonly, as an alternative to the criteria of minimum

[22] For example, the Finnish Act on Continuing Powers of Attorney (648/2007) and the Finnish Enforcement Act (705/2007).

[23] Finnish Act on the Dissolution of the Household of Cohabiting Partners (26/2011), the Finnish Adoption Act (22/2012), the Finnish Passport Act (671/2006) and the Finnish Securities Markets Act (746/2012).

[24] Finnish Act on Employment Pension Insurance Institutions (354/1997) and the Finnish Securities Markets Act (746/2012).

[25] Finnish Act on Reimbursements in the Foreign Service (596/2006), the Finnish Passport Act (671/2006), the Finnish Aliens Act (301/2004).

[26] Finnish Act on the Dissolution of the Household of Cohabiting Partners (26/2011), the Finnish Code of Inheritance (40/1965), the Finnish Inheritance and Gift Tax Act (378/1940, S. 11), the Finnish Act on the Recovery of Property to the Estate of a Bankrupt Person (758/1991), the Finnish Act on Certain Personal Data Files of Local Register Offices (57/2005).

[27] Finnish Employment Accidents Act, the Finnish Act on Military Benefits (781/1993).

duration.[28] 'A former marriage or a common child' has also been stated as one requirement for cohabitation to have legal effect in the area of tax law and agricultural benefits.[29] There is also one instance of 'a confirmed agreement of mutual support' being required, which is a precondition for having the right to a widow(er)'s pension after the death of one of the cohabiting partners. This criterion, however, is an alternative condition for having a common child.[30]

FRANCE

According to Art. 515-8 of the French Civil Code, a *concubinage* is *'une union de fait, caractérisée par une vie commune présentant un caractère de stabilité et de continuité, entre deux personnes, de sexe différent ou de même sexe, qui vivent en couple'* (a factual union, characterised by common life with the character of stability and continuity, between two persons of the opposite or same sex, living as a couple). This means that a *concubinage* cannot be of a short duration, since stability and continuity are required. Living together is also a condition to be fulfilled. What is defined in Art. 515-8 is *'concubinage'*, not any other kind of informal relationship. Only *concubinage* can lead to certain legal effects.

However, with regard to some legal effects which can possibly be derived from the informal relationship, the French civil courts do not always require that the condition of living together (*communauté d'habitation*) has to be fulfilled.[31]

The definitions, or at least the conditions to be fulfilled to obtain legal advantages, may vary. Thus, some specific provisions contain further (or different) requirements. See under Question 2: sometimes, it is required

---

28 Finnish Act on the Dissolution of the Household of Cohabiting Partners (26/2011), the Finnish Code of Inheritance (40/1965), the Finnish Inheritance and Gift Tax Act (378/1940, S. 11), the Finnish Act on the Recovery of Property to the Estate of a Bankrupt Person (758/1991), the Finnish Act on Certain Personal Data Files of Local Register Offices (758/1991), the Finnish Act on Reimbursements in the Foreign Service (596/2006), the Finnish Passport Act (671/2006), the Finnish Aliens Act (301/2004).

29 Finnish Income Tax Act (1535/1992), the Finnish Act on Direct Agricultural Subsidies by the European Union (193/2013), the Finnish Act on National Agricultural and Horticultural Subsidies (1559/2001), the Finnish Act on the Reimbursement for Crop Damages (1214/2000), the Finnish Act on Reimbursement for Natural Damages, the Finnish Act on Environmental Subsidies to Agriculture and Certain Other Subsidies related to the Improvement of the Countryside (1440/2006).

30 Finnish Employment Accidents Act (608/1948).

31 See e.g. CA DOUAI, 8 September 2011, no 10/09189, JurisData no 2011-018543; CA DOUAI, 12 December 2002, no. 01/03255, *Dr. Famille* 2003, comm. 86, with note H. LÉCUYER.

that both partners have been living together for at least two years (organ donation between partners who are both living), or one year for the transfer of the residential lease if the other partner dies or leaves the dwelling.

GERMANY

There are different definitions in various fields of law. On one occasion the Federal Constitutional Court has, in the context of social security law, given a definition for a 'community similar to marriage' (*eheähnliche Gemeinschaft*). According to this it is a 'community of life' (*Lebensgemeinschaft*) established with a 'permanent purpose' (*auf Dauer*) which does not allow for another coexisting 'community of life'. It is characterised by 'inner ties of commitment' with a reciprocal responsibility between the partners which is more than a pure accommodation and economic community.[32] This approach has been accepted by the Federal Supreme Courts in civil, administrative and social security matters.[33]

In the past it has sometimes been added to the definitions that a community of life exists between a man and a woman. Today, however, it is generally accepted that homosexual relationships are also covered.[34] Existing sexual relations between the partners are not a necessary element.[35] Living together at the same place and a common household are not necessary.[36] They are only indications of a *de facto* community.[37] A mutual commitment to a shared life is necessary.

There is no general statutory definition of cohabitation in civil law. A cohabitant has a right to succeed to a tenancy upon the death of the tenant with whom he resided (§ 563 para. 2 s. 4 German Civil Code). The statute mentions a person who maintains a joint household of a permanent nature with the tenant. The stable union (*verfestigte*

32 BVerfG, 17.11.1992, *BVerfGE*, 87, 234, 264 = *NJW*, 1993, 643.

33 For references see M. WELLENHOFER, 'Anh. zu § 1302', in: *Münchener Kommentar zum Bürgerlichen Gesetzbuch*, Beck, Munich, 2013, at No. 3.

34 M. WELLENHOFER, 'Anh. zu § 1302', in: *Münchener Kommentar zum Bürgerlichen Gesetzbuch*, Beck, Munich, 2013, at No. 4.

35 BVerfG, 17.11.1992, *BVerfGE*, 87, 234, 268 = *NJW*, 1993, 643; M. LÖHNIG, 'Anh. zu §§ 1297 et seq.', in: J. VON STAUDINGER, *Kommentar zum Bürgerlichen Gesetzbuch*, Sellier-de Gruyter, Berlin, 2012, at No. 15.

36 BGH, 24.10.2001, *NJW*, 2002, 217 = *FamRZ*, 2002, 23 with note D. SCHWAB (maintenance after divorce).

37 N. DETHLOFF, *Familienrecht*, Beck, Munich, 2012, at § 8 No. 6.

Lebensgemeinschaft) of the claimant and a cohabitant which excludes maintenance claims after divorce (§ 1579 No. 2 German Civil Code) must exist mainly in the economic sphere.[38]

In succession law the heir has a duty to grant maintenance to 'family members' of the deceased in the first thirty days after the devolution of the inheritance (§ 1969 para. 1 German Civil Code, see Question 48). According to the dominant view, a cohabitant is also such a person entitled to maintenance.[39] Despite failing to be a family member in the narrow sense of the law, legal maintenance claims are not barred because it is the factual dependency which is decisive.

However, in social security law in particular there are definitions (see Question 2). Support of the other partner solely in the form of a loan is not enough.[40]

GREECE

No variations are known concerning the definition of informal cohabitation in Greek law. Case law has defined a free union outside marriage as the informal cohabitation of persons of different gender who do not intend to marry. It is the element of a reciprocal promise to marry at some future time which distinguishes a state of engagement from one of free union or cohabitation, in which the partners not only have not agreed to marry, but have in fact made a conscious decision to eschew marriage.[41]

HUNGARY

Art. 6:514 of the Hungarian Civil Code provides a definition of cohabitation which does not differ from the definition used in the Civil Code of 1959. According to this provision cohabitants are two persons who live together without entering into a marriage, in a common

38 See G. HOHLOCH, '§ 1579', in: W. ERMAN, *BGB Kommentar*, O. Schmidt, Cologne, 2014, at No. 18 et seq.

39 Higher Regional Court (Oberlandesgericht; OLG) Düsseldorf, 14.12.1982, *NJW*, 1983, 1566; D. WEIDLICH, '§ 1969', in: O. PALANDT, *Bürgerliches Gesetzbuch*, Beck, Munich, 2015, at No. 1. For an application by way of an analogy, D. SCHWAB, *Familienrecht*, Beck, Munich, 2014, at No. 980.

40 Federal Administrative Court (Bundesverwaltungsgericht; BVerwG), 17.5.95, *Entscheidungen des Bundesverwaltungsgerichts (BVerwGE)*, 98, 195 = *NJW*, 1995, S.2802 = *FamRZ*, 1995, 1352 (social assistance).

41 Precisely as ruled by the Supreme Court - Areios Pagos in judgment No. 1141/2011.

household, in an emotional fellowship and in an economic partnership (a community of life). Neither of them can live in a matrimonial community of life or community of life within cohabitation or a registered partnership with a third person and they cannot be direct relatives or siblings.

Cohabitants can be both different-sex and same-sex persons and they cannot be either spouses or – analogously – registered partners. If either or both of them has/have an existing and valid marriage or registered partnership with a third person the existence of cohabitation is not excluded, but there is no cohabitation if either or both of them have not only a matrimonial bond (or a registered partnership 'bond') but also a community of life. (I have to remark that according to the demographic data it is not extraordinary that a person has a matrimonial bond but he or she nevertheless lives in cohabitation with a third partner.) Siblings and half-siblings also cannot live in cohabitation according to the explanatory provisions of the Hungarian Civil Code.

The elements of a community of life, namely living together in a common household, in an emotional fellowship and in an economic partnership, have always been scrutinised in legal debates so these requirements have become crystallised in the case law. I have to remark that this crystallisation has taken place concerning the old regime of cohabitation and this old regime will still be applied for a rather long time as a consequence of the transitory period (also see the answer to Question 1). There is, as yet, no experience concerning the application of the new regime under the Hungarian Civil Code. Although the definition of cohabitation has remained intact, other provisions on the property of the cohabitants, their maintenance obligations etc. have substantially changed and that is why I do not exclude some divergence in interpretation. However, after a number of years it will become apparent whether the Hungarian judiciary will have deviated from the interpretation being applied today.

Concerning the interpretation of certain elements of the definition, the judiciary and especially the Hungarian Curia (the former Supreme Court) have demonstrated a strict attitude up to now. They have not only developed the criteria for living together – an emotional and economic community – but have complemented this enumeration with other factors. One of these extra requirements is that the partners' belonging together must have been obvious to third persons, e.g. their relatives or neighbours, and the stable and/or marriage-like character of their partnership. An emotional fellowship is interpreted as mutuality, so the one-sided affection of one partner towards another is not satisfactory. An economic community as a criterion carries the greatest weight as it seems to be decisive. An economic community means economic co-operation so the partners have to co-operate in the interest of achieving a common aim, maintaining a common way of living and using their income for their common aim.[42]

According to the determined case law the lack of one element does not necessarily result in no cohabitation as all elements have to be investigated and weighed according to their complexity.

REPUBLIC OF IRELAND

Part 15 of the Irish 2010 Act sets out the law in respect of cohabitants. A 'cohabitant' is defined at S. 172 as being 'one of two adults (whether of the same or opposite sex) who live together as a couple in an intimate and committed relationship and are not related to each other within the prohibited degrees of a relationship or married to each other or civil partners of each other'. In determining whether or not two adults are cohabitants the court can take into account all the circumstances of the relationship and in particular the following as per S. 172(2):

'(a) the duration of the relationship;
(b) the basis on which the couple live together;
(c) the degree of financial dependence of either adult on the other and any agreements in respect of their finances;
(d) the degree and nature of any financial arrangements between the adults including any joint purchase of an estate or interest in land or joint acquisition of personal property;
(e) whether there are one or more dependent children;
(f) whether one of the adults cares for and supports the children of the other; and
(g) the degree to which the adults present themselves to others as a couple.'

Section 172(3) clarifies that a relationship does not cease to be an intimate relationship for the purpose of the Irish 2010 Act merely because it is no longer sexual in nature. Not only does the Irish 2010 Act provide for the

42 O. SZEIBERT-ERDŐS, 'Unmarried Partnerships in Hungary', in: K. BOELE-WOELKI (ed), *Common Core and Better Law in European Family Law*, Intersentia, Antwerp, 2005, at p. 324-327.; O. SZEIBERT, *Az élettársak és vagyoni viszonyaik (Cohabitants and their property relations)*, HVG-ORAC, Budapest, 2010, at p. 222-304.

category of cohabitants. It also introduces the concept of 'qualified cohabitants'. Section 172(5) states:

> 'For the purposes of this part, a qualified cohabitant means an adult who was in a relationship of cohabitation with another adult and who, immediately before the time that the relationship ended, whether through death or otherwise was living with the other adult as a couple for a period:
> (a) of two years or more, in the case where they are parents of one or more dependent children; and
> (b) of five years or more in any other case.'

The independent significance of the term 'cohabitant' is primarily that cohabitants are covered by the rules on cohabitation agreements in S. 202 of the Irish 2010 Act, irrespective of whether the duration of their relationship is such that they come within the definition of 'qualified cohabitants'. It is only a qualified cohabitant who is eligible to apply for redress from the other cohabitant upon the termination of the relationship through the redress scheme in the Act. Thus couples who have lived together for four years for example, and have no dependent children together, cannot apply to court for relief when their relationship ends.

ITALY

Legislation and case law do not provide any general definition of informal relationships. The definition thereof, whenever this is provided, then varies according to the context.[43] For instance, in the law on medically assisted reproduction cohabitation is not qualified at all, while in the rules on adoption it is specified that it must have lasted for at least three years. A significant indication, however, is contained in an old decision of the Court of Cassation which defined the task of the judge in ascertaining the real substance of a cohabitation as that of ensuring that the cohabitants had formed a 'reliable and stable' *de facto* family, going beyond 'the mere presence of sexual intercourse' between them.[44]

The existence, or not as the case may be, of an informal relationship is a matter of fact left to the discretional evaluation of the court. Its existence may be proved through any means provided by the law and often by

---

43 L. LENTI and J. LONG, *Diritto di famiglia e dei servizi sociali*, Laterza, Bari/Rome, Laterza, 2011, at p. 202.

44 Cass. 4 April 1998, n. 3503 in *Foro It.*, 1998, I, 2154. Compare L. BALESTRA, 'La famiglia di fatto', in: G. FERRANDO (ed.), *Il nuovo diritto di famiglia*, Zanichelli, Bologna, 2008, at p. 1039, n. 23.

witnesses. The burden of proof lies on the person who asserts the existence of the relationship.[45]

It should also be mentioned here that the Italian language has several words and expressions to indicate the idea of two partners sharing a household and their everyday life: *coabitazione* (the mere fact of living in the same home), which has its etymology in the Latin *cum habitatio* (inhabit together); *convivenza* (*cum vivere*, living together) having a meaning of sharing a common life; *convivenza more uxorio* (from the Latin 'similar to the matrimonial way of living'); *famiglia* or *unione* or *coppia di fatto; unioni libere;* and *convivenze senza matrimonio.*[46] Although these terms have different meanings and implications (sometimes significantly so), in everyday language and even in the legal doctrine and case law, however, they are frequently treated as synonyms and are interchangeable.

In any case, same-sex partnerships are included in these definitions just as different-sex unions are.[47]

LATVIA

Since Latvian national laws and other legislative acts do not contain a general legal order on informal relationships, there is also no general definition of informal relationships.

However, in previously mentioned cases when the court has had to assess whether there is an actual cohabitation between the parties, the focus was mostly on whether the persons had lived in a common household, how long they had so cohabited, whether there had been common expenses (common budget), and whether they had shared psychological and emotional links.[48] In certain cases, it was also taken into account as to whether children had been born in the course of the

45 Cass. 28 March 1994, n. 2988: compare L. BARDARO, 'Il convivente della vittima', in: P. CENDON (ed.), *Trattato dei nuovi danni*, Cedam, Padua, 2011, at p. 220 et seq.; G. OBERTO, *I diritti dei conviventi. Realtà e prospettive tra Italia ed Europa*, Cedam, Padua, 2012, at p. 208 et seq.

46 The old term *concubinato* – with its negative implication – is no longer used.

47 For instance Trib. Firenze 11 August 1986, in *Dir. eccl.*, 1989, II, p. 367 and Trib. Milano 1 July 1993, in *Gius*, 1994, p. 103. Compare L. BALESTRA, 'La famiglia di fatto', in: G. FERRANDO (ed.), *Il nuovo diritto di famiglia*, Zanichelli, Bologna, 2008, at p. 1044. Also C. Cost. 15 April 2010, n. 138, in *Fam.dir.* 2010, p. 653 (see infra the answer to question 6).

48 Senate of the Supreme Court of the Republic of Latvia, Department of Administrative Cases, judgment of 27 July 2010 No.SKA-307/2010. Available at: tiesas.lv/nolemumi.

cohabitation.[49] The Court[50] has taken the preconditions for establishing an actual cohabitation from the Latvian Civil Law S. 84 which states that 'Marriage creates a duty on the part of a husband and a wife to be faithful to each other, to live together, to take care of each other and to jointly ensure the welfare of their family'. The Court suggested that from this provision of law follows the obligation to live together in a single family dwelling and to conduct a *de facto* cohabitation. Accordingly, the Court assessed the existence of a common life and a common household, indicating that since partnership in Latvia is not defined, there are no other preconditions for detecting the existence of such relationship.

LITHUANIA

The current legislation does not provide a definition of informal relationships between couples. Individual legal acts contain a variety of terms mostly referring to family members, the family,[51] close relatives, persons engaged in joint household management, close persons, etc. An analysis of the legislation suggests that persons remaining in such a relationship are considered to be cohabitants, persons in a close relationship, partners, etc. For instance, the Lithuanian Law on Protection against Violence in a Proximate Environment uses the definition of a 'proximate environment' which means an environment consisting of individuals linked together by the present or past matrimonial, partnership, in-law or similar close relationship, as well as individuals living together and engaged in joint household management.[52] The Law on State Benefits for Families Raising Children[53] defines a family as 'spouses or cohabiting persons, as well as a married person with whom, by a court order, their children live because of the separation of the spouses, or one of the parents, their children and adopted children aged 18 and under'. The family shall also include persons between the ages of 18 and 24 who are unmarried and not cohabiting with another person:

49 Senate of the Supreme Court of the Republic of Latvia, Department of Administrative Cases, judgment of 27 July 2010 No.SKA-307/2010. Available at: tiesas.lv/nolemumi.

50 District Court of Jēkabpils judgment on 4 August 2011in case No.C16073311 (not published).

51 It was established that the terms 'family' or 'family members' are used in almost 200 laws, and the definitions of a 'family' or 'family members' are present in about 30 laws. K. Ambrazevičiūtė, E. Kavoliūnaitė-Ragauskienė, V. Mizaras, 'Šeimos kaip teisės kategorijos turinys Lietuvos Respublikos įstatymuose' (The substance of the family as a legal category in Lithuanian Legislation), *Teisės problemos*, Vol. 78, No. 4, 2012, at p. 81.

52 Extract from Art. 2, part 1 of the Law of the Republic of Lithuania on the Protection Against Violence in a Proximate Environment (*Lietuvos Respublikos apsaugos nuo smurto artimoje aplinkoje įstatymo straipsnio 1 dalis)* Official gazette, 2011, No. 72-3475.

53 Law on State Benefits to Families Raising Children, Official Gazette, 2004, No. 88-3208.

full-time school-children and students at secondary schools and other institutions of formal education, as well as persons from the day of graduating from a secondary school which they attended as full-time students until the 1st of September of the same year.

The case law suggests that the definitions depend upon the nature of the legal relationships,[54] therefore the following circumstances play an important role: the fact of cohabitation and its duration,[55] joint household management (including care and maintenance), the creation of joint property by contributing personal funds and joint labour, mutual health care and relaxation, agreements regarding common objectives (e.g. the acquisition of certain property for the fulfilment of mutual needs or undertaking joint liabilities), an open demonstration of close emotional relations and appearing in public as a couple.

LUXEMBOURG

No, this definition does not vary according to the context. Either it is an informal relationship or it is not, depending on whether the situation corresponds to the definition.

The case law in Luxembourg defines the informal relationship as: '*Le concubinage peut être défini comme étant une union de fait tenant à l'existence d'une vie commune stable et continue entre deux personnes formant un couple et un ménage*'.

---

54 For example, on the 26th of April 2005 the Board of the Supreme Administrative Court of Lithuania heard a case (Ruling of the Supreme Administrative Court of Lithuania in case *H.J. v. Pravieniškių 1 Correction House No. A* [10]*- 483-05)* and applied the provisions of the Lithuanian Civil Code concerning cohabitants, although they are not legally effective. In this case, the Court acknowledged the claimant's right to have his long-term relationship with his cohabitant recognised, although such a right is not incorporated in the internal rules of the correctional institutions (their living together (partnership) was not registered). Other possible criteria for acknowledging a long-term relationship were also absent (for example, a mutual child).

55 For example, on the 15th of September 2005 the Supreme Court of Lithuania delivered its ruling in civil case No. 3K-3-389/2005 where a dispute had arisen concerning the cohabitant of a deceased tenant of an apartment and a close relative (grandmother) with regard to their recognition as family members and their right to the apartment which belonged to the municipality. This case did not apply the norms of 'family law', but relied on the sixth book of the Lithuanian Civil Code (Art. 6.588), i.e. the Supreme Court held that it is not the registration of the partnership that is important, but rather the exact time when the claimants settled in the living accommodation and whether they had lived there for not less than one year.

Translated, this means that Luxembourg case law defines an informal relationship as a union between two persons who live together and form a couple in a stable and durable way.

THE NETHERLANDS

In this respect a distinction has to be made between the specific regulations in different areas of the law and the areas which are not covered by a specific provision.

In specific legislation different terms and definitions are used. There is a broad range of terms: (other) life partner,[56] the person having a joint stable household with a tenant for at least two years,[57] a joint durable household continuously for at least six months if a number of other conditions are met,[58] a partner, but only if a number of requirements are fulfilled,[59] 'began to live together with another as if they are married or as if they had registered their partnership',[60] and an unmarried person who shares a joint household.[61] The legislature is aware of the wide variety of the definitions of conditions and has expressed its intention to reduce this variety.[62] So far, this has been rather unsuccessful.

If no specific definition in the legislation applies, the courts do not use a typical definition. These cases generally concern disputes in relation to the law of obligations and property law. The courts state in the decision that the parties are (ex-)partners. If there is a cohabitation contract this will be mentioned as well.

---

56 In the provisions on the protection of vulnerable adults, but also in criminal law.

57 Art. 7:267 Dutch Civil Code.

58 A joint durable household will only be taken into account if the deceased and the surviving partner have been registered at the same address and if the partners concluded a cohabitation contract signed by a notary. In this contract a duty to take care of each other has to be included. In addition, the partners should have opted to be qualified as tax partners under the Dutch Income Tax Act 2001.

59 Art. 1a Dutch Inheritance Tax Act 1956, including a notarial cohabitation contract with a duty to support each other during the relationship, only with one person, registered at the same address; both adults, and no relatives, this being subject to a number of exceptions.

60 Art. 1:160 Dutch Civil Code on which there is a great deal of case law defining the exact conditions of this term.

61 Art. 3 para. 2 *Participatiewet*, only if they are not first-grade relatives and in a number of situations the partners are deemed to share a joint household, regardless of their intention.

62 *Aanwijzing voor de regelgeving* 72a, as amended in 2004, Stcrt. 2014, 213.

NORWAY

The Norwegian Inheritance Act 1972, S. 28(a) first paragraph, defines cohabitation as follows: 'Two people over the age of 18 who are neither married, registered partners nor cohabitants with others, living together in a marriage-like relationship.' This definition includes both opposite-sex and same-sex couples. The core of the definition is 'marriage-like', which means that they must constitute a couple, although it is not a condition that they must have a sexual relationship. Two students living together for practical reasons without being a couple are not, however, cohabitants in the sense of the law.[63] This definition of cohabitation is limited to the Norwegian Inheritance Act, but similar definitions would apply in case law concerning co-ownership and cohabitation.[64]

Pursuant to the Norwegian Inheritance Act, S. 28(a) second paragraph, the partners can still be considered cohabitants, even if they live apart for some time due to education, work, illness, a stay in an institution or other similar circumstances. The preparatory works state that a permanent stay in a nursing home does not in itself preclude inheritance rights. Professor John Asland considers that long prison terms should be considered in the same way.[65] Moreover, pursuant to S. 28(a) second paragraph, it is not considered to be a cohabitation when two persons who according to the Norwegian Marriage Act, S. 3 (prohibition against marriage between close relatives) cannot marry, live together.

PORTUGAL

The sole and persistent definition in recent laws is: 'The *de facto* union is the legal situation of two people, regardless of gender, living in conditions similar to those of marriage for over two years' (Law No. 7/2001, of 11 May, Art. 1, n. 2).

Since both *de facto* unions and marriages between same-sex couples are allowed, there is no problem in saying 'living in conditions similar to that of marriage'.

Nevertheless, there are circumstances in which cohabitation is taken into account even if that specific lapse of time has not occurred (e.g. parental

63 J. ASLAND, 'Gjenlevende samboers rettsstilling', in: J. ASLAND et al. (eds.), *Nordisk samboerrett*, Gyldendal Juridisk, Oslo, 2014, at p. 183-184.

64 P. LØDRUP and T. SVERDRUP, *Familieretten*, 2011, at p. 336-337.

65 J. ASLAND, 'Gjenlevende samboers rettsstilling', in: J. ASLAND et al. (eds.), *Nordisk samboerrett*, Gyldendal Juridisk, Oslo, 2014, at p. 185-186.

responsibilities regarding parents who cohabit - Art. 1911 of the Portuguese Civil Code), or in which a longer period of cohabitation is required (e.g. acquisition of nationality - Art. 3(3) of the Portuguese Nationality Act).

RUSSIA

There is no general legal definition of informal relationships either in statutory law or in the case law.

SCOTLAND

Informal relationships between couples are defined under the heading of 'cohabitation'. There are two principal statutory definitions within the scope of family law: in S. 18 of the Matrimonial Homes (Family Protection) (Scotland) Act 1981 and S. 25 of the Family Law (Scotland) Act 2006. Both initially relied on comparison with the model of living together as husband and wife but were extended to include living together as husband and wife, for opposite sex couples, and living together as civil partners, for same-sex couples. The effect of the Marriage and Civil Partnership (Scotland) Act 2014 is to change the legal meaning of marriage to include both same-sex and different-sex marriage and it is provided that cohabitation will be defined in relation to marriage for all couples.[66]

For the purposes of regulating occupancy of the family home, S. 18 of the Matrimonial Homes (Family Protection) (Scotland) Act 1981 defines cohabitants as two persons living together as if they were married. It is further provided that:

> 'In determining whether ... two persons are a cohabiting couple the court shall have regard to all the circumstances of the case including -
> (a) the time for which it appears they have been living together; and
> (b) whether there is any child -
> (i) of whom they are the parents; or
> (ii) who they have treated as a child of theirs.'[67]

In practice, there is little evidence of this definition being considered by the courts, with only a handful of reported cases on cohabitants since the Act came into force. The reported cases, which do consider the definition,

---

66 Marriage and Civil Partnership (Scotland) Act 2014, S. 4(2), (3) and (4).
67 Matrimonial Homes (Family Protection) (Scotland) Act 1981, S. 18(2).

do not look in detail at the relationship between the parties but focus instead on the date when the test for cohabitation requires to be met. If an applicant seeks to bring herself within the scope of the definition, does she need to show that she was still cohabiting at the time of application? A very literal interpretation of the words in S. 18, and the use therein of the present tense, was adopted in *Verity v Fenner*[68] where it was held that the test was not satisfied where the couple was not still 'living together as husband and wife' at the date of the proof. In *Armour v Anderson*,[69] both at first instance and on appeal, a more purposive approach was applied which acknowledged the underlying aim of the legislation and the undesirability of requiring a party to remain living together with an abusive partner in order to qualify under the terms of the Act. The court gave its opinion to the effect that the test under S. 18(3) was not whether they were still in fact living together at the point of application but whether they were cohabiting in the relevant home 'when the conduct which gave rise to the application occurred'.[70]

The second statutory definition is set out in S. 25 of the Family Law (Scotland) Act 2006 and it establishes the threshold for access to a range of property and financial awards in the context of cohabitation and the breakdown of cohabitation. S. 25(1) defines a cohabitant as either member of a couple who are living together as if they were married.[71] While this is a vague and highly discretionary test to apply, particularly in light of the fact that Scots law provides very little statutory definition or regulation of the marriage relationship, it is arguably a familiar test.[72] Facts and witnesses rather than legal principles are central and frequently the 'issue is a clear one of credibility and reliability'.[73]

Section 25 has been strongly criticised for its 'intellectually incoherent' drafting[74] due to the fact that the requirement in subsection (1) is followed by subsection (2), which provides:

> 'In determining ... whether a person ("A") is a cohabitant of another person ("B"), the court shall have regard to –

68 *Verity v Fenner* 1993 SCLR 223.
69 *Armour v Anderson* 1994 SLT 1127.
70 *Armour v Anderson* 1994 SLT 1127, at 1132.
71 For the avoidance of doubt, it is confirmed that such a couple must not be in a formal relationship with each other, i.e. either marriage or civil partnership: Marriage and Civil Partnership (Scotland) Act 2014, S. 4(3).
72 F. McCarthy, 'Defining cohabitants', *Scots Law Times*, 2014, pp. 143-145, at p. 143.
73 *Fairley v Fairley* 2008 Fam LR 112 at para. 3.
74 J.M. Thomson, *Family Law in Scotland*, Bloomsbury Professional, London, 2006, at p. 30.

(a) the length of the period during which A and B have been living together (or lived together);
(b) the nature of their relationship during that period; and
(c) the nature and extent of any financial arrangements subsisting, or which subsisted, during that period.'

The absence of any connecting word between subsections (1) and (2) has given rise to uncertainty. Is the test for cohabitation the broad test of living together as if married, in subsection (1), or must it include the specific factors set out in subsection (2)? To date, there have been relatively few applications under the Act, which have required the court to apply S. 25 as, in the majority of reported cases, it has been accepted or admitted that the parties were in fact cohabiting. Where the question has arisen, however, the uncertainties and inherently discretionary nature of the test emerge. In some cases it appears that the court is recognising the 'gatekeeping' function of S. 25 and is willing to accept the existence of cohabitation in order to enable the applicant to proceed with his or her claim.[75]

In *Garrad v Inglis*,[76] the sheriff took the view that the three factors listed in S. 25(1)(b) were not exclusive and suggested a longer list of factors which might be considered:

> '(1) the length of time during which the parties lived together, (2) the amount and nature of the time the parties spent together, (3) whether they lived under the same roof in the same household, (4) whether they slept together, (5) whether they had sexual intercourse, (6) whether they ate together, (7) whether they had a social life together, (8) whether they supported each other, talked to and were affectionate to each other, (9) outward appearances, (10) their financial arrangements, whether they shared resources, household and child-care tasks, (11) the intentions of each party and whether any of them were communicated to the other party, and (12) physical separation.'[77]

It was made clear in *Garrad v Inglis* that no single factor was conclusive and this is a point which has been stressed in several cases. In particular, the issue has arisen as to whether a couple must in fact be living together in the same house in order to satisfy the definition of cohabitation. On

75 As happened, e.g. in the first application under s29 where it was found that the applicant had title to make a claim but the court assessed the value of the claim at nil: *Savage v Purches* 2009 SLT (Sh Ct) 36, discussed further in F. MCCARTHY, 'Rights in succession for cohabitants: *Savage v Purches*', *Edinburgh Law Review*, 2009, pp. 325-329.
76 *Garrad v Inglis* 2014 GWD 1-17.
77 *Garrad v Inglis* 2014 GWD 1-17, at para. 9.

appeal in *B v B*,[78] the sheriff principal observed that 'undue concentration on the words *living together* is both wrong in law and inequitable. Strict application of the requirement that cohabitants live together ignores the realities of life.'[79]

SLOVAKIA

There is no legal definition of informal relationships between a couple.

SLOVENIA

Legislation in fields outside family law that ascribe legal consequences to an extramarital union, in the sense that extramarital partners often derive such consequences from the definition of an extramarital union determined in Art. 12 of the Slovenian Marriage Act, although an extramarital union and thus the conditions for the occurrence of the legal consequences of this union could also be defined otherwise than in Art. 12 of the Slovenian Marriage Act: under the Slovenian Penal Code, an extramarital union is considered to be a durable life union between a man and a woman who have not concluded a marriage.[80] It also occurs that legislation gives extramarital partners specific rights without checking the existence of the conditions for a legally recognised extramarital community under Art. 12 of the Slovenian Marriage Act: only partners that are in an extramarital union can request a fertilisation procedure with biomedical assistance – but the physician does not verify the existence of the extramarital union.[81]

SPAIN

The Spanish Civil Code system only has a limited number of provisions that refer to informal cohabitation without defining it. In special statutes that grant rights to partners in an informal relationship these may be defined for the specific purpose of the statute. The Spanish Law on

---

78 *B v B* 2014 GWD 30-593.

79 *B v B* 2014 GWD 30-593, at para. 36.

80 Para. 4 of Art. 99 of the Slovenian Penal Code, Uradni list RS (Official Journal) Nos 55/2008, 66/2008, 39/2009, 91/2011.

81 The Amending Act of the Act on the Treatment of Infertility and Procedures of Fertilisation with Biomedical Assistance, which guarantees a single woman the right to fertilisation with biomedical assistance, did not take effect because of a referendum decision of 17 June 2001.

leasehold requires partners, whether of the same or opposite sex, to have cohabited for a period of two years or to have a common child.[82]

Case law often uses the concept of cohabitation *more uxorio* which is defined as a cohabitation that has a certain stability, duration and public character and is marriage-like because the couple is united by feelings similar to those of spouses (*affectio maritalis*) and different from those of friendship. A decision by the Supreme Court dated 18 May 1992, which is often cited by lower instance courts, stated that *more uxorio* cohabitation requires 'cohabitation on a daily basis, stability and duration over some years as well as publicity, with partners performing joint acts vis-à-vis third parties'. Some decisions would seem to exclude same-sex couples from the concept, even though this would appear to be inconsistent with the constitutional principle of non-discrimination and the general evolution of Spanish family law and may be explained by the specific facts of the case.[83] As for duration it would seem that a two-year period is generally required.

In Catalan law a stable couple is a couple of same-sex or opposite-sex individuals who cohabit in a manner analogous to marriage. In order to qualify, couples need either (a) to have cohabited uninterruptedly for at least two years, or (b) to have a common child (Art. 234-1 Catalan Civil Code).

Social security law, which applies throughout the country, defines *de facto* couples for the purpose of survivor's pension. In order to qualify for survivor's pension, Art. 174 of the *Ley General de la Seguridad Social*,[84] requires cohabitation for at least five years prior to the worker's death. Cohabitation needs to be proved by city registration in the same dwelling. Additionally, the couple needs to have formalised their relationship either by notarial deed or by registration in one of the Registries of the Autonomous Community or Municipalities, where available, at least two years before the death. If partners are married to a third person or if there are other marriage impediments that would not allow the couple to enter into marriage, the couple does not qualify. A paragraph which referred to partnership provisions of Autonomous Communities was struck out by the Constitutional Court. STC 40/2014 of

82 Art, 12 Ley de arrendamientos urbanos (BOE núm 282 de 25 de Noviembre de 1994).

83 See STS of 21 October 1992, 27 May 1994, 27 March 2001 and 5 July 2001.

84 Real Decreto Legislativo 1/1994, de 20 de junio, por el que se aprueba el Texto Refundido de la Ley General de la Seguridad Social (BOE núm. 154 de 29 de Junio de 1994).

11 March 2014 found this provision to violate the principle of equality between Spaniards, since social security benefits could not vary depending on the applicable law.

SWEDEN

The most relevant statutory definition on informal relationships is found in the Swedish Cohabitation Act (2003:376) § 1 para. 2 defining the 'cohabitees' covered by the enactment as two people who live together as a couple on a habitual basis and who share a household. The neutral reference to 'two people' means that both opposite-sex and same-sex couples are covered. Paragraph 2 indicates that the given definition is not limited to the 2003 enactment, but includes other legislative provisions referring to cohabitees or persons living together under marriage-like circumstances. According to the provisions in para. 3-4 such relationships are only covered where neither of the parties is married or a registered partner.

Other legislation, such as the Swedish Social Insurance Code, refers to the definition above in the Swedish Cohabitation Act, but in addition to this sets out additional requirements for a cohabitee to qualify for the enactment's protection. To qualify for an adjustment pension from the deceased cohabitee, for example, the surviving cohabitee must have been previously married to the deceased, have or have had a child with the deceased or be pregnant with the deceased's child (Swedish Social Insurance Code, Chapter 80 § 4).

The requirement in the Cohabitation Act expecting the couple to live together on a habitual basis (in Swedish: *stadigvarande*) suggests that temporary relationships are not covered. No minimum period is given in the enactment itself, for the relationship to be counted as habitual, although six months has been given as a kind of 'benchmark' in the *travaux préparatoires* to the Act. Factors other than the duration of the cohabitation may also be of relevance, in the case of shorter relationships.[85] In the Court of Appeal judgment RH 2005:34, the court accepted the relationship as being subject to the Swedish Cohabitation Act even though the actual cohabitation had only lasted two and a half months.[86]

85 Government Bill, Prop. 1986/87:1, p. 253.
86 Court of Appeal judgment *RH 2005:34*.

The definition of cohabitants in the Swedish Cohabitation Act also includes that the couple needs to share the household. There is no absolute requirement that the two persons have to be registered as living at the same address, even if this is usually the case. In the Supreme Court judgment NJA 1994 s. 256, the Court regarded two people not registered as living at the same address as cohabitees, since they had shared the expenses of the household and had a joint dwelling where their common child had been cared for and had been raised by them both. Sharing a household requires cooperation between the partners in respect of costs and expenses of the household.

The criteria of having to live together as a couple means that the two people usually have a sexual intimacy with each other, even if it is not an absolute criterion. (No such requirement exists either in respect of formal relationships.) The aim of this criterion is to exclude people in other kinds of relationships from the scope of the Swedish Cohabitation Act, such as parents and grown-up children, siblings or friends living together.[87] Regarding the distinction between relationships that should be subject to the Swedish Cohabitation Act and relationships that fall outside it, the intention of the people in the relationship and their behaviour are to be taken into account. If the people in question are spending holidays together, attend celebrations together and otherwise act as a couple officially, that might be relevant for the classification of their relationship according to the Swedish Cohabitation Act.[88]

SWITZERLAND

There is no statutory definition of informal relationships in Switzerland. Rather, it is up to the courts to define informal relationships according to the respective legal question. The Swiss Federal Supreme Court still (mostly) uses the outdated and stigmatising term *Konkubinat* for informal relationships.

In 1992 the Swiss Federal Supreme Court developed a definition of informal relationships in family law with regard to the termination of spousal support (for the entitled person living in an informal relationship with another person). According to the Swiss Federal Supreme Court an informal relationship is a long-term, if not permanent, comprehensive and generally exclusive relationship between two persons of a different

[87] Government Bills, Prop. 1986/87:1 p. 252 and Prop. 2002/03:80 p. 26.

[88] Göran Lind, *Sambolagen, en kommentar*, Nordstedts Juridik, Stockholm, 2013, at § 1.

sex, which comprises an intellectual/emotional, a physical and a financial element and can also be described as a 'community of residence, table and bed'.[89] However, the Swiss Federal Supreme Court further held that not all of these three elements have the same importance. Rather, it is up to the judge to individually evaluate all (relevant) circumstances to determine the quality of an informal relationship.

This definition has, concerning certain parts thereof, been strongly criticised by legal doctrine.[90] First, it excludes same-sex relationships without any justified reason. Second, neither a sexual relationship nor the fact that a couple live together should be qualified as a mandatory requirement. Meanwhile, the Swiss Federal Supreme Court has held that the physical element ('community of bed') is not an indispensable element for an informal relationship.[91] All in all, the practical relevance of the definition is very limited.[92]

The definition has been adopted outside family law in cases regarding occupational pensions or with regard to the payment of an appropriate sum for pain and suffering in cases of homicide (Art. 47 Swiss Code of Obligations (*Genugtuung*)). However, in cases regarding occupational pensions, the Swiss Federal Supreme Court has held that also same-sex couples may qualify as an informal relationship and a residential community is not a mandatory element.[93]

---

89 Swiss Federal Supreme Court, BGE 118 II 235 E.3.b).

90 A. BÜCHLER, 'Vermögensrechtliche Probleme in der nichtehelichen Lebensgemeinschaft', in: A. RUMO-JUNGO and P. PICHONNAZ, *Familienvermögensrecht*, Stämpfli, Bern, 2003, at p. 59, 65 et seq. with further references.

91 Swiss Federal Supreme Court, BGer 5C.135/2002 (2.7.2002) E.2.5.

92 A. BÜCHLER, 'Vermögensrechtliche Probleme in der nichtehelichen Lebensgemeinschaft', in: A. RUMO-JUNGO and P. PICHONNAZ, *Familienvermögensrecht*, Stämpfli, Bern, 2003, at p. 66.

93 Swiss Federal Supreme Court, BGE 134 V 369 E.6.3.2 and E.7.1.

QUESTION 5

Where informal relationships between a couple have legal effect:

a. When does the relevant relationship begin?

b. When does the relevant relationship end?

AUSTRIA

a. When does the relevant relationship begin?

Due to the fact that there is no objective connecting factor such as entering into a marriage or registering the partnership, the precise date – since and until when an informal relationship lasts – is difficult, if not impossible, to determine.[1] However, for the application of the legal provisions referring to an informal relationship it is not crucial when the informal relationship has started, but whether it exists/has existed at a certain point in time. This in turn has to be examined as a preliminary step by assessing whether the three criteria explained above in the answer to Question 4 are met.[2]

b. When does the relevant relationship end?

Similarly to the beginning of an informal relationship also the termination can only be determined by assessing whether the requirements necessary to establish an informal relationship are still fulfilled or have already ceased to exist.

The provisions which currently refer to informal relationships neither link the beginning nor the termination of an informal relationship to specific legal consequences, but rather stipulate that the existence of the informal relationship entails certain legal effects. The existence of an informal relationship has to be assessed according to the established definition.[3]

---

1 Cf. P. RUMMEL, 'Ehe, Familie, Lebensgemeinschaft – Rechtsdogmatisches und Rechtspolitisches', *ÖJZ*, 1991, at p. 60.

2 Cf. P. RUMMEL, 'Ehe, Familie, Lebensgemeinschaft – Rechtsdogmatisches und Rechtspolitisches', *ÖJZ*, 1991, at p. 60.

3 See the answer to Question 4.

BELGIUM

a. When does the relevant relationship begin?

There is no uniform 'point of departure' for an informal relationship to have legal effect in the different legal provisions that regulate the consequences of such relationships. Some legal provisions use a formal 'connecting factor', such as registration in the population register (Art. 1.1.0.0.2, par. 5, 4°, c) Flemish Taxation Code). Other provisions furthermore require a certain continuous duration of the relationship, e.g. one year (Art. 1.1.0.0.2, par. 5, 4°, c) Flemish Taxation Code) or three years (Art. 343, § 1, b Belgian Civil Code). Various legal provisions finally use qualitative conditions for the informal relationship to be recognised, such as its affective and sexual nature (Art. 410 Belgian Criminal Code) or more generally cohabitation as if the couple were married (Art. 301, § 10 Belgian Civil Code). Interestingly, no legal provisions make the legal recognition of informal relationships dependent on a (*posthoc*) registration as informal partners. Some local authorities allow informal partners to register their notarial cohabitation agreement (Art. 1, 10° Royal Decree of 16 July 1992 on the population registers). Such registration, however, has no legal consequences in terms of the recognition of their informal relationship.

b. When does the relevant relationship end?

Just as there is no uniform 'point of departure', there is no uniform criterion regarding the end of an informal relationship. It will have to be determined whether, at the relevant time, the ad hoc conditions for the existence of an informal relationship are fulfilled or not. If not, the relationship will be considered to have ended.

BULGARIA

a. When does the relevant relationship begin?

None of the investigated pieces of legislation explicitly specifies a formal momentum or a fact establishing the start of the relationship. The beginning of the relationship could be proved by a common declaration by the partners, or by witness evidence. However, bearing in mind the definitions cited above, registration at a common address is the most obvious evidence of the commencement of the relationship, especially in cases of specific legal effects in the private interest (i.e. donorship, protection against domestic violence).

b. When does the relevant relationship end?

None of the investigated pieces of legislation explicitly specifies a formal momentum or a fact establishing the end of the relationship. It is presumed that the end of common living/separation of the partners terminates the relationship of the couple. It could be proved in the same way – a change in the registered address, a declaration to that effect or witness evidence.

CROATIA

The time of the commencement of a life union and the time of its termination are not laid down in the respective act. The time of the beginning and ending of a cohabitation or same-sex informal partnership is to be determined in proceedings which deal with a particular right or liability.

Cohabitation implies legal effects:
a. during the relationship: property rights and liabilities, personal rights and liabilities, adoption rights, medical reproduction rights, the right to protection against domestic violence, social rights and obligations, the right to be exempted from testifying in criminal proceedings etc.;
b. when the relationship ends: maintenance rights and liabilities, the right to protection against domestic violence, inheritance rights and liabilities, pension rights and liabilities etc.

A same-sex informal partnership implies legal effects:
a. during the relationship: property rights and liabilities, personal rights and liabilities, the right to protection against domestic violence, social rights and obligations, the right to be exempted from testifying in criminal proceedings etc.;
b. when the relationship ends: maintenance rights and liabilities, the right to protection against domestic violence, inheritance rights and liabilities, pension rights and liabilities etc.

It means that with the exception of adoption rights, a same-sex informal partnership and cohabitation entail the same legal effects.

CZECH REPUBLIC

a. When does the relevant relationship begin?

It is difficult to answer this question, because neither legislation nor case law deals with the beginning or the ending of an informal relationship.

A relevant relationship begins when two people start to live together. To fulfil the definition regarding the law of succession (S. 1475 et seq. Czech Civil Code), the partners to an informal relationship have to live together in the common household for at least one year before the death of one of the partners. If this condition is fulfilled, the living partner can inherit from his position in the second class of heirs or third class of heirs (S. 1636(1) and S. 1637(1) Czech Civil Code). For the purposes of the criminal law (see Czech Criminal Code, Act No. 40/2009 Coll.) where the term 'close person' is used, the condition of a long period of living together in a common household is not necessary, but it is only possible to use this term if the injury suffered by one of the partners is considered by the other partner as his own injury (S. 125 Czech Criminal Code).

b. When does the relevant relationship end?

It is difficult to answer this question, because neither legislation nor case law deals with the beginning or the ending of an informal relationship. Because an informal relationship is based on fact, it ends when the partners in an informal relationship stop living together.

DENMARK

a. When does the relevant relationship begin?

Danish Social Security Acts: A relationship similar to marriage is deemed to exist when the parties have a joint household and live together in a relationship that may lead to marriage. They need not be registered in the population register as residing at the same address. Special weight is given to the character of the parties' relationship and their housing circumstances. Even if they have different addresses and different homes, they can be deemed to be living in a relationship similar to marriage.

The Danish Inheritance Act, the Danish Inheritance Tax Act, and the Danish Insurance Contracts Act: At the time of the first partner's death the cohabitants must have been living together in a joint dwelling in a marriage-like relationship. Special weight is given to registration in the population register and the character of the parties' relationship.

b. When does the relevant relationship end?

Danish Social Security Acts: When the parties no longer live together and no longer share a household.

The Danish Inheritance Act, the Danish Inheritance Tax Act, the Danish Insurance Contracts Act: When the parties no longer live together.

ENGLAND AND WALES

a. When does the relevant relationship begin?

When the couple begin to cohabit in the same household. This is a question of fact which has to be determined in each case and proved on the balance of probabilities on the evidence adduced.

There are no explicit statutory provisions on this. However, if a couple do not agree the date, the court will have to take evidence and decide the date cohabitation began if this is relevant to the case, such as where a minimum period of cohabitation is specified to make a cohabitant eligible to make a claim.

b. When does the relevant relationship end?

When they separate and no longer live in the same household. This is a question of fact which has to be determined in each case and proved on the balance of probabilities on the evidence adduced.

There are no explicit statutory provisions on this. However, if a couple do not agree the date, the court will have to take evidence and decide the date cohabitation ended if this is relevant to the case, such as where a minimum period of cohabitation is specified to make a cohabitant eligible to make a claim.

ESTONIA

a. When does the relevant relationship begin?

In the case of an informal relationship there is no formal regulation on when such a relationship commences; in disputes regarding property rights the parties will often define when they consider their informaal relationship to have commenced.[4] One opportunity to evidence this in judicial proceedings is with the entry of the place of residence in the population register. The beginning of cohabitation is certainly of decisive importance when the provisions of a partnership contract are applied to mutual proprietary relations.

b. When does the relevant relationship end?

As regulations on the commencement of an informal relationship are lacking, in disputes relating to proprietary relations the parties themselves generally rely on when the cohabitation came to an end and if the provisions of a partnership contract are applied to the proprietary

[4] See the Decision of the Civil Chamber of the Supreme Court 3-2-1-109-14, at para. 12.

relations, the regulation of the end of the partnership as in the Estonian Law of Obligations Act shall be valid.[5]

FINLAND

a. When does the relevant relationship begin?

If the statutory provision does not require a minimum duration of the cohabitation, the legal consequences of cohabitation begin from the moment the couple may be deemed to live continuously in a common household.[6] The exact time of when cohabitation is deemed to be continuous is left for interpretation in the relevant context. As the relationship based on cohabitation is not registered before a religious community or a governmental body, one very significant element for the establishment of the commencement of the joint household is the date when one or both of the partners submitted a notification according to which the couple live at the same address (*muuttoilmoitus/flyttanmälan*). Submitting the notification of a change of address, which is then recorded in the population information system, is a statutory requirement according to the Finnish Act on Domicile (201/1994). The factual circumstances according to which the couple can be deemed to 'live continuously in a common household' may, however, have already begun before the date when the notification is made. The party seeking to rely on the fact that the cohabitation has begun earlier or later than is evidenced by the information contained in the population register has to provide evidence that supports his or her claim.

Information contained in the population register can also be used for the purpose of establishing the other statutory criteria that may be required for the cohabitation to have legal effect, such as the birth of a common child, the decision establishing common custody of the child or a former

---

5 See the Decision of the Civil Chamber of the Supreme Court 3-2-1-109-14, at para 20.

6 The Social Insurance Institution (*Kansaneläkelaitos/Folkpensionsanstalten*), which administers, e.g., the social insurance and social benefits schemes in Finland, has issued a number of guidelines related to the various schemes. According to the guidelines, the interpretation of a cohabitee relationship may vary according to the scheme in question. However, according to the national benefit schemes such as the housing benefit scheme and the widow(er)'s pension scheme, the cohabitation relationship is automatically presumed to exist without a waiting period if a man and a woman live together at the same address without being married and they are not closely related to each other. Evidence to the contrary is considered on a case by case basis. According to some other schemes, such as entitlement to the Finnish social insurance scheme or the study grant scheme, living together for at least six months is required in order to qualify as continuous cohabitation (www.kela.fi/kelan-etuusohjeet).

marriage, as all these circumstances are also recorded in the population information system (*väestötietojärjestelmä/befolkningsdata-systemet*).

b. When does the relevant relationship end?
The relationship based on cohabitation in a common household usually ends when the parties cease to live in a common household. In practice, this means that one of the partners moves away from the common address. Again, the establishment of this moment can be evidenced by the information contained in the population register. However, if the legal effects of cohabitation have been based on the fact that the couple have a common child or common custody of a child, the death of the child does not normally affect the legal status of the relationship.[7]

FRANCE

a. When does the relevant relationship begin?
No provision regulates when the relevant relationship begins.

This issue is considered to be purely factual, so that the commencement of the relationship can be established by any admissible means of evidence (witness testimony,[8] letters, official tax documents indicating a common address, *certificat de concubinage*[9] – which is a certificate issued by the town hall's administration, a lease contract, phone bills etc.).

---

7 Exceptions to this are, at least according to the letter of the statute, the benefits paid by the Finnish Act on Military Benefits (781/1993). Also the definition of cohabitation in the Finnish Aliens Act (301/2004) has been drafted in such a manner that if joint guardianship of a child ends, it may result in the conclusion of the legal effects of the cohabitation partnership unless the couple have by this time lived together for at least two years or there is some other weighty reason why the couple should be treated similarly to a married couple. The latter criterion may well be fulfilled by the former joint guardianship of a child.

8 CA Colmar, 8 February 2007, no. 2A04/01165.

9 A *certificat de concubinage* can be issued by the administration services of the town hall. The requirements which have to be fulfilled are not the same in all towns. The partners can be requested to testify that they have been living together in a stable way and to present proof of their joint address. Sometimes, the presence of two witnesses (of the age of majority and not relatives of the partners) is required. According to a ministerial answer, such certificates, however, do not have any legal effect (Rép. Min. no 40233, *JOAN* Q 2 September 1996). Such a certificate can be required when the partner requests certain social benefits or the right to remain in the dwelling. However, some institutions and administrations have stopped requiring any *certificat de concubinage* and are satisfied with a simple *declaration sur l'honneur* (an affidavit, a written sworn statement) by the partner(s).

b. When does the relevant relationship end?
No provision regulates when the relevant relationship ends.

This issue is considered to be purely factual, so that the termination of the relationship can be established by any admissible means of evidence. See under a).

GERMANY

a. When does the relevant relationship begin?
There is no statutory provision determining the exact point in time when an informal relationship begins. Since there is no precise definition of the informal relationship, it is also not possible to rely on only one element. Some indicators are proposed (see Question 4). Usually the partners live together. Therefore one indicator is the establishment of a common household[10] or the official registration of a common residence.[11] However, a common household is not necessary in every case. According to the dominant view, the determinative element is subjective, namely whether the parties have accepted a reciprocal responsibility for one another (see Question 4).[12] In practice one will look for a certain stability of the union.

b. When does the relevant relationship end?
There is no statutory provision specifying the point in time when the informal relationship is terminated. An indicator will often be the voluntary establishment of separate residences.[13]

GREECE

In principle there are no consequences in the law stemming from the decision of two persons, of the same or different gender, to cohabit. Such consequences are only generated during the period of cohabitation. There are substantive differences between a marriage and a free union, in respect, inter alia, of their establishment, functioning and termination, and the rights, obligations and commitments of the partners.[14] Free

---

10 M. WELLENHOFER, 'Anh. zu § 1302', in: *Münchener Kommentar zum Bürgerlichen Gesetzbuch*, Beck, Munich, 2013, at No. 3.
11 M. WELLENHOFER, 'Anh. zu § 1302', in: *Münchener Kommentar zum Bürgerlichen Gesetzbuch*, Beck, Munich, 2013, at No. 3.
12 M. WELLENHOFER, 'Anh. zu § 1302', in: *Münchener Kommentar zum Bürgerlichen Gesetzbuch*, Beck, Munich, 2013, at No. 3.
13 M. WELLENHOFER, 'Anh. zu § 1302', in: *Münchener Kommentar zum Bürgerlichen Gesetzbuch*, Beck, Munich, 2013, at No. 3.
14 See Supreme Court – Areios Pagos, judgment No. 1926/2013.

cohabitation, without offspring, is not recognised in Greek law, which does not recognise legal consequences of this specific form of relationship, which thus cannot be comprehended within the concept of the family, nor enjoy protection, since in effect those who choose such an arrangement are choosing not to subject themselves to legal provisions, and therefore commitments, and it would be contradictory if they were to enjoy protection without responsibility. On the other hand, the protection enjoyed by married heterosexuals and their offspring, pursuant to Art. 21 para. 1 of the Greek Constitution,[15] cannot impede or provide grounds for prohibiting the existence and functioning of this informal cohabitation of heterosexual or same-sex couples.

a. When does the relevant relationship begin?

And so the answer to the first question is that a couple entering into extra-marital cohabitation does not automatically entail the generating of legal effects.

b. When does the relevant relationship end?

In response to the second question, it might be said that the ending of the cohabitation, by a unilateral decision or mutual consent, or following the death of one partner, may have certain legal consequences, e.g. a claim to a share of the acquisitions, as is the case with the ending of a marriage, under Art. 1400 of the Greek Civil Code.[16] There might also be grounds for a claim of unjust enrichment.[17] The same applies in the case of the awarding of damages for emotional distress when a survivor's partner has died as the result of an accident.

The awarding of damages to such persons, pursuant to Art. 932 of the Greek Civil Code, as accepted by the Greek courts, is obviously conditional upon the existence, in the view of the judge assessing the facts of the case, of feelings of love and affection between the entitled person and the deceased, when the latter was alive. Should the court take the view that there were no such emotional ties, some or all of the

15 Article 21 para. 1 of the Greek Constitutions states: 'Family, being the cornerstone of the preservation and the advancement of the Nation, as well as marriage, motherhood and childhood, shall be under the protection of the State', translated into English by X. Papparigopoulos and S. Vassilouni, *The Constitution of Greece*, Athens, 2008, available at: www.parliament.gr.

16 Although our courts do not recognise such a claim; see Supreme Court – Areios Pagos, judgments 874/2008 and 206/2011.

17 But see, here too, the opposite view taken in the case law – Kozani Multi-Member Court of First Instance, judgment 163/2008.

persons may have their claim for damages dismissed.[18] It follows that the victim's family is not held to include those persons who lived with him in a state of free union with no intention of marrying. Thus, the law makes no provision for the awarding of damages for emotional distress caused to the survivor by the death of his or her partner. Nor, however, may damages be awarded by the application – *mutatis mutandis* – of the aforesaid provision of Art. 932(3) of the Greek Civil Code to compensate for adverse situations and consequences arising from the loss of the victim. A contrary view would not only be *contra legem*, but would subvert the constitutionally enshrined institution of marriage.

The same negative view is taken when the courts are asked to award maintenance in the event of the death of a partner, pursuant to Art. 928 of the Greek Civil Code.[19]

HUNGARY

a. When does the relevant relationship begin?

According to Art. 6:514(2) of the Hungarian Civil Code (Art 6:514(2) of Title XXIV, Third Part on special contracts, Sixth Book of Hungarian Civil Code) cohabitation comes into being upon the realisation of the conceptual elements determined in Art. 6:514(1) and by constituting a community of life and it terminates if the cohabitants enter into a marriage or a registered partnership with one another or their community of life ends. This has preserved the factual character of cohabitation and has not codified any change to the legal regime under the Civil Code of 1959. Earlier this factual character of cohabitation was not directly laid down but the Hungarian Civil Code refers to it with the aim of emphasizing that no formality is required either for establishing or terminating cohabitation. The 'factual model' has as a consequence that if either the existence of the cohabitation itself or the date when it began is contested it has to be proved by the party in question. In such case the elements of cohabitation must be proved.

Act No. XXIX 2009 on registered partnerships[20] contained provisions not only concerning a registered partnership but also concerning *de facto* cohabitation. It introduced a new register, namely the Register of Cohabitants' Statements which is kept by the Hungarian National

18 Supreme Court – Areios Pagos [Plenary Session], judgment 21/2000.
19 See Athens Court of Appeal, judgment 358/1997.
20 Act No. XXIX 2009 on Registered Partnership, Modification of Legal Rules in Connection with Registered Partnership and the Facilitation of Proof of Cohabitation.

Chamber of Notaries. The system operates according to an 'opt-in model' as there is no obligation for cohabitants to register their statement. As a consequence, the aim of the register is only to facilitate proof of cohabitation so the registration of the statement has no constitutive character but only a declaratory one. Cohabitation is constituted by living together under the circumstances prescribed in Art 6:514(1) and not by registering the statement of the cohabitants. Nevertheless, registration does create a presumption concerning the existence of cohabitation and the date of its commencement (if this date is incorporated in the statement). As the case law is strict when interpreting the existence of cohabitation, when there is a dispute between the partners the registration of the cohabitants' statement can be useful. However, as it only establishes a presumption the other partner may prove that cohabitation did not in fact exist or that the community of life only began at a later date.

It is useful to remark that originally one significant legal consequence, namely a paternal presumption, was connected to opting in as far as the register was concerned. If the mother had no marital bond in the period from conception until the child's birth, even for a short time, the man with whom the mother lived in cohabitation from the conception until the child's birth, even if this was for a short time, as evidenced by the Register of Cohabitants' Statements, had to be regarded as the child's father. Nevertheless, this presumption only existed concerning children born in 2010.[21]

The provisions in this register and the cohabitants' statements are contained in the Hungarian Act on Non-litigious Notarial Procedures.[22] Two capable persons who are over 18 years of age can make a statement before a notary that they are living in cohabitation under the terms of the Hungarian Civil Code[23] and this statement will be recorded in the register. The register of cohabitants' statements certifies that cohabitation exists between the couple whose common statement on cohabitation has been recorded in the register and that no statement on the non-existence thereof has been registered.[24] Although cohabitation does not create any personal status the register may certify only one cohabitation per

21 See in detail O. SZEIBERT, 'How Cohabitants and Registered Partners Can or Cannot Be a Child's Legal Parents in Hungary with a Special View to the 'Pater Est' Principle for Cohabitants', in: B. ATKIN (ed.), *The International Survey of Family Law 2011 Edition*, Jordan Publishing, Bristol, 2011, at p. 214-216.

22 Art. 36/E-36/G. of Act No. XLV 2008 on Non-litigious Notarial Procedures.

23 Art. 36/E(1) a) of Act No. XLV 2008.

24 Art. 36/E(2) of Act No. XLV 2008.

person.[25] If the register certifies someone's cohabitation, this person's statement on cohabitation with another man or woman cannot be registered until that person's earlier cohabitation is no longer certified.

b. When does the relevant relationship end?

According to Art. 6:514(2) of the Hungarian Civil Code (Art. 6:514(2) of Title XXIV, Third Part on special contracts, Sixth Book of Hungarian Civil Code) cohabitation comes into being upon the realisation of the conceptual elements laid down in Art. 6:514(1) and by constituting a community of life, and it will terminate if the cohabitants enter into a marriage or a registered partnership with one another or their community of life comes to an end. It is obvious that cohabitation ends by either partner's death and the Hungarian Civil Code further underlines that it will also come to an end with the termination of the community of life or entering into a marriage or establishing a registered partnership with one another. The Hungarian Civil Code emphasises the factual character of cohabitation and this prevails not only at the beginning of cohabitation but also when it terminates. As no formality is required when cohabitation terminates, if one partner contests the date up until when the cohabitation existed it is up to either partner to prove the date when the cohabitation ended. In such a case the lack of conceptual elements is decisive. Sometimes it is crucial that both the beginning and the end of cohabitation are determined.

The Act on registered partnerships mentioned under (a) introduced a new register, namely the Register of Cohabitants' Statements which is kept by the Hungarian National Chamber of Notaries. As there is no obligation for cohabitants to opt in, there is no obligation for them to register their statement on the non-existence of cohabitation. The register does not amount to irrebuttable proof. Cohabitation ends as is stated in Art 6:514(2) and not by recording a statement by cohabitants that their cohabitation no longer exists.

According to the Hungarian Act on Non-litigious Notarial Procedures[26] either the two persons whose statement of cohabitation was recorded or at least one of them can make a statement before a notary that their or his/her cohabitation which was recorded no longer exists.[27] If only one partner has made a statement on the non-existence of cohabitation the notary delivers a writ containing this statement to the other cohabitant *ex*

[25] Art. 36/E(3) of Act No. XLV 2008.

[26] Art. 36/E-36/G. of Act No. XLV 2008 on Non-litigious Notarial Procedure.

[27] Art. 36/E(1) b) of Act No. XLV 2008.

officio.[28] As the record creates a presumption concerning the existence of cohabitation and also the date of its ending the partners or partner may adduce evidence that the cohabitation did not terminate at the time when the statement on non-existence was made and that the community of life finished either earlier or later. The register does not certify the truth of the statement on cohabitation if the statement on the non-existence of cohabitation was registered later, if one cohabitant has died, or if either cohabitant has later entered into marriage or established registered partnership.[29]

As the case law is strict when interpreting the existence of cohabitation, including the dates of its beginning and ending, in the case of conflict between the partners the registration of the cohabitants' statement on the non-existence of cohabitation can amount to useful evidence. Nevertheless, the possibility of recording such statements on cohabitation is not extensively used. According to the experiences of notaries, at the time when 'opting in' resulted in the presumption of paternity it was much more frequently used by cohabitants.

REPUBLIC OF IRELAND

a. When does the relevant relationship begin?

To come within the definition of a 'cohabitant', there is no precise enumeration in the Act as to the required length of cohabitation. As seen above, however, the duration of the relationship is one of the circumstances that the court will take into account in determining whether two adults are cohabitants or not.

With regard to 'qualified cohabitants', S. 172 (5) of the Irish 2010 Act states the following:

> 'For the purposes of this Part, a qualified cohabitant means an adult who was in a relationship of cohabitation with another adult and who, immediately before the time that that relationship ended, whether through death or otherwise, was living with the other adult as a couple for a period –
> (a) of 2 years or more, in the case where they are the parents of one or more dependent children, and
> (b) of 5 years or more, in any other case.'

28 Art. 36/F(5) of Act No. XLV 2008.
29 Art. 36/E(2) of Act No. XLV 2008.

This suggests that the relationship in itself must have commenced either 2 years or more where children are involved, or 5 years or more if not. The relationship has legal importance in terms of gaining redress etc. beginning from such time as the relationship actually reaches those thresholds.

The categorisation of one as being a qualified cohabitant is significant in that it enables that person to apply to the court for redress in circumstances where he or she is financially dependent on the other cohabitant (S. 173). Where a court is satisfied that a qualified cohabitant is financially dependent on another cohabitant and that such financial dependency arises from the relationship, or termination of the relationship between the parties, the court may, if it is satisfied that it is 'just and equitable' to do so, make various ancillary Orders (S. 173(2)). Section 173(3) directs a court to take into account the following factors in considering whether or not it is just and equitable to make an Order in all the circumstances:

> '(a) The financial circumstances, needs and obligations of each qualified cohabitant existing as at the date of application or which are likely to arise in the future;
> (b) Subject to subsection (5), the rights and entitlements of any spouse or former spouse;
> (c) The rights and entitlements of any civil partner or former civil partner;
> (d) The rights and entitlements of any dependent child or of any child of a previous relationship of either cohabitant;
> (e) The duration of the parties' relationship, the basis on which the parties entered into the relationship and the degree of commitment of the parties to one another;
> (f) The contributions that each of the cohabitants made or is likely to make in the foreseeable future to the welfare of the cohabitants or either of them, including any contribution made by each of them to the income, earning capacity or property and financial resources of the other;
> (g) Any contribution made by either of them in looking after the home;
> (h) The effect on the earning capacity on each of the cohabitants on the responsibilities assumed by each of them during the period they lived together as a couple and the degree to which the future earning capacity of a cohabitant is impaired by reason of that qualified cohabitant having relinquished or forgone the opportunity of remunerative activity in order to look after the home;
> (i) Any physical or mental disability of the qualified cohabitant;
> (j) The conduct of each of the cohabitants, if the conduct is such that, in the opinion of the Court, it would be unjust to disregard it.'

Section 173(5) precludes the court from making any Order in favour of a qualified cohabitant that would affect any right of any person to whom the other cohabitant is or was married to. Ancillary Orders made under Part 15 in favour of qualified cohabitants can be varied in accordance with S. 173(6) of the Irish 2010 Act.

b. When does the relevant relationship end?

The statute does not explicitly define when a relationship of cohabitation ends, but it presumably is where the couple no longer live together in an intimate and committed relationship. Thus, for the purpose of having legal effect, it may be inferred that cohabitation ends when the disqualifying criteria such as marriage to another person are met, and in any case where the couple are no longer actually cohabiting. Regarding 'qualified cohabitants' the relationship must have ended after the lengthy cohabitation period specified in the above cited Irish 2010 Act (two or five years depending on whether or not the cohabitants have children together). There is a limitation period for seeking redress as a qualified cohabitant. Section 195 of the Act provides that an application for redress must be instituted within 2 years of when the relationship between the cohabitants ends, whether through death or otherwise, save in exceptional circumstances. Qualified cohabitants, therefore, cannot apply for redress once this limitation period has passed.

ITALY

As the relationship is a matter of fact, it is up to the judge, taking into account the specifics of the case, to identity the precise moment when it began or when it ended.

This principle is expressly laid down regarding adoption. Here, where the law requires, on the part of the would-be parents a 'continuity and stability of their living together' for a minimum duration of three years prior to the adoption is required[30] and the Tribunal for minors will in fact have to 'consider all the circumstances of the actual case' (*del caso concreto*) to check whether this prerequisite has been satisfied.

30 Art. 6 para. 4, law of 4 May 1983, n. 184, as modified by Art. 6 of the law of 28 March 2001, n. 149.

LATVIA

Latvian national laws and other legislative acts do not contain a legal order on informal relationships.

LITHUANIA

a. When does the relevant relationship begin?

No law defines the starting point of an informal relationship between a couple. On the other hand, Art. 3.299 of the Lithuanian Civil Code implies that legal consequences should occur as of the moment when a partnership is registered.

The case law suggests that an important detail is the moment from which the parties started living together and engaged in joint household management.[31]

b. When does the relevant relationship end?

No law defines the end point of an informal relationship between a couple. On the other hand, according to Art. 3.232 of the Lithuanian Civil Code, such a relationship could be considered as having been terminated when the couple starts living separately (the end of cohabitation) or upon the death of one of the partners.

LUXEMBOURG

a. When does the relevant relationship begin?

An informal relationship begins when there is a situation of stability and this is of a certain duration between a couple.

b. When does the relevant relationship end?

When there is no longer any duration or stability, the informal relationship ends; the separation of the couple or the death of one of the partners also ends the informal relationship.

THE NETHERLANDS

a. When does the relevant relationship begin?

This depends on the specific legal area involved. It is impossible to list all the definitions and the exact moment when such a relationship begins.

[31] Ruling of the Lithuanian Supreme Court of 9 January 2015, civil case no. 3K-3-62/2015.

Generally speaking, the relationship qualifies under a specific provision as soon as all the requirements are met.

b. When does the relevant relationship end?

This depends on the specific legal area involved. It is impossible to list all the definitions and the exact moment when such a relationship ends. Generally speaking, the relationship no longer qualifies under a specific provision as soon as one of the requirements is no longer met. However, there are some exceptions.[32]

NORWAY

a. When does the relevant relationship begin?

Pursuant to the Norwegian Inheritance Act, the cohabitation begins when the two parties are living together in a marriage-like relationship in accordance with the definition in S. 28(a), i.e. two people who are neither married, registered partners nor cohabitants with others. The partners can be considered cohabitants even if they live apart for some time due to education, work etc. However, only cohabitants who have common children[33] have the right to inherit and the right to undivided possession of assets, see S. 28(b) and 28(c).

b. When does the relevant relationship end?

Pursuant to the Inheritance Act 1972, for the cohabitation to end, there has to be a breach in the relationship, in other words, they are not a couple anymore. In exceptional cases, cohabitation may be deemed to have ended even if the parties have not ceased living together. Failure to move out may be due to the parties' fear of placing themselves in a disadvantageous position in terms of property distribution pursuant to the Norwegian Household Community Act. If a demand has been made to take over the joint dwelling before one of the parties dies, physical separation/moving apart should not be necessary.[34]

---

32 Such as Art. 5a para. 7 *Algemene Wet Rijksbelastingen* stating that if the partners are no longer registered at the same address, because one of them has had to be hospitalised or placed in a care home, they still qualify as partners with respect to taxation law, including inheritance tax.

33 More precisely 'have, have had or are expecting children together'.

34 J. ASLAND, 'Gjenlevende samboers rettsstilling', in: J. ASLAND et al. (eds.), *Nordisk samboerrett*, Gyldendal Juridisk, Oslo, 2014, at p. 185.

PORTUGAL

a. When does the relevant relationship begin?

The *de facto* union begins when its members start living as if they were a married couple. It is difficult for anyone to know the exact moment when this occurs besides the members themselves. This is why evidence is such an important issue, and Law No. 7/2001 clarifies some previously debated aspects. The main provisions are: any kind of evidence is permitted; the most common kind of evidence is a certificate from the local authority in the neighbourhood; false declarations to the local authority are punishable under the Portuguese Criminal Code.

b. When does the relevant relationship end?

Law No. 7/2001 (Art. 8, n. 1) determines that a *de facto* union ends by death (a) or by intention (b) or by marriage (c) of any of the members. Termination due to the first or the third reason is easily verifiable and produces its effects without any further specific formality. On the other hand, termination by intention ought to be judicially certified whenever any of the members wish to obtain some of the legal benefits.

RUSSIA

a. When does the relevant relationship begin?

The beginning of the relationship is never relevant.

b. When does the relevant relationship end?

The rules of inheritance law require cohabitation for at least one year. If cohabitation has lasted for at least one year and the surviving partner is unable to work and was maintained by the deceased partner, the surviving partner has a right of inheritance in the event of intestate succession (Art. 1148(2) Russian Civil Code).

The duration of the relationship is also relevant for a court decision on granting an informal partner the status of a member of the family of the other partner if the latter was the sole owner or the social tenant of the family home (see the answer to the Question 22).

SCOTLAND

a. When does the relevant relationship begin?

The statutory tests for cohabitation, discussed in Question 4 above, are based on assessment of the factual scenario of living together as husband and wife. It is a key feature of the Scottish provisions that there are no fixed time periods and no minimum requirements of a period of living together before the parties will be found to satisfy the test for cohabitation. If the question arises, it is a matter for the court to decide when the parties commenced living together as husband and wife: 'a question of objective fact to be determined having regard to the particular circumstances of the particular case.'[35]

b. When does the relevant relationship end?

As discussed in part (a), the question is one of fact for the court to decide. In terms of the Matrimonial Homes (Family Protection) (Scotland) Act 1981, the question which has arisen is whether the fact that the relationship has already ended prior to the court application is fatal to a finding that the applicant falls within the definition of cohabitant. A very literal interpretation of the words in S. 18, and the use therein of the present tense, was adopted in *Verity v Fenner*[36] where it was held that the test was not satisfied where the couple was not still 'living together as husband and wife' at the date of the proof. In *Armour v Anderson,*[37] a more purposive approach was applied which acknowledged the underlying protective aim of the legislation and the undesirability of requiring a party to remain living together with an abusive partner in order to qualify under the terms of the Act. The court gave its opinion to the effect that the test in S. 18(3) was not whether they were still in fact living together at the point of application but whether they were still cohabiting in the relevant home 'when the conduct which gave rise to the application occurred.'[38]

The date when cohabitation ends is a question of considerable importance in respect of claims under the 2006 Act as there is a strict time limit within which any such claims must be raised.[39] A significant proportion of cases which have been reported to date, are preliminary hearings dealing with the question of whether a claim has been submitted within the time limit of one year. The Court of Session on appeal in *Simpson v Downie* has confirmed that compliance with the statutory time limit is essential: 'it is only compliance with the time limit

[35] *Garrad v Inglis* 2014 GWD 1-17, at para. 8.
[36] *Verity v Fenner* 1993 SCLR 223.
[37] *Armour v Anderson* 1994 SLT 1127.
[38] *Armour v Anderson* 1994 SLT 1127, at 1132.
[39] Family Law (Scotland) Act 2006, S. 28(8).

which validates an application and clothes the court with the necessary jurisdiction.'[40]

Research into the views and experiences of legal practitioners concerning the provisions found that time limits were identified by 76% of the sample of 97 solicitors as being a problem.[41] Subsequent cases have tended to confirm this early view that the imposition of a short time limit does cause problems. Particularly in the context of a long relationship, it can be difficult to pinpoint the precise date at which cohabitation ceased. The sheriff principal, on appeal in *B v B*, cautioned against 'undue concentration' on physical living together in the same house. She observed, with reference to a couple who had cohabited over a period of 23 years, that:

> 'Physical separation is not conclusive of or determinative of the end of cohabitation ... The importance of the emotional and supportive qualities that characterise partnership or being husband and wife should not be underestimated.'[42]

SLOVAKIA

a. When does the relevant relationship begin?

Informal relationships can be described using the sociological aspect of the legal definitions in § 115 and § 116 of the Slovak Civil Code: An informal relationship commences when the persons in question start living in a common household permanently together and share their living costs and also if they start to build up a moral relationship. A moral relationship could be understood as a relationship between persons where one of the partners would reasonably feel the injury suffered by the other partner as his or her own injury.

b. When does the relevant relationship end?

When the aspects mentioned in (a) start to be absent.

---

[40] *Simpson v Downie* 2013 SLT 178, at para. 13.

[41] F. WASOFF, J. MILES and E. MORDAUNT, *Legal Practitioners' Perspectives on the Cohabitation Provisions of the Family Law (Scotland) Act 2006* (unpublished report), University of Cambridge, Nuffield Foundation, 2010, available at: crfr.ac.uk/assets/Cohabitation-final-report.pdf, at p. 55, Table 5.4.

[42] *B v B* 2014 GWD 30-593, at para. 36.

SLOVENIA

a. When does the relevant relationship begin?

The legal consequences of an extramarital union begin when the partners live together for an extended time, with retrospective effect (*ex tunc*), i.e., from the moment that the partners started living together.

b. When does the relevant relationship end?

An extramarital union ends when the partners cease to live together.

SPAIN

a. When does the relevant relationship begin?

Under the Spanish Civil Code system it is difficult to answer this question conclusively. There is however case law that suggests that a two-year period of permanent cohabitation is required and that relationships not meeting this requirement do not qualify. It is uncertain whether the couple qualifies retroactively once the requirement has been met.

Catalan law establishes that the couple has to cohabit for two years without interruption in order to qualify. Once this time limit has been met, the stable couple is deemed to have begun on the date when cohabitation started. If a child is born to or adopted by a cohabiting couple it also qualifies as a stable couple from the moment of birth or adoption (Art. 234-1 Catalan Civil Code).

b. When does the relevant relationship end?

Under the Spanish Civil Code there is no case law that would allow this question to be answered conclusively. In most cases that touch upon this issue the relationship ends either because of separation or because of the death of a partner. There is also no doubt that the relationship ends if one of the partners marries a third person, or changes its legal status if the partners marry each other.

According to Art. 234.4 Catalan Civil Code a stable couple ends: if the partners cease to cohabit and this puts an end to their personal relationship; if one of them dies or is declared to have died; if they marry (each other or a third person); if they so agree (the agreement needs to be formalised in a notarial deed); or at the unilateral will of one of the partners provided that it is notified to the other partner.

SWEDEN

a. When does the relevant relationship begin?

The Swedish Cohabitation Act (2003) does not explicitly establish the criteria for the 'beginning' of the relationship. However, the criterion 'living together on a permanent basis' (habitually) suggests that more temporary relationships are not covered. In the *travaux préparatoires* to the Act, to qualify for the 'habitually' test, usually at least a six-month long cohabitation is required. Even shorter periods may, nevertheless, qualify, depending on an overall assessment of the circumstances of the case.[43] In case law, for example in the Court of Appeal's judgment RH 2005:34, the relationship was considered to be covered by the 2003 enactment in spite of the fact that the couple had only lived together for two and a half months before they separated. When assessing whether the couple's living together could qualify as 'habitual', the court paid special regard to the fact that the couple had had a relationship with each other for a longer period before they moved in together and that they had made a joint will. It has been suggested in the legal literature that the 'subjective side' should be taken into account, that is, the parties' intentions towards their relationship.[44] This position finds support in case law, notably in the Court of Appeal's judgment RH 1993:91. In that case, a man and woman had been registered at two different addresses, in spite of having had a joint dwelling and household for a period of six years. The man had made a will in favour of the woman. In the court's opinion, it was evident that the couple had wished to be regarded as cohabitees. In his Commentary to the Swedish Cohabitation Act, Professor Göran Lind is of the opinion that if the couple, when moving in together, intended from that day on to be regarded as a cohabiting couple, then the relationship is to be counted as such from the date of their moving in together. The situation is different, if they merely start living together to test whether the relationship works. As time goes by, the relationship may well come to qualify as a habitual relationship, the duration of which is then to be calculated from the day they moved in together.[45]

---

[43] Government Bill, Prop. 1986/87:1 p. 253. See also M. JÄNTERÄ-JAREBORG, 'Rechtsregeln für nichteheliches Zusammenleben in Schweden' (in English), in: I. KROPPENBERG et al. (eds.), *Rechtsregeln für nichteheliches Zusammenleben*, Gieseking Verlag, Vienna, 2009, pp. 207-226, at p. 216-217 and G. LIND, 'Utvecklingen av samboförhållanden och samborätten i Norden', in: J. ASLAND et al., *Nordisk samboerrett*, Gyldendal, Oslo, 2014, at p. 55 (see Chapter 1.4.2, in the English version of the book, to be published by Intersentia in 2015).

[44] G. LIND, *Sambolagen, en kommentar*, Nordstedts Juridik, Stockholm, 2013, at § 1.

[45] G. LIND, *Sambolagen, en kommentar*, Nordstedts Juridik, Stockholm, 2013, at § 1.

b. When does the relevant relationship end?

The Swedish Cohabitation Act, § 2 para. 1, regulates when an informal relationship ends, if it is covered by the Act. The relationship ends, firstly, if the cohabitees or one of them marries. Secondly, it ends if the couple moves apart. This is often evident when the couple ceases to be registered as living in the same address.[46] Thirdly, it ends if one of the cohabitees dies. An additional provision, § 2 para. 2, gives a further ground to regard the relationship as terminated, namely when one of the cohabitees applies to court for the appointment of a property distributor or for the right to be entitled to reside alone in the joint dwelling or to take it over. This ground finds an explanation in the fact that the Swedish Cohabitation Act focuses on the regulation of the cohabiting couple's joint dwelling and joint household goods. (Assets which qualify as belonging to these categories are, according to the main rule of the enactment, to be divided jointly by the parties after the termination of the relationship; they are called 'cohabitation property'.)

The above-mentioned grounds all reflect objective criteria. In the case of fulfilment of any of these criteria, the cohabitation relationship should usually be viewed as having come to an end. However, in a case where the cohabitees for some reason have moved apart without intending to end their relationship, they may still qualify to be covered by the Act and be regarded as cohabitees. This might be the case if, for example, one of the cohabitees falls ill and needs to be hospitalised, or if one of them needs to spend time in another city because of work or education. The first example finds support in case law. In the Supreme Court judgment NJA 1994 p. 61, it was necessary for the man to move out of the couple's joint dwelling and spend his time in different health facilities, due to an accident which had disabled him. In the Court's opinion, the couple's motives for no longer living together had to be taken into account. An illness which requires one of the partners to move out of the joint dwelling should not result in the end of the cohabitation relationship against the intentions of the partners.

The cohabiting couple might also move apart temporarily, in a form of 'trial separation', without aiming to finally end their relationship. In those situations, their intentions concerning the separation and the circumstances are of relevance, and assessments may differ from case to case.[47] Another tricky situation is when the cohabiting couple wishes to end their relationship but have not yet moved apart, for example,

46 Statens Offentliga Utredningar, SOU 1999:104 p. 339.

47 G. LIND, *Sambolagen, en kommentar*, Nordstedts Juridik, Stockholm, 2013, at § 2.

because new accommodation has not yet been found for the cohabitee who is to move out of the joint dwelling. In the legal literature it has been suggested that, in a case like this, the cohabitation relationship should not to be considered to have ended until one of the objective criteria in the Swedish Cohabitation Act § 2 (above) has been fulfilled.[48] There is, however, no case law on the issue.

SWITZERLAND

a. When does the relevant relationship begin?

Depending on the subject and the case, importance is given to different factors. Regularly, major importance is attributed to cohabitation in terms of a common household.[49]

With regard to questions such as the termination of spousal support, social benefits or permission for residence in connection with aliens law, the duration is of great importance when determining whether or not legal effect is to be given to an informal relationship. The required duration may vary (mostly between two to five years) depending on the respective subject.[50]

However, with regard to damages where a surviving partner is deprived of his or her means of support as a result of homicide (Art. 45 para. 3 Swiss Code of Obligations (*Versorgerschaden*)), rather than the duration of the relationship, decisive is whether the deceased partner actually supported the surviving partner.[51] Similarly, representation in relation to medical procedures is only granted where the partner regularly and personally supports his or her partner.[52]

48 G. LIND, *Sambolagen, en kommentar*, Nordstedts Juridik, Stockholm, 2013, at § 2.

49 E.g. Art. 378 para. 1 No. 4 Swiss Civil Code.

50 After five years the Swiss Federal Supreme Court regularly assumes a qualified informal relationship which terminates spousal support, see e.g. BGE 109 II 188 E.2; BGE 118 II 235 E.3.a). Under the reformed divorce law the suspension of spousal support has in some cases already been granted after three years, see Swiss Federal Supreme Court, BGer 5C.296/2001 (12.3.2002); BGer 5A_81/2008 (11.6.2008). With regard to social benefits already two years were sufficient to give legal effect to the informal relationship. However, with regard to permission for residence (aliens law) an informal relationship of three years' duration did not suffice, see BGer 2C_97/2010 (4.11.2010).

51 The couple had only been cohabiting for 10 months, see Swiss Federal Supreme Court, BGE 114 II 144 E.2.

52 Art. 378 para. 1 No. 4 Swiss Civil Code.

In cases where the legal rules for simple partnership (Art. 530 et seq. Swiss Code of Obligations) are applied to the financial consequences upon the dissolution of the informal relationship, the parties' intention to enter into a legally binding relationship, their contributions and the common partnership goal pursued by the partners are decisive.

b. When does the relevant relationship end?

The relationship ends if one of the partners dies or the couple separate. The dissolution of the relationship is possible at any time, by mutual consent or unilaterally.

In cases where the legal rules for simple partnership are applied, the dissolution of the relationship does not, however, have to necessarily coincide with the dissolution of the simple partnership.[53]

53 Swiss Federal Supreme Court, BGer 4A_320/2010 (17.8.2010). See Arts. 545 and 546 Swiss Code of Obligations for the grounds for the dissolution of a simple partnership.

QUESTION 6

To what extent, if at all, has the national constitutional position been relevant to the legal position of informal relationships between a couple?

AUSTRIA

The Austrian Constitution does not contain a rule regulating the scope of protection of a marriage or an informal relationship.[1] Respective provisions are, however, contained in the European Convention on Human Rights (ECHR), which is directly applicable in Austria. In Article 12 ECHR the right to marriage is enshrined, whereby the concrete design of this right is left to the national laws. Informal relationships are protected by Article 8 ECHR, which contains the right to respect for family and private life.[2]

From a fundamental rights point of view, the Austrian legislator is not obliged to provide a legal framework for informal relationships.[3] The Austrian Supreme Court has held, for example, that the fact that the dependent's pension for partners in an informal relationship is not regulated by law is not unconstitutional.[4] If, however, rules are introduced, they have to comply with the principle of equality and must be objectively justified.[5] The Austrian Constitutional Court decided that the fact that same-sex couples can register their partnership, whereas for heterosexual couples the same possibility is not provided, does not violate the principle of equality, because those couples are entitled to

1 A. Deixler-Hübner, 'Die Regelung gleich- und verschiedengeschlechtlicher Lebenspartnerschaften', *iFamZ*, 2008, at p. 200.

2 A. Deixler-Hübner, 'Die Regelung gleich- und verschiedengeschlechtlicher Lebenspartnerschaften', *iFamZ*, 2008, at p. 201.

3 M. Hinteregger, 'Nichteheliche Lebensgemeinschaft und Grundrechte', in: Österreichischer Juristentag (ed.), *Zivilrecht – Neue Regelungen für nichteheliche Lebensgemeinschaften*, Manzsche Verlags- und Universitätsbuchhandlung, Vienna, 2013, pp. 58-76, at p. 66.

4 Austrian Supreme Court, Judgement of 25.11.2008, 10 ObS 123/08y.

5 M. Hinteregger, 'Nichteheliche Lebensgemeinschaft und Grundrechte', in: Österreichischer Juristentag (ed.), *Zivilrecht – Neue Regelungen für nichteheliche Lebensgemeinschaften*, Manzsche Verlags- und Universitätsbuchhandlung, Vienna, 2013, pp. 58-76, at p. 66.

enter into a marriage.[6] Further, according to established case law from the European Court of Human Rights and the Austrian Constitutional Court the legislator is not obliged to treat an informal relationship entirely equally with a marriage.[7]

Hence, the current situation in Austria that informal relationships are not subject to a comprehensive legal regime can be explained by the fact that from a constitutional point of view such a statute is not considered necessary.

BELGIUM

The Belgian Constitution does not explicitly protect formal relationships, particularly marriage, as legal institutions. In other words, there is no *Institutionsgarantie* that would exclude the (equal) statutory protection of informal relationships. Informal relationships are not protected in the Belgian Constitution. It does however warrant equality before the law and forbids discrimination (Art. 10 and 11 Belgian Constitution). It also encompasses the right to respect for private life and family life (Art. 22 Belgian Constitution). The courts have relied on the aforementioned provisions with regard to the (non-)protection of informal relationships. On the one hand, the Constitutional Court has exclusive power to assess legislative acts against the Constitution. It has inconsistently delineated the protection of informal relationships vis-à-vis marriage and legal cohabitation in numerous judgments.[8] On the other hand, all civil courts are competent to assess acts of the executive branch against the Constitution. This competence is less important for the development of the legal recognition of informal relationships.

BULGARIA

The Bulgarian Constitution (of 1991, last amended in 2007) is silent on the legal position of informal relationships. The family situation is not referred to among the grounds for the prohibition of discrimination (Art. 6, para. 2). The Bulgarian Constitution declares that the family is protected by the state and society, but the meaning of a family encompasses only the family established by a civil marriage.

---

6 Austrian Constitutional Court, Decision of 22.09.2011, B 1405/10, *iFamZ*, 2012/4.

7 ECtHR, *Johnston v. Ireland*, No. 9697/82, 18.12.1986; Austrian Constitutional Court, Decision of 22.09.2011, B 1405/10, *iFamZ*, 2012/4.

8 For an exhaustive and critical review: S. EGGERMONT, *De juridische bescherming van private relaties*, PhD, University of Antwerp, 2015.

CROATIA

Article 62 of the Constitution of the Republic of Croatia (Official Gazette no. 56/90, 135/97, 113/00, 28/01, 76/10, 5/14 (hereinafter: the Croatian Constitution)) places the family under the special protection of the state while, concerning family unions, it specifically refers to marriage and cohabitation and proclaims that they are regulated by law:

> 'The Family shall enjoy special protection of the State.
> Marriage is a life union of a woman and a man.[9]
> Marriage, common-law marriage and the family shall be regulated by law.'

According to the Croatian Family Act, cohabitation is a heterosexual union. It suggests that the Croatian Constitution specifically refers to informal heterosexual unions.

However, today the constitutional position is not particularly relevant for the legal position of informal relationships between a couple because both kinds of informal unions: a) heterosexual (cohabitation) as well as b) homosexual unions (same-sex informal partnerships) are regulated by the law in an almost equal way, regardless of the fact that the Croatian Constitution constrains itself to the legal regulation of heterosexual unions - cohabitations.

CZECH REPUBLIC

The Czech national Constitution and the Charter of Fundamental Rights and Freedoms are separate documents, but they are both considered to be a part of a constitutional system, or more precisely they both have a legal standing as a constitution and all other legal enactments have to be in conformity with them. The basic rule related to the matter of an informal relationship lies in Art. 2(4) of the Czech Constitution: 'Every citizen may do what is not prohibited by law and nobody may be forced to do what the law does not instruct them to do' and in Art. 2(3) of the Charter of Fundamental Rights and Freedoms: 'Everyone may do that which is not prohibited by law; and nobody may be compelled to do that which is not imposed upon her by law'. This is also one of the basic principles of private law (see S. 3(1) b Czech Civil Code: Private law primarily relies on the following principles: b) family, parenthood and

9 The definition of marriage as a life union between a woman and a man was incorporated by the Croatian Parliament pursuant to the referendum held on 1 December 2013. Judgement of the Constitutional Court of 14 January 2015, SuP-0-1/2014, Official Gazette 05/2014.

marriage enjoy special statutory protection). By these provisions, an individual's right to live in their own way is established, including the decision as to what kind of relationship (if any) a person wants to live in. Couples living in an informal relationship are given a great amount of freedom and they can be regarded as a family as well. On the other hand there are still some matters where they are considerably disadvantaged; for example, there is no specific property law concerning partners in an informal relationship, partners in an informal relationship do not have a duty to maintain and support each other, and they cannot adopt a child together.

It is also important to highlight the constitutional principle according to which children, whether born in or out of wedlock, enjoy equal rights (Art. 32(3) of Czech Charter of Fundamental Rights and Freedoms).

DENMARK

Article 75(2) of the Danish Constitution states that any person who is unable to support himself or herself or his or her dependants shall, where no other person is responsible for his or her of their maintenance, be entitled to receive public assistance, provided that he or she shall comply with the obligations imposed by statute in this respect.

In 2002 new rules were introduced for special (low) support payments to certain groups of foreigners (called 'Start help'). These were considered to be contrary to Art. 75(2) of the Danish Constitution.[10] If a person who received Start help lived together with a person who received a cash benefit (a higher level of social support), the two forms of social support would be combined as an amount corresponding to what they would obtain if they both received the lower Start help. This resulted in the Start help being reduced or lapsing entirely. Since a cohabitant does not have a duty to care for his or her partner it was regarded as unconstitutional to reduce the Start help, since a recipient of Start help must be ensured a sufficient basis for subsistence. The law was therefore amended so that the reduction of the combined support payments was not made by adjusting the Start help but by adjusting the cash benefit.

---

10 See I. LUND-ANDERSEN, *Familieøkonomien*, Jurist- og Økonomforbundets Forlag, Copenhagen, 2011, at p. 256-258.

ENGLAND AND WALES

Not at all.

ESTONIA

According to § 27(1) of the Estonian Constitution, the family is fundamental to the preservation and growth of the nation and constitutes the foundation of society and it therefore enjoys the protection of the government. As for personal protection, § 27 clause 1 of the Estonian Constitution ensures the right of all and everybody. This protection under § 27 clause 1 of the Estonian Constitution extends to citizens of Estonia as well as to citizens of foreign states and stateless persons who reside in Estonia (Estonian Constitution § 9).[11] Neither the Estonian Constitution nor any other Estonian laws provide a definition of the 'family'. The constitutional definition of family life definitely includes relations between officially married men and women. Taking into account the diversity of relations between people in contemporary society, it is not justified, according to the legal literature, to relate the constitutional definition of a family only with an official marriage.[12] This opinion voiced in the legal literature is also supported by the Supreme Court. On June 19, 2000, the Administrative Law Chamber of the Supreme Court found that subsection 1 of § 27 of the Estonian Constitution also protects an unregistered cohabitation between a man and a woman from unfounded intervention by the state as prescribed by law. The Supreme Court found that within the protection granted by § 27(3) of the Estonian Constitution parents have a right to raise their children. There must therefore be very sound reasons to restrict the right to live as a family and to raise children.[13]

§ 27(5) of the Estonian Constitution obligates the family to provide for those family members who are in need. In its decision of January 21, 2004,[14] the Supreme Court found that in deciding on social aid to be provided by the state and its scope, the provision of § 27 of the Estonian Constitution must be taken into account. In the same decision the Supreme Court also found that it thus follows from the Estonian Constitution that the right of a person in need to claim against the state

11 Decision of the Supreme Court 3-4-1-9-04, at para. 13.

12 Eesti Vabariigi Põhiseadus. Kommenteeritud väljaanne, 2012; available at: www.pohiseadus.ee/ptk-2/pg-27/ (in Estonian)

13 Decision of the Administrative Law Chamber of the Supreme Court 3-3-1-16-00, at para. 1.

14 Decision of the Supreme Court 3-4-1-7-03, at para. 18.

on the basis of clause 2 of § 28 of the Estonian Constitution shall completely or partially lapse if the needy person in question has family members who are able to care for him or her. The scope of the social aid provided by the state for 'needy persons', as stipulated in the first sentence of clause 2 of § 28 of the Estonian Constitution, should thus depend on the definition of a 'family', as referred to in clause 5, § 27 of the Estonian Constitution. In the same decision the Supreme Court found that maintenance relations between members of the family are regulated by several laws. Although the Supreme Court admitted that the Estonian Social Welfare Act[15] extends the definition of 'a family member' to persons who use one or more sources of income jointly, it did not take the opportunity to examine the effect of this law on maintenance obligations more closely.

Still, it is not correct and is legally unfounded to speak of the Estonian Constitution as being the basis for a claim relating to a maintenance obligation, as the Estonian Constitution also includes other provisions which regulate private law relations. Namely, § 25 of the Estonian Consitution provides the right to compensation for intangible as well as tangible harm that a person has suffered because of unlawful actions by any person and this has also been dealt with in the legal literature as a directly applicable claim.[16] But such a direct triple effect of fundamental rights is not correct and the Supreme Court already found in its decision of December 1, 1997, that civil law protective instruments are prescribed in civil law.[17]

In clauses 40-41 of its decision of May 5, 2014,[18] the Constitutional Review Chamber of the Supreme Court found that the second sentence of section 2 of § 22 of the Estonian Social Welfare Act provides a definition of a family for the purpose of granting subsistence benefits. But in the same decision the Supreme Court clearly stressed that no legal prerequisite can be derived from § 22(2) of the Estonian Social Welfare

15 Sotsiaalhoolekande seadus (adopted on 8 February 1995, entered into force on 1 April 1995). - RT I 1995, 21, 323; RT I, 29.06.2014, 71 (in Estonian), available in English at: www.riigiteataja.ee/en/eli/ee/Riigikogu/act/509072014019/consolide.

16 Eesti Vabariigi Põhiseadus, Kommneteeritud väljaanne, available at: www.pohiseadus.ee/ptk-2/pg-25/; See Decision of the Civil Chamber of the Supreme Court 3-2-1-37-06, para. 10; Critically see K. SEIN, P. VARUL, I. KULL, V. KÕVE, M. KÄERDI, and I. VÕLAÕIGUSSEADUS, *Kommenteeritud väljaanne* (Law of Obligations I. Commented Edition), Juura, Tallinn, 2006, at p. 455 (in Estonian).

17 Decision of the Civil Chamber of the Supreme Court 3-2-1-99-97.

18 Decision of the Supreme Court 3-4-1-67-13.

Act to the effect that people who live together must provide maintenance to each other.

FINLAND

There are at least two instances where Parliament's Constitutional Law Committee has addressed the status of cohabiting couples. The first involved the definition of cohabiting couples in the context of the legislative process of the Finnish Nationality Act in 2002 (359/2003)[19] and the second involved the definition of cohabiting couples in the context of processing the government proposal on the Finnish General Housing Benefits Act (938/2014) in 2014.[20]

In the first instance, the government proposal on the Finnish Nationality Act proposed that 'a spouse shall refer to a marital spouse, to a person living in circumstances akin to marriage, to spouses who have registered their relationship and to persons who live in a partnership similar to a partnership referred to in the Finnish Act on Registered Partnerships (950/2001) without registering their partnership.' Accordingly, the proposal would have equated marital and registered spouses with cohabitation partners irrespective of their sex.

However, the Constitutional Law Committee considered this to be problematic and deleted the reference to cohabitation partners of the same sex. It justified this by referring to a decision made by Parliament one year previously on the Finnish Act on Registered Partnerships. In the context of accepting the said Act, Parliament issued a statement according to which the Act is not applicable to same-sex cohabiting couples who do not register their relationship and that those provisions that exist in the legislation on relationships akin to marriage cannot be applied to same-sex cohabiting couples on the basis of the Finnish Act on Registered Partnerships. According to the Constitutional Law Committee, the definition of a spouse proposed by the government would have violated the rationale behind the Parliamentary statement which was issued in 2001.

In the context of examining the government proposal on the general housing benefits Act in 2014, the Committee again considered the

---

19 Report of the Constitutional Law Committee No. 8/2002, related to government proposal No. 235/2002.

20 Statement of the Constitutional Law Committee No. 17/2014, related to government proposal No. 52/2014.

definition of cohabitees. This time the proposal by the government was to limit the definition of a cohabitee to 'a man and a woman, who live in a cohabitation relationship, i.e. in a continuous common household in circumstances akin to marriage.' According to the detailed rationale of the proposal, if two persons of a different sex live together at the same address, it is presumed that they live in a cohabitation relationship regardless of whether they have entered into the rental contract amongst themselves or separately, unless the age of the persons involved, the size of the apartment or other similar matters point to the conclusion that it is not a cohabitation relationship.[21]

The Constitutional Law Committee found the rationale to be problematic, as, on the one hand, the criteria attached to the definition were too rigid leaving no room for the opinions of the benefit seekers themselves, but on the other hand, the criteria gave too much room for interpretation to the officials deciding on benefits in independent cases. The Committee did not comment on the fact that the definition only concerned cohabitees of a different sex. However, the Committee took the view that it was important that the government conducts a comprehensive study on the problems related to the definitions of cohabitation across various legislative instruments and the possibilities for solving them in a manner that better accounts for the fundamental rights involved.

FRANCE

The French Constitution does not contain any specific requirement with regard to spouses or partners in an informal relationship. Only the principle of equality (Art. 6 of the Declaration of Human and Civil Rights 1789, to which the French Constitution refers) can be mentioned with regard to possible discrimination between married and unmarried couples and/or between same-sex and opposite-sex partners. However, the French Constitutional Council held in 2011[22] that the principle of equality does not require that same-sex partners should be treated in the same way as opposite-sex partners. In particular, the right to normal family life does not imply the right to marriage for same-sex couples. The Constitutional Council accepted that the legislator could decide that the difference in the situation of same-sex and opposite-sex couples justified a different treatment with regard to family law rules.

---

21 Government proposal No. 52/2014, at p. 18.

22 CC, 28 January 2011, no. 2011-92. See also CC, 29 July 2011, no. 2011-155 QPC.

GERMANY

The most important constitutional provisions in this context are Article 6 para. 1 of the German Constitution (Grundgesetz; GG or Basic Law), granting special protection to marriage, and also, albeit to a lesser extent, Article 2 para. 1 of the German Basic Law, guaranteeing the right of self-determination.[23] Article 6 para. 1 German Basic Law is a 'guarantee of an institution' (*Institutsgarantie*) and states that marriage and family are to enjoy the special protection of the State. 'Family' includes the relationship between parents and their children, whether legitimate or illegitimate. This is understood not only as a constitutional guarantee of an institution and the expression of a basic value in the areas of public and private law, but also as a mandate to take action to benefit marriage and the family.[24] 'Marriage' is a freely entered, lasting legal relationship between a man and a woman.[25] Official participation in the marriage ceremony is an essential part of this conception of marriage. Cohabitation without a marriage ceremony is not a marriage in the constitutional sense.[26] However, according to the Federal Constitutional Court, Article 6 para. 1 does not prevent the legislature from granting certain benefits to cohabiting couples.[27]

According to the Federal Constitutional Court, non-marital cohabitation enjoys protection only under the general freedom of action clause (*allgemeine Handlungsfreiheit*) of Article 2 para. 1 German Basic Law.[28] Like any other human action that is not protected by a special constitutional right, cohabitation is protected by this provision, which

---

23 See for the guarantee of marriage and the family (Art. 6 Basic Law) N. WITZLEB, 'The German 'Registered Life Partnership' - A Marriage That Dares Not Speak Its Name?' *Austr. J. Fam. L.*, 2002, at p. 239 et seq.; K. VOGELSANG, 'Verfassungsrecht', in: R. HAUSMANN and G. HOHLOCH (eds.), *Das Recht der nichtehelichen Lebensgemeinschaft*, E. Schmidt, Berlin, 2004, at p. 193, 202 et seq. No. 13 et seq.

24 See in more detail A. SANDERS, 'Marriage, Same-Sex Partnership, and the German Constitution', *German Law Journal*, 2012, at p. 911 and 913 et seq.

25 BVerfG, 17.7.2002, *BVerfGE*, 105, 313, 345.

26 BVerfG, 16.12.1958, *BVerfGE*, 9, 20, 34–35; BVerfG, 7.10.1970, *BVerfGE*, 29, 166, 166; BVerfG, 11.11. 2004, *BVerfGE*, 112, 50, 65; K. VOGELSANG, 'Verfassungsrecht', in: R. HAUSMANN and G. HOHLOCH (eds.), *Das Recht der nichtehelichen Lebensgemeinschaft*, E. Schmidt, Berlin, 2004, at p. 193, 202 et seq. No. 13 et seq.

27 BVerfG, 3.4.1990, *BVerfGE*, 82, 6, 15.

28 BVerfG, 3. 4.1990, *BVerfGE*, 82, 6 (relating to the legislative protection of tenants' rights). Cf. also R. FRANK, 'The status of cohabitation in the legal systems of West Germany and other West European countries', *The American Journal of Comparative Law*, 1985, at p. 186; K. VOGELSANG, 'Verfassungsrecht', in: R. HAUSMANN and G. HOHLOCH (eds.), *Das Recht der nichtehelichen Lebensgemeinschaft*, E. Schmidt, Berlin, 2004, at p. 193, 210-211 No. 26 et seq.

guarantees that freedom can be restricted only by means of a proportionate law.

In the past, the debate in constitutional law very often dealt with the question whether the special protection granted to marriage in the Constitution meant that no other union should be even remotely granted protection and benefits like those afforded to marriage. It was argued that there should be a considerable distinction between marriage and other unions and that a 'distance rule' (*Abstandsgebot*)[29] was appropriate.[30] Accordingly, it was deemed not possible to give cohabitants the same legal rights as married couples.

However, a certain liberalisation was achieved in the context of civil partnerships. These partnerships are not marriages but legal relationships that do not compete with marriage. The Federal Constitutional Court rejected the claim that the wording of Article 6 para. 1 demanded that there remain a significant distinction between marriage and other relationships. It was held by the Court that while marriage should not be discriminated against, the Constitution did not require that other relationships be treated less favourably than marriage.[31] However, another constitutional argument which has been raised is that the Constitution also grants the freedom to decide whether or not to enter into a marriage and that this freedom would be infringed by codifying the consequences of cohabitation in the same way as in matrimonial law.[32]

In some Constitutions of the States (the *Länder*) there are provisions which are more favourable in granting cohabiting couples legal protection. For example, Article 26 of the Constitution of the State of Brandenburg additionally recognises the protection of other permanent

---

29 In literature, the terms 'duty to privilege marriage' (*Privilegierungsgebot*) and 'prohibition against opening marriage to other unions' (*Öffnungsverbot*) have been used, see W. PAULY, 'Sperrwirkungen des verfassungsrechtlichen Ehebegriffs', *NJW*, 1997, at p. 1956.

30 For a discussion of the 'distance rule' (*Abstandsgebot*), see BVerfG, 17.7.2002, *BVerfGE*, 105, 313, 348; see also id. at 357-359 (Papier, dissenting); id. at 359-365 (Haas, dissenting).

31 BVerfG, 17.7.2002, *BVerfGE*, 105, 313, 347 f. Cf. K. VOGELSANG, 'Verfassungsrecht', in: R. HAUSMANN and G. HOHLOCH (eds.), *Das Recht der nichtehelichen Lebensgemeinschaft*, E. Schmidt, Berlin, 2004, at p. 193, 213 et seq. No. 32 et seq.

32 M. LÖHNIG, 'Anh. zu §§ 1297 et seq.', in: J. VON STAUDINGER, *Kommentar zum Bürgerlichen Gesetzbuch*, Sellier-de-Gruyter, Berlin, 2012, at No. 20.

communities of life. Such provisions have, however, no influence on federal law.[33]

A certain degree of influence is to be found in Art. 6 para. 5 German Basic Law. Pursuant to this provision, legislation must provide children born outside marriage with the same opportunities for physical and mental development and for their position in society as are enjoyed by children born within marriage. Therefore discrimination against illegitimate children is prohibited under constitutional law and the parents' marital status is of only minor influence.

GREECE

The response is framed by the Supreme Court, which has ruled[34] that an informal, lasting relationship between two partners (usually of the opposite sex) is one of the '*de facto* family relationships', which is to say that it should be numbered among those atypical or, from a legal perspective, irregular situations which lie on the margins of legal life. Moreover, it follows from the complex of provisions of Art. 1444(2), 1456, 1457, 1471, 1479, 1350 et seq. and 1386 et seq. of the Greek Civil Code, in conjunction with Art. 21(1) of the Greek Constitution, which protects marriage, the family and children, that this is a conscious choice by the legislator, which – although aware of free unions from as far back as 1983[35] – had no desire to regulate the issues and legal questions arising therefrom. The institution of marriage is regulated and protected by the aforesaid Constitutional provision, and by the Greek legal system in general, whereas there is no corresponding recognition or matching protection for extra-marital cohabitation, nor is there any obligation of regulatory intervention on the part of the legislator. In fact, the lasting cohabitation of two partners, even if it were to be officially registered, cannot be compared with the institution of marriage. The two institutions differ in both name and substance, because they were created to meet different kinds of social needs.

Thus the so-called free union is one of the '*de facto* family relationships', which is to say that it belongs to those atypical or, from a legal

[33] In more detail H. GRZIWOTZ, *Nichteheliche Lebensgemeinschaft*, Beck, Munich, 2014, at § 4 No. 7 et seq.

[34] Supreme Court – Areios Pagos, judgment 775/2011.

[35] Before Law 1329/1983, which, as part of the more general reforms of family law, in the spirit of the principle of gender equality, under Art. 4(2) of the Greek Constitution, introduced certain amendments, among them an oblique recognition of a free union, through Art. 1444 of the Greek Civil Code.

perspective, irregular situations lying on the margins of legal life. Furthermore, it follows from the complex of provisions of Art. 1444(2), 1456, 1457, 1471, 1479, 1350 et seq. and 1386 et seq. of the Greek Civil Code, in conjunction with Art. 21(1) of the Greek Constitution, that this was a conscious decision by the legislator, which did not wish to regulate issues and legal questions arising from this informal cohabitation. The institution of marriage is regulated and protected by the aforesaid provisions of the Greek Constitution, and by the Greek legal system in general, whereas there is no corresponding recognition or matching protection for extra-marital cohabitation.

The latter, even if it were to be an officially registered relationship, could not be assimilated with the institution of marriage. The two institutions, i.e. that of the 'officially registered partnership' concerning cohabitation between heterosexuals or homosexuals, and that of marriage, do not only differ in name but also in substance, given that they were created to meet different social needs. Free cohabitation without offspring is not recognised in Greek law, which recognises no legal consequences of such an arrangement; it therefore cannot be comprehended within the concept of the family, nor can it be protected, because in effect those who choose such an arrangement do not wish to be subject to legal regulation, and therefore a commitment, and so it would be contradictory if they were to enjoy protection without responsibility.[36]

Furthermore, the European Court of Human Rights (ECtHR) dismissed an appeal in the case of *Korosidou v Greece* regarding the refusal to grant a widow's pension to Ms Korosidou, who had been the partner, for 39 consecutive years, of a deceased pensioner receiving a pension from the Greek Social Insurance Foundation, with whom she had had a large number of children.[37] Relying in particular on Art. 8 (the right to respect for private and family life) and 14 (the prohibition of discrimination) and Art. 1 of Protocol No. 1 (the protection of property), the applicant complained about a refusal to award her a survivor's pension as a widow on the ground that she had not been married to her deceased partner. It should be noted that the ECtHR ruled only that the Greek courts had been tardy in issuing a decision under Art. 6 § 1 (the right to a fair hearing within a reasonable time) and Art. 13 (the right to an effective remedy) and had not ventured into the substance of the case, i.e. that the applicant would not be allowed to continue collecting the pension of her deceased partner.

36 Supreme Court – Areios Pagos, judgment No. 775/2011.
37 ECtHR, *Korosidou v. Greece*, No. 9957/08, 10.2.11.

HUNGARY

The national constitutional position has always been relevant to the legal position of cohabitants, primarily in more recent years. A decision by the Constitutional Court[38] influenced the provision on cohabitation for the first time in 1996. In 1995 a petitioner requested the Constitutional Court to declare unconstitutional a provision in the Civil Code of 1959 which recognised only cohabitation between different-sex persons. [39] The Constitutional Court examined the legal rules which contained rights and obligations for cohabitants at that time and came to the conclusion that the law considered a cohabitant to be in the same position as a dependant and in these cases a differentiation between partners according to their gender violated the constitutional prohibition of discrimination, with some exceptions concerning either the common children or a marriage with a third person where it remains important to distinguish between the forms of cohabitation according to the gender of the partners. The Constitutional Court stayed the proceedings and the legislator extended the definition of cohabitation, contained in the Civil Code of 1959, to same-sex cohabitants. This stance has been retained in the Hungarian Civil Code, so both different-sex and same-sex partners may cohabit.

Two decisions by the Constitutional Court[40] have dealt with a registered partnership. Although these judgments compared and analysed marriage and a registered partnership as well as the rights and obligations emerging from marriage and a registered partnership, cohabitation was also mentioned when referring to the strong constitutional protection of marriage and the family based upon marriage. The decisions certainly confirmed the legal privilege given to marriage as compared to cohabitation.

A new piece of legislation, namely the Hungarian Act on the Protection of Families was approved by Parliament in 2011 and it stated that the family is a system of relations establishing an emotional and economic community between natural persons, the basis of which is a marriage between one man and one woman or lineal affinity or guardianship in a family. [41] This strict concept of a family was deemed to be

---

38 Decision of the Constitutional Court No. 14/1995 (III. 13).

39 This decision is dealt with in detail in: O. SZEIBERT-ERDŐS, 'Unmarried Partnerships in Hungary', in: K. BOELE-WOELKI (ed.), *Common Core and Better Law in European Family Law*, Intersentia, Antwerp, 2005, at p. 316-319.

40 Decision of Constitutional Court No. 154/2008 (XII. 17); decision of Constitutional Court No. 32/2010 (III. 25).

41 Art. 7(1) of Act No. CCXI of 2011 on the Protection of Families.

unconstitutional and it was repealed[42] in December 2012. At that time the Civil Code of 1959 was still in effect but the new Hungarian Basic Law[43] had already entered into force at that time. The procedure at the Constitutional Court had been initiated by the Hungarian Ombudsman and the Court had to apply the Hungarian Basic Law. The Hungarian Basic Law originally determined that 'Hungary shall protect the institution of marriage, the conjugal union of a man and a woman based on voluntary and mutual consent. Hungary shall also protect the institution of the family which is recognised as the basis for the survival of the nation.'[44] This Article was also evaluated by the Constitutional Court which concluded that when determining rights and obligations for families the existing level of the protection of partnerships, such as cohabitation, cannot be terminated or minimised, specifically with regard to the protection of the child's best interests. It is prohibited to discriminate against children either directly or indirectly upon the basis of whether their parents who are caring for them are spouses or cohabitants. As a result, Art. 7 of the Hungarian Act on the Protection of Families was deemed to be restrictive in comparison with Art. L of the Hungarian Basic Law.

In March 2013 the Hungarian Basic Law was amended[45] which resulted in a new provision, Art L. According to this modified text Hungary protects not only marriage but also the family and it is determined that 'The basis of the family is marriage and the parent-child relationship.' The solution in the Hungarian Civil Code which has provided provisions on cohabitation both as a contract and as a contract with family law consequences is in tandem with the attitude of the Basic Law (also see the answer to Question 8).

A brand new decision[46] has dealt with the difference between families based upon marriage and those based upon the parents' cohabitation. Although this decision cannot affect the legal position of cohabitants it may influence the judiciary, especially when cohabiting couples taking

---

42 Decision of the Constitutional Court No. 43/2012 (XII. 20)

43 The Hungarian Basic Law was approved in April 2011 and entered into force in January 2012.

44 Art. L of the Basic Law before its amendment. See also O. SZEIBERT, 'Parental Responsibilities and the Child's Best Interest in the New Hungarian Civil Code', in: B. ATKIN (ed.), *The International Survey of Family Law 2013 Edition*, Jordan Publishing, Bristol, 2013, at p. 143-146. The translation is the official one (CompLex Legal Database).

45 Fourth amendment of the Hungarian Basic Law; the new provisions became effective in April 2013.

46 Decision of the Constitutional Court No. 14/2014. (V. 13.).

care of children are to be dealt with. The Act of 1998 on supporting families did not provide the same amount of family allowances for families where the parents were spouses and cared for their children, but not only common children, and for families where the parents were cohabitants and cared for their own but not exclusively common children. In the earlier case the mentioned Act considered all the children together and provided a higher amount of family allowance while in the latter case the cohabitants were regarded not as two single parents but as creating a quasi-family without adding all the children together. The Constitutional Court confirmed that the obligation to protect marriage and the family originating from the Hungarian Basic Law cannot result in direct or indirect discrimination between children based upon whether their parents are spouses or live together in another kind of community of life and it stated that the alleged discrimination in the field of family allowances breaches the Hungarian Basic Law.

REPUBLIC OF IRELAND

It has been very significant and relevant. A precise definition of the family is not provided by the Irish Constitution and this has led to the courts formulating its own definition. They have interpreted the Constitution as only recognising the family unit as based upon marriage. Kelly J in *Ennis v Butterly* [1997] I.L.R.M. 28 held that 'non-marital cohabitation ... cannot have the same constitutional status as marriage' and 'that it would be contrary to public policy, as enunciated in the Constitution, to confer legal rights on persons in non-marital unions akin to those who are married'. While these judicial statements certainly reflect the aforementioned constitutional position, they appear to have left some flexibility for legal recognition of cohabitation, providing it was not equivalent to that afforded to traditional marriage. The leading judgment on this point was delivered by Walsh J in *The State (Nicolaou) v An Bord Uchtála* [1966] I.R. 567. In this case, Walsh J held that: 'While it is true that unmarried persons cohabiting together and the children of their union may be referred to as a family and have many, if not all, of the outward appearances of a family ... nevertheless so far as Article 41 is concerned the guarantees therein contained are confined to families based on marriage.'

Walsh J acknowledged the existence of other types of family units and their lack of Constitutional protection. As non-marital and less traditional family units become increasingly common in Ireland, the deficiencies of the Irish Constitution (or, perhaps more properly, the mode of interpretation favoured by the courts) in this regard have become more marked. This has necessitated the use of legislation to provide some protection and legal recognition for cohabiting couples.

The view taken by the courts in relation to cohabiting couples is a strict one and its origin is found, not only in the case law but more particularly in the Irish Constitution. Under Art. 41 the State recognises the family as the natural primary and fundamental unit group of society and further pledges to guard with special care the institution of marriage on which the family is founded and to protect it against attack. In *State (Nicolaou) v An Bord Uchtála* [1966] I.R. 567 Henchy J. in the High Court held that:

> 'for the State to award equal constitutional protection to the family founded on marriage and the 'family' founded on an extra-marital union would in effect be a disregard of the pledge which the State gives in Article 41.3.1 to guard with special care the institution of marriage.'

Further, on appeal, Walsh J. in the Supreme Court said that it was:

> 'quite clear ... that the family referred to in Article 41 is the family which is founded on the institution of marriage and, in the context of the Article, marriage means valid marriage under the law for the time being in force in the State.'

In the case of *W.O'R. v E.H. & An Bord Uchtála* [1996] 2 I.R. 248 this view was reiterated by Hamilton C.J. when he said that:

> 'a de facto family, or any rights arising therefrom is not recognised by the Constitution or by any of the enactments of the Oireachtas dealing with the custody of children.'

This position was more recently upheld by the Supreme Court in *McD v L* [2009] IESC 81 where it was emphatically stated that 'there is no institution in Ireland of a *de facto* family'.

As Irish society changes the social view in relation to cohabitation has also changed. It was not, however, until 2010 that the law in Ireland changed in respect of cohabiting couples and those in same-sex relationships. Arguably, the amendments do not go far enough in satisfying the degree of change advocated for by those who lobby for the rights of same-sex couples and cohabiting couples. Others see the Irish 2010 Act as a stepping stone to greater recognition and status in the future.

There is likely to be significant developments in this area with the Irish Government promising a referendum on same-sex marriage during 2015.

ITALY

As the Italian Constitution states in Art. 29 that 'The Republic recognises the rights of the family as a natural group founded on marriage', the legal recognition of cohabitation has been grounded in another article of the Italian Constitution, Art. 2: 'The Republic recognises and guarantees the inviolable rights of the person, as an individual and in the social groups where human personality is expressed.'

Cohabitation has indeed been held to be one of the groups where personality is expressed. This interpretation has been introduced by the Constitutional Court through many decisions, the oldest of which dates from 1977.[47]

More recently, the Constitutional Court has also included same-sex couples among the social groups deserving legal protection according to Art. 2 of the Italian Constitution.[48] This protection, however, has not resulted in dispensing with the discrepancy between the legitimate family and cohabitants in terms of their legal treatment, but simply in applying the general rules on contract and obligations to informal relations.[49]

LATVIA

With the amendments of 15 December 2005 to the Constitution of the Republic of Latvia the legislature amended Art. 110 to provide that 'The State shall protect and support marriage – a union between a man and a woman – the family, the rights of parents and rights of the child. The State shall provide special support to disabled children, children left without parental care or who have suffered from violence', and thus decided that the union of unmarried people cannot be equated to marriage. In the annotation of the amendments of 15 December 2005 to the Constitution of the Republic of Latvia it was indicated that Latvian national laws and other legislative acts do not define what marriage is.

---

47 C. Cost. 8 February 1977, n. 556 in *Giur. It.*, 1980, I, 1, 346. In the same sense C. Cost. 7 April 1988, n. 404 in *Foro It.*, 1988, I, 2515; C. Cost. 13 May 1998, n. 166 in *Giust. Civ.*, I, p. 1759 and many decisions by the Court of Cassation.

48 C. Cost. 15 April 2010, n. 138, in *Foro It.*, 2010, I, c. 1701.

49 Compare G. FERRANDO, *Diritto di famiglia*, Zanichelli, Bologna, 2013, at p. 151.

Therefore, taking into account the traditional views about marriage and family that have been established in the course of Latvian history and culture, as well as the continuous threats to this traditional value, it is important to include the definition of marriage in Latvian national laws.[50]

Nevertheless, it must be emphasised that Art. 110 of the Constitution of the Republic of Latvia contains the concept of family, which is wider than the concept of marriage. Section 214 of the Latvian Civil Law stipulates that, in the narrow sense of its definition, a family consists of the spouses and their children while they are still part of a common household, but from international human rights documents it follows that the concept is wider.

The Constitutional Court has indicated that, when interpreting the fundamental rights mentioned in the first part of Art. 110 of the Latvian Constitution, one must also take into account the norms of international human rights documents and their application in practice. The Constitutional Court followed this when it was assessing whether the prohibition to challenge or appeal a voluntary recognition of paternity can interfere with the right to family life, namely the court made a reference to the practice of the European Court of Human Rights (ECtHR). The ECtHR stated that, according to Art. 8 of the European Convention on Human Rights, it has been recognised that the concept of 'family' is not limited to relationships based on marriage; it can contain other *de facto* family ties such as in cases when people live together without entering into marriage. Thus, the ECtHR interprets the concept of family life more widely, emphasising that the conformity of a particular relationship to the concept of family life can be dependent on many factors, namely whether the couple is living together, the duration of the relationship, whether both parties are faithful to one another, or whether they have common children etc.[51]

Accordingly, in certain cases when there is a reference in the legal provision to family or members of the family, this explanation of the concept of family by the Constitutional Court can also cover unmarried persons living in a union.

---

50 Annotation of the draft law on ´Amendments in the Constitution of the Republic of Latvia'. Available at: helios-web.saeima.lv/bi8/lasa?dd=LP1400_0.

51 Constitutional Court of the Republic of Latvia judgment No. 2004-02-0106 of 11 October 2004. Available at: satv.tiesa.gov.lv/upload/spriedums_2004-02-0106.htm.

For example, in comparison with other procedural laws, the Latvian Civil Procedure Law holds a somewhat different legal order for the right to refuse to testify, namely the persons who may refuse the duty to testify are relatives in a direct line and of the first or second degree in a collateral line, spouses, spouse and affinity relatives of the first degree, and family members (*ģimenes locekļi*) of parties.[52] Similarly, the Ministry of Justice in its response letter on the legal order of actual cohabitation of 29 June 2012 to the Ombudsmen of the Republic of Latvia points out that, although S. 214 of the Latvian Civil Law stipulates the definition of family in the narrow sense, that does not prevent the legislature from including the wider concept of family in specific laws. Therefore, in the opinion of the Ministry of Justice the concept of family is not solely confined to the relationship based on marriage, but can also include other *de facto* family ties when people are living together without entering into marriage.[53]

For example, on the interpretation of para. 4 of the first part of S. 74 of the Latvian Labour Law (an employer has a duty to pay remuneration in the case where the employee does not perform work for not more than two working days due to the death of his or her spouse, parents, child or other close family member (*tuvs ģimenes loceklis*)), the Ministry of Welfare has indicated that the legislative acts do not contain the definition of the 'close family member' and hence the Ministry made a reference to the Constitutional Court's previously mentioned judgment and the ECtHR's interpretation of the concept of family. Accordingly, the Ministry of Welfare came to the conclusion that, within the context of the above-mentioned legal provision, a close family member can be regarded as any person with whom the employee maintains a close link and regular contact, including unmarried persons living in a union.[54]

State family policy guidelines 2011-2017 indicate that, in Latvia's legal system, referability to the explanations and the interpretation of the concept of family depends on the legal field in which the concept is applied. The concept of family is applied according to the above-mentioned practice of international law especially in those areas that are concerned with providing state aid in certain situations. It is applied

52 S. 450.[44] Latvian Civil Procedure Law.

53 The Ministry of Justice letter No.1-12/2448 of 29 June 2012. Available at: tiesibsargs.lv/par-mums/konsultativas-padomes/par-partnerattiecibu-tiesisko-regulejumu/.

54 Cabinet of Ministers of the Republic of Latvia letter No.18/TA-219 of 16 March 2012. Available at: tiesibsargs.lv/par-mums/konsultativas-padomes/par-partnerattiecibu-tiesisko-regulejumu/.

recognising legal reality, implementing the principle of legal equality and without discrimination against human rights. For instance, the first part of S. 33 of the Latvian Law on Social Services and Social Assistance on the recognition of a family (person) to be in need, stipulates that the Cabinet must determine the level of income and the material situation of a family, consisting of spouses, people who have common expenses for food and who live in one dwelling or a person living separately, who by failing to reach that level of income etc. is recognised to be in need and must also specify the procedures by which a family (person) is to be recognised as being in need.[55]

It has been indicated that, in order to successfully introduce the legal order of partnership, it is necessary not only to clearly define it, but also to clearly define the concept of family.[56]

LITHUANIA

The Constitution of the Republic of Lithuania provides no definition of a family, so some disputes have arisen as to whether cohabitants can be considered to be family members, followed by questions regarding the possible discrimination of families created outside of marriage. In this context, on 28 September 2011 the Constitutional Court of the Republic of Lithuania adopted a resolution 'On the compatibility of the provisions of the State Family Policy Concept approved by Resolution No. X-1569 of the Seimas of the Republic of Lithuania of 3 June 2008 'On the approval of the State Family Policy Concept' with the Constitution of the Republic of Lithuania'.[57] Among other things, this Court resolution states that the Constitution and, *inter alia*, the provisions of its Art. 38, part 1, offer protection also to families created on a different basis than marriage covering, *inter alia*, the cohabitation of a man and a woman outside marriage based on a continuous emotional attachment, mutual understanding, responsibility and respect, the joint nurturing of children and similar relations, as well as on a voluntary decision to assume certain rights and duties, which form the basis of the constitutional institutions of motherhood, fatherhood and childhood. Thus, as noted by the Lithuanian Constitutional Court, the State has a duty not only to

55 State family policy guidelines 2011-2017. Available at lm.gov.lv/upload/berns_gimene/lmpamn_200111_gvp.pdf.

56 Eversheds Bitans Law Office, Legal study on 'Male and female registered partnership legislation in Europe and Latvia' 2008.

57 Resolution No X-1569 of the Seimas of the Republic of Lithuania of 3 June 2008 On the Approval of the State Family Policy Concept, Official gazette, 2008, No. 69-2624.

'establish a legal regulation that, *inter alia*, creates preconditions for the proper functioning of a family, strengthens family relationships and protects the rights and legitimate interests of family members' but also a duty to 'regulate family relationship by way of laws and other legal acts in a way that leaves no grounds for discrimination against the parties to a family relationship (such as a man and a woman living together outside marriage, their children (foster children), a single parent raising a child (foster child), etc.)'. Bearing in mind the arguments presented by the Lithuanian Constitutional Court, there is an indisputable necessity to create legal premises for the functioning of the institution of a partnership.

LUXEMBOURG

The national constitutional position has not been relevant; an informal relationship does not have a legal position. An informal relationship may, in certain circumstances, produce some legal effects.

THE NETHERLANDS

In the Dutch legal system the courts are not permitted to scrutinise the constitutionality of acts pursuant to Art. 120 of the Dutch Constitution. Therefore, the Constitution has not played a role in the development of the law in this area.[58]

NORWAY

The national constitutional position has not been relevant to the legal position of informal relationship.

PORTUGAL

The Portuguese Constitution neither mentions nor directly regulates a *de facto* union.

However, some see the recognition of a *de facto* union as being implicit in 'the right to constitute a family', as foreseen in the Portuguese Constitution, while others understand that this norm is not intended to refer to a *de facto* union, but rather relates exclusively to questions of

---

58 W.M. SCHRAMA, *De niet-huwelijkse samenleving in het Nederlandse en Duitse recht*, Kluwer, Deventer, 2004, at p. 232-236 and at p. 243.

filiation: the 'right to constitute a family' is, firstly, a right to procreate, and, secondly, a right to establish corresponding relations of motherhood and fatherhood.

A *de facto* union is, however, included in the 'right to the development of personality' (Art. 26, n. 1). Legislation which would prohibit a *de facto* union, which would penalise it by imposing sanctions on members within the relationship and restrict, in an intolerable way, the right to live in a *de facto* union would therefore clearly be unconstitutional.

The principle of the protection of a *de facto* union arising from the 'right to the development of personality' does not demand, however, that the legislator grants the *de facto* union rights which are identical to those granted to marriage, thereby equalizing the rights of both.

We even believe that legislation which would entirely equalise a *de facto* union with a marriage would be unconstitutional, irrespective of how it was drawn up. Legislation which ceased to impose obligations upon spouses and allowed any spouse to marry without any formalities, etc., thus equalizing marriage with a *de facto* union, would violate Art. 36. n. 1 (part 2), which, by granting everyone the 'right to marry', guarantees the 'institution of matrimony', which, for that reason, the legislator cannot suppress, disfigure or essentially change its character. On the other hand, legislation which would equalise a *de facto* union with marriage, imposing the same duties upon people who live together in a marital fashion and affording them the same rights as those granted to married couples, would also be unconstitutional, insofar as it would violate the right not to marry, 'a negative side or dimension' of 'the right to contract marriage', which is recognised in Art. 36, n. 1 (part 2).

In conclusion, we believe that the Portuguese Constitution allows neither the penalization of a *de facto* union nor equalization with marriage: within these parameters, what should be applied is the democratic principle, which allows the ordinary legislator to freely adapt to the *de facto* union regime, in accordance with the most 'progressive' or 'conservative' option of the family policy adopted.

RUSSIA

Article 38 of the Constitution of the Russian Federation states that motherhood, childhood and the family are protected by the state. Neither the Russian Constitution nor the Russian Family Code contains a legal definition of the family. That has prompted some authors to conclude that a family made up of informal partners should be regarded as being protected by the state and that the legislation should be changed in order to ensure better protection for informal partners and their families.[59]

SCOTLAND

Neither Scotland nor the UK has a formal written constitution and so this question is not relevant. There is no particular protection provided for the family or family relationships.

SLOVAKIA

The Constitution of the Slovak Republic as the fundamental act of the Slovak Republic (460/1992 Coll.) provides in Art. 19 para. 2: Everyone has the right to protection against unauthorised interference in private and family life. Article 41 para. 1 provides: Marriage, parenthood and the family are under the protection of the law. The special protection of children and minors is guaranteed.

SLOVENIA

The Slovenian Constitution determines that legal relations in an extramarital union shall be regulated by law (para. 2 Art. 53 of the Slovenian Constitution).

SPAIN

The Spanish Constitution has been decisive in connection with the legal position of informal relationships. The constitutional principles of equality and non-discrimination, particularly on grounds of filiation or sexual orientation (Art. 14), of free development of one's personality (Art. 10) and of legal, social and economic protection of the family and children, regardless of filiation, and mothers, regardless of civil status (Art. 39.1 and 2) were instrumental in the first years after the enactment of the Constitution in 1978. Based on these provisions the Constitutional Court established a broad concept of family that includes informal relationships (STC 222/1992 and 116/1999).

---

59 А.С. КОВАЛЕВА, 'Гражданский брак как дестабилизатор семьи', *Власть и управление на Востоке России*, 2009, at p. 145.

The Constitutional Court however also consistently held that the fact that informal relationships were recognised and protected by the Constitution did not mean that partners had the same legal status as spouses in connection with, for example, social security pensions in the case of death of one of the partners, or in connection with leasehold contracts (STC 184/1990 and 156/1987). These decisions caused an enormous social uproar and pushed the legislature into becoming active and legislate. The Spanish Parliament opted for the modification of specific provisions in the law of leasehold and social security, whereas legislatures in the Autonomous Communities enacted comprehensive statutes that dealt with all matters within their competence. These statutes were very significant from a political point of view and were certainly decisive steps towards the opening up of marriage. There were, however, doubts as regards their constitutionality.

In 2013 the Constitutional Court delivered two decisions in connection with the domestic partnership laws of Madrid and Navarre. The constitutional issues arose not because of the absence of legislation, but, on the contrary, because of the content of the legislation enacted.[60]

The first decision, STC 81/2013, on the Law of the Autonomous Community of Madrid, decreed that the Autonomous Community had gone beyond its legislative competence. It is therefore of no interest for the present report, since it deals with the division of legislative powers within Spain. The second decision, STC 93/2013, found nine provisions of the legislation of the Autonomous Community of Navarre to be unconstitutional, because they were in breach of the right to free development of personality since the law did not provide an opt-out mechanism allowing partners to exclude their application by agreement. According to the Constitutional Court provisions containing detailed regulation that cannot be derogated by agreement are not in conformity with the couple's individual freedom.

The 2013 decisions of the Constitutional Court only refer to the partnership bills of two Autonomous Communities. If the constitutionality of other laws is challenged, judges need to request a new decision by

[60] M. ANDERSON, 'The Impact of the Spanish Constitutional Court's Judgments of Family Law and Succession in the Autonomous Communities', in: W. PINTENS and C. DECLERCK (eds.), *Patrimonium*, Intersentia, Antwerpen, 2013, pp. 379-394; Á. AMARCA MARQUES, 'The unconstitutionality of Cohabitation Regulation-Two decisions of the Spanish Constitutional Court', in: N. WITZLEB et al. (eds.), *Festschrift für Dieter Martiny zum 70. Geburtstag*, Mohr Siebeck, Tübingen, 2014, pp. 1141-1161.

the Constitutional Court. It is, however, only a matter of time until this happens.[61] In the meantime the legal situation of non-formalised relationships falling under the scope of application of the special statutes enacted by the Autonomous Communities of Aragon and Catalonia is uncertain.

SWEDEN

The position of the Swedish Constitution remains neutral in respect of whether the relationship of a couple is formal or informal. This position has facilitated Sweden's 'stance or ideology of neutrality', meaning that legislation should not contain provisions which create difficulties for persons who choose to found a family and have children without marrying.

SWITZERLAND

The Swiss Constitution[62] has not had a noteworthy influence on the legal position of informal relationships between couples. Nowadays, the informal relationship is protected by the Swiss Constitution.[63]

---

61 J. FERRER RIBA, 'Gemeinsames Sorgerecht, gleichgeschlechtliche Ehe und eheähnliche Gemeinschaften in der spanischen Verfassungsrechtsprechung', *FamRZ*, 2013, at p. 1464.

62 Bundesverfassung der Schweizerischen Eidgenossenschaft, SR 101.

63 See R. AEBI-MÜLLER and C. WIDMER, 'Rechtsregeln für nichteheliches Zusammenleben in der Schweiz', in: I. KROPPENBERG, D. SCHWAB, D. HENRICH, P. GOTTWALD and A. SPICKHOFF, *Rechtsregeln für nichteheliches Zusammenleben*, Gieseking, Bielefeld, 2009, at p. 65, 66.

QUESTION 7

To what extent, if at all, have international instruments (such as the European Convention on Human Rights) and European legislation (treaties, regulations and directives) been relevant in your jurisdiction to the legal position of informal relationships between a couple?

AUSTRIA

The relation between partners in an informal relationship is protected by Art. 8 European Convention on Human Rights, which directly applies in Austria.[1] However, even Art. 8 ECHR does not oblige the legislator to treat a marriage and an informal relationship equally.[2] To date, international instruments have had no effect on the position of heterosexual partners in an informal relationship.[3]

BELGIUM

The European Convention on Human Rights, particularly Art. 8 and 14, have been most relevant for the development of the legal recognition of informal relationships. Belgium is a 'monist state' and until the reform in 2009 all civil courts were competent to directly apply the ECHR over national legislation. This had led some courts to apply the primary matrimonial regime to cohabitants on the basis of Art. 8 ECHR.[4] But

---

1 Regarding heterosexual couples see ECtHR, *Johnston v. Ireland*, No. 9697/82, 18.12.1986; regarding same-sex couples see ECtHR, *Schalk and Kopf v. Austria*, No. 30141/04, 24.6.2010 and ECtHR, *P.B. and J.S. v. Austria*, No. 18984/02, 22.7.2010.

2 P. PERNTHALER and I. RATH-KATHREIN, 'Der grundrechtliche Schutz von Ehe und Familie', in: R. MACHACEK, W. PAHR and G. STADLER (eds.), *40 Jahre EMRK, Grund- und Menschenrechte in Österreich*, Engel, Kehl am Rhein, 1992, at p. 268 et seq.

3 Article 23 International Covenant on Civil and Political Rights is not directly applicable in Austria.

4 Divisional Court of Tongeren 1 April 1992, *Limb.Rechtsl.* 1993, 59; Justice of the Peace Aalst 11 June 1991, *RW* 1993-94, 1307; Justice of the Peace Aalst 1 September 1992, *T.Vred.* 1992, 326.

since 2009, civil courts in principle are obliged to refer a prejudicial question to the Constitutional Court on the compatibility of national legislation with international fundamental rights that are also guaranteed in the Belgian Constitution (Art. 26, § 4 Constitutional Court Act). Moreover, already in 2003 the Supreme Court determined that Art. 8 and 14 ECHR do not imply that all remaining differences between informal relationships and marriage should be eliminated.[5]

Other international instruments were relevant to a lesser extent. For example, Art. 3.2 b) of the Free Movement of Persons Directive (2004/38/EC) has been reproduced in Art. 47/3, para. 1 Belgian Aliens Act for the purposes of family reunification.

BULGARIA

Bulgaria is a state party to the following relevant UN treaties:

- International Covenant on Civil and Political Rights (1966) – ratified by Bulgaria in 1970;
- International Covenant on Economic, Social and Cultural Rights (1966) – ratified by Bulgaria in 1970;
- Convention on the elimination of all forms of Discrimination against Women – ratified by Bulgaria in 1982;
- Convention on the Rights of the Child (1989) – ratified by Bulgaria in 1991;
- International Convention on the Protection of the Rights of all Migrant Workers and Members of Their Families (1990) has still not been ratified by Bulgaria;
- The European Convention on Human Rights – ratified by Bulgaria in 1992.

The European legislation is also applicable since Bulgaria has been a member state of the EU from 1.01.2007.

CROATIA

Since couples in informal relationships (both same-sex and different-sex relationships) have a far greater number of rights and liabilities pursuant to the national legislation than in accordance with international instruments and European legislation, it is difficult to talk about the relevance

5 Cass. 17 November 2003, S.03.0018.N, www.cass.be.

of international instruments and European legislation for the legal position of informal relationships between Croatian couples.

Couples in informal relationships possess all the rights granted by the relevant international and European documents such as the right to respect for family life under Art. 8 of the European Convention for the Protection of Human Rights and Fundamental Freedoms. They also have those rights which, in accordance with European documents, can but do not have to be provided such as entry and residence according to Council Directive 2003/86/EC on the right to family reunification and Council Directive 2004/38/EC on the right of citizens of the Union and their family members to move and reside freely within the territory of the Member States.

Nevertheless, according to the national legislation, couples in informal relationships have numerous rights and liabilities which have been or should be granted, e.g. property rights, inheritance rights etc.

CZECH REPUBLIC

There are several international treaties and instruments that are binding on the Czech Republic and its jurisdiction, thus Czech legislation fully respects all the rights granted to a family, parents, children and other family-related matters. This fact provides a fundamental framework for legal protection to couples in an informal relationship. Amongst the most important international documents are, for example, International Covenant on Civil and Political Rights, International Covenant on Economic, Social and Cultural Rights, European Convention on Human Rights (especially Art. 8), Recommendations of the Committee of Ministers of the Council of Europe No. 3/1988, on validity of contracts between persons living together as an unmarried couple and their testamentary dispositions, Recommendations of the Committee of Ministers of the Council of Europe No. 4/1984, on parental responsibility, and European Convention on the Legal Status of Children born out of wedlock. All of them are in a way reflected in various provisions aiming to equate couples in an informal relationship with married couples as well as equate children born outside marriage with children born within marriage.

DENMARK

The Danish reservations from 1992 mean that Denmark does not participate in the supranational EU cooperation on justice and home affairs.

ENGLAND AND WALES

With regard to same-sex couples European Convention on Human Rights (ECHR) arguments under the English Human Rights Act 1998 have been very significant and culminated in the Court of Appeal case of *Mendoza v Ghaidan* [2002] EWCA Civ 1533, [2003] Ch 380 which was subsequently confirmed by the House of Lords in *Ghaidan v Godin-Mendoza* [2004] UKHL 30; [2004] 2 AC 557. This extended the same rights available to different-sex cohabiting couples to same-sex cohabiting couples in the Rent Act family home tenancy succession context. This extension of rights, along with amendment of all other statutes governing cohabitation relationships, was subsequently put on a statutory footing when the English Civil Partnership Act 2004 was passed, to avoid discrimination against same-sex cohabiting couples.

However, this trend to extend rights to same-sex couples had originally been started without reference to the ECHR. In point of fact the English Human Rights Act 1998 was not considered relevant in an earlier case on the same point *Fitzpatrick v Sterling Housing Association* [2001] 1 AC 27 before the implementation of the English Human Rights Act 1998. Yet the later case of *Mendoza v Ghaiden* (confirmed on appeal in *Ghaidan v Godin-Mendoza*) found the right to private and family life combined with the non-discrimination principle (Art. 8 plus Art. 14 ECHR) decisive, given different-sex couples had already acquired the same rights as married couples in this context.

ESTONIA

The explanatory memorandum to the Estonian Registered Partnership Act clearly refers to the fact that partners in an informal relationship (primarily, same-sex cohabitation) have so far not been given sufficient protection in Estonian legislation.[6] Persons in an informal relationship did not have sufficient protection as compared with the practice of the

6 Available at: www.riigikogu.ee/?op=ems&page=eelnou&eid=ea84e71c-291a-4c91-88b0-bd64af650d21& (in Estonian).

European Court of Human Rights. In the memorandum,[7] sent to the Minister of Justice in 2011, the Chancellor of Justice found that a permanent cohabitation between two persons of the same sex falls within the field of protection granted by the fundamental rights of the family, and therefore this form of cohabitation is legally unregulated, a situation which is not in conformity with the Estonian Constitution. Thus, it is in accordance with the principle of ensuring fundamental rights to establish an appropriate legal framework for the regulation of such legal relations. In particular, in the analysis by the Ministry of Justice it could be pointed out that the regulation concerning the adoption and the custody of a child may not guarantee a consideration of the child's interests. According to the Estonian Family Law Act § 148(1), a single person can only adopt alone. According to the first sentence of the Estonian Family Law Act § 148(2), only married persons can jointly adopt the same child. Thus, partners in an informal relationship do not have the right to adopt children together and custody is only given to the partner who adopts alone.[8]

After the adoption of the Estonian Registered Partnership Act the parties in an informal relationship now have the right to register their cohabitation and to be given the necessary legal recognition, but it cannot be predicted how many partners in an informal relationship will make use of this opportunity.

FINLAND

In Finland cohabitation was already given legal effect in social law and tax law in the 1970s. The rights and obligations involved in cohabitation relationships have gradually been extended to all administrative sectors and even to private law. The original impetus and the legislative model for the legal status of cohabitees mainly stems from the domestic law of the other Nordic and Central European countries rather than international instruments. Therefore, it cannot be said that the European instruments have, until recently, been the focus when the legal position of cohabiting couples has been discussed.

---

7 Available at: oiguskantsler.ee/sites/default/files/field_document2/6iguskantsleri_margukiri_samasooliste_isikute_peresuhe.pdf.

8 Perekonnaseadus (adopted on 18 November 2009). – RT I 2009, 60, 395; RT I, 29.06.2014, 104, available in English at: www.riigiteataja.ee/en/eli/ee/Riigikogu/act/522082014005/consolide.

Finland ratified the European Convention on Human Rights in 1990 and became a member of the European Union in 1995. The influence of the European instruments has gained increasing weight and today the case law of the European courts is closely followed.

FRANCE

The French *Cour de cassation, Conseil d'État* (State Council, the highest administrative court) and *Conseil constitutionnel* (Constitutional Council) increasingly take the case law of the European Court of Human Rights (ECtHR) into account. However, the legislator's decision to allow same-sex marriages was independent of the EtCHR's case law, which does not require contracting states to go that far.[9]

With regard to informal relationships, there has so far not been any specific influence by European legislation or case law on the legal position of informal relationships between a couple under French law.

GERMANY

The European Court of Human Rights interprets the term 'family life' in Art. 8 para. 1 European Convention on Human Rights (ECHR) autonomously. Where a man and a woman enjoyed a stable relationship which produced common children, the relationship between them amounts to family life even though they chose neither to marry nor to live together.[10] International instruments and European legislation are increasingly taken into account in determining the existence of informal relationships between a couple There are, however, no cases of the European Court of Human Rights or the Court of Justice of the European Union that deal with informal relationships and have an influence on German law.

GREECE

Article 8 of the European Convention on Human Rights (ECHR) might apply. According to the European Court of Human Rights (ECtHR) in Strasbourg the notion of family life has developed over time in accordance with changing social attitudes, so as to also include *de facto*

---

9 See e.g. ECtHR, *Schalk and Kopf v. Austria*, No. 30141/04, 24.6.2010.

10 ECtHR, *Kroon and others v. the Netherlands*, No. 18535/91, 27.10.1994; ECtHR (Grand Chamber), *K and T v. Finland*, No. 25702/94, 12.7.2001 = *NJW*, 2003, 809.

relationships.[11] The ECtHR may consider whether or not a couple live together, the length of their relationship, and whether or not they have demonstrated their commitment by having children or by any other means.[12] Another possible article could be Art. 14 of the ECHR on the principle on non-discrimination.[13]

In an EU context,[14] the Charter of Fundamental Rights of the EU contains provisions concerning family relations, which after the entry into force of the Lisbon Treaty have acquired the same legal value as the primary sources of EU law, namely the treaties. The Charter guarantees the protection of family life and the right to marry in Arts 7 and 9, respectively. Under Art. 7, 'Everyone has the right to respect for his private and family life, home and communications', whereas according to Art. 9, 'The right to marry and the right to found a family shall be guaranteed in accordance with the national laws governing the exercise of these rights'. Although both provisions are inspired by Arts 8(1) and 12 ECHR, they differ from the latter in so far as Art. 9, which guarantees the right to marry, makes no reference to 'men and women' in the way that Art. 12 ECHR does, and so offers more extensive protection to novel forms of the family (e.g. a registered partnership, a same-sex marriage, etc.) than the latter. Other provisions of the Charter concerning family law are: Art. 21 prohibiting discrimination on several grounds and, more particularly, on the basis of sexual orientation, Art. 24 guaranteeing the rights of the child and Art. 32 which proclaims the legal, economic and social protection of the family and guarantees the reconciliation of family and professional life. In the future these provisions may constitute the

---

11 Concerning the pragmatist approach to the concept of family life adopted by the ECtHR when interpreting Art. 8(1) ECHR and the diversification of this approach from that of the CJEU, see, H. STALFORD, 'Concepts of Family under EU Law – Lessons from the ECHR', *International Journal of Law, Policy and the Family*, 2002, pp. 410-434; C. MCGLYNN, *Families and the European Union: Law, Politics and Pluralism,* Cambridge University Press, Cambridge, 2006; C. DELIYIANNI-DIMITRAKOU, 'Le droit social de l'Union Européenne face aux nouvelles formes de famille', in: I. SCHÖMANN, *Mélange à la mémoire de Yota Kravaritou, A trilingual tribute,* European Trade Union Instituts, Brussels, 2012, pp. 71 et seq.

12 ECtHR, *X, Y and Z v. UK*, No. 21830/93, 5.12.2013. The Court recalled that the notion of 'family life' in Art. 8 is not confined solely to families based on marriage and may encompass other *de facto* relationships (see ECtHR, *Marckx v. Belgium*, No. 6833/74, 13.6.1979, para. 31; ECtHR, *Keegan v. Ireland*, No. 16969/90, 26.5.1994, para. 44; and ECtHR, *Kroon and Others v. the Netherlands*, No. 18535/91, 27.10.1994, para. 30).

13 In this respect see the case ECtHR, *Vallianatos and Others v Greece,* Nos. 29381/09 and 32684/09, 7.11.2013 as discussed below under Question 9.

14 For a detailed discussion on the Europeanisation of family law and the role of fundamental rights, see C. DELIYIANNI-DIMITRAKOU and C. AKRIVOPOULOU, *Fundamental Rights and Private Relations in Greek and European Law*, Sakkoulas, Thessaloniki/Athens, 2014.

relevant legal basis for reforms to the Greek legal system concerning free unions, registered partnerships, and marriage for same-sex partners.

As far as secondary EU law is concerned, relevant legislation, which may apply in the Greek legal context, is the so-called 'Citizenship Directive', i.e. Directive 2004/58,[15] which addresses the right of EU citizens and their family members to move and reside freely within EU territory, and Directives 2003/86[16] and 2003/9,[17] which address the right to family reunification and minimum standards for the reception of asylum seekers, respectively.[18]

Specifically, Directive 2004/58 on the right of EU citizens and their family members to freely move and reside provides that EU citizens of the same or the opposite sex living in a registered partnership, as well as married homosexuals, are considered to be members of the family solely in cases when the legislation of the host country recognises them as such. A relevant, yet not identical, provision is also contained in Directives 2003/86 [19] and 2003/9 [20] on the right to family reunification and minimum standards for the reception of asylum seekers, respectively.

More particularly, Directive 2003/86/EC [21] on family reunification outlines in detail the applicable rules for the entry of family members of lawfully resident third-country nationals. Similar to Directive 2004/58/EC on the free movement of persons, Directive 2003/86/EC adopts a restrictive definition of 'family members', limited to the nuclear family,

---

15 See Directive of the Parliament and of the Council 2004/58 EC of 29 April 2004 on the right of citizens of the EU and their family members to move and reside freely within the territory of the Member States [2004] OJ L 229/35.

16 See Council Directive 2003/86 EC of 22 September 2003 on the right to family reunification [2003] OJ L *251/12.*

17 See Council Directive 2003/9 EC of 27 January 2003 laying down minimum standards for the reception of asylum seekers [2003] OJ L 31/18.

18 Concerning the notion of 'European Social Citizenship', adopted by this legislation and the subsequent case law of the CJEU, see A. STERGIOU, European Social Citizenship, www.constitutionalism.gr/site/stergiou-koinoniki-ithageneia/*EDKA*_Stergiou_europaiki-koinoniki-ithageneia.pdf, and A.-M. KONSTA, 'Gender and Plastic Citizenship in European Social Law', in: M.-A. MOREAU (ed.), *Before and After the Economic Crisis: What implications for the European Social Model,* Edward Edgar Publishing Ltd, Cheltenham, 2011, p. 129 et seq.

19 See Art. 4(3) Council Directive 2003/86 EC on the right to family reunification.

20 See Art. 2(d-i) Council Directive 2003/9 EC establishing minimum standards for the reception of asylum seekers.

21 The Directive has been implemented in the Greek legal order through Presidential Decrees 131/2006 and 167/2008 on the right to family reunification and its application in cases concerning migration, refugees (the protection of international status) and subsidiary protection for third-country citizens.

namely, the spouse of the 'sponsor' and minor children solely dependent on the 'sponsor'. However, provisions relating to registered and unmarried partners are permissive, with only Art. 4(3) providing that Member States may authorise the entry and residence of an unmarried partner in a 'duly attested long-term stable relationship or a partner of a registered partnership'. Thus, unmarried partnerships are at least recognised by the Directive, even though there is no requirement that Member States should recognise such relationships.[22]

Accordingly, Directive 2003/86/EC on family reunification for third-country nationals incorporates a concept of the family that is more limited than the one adopted by Directive 2004/58/EC in relation to family members of Union citizens exercising their right to free movement, because unlike the latter it does not provide for the reciprocal obligation of Member States to authorise the entry of an 'unmarried partner living in a long-term relationship with the applicant, if the legislation of the Member State concerned treats the situation of unmarried couples as a situation corresponding to that of married couples'.[23]

Moreover, the introduction of Greek Law 3500/2006 on 'domestic violence' has been an attempt to align Greek law with the Equal Treatment Directive between men and women, 2006/54/EC,[24] and the relevant case law of the EU Court on gender equality.[25] The Greek Law provides for a *de facto* definition of the term 'family' stipulating that, apart from married couples, a family may comprise couples living in a free union and children born in free unions.[26]

---

22 See C. McGlynn, *Families and the European Union: Law, Politics and Pluralism*, Cambridge University Press, Cambridge, 2006, at p. 133.

23 See recitals 2 and 11, Council Directive 2003/86 EC.

24 Directive 2006/54 EC of 5 July 2006 on the implementation of the principle of equal opportunities and equal treatment of men and women in matters of employment and occupation [2006] OJ L 204/23.

25 C. Deliyianni-Dimitrakou and C. Akrivopoulou, *The Influence of Human Rights and Basic Rights on Greek Private Law*, National Report for the 19th International Congress of Comparative Law, Vienna, 20th to 27th July 2014, *Hellenic Review of International Law*, 2014, pp. 283 et seq. See, also C. Deliyianni, The Greek Civil Code, Greek Report May 2012, *Hellenic Review* on Thematic Congress of International Academy of Comparative Law in Taiwan, *of International Law*; 2012, pp. 417 -497.

26 It may also comprise children born within wedlock, adopted children and cohabiting relatives.

HUNGARY

When the recodification of a new civil code began in the late 1990s it was generally emphasised that the decisions of the European Court of Human Rights were to be taken into account when formulating the new regulations. (Besides, the need to reshape the rules which apply to cohabitants was also underlined, see also the answer to Question 8). These judgments are referred to in the commentary literature.[27]

REPUBLIC OF IRELAND

Ireland has a dualist approach to international instruments.

The European Convention on Human Rights Act 2003 was intended to give the Convention domestic effect in Ireland. It allowed litigants to rely directly upon the Convention in ways that had been previously precluded.

EU legislation has had a greater impact given the fact that regulations enjoy the status of supremacy.

The designation of the family in Art. 41 of the Irish Constitution as a private realm, which is virtually impenetrable, still endures, as can be seen from the Supreme Court case of *North Western Health Board v HW and CW* [2001] IESC 90. In the face of such a restrictive interpretation of the 'family', Irish litigants have sought redress under international law through international human rights treaties. However, our dualist approach to international law generally makes international human rights treaties binding on the State, though not on the courts, as such treaties have traditionally not been incorporated into Irish law. This has changed, to a limited extent, with the incorporation of the European Convention on Human Rights and Fundamental Freedom (ECHR) into domestic law.

The incorporation of the ECHR into Irish law has been by way of statute. As a result of incorporation, the provisions of the ECHR have become part of Irish domestic law. It is now possible to take proceedings before the Irish courts alleging a breach of the ECHR. Previously, to assert any

---

27 O. SZEIBERT, 'Alapelvek' ('Principles'), in: L.VEKÁS and P. GÁRDOS (eds.), *Kommentár a Polgári Törvénykönyvhöz (Commentary to Civil Code)*, Complex, Budapest, 2014, at p. 629-634.; A. KŐROS, 'Alapelvek' ('Principles'), in: A. KŐROS (ed.), *Polgári jog. Családjog. Az új Ptk.magyarázata (Civil law. Family law. Commentary to new Civil Code)*, HVG-ORAC, Budapest, 2013, at p. 24-26.

rights under the ECHR, an injured party had to first exhaust all domestic remedies before bringing the case to the European Court of Human Rights in Strasbourg, with the costs and delays associated with that process.

The indirect or interpretative mode of incorporation preserves the domestic primacy of the Constitution. Consequently, Art. 41 of the Irish Constitution continues to act an impediment to the effective implementation of the legal entitlements of children under the ECHR. In particular, incorporation of the ECHR at sub-constitutional level ensures that child rights remain subordinate to parental rights.

The impact of the revised Brussels II Regulation was highly significant in Ireland in several respects. It brought the so-called Brussels Convention directly into the corpus of EC law. As such it enjoyed the status of supremacy accorded to all binding EU laws. It rendered the measure directly applicable in Ireland as a matter of EC law. In other words, the measure became part of Irish law without the need for incorporation by the Irish State.

ITALY

International instruments and European legislation can hardly be said to be relevant in the Italian jurisdiction with regard to the legal position of informal partners. Taking into account the framework formed by Art. 29 of the Italian Constitution and the traditional, privileged recognition accorded to marriage - in its most narrow conception as a legal bond between a man and a woman - as opposed to all other kinds of unions, supranational sources provide at present merely general principles corroborating the legitimacy of cohabitation.[28]

Recommendations such as those contained in the Resolution of 16 March 2000 of the European Parliament calling on 'those States which have not yet granted legal recognition to amend their legislation to grant legal recognition of extramarital cohabitation, irrespective of gender', and the rules concerning the right to marry and to found a family contained in Art. 9 of the Charter of Fundamental Rights of the European Union are still awaiting implementation.

[28] Compare G. FERRANDO, *Diritto di famiglia*, Zanichelli, Bologna, 2013, at p. 140. A full and up to date discussion of this and related issues can be found in G. OBERTO, *I diritti dei conviventi. Realtà e prospettive tra Italia ed Europa*, Cedam, Padua, 2012, at p. 13 et seq. and p. 211 et seq.

LATVIA

With regard to the practice of the ECtHR, it has already been mentioned that Latvian courts have made references to the judgments of the ECtHR when clarifying the concept of family life within the context of Art. 8 of the European Convention on Human Rights.[29] At the same time it was indicated that the Convention does not oblige a country to provide to people living in a partnership the same rights as spouses.[30]

LITHUANIA

The State must equally guarantee effective respect for the family life of all participants in family-type relationships (spouses, cohabitants, parents and children, other persons linked by blood, in-law or other types of relationships (e.g. those of foster parents and foster children)). This value is protected by EU legal acts, the European Convention on Human Rights and other global and regional legal acts, of which the ECHR has been the most important and effective as far as Lithuania is concerned. For instance, on the basis of the case law of the European Court of Human Rights, the Law of the Republic of Lithuania on the legal status of foreign nationals[31] contains a norm that obliges migration officers dealing with the question of the deportation of a foreign national from the Republic of Lithuania to take into consideration, inter alia, his/her family relations with persons living in the Republic of Lithuania. Thus, from a human rights perspective, not only spouses but also cohabitants have the right to protection as laid down in Art. 8 of the ECHR if their relationship can be considered to be a family-type relationship in terms of its substance and quality.[32]

---

[29] Constitutional Court of the Republic of Latvia judgment No. 2004-02-0106 of 11 October 2004. Available at: satv.tiesa.gov.lv/upload/spriedums_2004-02-0106.htm. Senate of the Supreme Court of the Republic of Latvia, Department of Administrative Cases, judgment of 28 February 2008 No. SKA-53/2008. Available at: tiesas.lv/nolemumi.

[30] Senate of the Supreme Court of the Republic of Latvia, Department of Civil Cases, judgment of 1 February 2012 No. SKC-4/2012. Available at: at.gov.lv/lv/judikatura/judikaturas-nolemumu-arhivs/senata-civillietu-departaments/hronologiska-seciba_1/2012-hronologiska-seciba/.

[31] Lietuvos Respublikos įstatymas dėl užsieniečių teisinės padėties *(The Law of the Republic of Lithuania on the legal status of foreign nationals)*, Official gazette, 2004, No. 73-2539.

[32] G. SAGATYS, *Šeimos teisinių santykių turinys. Lietuvos Respublikos civilinio kodeksas: pirmieji dešimt galiojimo metų. Mokslo studija* (The Substance of Legal Relations Within Family/ Civil Code of the Republic of Lithuania: the first decade in force. Academic study) MRU, Vilnius, 2013, at p. 442-443.

LUXEMBOURG

An informal relationship may, in certain circumstances, produce legal effects; it does not have a legal position.

THE NETHERLANDS

In the light of the prohibition on the courts scrutinising acts as to their constitutional conformity, the influence of unwritten norms and of international instruments has been profound. Article 8 (respect for family life and private life) and Art. 14 ECHR and Art. 26 International Covenant on Civil and Political Rights (the principle of equality) have had a major impact on the development of the law in relation to non-marital cohabitants. However, there is a large variation between different areas of the law. In relation to the property and contract law aspects of the relationship, international instruments have played no role at all, which is basically in line with the case law of the European Court of Human Rights. However, for instance in parent-child relations, in social security law, and in taxation law, Art. 26 ICCPR, and Art. 8 and 14 ECHR have played a significant role in the case law, mostly during the 1980s and 1990s.[33]

NORWAY

International instruments (such as the European Convention on Human Rights) and European legislation have so far not been relevant to the legal position of informal couple relationship.

PORTUGAL

The legal regime of a *de facto* union does not refer to international case law as an explicit influence. Nevertheless, the options of the Portuguese legislature express the concern to conform to human rights.

RUSSIA

International instruments have so far not had any direct influence on the legal position of informal spouses. However, some authors note that by failing to protect informal relationships, Russia is violating its obligations

---

33 W.M. SCHRAMA, *De niet-huwelijkse samenleving in het Nederlandse en Duitse recht*, Kluwer, Deventer, 2004, at p. 232-236 and p. 581-596.

under Art. 8 ECHR.[34] In 2004, in the case of *Prokopovich v Russia*, the ECtHR ruled against Russia for violating Art. 8 ECHR. In this case the European Court decided that the informal relationship of Ms. Prokopovich and her deceased partner fell under the protection of Art. 8 ECHR and that Ms. Prokopovich was therefore entitled to succeed him in the tenancy.[35]

SCOTLAND

While international instruments have been of considerable significance to the legal recognition of same-sex relationships, the introduction of civil partnership and the redefinition of marriage to include both different and same-sex relationships, there is little direct evidence of their influence on the regulation of informal relationships.

SLOVAKIA

Slovak doctrine[36] and the case law of the Constitutional Court of the Slovak Republic[37] accept the broad concept of private and family life in accordance with the ECHR case law relating to Art. 8. This article protects the right to identity and personal development, and the right to establish and develop relationships with other human beings and the outside world. There is therefore a zone of interaction between a person and others, even in a public context, which may fall within the scope of 'private life'.

SLOVENIA

Slovenia has regulated extramarital unions since the Slovenian Marriage Act took effect in 1977. This legislation from 1977 has not been subsequently amended. International instruments did not affect its introduction.

---

34 И.А. КОСАРЕВА, 'Международное, зарубежное и российское право о статусе лиц, состоящих в фактических супружеских отношениях', *Семейное и жилищное право*, 2010, at p. 3.

35 ECtHR, *Prokopovich v. Russia*, No. 58255/00, 18.11.04, at § 29.

36 R. DOBROVODSKÝ, 'Europeizácia a internacionalizácia rodinného práva (Europeaisation and internationalisation of family law)', in: J. LAZAR et al. (eds.), *Občianske právo hmotné* (Substantive Slovak Civil Law), Iuris Libri, Bratislava, 2014, at p. 260-261.

37 D. KROŠLÁK, *Introduction to the Slovak Constitutional System*, Leges. Praha, 2014, at p. 111.

International instruments have also not had a major influence on the creation of the legal recognition of a life union between unregistered same-sex partners living together. Indirectly, the Resolution on equal rights for homosexuals and lesbians in the EC and the European Convention on Human Rights have had an impact (for example, in connection with the case of *Karner v Austria*), although the judicature of the European Court of Human Rights is fairly restrained in interpreting provisions to the benefit of persons with a same-sex orientation.

SPAIN

The partnership laws of the Spanish Autonomous Communities pursued two objectives. On the one hand, they sought the legal recognition of same-sex couples at a time when these individuals could not marry and, on the other hand, they intended to provide a legal framework for informal relationships. Whereas international instruments were relevant as regards the first objective, they have very rarely been relied upon in connection with the second. The Preamble to the first Catalan Law on stable couples, enacted by the Catalan Parliament in 1998, makes no reference to international instruments.

Case law has sometimes cited international instruments in order to justify new solutions. One of the oldest decisions of the Supreme Court accepting that partners may enter into an agreement and which establishes that their economic relationships are to be governed by the matrimonial property regime of community of acquisitions, STS of 18 May 1992, refers to Council of Europe Recommendation No. R (88) 3 on the validity of contracts between persons living together as an unmarried couple. These contracts were formerly held to be in breach of moral order.

SWEDEN

The European Convention on Human Rights (ECHR) enjoys in Sweden the status of higher ranking legislation, equal to that of the Swedish Constitution. The case law of the European Court of Human Rights (ECtHR) is taken into account in particular in the drafting of new legislation but also in case law. Considering that Sweden in comparison with other European countries is in the forefront as regards legal recognition of informal couples, irrespective of the couple's sexual orientation (on condition that they habitually cohabit with each other), the influence of the ECtHR's case law has remained limited. Yet, the

ECtHR's case law has the potential of improving in particular unmarried fathers' parental responsibilities. Fathers to children born in informal relationships lack, namely, *ex lege* parental rights under Swedish law. The impact of other European legislation has been limited, due to the higher level of protection generally provided by Swedish law.

SWITZERLAND

International instruments and European legislation have not had a noteworthy relevance for the Swiss jurisdiction with regard to the legal position of informal relationships between a couple.

QUESTION 8

Give a brief history of the main developments and the most recent reforms of the rules regarding informal relationships between a couple. Briefly indicate the purpose behind the law reforms and, where relevant, the main reasons for not adopting a proposal.

AUSTRIA

Until the end of the 19th century concubinage was deemed to be illegal in Austria and was prosecuted under administrative criminal law.[1] The first efforts to regulate informal relationships were undertaken at the beginning of the 20th century and after the First World War. However, these attempts were frustrated shortly thereafter by the legislation of the post-war period.[2]

Apart from the Austrian Victims Welfare Act *(Opferfürsorgegesetz)*, which already took informal relationships into consideration at the time of its introduction in 1947, the Austrian legislator has only in recent decades started to adopt rules equating, under certain conditions, informal relationships with marriages.[3] In terms of their practical importance, crucial provisions have been the introduction of S. 14 para. 3 Austrian Tenancy Act in 1967 and S. 5 para. 1 Austrian Condominium Act in 2002.[4] A further harmonization between marriages and informal

1 J. STABENTHEINER, 'Die nichteheliche Lebensgemeinschaft - ein Überblick', *NZ*, 1995, at p. 49.

2 For examples see J. STABENTHEINER, 'Die nichteheliche Lebensgemeinschaft - ein Überblick', *NZ*, 1995, at p. 49.

3 M. NEUMAYR, 'Neue Regeln für nichteheliche Lebensgemeinschaften? Von den öffentlich-rechtlichen Folgen einer Lebensgemeinschaft im Außenverhältnis bis zum "Zivilpakt"', in: Österreichischer Juristentag (ed.), *Zivilrecht - Neue Regelungen für nichteheliche Lebensgemeinschaften*, Manzsche Verlags- und Universitätsbuchhandlung, Vienna, 2013, pp. 119-136, at p. 129.

4 Section 14 Austrian Tenancy Act stipulates that after the death of one partner the other partner is entitled to step into the tenancy agreement. Section 5 para. 1 Austrian Condominium Act allows two natural persons to jointly purchase a condominium.

relationships gave rise to – at least partly – the act amending family law in 2009.[5]

In 2004 the Austrian Green Party presented its idea of a 'civil pact' *(Zivilpakt)* and submitted a proposal for a respective statute in 2005.[6] In contrast to a marriage the civil pact should have been easier to terminate without any significant consequences; in terms of inheritance the civil pact would have been treated similar to the marriage.[7] In 2009, the judicial committee finally voted on the proposal, but it did not reach the necessary majority and was therefore rejected.[8]

BELGIUM

Even though informal relationships are still not regulated in Belgian family law as such, 1989/1990 was an important turning point for their recognition.[9]

Before 1989, informal relationships were not recognised in Belgian law; reference was often made to a formula attributed to Napoleon Bonaparte during the preparatory works of the *Code civil*: '*Les concubins se passent de la loi, la loi se désintéresse d'eux*'.[10] But rather than being ignored as 'neutral', informal relationships were approached negatively. In 1958, the Supreme Court considered that the legislature had necessarily refused to consider the benefits from a *de facto* cohabitation as legitimate interests, as it had made marriage the essential foundation of the family.[11] In 1967 the Supreme Court considered that benefits from a non-adulterous *de facto* cohabitation were not necessarily illegitimate, even though informal

[5] See S. FERRARI, 'Rechtsregeln für nichteheliches Zusammenleben in Österreich', in: I. KROPPENBERG et al. (eds.), *Rechtsregeln für nichteheliches Zusammenleben*, Gieseking Verlag, Vienna, 2009, pp. 167-206, at p. 175.

[6] Available at: www.parlament.gv.at/PAKT/VHG/XXII/A/A_00712/imfname_049597.pdf.

[7] J. CORNIDES, 'Alles gleich? Gesetzesinitiativen zur Schaffung eines Zivilpaktes und einer Eingetragenen Partnerschaft', *JBl*, 2008, at p. 287; M. NEUMAYR, 'Neue Regeln für nichteheliche Lebensgemeinschaften? Von den öffentlich-rechtlichen Folgen einer Lebensgemeinschaft im Außenverhältnis bis zum "Zivilpakt"', in: Österreichischer Juristentag (ed.), *Zivilrecht – Neue Regelungen für nichteheliche Lebensgemeinschaften*, Manzsche Verlags- und Universitätsbuchhandlung, Vienna, 2013, pp. 119-136, at p. 131.

[8] Available at: www.parlament.gv.at/PAKT/VHG/XXIV/I/I_00562/fname_174191.pdf.

[9] A. HEYVAERT, *Het personen- en gezinsrecht ont(k)leed*, Kluwer, Mechelen, 2002, at n°s 434 et seq.; F. SWENNEN, *Het personen- en familierecht. Identiteit en verwantschap vanuit juridisch perspectief*, Intersentia, Antwerp, 2015, at n° 679.

[10] Ph. MALAURIE, 'Mariage et concubinage en droit français contemporain', *Arch. phil. dr.* 1975, at p. 19.

[11] Cass. 21 April 1958, *Pas.* 1958, I, 921.

relationships were not recognised by law.[12] Any benefit from an adulterous *de facto* cohabitation, however, was necessarily incompatible with public policy.[13] The surviving partner of a still married deceased partner consequently could not claim damages from the person liable for the car accident in which the partner had died.

In 1989, the Supreme Court concluded that the illegitimacy of an adulterous *de facto* cohabitation only existed vis-à-vis the spouse, and not vis-à-vis a third party who is liable in tort for a car accident in which a cohabitant died. The surviving cohabitant consequently had a legitimate interest in claiming damages.[14] The legitimacy of interests from an adulterous, and *a fortiori* non-adulterous, cohabitation was confirmed in 1990.[15] The legal recognition of *de facto* cohabitation is a logical pendant of a 1987 reform since which marital and extramarital parentage are treated equally, following the Marckx judment of the ECtHR.[16]

Since 1989, informal relationships are increasingly taken into account in public and private family law regulations. This evolution started in public family law, particularly in social security law and in tax law. By cohabiting instead of marrying, partners could avoid certain burdens and the legislature consequently equated cohabitation with marriage. Afterwards, equal treatment was introduced with regard to benefits too, and also in private family law.

BULGARIA

Until 1991 informal relationships between a couple were considered as a crime if this entailed a formal family being abandoned (Bulgarian Penal Code, Art. 180, repealed in 1991). The only legal effect of *de facto* relationships regulated by the family legislation was and still is the establishment of parental rights and duties only after the establishment of parenthood.

The debates among experts as to whether to enact legislation on factual relationships started at the end of the 1990s. The debates have been influenced by the doctrinal discussions and the changes in legislation in

12 Cass. 26 June 1967, *RW* 1967-68, 786.
13 Cass. 19 December 1978, *RW* 1978-79, 1709.
14 Cass. 1 February 1989, *Pas.* 1989, I, 582.
15 Cass. 15 February 1990, *JT* 1990, 216. Justice of the Peace Bilzen 30 September 1991, *T.vred.* 1992, 16 (an adulterous cohabitation was contrary to public policy and the cohabitants' joint tenancy was null and void).
16 ECtHR, *Marckx v. Belgium*, No. 6833/74, 13.6.1979.

European states.[17] An experts' group was established at the Ministry of Justice to prepare a Draft Family Code exactly on the eve of the accession of Bulgaria to the EU (2006-2007). The period was marked by the Europeanization of Bulgarian legislation during the pre-accession negotiations and the feeling of permissiveness was strong. Statistical data provided evidence of an increase in the number of factual relationships between couples of different sex. In such a context the Draft Family Code proposed a modest regulation on informal relationships: the registration of an informal relationship, no regulation of relations between partners and limited provisions concerning the consequences of the termination of an informal relationship:

> 'Article 12:
> (1) The factual spousal relationship between a man and a woman has legal consequences in cases stipulated by legislation.
> (2) The factual spousal relationship may be registered according to the stipulations of the Civil Registration Act. The application for registration should be submitted by both partners and the registration should be made with the recorded address.
> (3) The termination of the factual spousal relationship may be declared by one partner only.'

One of the admired proposals (and maybe the only one which was admired) was to extend the scope of application of the presumption of fatherhood to informal relationships. There was also a proposal to assign the maintenance obligation to a partner after the termination of the informal relationship.

The proposed regulation was challenged before the Commission on Protection against Discrimination on the ground of discrimination based on sex (Claim No. 12-20-30/11.04.2008 by Jemini – an NGO on the rights of same-sex partners). The Commission upheld the fact that the provisions in the Draft Family Code relating to the sex of the partners was discriminatory: Recommendation No. 2/01.07.2008. Its Chair declared: 'a same-sex factual relationship could be regulated in Bulgaria if the legislature would agree with the Commission's arguments', namely that the provisions related to marriage and a factual relationship had to remain gender neutral.

---

[17] A proposal was made in 1999 within the Draft Family Code that has never been publicly discussed.

Despite this strong intervention in support, the Draft invoked rather negative comments by some active proponents of the traditional family law institutions. The Christian Church also became involved by challenging the proposed regulation on the *de facto* family.[18] The debate was concentrated around two considerations: a weakening of the institution of marriage and opening the door to same-sex unions. The following sentiments were at the core of the debate:

- Informal relationships would jeopardise the institution of marriage – 'the message we send to society after providing legal effect to cohabitation is that marriage is useless and the heterosexual informal relationships would be followed by homosexual cohabitation or marriage';[19]
- The need to respect the choice of unmarried couples and not to intervene supported by the not very strong interest among informal couples in being involved in the debate;
- The new Code would legalise polygamy, incest, and same-sex relationships including their ability to adopt children.[20]

The debate resulted in the withdrawal of the proposals from the Bill by a consensus reached between the governing left-wing socialist party (a member of whom chaired the Parliamentary Legal Commission) and the opposition, the right-wing conservative party.[21]

CROATIA

Croatia legally recognised informal relationships between heterosexual couples – cohabitations – during the late 1970s when the Marriage and Family Relations Act (1978) was adopted. This Act provided couples who lived in a life union for a long period of time with property and maintenance rights identical to those provided to spouses.[22] At that time,

---

18 See: semeistvo.bg/index.php?option=com_content&task=view&id=238#, 20.11.2008.

19 For instance, see the post of 25.09.2008: www.legalworld.bg/11545.izhvyrliat-fakticheskoto-syjitelstvo-ot-noviia-semeen-kodeks.html.

20 Luben Dilov, an MP from the right-wing opposition, stated: 'If the idea of the informal family is a preface to the same-sex marriage, let us say this', at: www.mediapool.bg/deputati-v-spor-za-semeiniya-zhivot-bez-brak-i-gei-sazhitelstvoto-news144020.html.

21 Martin Dimitrov, an MP from the right-wing opposition, declared that as 70% of informal relationships end in marriages, the new regulation on cohabitation would make marriage less attractive, thus ruining the value of marriage at: www.mediapool.bg/deputati-v-spor-za-semeiniya-zhivot-bez-brak-i-gei-sazhitelstvoto-news144020.html.

22 M. ALINCIC and A. BAKARIC-MIHANOVIC, *Family Law*, Pravni fakultet Zagreb (Law School of Zagreb) Biblioteka Udžbenici i skripta, Zagreb, 1980, at p. 364.

Croatia was not an independent country but was part of the former Yugoslavia. It is possible that the socialist regime contributed to the fact that Croatia and other republics of the former Yugoslavia pioneered the development of the legal protection of informal relationships between heterosexual couples in Europe. Moreover, since the acquisition of its independence and a complete change of its political order, Croatia has been experiencing a constant expansion of the legal protection of informal relationships between heterosexual couples (cohabitations). Along with marriage, cohabitation is becoming a constitutional category which is legally regulated by the Croatian Constitution.[23] In substituting the Marriage and Family Relations Act (1978), the Family Act (1998) also gave cohabitants property and maintenance rights identical to those provided to spouses and the same rights and liabilities were retained in the 2003 Family Act.[24]

By now, cohabitation has taken its place not only in family law but in many other areas of the law as well. Since 2003, cohabitants have possessed the same inheritance rights and liabilities as spouses have,[25] since 2008 the same pension rights and obligations,[26] etc.

The constant extension of the legal effects of marriage to cohabitation has resulted in the full equality of marriage and cohabitation in the latest Croatian Family Act.[27] Art. 11 paragraph 2 of the Croatian Family Act prescribes that cohabitation:

> 'generates personal and property effects identical to those of a marital union and thus the former is, in an appropriate way, subject to the provisions of other laws governing the personal, property and other relations of spouses'.

Furthermore, Art. 11 paragraph 3 of the Croatian Family Act prescribes that:

---

23 Article 62, Croatian Constitution, Official Gazette 59/90.

24 M. Alincic, D. Hrabar, D. Jakovac-Lozic and A. Korac Graovac, *Family Law*, Narodne novine, Zagreb, 2007.

25 Official Gazette no. 48/03. See V. Belaj and A. Čulo, 'Inheritance Right of Cohabitants', *Pravni vjesnik*, 2007, pp. 121-137, and D. Hrabar, 'Family Law View on Inheritance Rights', *Hrvatska pravna revija*, 2003, pp. 74-84.

26 Supreme Court Judgment no. U-X/1457/2007, Official Gazette no. 43/07.

27 A full equalization of the legal effects of marriage and cohabitation has resulted from the amendment to the Draft Family Act 2013 proposed by social and liberal political parties. The purpose of the equalization of marriage and cohabitation referred to the abolition of any kind of discrimination which is based on the type of life union. www.sabor.hr/konacni-prijedlog-obiteljskog-zakona-drugo-citanje.

'unequal treatment of cohabitants in regard to an access to the benefits, privileges and liabilities provided to spouses, which is not justifiable on objective grounds and not necessary for their exercise, represents discrimination based on the family status'.

However, the Constitutional Court is currently deciding on the constitutionality of this legal provision.[28]

There are no significant proposals by relevant bodies for extending the legal protection of cohabitation that have failed to be adopted.

The legal protection of homosexual partners in same-sex informal partnerships was first introduced in Croatia in 2003 when the Same-Sex Unions Act (Official Gazette no. 116/03) was adopted. According to the Croatian Same-Sex Unions Act, same-sex partners who lived together in a stable relationship for at least three years had the same property and maintenance rights as spouses had. Since the Croatian Same-Sex Unions Act did not prescribe the possibility to formalise (register) same-sex unions which would put homosexual partners in a similar legal position as that of spouses, Croatia has recently replaced the Croatian Same-Sex Unions Act with the Croatian Partnership Act.

The Croatian Partnership Act puts same-sex partners and spouses in the same legal position regarding all of their rights and liabilities except for those referring to legal relations with children. According to the Croatian Partnership Act, same-sex partners who have not registered their union (same-sex informal partners) shall have the same property and personal rights and duties as same-sex registered partners have. Also, homosexual and heterosexual informal couples (cohabitation) have the same rights and liabilities concerning inheritance tax, the pension system, the social welfare system, compulsory health insurance and healthcare, rights and liabilities arising from employment, access to public and commercial services and a public legal position.

There are no significant proposals by relevant bodies for extending the legal protection of cohabitation that have failed to be adopted.

[28] Official Gazette No. 5/2014.

CZECH REPUBLIC

To begin with, it is important to look at the difference in understanding the concept of 'family' in the communist era and after 1989. In the past a family was a unit, a base for the whole socialist society and parents were obliged to raise, teach and prepare their children according to then communist ideology. People got married quite early and the first child was born after a year or two of marriage. The number of divorced couples was rather low. Of course, there were couples that lived in an informal relationship, mainly old and divorced or widowed, but not much attention was given to them because this kind of relationship did not perfectly fit the ideology. When Act no. 265/1949 Coll., on Family Law, was adopted, it was not possible to get a divorce without the other spouse's consent. This legislation resulted in disharmony between marital status *de facto* and *de iure* and in an increase in factual marriages, meaning that besides the marriage that could not be terminated, one or both of the spouses had lived with someone else in an informal relationship. Although informal relationships were tolerated, it was still a complete family that was considered as a 'guarantee' for social order. After the so-called 'Velvet revolution' in 1989 when the communist era ended and people learnt to live in a democratic system, social traditions and habits were turned upside down. The number of divorces went up rapidly as well as the number of people living in an informal relationship. Despite the fact that fewer children were born, the number of children born outside marriage increased. Nowadays marital status, family and informal relationship-related legislation is rather liberal. As was mentioned above, there are not many provisions referring directly to informal relationships, which means that there are even fewer opportunities for any reforms of this kind. It is possible to say that the legislature does not have a need to adopt any special law or to drastically change current legislation, since it does not show any crucial defects or gaps.

DENMARK

In 1980 the Danish Marriage Committee submitted a report on unmarried cohabitants. The committee rejected the idea of a comprehensive regulation for non-marital cohabitation, as the Committee did not want to create a 'second class marriage'. Instead the committee suggested the introduction of rules in a few areas where special protection was needed. These rules were less far-reaching than those applicable to married couples. Developments have shown that the attitude of the Marriage Committee was too conservative. Since then legislation on cohabitation has been gradually amended with consequences that the committee never imagined.

The Danish Inheritance Act Committee proposed provisions on inheritance for cohabitants in Report No. 1473/2006. The Committee proposed that cohabitants should be able to make an 'extended cohabitant's will' for each other's benefit. Such a regime would be very similar to that applicable to married spouses who have completely separate property. The Committee also proposed that relationships that could demonstrate a certain stability should qualify for a legal right of inheritance. In addition to the requirement for the parties to have, have had, or to be expecting a child together, the Committee proposed that they must have cohabited for at least two years. It was proposed that the lawful inheritance portion should amount to one-fourth of the estate, up to DKK 500,000. The rules on a legal right of inheritance should be dispositive. Where cohabitants had no children or had not lived together for two years, the commission proposed that it should be possible in exceptional cases for the surviving party to be granted a right of inheritance.

In considering the Committee's proposals, the Danish Ministry of Justice argued that there is a difference between marriage and unmarried cohabitation. By entering into a marriage, the parties are making a choice which has a number of legal consequences, both during their lives together and after the death of a spouse, while parties establishing an unmarried cohabitation relationship are making no such choice. Furthermore, the Ministry argued that there may be couples who have chosen unmarried cohabitation in order to avoid the legal consequences of marriage and that that choice must be respected. Finally, the Ministry pointed to the need for clear rules and to the difficulty of determining whether a cohabitation relationship was similar to a marriage.[29] For these reasons, the legal rights of inheritance for unmarried cohabitants were not incorporated in the bill that was submitted to the Danish Parliament. Thus, 'extended cohabitants' wills' were introduced.

ENGLAND AND WALES

Much of the developments in the heterosexual context were made through case law in Rent Act and Housing Act cases. This is a brief

[29] See also J. ASLAND et al., *Nordisk Samboerrett*, Gyldendal Norsk Forlag, Oslo, 2014, at p. 45-46.

summary of how progress was made in legally acknowledging informal (mainly couple) relationships 'as a member of the tenant's family' through the courts in the context of allowing the surviving partner to succeed to the tenancy of the family home:

- *Brock v Wollams* [1949] 2 KB 388
  Accepted informally adopted daughter of tenant as a member of the family
- *Gammans v Ekins* [1950] 2 KB 328
  Rejected cohabitant with no children
- *Hawes v Evenden* [1953] 2 All ER 737
  Accepted mistress of 12 years with children
- *Dyson Holdings Ltd v Fox* [1976] QB 503
  Lord Denning accepted cohabitant with no children
- *Joram Developments Ltd v Sharratt* [1979] 1 WLR 928
  Quasi aunt and nephew members of household not a family
- *Watson v Lucas* [1980] 3 All ER 607
  Accepted cohabitant lived with a man notwithstanding that he remained married to his wife
- *Chios Property Investment Ltd v Lopez* [1988] Fam Law 384
  Confirmed Denning approach, stressing the importance of a 'sufficient state of permanence and stability' having been reached to constitute a family
- *Fitzpatrick v Sterling H A Ltd* [2001] 1 AC 27
  House of Lords rejected same-sex cohabitant as 'spouse' but accepted him as 'member of tenant's family' (despite *Harrogate BC v Simpson* [1986] 2 FLR 91 approved by ECHR in *S v UK* 47 DR 275 in the secure council tenancy context)
- *Mendoza v Ghaidan* [2002] EWCA Civ 1533, [2003] Ch 380
  Court of Appeal accepted same-sex cohabitant as 'spouse' on the basis that not to do so was post-Human Rights Act 1998 in breach of Art. 8 and Art. 14 ECHR
- *Ghaidan v. Godin-Mendoza* [2004] UKHL 30, [2004] AC 557
  On 21st June 2004, the House of Lords dismissed the appeal and endorsed the decision of the Court of Appeal.

Other than the extension of the term 'cohabitant' to same-sex couples living as civil partners, which extended existing cohabitant rights to that community, the last substantive reforms extending new rights and remedies to different-sex cohabitants took place in the late 1980s to mid 1990s. The English Housing Act 1988 extended the definition of spouse to cohabiting couples in the private and independent housing sector tenancy succession context. Subsequently, an amendment to the English Inheritance (Provision for Family and Dependants) Act 1975 by the English Succession (Reform) Act 1995 extended those eligible to apply for financial provision to cohabiting partners of the deceased on less generous terms than that available to spouses. The English Family Law Act 1996 extended occupation order rights to cohabitants in the domestic violence context and also for the first time enabled a non-tenant cohabitant to apply for the rented family home to be transferred into their sole name on relationship breakdown, although applied different criteria to the married context.

ESTONIA

Already in his memorandum[30] sent to the Minister of Justice in 2011, the Chancellor of Justice remarked that a permanent cohabitation between persons of the same gender should fall within the protection granted by the fundamental rights of the family, so where such cohabitation is legally unregulated, this is not in accordance with the Estonian Constitution.

On October 9, 2014, the Estonian Parliament adopted the Estonian Registered Partnership Act,[31] which was validated by the President only a few hours after its adoption. The proceedings of the draft legislation in Parliament polarised society and attracted extraordinary public attention. It was the first draft legislation which gave an opportunity to partners in an informal relationship to regulate mutual legal relations and legal relations with third parties (a cohabitation is gender-neutral and a cohabitation contract can be concluded between two persons of the same as well as of different genders). Numerous appeals were made with regard to the draft legislation by citizens' associations, religious organisations, trade unions, different societies and private persons,[32] which were received by the leading committee before the first reading as well as beween the first and the second reading. As for the different opinions and appeals, they are mostly positions expressing a certain general mentality.[33] The Pro Patria and Res Publica Union fractions

---

30 Available at: oiguskantsler.ee/sites/default/files/field_document2/6iguskantsleri_margukiri_samasooliste_isikute_peresuhe.pdf.

31 Kooseluseadus. - RT I, 16.10.2014, 1 (in Estonian), available in English at: www.riigiteataja.ee/en/eli/ee/Riigikogu/act/527112014001/consolide.

32 The procedural course of the draft legislation can be followed in Estonian. Available at: www.riigikogu.ee/?op=ems&page=eelnou&eid=ea84e71c-291a-4c91-88b0-bd64af650d21&.

33 Explanatory memorandum to the draft legislation of the Estonian Registered

submitted a draft legislation to Parliament, according to which a referendum should have been organised with regard to the adoption of the Estonian Registered Partnership Act. This draft legislation was rejected by Parliament.

FINLAND

The status of cohabitees has already been discussed in Finland since the mid-1970s and 1980s, when the number of cohabitee relationships started to increase rapidly. In this time period, legal effect to cohabitee relationships was mainly given in the area of social law and tax law. In 1984, the rights and obligations of cohabitee partners were also taken into account in housing legislation. This concerned, at first, only rental apartments and since 1990 also right-of-occupancy housing (*asumisoikeus-asunto/bostadsrättsbostad*). However, cohabitation does not constitute rights or obligations according to the legislation on limited liability housing companies (*asunto-osakeyhtiö/bostadsaktiebolag*), which are, together with real estate housing, the most common housing options based on ownership.

In the main area of private law, cohabitation has not been recognised as a relationship that can be accorded rights or obligations according to legislation until very recently. There is, however, some case law from the 1980s and 1990s on long-lasting cohabitation partners being successful in bringing actions on the basis of unfair enrichment or ownership (e.g. KKO 1988:85 and KKO 1993:168). In the context of the reform of the Finnish Code of Inheritance in 1983, it was suggested that, similar to an engaged person, the surviving cohabitee partner could receive support from the estate of the deceased partner in order to ensure his or her subsistence, albeit not becoming an heir. However, this proposal was not accepted until almost 30 years later in 2011, when the general Finnish Act on the Dissolution of the Household of Cohabiting Partners (26/2011) was enacted and the related amendments to the Finnish Code of Inheritance (40/1965) were agreed upon. The Finnish Cohabitation Act also clarified the criteria for an action for unfair enrichment based on long-lasting informal relationships. Since then, no new steps have been taken, although calls for the need to harmonise the legal effects of cohabitation across all administrative sectors are frequently made.

Partnership Act. Procedure in the leading committee between the first and second reading. Available at: www.riigikogu.ee/?op=ems&page=eelnou&eid=ea84e71c-291a-4c91-88b0-bd64af650d21& (in Estonian).

FRANCE

Initially, the Code Napoléon 1804 did not regulate informal relationships at all. '*Concubins*' (the partners in an informal relationship) were supposed to 'ignore' the law, so that the law should also 'ignore' them. However, little by little, case law began to accept that some legal effects could be derived from the existence of a stable informal relationship. For the Court of cassation, until Law Act no. 99-944 of 15 November 1999, a '*concubinage*' could only be an informal relationship between a man and a woman.[34] The court recognised a right to compensation for the surviving partner in case of a fatal accident caused by a third person,[35] even if the relationship was adulterous.[36] Not only economic loss, but also non-pecuniary damage could be claimed.

The Court of cassation also held that in the case of the breakup of a relationship, a partner can claim compensation on the basis of general provisions (unjust enrichment, tort law, *de facto* partnership).

In 1999, Law Act no. 99-944 of 15 November 1999 created the *pacte civil de solidarité* (PACS), which is a registered partnership between opposite or same-sex partners. It was amended by Law Act no. 2006-728 of 23 June 2006,[37] which extended the effects of the PACS and therefore brought it more into line with a marriage.

Law Act no. 99-944 of 15 November 1999 also introduced in the French Civil Code a definition of 'informal relationships' (*concubinage)*. According to Art. 515-8, it is '*une union de fait, caractérisée par une vie commune présentant un caractère de stabilité et de continuité, entre deux personnes, de sexe différent ou de même sexe, qui vivent en couple*' (a factual union, characterised by common life with the character of stability and continuity, between two persons of the opposite or same sex, living as a couple). This new provision introduced an important change since now a

---

[34] Cass. Soc., 11 July 1989, two decisions, *JCP G* 1990, II, 21 553 with note MEUNIER; Cass. Civ. III, 17 December 1997, no. 95-20779, *Bull. Civ.* III, no 225 ('*Mais attendu qu'ayant retenu, à bon droit, que le concubinage ne pouvait résulter que d'une relation stable et continue ayant l'apparence du mariage, donc entre un homme et une femme, la cour d'appel n'a violé ni l'article 26 du Pacte international relatif aux droits civils et politiques, ni l'article 8, alinéa 1er, de la Convention européenne de sauvegarde des droits de l'homme et des libertés fondamentales*'). However, some first-instance courts had ruled that the partner in a same-sex relationship could claim compensation for the damage caused to him or her due to the accidental death of his or her partner (TGI Belfort, 21 July 1995).

[35] Cass. Ch. mixte, 27 February 1970, *Dangereux*.

[36] Cass. Crim., 19 June 1975, *Bérigaud*, *D.* 1975, jur., p. 679, with note TUNC.

[37] *JORF* 24 June 2006, at p. 9513.

concubinage can also be regarded as existing between two men or two women, which the Court of cassation refused to admit.[38]

In parallel with these evolutions in the civil law, several specific provisions contained in numerous pieces of legislation and Codes extended to partners in an informal relationship (*concubins*) and to partners in a PACS, rights which had already been granted to spouses (social security, labour law, judicial assistance and representation, assisted reproduction). See the examples provided under Question 2.

GERMANY

After 1949, the year in which the Basic Law entered into force, there has been a continual discussion on informal relationships. Case law and the discussion in literature strongly stressed constitutional law arguments. Particularly in the reform debate of the 1990s, the protection of marriage was not seen as an insurmountable bar to a reform. However, it was widely accepted that an informal cohabitation should only grant protection of a lesser degree than that granted by marriage under matrimonial law (see Question 6). The position that an informal relationship is not recognised by civil law and does not deserve protection is now no longer defended.[39] The former argument of immorality is similarly no longer put forward.[40]

The possibility of introducing a comprehensive statute has been discussed. However, the opinion that there should be only reforms on individual matters has dominated. The main question is generally whether a different treatment of marriage and of informatal cohabitation is justified. In the past the non-marital nature of cohabitation was discussed mainly under the heading of 'unmarried cohabitation' (*nichteheliches Zusammenleben* or *nichteheliche Lebensgemeinschaft*). Today increasingly more scholars prefer the more neutral *faktische Lebensgemein-*

[38] See also *Conseil d'État* (the highest administrative court), 4 May 2001, *Association Promouvoir,* D. 2002, somm. p. 537 with note LEMOULAND: the nullity of the measure taken by the SNCF (railway company) to issue a '*carte couple*' to same-sex partners in an informal relationship before the coming into force of the Law Act of 15 November 1999.

[39] In more detail H. GRZIWOTZ, *Nichteheliche Lebensgemeinschaft*, Beck, Munich, 2014, at § 5 No. 11.

[40] Cf. R. FRANK, 'The status of cohabitation in the legal systems of West Germany and other West European countries', *The American Journal of Comparative Law,* 1985, at p. 185 et seq.

schaft ('*de facto* community of life') which places a greater stress on the existence of a *de facto* relationship.[41]

The reform of the law of parent and child relations had an indirect effect on the issue. This reform basically led to a uniform law for all children which was adopted as of 1 July 1998.[42] There is also a trend towards equal treatment of all parents.

GREECE

Law 1329/1983 gave indirect recognition to extra-marital cohabitations as 'free unions', and this recognition was continued in Law 3500/2006 on protection from domestic violence. The most important legislative development to date has been Law 3719/2008, which introduced the cohabitation pact between heterosexual couples as a diluted form of marriage. The hesitancy one observes in this area is due, in our opinion, to the reaction of powerful political and social groups who see a threat to the institution of marriage in its traditional form.

HUNGARY

The first normative provisions on cohabitation based upon the Hungarian Supreme Court's case law were included the Civil Code of 1959 in 1977. The Act's explanation underlined that a specific regulation on persons living in a common household was justified by the frequency of this unmarried companionship. The Civil Code of 1959 had contained two provisions from 1977, one concerned the definition of cohabitation, another was concerned with the rules on cohabitants' community of property. These rules were amended in 1996 when the restriction of cohabitation to different-sex persons was terminated and the door was opened to same-sex persons (via a decision by the Constitutional Court, see in detail the answer to Question 6).[43] The rules under the Civil Code of 1959 were last modified in 2009. The definition was made more comprehensive and the Register on Cohabitant's Statements was established (this is dealt with in detail in the answer to Question 5).

---

41 See N. DETHLOFF, *Familienrecht*, Beck, Munich, 2012, at p. 239 et seq. § 8 No. 239 et seq.; M. LÖHNIG, 'Anh. zu §§ 1297 et seq.', in: J. VON STAUDINGER, *Kommentar zum Bürgerlichen Gesetzbuch*, Sellier-de-Gruyter, Berlin, 2012, at No. 10.

42 See N. DETHLOFF, 'Parental Rights and Responsibilities in Germany', *Family Law Quarterly*, 2005, at p. 315 et seq.

43 Concerning the detailed history of cohabitation in Hungary, see O. SZEIBERT-ERDŐS, 'Unmarried Partnerships in Hungary', in: K. BOELE-WOELKI (ed.), *Common Core and Better Law in European Family Law*, Intersentia, Antwerp, 2005, at p. 313-326.

The recodification of a new Civil Code began in the late 1990s. The Concept and the Regulation Programme for the Civil Code were published in 2003 and they expressed the necessity of guaranteeing further rights for cohabitants but only in such a way that the institution of marriage is not weakened. It has to be remarked that the aspect of provisions on cohabitation was one of the most debated issues from very early on, primarily due to the fact that a regulation on cohabitation was planned to be included, in its entirety, in the Family Law Book. The original idea which prevailed during the whole period of the recodification [44] was that the rules on cohabitation should follow matrimonial rules. This would have guaranteed the family-like feature of cohabitation.

According to the Programme the differences concerning the default property regime of cohabitants would have been retained. While the default matrimonial property regime was planned to preserve the community of property regime, the default property regime of cohabitants was to be drafted so as to avoid the community of property. The proposed regime prevailed so it is currently in effect in the Hungarian Civil Code just as the definition of cohabitation which was also retained.

Two aspects of financial rights were stressed in the Regulation, namely the maintenance of a former cohabitant and the use of the common dwelling after separation. Concerning both issues the proposed regulation aimed to reward both the common child of cohabitants and the long-lasting duration of the cohabitation. Only one year of community life was considered to be sufficient when having a common child, while without a common child ten years of living together would have been the basis of further legal consequences. When the draft Civil Code was submitted to Parliament the original ideas were contained in the draft. At a later stage before Parliament in late 2012, the necessity and rationale of regulating cohabitation as a family law relationship was questioned and debated as being in contrast with the attitude to marriage and any partnership outside of marriage. Lastly, the regulations on cohabitation were divided into two sections. The contractual character of cohabitation was held to be maintained while the importance of a common child was emphasised. The general rules are currently contained in the Sixth Book and the specific rules determining family law

[44] A. KŐROS and K. MAKAI, 'Családjog' ('Family Law'), in: L. VEKÁS(ed.), *Szakértői Javaslat az új Polgári Törvénykönyv tervezetéhez (Experts' Proposal for the Draft of the New Civil Code)*, Complex, Budapest, 2008, at p. 465-479.

consequences can be found in the Fourth Book (see also the answer to Question 2).

It has to be remarked that commentaries and the legal literature are of the opinion that cohabitation has a family-like character. The Regulation proposed some rights of inheritance in the case of intestate succession for the surviving cohabitant after at least ten years of cohabitation and mainly concerning the usage of the commonly used dwelling. This right was abandoned at the parliamentary stage which has been considered to be unequivocally unfair by judicial commentators.

REPUBLIC OF IRELAND

Informal relationships were not regulated or recognised in Irish law prior to the Irish 2010 Act. This Act was intended to recognise cohabitant status and give cohabitants rights in law.

The Irish Children and Family Relationships Bill is the most recent proposal for reform of the rules regarding informal relationships between couples. It represents the most significant change in family law in a generation and attempts to reflect the social reality of contemporary family life in Ireland. Until recent decades, family life in Ireland has been synonymous with marriage. However, increasing recognition of marriage breakdown, changes in relationship formation patterns, economic change and the influence of international law have all contributed to the increasing fluidity and diversification of family forms. The new framework that will be implemented following the passage of this Bill will not only radically overhaul many existing rules, it will create new rights for parents, both biological and social, and, most critically, for children. As a result, it represents an important milestone on the road to recognition of children as rights holders.

The Bill can be seen as providing various different pathways to parentage. This is connected to legal recognition of the changing family landscape in modern Ireland: diversity in families is ever more common. These families deserve recognition, security, and equity. Allowing for parentage to be legally confirmed and recognised is an important element in this. It is vital for children, in that it invests those who are already, or who are likely to, provide for, support and care for the child and their development with the rights, responsibilities and legally consequential duties attendant upon parenthood. This can be seen in such Heads as 5-7 and 8-13 of the Bill.

Issues that are addressed in the Bill include: presumptions of paternity; determination of parentage; declarations of parentage; parentage and legal issues in the context of assisted human reproduction ('AHR'); DNA testing to determine parentage; the establishment of a national donor-conceived persons register; issues relating to guardianship, custody, access and maintenance; reform of court practices and adoption, among other issues. For the first time, the Bill introduces automatic guardianship for non-marital fathers, provided certain cohabitation requirements have been satisfied.

Almost of all the proposals contained in the draft Bill are progressive and given that there has been only piecemeal reform to the Irish law in relation to the family outside marriage since the Irish Guardianship of Infants Act 1964, this consolidated approach is to be welcomed and should considerably improve the position regarding informal relationships between a couple.

ITALY

Many bills on informal partnerships have been proposed, but not passed, in recent legislatures. The Italian Parliament has up to now never shown a genuinely positive attitude toward passing a law on this matter.

During the XIVth legislature (30 May 2001-27 April 2006) two bills among all those presented must be recalled here. The first was proposal n. 3308 of the Acts of the *Camera dei deputati* (proposal by De Simone and others, 23 October 2002) which set forth the introduction of registered unions, civil unions, and *de facto* cohabitations (*convivenze di fatto*). The second bill (n. 3296, proposal by Grillini and others) envisaged 'civil solidarity agreements' (*patti civili di solidarietà*).

Subsequently, during the XVth legislature (18 April 2006-28 April 2008) ten draft bills were put before the *Camera dei deputati* and nine before the *Senato*, in addition to another proposal by the government of the time (signed by Bindi-Pollastrini, 7/8 February 2007).

The most convincing attempt to pass a law on informal partnerships was the latter of the above. Entitled 'The rights and duties of cohabiting couples' (*Diritti e doveri delle coppie stabilmente conviventi*, hence the proposed acronym Di.Co.), it was also intended to apply to same-sex couples and outlined a thorough regulation of cohabitation, foreseeing the rights and duties arising automatically therefrom. Under the proposal cohabitation was to be proved through the Civil Status Registry and rules were suggested on matters of succession, maintenance, lease contracts, and support in the event of illness. The project was eventually abandoned, however, after criticism from various sides had been aroused: there was substantial criticism of the very notion of regulating cohabitation by those who were against introducing any legal institution other than marriage. Moreover, many points regarding the machinery and technicalities of the bill – for instance, the requisites defining and the evidence proving cohabitation – appeared to be unclear and controversial.[45] Towards the end of the legislature, the president of the *Commissione giustizia* of the Senate, Cesare Salvi, elaborated a text unifying all the proposals presented in previous years. The resulting amalgamation referred to a 'contract of supportive union' (*contratto di unione solidale*) to be signed by the couple in the presence of a notary or a justice of the peace and then registered. This proposal was, however, never discussed in the Senate due to the prior dissolution of Parliament.

During the following legislature, the XVIth (29 April 2008-14 March 2013), no fewer than seven other proposals were presented, all having a similar content to one previous bill or another.

LATVIA

Though Latvian national legislation does not have a general legal order for informal relationships, this issue has been repeatedly raised in recent years.

The Ministry of Justice action strategy 2007-2009 indicated that the Latvian Civil Law lacks a legal order for unregistered partnerships. Thus, it was decided that someone should be given the task of preparing a concept about the legal order for unregistered partnerships.[46] In 2008 the Ministry of Justice signed a contract with Eversheds Bitans Law Office for the conducting of a legal study to identify the existing issues and challenges in the sphere of male/female unregistered partnerships, as well as to offer possible solutions to the identified issues in order to create an applicable legal order for unregistered partnerships in the

---

45 B. DE FILIPPIS, 'La famiglia non matrimoniale nelle storia del diritto', in: AA. VV., *La separazione nella famiglia di fatto*, Cedam, Padua, 2014, at p. 64 et seq.; for a more general overview see R. TOMMASINI, 'La famiglia di fatto', in: M. BESSONE (ed.), *Trattato di diritto privato*, Giappichelli, Turin, 1999, at p. 404 et seq.

46 The Ministry of Justice action strategy 2007-2009. Available at: jpa.gov.lv/uploads/filedir/strategjija.pdf.

Latvian legal system. As a result a legal study was made on 'Male and female registered partnership legislation in Europe and Latvia'.[47]

In May 2011 the Human Rights and Public Affairs Committee of the Saeima (Parliament of the Republic of Latvia) and non-governmental organisations called on the Ombudsman to pay attention to the legal order of partnership and a joint meeting was held.[48]

In 2011 the Ombudsman created the Advisory Council on the legal order for partnership. The aim of this Advisory Council was to evaluate, amongst lawyers and experts, the proposals on the legal order of partnership and the need for amendments to the national laws and other legislative acts. The Ombudsman also widened the issue to include unregistered cohabitation (union outside marriage), thus taking account of the broader interests of society. At that time it was indicated that, according to the statistics, in the past 20 years the number of children born outside marriage had increased from 17 to 45 percent.[49]

The work of the Ombudsman's Advisory Council concluded with the Ombudsman's opinion that the majority of Latvian society was not ready to equate same-sex partnerships to the institution of marriage nor to normatively recognise homosexual relationships as an acceptable lifestyle. Therefore it was suggested that amendments should be made in several legislative acts that would bring the legal protection of a people living together outside marriage closer to the legal protection accorded to spouses. On 26 January 2012 the Ombudsman sent his opinion on the legal order of partnership to the Human Rights and Public Affairs Committee of the Saeima and the Legal Affairs Committee of the Saeima, as well as to the Cabinet of Ministers and called for amendments in several legal provisions relevant to: the protection of the rights of patients; prevention of conflicts of interest; procedural law; a person's social rights; and the right to information.[50]

---

47 Eversheds Bitans Law Office, Legal study on 'Male and female registered partnership legislation in Europe and Latvia' 2008.

48 The Ombudsman of the Repubic of Latvia letter No.1-8/4. of 26 January 2012. Available at: tiesibsargs.lv/par-mums/konsultativas-padomes/par-partnerattiecibu-tiesisko-regulejumu/.

49 The Ombudsman of the Repubic of Latvia letter No.1-8/4. of 26 January 2012. Available at: tiesibsargs.lv/par-mums/konsultativas-padomes/par-partnerattiecibu-tiesisko-regulejumu/.

50 The Ombudsman of the Repubic of Latvia letter No.1-8/4. of 26 January 2012. Available at: tiesibsargs.lv/par-mums/konsultativas-padomes/par-partnerattiecibu-tiesisko-regulejumu/.

The Cabinet of Ministers, in the response letter to the Ombudsman, analysed the legal provisions suggested by the Ombudsman and indicated that, for most of them, no amendments were needed because it was possible to interpret the existing legal provisions in a way that would cover people living together in a union outside marriage. In certain cases it was noted that those applying the law could variously interpret the legal order contained in the law, for example, as previously mentioned, the right to refuse to testify in procedural laws. Consequently, amendments should be considered to the procedural laws to establish common procedural guarantees for persons who have a common household.

With regard to a person's social rights, an opinion was expressed that, in certain cases, legislative acts already provided legal protection for persons living together in a union outside marriage; for example, in Question 6, para. 4 of the first part of S. 74 of the Latvian Labour Law and the first part of S. 33 of the Latvian Law on Social Services and Social Assistance. At the same time it was indicated that it would be necessary to develop a concept for persons living together in a union outside marriage to be granted the right to receive the amounts of State social allowance calculated for disbursement that are not disbursed until the death of the recipient of the allowance (para. 5 S. 17 of the Latvian Law on State Social Allowances) and also the right to disbursement of a pension not received in relation to the death of the recipient of that pension and to a funeral allowance (para. 1 and 3, S. 37 of the Latvian Law on State Pensions).[51]

In turn, when the Ombudsman objected to the claim that the principle of legal equality could be ensured by way of interpretation (referencing the judgment of the Senate of the Supreme Court of the Republic of Latvia, Department of Civil Cases, of 1 February 2012 No. SKC-4/2012), the Cabinet of Ministers agreed that the issue of rights that should be assigned to the people living in a union outside marriage should be addressed through legislation, rather than being left to the Court. Also, it should be evaluated as to whether it was necessary to begin actively drafting a law on the legal order on partnership.[52]

---

51 Cabinet of Ministers letter No.18/TA-219 of 16 March 2012. Available at: tiesibsargs.lv/par-mums/konsultativas-padomes/par-partnerattiecibu-tiesisko-regulejumu/.

52 Cabinet of Ministers letter No.18/TA-219/5175 of 3 May 2012. Available at: tiesibsargs.lv/par-mums/konsultativas-padomes/par-partnerattiecibu-tiesisko-regulejumu/.

LITHUANIA

In analysing the legal regulation of informal relationships we should look at actual marital relations or what is otherwise called a factual marriage (cohabitation) in the context of the development of family law.[53] It has to be mentioned that the legislation in force in 1918-1940 did not regulate cohabitation at all. A factual marriage was most widely regulated in 1926 by the Code of Matrimony, Family and Foster Care, which was adopted in Lithuania on 1 December 1940. Its provisions accepted a factual marriage alongside the registered marriage. A factual marriage had to be established by a court ruling stating that 1) a man and a woman had kept house together, 2) did not hide their relationship from other persons, 3) the relationship was supported by documentary evidence, 4) they provided material support to each other, 5) they had children and raised and supported them. According to the norms of this Code a factual marriage could be established with reference to similar factors. However, the courts could only equate actual cohabitation with an actual marriage in two cases: 1) when establishing cohabitant's right to maintenance as a result of incapacity, and 2) when dividing property which had been acquired when living together. Not all relations were identified as a factual marriage, but only serious and enduring relations with the intention of forming a family. For several years a factual marriage was equated with a registered marriage, i.e. legal acts recognised both factual (not registered with the state institutions under the act of civil status) and registered marriages. In both cases the legal outcomes were the same. The legal regime of property acquired in a factual marriage obtained the same legal property status as in a registered marriage. On the 8th of July 1944 this situation was changed by a decree,[54] which abolished the legal recognition of factual marriages. Persons who had been living as factual cohabitants until the decree came into force, were allowed to register their marriage. In the process of registering their marriage they could indicate the beginning of their factual marriage. This date was then considered as the date on which marital rights and duties had originated. This legal act again acknowledged the importance of marriage registration bearing in mind that a factual marriage could endanger the

[53] I. KUDINAVIČIŪTĖ-MICHAILOVIENĖ, 'Unmarried cohabitation: Theoretical and Practical aspects', in: *The Seventh year as European Union Member States: Economics, Politics, Law*, Proceedings of the International Conference 6-7 May, Riga, 2011, at p. 271-28.

[54] USSR decree of the Praesidium of the Supreme Soviet 'On the increase of State aid to pregnant women, mothers with many children and single mothers, on strengthening measures for the protection of motherhood and childhood; on the establishment of the honorary title 'Mother Heroine' and foundation of the institution of the order 'Motherhood Glory' and 'Motherhood Medal', USSR Supreme Soviet News, 1944, No. 37.

principle of monogamy and could encourage polygamy. Factual cohabitation was seen as avoiding state control which determined the legal obstacles to marriage registration, since factual cohabitants did not apply to the Department of the record of the civil status act. Therefore, difficulties occurred while trying to set demographic tasks with regard to population records. Factual marriages were also considered to encourage frivolous relations.[55] Finally, factual cohabitation (any informal relationships) was not recognised by the valid norms of the Family and Marriage Code of the Republic of Lithuania (hereafter the Lithuanian Family and Marriage Code).[56]

The Civil Code of the Republic of Lithuania, which came into force in 2001, introduced a new institution – living together without the registration of marriage (cohabitation).

It must be mentioned that on 24 February 2004 a draft law on partnership (cohabitation without the registration of marriage) was presented; however, most of its provisions were not sufficiently grounded or finalised.[57] As the adoption of the legal act on partnerships (cohabitation) had failed, the Government of the Republic of Lithuania instructed the Ministry of Justice on 4 September 2006 to draft amendments to the Civil Code concerning the registration of a Partnership. On 22 August 2007, a Draft Law on the Amendment of the Civil Code[58] was introduced. This bill included a proposal to partly modify the definition of a partnership as presented in the existing Civil Code by stating that a 'partnership shall be cohabitation between a man and a woman (cohabitants) following the principle of monogamy on the basis of a joint declaration of partnership produced in writing and duly registered and thus having legal consequences for property rights'. The draft proposed a procedure whereby a partnership declaration would have to be validated by a notary and registered at the Registry of Marriage Contracts. The bill was subject to serious criticism and was eventually abandoned.

---

55 V. RIASENCEV, *Family Law* (in Russian), 1971, at p. 32.

56 Marriage and Family Code of the Republic of Lithuania, Ministry of Justice Press, Vilnius, 1990.

57 Draft Law on Partnership 14-07-2004, available at: www.lrs.lt; Report regarding the Law on Partnership (Committee on Legal Affairs of the Seimas of the Republic of Lithuania (IXP-3272)), available at: www.lrs.lt.

58 Draft Law on the Amendment of Art. 2.18, 2.19, 3.16, 3.229, 3.230, 3.232, 3.234 and 3.235 of the Civil Code and Supplementing thereof with New Articles 3.229(1) and 3.229(2), available at: www.lrs.lt.

On 20 November 2011 a third option for legal regulation was presented in the form of a Draft Law on the Amendment of Art. 2.18, 2.19, 3.140, 3.229, 3.230, 3.231, 3.232, 3.233, 3.234 and 3.235 of the Lithuanian Civil Code and Supplementing it with the new Art. 3.229(1), 3.234(1) and 3.234(2) prepared by the Ministry of Justice. An analysis of the provisions of this bill leads to the conclusion that the legal regulation scheme presented therein also lacked legal clarity, consistency and finalisation. For example, the draft included an unjustified proposal to divide any property jointly acquired by cohabitees into equal shares, with possible exceptions only being made in cases specified by the law, and another proposal that a cohabitee shall have no right to dispose of joint-partial property without the written consent of the other cohabitee. An usufruct option was proposed with an unjustified widening of the grounds for its application (lacking any specification). The draft also lacked a legal regulation linked to the civil liabilities of partners arising from their obligations, and left open certain aspects of paternity disputes, paternity verification, etc.[59]

On 21 February 2012, new provisions of the Lithuanian Civil Code on Cohabitation were drafted by Parliament (Draft XIP-4097). This final attempt to amend the Lithuanian Civil Code also failed.

The difficulties in legally regulating partnerships in Lithuania are likely to be caused by several major reasons. One of them is the position of the Church, another is the ambiguous and mixed public opinion.[60] On top of that, politicians do not support the model of a registered partnership and are of the opinion that cohabitanting couples (staying in informal relationship) should not enjoy the legal protection encompassing all the rights and privileges of marital partners. According to the prevailing political opinion regarding alternative forms of family relationships and their legal regulation, it is reasonable to regulate such relationships by way of the institution of a 'partnership by law', thereby applying its provisions within the limited scope of property interests to the extent

59 I. Kudinavičiūtė-Michailovienė, *Teisinė šeimos forma, Lietuvos Respublikos civilinis kodeksas: pirmieji dešimt galiojimo metų. Mokslo studija* (The Legal Form of a Family, Civil Code of the Republic of Lithuania: the first decade in force. Academic study), MRU, Vilnius, 2013, at p. 423-426.

60 For further details refer to: I. Kudinavičiūtė-Michailovienė, *Santuokos sąlygos ir jų vykdymas, Monografija* (Marriage Conditions and their Implementation, Monograph), Justitia, Vilnius, 2007. E. Nemaikštytė and M. Poškutė, 'Law on Partnership - which way Lithuania choose?', *Law News*, Vol. 17, No. 4, 2006.

which is necessary for the protection of the weaker party's property interests.[61]

LUXEMBOURG

Before the 1970s, no consideration was given to informal relationships and they could not produce legal effects.

Since the French decisions of the Cour de cassation of 1970 and 1975, an informal relationship, even if it is adulterous, may have legal consequences. It is taken into consideration as a fact.

It is also important to note that adultery was decriminalised by the law during the mid-1970s. And the fact that adultery was no longer a peremptory cause of divorce was also significant to the recognition of the effects of an informal relationship.

When the registered partnership was introduced by law in 2004, legislation provided an option for couples: to conclude a partnership was easier in some ways than the conclusion of a marriage. But even though this option now exists, there are more and more couples who want to constitute an informal relationship, without any formalities at all.

Legislation cannot prevent couples from constituting informal relationships, nor does it tend to dissuade them.

THE NETHERLANDS

Non-marital cohabitation has slowly and on a step-by-step basis been identified by the legislature as a lifestyle with important economic and emotional functions and therefore as relevant for legislation. This trend in which legal policy makers in the Netherlands chose the family function over the family form started as early as in the 1980s. The legislator mainly uses three models:[62] first, a model with one status for

---

61 An empirical study of political opinions took place on 16/10/2014 by way of sociological opinion poll. Opinions were expressed by 100 respondents (The Parliament of Lithuania (Seimas) consists of 141 members). Polling was done by L. GALINIENĖ, 'Heteroseksualių sugyventinių porų teisinio statuso reglamentavimas (lyginamasis aspektas)' (Regulation of the legal status of heterosexual cohabitant couples (a comparative aspect)).

62 The legislature appears not to be aware of this implicit policy, since each act is only considered within the specific context of the subject, without taking the broader picture into perspective.

all relationships with the same rights and duties for all couples;[63] secondly, a different status for formal and informal couples, but with some rights and duties for informal couples; and thirdly, a status for formal couples and no status for informal couples. In inheritance law and criminal and criminal procedural law the policy and the legislation shifted slowly from the third into the second model. Non-marital cohabitation is no longer completely ignored, although the family form is still very dominant.[64] Most striking is the complete ignorance of non-marital cohabitation in relation to family law and civil procedural law. The internal relationship between the partners has not been regulated, not in family law and not in family procedural law. One possible explanation for the lack of a *lex specialis* is that the focus of legal reform always has been on achieving equality for same-sex couples, thus overlooking informal cohabitation.[65] This started in 1991, when the Kortmann Committee recommended the introduction of two types of registration. The first would be with the local municipal administration and would mainly have public law effects.[66] The second would be in the civil status register and would bring about the same effects as a marriage. This was meant as an alternative to marriage for all couples, regardless of their sex. In 1993 the government agreed with the view of the committee that different lifestyles should be taken into account in the legislation, but it rejected the proposed municipal registration.[67] In 1998 the Dutch Registered Partnership Act entered into force, which was almost identical to the legislation on marriage and was open for both same-sex and opposite-sex couples. In 2001 marriage was made available to same-sex couples, but the registered partnership, after an evaluation of the registered partnership act, was not abolished.[68]

NORWAY

Unmarried cohabitation was punishable right up until the 1970s; however, the provision had not been enforced for a long time. Proposals

---

63 For instance, income tax law, inheritance tax law, social security law.

64 W.M. Schrama, 'The Dutch approach to informal lifestyles: Family function over family form?', *International Journal of Law, Policy and the Family*, 2008, pp. 311-332.

65 W.M. Schrama, 'Marriage and alternative status relationships in the Netherlands', in: J. Eekelaar and R. George (eds.), *Routlegde Handbook of Family Law and Policy*, Routledge, London, 2014, pp. 14-25.

66 For instance, in the field of social security. With regard to private law effects the partners would be obliged to maintain each other during the registration and for a short period thereafter.

67 This would be too expensive while the aim (the prevention of fraud) would not be met.

68 *Kamerstukken* II, 31 200 VI, no. 11, p. 2-3.

to repeal the criminal provision were put forward both in 1925 and in 1953, and the provision was finally repealed in 1972. [69] The increase in the number of cohabiting couples in the 1970s led to the appointment of the first law committee in 1976. Several public reports were published during the 1980s and 1990s; however, only minor changes in the legal position were suggested in the field of family law. The Norwegian Household Community Act 1991 gave members of a household a limited right to acquire the previous family home and household goods at market value. The Christian Democrats believed that legislation would undermine the status of marriage and the Social Democrats did not have any strong desire for legislation. The legislature's willingness to enact statutory regulation was stronger in the field of inheritance law. The law commission of 1999 as well as the White Paper in 2003 suggested that a surviving cohabitant should keep part of the deceased cohabitant's estate undivided if the cohabitants had had children together. In 2008, a law to this effect was enacted along with a limited right to inherit.

PORTUGAL

In Portugal a *de facto* union was to a certain extent 'institutionalised' in Law No. 135/99, of 28 August, abrogated by Law No. 7/2001, of 11 May, which substitutes it and 'adopts measures for the protection of *de facto* unions'. This law, in turn, was amended by Law No. 23/2010, of 30 August. The legislation of 1999, however, did not signal a break with previous legislation; Law No. 135/99, like Law No. 7/2001 which followed soon afterwards, was to a large extent a mere summary of the protective measures enshrined in previous legislation: in various places in Art. 3 the legislation simply recognises rights conferred 'under the law' to people who live in a *de facto* union, 'legislation' which in many cases already existed.

There was, however, some innovation in the legislation of 1999, the most significant of which permitted the joint adoption of minors by people of different sex who lived in a *de facto* union, under the terms established for spouses in Art. 1979, No. 1, of the Portuguese Civil Code (Art. 7). In addition, in the event of the death of the *de facto* union member who is the owner of the home where the couple lived, the law granted the surviving member the real right to remain in the house for a period of five years and a right of preference in the sale of the home for the same period (Art. 4, Nos. 1 and 2). Lastly, in relation to fiscal questions, Law

69 The Norwegian Criminal Code 1902, S. 379, NOU 1999: 25 chapter 8.3.1.

No. 7/2001 subjected *de facto* unions to the same legal rules relating to the taxation of personal income which were applicable to married couples living together (Art. 3.º, al. d)).

In 2010, Law No. 23, of 30 August, introduced amendments to Law No. 7/2001.

In the knowledge that various countries had recognised equalization between a *de facto* union and a marriage, the moderate option arrived at by Portuguese legislation represents a true choice. The legislator must have taken into consideration the fact that the interested parties might not have wanted extensive regulation of their lives, given that they had opted not to marry; and that since they had chosen a *de facto* union, they should organise their private life as they wished, rather than having to conform to laws in areas which they themselves could regulate. *De facto* unions should continue to be non-juridical. On the other hand, in spite of this, and despite the fact that it is the matrimonial model which continues to be preferred by society and its laws, the State, today, cannot ignore and scorn those citizens who, by virtue of choices which they have made, create situations of need; or those who, simply being unable to make choices, find themselves in situations of acute want. Having said this, the general aim of the amendments was to provide increased support following a death or a breakdown in the relationship, above all when agreed decisions are no longer possible and when the objective is the social protection of a surviving member who is left in a vulnerable position, above all with respect to housing needs, minimum sustenance, or during moments of acute suffering, such as in cases of life-threatening injury or illness.

It can be concluded that Portuguese law, in comparison with other juridical systems, is very modest in its recognition of *de facto* union rights, and when compared to those of married couples the relative difference is enormous, since the *de facto* union regime continues to lack norms relating to registration, constitutional invalidity, property regimes, the management of assets, the illegitimacy of certain provisions, debt liability, contract prohibitions, the regulation of participation in companies, extinction (besides Art. 8 of Law No. 7/2001), and rights of inheritance.

RUSSIA

The Second Russian Family Code of 1926[70] equated the legal consequences of a long-standing *de facto* cohabitation with those of a formal marriage.[71] The registration of marriage was preserved, but was no longer treated as a constitutive element of the formation of marriage. Consent alone was sufficient to create a valid marriage. The reasons for this far-reaching innovation were manifold. One rather utopian motive behind this deformalisation was the urge to build a Communist future, where formal marriage was supposed to 'die out'. A more down-to-earth incentive to equate registered and unregistered marriage was the aim of protecting 'proletarian' *de facto* wives from 'exploitation' by their usually more economically powerful *de facto* husbands.[72]

In 1944, cohabitation lost its legal standing and unmarried couples were summoned to formalise their relationships. From then onwards, and until *perestroika*, stable non-marital cohabitation all but disappeared in the Soviet Union.

SCOTLAND

Before setting out the recent reforms in Scotland in respect of informal relationships, it should be noted that until 2006 Scots law continued to recognise a form of irregular marriage, which might in itself be regarded as a type of informal relationship. Irregular marriage, of which there were originally three recognised forms, survived in Scotland much later than in other jurisdictions. Marriage by exchange of present consent and marriage *per verba futuro subsequente copula* were abolished by S. 5 of the Marriage (Scotland) Act 1939 and marriage by cohabitation with habit and repute survived until its abolition by S. 3 of the Family Law (Scotland) Act 2006. While this form of marriage, which required evidence of a substantial period of cohabitation as husband and wife together with general repute of marriage, was widely regarded as out of date and of little relevance, its continued existence is noteworthy in the context of increased recognition of informal relationships. Irregular marriage was a very pragmatic way of extending protection to couples who lived together as if they were married but without having complied

---

70 Кодекс законов о браке семье и опеке (Code on Marriage, Family and Guardianship) of 19 November 1926.

71 The Code, as such, did not treat the two institutions as being equal; this result was attained through the case law.

72 Д. ГЕНКИН, И. НОВИЦКИЙ and Н. РАБИНОВИЧ, *История советского гражданского 1917-1947*, Юридическая литература, Moscow, 1949, at p. 443.

with the formal requirements of legal ceremony and registration. It was principally the pretence or deceit involved in establishing repute that seemed out of date in contrast to the increasingly common practice of couples openly cohabiting without marriage.

Marriage by cohabitation with habit and repute was abolished by the Family Law (Scotland) Act 2006 which at the same introduced some new legal rights for cohabitants. The legal position of cohabiting couples was considered by the Scottish Law Commission in 'The Effects of Cohabitation in Private Law'.[73] Following consultation, recommendations were published in 1992 in their 'Report on Family Law'.[74] The Scottish Law Commission stated two initial conclusions: first, that there was a clearly established need for 'some limited reform' and secondly, that such reform 'should neither undermine marriage, nor undermine the freedom of those who have deliberately opted out of marriage.'[75] They were quite clear that cohabitation was not marriage and that it would be inappropriate to apply all of the legal consequences of marriage to it but some more limited provisions should be introduced. It was concluded, for example, that it would not be appropriate to extend the obligation of aliment (maintenance) to cohabitation.[76] The distinction between marriage and cohabitation was highlighted in particular in the context of financial provision on termination of the relationship. The Scottish Law Commission concluded that, while there should be some provision for discretionary awards, there should not be a comprehensive framework comparable to that which applies on divorce or dissolution of a civil partnership. Such an approach was firmly rejected on the basis that it would 'impose a regime of property sharing, and in some cases continuing financial support, on couples who may well have opted for cohabitation in order to avoid such consequences.'[77]

The Scottish Law Commission's draft Bill, published in 1992, was not taken forward and in fact it was not until 2005 that draft legislation, which was to become the Family Law (Scotland) Act 2006, was introduced by the Scottish government. The provisions which were finally included in the 2006 Act undeniably had their origins in the Commission's original Report but their form had changed.[78] While the

---

[73] Scot Law Com, No 86, 1990.

[74] Scot Law Com, No 135, 1992.

[75] Scot Law Com, No 135, 1992, para. 16.1.

[76] Scot Law Com, No 135, 1992, para. 16.5.

[77] Scot Law Com, No 135, 1992, para. 16.15.

[78] E.E. SUTHERLAND, 'From 'bidie-in' to cohabitant: the perils of legislative compromise', *International Journal of Law, Policy and the Family*, 2013, pp. 143-175.

idea of rights for cohabitants was broadly welcomed, the precise detail of the provisions which were finally adopted has been much criticised and concerns which were already being raised during the legislative process have subsequently given rise to questions in the courts 'which are not free from difficulty'. New statutory provisions can be expected to require a 'settling in' period but nine years later it is difficult to see much evidence of the provisions working well. Despite guidance from the UK Supreme Court in the case of *Gow v Grant*[79] there continues to be considerable uncertainty as to how to interpret and apply the key provisions, and in particular S. 28. The operation of strict statutory time limits is also seen as problematic.

SLOVAKIA

There have been no major reforms of the rules regarding informal relationships between couples in Slovakia. Slovakian society perceives marriage as a very essential and non-derogable legal construction. Especially the conservative parties in the Slovak Parliament are even trying to buttress marriage unions. There is national consensus across the whole spectrum of political parties concerning the supremacy of marriage in family law as manifested by the legal concept of marriage in the Slovak Family Act. The supremacy of marriage was also recently manifested by the National Council (Parliament) of Slovakia. On 4 June 2014, the Council adopted a Constitutional Law (no. 490/2014) amending the 1992 Constitution, which entered into force on 1 September 2014. Article 41 of the law defines marriage as 'a unique union between a man and a woman'. The explanatory memorandum that accompanies the law explicitly states that same-sex couples will not have the possibility to enter into a marriage. Of the 123 members of Slovakia's Parliament who voted on the measure, only 18 voted against adopting the amendment. The amendment specifically denies same-sex couples the legal protection associated with marriage by specifying that 'it will be impossible for the rights and duties associated with marriage to be conferred in any way other than a legally recognised union between a man and a woman.'

SLOVENIA

The legal regulation of extramarital unions has not changed since its introduction in 1977.

---

[79] *Gow v Grant* 2012 SLT 829.

On 16 June 2011 Parliament adopted a draft Family Code[80] but its entry into force was deferred because a referendum was demanded. The reason for the referendum was the decision of the legislator also to include the regulation of registered same-sex civil partnerships and unregistered actual life unions of same-sex partners, whereby a registered same-sex civil partnership, in terms of its legal consequences, was supposed to be akin to a marriage and an unregistered actual life union of same-sex partners was supposed to be akin to an extramarital union of heterosexual partners. The possibility of a referendum on the Slovenian Family Code, at the request of the National Assembly RS, which believed that anti-constitutional consequences would occur by the deferment of the implementation or the rejection of the Slovenian Family Code in a referendum, was soon submitted to the Constitutional Court for its decision. The Constitutional Court decided that the result of the referendum would not cause the creation of anti-constitutional consequences since the Slovenian Family Code would not take effect immediately but only one year after its introduction. This period was said to deviate only slightly from the same period in which the National Assembly is bound by the result of a referendum. The legal position would thus remain the same in the event of the Slovenian Family Code being rejected as in the case of its confirmation, i.e., that the Slovenian Marriage Act and the Slovenian Partnership Act would continue to be used for a further year after the proclamation of the referendum decision.[81]

In the referendum held on 25 March 2012, 55% of those who voted were against the Slovenian Family Code. This had the result that for one year after the proclamation of the referendum decision, the National Assembly could not adopt any new family arrangement that would be in conflict with the decision of the voters.[82]

SPAIN

The 1978 Spanish Constitution meant a radical change in Spanish family law, which had been very close to Roman Catholic standards and principles during the long period of the Franco dictatorship (1939-1975).

80 Available at: www.dz-rs.si/wps/portal/Home/deloDW?rs.si/wps/portal/Home/deloDZ/zakonodaja/izbranZakonAkt?uid=F7B438D711DE188FC12578A300523C14&db=pre_zak&mandat=V&tip=doc.

81 Decision of the Constitutional Court RS, No. U-II-3/11 of 8 December 2011, Uradni list RS (Official Journal) No. 109/2011.

82 See: B. NOVAK, 'Neueste Entwicklung des Slowenischen Familienrechts', *FamRZ*, No. 18, 2012, at p. 1456.

In the 1980s the Spanish Constitutional Court held, in various landmark decisions, that families not based on marriage were equally protected under Art. 39 of the Spanish Constitution. This did not mean that marriage and cohabitation were equal and the Spanish Constitutional Court held that it was therefore legitimate not to treat them alike. These findings of the Constitutional Court pushed the legislature into becoming active.

The Autonomous Communities with jurisdiction to legislate in private law matters enacted different laws between the late 1990s and 2006. The first was Catalonia in 1998 with a special law on stable couples[83] that applied both to informal relationships and to couples that formalised their relationship by notarial deed. It contained different chapters on opposite-sex and same-sex couples, with more far-reaching effects for the second, which were justified by the fact that they could not enter into marriage. The second Autonomous Community to become active, Aragon,[84] though closely following Catalan legislation, gave up this distinction. The Law enacted by the Autonomous Community of Navarre followed the same path.[85] It was, however, challenged on constitutional grounds by 40 members of the Parliament of the Autonomous Community. One of the arguments brought forward was that the legislation imposed mandatory provisions on unmarried couples, thus infringing their right to self-determination. Other Autonomous Communities with jurisdiction to legislate in private law matters, namely the Basque Country, Galicia, the Balearic Islands and Valencia decided to regulate only registered partnerships.[86]

In the rest of the country, where Autonomous Communities do not have jurisdiction to legislate in private law matters, two developments are noteworthy. First, Autonomous Communities such as Madrid, [87]

[83] Llei 10/1998, de 15 de juliol, d'unions estables de parella, (BOE núm. 198, 19 de agosto de 1998).

[84] Ley 6/1999, de 26 de marzo, de las Cortes de Aragón, relativa a Parejas estables no casadas (BOE núm. 95, 21 de abril de 1999).

[85] Ley Foral 6/2000, de 3 de julio, para la igualdad jurídica de las parejas estables (BOE núm. 214, de 6 de septiembre de 2000).

[86] Valencia (Ley 1/2001, de 6 de abril, por la que se regulan las uniones de hecho (BOE núm. 112, 10.05.2001)), Balearic Islands (Ley 18/2001, de 19 de diciembre, de Parejas Estables (BOE núm.14, 16.01.2002)), Basque Country (Ley 2/2003, de 7 de mayo, reguladora de las parejas de hecho (BOPV núm. 100, 23.05.2003)) and Galicia (provision in Ley 2/2006, de 14 de junio, de derecho civil de Galicia (BOE núm. 191, 11.08.2006)).

[87] Ley 11/2001, de 19 de diciembre, de Uniones de Hecho de la Comunidad de Madrid (BOE núm. 55. 05.03. 2002).

Asturias,[88] Andalusia,[89] Canary Islands,[90] Extremadura[91] and Cantabria[92] enacted legislation on unmarried couples. These laws are very often rather thin in substance, since they deal with very limited areas of public law that are open to regulation by the Autonomous Community, such as public housing, benefits for the family situation of civil servants and some aspects of tax law. Secondly, the Spanish Parliament, which has competence to legislate on private matters for these territories, did not approve any of the various bills that were presented[93] in the period between 1996 and 2004. This can be explained by the fact that large sectors of the party that governed, the Conservative *Partido popular*, strongly supported the views on family and morality of the Catholic Church. At the Spanish national level, the approach towards informal relationships has been a piecemeal approach – they were dealt with in the course of different reforms on single issues like adoption or leasehold.

In 2005, the Socialist Party won the elections. Family law became prominent on the political agenda. Marriage was opened up to same-sex couples; divorce law was reformed in order to make divorce more easily accessible to couples that no longer wished to be married. Informal relationships, though on the increase in Spanish society, were ignored in the period 2004-2011, when the Socialist party was in government, and later on, when the *Partido popular* regained power in 2011. Probably the need for specific legislation was felt to be less strong once all couples, regardless of sexual orientation, could get married.[94] From a political point of view, it may also have seemed unnecessary, given the different laws enacted by the Autonomous Communities.

---

88 Ley del Principado de Asturias 4/2002, de 23 de mayo, de Parejas Estables (BOE. Núm. 157, 02. 07.2002).

89 Ley 5/2002, de 16 de diciembre, de Parejas de Hecho (BOE núm.11., 13.01.2003).

90 Ley 5/2003, de 6 de marzo, para la regulación de las Parejas de Hecho en la Comunidad Autónoma de Canarias (BOC núm. 54, 19.03.2003).

91 Ley 5/2003, de 20 de marzo, de Parejas de Hecho de la Comunidad Autónoma de Extremadura, (DOE núm.42, 08.04.2003).

92 Ley de Cantabria 1/2005, de 16 de mayo, de Parejas de Hecho de la Comunidad Autónoma de Cantabria (BO Cantabria núm. 98, 16.05.2005).

93 There have been more than ten proposals. See J.M. Mata de Antonio, 'Parejas de hecho ¿equiparación o discriminación?: análisis de la normativa autonómica', *Acciones e investigaciones sociales*, 2002, pp. 187–254.

94 C. Gonzalez Beilfuss, 'Die Regelung der Paarbeziehungen im neuen spanischen Familienrecht', in: B. Heiderhoff and A. Röthel (eds.), *Regelungsaufgabe Paarbeziehung: Was kann, was darf, was will der Staat?*, Wolfgang Metzner Verlag, Frankfurt am Main, pp. 89-102; M. Navarro-Michel, 'Same sex couples in Spain and Catalonia', *International Journal of Legal Information*, 2014, pp. 47-54.

In 2010 the Catalan legislature decided to amend its 1998 Law. Originally, in 1998, the option had been to legislate about stable couples outside the family law book of the Catalan Civil Code. Twelve years later, when the Catalan Parliament decided to enact Book II of the Catalan Civil Code, containing all the regulations on Persons and Family Law, this separation could no longer be justified. The Catalan legislature also took the opportunity to revise its legislation on stable couples. Whereas originally matters during the relationship were also regulated, the present legislation mainly concentrates on the effects after break-up. In the Preamble this is justified by reference to sociological data, even though it is not clear how they were obtained. The legislature assumes that in Catalan law informal relationships are essentially trial marriages.

In 2013 the Constitutional Court delivered two decisions in connection with the domestic partnership laws of Madrid and Navarre. The second decision, STC 93/2013, is noteworthy because it found that provisions which contain detailed regulation which cannot be eliminated by an agreement between the parties (i.e., no possibility of opt-out), are unconstitutional because they interfere with individual freedom. In 2014 a new decision by the Constitutional Court, STC 40/2014, held that a provision on survivor's pension in the Law on Social Security which deferred to Autonomous Communities' regulations on partnerships, was unconstitutional because it infringed the principle of equality between Spaniards.

SWEDEN

A 'stance of neutrality' (above Question 6) was adopted towards the end of the 1960s, in a government mandate to a legislative committee appointed to consider necessary changes in Swedish family law, in particular within the field of marriage law. The committee's mandate was extended in 1969 to cover unmarried cohabitation, as a response to the ever increasing number of couples in Sweden living together (and even having children together) without marrying.[95]

---

95 See M. JÄNTERÄ-JAREBORG, 'Rechtsregeln für nichteheliches Zusammenleben in Schweden' (in English), in: I. KROPPENBERG et al. (eds.), *Rechtsregeln für nichteheliches Zusammenleben*, Gieseking Verlag, Vienna, 2009, pp. 207-226, at p. 209 et seq.; G. LIND, 'Utvecklingen av samboförhållanden och samborätten i Norden', in: J. ASLAND et al., *Nordisk samboerrett*, Gyldendal, Oslo, 2014, at p. 23 et seq. (see Chapter 1.3, in the English version of the book, to be published by Intersentia in 2015); C. SÖRGJERD, *Reconstructing Marriage -The Legal Status of Relationships in a Changing Society*, Intersentia, Cambridge, 2012, at p. 135 et seq.

The Swedish legislature's first enactment, specially designed for couples who lived together outside marriage, was the Act of Unmarried Cohabitants' Joint Dwelling (in Swedish, *Lagen 1973:651 om ogifta sambors gemensamma bostad*). The aim of this legislation was modest in the sense that it was limited to regulating which of the cohabitees, upon termination of the relationship, had the right to take over the occupation of the joint dwelling, but only in cases where the joint dwelling was a leased property or owned by the cohabitees or one of them on a tenant-basis (such as a condominium or a housing association apartment, but not real estate). The decision had to be made on the basis of the (former) cohabitees' needs of the dwelling, whereby the children's residence was a factor of utmost relevance. The 1973 Act (which entered into force on 1 January 1974) was intended as a provisional solution, to be soon replaced by more comprehensive legislation, but applied until 1 January 1988 when new legislation finally entered into force.

At that date, together with the new Swedish Marriage Code, a new enactment entitled Act on Cohabitees' Joint Home (in Swedish, *Lagen 1987:232 om sambors gemensamma hem*) became applicable. As with the previous legislation of 1973, this Act only applied to situations where an unmarried man and an unmarried woman lived together under marriage-like circumstances. This legislation was far more radical than its predecessor. In essence, it provided for the right for both cohabitees to share the net value of the joint dwelling and joint household goods upon termination of the relationship, on condition that this was property acquired for the couple's joint use (i.e., 'cohabitation property'), and unless otherwise agreed between them. The enactment also provided for the right to take over the occupation of such property upon the termination of the relationship and, during the relationship, protected each of the cohabitees against unilateral actions concerning this property by the other cohabitee. The clear influence of the provisions of the Swedish Marriage Code regarding matrimonial property relations is visible. As in the case of marriage, entering into unmarried cohabitation did not as such affect ownership rights to any property.[96] Cohabitees received instead a right to an equal division of the net value of property acquired for the purpose of being used as their joint dwelling or the net value of household goods. The difference from marital property rights is that only these two categories of property were of relevance for the property division, whereas in a marriage all the spouses' property will be

96 M. JÄNTERÄ-JAREBORG, 'Rechtsregeln für nichteheliches Zusammenleben in Schweden' (in English), in: I. KROPPENBERG et al. (eds.), *Rechtsregeln für nichteheliches Zusammenleben*, Gieseking Verlag, Vienna, 2009, pp. 207-226, at p. 215 et seq.

included, unless otherwise agreed by them (or stipulated by a third party). Through another piece of legislation, namely Act on Homosexual Cohabitees (in Swedish: *Lagen 1987:813 om homosexuella sambor*), the 1987 Act on Cohabitees' Joint Home was extended to cover same-sex cohabitees as well.

The currently applicable provisions are found in the Cohabitation Act of 2003 (in Swedish: *Sambolag 2003:376*). The bulk of the provisions of the 1987 Act on Cohabitees' Joint Home were transferred unchanged into the 2003 enactment in addition to certain important clarifications, largely in response to problems experienced in practice. The 2003 enactment covers both same-sex and opposite-sex couples, on the same conditions.

During the drafting procedure, much consideration was given to the issue whether the concept of cohabitation property, i.e., the property to be included in the property division, should be extended to cover motor vehicles, such as cars, acquired for the couple's joint use. This would have meant, as suggested by the law commission in charge of the proposals, that the parties to the relationship, upon its termination, would have had the right to equal division of the net value consisting not only of the joint dwelling and household goods acquired for their joint use, but also of motor vehicles. The proposal also included the right for the cohabitee in greater need of the vehicle to take it over, as is the case with the couple's joint dwelling and household goods. The proposal aimed to achieve a greater economic security for people living together in an informal relationship. The proposal was, however, turned down by the government which was not convinced that this was an optimal way of achieving increased protection, for example, because it could result in one of the cohabitees having to include cars owned by him or her in the property division while a car owned by the other cohabitee might not be included. [97] This discussion demonstrates two important characteristics of Swedish law, namely, that motor vehicles, such as cars, are not included within the scope of household goods and that, in respect of informal cohabitation, only property acquired for the couple's joint use can be included in a property division whereas, e.g., previously acquired property of the same kind is not covered. For example, if one of the partners moves to a dwelling owned by the other partner where the couple stills lives until they separate 10 years later, this dwelling will not qualify as 'cohabitation property' to be included in the property division, because it had not been acquired for the couple's joint use. If, on the other

[97] Government Bill, Prop. 2002/03:80, p. 25 and p. 31 et seq.

hand, this dwelling had been sold during the couple's relationship and the money received had been used by the owner to buy a new dwelling for the couple, that new dwelling would be included because it was acquired for the couple's joint use. The results can in fact be quite arbitrary.[98]

The government was also concerned about the general lack of knowledge regarding what rules apply to unmarried couples in the couple's mutual relationship, and that the couples concerned should not be confronted with the application of rules they had not counted upon.

In other areas of law, most importantly as regards parental rights, the legislative trend since the 1970s has been to place couples cohabiting informally with each other on an equal footing with married couples.[99] The child's birth status does not affect parental responsibilities. Certain differences of treatment exist, however, in some respects, such as the unmarried father's need to acknowledge his paternity whereas the married father is covered by the *pater est* rule. Cohabiting couples qualify for assisted fertilisation treatments under the general health care system of Sweden on the same conditions as couples in a formalised relationship. In a lesbian relationship, the birth-mother's same-sex partner (irrespective of the existence of marriage, registered partnership or cohabitation) always has to acknowledge her parentage in relation to the child, born through assisted fertilisation treatment to the couple. Under Swedish law only married couples and couples in a registered partnership may jointly adopt a child (Swedish Children and Parents Code, Chapter 4, § 4). Furthermore, if the parents are not in a formalised relationship with each other at the time of the child's birth (or later), parental rights belong to the birthmother alone (Swedish Children and Parents Code, Chapter 6 § 3). Shared parental rights require in that case a parental agreement or a court decree (Swedish Children and Parents Code, Chapter 6 § 4).

---

98 For concrete examples on how the Swedish Cohabitation Act works in practice, see M. BRATTSTRÖM, 'The Protection of a Vulnerable Party when a Cohabitee Relationship Ends - An Evaluation of the Swedish Cohabitees Act', in B. VERSCHRAEGEN (ed.), *Family Finances*, Jan Sramet Verlag, Vienna, 2008, at p. 345–354 and M. JÄNTERÄ-JAREBORG, 'Rechtsregeln für nichteheliches Zusammenleben in Schweden' (in English), in: I. KROPPENBERG et al. (eds.), *Rechtsregeln für nichteheliches Zusammenleben*, Gieseking Verlag, Vienna, 2009, pp. 207-226, at p. 218-221.

99 See further, M. JÄNTERÄ-JAREBORG, 'Rechtsregeln für nichteheliches Zusammenleben in Schweden' (in English), in: I. KROPPENBERG et al. (eds.), *Rechtsregeln für nichteheliches Zusammenleben*, Gieseking Verlag, Vienna, 2009, pp. 207-226, at p. 210 et seq. and A. SINGER, 'Samboendets föräldrarättsliga relevans', in: J. ASLAND et al., *Nordisk samboerrett*, Gyldendal, Oslo, 2014, at p. 225 et seq. (see Chapter 5, in the English version of the book, to be published by Intersentia in 2015).

When it comes to means-tested social welfare benefits, for instance living support and housing allowance, the income and means of both cohabitees are taken into account when deciding whether they can qualify for a benefit and to what extent.[100] The reason is that couples living in informal cohabitation could otherwise profit financially at the expense of society by choosing not to marry.

The survey above shows that the Swedish legislature's concern since the late 1960s has focused on couples living habitually together in an informal relationship. No attention has been given to any other kinds of informal relationships between couples. It has been under consideration, but in the end dismissed as not necessary, to draft legislation regarding the joint household of other people (than couples), such as the joint household of siblings or the joint household between a parent and a grown-up child.[101]

SWITZERLAND

Only a few decades ago, unmarried cohabitation had been a criminal offence in many of the Swiss cantons.[102] Although not necessarily implemented or enforced, it was not until 1995 that the last prohibition on unmarried cohabitation was abolished in the Valais canton.

Statutory rules on informal relationships have repeatedly been rejected by the Swiss legislature.[103] During the reform of the marriage law in 1984,[104] the need for the regulation of informal relationships in family law had been realised and discussed. The Swiss legislature then decided to postpone this discussion until the subsequently planned reform of the divorce law. There were different reasons for this decision: an in-depth analysis and discussion were seen as necessary, some wanted to await further developments and input from legal practice with regard to informal relationships and for others this question was not at all urgent

---

100 Government Bill, Prop. 1978/79:12, pp. 87 et seq. and Socialstyrelsen, *Ekonomiskt bistånd. Handbok för socialtjänsten*, 2013, at p. 98 et seq.

101 See Statens Offentliga Utredningar, SOU 1999:104, pp. 271-280.

102 In the 1970s around half of the Swiss cantons had a so-called *Konkubinatsverbot*, see R. FRANK, 'Kantonalrechtliche Konkubinatsverbote', in: R. FRANK, A. GIRSBERGER, N.P. VOGT, H.U. WALDER-BOHNER and R.H. WEBER, *Die eheähnliche Gemeinschaft (Konkubinat) im schweizerischen Recht*, Schulthess Juristische Medien, Zurich, 1984, at p. 6-8.

103 For further details and references, see D. DIEZI, *Nachlebensgemeinschaftlicher Unterhalt*, Stämpfli, Bern, 2014, at p. 157 et seq.

104 In force since 1988.

or necessary since the Swiss Federal Supreme Court was already addressing the most urgent financial problems upon dissolution (see Question 3).

During the reform of the divorce law in 1998,[105] the regulation of informal relationships in family law was, however, explicitly rejected. It was argued that couples in an informal relationship may contractually regulate their relationship. Apparently, the legal practice of the courts (applying the rules for a simple partnership) did not reveal any need for a comprehensive regulation of informal relationships. Furthermore, a regulation of informal relationships would only create a (unnecessary) 'marriage light'.[106]

Hence, the question of how to legally deal with informal relationships is still left to the courts and legal practice. Nevertheless, the informal relationship has found its way into a few more recent laws concerning questions such as procedural rights[107] or rights in connection with the reformed law of adult protection.[108]

105 In force since 2000.

106 See Divorce Reform Message, Botschaft Scheidungsrecht, Bundesblatt 1996 I, at p. 1, 16.

107 E.g. Art. 47 para. 1(c) and Art. 165 para. 1(a) Swiss Civil Procedure Code; Art. 56(c) and Art. 168 para. 1(a) Swiss Criminal Procedure Code.

108 Art. 378 para. 1 and 420 Swiss Civil Code.

QUESTION 9

Are there any recent proposals (e.g. by Parliament, law commissions or similar bodies) for reform in this area?

AUSTRIA

Although the need to clarify the legal status of persons who have opted for this novel form of union is generally recognised, no legislative proposals are currently under consideration.[1] Even in the working programme of the Austrian government for the years 2013-2018 the further development of the inheritance law - in particular the improvement of the status of partners in an informal relationship - is mentioned.[2] To date, however, no concrete proposals have been brought forward.[3]

BELGIUM

Paragraph 6.3.1. of the Coalition Agreement of 9 October 2014 explicitly states that the coalition will introduce a clear framework with regard to the patrimonial rights and obligations of *de facto* cohabitants. The Minister of Justice intends to regulate both the internal and the external dimensions of informal relationships. The emphasis will also lie on explaining the differences between marriage, legal cohabitation and *de facto* cohabitation to citizens.[4] It remains to be seen which priority will be given to this reform. Some individual parliamentary initiatives have also

---

1 Austrian Supreme Court, Legal Proposition RS0109605, Judgement of 01.04.1998, 9 Ob 96/98b; see C. FISCHER-CZERMAK and B. BECLIN, 'Neue Regeln für nichteheliche Lebensgemeinschaften?', in: Österreichischer Juristentag (ed.), *Zivilrecht - Neue Regelungen für nichteheliche Lebensgemeinschaften*, Manzsche Verlags- und Universitätsbuchhandlung, Vienna, 2012.

2 Available at: www.justiz.gv.at/web2013/file/2c94848642ec5e0d0142fac7f7b9019a.de.0/regprogramm.pdf.

3 According to the information provided by the Ministry of Justice by e-mail dated 04.02.2015.

4 Policy Statement in the Chamber of Representatives, *Parl.St.* Kamer 2014-15, n° 54-20/018, available at: www.lachambre.be.

been taken, but they are subsidiary to the execution of the coalition agreement.

BULGARIA

The most recent proposals to legalise some effects of informal relationships date from 2012. Some Members of Parliament from the governing party GERB declared an intention to start a wide public discussion on the need to equate some of the important effects of marriage and informal relationships.[5] The following were mentioned as being important to legalise: the adoption of children by two partners, the contracting of joint credits, and providing consent for medical treatment. An increase in the birth rate among children born outside wedlock to more than half of all children born annually was suggested as being a good reason for the proposed legal change. The opposition resurrected the old arguments: to legalise informal relationships would be against the customs and morals of Bulgarians.[6]

CROATIA

The latest proposals in this area were adopted by the Croatian Parliament on 6 June 2014.

CZECH REPUBLIC

There are no recent proposals for reform in this area. There are not many provisions referring directly to informal relationships, which means that there are fewer opportunities for any reforms of this kind. It is possible to say that the legislature does not have a need to adopt any special law or to drastically change the current legislation, since it does not show any crucial defects or gaps.

---

5 Emil Radev, a GERB MP, was a proponent of some legalisation of informal relationships: www.dnevnik.bg/live/debati/2012/07/11/1863770_da_se_legalizira_li_sujitelstvoto_bez_brak/.

6 Luben Kornezov, an MP from the Socialist Party, stated: 'Such a regulation would be the first step in legalising same-sex marriages ... it would confuse the property relations of partners and jeopardise the inheritance rights of children ... those who want to benefit from the rights of the Family Code have to enter into a marriage', at: www.dnevnik.bg/live/debati/2012/07/11/1863770_da_se_legalizira_li_sujitelstvoto_bez_brak/.

DENMARK

Denmark has rules on a public law mutual duty of care between cohabitants which is relevant to obtaining certain social benefits (educational assistance or social assistance). These rules were introduced in 2013 and came into force on 1 January 2014. Due to severe criticism the rules will be repealed as from 1 January 2016.[7]

ENGLAND AND WALES

Yes. There have been two recent Law Commission Reports which have recommended reform but both have been rejected by government for England and Wales, despite Scottish and Irish reform.

In 2007, the Law Commission for England and Wales recommended reform to provide a remedy for cohabitants on relationship breakdown to redress economic advantage and disadvantage incurred during the relationship, with a provision that couples could opt out of the scheme proposed and which was similar to Scottish legislation.[8] Their report[9] followed a thorough consultation process[10] and a previous attempt which rejected a property law-based reform and indicated that in their view, a family law-based reform of cohabitation law should be considered.[11] The 2007 proposals were formally rejected by the Coalition government in 2011. In 2011, the Law Commission published a further report regarding succession and proposed a cohabitant should succeed to a portion of a deceased cohabiting partner's estate on intestacy (see Intestacy and Family Provision Claims on Death, Law Com 331, London, TSO 2011). These proposals and the draft Inheritance (Cohabitants) Bill were rejected by the Coalition Government in March 2013.

A Private Members Cohabitation Bill put forward in 2009 by Lord Lester which aimed to provide a claim for the financial needs of a cohabitant partner against their former partners on relationship breakdown but this was rejected.

---

7 See Act No. 1522 of 27.12.2014.

8 The Family Law (Scotland) Act 2006 extended rights to cohabitants to redress economic disadvantage on relationship breakdown.

9 Law Commission, *Cohabitation: the financial consequences of relationship breakdown*, Law Com. No. 307, CM 7182, TSO, London, 2007.

10 See their consultation paper – Law Commission, *Cohabitation: the financial consequences of relationship breakdown*, Law Com No 179, TSO, London, 2006.

11 Law Commission, *Sharing Homes: a Discussion Paper*, TSO, London, 2002.

In 2014, another attempt was made through the Cohabitation Rights Bill 2014 which is Private Members Bill sponsored by Lord Marks. It has passed its second reading in the House of Lords and the planned legislation now proceeds to the committee stage, during which its provisions will be examined in greater detail by the House. If passed, the bill would give cohabiting couples similar rights to married ones, although these would not be as extensive. Amongst other measures, they would gain the right to apply for a financial settlement within two years of a relationship ending. As it is a private members bill, it is unlikely this will become law.

ESTONIA

Not at present. With regard to the fact that the Estonian Registered Partnership Act with its implementing provisions must enter into force on January 1, 2016, the legislator must include the Registered Partnership with other private as well as public legal acts, the marital property register must be rearranged etc. Thus, the implementation act of the Estonian Registered Partnership Act can be expected in the very near future.

FINLAND

It is currently being discussed whether female registered couples and female cohabiting couples should be allowed to have access to infertility treatment as a couple in the same manner as married couples and cohabiting couples of a different sex. Currently, fertility treatment can be given to couples of a different sex and single women. In practice, many of these single women actually live in a registered partnership or in a cohabiting partnership, which is, however, not recognised in the treatment process.

FRANCE

There has been no recent proposal for reform in the area of informal relationships. As already seen, little by little, specific provisions of social, labour, civil and criminal law,[12] which apply to spouses, have been extended to partners in an informal relationship (*concubinage*) and to

12 See e.g. Art. 132-80 of the French Criminal Code: the sanctions can be increased for some offences when they have been committed by a spouse, a partner in an informal relationship (*concubin*) or a partner in a PACS. Under some conditions, this can also apply to a *former* spouse or partner.

PACS partners. Recently, Law Act no. 2014-873 of 4 August 2014 has extended to partners in an informal relationship, or adapted for their benefit, certain regulations applying to spouses in the case of domestic violence, see under Question 23.

GERMANY

The German reform debate is still in its early stages. A reform has to be in line with both Art. 6 para. 1 of the German Basic Law granting special protection by the state to marriage as well as Art. 2 para. 1 of the German Basic Law guaranteeing the right of self-determination. Despite the fact that the existing situation is far from satisfactory in practice, the necessity of fundamental reform is denied by many. Up until now there has also been no visibly clear structure for reform legislation. In 1988 the 57th German Lawyers' Conference (*Deutscher Juristentag*) was in favour of a reform featuring individual measures.[13] In 1997, the party Alliance '90/The Greens put forward a draft dealing with the formation and status of a community of life as well as with compensation claims after its dissolution.[14] This draft is, however, now outdated and was never debated in Parliament.

The idea of registration for non-marital cohabitation does not have much support since marriage or registered partnership is open for couples, and it does not make much sense to offer a second set of rules – which also may not be accepted by the parties.[15] There is also scepticism about the introduction of an obligatory formal agreement to be entered into by the parties. A realistic alternative could be rules which would be applicable where there is factual cohabitation of a certain duration. One of the problems is, however, the definition of such a union and the delimitation of the issues to be regulated. It is also not clear if comprehensive

---

13 Cf. M. LÖHNIG, 'Anh. zu §§ 1297 et seq.', in: J. VON STAUDINGER, *Kommentar zum Bürgerlichen Gesetzbuch*, Sellier-de-Gruyter, Berlin, 2012, at No. 18 with references.

14 Draft for a law on the regulation of the legal relations of non-marital communities of life (*Entwurf eines Gesetzes zur Regelung der Rechtsverhältnisse nichtehelicher Lebensgemeinschaften; Nichteheliche-Lebensgemeinschaften-Gesetz* – NeLgG) of the parliamentary group Bündnis 90/Die Grünen, BT- Drucksache 13/7228 of 14.3.1997. Cf. K. Schumacher, 'Zum gesetzlichen Regelungsbedarf für nichteheliche Lebensgemeinschaften', FamRZ, 1994, at p. 857 et seq.; H. TRIMBACH and A. EL ALAMI, 'Die nichteheliche Lebensgemeinschaft – eine Herausforderung für den Gesetzgeber', Neue Justiz, 1996, at p. 57 et seq.

15 Cf. J.M. SCHERPE, 'Rechtsvergleichende Gesamtwürdigung – Empfehlungen zur Rechtsstellung nichtehelicher Lebensgemeinschaften', in: J.M. SCHERPE and N. YASSARI (eds.), *Die Rechtsstellung nichtehelicher Lebensgemeinschaften*, Mohr Siebeck, Tübingen, 2005, at p. 571, 580 et seq., and 603.

legislation on non-marital cohabitation is necessary or if a simple piecemeal approach is sufficient.[16] As regards an ongoing cohabitation, only a few provisions dealing with the internal relations of the partners seem to be necessary. In external relations, equal treatment with marriage seems in some respects to be appropriate.

GREECE

There was an attempt to regulate, in particular, permanent cohabitation arrangements between same-sex partners in the debate on the so-called 'anti-racist' legislation during the summer of 2014 (Law 4285/10-9-2014). However, the only part of the bill which finally became law was the criminalisation of actions against victims on grounds of their sexual orientation or actions motivated by racial hatred (Art. 10) in the aftermath of the ruling of the ECtHR of 7/11/2013 on appeals 29381/09 and 32684/09, in *Vallianatos and others v. Greece*. The Court found that Greece had violated Art. 8 and 14 of the European Convention on Human Rights because of its failure to regulate, through legislation, permanent homosexual relations/cohabitations, which constitutes discrimination on the grounds of sexual orientation. The appellants advanced the argument that the legislator had only made the cohabitation pact available to heterosexual couples, thereby failing to extend it to homosexuals. They referred in detail to the public consultation preceding the passage of the law, setting out the positions taken by the Greek Orthodox Church, the National Commission for Human Rights and other bodies, adducing evidence to show that Greece was the only state in Europe which, while regulating heterosexual relations outside marriage (since there is no legal obligation for those not wishing to marry or to become engaged to make use of the cohabitation pact), limits the provisions in question to heterosexual couples, and asking the ECtHR to explore the need for the regulation of homosexual relations. The appellants asked the ECtHR to rule that Law 3719/2008 on the cohabitation pact for heterosexual couples constitutes discriminatory treatment on grounds of sexual orientation and an infringement of Art. 8 and 14 of the Convention. They also claimed an infringement of Art. 13 of the Convention, in that there was no suitable legal avenue in the Greek system for an appeal against the covert discrimination introduced by Law 3719/2008. Finally, they invoked Art. 41 of the European Convention on Human Rights on the awarding of fair damages.

---

16 M. LÖHNIG, 'Anh. zu §§ 1297 et seq.', in: J. VON STAUDINGER, *Kommentar zum Bürgerlichen Gesetzbuch*, Sellier-de-Gruyter, Berlin, 2012, at No. 20 and 22.

As the ECtHR pointed out in its previous jurisprudence, same-sex stable relationships are included within the scope of family life under Art. 8 ECHR.[17] Accordingly, any discriminatory treatment of their right to enjoy privacy and family life would violate Arts 8 and 14 ECHR. In the Vallianatos case, after performing a proportionality test, the Court concluded that Law 3719/2008 was not pursuing any legitimate aim that could justify the exclusion of same-sex couples from its scope. In the Court's observations, there was a perfect analogy between opposite-sex and same-sex couples as far as their needs for mutual assistance, companionship and care were concerned, thus deeming their being banned from legislatively recognised civil unions unnecessary in a democratic society.[18]

According to research by journalists, the institution of the cohabitation pact for heterosexual couples has not been embraced by society. It is said that since the law came into effect, and in the region of Athens and Piraeus, where half the population of Greece is concentrated, no more than 127 of these pacts have been concluded.[19]

HUNGARY

As the new Hungarian Civil Code, which includes new provisions on cohabitation, entered into force in March 2014 there is currently no new proposal.

REPUBLIC OF IRELAND

The Irish Children and Family Relationships Bill contains provisions which increase the legal recognition of informal relationships by providing them with the rights, responsibilities and duties of guardianship, and which does the same for adoption through amending the relevant adoption legislation. This brings those couples in informal

---

17 ECtHR, *Shalk and Kopf v. Austria*, No. 30141/04, 24.6.2010.

18 C. Deliyianni-Dimitrakou and C. Akrivopoulou, *Fundamental Rights and Private Relations in Greek and European Law*, Sakkoulas, Thessaloniki-Athens, 2014.

19 See also the criticism of the legislator responsible for the cohabitation pacts in A. Koutsouradis, 'Nutzlose Reformen im griechischen Familienrecht - Am Beispiel der verschiedengeschlechtlichen eingetragenen Partnerschaft', in: A. Büchler and M. Müller-Chen (eds.), *Festschrift für Ingeborg Schwenzer*, Stämpfli Verlag, Bern, 2011, pp. 981 et seq.

relationships closer in legal provision and recognition to married couples.[20]

The Bill includes some far reaching provisions which will be examined below. These include the extension of automatic guardianship to non-marital fathers cohabiting for a specified period with the child's mother. Other major developments in the Bill include the provisions on Assisted Human Reproduction. Part 12 of the Bill allows same-sex couples, both civil partners and cohabiting couples, to adopt a child jointly subject to the requirement that they are suitable adopters. Part 7 of the Bill sets out various provisions by which a wider circle of people will be able to apply for guardianship, custody of, or access to a child. Part 9 of the Bill sets out various provisions which aim to help make 'parenting work'. The law relating to child maintenance is amended so that all children will be treated equally regardless of the circumstances of conception and birth, when making child support/lump sum orders. Mediation is encouraged to resolve disputes about children of estranged parents (Part 8).

ITALY

The XVIIth legislature began on 15 March 2013. Since then several bills[21] have been presented and many of them have been unified in the *disegno di legge* n. 1211 (the first to sign was on. Marcucci) entitled 'Modifications to the civil code in the matter of the regulation of civil unions and cohabitation agreements'.

This bill introduces two kinds of registers to be kept in each of the country's municipalities. The first of them, called the Register of Civil Unions, will only be available to adults of the same sex 'united by a reciprocal affective bond'. From the moment of registration the two partners – bound by a reciprocal duty of moral and material support and to contribute to their communal life – will have to choose the patrimonial regime of the union (if they do not choose, the regime of community of

[20] The author, Geoffrey Shannon, acts as the sole Government Rapporteur in this area and has made extensive proposals for reform which are reflected in the Children and Family Relationships Bill. See website of Department of Children and Youth Affairs.

[21] Disegno di legge N. 14 (Manconi and Corsini) Discipline of civil unions; 197 (Alberti Casellati and others) Modifications to the civil code in the matter of the regulation of the cohabitation agreement; 239 (Giovanardi and others) Introduction into the civil code of the contract of cohabitation and subsidiarity; 314 (Barani and Mussolini) Discipline of the reciprocal rights and duties of the cohabitants; 909 (Petraglia and others) Rules on civil unions and unions of reciprocal aid.

property will apply) and in case of death the rights provided for the civil partner are the same as those provided by the code for spouses. When a child is born to a partner - even through medically assisted reproduction - the other partner is considered to be his or her parent from the moment of conception. The union may be dissolved by both a common or unilateral decision.

The other register is the Register of Cohabitation Agreements (*patto di convivenza*) where adult persons of the same or different sex may ask to be registered in order 'to organise their life together'. They are bound by a reciprocal duty of moral and material support and to contribute to their communal life, but no legal regime regarding their property applies, nor any of the rules provided by the code in the matter of the law of succession. In contrast, the rights and duties stipulated for spouses in matters of healthcare and imprisonment do apply to registered partners.

The head of the current Italian government, Matteo Renzi, has declared his intention to intervene in the matter of informal partnerships, so this bill does appear to have the chance of becoming law.

LATVIA

In October 2014 the Judicial Policy Subcommittee of the Legal Affairs Committee of the Saeima assessed the proposal of the Council of Sworn Notaries of Latvia on entering into marriage by way of a procedure before a sworn notary besides procedures in the civil registry and in the church. Although this proposal is not directly related to the sphere of informal relationship, the Council of Sworn Notaries based its proposal on the results of a sociological inquiry about legal security in unregistered relationships and marriage. In the inquiry it was concluded that people choose to live in unregistered partnerships because they do not see the point of getting married. People feel discouraged from registering a marriage because of the supposed difficulty of the procedure, the large financial investment it would require and also because people have not yet faced a situation when the status of spouses would have been necessary. The inquiry also showed that 22% of respondents would feel encouraged to get married if entering into marriage was simple and quick. In the Subcommittee meeting no concrete decision was taken to support or to reject this proposal, but it was indicated that work on this issue must be continued and that it was necessary to have a wider discussion on such matters in society.[22]

In November 2014 the discussion in society and among politicians about the necessity for the legal order on unregistered relationships was stimulated by the already mentioned court judgment by which the application of IV to recognise a *de facto* marriage with ER who died fulfilling his duties at the State Fire and Rescue Service of Latvia, was refused. To date, no concrete proposals have been developed. However, in December 2014 when the law on the 'Medium Term Budget Framework for 2015, 2016 and 2017' was passed, financial means were marked out for conducting a study on the problems of unregistered marriage.

LITHUANIA

On 16 June 2014, the Ministry of Justice submitted to the Government a Draft Law on the Amendment of Art. 2.18, 2.19, 3.16, 3.140 and 3.150 as well as Chapter XV of Part VI, Book III and Art. 5.13 of the Lithuanian Civil Code.[23] According to this draft, a partnership is defined as cohabitation (living together) between a man and a woman (the partners) in order to build a family relationship without the registration of marriage. Partners must be adults, not linked by blood relations, and not married to each other or to any other person, and they cannot also be in a registered partnership with another person. Both partners must have legal capacity at the time of entering into the partnership. Partners shall be loyal to each other, show mutual respect, render moral and material support to each other, and contribute to the common family needs or the needs of the other partner. A partnership entails legal consequences from the moment of entering into cohabitation. A partnership entails legal consequences with respect to third parties if the Residents' Register Service of the Republic of Lithuania contains a corresponding record made on the basis of a joint declaration of partnership signed by both partners and duly notarised. Such data shall be notified to the Residents' Register Service by the notary within 3 working days. Any property acquired during the partnership in the name of both partners or one of them shall be considered to be the joint-partial property of the partners.

22 Judicial Policy Subcommittee of the Legal Affairs Committee of the Saeima, 14 October 2014 record of meeting (not published).

23 See: www.lrs.lt/pls/proj/dokpaieska.showdoc_l?p_id=241949&p_org=8&p_fix=n&p_gov=n.

The draft also includes the possibility of succession by law to the deceased partner's property.

LUXEMBOURG

No, there are no recent proposals at this time.

THE NETHERLANDS

In 2009 the Ministry of Security and Justice commissioned research on two subjects: couples married under a separation of property regime without a duty to net income or capital and non-marital cohabitants.[24] The research question in relation to non-marital cohabitants was limited to the nature and scale of problems resulting from a relationship breakdown and their solution. The research was limited to situations in which a separation of an informal couple resulted in serious financial problems or profound injustice due to investments (either in money or non-financial contributions) by one partner resulting in profit for the other partner. Whether the law as it stands is sufficiently capable of dealing with non-marital cohabitation was not included.[25] With respect to the first problem, the researchers estimated[26] that about 20,000 women with children suffer serious financial difficulties after a relationship breakdown. The number of couples who experienced an unfair dissolution of their non-marital relationship could not be estimated.[27]

As to the causes of the problems the report refers to the relationship-based reduction in the earning capacity of women and unfair effects encountered by child-caring women after a relationship breakdown. These effects are not compensated by the law (no statutory maintenance obligations, no relocation of unequal property relationships). Serious problems and unfair effects mainly occur when one partner's child-care and work in the business of the other partner is combined with the sole ownership of the business by the latter partner.

---

24 M.V. ANTOKOLSKAIA, B. BREEDERVELD, J.E. HULST, W.D KOLKMAN, F.R. SALOMONS and L.C.A. VERSTAPPEN, 'Koude uitsluiting, Materiële problemen en onbillijkheden na scheiding van in koude uitsluiting gehuwde echtgenoten en na scheiding van ongehuwd samenlevende partners, alsmede instrumenten voor de overheid om deze tegen te gaan', WODC, The Hague, 2011.

25 W.M. SCHRAMA, 'Een lex specialis voor ongehuwde samenlevers?', *Tijdschrift voor Familie- en Jeugdrecht*, 2012, pp. 242-248.

26 Hardly any empirical data were (and are) available.

27 See the English summary of the report at: wodc.nl/onderzoeksdatabase/koude-uitsluiting.aspx.

Based on extensive comparative law research, the report suggests that the legislature should consider the introduction of a number of specific legal instruments to mitigate the financial problems and unfair effects resulting from the termination of informal relationships, especially in the interest of the couples' children. Maintenance in all informal marriage-like relationships would allow a temporary mitigation of the reduction in the earning capacity of the child-caring partner. [28] Several other instruments, also suggested in relation to the problems of spouses, could be applied to informal partners: a provision on the household expenses as is applicable for married couples (Art. 1:84 Dutch Civil Code); a provision for the compensation for investments (like Art. 1:87 Dutch Civil Code for married couples); a regulation regarding fair compensation for unpaid work in the business of the other partner; a discretionary power of the court to amend a cohabitation contract; procedural rules regarding provisional orders and orders on ancillary matters in cases of separation.

At first the State Secretary's response was rather positive in relation to the recommendation to introduce a maintenance right/duty after a separation of an informal couple.[29] With respect to the other proposed instruments, he was rather hesitant. Later, after a number of organizations working in this field[30] had reflected on the proposals, many objections were raised. In 2012, the government declined to follow all the recommendations except one.[31] It argued that the suggested legal instruments were not necessary since the law of obligations, contract law and property law are sufficient. Moreover, the State Secretary concluded that the relevant organizations do not support the instruments. In 2011 civil procedural legislation was announced[32] introducing similar procedural means as apply to married couples in order to concentrate all disputes in one procedure on the basis of a petition procedure.[33] In addition, civil procedural law for informal couples would provide for the option of orders on ancillary matters pertaining to separation. In the spring of 2015 still no bill has been introduced to this effect.

---

28 Strongly opposed: J. VAN DUIJVENDIJK-BRAND, 'Ex-samenwonenden en het onderhoudsrecht', *FJR*, 2007. See also: A.R.J. MULDER and E.M. VAN LIEROP-SNUIF, 'Onderhoudsplichten en rechten voor ex-ongehuwd samenlevers', *FJR*, 2011.

29 *Kamerstukken* II 2011-2012, 28 867 no. 23, p. 13.

30 Raad voor de rechtspraak, the Nederlandse Orde van Advocaten, the Vereniging van Familierecht, Advocaten Scheidingsmediators (vFAS) and the Koninklijke Notariële Beroepsorganisatie.

31 *Kamerstukken* II 2011-2012, 28 678 no. 29.

32 *Kamerstukken* II 2011-2012, 28 867 no. 23.

33 Instead of the contentious procedure which has to be used by informal couples.

Whether a *lex specialis* is the right response to deal with the existing problems is a matter of balancing the different interests at stake. In the legal doctrine there is no consensus as to the outcome. Some researchers emphasise that the lack of legally prescribed solidarity resulting in unjust outcomes and poverty can only be remedied by specific legislation.[34] At the other end, the view is expressed that since there are no problems in relation to the application of contract and property law, there is nothing to be solved.[35] Others recognise the nature and extent of the problems, but are somewhat reluctant to see yet another *lex specialis*.[36] Preferably, alternatives should first be analysed, such as a better use of cohabitation contracts. Anyway, it is a missed opportunity that the government in 2011 did not present a coherent view on non-marital cohabitation, in particular given the fact that the current policy will inevitably result in a growing number of partners and children falling outside the scope of family law.

NORWAY

Currently no proposals exist for reform in this area.

PORTUGAL

None following the approval of Law No. 23/2010, of 30 August, amending Law No. 7/2001, of 11 May.

RUSSIA

No. There have been several attempts by members of the academic community to place legislation governing informal relationships on the

34 M.V. ANTOKOLSKAIA, B. BREEDERVELD, J.E. HULST, W.D KOLKMAN, F.R. SALOMONS, L.C.A. VERSTAPPEN, 'Koude uitsluiting, Materiële problemen en onbillijkheden na scheiding van in koude uitsluiting gehuwde echtgenoten en na scheiding van ongehuwd samenlevende partners, alsmede instrumenten voor de overheid om deze tegen te gaan', WODC, The Hague, 2011, at p. 233 et seq. C. FORDER and A.L.P.G. VERBEKE, *Gehuwd of niet: maakt het iets uit?*, Intersentia, Antwerp, 2005, at p. 638-640; A.N. LABOHM, 'Samenlevers met en zonder contract', *EB*, 2011.

35 C.G. BREEDVELD-DE VOOGD, 'Het huis waarin zij samenwoonden', *FJR*, 2007.

36 Y. QUISPEL, 'Niet-geregistreerde samenwoners vanuit het perspectief van het huwelijksvermogens- en erfrecht', *FJR*, 2005, who suggests to introduce a registration of a compulsory cohabitation contract of a couple at the *Basisregistratie Personen*. W.M. SCHRAMA, 'Een redelijk en billijk relatierecht', *TPR*, 2010, pp. 1703-1740 and W.M. SCHRAMA, 'Een lex specialis voor ongehuwde samenlevers?', *Tijdschrift voor Familie- en Jeugdrecht*, 2012, pp. 242-248.

agenda of the Duma (the Lower Chamber of the Russian Parliament), but these have so far been unsuccessful.

SCOTLAND

There are proposals for reform of the law of testate and intestate succession which would affect cohabitants. The Scottish Law Commission published its 'Report on Succession' in 2009[37] and the Scottish government has now indicated its intention to proceed with reform in this area. The proposed reform would involve repeal of the existing provision by which a surviving cohabitant may apply for a discretionary award on intestacy.[38] The current provision has been criticised for its strict time limit, its restriction to intestacy and its highly discretionary nature. To date there have been very few cases brought under S. 29 and thus there is very little guidance as to how the courts might deal with applications. This has heightened concern about the vague and discretionary nature of the provision. The Scottish Law Commission has proposed a new provision which would apply to both testate and intestate estates. The proposal is that, within one year of death, the surviving cohabitant could apply to court for financial provision which would be calculated on the basis of an 'appropriate percentage'. In assessing the appropriate percentage, the court would take into account three factors: the length of cohabitation, the interdependence, financial or otherwise, of the partners during cohabitation and what the survivor contributed to the couple's life together financial or otherwise.[39] The percentage could not exceed 100% of the share to which a surviving spouse or civil partner would have been entitled, and in the case of both a surviving spouse and cohabitant, the appropriate percentage would be applied to one half of the available estate.

SLOVAKIA

There are no recent proposals to reform the rules regarding informal relationships between a couple in Slovakia.

37 Scot Law Com, No 215, 2009.
38 Family Law (Scotland) Act 2006, S. 29.
39 Scot Law Com, No 215, para. 4.14.

SLOVENIA

In January 2015, the collegium of the president of the National Assembly, as a result of a proposal by the political party Združena levica (United Left) submitted on 15 December 2014, took the decision to adopt, by means of an accelerated legislative procedure, a proposed Act to amend the Slovenian Marriage Act,[40] which alters the definition of a marriage and an extramarital union into a sexually neutral definition: the draft amending act replaces the phrase 'community of a man and a woman' with the words 'community of two persons'.

SPAIN

There are no recent proposals for reform in this area in Spain.

SWEDEN

Even if the Swedish government, in connection with the 2003 law reform, was sympathetic towards future law reforms to strengthen the mutual rights and duties of unmarried cohabiting couples, no such proposals have in fact been presented by law commissions or the government to Parliament. Currently (2015), a law commission is considering how to amend the legislation so as to provide increased prospects for treating involuntary childlessness.[41] No differences are to be made on the basis of whether the relevant parties wishing to have a child are in a formalised or an informal relationship of cohabitation. In 2009, a law commission proposed extending the right to joint adoption of children to cohabiting couples.[42] This proposal is currently under consideration by the government and may result in a Bill to Parliament in 2015 or 2016.

In the legal literature, on the contrary, there is active debate on how to improve the mutual legal rights of people living together as a couple in an informal relationship. Nordic legal scholars have, furthermore, carried out joint research on how best to harmonise the Nordic laws (Denmark, Finland, Iceland, Norway and Sweden) on informal cohabitation. The proposals have been published in the book *Nordisk samboerrett*,[43] the

---

40 Proposed Act to amend the Marriage and Family Relations Act (ZZZDR-D), shortened procedure, EPA 257-VII, available at: imss.dz-rs.si/imis/4c9d4b6c7a20845698d5.pdf.

41 Utredningen om utökade möjligheter till behandling av ofrivillig barnlöshet, Dir. 2013:70 (Committee on increased prospects for treatment of involuntary childlessness).

42 Statens Offentliga Utredningar, SOU 2009:61.

43 J. ASLAND et al., *Nordisk samboerrett*, Gyldendal, Oslo, 2014.

English translation of which - *Nordic Cohabitation Law* - was published in 2015.

SWITZERLAND

There are no recent proposals with regard to a comprehensive reform in the area of informal relationships. However, there are a few reforms which are relevant, on some points, for informal relationships.

Currently, there is a legislative motion pending which requests the Swiss Federal Council to modernise the Swiss law of succession.[44] Accordingly, intestate succession and the right to a reserved share (*Pflichtteilsrecht*) shall be more flexible and adapted to the demographic, social and family-related changes and in particular shall include partners in an informal relationship. The legislature has accepted this motion; however, it has further included the condition that with regard to the law of succession no equal treatment between couples in an informal relationship and married couples should be granted.[45]

Furthermore, a major revision of child support is pending. According to the draft, child support shall encompass the costs incurred by the person caring for the child for forgoing gainful employment.[46] This means that child support would replace the support obligation towards the former spouse who is caring for the child (a similar regulation for the unmarried mother does not exist in Swiss law). Accordingly, an unmarried mother might soon receive financial support, at least indirectly, via child support.

Moreover, a draft allowing for step-parent adoption in informal relationships (as well as in registered same-sex relationships) is pending.[47] Currently, only adoption by a single person is open to partners living in an informal relationship. According to the draft, joint adoption is still only provided for married couples.

---

44 Motion 10.3524 Gutzwiller 'Für ein zeitgemässes Erbrecht'.

45 Amtliches Bulletin Nationalrat 2011, at p. 111 ('*keine erbrechtliche Gleichstellung der Konkubinatspaare mit den Ehepaaren*').

46 See Art. 276 para. 2 and Art. 285 para. 2 Draft Swiss Civil Code, available at: www.bj.admin.ch/bj/ de/home/gesellschaft/gesetzgebung/kindesunterhalt.html.

47 See Art. 264c para. 1 Draft Swiss Civil Code, available at: www.bj.admin.ch/bj/de/home/gesellschaft/gesetzgebung/adoptionsrecht.html.

Finally, the Swiss Federal Council has been requested to present a report on a modern and coherent civil and especially family law.[48] The referring expert opinions and discussions have - amongst other subjects - addressed the regulation of informal relationships.[49] The final report has just recently been published.[50] A comprehensive legal regulation of informal relationships has not been proposed. Rather, the Swiss Federal Council considers evaluating a regulation similar to the *pacte civil de solidarité* (PACS) as known in France or at least a regulation for informal relationships in cases of hardship.

48 Postulat 12.3607 Fehr 'Zeitgemässes kohärentes Zivil- und insbesondere Familienrecht'.

49 For the presentations and contributions to the discussions and expert opinion (I. SCHWENZER, 'Familienrecht und gesellschaftliche Veränderungen'), see *Die Praxis des Familienrechts*, 2014, at p. 779-1008.

50 Bericht des Bundesrates zum Postulat Fehr (12.3607), 'Modernisierung des Familienrechts', available at: www.ejpd.admin.ch/ejpd/de/home/aktuell/news/2015/Onderhoudsplichten 2015-03-250.html.

PART B
STATISTICS AND ESTIMATIONS

QUESTION 10

How many marriages and, if permissible, other formalised relationships (such as registered partnerships and civil unions) have been concluded per annum? How do these figures relate to the size of the population and the age profile? Where relevant and available, please provide information on the gender of the couple.

AUSTRIA

Marriages (available only for heterosexual couples) concluded per annum in Austria since 2003[1]

Year	Marriages	Total population	Average age at the first marriage female	Average age at the first marriage male
2003	37,195	8,118,245	27.7	30.4
2004	38,528	8,169,441	27.9	30.6
2005	39,153	8,225,278	28.1	30.9
2006	36,923	8,267,948	28.6	31.4
2007	35,996	8,295,189	28.8	31.6
2008	35,223	8,321,541	28.9	31.7
2009	35,469	8,341,483	29.1	31.8
2010	37,545	8,361,069	29.3	31.9
2011	36,426	8,388,534	29.5	32
2012	38,529	8,426,311	29.8	32.2
2013	36,140	8,477,230	29.8	32.2

Registered partnerships (available only for same-sex couples) concluded per annum in Austria since 2010[2]

	2010	2011	2012	2013
Total	705	433	386	368
Male	450	259	231	203

1 Statistik Austria, available at: www.statistik.at/web_de/statistiken/bevoelkerung/eheschliessungen/023945.html.

2 Statistik Austria, available at: www.statistik.at/web_de/statistiken/bevoelkerung/gleichgeschlechtliche_partnerschaften_eintragung_und_aufloesung/partnerschaftsbegruendungen/053657.html.

18-30 years	125	81	93	85
30-50 years	532	306	260	247
Over 50 years	243	131	109	74
Female	255	174	155	165
18-30	120	79	80	93
30-50	309	214	184	189
Over 50 years	81	55	46	48

BELGIUM

Over the years, there has been a slight decrease in the number of marriages in Belgium. Nevertheless, the total number of marriages remains quite high, compared to other European countries.

Number of marriages in Belgium per year (ADSEI)

Year	Number of marriages
2003	41,777
2004	43,296
2005	43,141
2006	44,813
2007	45,561
2008	45,613
2009	43,303
2010	42,159
2011	41,001
2012	42,198
2013	37,854

Informal relationships are not officially registered, but the National Statistics Office does provide statistics on legal cohabitations. Both statistics on different-sex and same-sex cohabitations are available, but do not distinguish between intra-family and other forms of cohabitation. From 2013 onwards, the number of legal cohabitations outweighs the number of marriages.

Number of persons who entered into a legal cohabitation in Belgium per year (ADSEI)

Year	Total	Different-sex	Same-sex
2002	544	4,397	747
2003	21,427	20,380	1047
2004	8,958	8,239	719
2005	11,263	10,470	793
2006	18,729	17,802	927
2007	30,961	29,811	1150
2008	34,605	33,366	1239

2009	49,515	47,790	1725
2010	64,021	61,900	2121
2011	67,561	65,406	2155
2012	72,191	69,946	2245
2013	78,392	75,954	2438

BULGARIA

The National Statistics Institute provides information only on the number of marriages concluded per annum. These are the only formalised heterosexual relationships regulated by law.

Two national censuses have been conducted by the National Statistics Institute for the period 2000-2014: in 2001 and in 2011. Most of the data below comes from these censuses.[3]

The population of Bulgaria decreased from 7,928,901 persons in 2001 to 7,364,570 persons in 2011. The age profile of the population also changed between the two national polls. There is an ageing population and this can be seen by the decrease in both the absolute number and the share of the young population (under 15 years of age) as well as in the increase among the elderly (above 65 years of age):

- In 2001 the share of children below 15 years of age in the total population was 15.3%. In 2011 this had decreased to 13.2%.
- The share of the population aged 15-64 increased insignificantly during 2001-2011 by 0.4% to reach 68.3% of the total population.
- The share of the elderly (65 and above) showed the largest increase: from 16.8% in 2001 to 18.5% in 2011.[4]

In such a context the statistics provide the following data on the behaviour of Bulgarians towards family creation and dissolution:

3 The information in its entirety is available at: www.nsi.bg/census2011/. Also in: Report on the Implementation of the Revised National Strategy on Demographic Development of the Population in Republic of Bulgaria (2012-2030), passed by the Council of Ministers, decision No. 40/ 1 October 2014: 2013. Available in Bulgarian at: www.mlsp.government.bg/bg/docs/indexstr.htm.

4 Available at: www.nsi.bg/census2011.

Number of marriages (and the marriage rate)[5]

Year	Marriages	Marriage rate[6]	Divorces	Divorce rate
2000	35,164	-	10,578	-
2001	31,974	4.0%	10,275	1.3%
2002	29,218	3.7%	10,203	1.3%
2003	30,645	3.9%	12,003	1.5%
2004	31,038	4.0%	14,669	1.9%
2005	33,501	4.3%	14,676	1.9%
2006	32,773	4.3%	14,828	1.9%
2007	29,640	3.9%	16,347	2.2%
2008	27,722	3.7%	14,104	1.9%
2009	25,923	3.5%	11,662	1.6%
2010	24,286	3.3%	11,012	1.5%
2011	21,448	2.9%	10,581	1.4%
2012	21,167	2.9%	11,947	2.9%
2013	21,943	3.0%	10,908	2.9%

Additional data is available on the number and structure of the families and households in Bulgaria.[7] It suggests an increase in the number of families by 289,807 (12.0%) and of their members by 658,843 (9.1%) for the period 1965-1985. Subsequently, a reverse trend can be seen: a total decrease in the number of families by 576,731 and of their members by 2,139,542. The largest decrease can be seen in the number of families between 2001 and 2011: by 1.02.2011 there were 245,876 (10.4%) fewer families in comparison with 2001.[8]

Structure of the households and formal families in 2011

Total number of households	3,006,376
Average number of family members in households	2.4
Total number of families based on marriage	2,123,224
Average number of family members	2.7
Families with unmarried children	996,446
Families without children	813,995
One-parent families with (unmarried) children	312,783

5 Specific information on marriages and divorces is available at: www.nsi.bg/bg/content/3044/бракоразводи-по-области-и-местоживеене/.

6 Source Eurostat: ec.europa.eu/eurostat/tgm/table.do?tab=table&init=1&language=en&pcode=tps00012&plugin=1.

7 Report on the Implementation of the Revised National Strategy on Demographic Development of the Population in the Republic of Bulgaria (2012-2030), 2012: 37; 2013: 18.

8 National Census 2011, Families. at: www.nsi.bg/census2011/pagebg2.php?p2=175&sp2=200.

Another trend is the significant decrease in the numbers of full nuclear families (spouses and unmarried children) during 1985-2011. Their share also decreased from 54.7% in 1985 to 50.8% in 2001 and to 46.9% in 2011. The share of persons who had entered into a marriage in 2011 had decreased by 10% compared to 2001. The share of persons living in informal relationships had doubled during the same period: from 4% in 2001 to almost 8% in 2011.

CROATIA

The number of concluded marriages per annum and its relation to the size of the population are shown in:

- Graph no. 1 (Marriages and Divorces, 1983-2012) and
- Graph no. 2 (Natural Change in the Population, 1993-2012).

Marriages and divorces, 1983-2012

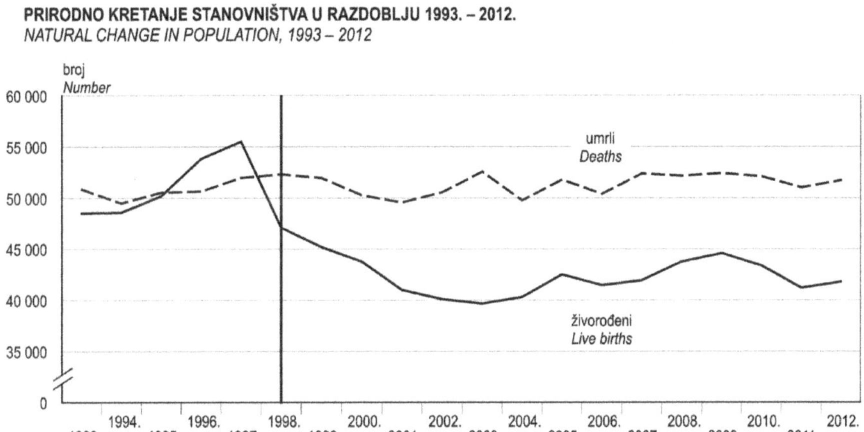

Source: Statistical Report of the Croatian Bureau of Statistics - Natural Change in the Population in 2012, available at: www.dzs.hr (as of 1 December 2014).

Natural change in the population, 1993-2012

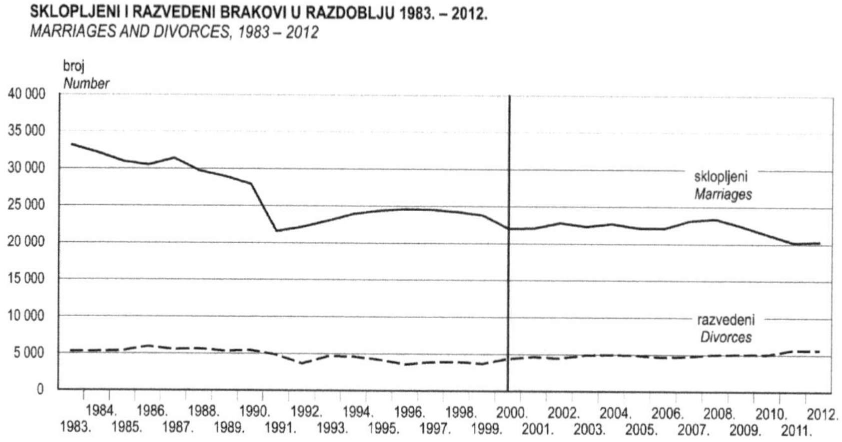

Source: Statistical Report of the Croatian Bureau of Statistics – Natural Change in the Population in 2012, available at: www.dzs.hr (as of 1 December 2014).

Same-sex registered partnerships were introduced in the Croatian legal system in September 2014, so there are still no annual statistical data.

Since a marriage can only be concluded by a heterosexual couple and a registered partnership by a homosexual couple, the gender of the couple is not relevant in this matter.

CZECH REPUBLIC

Year	Marriage	Registered partnership	Inhabitants
2006	52,860	235	10,287,189
2007	57,157	252	10,381,130
2008	52,457	231	11,467,500
2009	47,900	203	10,506,800
2010	46,700	195	10,532,770
2011	45,100	177	10,504,200
2012	45,200	206	10,513,100
2013	43,500	201	10,512,400
2014	45,600	233	10,538,300

From the table[9] above it is obvious that many couples wanted to get registered as soon as this legal option was given to them. Currently there are 1,295 male and 638 female couples registered in the Czech Republic.

[9] Data gathered from various articles and statistics published on the official website of the Czech Statistical Office, available at: www.czso.cz/csu/czso/domov.

As for marriage, the greatest number of people got married in 2007, in July, which could have been caused by the 'magic' date '07.07.07' and probably not by any demographic or legal reason. As the table shows, in 2013 there were only 43,500 marriages, which is the lowest number since 1918. Recent studies also show a representation of those countries that are most common in marriages with a foreigner. Czech men marry on the whole women from Slovakia, Ukraine and Russia; Czech women marry on the whole men from Slovakia, Germany and UK. Nowadays the average age of a man entering marriage for the first time is 29, and for women the average age is 27. For 67.5% of individuals it is their first formal relationship.

DENMARK

Marriages per annum[10]

Year	Concluded marriages
1990	31,513
2000	38,388
2007	36,476
2010	30,949
2013	27,503

On 1 January 2014 the population of Denmark was about 5.6 million, of whom about 1.1 million were under 18.

The average age for first-time marriages shows that the ages are increasing for both men and women:

Year	Men	Women
1990	30.2	27.6
2000	32.5	30.1
2013	34.9	32.2

Same-sex marriage was introduced on 15 June 2012. More women than men have entered into a marriage with a partner of the same sex:

Year	Same-sex marriage, both men	Same-sex marriage, both women
2012	104	164
2013	129	234

10 Unless otherwise stated, the statistical information in replies to Questions 10-17 is taken from Danmarks Statistik, Befolkning og Valg, Statistikbanken.

The number of registered partnerships entered into does not show a great variation:

Year	Registered partnerships
1990	457
1995	266
2000	310
2005	390
2011	346

ENGLAND AND WALES

Number of marriages and civil partnerships formed in England and Wales 2000-2012

Year	Marriages (heterosexual)[11]	Civil partnerships	CP male	CP female
2000	267,961	-	-	-
2001	249,227	-	-	-
2002	255,596	-	-	-
2003	270,109	-	-	-
2004	273,069	-	-	-
2005[12]	247,805	1,857	1,228	629
2006	239,454	14,943	9,003	5,940
2007	235,367	7,929	4,371	3,558
2008	235,794	6,558	3,536	3,022
2009	232,443	5,687	2,962	2,725
2010	243,808	5,804	2,868	2,936
2011	249,133	6,152	3,171	2,981
2012	262,240	6,362	3,138	3,224

Source: ONS.[13]

Marriages:

The provisional number of marriages registered in England and Wales rose by 5.3% in 2012 to 262,240, compared with 249,133 in 2011. This increase in the provisional marriage figure for 2012 continues the recent upward trend, following the low number recorded for 2009 which itself followed 20 years of decline in the number of marriages.

---

11 The figures for marriage relate to heterosexual marriage as same-sex marriage was only introduced in 2013 and no data are yet available.

12 Same-sex civil partnership was introduced on 5 December 2005 in England and Wales.

13 These data were compiled from tables in ONS 2013 on-line publications *Marriages in England and Wales (Provisional) 2012*, available at: www.ons.gov.uk/ons/dcp171778_366530.pdf and *Civil Partnerships in the UK*, 2012, available at: www.ons.gov.uk/ons/dcp171778_329457.pdf.

The provisional male General Marriage Rate (GMR) in 2012 was 23.2 men marrying per thousand unmarried men aged 16 and over, compared with 22.1 in 2011 and 27.4 in 2002. The provisional GMR for women in 2012 was 21.0 women marrying per thousand unmarried women aged 16 and over, compared with 19.9 in 2011 and 23.9 in 2002.

Since 1972 the mean age at first marriage has increased by almost eight years for both men and women. In 2012 the provisional mean age at marriage for never-married men was 32.4 years, while for never married women it was 30.3 years. This compares with 24.9 years and 22.9 years respectively in 1972.

Provisional figures show that in 2012, 175,040 marriages in England and Wales were first marriages for both partners. This accounted for 67% of all marriages. This number peaked in 1940 at 426,100 when 91% of all marriages were the first for both partners. Remarriages for both parties accounted for 15% of all marriages in 2012. The remaining 19% of marriages were of couples where only one partner had been married previously. The proportion of marriages that were the first for both parties has gradually increased since 1996 (rise of 9.1 percentage points), while remarriages for one or both parties have decreased over the same period (fall of 4.6 percentage points for both).

Civil partnerships:
The mean (average) age at formation of civil partnership in the UK fell slightly from 40.1 years in 2011 to 40.0 in 2012 for men, and for women from 38.3 years in 2011 to 37.6 in 2012. The average age at formation has been decreasing year on year as older couples who had waited for the introduction of the legislation took the opportunity to form a civil partnership early on.

In 2012, there were slightly more female civil partnerships (51%) in the UK than male, whereas in 2011 there were slightly more male civil partnerships (51%) than female. Initially the numbers of males forming civil partnerships were much higher than females, but the numbers of male and female civil partnerships converged in 2009/10.

ESTONIA

The number of concluded marriages and marriages per 1000 of the population, 2000–2013

Year	Concluded marriages	Marriages per 1,000 of the population
2000	5,485	3.93
2001	5,647	4.07
2002	5,853	4.24
2003	5,699	4.16
2004	6,009	4.41
2005	6,121	4.52
2006	6,954	5.16
2007	7,022	5.24
2008	6,127	4.58
2009	5,362	4.02
2010	5,066	3.80
2011	5,499	4.14
2012	5,888	4.45
2013	5,630	4.27

Source: Statistics Estonia.

Married people according to gender and age, 2000–2013

Age	2000	2001	2002	2003	2004	2005	2006
Men							
15-19	110	107	78	84	90	65	100
20-24	1,293	1,258	1,151	1,153	1,102	1,111	1,250
25-29	1,569	1,567	1,762	1,682	1,720	1,813	1,920
30-34	898	1,002	1,132	1,102	1,255	1,172	1,413
35-49	472	540	590	623	662	712	873
40-44	382	390	388	367	408	438	485
45-49	255	272	292	245	291	316	361
50-54	191	188	197	170	178	205	243
55-59	116	131	114	107	147	140	155
60+	199	192	149	166	156	149	154
Women							
15-19	492	475	414	407	388	369	417
20-24	1,773	1,737	1,751	1,706	1,737	1,772	1,929
25-29	1,327	1,426	1,604	1,563	1,626	1,679	1,879
30-34	672	705	864	835	925	889	1,110
35-49	375	423	414	423	474	527	632
40-44	264	312	274	289	305	327	348
45-49	233	240	237	191	220	216	266
50-54	155	148	151	118	172	163	190
55-59	67	75	65	75	80	91	96
60+	127	106	79	92	82	88	87

Age	2007	2008	2009	2010	2011	2012	2013
Men							
15-19	82	60	52	40	32	21	32
20-24	1,121	954	728	678	646	626	575
25-29	1,968	1,721	1,511	1,382	1,534	1,589	1,568
30-34	1,485	1,254	1,144	1,144	1,170	1,327	1,241
35-49	924	799	726	706	847	918	793
40-44	531	469	424	426	481	556	567
45-49	363	350	302	270	296	333	326
50-54	263	220	180	185	230	226	239
55-59	135	149	141	100	129	144	135
60+	150	151	154	135	134	148	154
Women							
15-19	367	312	184	162	137	123	137
20-24	1,851	1,536	1,284	1,145	1,187	1,157	1,106
25-29	1,942	1,716	1,577	1,545	1,669	1,792	1,647
30-34	1,187	1,036	927	916	1,003	1,104	1,107
35-49	662	608	542	537	590	738	671
40-44	367	354	307	293	379	412	379
45-49	286	252	219	196	220	223	235
50-54	178	144	141	134	164	162	165
55-59	107	84	100	68	84	101	96
60+	75	85	81	70	66	76	87

Source: Statistics Estonia.

Average age upon first marriage, 2000–2013

Year	Average age upon first marriage	
	Men	Women
2000	27.4	24.9
2001	27.7	25.2
2002	28.1	25.4
2003	28.1	25.6
2004	28.6	26
2005	28.6	26.2
2006	28.9	26.4
2007	29.3	26.8
2008	29.4	27.1
2009	29.9	27.5
2010	30.2	27.8
2011	30.6	28.1
2012	31	28.6
2013	30.8	28.4

Source: Statistics Estonia.

FINLAND

Number of concluded marriages and registered partnerships per annum related to the size of the population (marriages according to the female spouse)

Year	Marriages	Male registered partnerships	Female registered partnerships	Total	Pop. at the end of the year	Formalised relationship per pop. size
2000	26,150	-	-	26,150	5,181,115	0.50%
2001	24,830	-	-	24,830	5,194,901	0.48%
2002	26,969	240	206	27,415	5,206,295	0.53%
2003	25,815	84	106	26,005	5,219,732	0.50%
2004	29,342	84	102	29,528	5,236,611	0.56%
2005	29,283	100	100	29,483	5,255,580	0.56%
2006	28,236	84	107	28,427	5,276,955	0.54%
2007	29,497	93	120	29,710	5,300,484	0.56%
2008	31,014	91	158	31,263	5,326,314	0.59%
2009	29,836	91	155	30,085	5,351,427	0.56%
2010	29,952	124	198	30,274	5,375,276	0.56%
2011	28,408	111	222	28,741	5,401,267	0.53%
2012	28,878	110	219	29,207	5,426,674	0.54%
2013	25,119	126	247	25,492	5,451,270	0.47%

Source: Statistics Finland: Changes in marital status.

Number of concluded marriages in relation to the age profile according to the female spouse

Age	2000	2001	2002	2003	2004	2005	2006
≤19	813	813	779	704	779	773	735
20-24	5,648	5,100	5,047	4,663	4,826	5,002	4,626
25-29	7,575	7.340	8,262	8,110	8,876	8,892	8,585
30-34	4,931	4,518	4,756	4,587	5,175	5,358	5,207
35-39	2,838	2,614	2,956	2,878	3,598	3,300	3,105
40-44	1,630	1,673	1,851	1,798	2,148	2,168	2,164
45-49	1.302	1,308	1,597	1,420	1,818	1,784	1,754
50-54	781	791	876	825	1,023	974	959
55-59	304	361	469	489	666	609	620
60-64	160	178	209	191	240	242	288
≥65	168	134	167	150	193	181	193

Age	2007	2008	2009	2010	2011	2012	2013
≤19	703	700	715	705	640	631	576
20-24	4,688	4,608	4,489	4,350	3,998	3,952	3,679
25-29	8,900	9,256	8,952	8,984	8,191	8,282	7,139
30-34	5,641	5,938	5,867	6,014	5,802	5,591	5,196
35-39	3,092	3,285	3,017	3,127	3,097	3,188	2,735
40-44	2,256	2,497	2,182	2,270	2,109	2,167	1,697

45-49	2,018	2,334	2,171	2,133	2,158	2,409	1,890
50-54	1,003	1,127	1,071	1,014	1,075	1,141	940
55-59	658	706	701	671	679	761	639
60-64	326	331	423	437	394	444	342
≥65	212	232	248	247	265	312	286

Source: Statistics Finland: Changes in marital status.

Number of concluded marriages in relation to the age profile according to the male spouse

Age	2000	2001	2002	2003	2004	2005	2006
≤19	260	269	240	223	248	262	236
20-24	3,344	3,031	3,075	2,779	2,897	2,968	2,762
25-29	7,235	7,050	7,617	7,335	7,806	8,061	7,518
30-34	6,141	5,456	5,923	5,602	6,200	6,241	6,166
35-39	3,720	3,549	3,808	3,724	4,303	4,211	3,989
40-44	2,103	2,174	2,408	2,263	2,855	2,786	2,822
45-49	1,644	1,588	1,867	1,699	2,123	2,167	2,087
50-54	1,179	1,168	1,301	1,141	1,405	1,289	1,391
55-59	581	613	734	761	1,000	1,028	926
60-64	261	326	372	346	438	388	483
≥65	294	286	296	276	354	346	328

Age	2007	2008	2009	2010	2011	2012	2013
≤19	247	231	270	258	213	235	204
20-24	2,779	2,79	2,749	2,596	2,409	2,418	2,263
25-29	7,752	7,960	7,700	7,697	7,065	6,997	6,101
30-34	6,758	7,091	6,892	7,096	6,586	6,544	5,974
35-39	4,109	4,168	3,875	3,956	3,983	3,977	3,554
40-44	2,782	3,118	2,992	2,836	2,759	2,685	2,179
45-49	2,429	2,655	2,522	2,494	2,487	2,789	2,236
50-54	1,449	1,492	1,471	1,436	1,476	1,560	1,266
55-59	1,008	1,092	1,012	983	1,055	1,128	984
60-64	516	594	706	697	694	733	586
≥65	377	400	434	427	469	525	486

Source: Statistics Finland: Changes in marital status.

Number of married persons according to age group, 2000-2013 (both genders together)

Year	≤25	26-40	41-65	≥66	Total
2000	36,082 (1.8%)	485,601 (24.4%)	1,119,738 (56.4%)	344,961 (17.4%)	1,986,382 (100%)
2001	35,081 (1.8%)	471,915 (23.8%)	1,120,682 (56.6%)	352,676 (17.8%)	1,980,354 (100%)
2002	34,113 (1.7%)	461,595 (23.3%)	1,122,898 (56.8%)	359,888 (18.2%)	1,978,494 (100%)
2003	32,599 (1.6%)	451,747 (22.9%)	1,121,977 (56.8%)	368,404 (18.7%)	1,974,727 (100%)

2004	32,169 (1.6%)	444,931 (22.5%)	1,121,956 (56.7%)	379,815 (19.2%)	1,978,871 (100%)
2005	32,236 (1.6%)	439,346 (22.2%)	1,119,403 (56.4%)	392,309 (19.8%)	1,983,294 (100%)
2006	32,003 (1.6%)	433,843 (21.8%)	1,121,003 (56.5%)	398,924 (20.1%)	1,985,773 (100%)
2007	31,846 (1.6%)	430,593 (21.6%)	1,111,942 (55.8%)	416,891 (20.9%)	1,991,272 (100%)
2008	31,763 (1.6%)	429,398 (21.5%)	1,117,157 (55.9%)	421,437 (21.1%)	1,999,755 (100%)
2009	31,149 (1.6%)	428,089 (21.3%)	1,114,231 (55.6%)	432,066 (21.5%)	2,005,535 (100%)
2010	30,509 (1.5%)	429,398 (21.4%)	1,107,203 (55.1%)	442,698 (22.0%)	2,009,808 (100%)
2011	29,701 (1.5%)	429,686 (21.4%)	1,091,240 (54.2%)	461,837 (22.9%)	2,012,464 (100%)
2012	28,917 (1.4%)	430,979 (21.4%)	1,072,290 (53.2%)	485,078 (24.0%)	2,017,264 (100%)
2013	27,943 (1.4%)	428,123 (21.3%)	1,048,709 (52.1%)	508,392 (25.3%)	2,013,167 (100%)

Source: Statistics Finland: Population structure.

Number of persons living in a registered partnership according to age group, 2002-2013 (the registration of a partnership was made possible from 1.3.2002 onwards)

Year	≤25	26-40	41-65	≥66	Total
2000	48 (5.5%)	395 (45.4%)	403 (46.3%)	25 (2.9%)	871 (100%)
2001	80 (6.6%)	554 (45.6%)	551 (45.4%)	29 (2.4%)	1,214 (100%)
2002	83 (5.4%)	715 (46.6%)	697 (45.4%)	40 (2.6%)	1,535 (100%)
2003	88 (4.8%)	858 (46.4%)	855 (46.2%)	48 (2.6%)	1,849 (100%)
2004	103 (4.8%)	955 (44.6%)	1,022 (47.8%)	60 (2.8%)	2,140 (100%)
2005	121 (5.0%)	1,023 (42.2%)	1,207 (49.8%)	75 (3.1%)	2,426 (100%)
2006	148 (5.3%)	1,141 (40.7%)	1,424 (50.8%)	88 (3.1%)	2,801 (100%)
2007	146 (4.6%)	1,285 (40.6%)	1,624 (51.3%)	112 (3.5%)	3,167 (100%)
2008	164 (4.5%)	1,457 (40.3%)	1,860 (51.4%)	138 (3.8%)	3,619 (100%)
2009	225 (5.5%)	1,657 (40.4%)	2,070 (50.5%)	150 (3.7%)	4,102 (100%)
2010	276 (6.1%)	1,802 (39.9%)	2,269 (50.3%)	164 (3.6%)	4,511 (100%)
2011	317 (6.3%)	2,035 (40.5%)	2,481 (49.3%)	196 (3.9%)	5,029 (100%)

2012	48 (5.5%)	395 (45.4%)	403 (46.3%)	25 (2.9%)	871 (100%)
2013	80 (6.6%)	554 (45.6%)	551 (45.4%)	29 (2.4%)	1,214 (100%)

Source: Statistics Finland: Population structure.

FRANCE

On the 1st of January 2014, France had 66 million inhabitants.

At the beginning of 2011, 32 million adults were living as a couple in France. 72% of them were married. Of the non-married couples, 7.2 million were living in an informal relationship and 1.4 million were registered partners (PACS). Below the age of 25, 84% of the adults living as a couple were living in an informal relationship.[14]

Up to 2011 the number of marriages had decreased during the previous ten years. In 2012, however, it increased again (246,000). For 2013, the estimations indicate about 231,000 marriages.

In 2011 and 2012, there were 2 PACS for every 3 marriages entered into.[15]

With regard to same-sex marriages, in 2012 3 out of 5 couples were male couples. 54% of same-sex registered partnerships were entered into by male partners.[16]

Marriages and PACS (registered partnerships)

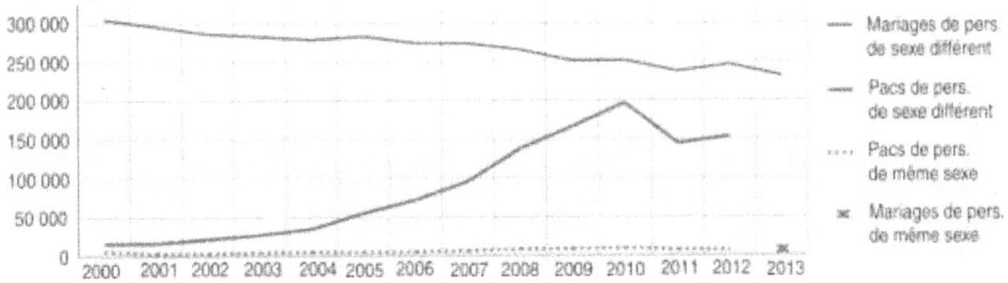

Champ: France hors Mayotte
Sources: Insee, statistiques de l'état civil (mariages); Ministère de la Justice (Pacs).

14 INSEE (National Institute for statistic and economic studies), TEF: ed. 2014.
15 INSEE Première, no. 1482, January 2014.
16 INSEE, TEF: ed. 2014.

Evolution of the number of marriages and PACS entered into 2004-2014

	2004	2005	2006	2007	2008	2009
Marriages						
Opposite-sex partners	278,439	283,036	273,914	273,669	265,404	251,478
Same-sex partners	N/A[17]	N/A	N/A	N/A	N/A	N/A
Total	278,439	283,036	273,914	273,669	265,404	251,478
PACS						
Opposite-sex partners	35,057	55,597	72,276	95,770	137,744	166,148
Same-sex partners	5,023	4,865	5,071	6,222	8,194	8,436
Total	40,080	60,462	77,347	101,992	145,938	174,584
Total marriages and PACS between opposite-sex partners	313,496	338,633	346,439	369,439	403,148	417,626

	2010	2011	2012	2013	2014[18]
Marriages					
Opposite-sex partners	251,654	236,826	245,930	231,225	231,000
Same-sex partners	N/A	N/A	N/A	7,367	10,000
Total	251,654	236,826	245,930	238,592	241,000
Pacs					
Opposite-sex partners	196,416	144,675	153,670	162,072	-[19]
Same-sex partners	9,145	7,492	6,969	6,054	-
Total	205,561	152,169	160,639	168,126	-
Total Marriages and PACS between opposite-sex partners	488,070	381,501	399,600	393,297	-

Scope: France without Mayotte until 2014 and with Mayotte for 2014.
Source: Insee, statistiques de l'état civil; SDSE, fichiers détails pacs, see www.insee.fr/fr/themes/tableau.asp?reg_id=0&ref_id=NATTEF02327.

Marriages:
In 2012, 80.2% of the men who married had not been previously married. 18.7 % of the women who married in 2012 were divorced of widows.

17 Not applicable, a marriage between same-sex partners has only been possible since May 2013.
18 Provisional statistics.
19 Not available.

	Year of marriage					
	2003	2009	2010	2011	2012	2013[20]
Total number of marriages	282,756	251,478	251,654	236,826	245,930	231,000
Former marital status of the spouses						
Men						
Single	81.4%	79.3%	79.4%	79.4%	80.2%	-
Widowed or divorced	18.6%	20.7%	20.6%	20.6%	19.8%	-
Female						
Single	82.6%	80.7%	80.8%	80.6%	81.3%	-
Widowed or divorced	17.4%	19.3%	19.2%	19.4%	18.7%	-
Average age upon first marriage						
Male	30.6	31.7	31.8	31.9	32.0	-
Female	28.5	29.8	30.0	30.1	30.2	-
Average age upon marriage						
Male	34.3	36.3	36.5	36.6	36.7	-
Female	31.6	33.5	33.8	34.0	34.0	-

Scope: France without Mayotte, and without same-sex marriages.
Source: Insee, estimations de population et statistiques de l'état civil.

GERMANY

In Germany in 2013 there were 373,655 marriages (in 2000: 418,550).[21] In 2013, there were 46.3 marriages per 10,000 inhabitants (2000: 51.0). This means that there has been a decline in marriage rates.

There are no federal statistics on how many registered partnerships have been concluded per year. In 2006 there were 12,000 registered partnerships in Germany (2010: 23,000).

The average marriage age is increasing. In 2012 it was 37.7 years for men (2000: 35.0) and 34.6 years for women (2000: 31.9).[22] In 2012, for the first marriage it was 33.5 for men (2000: 31.2) and 30.7 years for women (2000: 28.4).

---

20 Provisional statistics.

21 Federal Statistical Office (Statistisches Bundesamt), available at: www.statistik-portal.de/Statistik-Portal/de_jb01_jahrtab3a.asp.

22 Statistisches Bundesamt, *Statistisches Jahrbuch Deutschland und Internationales 2014*, Statistisches Bundesamt, Wiesbaden, 2014, at p. 54.

GREECE

Such official information could not be obtained.

HUNGARY

General – marriages, population

Year	Marriages in total	Marriages per 1,000 inhabitants	Population on the 1st of January in millions
2000	48,110	4.7	10.222
2001	43,583	4.3	10.200
2002	46,008	4.5	10.175
2003	45,398	4.5	10.142
2004	43,791	4.3	10.117
2005	44,234	4.4	10.098
2006	44,528	4.4	10.077
2007	40,842	4.1	10.066
2008	40,105	4.0	10.045
2009	36,730	3.7	10.031
2010	35,520	3.6	10.014
2011	35,812	3.6	9.986
2012	36,161	3.6	9.932
2013	36,986	3.7	9.909
2014	not yet reported	not yet reported	9.877

Data from the Hungarian Central Statistical Office.

Marriages – age-groups, men and women

Age	1990			2001		
	Men	Women	Total	Men	Women	Total
15-19	4,181	25,934	30,115	788	4,967	5,755
20-24	88,350	178,032	266,382	32,768	80,188	112,956
25-29	196,022	237,544	433,566	144,328	203,645	347,973
30-34	284,238	309,996	594,234	214,168	241,169	455,337
35-39	324,275	335,535	659,810	207,096	223,062	430,158
40-44	281,696	279,478	561,174	244,562	260,018	504,580
45-49	264,488	263,089	527,577	290,623	296,703	587,326
50-54	228,405	233,417	461,822	254,794	248,742	503,536
55-59	235,824	219,561	455,385	219,934	208,596	428,530
60-64	217,843	189,734	407,577	182,432	171,500	353,932
65-69	181,656	142,205	323,861	16,642	133,422	295,064
70-74	83,349	52,990	136,339	129,441	92,974	222,415
75-79	82,188	42,562	124,750	83,344	48,778	132,122
80-84	33,374	12,950	46,324	31,236	12,876	44,112

85+	10,033	2,727	12,760	16,609	5,309	21,918
Total	2,515,922	2,525,754	5,041,676	2,213,765	2,231,949	4,445,714

Age	2011		
	Men	Women	Total
15-19	342	1,689	2,031
20-24	5,672	16,214	21,886
25-29	40,153	80,782	120,935
30-34	138,891	184,112	323,003
35-39	207,875	229,710	437,585
40-44	205,886	215,643	421,529
45-49	180,968	188,640	369,608
50-54	200,471	211,070	411,541
55-59	246,324	246,354	492,678
60-64	211,856	197,295	409,151
65-69	166,345	143,664	310,009
70-74	121,503	95,651	217,154
75-79	82,965	52,785	135,750
80-84	47,164	22,262	69,426
85+	931	6,517	27,448
Total	1,877,346	1,892,388	3,769,734

Data from the Hungarian Central Statistical Office[23]

There are comparatively few registered partnerships in Hungary. The possibility of establishing a registered partnership has existed since July 2009. In the second half of 2009 67 registered partnerships were established and in 2010 the total was 80. This number has been consistently decreasing and in 2013 30 couples established this partnership. Among them 20 couples were made up of two men and 10 couples were made up of two women; more than half of the 30 couples were from Budapest, the capital of Hungary. Their average age upon initiating the procedure was 37.3 for men and 33.8 for women.[24]

REPUBLIC OF IRELAND

Modified table of statistics from the Irish Central Statistics Office website:

---

23 A 15 éves és idősebb házas népesség ötéves korcsoportok és nemek szerint. Demográfiai adatok a 2011. évi népszámlálást követően. (Married population over 15 years of age according to age groups and gender. Demographic data following the Census in 2011). Available at: www.ksh.hu.

24 *'Magyarország 2013' ('Hungary 2013')*, M. FREID (ed.), Központi Statisztikai Hivatal, Budapest, 2014, at p. 16.

Year	Marriages	
	Number[25]	Rates[26]
2000	19,168	5.1
2001	19,246	5.0
2002	20,556	5.2
2003	20,302	5.1
2004	20,979	5.2
2005	21,355	5.2
2006	22,089	5.2
2007	22,756	5.2
2008	22,187	5.0
2009	21,627	4.8
2010	20,594	4.5
2011	19,879	4.3
2012	21,245	4.6
2013	20,680 (338 civil partnerships)	4.5

Population estimates by age group and sex (rounded off to hundreds)

	2013	2014
Both sexes		
0-14 years	1,007,700	1,015,900
15-24 years	533,300	523,400
25-44 years	1,414,000	1,397,800
45-64 years	1,070,000	1,086,200
65 years and over	568,100	586,600
All ages	4,593,100	4,609,600
Male		
0-14 years	513,900	518,000
15-24 years	273,200	268,700
25-44 years	693,200	681,600
45-64 years	532,200	540,400
65 years and over	261,300	271,100
All ages	2,273,800	2,279,700
Female		
0-14 years	493,800	497,700
15-24 years	260,100	254,700
25-44 years	720,800	716,100
45-64 years	537,800	545,800
65 years and over	306,800	315,600
All ages	2,319,300	2,329,900

[25] Data for marriages are by year of registration. Births and deaths data up to and including 2010 are year of occurrence and are final, 2011 and 2012 data are year of registration and are preliminary.

[26] Rates per 1,000 of the estimated population.

According to the Irish Central Statistics Office in the past fifty years, the average age of grooms increased from 26.2 years in 1977 to a high of 34.7 years in 2012. The average age of grooms in 2013 was 34.9 years, 0.2 years more than the average age in 2012. A similar trend exists for brides - the average age increased from 24.0 in 1977 to a high of 32.8 in 2013.

The number of marriages registered in 2013 was 20,680 which equates to a marriage rate of 4.5 per 1,000 of the population. 20,713 marriages were registered in 2012, also equating to a marriage rate of 4.5 per 1,000 of the population. In 2011, 19,855 marriages were registered with a marriage rate of 4.3 per thousand of the population.

429 civil partnership ceremonies occurred in 2012 and 338 civil partnership ceremonies in 2013, with 208 male unions and 130 female unions. Almost 74% (249) of these same-sex couples reside in the Leinster area with 139 same-sex partnerships (41%) living in Dublin City and a further 22% residing in the greater Dublin area. Excluding the Dublin area, Cork County had the highest number of civil partnerships registered in 2013 (18) and accounted for over 5% of all civil partnerships registered in that year. In contrast, in 2012 Leitrim, Mayo, Roscommon or Sligo registered no civil partnerships and in 2013 there were no registered civil partnerships in Cavan, Leitrim, Longford, Monaghan, Offaly, Sligo or South Tipperary.

ITALY

Since 1972 the number of marriages in Italy has been in decline, but this decline has been steeper in recent years. In fact, while from 1991 to 2013 the overall average annual drop was -1.2% per year, from 2008 to 2013 the decrease amounted to -5%. In the year 2013[27] the total number of marriages was 194,057, a fall of 13,081 on the previous year.

According to the report entitled 'Indicatori demografici',[28] in 2013 about 200,000 marriages were celebrated, with a marriage rate of 3.3 per 1,000 persons, one of the lowest in Europe.

In 2012 statistics showed a slight increase in the number of marriages which was explained by the increase in the number of marriages between

27 Data released by the Istat (National Institute for Statistics), 'Il matrimonio in Italia (anno 2013)', published on 12 November 2014.

28 Published by the Istat on 26 June 2014.

spouses of which one was a foreign citizen. But this tendency was not confirmed in 2013.

However, it is marriages between Italian citizens which have been declining more steeply and steadily. This is true for both first and second marriages.

The reduction in the number of first marriages must of course be related to a fall in the birth rate which has been a demographic feature in Italy since the mid-1970s and which has resulted in a reduction in the number of 16- to 34-year-olds in the population, among whom first marriages are more frequent.

Those who have achieved lower levels of education show a more distinct tendency to avoid marriage: from 2003 to 2013 marriages involving men in this category fell from 612 per 1,000 inhabitants to 427 (which amounts to a decrease of 25%); marriages involving women with lower levels of education dropped from 740 to 499 per 1,000 inhabitants (a decrease of 33%). Over the same period, the decline in the number of marriages involving those with medium to high levels of education was 22% for men and 19% for women.

It is probable that this decrease in the marriage rate is, in part, due also to the economic crisis, which has made it harder to find work.

As the Italian legal system recognises not only civil marriages but also concordat marriages,[29] it may be of some interest to note that the numbers of concordat marriages have reduced in number too: in 2013, 42.5% of the total number of marriages across Italy were civil, peaking in the north (55%) and slightly lower at 51% in the centre. In comparison, in 2008 civil marriages represented 36.8%. The decrease in religious marriages may be explained, in part, by the increase in the number of second marriages and of marriages where one of the spouses is a foreign citizen.

An interesting point – though one which is difficult to explain – is that the propensity to enter into a civil marriage, which in the past was more widespread among more educated spouses, has recently seen a proportionately more pronounced growth among spouses with lower levels of education. In 2012 28.5% of husbands with a lower level of

[29] As is probably known, a concordat marriage is a marriage with legal effects under both the Italian legal system and the jurisdiction of the Holy See.

education chose a civil marriage (compared to 11.9% in 1995) while it was 20% of men with a university degree (compared to 12.7% in 1995). Similar values are reflected for wives: 29.8% of brides with a lower educational level (12.5% in 1995) and 21.1% with a university qualification (12.8% in 1995) opted for a civil marriage.[30]

Second marriages – which were on the increase up to 2008 – subsequently decreased by 10% in the years up to 2013, but remain more frequent in the north. Currently 15.8% of the total number of marriages are second marriages. Men remarry, on average, at the age of about 50 if they are divorced and 63 if they are widowed, while women are aged 44 if divorced and 51 if widowed.

In 2013 two marriages in three opted for the separation of property regime with no meaningful difference among the different areas of the country (69.5% of the total number of marriages in Italy in 2013). When both the spouses have a high level of education, this figure reaches 72%.

LATVIA

According to the Central Statistical Bureau of Latvia's database of information, from 2000 to 2007 the number of registered marriages has increased by an annual average 896 registered marriages. For example, in 2000 9,211 marriages were registered, in 2001 9,258 marriages were registered, in 2002 there were 9,738 registered marriages, and in 2003 there were 9,989 marriages. In turn, from 2007 a decline in the number of registered marriages can be observed. Up to 2010 the number of registered marriages had decreased to 9,290 and then increased to 11,436 in 2013.

The highest increase in the number of registered marriages can be observed in 2005 when the registration of marriages in comparison with 2004 had increased by 2,174. The highest number of concluded marriages was in 2007, namely 15,486 marriages.[31] In this same year a new marriage registration record was achieved when, in one day (07.07.07), 748 couples

30 Istat, 'Il matrimonio in Italia (2013)', at p. 9.

31 Central Statistical Bureau of Latvia database information: Number of concluded marriages and the average age of married person. Available at: data.csb.gov.lv/pxweb/lv/Sociala/Sociala__ikgad__iedz__laulibas/IL0020.px/table/tableViewLayout1/?rxid=cdcb978c-22b0-416a-aacc-aa650d3e2ce0.

registered their marriage.[32] On average 68 couples a day registered their marriage in July 2007.

Number of concluded marriages and the average age of married persons[33]

Year	Marriages	Average age of married persons	
		Men	Women
2004	10,370	32.1	29.4
2005	12,544	32.8	30.0
2006	14,616	33.0	30.4
2007	15,486	33.3	30.7
2008	12,946	33.5	30.9
2009	9,925	34.0	31.3
2010	9,290	34.1	31.4
2011	10,760	34.4	31.6
2012	11,244	34.8	32.0
2013	11,436	35.1	32.5

Population age structure[34]

Year	Total population	Age structure of population			
		20-24	25-29	30-34	35-39
2004	2,276,520	165,593	154,783	157,690	153,963
2005	2,249,724	168,612	152,140	156,450	151,168
2006	2,227,874	170,392	150,265	154,709	151,582
2007	2,208,840	173,133	149,340	151,690	151,758
2008	2,191,810	175,520	151,015	149,315	151,962
2009	2,162,834	171,794	152,409	145,528	149,783
2010	2,120,504	163,497	150,828	140,253	147,049
2011	2,074,605	155,706	147,966	135,044	142,973
2012	2,044,813	149,364	148,320	132,353	138,898
2013	2,023,825	143,614	149,365	132,349	135,424
2014	2,001,468	134,223	147,024	134,101	132,003

32 Central Statistical Bureau of Latvia database information, 'Nozīmīgākie fakti Latvijā pēc 1990. gada (Most important facts on Latvia after 1990 in the view of CSB)', available at: csb.gov.lv/sites/default/files/dati/csp_2012.pdf.

33 Central Statistical Bureau of Latvia database information: Concluded marriages and divorces. Number of concluded marriages and the average age of married person. Available at: data.csb.gov.lv/pxweb/lv/Sociala/Sociala__ikgad__iedz__laulibas/IL0010.px/table/tableViewLayout1/?rxid=cdcb978c-22b0-416a-aacc-aa650d3e2ce0.

34 Central Statistical Bureau of Latvia database information: Population by age, sex and marital status at the beginning of the year. Available at: data.csb.gov.lv/pxweb/lv/Sociala/Sociala__ikgad__iedz__iedzskaits/IS0110.px/?rxid=cdcb978c-22b0-416a-aacc-aa650d3e2ce0.

Number of married persons in certain age groups[35]

Year	20-24		25-29		30-34		35-39	
	Men	Women	Men	Women	Men	Women	Men	Women
2004	2,503	3,562	3,195	2,834	1,804	1,355	966	692
2005	2,733	4,036	3,778	3,430	2,314	1,754	1,164	923
2006	2,991	4,527	4,361	4,074	2,772	2,069	1,519	1,137
2007	3,058	4,666	4,575	4,188	2,864	3,058	4,666	4,575
2008	2,392	3,802	3,959	3,650	2,402	1,878	1,414	1,090
2009	1,570	2,634	3,135	3,003	1,850	1,498	1,139	870
2010	1,455	2,402	2,865	2,872	1,816	1,410	1,044	812
2011	1,389	2,539	3,456	3,465	2,143	1,709	1,278	993
2012	1,331	2,428	3,624	3,736	2,177	1,801	1,386	1,091
2013	1,161	2,163	3,488	3,811	2,488	1,912	1,412	1,190

LITHUANIA

In the past few years the number of marriages contracted per year has fluctuated at around 20,000 with the crude marriage rate (marriages per 1,000 population) reaching 6.9. The last decade has marked a gradual upward trend in the marriage rates and was preceded by a decade which saw a dramatic decrease in marriages in the 1990s. Between 1990 and 2000, the absolute number of marriages dropped from around 36,000 to 17,000 and the crude marriage rate from 9.8 to 4.8.[36] The year 2001 marked the lowest marriage rate at around 4.5. The reported upward trend is also reflected in the total first marriage rate that is gender- and age-specific.

Marriages in Lithuania, 2000–2013

Year	Number of marriages	Marriages per 1,000 population	Total first marriage rate	
			Male	Female
2000	16,906	4.8	-	-
2001	15,764	4.5	0.51	0.53
2002	16,151	4.7	0.53	0.55
2003	16,975	5	0.57	0.58
2004	19,130	5.7	0.64	0.65
2005	19,938	6	0.67	0.69
2006	21,246	6.5	0.73	0.74
2007	23,065	7.1	0.8	0.8

35 Central Statistical Bureau of Latvia database information: Population by age, sex and marital status at the beginning of the year. Available at: data.csb.gov.lv/pxweb/lv/Sociala/Sociala__ikgad__iedz__iedzskaits/IS0110.px/?rxid=cdcb978c-22b0-416a-aacc-aa650d3e2ce0.

36 *Demografijos metraštis 2013* (Demographic Yearbook 2013), Lietuvos statistikos departamentas, Vilnius, 2014, at p. 95.

2008	24,063	7.5	0.84	0.85
2009	20,542	6.5	0.74	0.75
2010	18,688	6	0.71	0.71
2011	19,221	6.3	0.75	0.76
2012	20,660	6.9	0.82	0.84
2013	20,469	6.9	0.81	0.83

Source: Statistics Lithuania, www.stat.gov.lt.

At the beginning of the 2000s, Lithuania experienced a secular turn towards the non-direct family formation model. Around 70% of all first partnerships started as cohabitations.[37]

There is no official statistical data on registered partnerships.

LUXEMBOURG

Marriage or cohabitation between couples with child(ren), according to the age of the father in 2001

	Less than 30 years old	**30-44 years old**	**45-59 years old**	**60 years and older**	**Total**
Marriage	82.9%	94.4%	97.0%	96.1%	94.8%
Cohabitation	17.1%	5.6%	3.0%	3.9%	5.2%
Total	100%	100%	100%	100%	100%

Source: Recensement de la population (STATEC). Calculated by: CEPS/INSTEAD.

Interpretation: 82.9% of fathers under the age of 30 who are living in a couple are married.

Evolution from 1960 to present day in the number of first marriages

	1960	**1970**	**1980**	**1990**	**2000**	**2006**
Marriages	2,236	2,156	2,149	2,312	2,148	1,948
First marriages (two unmarried spouses)	2,040	1,881	1,737	1,652	1,410	1,244

Source: Le Luxembourg en chiffres 2007 STATEC, et Statistiques historiques 1839-1989 STATEC.

THE NETHERLANDS

Number of marriages concluded per annum

Year	**Total**	**Man and woman**	**Two men**	**Two women**
2000	88,074	88,074	-	-

[37] A. MASLAUSKAITĖ, Development of cohabitation in Lithuania (Kohabitacijos raida Lietuvoje), *Lietuvos socialinė raida*, No. 1, 2012, at p. 102–119.

2001	82,091	79,677	1,339	1,075
2002	85,808	83,970	935	903
2003	80,427	78,928	735	764
2004	73,441	72,231	579	631
2005	71,263	71,113	570	580
2006	72,369	71,157	579	633
2007	72,485	71,114	663	708
2008	75,438	74,030	656	752
2009	73,477	72,119	573	785
2010	75,399	74,045	660	694
2011	71,572	70,217	601	754
2012	70,315	69,030	544	741
2013	64,549	63,327	522	700

Source: CBS Statistics Netherlands.

Amount of registered partnerships concluded per annum:

Year	Total	Man and woman	Two men	Two women
2000	2,922	1,322	815	785
2001	3,377	2,847	285	245
2002	8,321	7,774	269	278
2003	10,119	9,577	262	280
2004	11,156	10,573	261	322
2005	11,307	10,699	279	329
2006	10,801	10,182	295	324
2007	10,550	9,945	269	336
2008	10,842	10,231	298	313
2009	9,497	9,002	221	274
2010	9,571	9,084	234	253
2011	9,945	9,464	235	246
2012	9,224	8,789	217	218
2013	9,445	9,038	208	199

Source: CBS Statistics Netherlands.

Number of concluded formal relationships as a percentage of the Dutch population

Year	Marriages	Registered partnerships
2000	0.55%	0.018%
2001	0.51%	0.021%
2002	0.53%	0.052%
2003	0.50%	0.062%
2004	0.45%	0.069%
2005	0.44%	0.069%
2006	0.44%	0.066%
2007	0.44%	0.064%
2008	0.46%	0.066%
2009	0.44%	0.057%

2010	0.45%	0.058%
2011	0.43%	0.060%
2012	0.42%	0.055%
2013	0.38%	0.056%

Average age upon marriage

Year	Men	Women
2000	34.1	31.1
2001	34.6	31.5
2002	34.7	31.6
2003	35.0	31.9
2004	35.4	32.2
2005	35.8	32.7
2006	36.1	33.0
2007	36.3	33.2
2008	36.4	33.4
2009	36.5	33.4
2010	36.6	33.4
2011	36.9	33.8
2012	37.0	33.8
2013	37.0	33.8

Source: CBS Statistics Netherlands.

NORWAY

A total of 22,887 couples got married in 2014, which is 523 fewer marriages than in 2013.[38]

At the end of 2014, the total population of Norway was 5,165,000 people.[39] Approximately 344,000 people were between 20–24 years old, and of these only 10,700 were married. The age group 24-29 consisted of about 355,000 people and 62,500 of them were marred. In comparison, for the age group 55-59 about 189,000 out of 315,000 people were married.[40]

From 1992 to 2000, the number of contracted marriages increased from 18,600 to a peak of 25,500 couples in 2000. In the period 2001-2005 the

38 Statistics Norway, 'Marriages and divorces 2014', available at: www.ssb.no/en/befolkning/statistikker/ekteskap.

39 Statistics Norway, 'Population and population changes, Q4 2014', available at: www.ssb.no/en/befolkning/statistikker/folkendrkv/kvartal.

40 Statistics Norway, 'Population, 1 January 2015', available at: www.ssb.no/en/befolkning/statistikker/folkemengde/aar/2015-02-19?fane=tabell&sort=nummer&tabell=218740.

annual average was 23,000 and in the period 2006-2010 the annual average was 23,800 married couples.[41]

In 2014, a total of 269 same-sex couples got married – 106 of them were male couples and 163 female couples.[42] The number of married same-sex couples has remained stable since the new marriage legislation was introduced on 1 January 2009. Earlier, between 1993 and 2008, same-sex couples could register their partnerships. Between 2001 and 2007 there were an average of 207 registered partnerships per year.[43]

PORTUGAL

Year	Number of marriages	Overall population
2007	46,329	-
2008	43,228	-
2009	40,391	-
2010	39,993	10,356,117
2011	36,035	10,562,178
2012	34,423	-

RUSSIA

Year	Number of marriages	Marriages per 1,000 of the population
1950	1,222,971	12.0
1960	1,499,581	12.5
1970	1,319,227	10.1
1980	1,464,579	10.6
1990	1,319,928	8.9
1995	1,075,219	7.3
2000	897,327	6.2
2001	1,001,589	6.9
2002	1,019,762	7.1
2003	1,091,778	7.5
2004	979,667	6.8
2005	1,066,366	7.4

41 Statistics Norway, 'Marriages and divorces 2014', available at: www.ssb.no/en/befolkning/statistikker/ekteskap.

42 Statistics Norway, 'Marriages and divorces 2014', available at: www.ssb.no/en/befolkning/statistikker/ekteskap.

43 Statistics Norway, 'Fra registret partnerskap til felles ekteskapslov', available at: www.ssb.no/befolkning/artikler-og-publikasjoner/fra-registrert-partnerskap-til-felles-ekteskapslov.

2006	1,113,562	7.8
2007	1,262,500	8.8
2008	1,179,007	8.3
2009	1,199,446	8.4
2010	1,215,066	8.5
2011	1,316,011	9.2
2012	1,213,598	8.5
2013	1,225,501	8.5

SCOTLAND

There has been a significant decline in marriage in Scotland since the 1970s, although since the mid-1990s the rate appears to have stabilised to some extent. In 1974, 41,171 marriages were registered, in 2000 there were 30,367 and in 2013, 27,547.[44] Civil partnership was introduced during 2005 and in the first partial year, 84 partnerships were registered. The numbers peaked in 2006 at 1,047 and in 2013 there were 530 registered civil partnerships. The numbers are roughly equal between male and female same-sex couples. The population in Scotland has been relatively stable over the past 50 years, with a total in 2013 of 5,327,700.

In terms of age at marriage, there is a very clear trend towards couples postponing marriage with the average age in 2013, at first marriage, being 33 for men and 31 for women. In 1974, 5,156 men and 11,963 females entered into marriage between the ages of 16 and 19. For this age group, by 2013 the numbers had reduced to 53 men and 186 women. Between the 1970s and the mid-90s, the most common age range for couples to marry was between 20 and 24 but since then it has shifted to 25-34. In 2013, 14,313 women and 13,199 men married between the ages of 25 and 34.[45]

SLOVAKIA

In 2013 a total of 25,491 marriages were concluded. Compared to 2003, there were 511 fewer marriages concluded in 2013. The average age of the spouses was men: 29.5, women: 26.5 in 2003 and in 2013 it was men: 32.9, women: 29.9.[46]

---

44 General Registry Office of Scotland, *Marriage and Civil Partnership Time Series Data*, 2014.

45 General Registry Office of Scotland, *Marriage and Civil Partnership Time Series Data*, 2014.

46 Statistical Office of the Slovak Republic: Slovak Statistics and Demography 2003-2013, at p. 6. Available at: www7.statistics.sk/PortalTraffic/fileServlet?Dokument=b653d111-8505-46ba-933b-7b2397a33bf3.

SLOVENIA

According to data by the Statistical Office RS, on 1 January 2011 in Slovenia, with a population of 2,050,189, there were 362,911 marriages (of which 237,422 couples had children) and 61,307 extramarital unions (of which 49,122 couples had children). Following the legalisation of registered same-sex civil partnerships, 55 couples were registered between 2005 and 2011.[47]

There were 6,671 marriages concluded in 2011. The average age of the groom was 34 years. The average age of the bride was 31.2 years.

In 2011, there were 15 same-sex partnerships registered, of which 7 were male and 8 were female same-sex partnerships. There are no data on the age of the persons who registered same-sex partnerships.[48]

An extramarital union is a *de facto* life union, which is not created on a formal level with registration, so there are no data on how many such unions were formed in 2011. Similarly, there are no data on *de facto* life unions between same-sex couples.

SPAIN

Year	**Total number of marriages**[49]	**Marriage rate (per 1,000 inhabitants)**	**Civil unions (formalised before a notary)**[50]
2000	216,451	5.33	-
2001	208,057	5.07	-
2002	211,522	5.06	-
2003	212,300	4.99	-
2004	216,149	5.00	-
2005	209,415	4.76	-
2006	207,766	4.64	-
2007	204,772	4.48	1,598
2008	197,216	4.25	1,853
2009	177,144	3.78	2,327
2010	170,440	3.62	2,389
2011	163,338	3.46	6,014

47 Available at: www.stat.si/novica_prikazi.aspx?id=4029.

48 Available at: www.stat.si/novica_prikazi.aspx?id=4814.

49 Statistics are from the National Institute of Statistics (*Instituto Nacional de Estadística*), Latest report 2014 (*Anuario Estadística de España 2014*), available at: www.ine.es. Includes data up to 1 January 2013.

50 Statistics are from the Centro de información estadística del notariado, del Consejo General del Notariado, available at: www.cienotariado.org.

2012	168,556	3.56	5,803
2013	-	-	5,026

Same-sex marriage has been legal since Law 13/2005, 1 July, which modifies the Civil Code on the right to marriage. The total number of marriages since 2005 therefore includes both heterosexual and same-sex marriages.

SWEDEN

By the end of 2012, the population of Sweden consisted of 9,555,893 inhabitants. The civil status of the population was as follows. Approximately one third were married (3,233,934); one half were registered as single (4,943,573) even if many of these people were living in an unmarried cohabitation relationship;[51] one tenth were divorced (916,856) and one twentieth (451,530) were widowed.[52] Marriage is the most common civil status for men between the ages of 39 to 91 and for women between the ages of 34 to 78. Younger persons are often unmarried. Among the oldest groups in the population, being widowed is the most common civil status, especially for women whose average life expectancy exceeds that of men. In 2012, the average age of marrying was 39.1 years for men and 36.1 years for women. That can be compared with the year 1991, when the male and female average ages for marriage were 33.5 years and 30.5 years, respectively.[53]

The number of concluded marriages in Sweden, from 2000 to 2013, is stated in the table below.[54]

Year	**Marriages**
2000	39,895
2001	35,778
2002	38,012
2003	39,041
2004	43,088

51 Statistics Sweden, 'Nästan halva befolkningen lever i parrelation', available at: www.scb.se/sv_/Hitta-statistik/Artiklar/Nastan-halva-befolkningen-lever-i-parrelation/.

52 Statistics Sweden, 'Statistisk årsbok 2014: Befolkning', available at: www.scb.se/Statistik/_Publikationer/OV0904_2014A01_BR_06_A01BR1401.pdf, at p. 96-97. The figures for married people includes those who have registered partnerships.

53 Statistics Sweden, 'Statistisk årsbok 2014: Befolkning', available at: www.scb.se/Statistik/_Publikationer/OV0904_2014A01_BR_06_A01BR1401.pdf, at p. 77.

54 Statistics Sweden, 'Befolkningsutveckling', available at: www.scb.se/sv_/Hitta-statistik/Statistik-efter-amne/Befolkning/Befolkningens-sammansattning/Befolknings statistik/25788/25795/Helarsstatistik---Riket/26046/.

2005	44,381
2006	45,551
2007	47,898
2008	50,332
2009	48,033
2010	50,730
2011	47,564
2012	50,616
2013	45,703

Between 1 January 1995 and 30 April 2009 same-sex couples could enter into a registered partnership in Sweden, which was regulated by rules essentially corresponding to those applicable to marriages and spouses. The Registered Partnership Act was abolished as of 1 May 2009, when it became possible for same-sex couples to marry or to have their registered partnership converted into a marriage through a simple administrative act. By the end of 2013 there were 4,883 women and 3,962 men in Sweden who lived in a same-sex marriage or in a registered partnership.[55] The number of registered partnerships concluded in Sweden is stated in the table below.[56]

Year	Registered partnerships
1995	665
1996	319
1997	262
1998	250
1999	287
2000	357
2001	381
2002	422
2003	497
2004	567
2005	593
2006	660
2007	650
2008	814
2009	148

55 Statistics Sweden, 'Giftermål mer populärt än partnerskap', available at: www.scb.se/sv_/Hitta-statistik/Artiklar/Giftermal-mer-populart-an-partnerskap/.

56 Statistics Sweden, 'Partnerskapsförändringar efter region, civilstånd och kön', available at: www.statistikdatabasen.scb.se/pxweb/sv/ssd/START__BE__BE0101__BE0101O/PartnerskapAndring/table/tableViewLayout1/?rxid=fbda2c7f-db3b-419c-8962-9298c4ff0eaf.

SWITZERLAND

Marriages concluded per annum in Switzerland

Year	Total[57]	Crude marriage rate[58]
2000	39,758	5.5
2001	39,244	5.4
2002	40,213	5.5
2003	40,056	5.5
2004	39,460	5.3
2005	40,139	5.4
2006	39,817	5.3
2007	40,330	5.3
2008	41,534	5.4
2009	41,918	5.4
2010	43,257	5.5
2011	42,083	5.3
2012	42,654	5.3
2013	39,794	4.9

Average age at first marriage in Switzerland[59]

Year	Men	Women
2000	30.3	27.9
2001	30.4	28.0
2002	30.5	28.1
2003	30.6	28.4
2004	30.8	28.6
2005	31.0	28.7
2006	31.0	28.7
2007	31.2	28.9
2008	31.4	29.1
2009	31.5	29.2
2010	31.6	29.4
2011	31.8	29.5
2012	31.7	29.5
2013	31.8	29.6

57 Swiss Federal Statistical Office, available at: www.bfs.admin.ch/bfs/portal/en/index/themen/ 01/06/blank/key/05/01.html.

58 The crude marriage rate is the total number of marriages registered during the year among the average permanent resident population. This indicator is expressed by the number of marriages per thousand inhabitants. Swiss Federal Statistical Office, available at: www.bfs.admin.ch/bfs/ portal/en/index/themen/01/06/blank/key/05/02.html.

59 Swiss Federal Statistical Office, available at: www.bfs.admin.ch/bfs/portal/en/index/themen/ 01/06/blank/key/05/04.html.

Registered partnerships[60] concluded per annum in Switzerland (the Swiss law on registered partnership entered into force in 2007)

Year	Total	Male couples	Female couples
2007	2,004	1,431	573
2008	931	660	271
2009	872	588	284
2010	720	499	221
2011	672	426	246
2012	695	428	267
2013	693	463	230

60 Swiss Federal Statistical Office, available at: www.bfs.admin.ch/bfs/portal/en/index/themen/01/06/blank/key/07.html.

QUESTION 11

How many couples are living in an informal relationship in your jurisdiction? Where possible, indicate trends.

AUSTRIA

In 2013, there were 353,000 informal relationships in Austria.[1] This number has more than doubled in the last twenty years (compared to 169,000 informal relationships in 1995).

BELGIUM

Informal relationships are not officially registered in Belgium. Therefore, we need survey data to get an idea of the prevalence of informal relationships.

The European Social Survey allows us to see the spread of informal relationships across time. Unfortunately, the question on civil status has changed twice. This leads to instability with regard to the time series.

In 2002 and 2004, only the official civil status was asked. With the help of the presence of a partner in the household, non-married persons with partners in the household could be identified as cohabiting.

In 2006 and 2008, respondents were asked whether they lived in a 'civil partnership'. No possibility existed to determine whether this was legally recognised or not.

Only from 2010 onwards could respondents indicate whether they cohabited in a legally recognised partnership or not. To enhance comparability with 2006 and 2008, we give both the aggregated numbers

---

1 Statistik Austria, available at: www.statistik.at/web_de/statistiken/bevoelkerung/haushalte_ familien_lebensformen/familien/023079.html.

of cohabiting respondents and the more detailed division into legally recognised or not.

Formal and informal relationships in Belgium (ESS 2002-2012)

	2002	2004	2006	2008	2010	2011
Single	39.8%	35.4%	40.8%	42.7%	38.9%	40.8%
Married	51.5%	50.8%	52.7%	49.4%	48.8%	48.7%
Cohabiting	8.8%	13.8%	-	-	-	-
Civil partnership	-	-	6.5%	7.9%	12.3%	10.5%
Civil partnership (registered)	-	-	-	-	6.6%	3.6%
Civil partnership (unregistered)	-	-	-	-	5.7%	6.8%

BULGARIA

An informal relationship as a family pattern has increased in Bulgaria during the last 20-25 years. The number of couples living in an informal relationship doubled during a 10-year period – 2001-2011. In 2011, the number of couples living in an informal relationship was 289,893 (13.7%). Family members among these couples was 888,818, that is 15.3% of the total number of persons living in families. This number was 314,718 people in 2001.[2] The share of informal relationships in the total number of families was 6.6% in 2001. This share had doubled by 2011 – 13.7% of the total number of families.

CROATIA

The only data on informal relationships which are available at the Croatian Bureau of Statistics relate to different-sex informal relationships and not to same-sex informal partnerships.

In compliance with the data obtained by the latest census and published by the Croatian Bureau of Statistics,[3] a total of 97,912 people lived in informal partnerships (cohabitations) in 2011, which constitutes 2.6% of the entire population.

2 See: 'Population of Bulgaria at the beginning of XXIst century. Status and Trends', Bulgarian Academy of Sciences, Institute for the Study of Population and Mankind, 2011, at p. 115, available at: www.nsi.bg/census2011/pagebg2.php?p2=175&sp2=200&SSPP2=204.

3 www.dzs.hr/Hrv/censuses/census2011/results/htm/h01_01_17/H01_01_17.html.

However, there is ongoing research and the first results thereof show that the real number of people living in cohabitations is much larger. Indeed, a great number of people living in cohabitations do not have a registered residence at the same address. Notably, younger partners with a registered residence at their parents' address were registered as singles in the census although they might live in an informal partnership in a rented flat. Likewise, partners in informal relationships, particularly those who live in permanent and stable unions are more likely to reveal their extra-marital status in unofficial surveys than in censuses. Therefore, more accurate data on the number of people living in cohabitations are expected to be obtained after the completion of the ongoing research (the results will be available soon).

CZECH REPUBLIC

In 2011 there were 234,346 couples living in an informal relationship. Since then, there has been no such record of this matter. Looking at statistics from the previous decade, it is possible to say that the trend is increasing.[4]

DENMARK

Year	Adult unmarried cohabitants	Percent of all couples (married, cohabiting and registered partners)
1979	371,000	13%
1994	537,730	20%
2003	583,656	22%
2014	633,702	23.6%

The increase in the number of unmarried cohabitants has not been so great in recent years, though there has been a small increase every year.

The number of adults cohabiting with a child in common is high and growing:

Year	Number of adults cohabiting with a child in common
1990	153,284
2000	209,108
2014	230,430

4 Data gathered from various articles and statistics published on the official website of the Czech Statistical Office, available at: www.czso.cz/csu/czso/domov.

The number of adults cohabiting without a child in common is the largest group of unmarried cohabitants, and the number is growing:

Year	Number of adults cohabiting without a child in common
1990	355,108
2000	386,056
2014	403,272

ENGLAND AND WALES

Cohabiting couples:

The most recent statistics published by ONS (ONS, *Families and Households 2014*)[5] in relation to informal cohabiting couples are, in contrast to data for marriage and civil partnership, only available for the whole of the UK (rather than England and Wales). Generally, however, although the trends in Northern Ireland are different due to far greater religious adherence than the rest of the UK, this is a small element of the UK population. Trends in England and Wales tend to coincide with those in Scotland and for the UK as a whole and would not be significantly different in the statistical sense from those described below.

There were nearly 6 million people cohabiting in opposite sex cohabiting couple families in 2014 or just under 3 million couples (more than double the 1996 figure of 1.5 million). In addition, there were 84,000 same-sex cohabiting couple families in the UK in 2014. Together cohabiting couple families account for 16.4% of all families in the UK. For opposite-sex cohabiting couple families there has been a statistically significant increase from 13% of all families in 2004 to 16% in 2014. Same-sex cohabiting couple families as a percentage of all families also increased over the same time period but this was not a statistically significant change (0.4% to 0.5%).

Cohabiting couple families are the fastest growing family type in the UK.

Significant trends:

- The number of dependent children living in opposite sex cohabiting couple families doubled from 0.9 million in 1996 to 1.8 million in 2012.

[5] ONS, 2015, available at: www.ons.gov.uk/ons/dcp171778_393133.pdf.

- Over the same period, the percentage of people aged 16 or over who were cohabiting steadily increased, from 6.5% in 1996 to 11.7% in 2012. This makes cohabitation the fastest growing family type in the UK.
- Between 1996 and 2013 the number of same-sex cohabiting couples increased from around 16,000 to 89,000, which is an increase of around 450%. (However, note that this figure understates the true extent of growth in same sex couple families, because the introduction of civil partnerships means some same sex couple families are no longer recorded as cohabiting.)

In 2014, 39% of all opposite sex cohabiting couple families had dependent children in the household, in contrast to only 11% of same-sex cohabiting couple families.

The largest group of opposite sex cohabiting couple families are those with no children in the household (61%). This could be associated with young couples choosing to cohabit before getting married and starting a family. However, some young cohabiting couples may choose to have a child before getting married; this is demonstrated in the age at first marriage being higher (30.3 years) than the average age of women at the birth of their first child (28.3 years).

The table below shows how families are spread across different family type within the UK.

Families in the UK: by family type in 2004 and 2014[6] (in thousands)

Family type	2004		
	With dependent children	**Without dependent children[7]**	**Total**
Married couple family	4,689	7,521	12,210
Civil partner couple family[8]	N/A	N/A	N/A
Opposite-sex cohabiting couple family	885	1,412	2,298
Same-sex cohabiting couple family	...[9]	60	61

6 This table appears as Figure 1 in ONS, 2015, *Families and Households 2014*, available at: www.ons.gov.uk/ons/dcp171778_393133.pdf.

7 Families without dependent children have only non-dependent children or no children in the household.

8 Civil partnerships were introduced in the UK in December 2005.

9 Indicates that estimates are not sufficiently reliable to be published.

Lone parent family	1,869	817	2,685
All families	7,444	9,811	17,254

Family type	2014		
	With dependent children	Without dependent children[10]	Total
Married couple family	4,751	7,725	12,476
Civil partner couple family[11]	12	49	61
Opposite-sex cohabiting couple family	1,163	1,812	2,975
Same-sex cohabiting couple family	9	75	84
Lone parent family	1,981	1,024	3,005
All families	7,916	10,684	18,601

Note: Totals may not sum due to rounding.
Source: Labour Force Survey, Office for National Statistics.

The types of families in which dependent children live have changed significantly.

The biggest change is for dependent children living in opposite sex cohabiting couple families.

In 2004 11% of dependent children lived in such families, and this rose to 14% by 2014. Over the same period, the percentage of dependent children living in a married couple family fell by three percentage points to 63% by 2014. (The percentage of dependent children living in lone parent families changed little over the decade; 23% lived in lone parent families in 2014.)

Living Apart Together Couples:
A recent study using the nationally representative British Social Attitudes Survey 2011, estimates that 9% of the adult population of the UK classify themselves as 'Living Apart Together' and this confirms earlier findings from the British Social Attitudes Survey 2006. However, this study's use of a self-definition approach means that a wide range of relationships are likely to be included in this figure as the criteria for inclusion were not

10 Families without dependent children have only non-dependent children or no children in the household.
11 Civil partnerships were introduced in the UK in December 2005.

specified precisely by the study but rather left to whether people considered they were living in this style of relationship.[12]

ESTONIA

According to the population and dwelling census in 2000 (reference period: 31 March 2000), there were 61,223 couples in an informal relationship[13] (21.5% of all persons living with partners) (Statistics Estonia 2000).

According to the population and dwelling census in 2011 (reference period 31 December 2011), there were 85,107 couples in an informal relationship (31% of all people living with partners) (Eurostat, 2011 Census).

FINLAND

Number of unmarried cohabiting couples 2000-2013

Year	Number of cohabiting couples
2000	262,713
2001	272,000
2002	277,811
2003	283,389
2004	288,389
2005	293,437
2006	299,403
2007	304,032
2008	307,143
2009	310,691
2010	313,221
2011	318,225
2012	321,470
2013	328,304

Note: in order to have the number of persons living in a cohabiting partnership according to female gender, the number should be doubled.
Source: Statistics Finland: Families.

FRANCE

The INSEE has carried out an investigation relating to couples. The chart below relates to adults who declared that they lived as a couple.

12 See further, M. PHILLIPS, S. DUNCAN, S. ROSENEIL, J. CARTER and M. STOILOVA, *Living Apart Together Sourcebook: National survey of people who Live Apart Together (LAT)*, Britain, 2011, available at: www.applied-social-research.brad.ac.uk/current-projects/living-apart-together/.

13 Couples – persons aged 15 years or older and whose age is unknown.

In 2011, in metropolitan France, 23 million adult persons declared that they lived as a couple. 72% of them indicated that they were married and shared the same home with their opposite-sex spouse. 7 million were living in a so-called *'union libre'* (*concubinage,* an informal relationship) and 1.4 million had entered into a registered partnership.

The number of couples living in an informal relationship has been consistently increasing for the last 40 years.[14]

4% of the adults who declared that they lived as a couple did not live in the same home as their partner. More than half of those persons not living together were below the age of 30. Between the ages of 30 and 59, one out of ten persons did not live together with hir or her partner in the absence of common children. Most couples who did not live together were partners in an informal relationship.

In 2011, 200,000 persons were living as a couple with a same-sex partner. 16% of those couples were not living in the same home. 6 out of 10 such couples were male. 43% were registered partners (*pacsés*).

	Total number of persons living as a couple	**Cohabitant (living together)**	**Non-cohabitant (not living together)**
Married	23,202,000 (73.1%)	23,001,000 (72.4%)	201,000 (0.6%)
PACS (registered partnership)	1,377,000 (4.3%)	1,354,000 (4.3%)	23,000 (0.1%)
Union libre (informal relationship)	7,169,000 (22.6%)	6,079,000 (19.2%)	1,090,000 (3.4%)
Total	31,748,000 (100%)	30,434,000 (95.9%)	1,314,000 (4.1%)

Source: INSEE, enquête Famille et logements 2011,[15] with an update: 26 February 2013.

GERMANY

In 2013 there were 2.83 million cohabiting couples in Germany. In 2010, 11.01% of all couples cohabited without getting married or registering a

[14] See INSEE (National Institute for statistic and economic studies), www.insee.fr/fr/themes/document.asp?ref_id=ip1435.

[15] See INSEE (National Institute for statistic and economic studies), www.insee.fr/fr/themes/document.asp?ref_id=ip1435#inter1.

civil partnership.[16] There is a trend towards more informal unions, this having already started in West Germany already in the 1970s.

Number of informal 'communities of life' (*Lebensgemeinschaften*) in Germany (1,000s)[17]

	2000	2010	2011	2012	2013
Number of couples (total)	2,130	2,648	2,732	2,697	2,823
Number of couples of opposite sex	2,083	2,585	2,668	2,627	2,745

GREECE

Such official information could not be obtained.

HUNGARY

Cohabitants

Age	1990			2001		
	Men	Women	Total	Men	Women	Total
15-19	2,607	6,934	9,541	3,947	12,055	16,002
20-24	9,051	12,233	21,284	35,375	53,898	89,273
25-29	12,167	12,516	24,683	56,949	56,513	113,462
30-34	16,804	15,390	32,194	42,734	36,104	78,,838
35-39	18,305	17,251	35,556	30,332	26,175	56,507
40-44	15,183	14,519	29,702	31,430	27,522	58,952
45-49	13,518	13,010	26,528	32,477	28,877	61,354
50-54	10,298	10,397	20,695	23,798	20,869	44,667
55-59	8,710	8,083	16,793	16,325	13,728	30,053
60+	18,750	14,926	33,676	28,886	21,881	50,767
Total	125,393	125,259	250,652	302,253	297,622	599,875

Age	2011		
	Men	Women	Total
15-19	3,497	10,048	13,545
20-24	27,745	50,788	78,533
25-29	60,921	76,086	137,007
30-34	84,472	81,471	165,943
35-39	78,023	67,534	145,557
40-44	54,066	44,920	98,986
45-49	36,549	31,150	67,699

[16] Statistisches Bundesamt, Statistisches Jahrbuch Deutschland und Internationales tbl. 2.16 (2011), available at: www.destatis.de/DE/Publikationen/StatistischesJahrbuch/Bevoelkerung.pdf?__blob=publicationFile.

[17] Gesundheitsberichterstattung des Bundes, Rahmenbedingungen, Lebensgemeinschaften, available at: www.gbe-bund.de.

50-54	32,747	27,863	60,610
55-59	32,243	26,596	58,839
60+	48,369	35,204	83,573
Total	**458,632**	**451,660**	**910,292**

Data from the Hungarian Central Statistical Office.[18]

REPUBLIC OF IRELAND

Cohabitation has increased substantially in Ireland over the last decade. Indications are that it nearly tripled in incidence between 1994 and 2002. It is associated with being young, urban and in the labour market. Most cohabitations are short, and over 40% of new marriages are preceded by cohabitation, reflecting its position as an accepted mainstream practice in contemporary Ireland.

Of the 1.18 million families in Ireland, the 2011 census showed that 143,600 were cohabiting couples. This was an increase of 21,800 on the 2006 figure, but shows a slower rate of growth than in previous years. (From 2002 to 2006 cohabiting relationships grew by an average of 11,000 per year).

While the majority (57.8%) of those couples had no children, the average number of children in this family type was rising. There were 0.7 children per cohabiting couple in 2011, up from 0.6 in 2006. Cohabiting couples with children had an average of 1.74 children. As cohabitation is often a precursor to marriage in Ireland, these couples tend to be younger on average than married couples (35.1 years as opposed to 50.4 for married).

Relevant data is as follows:
Cohabiting couple without children: 83,292
Cohabiting couple with children (of any age)
All children under 15 years: 49,005
All children aged 15 years and over: 5,717
Remainder: 5,547
Total: 60,269

18 A 15 éves és idősebb népesség élettársi kapcsolat, ötéves korcsoportok és nemek szerint. Demográfiai adatok a 2011. évi népszámlálást követően. (Population in cohabitation over 15 years of age according to age groups and gender. Demographic data following the Census in 2011). Available at: www.ksh.hu.

ITALY

According to the last census (2011) cohabiting couples comprised 8.9% of the total number of couples (they were 3.6% pursuant to the previous census in 2001).[19] Currently, there are more cohabitations in the North of Italy (10.0% of the couples) and in the Centre (9.4%) than in the South (5.2%) and the Islands (6.3%).[20] However, the rate of increase in the South and on the Islands has been considerably higher than the average, showing a tendency towards conformity across the regions.[21]

Historical data show a tendency towards an increase in the number of cohabitations, as shown by the following table, published by the Italian Institute for Statistics (ISTAT).

Data referring to the whole of Italy[22]

Years	Unmarried couples[23]
1994-1995	1.8%
1998-1999	2.4%
2002-2003	3.9%
2006-2007	4.6%
2008-2009	5.5%

The 2011 census also considered same-sex couples for the first time. Although many people preferred not to openly declare their cohabitation, same-sex partnerships amounted to 7,513, the greater proportion thereof (41.7%) living in the North-west of the country.

On the whole, according to the survey entitled *Come cambiano le forme familiari* (How family forms change) published by Istat,[24] 5,910,000 Italians have cohabited at some time in their lives (amounting to 11.5% of people aged over 15), including those who are still cohabiting (30.3%), those who have subsequently married (53.2%) and those who in the end separated from their partner (25.2%). Moreover, 24% of the total number of current informal partners are separated and 41.7% are divorced.

19 Their total number was 510,251 in 2001, compared with 1,242,434 according to the 2011 census.

20 'Islands' refers to Sardinia and Sicily.

21 The authors will only quote the data referring to the South: cohabitants comprised 1.6% of the total number of couples in the 2001 census, but amounted to 5.2% in that of 2011.

22 Istat, 'La misurazione delle tipologie familiari nelle indagini di popolazione', 2010, at p. 18; Istat, 'La vita quotidiana nel 2009', 2010, at p. 16.

23 Percentage of the total number of couples. Each figure on the right indicates the average for the years indicated on the left.

24 The survey was published on 15 September 2011 but it referred to 2009.

Cohabiting women show a higher level of education than married women (16.1% of them have a university degree compared with 12.3% of wives). Moreover, it is more frequent among cohabitants that the female partner is academically better qualified than the male (29.5% of cases, against 25.0% of married women).

As for the work situation of partners, both work in 58.0% of cases against 31.3% of married couples.

LATVIA

According to the Central Statistical Bureau of Latvia's database of information, in 2011 76,780 families were living in informal relationships and 26,564 of them had at least one child.

Family nuclei belonging to private households in statistical regions, cities under state jurisdiction and counties by type and number of children, March 2011[25]

	Total number of families	Married couples	Cohabitating partners	Single parent (father)	Single parent (mother)
Total number of families	587,691	314,739	76,780	25,301	170,871
No (under-age) children	156,000	124,956	31,044	0	0
1 child	276,809	101,218	26,564	20,667	128,360
2 children	122,084	69,523	13,857	3,996	34,708
3 children	25,270	15,095	3,719	511	5,945
4 children	5,075	2,682	1,034	90	1,269
5 children	1,547	802	342	27	376
6 children	544	252	135	7	150
7 children	200	123	42	1	34

In 2011, compared with the Population Census of 2000, the proportion of unregistered cohabiting partners/families had increased, but the proportion of married couples/families had decreased. In 2000 unregistered

[25] Central Statistical Bureau of Latvia database information: Family nuclei belonging to private households in statistical regions, cities under state jurisdiction and counties by type and number of children; in March 2011. Type of family nucleus, Indicators, Number of children. Available at: data.csb.gov.lv/pxweb/lv/tautassk_11/tautassk_11__tsk2011/TSG11-281.px/table/tableViewLayout1/?rxid=cdcb978c-22b0-416a-aacc-aa650d3e2ce.

cohabiting couples with or without children was 6% of the total number of families; in 2011 it was 13% of the total number of families.[26]

In 2011 in Latvia 153,560 people lived in unregistered cohabitation while 629,478 people lived in registered marriage.

Resident population in statistical regions, cities under state jurisdiction and counties by gender and family status, on 1 March 2011[27]

	Sum total	Men	Women
All inhabitants	2,070,371	946,102	1,124,269
Married couples	629,478	314,739	314,739
Partners in unregistered cohabitation	153,560	76,752	76,808

In a joint study between the Latvian Sworn Notary Council and the marketing and public opinion research centre SKDS in 2014, the majority, i.e. 52.5%, of respondents who live together with their partners, but are not married, indicate that they are not certain (30.9%) or they are somewhat uncertain (21.3%) that a legal form of partnership would provide them with protection in problematic situations.[28]

The results of this particular research show that the most common reason (in 41% of cases) why people choose to live in unregistered partnerships, is the opinion that there is no need to get married because marriage will not change their relationship. This kind of view is more common amongst men. A slightly smaller number of respondents (32%) indicate that the marriage ceremony is a complex process, requiring a large financial investment. The same number of respondents indicate that there has not yet been a situation in their lives where marital status would have been necessary. 26% of respondents indicated that they live in an unregistered partnership only temporarily and soon plan to get married.[29]

26 Central Statistical Bureau of Latvia, '2011.gada tauatas skaitīšana - Galvenie rādītāji (Population census 2011 - Main indicators)', 11.04.2014, available at: csb.gov.lv/statistikas-temas/2011gada-tautas-skaitisana-galvenie-raditaji-33608.html.

27 Central Statistical Bureau of Latvia database information: Resident population in statistical regions, cities under state jurisdiction and counties by gender and family status; on 1 March 2011 - Names of statistical regions and administrative territories, family status, and gender. Available at: data.csb.gov.lv/pxweb/lv/tautassk_11/tautassk_11__tsk2011/TSG11-27.px/?rxid=cdcb978c-22b0-416a-aacc-aa650d3e2ce.

28 In 2014 a joint study was made between the Latvian Sworn Notary Council and the marketing and public opinion research centre SKDS, 'Legal security of non-marital relationship and marriage, population experience'.

29 The Latvian Sworn Notary Council and research centre SKDS, 'Legal security of non-marital relationship and marriage, population experience'.

LITHUANIA

According to the last official Census of 2011, there were 75,201 couples living in informal relationships in Lithuania; cohabitants constituted 5% of the total household population.[30] The Census of 2001 registered 55,222 couples living in informal relationships and cohabitants represented 3.1% of the total household population.[31] Thus there was an increase in the prevalence of cohabitation in the first decade of the 21st century in Lithuania.

LUXEMBOURG

The percentage of couples who cohabitate of all the individuals stating to live as a couple in 2006, by generation and nationality

Age	Luxembourgers	Portugese	French, Belgians, Germans	Others	Total
< 30 years	50%	29%	61%	28%	**41%**
30-44 years	11%	15%	22%	15%	**14%**
45-59 years	7%	3%	12%	6%	**7%**
60 ≥ years	2%	*	4%	1%	**2%**
Total	**9%**	**14%**	**21%**	**10%**	**11%**

* The amount in this category is too small (28) for the percentages discussed.
Source: PSELL-3/EU-SILC.

Interpretation: Of the Luxembourgers under the age of 30 who were in a union in 2006, 50% stated that they were cohabitating.

The percentage of marriages and cohabitations according to the time of formation of the marriage and/or cohabitation

Year	Marriage	Cohabitation
Before 1967	99%	1%
1968-1972	98%	2%
1973-1977	89%	11%
1978-1982	81%	19%
1983-1987	67%	33%
1988-1992	61%	39%
1993-1997	57%	44%

30 *Results of the 2011 Population and Housing Census of the Republic of Lithuania*, Statistics Lithuania 2013, at p. 356–357.

31 A. MASLAUSKAITĖ, 'Household status of members of the private households', in: D. AMBROZAITIENĖ, V. STANKŪNIENĖ, A. MASLAUSKAITĖ and R. BALANDIENĖ (eds.), *Population of Lithuania: Composition and Demographic Development*, Statistics Lithuania, Vilnius, at p. 94.

1998-2002	53%	47%
After 2003	64%	36%

Source: PSELL-3/EU-SILC.

Interpretation: Between 1973 and 1977, cohabitation was 11% of the first unions formed. Between 1988 and 2002, most of the first unions were cohabitation (53%) at the expense of marriage (47%).

Number of people living as a couple by nationality and type of union on the 1st of February 2011

Type of union	Luxembourgers	Foreigners	Total
Married persons	112,808	91,136	203,944
PACS partners	3,922	2,438	6,360
Cohabitating persons	9,844	11,324	21,168
Total	**126,574**	**104,898**	**231,472**
Married persons	89.1%	86.9%	88.1%
PACS partners	3.1%	2.3%	2.7%
Cohabitating persons	7.8%	10.8%	9.1%
Total	**100%**	**100%**	**100%**

Source: STATEC - RP2011.

THE NETHERLANDS

On the 1st of January 2014 there were 916,991 households consisting of a couple in an informal relationship. There is a clear trend showing an increase in households consisting of a couple in an informal relationship. Each year since 2000 there has been a steady increase of 2-3%, while the total household growth has only been 1% per year. Between 2000 and 2014 there was a total increase of 39.45%.

Amount of households consisting of a couple in an informal relationship

Year	Number of households
2000	657,579
2002	696,290
2004	726,722
2006	759,189
2008	800,022
2010	836,339
2012	872,962
2014	916,991

Source: CBS Statistics Netherlands.

NORWAY

In 2014, about 315,000 couples (630,000 people) were living in an informal relationship.[32]

Among the country's 3.9 million inhabitants aged 18 years and over, 2.34 million people were living in a relationship as a couple. Of these, 73% were married and 27% were cohabiting couples. Not surprisingly, informal relationships are more popular among the younger age groups. 72% of all people aged between 18 and 29 who are living as part of a couple are cohabiting. For the age group 30-44, 63% of the couples are married couples. Among those 67 years and over, 95% of the couples are married couples.[33]

The proportion of cohabitants compared with married people has risen steadily. Between the years 1993-95, 20% of all couples were cohabiting couples. The proportion increased to 25% in 2004, 26%in 2011[34] and 27% in 2014.

PORTUGAL

2012: 729,832.

RUSSIA

The most recent[35] reliable data are provided by the 2002 population census. As part of the census, respondents were asked whether their marriage was registered. According to the response,[36] 11% of marriages were not registered.[37] This response does not, however, indicate what respondents consider to be a 'non-registered marriage'. Another repre-

32 Statistics Norway, available at: www.ssb.no/statistikkbanken. The number of cohabitants in 2013 was 573,000, but figures from 2014 cannot easily be compared with figures from 2013 and earlier, as changes have resulted in a break in the time series.

33 Statistics Norway, 'Families and households, 1 January 2014', available at: www.ssb.no/en/befolkning/statistikker/familie/.

34 Statistics Norway, 'Cohabitants, 2011', available at: www.ssb.no/en/befolkning/statistikker/samboer.

35 The results of the most recent census of 2010 are unfortunately not yet available.

36 The data have been obtained from self-reporting rather than being official data from marriage registers and the like.

37 Calculated by E. Вовк on the basis of the data from the 2002 census. E. ВОВК, 'Незарегистрированные интимные союзы: "разновидности" брака или "альтернативы" ему? (Часть 1)', *Демоскоп Weekly*, 229-2230, 1-22 January 2006, available at: bd.fom.ru/report/cat/journ_socrea/number_1_05/gur050103 and perepis2002.ru/index.html?id=7.

sentative survey provides more specific data on various types of informal unions. In a 2005 nationwide ('All-Russia') survey, with an extensive selection in Moscow,[38] 9% of all the respondents indicated that they 'maintain a stable close intimate relationship with a man/woman without being married to him/her'. According to this survey, only half of these couples live under the same roof, while a quarter do not live together, and the rest 'live sometimes together, sometimes apart'.[39]

SCOTLAND

In the most recent statistics for the UK as a whole, in 2014 there were 18.6 million families in the UK and of these 12.5 million were married couple families. Clearly, marriage based families remain the most common form. Cohabiting couple families are, however, the fastest growing type of family, having increased by 29.7% since 2004.[40] In 1990, when the Scottish Law Commission proposed the introduction of some legal rights for cohabitants, they noted that around '2% of households are now headed by a cohabitant.'[41] More recently, census figures indicate that in 2001, 7% of households in Scotland were cohabiting couples and this had risen to 9% by 2011.

SLOVAKIA

There are no official statistics available.

SLOVENIA

On 1 January 2011, when the first population census was carried out, there were 122,614 people living in extramarital unions. The number of extramarital unions is growing although official statistics on this are lacking.[42]

---

38 E. BOBK, 'Незарегистрированные интимные союзы: "разновидности" брака или "альтернативы" ему? (Часть 1)', *Демоскоп Weekly*, 229-2230, 1-22 January 2006, available at: bd.fom.ru/report/cat/journ_socrea/number_1_05/gur050103.

39 E. BOBK, 'Незарегистрированные интимные союзы: 'разновидности' брака или ' 'альтернативы' ему? (Часть 1)', *Демоскоп Weekly*, 229-2230, 1-22 January 2006, available at: bd.fom.ru/report/cat/journ_socrea/number_1_05/gur050103.

40 Office for National Statistics (ONS), *Social Trends: Families and Households 2014*, Statistical Bulletin, January 2015.

41 Scot Law Com, No 86, *The Effects of Cohabitation in Private Law*, 1990, para. 1.3.

42 Z. ĐOKIĆ, 'Časopis Dnevnik: Poroka se (ne) splača (Marriage (doesn't) pay)', *Dnevnik*, 6 October 2010, available at: www.dnevnik.si/clanek/1042394903.

SPAIN

There are no official statistics available for informal relationships.

According to the population census of 2011, the number of couples living together has increased 195.8% since 2001. However, this information does not make a distinction between couples in a civil union or an informal partnership.[43]

Year	Total number of marriages	Same-sex marriages	Male marriages	Female marriages
2005	209,415	1,269	914	355
2006	207,766	4,313	3,000	1,313
2007	204,772	3,193	2,141	1,052
2008	197,216	3,194	2,051	1,143
2009	177,144	3,082	1,984	1,098
2010	170,440	3,193	1,955	1,238
2011	163,338	3,540	2,073	1,467
2012	168,556	3,455	1,935	1,520

According to research conducted by Domínguez-Folgueras and Mastro-Martín[44] cohabitation has spread significantly since 2006 among younger age groups and hence can no longer be considered as playing a marginal role in the family formation process. The authors used data from the 2006 Spanish Fertility, Family and Values Survey.

For Meil Landwerlin,[45] most partnerships are trial marriages, particularly in cases where it is the first shared life project with cohabitation; and becomes an alternative to marriage if it is a second or subsequent relationship. This author also highlights that the probability of women entering into a partnership rather than a marriage is three times higher for women with a university degree.[46] However, men present the same statistics even though their job or professional prospects are not affected by their family situation (fatherhood and division of tasks in the household).

43 See Instituto Nacional de Estadística, 'Censos de Población y Viviendas 2011, Datos detallados', *Notas de prensa*, 12 December 2013.

44 M. Domínguez-Folgueras and T. Castro-Martín, 'Cohabitation in Spain: no Longer a Marginal Path to Family Formation', *Journal of Marriage and Family*, 2013, pp. 422-437.

45 G. Meil Landwerlin, 'Actitudes y uso social de las uniones de hecho en España', *Anuario de la Facultad de Derecho de la Universidad Autónoma de Madrid*, 2006, pp. 95-111, at p. 107.

46 G. Meil Landwerlin, 'Actitudes y uso social de las uniones de hecho en España', *Anuario de la Facultad de Derecho de la Universidad Autónoma de Madrid*, 2006, pp. 95-111 at p. 109.

The Preamble to the Catalan Civil Code also deems informal relationships to be trial marriages.

SWEDEN

To live in an informal relationship, such as cohabitation covered by the Swedish Cohabitation Act of 2003, is not a civil status. Consequently, information in the population records (civil register) only mentions if a person is married, divorced, widow/widower or single. Official Swedish statistics indicate, however, that approximately one third of all couples living together in Sweden 2013 were in an informal relationship, as cohabitants (1,390,464).[47]

In this connection, one should also mention a survey carried out by Dr. Kajsa Walleng for her PhD thesis in law (defended in May 2015) about cohabitation relationships in Sweden. The survey includes data collected through a questionnaire from a number of people between the ages of 20 to 70 who were registered as single in the population records. This survey indicates that 40% of all couples living together in Sweden are in an informal relationship, as cohabitees.[48]

In Sweden, the development of modern cohabitation outside marriage dates back to the 1960s, when the marriage rates fell sharply, while at the same time the number of informal relationships and the number of children born outside marriage rose dramatically. The proportion of couples living together outside marriage was estimated in 1969 to be 6-7%, in 1985 to be 20% and in the early 2000s to be slightly more than one third of all couples living together.[49]

SWITZERLAND

There is no detailed information available with regard to this question.

---

[47] Statistics Sweden, 'Nästan halva befolkningen lever i parrelation', available at: www.scb.se/sv_/Hitta-statistik/Artiklar/Nastan-halva-befolkningen-lever-i-parrelation/. Since 2012, register-based census household statistics have been available in Sweden. This means that statistics based on census data can show both family relationships and the sharing of accommodation. According to the model used, a couple was classified as cohabitees if the people were registered in the same dwelling, were at least 18 years of age, of different sexes, not closely related to each other and the age difference between the persons did not exceed 15 years.

[48] K. WALLENG, *Att leva som sambo*, Iustus Förlag, Uppsala, 2015, at p. 81 and p. 88–91.

[49] Government Bill, Prop. 2002/03:80 p. 24; A. AGELL and M. BRATTSTRÖM, *Äktenskap Samboende Partnerskap*, Iustus Förlag, Uppsala, 2011, at p. 18.

There is, however, information available with regard to household forms in Switzerland.[50] According to those numbers, it can be said that the number of informal relationships has grown during the last few decades. Whereas in 1980 around 96% of all households consisting of couples (*Paarhaushalte*) were married couples, in 2011 this number was only around 84.2%. Thus, 15.2% of households made up of couples in 2011 were formed by informal relationships between persons of a different sex (with or without children) and 0.6% by same-sex couples (registered and informal relationships).[51]

50 Hence, these numbers do not include informal relationships which do not have a common household (living apart together).

51 Swiss Federal Statistical Office, 'Informationen aus der Demographie', *Newsletter No. 1 May 2014*, at p. 2 et seq.

QUESTION 12

What percentage of the persons living in an informal relationship are:

a. Under 25 years of age?

b. Between 26-40 years of age?

c. Between 41-50 years of age?

d. Between 51-65 years of age?

e. Older?

AUSTRIA

The following data is only available for the year 2012.[1] The table below shows the number of persons living in an informal relationship in 2012, according to their age:

Age	Total persons	Percentage
Under 25 years of age	83,906	0.99%
Between 26-40 years of age	303,476	3.6%
Between 41-50 years of age	143,323	1.7%
Between 51-65 years of age	85,916	1.01%
Older	32,757	0.38%
Total	649,378	7.7%

BELGIUM

The numbers from the European Social Survey are too low to generate reliable tables according to age. Therefore, we refer to the Belgian Census data of 2011 to give an age distribution of the household position. Unfortunately, it is not possible to provide any trends here since the

1 This data was made available upon request. Many thanks to Mag. Karin Klapfer from Statistik Austria for her assistance in this regard.

census was only compiled for 2011. The age classes are not exactly what is asked in Question 12 but these are the only available age classes.

Household positions in Belgium (Census 2011)

Age	Married		Registered partnership		Cohabiting	Single
	Different-sex	Same-sex	Different-sex	Same-sex		
< 15	-	-	-	-	1 (0.0%)	-
15-29	193,798 (9.5%)	1,557 (0.1%)	72,797 (3.6%)	1,333 (0.1%)	218,253 (10.7%)	205,797 (10.1%)
30-49	1,575,446 (51.1%)	8,523 (0.3%)	149,730 (4.9%)	4,562 (0.1%)	380,947 (12.4%)	453,986 (14.7%)
50-64	1,392,522 (65.2%)	3,001 (0.1%)	29,182 (1.4%)	1,546 (0.1%)	100,439 (4.7%)	382,267 (17.9%)
65-84	972,345 (59.5%)	522 (0.0%)	8,202 (0.5%)	562 (0.0%)	27,990 (1.7%)	456,442 (27.9%)
85 ≤	54,833 (22.1%)	11 (0.0%)	443 (0.2%)	51 (0.0%)	2,180 (0.9%)	109,249 (44.0%)
Total	**4,188,944 (38.1%)**	**13,614 (0.1%)**	**260,354 (2.4%)**	**8,054 (0.1%)**	**729,810 (6.6%)**	**1,607,741 (14.6%)**

Age	Single parent	Child of non-single parents	Child of single parents
< 15	8 (0.00%)	1,478,885 (79.2%)	362,818 (19.4%)
15-29	41,124 (2.0%)	904,603 (44.5%)	308,054 (15.1%)
30-49	267,931 (8.7%)	88,221 (2.9%)	62,063 (2.0%)
50-64	118,103 (5.5%)	8,871 (0.4%)	31,176 (1.5%)
65-84	55,577 (3.4%)	87 (0.0%)	2.275 (0.1%)
85 ≤	14,511 (5.8%)	-	2 (0.0%)
Total	**497,254 (4.5%)**	**2,480,667 (22.6%)**	**766,388 (7.0%)**

Age	Person in household with family members	Person in household without family members	Institutionalised person	Unknown household
< 15	12,651 (0.7%)	8,108 (0.4%)	2,267 (0.1%)	2,559 (0.1%)
15-29	33,844 (1.7%)	43,603 (2.1%)	8,721 (0.4%)	-
30-49	27,421 (0.9%)	50,411 (1.6%)	12,961 (0.4%)	-
50-64	31,441 (1.5%)	23,416 (1.1%)	12,511 (0.6%)	-

65-84	43,131 (2.6%)	20,027 (1.2%)	47,795 (2.9%)	-
85 ≤	12,784 (5.2%)	2,082 (0.8%)	52,079 (21.0)	-
Total	**161,272 (1.5%)**	**147,647 (1.3%)**	**136,334 (1.2%)**	**2,559 (0.1%)**

BULGARIA

There is no disaggregated data on the age structure of informal relationships in Bulgaria.

The general trend in the family structure in Bulgaria for the 10-year period in question (2001-2011) is a decrease in marriage-based families and an increase in informal relationships. As per the final results of the 2011 national census, 70% of all informal relationships are composed by young people aged 16-39 years. This share decreases when the age of the persons in question increases – among the age group 40-49 some 16% live in an informal relationship, and among the age group above 50 years the share of informal relationships is 14%.[2]

There is disaggregated data on the age structure of the family status of the total population in Bulgaria. It suggests that:

a. Under 25 years of age?

14.6% of this age group live in informal relationships.

b. Between 26-40 years of age?

55.3% of this age group live in informal relationships.

c. Between 41-50 years of age?

16.3% of this age group live in informal relationships.

d. Between 51-65 years of age?

13.8% of this age group live in informal relationships.[3]

2 www.nsi.bg/sites/default/files/files/pressreleases/Census2011final.pdf.

3 www.nsi.bg/sites/default/files/files/pressreleases/Census2011final.pdf.

CROATIA

Currently there is no statistical data on people living in informal relationships according to age. (Research is currently in progress. The results will be available soon).

CZECH REPUBLIC

The percentage of people living in an informal relationship according to age is as follows:

Age	Percentage of people living in an informal relationship
≤ 25 years	7.3%
26-40 years	52.8%
41-50 years	17.9%
51-65 years	16.8%
≥ 65 years	5.2%

The representation of each age category can be quite easily explained. Young couples tend to start living together and they share household costs as a relationship test. After some time of being partners in an informal relationship, they usually decide to get married. Most people living in an informal relationship are in their thirties. This could be because they are already divorced or just do not accept the general idea of formalised relationships. The same reason can be applied to the following category with a hypothesis that older people who have lost their spouse do not want to stay on their own. On the other hand the idea of a different (new) spouse or partner, when the previous one has died, is not generally accepted by older people, because they belong to the generation that tends to think in a more traditional way.

DENMARK

The following totals are as per 1 January 2009:

Age	Cohabiting couples with a child in common		Cohabiting couples without a child in common	
	Men	Women	Men	Women
Up to 25	2,761	6,236	30,388	47,243
25-34	34,883	41,214	54,492	59,314
35-44	37,059	34,251	32,210	28,083
45-54	18,990	15,750	25,801	26,370
55-64	7,852	5,076	9,187	17,442

65-74	1,706	940	9,569	8,534
75+	345	123	4,349	3,286

Source: Danmarks Statistik, Befolkning og valg 2009:7.

In the age groups below 25 and above 45 there is a clear predominance of cohabiting couples without a child in common. Most of those who live as cohabiting couples with a child in common are between the ages of 25 and 44, totalling 147,407 (corresponding to 25% of all cohabiting couples). The number of older people who live as cohabiting couples falls significantly after they have reached the age of 65. On average women are younger than the men they cohabit with.

ENGLAND AND WALES

a. Under 25 years of age?

Of cohabitants, this was 18.8% in England and Wales according to the 2011 census.

b. Between 26-40 years of age?

Of cohabitants, this was 67.1% in England and Wales according to the 2011 census.

c. Between 41-50 years of age?

Of cohabitants, this was is 27.2% in England and Wales according to the 2011 census.

d. Between 51-65 years of age?

Of cohabitants, this is 23.2% in England and Wales according to the 2011 census.

e. Older?

Cohabitants over 65 are 13.2% of that population in England and Wales according to the 2011 census.

The data above refers to opposite sex cohabitation relationships and are taken from the table below based on 2011 census analysis.

Age	2001	2011
16-19	3.4%	2.2%
20-24	17.3%	16.6%
25-29	25.5%	27.1%
30-34	19.0%	22.5%

35-39	13.8%	17.5%
40-44	10.4%	14.8%
45-49	8.3%	12.4%
50-54	6.3%	10.0%
55-59	4.7%	7.6%
60-64	3.4%	5.6%
65-69	2.4%	4.3%
70-74	1.7%	3.2%
75-79	1.3%	2.4%
80-84	1.2%	1.8%
85+	0.9%	1.5%

Source: Office for National Statistics, 2014.[4]

In terms of the proportions within the UK population who are cohabiting,[5] in 1996, 15%of people aged 25 to 34 were cohabiting, and this rose to 27% in 2012. This makes people in this age group the most likely to cohabit, often living together before getting married. The percentage of those in the 35 to 44 year age group who are cohabiting also increased, from 7% in 1996 to 15% in 2012. This may be related to the increasing age at marriage. Four-fifths of people marrying (80%) were living together before their marriage.

ESTONIA

The publicly available statistics do not enable an in-depth abstract of the required age groups to be made.

2000

Persons in an informal relationship according to age groups, 2000
Total number of couples in an informal relationship: 61,223
Total number of persons in an informal relationship: 122,446

	Men	Women	Total	% of persons in an informal relationship
15-25	8,832	14,387	23,219	18.96%
26-40	28,079	25,007	53,086	43.36%
41-49	10,218	9,257	19,475	15.90%
50-64	10,223	9,110	19,333	15.79%

4 The census analysis informs Figure 8 in the ONS paper, 'How Have Living Arrangements and Marital Status in England and Wales Changed Since 2001?', published online, available at: www.ons.gov.uk/ons/dcp171776_356002.pdf.

5 These figures are UK wide, refer to heterosexual cohabitation and taken from ONS, *Short Report: Cohabitation in the UK, 2012*, 2012, available at: www.ons.gov.uk/ons/dcp171776_284888.pdf.

65+	3,835	3,443	7,278	5.94%
Age unknown	36	19	55	0.04%
Total	61,223	61,223	122,446	

Source: Statistics Estonia, Population and dwelling census 2000.

2011

Persons in an informal relationship according to age groups, 2011
Total number of couples in an informal relationship: 84,893
Total number of persons in an informal relationship: 169,786

	Men	Women	Total	% of persons in an informal relationship
15-25	6,804	12,829	19,633	11.56%
26-40	40,657	40,269	80,926	47.66%
41-49	17,858	15,080	32,938	19.40%
50-64	14,336	12,426	26,762	15.76%
65+	5,238	4,289	9,527	5.61%
Total	84,893	84,893	169,786	

* The table does not include the informal relationships of couples of the same gender.
Source: Statistics Estonia, Population and dwelling census 2011.

FINLAND

Number of persons living in a cohabiting partnership according to age group 2000-2013 (both genders together)

Year	≤25	26-40	41-50	51-65	≥66	Total
2000	120,723 (23.0%)	233,708 (44.5%)	94,656 (18.0%)	62,261 (11.8%)	14,078 (2.7%)	525,326 (100%)
2001	123,253 (22.7%)	239,957 (44.1%)	98,192 (18.1%)	67,642 (12.4%)	14,956 (2.7%)	543,900 (100%)
2002	122,893 (22.1%)	243,624 (43.8%)	100,743 (18.1%)	72,533 (13.1%)	15,829 (2.9%)	555,522 (100%)
2003	122,529 (21.6%)	246,717 (43.4%)	103,672 (18.3%)	77,822 (13.7%)	16,892 (3.0%)	567,532 (100%)
2004	123,820 (21.5%)	246,451 (42.7%)	105,789 (18.3%)	82,430 (14.3%)	18,288 (3.2%)	576,678 (100%)
2005	125,017 (21.3%)	246,524 (42.0%)	108,434 (18.5%)	87,105 (14.8%)	19,794 (3.4%)	586,774 (100%)
2006	126,209 (21.1%)	248,634 (41.5%)	110,691 (18.5%)	92,312 (15.4%)	20,960 (3.5%)	598,706 (100%)
2007	126,125 (20.7%)	249,906 (41.1%)	112,512 (18.5%)	96,561 (15.9%)	22,960 (3.8%)	607,964 (100%)
2008	125,985 (20.5%)	249,723 (40.7%)	112,894 (18.4%)	101,584 (16.5%)	24,100 (3.9%)	614,186 (100%)
2009	125,866 (20.2%)	250,866 (40.4%)	113,416 (18.3%)	105,591 (17.0%)	25,643 (4.1%)	621,282 (100%)

2010	125,273 (20.0%)	251,478 (40.1%)	112,687 (18.0%)	109,360 (17.5%)	27,644 (4.4%)	626,342 (100%)
2011	126,117 (19.8%)	255,372 (40.1%)	111,687 (17.5%)	112,842 (17.7%)	30,432 (4.8%)	636,450 (100%)
2012	127,253 (19.8%)	256,777 (39.9%)	109,806 (17.1%)	115,378 (17.9%)	33,726 (5.3%)	642,840 (100%)
2013	128,912 (19.6%)	262,483 (40.0%)	108,779 (16.6%)	118,823 (18.1%)	37,611 (5.7%)	656,508 (100%)

Source: Statistics Finland: Families.

FRANCE

For young people between the ages of 18 and 24, see the chart below.

Cohabitation mode of young people (18-24 years) in 2011

Cohabitation mode	Number	Distribution		
		Total	Male	Female
Child of a couple	2,053,200	36.7%	41.0%	32.3%
Child in a single-parent family	774,800	13.8%	15.5%	12.2%
Living as a couple without children	708,400	12.7%	9.3%	16.1%
Living as a couple with children	259,900	4.6%	2.7%	6.6%
Single parent	76,000	1.4%	0.1%	2.6%
Living together with other persons	527,000	9.4%	9.7%	9.2%
Single	883,700	15.8%	14.9%	16.7%
Total	5,595,100	100%	100%	100%

Source: Insee, RP2011 exploitation complémentaire.

See also the chart below which differentiates between:

- Same-sex and opposite-sex couples
- Married, registered partners and partners in an informal relationship
- Age of partners

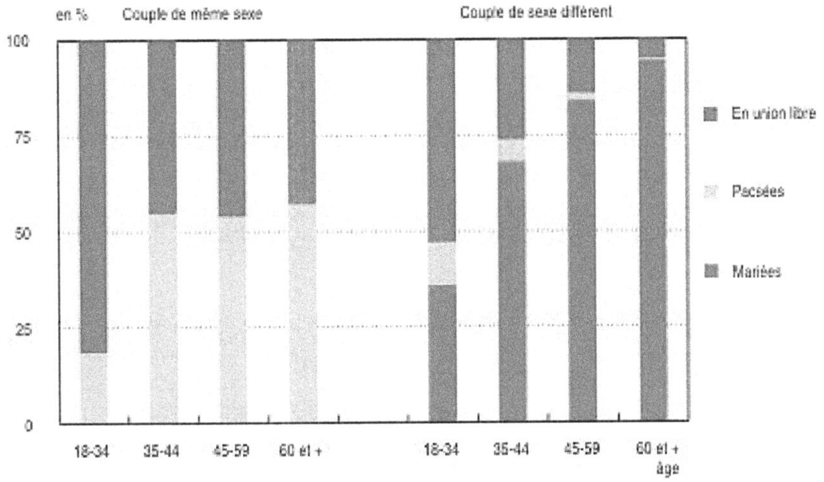

Source: Insee, enquête Famille et logements 2011.

GERMANY

People in informal relationships tend to be younger than people in marital relationships. The percentage of persons aged under 25 years for all cohabiting couples was 66% in 2010. For persons between 25-44 years of age it was 23%, between 45-64 years of age it was 10% and over 65 years of age it was 4%.[6]

GREECE

Such official information could not be obtained.

HUNGARY

a. Under 25 years of age?

	1990	2001	2011
Between 15-24 years of age	12.29%	17.54%	10.11%

b. Between 26-40 years of age?

	1990	2001	2011
Between 25-39 years of age	36.87%	41.47%	49.27%

6 N. SANCHEZ GASSEN and B. PERELLI-HARRIS, *The increase in cohabitation and the role of marital status in family policies: A comparison of 12 European countries*, ESRC Centre for Population Change, Southampton, 2014, at p. 9.

c. Between 41-50 years of age?

	1990	2001	2011
Between 40-49 years of age	22.43%	20.08%	18.31%

d. Between 51-65 years of age?

	1990	2001	2011
Between 50-59 years of age	14.95%	12.45%	12.12%

e. Older?

	1990	2001	2011
Above 60 years of age	13.43%	8.46%	9.18%

Data from the Hungarian Central Statistical Office.[7]

REPUBLIC OF IRELAND

All that is known is that men in cohabiting couples are on average 2.35 years older than their female partner.

As cohabitation is often a precursor to marriage in Ireland, cohabiting couples tend to be younger on average than married couples (35.1 years as opposed to 50.4 for married).

ITALY

The data for a precise answer are not available. According to the Istat 2009 survey quoted above,[8] however, among those Italians who have lived in a partnership at some time in their lives, 21.1% of them are between 35 and 44 years, and 20.2% between 25 and 34.

We know more about women: among those who cohabit 39.8% of them are up to 34 years of age, 49.9% are between 35 and 54 and 10.2% are 55 and over.

One issue related to the question of the age of the partners is that by 2009 the number of partners who were in an informal partnership, having never been married before (53.9%),[9] had exceeded the number of those

[7] A 15 éves és idősebb népesség élettársi kapcsolat, ötéves korcsoportok és nemek szerint. Demográfiai adatok a 2011. évi népszámlálást követően. (Population in cohabitation over 15 years of age according to age groups and gender. Demographic data following the Census in 2011). Available at: www.ksh.hu.

[8] Istat, 'Come cambiano le forme familiari', 2011, *Tavole*.

[9] *Celibi* or *nubili*.

legally separated or divorced before starting their current partnership (41.8%). This represents a significant shift compared with previous years; unmarried persons comprised only 45% in 2003 and 47.9% in 1998. The pattern of informal partnerships therefore seems to be changing, and now involves more young people than in the past.

The reasons for the forming of informal partnerships, however, may vary significantly according to the age and the different legal and personal situations of the partners. Some reasons are indeed peculiar to the Italian legal system and society.

Young people may simply desire to experience living together before deciding to marry; those who have already been married may opt to cohabit during the long period of time and the two legal procedures required in order to divorce;[10] others may choose a partnership for ideological reasons; in some cases the very ceremony of marriage, which involves families, social duties and considerable preparation, may appear too burdensome, especially in the current climate of economic crisis.[11] Some older couples, with sons and daughters from previous unions, do not want to incur the unavoidable consequences of remarriage especially those pertaining to succession law.[12]

LATVIA

There are no such statistics available. However, in evaluating attitudes to unregistered partnership, the following tendencies have been observed: the living together of two opposite sex partners without marriage is acceptable to 70% of respondents (fully acceptable 29.7% and partially acceptable 40.5%). This kind of relationship model is more acceptable to the age range 25 to 34, where cohabitation is fully acceptable to 44% of

---

10 It is well known that the Italian jurisdiction requires three years of legal separation and two legal proceedings in order to obtain a divorce. However, the Italian Parliament seems to be about to approve a law to curtail the time and to simplify the procedure for couples having no issue under 26.

11 According to the Istat report 'La vita di coppia', while before 1964 only 76.5% of Italian spouses had a wedding reception, after 1993 receptions were offered by 94.2% of marrying couples. Parties with more than 100 guests, moreover, were 13% in 1964, but 55.5% in 1993. Similar trends apply to honeymoons. Marriage has indeed become a very expensive matter.

12 That Italian succession law imposes very severe limits on testamentary succession is a significant consideration. Sons and daughters of a first marriage, for instance, in the event of their parent remarrying, will have to divide their inheritance share with the new spouse, with no possibility for the testator to circumvent this outcome, however unfair it may appear in some circumstances.

respondents, and to the age range 35 to 44, where cohabitation is fully acceptable to 39% of respondents. However, 32% of respondents, who are in a marriage, indicate that cohabitation without marriage is partially or fully unacceptable.[13]

LITHUANIA

The age distribution of the population living in informal relationships proves that among the cohabitants young, middle-aged and older middle-aged groups are equally frequent. The share of cohabitants aged 20-29, 30-39, 40-49 is around 23% in each group respectively. People aged 50-59 constitute around 17% of those in informal relationships and 60 years and older represented 12.3%. The age distribution of the cohabit-tants did not experience any significant changes between the 2001 and 2011 Censuses.

Age composition of persons living in informal relationships in Lithuania in 2001 and 2011

Age	2001	2011
Under 19	1.4%	1.11%
20-29	23.4%	22.93%
30-39	26.3%	23%
40-49	23.45%	23.09%
50-59	15%	17.57%
60 and older	10.48%	12.3%
Total	100%	100%

Source: Results of the 2011 Population and Housing Census of the Republic of Lithuania, 2013; A. MASLAUSKAITĖ, 2006.

LUXEMBOURG

Persons living as couples by age, gender, type of union and nationality on the 1st of February 2011

	Luxembourgers			Foreigners		
	Married persons	PACS partners	Cohabitating persons	Married persons	PACS partners	Cohabitating persons
Men						
20-24	25.5%	24.1%	50.4%	47.3%	6.9%	45.8%
25-29	43.2%	20.1%	36.7%	61.6%	7.1%	31.2%
30-39	73.6%	8.1%	18.2%	80.2%	3.5%	16.3%
40-49	88.9%	2.8%	8.4%	89.2%	2.0%	8.8%

13 The Latvian Sworn Notary Council and research centre SKDS, 'Legal security of non-marital relationship and marriage, population experience', at p. 4-5.

50-64	95.0%	1.2%	3.8%	94.2%	0.9%	4.8%
65+	96.0%	0.5%	1.5%	97.4%	0.7%	1.9%
Total	**89.2%**	**3.1%**	**7.6%**	**86.5%**	**2.4%**	**11.1%**
Women						
20-24	34.2%	20.2%	45.6%	57.4%	6.7%	35.9%
25-29	52.6%	15.7%	31.7%	69.0%	6.1%	24.9%
30-39	78.6%	6.1%	15.3%	83.6%	3.0%	13.4%
40-49	91.0%	2.0%	7.0%	91.4%	1.3%	7.3%
50-64	95.7%	1.1%	3.2%	95.4%	0.7%	3.8%
65+	97.8%	0.4%	1.8%	98.2%	0.5%	1.3%
Total	**89.0%**	**3.1%**	**77.9%**	**87.3%**	**2.3%**	**10.5%**

Source: STATEC – RP2011.

THE NETHERLANDS

Percentage of persons living in an informal relationship by age

Year	Under 25	26-40	41-50	51-65	Over 65
2000	13.90%	58.49%	13.87%	9.34%	4.41%
2001	13.60%	58.04%	14.47%	9.60%	4.30%
2002	13.22%	57.80%	15.08%	9.78%	4.12%
2003	12.80%	57.22%	15.80%	10.12%	4.05%
2004	12.23%	56.47%	16.68%	10.52%	4.10%
2005	11.79%	55.56%	17.55%	10.95%	4.14%
2006	11.22%	54.95%	18.37%	11.33%	4.13%
2007	10.93%	54.15%	19.05%	11.76%	4.11%
2008	10.73%	53.16%	19.72%	12.24%	4.16%
2009	10.69%	51.97%	20.40%	12.75%	4.20%
2010	10.52%	50.64%	21.22%	13.32%	4.30%
2011	9.87%	49.56%	22.06%	14.17%	4.34%
2012	9.43%	48.60%	22.63%	14.69%	4.65%
2013	9.19%	47.82%	22.91%	15.20%	4.89%
2014	9.08%	47.25%	22.83%	15.78%	5.06%

Source: CBS Statistics Netherlands.

NORWAY

a. Under 25 years of age?

'Under 25 years', i.e. age group 16–24: 14.5 percent are living in an informal relationship.[14]

---

14 See T. NOACK, *En stille revolusjon. Det moderne samboerskapet i Norge*, Unipub, Olso, 2010, at p. 96-97.

b. Between 26-40 years of age?
Age group 25–39: 50.7 percent are living in an informal relationship.

c. Between 41-50 years of age?
Age group 40–49: 19.5 percent are living in an informal relationship.

d. Between 51-65 years of age?
Age group 50–64: 12 percent are living in an informal relationship.

e. Older?
Age group 65–79: 3 percent are living in an informal relationship, and amongst people of 80 years and over, 0.3 percent are living in an informal relationship.

PORTUGAL

a. Under 25 years of age?
8.8%

b. Between 26-40 years of age?
52%

c. Between 41-50 years of age?
19.9%

d. Between 51-65 years of age?
14.7%

e. Older?
4.7%

RUSSIA

The general 2002 census provided the following data:[15]

[15] Rosstat, available at: www.perepis2002.ru/index.html?id=87.

		Males			
		Total population	Total married	Registered marriage	Not registered marriage
Population 16 years old and over, incl. persons under 16 who stated their marital status		54,154,219	33,916,617	30,594,556	3,322,061
At ages, years	< 16	1,116	953	554	399
	16-17	2,557,374	10,602	4,614	5,988
	18-19	2,632,472	68,884	43,012	25,872
	20-24	5,783,137	1,376,808	1,074,974	301,834
	25-29	5,314,150	3,063,210	2,581,611	481,599
	30-34	4,914,529	3,480,011	3,024,425	455,586
	35-39	5,024,854	3,836,392	3,420,919	415,473
	40-44	6,084,104	4,799,369	4,357,755	441,614
	45-49	5,493,467	4,404,996	4,039,636	365,360
	50-54	4,642,046	3,766,486	3,485,729	280,757
	55-59	2,365,925	1,928,128	1,796,934	131,194
	60-64	3,250,993	2,637,999	2,465,305	172,694
	65-69	2,444,084	1,976,755	1,862,310	114,445
	70 ≤	3,585,602	2,551,936	2,424,266	127,670
	Age not stated	60,366	14,088	12,512	1,576

		Females			
		Total population	Total married	Registered marriage	Not registered marriage
Population 16 years old and over, incl. persons under 16 who stated their marital status		64,689,355	33,984,049	30,676,598	3,307,451
At ages, years	< 16	3,010	2,761	942	1,819
	16-17	2,485,198	55,355	25,805	29,550
	18-19	2,544,902	313,903	211,557	102,346
	20-24	5,683,267	2,404,700	1,947,336	457,364
	25-29	5,298,826	3,464,715	2,971,937	492,778
	30-34	4,921,845	3,474,022	3,063,712	410,310
	35-39	5,191,530	3,760,813	3,412,349	348,464
	40-44	6,462,366	4,658,090	4,285,046	373,044
	45-49	6,112,425	4,264,139	3,936,847	327,292
	50-54	5,429,152	3,561,693	3,301,843	259,850
	55-59	2,981,474	1,785,260	1,666,453	118,807
	60-64	4,732,069	2,459,482	2,305,622	153,860
	65-69	3,900,492	1,731,827	1,626,005	105,822
	70 ≤	8,883,270	2,032,952	1,908,217	124,735
	Age not stated	59,529	14,337	12,927	1,410

Less detailed, but more easily intelligible data are provided by the above-mentioned 2005 survey.[16] According to this survey, half of all relationships in the sample in the 18-24 age group were informal relationships, while the share of informal relationships in the older age groups was gradually diminishing, but was still present.

	Age				
	18-24	25-34	35-44	45-54	>55
Marriages	15%	60%	61%	67%	51%
Informal relationships	15%	15%	17%	6%	2%
Percentage of informal relationships from all relationships	50%	20%	22%	9%	5%

SCOTLAND

The 2011 Census indicates the percentage of cohabiting couples in Scotland according to age, although the age ranges used (indicated below) do not match exactly with those requested.[17]

a. Under 25 years of age?

Census 2011: under 24: 9%.

b. Between 26-40 years of age?

Census 2011: 25-34: 35%.

c. Between 41-50 years of age?

Census 2011: under 35-49: 36%.

d. Between 51-65 years of age?

Census 2011: under 50-64: 17%.

e. Older?

Census 2011: 65-74 years of age: 3%, 75-84 years of age: 1%, and 85 years of age and above: less than 0.5%.

---

16 E. Вовк, 'Незарегистрированные интимные союзы: 'разновидности' брака или 'альтернативы' ему? (Часть 1)', *Демоскоп Weekly*, 229-2230, 1-22 January 2006, available at: bd.fom.ru/report/cat/journ_socrea/number_1_05/gur050103.

17 National Records of Scotland, *Scotland's Census 2011*: accessible at scotlandscensus.gov.uk/bulletin-figures-and-tables.

SLOVAKIA

There are no official statistics available.

SLOVENIA

a. Under 25 years of age?
2.28%[18]

b. Between 26-40 years of age?
51.29%

c. Between 41-50 years of age?
26.94%

d. Between 51-65 years of age?
16.48%

e. Older?
3.01%

In general it is the case that extramarital unions are more characteristic of the younger population.[19]

SPAIN

a. Under 25 years of age?
There is no information available for informal relationships.

b. Between 26-40 years of age?
There is no information available for informal relationships.

According to the population census of 2011 the percentage of people between 25 and 34 years of age who live in a partnership without children is 20%; the percentage of people between 25 and 34 years of age who live in a partnership with children is 22%. However, this information does not make a distinction between married couples, people in a civil partnership or in an informal partnership.[20]

[18] All answers to the above questions are based on data from the first population census in 2011, published on pxweb.stat.si/pxweb/Dialog/Saveshow.asp.

[19] Available: www.stat.si/doc/pub/Ljudje_druzine_stanovanja.pdf.

[20] See Instituto Nacional de Estadística, 'Censos de Población y Viviendas 2011, Datos detallados', *Notas de prensa*, 12 December 2013.

c. Between 41-50 years of age?
There is no information available for informal relationships.

d. Between 51-65 years of age?
There is no information available for informal relationships.

e. Older?
There is no information available for informal relationships.

SWEDEN

There are no official statistics on details such as these. It is, however, estimated that on average a woman is just under 25 years of age and a man just under 27 years of age when the informal cohabitation relationship starts. These figures can be compared with the average age of marriage, which for a woman is 36 years and for a man 39 years.[21]

In the survey included in Kajsa Walleng's above-mentioned study (Question 11), the people who answered the questionnaire and regarded themselves to be in an informal cohabitation relationship were divided into groups as follows.[22]

20-29 years	28%
30-39 years	27%
40-49 years	22%
50-59 years	13%
60-70 years	10%

SWITZERLAND

a. Under 25 years of age?
There is no information available with regard to this question.

b. Between 26-40 years of age?
There is no detailed information available with regard to this question.

From the population census of 2000 it can be said that most of the couples in an informal relationship without children are around 25-35 years of age. From 35 years onwards there is a sharp decline in informal relation-

21 Statistics Sweden, 'Statistisk årsbok 2014: Befolkning', available at: www.scb.se/Statistik/_Publikationer/OV0904_2014A01_BR_06_A01BR1401.pdf, at p. 77.

22 K. WALLENG, *Att leva som sambo*, Iustus Förlag, Uppsala, 2015, at p. 83.

ships, which is (commonly) the time of a transfer to parentage.[23] Hence, it can be said that child-oriented marriage is (still) a very common phenomenon in Switzerland.

c. Between 41-50 years of age?

There is no information available with regard to this question.

d. Between 51-65 years of age?

There is no information available with regard to this question.

e. Older?

There is no information available with regard to this question.

23 B. FUX, *Familiale Lebensformen im Wandel (Eidgenössische Volkszählung 2000)*, Bundesamt für Statistik, Neuchâtel, 2005, at p. 45.

QUESTION 13

How many couples living in an informal relationship enter into a formal relationship with each other:

a. Where there is a common child?

b. Where there is no common child?

AUSTRIA

The Generations and Gender Programme[1] has found that 'the presence of children promotes the increasing incidence of marriage. When there are children in the household, over two thirds of respondents are married, another 21% live in cohabitation.'[2] Although without any reference to children it can further be stated that in 2012 73% of all persons entering into a marriage had previously lived together at the same address – highly likely as partners in an informal relationship.[3] Unfortunately, other statistics, estimations or research studies do not exist on this issue. Also, an enquiry directed towards the family sociologist and family judge Dr. Thomas Bauer (Regional Appellate Court Linz/Upper Austria) did not provide any further information.

BELGIUM

This is a question that can only be answered with longitudinal data. Unfortunately, Belgium has never invested in a nationally representative

1 The Generations and Gender Programme is a longitudinal survey of 18-79 year olds in 19 countries. In Austria the second survey was conducted in 2012/2013 with 5,000 persons between the ages of 18-44. I. BUBER-ENNSER, N. NEUWIRTH and M.R. TESTA (eds.), *Families in Austria 2009-2013*, AV-Astoria, Vienna, 2013, at p. 9, available at: www.ggp-austria.at.

2 I. BUBER-ENNSER, N. NEUWIRTH and M.R. TESTA (eds.), *Families in Austria 2009-2013*, AV-Astoria, Vienna, 2013, available at: www.ggp-austria.at.

3 Statistik Austria, *Demographisches Jahrbuch 2012*, Bundesanstalt Statistik Österreich, Vienna, 2013, at p. 28, available at: www.statistik.at/dynamic/wcmsprod/idcplg?IdcService=GET_NATIVE_FILE&dID=177261&dDocName=080293.

panel. Only the Research Department of the Flemish Government or the National Register might be able to answer this question appropriately.

BULGARIA

There is no information available to answer this question.

CROATIA

There are no statistical data on these matters.

CZECH REPUBLIC

This question cannot be answered precisely, because there are no relevant data. The only figure available is that 37.4% of women who live in an informal relationship and get pregnant, later enter into a marriage with the father of their child.[4]

DENMARK

The great majority of weddings in both 2003 and 2013 involved couples who were already cohabiting at the time when they became married (2003: 86% and 2013: 82%).[5] As for the duration of the preceding cohabitation, the figures show that in both 2003 and 2013 most of the couples who had lived together before marrying had done so for less than 2 years. In 2013 51% of these couples were living together on their wedding day.

a. Where there is a common child?

Figures from 2011 show that half of all couples who had a child in common, and whose oldest child was under two years old, were married to each other. The older the child, the higher this percentage. 75% of couples were married when their oldest child was 4 years old, and 93% were married when their oldest child was 17.[6]

---

4 Data gathered from various articles and statistics published on the official website of the Czech Statistical Office, available at: www.czso.cz/csu/czso/domov.

5 Commission Report No. 1552/2015, *Ægtefællers økonomiske forhold* (Financial relations between spouses), at p. 188.

6 Nyt fra Danmarks statistik, *Børn og familier* (Children and families), 2011, No. 232, 2 May 2012.

b. Where there is no common child?
There is no information available on this.

ENGLAND AND WALES

There does not appear to be data collected on this at the point of marriage/civil partnership. We know what proportion of those who marry were living together before marriage (80%) but no further information seems to be available.

However, research cited by ONS by Beaujouan and Bhrolcháin published in 2011and based on the General Household Survey (GHS) suggests that around 40% of cohabiting couples are estimated to marry within 5 years, based on cohabiting unions which started between 2000 and 2004.[7] They go on to say that after 10 years cohabitation, 50% of these unions have converted to marriage.

There is no information about separating cohabitants with and without children at marriage or civil partnership entry. However, in 2012, the majority of cohabitants (56%) had no children in their household, while 4% had only non-dependent (adult) children. We also know from the table in Question 11 above[8] that 39% of all different-sex cohabitants in the UK had dependent children living with them.

ESTONIA

Married persons having been in an informal relationship before marriage and the number of common children involved, 2000–2013

Year	No common children	Having common children	Total
2000	3,026	1,106	4,132
2001	3,112	1,079	4,191
2002	2,828	1,105	3,933
2003	2,498	1,180	3,678
2004	2,319	1,254	3,573
2005	2,336	1,321	3,657
2006	3,071	1,580	4,651
2007	3,353	1,753	5,106
2008	3,092	1,556	4,648

7 See E. Beaujouan and M. Bhrolcháin, 'Cohabitation and Mariage in Britain since the 1970s', *Population Trends no. 145*, 1-25, 2011, available at: eprints.soton.ac.uk/198915/1/06poptrends145beaujoua_tcm77-227428.pdf.

8 This is taken from ONS, 2015, *Families and Households 2014*, ONS, 2015, available at: www.ons.gov.uk/ons/dcp171778_393133.pdf.

2009	2,706	1,472	4,178
2010	2,571	1,360	3,931
2011	2,596	1,514	4,110
2012	2,820	1,673	4,493
2013	2,601	1,540	4,141

Source: Statistics Estonia.

FINLAND

This information is not available from the statistics, as detailed information on cohabiting partnerships is not available due to the nature of the relationship.

However, according to the questionnaire sent to 2,000 persons in 1997 and to 3,000 persons in 2007 by the Family Federation of Finland (*Väestöliitto*), acquiring children was reported amongst the six most important reasons for the conclusion of marriage by cohabitee respondents who were anticipating concluding a marriage in the near future. More or equally important reasons for concluding a marriage were (in the order of importance): 1) 'I have found a person who I want to share my life with', 2) 'Marriage is financially more secure', 3) 'I want to show that this relationship is permanent', 4) 'Marriage brings security', and 5) 'The time is ripe'. Of the persons already married, pregnancy was stated as the fourth most important reason for concluding the marriage after 1) 'I had found a person who I want to share my life with', 2) 'I wanted to show that this relationship is permanent', and 3) 'I thought that the conclusion of a marriage was appropriate in a long relationship'.[9]

FRANCE

No information could be found.

GERMANY

a. Where there is a common child?

The majority of the approximately 2.83 million unmarried couples living together are younger couples in a 'trial marriage' which often leads to a formal marriage or a registration of a life partnership. There is an

[9] P. PAAJANEN, 'Mikä on minun perheeni? Suomalaisten käsityksiä perheestä vuosilta 2007 ja 1997', Perhebarometri 2007, Väestöliitto - Väestöntutkimuslaitos Katsauksia E 30/2007, at p. 41-45.

identifiable pattern of behaviour whereby cohabitants often marry in connection with the birth of their first child. However, the impact of the birth of a child is decreasing in that the birth of a child no longer correlates as strongly to marriage as it did formerly.[10]

b. Where there is no common child?

In the majority of informal relationships there are no children. Couples tend to abandon cohabitation when children are in the immediate future. They marry particularly when the female partner gets pregnant. It is not known, however, how many partners enter or stay in an informal relationship where there is no common child.

GREECE

Such official information could not be obtained.

HUNGARY

Unfortunately we do not have exact statistics. Although demography deals with categories such as cohabitation in Hungary, marriage and having a common child or taking care of one's partner's child are not connected to each other in the statistics. The phenomenon of being 'born out of wedlock' is used in surveys, although 'being born out of wedlock' does not necessarily mean that the mother is alone.

The attitude of Hungarian society can be shown via the results of public opinion surveys.

The marriage plans of cohabiting men and women were surveyed in 2008. 58.7% of men living in cohabitation did not want to marry their partner and 41.3% wanted to marry their cohabitant. Concerning women, 61.7% did not want to marry their current partner while 38.3% wanted to marry that person.[11]

The following percentages are according to age groups:

---

10 K. KÖPPEN, *Marriage and Cohabitation in Western Germany and France*, Universität Rostock, Rostock, 2011, at p. 100 et seq. and 188.

11 Source: Turning Points in the Course of Life. Survey by the Demographic Research Institute, 2008-9, 3rd wave. In: M. PONGRÁCZ, 'Characteristics of partnership', in: Zs. SPÉDER and P. ŐRI (eds.), *Demographic Portrait of Hungary 2012*, Demographic Research Institute, HCSO, Budapest,2012, at p. 14.

Age group	Does not want to marry his/her partner	Wants to marry his/her recent partner
20-29	41.4%	58.6%
30-39	56.5%	43.5%
40-49	71.7%	28.3%
50-59	80.8%	19.2%
60+	90.5%	9.5%

Source: Turning Points in the Course of Life. Survey by the Demographic Research Institute, 2008-9, 3rd wave.[12]

Two surveys were carried out in 2004 and 2008 and the findings of this representative panel survey showed that 15% of persons who lived in cohabitation in 2004 had married by 2008, while 63% of them still lived in cohabitation and 20% had terminated their partnership between 2004 and 2008. When it comes to marrying after cohabitation it was obvious that marriage is almost the only preferred way of living together and two-thirds of people interviewed in 1991 and 1997 found it important that couples expecting children should marry before the child is born. Nowadays both the public opinion and the actual demographic situation are different as the percentage of those considering that marriage is important and those considering that it is not so important has become more evenly balanced.[13]

'How important is it to marry in the event of pregnancy?' opinions of men and women between 18 and 50 years of age, 2001, 2009.[14]

Getting married is...	**2001**	**2009**
Important	57.7%	50.2%
Before birth	83.3%	65.2%
After birth	14.7%	10.9%
Does not matter when	-	23.8%
Not important	41.1%	49.0%
Do not know	1.2%	0.8%
Number of cases	10,089	1,616

12 M. PONGRÁCZ, 'Characteristics of partnership', in: Zs. SPÉDER and P. ŐRI (eds.), *Demographic Portrait of Hungary 2012*, Demographic Research Institute, HCSO, Budapest, 2012, at p. 14.

13 M. PONGRÁCZ, 'Characteristics of partnership', in: Zs. SPÉDER and P. ŐRI (eds.), *Demographic Portrait of Hungary 2012*, Demographic Research Institute, HCSO, Budapest, 2012, at p. 17.

14 M. PONGRÁCZ, 'Characteristics of partnership', in: Zs. SPÉDER and P. ŐRI (eds.), *Demographic Portrait of Hungary 2012*, Demographic Research Institute, HCSO, Budapest, 2012, at p. 18.

Even if fewer people consider it important to marry when pregnant, the percentage of cohabiting couples who 'develop' their cohabitation into a marriage specifically when planning to have or expecting a child is important.[15]

REPUBLIC OF IRELAND

The 2011 census simply demonstrated that 'pre-family' couples (defined for census purposes as couples without children where the woman was aged under 45) accounted for the vast majority (85.8%) of childless cohabiting couples. A further 12.6% were 'empty nest' families (i.e. where the woman was aged 45 to 64), and less than 2% were retired couples (woman aged 65 or over).

ITALY

According to data published in 2011,[16] 7.9% of the total number of marriages celebrated in Italy up to that year had been preceded by cohabitations. Informal partnerships had preceded more or less half of the second marriages and 7% of the first.

Among the cohorts between 2004 and 2009, about 33% of the first marriages were preceded by cohabitation and more than 70% of the second ones. With reference to the distinction between civil and concordat marriages, 50.0% of first civil marriages were preceded by cohabitation (the highest value in the Centre, 60.9%), and 26.8% of religious ones.

If we look at this data the other way round, among those who have lived in an informal partnership, 53.2% have subsequently married. The remaining 30.3% have continued to cohabit.

More accurate data – especially data linking the birth of a child with a partnership leading to a marriage – are not available. Still, some conclusions may be drawn from the Istat report entitled 'La vita di coppia' (published in 2006 but referring to data pertaining to 2003). A question was posed to cohabiting respondents who subsequently

[15] I. HARCSA and J. MONOSTORI, 'Demográfiai folyamatok és a családformák pluralizációja Magyarországon' ('Demographic trends and the pluralisation of family forms in Hungary'), in: T. KOLOSI and I. GY. TÓTH, *Társadalmi riport 2014 (Society Report 2014)*, TARKI, Budapest, 2014, at p. 15.

[16] Istat, 'Come cambiano le forme familiari', 2011, at p. 6.

married, but had not decided to do so at the outset of their relationship. They were asked what had made them change their minds and convinced them to marry: the more frequent answers were that 'life in common showed us that we could marry' (60.5% of the total number of cases) and that 'we were expecting, or we wanted a baby' (14.6%). It may be of some interest to add that the former motive has become more prevalent in recent years (it was indicated by 54% of those who married before 1974, but by 64.9% of those who married in the years up to 2003), while the second motive is cited less: from 17.3% (for marriages up to 1974) to 9.1% (of the more recent marriages).[17]

Finally, 8.4% of informal relationships led to marriages in order 'to meet the parents' expectations', and 6.3% 'because of the social difficulties encountered as unmarried cohabitants'.

LATVIA

Such statistics are not collected. However, in 2014 the joint study between the Latvian Sworn Notary Council and the marketing and public opinion research centre SKDS showed that 23% of respondents name pregnancy as one of the reasons that could encourage them to officially register their relationship. This kind of view is held by 20% of female respondents and 27% of male respondents.[18]

LITHUANIA

There is no official statistical data on the transition from cohabitation to marriage according to the status of common children. Some estimations could be provided on the basis of the 'Generations and Gender Survey'[19] on the transition rate for first partnerships as cohabitations. Out of all cohabitations entered into in the 2000-2009 period as first partnerships, 25% had been transformed into a marriage by the end of the first year of cohabitation and by the end of the third year this was around 40%.[20]

---

17 Istat, 'La vita di coppia', 2006, at p. 3.

18 The Latvian Sworn Notary Council and research centre SKDS, 'Legal security of non-marital relationship and marriage, population experience', at p. 13-14.

19 UNECE, *Generations and gender Programme: Survey Instruments*, United Nations Economic Commision for Europe, Geneva, 2005.

20 A. MASLAUSKAITĖ, 'Kohabitacija Lietuvoje: šeimos formavimo etapas ar 'nauja šeima'?' (Cohabitation in Lithuania: a stage in family formation or 'the new family'?), in: V. STANKŪNIENĖ and A. MASLAUSKAITĖ (eds.), *Lietuvos šeima: tarp tradicijos ir naujos realybės* (The Lithuanian Family: between tradition and new reality), LSTC, Vilnius, 2009, at p. 37-98.

LUXEMBOURG

No figures found at this time.

THE NETHERLANDS

Unknown, there are no available statistics concerning this topic.

NORWAY

a. Where there is a common child?

Of women born between 1945 and 1968 who had their first child in an informal relationship, more than 50 percent were married within five years after the child was born.[21]

b. Where there is no common child?

No available statistics.

For both a and b, of women born between 1960 and 1969, 42 percent of them who had lived in an informal relationship were married before 1997. Of women born between 1950 and 1959 the corresponding figure was 64 percent and of women born between 1940 and 1949 75 percent of them were married before 1997.[22]

PORTUGAL

There are no statistics available for this question.

RUSSIA

According to the results of the 2005 All-Russia survey, 11% of all currently married respondents had cohabited informally with their present spouse before they married.[23] According to a recent survey ('Parents and Children, Men and Women in the Family and in Society',

---

21 T. NOACK, *En stille revolusjon. Det moderne samboerskapet i Norge*, Unipub, Olso, 2010, at p. 103.

22 T. NOACK, *En stille revolusjon. Det moderne samboerskapet i Norge*, Unipub, Olso, 2010, at p. 116 with further references.

23 E. BOBK, 'Незарегистрированные интимные союзы: "разновидности" брака или "альтернативы" ему? (Часть 1)', *Демоскоп Weekly*, 229-2230, 1-22 January 2006, available at: bd.fom.ru/report/cat/journ_socrea/number_1_05/gur050103.

which covers the age range of 18-79), informal partners ultimately married each other in 15% of cases.[24]

a. Where there is a common child?
No specific data available.

b. Where there is no common child?
No specific data available.

SCOTLAND

There are no detailed statistics available on these specific questions although a recent report into cohabitation observed that, across the UK as a whole, analysis of British Household Panel Survey data indicated that 'about 60% of cohabitations result in marriage.'[25]

SLOVAKIA

There are no official statistics available.

SLOVENIA

a. Where there is a common child?
There are no statistical data on how many couples living in an informal relationship and having a common child enter into a formal relationship with each other. However, in view of the legal equality of legitimate and illegitimate children, the decision on having common children does not significantly influence the decision on the formalisation of the life union of the partners.

b. Where there is no common child?
There are no statistical data on how many couples living in an informal relationship without a common child enter into a formal relationship with each other.

---

24 A.B АРТАМОНОВА and E.C. МИТРОФАНОВА, 'Незарегистрированный союз в России как пробная версия брака', *Демоскоп Weekly*, 625-626, 1-25 January 2015, available at: demoscope.ru/weekly/2015/0625/analit03.php.

25 F. WASOFF, J. MILES and E. MORDAUNT, *Legal Practitioners' Perspectives on the Cohabitation Provisions of the Family Law (Scotland) Act 2006* (unpublished report), University of Cambridge, Nuffield Foundation, 2010, available at: crfr.ac.uk/assets/Cohabitation-final-report.pdf, at p. 14.

SPAIN

This information is not available.

SWEDEN

a. Where there is a common child?

There are no specific official statistics on this. However, a demographic report (by the Swedish state's agency for statistical information, published in 2012) about family structures and separations among first-time parents with children born in 2000 includes some figures of interest. Approximately one third of the couples were already married when the first child was born and approximately an additional third of the couples married before the end of 2010.[26] In the legal literature, a survey by Professor Margareta Brattström indicated that 74% of the married couples surveyed (who later on had divorced) had been in an informal relationship of cohabitation with each other, on average for more than four years, before they married.[27]

b. Where there is no common child?

Again, there are no specific official statistics on this question. Brattström's above-mentioned survey gave as a result that 74% of the interviewed persons had been in a cohabitation relationship with each other before marriage, see above under a.[28] According to the same survey, when a divorced person enters into a new relationship this is more commonly of an informal than formal nature.[29]

---

26 Statistics Sweden, 'Sambo, barn, gift, isär? Demografiska rapporter 2012:1', available at: www.scb.se/statistik/_publikationer/BE0701_2012A01_BR_BE51BR1201.pdf, at p. 9 and 82.

27 M. BRATTSTRÖM, 'Bodelning mellan makar – verklighetens betydelse för framtidens regelutformning', *Tidskrift för Familierett, Arverett og Barnevernsrettslige spørsmål* (FAB), 2011, at p. 71.

28 M. BRATTSTRÖM, 'Bodelning mellan makar – verklighetens betydelse för framtidens regelutformning', *Tidskrift för Familierett, Arverett og Barnevernsrettslige spørsmål* (FAB), 2011, at p. 71.

29 M. BRATTSTRÖM, 'Bodelning mellan makar – verklighetens betydelse för framtidens regelutformning', *Tidskrift för Familierett, Arverett og Barnevernsrettslige spørsmål* (FAB), 2011, at p. 76.

SWITZERLAND

a. Where there is a common child?

Couples in Switzerland with common children before their marriage[30]

Year	Total
2000	2,763
2001	2,745
2002	3,050
2003	3,149
2004	3,226
2005	3,526
2006	3,654
2007	3,885
2008	4,260
2009	4,581
2010	4,992
2011	5,127
2012	5,163
2013	4,864

There is no information available with regard to this question concerning registered partnerships.

b. Where there is no common child?

There is no detailed information available with regard to this question.

However, it can be said that child-oriented marriage is (still) a very common phenomenon in Switzerland. Hence, a child's birth enhances a formalisation of the relationship.[31]

[30] Swiss Federal Statistical Office, table su-d-1.5.3.6 (Paare mit gemeinsamen Kindern vor der Heirat, 1980-2013).

[31] B. FUX, *Familiale Lebensformen im Wandel (Eidgenössische Volkszählung 2000)*, Bundesamt für Statistik, Neuchâtel, 2005, at p. 45.

QUESTION 14

How many informal relationships are terminated:

a. Through separation of the partners?

b. Through the death of one of the partners?

AUSTRIA

Neither the beginning nor the termination of informal relationships is statistically recorded. Unfortunately, also no official estimations or research studies on this issue exist. Also, an enquiry with the family sociologist and family judge Dr. Thomas Bauer (Regional Appellate Court Linz/Upper Austria) did not provide any further information. Therefore, no information regarding the duration or the reason for the termination of the informal relationship is available.[1]

BELGIUM

The National Statistics Office of Belgium only provides statistics on the numbers of divorces and the 'discontinuance' of legal cohabitations per year. It is unclear which causes of 'discontinuance' are included in the latter. No statistics are available on the number of terminations of informal relationships.

BULGARIA

There is no information available to answer this question.

CROATIA

There are no statistical data on these matters.

---

1 According to the information provided by Statistics Austria, the Austrian Institute for Family Studies and the Vienna Institute for Demography by e-mails dated 02.02.2015 and 03.02.2015.

CZECH REPUBLIC

There is no such record. Although informal relationships are defined neither by law nor by case law, there are a few theoretical categories. According to one of them, informal relationship can exist as a pre-marital form of living, when partners use it as a preparation for the real marriage. On this ground therefore a third factor could also be considered as a reason for terminating an informal relationship, and that is entering into a formal relationship, meaning a marriage or civil union.

DENMARK

There is no information available on this.

ENGLAND AND WALES

a. Through separation of the partners?

There is no record of separation from informal cohabitation.

It is estimated by Beaujouan and Bhrolcháin (2011) that of couples who began cohabiting between 2000-2004, 38% of cohabitants had separated after 5 years and 50% had separated after 10 years, based on data from GHS, 2000-2007.

b. Through the death of one of the partners?

There are no data on this. The mortality statistics only record death by formal marital status and a cohabitant is not entitled to register the death. There do not seem to be any estimates. However, the biggest percentage increase in cohabitation is found in the over 65 age group, indicating that death of a partner is likely to become a more common reason for a cohabitation relationship to end.

ESTONIA

There are no official statistics available.

FINLAND

a. Through separation of the partners?

This information is not available from the statistics, as detailed information on cohabiting partnerships is not available due to the informal nature of the relationship.

b. Through the death of one of the partners?

This information is not available from the statistics, as detailed information on cohabiting partnerships is not available due to the informal nature of the relationship. However, as can be seen from the table in Question 12, cohabiting partnerships are becoming more frequent also among the older population.

FRANCE

INSEE carried out investigations which showed that in 1988, ten years after they started to live as a couple, 28% of the partners had separated, 1% had lost their partner (due to death), 53% were married and 18% were still living in an informal relationship (*union libre, concubinage*). However, these results are relatively old (1999).

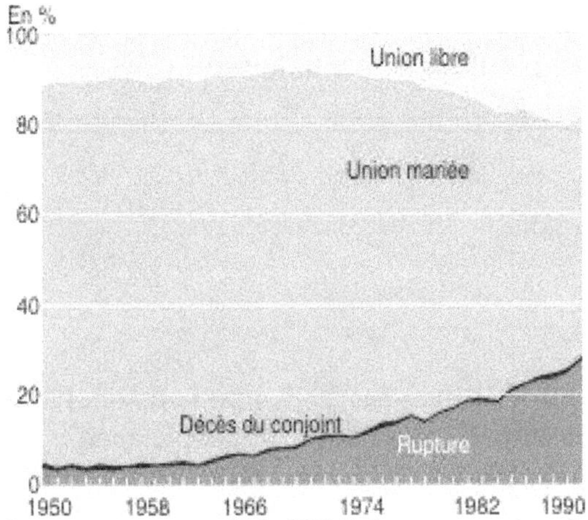

Scope: persons over 18 in 1999 living as a couple or having lived as a couple.
Explanation: *rupture*: breakup; *décès du conjoint:* death of the partner; *union mariée*: marriage; *union libre*: informal relationship.
Source: enquête sur l'Étude de l'histoire familiale de 1999, Insee.[2]

GERMANY

There are no statistical data on this matter.

GREECE

Such official information could not be obtained.

[2] See INSEE (National Institute for statistic and economic studies), www.insee.fr/fr/themes/document.asp?reg_id=0&ref_id=IP1107&page=graph#graphique1aetb.

HUNGARY

According to demographic surveys, although data collection concerning cohabitation already began in the 1970 census, the duration, beginning and end of cohabitation cannot be easily determined, so no statistical data are available concerning the dissolution of cohabitation either through separation or death.[3] There are only estimations concerning the rate of the dissolution of cohabitations. The longitudinal panel data survey Turning Points in the Course of Life (2008-2009) shows that cohabitations tend to terminate within a relatively short period of time or are transformed into a marriage. Every third cohabitation comes to an end within 5 years, whereas the rate of marriages terminated within 5 years is below 10 percent. Twenty-eight percent of all cohabiting couples continue to live in this kind of partnership after 5 years, while nearly 40 percent of them have married their partners in the meantime. (0.2% of marriages contracted after cohabitation came to an end in the first five years due to the death of one of the spouses, while the respective figure for those marrying without previous cohabitation was 0.6%.)[4]

REPUBLIC OF IRELAND

Statistical information is not available.

ITALY

Among those 5,910,000 Italians alive in the year 2009 who had cohabited at some time in their lives (amounting to nearly 15% of people aged over 15),[5] in 25.2% of the cases the relationship had come to an end without being formalised. No more accurate data are available to ascertain whether the termination came through separation or a partner's death.

LATVIA

There are no such statistics available.

3 E. FÖLDHÁZI, 'Divorce', in: Zs. SPÉDER and P. ŐRI (eds.), *Demographic Portrait of Hungary 2012*, Demographic Research Institute, HCSO, Budapest, 2012, at p. 27.

4 E. FÖLDHÁZI, 'Divorce', in: Zs. SPÉDER and P. ŐRI (eds.), *Demographic Portrait of Hungary 2012*, Demographic Research Institute, HCSO, Budapest, 2012, at p. 28-29.

5 Istat, 'Come cambiano le forme familiari', 2011, at p. 4.

LITHUANIA

a. Through separation of the partners?

There is no official statistical data on the termination of cohabitations; however, some survey-based estimations could be provided for first partnerships. 25 percent of first partnerships that started as cohabitation and were not converted into a marriage by the end of the third year were terminated.[6] The rate is not specified according to the calendar period due to data limitations, thus the rate is very crude.

b. Through the death of one of the partners?

No information available.

LUXEMBOURG

No figures found at this time.

THE NETHERLANDS

a. Through separation of the partners?

There are no recent, reliable and publicly available data. A number of 60,000 separations per year is often used.[7]

b. Through the death of one of the partners?

Unknown, there are no available statistics concerning this topic.

NORWAY

a. Through separation of the partners?

Among couples with children that were cohabiting in 2005, about 189 cohabitants per 1,000 cohabitants had experienced termination of the relationship through separation during the eight-year period 2005–2013.

The corresponding number among cohabitants without children was much higher, 301 per 1,000 cohabitants.

---

6 A. MASLAUSKAITĖ, 'Development of cohabitation in Lithuania (Kohabitacijos raida Lietuvoje)', *Lietuvos socialinė raida*, No. 1, 2012, at p. 102–119.

7 L. STEENHOF and C. HARMSEN, 'Ex-samenwoners', *Maandstatistiek van de Bevolking*, 2002, at p. 17-20.

b. Through the death of one of the partners?

Among couples with children that were cohabiting in 2005, about 7 cohabitants per 1,000 cohabitants had experienced termination of the relationship through death during the eight-year period of 2005–2013. The corresponding number among cohabitants without children was 40 per 1,000 cohabitants.[8]

PORTUGAL

There are no statistics available for this question.

RUSSIA

a. Through separation of the partners?

According to the above recent survey ('Parents and Children, Men and Women in the Family and in Society'), partnerships ended through termination in 76% of cases.[9]

b. Through the death of one of the partners?

No data available.

SCOTLAND

No statistics are available on this question in Scotland and the author is not aware of any relevant research evidence.

SLOVAKIA

There are no official statistics available.

SLOVENIA

There are no statistical data on these questions because a life union of extramarital partners is formed and ceases without this being particularly registered anywhere.

---

8 Register-based statistics from Statistics Norway processed in E. GOPLEN, *Barn i det moderne samboerskap – en bindende eller splittende faktor?*, Master's thesis, University of Oslo, 2014, table 3 at p. 32.

9 А.В АРТАМОНОВА and Е.С. МИТРОФАНОВА, 'Незарегистрированный союз в России как пробная версия брака', *Демоскоп Weekly*, 625-626, 1-25 January 2015, available at: demoscope.ru/weekly/2015/0625/analit03.php.

SPAIN

This information is not available for informal relationships.

SWEDEN

a. Through separation of the partners?

There are no official statistics on how many informal relationships are terminated by the couple separating. According to a Government Bill from the early 2000s, it had been twice as common for children with merely cohabiting parents to experience their parents' separation than children whose parents were married.[10] Later data indicates, however, that both unmarried cohabitation and marital relationships tend to be more stable, in terms of duration, in the 2000s than in the 1990s.[11]

b. Through the death of one of the partners?

There are no official statistics about how many informal relationships are terminated through the death of one of the cohabitees. As mentioned before, unmarried cohabitation does not qualify as a civil status so as to be specially mentioned in the population records, and it is therefore not possible to use any general statistics to answer the question. However, Dr. Oscar Erixson analysed in his PhD thesis (defended in national economics in 2013) the information in a Swedish administrative dataset containing estate inventories of almost 70,000 people in Sweden who had died between the years 2002-2004. His conclusion was that about 3% of the deceased had been in an informal relationship of cohabitation at the time of death.[12] The figure seems reasonable; the average life expectancy is approximately 80 years in Sweden.[13] Cohabitation outside marriage is not very common at that age.[14]

SWITZERLAND

There is no information available with regard to this question.

---

10 Government Bill, Prop. 2002/03:80, p. 24.

11 Statistics Sweden, 'Kärnfamiljen vinner mark', available at: www.scb.se/sv_/Hitta-statistik/Artiklar/Karnfamiljen-vinner-mark/.

12 O. ERIXSON, *Economic Decisions and Social Norms in Life and Death Situations* [diss. Uppsala University], 2013, at p. 59 and 64.

13 Statistics Sweden, 'Medellivslängden ökar stadigt', available at: www.scb.se/sv_/Hitta-statistik/Artiklar/Medellivslangden-okar-stadigt/.

14 G. LIND, 'Utvecklingen av samboförhållanden och samborätten i Norden', in: J. ASLAND et al., *Nordisk samboerrett*, Gyldendal, Oslo, 2014, at p. 19 (see Chapter 1.2.4, in the English version of the book, to be published by Intersentia in 2015).

QUESTION 15

What is the average duration of an informal relationship before its termination? How does this compare with the average duration of formalised relationships?

AUSTRIA

In 2013, the average duration of a marriage was 13.2 years. In contrast, in 2003, a divorce claim was filed after an average of 12 years.[1] The possibility of same-sex couples registering their partnership has existed since 1st January 2010. Hence, no figures as to the average duration of these relationships exist, only the numbers of dissolutions of registered partnerships are available:

	2010	2011	2012	2013
Dissolution of registered partnerships	1	13	26	37

Unfortunately, neither official statistics nor official estimations nor research studies exist and therefore no comparisons can be made.[2] Also, an enquiry with the family sociologist and family judge Dr. Thomas Bauer (Regional Appellate Court Linz/Upper Austria) did not provide any further information.

BELGIUM

This requires longitudinal data, which are not available for informal relationships.

1 Statistik Austria, available at: www.statistik.at/web_de/statistiken/bevoelkerung/scheidungen/022912.html.

2 According to the information provided by Statistics Austria, the Austrian Institute for Family Studies and the Vienna Institute for Demography by e-mails dated 02.02.2015 and 03.02.2015.

BULGARIA

There is no information available to answer this question.

CROATIA

There are no statistical data on these matters.

CZECH REPUBLIC

The average duration of an informal relationship before termination is approximately 3.5 years. The average duration of a marriage before termination is much longer, about 13 years.[3]

DENMARK

Danish research based on annual interviews with a representative sample of the adult population from 1985-1991 showed that the average duration of unmarried cohabitation was 5-6 years, while married couples had lived together for 23-25 years on average.[4]

The figures from 2013 show that most divorces occur in the first 10 years of a marriage (55%). The number divorces in the first 5 years of marriage is notable (28%).[5]

ENGLAND AND WALES

The nationally representative British Social Attitudes Survey showed that the mean average length of a cohabitation relationship for those cohabiting in 2006 was 7 years as compared with 6.5 years in 2000. For cohabitants with children this increased to 8.5 years (with a median of 7 years).[6] The average length of a marriage which does not end in divorce is calculated by ONS to be 32 years.[7]

---

3 Data gathered from various articles and statistics published on the official website of the Czech Statistical Office, available at: www.czso.cz/csu/czso/domov.

4 M. Nygaard Christoffersen, *Familiens udvikling i det 20. århundrede* (The development of the family in the 20th century), Socialforskningsinstituttet, Copenhagen, 2004, p. 46.

5 Commission Report No. 1552/2015, *Ægtefællers økonomiske forhold*, (Financial relations between spouses), p. 190.

6 A. Barlow, C. Burgoyne, E. Clery and J. Smithson, 'Cohabitation and the law: myths, money and the media', in: A. Park, J. Curtice, K. Thomson, M. Phillips, M. Johnson, E. Clery (eds.), *British Social Attitudes: the 24th report*, Sage, London, 2008, pp. 29-52.

7 See, ONS 2014, *Divorces in England and Wales 2012*, available at: www.ons.gov.uk/ons/dcp171778_351693.pdf.

The average length of a marriage which does end in divorce is 11.5 years.[8]

ESTONIA

There are no official statistics available as to what is the average duration of informal relationships before their termination. There were no questions on this aspect in the population census in 2011.

FINLAND

This information is not available from the statistics, as detailed information on cohabiting partnerships is not available due to the informal nature of the relationship.

FRANCE

No statistics could be found in this respect. The statistics only indicate that the average age of the partners in an informal relationship is lower than the average age of married partners. According to an inquiry, the average duration of a partnership at the time when the inquiry was carried out (2005) was much shorter for informal relationships (7½ years) than for marriages (26 years).[9] Informal relationships do not last as long as marriages.

GERMANY

In 2013, the average duration of a marriage which ended with a divorce was 14 years and 8 months. There is a trend toward a longer marriage duration before divorce. In 1983, for example, the average duration of a marriage ended was 11 years and 7 months.[10]

Informal relationships often occur at a stage of life before marriage, but many of these relationships subsequently dissolve. Stability in informal relationships is much less than in formal relationships. According to data

---

8 See ONS 2014, *Divorces in England and Wales 2012*, available at: www.ons.gov.uk/ons/dcp171778_351693.pdf.

9 F. PRIOUX, 'Les couples non mariés en 2005: quelles différences avec les couples mariés ?', *Politiques sociales et familiales*, 2009, at p. 90, available at: www.ined.fr/fichier/s_rubrique/185/psf96.fprioux.fr.pdf.

10 See Statistisches Bundesamt, available at: www.destatis.de/DE/ZahlenFakten/GesellschaftStaat/Bevoelkerung/Ehescheidungen/ScheidungenDeutschland.html.

from the 1990s, 20% of informal relationships terminated after two years and 50% had terminated after six years.[11] However, cohabitation is becoming more and more stable.[12] There are no specific statistical data available for the average duration of an informal relationship.

GREECE

Such official information could not be obtained.

HUNGARY

There are only few statistical data, mostly estimations. See also the answer to Question 14. Every third cohabitation comes to an end within 5 years, whereas the rate of marriages which are terminated within 5 years is below 10%.[13]

REPUBLIC OF IRELAND

Statistical information is not available.

ITALY

Data are only available for informal relationships leading to marriage. Among the cohorts for 2004-2009 the average duration was 2.6 years but tending to increase,[14] and 64% of the couples had lived together for at least 2 years before marriage. As for second marriages, they were generally preceded by cohabitations lasting about 5 years.

The average duration of a marriage, on the contrary,[15] is 16 years at the moment of the initiation of the judicial proceeding for separation and 19 for divorce (the data referred to 2012). But the more recent marriages are shorter: while in 1985 marriages interrupted after only 7 years comprised 4.5% of the total, in 2005 this figure had increased to 9.3%.

---

11 R. NAVE-HERZ, 'Die nichteheliche Lebensgemeinschaft: eine soziologische Analyse', *Familie Partnerschaft Recht*, 2001, at p. 3 and 5 with references.

12 K. KÖPPEN, *Marriage and Cohabitation in Western Germany and France*, Universität Rostock, Rostock, 2011, at p. 141 et seq.

13 E. FÖLDHÁZI, 'Divorce', in: Zs. SPÉDER and P. ŐRI (eds.), *Demographic Portrait of Hungary 2012*, Demographic Research Institute, HCSO, Budapest, 2012, at p. 28-29.

14 Istat, 'Come cambiano le forme familiari', 2011, at p. 6.

15 Istat, 'Separazioni e divorzi in Italia', 2012, 2014, at p. 5.

Concordat marriages are more stable than lay ones: of every 1,000 religious marriages celebrated in 2005, 933 of them still endured in 2012, while for every 1,000 civil marriages celebrated in 2005, the figure, by 2012, was only 880.

LATVIA

There are no statistics on the average duration of informal relationships. The table presents the number of divorces by duration of marriage.

Divorces by duration of marriage[16]

Year	Duration of marriage in years							
	0	1-2	3-4	5-9	10-14	15-19	20-29	30+
2004	6	247	463	1,311	1,250	980	821	193
2005	19	371	618	1,410	1,436	1,250	994	243
2006	24	445	689	1,532	1,414	1,435	1,415	295
2007	29	519	698	1,559	1,257	1,447	1,534	360
2008	24	538	681	1,271	908	1,135	1,321	336
2009	21	404	724	,106	758	780	1,012	294
2010	3	364	803	1,180	655	638	1,009	278
2011	26	491	1,247	2,215	1,066	907	1,733	617
2012	66	425	785	2,094	931	795	1,617	598
2013	38	457	684	2,217	970	695	1,970	553

LITHUANIA

The average duration of unions that start as cohabitations and are dissolved due to a break-up is 4.3 years for men and 7.4 years for women; for marriages the corresponding rate is 12.2 years for men and 21.3 years for women.[17]

LUXEMBOURG

Here are some figures on the duration of marriages:

16 Central Statistical Bureau of Latvia database information: Divorces by duration of marriage. Available at: data.csb.gov.lv/pxweb/lv/Sociala/Sociala__ikgad__iedz__laulibas/IL0061.px/table/tableViewLayout1/?rxid=cdcb978c-22b0-416a-aacc-aa650d3e2ce0.

17 V. STANKUNIENE and M. BAUBLYTE, *Parents and Children, Men and women in Family and Society. Standard tabulations. Generations and Gender Survey in Lithuania*, LSTC, Vilnius, 2008, at p. 135.

Amount of marriages and the dissolution of marriages, 1994 to 2008

Year	Marriages	Dissolution by divorce	Dissolution by the death of the husband	Dissolution by the death of the wife
1994	2,352	700	1,058	391
1995	2,074	727	1,186	427
1996	2,105	817	1,117	453
1997	2,007	1,001	1,118	504
1998	2,040	1,017	1,117	456
1999	2,090	1,043	1,079	433
2000	2,148	1,030	1,073	444
2001	1,983	1,029	1,009	429
2002	2,022	1,092	1,067	413
2003	2,001	1,026	1,149	468
2004	1,999	1,055	1,057	373
2005	2,032	1,046	991	450
2006	1,948	1,182	1,069	445
2007	1,969	1,106	1,130	461
2008	1,917	977	1,046	446

Source: STATEC.

The following is an extract from a study analysing the duration of informal relationships between 1970 and 2000:

'La typologie des unions libres établie par Villeneuve-Gokalp en 1990 distingue quatre types d'unions libres:

- Si la durée de cohabitation est inférieure à trois ans (cohabitation suivie par une rupture), on parle d'unions éphémères; leur part est restée stable dans le temps (cf. tableau).
- Si la durée de cohabitation est inférieure à trois ans mais qu'un mariage suit cette période, on parle alors de test ou prélude au mariage. Au Luxembourg, ce type de cohabitation a fortement diminué depuis 1970. En analysant les premières unions libres des individus, on constant ainsi que près de la moitié (49%) des unions libres constituées entre 1970 et 1979 formaient un test ou prélude au mariage, alors qu'elles ne sont plus que 27% de celles établies dans les années 2000.
- Si la durée de cohabitation est supérieure à trois ans mais s'il n'y a ni mariage ni naissance dans ces trois ans, il s'agit d'unions libres stables sans engagement. Au Luxembourg, c'est à ces unions-là surtout qu'a profité la baisse des préludes au mariage. Ainsi, ce type d'union, qui ne représentait que 16% des unions libres dans les années 70, a doublé dans les années 2000 (33%). Elles représentent d'ailleurs aujourd'hui le type d'union libre le plus fréquent.
- Enfin, si la durée de cohabitation est supérieure à trois ans, et s'il y a un naissance au cours de ces trois premières années, alors il s'agit d'unions libres stables avec engagement. Le comportement des individus optant

pour ce statut s'apparente fortement à celui des individus qui se marient. Au Luxembourg l'évolution de ce statut est discontinue: après un recul dans les années 80 et 90, il constitue environ 20% des unions libres dans les années 2000.'

Typology of first cohabitations by the date of commencement

	Date of commencement of the first cohabitation			
	1970-1979	1980-1989	1990-1999	After 2000*
Prelude or test for marriage	49%	43%	38%	27%
Ephemeral cohabitation	14%	10%	13%	18%
Cohabitation without engagement	16%	33%	36%	33%
Cohabitation with engagement	21%	14%	13%	22%

* The cohabitations considered here all started at the latest in 2003, showing the developments of the relationship only until 2006.
Source: PSELL-3/EU-SILC.

Interpretation: Among the first cohabitations formed in the 1970s, 49% were a test for marriage, 14% failed within 3 years from the start of the cohabitation, while 21% and 16% became stable relationships with or without children.

THE NETHERLANDS

The average duration of a marriage which is terminated by divorce is 14.4 years; the average duration of a marriage which is terminated by the death of one of the spouses is approximately 45 years. There are no recent data in relation to informal relationships.

NORWAY

A survey[18] in 2001 found that 77 percent of cohabiting relationships lasted between 0 and 9 years, 22 percent lasted between 10 and 24 years and 1 percent lasted 25 years or more. The corresponding numbers for spouses were 24 percent, 29 percent and 40 percent respectively.

PORTUGAL

There are no statistics available for this question.

18 Statistics Norway's Omnibus survey 2001, available at: www.ssb.no/a/samfunnsspeilet/utg/200301/05/.

RUSSIA

The 2005 All-Russia survey provides the following information on the duration of marriages and informal relationships:[19]

	Duration of relationships (years)						
	< 1	1-3	4-5	6-10	11-15	16-20	> 20
Marriages	27%	54%	57%	84%	89%	94%	98%
Informal relationships	73%	46%	43%	16%	10%	6%	2%

SCOTLAND

UK research tends to indicate that informal relationships are likely to be of shorter duration than marriage.[20] It is also indicated that the 'duration of cohabitation has lengthened over time, from a median of just over two years in the early 1980s to nearly three years' in the period 2000-04.[21]

There is an absence of detailed data relating to Scotland but researchers in 2010 summarised a range of relevant sources as follows:

> 'Analysis of British Household Panel Survey data suggests that cohabiting unions last for a median length of two years before either making a transition into marriage, or dissolving. About 60% of cohabitations result in marriage and the majority of the remainder dissolve within 10 years. Data from the Scottish Social Attitudes Survey in 2000 suggest that the median length of cohabitation in Scotland is three years before moving to either marriage or separation.'[22]

SLOVAKIA

There are no official statistics available on the average duration of an informal relationship before its termination. But according to official statistics concerning the average duration of formalised relationships (in Slovakia this means only a marriage) in 2013 more than 69.2% of

---

19 Е. Вовк, 'Смыслы и значения незарегистрированных отношений: разновидности брака или альтернативы ему? (Часть 2)', *Демоскоп Weekly*, 229-2230, 1–22, available at: demoscope.ru/weekly/2006/0229/analit03.php.

20 J. Haskey, 'Demographic Aspects of Cohabitation in Great Britain' *International Journal of Law, Policy and the Family*, 2001, pp.51-67 at p.58.

21 E. Beaujouan and M.N. Brolchain, 'Cohabitation and marriage since the 1970s', *Population Trends*, 2011, pp. 31-55, at p. 44.

22 F. Wasoff, J. Miles and E. Mordaunt, *Legal Practitioners' Perspectives on the Cohabitation Provisions of the Family Law (Scotland) Act 2006* (unpublished report), University of Cambridge, Nuffield Foundation, 2010, available at: crfr.ac.uk/assets/Cohabitation-final-report.pdf, at p. 14.

divorced marriages had come to an end after more than 9 years of marriage.[23]

SLOVENIA

There are no statistical data on the average duration of an informal relationship but it is the case that extramarital unions are no less stable than marriages.[24] Statistical data show that marriages do last longer. Data for 2011 show that married couples, on average, divorce after 15 years of marriage.

SPAIN

There is no information available for informal relationships.

As regards formalised relationships, there are no Spanish statistics on their duration.

SWEDEN

There are no official statistics about the average duration of informal relationships of cohabitation. Certain available figures indicate, however, that it is more likely that cohabiting couples separate than married couples.[25]

According to Kajsa Walleng's above-mentioned (Question 11) survey on cohabitation relationships in Sweden, 51% of these relationships had lasted less than 7 years. On the other hand, 13% of the cohabiting relationships had lasted more than 20 years.[26]

The average duration of a marriage in Sweden is 24 years.[27] The chart below shows the number of dissolved marriages in Sweden in 2013 and their duration in years, both for cases of divorce (in Swedish: *skilsmässor*)

---

23 Statistical Office of the Slovak Republic: Slovak Statistics and Demography 2003-2013, at p. 21. Available at: www7.statistics.sk/PortalTraffic/fileServlet?Dokument=b653d111-8505-46ba-933b-7b2397a33bf3.

24 K. ZUPANČIČ, 'Družinsko pravo (Family Law)', *Uradni list (Official Journal) RS*, Ljubljana, 1999, at p. 123.

25 Statistics Sweden, 'Sambo, barn, gift, isär? Demografiska rapporter 2012:1', available at: www.scb.se/statistik/_publikationer/BE0701_2012A01_BR_BE51BR1201.pdf, at p. 24.

26 K. WALLENG, *Att leva som sambo*, Iustus Förlag, Uppsala, 2015, at p. 84.

27 Statistics Sweden, 'Nästan 54 000 äktenskap tog slut 2013', available at: www.scb.se/sv_/Hitta-statistik/Artiklar/Nastan-54-000-aktenskap-tog-slut-2013/.

and for cases where the marriage was terminated through the death of a spouse (in Swedish: *dödsfall*).[28] The marriages which ended in a divorce in 2013 had lasted on average 11 years, while those terminated through the death of a spouse had lasted 47 years on average. The majority of all marriages in Sweden are lifelong.

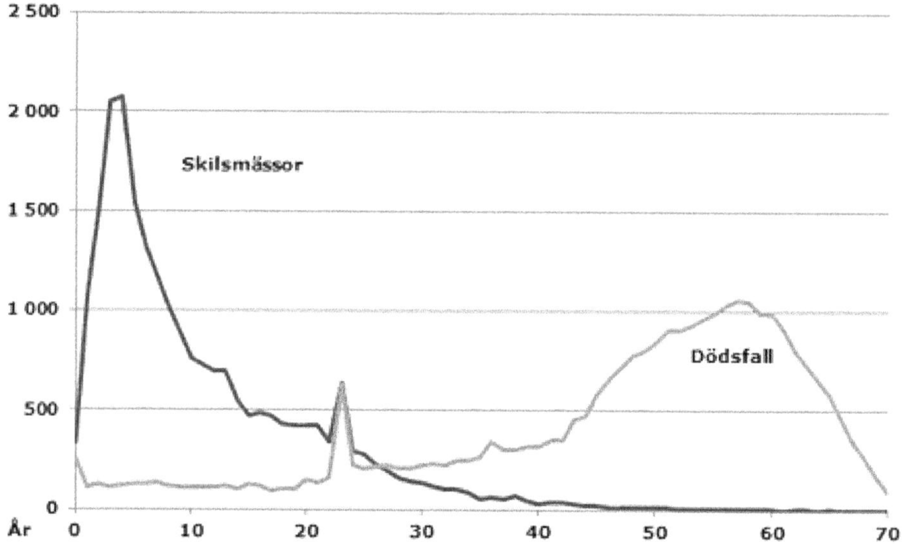

There are no official statistics about the duration of partnerships registered in Sweden. In 2013, 130 registered partnerships were dissolved through a court decree ('partnership divorce') and 19 registered partnerships ended through the death of one of the partners.[29] The same figures for 2008, i.e., the last full year when it was possible to register a partnership in Sweden, were 181 partnership divorces and 21 partnerships which ended through the death of a registered partner. Swedish law does not require a partnership divorce for the couple to marry each other.[30]

[28] The chart is Statistics Sweden, 'Nästan 54 000 äktenskap tog slut 2013', available at: www.scb.se/sv_/Hitta-statistik/Artiklar/Nastan-54-000-aktenskap-tog-slut-2013/. Unfortunately, it has not been possible to change from a chart to a table.

[29] Statistics Sweden, 'Partnerskapsförändringar efter region, civilstånd och kön', available at: www.statistikdatabasen.scb.se/pxweb/sv/ssd/START__BE__BE0101__BE0101O/PartnerskapAndring/table/tableViewLayout1/?rxid=fbda2c7f-db3b-419c-8962-9298c4ff0eaf.

[30] Registered partners are permitted to marry – or to convert their registered partnership into a marriage through a simple administrative act – now that the Swedish Act on Registered Partnerships no longer (since 1 May 2009) applies.

SWITZERLAND

There is no information available for informal relationships as well as for registered partners with regard to this question.

The average duration of a marriage increased from 13.1 years in 2000 to 14.7 years in 2013.[31]

[31] Swiss Federal Statistical Office, available at: www.bfs.admin.ch/bfs/portal/en/index/themen/01/06/blank/key/06/04.html.

QUESTION 16

What percentage of children are born outside a formal relationship? Of these children, what percentage are born in an informal relationship? Where possible, indicate trends.

AUSTRIA

The available statistics merely distinguish between children born within a marriage and children born out of wedlock. The latter category includes children born in an informal relationship, but also single mothers.

Year	Children born within a marriage	Children born out of wedlock	Percentage of children born out of wedlock
2003	49,803	27,141	35.3%
2005	49,621	28,569	36.5%
2007	47,122	29,128	38.2%
2009	46,356	29,988	39.3%
2010	47,131	31,611	40.1%
2011	46,587	31,522	40.4%
2012	46,183	32,769	41.5%
2013	46,477	32,853	41.4%

The figures clearly indicate that the number of children born out of wedlock is steadily increasing, whereas concurrently the number of children born within a marriage has fallen consistently over the last ten years. Although scientific evidence is lacking in this regard, it is highly likely that there is a relation between the increasing number of informal relationships and the number of children born out of wedlock. [1] Unfortunately, other official statistics, estimations or research studies on this issue do not exist. Also, an enquiry with the family sociologist and family judge Dr. Thomas Bauer (Regional Appellate Court Linz/Upper Austria) did not provide any further information.

1 Statistik Austria, available at: www.statistik.at/web_de/statistiken/bevoelkerung/geburten/022899.html.

BELGIUM

Eurostat statistics only reflect the number of births outside marriage, not further specified.

Live births by mother's age and legal marital status (EUROSTAT)

Year	Live births total	Live births outside marriage	Percentage of births outside marriage
2003	114,005	39,594	34.73%
2004	117,295	43,269	36.89%
2005	119,622	47,100	39.37%
2006	122,529	50,066	40.86%
2007	124,095	53,634	43.22%
2008	127,205	56,779	44.64%
2009	127,198	57,921	45.54%
2010	130,100	59,509	45.74%

We also found this table in Lodewijckx (2008) for Flanders only.[2] No comparable table is available for Belgium as a whole.

Private households (Flanders, 2007) (numbers rounded to hundreds)

	1990	2007	Difference 1990-2007	Increase 1990-2007
Singles	551,600	758,400	551,600	38%
Married without children	554,800	611,300	554,800	12%
Married with children	881,800	709,300	881,800	-20%
Youngest 0-19	684,400	511,400	684,400	-25%
Youngest 20-24	115,700	94,000	115,700	-19%
Youngest 25 and older	81,800	104,000	81,800	27%
Cohabiting without children	35,500	127,800	35,500	260%
Cohabiting with children	22,900	108,900	22,900	376%
Youngest 0-19	20,100	100,200	20,100	399%
Youngest 20-24	1,700	5,100	1,700	204%
Youngest 25 and older	1,100	3,600	1,100	220%
Single parent household	146,800	205,100	146,800	40%
Youngest 0-19	76,600	120,300	76,600	57%
Youngest 20-24	21,300	25,600	21,300	20%
Youngest 25 and older	48,900	59,200	48,900	21%

2 E. LODEWYCKX, (2008), Veranderende leefvormen in het Vlaamse Gewest 1990-2007 (en 2021). Een analyse van gegevens uit het Rijksregister. *SVR-Rapport 2008/3* at p. 8.

Other type of household	29,200	36,200	29,200	24%
Total	2212,600	2557,000	2212,600	16%

Source: Research Department of the Flemish Government in datafile of the National Register.

BULGARIA

Percentage of children born outside a formal relationship[3]

Year	Percentage of children born outside marriage
2001	42.0%
2002	42.8%
2003	46.1%
2004	48.7%
2005	49.0%
2006	50.8%
2007	50.3%
2008	51.2%
2009	53.4%
2010	54.1%
2011	56.1%
2012	57.4%
2013	59.1%

The trend is an increase in the share of children born outside a formal relationship. This started after the start of the political and economic transformation of Bulgarian society in 1989-1990. In 1992 the share of these children was 18.5% and it reached its peak in 2013 at nearly 60% of all newborn children. The official statistics suggest that the share of children born outside a formal relationship is higher in rural areas (68.4%) and among the most poor than in the urban areas of Bulgaria (56%).

According to the Reports on the Implementation of the Revised National Strategy on Demographic Development of the Population in the Republic of Bulgaria (2012-2030) of 2012 and 2013 the high share of children born outside a formal relationship is the result of a significant increase in the number of informal relationships among younger members of the

[3] Report on the Implementation of the Revised National Strategy on Demographic Development of the Population in the Republic of Bulgaria (2012-2030), 2013, at p. 15, available at: www.nsi.bg/bg/content/2963/живородени-брачни-и-извънбрачни-по-области-общини-и-местоживеене/.

population.[4] This is evidence of a change in the traditional family pattern in Bulgaria – from marriage to cohabitation.

The same source suggests that for 69.9% of children born outside a formal relationship fatherhood is established (69% in 2011 and 69.8% in 2012). From this we can conclude that these 69.8% are born in an informal relationship. It could be estimated that approximately 40% of all newborn children are born in an informal relationship and the trend is for their share to increase.

CROATIA

In Croatia, like in most European countries, the number of extramarital births is constantly increasing. The percentage of children born outside a formal relationship is shown in the figure below.

Proportion of live births outside marriage

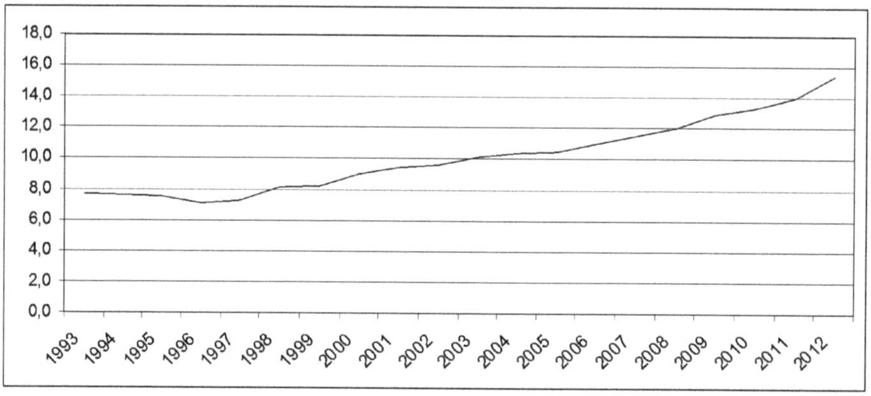

Source: Eurostat.[5]

However, when it comes to extramarital births, Croatia is ranked far below the European average. Whereas in many other European countries, the percentage of children born outside marriage has been experiencing a sharp rise in the last two decades, the upward tendency of extramarital births in Croatia has not been so prominent.

4 Report on the Implementation of the Revised National Strategy on Demographic Development of the Population in the Republic of Bulgaria (2012-2030), 2013, available at: www.nsi.bg/bg/content/2963/живородени-брачни-и-извънбрачни-по-области-общини-и-местоживеене/. See also the same Report for the year 2012 at p. 17.

5 Available at: epp.eurostat.ec.europa.eu/tgm/table.do?tab=table&init=1&language=en&pcode=tps00018&plugin=1.

There are no data on the number of extramarital children born in cohabitations.

CZECH REPUBLIC

In the last 15 years the percentage of children born outside a formal relationship has increased approximately by 20%, now 43% of all new born children are born outside a formal relationship.[6]

DENMARK

The proportion of children born outside marriage rose from 1% in 1970 to 45% in 1987. In 2007 it was 46% and this went up to 51% in 2013. A natural explanation for why the level has more or less stabilised is that many couples wait until after they have had their first child before marrying. Thus a second child will more often be born to married parents.[7]

Few women choose to have a child without living with the child's father. Information from interviews in connection with research on midwives shows that the proportion of children born to single parents rose from about 3.4% in 1982 to 5.0% in 1990-92.[8]

ENGLAND AND WALES

47.4% of all live births were born outside a formal relationship in 2013[9], of which 75% are to parents who live at the same address and are assumed to be cohabiting. The trends show an annual increase in the number of births outside marriage. In 2000, 40% of all births were outside marriage.

6 V. JEDRZEJCZYKOVÁ, *Commitment in marriages and in informal relationships between young adults* [diss. Masaryk University], Brno, 2009. See for statistics: K. ŠIMEK, 'Současné demografické trendy z křesťanské perspektivy', 29 July 2013, available at: www.stjoseph.cz/soucasne-demograficke-trendy-z-krestanske-perspektivy/.

7 Commission Report No. 1552/2015, *Ægtefællers økonomiske forhold*, (Financial relations between spouses), at p. 52.

8 Commission Report No. 1552/2015, *Ægtefællers økonomiske forhold*, (Financial relations between spouses), at p. 53.

9 ONS 2014, *Births in England and Wales 2013*, available at: www.ons.gov.uk/ons/dcp171778_371129.pdf.

In 2012, 39% of opposite sex cohabiting couples had dependent children, compared with 38%of married couples.[10]

ESTONIA

Number of live births outside marriage and in an informal relationship,[11] 2000–2013

Year	Live births outside marriage	Percentage of live births outside marriage	Amount of live births in an informal relationship	Percentage of live births in an informal relationship of those born outside a marriage
2000	7,115	54.45%	3,675	51.65%
2001	7,101	56.21%	3,804	53.57%
2002	7,318	56.29%	2,642	36.10%
2003	7,538	57.82%	2,891	38.35%
2004	8,111	57.97%	5,730	70.64%
2005	8,396	58.51%	6,103	72.69%
2006	8,665	58.24%	6,799	78.47%
2007	9,159	58.06%	7,363	80.39%
2008	9,467	59.07%	7,754	81.91%
2009	9,328	59.18%	7,717	82.73%
2010	9,359	59.14%	7,721	82.50%
2011	8,759	59.67%	7,555	86.25%
2012	8,209	58.40%	7,301	88.94%
2013	7,975	58.94%	7,161	89.79%

* The number of births in informal relationships in the years 2000–2003 has been underestimated due to the amendments to the data collection.
* Birth in an informal relationship – a child whose parents are not officially married at the moment of registering the birth, but who have defined their cohabitation as an informal relationship.
Source: Statistics Estonia.

The percentage of children born outside a marriage has been increasing since the end of the 1980s, when the percentage of children born within a marriage decreased.[12] As for births outside a marriage, the percentage of births in which the parents have defined their cohabitation as an informal relationship is increasing. It is important to note here that the number of births in an informal relationship in the years 2000-2003 has been underestimated due to the amendments to the data collection, thus the share of these children in these years is remarkably smaller.

[10] See ONS 2012, *Short Report: Cohabitation in the UK 2012,* available online at: www.ons.gov.uk/ons/dcp171776_284888.pdf.

[11] Child born from an informal relationship – a child whose parents are not officially married at the moment of registering the birth, but have defined their cohabitation as an informal relationship.

[12] L. Järviste, K. Kasearu and A. Reinomägi, 'Abielu ja vaba kooselu: trendid, regulatsioonid, hoiakud', Sotsiaalministeeriumi toimetised, 2008, at no. 4.

FINLAND

All newborn children, children born outside marriage and the percentage of children born outside marriage 2000-2013 according to the statistics on all live births

Year	Born total	Born outside marriage	Percentage of children born outside marriage
2000	56,742	22,247	39.2%
2001	56,189	22,222	39.5%
2002	55,555	22,156	39.9%
2003	56,630	22,649	40.0%
2004	57,758	23,554	40.8%
2005	57,745	23,319	40.4%
2006	58,840	23,858	40.5%
2007	58,729	23,824	40.6%
2008	59,530	24,246	40.7%
2009	60,430	24,697	40.9%
2010	60,980	25,066	41.1%
2011	59,961	24,498	40.9%
2012	59,493	24,695	41.5%
2013	58,134	24,488	42.1%

Source: National Institute for Health and Welfare: Register of newborn children.

Mothers giving birth, unmarried mothers,[13] cohabitee mothers and the percentage of cohabitee mothers in relation to unmarried mothers 2000-2013 according to information derived from maternity hospitals

Year	Mothers total	Unmarried mothers	Cohabitee mothers	Percentage of cohabitee mothers of unmarried mothers
2000	55,851	23,361 (41.8%)	15,440 (27.6%)	66.1%
2001	55,135	23,578 (42.8%)	15,332 (27.8%)	65.0%
2002	54,698	21,551 (39.4%)	14,103 (25.8%)	65.4%
2003	55,788	21,792 (39.1%)	14,688 (26.3%)	67.4%
2004	56,878	22,891 (40.2%)	18,055 (31.7%)	78.9%
2005	56,961	22,814 (40.1%)	17,752 (31.2%)	77.8%
2006	58,158	23,275 (40.0%)	17,637 (30.3%)	75.8%
2007	58,025	23,597 (40.7%)	19,029 (32.8%)	80.6%
2008	58,925	24,334 (41.3%)	19,817 (33.6%)	81.4%
2009	59,918	25,209 (42.1%)	19,434 (32.4%)	77.1%
2010	60,422	25,471 (42.2%)	19,648 (32.5%)	77.1%
2011	59,385	24,979 (42.1%)	19,033 (32.1%)	76.2%
2012	59,039	24,985 (42.3%)	18,814 (31.9%)	75.3%
2013	57,728	24,664 (42.7%)	19,205 (33.3%)	77.9%

Source: National Institute for Health and Welfare: Register of newborn children.

[13] Unmarried mothers means, in this context, mothers who are not married and not in a registered partnership.

FRANCE

In 2013, 811,510 children were born in France. 57.2% of them were born outside a formal relationship.[14] The percentage of children born outside a formal relationship has been consistently increasing (47.4% in 2004; 51.7% in 2007; 54.9% in 2010). The most recent statistics for 2014 indicate that 820,000 children (58.2%) were born outside marriage.

The average age of the mother was 30.3 years in 2013. It has been consistently increasing since 1950 (27.7 years in 1950).

GERMANY

In 2012 673,544 children were born (2010: 677,947; 2000: 766,999).[15] The parents of 232,383 children were not married (2010: 225,473: 2000: 179,574).[16] This means that in 2012, 34.8% of the children were born outside a formal relationship (2010: 33.3%; 2000: 23.4%). There is more non-marital childbearing in the east of Germany than in the west of the country. In some regions there are even more children born in an informal relationship than within a marriage. The percentage of children born in informal relationships is rising in all parts of Germany. The rise in informal relationships, a later age for getting married, and a growing tendency to remain unmarried contribute to the increasing trend of non-marital childbearing. There are, however, no specific statistical data available which allow a differentiation to be made between children living within an informal relationship and those living with a lone parent.

GREECE

Such official information could not be obtained.

HUNGARY

The trend is obvious as the number of children born outside a formal relationship is continuously increasing. According to data provided by

---

14 See INSEE (National Institute for statistic and economic studies), www.insee.fr/fr/themes/tableau.asp?reg_id=0&ref_id=NATnon02231.

15 Statistisches Bundesamt, *Statistisches Jahrbuch Deutschland und Internationales 2014*, Statistisches Bundesamt, Wiesbaden, 2014, at p. 33.

16 Statistisches Bundesamt, *Statistisches Jahrbuch Deutschland und Internationales 2014*, Statistisches Bundesamt, Wiesbaden, 2014, at p. 33.

the Demographic Research Institute the rate of children born out of wedlock certainly increased between 1990 and 2004.

Year	Approximate rate of children born out of wedlock
1990	13%
1991	14%
1992	15.5%
1993	17.5%
1994	19.5%
1995	20.5%
1996	22.5%
1997	25%
1998	26.5%
1999	28%
2000	29%
2001	30.5%
2002	31%
2003	32.5%
2004	34%
2005	35%
2006	36%
2007	39%
2008	40%
2009	41%
2010	41%
2011	43%
2012	45%
2013	46.2%

Source: Data from the Demographic Research Institute.[17]

Against the background of the increasing number of children being born outside of marriage there is the decrease in the number of cohabitations. Whereas, previously, children born out of wedlock tended to be born to a single mother, nowadays, according to estimations, only one-tenth of all births involve a single mother. This means that one-third of all births involve cohabiting couples.[18] According to a survey in the 1990s 30% of

17 B. KAPITÁNY, 'Átalakuló gyermekvállalási szokások' ('Changes in the habits of having children'), *KorFa*, 2006, at p. 2; Zs. SPÉDER, 'Demográfiai folyamatok: születések, halálozások, korösszetétel' (Demographic trends: births, deaths, age structure'), in: T. KOLOSI and I. GY. TÓTH (eds.), *Társadalmi Riport 2014 (Society Report 2014)*, TARKI, Budapest, 2014, at p. 69.

18 Zs. SPÉDER, 'Demográfiai folyamatok: születések, halálozások, korösszetétel', in: T. KOLOSI and I. GY. TÓTH, *Társadalmi riport 2014 (Society Report 2014)*, TARKI, Budapest, 2014, at p. 69-70.

children born out of wedlock were taken care of by their mother only, so the mothers of 70% of those children lived in a later established marriage or cohabitation with the father.[19]

REPUBLIC OF IRELAND

Statistical information is not available.

ITALY

In general, children may be born outside a formal relationship under several circumstances: for instance, to a single mother who recognises the baby as her own, to a mother who chooses not to be nominated according to the Decree of the President of the Italian Republic 3 November 2000, n. 356 and the law of 15 May 1997, n. 127, or to an unmarried couple. In the latter case, the baby may be recognised by both or just one of his or her parents.

Unfortunately, available data only refer to children born to unmarried parents, and no other statistical data are available for children born in other situations.

In 2012 children born to unmarried parents comprised 24.8% of the total number of births (about 132,000 newborn babies).[20] One baby out of four is therefore born within an informal relationship. But their distribution throughout the country is not uniform: in the North and the Centre they amount to almost 30% (with peak values of 44% in the province of Bolzano, and 36.2% in Valle d'Aosta). In these parts of Italy, considered together, the corresponding values in 1995 amounted to 9.7%. The trend is rising steeply.

The South and Sicily show lower numbers of births outside marriage, but here too the trend is rising: from 5.2% in 1995 to 16.4% in 2012 in the South, and from 8.7% to 19.5% in Sicily. Sardinia has percentages similar to the North (28.2% in 2012).

It may be of interest to note that the proportion of children born outside marriage does not change if we refer only to parents who are both Italian

---

19 B. KAPITÁNY, 'Átalakuló gyermekvállalási szokások' ('Changes in the habits of having children'), *KorFa*, 2006, at p. 3.

20 Istat, 'Natalità e fecondità della popolazione residente (2012)', 2013, at p. 7; Istat, 'Indicatori demografici. Stime per l'anno 2013', 2014, at p. 5.

(25.4% of the total number of births), while it is lower if we consider parents who are both foreigners (16.8%). Among mixed couples, on the contrary, the value is higher (about 35%) because most of these couples are reconstituted families where marriage is in general rarer.

LATVIA

Data of the Central Statistical Bureau (CSB)[21] show that in 2013, a total of 20,600 children were born in Latvia, 9,200 or 44.6% of which were extra-marital births. The majority (53%) of first-born children were born outside marriage.

11,400 or 55.4% of children were born in a registered marriage. Compared with 2012, the number of marital births out of the total number of births increased by just 0.4%. In 2013 the increased number of babies born in a registered marriage can be explained by the growth in the number of second and third children. Out of the total number of second and third children, 62.6% and 64.6% respectively, were born to a married couple.

In 2013 a larger number of extramarital births were registered to women under 26 years of age, when usually the first baby is born.

Number of births by marital status and age of the mother in 2013

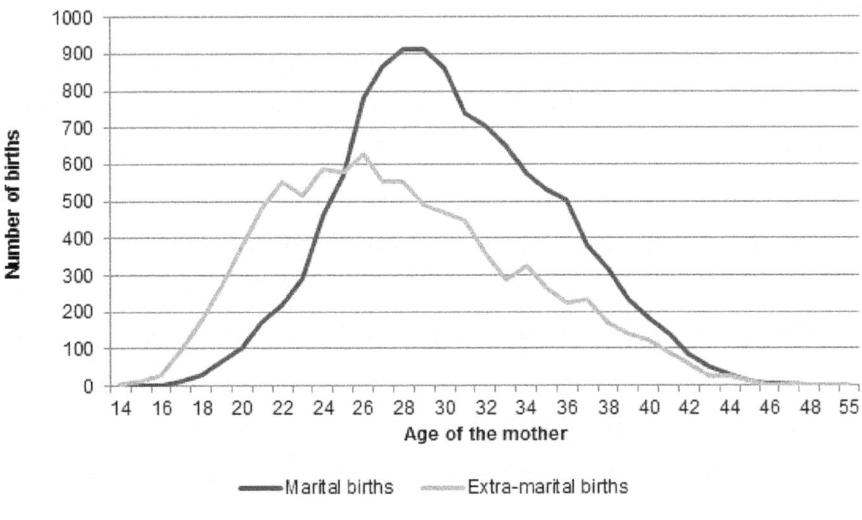

Source: Central Statistical Bureau of Latvia.

[21] Central Statistical Bureau of Latvia, 'Last year 53% of the first-born children were born outside marriage', 29.10.2014, available at: csb.gov.lv/notikumi/pern-53-pirmo-bernu-dzimusi-arpus-laulibas-40972.html.

In 1990, 83.1% of all babies were born to a married family; in 2000 this was 59.6%, and in 2013 it was only 55.4%. Since 1980, when 87.5% of all children were born in a registered marriage, the share of marital births has been decreasing nearly every year. A slight growth was registered only between 2005 and 2008, when the share of marital births reached 56.8% (an increase of 1.5% compared with 2005).

Share of marital and extra-marital births (1990-2013)

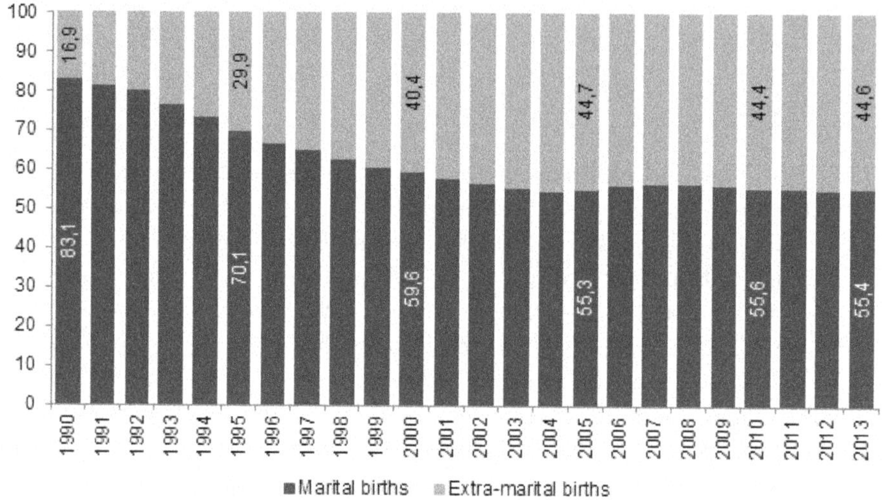

Source: Central Statistical Bureau of Latvia.

Before 1996 there was no distinct difference between the average age of women at the birth of the first child and the average age at entering marriage. Since 1997 the average age at the birth of the first child has been lower than that at the first marriage.

In 2000 the average age of women at the first marriage was 24.9 years, and at the birth of the first child – it was 24.4 years. In turn, in 2013 the average age of women at the first marriage was 28.5 years, and at the birth of the first child it was 26.9 years.

Average age of women at the first marriage and average age of mother at the first childbearing (1990-2013)

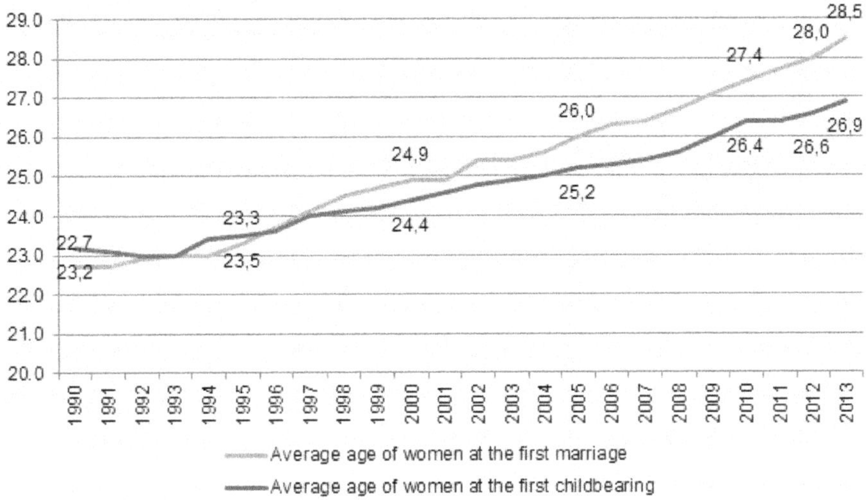

Source: Central Statistical Bureau of Latvia.

Data of the Population Census show that a total of 587,700 families were registered in Latvia in 2013, of which 232,700 (39.6%) were families with underage children. Of the total number of families with underage children, 106,500 (45.8%) were families of a married couple, 35,700 (15.3%) were families of cohabiting partners, 12,400 (5.3%) were families of a single father, and 78,200 (33.6%) were families of a single mother.

In 2011, 340,400 underage children were living in families. Of these 49% lived in a family of a married couple, 31% in a family of a single mother, 16% in a family of cohabiting partners, and 4% in a family of a single father.

Extramarital births in 2004 were 9,307, in 2005 they were 9,780, in 2006 they were 10,012, in 2007 they were 10,348, in 2008 they were 10,542, in 2009 they were 9,578, in 2010 they were 8,761, in 2011 they were 8,367, in 2012 they were 8,938, and in 2013 they were 9,181.

Live births by marital status and age of mother[22]

Year	Age of the mother	Total births	Marital births	Extra-marital births	Percentage of extra-marital births
2004	≤ 19	1,462	357	1,105	75.58%
	20-24	5,957	2,619	3,338	56.03%
	25-29	6,237	3,814	2,423	38.84%
	30-34	4,361	2,839	1,522	34.90%
	35-49	1,981	1,282	699	35.28%
	40-44	519	312	207	39.88%
	≥ 45	29	16	13	44.82%
2005	≤ 19	1,443	323	1,120	77.61%
	20-24	5,949	2,561	3,388	56.95%
	25-29	6,743	4,788	2,555	37.89%
	30-34	4,955	3,223	1,732	34.95%
	35-49	2,245	1,466	779	34.69%
	40-44	504	309	195	38.69%
	≥ 45	34	23	11	32.35%
2006	≤ 19	1,572	354	1,218	77.48%
	20-24	6,187	2,717	3,470	56.08%
	25-29	7,004	4,346	2,658	37.94%
	30-34	5,089	3,435	1,654	32.50%
	35-49	2,411	1,612	799	33.14%
	40-44	572	373	199	34.79%
	≥ 45	32	18	14	43.75%
2007	≤ 19	1,519	349	1,170	77.02%
	20-24	6,354	2,815	3,539	55.69%
	25-29	7,445	4,721	2,724	36.58%
	30-34	5,272	3,515	1,757	33.32%
	35-49	2,708	1,776	932	34.41%
	40-44	618	407	211	34.14%
	≥ 45	33	18	15	45.45%
2008	≤ 19	1,500	291	1,209	80.60%
	20-24	6,151	2,655	3,496	56.83%
	25-29	7,709	4,893	2,816	36.52%
	30-34	5,521	3,688	1,833	33.20%
	35-49	2,847	1,896	951	33.40%
	40-44	634	415	219	34.54%
	≥ 45	33	15	18	54.54%

22 The number of births also includes children born abroad to a mother (permanent resident of the Republic of Latvia) temporarily residing in a country outside the Republic of Latvia. Central Statistical Bureau of Latvia database information. Available at: data.csb.gov.lv/pxweb/lv/Sociala/Sociala__ikgad__iedz__dzimst/ID0030.px/table/tableViewLayout1/?rxid=cdcb978c-22b0-416a-aacc-aa650d3e2ce0.

2009	≤ 19	1,142	186	956	83.71%
	20-24	5,145	2,141	3,004	58.38%
	25-29	7,132	4,426	2,706	37.94%
	30-34	5,110	3,446	1,664	32.56%
	35-49	2,779	1,803	976	35.12%
	40-44	681	423	258	37.88%
	≥ 45	42	27	15	35.71%
2010	≤ 19	860	124	736	85.58%
	20-24	4,363	1,656	2,707	62.04%
	25-29	6,481	4,011	2,470	38.11%
	30-34	4,837	3,168	1,669	34.50%
	35-49	2,492	1,588	904	36.27%
	40-44	692	434	258	37.28%
	≥ 45	40	23	17	42.50%
2011	≤ 19	831	136	695	83.63%
	20-24	3,883	1,425	2,458	63.30%
	25-29	6,146	3,746	2,400	39.05%
	30-34	4,726	3,118	1,608	34.02%
	35-49	2,531	1,599	932	36.82%
	40-44	656	394	262	39.93%
	≥ 45	29	17	16	55.17%
2012	≤ 19	783	118	665	84.93%
	20-24	3,908	1,354	2,554	65.35%
	25-29	6,632	3,911	2,721	41.03%
	30-34	5,057	3,332	1,725	34.11%
	35-49	2,788	1,790	998	35.79%
	40-44	683	424	259	37.92%
	≥ 45	33	17	16	48.48%
2013	≤ 19	710	115	595	83.80%
	20-24	3,759	1,243	2,516	66.93%
	25-29	6,848	4,040	2,808	41.00%
	30-34	5,417	3,529	1,888	34.85%
	35-49	2,997	1,965	1,032	34.43%
	40-44	811	489	322	39.70%
	≥ 45	45	25	20	44.44%

LITHUANIA

The percentage of children born out of wedlock in Lithuania is 29.3% and in the last decade (2003-2013) this figure has been more or less stable with the exception of a short-term fluctuation in 2009-2010. The secular increase in non-marital fertility in Lithuania started at the beginning of the 1990s when the long-term stable rate of non-marital fertility (6-7% in the period 1922–1990) started to move gradually upwards after 1992 and increased by more than three times in the period of 1992–2001.[23]

Recently, the majority of children born out of wedlock are registered to parents living in cohabitation and only a small fraction to single mothers. In 2013, out of all children born out of wedlock, 81% were registered by both non-married parents and 19% by single mothers. Moreover, in recent years, the share of children born to single mothers has decreased; the share of children born to cohabiting parents, in contrast, has increased.[24]

The composition of non-marital fertility by the partnership status of the parents significantly changed after 2004. Before this, the majority of non-marital fertility cases had been attributed to single mothers, while after 2004 this was to cohabiting parents. This trend has been generated by the legislative changes in the social support policies in 2004 and not the demographic factors.

Non-marital fertility, totals and according to type of the parental partnership status, 2000–2013

Year	Non-marital births, total	Non-marital births registered by the statement of both non-married parents	Non-marital births registered by the statement of the mother	Non-marital birth registered by the statement of a guardian
2000	22.3%	6.8%	15.8%	0%
2001	25.4%	8.3%	17%	0.1%
2002	28%	9.5%	18.4%	0.1%
2003	29.5%	13.2%	16.2%	0.1%
2004	28.5%	19.3%	9%	0.2%
2005	28%	18.9%	8.9%	0.2%
2006	28.7%	19.9%	8.7%	0.2%
2007	27.8%	19.9%	7.8%	0.2%
2008	26.5%	19.6%	6.8%	0.2%
2009	25.4%	18.8%	6.4%	0.1%
2010	25.6%	19.3%	6.2%	0.2%
2011	27.7%	20.9%	6.6%	0.2%
2012	28.8%	23%	5.7%	0.1%
2013	29.3%	24%	5.2%	0.1%

Source: Statistics Lithuania database (www.stat.gov.lt).

23 A. MASLAUSKAITĖ, 'Nesantuokinis gimstamumas Lietuvoje: raida ir erdvinė diferenciacija' (Non-marital fertility in Lithuania: trends and spatial differentiation), *Lietuvos socialinė raida*, 2014 (in press).

24 A. MASLAUSKAITĖ, 'Nesantuokinis gimstamumas Lietuvoje: raida ir erdvinė diferenciacija' (Non-marital fertility in Lithuania: trends and spatial differentiation), *Lietuvos socialinė raida*, 2014 (in press).

LUXEMBOURG

Persons living as a couple with or without child(ren) on the 1st of February 2011

Type of union	Amount	Percentage	Mean age	Median age
Total married persons	**203,944**	**100.0%**	**50.8**	**49.0**
Married persons without children	76,466	38.5%	59.7	62.0
Married persons with children	125,478	61.5%	45.2	45.0
Total PACS partners	**6,360**	**100.0%**	**36.9**	**34.0**
PACS partners without children	3,910	61.5%	36.8	32.0
PACS partners with children	2,450	38.5%	37.1	36.0
Total cohabitating persons	**21,168**	**100%**	**37.7**	**35.0**
Cohabitating persons without children	9,910	46.8%	37.6	**33.0**
Cohabitating persons with children	11,258	53.2%	37.8	37.0

Source: STATEC - RP2011.

Amount of live births within a marriage by age of the mother

		Age							
	Total	**<20**	**20-24**	**25-29**	**30-34**	**35-39**	**40-44**	**≥ 45**	**Unknown**
1950	4,252	130	1,065	1,517	873	514	144	9	-
1960	4,860	191	1,417	1,624	1,080	431	106	11	-
1970	4,234	292	1,432	1,322	706	367	109	5	1
1980	3,920	182	1,144	1,546	796	206	43	3	-
1990	4,300	90	777	1,815	1,224	346	47	-	1
2000	4,470	61	569	1,452	1,611	684	90	3	-
2010	3,878	21	275	1,031	1,587	768	186	8	2
2011	3,716	18	293	944	1,503	778	168	11	1
2012	3,775	18	276	914	1,536	840	179	10	2
2013	3,841	14	247	973	1,531	871	195	8	2

Amount of live births outside of a marriage by age of the mother

		Age							
	Total	**<20**	**20-24**	**25-29**	**30-34**	**35-39**	**40-44**	**≥ 45**	**Unknown**
1950	149	34	58	30	11	11	5	-	-
1960	159	38	69	22	18	7	5	-	-
1970	177	40	59	33	24	13	7	1	-
1980	249	46	87	44	35	13	3	-	21
1990	636	59	183	194	130	57	8	-	5
2000	1,253	85	270	376	325	159	31	3	4
2010	1,996	90	347	553	565	339	93	6	3
2011	1,923	91	339	525	561	320	73	9	5
2012	2,251	83	378	595	730	358	91	6	10
2013	2,274	70	308	629	714	440	102	7	4

THE NETHERLANDS

Percentage of children born outside a formal relationship

Year	Born outside a formal relationship
2000	24.94%
2001	27.20%
2002	28.96%
2003	30.67%
2004	32.49%
2005	34.89%
2006	37.06%
2007	39.46%
2008	41.24%
2009	43.28%
2010	41.08%
2011	41.76%
2012	42.64%
2013	43.19%

Source: CBS Statistics Netherlands.

There has been a steady increase in the amount of children born outside a formal relationships in the past 13 years. In the 1950s up until 1980 the percentage of children born outside a formal relationship was only approximately between 1 to 3%. From 1980 to 1990 it more than doubled from 4.11% to 11.38%, and from 1990 to 2000 it again more than doubled to 24.94%. From 2000 to 2008 the percentage increased to the 40%. From 2008 onwards the percentage appears to have stabilised. It is unknown what percentage of the children born outside a formal relationship are born within an informal relationship of a cohabiting couple.

NORWAY

A total of about 57,000 children were born in 2014, and about 30,000 of these children were born outside a formal relationship, that is, 52 percent of the children were born outside marriage. Of these children, 22,756 children were born in a cohabiting relationship, and 6,869 children to a single mother. By comparison, in 2013, 56 percent of the children were born outside marriage. However, the long-term trend has been going in the opposite direction – more children are born outside a formal relationship. Compared to the period average of the ten-year period 2003-2013, the number of children born inside marriage has decreased by

8.6 percent, and the number of children born to a cohabiting mother has increased by 18.6 percent.[25]

PORTUGAL

Year	Born outside of marriage	Born in an informal relationship
2005	30.7%	24.8%
2010	41.3%	32.0%
2013	47.6%	33.0%

RUSSIA

The increasing popularity of informal relationships has led to a spectacular increase in the number of children born outside marriage. Between 1989 and 2002 the number of children born out of wedlock doubled and now amounts to around 30% of all births. Almost half of these children are registered by their parents jointly, which suggests that their parents have a stable relationship.[26]

SCOTLAND

There has been a marked increase in Scotland in the percentage of children born outside marriage over recent decades. In 1971, 8% of children were born outside marriage, with this rising to 42% by 2000. The majority of children are now born outside marriage: 51% in 2013.[27] The Registrar General observed in his most recent annual review that: '[t]he proportion of births registered solely in the mother's name - generally around 6-7% in the 1980s and 1990s - has fallen over the past 13 years to 5% in 2013, suggesting that the increase in births to unmarried parents has been in babies born to unmarried parents who are in a relationship.'[28]

---

25 Statistics Norway, 'Births, 2014', available at: www.ssb.no/en/befolkning/statistikker/fodte.

26 According to the census of 2002, available at: perepis2002.ru/index.html?id=7.

27 National Records of Scotland, *Scotland's Population: The Registrar General's Annual Review of Demographic Trends*, 2013, available at: nrscotland.gov.uk/files//statistics/annual-review-2013/rgar-2013.pdf, at p. 20.

28 National Records of Scotland, *Scotland's Population: The Registrar General's Annual Review of Demographic Trends*, 2013, available at: nrscotland.gov.uk/files//statistics/annual-review-2013/rgar-2013.pdf, at p. 20.

SLOVAKIA

In 2013 54,986[29] children were born in Slovakia (compared with 2003: 51,713).[30]

SLOVENIA

Slovene families have an average of 1.18 children: families in marriage predominate (64.2%), families in extramarital unions represent 10.8% of all families and single parent families account for 25% of all Slovene families.[31]

SPAIN

The Spanish National Institute of Statistics provides information on the percentage of children born outside marriage.[32]

Year	Percentage of children born outside marriage
2005	26.5%
2006	28.4%
2007	30.2%
2008	33.2%
2009	34.5%
2010	35.5%
2011	37.3%
2012	38.9%

The percentage of children born outside marriage is on the increase. However, there is no information as regards the relationship which the mothers are in, namely whether they are in a formal relationship (besides marriage) or an informal relationship.

---

29 Statistical Office of the Slovak Republic: Slovak Statistics and Demography 2003-2013, at p. 9. Available at: www7.statistics.sk/PortalTraffic/fileServlet?Dokument=b653d111-8505-46ba-933b-7b2397a33bf3.

30 Statistical Office of the Slovak Republic: Slovak Statistics and Demography 2003-2013, at p. 12. Available at: www7.statistics.sk/PortalTraffic/fileServlet?Dokument=b653d111-8505-46ba-933b-7b2397a33bf3.

31 Available at: www.stat.si/novica_prikazi.aspx?id=4029.

32 See the 2014 Report, available at: www.ine.es/prodyser/pubweb/anuario14/anu14_02demog.pdf.

SWEDEN

The latest available official statistics about the percentage of children born outside a formal relationship are from 2009. In that year 55% of all children were born outside a formal relationship, but as many as 46% had a birthmother who at the time of the child's birth cohabited with the father of the child.[33] As indicated above in Question 14a, it is not unusual in Sweden that cohabitants with a common child later marry each other. Of all children living together with both their parents in Sweden in 2011, 70% of the parents were married and 30% were cohabiting.[34]

In Kajsa Walleng's survey (above Question 11), 81% of the cohabiting couples were living together with joint children. Among them, 74% had only joint children and 7% had both joint children and children who were not the couple's joint children.[35]

SWITZERLAND

Percentage of children born out of wedlock in Switzerland[36]

Year	Percentage
2000	10.7%
2001	11.2%
2002	11.7%
2003	12.4%
2004	13.3%
2005	13.7%
2006	15.4%
2007	16.2%
2008	17.1%
2009	17.9%
2010	18.6%
2011	19.3%
2012	20.2%
2013	21.1%

There is no detailed information available with regard to the number of children born in an informal relationship. However, according to the

33 Statistics Sweden, *Tabeller över Sveriges befolkning 2009* s. 213.

34 Statistics Sweden, '50 000 barn är med om en separation varje år', available at: www.scb.se/sv_/Hitta-statistik/Artiklar/50-000-barn-ar-med-om-en-separation-varje-ar/.

35 K. WALLENG, *Att leva som sambo*, Iustus Förlag, Uppsala, 2015, at p. 85.

36 Swiss Federal Statistical Office, available at: www.bfs.admin.ch/bfs/portal/en/index/themen/01/06/blank/key/02/03.html.

Swiss Federal Statistical Office, the growing number of births out of wedlock generally indicates that these births are wanted births by unmarried women, mostly in an informal relationship.[37]

Furthermore, the statistics concerning household forms in Switzerland show that 3.7% of all households formed by couples were informal relationships with children (11.5% were informal relationships without children, 45% were married couples with children, 39.2% married couples without children and 0.6% were same-sex couples with or without children).[38]

---

37 Swiss Federal Statistical Office, available at: www.bfs.admin.ch/bfs/portal/en/index/themen/ 01/06/blank/key/02/03.html.

38 Swiss Federal Statistical Office, 'Informationen aus der Demographie', *Newsletter No. 1 May 2014*, at p. 2 et seq.

QUESTION 17

What is the proportion of children living within an informal relationship who are not the couple's common children (excluding foster children)?

AUSTRIA

In 2013, there were 352,000 informal relationships in Austria.[1] Of these, 152,000 informal relationships had children, whereby 149,000 informal relationships had children under the age of 27 years. From these 149,000 informal relationships 39.6% were so-called 'patchwork families', which means that at least one partner brought his/her children from previous relations into the new 'patchwork family'.[2]

BELGIUM

There are no statistics available for this question.

BULGARIA

There is no information available to answer this question.

CROATIA

There are no statistical data on these matters.

CZECH REPUBLIC

There is no such precise record, although it is well-known that the number of children living with only one parent due to the fact that the parents' relationship has ended, is increasing. Nowadays almost 20% of

[1] Statistik Austria, available at: www.statistik.at/web_de/statistiken/bevoelkerung/haushalte_familien_lebensformen/familien/023079.html.

[2] Statistik Austria, available at: www.statistik.at/web_de/statistiken/bevoelkerung/haushalte_familien_lebensformen/familien/044931.html.

all children live in a single-parent family. The main reason is divorce, because marriage can be ended this way quite easily and the divorce rate has reached 50%.[3] When the marriage is ended by divorce, children are usually entrusted into one parent's care. However it has not yet been assessed how many parents, to whom a child has been entrusted, live in an informal relationship.

DENMARK

On 1 January 2009 there were 190,272 cohabiting couples without a child in common (380,544 individuals), of whom 28,423 had a child not from the relationship.[4]

ENGLAND AND WALES

There are no available data or estimates on this for England and Wales or the UK.

ESTONIA

There are no publicly available official statistics on this.

FINLAND

Children living in cohabitation families, non-common children and the proportion of non-common children living within cohabitation families

Year	Children living in cohabitation families	Non-common children	Percentage of non-common children living within a cohabitation family
2000	156,411	67,091	42.9%
2001	161,502	69,188	42.8%
2002	164,954	70,936	43.0%
2003	168,479	72,269	42.9%
2004	170,584	73,869	43.3%
2005	172,898	75,974	43.9%
2006	175,516	77,254	44.0%
2007	176,801	77,906	44.0%
2008	175,986	77,841	44.2%
2009	175,951	77,671	44.1%

3 Czech Statistical Office, 'Demographic motion – year 2014. Brief information', 23 March 2015, available at: www.czso.cz.

4 See I. LUND-ANDERSEN, *Familieøkonomien,* Jurist- og Økonomforbundets Forlag, Copenhagen, 2011, at p. 48

2010	175,563	76,925	43.8%
2011	175,981	76,896	43.7%
2012	176,104	76,392	43.4%
2013	178,899	75,957	42.5%

Source: Statistics Finland: Families.

FRANCE

Any statistics on this specific point, if they exist at all, are very hard to find. Nevertheless, some relevant figures from 2011 can be found on children living in stepfamilies.[5] In 2011, a total of 960,000 children were living on a regular basis in stepfamilies, without regard to the matrimonial situation of the couple. Amongst them, 210,000 were living regularly with their father and his spouse, partner or cohabitant. The remaining 750,000 were living with their mother and her spouse, partner or cohabitant.

GERMANY

The proportion of children living within an informal relationship who are not the couple's common children but who are marital or non-marital children of only one of the cohabitants cannot be quantified.

GREECE

Such official information could not be obtained.

HUNGARY

Unfortunately we do not have any statistical data on this.

REPUBLIC OF IRELAND

Year	Births outside marriage	Births registered to parents at the same address	Births outside marriage as a % of all births
2002	18,815	-	31.1%
2003	19,313	-	31.4%
2004	19,938	-	32.3%
2005	19,528	-	32.0%

5 INSEE (National Institute for statistic and economic studies), www.insee.fr/fr/themes/document.asp?ref_id=ip1470.

2006	21,295	-	33.2%
2007	23,170	11,932	32.8%
2008	24,844	12,859	33.1%
2009	24,532	13,647	33.0%
2010	24,860	13,498	33.7%
2011	25,190	13,822	34.0%
2012	25,344	14,321	35.1%

There were 6,406 births registered as outside marriage/civil partnership in quarter 1 of 2013. This accounted for 36.5% of all births, an increase of 0.6 percentage points on the first quarter of 2012. Ten years earlier, in quarter 1 of 2004, 5,181 births were registered outside marriage or 33.2% of all births. (CSO, Vital Statistics, First Quarter 2013.)

This provides a basic insight, but it does not differentiate between lone parents and cohabitants where only one cohabitant is the parent.

ITALY

In 2009, 49.7% of the cohabiting couples had at least one child[6] – they were 40.1% in 1998. Among those couples, 36.4% had children common to both partners; while 6.5% had children of only one partner; and 6.9% had both children of one partner and children together.

In the same year married couples with children comprised 36.4% of the total number of families (compared with 46.2% in 1998).

LATVIA

Such statistics are not collected.

LITHUANIA

There is no official statistical information available on the proportion of children in cohabiting families that are not the couple's common children. According to the Census of 2011, 9.2% of children were living in cohabiting families in Lithuania in total, and the number was higher in rural areas (12.3%) than in urban areas (7.5%).[7]

---

6 Istat, 'Come cambiano le forme familiari', 2011, at p. 5.

7 *Results of the 2011 Population and Housing Census of the Republic of Lithuania*, Statistics Lithuania 2013, at p. 360.

LUXEMBOURG

5% of children lived in reconstituted families in 2008.

This results from a study by CEPSINSTEAD carried out in 2008: *'Il y aurait aujourd'hui au Luxembourg environ 5% d'enfants vivant dans un ménage recomposé, c'est-à-dire dans un ménage dans lequel vit au moins un enfant issu d'une union précédente de l'un des conjoints. Mais nous ne disposons pas pour le moment d'information quant à sa progression dans le temps.'*

Hereunder are some figures concerning children living in different family structures.

Children in family structures in 1991 and 2001

	1991	2001
Households with two parents	**91.1%**	**87.7%**
Married couples	71.0%	70.6%
Cohabitating couples	2.1%	3.3%
Married couples and other people	16.9%	12.8%
Cohabitating couples and other people	1.1%	1.0%
Single parents households	**8.9%**	**12.3%**
Mothers	5.2%	7.9%
Fathers	0.8%	1.0%
Mothers and other people	2.1%	2.1%
Fathers and other people	0.8%	1.3%

Sources: Recensements de la population (STATEC). Calculated by: CEPS/INSTEAD.

THE NETHERLANDS

Unknown, there are no available statistics concerning this topic.

NORWAY

No available data.

PORTUGAL

There are no statistics available for this question.

RUSSIA

No data available.

SCOTLAND

According to the 2011 Census, 6% of all family types within Scotland were made up of cohabiting couples with dependent children.[8] Looking only at families with dependent children, marriage based families were still by far the most common: 54% compared to 15% based around a cohabiting couple. Within cohabiting couple families with dependent children, approximately two-thirds comprised common children of the couple and one-third comprised children of one partner only.[9]

SLOVAKIA

37% of children were born out of wedlock.[10] But the statistical data do not provide exact data on children living in a so-called one-parent family (a nuclear family) or within an informal relationship between the child's parents.

SLOVENIA

Every fifth family of extramarital partners (i.e. 4.1% of all families) is a so-called re-established family, in which, on average, one non-common child that is the biological child of the female partner lives in 86% of such families with partners.[11]

SPAIN

This information is not available.

SWEDEN

There are no updated official statistics in Sweden about the proportion of children living within a relationship of informal cohabitation who are not the couple´s common children. Of all children who lived with two adults in 2011, approximately 10% did not live in their original nuclear families but in blended families, with a step-father or a step-mother, with or

---

8 National Records of Scotland, *Scotland's Census 2011*, TableDC1109SC.

9 National Records of Scotland, *Scotland's Census 2011*, Table DC1114SC.

10 Statistical Office of the Slovak Republic: Slovak Statistics and Demography 2003-2013, at p. 12. Available at: www7.statistics.sk/PortalTraffic/fileServlet?Dokument=b653d111-8505-46ba-933b-7b2397a33bf3.

11 Available at: www.stat.si/novica_prikazi.aspx?id=4029.

without half-siblings or step-siblings.[12] It can be assumed that informal cohabitation is more common than marriage among blended families. The given figure coincides with the results of Kajsa Walleng's survey (Question 11). Among those who answered the questionnaire in 2010 and counted themselves as cohabitees, 18% said that they were living with children who were not the couple´s common children.[13]

SWITZERLAND

There is no information available with regard to the proportion of children living within an informal relationship who are not the couple's common children. There are, however, numbers available with regard to the household forms in Switzerland including the number of reconstituted families.[14]

One-family households with children in Switzerland in 2012:[15]

	Number of households	**Confidence interval ± (in %)**
Total one-family households with child(ren)	1,163,167	0.5%
Unmarried couples with at least one child under 25 years, not reconstituted families (original families)	49,421	3.5%
Unmarried couples with at least one child under 25 years, reconstituted families	25,837	4.4%
Unmarried couples with youngest child aged 25 years or older	2,140	15.2%

12 Statistics Sweden, '50 000 barn är med om en separation varje år', available at: www.scb.se/sv_/Hitta-statistik/Artiklar/50-000-barn-ar-med-om-en-separation-varje-ar/.

13 K. Walleng, *Att leva som sambo*, Iustus Förlag, Uppsala, 2015, at p. 86.

14 A reconstituted family is a family consisting of a couple and child(ren), of which at least one child is from a previous relationship.

15 Shortened version of the table, see Swiss Federal Statistical Office, available at: www.bfs.admin.ch/ bfs/portal/en/index/themen/01/04/blank/key/01/06.html.

QUESTION 18

How many children are adopted within an informal relationship:

a. By one partner only?

b. Jointly by the couple?

c. Where one partner adopted the child of the other?

AUSTRIA

In 2013, 91 adoptions within Austria *(Adoptionsvermittlungen im Inland)* were completed, whereby no distinction was made with respect to the adopting person.[1] Unfortunately, other official statistics, estimations or research studies on this issue do not exist. Also, an enquiry with the family sociologist and family judge Dr. Thomas Bauer (Regional Appellate Court Linz/Upper Austria) did not provide any further information.

In Austria, either a single person or spouses can adopt a child.[2] Thus, in informal relationships only one partner can adopt a child; they cannot jointly adopt a child. Due to the fact that single persons are allowed to adopt children, it follows that also one partner in an informal relationship can adopt the child of the other partner. The adopting person has to have attained the age of 25.[3] The provision according to which the adopting person has to be at least 16 years older than the adoptee was held unconstitutional by the Austrian Constitutional Court in December 2014.[4] On an interim basis this provision will remain valid until 31st December 2015. The adoption must be agreed upon between the

1 Bundesministerium für Familien und Jugend, *Jugendwohlfahrtsbericht*, Vienna, 2013, at p. 9, available at: www.bmfj.gv.at/familie/kinder-jugendhilfe/statistik.html.

2 A. DEIXLER-HÜBNER, 'section 191 General Austrian Civil Code', in: A. KLETEČKA and M. SCHAUER, *ABGB-ON 1.01*, Manz Verlag, Vienna, 2013, at marg. No. 3.

3 Section 193 para. 1 General Austrian Civil Code.

4 Austrian Constitutional Court, Decision of 11.12.2014, G 18/2014-14.

adopter and the adoptee in a written contract, which requires the court's approval in order to be effective.[5]

BELGIUM

The National Office of Statistics provides general adoption statistics. We have indications of the number of adoptions by one parent and by two parents (same- and different-sex). We do not know whether the single parent adoptions are in fact second parent adoptions. Nevertheless, the figures where one parent adopts a child strongly relate to this question.

Number of adoptions in 2013 (ADSEI)

	Total number of adoptions	Adoptions from abroad	Internal adoptions
Total	819	237	582
Man	236	27	209
Woman	314	16	298
Same-sex male couple	7	0	7
Same-sex female couple	5	2	3
Heterosexual couple	257	192	65

BULGARIA

a. By one partner only?

Bulgarian family law allows adoption by one person but not by two persons living in an informal relationship. Two persons may adopt a child jointly or one of them only if they are married (Art. 81, para. 1 of the Bulgarian Family Code).

There is no disaggregated data on the family status of adopters – in particular on one-parent adoptions.[6]

b. Jointly by the couple?

Couples in informal relationship cannot adopt a child together.

c. Where one partner adopted the child of the other?

Adopting the child of a partner is only possible when the couple are married (Art. 81, paras 1 and 3 of the Bulgarian Family Code).

5 Section 192 para. 1 General Austrian Civil Code.

6 According to the official response to my inquiry received from the Bulgarian Agency for Social Assistance (No. 94BB/0172 of 28.11.2014).

CROATIA

a. By one partner only?

Article 185 of the Croatian Family Act prescribes that children can be adopted 'by both spouses or both cohabitants (jointly), by only one spouse or cohabitant if the other partner is a parent or adoptive parent of the child, by only one spouse with the consent of the other spouse or by an unmarried (single) person'.

Considering that the new Croatian Family Act envisages the possibility that one cohabitant adopts a child if the other cohabitant gives consent thereto, there are still no data on adopted children in such circumstances.

Since the former Croatian Family Act (2003) foresaw the possibility that children are adopted by only one person, irrespective of their marital or extramarital status, there have also been no data on the adoption of children by one cohabitant pursuant to the former Croatian Family Act (2003).

There are no data on the adoption of children by one partner living in a formal or informal union.

b. Jointly by the couple?

Article 185 of the Croatian Family Act prescribes that a child can be adopted by spouses or cohabitants as a couple.

Due to the fact that the Croatian Family Act has only recently granted adoption rights to cohabitants, there are still no data on the adoption of children by couples in informal relationships.

Partners in homosexual unions (both in registered and informal partnerships) do not have adoption rights.

c. Where one partner adopted the child of the other?

Article 185 of the Croatian Family Act prescribes that a child can be adopted by one spouse or cohabitant if the other parent is its real or adoptive parent.

Due to the fact that the Croatian Family Act has only recently granted adoption rights to cohabitants, there are still no data on the adoption of children by couples in informal relationships.

Partners in homosexual unions (both in registered and informal partnerships) do not have adoption rights.

CZECH REPUBLIC

In the Czech Republic it is only possible for two people to adopt a child together if they are man and wife. It means that partners in a registered relationship cannot adopt a child together, nor can partners in an informal relationship. Only within marriage is there a possibility of adopting a child by the wife/husband who is not a parent of the child.

Given the fact that no official statistics for 2014 are yet available, it is quite difficult to consider all the changes and reforms that the new Civil Code has brought. In earlier years data concerning such matters were not analysed in detail.

To be precise, for adoption in 2013 the total amount of children who were adopted was 504 and only one of them was older than 15. Another 426 children were handed over into the care of prospective adoptive parents.[7]

DENMARK

On 1 January 2015 an amendment was made to the law according to which unmarried cohabitants were permitted to adopt together on an equal footing with married couples, if the conditions for doing so are otherwise fulfilled.[8] Among other things, there is a requirement that the cohabitants should have lived together for 2½ years. This right of unmarried cohabitants to adopt together only applies to applications made after the law's entry into force. So far there has been no completed adoption where unmarried cohabitants have been granted permission to adopt together or to adopt the children of one of the cohabitants.[9]

a. By one partner only?
No, but see (b).

b. Jointly by the couple?
Persons who live together can only adopt together with their partner, apart from stepchild adoption, unless that person's partner cannot be found or is, by reason of insanity, a mental deficiency or any similar condition, incapable of managing his or her own affairs; see S. 5 of the Danish Adoption (Consolidating) Act.

---

7 Ministry of Labour and Social Affairs, 'Annual Statement of Performance of Child Protection in 2013', available at: www.mpsv.cz/cs/7260.
8 Act No. 1525 of 27 December 2014.
9 Information from the Social Appeals Board, 22 January 2015.

c. Where one partner adopted the child of the other?
Persons who live together may adopt the child or adoptive child of the other partner (stepchild adoption); see S. 5a of the Danish Adoption (Consolidating) Act. Furthermore, there may be the stepchild adoption of the child or adopted child of a former partner.

ENGLAND AND WALES

There are no data that reveal this. Court statistics are collected according to whether adopters are a male and female couple, a same-sex couple or a sole adopter.

According to ONS, the Adopted Children Register does not hold any information on the marital status of the adopting parents. Consequently, it is not possible to measure the impact of the implementation of the English Adoption and Children Act 2002 on 30 December 2005 which for the first time allowed civil partners, same-sex couples and unmarried couples (if in an enduring relationship) to adopt.

ESTONIA

According to § 148(1) of the Estonian Family Law Act, a single person may only adopt a child alone. Married persons may adopt a child jointly. A child may also be adopted by one spouse only if: 1) he or she adopts the child of the other spouse; 2) the other spouse cannot adopt because he or she has restricted active legal capacity (§ 148 (2)). Thus, the partners in an informal relationship do not have the right to adopt children together and custody is only given to the partner who adopts alone. The available statistics relate to single persons adopting a child, but they do not refer to the relationship status of the adopting person. From January 1, 2016, when the Estonian Registered Partnership Act will enter into force, a registered partner who is not a parent of the other registered partner's child will have the right of access to the other registered partner's child on the basis of subsection 143(4) of the Estonian Family Law Act.

FINLAND

a. By one partner only?
No exact figures are available on this, but according to the Finnish Adoption Board, these cases are very rare. Their estimate for adoptions within a cohabitation partnership is five cases in 2000-2013. According to Statistics Finland, no adoptions of this kind took place in the year 2013.

b. Jointly by the couple?

According to the Finnish Adoption Act (22/2012), it is not possible for cohabiting partners to adopt jointly. It is only possible to adopt a child jointly if the couple are married.

c. Where one partner adopted the child of the other?

According to the Finnish Adoption Act (22/2012), it is not possible for one cohabiting partner to adopt the child of the other. It is only possible to adopt the child of the other partner if the couple are married or living in a registered partnership.

FRANCE

a. By one partner only?

Adoption by one registered partner or one cohabitant only is possible according to French legal provisions.[10] The prospective adopter must be over 28 years of age, which is a legal prerequisite.[11] If international adoption or the adoption of a ward of the State is contemplated, administrative consent for the adoption is compulsory.[12]

The fact that the prospective adopter is living with a partner or cohabitant will be taken into account by the social services. This element will be recorded in the welfare report that must be completed for the purposes of the administrative consent.

The French legal system has regulated two adoption schemes: plenary and simple adoption.

A plenary adoption annuls the original filiation of the child with his or her biological parent(s) and exclusively substitutes it with adoptive filiation.

A simple adoption creates adoptive filiation in addition to the pre-existing biological or adoptive filiation. The simple adoption scheme is possible regardless of the age of the child and in 86% of cases this concerns persons over 18 years of age, whereas, according to the French legal provisions, a plenary adoption can only be contemplated when the child is under 15 years of age.[13]

---

10 Art. 343-1 of the French Civil Code.

11 Art. 343-1 of the French Civil Code.

12 Art. R225-1 to R225-11 of the French Social Welfare and Family Code.

13 Art. 345 of the French Civil Code.

In 2007, adoption by one person only represented 18% of plenary adoption orders (12% were female adopters and 6% were male adopters), and 93% of them were not family adoptions.[14]

Plenary adoptees considering the nature of the adoption and the adopter

Nature of adoption	Total adoptees	Single male adopter	Single female adopter	Couple adopting
Altogether	3,964 (100%)	242 (6.1%)	468 (11.8%)	3,254 (82.1%)
International adoption	2,824 (100%)	26 (0.9%)	422 (14.9%)	2,376 (84.1%)
National adoption	882 (100%)	0 (0%)	24 (2.7%)	858 (97.3%)
Family adoption	258 (100%)	216 (83.7%)	22 (8.5%)	20 (7.8%)

Source: Ministry of Justice – 2007 adoption enquiry.

In 2007, adoption by one person only represented 94% of simple adoption orders (72% were male adopters and 22% were female adopters), yet only 5% of them were not family adoptions, i.e. by a single person who was not the spouse of the child's parent.[15]

b. Jointly by the couple?

A joint adoption in an informal relationship is prohibited under French law.[16]

c. Where one partner adopted the child of the other?

According to the French legal provisions adoption is a privilege granted to a marriage.[17] Indeed, only marriage with the child's parent opens up the possibility for the prospective adopter to adopt the child of his or her spouse. In 2007, the adoption of the child of the spouse represented 7% of plenary adoption orders and 95% of simple adoption orders.[18]

14 472 plenary adoptions by one person only had been ordered in 2007 where the adoptee was not the child of the adopter's spouse. Z. BELMOKTHAR, 'Les adoptions simples et plénières en 2007', 2009 report for the Director of civil affairs (*Direction des affaires civiles et du sceau*) by the French Ministry of Justice, available at: www.adoption.gouv.fr/IMG/pdf_1_1_stat_adoptions07_20090611.pdf.

15 1,176 simple adoptions by one person only had been ordered in 2007 where the adoptee was not the child of the adopter's spouse. Z. BELMOKTHAR, 'Les adoptions simples et plénières en 2007', 2009 report for the Director of civil affairs (*Direction des affaires civiles et du sceau*) by the French Ministry of Justice, available at: www.adoption.gouv.fr/IMG/pdf_1_1_stat_adoptions07_20090611.pdf.

16 Art. 343 and 346 of the French Civil Code.

17 Art. 343 and 346 of the French Civil Code.

18 Z. BELMOKTHAR, 'Les adoptions simples et plénières en 2007', 2009 report for the Director of civil affairs (*Direction des affaires civiles et du sceau*) by the French Ministry of

In a prospective adoption as far as minor children are concerned, plenary and simple adoptions must be distinguished.

Indeed, the plenary adoption of a minor child by the spouse of his or her parent has an identical effect compared to joint adoption by a couple. The joint exercise of parental responsibilities is granted to the initial parent (either biological or adoptive[19]) and the second adoptive parent.[20]

Regarding the same situation in the simple adoption scheme, however, parental responsibilities are vested in the adoptive parent too, but the joint exercise of parental responsibilities, by the initial parent with the adoptive parent, is subject to certain conditions. Indeed, parents must file a joint declaration of the joint exercise of parental responsibilities regarding the minor child.[21]

Without marriage, the adoption of the child by the parent's partner or cohabitant has consistently been held by the *Cour de cassation* as being against the best interests of the child when the initial parent wants to continue to raise the child after adoption.[22] Indeed, where the adopter and the initial parent are not married the first effect of a simple adoption of a minor child is to automatically deprive the initial parent of the exercise of parental responsibilities and to transfer them exclusively to the adoptive parent. As a consequence, the initial parent automatically loses the possibility to take any decision concerning the child's life, and this has been held to contradict the best interests of the child and to be inconsistent with the project of jointly raising a child. Although all the cases concerned same-sex couples who were not allowed to marry at that time,[23] the sexual orientation of the prospective adopter and of the initial parent was not at stake in the *Cour de cassation's* reasoning on this issue.

Justice, available at: www.adoption.gouv.fr/IMG/pdf_1_1_stat_adoptions07_2009 0611.pdf.

19 Art. 345-1 and 360 of the French Civil Code open up the possibility to adopt the child of one's spouse irrespective of the nature of the filiation (either biological or adoptive) of the child with his or her initial parent.

20 Art. 356 of the French Civil Code.

21 Art. 365 of the French Civil Code.

22 Cass. Civ 1, 20 February 2007, no. 06-15.647 and no. 06-15.676, available at: www.legifrance.gouv.fr.

23 Same-sex marriages were legalised by the 2013 Act allowing same-sex couples to marry on an equal basis with heterosexual couples, Act no. 2013-404 of 17 May 2013.

GERMANY

a. By one partner only?

In 2013 there were 3,793 adoptions (2000: 6,373).[24] Only a minority were adoptions by single persons. Step-child adoption is very common in Germany. Nearly two-thirds of all adoptions are step-child adoptions. However, an adoption by a cohabitant is not a step-child adoption in the legal sense. Official statistical data conceptualise married step-parents and 'life partners' together.[25] There are no statistical data giving more information on adoptions in informal relationships.

b. Jointly by the couple?

A joint adoption by an unmarried couple is not possible under German law.[26]

c. Where one partner adopted the child of the other?

If one partner adopts the child of the other partner, the parent-child relationship between the biological parent and the child is terminated. Therefore such an adoption occurs only in rare cases.

GREECE

Such official information could not be obtained.

HUNGARY

a. By one partner only?

In Hungary spouses can adopt a child or one adult person can himself or herself adopt a child, but since the early 2000s spouses have been in a privileged position in this respect. Although only one person can adopt a child there is no public information as to whether he or rather she lives in a marriage or cohabitation. If somebody adopts a child alone but lives in a marital community of life the spouse of this person is heard during the procedure preceding the authorization of the adoption because if they live in a common household the child is going to live not only with the adoptive parent but also with this parent's spouse. There is no such obligation if somebody is living in cohabitation.

---

24 Statistisches Bundesamt, *Statistiken der Kinder- und Jugendhilfe, Adoptionen 2013*, Statistisches Bundesamt, Wiesbaden, 2014, at p. 23.

25 Statistisches Bundesamt, *Statistiken der Kinder- und Jugendhilfe, Adoptionen 2013*, Statistisches Bundesamt, Wiesbaden, 2014, at p. 7.

26 I. GÖTZ, '§ 1741', in: O. PALANDT, *Bürgerliches Gesetzbuch*, Beck, Munich, 2015, at No. 8.

b. Jointly by the couple?
Joint adoptions by cohabitants is forbidden in Hungary. Only spouses can adopt a child together.

c. Where one partner adopted the child of the other?
It is not permitted for cohabitants to adopt their partner's child.

REPUBLIC OF IRELAND

a. By one partner only?
Statistical information is not available. Adoption is only possible in very specific cases.

b. Jointly by the couple?
This is not possible under the Irish Adoption Act 2010.

In Ireland, at present the following persons are eligible to adopt:

- A married couple living together;
- A married person alone. The other spouse's consent to adopt must be obtained unless the couple is living apart and separated under a court decree or a deed of separation, or the other spouse has deserted the prospective adoptive parent or the other spouse's conduct has resulted in the prospective adoptive parent, with just cause, leaving the other spouse;
- The mother, father or relative of the child (relative meaning a grandparent, brother, sister, uncle or aunt of the child and/or the spouse of any such person, the relationship to the child being traced through the mother or the father);
- A widow or widower;
- A sole applicant who is not in one of the categories listed above may only adopt where the Adoption Authority is satisfied that, in the particular circumstances of the case, it is desirable.

It is not possible for two unmarried persons to adopt jointly. This, however, is due to change with the Irish Children and Family Relationships Bill. Part 11 of the Bill allows same-sex couples, both civil partners and couples cohabiting for three years or more, to adopt a child jointly subject to the requirement that they are suitable adopters.

c. Where one partner adopted the child of the other?
Statistical information is not available.

ITALY

Adoption is only possible for married couples (Art. 6, Law of 4 May 1983, n. 184[27] as modified by several statutory instruments, the most important of which is the Law of 28 March, n. 149). This clearly excludes same-sex couples and cohabitants.

a. By one partner only?

While it is impossible for a *de facto* couple to adopt, a single person, irrespective of being in an informal partnership or not, can adopt a child under very specific circumstances (Art. 44 Italian Law on Adoption quoted supra).[28] This may occur when the child – who must necessarily be an orphan – is a relative of the adopter within the sixth degree; when the adopter and the adoptee were linked by a stable lasting bond prior to the parent's death (same article, sub a); when the child is an orphan and has a physical handicap (sub c); and when it has proved impossible to place that child in pre-adoptive fostering (sub d).

This kind of adoption, called 'adoption in particular cases', has several peculiarities: it does not interrupt the relationship between the adoptee and his or her original family; its effects do not extend to the adopter's family so that the child does not become a niece or nephew;[29] it does not require that the child has been abandoned; and the child has succession rights with respect to both the original and the new family.

b. Jointly by the couple?

Not applicable.

c. Where one partner adopted the child of the other?

Not applicable to unmarried couples.

On the contrary, stepfamilies where the new couple are married may have recourse to another form of 'adoption in particular cases' regulated by Art. 44(b) of the Law of 4 May 1983, n. 184. A child, even if adopted, can be adopted by the spouse of his or her parent. Lacking a comprehensive legal rule for stepfamilies under the Italian jurisdiction,

---

27 The law, now entitled 'Right of the minor to a family', is a comprehensive discipline of adoption and foster care, applying also, with a few exceptions, to international adoptions.

28 This rule has been extended also to international adoption: C. Cost. 2005, n. 347.

29 It is not yet clear if the new text of Art. 74 of the Italian Civil Code, modified by the Law of 10 December 2012, n. 219, applies also to 'adoption in particular cases', but if it does, then the adoptee will also establish bonds with the adopter's relatives.

this rule helps to establish a legal bond between the step-parent and the child. The consent of the biological parent is however essential.

LATVIA

Such statistics are not collected.

LITHUANIA

No data available.

According to Art. 3.210 of the Lithuanian Civil Code, the right to adopt a child may be exercised by married couples. In exceptional cases, an unmarried person or one of the spouses may be allowed to adopt a child. Unmarried persons may not adopt the same child. As a consequence of this regulation, the State Child Rights Protection and Adoption Service under the Ministry of Social Security and Labour reports on the number of children adopted through the Service by spouses, one of the spouses and unmarried (single) individuals. The statistics suggest that up to 10 children, on average are adopted annually by single individuals.[30] It should be noted that there are no data available on possible cohabitation or other forms of informal relationships by these individuals.

LUXEMBOURG

The law distinguishes between simple adoption (*adoption simple*) and full adoption (*adoption plénière*).

At this point in time (there are proposals for change) only spouses can adopt by *adoption plénière* (this form of adoption erases the former filiation of the child and the child becomes a full member of his or her new family; the *adoption simple*, on the other hand, does not erase the former filiation of the child, but adds the new filiation to the original one).

A simple adoption is also possible for one person wishing to adopt or for two partners.

[30] The highest adoption rate by single individuals adopting children deprived of parental care was registered in 2007 (16 cases), while the lowest was in 2004 and 2010 (4 cases each). In 2008 and 2011, 6 adoptions by single individuals were registered. One may assert that adoption by single individuals shows a declining trend since 2007. Available at: www.vaikoteises.lt/en/.

As the number of reconstituted families is increasing, one partner often wants to adopt the child of his or her partner. This is only possible by a simple adoption.

A judge will determine if an adoption is in the interest of the child as he or she does with every request for adoption (Art. 343 of Luxembourg Civil Code).

Hereunder are some figures, even if they do not exactly correspond to the mentioned question.

Adoptions 1997-2012

	1997	2000	2003	2004	2005	2006
District Court of and in Luxembourg						
Number of applications	-	-	122	127	103	99
Applications received	123	110	85	125	98	98
Adoptions simples	24	33	18	51	31	33
Adoptions plénières	79	57	59	47	35	54
Adoptions rectificatives	-	5	4	4	2	0
Interlocutory decision	-	14	19	20	20	11
Rejection decision	-	6	1	1	3	1
Adoptions on the basis of Art. 5 of the Hague Convention 1993	-	-	8	27	32	22
District Court of and in Diekirch						
Number of applications	26	29	20	14	20	21
Applications received	25	29	20	17	9	23
Adoptions simples	11	5	5	1	2	4
Adoptions plénières	17	19	12	16	7	10
Adoptions rectificatives	0	1	0	1	0	3
Interlocutory decision	1	4	2	0	0	2
Rejection decision	1	1	1	0	1	5
Adoptions on the basis of Art. 5 of the Hague Convention 1993	-	-	-	4	0	2

	2007	2008	2009	2010	2011	2012
District Court of and in Luxembourg						
Number of applications	95	88	87	67	-	-
Applications received	93	82	80	61	-	-
Adoptions simples	32	23	11	22	-	-
Adoptions plénières	33	37	53	15	-	-
Adoptions rectificatives	3	2	1	2	-	-
Interlocutory decision	11	4	20	18	-	-
Rejection decision	2	6	8	6	-	-
Adoptions on the basis of Art. 5 of the Hague Convention 1993	14	16	7	4	-	-

District Court of and in Diekirch						
Number of applications	13	13	19	13	12	13
Applications received	13	12	19	9	12	11
Adoptions simples	2	5	5	1	2	4
Adoptions plénières	7	9	4	2	5	7
Adoptions rectificatives	1	1	2	0	0	1
Interlocutory decision	0	1	1	3	2	0
Rejection decision	0	0	0	0	0	1
Adoptions on the basis of Art. 5 of the Hague Convention 1993	0	0	3	1	1	2

THE NETHERLANDS

Unknown, there are no available statistics concerning this topic.

NORWAY

a. By one partner only?

No available data. Pursuant to the Norwegian Adoption Act 1986, a cohabitant could adopt individually until 1 October 2014. After this date such adoption is not allowed, see the Norwegian Adoption Act, S. 5.

b. Jointly by the couple?

No available data. Until 1 October 2014, cohabiting couples were not eligible to adopt a child jointly. After this date, cohabitants can adopt jointly, see the Norwegian Adoption Act, S. 5.

c. Where one partner adopted the child of the other?

No available data. Until 1 October 2014, a cohabitant could not adopt the child of the other cohabitant. After this date, stepchild adoption is allowed, see the Norwegian Adoption Act, S. 5(b).

PORTUGAL

There are no statistics available for this question.

RUSSIA

a. By one partner only?

No data available.

b. Jointly by the couple?
According to Art. 127(2) Russian Family Code, an unmarried couple cannot jointly adopt a child.

c. Where one partner adopted the child of the other?
No data available.

SCOTLAND

There are no statistics available in Scotland to answer this question. It should be noted, however, that this is an area of law which has changed relatively recently as a result of the Adoption and Children (Scotland) Act 2007. Prior to the 2007 reforms, joint adoption was only open to spouses or civil partners and in any other case there could only be sole adoption. The key concept which now applies in respect of prospective adopters is that of 'a relevant couple' and where prospective adopters are part of a relevant couple, the default position is that they will adopt jointly. There are only limited exceptions which would permit either party to adopt alone. A 'relevant couple' includes parties who are (1) married to each other; (2) civil partners; or (3) living together as if husband and wife in an enduring relationship.[31] In 2013, there were 489 registered adoptions in Scotland of which the vast majority were by couples: 350 (different-sex) and 14 (same-sex).[32]

a. By one partner only?
Where a prospective adopter is part of a 'relevant couple' then he or she would normally have to adopt a child jointly with his or her partner. Adoption by one partner only is possible where the other partner is incapable of applying for adoption by reason of physical or mental ill health.[33]

b. Jointly by the couple?
Since the Scots Adoption and Children Act 2007, where the prospective adopter is part of a 'relevant couple' the adoption will usually be a joint adoption.[34] The only exceptions to this are where the other party either is

---

31 Adoption and Children (Scotland) Act 2007, S. 29(3).
32 General Register Office for Scotland, *Vital Events Reference Tables 2013*, available at: gro-scotland.gov.uk/statistics/theme/vital-events/general/ref-tables/2013.
33 Adoption and Children (Scotland) Act 2007, S. 30(1) and (5).
34 Adoption and Children (Scotland) Act 2007, S. 29.

incapable of applying for adoption due to ill health[35] or is the parent of the child.[36]

c. Where one partner adopted the child of the other?
One partner to a relevant couple may adopt where the other partner is the parent of the child concerned.[37]

SLOVAKIA

There are no official statistics available.

SLOVENIA

a. By one partner only?
0. Each of the partners may adopt a child separately, but there are practically no children available for adoption in Slovenia (see explanation below).

b. Jointly by the couple?
0. Extramarital partners may not adopt a child together (see explanation below).

c. Where one partner adopted the child of the other?
1. One partner may adopt the child of his or her partner, but there are not many such cases per year.

In compliance with regulations that state that nobody may be adopted by more than one person, unless the adopters are a married couple, extra-marital partners may not adopt a child together; each may adopt a child separately or one partner may adopt the child of his or her partner. Because there are practically no children available for adoption in Slovenia, only the child of the partner enters into consideration. There are no exact data on how many such adoptions there are by an extramarital partner or a partner from a *de facto* life union of partners of a different sex, to whom the case law recently recognised the right to unilateral adoption.[38]

---

35 Adoption and Children (Scotland) Act 2007, S. 30(5).
36 Adoption and Children (Scotland) Act 2007, S. 30(3).
37 Adoption and Children (Scotland) Act 2007, S. 30(3).
38 In 2011 there were also 19 children adopted from abroad but there are no data on who their adopters were: www.mddsz.gov.si/si/delovna_podrocja/druzina/posvojitve/.

SPAIN

a. By one partner only?
Statistical information is not available.

Both the Spanish Civil Code (Art. 175 Spanish Civil Code) and the Catalan Civil Code (Art. 235-30 Catalan Civil Code) allow adoption by a single person.

b. Jointly by the couple?
Statistical information is not available.

A couple in an informal relationship may adopt jointly. Spain has allowed this since the passing of law 21/1987, 11 November. The Catalan Civil Code mentions this possibility in Art. 235-30.2 Catalan Civil Code.

c. Where one partner adopted the child of the other?
Statistical information is not available.

One partner may adopt the child of the other, both in Spain and in Catalonia. See Art. 175.4 Spanish Civil Code, and Art. 235-32.1 Catalan Civil Code.

SWEDEN

a. By one partner only?
There are no statistics about this in Sweden. Since single people may adopt under Swedish law and people living in an informal cohabitation relationship are regarded as single people in Swedish population records in respect of civil status, such adoptions could at least theoretically take place. Considering, however, that the prospects for adopting a child are much greater when the prospective adoptive parent lives in a formalised relationship and adopts jointly with his or her spouse or registered partner, the number of adoptions by a sole person in an unmarried cohabitation can be expected to be low. Couples wishing to adopt a child usually formalise their relationship, since this is the only way to be able to adopt jointly under Swedish law (Swedish Children and Parents Code, in Swedish: *Föräldrabalken 1949:381*), Chapter 4, § 4.

b. Jointly by the couple?
Under current Swedish law, only couples who have formalised their relationship may jointly adopt a child (see above under a). Hence, there are no statistics on this.

c. Where one partner adopted the child of the other?

Under the current Swedish law, only persons living in a formalised relationship, i.e., in a marriage or registered partnership, may adopt the other partner's child Swedish Children and Parents Code, Chapter 4, § 1. Therefore, there are no statistics about this.

SWITZERLAND

a. By one partner only?

There is no information available with regard to the relationship status of a single adopter. Since 2000 only around 10-31 adoptions by a single person per year have been counted in Switzerland.[39]

b. Jointly by the couple?

In Switzerland, joint adoption by a couple is only possible for married couples (Art. 264a para. 1 Swiss Civil Code).

c. Where one partner adopted the child of the other?

Adoption of the partner's child is only allowed for married couples (Art. 264a para. 3 Swiss Civil Code). Currently, a draft Swiss Civil Code allowing for step-parent adoption in informal relationships is pending.

---

39 Swiss Federal Statistical Office, table T 1.2.2.2.5.1 (Adoptionen).

QUESTION 19

How many partners in an informal relationship have been in a formal or an informal relationship previously?

AUSTRIA

In the course of the Generations and Gender Programme respondents were asked about the number of their previous partnerships. It was found that 'one-half were living together with a partner for the first time, while for approximately one in seven it was already the second time. Only some four percent of respondents reported to have lived together with a partner three times or more often.'[1] Unfortunately, other official statistics, estimations or research studies on this issue do not exist. Also, an enquiry with the family sociologist and family judge Dr. Thomas Bauer (Regional Appellate Court Linz/Upper Austria) did not provide any further information.

BELGIUM

We present the repartnering chances of formerly married people. We do not have statistics on the repartnering chances of formerly cohabiting people. This table only applies to Flanders.

Repartnering chances on specific durations after divorce since the actual divorce, separate for men and women, according to divorce cohort[2]

A new relationship

Time in years	Men				Women			
	1981-2005	**1981-1990**	**1991-2000**	**2001-2005**	**1981-2005**	**1981-1990**	**1991-2000**	**2001-2005**
0	20%	23%	20%	19%	20%	16%	19%	22%
1	45%	39%	48%	43%	46%	32%	43%	51%

1 I. BUBER-ENNSER, N. NEUWIRTH and M.R. TESTA (eds.), *Families in Austria 2009-2013*, AV-Astoria, Vienna, 2013, at p. 9, available at: www.ggp-austria.at.

2 I. PASTEELS and D. MORTELMANS, 'What after divorce? Repartnering in Flanders in 2010', *Relaties en Nieuwe gezinnen*, 2013, at p. 66.

2	62%	61%	64%	59%	58%	53%	56%	64%
5	78%	79%	79%	77%	78%	74%	77%	80%
10	86%	89%	87%	83%	86%	84%	86%	86%

		Median duration in months
Men	1981-2005	15
	1981-1990	18
	1991-2000	13
	2001-2005	13
Women	1981-2005	15
	1981-1990	23
	1991-2000	19
	2001-2005	12

Cohabiting after divorce

Time in years	Men				Women			
	1981-2005	**1981-1990**	**1991-2000**	**2001-2005**	**1981-2005**	**1981-1990**	**1991-2000**	**2001-2005**
0	24%	22%	24%	25%	24%	19%	22%	27%
1	37%	38%	38%	36%	38%	32%	37%	40%
2	61%	65%	63%	57%	63%	65%	61%	64%
5	74%	80%	75%	72%	75%	82%	74%	73%
10	39%	38%	37%	43%	36%	36%	38%	34%

Median duration in months

Time in years	Men				Women			
	1981-2005	**1981-1990**	**1991-2000**	**2001-2005**	**1981-2005**	**1981-1990**	**1991-2000**	**2001-2005**
2	5	4	4	4	4	1	5	3
5	20	24	20	19	19	23	19	17
10	35	48	34	31	35	46	34	31

BULGARIA

There is no information available to answer this question.

The national statistics reveal that informal relationships are most popular among persons who have never married: 76.4% of all partners living in informal relationships; 16.7% of partners in informal relationships have been married before (i.e., they are divorced); 3.2% are widows/widowers and 3.7% are married.

CROATIA

There are no statistical data on these matters.

CZECH REPUBLIC

There is no such evidence. Given modern times and the lack of definition of any informal relationship, it is basically impossible to track a number of previous partners either in formal or informal relationships. On the other hand statistics show that a great number of couples in an informal relationship are divorced or widowed individuals.

DENMARK

There is no information available on this.

ENGLAND AND WALES

This varies by age. Of those under 35, the vast majority of cohabitants (over 95%) are single and never married. Of those, 35-44, 25% are divorced; of those aged 45-54 - 50% are divorced and of the over 65s, 66% are divorced.

There are no data on what percentage have had a previous informal relationship, but this is likely to increase over the age bands, other than perhaps the over 65s.

Percentage of cohabiting people in each age group in the UK by marital or civil partnership status, 2012

Marital or civil partnership status	Age group					
	16-24	**25-34**	**35-44**	**45-64**	**65-74**	**75+**
Single	99.5%	95.7%	74.8%	41.3%	13.1%	2.0%
Married/civil partnership (separated)	0.3%	0.9%	4.4%	6.8%	3.2%	2.2%
Divorced/dissolved civil partnership	0.3%	3.3%	20.3%	48.5%	64.5%	44.6%
Widowed/survived civil partner	0.0%	0.1%	0.5%	3.4%	19.2%	48.0%

Source: Labour Force Survey, Office for National Statistics.

ESTONIA

The official marital status of persons in an informal relationship (N= 122 446), 2000

	2000
Have never been officially married	67,537
In an official marriage	8,778
Divorced	37,441
Widowed	7,160

* 15 years of age and older, also persons whose age is unknown.
Statistics: Statistics Estonia, Population and dwelling census 2000.

In the population and dwelling census in 2000, there were 122,446 persons in an informal relationship, 67,537 of them had not been in an official marriage before, i.e. their marital status was 'single' (including also in an informal relationship and in free cohabitation). There were 37,441 persons in an informal relationship who were divorced and 7,160 were widowed. Thus, in the population census of 2000 there were 44,601 persons who had previously been in a registered relationship, i.e. in a marriage. A total of 8,778 persons who had marked their marital status as being 'in an informal relationship' in the population census in 2000 were actually still in an official marriage (this included persons who factually lived separately but had not officially divorced).

Official marital status of persons in an informal relationship[3] (N=170,214), 2011

	2011
Have never been officially married	117,403
In an official marriage	5,556
Divorced	40,758
Widowed	5,801

* Persons who are at least 15 years old.
Source: Statistics Estonia, Population and dwelling census 2011.

According to the population and dwelling census in 2011, there were at least 170,214 persons aged 15 years and older whose marital status was 'in an informal relationship' or whose status in the household was a 'partner in an informal relationship'. 117,403 of them had not previously been in an official marriage, i.e. their official marital status was single (including also in an informal relationship in in free cohabitation). 40,758 of the persons in an informal relationship were divorced and 5,801 were widowed. Thus, in the population and dwelling census in 2011, 46,559 persons in an informal relationship were previously in an official relationship, i.e. were married. 5,556 persons who in the population and

3 Status of a person in the household as a 'partner in an informal relationship'.

dwelling census of 2011 marked their actual marital status as being 'in an informal relationship' had an official marital status as being 'in an official marriage' (this number includes, for example, persons who factually lived separately, but had not officially divorced).

FINLAND

Only information on previous marriages is available and only from 2005 onwards.

Number of previous marriages of men and women living in a cohabiting partnership at the end of the year 2005-2013

			Previous marriages (female)		
	Previous marriages (male)	Total	0	1+	Unknown
2005	Total	**293,437**	218,079	74,560	798
	0	222,578	193,212	29,097	269
	1+	69,963	24,523	45,119	321
	Unknown	896	344	344	208
2006	Total	**299,403**	223,089	75,436	878
	0	227,260	197,587	29,357	316
	1+	71,147	25,097	45,729	321
	Unknown	996	405	350	241
2007	Total	**304,032**	226,956	76,135	941
	0	230,947	201,120	29,476	351
	1+	71,991	25,383	46,288	320
	Unknown	1,094	453	371	270
2008	Total	**307,143**	229,781	76,293	1,069
	0	233,560	203,690	29,452	418
	1+	72,329	25,535	46,466	328
	Unknown	1,254	556	375	323
2009	Total	**310,691**	232,992	76,522	1,177
	0	236,636	206,673	29,491	472
	1+	72,608	25,621	46,655	332
	Unknown	1,447	698	376	373
2010	Total	**313,221**	235,364	76,554	1,303
	0	238,674	208,782	29,386	506
	1+	72,892	25,758	46,783	351
	Unknown	1,655	824	385	446
2011	Total	**318,225**	239,665	77,079	1,481
	0	242,708	212,588	29,543	577
	1+	73,526	26,042	47,123	361
	Unknown	1,991	1,035	413	543
2012	Total	**321,470**	242,600	77,156	1,714
	0	245,525	215,262	29,591	672

	1+	73,593	26,123	47,110	360
	Unknown	2,352	1,215	455	682
2013	**Total**	**328,304**	248,124	78,364	1,816
	0	250,530	219,978	29,878	674
	1+	75,050	26,679	47,996	375
	Unknown	2,724	1,467	490	767

Source: Statistics Finland: Families.

FRANCE

The most recent figures found on this issue are statistics from 2005 but this specific point was not directly dealt with. Nevertheless, it emerges from the statistics that the proportion of informal relationships is much more important amongst second and following unions in one person's matrimonial life. The curve is exponential as far as the members of the couple are becoming older.[4]

Graphique 3 - Pourcentage d'hommes et de femmes en couple dans une union de rang 2 (ou plus) selon leur âge et leur situation matrimoniale.

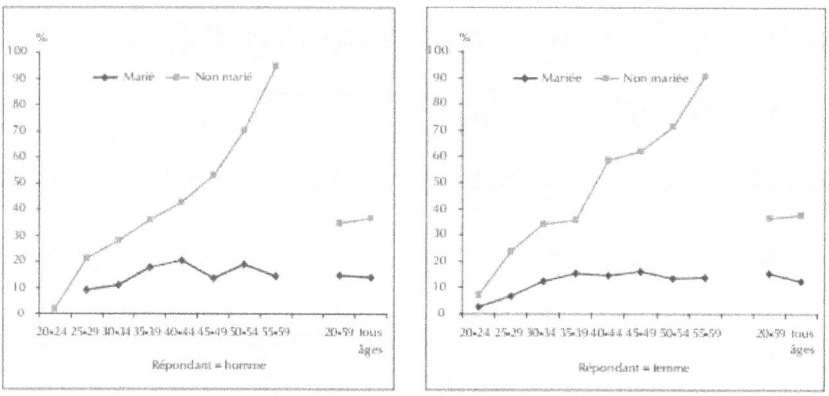

Source : enquête ERFI-GGS, INED-INSEE, 2005.
Champ : ensemble des répondants à l'enquête vivant en couple.

GERMANY

Cohabitation is mainly a life arrangement of younger couples. However, as the age of the partners increases, there will be more partners who have previously lived in an informal relationship, who are divorced or separated.

[4] F. PRIOUX, 'Les couples non mariés en 2005: quelles différences avec les couples mariés?', *Politiques sociales et familiales*, 2009, at p. 91, available at: www.ined.fr/fichier/s_rubrique/185/psf96.fprioux.fr.pdf.

GREECE

Such official information could not be obtained.

HUNGARY

The fact that a cohabitant has lived in an earlier informal relationship cannot be determined from the statistics. Nevertheless, the personal or family status of the population has been surveyed. Those statistics show whether somebody who lives in cohabitation is single (unmarried), married, divorced or widowed. The number of persons being unmarried includes those who had lived in a previous cohabitation.

	Unmarried	Married	Divorced	Widowed	Total
1990					
Men	42,779	12,863	11,763	57,988	125,393
Women	32,439	12,334	24,400	56,086	125,259
Total	75,218	25,197	36,163	114,074	250,652
2001					
Men	168,195	11,884	16,991	105,183	302,253
Women	152,596	9,919	34,580	100,527	297,622
Total	320,791	21,803	51,571	205,710	599,875
2011					
Men	299,889	9,761	15,802	133,180	458,632
Women	284,260	8,041	30,948	128,411	451,660
Total	584,149	17,802	46,750	261,591	910,292

Data from the Hungarian Central Statistical Office.[5]

REPUBLIC OF IRELAND

Statistical information is not available.

ITALY

No data exists for those cohabitants who have been in a previous informal relationship terminated in the past.

On the contrary, we only know that reconstituted families formed by persons who are divorced and have remarried constituted 3.3% of the

[5] A 15 éves és idősebb népesség élettársi kapcsolat, ötéves korcsoportok és nemek szerint. Demográfiai adatok a 2011. évi népszámlálást követően. (Population in cohabitation over 15 years of age according to age groups and gender. Demographic data following the Census in 2011). Available at: www.ksh.hu.

total number of families in 2009, compared with 2.0% in 1998.[6] Married and unmarried reconstituted families together formed 7.0% of the total number of families in 2009.

LATVIA

Such statistics are not collected.

LITHUANIA

43.4% of men and 39.9% of women registered in the 2011 Census as cohabitants were divorced, 44.7% of men and 41.6% of women were not married.[7] The composition of those in informal relationships by marital status in the 2001 Census was similar: 47.7% divorced men and 43.2% divorced women, 37.3% non-married men and 32.1% non-married women, 6.6% widowed men and 17.1% widowed women, 8.1% married men and 7.4% married women living in cohabitation.[8]

Thus, despite the moderate fluctuations, the composition of cohabitants by marital status did not experience any substantial changes between the two last censuses. The informal relationships are more often the re-constitution of the family after the dissolution of a previous marriage than the first partnership.

LUXEMBOURG

Distribution of type of union no later than six years after the divorce, by the date of the divorce

After the divorce	Date of divorce	
	Prior to 1985	1985-1999
Marriage not preceded by a period of cohabitation	48%	34%
Cohabitation for more than 3 years	31%	51%
Cohabitation and remarriage within 3 years	16%	10%
Cohabitation and dissolution within 3 years	6%	5%

Source: PSELL-3/EU-SILC.

6 Istat, 'Come cambiano le forme familiari', 2011, at p. 1 and p. 3.

7 *Results of the 2011 Population and Housing Census of the Republic of Lithuania*, Statistics Lithuania 2013, at p. 334.

8 A. Maslauskaitė, 'Household status of members of the private households', in: D. Ambrozaitienė, V. Stankūnienė, A. Maslauskaitė and R. Balandienė (eds.), *Population of Lithuania: Composition and Demographic Development*, Statistics Lithuania, Vilnius, 2006, at p. 103.

Interpretation: Almost half of the new unions following divorce before 1985 were marriages. This percentage is only 34% if the divorce took place between 1985 and 1999.

The amount of individuals who cohabitate, amongst those who are already a couple, by age group in 2006

	Amount of individuals who cohabitate
Less than 30 years old	67%
30-44 years old	49%
45-59 years old	25%
60 years and older	6%

Source: PSELL-3/EU-SILC.

Interpretation: Among individuals under the age of 30 who have already lived together as a couple, 67% say that they cohabitate.

THE NETHERLANDS

Unknown, there are no (publicly) available data.

NORWAY

No available data.

PORTUGAL

There are no statistics available for this question.

RUSSIA

According to the results of the 2005 All-Russia survey, at least 22% of all respondents have been in informal relationships in the past.[9]

SCOTLAND

Information on this question is not available for Scotland but some indication can be found in statistics concerning cohabiting couples across the UK as a whole. The Office for National Statistics in a report on

9 Е. ВОБК, 'Смыслы и значения незарегистрированных отношений: разновидности брака или альтернативы ему? (Часть 2)', *Демоскоп Weekly*, 229-2230, 1-22, available at: http://demoscope.ru/weekly/2006/0229/analit03.php.

cohabitation in 2012 indicated clear distinctions in terms of age. While 95% of cohabiting couples between the ages of 25 and 35 had never been married, this declined significantly across older age groups: 75% between 35 and 44; 41% between 45 and 64 and 13% between 65 and 74. Of cohabiting couples who had previously been married or in a civil partnership, but were now divorced/dissolved, the percentages were 3% in the age range 25-34; 20% in the age range 35-44; 48% in the age range 45-64; 64% in the age range 65-74 and 44% above 75.[10]

SLOVAKIA

There are no official statistics available.

SLOVENIA

There are no statistical data on this question.

SPAIN

This information is not available.

SWEDEN

There are no official statistics in Sweden about how many cohabitees in an informal relationship had previously been in a formal or an informal relationship. In Kajsa Walleng's survey concerning the year 2010, 22% of the people regarding themselves as living in an unmarried cohabitation reported that they had been previously married and 35% reported that they had previously cohabited in an informal relationship.[11] See also the answer to Question 13.

SWITZERLAND

There is no information available with regard to this question.

[10] Office for National Statistics, *Short Report: Cohabitation in the UK 2012.*

[11] K. WALLENG, *Att leva som sambo*, Iustus Förlag, Uppsala, 2015, at p. 86.

PART C
DURING THE RELATIONSHIP

QUESTION 20

Are partners in an informal relationship under a duty to support each other, financially or otherwise:

a. Where there are no children in the household?

b. Where there are common children in the household?

c. Where there are other children in the household?

AUSTRIA

Partners in an informal relationship are not obliged to mutually support each other, regardless of whether there are no, common or other children living in the same household.[1] Since the amendment of the General Austrian Civil Code in 2009 S. 139 para. 2 General Austrian Civil Code obliges partners to undertake any effort to support minor stepchildren in order to protect the child's welfare. However, no similar obligation exists as between the partners themselves.

BELGIUM

a. Where there are no children in the household?

Informal partners are not under a duty to support each other in the absence of an (implicit) agreement to that end.[2] A natural obligation of support has not yet been recognised.[3]

b. Where there are common children in the household?

See the answer to sub a – there is no difference: no duty exists.

---

1 Austrian Supreme Court, Legal Proposition RS0096997, see Judgement of 29.01.1966, 5 Ob 1508/96.

2 Bergen 6 October 1994, *JT* 1995, 300. Implicitly: Cass. 11 April 1975, *AC* 1975, 881. Also see F. SWENNEN, 'Alimentatie tussen partners', in A. VERBEKE and C. FORDER, *Gehuwd of niet: maakt het iets uit?*, Intersentia, Antwerp, 2005, at p. 285.

3 K. WILLEMS, *De natuurlijke verbintenis*, die Keure, Bruges, 2011, at p. 255-258.

c. Where there are other children in the household?
See the answer to sub a – there is no difference: no duty exists.

BULGARIA

Partners in an informal relationship are not under a (legal) duty to support each other, neither financially nor otherwise in any of the above cases. Obligations to provide mutual financial and other support only arise from a marriage (Art. 17 and 140-141 of the Bulgarian Family Code).[4]

CROATIA

a. Where there are no children in the household?
According to Art. 31 paragraph 2 in relation to Art. 11 paragraph 2 of the Croatian Family Act, cohabitants are under a duty to support each other regardless of whether there are any children in the household or not. This means that they are bound to be loyal to each other, to help each other, to respect each other and to maintain harmonious family relationships. This obligation is not financial but rather personal.

According to Art. 37 paragraph 3 in relation to Art. 4 paragraph 1 of the Croatian Partnership Act, same-sex informal partners have a duty to support each other and to provide care and aid if they suffer from an illness regardless of whether there are any children in the household or not. This obligation is not financial but rather personal.

Pursuant to the Croatian Family Act, cohabitants are not provided with maintenance rights and liabilities during their relationship, regardless of the possible presence of children in the household.

According to Art. 37 paragraph 3 in relation to Art. 4 paragraph 1 of the Croatian Partnership Act, same-sex informal partners do have maintenance rights and liabilities during their relationship, regardless of the possible presence of children in the household.

4 See the same and more on the subject matter of the following questions: T. Tzankova, *The Factual Spousal Relationship and the Bulgarian Family Law*, Feneya, Sofia, 2000, at p. 124 et seq. Also in: M. Ekimdjiev, 'The Rights of Heterosexual Couples Living as a Family in Bulgaria in the Light of Article 14 of the ECHR', 16.08.2013, available at: eurorights-bg.org/?p=775.

The discrepancy that same-sex informal partners have maintenance rights and liabilities during their life union while cohabitants do not have maintenance rights and liabilities during their life union originate from a lack of harmonization between the laws (Croatian Family Act and Croatian Partnership Act).

b. Where there are common children in the household?

According to Art. 31 paragraph 2 in relation to Art. 11 paragraph 2 of the Croatian Family Act, cohabitants have a duty to support each other regardless of whether there are any children in the household or not. This obligation is not financial but rather personal.

According to Art. 37 paragraph 3 in relation to Art. 4 paragraph 1 of the Croatian Partnership Act, same-sex informal partners have a duty to support each other and to provide care and aid if they suffer from an illness regardless of whether there are any children in the household or not. This obligation is not financial but rather personal.

Cohabitants are not provided with maintenance rights and liabilities during their relationship, regardless of the possible presence of children in the household.

According to Art. 39 paragraph 2 in relation to Art. 4 paragraph 1 of the Croatian Partnership Act, same-sex informal partners do have maintenance rights and liabilities during their relationship, regardless of the possible presence of children in the household.

The discrepancy that same-sex informal partners have maintenance rights and liabilities during their life union while cohabitants are not provided therewith originates from a lack of harmonization between the laws (Croatian Family Act and Croatian Partnership Act).

c. Where there are other children in the household?

According to Art. 31 paragraph 2 in relation to Art. 11 paragraph 2 of the Croatian Family Act, cohabitants are under a duty to support each other regardless of whether there are any children in the household or not.

According to Art. 37 paragraph 3 in relation to Art. 4 paragraph 1 of the Croatian Partnership Act, same-sex informal partners have a duty to support each other and to provide care and aid if they suffer from an illness regardless of whether there are any children in the household or not. This obligation is not financial but rather personal.

Cohabitants are not provided with maintenance rights and liabilities during their relationship, regardless of the possible presence of children in the household.

According to Art. 39 paragraph 2 in relation to Art. 4 paragraph 1 of the Croatian Partnership Act, same-sex informal partners do have maintenance rights and liabilities during their relationship, regardless of the possible presence of children in the household.

The discrepancy that same-sex informal partners have maintenance rights and liabilities during their life union while cohabitants are not provided therewith originates from a lack of harmonization between the laws (Croatian Family Act and Croatian Partnership Act).

CZECH REPUBLIC

a. Where there are no children in the household?

Where the partners in the informal relationship do not have children in the household, they are not under a duty to support each other. There is no maintenance obligation nor is there an obligation to take care of each other.

b. Where there are common children in the household?

Because children born outside marriage have equal rights with children born within marriage, partners in an informal relationship have legal obligations to their children, although not to each other. A woman also has a right to obtain, from the father of her child, maintenance and support, and provision for the payment of certain costs for an unmarried mother. In accordance with S. 920 Czech Civil Code: if the child's mother is not married to the child's father, the child's father must provide her with maintenance for two years from the birth of the child and provide her with a reasonable contribution to cover the costs associated with pregnancy and childbirth. The man whose paternity is presumed has a duty to reimburse the costs associated with pregnancy and childbirth even if the child is not born alive. A court may, on the application of a pregnant woman, order the man whose paternity is presumed to provide an amount needed for maintenance and a contribution to cover the costs associated with pregnancy and childbirth in advance. A court may, on the application of a pregnant woman, also order the man whose paternity is presumed to provide in advance an amount needed to provide for the maintenance of the child for a period for which the woman would be entitled to maternity leave as an employee under another legal regulation.

c. Where there are other children in the household?

If there are other children in the household, a maintenance obligation only exists for their parents. The partners in an informal relationship have no duty to support each other under Czech law. According to S. 885 Czech Civil Code: where only one parent cares for a child, the parent's spouse or partner is involved in the care for and upbringing of the child if he lives in the family household with the child. This also applies to a person who lives with the child's parent without having entered into marriage or registered partnership with him, provided that the person lives in the family household with the child.

DENMARK

As a general rule, cohabitants do not have a legal obligation to contribute to their mutual maintenance, either during cohabitation or after separation.

On 1 January 2014 a mutual maintenance obligation was introduced for cohabitants aged 25 and over who live in a marriage-like relationship.[5] If a cohabitant has the means to provide for his or her partner, the latter – as with the rule that applies to married spouses – is not entitled to receive a cash benefit or educational assistance from the public authorities. In December 2014, the Danish government abolished these rules because of protests by cohabitants and the government's public-law responsibility to support cohabitants and their families.[6]

a. Where there are no children in the household?

According to the new rules from 2014 mentioned above, it is important whether the cohabitants are in a relationship similar to marriage.

b. Where there are common children in the household?

According to the new rules from 2014 mentioned above, if a cohabiting couple have children in common they are in a relationship similar to marriage and have a statutory obligation to maintain each other.

---

5 See Act No. 894 of 4 July 2013.

6 See Act No. 1522 of 2 December 2014 with effect from 1 January 2016.

c. Where there are other children in the household?
This is not important in relation to the new 2014 rules mentioned above.

ENGLAND AND WALES

a. Where there are no children in the household?
No.

b. Where there are common children in the household?
No, although it is possible to claim financial provision for the benefit of the child (in addition to child support) which can include an element for the other parent's care of the child or the cost of child care so that the partner can work, under Schedule 1 English Children Act 1989; *Re P (Child: Financial Provision)* [2003] EWCA Civ 837, [2003] 2 FLR 865.

c. Where there are other children in the household?
No.

ESTONIA

a. Where there are no children in the household?
According to Estonian law, the partners in an informal relationship do not have mutual maintenance obligations if they have no common children. The Estonian Social Welfare Act[7] § 22(2) stipulates that the granting of a subsistence benefit is based on the income of the benefit applicant and his or her family members. For the purpose of granting a subsistence benefit, persons who are married or living in the same dwelling in a conjugal relationship, their children and parents in need of assistance or other persons using one or more sources of income jointly or with a shared household are deemed to be family members. In clauses 40-41 of its decision of May 5, 2014,[8] the Constitutional Review Chamber of the Supreme Court found that the second sentence of section 2 of § 22 of the Social Welfare Act provides a definition of a family for the purpose of granting subsistence benefits. But in the same decision the Supreme Court clearly stressed that no legal prerequisite can be derived from § 22(2) of the Estonian Social Welfare Act to the effect that people who live together must provide maintenance to each other.

---

7 Sotsiaalhoolekande seadus (adopted on 8 February 1995, entered into force on 1 April 1995). – RT I 1995, 21, 323; RT I, 13.12.2014, 44 (in Estonian), available in English at: www.riigiteataja.ee/en/eli/ee/Riigikogu/act/509072014019/consolide.

8 Decision of the Supreme Court 3-4-1-67-13.

b. Where there are common children in the household?

The Estonian Family Law Act comprises the rules on the provision of maintenance in case of the birth of a child. The father of a child is required to provide maintenance to the mother of the child eight weeks before and twelve weeks after the birth of the child (§ 111(1) Estonian Family Law Act). If a mother is unable to maintain herself due to a health disorder caused by pregnancy or childbirth, the father is required to provide maintenance until there is an improvement in her state of health. The same applies if a mother is unable to receive an income due to having to care for a child (§ 111(2) Estonian Family Law Act). If the father cares for and raises a child and he is unable to receive an income due to having to care for the child, he has the right to file a claim against the mother (§ 111(3) Estonian Family Law Act). The obligation to provide maintenance commences no earlier than four months before the birth of a child and terminates after three years have passed since the birth of the child (§ 111(2) Estonian Family Law Act). The child's post-birth maintenance obligation does not depend on the cohabitation of the parties.

c. Where there are other children in the household?

According to Estonian law, the partners in an informal relationship do not have mutual maintenance obligations if they have other children in their household.

FINLAND

a. Where there are no children in the household?

Cohabitees are under no duty to support each other by law. However, the partners can enter into voluntary maintenance agreements.

b. Where there are common children in the household?

Cohabitees are not under a duty to support the other partner even if there are common children in the household. The parental duty to support one's children is limited to children and it does not extend to the parent of the child unless a separate contract has been entered into.

c. Where there are other children in the household?

Cohabitees are not under a duty to support the other partner even if there are common children in the household. The legal duty to support one's children is limited to one's own children and it does not extend to the parent of the common or non-common children living in the household.

FRANCE

a. Where there are no children in the household?

Partners in an informal relationship are not under a duty to support each other, financially or otherwise, when there are no children in the household.

b. Where there are common children in the household?

Partners in an informal relationship are not under a duty to support each other, financially or otherwise, when there are common children in the household. By contrast, each partner is under a duty to contribute to the maintenance of the common children (and of his or her own child).

c. Where there are other children in the household?

Partners in an informal relationship are not under a duty to support each other, financially or otherwise, when there are other children in the household. The parent of the child or of the children has to maintain them; the partner has no maintenance duty neither towards his or her partner nor with regard to the partner's children.

French law does not impose any maintenance obligation between partners in an informal relationship. However, the partners may agree on the payment of maintenance. According to the case law, if such a contractual obligation has been entered into by one of the partners, he or she has to fulfil it. Otherwise, it can be enforced. The French courts have often held that the purely natural obligation (*obligation naturelle)* on the part of the partners to provide mutual moral and financial support[9] can become a legal duty if the debtor spontaneously enforces this obligation.[10] This is for example the case where one of the partners has taken on the obligation to pay the rent for the common home[11] or to grant his or her partner the right to live in a dwelling for the rest of his or her life.[12]

GERMANY

a. Where there are no children in the household?

There is no statutory duty to support each other (i.e. a duty of maintenance) either during cohabitation or after the breakdown of the

9 See Cass. Civ. I, 17 November 1999, no. 97-17541; Civ. I, 19 February 2002, no. 99-18928.

10 Cass. Civ. I, 5 April 1993, no. 90-21734.

11 Cass. Civ. I, 3 June 1998, no. 93-16664.

12 Cass. Civ. I, 17 November 1999, no. 97-17541.

relationship. The only exception is maintenance in the case of care for a common child (§ 1615l of the German Civil Code).

b. Where there are common children in the household?

The father must pay the mother maintenance for a period of six weeks before and eight weeks after the birth of a child (§ 1615l para. 1 s. 1 of the German Civil Code). To the extent that the mother is not engaged in gainful employment because she is incapable of doing so as a result of either the pregnancy or an illness caused by the pregnancy or the delivery, the father is obliged to pay her maintenance for a period exceeding this period of time (§ 1615l para. 2 s. 1 of the German Civil Code). A claim for maintenance can also be filed to the extent that the mother or the father cannot be expected to be engaged in gainful employment by reason of the care or upbringing of the child (§ 1615l para. 2 s. 2 of the German Civil Code). The obligation to maintain begins, at the earliest, four months before the birth and continues for at least three years after the birth (§ 1615l para. 2 s. 3 of the German Civil Code). It is extended as long as and to the extent that this is equitable. Here, particular account is to be taken of the concerns of the child and the existing possibilities of childcare (§ 1615l para. 2 s. 4 of the German Civil Code). However, the sole basis for such a maintenance obligation is parentage. It does not depend on the place of living of the partners or a common household of the partners or cohabitation.[13]

c. Where there are other children in the household?

Step-parents and step-children (despite their special status in some social security statutes) are not obliged to support one another.[14] Therefore, a child living in an informal relationship retains his maintenance claim against his biological parent. The *de facto* partner is not obliged to maintain the children of his or her partner.[15] However, the ability to pay can be deemed to increase if the debtor lives in an informal relationship which gives him or her economic advantages.[16]

---

13 N. DETHLOFF, *Familienrecht*, Beck, Munich, 2012, at § 8 No. 6; D. SCHWAB, *Familienrecht*, Beck, Munich, 2014, at No. 998.

14 BGH, 24.6.1969, *NJW*, 1969, 2007; G. BRUDERMÜLLER, '§ 1601', in: O. PALANDT, *Bürgerliches Gesetzbuch*, Beck, Munich, 2015, at No. 2.

15 D. SCHWAB, *Familienrecht*, Beck, Munich, 2014, at No. 851.

16 See D. MARTINY, *Unterhaltsrang und -rückgriff I*, Mohr Siebeck, Tübingen, 2000, at p. 679 et seq.

GREECE

a. Where there are no children in the household?
No.

b. Where there are common children in the household?
No. Each partner has a legal duty only towards the common children, pursuant to Art. 1489 of the Greek Civil Code.

c. Where there are other children in the household?
No.

HUNGARY

a. Where there are no children in the household?
Cohabitants seem to be obliged to support each other while living in a community of life. Some uncertainty emerges from the fact that they are expected to support each other in the case law but this is not determined in any legal provision. Under the regime of the Civil Code of 1959 no such duty was prescribed for cohabitants but, according to the courts, taking care of each other during the community of life was an inseparable element of cohabitation. The Hungarian Supreme Court (later the Hungarian Curia) developed a practice according to which cohabitants are expected to support and maintain each other according to Hungarian social attitudes. The cases in which this statement was directly made dealt with maintenance contracts between cohabitants. In these cases the validity of the cohabitants' maintenance contract was contested (typically by third persons) and, according to the judges, it had to be scrutinised whether the services rendered by one partner went above and beyond the sphere of activity which was inseparable from cohabitation itself.

The Hungarian Civil Code contains provisions on cohabitants in the Sixth Book (Book on the Law of Obligations) and in the Family Law Book but neither book provides any regulation on the support that cohabitants should provide towards one another. The original concept and the normative text of the Civil Code proposed the inclusion of a rule on the maintenance of cohabitants in the course of the cohabitation. Nevertheless, this rule never went beyond the parliamentary stage. The commentaries on the Hungarian Civil Code emphasise the settled judicial practice but it still has to be seen whether the judges, in applying the provisions under the new regime, will follow this rule.

b. Where there are common children in the household?

The existence of common children does not directly influence the obligation of cohabitants to provide support.

c. Where there are other children in the household?

The existence of other children in the household does not directly influence the obligation of cohabitants to provide support.

REPUBLIC OF IRELAND

a. Where there are no children in the household?

Qualified Cohabitants (having been in a relationship of cohabitation of 5 years or more where they have no children together) may be under a legal duty to support each other upon the termination of the relationship, where one is financially dependent on the other, should the court accede to an application for redress under Part 15 of the Irish 2010 Act.

There is no entitlement under the Irish Family Law (Maintenance of Spouses and Children) Act 1976 for one cohabitee to apply for maintenance from the other for their own benefit.

b. Where there are common children in the household?

Qualified Cohabitants (having been in a relationship of cohabitation for 2 years or more and having one or more dependent children together) may be under a legal duty to support each other upon the termination of the relationship, where one is financially dependent on the other, should the court accede to an application for redress under Part 15 of the Irish 2010 Act.

There is a duty upon parents to support the dependent children of the informal relationship under S. 5A of the Irish Family Law (Maintenance of Spouses and Children) Act 1976. In respect of a dependent child whose parents are not married to each other, one parent may apply to court for a maintenance order to support any dependent children where there has been a failure to provide reasonable maintenance by the other parent.

c. Where there are other children in the household?

Qualified Cohabitants (having been in a relationship of cohabitation of 5 years or more where they have no dependent children together) may be under a legal duty to support each other upon the termination of the relationship, where one is financially dependent on the other, should the court accede to an application for redress under Part 15 of the Act.

A parent can only seek maintenance for their child from the other parent of the child under the Irish 1976 Act and cannot apply for same from their partner who is not the child's parent, although this may change under pending legislation.

The treatment of these issues in the legislation renders it difficult to answer the above questions separately. The court has regard to all of the above issues, when deciding on orders for maintenance, property etc.

Section 173 of the Irish Civil Partnership and Cohabitants Act 2010 provides as follows:

> '173— (1) A qualified cohabitant may, subject to any agreement under section 202, apply to the court, on notice to the other cohabitant, for an order under Sections 174, 175 and 187 or any of them.
> (2) If the qualified cohabitant satisfies the court that he or she is financially dependent on the other cohabitant and that the financial dependence arises from the relationship or the ending of the relationship, the court may, if satisfied that it is just and equitable to do so in all the circumstances, make the order concerned.
> (3) In determining whether or not it is just and equitable to make an order in all the circumstances, the court shall have regard to—
> (a) The financial circumstances, needs and obligations of each qualified cohabitant existing as at the date of the application or which are likely to arise in the future,
> (b) Subject to subsection (5), the rights and entitlements of any spouse or former spouse,
> (c) The rights and entitlements of any civil partner or former civil partner,
> (d) The rights and entitlements of any dependent child or of any child of a previous relationship of either cohabitant,
> (e) The duration of the parties' relationship, the basis on which the parties entered into the relationship and the degree of commitment of the parties to one another,
> (f) The contributions that each of the cohabitants made or is likely to make in the foreseeable future to the welfare of the cohabitants or either of them including any contribution made by each of them to the income, earning capacity or property and financial resources of the other,
> (g) Any contributions made by either of them in looking after the home,
> (h) The effect on the earning capacity of each of the cohabitants of the responsibilities assumed by each of them during the period they lived together as a couple and the degree to which the future earning capacity of a qualified cohabitant is impaired by reason of that qualified cohabitant having relinquished or foregone the opportunity of remunerative activity in order to look after the home,

(i) Any physical or mental disability of the qualified cohabitant, and
(j) The conduct of each of the cohabitants, if the conduct is such that, in the opinion of the court, it would be unjust to disregard it.'

As stated above, the categorisation of an individual as being a 'qualified cohabitant' is significant in that it enables that person to apply to the court for redress in circumstances where he or she is financially dependent on the other cohabitant (S. 173). Where a court is satisfied that a qualified cohabitant is financially dependent on another cohabitant and that such financial dependency arises from the relationship, or termination of the relationship between the parties, the court may, if it is satisfied that is it 'just and equitable' to do so, make various ancillary Orders (S. 173(2)).

Under the Irish 2010 Act, there are 4 main types of orders that a qualified cohabitant may seek from the court:

- Section 174 provides for the making of property adjustment orders, which enables the transfer or settlement of specified property in which the cohabitant has an interest.
- Section 175 provides for the making of Compensatory Maintenance Orders. This enables the court to make Periodical Payment Orders, Secured Periodical Payments Orders, or Lump Sum Orders in favour of a financially dependent qualified cohabitant. Periodic Orders cease to have effect upon the marriage or registration of a civil partnership of the recipient qualified cohabitant (S. 175(5)). Further, no such Order can be made in favour of a qualified cohabitant who has married or registered a civil partnership (S. 175(6)). In terms of the safeguarding of such payments, Attachment of Earnings Orders are available to qualified cohabitants as per S. 176-186. Further, in the event of a maintenance debtor failing to comply with any such Order, the maintenance creditor may sue by way of simple contract debt before a court of competent jurisdiction so as to enforce the Order.
- A qualified cohabitant may apply to the court for a Pension Adjustment Order as per S. 188 to 192 of the Irish 2010 Act.
- Section 194 provides that a qualified cohabitant may, after the death of his or her cohabitant, apply for an order for provision out of the net estate.

Where a qualified cohabitant institutes proceedings pursuant to S. 173 of the Irish 2010 Act seeking redress, the court may adjourn such proceedings so as to enable the parties to attempt to reconcile or reach an agreement as to the issue before them.

ITALY

Strictly speaking, partners in informal relationships are under no financial or moral obligation to support each other.[17] Nevertheless, support, assistance and contributions to the common needs of the partners and of the household are not without relevance as – in the absence of a legal regulation of informal relationships – they may be said to form the actual basis of the relationship, and constitute the evidence of its existence.[18]

The position of one partner vis-à-vis the other does not change if there are no children, or common children or when there are other children in the household. In the case of children common to both, of course, the responsibility toward them lies with the parents according to the general rules regarding maintenance, support and education which constitute the parents' responsibility toward their children (Art. 315 and 315 *bis* Italian Civil Code as amended by the law of 10 December 2012, n. 219). Therefore each partner is under an obligation to maintain and support his or her children with no effect on his or her duties toward the partner.

LATVIA

In Latvia there is no such specific legal order on informal relationships.

By way of comparison one can consider the following. In connection with marriage in the Latvian Civil Law this legal order is included: marriage creates a duty on the part of a husband and a wife to be faithful to each other, to live together, to take care of each other and to jointly ensure the welfare of their family.[19]

---

17 Only a few decisions have affirmed that informal partners have a duty to contribute to the common life: Trib. Savona, 29 June 2002, applying Art. 143 of the Italian Civil Code (which refers to married couples); Pret. Genova 21 May 1981, in *Foro it.*, 1982, I, c. 1459, extending to cohabiting couples the application of Art. 145 Italian Civil Code on the possibility to request judicial intervention when spouses disagree; Trib. Roma 13 December 1993, in *Dir. Fam. Pers.*, 1994, p. 1059; Trib. Messina 10 May 1991, in *Giust. Civ.*, 1992, I, p. 2899. See R. BASSETTI, *Contratti di convivenza e di unione civile*, Giappichelli, Turin, 2014, at p. 55 and L. BALESTRA, 'La famiglia di fatto', in: G. FERRANDO (ed.), *Il nuovo diritto di famiglia*, Zanichelli, Bologna, 2008, at p. 1046.

18 See, among others, G. FERRANDO, *Diritto di famiglia*, Zanichelli, Bologna, 2013, at p. 146.

19 S. 84 Latvian Civil Law.

Personal relations of parents and children are regulated by the Latvian Family Law (Chapter 2. 'Personal Relations of Parents and Children'). Section 179 of the Latvian Civil Law determines that parents, commensurate with their financial state, have a duty to maintain their child. Such duty lies upon the father and the mother until such time as the child is able to provide for itself.[20]

LITHUANIA

a. Where there are no children in the household?

There is no legal provision which imposes an obligation on partners in an informal relationship to support each other.

b. Where there are common children in the household?

There is no legal provision which imposes an obligation on partners in an informal relationship to support each other.

The maintenance of common children is regulated separately (Art. 3.192–3.204 of the Lithuanian Civil Code). The duty to support a child is universal and does not depend on the matrimonial status of the parents (married or non-married), i.e. Art. 3.156 of the Lithuanian Civil Code stipulates that parents shall have equal rights and duties with respect to their children irrespective of whether the child was born to a married or unmarried couple.

c. Where there are other children in the household?

There is no legal provision which imposes an obligation on partners in an informal relationship to support each other.

LUXEMBOURG

Partners in an informal relationship do not have any duty to support each other, whether there are children in the household or not.

Of course, if the couple have common children, each of them has a duty to support the children.

---

[20] S. 84 Latvian Civil Law.

THE NETHERLANDS

a. Where there are no children in the household?

There is no legal duty to support the other partner during the relationship, regardless of whether children are present. This follows from the Dutch Civil Code which only recognises a duty to support a partner in relation to married and registered partners, but not for non-marital cohabitants.

Partners may contract otherwise in a cohabitation contract. Research among non-marital cohabitants indicates that in 2010 about 50 percent of all non-marital cohabitants had concluded a notarial cohabitation contract.[21] Empirical research among notaries suggests that in many notarial cohabitation contracts a duty is included to provide support and the necessary means to each other during the relationship.[22] That is the same obligation as spouses have on the basis of Art. 1:81 Dutch Civil Code. This is almost a standard clause in notarial cohabitation contracts. Its use is stimulated by the condition laid down in the Dutch Inheritance Taxation Act and pension schemes which require a duty to support in a notarial contract in order to qualify as a partner.[23] Besides, as a result of such a contractual duty, payments during the relationship by one partner to the other will not qualify as a gift and will not be taxable.[24]

b. Where there are common children in the household?

There is no legal duty to support the other partner during the relationship, regardless of whether children (common or otherwise) are present. Partners may contract otherwise in a cohabitation contract. Research among non-marital cohabitants indicates that in 2010 about 50 percent of all non-marital cohabitants had concluded a cohabitation contract.[25] Empirical research among notaries suggests that in many notarial cohabitation contracts a duty is included to provide support and the necessary means to each other during the relationship.[26] It is not

---

21 A. DE GRAAF, 'Steeds meer samenwoners hebben een samenlevingscontract', *CBS Webmagazine* 10 February 2010.

22 W.M. SCHRAMA, P. KUIK and L.C.A. VERSTAPPEN, 'Samenlevingsovereenkomsten in de notariële praktijk', *Familie&Recht*, 2014, available at: familieenrecht.nl, at 14.1 and 14.2.

23 Each pension fund sets its own conditions. An example of one of the biggest funds in the Netherlands: www.abp.nl/relatie/trouwen-samenwonen/nabestaandenpensioen-partner-aanmelden.asp.

24 P. BLOKLAND, in: W.D. KOLKMAN and L.C.A. VERSTAPPEN (eds.), *Handboek Familievermogensrecht*, Walburg Pers, Zutphen, 2013, at 4.2.1.

25 A. DE GRAAF, 'Steeds meer samenwoners hebben een samenlevingscontract', *CBS Webmagazine* 10 February 2010.

26 W.M. SCHRAMA, P. KUIK and L.C.A. VERSTAPPEN, 'Samenlevingsovereenkomsten in de notariële praktijk', *Familie&Recht*, 2014, available at: familieenrecht.nl, at 14.1 and 14.2.

clear whether partners contract such a duty more often when they have common children, but there seems to be only a minor difference with regard to the prevalence of such a duty in notarial cohabitation contracts between, on the one hand, couples without children and, on the other, couples with children.[27]

c. Where there are other children in the household?

There is no legal duty to support the other partner during the relationship, regardless of whether children (common or otherwise) are present. Partners may contract otherwise in a cohabitation contract. Research among non-marital cohabitants indicates that in 2010 about 50 percent of all non-marital cohabitants had concluded a cohabitation contract.[28] Empirical research among notaries suggests that in many notarial cohabitation contracts a duty is included to provide support and the necessary means to each other during the relationship.[29] It is not clear whether partners contract such a duty more often when they have common children, but there seems to be only a minor difference with regard to the prevalence of such a duty in notarial cohabitation contracts between, on the one hand, couples without children and, on the other, couples with children.[30]

NORWAY

a. Where there are no children in the household?

Partners to an informal relationship are not under a duty to support each other in relationships where there are no children in the household.

b. Where there are common children in the household?

Partners to an informal relationship are not under a duty to support each other in relationships where there are children in the household.

c. Where there are other children in the household?

Partners to an informal relationship are not under a duty to support each other in relationships where there are other children in the household.

---

[27] W.M. SCHRAMA, P. KUIK and L.C.A. VERSTAPPEN, 'Samenlevingsovereenkomsten in de notariële praktijk', *Familie&Recht*, 2014, available at: familieenrecht.nl, at 14.1 and 14.2.

[28] A. DE GRAAF, 'Steeds meer samenwoners hebben een samenlevingscontract', *CBS Webmagazine* 10 February 2010.

[29] W.M. SCHRAMA, P. KUIK and L.C.A. VERSTAPPEN, 'Samenlevingsovereenkomsten in de notariële praktijk', *Familie&Recht*, 2014, available at: familieenrecht.nl, at 14.1 and 14.2.

[30] W.M. SCHRAMA, P. KUIK and L.C.A. VERSTAPPEN, 'Samenlevingsovereenkomsten in de notariële praktijk', *Familie&Recht*, 2014, available at: familieenrecht.nl, at 14.1 and 14.2.

PORTUGAL

a. Where there are no children in the household?
There is no duty to support each other in any case.

b. Where there are common children in the household?
There is no duty to support each other in any case, although each parent must contribute to the child's maintenance.

c. Where there are other children in the household?
There is no duty to support each other in any case, although each parent must contribute to the child's maintenance.

RUSSIA

a. Where there are no children in the household?
No.

b. Where there are common children in the household?
No.

c. Where there are other children in the household?
No.

SCOTLAND

In Scots law, the private law duty of support is known as the obligation of aliment.[31] The presence of this obligation is one of the key legal distinctions between formal and informal relationships. While there is an obligation of aliment between spouses and partners in marriage and civil partnership,[32] there is no such obligation between cohabitants. Extending the obligation of aliment to cohabiting couples was an option considered by the Scottish Law Commission, both in its Discussion Paper and Report, but it was concluded that it was not appropriate to extend aliment to informal relationships.[33]

There is no legal obligation to provide mutual support between spouses and civil partners, other than the financial obligation of aliment, and

---

31 Family Law (Scotland) Act 1985, S. 1.
32 Family Law (Scotland) Act 1985, S. 1(1)(a) – (bb).
33 Scot Law Com, *Report on Family Law*, No 135, 1992, paras 16.5–16.6.

similarly there is no such obligation in the context of informal relationships.

a. Where there are no children in the household?

As explained above, the general position is that there is no legal obligation on partners to an informal relationship to support each other. This is distinct from the obligation of aliment, which applies between spouses and between civil partners, regardless of the presence or absence of children.[34]

b. Where there are common children in the household?

As explained above, there is no duty of support between partners to an informal relationship and this is unaffected by the presence of children. All parents, however, owe a duty of support to their children in terms of the private law obligation of aliment[35] and this will apply in the context of an informal relationship. The duty to support arises because of the parent/child relationship and is not affected by the nature of the relationship between the adults. The private law obligation of aliment exists in conjunction with a public law system of child support,[36] which is intended to ensure that non-resident parents contribute appropriately to the maintenance of their children.

c. Where there are other children in the household?

As explained above, parties to an informal relationship owe no obligation to support each other. Parents do however owe an obligation to their children and the obligation of aliment extends to any child who has been 'accepted' as a child of the family.[37] While a cohabitant does not therefore owe any legal duty of support to his or her partner, he or she does owe a duty of aliment to the child of such a partner if that child has been accepted as a child of the family.

SLOVAKIA

a. Where there are no children in the household?

No, there is no duty to support each other.

---

34 Family Law (Scotland) Act 1985, S. 1.
35 Family Law (Scotland) Act 1985, S. 1(1)(c).
36 Child Support Act 1991.
37 Family Law (Scotland) Act 1985, S. 1(1)(d).

b. Where there are common children in the household?
No, there is no direct duty to support each other even if there are common children in the household. The Slovak Family Act provides for the following maintenance duties:

- duty of maintenance by parents towards children,
- duty of maintenance by children towards parents,
- duty of maintenance between other relatives,
- duty of maintenance between spouses,
- contribution to the maintenance of a divorced spouse, and
- contribution to the maintenance of and the reimbursement of certain costs incurred by an unmarried mother.

In a situation where there is a common child in the household an unmarried mother can claim a contribution towards her maintenance and a reimbursement of certain costs incurred by her. The father of a child whose mother is not married to him has to provide adequate contributions towards the mother's maintenance costs and to contribute to her costs related to pregnancy and birth. The father has to provide these contributions for a period of no longer than two years after the child's birth.

c. Where there are other children in the household?
No, there is no duty to support each other.

SLOVENIA

a. Where there are no children in the household?
A partner who does not have the necessary means for subsistence, and through no fault of his or her own is unemployed, remains entitled to claim maintenance from the other partner, even after the termination of the life union.

b. Where there are common children in the household?
The fact of having common children or not is irrelevant for the existence of a duty to maintain the other partner.

c. Where there are other children in the household?
The fact of having children in a household or not is irrelevant for the existence of a duty to maintain the other partner. However, an extramarital partner has a duty to support the underage children of the other partner if the child(ren) has/have no parent able to support

it/them. This duty is limited only to the children of a partner that live with the partners. The duty of an extramarital partner to support the children of her or his partner ceases with the termination of their extramarital union, unless the extramarital union ceased because of the death of the child's mother or father. The extramarital partner then has a duty to support the child of her or his deceased extramarital partner only if the extramarital partner lived with the child at the time of his or her death. This duty is not mutual; so children who have attained the age of majority do not have a duty to support the unsupported extramarital partner of their parent who cared for them or supported them for an extended period.

SPAIN

a. Where there are no children in the household?

In the absence of an agreement, there is no legal duty in the Spanish Civil Code for partners to an informal relationship to support each other. Partners are neither relatives nor spouses and therefore do not fulfil the requirements of Art. 143 Spanish Civil Code. A claim for maintenance between partners to an informal relationship would be dismissed in court. If, however, partners support each other spontaneously, this is considered as performance of a so-called 'natural obligation' or moral duty. This means that there is no possibility of requesting reimbursement of payments made.

The same holds for Catalan law. The legal provisions contained in the Catalan Civil Code concentrate on the effects after break-up and do not regulate matters during the relationship. Article 234-3 Catalan Civil Code establishes that during the relationship matters are governed by the partners' agreements. In the absence of an agreement, there is no legal duty for partners to support each other since they do not qualify under Art. 237-2 Catalan Civil Code.

b. Where there are common children in the household?

Parents have a duty to support their children, but not each other if they are not married.

c. Where there are other children in the household?

Partners have no duty to support each other. The fact that there are children in the household is irrelevant as to the relationship between the partners. It may give rise to maintenance duties towards the children.

SWEDEN

a. Where there are no children in the household?

Under Swedish legislation, no obligation exists for the cohabiting couple to support each other or to contribute to the shared household. In reality cohabitees usually cooperate to meet at least the joint needs, in equal shares or in relation to each cohabitee's income. Often they have an implied agreement or common understanding on this. And interestingly enough, in the practice of social welfare authorities, the existence of unmarried cohabitation is taken into account when assessing a partner's or the couple's rights to various social welfare benefits, such as living support, funded by the public sector. This means that even if there is no legal duty of mutual support, in practice parties in a cohabiting relationship are expected to financially support each other.

b. Where there are common children in the household?

See above, under a, indicating a negative answer. However, parents have a legal duty to maintain their children, irrespective of their own civil status and whether they live together or apart (Swedish Children and Parents Code, Chapter 7, § 1). The existence of common children in an unmarried cohabitation is at the same time not completely without relevance for a mutual duty of maintenance. Exceptionally, a cohabiting person's duty to maintain his or her children living in another residence may be reduced having regard to his or her need to maintain a partner with whom he or she is habitually living in an informal relationship, Swedish Children and Parents Code, Chapter 7, § 3.

c. Where there are other children in the household?

No. See above, under a and b. On the other hand, a person who lives on a habitual basis with a child and the child's parent may have a duty of maintenance in respect of the child. For this to be the case, the step-parent must either be married to the parent or have a joint child with the parent.[38] A step-parent's duty of maintenance lasts only for the duration of the cohabitation with the child's parent and it is subsidiary to the duty of maintenance owed by the child's other (non-residential) parent. The justification for extending the maintenance obligation to include the other partner's child in a cohabitation relationship, provided that the

[38] Swedish Children and Parents Code (in Swedish *Föräldrabalken* 1949:381), Chapter 7, Section 5.

cohabitants also had a child in common, was to safeguard for all the children in the family the right to enjoy the same standard of living.[39]

SWITZERLAND

a. Where there are no children in the household?

In Switzerland, partners in an informal relationship are under no duty to (financially) support each other.[40] Any support provided is to be qualified as a favour, a gift or as a fulfilment of moral obligations.[41]

Partners in an informal relationship may, however, contractually agree upon mutual financial support. Such an agreement can be concluded explicitly or impliedly and may be judicially enforced.[42]

If the partners have formed a simple partnership (Art. 530 et seq. Swiss Code of Obligations, see Question 3), they have to contribute (e.g. financially or through work and labour) to the partnership to achieve their common goal.[43] The simple partnership further entails a loyalty relationship between the partners, which obliges them to provide certain support and consideration.[44]

b. Where there are common children in the household?

Generally, there is no duty to (financially) support each other in an informal relationship, except where this has been contractually agreed (see Question 20(a)).

---

39 A. SINGER, 'Samboendets föräldrarättsliga relevans', in: J. ASLAND et al., *Nordisk samboerrett*, Gyldendal, Oslo, 2014, at p. 245 (see Chapter 3.5.5, in the English version of the book, to be published by Intersentia in 2015).

40 B. PULVER, *Unverheiratete Paare*, Helbing Lichtenhahn Verlag, Basel, 2000, at p. 50.

41 P. LIATOWITSCH and A. RUMO-JUNGO, 'Nichteheliche Lebensgemeinschaft: vermögens- und kindesrechtliche Belange', *Die Praxis des Familienrechts*, 2004, at p. 895, 904; R. AEBI-MÜLLER and C. WIDMER, 'Rechtsregeln für nichteheliches Zusammenleben in der Schweiz', in: I. KROPPENBERG, D. SCHWAB, D. HENRICH, P. GOTTWALD and A. SPICKHOFF, *Rechtsregeln für nichteheliches Zusammenleben*, Gieseking, Bielefeld, 2009, at p. 65, 72.

42 A. BÜCHLER, 'Vermögensrechtliche Probleme in der nichtehelichen Lebensgemeinschaft', in: A. RUMO-JUNGO and P. PICHONNAZ, *Familienvermögensrecht*, Stämpfli, Bern, 2003, at p. 59,75.

43 R. AEBI-MÜLLER and C. WIDMER, 'Rechtsregeln für nichteheliches Zusammenleben in der Schweiz', in: I. KROPPENBERG, D. SCHWAB, D. HENRICH, P. GOTTWALD and A. SPICKHOFF, *Rechtsregeln für nichteheliches Zusammenleben*, Gieseking, Bielefeld, 2009, at p. 65, 72.

44 R.D. DUSSY, *Ausgleichsansprüche für Vermögensinvestitionen nach Auflösung von Lebensbeziehungen*, Helbing Lichtenhahn Verlag, Basel, 1994, at p. 57.

The unmarried mother may only claim compensation against the father of the child for confinement costs, the costs of maintenance for at least four weeks prior to and at least eight weeks after the birth of the child and other expenses rendered necessary by the pregnancy or confinement, including the initial equipment for the child (Art. 295 para. 1 Swiss Civil Code).

Currently, a major revision of child support is pending. According to the draft, child support shall encompass the costs incurred by the person caring for the child for forgoing gainful employment. Accordingly, an unmarried mother may receive financial support, at least indirectly, via child support.

c. Where there are other children in the household?

Generally, there is no duty to (financially) support each other in an informal relationship, except where this has been contractually agreed (see Question 20(a)).

According to Art. 299 Swiss Civil Code, each spouse must give the other reasonable support in exercising parental responsibility over the latter's children and must represent the other spouse as the circumstances require. This provision may be applied by analogy to partners in an informal relationship.[45]

---

[45] I. SCHWENZER and M. COTTIER, in: H. HONSELL, N.P. VOGT and T. GEISER, *Basler Kommentar Zivilgesetzbuch I (Art. 1-456 ZGB)*, Helbing Lichtenhahn Verlag, Basel, 2014, at Art. 299 N 1.

QUESTION 21

Are partners in an informal relationship under a general duty to contribute to the costs and expenses of their household?

AUSTRIA

The Austrian Supreme Court has decided that an informal relationship does not entail a duty of mutual assistance *(Beistandspflicht)*.[1] The partners do not have to contribute financially to the partnership.[2] In contrast, S. 90 para. 1 General Austrian Civil Code states that spouses are obliged to mutually assist each other. In this regard mutual assistance is understood as any material and non-material support including contributions to the joint household.[3] In 2009 the Austrian legislator introduced a duty to support the child of the other partner, but refrained from laying down a similar obligation as between the partners.[4]

Although no respective obligation is stipulated, it has to be borne in mind that case law has defined an economic community - which constitutes one element of an informal relationship - as a community in which both partners have to support each other in case of hardship, have to contribute to maintenance and have to share its assets.[5] Further, the Austrian Supreme Court has decided that partners in an informal relationship have to jointly bear the costs of living or that one partner

1 Austrian Supreme Court, Judgement of 29.01.1996, 5 Ob 1508/96; A. DEIXLER-HÜBNER, *Scheidung, Ehe und Lebensgemeinschaft*, LexisNexis ARD ORAC, Vienna, 2013, at marg. No. 240.

2 Cf. P. RUMMEL, 'Ehe, Familie, Lebensgemeinschaft - Rechtsdogmatisches und Rechtspolitisches', *ÖJZ*, 1991, at p. 60.

3 Regional Court Salzburg, Judgement of 20.02.2012, 21 R 414/11w; Regional Court for Civil Matters Vienna, Judgement of 17.07.2012, 44 R 227/12a; P. SMUTNY, 'section 90 General Austrian Civil Code', in: A. KLETEČKA and M. SCHAUER, *ABGB-ON 1.02*, Manz Verlag, Vienna, 2014, at marg. No. 26, 31.

4 F. LINDER, in: E. GITSCHTHALER and J. HÖLLWERTH (eds.), *Kommentar zum Ehe- und Partnerschaftsrecht*, Springer, Vienna, 2011, at p. 1089.

5 Austrian Supreme Court, Legal Proposition RS0047035, see e.g. Judgement of 08.07.1981, 3 Ob 186/09p; U. AICHHORN, *Das Recht der Lebenspartnerschaften, Ehe und Lebensgemeinschaft*, Springer, Vienna, 2003, at p. 13.

contributes to the maintenance of the other.[6] Besides, it must be noted that the maintenance claim of a partner living in an informal relationship against his/her ex-spouse is suspended for the duration of the informal relationship.[7] Due to the hybrid definition of informal relationships in Austria, it should however be borne in mind that the economic community criterion - although vital - is not a mandatory prerequisite for all informal relationships.[8]

BELGIUM

Informal partners are not obliged, on a civil basis, to contribute to household expenses in the absence of an (implicit) agreement to that end. A (limited)[9] natural obligation to contribute has been recognised,[10] but its enforcement presupposes voluntary execution by the debtor or the promise to execute.[11] In the absence thereof, the partner who has solely or excessively contributed to the household expenses can subsequently reclaim the overpayment from the other partner on the basis of unjust enrichment.[12]

BULGARIA

Partners in an informal relationship are not under a general duty to contribute to the costs and expenses of their household. Such a duty only arises from a marriage (Art. 17 of the Bulgarian Family Code).

CROATIA

There is no legal provision that expressly lays down a duty to contribute to the costs and expenses of the household.

---

6 Austrian Supreme Court, Judgement of 09.10.1997, 2 Ob 258/97y.

7 Austrian Supreme Court, Legal Proposition RS0047108, see Judgement of 21.05.2014, 3 Ob 31/14a.

8 Austrian Supreme Court, Legal Proposition RS0021733, see e.g. Judgement of 30.08.1972, 1 Ob 188/72.

9 Justice of the Peace Wavre (2) 23 January 2007, *T. Vred.* 2009, 364.

10 For example Liège 20 June 1990, *JLMB* 1991, 157; District Court of Brussels 31 October 1996, *JLMB* 1997, 1044 and K. WILLEMS, *De natuurlijke verbintenis*, die Keure, Bruges, 2011, at p. 255-258.

11 Justice of the Peace Charleroi (4) 26 October 2001, *JLMB* 2002, 655.

12 Liège 28 April 2009, *RTDF* 2010, 43; District Court of Nivelles 25 October 2012, *Le Pli Juridique* 2013, N° 25, p. 7, with note JASSOGNE. Furthermore V. DEHALLEUX, 'La répétition de la contribution excessive aux charges du ménage: proposition d'une nouvelle issue aux conflits entre cohabitants de fait', *TBBR* 2009, at p. 144.

CZECH REPUBLIC

Partners to an informal relationship are not under a general duty to contribute to the costs and expenses of their household. Whatever each partner buys falls exclusively within that partner's ownership, as there is no community property or so-called 'usual family household equipment' as between spouses (S. 698(1) Czech Civil Code: usual family household equipment consists of a set of movable things which normally serve for the usual essential needs of the life of the family and its members; whether individual things belong to both spouses or just one of them is not decided).

DENMARK

There is no general duty.

Upon the termination of cohabitation a cohabitant can make claims under property law against his or her former partner. Any such claim must be judged in the light of the couple's community of interests, so there must be a clear basis for allowing such a claim. A claim can be rejected if the transfer of money between cohabitants must be regarded as a contribution to the shared household expenses and thus part of a joint financial arrangement. It is relevant whether the cohabitation has been of longer duration with joint finances.

ENGLAND AND WALES

No.

ESTONIA

Estonian laws do not stipulate a family maintenance obligation for partners in an informal relationship as prescribed in the Estonian Family Law Act.

FINLAND

No. If one partner does not contribute to the costs and expenses of their household, the other partner does not have a general legal right to force the other to contribute.

FRANCE

No. There is no legal obligation for partners in an informal relationship to contribute to the costs and expenses of their household.[13] On several occasions, the Court of cassation has held that the mandatory provisions called *régime primaire impératif* which apply to spouses (Art. 212 et seq. of the French Civil Code) cannot be extended to partners in an informal relationship.

However, the partners in an informal relationship can enter into an agreement (*convention de concubinage*) relating to their contribution to the costs and expenses of their household.[14]

As for the refusal of the Court of cassation to apply to partners in an informal relationship Art. 220 of the French Civil Code,[15] which makes the spouse jointly and severally liable for any debts incurred by one spouse for the joint household and the raising of the children,[16] see under Question 31.

GERMANY

The duty to contribute to the costs and expenses of the family household is regulated in §§ 1360-1360b German Civil Code. Pursuant to § 1360 s. 1 German Civil Code, both spouses are obliged to contribute through their work and their property to the reasonable maintenance of the family. However, the partners to an informal relationship are under no general duty to contribute to the costs and expenses of their household.[17] A partner normally cannot claim compensation for services after the cessation of cohabitation (see Question 46).

---

13 Cass. civ. I, 19 April 2005, no. 01-17226, *Bull. Civ.* I, no. 187; *Dr. Fam.* 2005, no. 127 with note LARRIBAU-TERNEYRE; Civ. I, 28 November 2006, no. 04-15480, *Bull. Civ.* I, no. 517.

14 Cass. Civ. I, 28 June 2005, no. 02-12767, *Bull. Civ.* I, no. 278.

15 Cass. Civ. I, 27 April 2004, no. 02-16291, *Bull. Civ.* I, no. 113; Civ. I, 17 October 2000, no. 98-19527, *Bull. Civ.* no. 244: *'aucune disposition légale ne réglant la contribution des concubins aux charges de la vie commune, chacun d'eux doit, en l'absence de volonté exprimée à cet égard, supporter les dépenses de la vie courante qu'il a exposées'* (As no statutory provision regulates the *concubins'* contribution to the household expenses, each of them must - in the absence of a specific intention expressed in this regard - bear the household expenses he or she has incurred).

16 For PACS partners, see Art. 515-4 of the French Civil code: they are jointly and severally liable towards third parties for any debts incurred by one partner for *'besoins de la vie courante'* (everyday needs).

17 D. MARTINY, 'Rechtsprobleme der nichtehelichen Lebensgemeinschaft während ihres Bestehens nach deutschem Recht', in: J.M. SCHERPE and N. YASSARI (eds.), *Die Rechtsstellung nichtehelicher Lebensgemeinschaften*, Mohr Siebeck, Tübingen, 2005, at p. 79 and 87 with references.

GREECE

Not on the basis of family law. In the spirit of freedom of contract (Art. 361 Greek Civil Code), the partners may agree on a different contractual arrangement. A contractual duty by one towards the other may also be recognised (Art. 873 et seq. Greek Civil Code), or even lifetime income, under Art. 840 et seq. of the Greek Civil Code.

HUNGARY

Living together in a household is one element of the definition of cohabitation but there is no normative obligation for cohabitants to contribute to the costs of the household. This issue may only emerge when there is a dispute between cohabitants concerning a property issue.

REPUBLIC OF IRELAND

There is no general duty on partners in an informal relationship to contribute to the costs and expenses of their household. This only becomes an issue if the matter is raised in the courts as above.

Cohabitants can, however, voluntarily enter into a 'cohabitants' agreement' to regulate their joint financial affairs during their relationship and for when their relationship ends. This could obviously include terms regarding the costs and expenses of their household. Section 202 of the Irish 2010 Act provides that this agreement will be recognised as valid and enforceable, as long as the cohabitants have each received independent legal advice prior to entry, or if they have received legal advice together, they have waived in writing their right to individual advice. The agreement must be in writing and signed by both, and the general law of contract must be complied with.

The agreement can include a full or partial opt-out of the redress and maintenance schemes.

The courts have the power to vary or set aside a cohabitants' agreement or part of an agreement if putting it into action would cause serious injustice.

The fact that such agreements are optional suggests that there is not necessarily such a duty on cohabitants to contribute to the costs and expenses of the household absent a valid cohabitants' agreement. While in an application under the redress scheme, the court may well find that maintenance is due, this is by no means guaranteed. The redress scheme only provides qualified cohabitants who meet the requirements in the Act with the right to apply for such orders in court and does not necessarily guarantee them success in their applications.

ITALY

No. No general duty to contribute is laid down by the law or can be inferred from the case law.

LATVIA

In Latvia there is no such specific legal order on informal relationships.

By way of comparison one can consider the following. In connection with marriage in the Latvian Civil Law it is determined that both spouses have a duty to cover the family and joint household expenses out of the joint property of the spouses. If the joint property of the spouses is insufficient to support the family, each spouse may require that the other spouse share the family and joint household expenses commensurately with his or her own separate financial resources.[18]

LITHUANIA

The provisions of Book III of the Lithuanian Civil Code (Art. 3.229-3.236) do not impose a direct obligation of this kind; however, considering the substance of these provisions (e.g. the legal regime of assets used by the cohabitees together; the division of assets acquired and used together, etc.), one may find an indirect implication that the partners in an informal relationship should contribute to the costs and expenses of their household. The existing case law suggests that an analysis of the circumstances presupposing a common household and the contributions to the family needs, as well as the generation of wealth from the personal revenues of the partners and also the revenues gained from the common household and through common efforts could be a sufficient ground for the court to recognise the existence of a (non-written) agreement between[19] the

18 S. 95 Latvian Civil Law.

19 Article 6.974 of the Lithuanian Civil Code: Joint expenses and joint damages: the distribution of joint expenses and joint damages, related to the joint activities, shall be established in the agreement on joint activities. Absent such agreement, each partner shall be liable for the joint expenses and joint damages in proportion to the amount of his part of such expenses or damages.

partners aimed at the creation of common partial ownership (Art. 4.76 of the Lithuanian Civil Code: 'Rights and duties of co-owners in possession and maintenance of common partial ownership').[20] In cases such as these, the court will analyse a property dispute by applying the general provisions of Lithuanian Property Law and Obligations Law rather than those of Family Law. It is also worth mentioning that if partners (cohabitants) rent an apartment, they will be subject to the general rules regarding the leasing of dwellings (Art. 6.589 of the Lithuanian Civil Code: 'Rights and duties of the lessee's family members').

LUXEMBOURG

As a principle, they are under no duty. However, If they have contributed to the costs of the household, they are not allowed to claim any reimbursement, because this contribution is the counterparty of the relationship. Only when one of the partners has met, during the informal relationship, some extraordinary expenses, which are of a substantial amount, may he or she claim a reimbursement (for more details see the answers to Part D. Separation).

THE NETHERLANDS

The Dutch Civil Code contains only a duty to contribute to the costs and expenses of the household for married and registered partners (Art. 1:84 Dutch Civil Code). Partners in such a formal relationship are under a duty to contribute to the costs and expenses according to their respective financial means.[21]

Such a statutory provision does not exist in the Dutch Civil Code for informal couples. It has been argued in the literature that there is room for the analogous application of Art. 1:84 Dutch Civil Code.[22] However, in this respect it is problematic that this analogous application cannot be

---

[20] Article 4.76 of the Lithuanian Civil Code: Rights and duties of co-owners in possession and maintenance of common partial ownership: Each of the co-owners in proportion to their respective shares shall have the right to the profits obtained from a thing (property), shall be accountable to third persons in relation to duties related to a thing (property), held in co-ownership and shall pay expenses related to its maintenance and preservation, taxes, dues and other payments. If one of the co-owners fails to fulfil the obligation to maintain and take care of a thing (property), the other co-owners shall have the right to a compensation for losses thus incurred.

[21] See K. BOELE-WOELKI, F. SCHONEWILLE and W. SCHRAMA, 'National report: The Netherlands', The property relations between the spouses, available at: ceflonline.net/country-reports-for-the-netherlands/, at p. 6-7.

[22] J. DE BOER, *Asser/De Boer, Personen- en familierecht*, Kluwer, Deventer, 2010, at no. 569.

enforced. Whether or not a court decides to base its decision on a provision by analogy falls within the discretion of the court. So far, the courts have not explicitly used Art. 1:84 Dutch Civil Code by analogy.

Contractual freedom and party autonomy are thus the leading principles in this respect, rather than the solidarity model for couples in a formal relationship. Notarial cohabitation contracts often include a clause on household expenses.[23] Mostly, these contracts seem to use a pro rata division of these costs. Practically more important is a clause in notarial cohabitation contracts that a claim for the reimbursement of paid costs for the household is limited in time, mostly a year.[24] This is especially relevant after a separation of the partners, since claims are limited to a short period of time.

Without a cohabitation contract, no specific rules apply, leaving the partners in an unclear position, even though the amounts of money involved are usually substantial. As long as the couple are happy together, generally no problems arise. However, after a separation partners might wish to reclaim certain amounts they contributed to the household expenses, especially in the case of an uneven division of these costs. The duty to contribute is governed by the law of obligations, which primarily regulates economic transactions between contract parties and which is not particularly suitable for the situation of partners in a loving relationship. Do cohabiting partners, just like married and registered couples, have to contribute according to their respective financial situations? Or is the rule that both partners have to pay half of all the costs, irrespective of their financial means, as would follow from the strict application of contract law? This is not clear and a growing body of case law demonstrates that it is an issue worth fighting for, since it is uncertain what the courts will rule.[25] In the legal doctrine it has been argued that although on the basis of contract law both partners are under a duty to contribute half of the expenses, it is more realistic to use a basic rule of an income-related approach.[26]

---

[23] W.M. SCHRAMA, P. KUIK and L.C.A. VERSTAPPEN, 'Samenlevingsovereenkomsten in de notariële praktijk', *Familie&Recht*, 2014, available at: familieenrecht.nl, at 14.1 and 14.2.

[24] P. BLOKLAND, in: W.D. KOLKMAN and L.C.A. VERSTAPPEN (eds.), *Handboek Familie-vermogensrecht*, Walburg pers, Zutphen, 2013, at 4.2.1.4.

[25] Hof Amsterdam 19 June 2007, LJN BA9165; Hof 's-Gravenhage 24 November 2009, LJN BK474; Hof 's-Gravenhage 17 August 2010, LJN BN4682; Hof Amsterdam 31 July 2012, ECLI:NL:GHAMS:2012:CA3064. See about the different issues to be discerned: W.M. SCHRAMA, 'Ongehuwd samenwonen en kosten van de huishouding', *Tijdschrift voor Erfrecht*, 2011, pp. 78-82.

[26] W.M. SCHRAMA, 'Rechten en plichten van informele partners', in: M.L.C.C. DE BRUIJN-LÜCKERS et al. (eds.), *Relatierecht, SDUCommentaar*, SDU, The Hague, 2014, at

Of crucial importance is whether it is possible to reclaim these costs after a relationship breakdown. If the answer is that is not, the issue of how these costs should be borne by the partners during their relationship is less relevant. In some cases the courts rule that it is possible to reclaim these costs only for the year prior to the separation.[27] However, in other cases, claims are in principle accepted by the courts.[28] The Supreme Court has not yet been in the position to provide any clarity in this respect.

NORWAY

Partners to an informal relationship are not under any general duty to contribute to the costs and expenses of their household.

PORTUGAL

There is no such general legal duty.

RUSSIA

No. There is no general duty under Russian law to contribute to the costs and expenses of the household. Even spouses have no such general duty. Partners are, however, jointly and severally liable for the costs related to the family home, in particular:

- Costs related to the home owned by one of the partners, provided that the other partner is acknowledged as a member of the owner's family under Art. 31 Russian Housing Code. In such cases, the partners are jointly and severally liable for all the costs related to the use of the home (Art. 292(1) Russian Civil Code, Art. 31(3) Russian Housing Code);
- Costs related to a home rented by one of the partners as a social tenant, provided that the other partner is acknowledged as a member of the social tenant's family under Art. 69 Russian Housing Code. In

p.1991-2004; W.M. SCHRAMA, 'Ongehuwd samenwonen en kosten van de huishouding', *Tijdschrift voor Erfrecht*, 2011, pp. 78-82.

27 Hof 's-Hertogenbosch 23 June 2009, LJN BI9975 ruled that case law of the Supreme Court (HR 29 April 1994, NJ 1995, 561) on the conditions for reclaiming costs after a relationship breakdown is equally applicable to non-marital partners; Hof Amsterdam 16 October 2012, ECLI:NL:GHAMS:2012:CA298; Hof 's-Gravenhage 17 August 2010, LJN BN46782.

28 Hof Den Bosch 28 January 2014, ECLI:NL:GHSHE:2014:173.

such cases, the partners are jointly and severally liable for all debts arising from the social rental contract (Art. 69(2) Russian Housing Code);
- Costs related to a home rented by one of the partners as a commercial tenant, provided that the partners have entered into an agreement on joint and several liability for all debts arising from the commercial tenancy (Art. 677(4) Russian Civil Code).

SCOTLAND

Scots law imposes no legal duty on parties to an informal relationship to contribute to household costs but nor is there any such obligation on couples in formal relationships. This is entirely a matter for individual agreement. There is some commentary in cohabitation cases, which reiterates this point. It is observed, for example, in *Harley v Thompson*[29] where, one partner was financially better off than the other and as a result contributed more to living costs of the couple:

> 'The pursuer has deeper pockets and she knowingly committed to a relationship where she would inevitably be the main breadwinner. Any negative impact on the pursuer's financial position is part and parcel of family life ... Any loss should lie where it falls.'[30]

SLOVAKIA

No.

SLOVENIA

Legislation does not have such an explicit provision for marital partners that could also be used for extramarital partners, but a duty to contribute to the costs and expenses of their household derives from general rules by which partners have a duty of mutual assistance (Art. 44 of the Slovenian Marriage Act) and to contribute within their means to the maintenance of the family (Art. 49 of the Slovenian Marriage Act).

---

29 *Harley v Thompson* 2014 GWD 36-673.

30 *Harley v Thompson* 2014 GWD 36-673, at para. 8.

SPAIN

Neither the Spanish nor the Catalan Civil Codes foresee any general duty to contribute to the costs and expenses of the common household in the absence of agreement. The Catalan Law on stable couples (1998), that was in force before the enactment of Book II Catalan Civil Code (2010), established a duty to contribute to common expenses, for which the partners were jointly and severally liable. This provision was removed and present legislation concentrates mainly on the effects after break-up.

SWEDEN

No, there is no general duty to contribute to costs and expenses of the household when living together in an informal relationship. In practice, see under Question 20, the cohabitees usually contribute to these costs, in equal shares or in relation to their ability to pay. As indicated in the previous answers (in particular to Question 8), the focus in Swedish legislation on unmarried cohabitation has been to protect the mutual rights in respect of a joint dwelling and household goods acquired for the couple's joint use.

SWITZERLAND

In Switzerland, partners in an informal relationship are under no general duty to contribute to the costs and expenses of their household.

QUESTION 22

Does a partner in an informal relationship have a right to remain in the home against the will of the partner who is the owner or the tenant of the home?

AUSTRIA

In general, no obligation to live together arises from an informal relationship. Accordingly, a right of residence cannot be assumed.[1] After the informal relationship has terminated, the partner who is the owner or the tenant of the home can seek the vacation of the apartment and is entitled to file an action for possession.[2] Such a claim will only be dismissed if the court considers it frivolous, e.g. the claim was only filed in order to harm the ex-partner.[3]

Hence, a partner, who has no independent right concerning the home, is not entitled to remain in this home against the will of the other partner, rather he/she has to move out voluntarily, if he/she does not want to be confronted with a respective claim.

BELGIUM

A partner is not entitled to remain in the other partner's home against the latter's will in the absence of specific legal provisions or of a (lease) agreement. Some of the case law does however consider the partner to be a tenant at will and would grant him some respite during which he is entitled to remain in the home (against payment).[4]

---

1 A. DEIXLER-HÜBNER, 'Rechtliche Regelungen für Lebensgemeinschaften im Innenverhältnis', *iFamZ*, 2012, at p. 194.

2 Austrian Supreme Court, Legal Propositions RS0011874 and RS0010337, see e.g. Judgement of 22.10.2010, 9 Ob 69/10b, Judgement of 19.11.2008, 3 Ob 202/08i.

3 Austrian Supreme Court, Legal Proposition RS0010345, see e.g. Judgement of 21.11.2013, 1 Ob 181/13v.

4 Justice of the Peace Bruges (1) 2 June 2005, *TGR-TWVR* 2005, 170; Justice of the Peace Wavre (2) 23 January 2007, *T.Vred.* 2009, 364; Justice of the Peace Halle 23 July 2008, *NJW* 2009, 136, with note VERSCHELDEN. Cf. on the basis of a right of habitation: Justice of the Peace Waremme 16 April 1987, *JL* 1987, 1987, 1577.

BULGARIA

The partner in an informal relationship does not have a right to remain in the home against the will of the partner who is the owner of the home. These relations are not the subject of a specific regulation and the ordinary legislation should apply. The Bulgarian Property Law (1951, last amended in 2014) provides protection for the owner to dispose of his/her property or to evict anyone who hinders his/her property rights (Art. 108-109, para. 1).

The legislation on the renting of homes in Bulgaria does not regulate the rights of partners in an informal relationship. The rights of tenants are governed by the general legislation – the Bulgarian Obligations and Contracts Law (Art. 228-239).

In case the home is a state property, the Bulgarian State Property Act (1996, last amended in 2014) will apply. Only a civil servant and his/her family can apply to rent a state owned home conditional to the existence of the circumstances listed in the Bulgarian State Property Act (Art. 22). The Act does not provide for a legal definition of the terms 'family' and 'family member' but the interpretation of some relevant provisions suggests that the meaning is only 'family based on a marriage' (see Art. 29 of the Implementing Regulations to the Act).

The regulations of the Bulgarian Municipal Property Act (1996, last amended in 2014) are similar. Each municipality passes its own regulations on municipal housing policy. Usually, the access to municipal housing is based on proven individual or family (married) needs. The Act sets out grounds for the termination of the rental contract. In addition, the rental contract determines the rights and obligations of tenants.

CROATIA

A partner in an informal relationship (a cohabitant as well as a same-sex partner) does not have the right to remain in the home against the will of the partner who is the owner or the tenant of the home.

CZECH REPUBLIC

A partner to an informal relationship does not generally have a right to remain in the home against the will of the partner who is the owner or the tenant of the home.

Only in a case of domestic violence, if one of the partners is a victim of domestic violence (even if this partner is not the owner or the tenant of the home), according to S. 400 et seq. of the Czech Act on special judicial proceedings, Act n. 292/2013 Col. does that partner have a right to ask for court protection or, according to S. 44(2) of the Act No. 273/2008 Coll., on the Police of the Czech Republic, have a right to ask for police protection.

Court protection: an application for a preliminary injunction must also include a statement of the facts showing that the petitioner and the respondent live together in a house or apartment in which there is a shared household which, for the petitioner, has become unbearable because of physical or mental violence against the petitioner or another who lives in the common household, or a statement of the facts which demonstrates the unwanted stalking or harassing of the petitioner (S. 402(1) Czech Act on special judicial proceedings). The court has a duty to decide about the proposal of the victim within 48 hours without a hearing. A preliminary injunction lasts one month from its inception but can be extended.

Court protection and police protection for the victims of domestic violence are independent of each other.

DENMARK

Owner: The owner of property has a right to remain in his or her property and can have his or her cohabitant removed from the property with the help of a bailiff.

Tenant: A tenant can have his or her cohabitant removed from the property with the help of a bailiff, unless the cohabitant can show that it is probable that there are such special reasons that he or she should be entitled to continue the tenancy pursuant to S. 77a of the Danish Tenancy Act, i.e. that there has been at least 2 years' cohabitation and that consideration for the interests of young children favour the cohabitant continuing to live in the rented property.[5]

5 See *Ugeskrift for Retsvæsen* (Weekly Law Journal) 2001, at p. 1907.

ENGLAND AND WALES

They do not have such a right but that partner can apply for an occupation order under S. 36 English Family Law Act 1996. This is commonly used where there is domestic violence although in theory violence is not a pre-requisite. The court is guided by the criteria in S. 36(6), namely, it must have regard to all the circumstances including:

- each party's housing needs and resources and of any relevant child;
- the financial resources of each of the parties;
- the likely effect of the decision of the court on the health, safety or well-being of the parties and any relevant child;
- the conduct of the parties;
- the length of time since they lived together;
- the nature of the parties relationship and the level of commitment involved in it;
- the length of the cohabitation;
- whether they have children together; the length of time since they separated, and
- the existence of any Children Act 1989 or property proceedings.

Only if they successfully apply for an occupation order to remain in the home, which can only be granted for a maximum of 12 months (6 months with a possible extension for a further maximum of 6 months) if the cohabitant is not a joint owner (or tenant), can they remain in the home. The only other possibility is to apply for a transfer of tenancy order.

- Rented family home
  Schedule VII English Family Law Act 1996 also allows applications for a transfer of tenancy order between cohabitants of the rented family home on relationship breakdown. This is also at the discretion of the court. A big issue is that this needs to be filed at court before the tenant or joint tenant partner gives notice to quit the tenancy to the landlord as this will determine the tenancy. (If the home is jointly rented either partner can give notice and terminate the whole tenancy.) The court applies the same criteria as for an occupation order under S. 36(6) above plus the circumstances in which the tenancy was granted and the suitability of the parties as tenants must be considered.

- Owner-occupied family home
  With regard to the owner occupied home, the only possibility of the non-owner remaining in occupation longer term is to show they have

a beneficial interest in the home under a constructive trust by making an application under S. 14 of the English Trusts of Land and Appointment of Trustees Act 1996 and even then, it will be difficult to remain in the home as the court will be likely to order sale and a division of the proceeds, particularly if there are no children.

This statutory provision and the criteria for determining applications set out in S. 15 are considered by the court alongside the law developed by the courts around common intention constructive trusts and previously, (and perhaps still where there is a mixed family and commercial investment) resulting trusts, where the respective proportion of the parties' financial contributions alone would indicate the likely shares, to determine whether a cohabitant has a beneficial share in a property which is formally legally owned by their partner/former partner. (This is typically the family home although it can be used in respect of any property.) If this is established, then the formal legal owner holds the home on trust for themselves and their partner in the shares determined by the court. This beneficial interest gives a right of occupation.

Where there are children of the relationship under 18, applications can be made under S. 15 and Schedule 1 English Children Act 1989 for a transfer of property order or a settlement of property for the benefit of the child.

The most common order under Schedule 1 English Children Act 1989 is for the home to be retained by the owner but held on trust to permit the occupation by the ex-partner and children of the family until the youngest child reaches the age of 18 or finishes their full-time education. This is known as a *Mesher* order and is at the discretion of the court. At the end of the *Mesher* period, the home will revert to the owner partner and the non-owner partner can gain no share in the home. It does provide for occupation after the separation where the resources of the parties permit this.

ESTONIA

According to Estonian laws, the partner in an informal relationship has no right under the law to remain in the home after the end of the cohabitation if the partner, who is the owner of the dwelling or the person who is entitled to use it, does not consent to this.

FINLAND

Generally not, if the home is owned solely by the unwilling partner and the home is in the form of a limited liability housing company (*asunto-osakeyhtiö/bostadsaktiebolag*) or real estate. However, according to S. 53 of the Finnish Act on Residential Leases (481/1995), one spouse alone cannot terminate a lease agreement without the other spouse's consent. According to the Act, persons living together as husband and wife without marriage are also considered as spouses and both spouses shall be heard in any matter related to the apartment where they both live, if this is considered necessary (S. 11). If the spouse withholds his or her consent without acceptable cause, the court may nevertheless authorise the termination of the lease agreement. If persons who are not marital spouses have rented the apartment for use as their joint home, the court may, upon request, order that the person or persons who have the greatest need for the apartment shall continue to hold the lease (S. 48). However, this option can only be used if the cohabiting spouses have rented the apartment together. If the spouses were married, the Court could issue the order regardless of who has signed the lease agreement.

Similarly, according to S. 41 of the Finnish Right-of-Occupancy Housing Act (650/1990), both spouses must be given a hearing in matters concerning the apartment they use as their joint residence, regardless of the fact that the right is owned by one partner alone.

FRANCE

No. If the relationship comes to an end, French law does not give the partner who is not the owner or the tenant of the home the right to remain in the home against the will of the partner who is the owner. Whether the partners have common children or not does not make any difference.

However, Art. 373-2-2 of the French Civil Code states that child maintenance can take the form of a right of use (*droit d'usage*) or a housing right (*droit d'habitation*), so that indirectly through the maintenance of the child, the other partner living with the child can remain in the home belonging to the other partner. However, this cannot happen against the will of the partner who is the owner or the tenant of the home.

Where the partner who is the owner of the home claims for compensation for occupancy because the female partner is staying in the home with the common children, the Court of cassation has held that the lower court must examine whether this free occupancy is a way in which the father fulfils (or enforces) his duty to maintain the children.[6]

GERMANY

A partner to an informal relationship does not have a right to remain in the home against the will of the partner who is the owner or the tenant of the home. A partner does not have a legal position (ownership) of his or her own against the other partner. The partner is a co-possessor in the sense of §§ 854 et seq. German Civil Code even if he or she is not a party to the tenancy (cf. Question 23).[7] This, however, gives the partner a claim for the protection of this co-possession and a claim against a forceful ejection, but not a right to stay.

GREECE

No, unless there is a pre-existing agreement on concessional use (e.g. as a loan of use or a lease) and the said agreement has not been terminated. In all other cases, the partner is regarded as a guest, with no consequences in the law.

HUNGARY

Although the Family Law Book regulates the use of the common dwelling even when one cohabitant is the owner or tenant, there is no rule on the use of the other cohabitant's own dwelling or where he or she is the only tenant during the community of life.

REPUBLIC OF IRELAND

A partner in an informal relationship has no automatic right to remain in the home against the will of the other partner who is the owner/tenant of the home. Their relationship alone does not give rise to any property rights in the home or rights of occupation.

Furthermore, cohabiting families do not have the benefit of the Irish Family Home Protection Act 1976 which applies only to married families. This means that property owned solely by one parent and being used as a

---

6 Cass. Civ. I, 6 July 2011, no. 10-27070, *RTD civ.* 2011, p. 749, with note HAUSER.

7 G. BRUDERMÜLLER, 'Einl. vor § 1297', in: O. PALANDT, *Bürgerliches Gesetzbuch*, Beck, Munich, 2015, at No. 18.

family home by the cohabiting couple can be sold without the consent of the other parent.

Section 174 of the Irish Civil Partnership and Certain Rights and Obligations of Cohabitants Act 2010, however, provides for the making of Property Adjustment Orders in respect of qualified cohabitants. The gives the court power to transfer the interest which one qualified cohabitant holds in a property to the other partner. It may also vary, extinguish or reduce the interest of either of the cohabitants under an agreement they made pursuant to S. 202 of the Irish 2010 Act. Section 74(2) provides, however, that before the court makes any Property Adjustment Order that it considers whether the financial needs of the qualified cohabitant would be met by either a Compensatory Maintenance Order (S. 175) or a Pension Adjustment Order (S. 187).

ITALY

At the end of the relationship, the partner who is not the owner of the home may be asked to leave by the other partner. The latter, however, in case the non-owner refuses to leave, cannot make use of the actions to recover possession provided by Art. 1168 Italian Civil Code,[8] because the cohabitant is considered to be a qualified holder (*detentore qualificato*) and not just a licensee.[9]

Possessory action being precluded, the owner can therefore make use of an ordinary action to contest the partner's occupation on the grounds of being without title. However, if the cohabitation has become unsustainable, the owner can start urgent proceedings (Art. 700 of the Italian Code of Civil Procedure).[10]

These rules also apply when a partner is the sole tenant of the home. It would then be advisable, in order to protect the informal partner's right to housing, that the lease contract be signed by both partners.

---

8 Only a rather old decision, given the specific circumstances of the case, allowed the owner to make use of a possessory action (Pret. Firenze 26 October 1990, in *Giur. Merito*, 1992, p. 861).

9 This interpretative trend is now prevailing, although some decisions still deny the cohabitant the designation of qualified possessor. The debate and the current solutions are discussed by G. OBERTO, *I diritti dei conviventi. Realtà e prospettive tra Italia ed Europa*, Cedam, Padua, 2012, at p. 189.

10 Pret. Milano 31 March 1990, in *Foro Pad.* 1990, I, c. 363; Trib. Messina 10 September 1997, in *Fam. Dir.* 1998, p. 255; Pret. Pisa 30 March 1990, in *Foro. It.* 1991, I, c. 329.

This is completely different, however, if the couple have children. See infra the answer to Question 43.

LATVIA

In Latvia there is no such specific legal order on informal relationships.

LITHUANIA

Article 3.234 of the Lithuanian Civil Code, part 5, provides that the dwelling or the apartment which belonged to one of the cohabitees before their life together can be occupied by the other cohabitee under a right of usufruct if he or she has underage children born to the cohabitation or due to health, age or other important reasons does not have his or her own dwelling.

Article 3.235 of the Lithuanian Civil Code defines the right to use a dwelling: Having regard to the duration of the cohabitation, the interests of the minor children of the cohabitees, the age, health, financial situation of the cohabitees and other important circumstances, the court shall have a right to award the use of the rented dwelling to the cohabitee who is in greater need of that dwelling. Having regard to the circumstances of the case, the court may oblige the cohabitee who has been awarded the right to use the rented dwelling to pay compensation to the other cohabitee for the expenses incurred in looking for and moving to another dwelling.

We should note that these rules are not applied in practice, therefore there have been cases when the courts have applied different legal norms by a parity of reasoning with exclusive consideration being given to the interests of minors. For instance, in 2006 the Lithuanian Supreme Court examined a case where the claimant (the child's mother), with whom the child was determined to reside, had requested that a right of usufruct to the apartment owned by the defendant (the child's father) be established. As the child's father and mother had never been married, the Court had to decide whether Art. 3.71 of the Lithuanian Civil Code[11] could also be

[11] In order to protect the child's right to a place to live, Art. 3.71 of the Lithuanian Civil Code provides for the right of an underage child to use a dwelling when the child's parents divorce: '[w]here the matrimonial dwelling is owned by one of the spouses, the court may make an usufruct order and allow the other spouse to remain in the matrimonial dwelling if their minor children live with him or her. The usufruct order shall be valid until the child (children) attain majority.' This legal regime may not be changed by an agreement of the spouses.

applicable when a child is born out of wedlock; therefore, the Lithuanian Supreme Court stated that '[t]he European Convention on the Legal Status of Children Born out of Wedlock, and the constitutional principle of equality between persons (paragraph 1 of Art. 29 of the Lithuanian Constitution), substantiate the necessity to equally defend the rights of children belonging to both married and unmarried parents ... Taking into account that there is no rule of law directly providing for guarantees for the rights of children belonging to unmarried parents and parents who have not registered their partnership with regard to the right to use a dwelling place, ... the effective Art. 3.71 of the Lithuanian Civil Code, which provides for such guarantees protecting children's rights when the child's parents are married, is to be applied by analogy'. In rejecting the respondent's arguments that the establishment of a usufruct would be in conflict with the principle of the inviolability of his property provided for in Art. 23 of the Lithuanian Constitution, the Court noted that 'this principle is not absolute and the restriction can be imposed on a person's property on the grounds provided for in the law, inter alia for protection of children's rights and interests, giving an underage child the right to use a dwelling by the right of usufruct.'[12]

LUXEMBOURG

No, the partner does not have a right to remain in the home as a principle (for exceptions see the answer to Question 23).

THE NETHERLANDS

There is no specific rule in the Dutch Civil Code to this effect. One could argue that given the special nature of the relationship between partners, the partner who owns or rents the home is not entitled to refuse access to the house to his partner. Maybe, the general provision (Art. 3:13 Dutch Civil Code) on abuse of right could play a role. However, there is no case law on this subject, which might be explained by the fact that partners do not usually go to court during their relationship.

NORWAY

When 'strong reasons' so indicate, a partner to an informal relationship (and other people living together in a household) may purchase what was previously the common residence and household goods at market

[12] Ruling of the Lithuanian Supreme Court of 26 April 2006, civil case No. 3K-3-302/2006.

value upon the termination of the household, pursuant to the Norwegian Household Community Act, S. 3. On the same strict conditions, a cohabitant may obtain the right to enter into a tenancy agreement even if the contract is established in the name of the other cohabitant. As the cohabitant is obliged to pay the market price and the conditions – 'strong reasons' – are strict, the Norwegian Household Community Act is not used very often. Sometimes the act is misused to permit one party to remain in the home even if there is no intention to buy out the other party.

PORTUGAL

The partner who wants to remain in the home against the will of the partner who is the owner may file a petition at the courts, on the grounds of Art. 4, of Law No. 7/2001 and Art. 1793 of the Portuguese Civil Code. The court will consider the necessity of both partners and their children. The rules are also applicable if the house is jointly owned. The petitioner may remain as a tenant.

The partner who wants to remain in the home against the will of the partner who is the tenant may file a petition at the courts, on the grounds of Art. 4, of Law No. 7/2001 and Art. 1105 of the Portuguese Civil Code. The court will consider the necessities of both partners and their children besides 'other relevant factors'. The rules are also applicable if both are equally tenants. The petitioner may remain as the tenant or the sole tenant.

RUSSIA

The position of an informal partner varies, depending on whether the other partner is the owner or the tenant of the home, and then depending on the type of tenancy.

If the other partner is the owner of the home, the right of the non-owning partner depends on whether he/she is granted the status of being a member of the owner's family [13] and thus covered by the regime provided for in Art. 292 Russian Civil Code and Art. 31 Russian Housing Code.[14]

---

13 See М.А. Димитраев, 'Особенности правового положения членов семьи собственника жилого помещения', *Семейное и жилищное право*, 2011, at p. 12-16.

14 Жилищный кодекс РФ (ЖК РФ) от 29.12.2004 N 188-ФЗ. Available at: www.consultant.ru/popular/housing/55_6.html#p565.

Under Art. 31(1) Russian Housing Code, the owner's spouse, children and parents, provided that they reside with him/her, are unconditionally regarded as family members. Other relatives and disabled dependants residing with the owner and, under exceptional circumstances, also other persons residing with the owner may be recognised as family members. The informal partner of the owner falls into this latter, more problematic category and may be granted the status of a family member of the owner, either in an agreement between the partners or, in the event of a dispute, by a court order. The Russian Supreme Court has stressed that, in the absence of a clear agreement, it is not the factual instalment of the informal partner in the home, but rather the partner-owner's intention to install him or her in the home as a member of his/her family that is decisive for being granted the status of a family member.[15] According to the Russian Supreme Court, such intention can be derived from the nature of the relationship between the partners (joint household, mutual support) and this can be proved by all forms of evidence admitted by the Russian Code of Civil Procedure.[16]

An informal partner who is not granted the status of a family member of the owner enjoys no protection at all. An informal partner who is granted such a status enjoys relatively extensive protection.

An informal partner of the owner who is acknowledged as a member of the owner's family has the same right to occupy the home as the owner, unless stated otherwise in an agreement between the partners (Art. 31(2) Russian Housing Code). If the right of the partner to occupy the home is violated, he/she may seek protection against any person causing this violation, including the owner (Art. 292(3) Russian Civil Code). That means that as long as the relationship lasts, the non-owning partner may remain in the home, even against the will of the partner-owner.

Under Art. 31(4) Russian Housing Code, however, the rights of a member of the owner's family to occupy the home cease to exist once the family relationship ends. According to the Russian Supreme Court,[17] proof of

---

15 Постановление Пленума Верховного Суда РСФСР от 2 июля 2009 года № 14 'О некоторых вопросах, возникших в судебной практике при применении Жилищного кодекса Российской Федерации', at p. 11.

16 Постановление Пленума Верховного Суда РСФСР от 2 июля 2009 года № 14 'О некоторых вопросах, возникших в судебной практике при применении Жилищного кодекса Российской Федерации', at p. 11.

17 Постановление Пленума Верховного Суда РСФСР от 2 июля 2009 года № 14 'О некоторых вопросах, возникших в судебной практике при применении Жилищного кодекса Российской Федерации', at p. 13.

the end of a marital relationship is demonstrated by divorce, while the end of an informal relationship can be proven by circumstances such as the partners no longer living together, no longer running a joint household and/or no longer supporting each other. However, as Art. 31(1) Russian Housing Code does not require the running of the same household for a partner to be acknowledged as a member of the owner's family, a decision by partners to divide their household can only constitute proof of the end of their family relationship if this occurs in conjunction with the other circumstances.[18] To sum up: unless the agreement between the partners provides otherwise, partners cease to be regarded as family members once they separate and the non-owing partner then loses his/her right to occupy the home owned by the other partner (Art. 35(1) Russian Housing Code). He/she can then be evicted by a court order upon an application to this effect by the partner-owner.

However, Art. 35(1) Russian Housing Code also provides for an exception to this rule, whereby protection is granted to a member of the owner's family if that person has neither any other home nor any entitlement to acquire one, if he/she is unable to provide him/herself with another home due to his/her financial situation (insufficient income or property) or other circumstances (e.g. unemployment, disability, study or the need to care for young children).[19] A non-owning partner who falls within this category can request the court to grant him or her a right of temporary occupation of the home owned by the other (ex)-partner. The court will then determine the permitted duration of such occupation by taking account of all circumstances of the case and the principles of reasonableness and fairness.[20]

If the other partner is a tenant, the rights of the non-tenant partner depend on whether the tenancy is a commercial tenancy or a social tenancy.

If the other partner is a social tenant (i.e. he/she rents a home belonging to the state or municipal housing fund and that is designated for social

18 Постановление Пленума Верховного Суда РСФСР от 2 июля 2009 года № 14 'О некоторых вопросах, возникших в судебной практике при применении Жилищного кодекса Российской Федерации', at p. 13.

19 Постановление Пленума Верховного Суда РСФСР от 2 июля 2009 года № 14 'О некоторых вопросах, возникших в судебной практике при применении Жилищного кодекса Российской Федерации', at p. 15 (b).

20 Постановление Пленума Верховного Суда РСФСР от 2 июля 2009 года № 14 'О некоторых вопросах, возникших в судебной практике при применении Жилищного кодекса Российской Федерации', at p. 15 (b).

use), the rights of the non-tenant partner depend on whether he/she is granted the status of a member of the tenant's family and, therefore, is covered by the regime provided for in Art. 69-71 of the Russian Housing Code.

Under Art. 69(1) Russian Housing Code, the tenant's spouse, children and parents residing with him/her are unconditionally regarded as family members. Other relatives and disabled dependants residing with the tenant are regarded as family members if they live in the home as family members of the tenant and run a joint household with the tenant. Under exceptional circumstances, other persons residing with the tenant may also be acknowledged as family members. The informal partner of the tenant again falls within this last, more problematic category and may be granted the status of a family member of the tenant only if the following conditions (as stated in Art. 70 Russian Housing Code) are met:

- The partners live together;
- The partners run a joint household. As this rule is designated not just for informal partners but for any persons, the law does not require affective or marriage-like relationships. However, the case law does take account of the nature of personal relationships [21] and an informal partner may therefore have a greater possibility of being recognised as a family member than, for instance, a nanny;
- The partner has been formally installed in the home by the tenant. This can occur in two ways:
    - At the moment of entering into the social tenancy contract: by listing the partner in the contract as a member of the tenant's family who intends to occupy the home with him/her (Art. 69(3) Russian Housing Code);
    - At a later moment: with the consent of all family members residing in the home and the consent of the landlord (Art. 70(1) Russian Housing Code). The landlord therefore has the right to refuse the instalment if the home is too small for the requested number of people (according to the municipal norms for social tenancies). The refusal of consent by family members cannot be overruled by a court order, while the refusal of consent by the landlord can be overruled by a court.[22]

---

[21] Е.А. СУХАНОВ (ed.), *Гражданское право*, Т. 3, Wolters Kluwer, Moscow, 2008, at p. 567.

[22] Постановление Пленума Верховного Суда РСФСР от 2 июля 2009 года № 14 'О некоторых вопросах, возникших в судебной практике при применении Жилищного кодекса Российской Федерации', at p. 26.

- The partner is granted the status of a member of the tenant's family by a court order.

The Russian Supreme Court has stressed that, according to the law, an informal partner can be acknowledged as a member of the tenant's family only in exceptional circumstances and only by means of a court order. When deciding on such cases, the courts must take into consideration circumstances such as the intention of the tenant to install the partner in the home as a member of his/her family, the duration of the cohabitation, the fact of sharing the same household, and whether the non-tenant partner has another home.[23]

An informal partner who has acquired the status of a member of the tenant's family enjoys exactly the same rights as the tenant (Art. 672 Russian Civil Code). This rule is mandatory and cannot be set aside by an agreement.

Therefore, although the law refers to the tenant and his/her family members, the literature rightly speaks of the joint tenancy of all family members.[24]

If the family relationship between the tenant and the family member ends and the ex-family member continues to occupy the home, he/she retains the occupational rights (Art. 69(4) Russian Housing Code). Therefore, once an informal partner acquires the status of being a member of the tenant's family, he/she retains the right to occupy (part of) the home, independent of the will of the partner-tenant, even after the relationship has ended.

If the other partner is a commercial tenant (i.e. rents a home in the private housing market), the rights of the non-tenant partner depend on the intention of the partner-tenant. The non-tenant partner's entitlement is based on the contract between the partner-tenant and the landlord.[25] The partner-tenant can list his/her informal partner in the initial rental contact as one of the people intending to occupy the home (Art. 677(2) Russian Civil Code) or can install him/her at a later date, subject to the

23 Постановление Пленума Верховного Суда РСФСР от 2 июля 2009 года № 14 'О некоторых вопросах, возникших в судебной практике при применении Жилищного кодекса Российской Федерации', at p. 25.

24 Е.А. Суханов (ed.), *Гражданское право*, Т. 3, Wolters Kluwer, Moscow, 2008, at p. 565.

25 Е.С. Крюкова, 'Правовое положение лиц, проживающих с нанимателем по договорам социального и коммерческого найма: сравнительный анализ', *Семейное и жилищное право*, 2006, at p. 17.

consent of the landlord (Art. 679 Russian Civil Code). In both cases the non-tenant partner will then have the same right to occupy the home as the tenant-partner (Art. 677(2) Russian Civil Code). The right of the non-tenant partner to occupy the home after separation will depend on the provisions of the tenancy agreement and any agreement that may be reached between the partners. If no such provisions have been made, the non-tenant partner will retain his/her occupancy rights even against the will of the other partner.

The restrictive approach to acknowledging an informal partner as a member of the family of his/her partner who is a sole owner or sole tenant of the family home is not in compliance with the ECtHR's decision in the 2004 case of *Prokopovich v Russia*. Although this case was governed by the old 1983 Russian Housing Code, it continues to remain relevant. In this case, the European Court decided that the ten-year informal relationship between Ms. Prokopovich and her deceased partner fell under the protection of Art. 8 ECHR. Therefore Ms. Prokopovich was entitled to take over her deceased partner's social tenancy despite the fact that her instalment in the home did not satisfy the legal requirements of the old law (official registration).[26]

SCOTLAND

According to the general law of property, a non-entitled person has no legal right to remain in the home without the consent of the owner or tenant. The strict application of this rule, within the context of marriage, could be seen in the cases of *MacLure v MacLure* 1911 SC 200 and *Millar v Millar* 1940 SC 56 where the Scottish courts made it clear that in any dispute it was the patrimonial rather than the matrimonial relationship which was relevant. The entitled spouse could have the non-entitled spouse legally removed from the home in exactly the same way that he or she could remove a stranger. This approach applies equally to partners in an informal relationship. The only situation where a non-entitled cohabitant has the right to remain in the home against the will of the entitled cohabitant is where he or she has obtained statutory occupancy rights in terms of the Matrimonial Homes (Family Protection) (Scotland) Act 1981. These are discussed more fully in the answer to Question 23.

---

26 ECtHR, *Prokopovich v. Russia*, No. 58255/00, 18.11.04, at § 29.

SLOVAKIA

No.

SLOVENIA

After the cessation of a life union, a partner who is not the owner cannot remain in the home in which the partners lived during the extramarital union against the will of the partner who is the owner.

Partners who lived in rented accommodation must agree which of them will remain in that dwelling when both partners are named as tenants in the rental contract, or become the tenant of the accommodation when only one of the partners is named as the tenant in the rental contract and the other partner as a person who will use the accommodation with the tenant. If there is no agreement the courts will decide in a non-litigious procedure.

SPAIN

No, at least not during the relationship. After its termination, the partner might have a right to remain in the home, particularly if there are children and the partner who is not the owner or tenant is granted custody rights.

SWEDEN

Yes, if the relationship is subject to the Swedish Cohabitation Act (2003), (see above, answers to Question 2, 4 and 8) this situation is specially regulated. According to § 28 of the Swedish Cohabitation Act, a cohabitee may apply to court to be granted the right to remain in the home until the property distribution is carried out, but only on condition that the home is to be included in the property division. This is the case, according to § 3, if the home was acquired for the couple's joint use as their joint home. It does not matter which of the cohabitants is the owner or tenant of the home, or in charge of payments. If the home was acquired to serve as a joint home for the cohabitants, it will be subject to the division of the property upon the termination of the relationship.

There is also a rule in the Cohabitation Act, § 22, which gives the cohabitant in greater need of the dwelling the right to take it over, even when the dwelling is owned by the other cohabitee and even if it is not subject to the division of the property: however, this only applies on the condition that such a taking over can be regarded as reasonable. The owner must, however, be compensated for the dwelling's value. Mostly, the cohabitant in greater need of the home is considered to be the one who will have the custody, or the actual care, of the children, though this is not an absolute requirement. This provision is only applicable to a home that is subject to a tenancy or is an apartment in a cooperatively owned building. If the dwelling qualifies as 'real estate property' under Swedish law, usually a house with a piece of land, it is excluded from the scope of § 22.

SWITZERLAND

A partner in an informal relationship does not have a right to remain in the home against the will of the partner who is the sole owner or the sole tenant of the dwelling.

Rather, the entitled partner may evict the other partner at any time, having regard to the period of notice possibly given.[27] The relationship may be qualified as sub-letting (Art. 262 Swiss Code of Obligations), with the usual three-month period of notice (Art. 266c Swiss Code of Obligations). An extension of the sub-lease may be possible under certain circumstances (Art. 272 Swiss Code of Obligations). The relationship may further be qualified as a simple partnership (Art. 530 et seq. Swiss Code of Obligations), with the usual six-month period of notice (Art. 546 para. 1 Swiss Code of Obligations). Finally, it may be qualified as a loan for use, which is free of charge (Art. 305 et seq. Swiss Code of Obligations). However, in the case of a loan for use, dismissal without notice is possible (Art. 310 Swiss Code of Obligations), unless otherwise agreed.

[27] For details see H. HAUSHEER, T. GEISER and R. AEBI-MÜLLER, *Das Familienrecht des Schweizerischen Zivilgesetzbuches*, Stämpfli, Bern, 2014, at N 03.31 et seq.

QUESTION 23

Are there specific rules on a partner's right of occupancy of the home:

a. In cases of domestic violence?

b. In cases where the partner owing or renting the home is absent?

AUSTRIA

a. In cases of domestic violence?

Interim orders for protection against domestic violence can be requested by close relatives, including partners in an informal relationship under S. 382b Austrian Enforcement Act.[1] The interim order will be granted – irrespective of whether a title belongs to the applicant with regard to the home[2] – when physical attacks, threats of physical attacks or any conduct that severely affects the mental health of the applicant render a further cohabitation unbearable and the home is urgently needed by the applicant for his/her accommodation. The respondent is either ordered to leave the home or is prohibited from returning to the home. In most cases both orders are issued accumulatively.[3] The effect of such interim orders is limited to three months and will only be prolonged if proceedings have been commenced on the question of who is entitled to use the home.[4] If such proceedings have been initiated before the interim order was requested, the court has to determine its term of validity, at most until the end of the proceedings. In this time period the applicant

1 J. GEBERT and A. KOLLER, 'Die einstweilige Verfügung nach § 382b EO – effektiver Rechtsschutz gegen Gewalt in der nichtehelichen Lebensgemeinschaft?', *iFamZ*, 2008, at p. 154.

2 E. KODEK, 'section 382b Austrian Enforcement Act', in: P. ANGST, *Exekutionsordnung*, Manz Verlag, Vienna, 2008, at marg. No. 16.

3 E. KODEK, 'section 382b Austrian Enforcement Act', in: P. ANGST, *Exekutionsordnung*, Manz Verlag, Vienna, 2008, at marg. No. 10.

4 J. GEBERT and A. KOLLER, 'Die einstweilige Verfügung nach § 382b EO – effektiver Rechtsschutz gegen Gewalt in der nichtehelichen Lebensgemeinschaft?', *iFamZ*, 2008, at p. 154.

has a right to occupy the home, regardless of whether a title belongs to him/her regarding the home.

b. In cases where the partner owning or renting the home is absent?
A person's long absence does not affect the ownership structure or any other rights of disposal. Hence, if a partner in an informal relationship does not have his or her own title with regard to the home, no rights can be derived from the fact of being a partner in an informal relationship. Even if it can be presumed that the partners have concluded a sublease agreement, this agreement is only binding as between the partners and does not have any effect in relation to the tenant.[5] The only remedy available to the partner, who does not have a legal title, is the so-called trespass action *(Besitzstörungsklage)*, which protects the concrete possession regardless of the actual entitlement.[6] Accordingly, if someone disturbs or precludes the partner's possession without authorization (e.g. by changing the door locks), that partner can submit a trespass action, which does not however create any substantive rights.

BELGIUM

a. In cases of domestic violence?
The Public Prosecutor is competent to issue a temporary domestic exclusion order in case of a serious and imminent danger of domestic violence against another person who 'occupies the same residence' (*'occupe la meme residence'* Art. 3, § 1 Act of 15 May 2012). The order applies for 10 days and can be extended once with a maximum of three months by the Family Court (Art. 5, § 2 Act of 15 May 2012).

The Act does not regulate the occupant's right to remain in the residence, though. It refers to the applicable procedures to obtain an interim order between spouses and between legal cohabitants. Such a procedure does not exist between informal cohabitants and the general rules apply.

b. In cases where the partner owning or renting the home is absent?
Legal absence. The court may establish a presumption of absence when a person has not appeared at his/her domicile or residence for more than three months and no news has been received from him/her, so that uncertainty arises as to whether that person is alive or dead (Art. 112 Belgian Civil Code). If the presumably absent person did not appoint an

5 See S. PERNER, M. SPITZER and E. KODEK, *Bürgerliches Recht*, Manz Verlag, Vienna, 2012, at p. 232.
6 Section 339 General Austrian Civil Code; section 454 Austrian Code of Civil Procedure.

agent, the court may appoint an administrator (Art. 113 Belgian Civil Code). Contrary to guardianship over incapacitated adults (Art. 496/3 Belgian Civil Code), the informal partner is not preferably appointed as the administrator. There are no specific rules on the occupancy of the home. The administrator is nevertheless obliged to further execute the absent person's rights and obligations, also those arising from any natural obligation.[7]

De facto absence. No specific rules apply in case of a '*de facto* absence', for example hospitalisation or imprisonment. The hospitalised or imprisoned partner retains his/her legal capacity and, if necessary, protection as an incapacitated adult will have to be applied. The other partner will at least be considered as a tenant at will, in the absence of other applicable categories such as a right to habitation.[8]

BULGARIA

a. In cases of domestic violence?

Yes, there are such regulations. In cases of domestic violence the court may order the expulsion of the perpetrator (regardless of the kind of relationship – formal or informal) from the common home for a certain period of time (Art. 5, para. 1, point 2 of the Bulgarian Protection against Domestic Violence Act). Such an expulsion does not affect the property rights of the owner, but rather the court order should guarantee a temporary safe occupancy of the home by the victim of domestic violence.

b. In cases where the partner owning or renting the home is absent?

No, there is no specific regulation when the partner who owns or rents the home is absent, no matter what the reason for this absence may be. There are also no generally applicable rules – these are private matters.

CROATIA

a. In cases of domestic violence?

In line with Art. 3 paragraph 1 of the Act on Protection against Domestic Violence (Official Gazette no. 137/09, 14/10, 60/10), a family means,

7 Cf. with regard to guardianship Justice of the Peace Kortrijk (2) 16 August 1999, *RW* 2000-01, 667.

8 Justice of the Peace Waremme 16 April 1987, *JL* 1987, 1987, 1577; Justice of the Peace Bruges (1) 2 June 2005, *TGR-TWVR* 2005, 170; Justice of the Peace Halle 23 July 2008, *NJW* 2009, 136, with note VERSCHELDEN.

among other things, a woman and a man in cohabitation. A perpetrator of domestic violence may face a protection (restraining) order ordering him/her to move out of the apartment, house or other housing area (Art. 11 paragraph 2). Such a protection order is applicable to perpetrators of domestic violence who have acted violently towards another family member living in the same apartment, house or other housing area in case there is a danger that the perpetrator will behave abusively again (Art. 15 paragraph 1). This measure shall apply for at least one month and not longer than two years (Art. 15 paragraph 3).

According to Art. 6 paragraph 2 Croatian Partnership Act, this legal provision is also applicable to same-sex informal partners.

b. In cases where the partner owning or renting the home is absent?
There are no specific rules on a partner's rights of occupancy of the home in cases where the partner owning or renting the home is absent.

CZECH REPUBLIC

a. In cases of domestic violence?
No, there are no specific rules on a partner's right of occupancy of the home in cases of domestic violence, but there are general rules which could be used. If one of the partners is a victim of domestic violence, according to S. 400 et seq. of the Czech Act on special judicial proceedings, that partner has a right to ask for court protection. An application for a preliminary injunction must also include a statement of the facts showing that the petitioner and the respondent live together in a house or apartment in which there is a shared household which, for the petitioner, has become unbearable because of physical or mental violence against the petitioner or another who lives in the common household, or a statement of the facts which demonstrates the unwanted stalking or harassing of the petitioner (S. 402(1) Czech Act on special judicial proceedings). The court has a duty to decide about the proposal of the victim within 48 hours without a hearing. A preliminary injunction lasts one month from its inception but can be extended.

The substantive regulation is in S. 751-753 of the Czech Civil Code (Special provisions against domestic violence) which, in accordance with S. 3021 Czech Civil Code, is also applicable to partners in an informal relationship (S. 3021 Czech Civil Code: the provisions of S. 751-753 on domestic violence also apply to cohabitation of persons other than spouses).

According to S. 44(2) of the Act No. 273/2008 Coll., on the Police of the Czech Republic a victim of domestic violence also has a right to ask for police protection.

b. In cases where the partner owning or renting the home is absent?

No, there are no specific rules on a partner's right of occupancy of the home in cases where the partner owning or renting the home is absent. If the partner owning or renting the home is absent, the second partner has a right to stay in the home, because there is an assumption that the partner owning or renting the home is still alive. When the death is declared of an individual (S. 71(1) Czech Civil Code): On the application of a person with a legal interest in declaring an individual dead, a court is to declare the death of an individual who may be reasonably presumed to have died, and is to determine the date established as the date of his death), it negates the assumption that he is still alive for the purposes of occupancy by the other partner. As for S. 1669 Czech Civil Code: persons who enjoyed gratuitous provision for life in the household of the deceased until his death are entitled to the same provision for life for another three weeks after the deceased's death.

As for a lease, if one of the partners who is the lessee dies and there is no joint lease of the apartment, the lease passes to a member of the lessee's household who lived in the apartment on the day of the lessee's death and has no apartment of his own. If such a person is someone other than the lessee's spouse, partner, parent, sibling, son-in-law, daughter-in-law, child or grandchild, the lease passes to such a person only if the lessor consents to the passage of the lease to that person (S. 2279(1) Czech Civil Code). It means that in case of the death of one partner, the other has a right to stay in the apartment without the permission of the lessor. A lease of an apartment in such cases is to end no later than two years from the date of the passage of the lease (S. 2279(2) Czech Civil Code).

DENMARK

a. In cases of domestic violence?

In the event of violence or a threat of violence a member of the household can have the perpetrator ejected, i.e. the perpetrator can be prohibited from staying in their own home.[9] The prohibition is for a specified period of up to 4 weeks. In dealing with such an ejection, the police can detain a person who can reasonably be assumed to have behaved in a

9 See S. 8-10 of Act No. 112 of 3 February 2012.

threatening manner against a member of his or her household. Such detention may not be for longer than 24 hours.

Women who are victims of violence can obtain help from one of the 40 crisis centres for women that are spread across the country. The crisis centres offer temporary accommodation for women who are unable to stay in their own homes because of violence or the threat of violence. They can also bring their children. The crisis centres do not offer treatment. The women pay a small amount to stay in a crisis centre.

A recent report by a committee has pointed out that situations can arise where it can be appropriate to give a spouse or one of an unmarried cohabiting couple a right to have a decision made giving him or her the possibility of continuing to live, for a short period, in the residence where he or she have been living following the termination of their marriage or cohabitation, regardless of whether the party in question is not the owner (joint owner) or tenant (joint tenant) of the residence.[10] Such an interim decision on residence can be relevant where one of the spouses or cohabitants has been ejected from the residence and where there are children in common under the age of 18.

b. In cases where the partner owning or renting the home is absent?

A tenant is entitled to sublet a flat which is let exclusively for residential purposes, for a period not exceeding 2 years, where the absence of the tenant is temporary and is due to illness, business, studies, placement, etc., see S. 70(1) of the Danish Consolidating Act on Rent.[11]

If the tenant of a flat moves to a nursing home, sheltered housing, a care home or the like due to old age or illness, his or her partner has a right to continue the lease if the partners shared a household for at least two years immediately before the first partner moved; see S. 76 and 75(2) of the Danish Consolidating Act on Rent.

ENGLAND AND WALES

a. In cases of domestic violence?

Yes – under S. 36 English Family Law Act 1996 the non-owner may apply to remain in occupation and to exclude the partner. If the grounds are

10 See Commission Report No. 1552/2015, *Ægtefællers økonomiske forhold* (Financial relations between spouses), at p. 554-560.

11 An Act to consolidate the Rent Act; see Danish Consolidating Act No. 920 of 10 September 2004.

made out, occupation/exclusion can be ordered for up to 12 months – 6 months renewable for a further maximum period of 6 months.

The criteria are set out in S. 36(6): the court must have regard to all the circumstances including:

- each party's housing needs and resources and of any relevant child;
- the financial resources of each of the parties;
- the likely effect of the decision of the court on the health, safety or well-being of the parties and any relevant child;
- the conduct of the parties; the length of time since they lived together;
- the nature of the parties relationship and the level of commitment involved in it;
- the length of the cohabitation;
- whether they have children together;
- the length of time since they separated, and
- the existence of any Children Act 1989 or property proceedings.

The court must also have regard to the 'balance of harm test' to consider whether the applicant or child will suffer significant harm attributable to the respondent ex-partner if the order is not made; and whether the harm suffered by the applicant or child is likely to be as great or greater than the harm attributable to the conduct of the respondent ex-partner or child.

b. In cases where the partner owning or renting the home is absent?

It is a matter of speculation whether an application under S. 36 English Family Law Act 1996 could be made outside the domestic violence context, for example, upon the basis of the owner's absence. Whilst the Act does not specifically require violence or threats to have occurred to make an occupation order, the court must apply the criteria in S. 36(6) and consider the balance of harm test. This is a matter which is in the discretion of the court but it is likely to be more difficult to establish a successful claim outside the domestic violence context generally. More specifically the likelihood of significant harm attributable to the respondent ex-partner within the balance of harm test, may be difficult to show. The order can only last for a maximum of 12 months.

ESTONIA

a. In cases of domestic violence?

In the Estonian legislation there is no legal basis to continue to use the dwelling against the will of the owner of the dwelling or the person entitled to use it, if the parties live in an informal relationship.

b. In cases where the partner owning or renting the home is absent?

According to § 289 of Estonian Law of Obligations Act, in residential leasehold relationships the lessee of a dwelling has the right to accommodate in the leased dwelling his or her spouse, minor children and parents who are incapacitated for work without the consent of the lessor unless it is agreed in the leasehold contract that the lessee may only do so with the consent of the lessor. The partner in an informal relationship is not included in this list. At the same time, § 289 has been entitled 'Accommodation of family members of the lessee of a dwelling' and the partner in an informal relationship should be included within the term 'family member'. The legal literature has not adopted a certain stance with regard to whether the accommodation of a person who is not included in the list is an infringement of the lease contract – the right of the lessee to accommodate other people may be inferred from the nature of the lease contract.[12]

Upon the death of a lessee of a dwelling, the spouse who lived in the dwelling together with the lessee has the right to take the place of the lessee in the lease contract. If the lessee did not have a spouse who has this right or if the spouse does not wish to take the place of the lessee in the lease contract, other family members who lived in the dwelling together with the lessee have the right to take the place of the lessee in the lease contract pursuant to an agreement between them (§ 321(1) Estonian Law of Obligations Act). A spouse or other family member may take the place of the lessee in a lease contract within one month of the death of the lessee by submitting a corresponding notice to the lessor (§ 321(2) Estonian Law of Obligations Act).

The family members of a person who lived with him or her and received maintenance from him or her until his or her death have the right to continue using the objects of the shared household and to receive maintenance from the estate for one month after the death of the person

12 P. VARUL, I. KULL, V. KÕVE and M. KÄERDI, *Võlaõigusseadus II. Kommenteeritud väljaanne* (Law of Obligations II. Commented Edition), Juura, Tallinn, 2007, at p. 187 (in Estonian).

in question (§ 132 Law of Succession Act). The partners in an informal relationship can be treated as members of the family.

FINLAND

a. In cases of domestic violence?

There are no specific rules concerning cohabiting partners in the Finnish Act on Restraining Orders (898/1998), but the rules on within-the-family restraining orders apply equally to all family members who live permanently in the same residence. According to the Act (S. 3), a person on whom a within-the-family restraining order has been imposed must leave the residence where he or she and the person protected permanently live together, and he or she may not return for the duration of the order. The restraining order does not have any effect on the financial responsibilities of the parties. For example, the partner who is a party to a lease agreement remains liable for the rent to be paid also for the duration of the order as well as the partner who remains in the home.

b. In cases where the partner owning or renting the home is absent?

There are no specific rules concerning cohabiting partners if one cohabitee owns the home but is absent, for example, due to hospitalization or imprisonment. The owner can allow anyone, including his or her cohabitee, to stay in the home. If the owner of the home does not wish the current occupant to remain in the home and the occupant does not leave the premises voluntarily, he or she can bring a claim to the District Court in order to apply for a ground for eviction. The same rules on hearing and consent apply as under Question 22 with regard to the Finnish Act on Residential Leases (481/1995) and the Finnish Right-of-Occupancy Act (650/1990).

There are no specific rules on the partner's right to occupy the home in cases where the owner is missing. According to the Finnish Act on the Declaration of a Person's Death (127/2005), the waiting period before a person can be declared dead varies from one year to five years according to the circumstances of the person's disappearance.

FRANCE

a. In cases of domestic violence?

Law Act no. 2010-769 of 9 July 2010 introduced Title XIV to the French Civil Code which deals with protection measures in favour of victims of domestic violence (Art. 515-9 et seq. French Civil Code). According to

Art. 515-9, if violence committed between a couple, or by a former spouse, a former registered partner or a former partner in an informal relationship (*concubin*) endangers the victim and/or one or several of the children, the family judge can issue a protection order in favour of the victim.

The recent Law Act no. 2014-873 of 4 August 2014 has extended some regulations applying to spouses in the case of domestic violence to partners in an informal relationship or has adapted those regulations concerning such partners.[13] Now, the family judge can issue a protection order (*ordonnance de protection*) not only if domestic violence is established, but also if there are 'serious reasons' to consider that the alleged violence is 'plausible' (*vraisemblable*), see Art. 515-11 of the French Civil Code. The protection order must be delivered as soon as possible. Since August 2014, similar rules apply to spouses and non-married partners with regard to the attribution of the home. Thus, Art. 515-11, no. 4 of the French Civil Code states that the family judge shall specify which of the registered partners or of the partners in an informal relationship (*concubins*) will remain in the family home and who will pay the costs of the home. In the absence of special circumstances, the enjoyment of the home should be allocated to the partner who is not the offender, even if he or she has obtained emergency housing. If there are common children, the family judge must also decide on the way in which parental responsibilities (Art. 515-11, no. 5) can be exercised and on child maintenance. The victim can be authorised by the family judge to conceal his or her address and to indicate his or her attorney's address as his or her residence, or the address of the Public Prosecutor for all civil claims to which he or she is a party (Art. 515-11, no. 6). For everyday needs, the victim can also be authorised by the family judge to indicate as his or her residence the address of a 'qualified legal entity'. The protection order can now be issued for six months (Art. 515-12 of the French Civil Code. Until the Law Act of 4 August 2014, it was only four months).

b. In cases where the partner owning or renting the home is absent?
No, there is no specific provision in that case. Art. 112 et seq. of the French Civil Code contains general provisions on the legal meaning of absence (meaning doubts as to whether the absent person is still alive or not). The civil court can appoint relatives or 'any other person' to represent the person who is deemed to be absent (*presume absente*) and to

[13] See also *Circulaire* no. JUSCO1419203C of 7 August 2014, which explains the legal consequences of the Law Act of 4 August 2014.

administer his or her assets. There is no specific rule regulating the case of a simple absence.

GERMANY

a. In cases of domestic violence?

There has been a special Protection against Violence Act (*Gewaltschutzgesetz*; GewSchG) from 11 December 2001. The statute allows spouses and cohabitants to have a violent partner removed from the common household. The cohabitant can obtain a temporary order vesting him or her with the sole right to use the home (§ 2 German Protection against Violence Act).

b. In cases where the partner owning or renting the home is absent?

If a cohabitant lives in the home owned by the other partner, his or her legal position is determined by general rules. The same is true if he or she lives in a rented home. According to these rules the partner has possession and, if there is a tenancy, the position of a tenant.[14] However, if there is no contractual arrangement one cohabitant may ask the other to leave the home. This is possible even if a common child lives together with the caring parent in the home. The protecting provision found in matrimonial law (§ 1361b German Civil Code) is very often not applied by analogy,[15] and there is no specific legal protection for informal cohabitation.[16] This lack of protection is regarded as unsatisfactory.[17] There are proposals to introduce a special provision,[18] but there has been no recent reform proposal.

However, if the other partner is the tenant, then the *de facto* partner is protected, against the landlord as a person who maintains a joint household of a permanent nature in the sense of § 563 para. 2 s. 4 German Civil Code.

---

14 M. LÖHNIG, 'Anh. zu §§ 1297 et seq.', in: J. VON STAUDINGER, *Kommentar zum Bürgerlichen Gesetzbuch*, Sellier-de-Gruyter, Berlin, 2012, at No. 188.

15 But where there are common children, see for an analogous application of § 1361b German Civil Code, Regional Court (Landgericht; LG) München I, 1.6.1990, *NJW Rechtsprechungs-Report Zivilrecht (NJW-RR)*, 1991, 834; M. LÖHNIG, 'Anh. zu §§ 1297 et seq.', in: J. VON STAUDINGER, *Kommentar zum Bürgerlichen Gesetzbuch*, Sellier-de Gruyter, Berlin, 2012, at No. 207.

16 D. SCHWAB, *Familienrecht*, Beck, Munich, 2014, at No. 986 and 991; G. BRUDERMÜLLER, '§ 1361b', in: O. PALANDT, *Bürgerliches Gesetzbuch*, Beck, Munich, 2015, at No. 5.

17 G. BRUDERMÜLLER, '§ 1361b', in: O. PALANDT, *Bürgerliches Gesetzbuch*, Beck, Munich, 2015, at No. 5.

18 M. LÖHNIG, 'Anh. zu §§ 1297 et seq.', in: J. VON STAUDINGER, *Kommentar zum Bürgerlichen Gesetzbuch*, Sellier-de-Gruyter, Berlin, 2012, at No. 207.

GREECE

a. In cases of domestic violence?
No.

b. In cases where the partner owning or renting the home is absent?
No.

The related issues are resolved on the basis of the general rules of the law of obligations and property law. Thus the partner owning the property has the authority (Art. 1000 Greek Civil Code) to allow or forbid the use or possession of all or part of the property by the other party, or to allow common use and to lay down particular rules to govern that use.

If the property is rented by one partner, it depends on the agreement with the landlord/owner whether use may be made by the other partner.

If there is a cohabitation pact, then under Art. 6 of Law 3719/2008 the partners are free to regulate the sharing or division of their assets as they see fit, by means of a notarized document, either upon the commencement of their cohabitation or at a later date.

HUNGARY

a. In cases of domestic violence?
Domestic violence is partly dealt with in the Hungarian Code on Penal Procedure and partly in Act No. LXXII of 2009.[19] This Act applies to both cohabitants and former cohabitants. (Relatives fall under the scope of the Act and cohabitants belong to the category of relatives according to the Hungarian Civil Code. However, in the beginning the Act was not applicable to former cohabitants, but in 2013 the scope of the Act was extended to former cohabitants.) Two kinds of injunctions are regulated, namely the preventive ouster injunction (i.e. an occupation order which excludes an abusive partner from the property) and the provisional preventive ouster injunction and, within the framework of both orders, the abusive partner may be obliged to stay away from the dwelling where the abused person habitually resides.[20] Nevertheless, there is no provision which gives a direct right to a recent cohabitant to occupy the home. In the case of former cohabitants one partner may apply to the

---

19 Act No. LXXII of 2009 on Occupation Injunctions in the case of Domestic Violence between Relatives entered into force in October 2009.

20 Art. 5(1)b) of Act No. LXXII of 2009.

courts for an order that he or she may remain in the common dwelling, but this is not directly connected to domestic violence.

b. In cases where the partner owning or renting the home is absent?
The cohabitant's right to occupy the home which is owned by the other cohabitant is not specifically regulated. In the case of separation (and not only being absent while preserving the cohabitation) there are certain provisions in the Hungarian Civil Code regulating the family law consequences of cohabitation.

An independent Act contains rules on the renting of apartments according to which a cohabitant can only live habitually in the apartment with the lessor's written permission.[21]

REPUBLIC OF IRELAND

The generally applicable rules are as in Question 22 above. These rules apply where the partner owning or renting the home is absent.

If domestic violence exists within an informal relationship, a barring order application may be made under the Irish Domestic Violence Act 1996. This secures the removal of the abusive respondent from the home and may impact upon a partner's right of occupancy of the home. There are, however, certain pre-conditions a person in an informal relationship must satisfy in order to bring such an application. A person can only apply for a barring order against a cohabitant, where the applicant and the respondent have lived together in an intimate and committed relationship for six months in aggregate out of the previous nine months. In addition, as a barring order effectively removes the respondent from his or her home, cohabitants can only apply for same where they have an equal or greater interest in the property in question than the respondent. If a cohabitant has no interest in the home, therefore, the cohabitant cannot obtain a barring order and has no entitlement to relief under the Irish Domestic Violence Act.

---

[21] Art. 21 of Act No. LXXVIII of 1993 on Certain Provisions Concerning Flat-letting and the Alienation of Flats.

ITALY

a. In cases of domestic violence?

Yes, such rules do exist. Some of them apply to adult cohabitants and others to the child or children living with the couple.

In cases of abuse against a partner the judge may employ specific remedies, provided by Art. 342 *bis* and 342 *ter* of the Italian Civil Code (introduced by the Law of 4 April 2001, n. 154), called 'protection orders' (*ordini di protezione*). These measures may include orders varying from an injunction to stop the offending behaviour, to the removal of the wrongdoer from the family home and measures prohibiting him/her from approaching the place where the other family members live. The duration of the order cannot exceed one year, but it can be extended, subject to a petition by the other party, for 'no longer than is strictly necessary' and 'only when there are serious grounds'. These rules apply to spouses and expressly to cohabitants.

In the case of abuse against the child or the children, 'when the conduct of one or both of the parents ... is ... harmful to the child, then the judge, according to the circumstances of the case, may take appropriate measures. The judge may also arrange for the child's removal from the home or for the removal of the parent or the cohabitant who mistreats or abuses the child' (Art. 333 Italian Civil Code: the words 'or the removal of the parent or the cohabitant who mistreats or abuses the child' were added by the law of 28 March 2001, n. 149).

b. In cases where the partner owning or renting the home is absent?

There are no specific rules. As the cohabiting partner can now be defined as a qualified holder,[22] his or her connection with the home exists autonomously even in the absence of the holder of the title to the home, resulting in a *de facto* occupation protected by the law against any intrusion or nuisance.

LATVIA

a. In cases of domestic violence?

From 31 March 2013 the rule on temporary protection against violence has been in force in the Latvian Civil Procedure Law. It provides that an application for temporary protection against violence may be submitted not only by spouses but also by: people who, for example, live or have

[22] But see the answer to Question 22.

lived in the same household; people who have or are expected to have children, irrespective of whether these people have been married or have lived together; and people between whom personal or intimate relations exist or have existed.[23] An order for the violent person to leave the habitual residence of the victim may be established as a temporary protection, as well as a prohibition against staying in specified places and within a specified distance of the victim's house.

b. In cases where the partner owning or renting the home is absent?
In Latvia there is no such specific legal order on informal relationships.

LITHUANIA

a. In cases of domestic violence?
Article 5 of the Lithuanian Law on Protection Against Violence in Proximate Environment stipulates that:

> 'Upon confirmation of the occurrence of violence in a proximate environment, protective measures shall be introduced to protect the victim of the violence:
> 1) the obligation for the perpetrator to temporarily move out of the place of residence if he/she shares a common dwelling with the victim;
> 2) the obligation for the perpetrator to stay away from the victim, and to refrain from any communication and seeking contact.'[24]

The above-mentioned measures will apply until the judicial scrutiny of the case comes to an end, unless the investigating judge or the Court imposes preventive measures as laid down in the Code of Criminal Procedure of the Republic of Lithuania: the transgressor may be remanded in custody or be ordered to live separately from the victim. These measures shall be imposed by the court within 48 hours at the latest.

b. In cases where the partner owning or renting the home is absent?
There are no specific rules, except Art. 3.234-3.235 of the Lithuanian Civil Code mentioned in Question 22. So in this case the general rules apply, the family members of the lessee of a dwelling shall have the same rights and duties arising from the lease contract as the lessee himself. Upon having ceased to be members of the lessee's family while continuing to reside in the leased dwelling, natural persons shall have the same rights

23 S. 450^{44} Civil Procedure Law.
24 Law of the Republic of Lithuania on Protection Against Violence in a Proximate Environment, Official gazette, 2011, No. 77-3475.

and duties as the lessee and his or her family members (Art. 6.589. Rights and duties of the lessee's family members).

Article 6.590 of the Lithuanian Civil Code provides a right for family members to occupy the leased dwelling:

> '1. In accordance with the lease contract, the right to occupy the dwelling shall be enjoyed by those family member of the lessee as well as former family members who are indicated in the contract. In the event of those persons failing to occupy the dwelling within six months from the date of the formation of the contract, they shall forfeit the right of occupancy. In respect of persons who are temporarily absent, this term shall start to run upon the expiry of the time-limit established in Art. 6.591 of this Code, in the event of an earlier return of these persons, it shall start from the date of their return.'

LUXEMBOURG

a. In cases of domestic violence?

The law against domestic violence is gender-neutral and provides that an abuser will be removed from his or her residence even if he or she is the owner of the residence. Thus also a partner in an informal relationship may be removed from the partner's residence even though he or she is the sole owner of the residence.

b. In cases where the partner owning or renting the home is absent?

The absence of the partner (a legal absence or an absence of long duration) does not confer any rights of occupancy on the other partner in cases where the partner owning the home is absent (unless there is an agreement to the contrary between the two of them).

Where the absent partner is renting the house, the other partner is protected by Art. 13 of the law of September 21st, 2006. This law states that the other partner may remain in the house when the tenant has abandoned the residence or when the tenant has died.

A legal absence or an absence of long duration coincides with the abandonment of the residence; in the first case, it is not necessarily voluntary, in the second it is voluntary. Here is an extract from the original text: '*En cas d'abandon du domicile par le locataire ou en cas de décès du locataire, le contrat de bail continue à durée indéterminée au profit du concubin, qui vivait avec lui en communauté domestique depuis au moins six mois à la date de l'abandon du domicile ou du décès et qui avait déclaré son domicile à la commune dans le logement pendant cette période.'*

THE NETHERLANDS

a. In cases of domestic violence?

There are no specific rules on a partner's right of occupancy, but there are specific provisions on the non-occupancy of the home in the case of domestic violence. On the basis of the *Wet Tijdelijk Huisverbod,* the partner using violence may be banned from the home for a specific period of time. It is not relevant whether he/she owns or rents the premises or not. The mayor may impose a temporary restraining order for ten days if the partner's presence causes a serious and immediate danger for the safety of a person who lives in the house. Whether the person sharing a household with the partner is married or not is irrelevant.[25]

b. In cases where the partner owning or renting the home is absent?

There are no specific rules which deal with the impact of the absence of a partner for a long duration on the rights of occupancy of the other partner. General provisions of the law of obligations and property law apply. When the partner owning/renting the house is sentenced to a term of imprisonment, the other partner has a right of occupancy as the result of an implicit consent to this extent.

If the partner entitled to the home becomes a missing person according to the missing persons Articles of the Dutch Civil Code, these rules on missing persons will apply. Whether someone is a married or a non-marital partner is not relevant.[26]

NORWAY

a. In cases of domestic violence?

There are no specific rules on a partner's rights of occupancy of the home in cases of domestic violence. The prosecuting authority may impose a ban not exceeding three months on visits to a person's own home if there is an imminent risk of domestic violence pursuant to the Norwegian Criminal Procedure Act 1981, S. 222a. Domestic violence might also be factor when assessing whether the non-owning cohabitant is to have the

---

25 Art. 2 *Wet Tijdelijk huisverbod.*

26 Both qualify as an interested party (Art. 1:409 and 413 Dutch Civil Code).

right to purchase or enter into a tenancy agreement pursuant to the Norwegian Household Community Act, S. 3.

b. In cases where the partner owning or renting the home is absent?
There are no specific rules on a partner's rights of occupancy of the home in cases where the partner owning or renting the home is absent. Pursuant to the Norwegian Missing Persons Act 2015, the remaining cohabitant has a duty to notify the district court about the absence and the court or the appointed guardian may decide on a partner's rights of occupancy of the home as well as on support. Moreover, pursuant to the Norwegian Household Community Act, absence could also be a factor in the assessment of whether to give the remaining cohabitant a right to purchase or enter into a tenancy agreement.

PORTUGAL

a. In cases of domestic violence?
In cases of a conviction for domestic violence, the court may forbid any contact between the perpetrator and the victim; in the event of doing so, this additional penalty mandatorily includes a prohibition on entering the victim's residence, regardless of the title of occupation (Portuguese Penal Code, Art. 152(4) and (5)). This article expressly applies to domestic violence against spouses and cohabitants.

When proceedings are ongoing, the court may impose upon the defendant the duty not to approach the victim or his/her relatives (Portuguese Penal Procedure Code, Art. 200, n. 1,a)). This is, however, a general rule which is applicable to any persons, regardless of their social or family relationships

b. In cases where the partner owning or renting the home is absent?
Whenever one of the members of the *de facto* union is absent without any notice (e.g. a missing person) and without a guardian or an agent under a power of attorney, a special manager may be nominated in order to manage the assets of the absent party (Art. 89 et seq. of the Portuguese Civil Code). This includes the home owned by the absent cohabitant or the right of lease entitled by him/her. In this way the other member of the *de facto* union may occupy the home when this is in accordance with this management.

In other cases of a long absence by one of the partners, there is no special provision. If that partner is capable of expressing his or her will (e.g. he or she has been imprisoned), it is expected that he or she does so; if not, (e.g. he or she is lying unconscious in a hospital) Portuguese law lacks any rule, unless a legal guardian is nominated.

RUSSIA

a. In cases of domestic violence?
No.

b. In cases where the partner owning or renting the home is absent?
If the partner-owner's absence is temporary, it has no effect on the occupancy rights of the other partner, except if the home has been bought with the help of a mortgage and the mortgage cannot be transferred to the other partner (for instance, because he/she does not have a sufficient income). If the absence is permanent due to death or other reasons, the home will pass to the deceased partner's heirs and the other partner will then have no right of occupancy.

The position of the informal partner of a tenant depends on whether their home is a social or commercial tenancy.

If the absent partner is a social tenant and a court has granted his/her informal partner the status of a family member, the temporary absence of the tenant will not affect the occupancy rights of his/her family members (Art. 71 Russian Housing Code). In the event of the death or permanent absence of the tenant, an adult family member (thus also the informal partner) can require the transfer of the tenancy to him/her (Art. 672(2) Russian Civil Code and 82(2) Russian Housing Code).

In the event of the death or permanent absence of a partner who is a commercial tenant, an informal partner can claim the transfer of the tenancy to him/her subject to the same conditions as those enjoyed by the absent partner, provided that the informal partner has been properly installed. If the home is occupied by other properly installed adults in addition to the informal partner, all those adults will have to agree on who is to take over the tenancy of the absent tenant. If no agreement can be reached, all the adults will become joint tenants (Art. 686(2) Russian Civil Code).

SCOTLAND

In terms of the Matrimonial Homes (Family Protection) (Scotland) Act 1981, a cohabitant, who does not have legal title to the family home, is entitled to apply to the court for statutory occupancy rights. Where a couple is living together as if they were married, S. 18 provides that:

> 'the court may, on the application of the non-entitled partner, if it appears that the entitled partner and the non-entitled partner are a cohabiting couple in that house, grant occupancy rights therein to the applicant for such period, not exceeding six months, as the court may specify.'

Unlike the automatic occupancy rights of a non-entitled spouse,[27] the grant of these rights to a cohabitant is discretionary and limited to a maximum period of six months although this can be extended, for further period or periods of six months.[28]

a. In cases of domestic violence?

The right to apply for statutory occupancy rights is not restricted to the situation of domestic violence although that is the context in which it is most likely to be exercised. The 1981 Act also sets out a range of orders which the court may make to regulate occupancy of the house, including regulatory orders and an order to exclude the non-applicant from the property where it is considered necessary in order to protect the applicant, or any child of the family, from harmful conduct and domestic interdicts.[29] These orders can be sought and made, either where there is one entitled and one non-entitled partner, who has obtained statutory occupancy rights, or where there are jointly entitled partners.

While these are important and significant statutory rights, in theory, there is a doubt as to the extent to which they are used in practice. Even in the case of marriage, where spouses automatically have occupancy rights, there is relatively little evidence of regulatory orders and exclusion orders being sought and it seems likely that they are even rarer in the context of informal relationships where the cohabitant may first have to obtain statutory occupancy rights.

b. In cases where the partner owning or renting the home is absent?

As explained in (a) above, the possibility of seeking occupancy rights is not limited to the situation of domestic violence and therefore a

27 Matrimonial Homes (Family Protection) (Scotland) Act 1981, S. 1.
28 Matrimonial Homes (Family Protection) (Scotland) Act 1981, S. 18(1)(b).
29 Matrimonial Homes (Family Protection) (Scotland) Act 1981, S. 18(3).

cohabitant could make an application where their partner is for some reason absent from the home. There are no reported cases to show how the courts would approach such an application but one issue might be interpretation of the requirement that the parties are indeed 'living with each other'.[30]

Although relatively little use has been made of the regulatory orders set out in the 1981 Act, and in particular of exclusion orders, one provision which has been more frequently used is S. 13 which provides for the transfer of tenancy. By means of this section, the court may order transfer of tenancy from the entitled to the non-entitled spouse or civil partner and by means of S. 18(3) this is extended to apply to a non-entitled cohabitant who has secured occupancy rights. Where such an order is made, provision can also be made for just and reasonable compensation to be paid to the entitled party.[31] This might be useful as a means of providing long-term security to the non-entitled cohabitant in the situation where their partner is absent.

SLOVAKIA

a. In cases of domestic violence?

On 15th December 2008 the Slovak Law on the Amendment of the Police Force entered into effect and it introduced into the Slovak legal system the authority of police officers to make use of a restraining order (*vykázanie*) and to expel a violent person from the common household.[32] This competence can be used based on legal grounds and in the situation where, on the basis of certain facts, it can be assumed that a dangerous attack against life, health or freedom is imminent. Using the order should prevent a violent partner from committing crimes such as: making death threats, bodily harm, abuse of a close person and a person in custody, extortion, rape, sexual violence, and sexual abuse. The aim of the police restraining order is to provide protection to a victim during the period between the escalation of violence and the day when a protective interlocutory judgment is delivered by the civil court. The protected

30 Matrimonial Homes (Family Protection) (Scotland) Act 1981, S. 18(1).

31 Matrimonial Homes (Family Protection) (Scotland) Act 1981, S. 18(1).

32 R. DOBROVODSKÝ, 'K inštitútu vykázania násilníckej osoby z obydlia a k iným zmenám pri ochrane obetí násilia páchaného v rodine (On the institution of the restraining order against violent persons in the common household and on other legal amendments for the protection of domestic violence victims)', *Justičná revue*, 2009, at p. 138 et seq.; M. DESET, 'Prevencia domáceho násilia inštitútom vykázania (Prevention of domestic violence using the restraining order)', *Bulletin slovenskej advokácie*, 2008, at p. 32.

person can be the partner of the violent person living in an informal relationship with him or her.

b. In cases where the partner owning or renting the home is absent?
Police officers are not obliged to examine (evidence of) the legal validity of a common home.[33] Police officers do not have to distinguish whether the violent partner owns or rents the home or whether the premises are common property or matrimonial property.

SLOVENIA

a. In cases of domestic violence?
A partner who is the victim of violence can propose to a court that it should decide on the abandonment of a home in common use. The court is limited in the duration of such a measure if the partners are co-owners or the common owner of the home, if they have building rights, the right of enjoyment or use of the land on which the home is located or if they have rented the home together. At the proposal of the partner who is a victim of violence and who cannot find other accommodation, the court may prolong the right for six months unless this would cause a disproportionately heavy burden on a third person. The partner to whom the home is awarded for use during the time of use bears the costs of the regular maintenance of the home. At the request of the partner who was responsible for the violence, she or he must pay suitable compensation for the use of the home if this is in accordance with the principle of fairness (Art. 21 of the Prevention of Violence within the Slovenian Family Act).

b. In cases where the partner owning or renting the home is absent?
There is no special rule in that case. There is only the rule by which the lessor is obliged in the case of the (permanent) cessation of a life union with a partner who will remain in the home to continue the rental relationship under the same conditions as were applicable up until then. This provision is especially important when the partners live in a home with a rental contract for an indefinite period of time and a non-profit

33 For more details see R. DOBROVODSKÝ, 'Procesné a hmotnoprávne predpoklady slovenského občianskeho práva k ratifikácii Dohovoru Rady Európy o predchádzaní násiliu na ženách a domácemu násiliu a o boji proti nemu (The civil procedural and substantive law regulation in Slovakia and the legal conditions for the ratification of the Council of Europe Convention on preventing and combating violence against women by Slovakia)', Psychológ medzi právnikmi. Pocta profesorovi Gustávovi Dianiškovi k 75. narodeninám, Trnavská univerzita v Trnave, Právnická fakulta, Trnava 2015.

lease. The rule does not apply to a service home (Art. 110 of the Slovenian Housing Act).[34]

SPAIN

a. In cases of domestic violence?

In cases of domestic violence a judge can order the perpetrator to leave the home and can prohibit return (Art. 64.1 *Ley de Proteccion Integral contra la Violencia de Género*).[35]

b. In cases where the partner owning or renting the home is absent?

Under the Spanish Law of leasehold[36] there are special rules that apply where the partner renting the home abandons the home. The partner to an informal relationship has the right to notify the owner within a month that he or she wishes to substitute his or her name for that of the absent partner in the contract. For this purpose an informal relationship is required to have lasted for at least two years unless there are common children.

If the home is owned by the absent partner, the partner might be able to stay without title under a so-called *derecho de precario* which would equate to possession. This situation entails that the partner can be ousted by the title-holder.

Under Spanish law a declaration of absence can be requested in cases where a person disappears from his or her habitual residence for more than one year and there is no information about his or her whereabouts. Such declaration can be requested by a spouse, but not by a partner, unless the partners entered into a prior specific agreement to this effect. The spouse would be the first person to be called upon by the judge in order to administer the property, which would guarantee that he or she could continue to occupy the family home. If the person declared to be absent lived in an informal relationship, his adult children and failing them, his parents, would be called upon to represent and administer, which might have as a consequence that the partner would be ousted from the home.

---

[34] Uradni list RS (Official Journal) Nos 69/2003, 18/2004, 47/2006, 45/2008, 57/2008, 90/2009, 62/2010, 40/2011, 56/2011, 87/2011, 40/2012.

[35] Ley Orgánica 1/2004, de 28 de diciembre, de Medidas de Proteccion Integral contra la Violencia de Género (BOE núm. 313, de 29 de diciembre de 2004).

[36] Ley de Arrendamientos Urbanos (BOE núm 282 de 25 de Noviembre de 1994), at Art. 12.

If the partner declared to be absent held the home on lease, the other partner would have the right to notify the owner that he or she wished to subrogate under Art. 12 of the Spanish Law on leasehold.

SWEDEN

a. In cases of domestic violence?

Yes, if the relationship is subject to the Swedish Cohabitation Act (see above, answers to Question 2 and 4), § 28, para. 2 which grants a cohabitee not only the right, by court order, to remain in the joint home (above Question 22), but also to apply the court to forbid the partners from visiting each other. The aim of this provision is to protect the integrity of the (former) cohabitees and to prevent domestic violence, but it applies only upon termination of the relationship and only until the property division. The court may also prohibit a partner from remaining in the couple's joint home, when the other partner's life, health or liberty is under threat, Swedish Act (1988:688) on Prohibition of Contact, § 1 a. Usually, this prohibition is limited to a period of two months, § 4.

b. In cases where the partner owning or renting the home is absent?

No specific rules apply concerning this situation. If the partners' relationship is classified as a cohabitation relationship and, therefore, is subject to the Swedish Cohabitation Act (see above, under Question 2 and 4), a permanent or long absence of one of the partners might lead to the conclusion that the relationship has ended (see above, Question 5 b). In that case, the other partner has the opportunity to apply to the court for the right to remain in the home until the property distribution has been carried out (see above, Question 22).

SWITZERLAND

a. In cases of domestic violence?

Civil law remedies in cases of domestic violence were enacted in Switzerland in 2007.[37] They are found in the chapter on the protection of personality rights. This ensures that these provisions apply irrespective of the legal status of the persons involved, and even encompass stalking by persons who are wholly unrelated to the victim.

---

37 For details see see I. SCHWENZER and A. BOCK, 'New Statutory Rules on Registered Partnerships and Protection Against Domestic Violence', in: B. ATKIN, *The International Survey of Family Law*, Jordan Publishing, Bristol, 2008, at p. 445 et seq.

In cases of violence, threats or harassment, the court may order the offender to leave the common home for a certain period of time if the victim and the offender share the same residence (Art. 28b para. 2 Swiss Civil Code). This eviction may be ordered irrespective of the offender's legal rights to the dwelling.[38] The period may be extended once only.

Furthermore, and where justified by the circumstances, the court may - with the landlord's consent - transfer the rights and obligations under the tenancy agreement to the victim alone (Art. 28b para. 3 No. 2 Swiss Civil Code).

b. In cases where the partner owning or renting the home is absent?

There are no specific rules on a partner's rights to occupy the home in cases where the partner owning or renting the home is absent.

In cases of an absence for a long duration by one of the partners (hospitalization or imprisonment), the partner may remain in the common home as long as the absent partner consents to this and in cases of a lease as long as the renting partner is not violating the lease contract.

Where the person (temporarily) lacks the capacity of judgement or is absent (e.g. unknown whereabouts) a deputy may be appointed by the adult protection authority (Art. 390 para. 1 Swiss Civil Code),[39] unless the informal partner has been appointed as the competent representative (in a respective directive). The deputy has to deal with further proceedings within his or her scope of competence. The consent of the adult protection authority is required before the deputy may carry out a liquidation of the household and/or terminate the lease on a dwelling where the client lives (Art. 416 para. 1 No. 1 Swiss Civil Code).

---

38 H. HAUSHEER, T. GEISER and R. AEBI-MÜLLER, *Das Familienrecht des Schweizerischen Zivilgesetzbuches*, Stämpfli, Bern, 2014, at N 03.34.

39 For details see H.HENKEL, in: H. HONSELL, N.P. VOGT and T. GEISER, *Basler Kommentar Zivilgesetzbuch I (Art. 1-456 ZGB)*, Helbing Lichtenhahn Verlag, Basel, 2014, at Art. 390 N 8 et seq., 16 et seq.

QUESTION 24

Are there specific rules on transactions (e.g. disposal, mortgaging, subletting) concerning the home of partners in an informal relationship:

a. Where the home is jointly owned by the partners?

b. Where the home is owned by one of the partners?

c. Where the home is jointly rented by the partners?

d. Where the home is rented by one of the partners?

AUSTRIA

There are no specific rules on transactions concerning the home of the partners in an informal relationship. The answers below are therefore based on the general rules of the law of obligations and property law.

a. Where the home is jointly owned by the partners?

In the case of ordinary joint ownership both parties are authorised to dispose of their share, e.g. each owner can sell, mortgage or bequeath his/her share, as far as he/she does not infringe the rights of the other owner.[1] Although the asset in question is shared, each co-owner nonetheless remains the sole proprietor of his/her share.[2] However, the joint owner cannot let his or her share, because this requires a 'real asset'.[3] The letting of a jointly owned home belongs to the ordinary administration, which will be decided by the majority of the votes, which

1 Section 829 General Austrian Civil Code; H. GAMERITH, 'section 829 General Austrian Civil Code', in: P. RUMMEL (ed.), *Kommentar zum Allgemeinen Bürgerlichen Gesetzbuch*, Manz Verlag, Vienna, 2000, at marg. No. 1.

2 Section 361 General Austrian Civil Code; H. BÖHM, 'section 829 General Austrian Civil Code', in: A. KLETEČKA and M. SCHAUER, *ABGB-ON 1.01*, Manz Verlag, Vienna, 2013, at marg. No. 1.

3 H. GAMERITH, 'section 829 General Austrian Civil Code', in: P. RUMMEL (ed.), *Kommentar zum Allgemeinen Bürgerlichen Gesetzbuch*, Manz Verlag, Vienna, 2000, at marg. No. 1; H. BÖHM, 'section 829 General Austrian Civil Code', in: A. KLETEČKA and M. SCHAUER, *ABGB-ON 1.01*, Manz Verlag, Vienna, 2013, at marg. No. 7.

is not counted according to the number of persons being joint owners, but according to their shares.[4] In the event of a tie, the court has to decide.[5] Hence, if the partners own the home with equal shares, they have to agree whether they want to let their home or not. In the case of disagreement one party refrains from letting their home or submits the issue to the court.

One has to distinguish between regular joint ownership and a condominium, which results in a so-called partnership of owners *(Eigentümerpartnerschaft)*. The shares belonging to the joint owners can only jointly be sold, mortgaged or submitted to execution;[6] all transactions require the consent of both owners.[7]

b. Where the home is owned by one of the partners?

The sole owner of the home can freely dispose of his/her property. He/she may sell or let the object in accordance with the general rules on the law of obligations or grant other persons limited *rights in rem* (e.g. servitudes, mortgage). This follows from the broad definition of ownership, which is the right to dispose arbitrarily of the substance and fruits of the property and to exclude everyone else from it, subject to limitations imposed by law or the rights of other parties.[8] Hence, if the other partner does not have any rights as regards their home, the other party is not restricted in his/her transactions.

c. Where the home is jointly rented by the partners?

Joint tenants are equally entitled and obliged: One tenant cannot dispose of his/her right on his/her own.[9] It follows that subletting is only possible if both tenants agree to this. Generally, the landlord cannot prohibit subletting, apart from a few exceptions.[10] In the case of a breakdown of an informal relationship the joint tenants either have to terminate the contract or reach an agreement – with the consent of the landlord – on which partner will remain in the home.[11] Joint tenants can

---

4 Section 833 General Austrian Civil Code.

5 H. BÖHM, 'section 833 General Austrian Civil Code', in: A. KLETEČKA and M. SCHAUER, *ABGB-ON 1.01*, Manz Verlag, Vienna, 2013, at marg. No. 21.

6 Section 13 para. 3 Austrian Condominium Act.

7 H. WÜRTH, 'section 13 Austrian Condominium Act', in: P. RUMMEL (ed.), *Kommentar zum Allgemeinen Bürgerlichen Gesetzbuch*, Manz Verlag, Vienna, 2003, at marg. No. 6.

8 Section 364 General Austrian Civil Code.

9 Regional Court for Civil Matters Vienna, Judgement of 29.10.1997, 41 R 633/97k.

10 Section 1098 General Austrian Civil Code; section 11 Austrian Tenancy Act.

11 Austrian Supreme Court, Judgement of 28.4.1999, 3 Ob 12/99g.

only terminate the contract together.[12] One tenant cannot file an action for possession *(Räumungsklage)* against the other tenant.[13] If the partners are joint tenants, the rules regarding joint ownership apply by analogy with the restriction that the possibility of transferring the right to rent the home of one tenant is excluded (S. 825 et seq. General Austrian Civil Code).[14]

d. Where the home is rented by one of the partners?

When the home is rented by one partner only, he/she can autonomously exercise his/her right without obtaining the consent of the other partner. Hence, the tenant may e.g. sublet his/her home or terminate the contract according to the rental agreement, but his/her transactions are not somehow restricted by the fact that the rental property also serves as the home of the other partner.

BELGIUM

a. Where the home is jointly owned by the partners?

No specific rules apply. In case the home is jointly owned, either the default rules on coincidental joint ownership or the rules on conventional joint property apply. In the case of coincidental joint property, each owner may dispose of his undivided part in the property (Art. 577-2, § 4 Belgian Civil Code).[15] The disposal is not opposable by the other undivided owners, which is particularly relevant in case an indivision agreement was concluded that was registered in the Mortgage Office. All undivided owners have to consent to the disposal regarding the home as a whole (Art. 577-2, § 6 Belgian civil Code).

b. Where the home is owned by one of the partners?

No specific rules apply in the absence of an agreement that would only be valid between the parties.[16] The sole owner is entitled to dispose of his property and to administer it. According to a minority position in the

12 E. MÖSCHL, *Die nichteheliche Lebensgemeinschaft*, LexisNexis ARD ORAC, Vienna, 2007, at marg. No. 47.

13 E. MÖSCHL, *Die nichteheliche Lebensgemeinschaft*, LexisNexis ARD ORAC, Vienna, 2007, at marg. No. 47.

14 H. BÖHM, 'section 825 General Austrian Civil Code', in: A. KLETEČKA and M. SCHAUER, *ABGB-ON 1.01*, Manz Verlag, Vienna, 2013, at marg. No. 32.

15 Cass. 22 December 2006, *RW* 2006-07, 711, with note MOSSELMANS.

16 W. PINTENS, C. DECLERCK, J. DU MONGH, K. VANWINCKELEN, *Familiaal vermogensrecht*, Intersentia, Antwerp, 2010, at n° 1015.

case law[17] and doctrine,[18] the same protection as between spouses and legal cohabitants should be accepted on the basis of Art. 8 and 14 ECHR, but that protection, even then, would not be relevant upon separation.[19]

c. Where the home is jointly rented by the partners?
No specific rules apply. If the home is jointly rented, then the tenancy must be terminated by both partners jointly or by one of them also acting for the other on the basis of (implicit) agency.[20] In case neither partner wants to leave the rented home upon separation, the court is only competent to temporarily organise occupancy in an (interim) order until the rental agreement is duly terminated. This includes the power to temporarily evict one of the partners.[21]

d. Where the home is rented by one of the partners?
No specific rules apply. The tenant is entitled to terminate the rental agreement. According to a minority position in the case law[22] and doctrine,[23] the same protection as between spouses and legal cohabitants should be accepted on the basis of Art. 8 and 14 ECHR, but that protection, even then, would not be relevant upon separation.[24]

BULGARIA

There are no specific rules on transactions concerning the home of the partners in an informal relationship. The common regulations on property (Bulgarian Property Law) and on contracts (Bulgarian Obligations and Contracts Law) should be applicable.

---

17 Divisional Court Tongeren 1 April 1992, *Limb.Rechtsl.* 1993, 59; Justice of the Peace Aalst 1 September 1992, *T.Vred.* 1992, 326.

18 A. HEYVAERT, *Het personen- en gezinsrecht ont(k)leed*, Kluwer, Mechelen, 2002, at n° 698.

19 S. EGGERMONT, *De juridische bescherming van private relaties*, PhD, University of Antwerp, 2015, at n° 169.

20 Justice of the Peace Herzele 19 December 2012, *RW* 2013-14, 273.

21 President of the District Court of Arlon 16 October 1985, *RTDF* 1985 185 (domestic violence); Justice of the Peace Hamme 21 November 1989, *RW* 1990-91, 514, with note PAUWELS; Justice of the Peace Bruges (1) 2 June 2005, *TGR-TWVR* 2005, 170 (domestic violence); Justice of the Peace Oudenaarde 2 February 2006, *NJW* 2006, 138, with note VERSCHELDEN. *Contra*: Justice of the Peace Kortrijk (2) 9 February 1988, *T.vred.* 1989, 50 (eviction contrary to art. 8 ECHR); Justice of the Peace Bilzen 30 September 1991, *T.vred.* 1992, 16 (adulterous cohabitation contrary to public policy).

22 District Court Liège 26 June 1980, *JL* 1981, 86, with note LIÉNARD; Divisional Court of Tongeren 1 April 1992, *Limb.Rechtsl.* 1993, 59; Justice of the Peace Aalst 1 September 1992, *T.Vred.* 1992, 326.

23 A. HEYVAERT, *Het personen- en gezinsrecht ont(k)leed*, Kluwer, Mechelen, 2002, at n° 698.

24 S. EGGERMONT, *De juridische bescherming van private relaties*, PhD, University of Antwerp, 2015, at n° 169.

a. Where the home is jointly owned by the partners?

When the home is jointly owned by the partners and they are co-owners with known shares (depending on the means of acquisition) the Bulgarian Property Law lays down joint actions for the disposal of the property (Art. 32 of the Bulgarian Property Law). In addition, any partner can dispose/sell his/her share of the immovable property only after proving that this share has first been offered to the other partner (Art. 33 of the Bulgarian Property Law). Any partner can claim a division of the property (Art. 34 of the Bulgarian Property Law).

b. Where the home is owned by one of the partners?

If the home is owned by one of the partners, the owner has the right to dispose of the property – the rights of the owner are specified in the related general legislation (e.g. Art. 183 and 188 (disposal of the home), Art. 167, para. 3 (mortgaging of the home), and Art. 228 (the renting of the home) of the Bulgarian Obligations and Contracts Law).

c. Where the home is jointly rented by the partners?

When the home is jointly rented any specific transaction depends on what has been agreed upon in the contract. Under the general law, Art. 234 of the Bulgarian Obligations and Contracts Law allows for the subletting of parts of the rented home if the contrary has not been agreed upon. If both partners are parties to the contract they both have to agree on any sub-renting. No other transactions apart from the payment of the rent (Art. 228) and the basic maintenance of the home are possible for tenants (Art. 231).

d. Where the home is rented by one of the partners?

If the home is rented by one of the partners the partner who is party to the contract should be empowered to take actions for sub-renting. No other transactions apart from the payment of the rent (Art. 228) and the basic maintenance of the home are possible for tenants (Art. 231).

CROATIA

All the answers from a. to d. equally refer to both cohabitants and same-sex informal partners. Indeed, Art. 54 of the Croatian Partnership Act stipulates that all the provisions regulating property relations between cohabitants shall also be applicable to property relations between same-sex informal partners.

a. Where the home is jointly owned by the partners?

According to Art. 32 paragraph 2 in relation to Art. 11 of the Croatian Family Act, one partner may not, without the written consent of the other partner whose respective signature shall be authenticated by a notary public, anyhow dispose of the family house or apartment that represents their community of property and family home. A family home means a family house or apartment where the partners and the children over whom they exercise their parental responsibility actually live.

b. Where the home is owned by one of the partners?

There are no specific rules on transactions concerning the home of partners in an informal relationship where the home is owned by one of the partners. It implies that one parent who is the sole owner of the family home can freely and without limitation dispose of his/her own property.

c. Where the home is jointly rented by the partners?

There are no specific rules on transactions concerning the home of partners in an informal relationship where the home is jointly rented by the partners.

d. Where the home is rented by one of the partners?

According to Art. 32 paragraph 3 in relation to Art. 11 of the Croatian Family Act, if a family home in which partners live together with the children over whom they exercise their parental responsibility is rented by only one of the partners, he/she may not cancel the lease agreement without the written consent of the other partner, unless the lease refers to a service flat (apartment) which is subject to special regulations (e.g. the official flat of MPs).

This provision entails that the partner who has leased the flat or house which represents the partners' family home is entitled to independently exercise his/her right to lease, regardless of the will of the other partner if they do not live with minor children.

CZECH REPUBLIC

a. Where the home is jointly owned by the partners?

Where the home is jointly owned by the partners, there are no specific rules on transactions (e.g. disposal, mortgaging, subletting). If the home is jointly owned by the partners, they are co-owners in the sense of S. 1115 Czech Civil Code et seq. As for S. 1117 Czech Civil Code: each co-owner has the right to the entire object. This right is limited by the same right of each of the other co-owners. With respect to the object as a whole, co-owners are considered to dispose of the object as a single person (S. 1116 Czech Civil Code). Consent of all co-owners is necessary if an undivided object is to be encumbered or such an encumbrance is to be cancelled; a decision forming the basis on which the rights of the co-owners are to be limited for more than ten years, requires the consent of all co-owners (S. 1132 Czech Civil Code). The only exception concerns a pledge or other similar security to secure a pecuniary claim arising from the improvement or renewal of an undivided object, then the decision of at least a two-thirds majority of the co-owners suffices (S. 1133 Czech Civil Code).

b. Where the home is owned by one of the partners?

Where the home is owned by one of the partners, there are no specific rules on transactions (e.g. disposal, mortgaging, subletting). The partner who is the sole owner has the full right of disposition of the home. Everything belongs to someone, thus all his corporeal and incorporeal things constitute the person's ownership (S. 1011 Czech Civil Code). An owner has the right to freely dispose of his property within the limits of the legal order and to exclude other persons from such disposal. An owner may not, beyond what is reasonable given the circumstances, seriously disturb the rights of others or perform such acts whose main purpose is to cause nuisance or harm to others (S. 1012 Czech Civil Code). The partner who is not the owner could have a title to live in the home under a contract with the partner who is the owner, e.g. a lease contract, establishing the habitation according to S. 1297-1298 of the Czech Civil Code.

c. Where the home is jointly rented by the partners?

Where the home is jointly rented by the partners, there are no specific rules on transactions (e.g. disposal, mortgaging, subletting). It is a joint lease according to S. 2270 and 2271 Czech Civil Code:

- S. 2270: (1) Where several persons conclude a lease contract with the lessor, they become joint lessees of the apartment; a person who, with the consent of the parties, accedes to the contract, also becomes a joint lessee. (2) Provisions on a lessee apply by analogy to joint lessees, unless otherwise provided below.
- S. 2271: Joint lessees have equal rights and duties. The provisions on a partnership apply with the necessary modifications.

- As for a sublease, if a lessee permanently resides in an apartment, he may sublease part of it to a third person even without the consent of the lessor (S. 2274 Czech Civil Code).

d. Where the home is rented by one of the partners?

Where the home is rented by one of the partners, there are no specific rules on transactions (e.g. disposal, mortgaging, subletting). According to S. 2272 Czech Civil Code the lessee has the right to receive anyone into his household. If a lessee receives a new member into his household, he must notify the lessor of the increase in the number of people living in the apartment without undue delay; if the lessee fails to do so within two months after the change, he is presumed to have seriously breached his duty. With the permission of the lessor, the second partner, who is not the lessee, can live with the lessee in the home.

If one of the partners who is the lessee dies and there is no joint lease of the apartment, the lease passes to a member of the lessee's household who was living in the apartment on the day of the lessee's death and has no apartment of his own. If such a person is someone other than the lessee's spouse, partner, parent, sibling, son-in-law, daughter-in-law, child or grandchild, the lease passes to such a person only if the lessor consents to the passage of the lease to that person (S. 2279(1) Czech Civil Code). It means that in case of the death of one partner, the other has a right to stay in the apartment without the permission of the lessor. A lease of an apartment in such cases must end no later than two years from the date of the passage of the lease (S. 2279(2) Czech Civil Code).

DENMARK

a. Where the home is jointly owned by the partners?

There are no specific laws regulating joint ownership in Denmark.

In principle, a cohabiting couple who own an asset jointly must agree on the legal decisions taken on the joint estate, such as selling, pledging as security and subletting. However, one of the parties can make normal minor arrangements and engage professional help to prevent damage to the property or take measures required by law.[25] If one of the parties incurs costs on behalf of the joint estate it is usually possible to claim the repayment of a proportionate amount from the joint owner.

---

[25] See I. LUND-ANDERSEN, *Familieøkonomien*, Jurist- og Økonomforbundets Forlag, Copenhagen 2011, at p. 208.

In relation to third parties, each of the parties is free to pledge his or her own share of the property as security. In the case of the sale of a jointly-owned asset, such as a holiday cottage which both parties use, the personal relations between the joint owners will be so significant that one party will generally not be entitled to sell his or her share of the property without the consent of the other; see *Ugeskrift for Retsvæsen* (Weekly Law Journal) 2008, p. 11. In this case a majority of the Supreme Court presumably interpreted this as being a shared presumption for the acquisition of the asset that there should be agreement between the joint owners as to the sale, as the other party would have a significant interest in who becomes his or her joint owner.

A joint ownership contract is often drawn up by the lawyer who helped an unmarried couple to buy a residence together.[26] The contract will govern ownership relations, the right to control the property, liability and the conditions for dissolving the joint ownership etc. It is possible to include a provision on subletting.

b. Where the home is owned by one of the partners?

Each of the parties in an unmarried cohabiting relationship is entitled to dispose of his or her own assets, both legally and factually, without the consent of the other party, even though the assets are used by the other party or form a natural part of the cohabitation home. This applies to selling, pledging as security and renting out property and household goods.

c. Where the home is jointly rented by the partners?

If a cohabiting couple rent a flat together, they are joint tenants, and in this situation one partner cannot terminate the lease without the consent of the other. A dispute between the parties will be decided by the courts on the basis of the respective needs and equitable considerations, in the same way as with married couples.[27]

d. Where the home is rented by one of the partners?

If only one of the cohabitants signs the tenancy agreement, he or she can dispose of the home on his or her own without the consent of the other partner. According to the Danish Tenancy Act S. 75(2), if one of the partners dies, the other has a right to continue the lease if the partners

[26] I. LUND-ANDERSEN, *Familieøkonomien*, Jurist- og Økonomforbundets Forlag, Copenhagen 2011, at p. 256-257 and at p. 526-527.

[27] See I. LUND-ANDERSEN and I. NØRGAARD, *Familieret*, Jurist- og Økonomforbundets Forlag, Copenhagen, 2012, at p. 332-333.

shared a household for at least two years immediately before the death of the partner, provided that the deceased does not leave a husband or wife behind.

If cohabitants stop living together for reasons other than the death of one of them, the partner who has not signed the tenancy agreement may continue the lease without the consent of the owner, provided the partner who is the tenant under the lease agrees; see the Danish Tenancy Act S. 77a. If the other tenant does not agree, it is for the courts to decide who is to continue the tenancy. A court will especially consider the welfare of children under 18, whether or not they are children in common or one of the partner's children from another relationship.[28]

ENGLAND AND WALES

The owner occupied family home is not considered special property as such in England and Wales outside the married/civil partnership context. General property law applies although in the owner occupied context the law of trusts can sometimes be used to establish a beneficial interest in the family home on behalf of the non-owning spouse.

The rented family home can be transferred between partners at the end of a cohabitation relationship regardless of ownership providing the tenancy is still in existence and at the discretion of the court, in accordance with the statutory criteria in Schedule 7 English Family Law Act 1996.

a. Where the home is jointly owned by the partners?

Joint ownership requires both partners' consent to sell, dispose or mortgage the home. In the absence of consent, an order of the court must be obtained. In joint ownership cases of dispute, the court has power to decide whether to order a sale and the presumption is that sale will be ordered (English Trusts of Land and Appointment of Trustees Act 1996). Sale or other disposal can be delayed when there are children and a Schedule 1 English Children Act 1989 application is possible seeking to transfer the home to one partner for the benefit of the child. The grant of an occupation order can delay the sale where there are grounds under S. 33 English Family Law Act 1996, which applies to joint owners and is typically applicable in the domestic violence context. Here, the fact of

28 I. LUND-ANDERSEN and I. NØRGAARD, *Familieret*, Jurist- og Økonomforbundets Forlag, Copenhagen, 2012, at p. 333-334.

joint ownership means in principle that the court can make an order excluding the other partner indefinitely, although this is not normally considered good practice.

b. Where the home is owned by one of the partners?

The sole owner has the right to sell or mortgage the home although if a partner is in 'actual occupation' they may have an overriding interest to remain in occupation where a third party is seeking to repossess the property as decided in *Williams & Glyn's Bank v Boland* [1981] AC 487. As a consequence of this rule, a partner will normally be asked to consent to any disposal or sale as the owner will be required to give vacant possession on sale and the mortgagee will want clarification of the occupant's rights if any in the home before proceeding. However, on relationship breakdown, if the non-owner's partner's permission/licence to occupy is terminated by their partner which is easy to do, they can be evicted by them. Only under a S. 36 English Family Law Act 1996 application, can this be delayed if there is an occupation order granted. Normally this will be for 6 months or 12 months absolute maximum and is most likely where there is domestic violence.

c. Where the home is jointly rented by the partners?

Joint tenancy rented homes - either joint tenant can terminate the tenancy of the family home by giving notice to quit to the Landlord as decided in *Hammersmith and Fulham BC v Monk* [1992] 1 AC 478. The tenancy of the home can be transferred to one cohabitant partner who is a joint tenant, depriving the other partner of their tenancy on relationship breakdown under Schedule 7 English Family Law Act 1996. This is at the discretion of the court when one cohabiting partner makes an application under the Act. However, this must be filed at court before the joint tenant partner gives notice to quit the tenancy to the Landlord, or there will be no tenancy left in existence to transfer. The court applies the same criteria as for an occupation order under S. 33(6) and, in addition, must have regard to the circumstances in which the tenancy was granted and the suitability of the parties as tenants.

The S. 33(6) criteria include:

- each party's housing needs and resources and those of any relevant child;
- the financial resources of each of the parties;
- the likely effect of the decision of the court on the health, safety or well-being of the parties and any relevant child;

- the conduct of the parties;
- the length of time since they lived together;
- the existence of any Children Act 1989 or property proceedings.

d. Where the home is rented by one of the partners?

Sole tenancy rented homes:

Schedule 7 English Family Law Act 1996 also allows applications for transfer of tenancy order between cohabitants of the rented family home on relationship breakdown in cases where the tenancy of the home is rented in the sole name of the other partner. This is also at the discretion of the court. Similarly, the application needs to be filed at court before the tenant partner gives notice to quit the home to the Landlord as this will extinguish the tenancy. The court applies the same criteria as for an occupation order under S. 36(6) as well as having regard to the circumstances in which the tenancy was granted and the suitability of the parties as tenants.

The S. 36(6) criteria are more extensive than those in S. 33(6) applying to joint tenant partners and require greater scrutiny of the relationship. They include:

- each party's housing needs and resources and those of any relevant child;
- the financial resources of each of the parties;
- the likely effect of the decision of the court on the health, safety or well-being of the parties and any relevant child;
- the conduct of the parties;
- the length of time since they lived together;
- the nature of the parties relationship and the level of commitment involved in it; the length of the cohabitation;
- whether they have children together;
- the length of time since they separated, and
- the existence of any Children Act 1989 or property proceedings.

ESTONIA

a. Where the home is jointly owned by the partners?

There is no separate regulation in Estonian legislation on the dispossession or encumbrance of joint ownership or common ownership with regard to whether it involves the partners in an informal relationship. According to § 73(1) of the Estonian Law of Property Act, a co-owner may transfer, bequeath, pledge or in any other manner dispose of the legal share in a shared thing belonging to the co-owner. Upon the sale of a legal share in immovable property to a person who is neither a co-owner nor is privileged pursuant to the law, the other co-owners have the right of pre-emption to the legal share being sold (§ 73(1) Estonian Law of Property Act).

b. Where the home is owned by one of the partners?

There is no separate regulation in Estonian legislation on the dispossession or encumbrance of sole ownership with regard to whether it involves the partners in an informal relationship. In civil issues, the partners in an informal relationship are akin to unmarried persons. According to § 69(1) of the Estonian Law of Property Act an owner has the right to possess, use and dispose of a thing, and to demand, as far as all other persons are concerned, the prevention of any violation of these rights and the elimination of the consequences of any violation.

c. Where the home is jointly rented by the partners?

There is no separate regulation of the sub-lease contract in Estonian legislation concerning the case when the parties are partners in an informal relationship. A lessee may, with the consent of the lessor, transfer the use of a thing fully or partially to a third party (sublease), particularly to sublet the thing (§ 288(1) Estonian Law of Obligations Act).

d. Where the home is rented by one of the partners?

Estonian legislation does not have a separate regulation on the lease contract with regard to whether they are partners in an informal relationship. According to § 289 of the Estonian Law of Obligations Act, the lessee of a dwelling has the right to accommodate in the leased dwelling his or her spouse, minor children and parents who are incapacitated for work without the consent of the lessor, unless it is agreed in the leasehold contract that the lessee may do so only with the consent of the lessor. It is a lessee's right before the lessor, not the mutual right of partners in an informal relationship.

FINLAND

a. Where the home is jointly owned by the partners?

The provisions of the Finnish Marriage Act that prevent one of the spouses from disposing of the joint home without the consent of the other spouse do not apply to cohabitees. However, the general provisions of the Finnish Act on Certain Joint Ownership (180/1958) apply instead.

The Act is applied to all joint owners independent of their partnership status. This Act states that a joint owner can dispose of or otherwise dictate his or her share of the property, if his or her actions do not affect the rights and benefits of the other owners. The joint owner of the property has the right to make an application to the District Court for an order to sell the property, if the owners cannot agree on the use of the property.

b. Where the home is owned by one of the partners?
Again, the provisions of the Finnish Marriage Act that prevent the spouse from disposing of the joint home without the consent of the other spouse do not apply to cohabitees. Generally, a partner can freely sell, mortgage or sublet the home if he or she is the sole owner the property. However, if the home is in a right-of-occupancy building under the Finnish Right-of-Occupancy Housing Act (650/1990), where the right of occupancy is purchased against payment, also a person living in circumstances similar to a marriage with the holder of the occupancy rights shall be given an opportunity to be heard in matters concerning the apartment. It is to be noted that this housing scheme is not to be confused with the limited liability housing companies (*asunto-osakeyhtiö/bostadsaktiebolag*), which is a much more common type of housing in Finland.

b. Where the home is jointly rented by the partners?
According to the Finnish Act on Residential Leases (S. 53), one spouse alone cannot terminate a lease agreement without the other spouse's consent regardless of who has signed the lease agreement. Such consent will not, however, be necessary if it cannot be obtained without undue inconvenience. Persons living together as husband and wife without marriage are considered as being equivalent to married spouses according to the Act (S. 11). The Act does not include specific provisions on subletting with regard to cohabitees.

c. Where the home is rented by one of the partners?
According to the Finnish Act on Residential Leases (S. 53), if the spouses live in an apartment which they have rented jointly or which one of them has rented, one spouse alone cannot terminate the lease agreement without the other spouse's consent. Such consent will not, however, be necessary if it cannot be obtained without undue inconvenience. Persons living together as husband and wife without marriage are considered as being equivalent to married spouses according to the Act (S. 11). The Act does not include specific provisions on subletting with regard to cohabitees.

FRANCE

a. Where the home is jointly owned by the partners?

Where the home is jointly owned by the partners: In this case, both partners' consent is necessary to dispose of the property (by means of a sale or donation). Both partners' consent is also required for a leasing agreement. There is no specific provision in the French Civil Code, so that the general rules apply. Several situations may arise with regard to mortgaging: 1) if both partners have agreed upon mortgaging (*hypothèque*), the mortgagee – in the absence of payment – can seize the property, which will be sold;[29] 2) if only one partner has obtained a mortgage on the home without the other partner's consent, the mortgagee cannot seize the property. He or she can only request the termination of the joint ownership before the courts (*indivision*);[30] 3) if one partner has entered into a mortgage only with regard to his or her share of the property, the same solution as under 2) applies: the mortgagee cannot directly seize the property but only request the termination of the joint ownership before the courts (the property will then be sold and the proceeds will be shared between the two partners), see Art. 815-7 of the French Civil Code, which is a general provision that applies in the case of joint ownership.

b. Where the home is owned by one of the partners?

Where the home is owned by one of the partners: The partner who is the owner of the property can sell or rent the home without the other partner's agreement. There is no specific provision in the French Civil Code. The general rules apply.

c. Where the home is jointly rented by the partners?

Where the home is jointly rented by the partners: Each partner is a party to the lease agreement (a lessee). Both partners are under a duty to pay the rent and rates (the lease contract can also include a clause making both partners jointly and severally liable. Such liability does not occur *ex lege*). If one wishes to terminate the lease, this has no effect with regard to the other partner who can remain in the home since he or she is also a leaseholder. The agreement of both partners is required for subletting.

d. Where the home is rented by one of the partners?

Where the home is rented by one of the partners: The partner who has rented the property can sublet the home without the other partner's

29 Cass. Com., 18 February 2003, no. 00-11008, *Bull. Civ.* IV, no. 21.

30 Cass. Civ. I, 19 November 1996, no. 94-22052.

agreement. He or she can also terminate the lease. In this latter case, however, under Art. 14 of Law Act no. 89-462 of 6 July 1989 the recognised partner (*concubin notoire*) can request the benefit of the transfer of the residential lease, subject to the condition that the partners have lived together for at least one year.[31]

GERMANY

a. Where the home is jointly owned by the partners?

Where the home is jointly owned by the partners the general rules of civil law apply. The partners are co-owners in equal proportions or unequal proportions (§ 1008 German Civil Code). Co-owners form a community (*Gemeinschaft*) in the sense of the law's obligations, § 741 German Civil Code (see as well Question 41). There is a common administration of the asset (§ 744 para. 1 German Civil Code). However, a co-owner may dispose separately of his share (§ 747 para. 1 s. 1 German Civil Code). Consent of the other co-owner is not necessary.

Regarding the common object as a whole, both co-owners can dispose jointly (§ 747 para. 1 s. 2 German Civil Code). This concerns dispositions in respect of the home and mortgaging.[32]

In the case of major transactions, such as the construction of a common family home, a compensation claim based on the statutory rules of (commercial) partnership law (§§ 705 et seq. of the German Civil Code) or the rules on unjust enrichment (§ 812 para. 1 s. 2 of the German Civil Code) may be made (see Question 46).[33]

b. Where the home is owned by one of the partners?

Where the home is owned by only one of the partners the general rules apply. Only this partner is the owner. The other partner has no legal position to block transactions such as dispositions in respect of the home, mortgaging and subletting.

---

31 This also applies to a same-sex partner and is therefore in line with the ECtHR's case law, see ECtHR, *Karner v. Austria*, No. 40016/98, 14.7.2003.

32 H. SPRAU, '§ 747', in: O. PALANDT, *Bürgerliches Gesetzbuch*, Beck, Munich, 2015, at No. 3.

33 A SANDERS, 'Cohabitants in Private Law: Trust, Frustration and Unjust Enrichment in England, Germany and Canada', *International & Comparative Law Quarterly*, 2013, at p. 641 et seq.; D. SCHWAB, *Familienrecht*, Beck, Munich, 2014, at No. 1006 et seq. and 1015.

c. Where the home is jointly rented by the partners?
Where the home is jointly rented by the partners the general rules apply. The partners are joint tenants. Each partner has the position of a joint tenant and has to co-decide on subletting.[34]

d. Where the home is rented by one of the partners?
Where the home is rented by only one of the partners the general rules apply. Only this partner is a tenant.[35] The other partner has no legal position to block transactions such as subletting. It is possible, however, for there to be a separate subletting contract between the partners.[36]

GREECE

a. Where the home is jointly owned by the partners?
No.

b. Where the home is owned by one of the partners?
No.

c. Where the home is jointly rented by the partners?
No.

d. Where the home is rented by one of the partners?
No.

All related issues are resolved on the basis of the general rules of the law of obligations and property law. In the event of joint ownership, the rules on joint ownership *pro indiviso* are applied (Art. 1113 et seq. and 785 et seq. of the Greek Civil Code). In a case where the partners merely have a shared lease, the rules of Art. 785 et seq. of the Greek Civil Code on shared (contractual) rights are applied.

---

34 F. STERNEL, 'Mietrecht', in: R. HAUSMANN and G. HOHLOCH (eds.), *Das Recht der nichtehelichen Lebensgemeinschaft*, E. Schmidt, Berlin, 2004, at p. 363 and 372 No. 12.

35 G. BRUDERMÜLLER, 'Einl. vor § 1297', in: O. PALANDT, *Bürgerliches Gesetzbuch*, Beck, Munich, 2015, at No. 18.

36 F. STERNEL, 'Mietrecht', in: R. HAUSMANN and G. HOHLOCH (eds.), *Das Recht der nichtehelichen Lebensgemeinschaft*, E. Schmidt, Berlin, 2004, at p. 363, 373, 378 et seq. No. 14, 30 et seq.

HUNGARY

a. Where the home is jointly owned by the partners?

There is no specific rule which mirrors the legal position of spouses. According to the general rules contained in the Fifth Book of the Hungarian Civil Code, if the dwelling is the partners' joint property their common (unanimous) decision is needed for transactions[37] such as the disposal, mortgaging or subletting of the whole dwelling.

b. Where the home is owned by one of the partners?

The cohabitant who is the owner of the dwelling can enter into transactions according to the general rules on ownership. This possibility diverges from that of spouses as the Hungarian Civil Code protects the family home if the spouses reside there.

c. Where the home is jointly rented by the partners?

In the case of a dwelling being jointly rented there is no specific rule. The cohabitants' possibilities, just as those of other renters, are severely restricted in the Hungarian Civil Code and Act No. LXXVIII of 1993 on Certain Provisions Concerning Flat-letting and the Alienation of Flats.

d. Where the home is rented by one of the partners?

There is no specific rule. The renter's rights are restricted in the Hungarian Civil Code and Act No. LXXVIII of 1993 on Certain Provisions Concerning Flat-letting and the Alienation of Flats.

REPUBLIC OF IRELAND

There are no specific rules on such transactions. See the previous answer to Question 22. If the home is jointly owned by the partners, both parties must join in the transaction.

ITALY

a. Where the home is jointly owned by the partners?

No specific rules apply to the home which is jointly owned by the two partners in an informal relationship. Ordinary rules on common ownership apply (*comunione ordinaria* or *comproprietà*) only when the home has been jointly purchased by the two partners and registered in both their names. In no case, in fact, can common ownership automatically result from the mere fact of cohabiting.

[37] Art. 5:78(2) of Hungarian Civil Code.

Pursuant to Art. 1100 et seq. Italian Civil Code, then, transactions exceeding ordinary administration like the disposal and mortgaging of a property must therefore be agreed upon by both partners and each co-owner can freely sell his or her share of the asset.

b. Where the home is owned by one of the partners?

When the home is owned by one of the partners, the fact that he or she are partners in an informal relationship has no relevance. Every transaction of ordinary or extraordinary administration will be decided by the homeowner alone.

c. Where the home is jointly rented by the partners?

As under Italian law a lease is a contract which gives rise only to personal rights of enjoyment, if the home is rented – regardless of whether by one or both of the partners – disposal and mortgage are not allowed. Subletting – although subject to restrictions (Art. 2 Law of 27 July 1978, n. 392) – is possible under the general law of contract, but there is no specific rule regarding a home which is jointly rented by the two partners in an informal relationship. Both lessors will therefore have to agree on the sublease.

d. Where the home is rented by one of the partners?

No specific rule is provided when the home is rented by one of the informal partners. Disposal and mortgages are excluded by the general law, and the lessor will be the sole person entitled to sublet the premises.

LATVIA

In Latvia there is no such specific legal order on informal relationships.

However, if the home is in the joint ownership of both partners, the general legal order of property rights as stated in the Latvian Civil Law would be applicable. Section 1067 of the Latvian Civil Law determines that ownership rights which belong to several people in respect of one undivided property, not as shares divided in actuality but as undivided shares – so that only the substance of the rights is divided – are joint ownership rights (*kopīpašuma tiesības*). Section 1068 of the Latvian Civil Law states that the consent of all the joint owners is required in order to deal with the subject-matter of the joint ownership, either as a whole or with respect to stated individual shares and if one of the joint owners acts separately then such action not only has no effect, but also imposes a duty on that joint owner to compensate the others for losses caused to them by the sole action. No individual joint owner may, without the consent of the others, encumber the subject-matter of joint ownership with property rights, nor alienate it as a whole or in part, nor alter it in some way. Therefore, every joint owner has the right to protest against such actions by one or all of the other joint owners, and this right may not be revoked by a majority vote. Section 1072 of the Latvian Civil Law provides that each joint owner's undivided share of a joint property belongs exclusively to such joint owner. Therefore, the joint owner is allowed to act with it in every way which conforms with its substance, as long as this action does not apply to the shares of the other joint owners. On this basis, each joint owner also has the right to alienate or pledge the share of the common property belonging to such joint owner. Section 1073 provides that if any of the joint owners of an immovable property alienate his or her share to a person who is not a joint owner, then the rest of the joint owners are to have a right of first refusal for a period of two months, calculated from the date that a copy of the purchase agreement is received, but in cases where it has not been possible to exercise the right of first refusal due to the fault of the alienor, then there is to be a right of pre-emption. If several joint owners apply at the same time to exercise rights of first refusal or pre-emption then they will acquire the alienated share jointly and must divide it among themselves in equal shares, unless they themselves agree otherwise.[38]

If living accommodation is rented only by one partner, then S. 17 of the Latvian Law on Residential Tenancy determines that a tenant has the right to sub-rent all the residential space or a part of it that he or she occupies, only with the consent of the landlord and the adult family members living together with the tenant. [39] However, it must be taken into account that, according to the first part of S. 9 of the Latvian Law on Residential Tenancy, a cohabiting partner (i.e. not a spouse) is not considered to be a family member (analysed in response to Question 3).

LITHUANIA

a. Where the home is jointly owned by the partners?

There are special rules: according to Art. 3.233 of the Lithuanian Civil Code, without the written consent of the other cohabitee a cohabitee shall have no right to sell, donate or alienate in any other way, or to lease or

38 Civil Law. Part Three. Property rights. Law of Republic of Latvia. "Valdības Vēstnesis", 24 February 1937, no.44.
39 Law On Residential Tenancy. Law of Republic of Latvia. "Latvijas Vēstnesis", 29 February 1993, no.19.

charge the assets acquired and used together or to encumber the rights to such assets in any other way.[40] If a cohabitee is incapable of giving such consent due to incompetence or the consent of the other cohabitee is impossible to achieve due to other important reasons, permission to make a transaction may be granted by the courts at the request of the other cohabitee.

A transaction entered into in violation of the rules laid down in Art. 233 may be declared null and void in an action brought by the cohabitee who has not given his or her consent to the transaction except in cases where a third party recipient of the assets sold, charged or leased had acted in good faith. The time limit for bringing an action to avoid such a transaction shall be one year from the day when the cohabitee knew or should have known about the transaction.

Considering the fact that these specific rules are not yet effective, informal relationships (*de facto* relations) between partners are not subject to a special legal regulation, and separate elements of such relations are subject to the rules of the general civil law under Book IV, 'Material Law', of the Lithuanian Civil Code, which regulates relations between co-owners. So in this case Art. 4.88 of the Lithuanian Civil Code defines a right of a co-owner to transfer or limit the right to the part held in joint common ownership:

- An asset (property) which is the object of common joint ownership is possessed, used and disposed of only upon agreement between the co-owners.
- Agreement between the co-owners is necessary in order to transfer immovable property to the ownership of another person, to rent or to give for use in some other way, to mortgage or otherwise to encumber the right to the asset. If a co-owner is a minor, permission may be given by his or her parents, guardians, or carer.
- A co-owner shall have no right to transfer to the ownership of another person his or her share of the commonly owned joint property until that share has been established in the common property, with the exception of cases where the property is being inherited, and in other cases established by law.

40 According to Art. 3.230 of the Lithuanian Civil Code, the community property of cohabitees shall include: '1) a house or an apartment acquired and used together by cohabitees for their life together; 2) the rental, usufruct or any other right of one of the cohabitees to use the dwelling house or the flat which the cohabitees use for their life together'.

b. Where the home is owned by one of the partners?

There are no specific rules. The case law contains some examples[41] when the Court's permission was necessary for transactions involving a family dwelling in cases where the partners had common children.[42] Such an approach is based on the provisions of the Law on the Fundamental Protection of the Rights of the Child,[43] the United Nations Convention on the Rights of the Child, and the 1975 European Convention on the Legal Status of Children Born out of Wedlock.

c. Where the home is jointly rented by the partners?

d. Where the home is rented by one of the partners?

Article 3.233 (see answer to Question 24(a)). Moreover, the lessee of a dwelling shall have the right to sublease that dwelling upon the written consent of all the family members residing together with him or her as well as that of the lessor. Upon concluding a contract to sublease, the lessee shall continue to be liable towards the lessor under the lease contract (Art. 6.595).

LUXEMBOURG

No, there are no specific rules; the partners are submitted to the general principles of contract law.

a. Where the home is jointly owned by the partners?

Where the home is jointly owned by the partners, one of them cannot dispose of or raise a mortgage without the consent of the other owning partner.

---

41 For example, in a case examined in 2008 the Lithuanian Supreme Court admitted that 'both parents must ensure a home for the child irrespective of whether or not the father is registered as the child's father in the statements of civil status, as the child's origin from his parents, on which the mutual rights and duties of the child and parents are founded, is confirmed from the date of the child's birth and creates related rights and duties under the law from that date'. In the Court's view, a breach of this duty is a basis for subjecting the father to civil liability; therefore, compensation was awarded to the child's mother for part of the expenses incurred in acquiring a dwelling for the child and herself. Ruling of the Lithuanian Supreme Court of 9 October 2008, civil case No. 3K-3-383/2008.

42 I. KUDINAVIČIŪTĖ-MICHAILOVIENĖ, 'Šeimos narių teisės į gyvenamąją patalpą įgyvendinimas ir gynimas' (The Realization and Protection of the Right of Family Members to the Dwelling), *Socialinių mokslų studijos*, Vol. 3, No. 3, 2009, at p. 193-212.

43 Official gazette, 1996, No. 33-807.

b. Where the home is owned by one of the partners?
Where the home is owned by one of the partners, the owner can dispose of or take out a mortgage.

c. Where the home is jointly rented by the partners?
Where the home is jointly rented by the partners, one of them may only sublet it with the consent of the other (and, of course, the consent of the lessor).

d. Where the home is rented by one of the partners?
Where the home is rented by one of the partners, this partner is the tenant and may sublet if his contract allows for subletting.

THE NETHERLANDS

a. Where the home is jointly owned by the partners?
Joint ownership. There are no specific rules which are applicable, such as the provisions of Art. 1:88 and 1:89 Dutch Civil Code which provide protection to married and registered partners during their relationship.[44] A spouse requires the written consent of the other spouse for a number of legal transactions which potentially affect the matrimonial home, regardless of whether it is the private or joint property of the spouses. These rules do not apply to non-marital partners, not directly and not by way of analogy.[45]

General contract and property law thus govern the issue of whether consent is required. Co-ownership of a house is subject to the general provisions on joint ownership in title 3.7 Dutch Civil Code. Two situations have to be discerned: first, the situation in which a partner wishes to contract and of dispose his/her share in the joint property and the second situation relates to transactions involving the joint property (thus not only a share).

Situation 1: Whether a partner is allowed to contract and to dispose of his/her share in the house is governed by Art. 3:175 Dutch Civil Code. The first paragraph states that each co-owner is allowed to convey his share in the community. Paragraph 2, however, lays down the rule that

[44] See K. BOELE-WOELKI, F. SCHONEWILLE and W. SCHRAMA, 'National report: The Netherlands', The property relations between the spouses, available at: ceflonline.net/country-reports-for-the-netherlands/, at p. 8.

[45] W.M. SCHRAMA, *Vermogensrecht voor ongehuwde samenlevers*, Kluwer, Deventer, 2000, at p. 66-67.

this is not allowed when it is contrary to the nature of the legal relationship between the co-owners. In the legal literature it has been argued that the legal relationship between cohabiting partners opposes this option, in particular since the relation between the co-owners is subject to the principle of reasonableness and fairness (Art. 3:166 para. 3 Dutch Civil Code).[46] It is contrary to this principle to confront a partner with a new co-owner of the house. There is no case law on this subject, however.

Situation 2: All transactions (disposing, mortgaging etc.) in relation to the community will have to be performed jointly by the co-owners (Art. 3:170 para. 3 Dutch Civil Code).[47]

b. Where the home is owned by one of the partners?

Sole ownership: There are no specific rules which are applicable, such as the provisions of Art. 1:88 and 1:89 Dutch Civil Code which provide protection to married and registered partners during their relationship.[48] A spouse requires the written consent of the other spouse for a number of legal transactions which potentially affect the matrimonial home, regardless of whether it is the private or joint property of the spouses. These rules do not apply to non-marital partners, not directly and not by way of analogy.[49]

General contract and property law thus govern the issue of whether the consent of the partner who is not an owner is required. As a result of these rules (Art. 5:1 para. 1 Dutch Civil Code) an owner has the most comprehensive property right to an asset. Para. 2 determines that the owner is free to use the asset to the exclusion of everyone else, provided that he/she respects the rights and entitlements of others to the asset and observes the restrictions based on rules of written and unwritten law. One could perhaps argue that given the special relationship between cohabiting partners the partner/owner should take into account the other partner's interest. There is no case law to this effect. However, even then,

---

46 W.M. SCHRAMA, 'Goederenrecht: mede-eigendom', in: M.L.C.C. DE BRUIJN-LÜCKERS et al. (eds.), *Relatierecht, SDUCommentaar*, SDU, The Hague, 2014, at p. 2025-2040.

47 The rule is more complicated, but for the purpose of this question this answer is sufficient.

48 See K. BOELE-WOELKI, F. SCHONEWILLE and W. SCHRAMA, 'National report: The Netherlands', The property relations between the spouses, available at: ceflonline.net/country-reports-for-the-netherlands/, at p. 8.

49 W.M. SCHRAMA, *Vermogensrecht voor ongehuwde samenlevers*, Kluwer, Deventer, 2000, at p. 66-67.

this would not imply that the consent of the partner is required for legal acts and transactions.

c. Where the home is jointly rented by the partners?
Jointly rented property. There are no specific rules which are applicable, such as the provisions of Art. 1:88 and 1:89 Dutch Civil Code which provide protection to married and registered partners during their relationship.[50] A spouse requires the written consent of the other spouse for a number of legal transactions which potentially affect the matrimonial home, regardless whether it is private or joint property of the spouses. These rules do not apply to non-marital partners, not directly and not by way of analogy.[51]

As the partners are only entitled to the house on the basis of a tenancy agreement, neither of them (nor together) is not allowed to transfer the title to the property. Whether the partners are allowed to sublet the house or a part thereof, depends on the specific agreement with the landlord.

d. Where the home is rented by one of the partners?
Sole rented property. There are no specific rules which are applicable, such as the provisions of Art. 1:88 and 1:89 Dutch Civil Code which provide protection to married and registered partners during their relationship.[52] A spouse requires the written consent of the other spouse for a number of legal transactions which potentially affect the matrimonial home, regardless of whether it is the private or joint property of the spouses. These rules do not apply to non-marital partners, not directly and not by way of analogy.[53]

As the partner is only entitled to the house on the basis of a tenancy agreement, the tenant is not allowed to transfer the title to the property. Whether the partner is allowed to sublet the house or a part thereof, depends on the specific agreement with the landlord.

---

50 See K. BOELE-WOELKI, F. SCHONEWILLE and W. SCHRAMA, 'National report: The Netherlands', The property relations between the spouses, available at: ceflonline.net/country-reports-for-the-netherlands/, at p. 8.

51 W.M. SCHRAMA, *Vermogensrecht voor ongehuwde samenlevers*, Kluwer, Deventer, 2000, at p. 66-67.

52 See K. BOELE-WOELKI, F. SCHONEWILLE and W. SCHRAMA, 'National report: The Netherlands', The property relations between the spouses, available at: ceflonline.net/country-reports-for-the-netherlands/, at p. 8.

53 W.M. SCHRAMA, *Vermogensrecht voor ongehuwde samenlevers*, Kluwer, Deventer, 2000, at p. 66-67.

NORWAY

a. Where the home is jointly owned by the partners?

During the relationship, there are no specific rules on transactions concerning the home of partners to an informal relationship where the home is jointly owned by the partners. Unless otherwise agreed, a co-owner may freely dispose of his or her undivided share in the property pursuant to the Norwegian Act on Co-ownership, 1965, S. 10. (In these cases, the other co-owner has a pre-emptive right of purchase, S. 11.) However, special circumstances might lead to a restricted right to dispose of an item, pursuant to the Norwegian Act on Co-ownership, S. 1. This could well be the case when the property in question is the home of the partners.

b. Where the home is owned by one of the partners?

During the relationship, there are no specific rules on transactions concerning the home of partners to an informal relationship where the home is owned by one of the partners. Thus, the owners may freely sell or mortgage their homes, whether or not they are partners to an informal relationship.

c. Where the home is jointly rented by the partners?

During the relationship, there are no specific rules on transactions concerning the home of partners to an informal relationship where the home is jointly rented by the partners. When two people rent a dwelling together, one of them may terminate the tenancy, unless otherwise agreed. The right to sublet etc. depends on the agreement between the two tenants and between the tenants and the landlord.

d. Where the home is rented by one of the partners?

During the relationship, there are no specific rules on transactions concerning the home of partners to an informal relationship where the home is rented by one of the partners. The tenant is entitled to include a cohabitant as a member of his or her household, under the provisions of the Norwegian Tenancy Act 1999, S. 7-1. As a rule, a tenant has no right to sub-let or in any other way transfer his or her right of use to other people without the consent of the landlord unless otherwise provided in an agreement, S. 7-2.

PORTUGAL

No. There are no specific rules, unlike marriage in which any transaction regarding the family home must be subjected to the consent of the other spouse, even if he/she does not own it or has rented it (Art. 1682-A and 1682-B of the Portuguese Civil Code).

a. Where the home is jointly owned by the partners?
The general rules of joint ownership apply (Art. 1403 et seq. of the Portuguese Civil Code).

b. Where the home is owned by one of the partners?
The general rules of ownership apply (Art. 1305 et seq. of the Portuguese Civil Code).

c. Where the home is jointly rented by the partners?
The general rules of leasing apply (Art. 1060 et seq. of the Portuguese Civil Code).

d. Where the home is rented by one of the partners?
The general rules of leasing apply (Art. 1060 et seq. of the Portuguese Civil Code).

RUSSIA

a. Where the home is jointly owned by the partners?
There are no specific rules governing transactions related to a home which is jointly owned by partners in an informal relationship. The general rule in Art. 246(1) of the Russian Civil Code is that joint owners enter into transactions related to their entire home jointly. That means that any transaction related to the home requires the written consent of both partners, irrespective of the size of their shares in the home. Under Art. 246(2) Russian Civil Code, each of the joint owners can independently dispose of (sell, donate, dispose of by will, mortgage or dispose of in any other way) his or her share in the jointly owned home. He/she is restricted in this respect, however, by the provisions of Art. 250(1) Russian Civil Code; under these provisions, a joint owner who wishes to sell a share in a jointly owned home to a third person must first offer this share to the co-owner subject to the same conditions as agreed upon with the third person. Under Art. 250(2) Russian Civil Code, a joint owner who wishes to sell his/her share to a third person has to send the other joint owner(s) written notification containing all the conditions which pertain to the transaction. He/she is free to sell the share to a third person if the co-owner does not agree to buy the share in the home within one month.

This means that a partner has a preferential right of purchase if his/her partner intends to sell his/her share in a jointly owned home to a third party. This right applies only to a sale, and does not protect the partner if the other partner decides to donate, dispose of by will or mortgage his/her share in the jointly owned home.

b. Where the home is owned by one of the partners?
In the absence of any specific rules, the partner-owner is free to dispose of the home solely owned by him/her.

c. Where the home is jointly rented by the partners?
In the case of a social tenancy the rights of a non-tenant partner to whom the court has granted the status of a member of the tenant's family are equal to those of the tenant.

d. Where the home is rented by one of the partners?
If the partner is a social tenant and his/her informal partner has been granted the status of a family member of the tenant by the court, his/her written consent is required for any transactions related to the tenancy (Art. 70 (instalment of other persons), 72 (swap), 76 (sublease), 82 (alteration of rental contract) and 82(2) (termination of the tenancy) Russian Housing Code).

If the absent partner is a commercial tenant and the informal partner is either mentioned in the initial tenancy contract or is later installed with the consent of the landlord, his/her written consent is required for any transactions related to the tenancy (Art. 679-680 Russian Civil Code (instalment of other persons) and Art. 687(1) Russian Civil Code (termination of the tenancy)).

SCOTLAND

a. Where the home is jointly owned by the partners?
Where a property is jointly owned, the parties may dispose of it by mutual agreement or, if they cannot agree, either may apply to the court for an order of division and sale. This is part of the general law of property and the court has no discretion in the matter.[54] Where the home is jointly owned by spouses or civil partners, the court does have discretion in terms of S. 19 of the Matrimonial Homes (Family Protection) (Scotland) Act 1981 and may refuse or postpone the granting of decree.

---

54 *Grant v The Governors of George Heriot's Trust and Others* 1906 13 SLT 986.

There is, however, no equivalent provision in respect of partners to an informal relationship. They are treated in the same way as any other owners in common and are entitled to order of division and sale.

b. Where the home is owned by one of the partners?

Where the home is owned by one of the partners, the other has no legal right to remain in the home against the wishes of the owner. There is some modification of this strict property law approach in terms of S. 18 of the Matrimonial Homes (Family Protection) (Scotland) Act 1981 which enables a cohabitant to apply to the court for grant of statutory occupancy rights. While statutory occupancy rights grant some legal security to a non-entitled cohabitant, their effect is limited and in particular they do not offer any protection against third party dealings.[55] In the context of marriage or civil partnership, the occupancy rights of a non-entitled spouse are protected against any dealings of the entitled spouse with a third party and, even where the entitled spouse has sold the property to a third party, the third party has no right to occupy the property.[56] There is no similar protection available to cohabitants. Even if a non-entitled cohabitant has obtained statutory occupancy rights in the family home, those rights will be defeated if the entitled partner disposes of the home.

c. Where the home is jointly rented by the partners?

Where the home is jointly rented by the partners, either partner may apply to the court for an order vesting the tenancy in their name solely, in terms of S. 13(9) of the Scots Matrimonial Homes (Family Protection) Act 1981. If the court grants such an order, it may provide for the payment by the applicant of just and reasonable compensation to the non-applicant.

d. Where the home is rented by one of the partners?

Where the home is rented by one of the partners, the non-entitled partner may apply to the court for an order transferring the tenancy into their name, in terms of S. 13(9) of the Matrimonial Homes (Family Protection) (Scotland) Act 1981. In deciding whether to grant such an order, the court shall have regard to all of the circumstances of the case, the suitability of the applicant to become the tenant and his or her capacity to fulfil the obligations of the lease.[57] Circumstances for consideration include:

---

55 Matrimonial Homes (Family Protection) (Scotland) Act 1981, S. 18(5).

56 Matrimonial Homes (Family Protection) (Scotland) Act 1981, S. 6.

57 Matrimonial Homes (Family Protection) (Scotland) Act 1981, S. 13(3).

- the conduct of the cohabitants in relation to each other and otherwise;
- their respective needs and resources;
- the needs of any child of the family;
- the extent to which the home is used in connection with either cohabitant's trade, business or profession;
- whether the non-applicant has offered to make available any suitable alternative accommodation.[58]

SLOVAKIA

In general within the limits of the law, the owner may: be in possession of his or her property (*ius possidendi*), use it and benefit from its proceeds (*ius utendi et fruendi*), and dispose of it (*ius disponendi*) (§ 123 Slovak Civil Code).[59] All owners have the same rights and duties and are granted the same legal protection (§ 124 Slovak Civil Code). According to the Slovak Civil Code an asset may be co-owned by more than one owner and the home can also be jointly owned by the partners.

Co-ownership may be divided or undivided. Undivided co-ownership may arise only between spouses (§ 136 para. 2 Slovak Civil Code).

a. Where the home is jointly owned by the partners?

In divided co-ownership (joint ownership), the co-owners have specific shares in the common asset (§ 137 para. 2 Slovak Civil Code). The shares specify the extent of the rights and duties resulting from the co-ownership of the common asset. Unless provided otherwise by statute or agreement, the shares of all co-owners are equal (§ 137 para. 2 Slovak Civil Code). All co-owners are jointly and severally entitled and obliged by juridical acts relating to the common asset.

Decisions concerning the management of the common asset are taken by a majority of votes determined according to the size of the shares (§ 139 para. 2 Slovak Civil Code). If the votes are equal or if no majority or agreement can be achieved, the courts will decide. Moreover, if there is an important change to the common asset, the minority co-owners may request a court decision as well (§ 139 para. 3 Slovak Civil Code). An 'important change' is not defined by the Slovak Civil Code, although

---

58 Matrimonial Homes (Family Protection) (Scotland) Act 1981, S. 3(3)(a)-(e).

59 See principally J. LAZAR, in: J. LAZAR et al. (eds.), *Občianske právo hmotné* (Substantive Slovak Civil Law), Iuris Libri, Bratislava, 2014, at p. 463-464.

doctrine has interpreted an important change to mean, for example, a rebuilding of the common home.[60]

If the share is transferred, the co-owners have a a right of pre-emption, unless the share is transferred to a relative (§ 140 Slovak Civil Code). The co-owners may agree on the cancellation of co-ownership and on a mutual settlement. The settlement agreement must be made in writing if it concerns immovables. In the case of movables, it need not be made in writing, but each co-owner must give the other co-owners a written confirmation of the settlement if requested to do so (§ 141 Slovak Civil Code). If the co-owners cannot reach an agreement, the co-ownership will be cancelled and will be settled by the courts upon a petition by any of the co-owners (§ 142 Slovak Civil Code). In this respect, the court will take into account the size of the shares and the use of the asset in question. The settlement may take various forms. If the common asset can be divided, it will be divided between the co-owners. If a new immovable is created by this settlement, the court may establish an easement in favour of the owner of the new immovable. If a division of the common asset is not possible, the court may grant ownership of the common asset to one or several co-owners against compensation. If none of the co-owners wants the asset, the court will order that the common asset be sold and the proceeds will be divided according to the size of shares.

However, if there are specific reasons (e.g. an elderly person is a co-owner of a house where he or she has lived for most of his or her life), the court will not cancel and settle the co-ownership by granting ownership of the asset to one or more co-owners against compensation or by selling the common asset and dividing the proceeds between them.

b. Where the home is owned by one of the partners?
The are no specific rules on transactions and no generally applicable rules for this legal situation.

c. Where the home is jointly rented by the partners?
The rules on the joint leasing of an apartment by the partners (a so-called co-tenancy: *spoločný nájom bytu*) do not generally prescribe any formal requirements for a valid conclusion of a contract. It may be concluded orally, implicitly or in writing, which is indeed recommended, as the

---

[60] See J. LAZAR, in: J. LAZAR et al. (eds.), *Občianske právo hmotné* (Substantive Slovak Civil Law), Iuris Libri, Bratislava, 2014, at p. 503.

lease contract is normally meant to regulate long-term relations.[61] Only the partners who have jointly concluded a contract have a direct right to use the apartment and the services connected therewith. Specifically, the members of the tenant's household (persons who live together permanently and together cover the costs of their needs) are expressly permitted to be the co-users of the apartment.

The law anticipates that ex-partners will agree on who will continue the lease of the common apartment as a tenant and who will leave. Such an agreement between the ex-partners will bring the joint lease to an end. If, however, the ex-partners cannot reach an agreement, either of them may apply for a court decision to terminate the right of co-tenancy and the court will then select the future tenant.

d. Where the home is rented by one of the partners?

The partner who is the tenant of the apartment will be able to continue to use the apartment without the need to provide replacement housing or other duties towards the co-habiting ex-partner. If, on the other hand, the partners are using the apartment as co-tenants, the fact that they have separated does not lessen their individual rights under the lease contract and they would both be able to continue the lease.

SLOVENIA

a. Where the home is jointly owned by the partners?

Partners manage and dispose of common property together. A legal transaction that one partner concludes in relation to common property without the necessary agreement of the other partner may be challenged by the other partner.

b. Where the home is owned by one of the partners?

There is no specific rule. A partner disposes of individual property independently.

c. Where the home is jointly rented by the partners?

There is no specific rule. Under the general rules partners who are joint lessees of a home may only jointly renounce rental relations.

---

61 See M. JURČOVÁ and J. ŠTEFANKO, 'TENLAW: Tenancy Law and Housing Policy in Multi-level Europe. Tenant's Rights Brochure for Slovakia', available at: www.tenlaw.uni-bremen.de/Brochures/SlovakiaBrochure_31052014.pdf, at p. 8.

d. Where the home is rented by one of the partners?
There is no specific rule. A partner who is the only lessee may renounce rental relations without the agreement of the other partner.

SPAIN

a. Where the home is jointly owned by the partners?
In the Spanish Civil Code there are no special rules on transactions concerning the home of partners. If the home is jointly owned, the ordinary rules of joint ownership apply. Under Art. 399 Spanish Civil Code each partner may conclude transactions concerning his or her property rights in the home. If the partners are married, any transaction concerning the home would require both spouses' consent and failing that, authorization by the judge (Art. 1320 Spanish Civil Code). This provision may also apply to partners to an informal relationship by analogy, but this is by no means certain.

According to Art. 231-9 Catalan Civil Code, neither spouse is allowed to dispose of, mortgage, or carry out any other transaction on the family home without consent, even of their individual share of the property. Such consent may not be excluded by agreement or granted in general. In the absence of consent, the judicial authority may authorise the act, taking account of the interests of the family, or if there is another just cause.

An act performed without consent or authorisation is voidable, at the request of the other spouse if the other spouse is living in the same dwelling, within four years of having knowledge thereof or from the time that the act is recorded in the Property Registry.

An act remains effective if the purchaser acts in good faith and for consideration and the owner stated that the property was not a family dwelling, even though it was an inaccurate representation. There is no good faith if the purchaser knew or could reasonably have known at the time of the acquisition that it was a family dwelling. In any case, the spouse who disposed thereof is liable for the damages caused, in accordance with the applicable laws.

This provision is also applicable to informal partnerships (Art. 234-3.2 Catalan Civil Code).

b. Where the home is owned by one of the partners?

There are no special rules protecting the family home in the Spanish Civil Code that apply to partners to an informal relationship. The partner who owns the home is therefore free to conclude any transactions on the home. Article 1320 Spanish Civil Code, which requires that the consent of both spouses for acts of disposal on the matrimonial home, may apply by analogy, but this is by no means certain.

According to Art. 231-9 Catalan Civil Code, neither spouse is allowed to dispose of, mortgage, or carry out any other transaction on the family home without consent. Such consent may not be excluded by agreement or granted in general. In the absence of consent, the judicial authority may authorise the act, taking account of the interests of the family, or if there is another just cause.

An act performed without consent or authorisation is voidable, at the request of the other spouse if the other spouse is living in the same dwelling, within four years of having knowledge thereof or from the time that the act is recorded in the Property Registry.

An act remains effective if the purchaser acts in good faith and for consideration and the owner stated that the property was not a family dwelling, even though it was an inaccurate representation. There is no good faith if the purchaser knew or could reasonably have known at the time of the acquisition that it was a family dwelling. In any case, the spouse who disposed thereof is liable for the damages caused, in accordance with the applicable laws.

This provision is also applicable to informal partnerships (Art. 234-3.2 Catalan Civil Code).

A spouse or partner who wants to obtain a mortgage on their right in the family home must obtain the non-owner spouse's or partner's consent (Art. 569-31 Catalan Civil Code). In the absence of consent, judicial authorisation may be sought.

c. Where the home is jointly rented by the partners?

If the partners are married, any transaction concerning the home would require the consent of both spouses and, failing that, authorization by the judge (Art. 1320 Spanish Civil Code). This provision may also apply to partners to an informal relationship by analogy, but this is by no means certain.

According to article 231-9 Catalan Civil Code, neither spouse is allowed to dispose of, mortgage, or carry out any other transaction on the family home without consent. This provision applies as well to the rented family home. Such consent may not be excluded by agreement or granted in general. In the absence of consent, the judicial authority may authorise the act, taking account of the interests of the family, or if there is another just cause.

This provision is also applicable to informal partnerships (Art. 234-3.2 Catalan Civil Code).

d. Where the home is rented by one of the partners?

The Law on Urban Leasehold, applicable throughout Spain, establishes in Art. 12 that when the household is rented, if the tenant does not wish to renew, or decides to terminate the agreement, the cohabitant spouse or partner may continue in the household, under the same conditions. The same will apply if the tenant abandons the household without any express declaration as to renewal or termination of the agreement.

SWEDEN

a. Where the home is jointly owned by the partners?

When two people own something jointly, general rules in the Swedish Co-ownership Act (in Swedish: *Lag 1904:48 s. 1 om samäganderätt*) are applicable. According to § 2 any disposal over a jointly owned asset requires the consent of all co-owners, unless it is not possible to acquire such consent due to illness or absence. If the partners qualify as cohabitees under the Swedish Cohabitation Act, special restrictions apply under its § 23, requiring the other partner's consent for dispositions such as any disposal, mortgage, lease and subletting of the joint dwelling acquired for the cohabitees' joint use, or for pawning it. A cohabitee is not permitted to divest, sublet, grant tenancies or pawn the joint home acquired for the couple's joint use and thus to be included in a property division. This also applies to any other joint dwelling to which the other cohabitee might be granted the right to take it over upon the ending of the relationship (under § 22). If a cohabitee refuses to consent, the court may upon application by the other cohabitee grant permission for the transaction, § 24.

b. Where the home is owned by one of the partners?

If the home qualifies as 'cohabitation property', meaning that it has been acquired for the cohabitees' joint use, the above-mentioned restrictions in the Swedish Cohabitation Act, § 23 apply. This has to do with the fact that the formal ownership of the joint dwelling is irrelevant under this enactment; what counts is that the home has been acquired for the couple's joint use. The partner owning the home must respect these restrictions. If cohabitees live in property to which one of them holds the title or lease, they may have the property registered as their joint dwelling by notifying Lantmäteriet (The National Land Survey). Notification to this effect can be a guarantee that the cohabitee who owns the property does not sell or mortgage it without the consent of the other cohabitee.

c. Where the home is jointly rented by the partners?

The same restrictions under the Swedish Cohabitation Act, requiring the consent of the other cohabitee, also apply when the home is a rented property just as when it is owned, by one of the cohabitees or both of them. See above, answers to Question 24a and b.

d. Where the home is rented by one of the partners?

See answers above, under a-c. It does not matter if the home is rented by one of the partners or by them both.

SWITZERLAND

a. Where the home is jointly owned by the partners?

There are no specific rules on transactions concerning the home of the partners in an informal relationship where the home is jointly owned by the partners.

In Switzerland, there are two kinds of collective ownership: co-ownership (*Miteigentum*) and joint ownership (*Gesamteigentum*). Depending on the type of ownership of the home, different rules regarding transactions apply.

A co-ownership exists where several persons own a share in an object which is physically undivided (Art. 646 para. 1 Swiss Civil Code). Each co-owner has the rights and obligations of ownership in respect of his or her share in the object (Art. 646 para. 3 Swiss Civil Code). Hence, unless otherwise agreed, each partner in an informal relationship may freely dispose of his or her share,[62] may encumber it with a mortgage or rent it

[62] However, co-owners do have the right of pre-emption against any person acquiring a share who is not a co-owner, Art. 682 para. 1 Swiss Civil Code.

to a third party, as long as it is compatible with the rights of the other co-owners (Art. 648 para. 1 Swiss Civil Code). The disposition or encumbrance of the (entire) object and the modification of its designated purpose require the consent of all co-owners, unless unanimously agreed otherwise (Art. 648 para. 2 Swiss Civil Code).

If several persons bound together in a community by a legal provision or contract own an object by virtue of that community, they are joint owners and the rights of each joint owner attach to the whole object (Art. 652 Swiss Civil Code). Such a community might, for example, be created if the persons build a community of heirs (Art. 602 para. 2 Swiss Civil Code) or in case of informal relationships if the partners form a simple partnership (Art. 544 para. 1 Swiss Code of Obligations).[63] Unless otherwise provided, the unanimous decision of all the joint owners is required in order to exercise ownership rights and in particular to dispose of the object in any way (Art. 653 para. 2 Swiss Civil Code). Further, the right to divide the object or make dispositions relating to a portion thereof is excluded for the duration of the community (Art. 653 para. 3 Swiss Civil Code).

b. Where the home is owned by one of the partners?

There are no specific rules on transactions concerning the home of partners in an informal relationship where the home is owned by only one of the partners. Unless otherwise agreed, the partner owning the home is free to dispose, mortgage or sublet the home as he or she wishes.

c. Where the home is jointly rented by the partners?

There are no specific rules on transactions concerning the home of partners in an informal relationship where the home is rented by both partners.

If both partners are tenants, they are jointly liable for the rent. With regard to the termination of a lease, they jointly have to terminate the lease contract and likewise the landlord has to give notice of termination to both partners.

The legal situation between the partners if they separate and one of them wants to leave the rented home is unclear. Without the landlord's

[63] Joint ownership of property requires the recording of the legal relationship (e.g. simple partnership) in the land register (*Grundbuch*), Art. 51 para. 1(c) and para. 3 provisions on the land register, Grundbuchverordnung, SR 211.432.1.

consent, the parties cannot assign the lease contract to one partner only.[64] Furthermore, the law does not provide efficient proceedings with the possibility of assigning the lease to one partner in the case of a dispute.[65]

d. Where the home is rented by one of the partners?

There are no specific rules on transactions concerning the home of partners in an informal relationship where the home is rented by only one of the partners. Unless otherwise agreed, the partner renting the home may terminate or sublet the home as he or she wishes.

Where a termination of the lease would cause hardship for the tenant or his or her family that cannot be justified by the interests of the landlord, the tenant may request an extension of the lease (Art. 272 para. 1 Swiss Code of Obligations). In 1979 the Swiss Federal Supreme Court decided that a partner in an informal relationship does not belong to the family in this regard.[66] However, this case law can now be considered to be outdated and no longer applicable.[67]

---

64 M. MONTINI and M. MONTINI, 'Protection du logement de famille: l'état civil doit-il (encore) jouer un rôle', in: O. GUILLOD and C. MÜLLER, *Pour un droit équitable, engagé et chaleureux*, Helbing Lichtenhahn Verlag, Basel, 2011, at p. 363, 394.

65 H. HAUSHEER, T. GEISER and R. AEBI-MÜLLER, *Das Familienrecht des Schweizerischen Zivilgesetzbuches*, Stämpfli, Bern, 2014, at N 03.30.

66 See Swiss Federal Supreme Court, BGE 105 II 197 E.3.c) referring to the former Art. 331 Swiss Code of Obligations, which corresponds to the currently applicable Art. 272 Swiss Code of Obligations.

67 M. MONTINI and M. MONTINI, 'Protection du logement de famille: l'état civil doit-il (encore) jouer un rôle', in: O. GUILLOD and C. MÜLLER, *Pour un droit équitable, engagé et chaleureux*, Helbing Lichtenhahn Verlag, Basel, 2011, at p. 363, 388; B. PULVER, *Unverheiratete Paare*, Helbing Lichtenhahn Verlag, Basel, 2000, at p. 59.

QUESTION 25

Under what circumstances and to what extent can one partner act as an agent for the other?

AUSTRIA

Section 96 General Austrian Civil Code stipulates that the spouse who manages the household and earns no income of his or her own represents the other spouse in legal transactions of daily life *(Schlüsselgewalt)*. Since a similar provision has not yet been introduced for informal relationships and S. 96 General Austrian Civil Code cannot be applied by analogy, the issue of representation has to be decided according to the general rules, S. 1002 et seq. General Austrian Civil Code.[1] The authorization to act as an agent for another person is an unilateral declaration of will. Generally, no formal requirements have to be considered when authorizing another person. The agent can be authorised to various extents:

- general authorization *(Generalvollmacht)*, which allows him/her to conclude all possible transactions as long as they are not of a highly personal nature
- authorization for particular types of transactions (Gattungsvollmacht)
- authorization for a particular transaction *(Spezialvollmacht)*.[2]

Besides the authorization, it is necessary that the agent has at least a limited capacity to contract and discloses the fact that the transaction is made for another person.[3] Section 1029 General Austrian Civil Code regulates the *prima facie* authorization *(Anscheinsvollmacht)*. In applying this provision the Austrian Supreme Court has decided that a man who – through his behaviour – entitled a third person to rely on the fact that he had previously authorised his partner to conclude transactions, which

1 U. AICHHORN, *Das Recht der Lebenspartnerschaften, Ehe und Lebensgemeinschaft*, Springer, Vienna, 2003, at p. 431.

2 S. PERNER, M. SPITZER and E. KODEK, *Bürgerliches Recht*, Manz Verlag, Vienna, 2012, at p. 124 et seq.

3 Sections 1017 et seq. General Austrian Civil Code; D. RUBIN, 'section 1002 General Austrian Civil Code', in: A. KLETEČKA and M. SCHAUER, *ABGB-ON 1.01*, Manz Verlag, Vienna, 2013, at marg. No. 46 et seq.

could also concern him, had to undertake the liabilities resulting from this contract.[4] Hence, if there are sufficient circumstances arising from the conduct of the authorising party, the other partner in an informal relationship can be entitled to act as an agent for him/her.

Further, if a person over the age of 18 years cannot conclude contracts of daily life due to a mental illness or mental disability and has no guardian or a legal or appointed representative, his or her immediate relatives, including his/her partner in an informal relationship, may represent him/her in these transactions provided that the concluded contracts are in accordance with the lifestyle of the represented person.[5] However, the partner is only allowed to represent the other partner if they have lived together for three years in the same household.[6]

BELGIUM

No specific rules apply. According to the general rules on agency, one partner can appoint the other as an agent under a general or specific agency, either for a definite or an indefinite period. An agency agreement can be implicit and such implicit agreements between informal cohabitants have been accepted in the case law.[7] Contrary to spouses, custom is not accepted as the sole basis for implicit agency.[8] Besides, third parties may invoke the existence of an apparent agency, which is an application of the theory on legitimate expectation.

BULGARIA

Either partner can act as an agent for the other (for the exercise of legal transactions) only on the basis of a power of attorney (if this is specifically authorised by the other partner). Again, in the absence of specific provisions, the general law is applicable – Art. 36 of the Bulgarian Obligations and Contracts Law. In contrast, either spouse can act as an agent for the other *ex lege* in actions involving the administration

4 Austrian Supreme Court, Judgement of 15.04.1971, 1 Ob 94/71.

5 Sections 284b, 284c para. 1 General Austrian Civil Code; S. FERRARI, 'Rechtsregeln für nichteheliches Zusammenleben in Österreich', in: I. KROPPENBERG et al. (eds.), *Rechtsregeln für nichteheliches Zusammenleben*, Gieseking Verlag, Vienna, 2009, pp. 167-206, at p. 173.

6 Section 284c para. 1 General Austrian Civil Code.

7 Internal dimension: District Court of Brussels 27 January 2000, *JLMB* 2000, 1088, with note SACE (withdrawal of money). External dimension: Justice of the Peace Herzele 19 December 2012, *RW* 2013-14, 273 (termination of tenancy).

8 B. TILLEMAN, *Lastgeving*, Story Scientia, Brussel, 1997, at n° 164.

of the common property or in carrying out family obligations (Art. 24, para. 2 and Art. 32, para. 2 of the Bulgarian Family Code).

CROATIA

There are no special legal regulations prescribing this.

CZECH REPUBLIC

There is no legal representation between partners to an informal relationship as there is between spouses in a marriage (see S. 696 Czech Civil Code). But they can represent each other according to the law of contract (contractual representation, S. 441 et seq. Czech Civil Code). If so stipulated by the parties, one represents the other as an agent to the stipulated extent (S. 441(1) Czech Civil Code). The principal must state the scope of the authority to represent in a power of attorney. Unless representation is only related to a particular juridical act, the power of attorney is granted in writing. Where a special form is required for juridical acts, the power of attorney is granted in the same form (S. 441(1) Czech Civil Code).

If the partners in an informal relationship have a common child, they can represent each other in juridical acts for which the child lacks legal capacity (see S. 892(1) and (2) Czech Civil Code).

DENMARK

The general law of agency applies to cohabitants and, as in the case of spouses, the rules can be adjusted to take account of the special community of interests between the partners. In certain situations an agency will be established by the partners' conduct, if their conduct rightfully gives a third party a reason to believe that one partner has authority to act on the other's behalf.[9] For example, an agency may be established if a cohabitant, without the distinct agreement of the partner who is the owner, orders work to be carried out on the owner's property and both cohabitants were present during the initial discussions with the tradesman. If the owner does not react, his or her passivity will justify the tradesman's belief that the person ordering the work had authority to do so.

[9] See in more detail I. LUND-ANDERSEN, *Familieøkonomien*, Jurist- og Økonomforbundets Forlag, Copenhagen, 2011, at p. 229-250.

Likewise, if a couple lead a third party to believe they are married, the special rules on spousal liability will apply.[10] For instance, a husband is liable for his wife's medical care as a doctor is an 'ordinary legal transaction in satisfaction of the wife's special needs'; see Legal Effect of the Danish Marriage Act S. 11(1).

ENGLAND AND WALES

There is no special rule of agency and so one partner can act as an agent for the other partner if he or she has the other's formal consent. Joint owners of property can usually act as agent for both owners in some matters but not for the sale or disposal of real property (i.e. immovable property) such as the owner occupied family home.

ESTONIA

There is no separate regulation in the Estonian legislation on representation dealing with the case when the representative is the partner in an informal relationship. The representation is regulated by chapter 8 of the General Part of the Estonian Civil Code Act. According to § 117(2), a right of representation may be granted by a transaction (authorisation) or it may arise under the law (the right of representation arising from the law). A principal grants authorisation by making a corresponding declaration of intention to the representative, to the person with whom the transaction requiring authorisation is to be entered into, or towards the public in general (§ 118(1)). According to § 767(1) of the Estonian Law of Obligations Act, if healthcare services are provided to a patient who is unconscious or is incapable of exercising his or her free will for any other reason, the immediate family of the patient must be informed about the patient's state of health. Immediate family means the spouse, parents, children and siblings of the patient. Other persons who are close to the patient may also be deemed to be immediate family if this can be concluded from the patient's way of life (§ 767(2) of the Estonian Law of Obligations Act).

FINLAND

Normally, one cohabiting partner can act as an agent for the other only according to the general rules on agency. For example, one cohabiting partner requires a power of attorney from the other partner in order to,

[10] See *Ugeskrift for Retsvæsen* (Weekly Law Journal) 1930, at p. 540.

e.g., deal with a bank, post office or any other financial transaction on behalf of the other partner. However, specific rules may apply. For example, when a process server has sought a person with a known residence in Finland, but has not found him or her or any persons competent to receive service in his or her place, the process server may serve the notice by delivering the documents to any household member, including a cohabiting partner, who has attained fifteen years of age (Finnish Code of Judicial Procedure, Chapter 11, S. 7).

FRANCE

There is no specific provision in this respect. Therefore, the general rules apply. A partner can allow the other partner to act as an agent for him or her. This falls under the general '*contrat de mandat*' (contract of agency).

GERMANY

Each spouse is entitled to enter into transactions for the appropriate provision of the necessities of life for the family. Within these limits, each spouse possesses a 'power of the key' (*Schlüsselgewalt*), a special kind of statutory authority. The resulting obligations bind both spouses (§ 1357 German Civil Code). However, if the spouses are separated or if one of them wants to live separately, such a statutory authority does not exist (§ 1357 s. 2 German Civil Code).

Unlike the provision in § 1357 German Civil Code for spouses, there is no liability for debts incurred by the other cohabitant. § 1357 German Civil Code is not applied by analogy.[11] One cohabitant can act, however, as an agent (*Stellvertreter*) on behalf of the other under the rules of agency law (§§ 164 et seq. German Civil Code; compare also Question 27). An undisclosed agency is recognised in cases of 'appearance of authority' (*Anscheinsvollmacht*)[12] and 'authority by estoppel' (*Duldungsvollmacht*) where one cohabitant acts without explicit authorisation.

GREECE

The general rules on voluntary representation apply (Art. 211 et seq. and 216 et seq. Greek Civil Code). Therefore it will be necessary for one

[11] N. DETHLOFF, *Familienrecht*, Beck, Munich, 2012, at § 8 No. 9; G. BRUDERMÜLLER, 'Einl. vor § 1297', in: O. PALANDT, *Bürgerliches Gesetzbuch*, Beck, Munich, 2015, at No. 23.

[12] D. SCHWAB, *Familienrecht*, Beck, Munich, 2014, at No. 995.

partner to grant the other instructions and authority to represent him. Such authority is often given tacitly, especially in the case of the so-called 'power of attorney on sufferance', i.e. the case where one partner appears before third parties as the representative of the other, without really being so, and this situation is accepted. Also, a statement 'to whom it may concern', to meet the needs of everyday transactions, might be used for legal transactions conducted by one partner on behalf of the other.

HUNGARY

There is no special rule for cohabitants.

REPUBLIC OF IRELAND

Cohabitants are in a position to act as agents for one another through the mechanism of power of attorney. This is a legal device set up by a person (the donor) during his/her life when he/she is not incapacitated by mental illness. It allows an appointed person (the attorney) to take actions on the donor's behalf if he/she is absent, abroad or incapacitated through illness. The legislation governing this power is set out in the Irish Powers of Attorney Act 1996 and the Irish Enduring Powers of Attorney Regulations 1996 (SI No. 196/1996) as amended by SI No. 287/1996.

The two types of power of attorney allowed under Irish law are power of attorney and enduring power of attorney. Power of attorney gives either a specific or a general power and ceases as soon as the donor becomes incapacitated. Donors can name any person as their attorney; this is therefore open to cohabitants. The enduring power of attorney takes effect on the incapacity of the donor. Cohabitants are eligible for this power only if they are aged 18 or over, not bankrupt, free of convictions for offences which involve fraud or dishonesty, and not disqualified under the Irish Companies Acts.

ITALY

No special provision to this effect is available to partners. In general, the simple fact of cohabiting does not in itself give any power of attorney to the partner.

According to the general rules, however, one partner may nominate the other as his or her agent through a specific legal act called *procura*. In this case, when the agent negotiates with a third party, the effects of the transaction rest on the principal, provided the agent identifies him or herself as acting in the name of the other partner.[13]

LATVIA

In Latvia there is no such specific legal order on informal relationships.

Therefore the general legal order of the management of property of other people as laid down in the Latvian Civil Law is applicable.[14]

Section 2289 of the Latvian Civil Law determines that, pursuant to an authorisation contract, one party (authorised person, assignee) undertakes to perform a certain assignment for the other party (person granting the authorisation, authorising person, assignor), and the person granting the authorisation undertakes to recognise the activity of the authorised person as binding on him or her. The legal order of unauthorised management may also be applicable. Accordingly, S. 2325 of the Latvian Civil Law, which provides that if a person undertakes, without being invited to do so, to manage another person's affairs in accordance with the true interests of such person and under such circumstances as where it could be accepted that such person, if he or she had been given an opportunity to express his or her volition, would have consented to this agency, then with such management legal relations are established, similar to those regarding a contract, between the manager and the represented person.

In 2013 a new legal order on continuing powers of attorney came into force. With continuing powers of attorney the assignor gives the assignee the right to manage his or her effects, in the case where the assignor, due to health problems or other reasons or circumstances, will not be able to understand the meaning of his or her actions and would not be able to manage his or her affairs.[15]

---

13 G. OBERTO, *I diritti dei conviventi. Realtà e prospettive tra Italia ed Europa*, Cedam, Padua, 2012, at p. 159.

14 Civil Law. Part Four. Law of Obligations. Law of Republic of Latvia. "Valdības Vēstnesis", 26 February 1937, no.46.

15 S. 2317[1] Latvian Civil Law.

LITHUANIA

There are no special rules, so the general rules of Art. 2.132-2.151 of the Lithuanian Civil Code apply.

Persons shall enjoy the right to conclude contracts through agents with the exception of those contracts which, due to their character, may only be concluded personally as well as other contracts prescribed by law. An agent may not conclude contracts in the principal's name either with himself or with a person whom he represents at the given time, as well as his spouse, parents, children or other close relatives. Such contracts, upon the principal's request, may be deemed null and void. An authorised agent whose rights are not clearly defined in the power of attorney shall enjoy the right to perform only those actions which are necessary for the protection of the principal's property and property interests as well as the supervision of the principal's property.

LUXEMBOURG

The rules of joint ownership (*les règles de l'indivision*) allow one partner to represent the other when administering joint assets but only if he or she has procuration (*mandat d'administration général*, compare the answer to Question 33).

The rules of quasi-contracts, especially of the management of the affairs of another (*gestion d'affaire*), may often be applied to partners in informal relationships.

THE NETHERLANDS

There are no specific statutory provisions concerning one cohabiting partner acting as an agent for the other. The general rules of Book 3 of the Dutch Civil Code are applicable. According to Art. 3:60-61 Dutch Civil Code a person may give a power of attorney to another person, either explicitly or implicitly. In notarial cohabitation contracts partners may agree to give each other a power of attorney in respect of specific transactions, e.g. the acquiring of movable assets.[16] In the case law questions in relation to agency do not play a role and in the legal doctrine little attention has been given to this subject.

---

16 P. BLOKLAND, in: W.D. KOLKMAN and L.C.A. VERSTAPPEN (eds.), *Handboek Familie-vermogensrecht*, Walburg Pers, Zutphen, 2013, at 4.2.4.5.

NORWAY

Partners to an informal relationship may - like others - agree that one partner is to act as an agent for the other. However, such agreements must apply to specific and limited areas - a broad authorisation to act on behalf of the other party in all matters would be unlawful. General principles of agency, like agency without specific authorisation (*negotiorum gestio*), will also apply between cohabitants.

PORTUGAL

There are no specific rules regarding the cohabitant as the agent of the partner. One partner can act as an agent for the other whenever a power of attorney has been granted (Art. 262 et seq. of the Portuguese Civil Code), which may or not be associated with a mandate (Art. 1157 et seq. of the Portuguese Civil Code).

RUSSIA

There are no specific rules governing partners in informal relationships who act as each other's agent. A partner can act as an agent for the other partner under the same circumstances as any unrelated person can, namely when the other partner has given him/her a power of attorney.

SCOTLAND

It is possible that one partner might act as agent for the other but this is regulated entirely by the general law of agency. There is no specific provision for cohabitants.

SLOVAKIA

It is possible for one partner to be represented by the other partner acting on his or her behalf. According to Slovak Civil Law this representation allows natural and legal persons that are not legally competent or cannot or do not want to act in person for any other reason to be represented by representatives acting on their behalf. With regard to the resulting legal effects, direct and indirect representation may be distinguished.[17] A direct representative expresses his will in the name of the principal. The representative's juridical acts directly establish the rights and duties of

[17] See principally M. JURČOVÁ, in: M. JURČOVÁ et al. (eds.), *Zastúpenie v súkromnom práve* (Representation in Private Law), C.H. Beck, Praha, 2012.

the principal. An indirect representative expresses his or her will on the principal's behalf. Subsequently, an indirect representative has to transfer the rights and duties acquired by him or her to the principal by means of another juridical act. The General Part of the Slovak Civil Code only deals with direct representation (§ 22 et seq. Slovak Civil Code). With respect to the legal title of representation, the Slovak Civil Code distinguishes statutory and contractual representation.

A representative is a person authorised to act instead and on behalf of someone else, whereby his acts directly establish the rights and duties of the principal. A representative may be a natural person or a legal person.

Any representative has to meet the following general requirements:

- the representative has to be competent to perform the juridical act covered by representation,
- the representative's interests must not be in conflict with those of the principal, and
- the representative has to act in person; he or she may only appoint another representative (a delegate) if this is provided by statute or is agreed by the parties.[18]

One partner as a principal may grant a power of attorney to a representative (the other partner) on the basis of a representation agreement (e.g. a contract of mandate). A power of attorney is a unilateral juridical act by which a principal expresses his or her will to authorise a representative to perform juridical acts on his or her behalf.[19] A power of attorney may also be granted to several representatives at the same time. It may be granted orally or in writing, or indeed in any other form as long as this does not result in unclarity. A power of attorney must be granted in writing if the juridical act covered by the representation requires a written form or if the power of attorney covers multiple juridical acts (§ 31 para. 4 Slovak Civil Code). As far as its contents are concerned, a power of attorney has to include at least the identification of the representative and the scope of his or her authority. Any instructions given to the representative and not included in the power of attorney do not affect the legal effects of the representative's acts, unless such instructions are known to the other party involved in

18 M. JURČOVÁ, in: M. JANČO et al. (eds.), *Introduction to Slovak Civil Law*, C.H. Beck, Plzeň, 2012.

19 See M. JURČOVÁ, in: J. LAZAR et al. (eds.), *Občianske právo hmotné* (Substantive Slovak Civil Law), Iuris Libri, Bratislava, 2014, at p. 171.

the juridical act performed by the representative. If the acts of a purported representative are not in compliance with the power of attorney granted by a principal, two situations are distinguished by statute with respect to legal effects of such acts:

- the representative has exceeded his or her authority arising from the power of attorney. In this case the principal is only legally bound by such acts if he or she approves the excess power of attorney (ratification) with retroactive effect (ex tunc) on the juridical acts performed. An irrefutable legal presumption [20] is established by statute, according to which the principal is deemed to have approved the excess power of attorney, unless the principal notifies his or her disapproval to the party to the juridical act performed by the representative without any delay once the principal becomes aware of such an act;
- the representative has exceeded his or her authority to act on the principal's behalf or the representative has acted on someone else's behalf without any power of attorney. The person having performed such an act is legally bound by this act. The irrefutable legal presumption of the principal's approval does not apply in this case; the principal may only be legally bound by such a juridical act if he or she actually approves it. A third party may require from the person having performed such an act either performance or damages provided that this party has acted in good faith, i.e. was unaware of the lacking power of attorney (§ 33 para. 2 Slovak Civil Code).

A contractual representation will terminate in certain given cases (§ 33b Slovak Civil Code). These cases include the performance of the act covered by the representation, the revocation of the power of attorney by the principal, the termination of the power of attorney by the representative, the representative's death and, in principle, also the principal's death.

SLOVENIA

Partners may agree that only one of them shall manage the common property or a part thereof, or that only one of them shall manage and also dispose of the common property (Art. 52 of the Slovenian Marriage Act). Unless otherwise agreed, the partner to whom management is entrusted

[20] See M. JURČOVÁ, in: J. LAZAR et al. (eds.), *Občianske právo hmotné* (Substantive Slovak Civil Law), Iuris Libri, Bratislava, 2014, at p. 175.

within the framework of regular administration may also dispose of common property or a part thereof (Art. 53 of the Slovenian Marriage Act). The general rules of the law of obligations on representation apply for all other authorisations.

SPAIN

There are no special rules in this regard. The ordinary rules of the contract of mandate apply (see Art. 1709-1739 Spanish Civil Code).

There is a general rule that establishes that nobody can act as an agent for another, unless authorisation is given (Art. 1259 Spanish Civil Code). Authorisation may be tacit, derived from conclusive acts (Art. 1710 Spanish Civil Code); but an informal relationship, per se, does not establish agency.

SWEDEN

In Swedish law, general rules on agency are applicable in situations where one of the cohabiting partners acts as an agent for the other partner. There are, in other words, no specific rules concerning agency in any kinds of informal relationships.

SWITZERLAND

In Switzerland, the general provisions on agency in the Swiss Code of Obligations apply to informal relationships (Art. 32 et seq. and in the case of a simple partnership Art. 543 para. 2 Swiss Code of Obligations). A distinction can be made between an agency with or without authorisation. The latter may be authorised subsequently (Art. 38 para. 1 Swiss Code of Obligations) or may be covered by the agency without authority (*Geschäftsführung ohne Auftrag*, Art. 419 et seq. Swiss Code of Obligations). In case of authorisation, the extent of the agency depends on the extent of the authorisation provided by the represented partner (Art. 33 para. 2 Swiss Code of Obligations).

A partner in an informal relationship may further be entitled to represent his or her partner in relation to medical procedures (Art. 378 para. 1 No. 4 Swiss Civil Code: representation may be assigned to any person who cohabits with the person lacking the capacity of judgement and regularly and personally provides him or her with support). However, the partner in an informal relationship – unlike the spouse or registered partner – is not statutorily entitled to represent the partner who is no longer capable of sound judgement (Art. 374 Swiss Civil Code). Partners in an informal relationship may certainly appoint each other as deputies in the respective directives.

QUESTION 26

Under what circumstances can partners in an informal relationship become joint owners of assets?

AUSTRIA

Section 825 General Austrian Civil Code provides four different possibilities as to how joint ownership can be established: (i) coincidence, (ii) statute, (iii) last will or (iv) contract. Practically speaking, joint ownership is most often created by last wills or contracts, whereby in terms of informal relationships the latter will be even more important.[1] If the partners together purchase a certain asset, they become the joint owners of it. Further, partners form a so-called partnership of owners *(Eigentümerpartnerschaft)* if they are acquiring condominium ownership together according to S. 13 et seq. Austrian Condominium Act *(Wohnungseigentumsgesetz)*.[2] This requires that every partner has an equal share of the minimum proportion, which is necessary for acquiring condominium ownership.[3]

BELGIUM

No specific rules apply. Informal partners usually become joint owners through joint acquisition.[4]

BULGARIA

Only on the basis of a joint acquisition: via original or derivative means (e.g. by purchase, under a will).

1 H. BÖHM, 'section 825 General Austrian Civil Code', in: A. KLETEČKA and M. SCHAUER, *ABGB-ON 1.01*, Manz Verlag, Vienna, 2013, at marg. No. 11.

2 J. STABENTHEINER, 'Das neue Wohnungseigentumsrecht im Überblick', *immolex*, 2002, at p. 163.

3 H. WÜRTH, 'section 14 Austrian Tenancy Act', in: P. RUMMEL (ed.), *Kommentar zum Allgemeinen Bürgerlichen Gesetzbuch*, Manz Verlag, Vienna, 2003, at marg. No. 4.

4 B. TILLEMAN, *Lastgeving*, Story Scientia, Brussel, 1997, at n° 164.

CROATIA

Art. 11 paragraph 2 of the Croatian Family Act sets forth that the effects of marriage concerning property shall apply to cohabitation too. According to Art. 4 paragraph 1 and Art. 54 of the Croatian Partnership Act, the effects of cohabitation with regard to property shall apply to same-sex informal partnerships. It means that the effects of marriage with respect to property shall apply to both cohabitants and same-sex informal partners.

So, the answer equally relates to both cohabitants and same-sex informal partners.

Accordingly, all the assets that partners have acquired on the basis of their work during the partnership or the assets that have been derived from such property represent the partners' community of property, co-owned in equal parts (Art. 36 paragraphs 1 and 3 of the Croatian Family Act and Art. 51 paragraphs 1 and 2 of the Croatian Partnership Act). Work is a constitutive element of the community of property. It can be individual, work done by each partner separately, e.g. on the basis of employment, housekeeping, the performance of copyright-related work or their joint work, e.g. work on an estate, within a trade, or a notary or law firm. Work can manifest itself as a direct or indirect contribution, such as taking care of children, organizing and housekeeping, cooking, moral support etc.[5]

Community of property also includes lottery prizes and income from intellectual and related rights acquired during the life union (Art. 36 paragraph 2 of the Croatian Family Act and Art. 51 paragraphs 3 and 4 of the Croatian Partnership Act).

CZECH REPUBLIC

Partners to an informal relationship become joint owners of assets according to S. 1115 et seq. Czech Civil Code. There is no special regulation concerning an informal relationship as there is in a marriage where community property is established. When partners in an informal relationship acquire something together, they are co-owners.

5 M. ALINČIĆ, D. HRABAR, D. JAKOVAC-LOZIĆ, A. KORAĆ GRAOVAC, *Family Law*, Narodne novine, Zagreb, 2007, at p. 501-502; B. REŠETAR and U. JOSIPOVIĆ, 'Issues of Dispute in Marital Contracts with Particular Attention to Marital Partners' Bank Contracts', *Zbornik radova Pravnog fakulteta u Splitu*, 2013, pp. 115-138, at p. 116-118.

DENMARK

In determining the ownership of an asset, what matters in the first instance is what the parties have agreed or assumed or otherwise intended. There can be evidentiary problems concerning what the parties have agreed.

When cohabiting couples enter into an ownership agreement, they can either agree on the ownership of specific assets, for example that they should both be recorded on the deed of their property, or they can agree to be the joint owners of a group of assets, or they can agree more generally on the ownership of assets which the couple bring into the relationship or later acquire. Such agreements can be included in a more comprehensive contract covering their cohabitation. The parties will typically agree to establish a joint ownership of assets to a wider extent than would apply under the general rules of property law.[6] For example, in a cohabitation contract it is often agreed that all assets acquired during the cohabitation are jointly owned, other than assets acquired by inheritance, as a gift or objects bought for personal use, education or work tools. As for the assets which each party brings into the cohabitation when it commences, it is generally agreed that each party retains full ownership of such assets.

If the parties have not entered into any express agreement on the ownership of an asset and if one of the parties is registered as the owner, as for married couples the assumption is that the registered ownership reflects the cohabitants' attitude to the ownership.[7] The evidentiary value of registration is assessed differently according to the kind of ownership. If registration involves legal obligations, for example liability for loans, tax etc., it will usually be assumed that the party's choice of who is registered is not a random decision. If only the name of one of the parties is entered in a property deed, this is usually regarded as a considered decision.

ENGLAND AND WALES

Joint ownership of assets is an accepted form of ownership between two or more individuals and is simple to achieve and very common. Joint purchase will normally result in joint legal and beneficial ownership of any asset including real property such as the family home (although if

---

6 See I. LUND-ANDERSEN, *Familieøkonomien*, Jurist- og Økonomforbundets Forlag, Copenhagen, 2011, at p. 256.

7 I. LUND-ANDERSEN, *Familieøkonomien*, Jurist- og Økonomforbundets Forlag, Copenhagen, 2011, at p. 257.

legal ownership is not in joint names, a declaration of trust by the court will be needed based on proof of joint contribution to acquisition costs or other express agreement between the parties). For real property, the transaction must be recorded in writing in the proper form, subject to the possibility of an implied common intention constructive or resulting trust being proved to the satisfaction of the court showing joint beneficial ownership.

ESTONIA

There is no separate regulation in Estonian legislation regarding the opportunity of the partners in an informal relationship to acquire assets in common or joint ownership. An informal relationship does not change ownership relations. Either person shall remain the owner of his or her assets. The assets acquired during the cohabitation shall be acquired according to the general rules of property law, i.e. either under sole ownership or joint ownership. If a partnership contract exists, contributions made by the partners and assets acquired for the partnership shall be transferred to the joint property of the partnership according to § 589(1) of the Estonian Law of Obligations Act.[8] The transfer of security is regulated in the Estonian Law of Obligations Act § 921. According to § 90(1) of the Estonian Law of Property Act,[9] possessor of a movable and any earlier possessor shall be deemed to be the owners of the asset during the possessor's possession until the contrary is proved. The presumption of ownership by the possessor of movable property arising from § 90 includes, as a rule, also the presumption of common ownership by the co-possessor, which provides certain protection to a (non-possesor) spouse as well as to the other partner in an informal relationship. In the case of immovable property this presumption is irrelevant.[10]

FINLAND

With regard to immovable assets, there are no specific rules concerning cohabitees: the partners can only become joint owners of immovable assets if they have acquired and recorded the property jointly or if it can be shown in court that their intention was to acquire the property jointly.

---

8 Decision of the Civil Chamber of the Supreme Court 3-2-1-109-14, at para. 17.

9 Asjaõigusseadus (adopted on 9 June 1993, entered into force on 1 December 1993). – RT I 1993, 39, 590; RT I, 08.07.2014, 7 (in Estonian), available in English at: www.riigiteataja.ee/en/eli/ee/Riigikogu/act/510072014007/consolide.

10 K. KAMA and K. KULLERKUPP, 'Vabaabielu versus abielu: varalised suhted muutuvate kooseluvormide kontekstis', *Juridica*, 2002, No. 6, pp. 359-368.

With regard to movable assets, there is a provision in the Finnish Act on the Dissolution of the Household of Cohabiting Partners (26/2011) that creates the presumed co-ownership of movable assets if it cannot be proven which cohabiting partner a particular movable object belongs to (S. 6). However, this Act only applies to cohabiting partners who have lived in a common household for a minimum period of five years or who have (or have had) a joint child. The provision applies only to situations where the property is being separated in the context of the dissolution of the common household.

FRANCE

Partners in an informal relationship become the joint owners of assets if they buy those assets jointly (*en indivision*) or receive them jointly, for example through a donation, bequest or will.

In the case of joint acquisition, each partner's ownership is determined regarding the specific contribution of each partner thereto. Where the issue is contested, and proof cannot be provided, an indivisible joint ownership (*indivision*) of 50/50 is presumed.[11]

GERMANY

There are no specific rules dealing with the property of the partners; the general civil law rules of the German Civil Code apply. All property, real or personal, owned by one of the cohabitants remains the personal property of that cohabitant.[12] Each of the partners manages his or her property independently. Property acquired by the parties with joint resources and funds will be considered joint property only if there is an appropriate agreement.[13] However, in the case of major transactions (e.g. construction of a common family home), a compensation claim based on the statutory rules of partnership law (§§ 705 et seq. German Civil Code) or the rules on unjust enrichment (§ 812 para. 1 s. 2 German Civil Code) may be made (see Question 46).

---

11 Case law has extended to cohabitants the legal presumption of the undivided right of ownership that is organised between spouses (art. 1538 of the French Civil Code) and between partners in a *pacte civil de solidarité* (art. 515-5 al. 2 of the French Civil Code).

12 M. LÖHNIG, 'Anh. zu §§ 1297 et seq.', in: J. VON STAUDINGER, *Kommentar zum Bürgerlichen Gesetzbuch*, Sellier-de-Gruyter, Berlin, 2012, at No. 52.

13 OLG Hamm, 7.6.2002, *FamRZ*, 2003, 529 (co-ownership of a recreational vehicle deemed in equal parts despite being financed mainly by one of the cohabitants); M. LÖHNIG, 'Anh. zu §§ 1297 et seq.', in: J. VON STAUDINGER, *Kommentar zum Bürgerlichen Gesetzbuch*, Sellier-de-Gruyter, Berlin, 2012, at No. 56.

GREECE

On the basis of the general provisions of the law of obligations and property law. They might also share a joint bequest, through the will of a relative or a friend.

HUNGARY

The Civil Code of 1959 provided for a default property regime which resembled that of spouses. According to that provision[14] cohabitants acquired common property in proportion to the contribution they had made in acquiring such property and when this proportion could not be calculated the property was considered to have been equally acquired. The work done in the household was considered to be a contribution to acquiring that property. Although this rule belongs to the old regime, it still has to be applied by the courts during the current transitional period. The Hungarian Act on Transitory Regulations in Connection with the Civil Code[15] provides that the rules which were effective before March 2014 are to be applied to obligations which already existed when the (new) Hungarian Civil Code entered into force. Henceforth, the old rules have to be applied in the case of cohabitation which came into existence before March 2014.

The Hungarian Civil Code regulates another default property regime for cohabitants which does not result in common property being acquired. According to the new regime cohabitants become joint owners of an asset, just like any other persons, namely if they are both parties to a contract.

REPUBLIC OF IRELAND

Partners in an informal relationship can become joint owners of assets by entering into a cohabitants' agreement. Section 202(1) of the Irish Civil Partnership and Cohabitants Act 2010 provides that cohabitants may enter into an agreement to provide for financial matters during their relationship or when the relationship ends. Partners can additionally become joint owners of assets by ordinary transfer of their assets or by jointly purchasing property together.

---

14 Art. 578/G(1) of the Civil Code of 1959.
15 Act No. CLXXVII 2013.

ITALY

For partners in an informal relationship no special rule on the joint purchasing of assets exists. No regime, similar to that of community of property (*comunione dei beni,* Art. 177 et seq. Italian Civil Code) provided for in marriage, exists and therefore each partner is the exclusive owner of assets they have personally purchased. The arrangement resembles the separation of property regime provided for spouses.

Thus, the only way for partners to become joint owners is to acquire the asset together. In the case of immovables, both partners must then be the registered owners of the land; in the case of movable property, proof must be provided that the transaction is ascribed to both partners. Assets will then be regulated by the general rules of common ownership (Art. 1100 et seq. Italian Civil Code).

The possibility to automatically apply rules on community of property to civil unions, on the basis of the very fact of cohabitation, has been discussed and excluded by legal doctrine on the grounds that one of the main reasons for cohabitation is to avoid the patrimonial consequences of marriage.[16]

It must also be considered that even married Italian couples often do not choose the community of property regime and prefer separation. According to the most recent Istat report '*Il matrimonio in Italia*',[17] in fact, a good 69.5% of the couples who married in 2013 chose the separation of property regime (72.6% of the couples in the South of Italy, only 66.1% in the North East). It would then be very unpopular to subject unmarried couples to the community of property regime without them expressly opting for it.

LATVIA

In Latvia there is no such specific legal order on informal relationship. A general legal order on obligation rights is applicable.

[16] L. BALESTRA, 'La famiglia di fatto', in: G. FERRANDO (ed.), *Il nuovo diritto di famiglia,* Zanichelli, Bologna, 2008, at p. 1055.; R. BASSETTI, *Contratti di convivenza e di unione civile,* Giappichelli, Turin, 2014, at p. 62.

[17] R. BASSETTI, *Contratti di convivenza e di unione civile,* Giappichelli, Turin, 2014, at p. 10.

LITHUANIA

Partners in an informal relationship can become joint owners of assets if documented proof of the acquisition of those assets can be established in accordance with Art. 4.47 of the Lithuanian Civil Code. Such proof could be a procurement contract indicating the acquisition of the asset as joint-partial property, or some evidence of an in-kind contribution to the creation of such assets with personal funds, labour or initiative in asset management. Also see the answer to Question 3.

LUXEMBOURG

Partners in an informal relationship may become joint owners just as two other persons, even strangers, can become such joint owners. There are no additional possibilities for partners in an informal relationship.

THE NETHERLANDS

In accordance with Art. 3:84 para. 1 Dutch Civil Code the transfer of title (*overdracht*) to an asset requires the delivery (*traditio*) of the asset by a person who has the power to dispose of the property on the basis of a title (such as a sales contract). When parties both act together (or one of them for both on the basis of a power of attorney)[18] and the property is delivered to both of them (or to one of them acting for both of them), they will be joint owners of the acquired asset.[19]

In some notarial cohabitation contracts partners are under a duty to use a power of attorney for the other partner in relation to the acquisition of certain assets (mostly inventory and other assets to be used in daily life). When a partner does use a power of attorney, both partners will co-own the acquired property.

The title for joint ownership may, under certain circumstances, be found in an implicit agreement that the partners will be the joint owners of a specific asset. In a famous Supreme Court case, Bruinsma claimed half of the savings in her (deceased) partner's bank account. She asserted that the savings were joint property, since the parties had implicitly agreed on

---

18 As a power of attorney is not bound to a formal requirement, this is an option without a cohabitation contract as well, but is difficult to prove.

19 W.M. SCHRAMA, 'Goederenrechtelijke afwikkeling: eigendomsvraag', in: M.L.C.C. DE BRUIJN-LÜCKERS et al. (eds.), *Relatierecht, SDUCommentaar*, SDU, The Hague, 2014, at p. 2005-2014.

this.[20] The partners had saved the money for a common purpose and Bruinsma had always paid the household expenses as a result of which the money could be saved in Smit's account. The Supreme Court ruled that whether a community exists will have to be answered on the basis of what the parties have agreed thereon, either explicitly or implicitly. The fact that both partners had their own bank account and that both paid for specific expenses of the household did not contradict an intention to be a co-owner. A title for joint ownership may thus be implicit and the intention of the parties can be derived from the actual financial organisation and plans (rather than a binding agreement) of the partners, thus leaving room for tailor-made judgements.[21]

Partners with a notarial cohabitation contract may also become joint owners of inventory and other movable goods as a result of a clause in their contract which obliges them to swap shares in each other's movable property.[22]

NORWAY

In Norway, ownership is obtained regardless of registered title; a legal, enforceable agreement relating to land does not even have to be in writing. Partners to an informal relationship may become joint owners of assets in the same way as other people (contract, gift etc.) but, in addition, special rules for acquiring co-ownership in items for common personal use developed through Supreme Court practice in the 1970s and 80s, first in marriage and then in cohabitation, see Rt. 1978 p. 1352 and Rt. 1984 p. 497. These case-law rules apply unless the cohabitants have expressly agreed who is to be considered the owner.

As long as the cohabitants have not expressly agreed upon ownership, co-ownership in items for personal common use is based on what the parties contributed to the acquisition. Not only direct, but also indirect contributions in the form of domestic work and/or payment of the family's expenses are acknowledged. In order to establish co-ownership,

---

20 HR 16 January 1987, NJ 1987, 912 (Bruinsma/Erven Smit).

21 However, a title alone is not sufficient for a transfer of title (overdracht), thus such an agreement alone does not result in a real property right, but a personal right: See W.M. SCHRAMA, 'Goederenrechtelijke afwikkeling: eigendomsvraag', in: M.L.C.C. DE BRUIJN-LÜCKERS et al. (eds.), *Relatierecht, SDUCommentaar*, SDU, The Hague, 2014, at p. 2005-2014.

22 P. BLOKLAND, in: W.D. KOLKMAN and L.C.A. VERSTAPPEN (eds.), *Handboek Familievermogensrecht*, Walburg Pers, Zutphen, 2013, at 4.2.5.

the acquisition must constitute a joint project.[23] Co-ownership is determined on the basis of a discretionary assessment of these factors. Assuming the conclusion is co-ownership, the partners own an equal part unless circumstances justify a different fraction of ownership, the Norwegian Co-ownership Act, S. 2.

PORTUGAL

They become joint owners of an asset any time they validly acquire the asset, in the same way as any other two persons would become joint owners. They share the asset in the proportion defined by the act of acquisition, or in equal parts if nothing has been settled, on the grounds of the generally applicable regime of co-ownership/joint ownership.

RUSSIA

Informal relationships do not as such give rise to the joint ownership of assets.[24] In order to become joint owners of assets, informal partners have to either:

- create joint ownership by agreement. According to Art. 244(4) Russian Civil Code, parties can create a regime of joint ownership by agreement; or
- acquire together, in both names, an undividable asset (Art. 244(4) Russian Civil Code).

SCOTLAND

Joint ownership is an option available to any parties under the general law of property. There are no special rules in relation to couples, whether in informal or formal relationships, and their position as owners is unaffected by their personal relationship. The approach has been summed up as follows: 'Where the couple buys property together, they are treated no differently to strangers and they own the property in proportion to their contributions to the price.'[25] It is a fundamental

---

23 P. LØDRUP and T. SVERDRUP, *Familieretten*, 2011, at p. 342-343.

24 Постановление президиума Челябинского областного суда от 8 июня 2005 г. (надзорное производство № 4г05-1168) / not officially published, available at Гарант. Cited by В.С. ПАНИН, *Проблемы правового регулирования фактических брачных отношений в России*, dissertation, Moscow, 2012, at p. 101.

25 E.E. SUTHERLAND, *Child and Family Law*, W. Green/Thomson, Edinburgh, 2008, at para. 13-060.

principle of the law of marriage that it has no effect on the property or legal capacity of the parties.[26] It is therefore not surprising that there are no special rules in respect of cohabitants.

SLOVAKIA

The acquisition of assets within divided co-ownership (joint ownership) is subject to generally applicable rules on acquisition. Ownership may be acquired *inter vivos* (by transfer) or *mortis causa* (by succession). In the process of the transfer of ownership (the acquisition of assets), two elements may be distinguished:

- the title of acquisition (*titulus adquirendi),* and
- the mode of acquisition (*modus adquirendi*).[27]

The title of acquisition is the title recognised by statute as a valid reason for acquiring ownership.

According to Slovak law the partners in an informal relationship can become the joint owners of assets by titles of acquisition such as:

- a contract of sale,
- a donation contract,
- and other contracts,
- succession,
- a decision by a state authority,
- acquisitive prescription,
- accession,
- processing and other facts stipulated by statute.

The mode of acquisition is the mode recognised by statute as a valid way of acquiring ownership. If movables are transferred on the basis of a contract, ownership is acquired by handing over and accepting the asset (tradition), unless the partners have agreed or stipulated otherwise. However, if immovables are transferred on the basis of a contract, ownership is acquired by registration in the Cadastre of Immovables. The Cadastre of Immovables is a special registry which registers ownership rights and other rights pertaining to immovables.

---

26 Family Law (Scotland) Act 1985, S. 24.

27 See J. LAZAR, in: J. LAZAR et al. (eds.), *Občianske právo hmotné* (Substantive Slovak Civil Law), Iuris Libri, Bratislava, 2014, at p. 483.

A specific title of acquisition of property is acquisitive prescription. A legitimate possessor (partners in an informal relationship) becomes the owner of the asset in his or her possession after 3 years of possession in the case of movables and after 10 years of possession in the case of immovables (§ 134 para. 1 Slovak Civil Code). The period of possession must not be interrupted. However, it also includes the period of the legitimate possession of the possessor's legal predecessors.

It is not possible for partners to acquire ownership of an asset that is lost, hidden or abandoned. According to Slovak law if the partners find a lost object, it must be returned to the owner. If the owner is not known, the finder must hand it over to the competent state authority (§ 135 para. 1 Slovak Civil Code). If the lost object is not claimed by the owner within one year, ownership will passes to the state. The partners as the finders have a right to the reimbursement of necessary expenses and to a reward corresponding to 10% of the value of the object found (§ 135 para. 2 Slovak Civil Code).

If the partners have acquired assets within divided co-ownership (joint ownership) the co-owners have specific shares in the common asset (§ 137 para. 2 Slovak Civil Code). The shares specify the extent of the rights and duties resulting from the co-ownership of the common asset. Unless provided otherwise by statute or otherwise agreed, the shares of all co-owners are equal (§ 137 para. 2 Slovak Civil Code). All co-owners are jointly and severally entitled and obliged by juridical acts concerning the common asset.

SLOVENIA

All assets that the partners obtain through work during the extramarital union are considered to be the common property of the partners (para. 2 of Art. 51 of the Slovenian Marriage Act). Common property includes, for example, pay, authors' honoraria, and payment on the basis of a work contract. Even a partner who does not engage in employment, or works part time, works and contributes to the creation of assets and is therefore also entitled to a suitable share of the common property; for example, such a partner by his or her housework saves the costs of childcare, household assistance, and enables the other partner to devote himself or herself more fully to his or her work and thus earns more. The rule on common property is of a compulsory nature.

Assets that a partner brings to an extramarital union, as well as assets that she or he obtains during the extramarital union other than by work, such as by inheritance or a gift, are considered to be her or his personal property (para. 1 of Art. 51 of the Slovenian Marriage Act).

SPAIN

Partners can acquire assets jointly under the ordinary rules of joint acquisition both in Catalan civil law and in Spanish civil law. This is the common situation when partners acquire an immovable.

Even though it has been disputed in academic legal writing, case law establishes that partners are free to agree that their property relations are to be governed by the matrimonial property regime of community of acquisitions (STS 18-5-1998, 21-10-1992, 23-07-1998). This would entail that assets acquired by any of them during the relationship would belong to the community and would be subject to division upon termination of the relationship. Such an agreement would be based upon the general principle of party autonomy (Art. 1255 Spanish Civil Code) in the Spanish Civil Code system and upon a special provision about party autonomy contained in Art. 234-3.1 Catalan Civil Code, which applies to informal relationships qualifying as a stable couple.

Case law related to the separation of a couple has sometimes held that partners to an informal relationship had created a community of property over an asset, or the assets acquired during the relationship, even though there was no express agreement to this effect, when there were conclusive facts which revealed that the partners actually wanted to create such a community (STS 22-02-2006).This would however require a decision by a judge and in practice would apply retroactively in order to distribute property when the relationship has broken up.

SWEDEN

Cohabitees can, just like anyone else, become co-owners by acquiring property together. This is the case when they buy something together, for example real estate, both receiving a title to it, or when they have received a common gift from a third party. If one of the cohabitees is the sole owner, they can become co-owners through transference of a share of the property to the other cohabitee, by sale or gift. Importantly, however, Swedish case law provides that having regard to the realities of family life, in particular the cohabitees' or spouses' contributions and intentions, it may in some cases be more reasonable to determine issues of ownership of property acquired for joint use, in a less formal manner than following the general principles of property law where emphasis is on the formal title.[28] As a result, two rebuttable presumptions have been developed, the one concerning primarily household goods, and the other for other types of property, both presumptions often resulting in co-ownership for cohabitees (or spouses/registered partners). The latter presumption is commonly called 'joint caveat ownership' or 'hidden co-ownership', and can be of significant economic relevance.[29] See further below, under Question 27 and Question 28.

SWITZERLAND

With regard to ownership in informal relationships the general rules on the law of property apply (Art. 641 et seq. Swiss Civil Code). Being in an informal relationship generally does not change the ownership of assets. Hence, ownership belongs to the person who has brought in, acquired or received the respective asset. However, if a simple partnership between the partners in an informal relationship exists and the asset is brought in (*quoad dominium*),[30] joint ownership is established.[31] The ownership remains with the sole owner of a simple partnership in case the asset is brought in only for use (*quoad usum*).

If the partners in an informal relationship jointly acquire assets they become co-owners (*Miteigentümer*) of those assets (Art. 646 et seq. Swiss Civil Code), unless otherwise agreed. Only if the partners are bound together in a community by a legal provision or contract do they become joint owners (*Gesamteigentümer*) (Art. 652 et seq. Swiss Civil Code), unless otherwise agreed. Such a community is in place if a simple partnership

---

28 See the preparatory works in NJA II 1921 p. 89, the Swedish Supreme Court decision *NJA 2002 p. 142* and M. BRATTSTRÖM, 'Egendomsförhållanden under bestående samboende', in: J. ASLAND et al., *Nordisk samboerrett*, Gyldendal, Oslo, 2014, at p. 71 et seq. (see chapter 2.2, in the English version of the book, to be published by Intersentia in 2015).

29 See M. BRATTSTRÖM, 'The Protection of a Vulnerable Party when a Cohabitee Relationship Ends – An Evaluation of the Swedish Cohabitees Act', in B. VERSCHRAEGEN (ed.), *Family Finances*, Jan Sramet Verlag, Vienna, 2008, at p. 350 and M. JÄNTERÄ-JAREBORG, 'Rechtsregeln für nichteheliches Zusammenleben in Schweden' (in English), in: I. KROPPENBERG et al. (eds.), *Rechtsregeln für nichteheliches Zusammenleben*, Gieseking Verlag, Vienna, 2009, pp. 207-226, at p. 222 et seq.

30 For property (*Grundeigentum*) the formal requirements for the transfer of ownership have to be followed, see Art. 657 para. 1 Swiss Civil Code.

31 For details see M. COTTIER and C. CREVOSIER, 'Die nichteheliche Lebensgemeinschaft als einfache Gesellschaft', *Aktuelle Juristische Praxis*, 2012, at p. 33, 39 et seq.

between the partners exists (either entirely or only with regard to the respective assets).[32]

[32] A. BÜCHLER, 'Vermögensrechtliche Probleme in der nichtehelichen Lebensgemeinschaft', in: A. RUMO-JUNGO and P. PICHONNAZ, *Familienvermögensrecht*, Stämpfli, Bern, 2003, at p. 59, 74.

QUESTION 27

To what extent, if at all, are there specific rules governing acquisitions and/or transactions in respect of household goods? In answering this question briefly explain what is meant by household goods.

AUSTRIA

There are currently no specific rules governing acquisitions and/or transactions of household goods in force. Partners in an informal relationship may therefore either separately or jointly purchase household goods.[1] If a partner has had an asset before entering into the informal relationship and makes it available for the joint household, he/she nonetheless remains the sole owner of the asset.[2] If the partners are the joint owners of an asset, they have to agree on the administration, use or possible sale of the asset, otherwise the court has to decide on disputed issues upon request.[3]

In terms of marriage, case law has defined household goods *(Hausrat)* pursuant to S. 758 General Austrian Civil Code as all movables belonging to the marital household.[4] This definition does not merely include furniture and household devices, but also luxury goods, such as oriental carpets.[5] With regard to an informal relationship no respective definition exists.

---

1 Cf. H. BÖHM, 'section 825 General Austrian Civil Code', in: A. KLETEČKA and M. SCHAUER, *ABGB-ON 1.01*, Manz Verlag, Vienna, 2013, at marg. No. 1, 10.

2 Section 354 General Austrian Civil Code.

3 H. BÖHM, 'section 833 General Austrian Civil Code', in: A. KLETEČKA and M. SCHAUER, *ABGB-ON 1.01*, Manz Verlag, Vienna, 2013, at marg. No. 21.

4 Austrian Supreme Court, Judgement of 20.12.1984, 6 Ob 716/84.

5 E. MÖSCHL, *Die nichteheliche Lebensgemeinschaft*, LexisNexis ARD ORAC, Vienna, 2007, at marg. No. 86.

BELGIUM

Art. 534 Belgian Civil Code defines household goods as all movables that serve to use and decorate the rooms in the home, excluding art collections that are not part of the everyday living surroundings.[6] This definition is also used in the context of marriage and legal cohabitation.

No specific rules apply regarding acquisitions and transactions in respect of household goods in a *de facto* cohabitation. In the internal dimension, between the partners, implicit agency may however be relevant. In the external dimension, third parties may rely on apparent agency[7] or, more generally, on the theory of legitimate expectation.[8] Furthermore, a minority position in the case law considers the primary regime of spouses to be applicable to informal partners on the basis of Art. 8 and 12 ECHR.[9]

BULGARIA

Bulgarian legislation does not provide a definition of 'household goods'. There are two specific rules which govern acquisitions and transactions in respect of household goods. These are not however relevant to partners in an informal relationship. Intestate heirs have the right to acquire the common household goods when they have lived together and have cared for the testator (Art. 12, para. 1 of the Bulgarian Inheritance Law of 1949, last amended in 2009). The term 'household goods' has been interpreted in the case law. According to the Supreme Court, household goods are 'all goods that have served the everyday needs of the family of the testator. These include the usual furniture, movables, kitchen equipment, TV sets, washing machines and dishwashers, fridges and similar utensils. All these should not be luxury goods in which the given family has invested a substantial amount of money' (Decision No. 485/ 1988, case No 396/88, Ist Division of the Supreme Court).[10] Household goods should be excluded from the inheritance and provided to the person with whom the deceased has shared a common life – i.e., the surviving spouse. Household goods may be disposed of by will and in

---

6 Gent 17 September 2008, *TGR-TWVR* 2009, 104.

7 B. TILLEMAN, *Lastgeving*, Story-Scientia, Deurne, 1997, at n° 164.

8 G. COPS and K. SABBE, 'Niet getrouwd, wel gescheiden. Juridische aspecten van de beëindiging van de samenwoning', *NFM* 2002, at p. 10.

9 Divisional Court of Tongeren 1 April 1992, *Limb.Rechtsl.* 1993, 59; Justice of the Peace Aalst 11 June 1991, *RW* 1993-94, 1307; Justice of the Peace Aalst 1 September 1992, *T.Vred.* 1992, 326.

10 This is the consistent interpretation within the case law. See the same in: PPVS No. 7/1973, p.2; SP Interpretative Decision No. 28/1970; Decision No. 1200/73-I.

such a case it is possible for the partner in the informal relationship to acquire (i.e., to inherit) them.[11]

The Bulgarian Family Code governs (but does not define household goods) the acquisition of and transactions involving movable goods as part of the joint ownership of the spouses. Household goods acquired during the marriage belong jointly to the spouses regardless of the title in acquisition (Art. 21, para. 1). Any transaction should take place jointly by the spouses (Art. 24, para. 3). In the case of a single transaction the law provides for certain remedies (Art. 24, para. 5 of the Bulgarian Family Code).

There is no specific regulation on the acquisition of and transactions in respect of household goods by partners in an informal relationship.

CROATIA

There are no specific rules governing acquisitions and/or transactions in respect of household goods.

CZECH REPUBLIC

There is no definition of the term 'household goods', but in the part of the Czech Civil Code concerning matrimonial property law (S. 708 et seq. Czech Civil Code) the term 'usual equipment of a family household' (S. 698 Czech Civil Code) is used. Usual family household equipment consists of a set of movable things which normally serve for the usual essential needs of the life of the family and its members; whether individual things belong to both spouses or just one of them is not decided (S. 698(1) Czech Civil Code). But this term is connected only with marriage, there is no specific property law concerning an informal relationship.

DENMARK

This is not relevant. There are no specific rules governing acquisitions and/or transactions in respect of household goods.

11 See: Supreme Court: Decision No. 1519/80-I; Decision No. 326/84-I; Decision No. 693/85-I. See also: T. TZANKOVA, *The Factual Spousal Relationship and the Bulgarian Family Law*, Feneya, Sofia, 2000, at p. 130-131.

ENGLAND AND WALES

There are no rules which relate to cohabitants in informal relationships other than the general rules of sole or joint ownership in relation to household goods. There is no separate law relating to household goods.

ESTONIA

Under Estonian law there is no separate definition of what should be deemed to be household goods. § 69(1) of the Estonian Family Law Act, although it does not apply to an informal relationship, defines property which is connected with the housing of a family in the case of divorce. According to the aforementioned provision, objects of the common household of the spouses can be described as objects of standard furnishings connected with the housing of the family for use in their shared household.

According to § 90(1) of the Estonian Law of Property Act, a possessor of a movable and any earlier possessor shall be deemed to be the owners of the asset during the possessor's possession until the contrary is proved. The presumption of ownership by the possessor of movable property, arising from § 90, includes, as a rule, also the presumption of common ownership by the co-possessor, which provides certain protection to a (non-possesor) spouse as well as to the other partner in an informal relationship. The aforementioned is important particularly with regard to the household and other goods used for daily living.

FINLAND

There are no specific rules governing cohabitees' acquisitions and/or transactions in respect of household goods.

FRANCE

Household goods are not subject to specific provisions with regard to partners in an informal relationship. Therefore, acquisitions and/or transactions in respect of household goods are not regulated, in contrast to spouses. Whereas, according to Art. 215 para. 3 of the French Civil Code, a spouse cannot dispose of the rights relating to the family home and of the household goods in the family home without the consent of the other spouse,[12] there is no such provision which applies to partners in an informal relationship. Therefore, each partner can freely dispose of the household goods which belong to him or her.

GERMANY

In matrimonial law, the term 'household goods' (*Haushaltsgegenstände*) covers all movable items (the definition of movable items can be found in § 90 German Civil Code) which are, according to the circumstances of the spouses and their children, designed to enable their cohabitation. However, the relevant provisions in matrimonial law (§ 1361a German Civil Code in the case of separation, § 1568b German Civil Code for divorce) do not apply to informal cohabitation.[13]

Since there are no special rules dealing with property, the general rules of civil law apply. Under the general rules either one or both of the cohabitants can acquire property. It is often assumed that both cohabitants acquire co-ownership and generally in equal half shares.[14] This is also possible if only one of the cohabitants enters into a sales agreement. There may be an explicit or implicit agreement of the cohabitants whereby one acts as an agent for the other cohabitant (see Question 25). The doctrine of 'transaction for whom it concerns' (*Geschäft für wen es angeht*) may also lead to joint property or even property of the other cohabitant.[15] According to one view, financing by one of the cohabitants generally leads to sole ownership of the financing cohabitant.[16] The opposite view argues that the mere fact that one of the cohabitants financed the transaction is not decisive.[17] The intention of the parties to a sales contract and its interpretation determine who will become owner.

---

12 The spouse who has not agreed may claim for nullity within one year from the day on which he or she was informed about the act of disposal.

13 W. SCHULZ, 'Die vorläufige Verteilung der Haushaltsgegenstände nach § 1361a BGB', *Neue Zeitschrift für Familienrecht*, 2014, at p. 486; G. BRUDERMÜLLER, '§ 1361a', in: O. PALANDT, *Bürgerliches Gesetzbuch*, Beck, Munich, 2015, at No. 1.

14 D. SCHWAB, *Familienrecht*, Beck, Munich, 2014, at No. 994; G. BRUDERMÜLLER, 'Einl. vor § 1297', in: O. PALANDT, *Bürgerliches Gesetzbuch*, Beck, Munich, 2015, at No. 20. Cf. for spouses BGH, 13.3.1991, *Entscheidungen des Bundesgerichtshofs in Zivilsachen (BGHZ)*, 114, 74 = *NJW*, 1991, 2283 = *FamRZ*, 1991, 923.

15 D. SCHWAB, *Familienrecht*, Beck, Munich, 2014, at No. 994; G. WEINREICH, 'vor § 1297', in: H. PRÜTTING, G. WEGEN and G. WEINREICH (eds.), *BGB-Kommentar*, Luchterhand, Cologne, 2014, at No. 46.

16 OLG Hamm, 28.09.1988, *NJW*, 1989, 909; P. BASSENGE, '§ 929', in: O. PALANDT, *Bürgerliches Gesetzbuch*, Beck, Munich, 2015, at No. 6.

17 OLG Düsseldorf, 18.12.1991, *NJW*, 1992, 1706.

GREECE

There are no specific rules.

HUNGARY

There are no specific rules.

REPUBLIC OF IRELAND

There are no specific rules governing acquisitions and/or transactions in respect of household goods. The case law on direct and indirect contributions, however, may be of relevance in this regard.

Where spouses or cohabitees separate, or it becomes necessary for any other reason to determine their respective beneficial interests in property, the courts often apply a resulting trust in favour of the party who does not legally own the property. Where property is purchased in one spouses' name but the other party has made direct financial contributions either to the purchase price or by paying the mortgage, the property will be held on resulting trust for the non-owning spouse to the extent of these contributions, unless there is an agreement between the parties to the contrary (*C v C* [1976] IR 254).

Where a spouse contributes indirectly to the general family fund, for example by paying the household bills through her own earnings, the court will infer a trust in her favour in the absence of an express or implied agreement to the contrary. This is because that spouse relieves the owning spouse from certain obligations, thereby permitting him to repay the mortgage (*McC v McC* [1986] ILRM 1). The non-owning spouse will have an equitable share in the property in proportion to her contributions.

The courts in Ireland, however, refuse to accept that a spouse's contribution to the household by working in the home, whether by looking after children or performing household duties, may give rise to a beneficial interest (*L v L* [1992] ILRM 115). Similarly, where one partner makes a direct contribution to an improvement on a home owned solely by the other partner, this will not give rise to a beneficial interest in the property unless there was an express or implied agreement that it would (*EN v RN* [1992] 2 IR 116).

Most of the above-mentioned case law concerns disputes between married couples. In *McGill v Snodgrass* [1978] I.R. 283, a situation of cohabitation was at issue. Here, the plaintiff left his wife, bought a new house and was registered as owner. The defendant, whom he was in a relationship with, moved in. In later proceedings for possession, the defendant claimed a beneficial interest in the property based on an indirect contribution of £1,000 and work she had done on the home. Gannon J declined to hold that she had any interest, on the ground that there no evidence of an agreement before the purchase of the house that the contributions should give her an interest, nor was there anything to connect the contributions with the purchase itself.

Gannon J stated as follows:

> '[I]n the case of two persons who are not spouses, evidence of a consensus derived from words or conduct and intended to have legal consequences would support a trust expressed or implied or constructive. But whether the party having the legal estate and the party claiming an equitable interest be spouses or not, the Court will not impute a relationship of trustee and *cestui que* trust from the facts of a couple living together in (or seemingly in) the married state and sharing expenses without any more cogent evidence.
> … As the counter-claiming defendant is not a spouse but claims to be a *cestui que* trust by virtue of indirect contributions in circumstances of a close domestic relationship corresponding to that between spouses, I think it necessary to point out that indirect contributions which are unrelated to the acquisition of the property cannot found an equitable interest in it.
> … the evidence of the defendant in support of her claim falls far short of what is required to enable the Court to hold, by the implication of a trust for her benefit, that she has acquired any beneficial interest in the property which is the subject of the claim. In spite of having the means and the opportunity, she took no part in the negotiations and contributed no amount of the purchase price for the acquisition of the property of which the plaintiff is sole owner. Such as were her indirect contributions all came after the acquisition of the property had been completed (without continuing instalment payments) and did not bear any significant relationship whatever to either the capital sum of £1,775 or to the sum of £9,750 spent by the plaintiff.'

From this judgment, it appears that a cohabitant in an informal relationship may have a more difficult task in persuading an Irish court that he or she has acquired a beneficial interest in property by virtue of indirect contributions, given the absence of a duty on one cohabitant to maintain the other (compared to spouses).

On the other hand, in *Power v Conroy* [1980] ILRM 31, the plaintiff claimed a beneficial interest in a house purchased in the name of the man with whom she had been living. The financial arrangements of the parties are not entirely clear from the judgment, but it appears that the plaintiff contributed an initial £2,750 to the purchase price of £10,760 together with a further indefinite sum by way of contribution to the joint living expenses while the mortgage was being repaid. McWilliam J. awarded the plaintiff a 55% share of the property. He did not treat the situation different from that of a married couple.

On the specific issue of household goods, *McC v McC* [1986] ILRM 1 is instructive. In this case, the wife had contributed to the cost of a previous family home. When this home was sold, this amount was put towards the cost of furniture in the parties' new house, the purchase of which was financed by the husband. The Supreme Court held that as the wife's contribution was not applied to the purchase price of the second property either directly or indirectly and had not been part of a general family fund, she was not entitled to a beneficial interest in the property. She was only entitled to a one-third share in the furniture and fittings. Although the couple in this case were married, it is likely a similar approach would be taken regarding cohabitants in an informal relationship.

ITALY

There are no specific rules on household goods within the context of informal partnerships. They are covered by the rules on movable property.

Household goods, according to an old decision by the Constitutional Court, include items of furniture, fittings, furnishings, electrical appliances, but also parking spaces and services.[18]

LATVIA

In Latvia there is no such specific legal order on informal relationships.

LITHUANIA

There are no specific rules governing acquisitions and/or transactions in respect of household goods. According to Art. 3.35 of the Lithuanian

[18] C. Cost. 27 July 1989, n. 454, in *Foro. it.* 1989, I, c. 3336.

Civil Code, movable property for the use of the household shall include household utensils and furniture, except for works of art, personal collections or home libraries. Article 4.8 of the Lithuanian Civil Code defines household objects are all things used in household activities such as movable things, furniture and decorative items, with the exception of book collections (libraries), collections of art works and other valuable collections, as well as items of scientific or historic value.

LUXEMBOURG

There are no specific rules governing acquisitions in respect of household goods.

THE NETHERLANDS

No specific rules exist governing acquisitions and transactions with respect to any goods at all. For married couples the Dutch Civil Code includes a number of specific provisions, but these do not apply to informal couples. This implies that each partner is entitled to act alone in relation to his or her goods. In relation to goods to be acquired, each partner may contract but only binds him or herself, unless he/she also represents the other partner.

NORWAY

During the relationship, no specific rules govern acquisitions or transactions in respect of household goods. Household goods are items of property that are usually kept inside a home, like furniture, household utilities, paintings etc. Assets that are in fact capital investments, e.g. expensive paintings and antiques, are not household goods.

PORTUGAL

Household goods are those assets that can be found in all common homes and that are almost used daily for the various purposes shared by people living in common.

There are no specific rules governing acquisitions and/or transactions in respect of household goods.

RUSSIA

There are no special provisions on household goods under Russian law. No such provisions even exist in respect of spouses.

SCOTLAND

There are no rules governing acquisition or transactions in respect of household goods. The acquisition of household goods is regulated, as is the acquisition of any other assets, according to the general rules of property law. There is, however, a rebuttable presumption of equal shares in household goods.[19] Household goods are defined in S. 26(4) of the Family Law (Scotland) Act 2006 as follows:

> 'any goods (including decorative or ornamental goods) kept or used at any time during the cohabitation in any residence in which the cohabitants are (or were) cohabiting for their joint domestic purposes, but does not include –
> (a) money;
> (b) securities;
> (c) any motor car, caravan or other road vehicle; or
> (d) any domestic animal.'

It is notable that it is easier to rebut this presumption than the similar presumption which applies in the context of marriage and civil partnership.[20] The latter provides that the presumption shall not be rebutted simply on the basis of evidence to the effect that 'the goods in question were purchased from a third party by either party alone or by both in unequal shares'.[21] No such exception applies to cohabitants and therefore the presumption may be easily rebutted by evidence of purchase or intention.

SLOVAKIA

The are no specific rules governing acquisitions (transactions) in respect of household goods. Therefore for acquisitions (transactions) in respect of household goods the provision of § 137 para. 2 Slovak Civil Code is applicable. It determines that unless provided otherwise by statute or otherwise agreed, the shares of all co-owners are equal.

19 Family Law (Scotland) Act 2006, S. 26.
20 Family Law (Scotland) Act 2006, S. 25.
21 Family Law (Scotland) Act 2006, S. 25(2).

SLOVENIA

Slovene legislation does not recognise the special concept and protection of household goods, as is familiar in some other countries. It contains only the concept of common property, which includes household goods, if they correspond to the general criteria of common property.

SPAIN

There are no specific rules on household goods that apply to partners to an informal relationship in Spanish or Catalan law. In some cases it has been held that partners may tacitly agree to create a community of property under ordinary civil law provisions (see Art. 392 Spanish Civil Code and 552-1 Catalan Civil Code). Partners would have equal shares in the household goods, unless there is proof to the contrary.

Household goods are defined in provisions related to the general rights and duties of marriage. They are described as movables for the ordinary use of the family (Art. 1320 Spanish Civil Code; Art. 231-9 Catalan Civil Code). Jewellery, works of art and antiques are excluded, as are any goods of outstanding value (Art. 1321.2 Spanish Civil Code and Art. 346 Catalan Civil Code).

SWEDEN

When it comes to acquisitions of movable assets, primarily in the form of household goods, cohabitees – as well as spouses and registered partners – are presumed to have acquired the property as co-owners, irrespective of the formal title to the property. The presumption can be used for items that have been acquired for the use of both cohabitees, on the condition that they both have contributed to the expenses of the joint household.[22] However, the presumption can be set aside if the holder of the title can show that the intention was not to acquire the property for the couple's joint use or that the cohabitee's (or spouse's) financial contribution for the acquisition was intended as a loan or a gift for the other cohabitee, to enable his or her acquisition of the property.[23]

---

22 See M. BRATTSTRÖM, 'Egendomsförhållanden under bestående samboende', in: J. ASLAND et al., *Nordisk samboerrett*, Gyldendal, Oslo, 2014, at p. 71 et seq. (see Chapter 2.2, in the English version of the book, to be published by Intersentia in 2015).

23 See M. BRATTSTRÖM, 'Egendomsförhållanden under bestående samboende', in: J. ASLAND et al., *Nordisk samboerrett*, Gyldendal, Oslo, 2014, at p. 75.

The definition or label of 'joint household goods' (in Swedish: *gemensamt bohag*) in the Swedish Cohabitation Act is independent of issues of ownership. Instead, the property must be intended for, and also used by, both cohabitees in their joint home. The owner cohabitee may not, without the consent of the other cohabitee, dispose of these goods, for example, in the form of alienation or pledging them as security, § 23. If the other cohabitee refuses to consent, the court may, upon application by the owner, permit the disposition, § 24. In the case where such dispositions have taken place without the required consent or permission by court, court proceedings can be initiated in order to have the transaction declared void and title or use restored, § 25, para. 1. The proceedings must be commenced within three months from the time when the other cohabitee learnt about the transaction, § 25 para. 2.

The owner cohabitee's right to dispose of household goods can be subject to restrictions under the Swedish Cohabitation Act, § 23, on condition that the assets qualify to be covered in the property division following the termination of the relationship. The basic requirement in this respect is that they have been acquired for the cohabitees' joint use (see § 3 and Question 24).[24] Joint household goods are defined in § 6 as furniture, domestic appliances and other corporeal chattels intended for the joint home. Goods which are exclusively used by one cohabitee are not included in the category of joint household goods. According to § 7, goods used mainly for recreational purposes do not qualify as joint household goods.

SWITZERLAND

There are no specific rules governing acquisitions and/or transactions in respect of household goods with regard to informal relationships.

24 This excludes previously (i.e. before the relationship) acquired household goods and assets received by a cohabitee from a third party, as a gift or bequest or by a will, on condition that the assets must be the recipient's separate property, to be kept outside a property division, see Swedish Cohabitation Act § 4.

QUESTION 28

Are there circumstances under which partners in an informal relationship can be regarded as joint owners, even if the title belongs to one partner only?

AUSTRIA

Section 380 General Austrian Civil Code provides that ownership can only be acquired with a legal title and a legal mode of acquisition.[1] This excludes the possibility that someone is regarded as an owner even if no title belongs to the person. It follows that partners in an informal relationship are only considered to be joint owners if they have acquired the item together.[2] In this case also the title belongs to both partners.

BELGIUM

There are different ways through which informal partners can be regarded as joint owners, both in the internal and external dimensions of the relationship.

In the internal dimension of the relationship, a partner may prove with all forms of evidence that a title does not correspond with ownership.[3] On the one hand, this evidence may relate to an underlying legal act, such as (implicit) agency or simulation, for example a nominee agreement.[4] On the other hand, it may relate to underlying facts, such as a cash deposit into an account of which the other partner is the holder.[5]

1 P. MADER, 'section 380 General Austrian Civil Code', in: A. KLETEČKA and M. SCHAUER, *ABGB-ON 1.01*, Manz Verlag, Vienna, 2014, at marg. No. 1.

2 Cf. U. AICHHORN, 'Vermögensaufteilung und Erbrecht bei nichtehelicher Lebensgemeinschaft', in: M. GRUBER et al. (eds.), *Erbrecht und Vermögensnachfolge*, Verlag Österreich, Vienna, 2010, at marg. No. 78.

3 Liège 25 March 2009, *RTDF* 2010, 335.

4 S. EGGERMONT, *De juridische bescherming van private relaties*, PhD, University of Antwerp, 2015, at n° 324; W. PINTENS, C. DECLERCK, J. DU MONGH, K. VANWINCKELEN, *Familiaal vermogensrecht*, Intersentia, Antwerp, 2010, at n° 958.

5 S. EGGERMONT, *De juridische bescherming van private relaties*, PhD, University of Antwerp, 2015, at n° 344; W. PINTENS, C. DECLERCK, J. DU MONGH, K. VANWINCKELEN, *Familiaal vermogensrecht*, Intersentia, Antwerp, 2010.

In the external dimension, third parties may try to rely on apparent agency[6] or, more generally, on the theory of legitimate expectation.[7]

BULGARIA

No, there are no such circumstances. In contrast the Bulgarian Family Code regulates the joint ownership of spouses irrespective of the title (Art. 21, para. 1 of the Bulgarian Family Code).

CROATIA

In line with Art. 11 paragraph 2 and Art. 36 of the Croatian Family Act and Art. 4 paragraph 1 and Art. 54 of the Croatian Partnership Act, the answer equally relates to both cohabitants and same-sex informal partners.

Partners in informal relationships are the co-owners of their community of property in equal parts *ex lege*, unless they have agreed otherwise (Art. 36 of the Croatian Family Act). Although the title itself belongs to one partner only, the other partner is also an owner of the partners' community of property, although an unregistered one.

If there is a dispute between the partners regarding their co-ownership, the partner who is not the title holder shall prove before the courts that he/she is a co-owner of the appertaining item which is registered in a public register (e.g. the land register).

CZECH REPUBLIC

No, there are no circumstances under which partners in an informal relationship can be regarded as joint owners even if the title belongs to one partner only. There is no specific property law concerning an informal relationship.

DENMARK

If one cohabitant has made a significant contribution to the acquisition of an asset of which the other cohabitant is the formal owner, it can be

---

6 B. TILLEMAN, *Lastgeving*, Story-Scientia, Deurne, 1997, at n° 164.

7 G. COPS and K. SABBE, 'Niet getrouwd, wel gescheiden. Juridische aspecten van de beëindiging van de samenwoning', *NFM* 2002, at p. 10.

doubted whether the formal ownership reflects the real ownership. This applies particularly if one of the parties is the purchaser in a purchase contract or in the case of a receipt where the registration of ownership does not have legal consequences. In this case a court could find that the assets have been bought jointly and the formal ownership by one owner will be disregarded.[8]

Formal ownership can also be disregarded if ownership is seen as being purely formal. It is usually difficult to succeed in a claim of pro forma ownership.[9]

ENGLAND AND WALES

Yes. If an express trust or an implied common intention constructive or resulting trust is shown to exist to the satisfaction of the court then the owning partner holds the property on trust for the other to the extent of their beneficial share. With regard to personal (i.e. movable) property, resulting trust principles, which look at the proportionate contributions of the parties and reflect that in shares of beneficial ownership, are likely to apply. The non-owner would normally have to prove that they contributed to the purchase or provide other proof that there was a common intention to share ownership and that that has been relied upon to their detriment, in which case a constructive trust could be found. In *Rowe v Prance* [1999] 2 FLR 787 a man used the proceeds of sale from his former matrimonial home to purchase a yacht in his sole name, but falsely told his new partner she could not own it jointly with him as she did not have an Ocean Master's Certificate. He promised her that they were going to sail around the world together which caused her to give up the tenancy of her home and put her furniture in storage. He then left her but on her claim for a declaration as to the ownership of the yacht, the court decided that the man held the yacht on trust for both of them in equal shares, giving her a 50% beneficial interest. In another case *The 'Up Yaws'* [2007] EWHC 210 (Admlty), [2007] 2 FLR 444 the woman of a cohabiting couple had purchased the home in her sole name and her partner had purchased a boat in his sole name. He then sold the boat, purchasing another more expensive boat with the help of monies from a

---

8 See e.g. *Tidsskrift for Familie- og arveret* (Journal of Family and Succession Law), 1999, at p. 101.

9 However, pro forma ownership was accepted in *Tidsskrift for Familie- og arveret* (Journal of Family and Succession Law), 2009, at p. 522, where the woman in a cohabiting relationship was formally the owner of a car for insurance purposes, while the man paid all the costs of the car. Because of his previous accidents the man had difficulty in obtaining insurance. The court found that the man was the sole owner of the car.

mortgage raised in the woman's sole name. The fact they had not discussed how the second boat would be owned resulted in the court finding a resulting trust under which they owned the second boat in proportion to their respective financial contributions.

ESTONIA

According to Estonian law, it is impossible for the partner in an informal relationship to become a joint owner of possessions, if there is no respective agreement to that effect.

FINLAND

The general rules of ownership also apply to cohabiting partners. As was explained under Question 26, the presumption of the co-ownership of movable property does not apply if it can be proven that the title of the movable asset belongs to one partner only. In cases involving the ownership of property, in addition to the title, the Supreme Court has paid attention to the intention of the partners and the payments made by them (for example, KKO 1985-II-167, KKO 1988:85, KKO 1992:48).

FRANCE

No.

GERMANY

There are no special rules dealing with property within an informal relationship; the general rules of the German Civil Code apply. Each cohabitant is owner of his or her own assets.[10] For immovable property the land register evidences ownership.[11] The title as such cannot be questioned. However, despite sole ownership of an asset, a compensation claim by the other cohabitant may be made after separation (see Question 46).

---

10 D. SCHWAB, *Familienrecht*, Beck, Munich, 2014, at No. 1001; M. LÖHNIG, 'Anh. zu §§ 1297 et seq.', in: J. VON STAUDINGER, *Kommentar zum Bürgerlichen Gesetzbuch*, Sellier-de Gruyter, Berlin, 2012, at No. 52.

11 D. SCHWAB, *Familienrecht*, Beck, Munich, 2014, at No. 1001.

GREECE

There are special rules or presumptions of joint ownership only for married partners (Art. 1398 of the Greek Civil Code). Partners in informal relationships are subject to the general rebuttable presumptions of Art. 1110-1111 of the Greek Civil Code. In both cases the presumptions relate only to moveable property.

HUNGARY

See the answer to Question 16.

REPUBLIC OF IRELAND

Where one partner to an informal relationship is the legal owner of property, the partners will not be regarded as joint owners solely by virtue of their relationship or due to their cohabitation. No property rights accrue to the non-owning partner by virtue of their relationship alone. However, the non-owning partner may claim a beneficial interest in the property even though title belongs to the other partner where he or she has made direct financial contributions to the purchase price, the mortgage or the general family fund. (See the law on direct and indirect contributions as set out in Question 27). This is dependent upon the non-owning partner making an application to court for a beneficial interest and the court making an order reflecting same if the circumstances demand it - it is not an automatic right. Where the non-owning partner is held to have a beneficial interest in the property, this interest will be in proportion to the contribution made and will not necessarily be an equal interest to that of the legal owner.

ITALY

If a partner has purchased an asset (movable or immovable) after the beginning of the partnership and is the sole legal holder of the right of ownership, in no case can the other partner become a joint owner.

However, when it can be proved that the purchase has been made possible through the partner's contribution in the form of housework, then the rule on unjust enrichment applies (Art. 2041):[12] '[a] person who

[12] Compare R. TOMMASINI, 'La famiglia di fatto', in: M. BESSONE (ed.), *Trattato di diritto privato*, Giappichelli, Turin, 1999, at p. 414; G. FERRANDO, *Il matrimonio*, in *Trattato Cicu-Messineo*, Giuffré, Milan, 2002, at p. 230.

has enriched himself without just cause at the expense of another shall, to the extent of the enrichment, indemnify the other for his correlative loss'.

LATVIA

As there is no legal order on informal relationships in Latvia, there is no such legal order on property relations of the partners in an informal relationship.

LITHUANIA

Article 3.231 of the Lithuanian Civil Code provides that where immovables or the rights to immovables are registered in the name of one of the cohabitees, both cohabitees may require, by submitting a joint application to the public registrar, the addition of a record to the effect that the cohabitees use these immovables or the rights to these immovable together. The signatures of the cohabitees added to such an application must be attested by a notary public.

The case law has developed practice to the effect that a certain asset of the cohabitees could be acknowledged as their joint-partial property despite its ownership being registered in the name of one of them if evidence exists that the asset was acquired by both cohabitees from their common funds and is used jointly, as well as in the case of legal relations based on contractual joint activities [13] leading towards a common objective, for instance, to acquire immovables by way of procurement contracts with the aim of subsequently renovating, building (/rebuilding) and using and managing them as joint-partial property, and also contributing to the creation of such assets with their labour.[14]

LUXEMBOURG

No.

THE NETHERLANDS

This is a difficult question without a clear-cut answer. A first remark is that according to property law the title is not decisive for assessing the property relations between the partners. What is relevant, in theory, is to

[13] Ruling of the Lithuanian Supreme Court of 9 January 2015, civil case no. 3K-3-62/2015.

[14] Ruling of the Lithuanian Supreme Court of 28 March 2011, civil case no. 3K-3-134/2011.

whom the asset has been delivered. For instance, in relation to movable goods, the partner to whom the asset is delivered is the owner (unless he/she has also represented the other partner, for instance pursuant to a provision in a cohabitation contract).

In practice, property relations become convoluted during cohabitation. When the relationship breaks down, it is often unclear who owns what property. Partners will generally claim that the contested asset is their private property (and not their joint property). There are not so many decisions which shed light on the circumstances under which property is considered to be co-owned. If there is no evidence as to the delivery or ownership of an asset, the courts sometimes decide that a movable asset is joint property.[15]

In relation to registered property the partner who is registered is the owner. There is no way to avoid this rule, since the Supreme Court has decided that it is impossible that the principal will become the owner of the house when his/her partner acted in his/her own name but as an agent for the principal.[16] As a result there is no possibility that the other partner will be entitled to the registered property.

In relation to savings in bank accounts, even if the account is registered in the name of one of the partners only, the question of which of the partners in their internal relationship is entitled to the savings has to be answered by taking into account what the intention of the partners was when the account was registered in the name of only one of them.[17] The registration is therefore not per se decisive.

NORWAY

As mentioned in the answer to Question 26, ownership is obtained regardless of judicial registration of title. Therefore, partners to an informal relationship can be regarded as joint owners even if the registered title belongs to one partner only.

Even though formal ownership (registered title) is not decisive, a good faith purchaser of land may rely on the registration. To obtain protection from a good faith purchaser, the real co-owner must have the property

15 W.M. SCHRAMA, 'Vermogensrechtelijke geschillen tussen ongehuwde samenlevers', *FJR*, 2003, at p. 7-8.
16 HR 2 April 1976, NJ 1976, 450 (Modehuis Nolly I).
17 HR 9 February 2007, LJN AZ6525 (not in relation to informal partners).

registered by the registrar for judicial registration of title pursuant to the Norwegian Land Registration Act.[18] This also holds true in cases where joint ownership is based on indirect contributions.[19]

Creditors, on the other hand, must accept real ownership as a rule.[20] This also applies in cases where joint ownership is based on indirect contributions.[21] However, when property is transferred from one partner to the other by contract, registration is necessary. To be protected from the creditors of the old owner, the new owner must see to it that the property is registered by the registrar for judicial registration of title pursuant to the Norwegian Land Registration Act.[22]

PORTUGAL

No, there are no such circumstances.

RUSSIA

Partners can provide by agreement for all or some of the assets that they already own and/or all or some of the assets that they later acquire during their relationship to be designated as their joint property, irrespective of the name in which these assets are acquired.

Panin suggests in his recent dissertation that an implied agreement can be derived from the fact that the parties live together, run a joint household and commonly use the assets acquired by either of them for the needs of the family.[23] However, it is unclear as to whether the courts will be prepared to regard such 'implicit' agreements as cohabitation agreements.

---

18 The Land Registration Act 1935, sections 20, 21 and 27.

19 Rt. 1996 s. 918, see T. SVERDRUP, *Stiftelse av sameie i ekteskap og ugift samliv*, Universiteitsforlaget, Oslo, 1997, at p. 36-37.

20 K. LILLEHOLT, *Allmenn formuerett. Fleire rettar til same formuesgode*, Universiteitsforlaget, Oslo, 2012, at p. 277 and T. SVERDRUP, *Stiftelse av sameie i ekteskap og ugift samliv*, Universiteitsforlaget, Oslo, 1997, at p. 34.

21 See K. LILLEHOLT, *Allmenn formuerett. Fleire rettar til same formuesgode*, Universiteitsforlaget, Oslo, 2012, at p. 276 and T. SVERDRUP, *Stiftelse av sameie i ekteskap og ugift samliv*, Universiteitsforlaget, Oslo, 1997, at p. 34-36.

22 The Norwegian Land Registration Act 1935, S. 20 and 23.

23 В.С. ПАНИН, *Проблемы правового регулирования фактических брачных отношений в России*, dissertation, Moscow, 2012, at p. 90, note 1.

SCOTLAND

In respect of heritable property, ownership depends on registered title and there is no special provision for the situation of partners in an informal relationship. It should be noted, however, that there is similarly no special treatment of partners in a formal relationship: marriage or civil partnership. Ownership is a matter for the general rules of property and takes no account of the personal relationship between the parties. There may be a possibility of arguing that, although title is registered in the name of one partner, it is held in trust for the other or for the couple.[24] This is not however a possibility which has been explored or developed to any extent in Scots law.

SLOVAKIA

No, there are none.

SLOVENIA

There are no such circumstances.

SPAIN

Case law related to a couple's separation has sometimes held that partners to an informal relationship had created a community of property over an asset or assets acquired during the relationship, even though title belonged to one partner only. In order to reach this conclusion, there had to be conclusive facts revealing that the partners actually wanted to create such a community (STS 22-02-2006). However, this would require a decision by a judge and in practice would apply retroactively in order to distribute property when the relationship has broken up. In cases in which the non-owner financed the acquisition of an asset by his or her partner, the non-owner might argue that he or she is a fiduciary owner. Case law however has sometimes held that the financial contribution was a donation (STSJ of Catalonia 22-05-2003, STS 13-02-2003) or compensated for other contributions (STS of 5-12-2005).

---

24 See *Barbour v Marriott* 2012 GWD 18-398.

SWEDEN

Swedish courts have in a number of cases accepted that a concealed ('hidden' or 'caveat') co-ownership can arise between cohabitees (and spouses) when the requirements of general principles on the law of obligations or property are not fulfilled.[25] The Supreme Court decisions NJA 1980 p. 705, NJA 1981 p. 693, NJA 1982 p. 589 and NJA 2013 p. 242 constitute important examples of this.[26] Although in these cases the property in question had been acquired only in the name of one cohabiting partner, the court concluded that at the time of acquisition the partners must have intended that the property would be co-owned by them. Such common intention has been considered to exist when it is shown that the property was, actually, acquired for the joint use of the cohabitees and that the other cohabitee (the 'hidden' co-owner) had made some financial contribution for the acquisition with the aim of becoming a joint owner. The Swedish Supreme Court has, in NJA 2002 p. 142, developed the justification behind this case law by stating that 'the construction of co-ownership gives financial protection to the cohabitee who was not the formal purchaser. With regard to the special community that arises in a cohabitation relationship, often with joint possession, and where non-formalised and implicit agreements are common, a natural point of departure is to presume that property which is purchased for the couple's joint use, formally by one spouse or cohabitee but with financial contribution from the other, is to be co-owned'. The hidden co-owner's contribution must, however, have been made at the time the property was acquired, in order to result in co-ownership. It is not possible for a cohabitee to achieve co-ownership (through the principle of the concealed right of co-ownership) by making successive payments in arrears - for example by paying in the form of instalments when the other cohabitee has already been the owner of the property for some time.

---

25 This case law includes spouses. The principle of concealed co-ownership is, however, of relevance in particular for cohabitees since their relationship is not covered by family law rules to the same extent as for spouses. See M. BRATTSTRÖM, 'The Protection of a Vulnerable Party when a Cohabitee Relationship Ends - An Evaluation of the Swedish Cohabitees Act', in: B. VERSCHRAEGEN (ed.), *Family Finances*, Jan Sramet Verlag, Vienna, 2008, at p. 350 and M. JÄNTERÄ-JAREBORG, 'Rechtsregeln für nichteheliches Zusammenleben in Schweden' (in English), in: I. KROPPENBERG et al. (eds.), *Rechtsregeln für nichteheliches Zusammenleben*, Gieseking Verlag, Vienna, 2009, pp. 207-226, at p. 222 et seq.

26 See also A. AGELL, *Äganderätten till fastighet för makar och samboende*, Norstedt, Stockholm, 1985, at p. 19 and M. BRATTSTRÖM, 'Egendomsförhållanden under bestående samboende', in: J. ASLAND et al., *Nordisk samboerrett*, Gyldendal, Oslo, 2014, at p. 78 et seq. (see Chapter 2.2.3, in the English version of the book, to be published by Intersentia in 2015).

In most cases, the principle of concealed co-ownership has been applied to real estate property (i.e., in this case, land property with a house) used as the cohabitees' joint dwelling. Case law confirms, however, that it can also arise in relation to real property used only for recreational purposes, to apartments in cooperatively owned buildings (in Swedish: *bostadsrätt*) used as the couple's joint dwelling, and to movable property such as boats, horses, etc. Of relevance in this respect are the Swedish Supreme Court decisions NJA 1992 p. 163, NJA 2002 p. 3, NJA 2008 p. 826 and NJA 2008 p. 1053.

If the formal owner is able to show that the intention was that only one of the cohabitees would own the property, or that the financial contribution by the other was a loan or a gift, the presumption of co-ownership can be set aside; see the Swedish Supreme Court decisions NJA 2004 p. 397 and NJA 2008 p. 1053 and the Court of Appeal decision RH 1991:23.[27]

SWITZERLAND

There are no circumstances under which partners in an informal relationship can be regarded as joint owners if the title belongs to one partner only.

[27] M. Brattström, 'Egendomsförhållanden under bestående samboende', in: J. Asland et al., *Nordisk samboerrett*, Gyldendal, Oslo, 2014, at p. 75 and p. 82 (see Chapter 2.2.2 and 2.2.3 in the English version of the book, to be published by Intersentia in 2015).

QUESTION 29

How is the ownership of assets proved as between partners in an informal relationship? Are there rebuttable presumptions?

AUSTRIA

Due to the lack of specific rules which are applicable to informal relationships the general rules on property law apply.[1] In case of a dispute the person who claims to be the owner has to prove that he/she has acquired the ownership of the item with a legal title and a respective mode of acquisition and that currently the defendant possesses the item; the claimant has to describe the item.[2] Section 323 General Austrian Civil Code contains the presumption that the possessor *(Besitzer)* of an item has also a valid legal title and cannot be requested to provide this title. Besides the possibility to prove ownership, S. 372 General Austrian Civil Code grants a facilitated option, where a person claiming his/her ownership only has to prove a 'better right to possession' against the other person *(actio publiciana).*[3]

Indications as to whether one or the other partner in an informal relationship has become the owner of the item are e.g. who was present at the time of purchasing the asset, who made the decision to purchase, who paid for the asset, which name is written on the invoice.[4] In the case of doubt it is presumed that both partners are joint owners.[5] Since it can turn out to be very difficult to prove ownership after many years, it is

1 Sections 369 et seq. General Austrian Civil Code.
2 Section 370 General Austrian Civil Code.
3 Only a qualified (honest, real and legitimate) possessor is entitled to file an *actio publiciana.*
4 E. MÖSCHL, *Die nichteheliche Lebensgemeinschaft,* LexisNexis ARD ORAC, Vienna, 2007, at marg. No. 86.
5 E. MÖSCHL, *Die nichteheliche Lebensgemeinschaft,* LexisNexis ARD ORAC, Vienna, 2007, at marg. No. 86.

recommended to keep all receipts and to maintain lists, which in case of doubt provide information on the question of who is the owner of what.[6]

BELGIUM

With regard to immovable property, the necessary authentic instrument will prove ownership between the partners. Authenticity does not apply to the sincerity of the parties' declarations; evidence in rebuttal is consequently allowed between the parties.[7]

With regard to movable property, all means of providing evidence of ownership are accepted. Particularly relevant is the presumption that possession amounts to title (Art. 2279 Belgian Civil Code). A partner may rely on joint possession to prove joint property.[8] On the contrary, it is debated whether a partner may rely on Art. 2279 Belgian Civil Code to prove sole ownership. According to some of the case law[9] and authors,[10] possession in this case is necessarily ambiguous. Other authors are of the opinion that *de facto* cohabitation does not necessarily create ambiguous possession.[11] This depends on the circumstances of the case. Ambiguity of possession, however, is often accepted in the case law.[12] In sum, even though there is no presumption of joint ownership between informal partners,[13] the rules on evidence will often persuade the court to reach such a conclusion. Anyhow, Art. 2279 Belgian Civil Code does not apply to bank accounts. The presumption that the holder of the account owns the balance[14] can be rebutted with all forms of evidence.[15]

---

6 U. AICHHORN, *Das Recht der Lebenspartnerschaften, Ehe und Lebensgemeinschaft,* Springer, Vienna, 2003, at p. 429.

7 Liège 25 March 2009, *RTDF* 2010, 335.

8 Liège 12 February 1988, *Ann.dr.Liège* 1989, 36, with note JOISTEN; Mons 4 October 2004, *RTDF* 2005, 885.

9 Justice of the Peace Oudenaarde 7 June 2007, *T.Vred.* 2009, 163.

10 W. PINTENS, C. DECLERCK, J. DU MONGH, K. VANWINCKELEN, *Familiaal vermogensrecht,* Intersentia, Antwerp, 2010, at n° 960.

11 S. EGGERMONT, *De juridische bescherming van private relaties,* PhD, University of Antwerp, 2015, at n° 328.

12 E.g. Liège 24 December 2003, *JT* 2004, 406; Antwerp 5 December 2006, *NJW* 2007, 414, with note VERSCHELDEN; District Court of Hasselt 10 March 1987, *TBBR* 1988, 131; District Court of Bruges 5 December 1988, *RW* 1989-90, 201; Justice of the Peace Oudenaarde 7 June 2007, *T.Vred.* 2009, 163.

13 Antwerp 5 December 2006, *NJW* 2007, 414, with note VERSCHELDEN.

14 Liège 9 February 2011, *RTDF* 2011, 743; Justice of the Peace Westerlo 11 December 2006, *T.Vred.* 2007, 354. But compare Liège 18 January 2005, *RTDF* 2007, 562, with note TAINMONT.

15 Mons 4 October 2004, *RTDF* 2005, 885.

BULGARIA

The ownership of assets between the partners in an informal relationship can only be proved on the basis of the title therein. There are no rebuttable presumptions in this respect.

CROATIA

In line with Art. 11 paragraph 2 and Art. 36 of the Croatian Family Act and Art. 4 paragraph 1 and Art. 54 of the Croatian Partnership Act, the answer equally relates to both cohabitants and same-sex informal partners.

There are no rebuttable presumptions between partners in an informal relationship with regard to the partner's ownership. It is very easy to prove ownership of assets if the ownership is registered in public registers. Still, there are so many open questions in proving the ownership of assets that belong to the community of property when only one partner is registered in a public register as the owner of the item in question.

What needs to be proven if co-ownership is not registered depends on the legal determination of the community of property and the personal property of the partners. Community of property which is co-owned in equal parts comprises assets acquired by the partners on the basis of their work during their life union as well as lottery prizes and income from intellectual and related rights (Art. 36 of the Croatian Family Act and 51 of the Croatian Partnership Act). Personal property means property owned by the partners at the time of the beginning of the life union, including assets acquired during the life union from sources other than work (e.g. inheritance, gifts etc.) Namely, what needs to be proven is as follows:

- the existence of a life union,
- the time of acquisition,
- the legal basis of the acquisition.[16]

These three determinants could be demonstrated using a different kind of evidence. Judicial practice shows that the existence of a life union, the

[16] B. REŠETAR and U. JOSIPOVIĆ, 'Issues of Dispute in Marital Contracts with Particular Attention to Marital Partners' Bank Contracts', *Zbornik radova Pravnog fakulteta u Splitu*, 2013, pp. 115-138, at p. 118-120.

exact time of its commencement and termination are the most difficult things to prove. The law does not stipulate what constitutes a life union, thus leaving this matter for the courts to decide on a case-by-case basis. In the absence of other forms of evidence, life unions are most often proved by the testimony of a large number of witnesses.[17]

CZECH REPUBLIC

There is no specific property law concerning an informal relationship. If partners in an informal relationship are co-owners according to S. 1115 et seq. Czech Civil Code of an immovable object, this fact is visible from the public register. If nothing special is declared, shares are presumed to be equal (S. 1122(3) Czech Civil Code).

If the partners in an informal relationship have a joint account (i.e. containing their joint funds) and they buy something with funds from this account, it is presumed that they are co-owners with an equal share.

DENMARK

When determining ownership an attempt is made to clarify the parties' subjective views. Their views may be apparent from an ownership agreement between the parties, or their assumptions may be documented in other ways. The assessment of the evidence takes account of two elements: formal ownership which can be objectively shown, and which of the parties has paid for the asset. In principle only direct contributions count, and there is generally a requirement for a clear connection between the payment and the acquisition. However, this requirement does not apply if there is no clear evidence of ownership because of the combining of the parties' finances. In these cases, if both parties had such favourable financial circumstances that they could both have contributed substantially to the acquisition, a court could rule that there is equal joint ownership. Such a 'chance' joint ownership may be relevant to the household goods of a shared home. Indirect contributions in the form of housework and the provision of care are not relevant.

---

[17] On the occasion of the verification of the existence of a life union, the courts mostly examine the existence of joint life at the same address, property ties, emotional and sexual bonds, joint travel, meeting the partner's relatives and friends and similar. Judgement of the Supreme Court, 22.11.2007., Rev 1121/2007-2; Judgement of the Supreme Court, 28.03.2007, Rev 1038/2006-2; Judgement of the Supreme Court, 29.12.2004., Rev 1024/2004-2.

ENGLAND AND WALES

Proof of purchase of any asset by one partner or property purchased with joint monies for the personal use of one partner will be presumed to be the property of that partner. However, this can be rebutted by proof of contributions to the purchase price for property for joint use by the other partner. The standard of proof is on the balance of probabilities and the burden of proof is on the non-legal owner partner. Evidence will be taken in court on the issue in the normal way, examining receipts, hearing from witnesses including the couple to enable the court to make a declaration of trust relating to the joint beneficial ownership if proven.

Jointly purchased property or property of which the title is vested in joint names is presumed to be owned in equal shares unless a contrary common intention is proved. Gifts are owned by the donee.

In the case of real property, the title deeds will evidence legal ownership and the law presumes that the beneficial ownership is the same, unless an implied common intention resulting or constructive trust is proved to the satisfaction of the court.

ESTONIA

An informal relationship itself does not alter ownership relations. Both persons shall remain the owners of their possessions.

FINLAND

The ownership of assets is normally proven according to the general rules. As for assets that require registration, e.g. immovable assets, flats, shares, cars, boats, motorcycles and firearms, the registration information acts as a strong presumption of ownership. However, with regard to movable assets that are not registered, the title may be more difficult to prove as the property is usually located in the common home and is controlled by the partners jointly. For this purpose, the Finnish Act on the Dissolution of the Household of Cohabiting Partners (26/2011) contains a provision that creates a presumption of co-ownership if it cannot be proven which partner a particular movable object belongs to (S. 6). However, this Act only applies to cohabiting partners who have lived in a common household for a minimum period of five years or who have (or have had) a joint child. The provision applies only to situations where the property is being separated in the context of the dissolution of the common household.

FRANCE

The ownership of assets as between the partners in an informal relationship is not regulated by specific statutory provisions. Therefore, the general rules apply.

In respect of movables, proof of ownership can be established by any kind of written document (an invoice, purchase order etc.). If there is no written document, Art. 2276 of the French Civil Code states that for tangible assets (*meubles corporels*) '*en fait de meubles, la possession vaut titre*'. This means that in matters concerning (tangible) movables, possession is equivalent to title. This provision contains a rule of evidence (a rebuttable presumption according to which the person who possesses the movable is presumed to be the owner). This presumption, however, only applies if the possession is not ambiguous (*équivoque*). [18] In a judgment of 24 October 2012,[19] the Court of cassation held that this presumption arising out of possession cannot be rebutted by the sole evidence that a vehicle was wholly financed by the other partner.

Each former cohabitant owns the asset that is in his or her possession. Indeed, according to the general principles of property law, possession of an asset determines its ownership.[20] This principle is also applicable to money deposited in bank accounts. This presumption of ownership based on possession can be rebutted by proof of ownership (a bill, receipt, etc.), but the burden of proof is a heavy one, and one cohabitant can face some difficulties in rebutting it. Indeed, the *Cour de cassation* has held that the exclusive financing of an asset does not amount to proof of ownership.[21]

As for intangible assets (*meubles incorporels*), the presumption laid down in Art. 2276 of the French Civil Code does not apply. Ownership can be proved by any means of evidence.[22]

---

[18] As regards personal belongings, jewellery, professional instruments, etc., possession will probably not be ambiguous, whereas this will be the case for household goods.

[19] Cass. Civ. I, 24 October 2012, no 11-16431, *Bull. Civ.* I, no 214: '*la présomption qui résulte de la possession implique pour le demandeur en revendication de prouver le titre précaire en vertu duquel le prétendu possesseur détient un meuble ou le vice affectant sa possession, que ne suffit pas à caractériser le paiement du prix par le revendiquant, à défaut de quoi ce défendeur a titre pour le conserver*'.

[20] Art. 2276 of the French Civil Code.

[21] Cass. Civ. 1, 24 October 2012, no.11.16431.

[22] Cass. Civ. I, 21 February 2006, no. 04-19667 and I. BARRIÈRE-BROUSSE and M. DOUCHY-OUDOT, *Les contentieux familiaux,* Lextenso, Paris, 2013, at no. 609.

If a partner cannot prove that he or she is the owner of a movable, the asset is deemed to belong jointly to both partners (50/50). This mainly applies to movables which are in the common home.

In respect of immovable property, proof is provided by the title drawn up by the notary public. In a case where a property had been jointly purchased by the cohabitants (50/50) but the loan was only being repaid by the man (the woman was unemployed and had no earnings of her own), the Court of cassation[23] held that after the breakup the man had no claim against his former partner since it followed from the factual circumstances of the case that his intention had been to favour and reward his partner.

GERMANY

There is a rebuttable presumption as to ownership in marriage. In respect of movables intended for the exclusive personal use of either spouse, it is, between the spouses and in relation to creditors, presumed that they belong to the spouse for whose use they were intended (§ 1362 German Civil Code).

As to informal cohabitation, there are no special rules dealing with property. The general presumption of ownership of the possessor applies. It is presumed, in favour of the possessor of a movable, that he or she is the owner of that property (§ 1006 para. 1 German Civil Code). This will often mean co-ownership.[24] It is also presumed, in favour of a former possessor, that he or she was the owner of the thing during possession (§ 1006 para. 2 German Civil Code). After a break-up of the relationship, this will also often lead to the presumption of co-ownership (see Question 41).[25]

GREECE

With the exception of moveable items in the possession of each partner and in respect of which partner there is a rebuttable presumption of ownership, there is no special provision.

---

23 Cass. Civ. I, 2 April 2014, no. 13-11025, *RTD civ.* 2014, at p. 702.

24 J. GERNHUBER and D. COESTER-WALTJEN, *Familienrecht*, Beck, Munich, 2010, at p. 503.

25 M. LÖHNIG, 'Anh. zu §§ 1297 et seq.', in: J. VON STAUDINGER, *Kommentar zum Bürgerlichen Gesetzbuch*, Sellier-de-Gruyter, Berlin, 2012, at No. 89.

HUNGARY

See the answer to Question 16 concerning the property relations of cohabitants in the Civil Code of 1959 which made it possible for cohabitants to acquire common property. Work done in the household was considered to be a contribution to acquiring that property. There is no rebuttable presumption in the Hungarian Civil Code.

REPUBLIC OF IRELAND

This is normally achieved through the law on direct and indirect contributions.

ITALY

As for immovables, ownership can only be proved through written instruments, especially the registered deed of sale.

As for movables, proof can be provided through any means, even by witnesses.

If, however, the party is not able to prove exclusive ownership of an asset, then the asset is considered to be the common property of both partners and is divided on an equal basis.[26] This rule has also been applied to current bank accounts opened in both partners' names.[27]

No other presumption is foreseen.

LATVIA

In Latvia there is no such specific legal order on informal relationships.

By way of comparison one can consider the following. In lawful property relations of spouses, everything acquired during the marriage by the spouses together, or by one of them but from the resources of both

26 Trib. Pavia 20 November 1979 in *Giur. It.* 1980, I, 2, p. 431; Pret. Torino 17 March 1988 in *Dir. Fam. Pers.* 1990, 1314. Compare G. FERRANDO, *Diritto di famiglia*, Zanichelli, Bologna, 2013, at p. 149.

27 In an often cited case, only the man had made bank deposits as he was the sole wage earner, while the woman was a housewife. Her work was nevertheless considered by the court to entitle her to half of the money. See Trib. Bolzano 20 January 2000, in *Giur. Mer.*, 2000, p. 818; AA. VV., *La separazione nella famiglia di fatto*, Cedam, Padua, 2014, at p. 171.

spouses, or with the assistance of the actions of the other spouse, is the joint property of both spouses; in a case of uncertainty, it is to be presumed that such property belongs equally to both spouses.[28] The burden of establishing that certain property is separate lies upon the spouse who asserts that fact. The fact that immovable property is the separate property of one spouse is to be recorded in the Land Register.[29]

LITHUANIA

According to Art. 177 of the Code of Civil Procedure of the Republic of Lithuania, evidence shall be any factual data on the basis of which the Court, following the procedures established by the Law, can issue a statement regarding the presence or absence of circumstances serving as grounds for the claims and rebuttals of the parties, as well as other circumstances relevant for a fair resolution of the case. Factual data can be obtained by the following means: explanations by the parties to the case and third parties, witness testimonies, documentary evidence, physical evidence, inspection protocols, expert evidence, visual and audio material legally obtained and other means of proof.

According to the practice of the Court of Cassation, the applicability of the principles of honesty, fairness and prudence to the rules on the admissibility of evidence in cases of this type means that the courts may remove any restrictions on the admissibility of evidence when they see a ground to admit that the property rights of cohabitees outside marriage who jointly managed the common household would not be protected merely because of a lack of a written agreement on joint activities, although practical relations between the parties, the evolved situation, the intentions of the parties, their goal-oriented behaviour and other actions would allow their legal relation to be qualified as joint activity.

As in the case of any other civil agreement, it is mandatory to establish the objective of the parties to the agreement, i.e. what particular asset (or all assets acquired during the entire period of the partners' relationship) was covered by the agreement on the acquisition of joint-partial property.[30]

The Court of Cassation has noted that the admissibility of evidence is an important aspect in the context of such cases because notarised

28 S. 89 para. 2 Latvian Civil Law.
29 S. 91 para. 2 Latvian Civil Law.
30 Ruling of the Lithuanian Supreme Court of 6 October 2008, civil case no. 3K-3-479/2008.

documents and records at the Registry of Immovable Property are *prima facie* evidence, therefore an established legal fact can be contested in accordance with the rules on the admissibility of evidence as defined in Art. 197, part 2, of the Lithuanian Code of Civil Procedure. Circumstances related to the legal regime of property supported by official documentary evidence are deemed to have been fully proven unless they are refuted by other evidence in the case, except for witness testimonies whereby restrictions on the use thereof may be lifted if they would contradict the principles of honesty, fairness and prudence.

The Supreme Court of Lithuania follows standard practice that cohabitation between a non-married couple, joint household management and the creation of joint assets by using common funds generated from the joint household, as well as personal funds, and by their own labour, can serve as a sufficient ground to recognise the existence of an agreement between the parties on joint activities for the creation of joint-partial property.[31]

It is presumed that the contributions of the partners are equal unless established otherwise in the agreement on joint activities (Art. 6.970 of the Lithuanian Civil Code), and each participant is allocated a corresponding share of the property rights, depending on the partners' contributions in terms of money, assets, personal input and with consideration being given to the joint household management (Rulings of the Lithuanian Supreme Court in civil cases No. 3K-3-37/2004, No. 3K-3-235/2008).

LUXEMBOURG

Each partner needs to prove ownership according to the principles of the law (the evidentiary measures determined by the rules of the Luxembourg Civil Code).

However, Art. 1348 of the Luxembourg Civil Code dispenses with such evidence in certain circumstances, due to the close position of the partners to each other. This article facilitates proof-taking for the partners.

---

31 Ruling of the Lithuanian Supreme Court of 8 April 2008, civil case no. 3K-3-235/2008; Ruling of the SCL of 28 September 2009, civil case no. 3K-3-336/2009; Ruling of the SCL of 21 December 2010, civil case no. 3K-3-553/2010.

The partner who claims to be the only owner of an asset bears the burden of proof.

If evidence of sole ownership cannot be produced, there is a rebuttable presumption of joint ownership.

THE NETHERLANDS

The general provisions of Books 3 and 5 of the Dutch Civil Code apply. In relation to movable goods, a rebuttable presumption of ownership applies. The partner who has power/control over an asset is presumed to be its possessor on the basis of Art. 3:109 Dutch Civil Code and a possessor is presumed to be the owner of the asset under Art. 3:119 Dutch Civil Code. This is, however, mostly relevant after a separation.

NORWAY

The documentation that is required depends on the basis for the claim of ownership. If the alleged basis is an agreement between the parties, the registered title, together with other factors, may serve as proof of an agreement, but the title in itself is not sufficient proof of ownership.[32]

If there is no express agreement and both cohabitants have made a direct financial contribution to the cost of an item of property for common personal use, the presumption is that the cohabitants have made a tacit agreement of co-ownership even if only one of the cohabitants is the buyer. This presumption is rebuttable - specific circumstances might suggest that the financial contribution was a gift or a loan. As mentioned under Question 26, not only direct, but also indirect contributions are acknowledged. No specific presumption applies in this assessment.

Assuming the conclusion is co-ownership, the rebuttable presumption is that the co-owners own equal parts unless circumstances justify a different fraction of ownership, the Norwegian Co-ownership Act S. 2.

PORTUGAL

There are no specific rules which are applicable to partners in an informal relationship. They may use all means acceptable in law, just as any citizen can.

---

[32] Rt. 1980, p. 1403.

When it is a case of co-ownership/joint ownership, a rebuttable presumption of an equal share is applicable whenever the title omits any difference between co-owners. Taking into account the difficulties raised by proof of the ownership of assets Parliamentary Bill n. 349/X, which preceded Act 23/2010, foresaw the possibility of stipulating clauses concerning the ownership of the assets acquired during cohabitation (Art. 5-A, n. 1). Moreover, it established a rebuttable presumption: movable assets would be presumed to be jointly owned by both partners (Art. 5-A, n. 2). These solutions, however, did not become law, due to the veto by the President of the Republic.

RUSSIA

By all means of proof admitted by the Russian Code of Civil Procedure. There are no rebuttable presumptions.

SCOTLAND

In general, ownership is established according to the ordinary rules of property law. In respect of heritable property, ownership is established on the basis of registered legal title to the property and, in respect of moveable property, it will be established by evidence of acquisition. There are two exceptions, both contained in the Family Law (Scotland) Act 2006, which apply to establishing ownership of assets within the context of an informal relationship of cohabitation.

Section 26 of the Family Law (Scotland) Act 2006 provides that: 'It shall be presumed that each cohabitant has a right to an equal share in household goods acquired (other than by gift or succession from a third party) during the period of cohabitation.'[33] The presumption applies where any question of ownership arises during or after cohabitation.[34] Household goods are defined in S. 26(4) as follows:

> 'any goods (including decorative or ornamental goods) kept or used at any time during the cohabitation in any residence in which the cohabitants are (or were) cohabiting for their joint domestic purposes, but does not include –
> (a) money;
> (b) securities;
> (c) any motor car, caravan or other road vehicle; or
> (d) any domestic animal.'

[33] Family Law (Scotland) Act 1985, S. 26(2).
[34] Family Law (Scotland) Act 1985, S. 26(1).

While this presumption is similar to one which applies in the context of marriage and civil partnership,[35] it should be noted that it is more limited. The scope of household goods applies only in respect of items acquired during the period of cohabitation and does not extend, as it does in the context of formal relationships, to goods acquired in prospect of the relationship. It is also significantly easier to rebut the presumption in the context of cohabitation than it is in marriage or civil partnership. The equivalent presumption of equal ownership in respect of spouses or civil partners provides that it shall not be rebutted simply on the basis of evidence to the effect that 'the goods in question were purchased from a third party by either party alone or by both in unequal shares'.[36] No such exception applies to cohabitants and therefore the presumption may be easily rebutted by evidence of purchase.

A second presumption is set out in S. 27 of the Family Law (Scotland) Act 2006. It applies where:

> 'Any question arises (whether during or after cohabitation) as to the right of a cohabitant to –
> (a) money derived from any allowance made by either cohabitant for their joint household expenses or for similar purposes; or
> (b) any property acquired out of such money.'[37]

In such circumstances, and 'subject to any agreement between the cohabitants to the contrary, the money or property shall be treated as belonging to each cohabitant in equal shares.'[38] The parties' sole or main residence is expressly excluded from the scope of 'property' in this provision.[39]

SLOVAKIA

No, there are no rebuttable presumptions concerning the ownership of assets between partners in an informal relationship. For the internal relationships between partners as co-owners the rules on decisions concerning the management of assets are applicable. Decisions concerning the management of the common assets are taken by a majority of the votes determined according to the size of the shares (§ 139

35 Family Law (Scotland) Act 1985, S. 25.
36 Family Law (Scotland) Act 1985, S. 25(2).
37 Family Law (Scotland) Act 2006, S. 27(1).
38 Family Law (Scotland) Act 2006, S. 27(2).
39 Family Law (Scotland) Act 2006, S. 27(3).

para. 2 Slovak Civil Code). If the votes are equal or if no majority or agreement can be achieved, the courts will decide. Moreover, in the case of an important change to a common asset, the minority co-owners may request a court decision as well (§ 139 para. 3 Slovak Civil Code). An 'important change' is not defined by the Slovak Civil Code, although doctrine interprets an important change as meaning, for example, rebuilding the common home.[40]

SLOVENIA

A legal assumption applies in the division of common property (all assets that the partners obtain through work during the life union) that the shares in the common property are equal.

SPAIN

There are no specific rules as regards property between partners to an informal relationship. As regards movables, the ordinary means of proof of ownership is the title of acquisition of the asset. The assets belong to the partner who appears as purchaser in the title of acquisition or as the owner in the documents resulting from the transaction. If no title can be found, possession will be taken into account.

As regards immovables, the registered owner will be considered to all effects and purposes to be the owner, unless challenged. Immovable property, if not registered in the Land Registry, will be owned by the person who has the latest title of acquisition.

SWEDEN

If both partners are not title holders – or if the criteria for the assumption of joint ownership in other cases (Question 27-28) are not fulfilled – general principles of the law of property apply. Where something is purchased or otherwise acquired, it usually means that the person who was a party to the contract or other transaction becomes the owner. Whose money is used to pay for the property, or who incurred the debt to acquire it, is of relevance for deciding on issues of ownership. Public registers such as land registers on real property or motor vehicle registers usually provide a good indication as to who the owner is.

---

[40] See J. LAZAR, in: J. LAZAR et al. (eds.), *Občianske právo hmotné* (Substantive Slovak Civil Law), Iuris Libri, Bratislava, 2014, at p. 503.

SWITZERLAND

If the ownership of an asset is unclear - because neither of the partners in the informal relationship can prove sole ownership (e.g. by an inventory or other documents) or joint ownership because of a simple partnership - the possessor of a chattel is presumed to be its owner (Art. 930 Swiss Civil Code). If the chattel is jointly possessed, co-ownership (in equal parts) is presumed.[41]

With regard to (immovable) property the record in the land register (*Grundbuch*) is decisive.

[41] A. BÜCHLER, 'Vermögensrechtliche Probleme in der nichtehelichen Lebensgemeinschaft', in: A. RUMO-JUNGO and P. PICHONNAZ, *Familienvermögensrecht*, Stämpfli, Bern, 2003, at p. 59, 74.

QUESTION 30

How is the ownership of assets proved as regards third parties? Are there rebuttable presumptions?

AUSTRIA

When it comes to proving ownership, no distinction is made as to whether it has to be proved as between the partners in an informal relationship or in relation to third parties. Accordingly, reference can be made to the answer to Question 29.

BELGIUM

With regard to immovable property, third parties may rely on the title published in the Mortgage Register as proof of ownership. In case of simulation, they may also choose to rely on the underlying legal situation.[1]

With regard to movable property, all forms of evidence are accepted. Particularly important is that third parties may rely on the presumption that possession amounts to title of the sole ownership (Art. 2279 Belgian Civil Code) of all movables, even during the informal relationship. Evidence in rebuttal of joint ownership or sole ownership by the other party is however allowed.[2]

BULGARIA

The ownership of assets as regards third parties can only be proved on the basis of the title therein. There are no rebuttable presumptions in this respect.

---

1 W. PINTENS, C. DECLERCK, J. DU MONGH, K. VANWINCKELEN, *Familiaal vermogensrecht*, Intersentia, Antwerp, 2010, at n°s 958, 987 and 997.

2 W. PINTENS, C. DECLERCK, J. DU MONGH, K. VANWINCKELEN, *Familiaal vermogensrecht*, Intersentia, Antwerp, 2010, at n° 998.

CROATIA

In line with Art. 11 paragraph 2 and Art. 36 of the Croatian Family Act and Art. 4 paragraph 1 and Art. 54 of the Croatian Partnership Act, the answer equally relates to both cohabitants and same-sex informal partners.

There are no rebuttable presumptions concerning a partner's ownership of assets.

In terms of third parties, the ownership of assets (real estate) can be proved through its registration in public registers (the land register), according to the principle of confidence in land register protection.[3]

CZECH REPUBLIC

There is no specific property law concerning an informal relationship. If partners in an informal relationship are co-owners according to S. 1115 et seq. Czech Civil Code of an immovable object, this fact is visible from the public register. If nothing special is declared and both partners are contracting parties, shares are presumed to be equal (S. 1122(3) Czech Civil Code).

DENMARK

In principle, the formal registration of the ownership of a significant asset, such as real property or a car, must be assumed to correspond to what the cohabitants have agreed and thus it expresses their view of ownership.[4] A party who claims that the registration is not in accordance with the facts must prove that the registration is not decisive.

Evidence is required of what the cohabitants have agreed or presumed about ownership, whether a conflict arises between the cohabitants or between a cohabitant and a creditor. Where there is doubt, the

---

[3] However, prior to the adoption of the Croatian Family Act 2014, case law in the sphere of matrimonial property (relating to both cohabitants and same-sex informal partners) had not always been consistent. Some groups of high court decisions attached a more powerful role to the land register in matrimonial property while other groups of high court decisions attached a more powerful role to confidence in the spouses' (partners') property. T. JOSIPOVIĆ and H. ERNST, 'The Role of Land Register in Matrimonial Property', in: *Liber amicourm in honorem Jadranko Crnić*, Novi informator, Zagreb, 2009, at p. 591.

[4] This is also the situation as regards spouses; see I. LUND-ANDERSEN and I. NØRGAARD, *Familieret*, Jurist- og Økonomforbundets Forlag, Copenhagen, 2012, at p. 116-117.

assessment of the evidence may vary depending on whether a creditor is a party to the conflict or the conflict is between cohabitants. Cohabitants will often have shared interests in a conflict with a creditor, and this will affect the assessment of their statements. The cohabitants will also have the possibility of securing evidence of ownership, which is not open to creditors.

ENGLAND AND WALES

Ownership of gifts from third parties depends on the donor's intention but the normal rule is that the donee will own a gift made to them. Otherwise the third party has to go to court for a declaration of ownership if this is not clear and is in dispute. The court will rule on the beneficial ownership under trust law if legal ownership is claimed not to reflect the beneficial ownership and is challenged.

The rebuttable presumptions around ownership are the same as for a dispute between the couple.

ESTONIA

According to § 90(1) of the Estonian Law of Property Act a possessor of movable property and any earlier possessor shall be deemed to be the owners of the asset during the possessor's possession until the contrary is proved. The presumption of ownership by the possessor of movable property, arising from § 90, includes, as a rule, also the presumption of common ownership by the co-possessor, which provides certain protection to a (non-possesor) spouse as well as to the other partner to an informal relationship. In the case of immovable property this presumption is irrelevant as this concerns mostly the household and other goods used in daily living. This presumption is based, *inter alia,* on the rule according to which the presumption of the transfer of the ownership of movable property is the transfer of possession with regard to this. In case of doubt, it should be presumed in the transfer of the possession that the right of ownership was also transferred to the possessor. The principle of sharing the burden of proof indirectly proceeds from this, which will always be of significance when there exists a dispute over the right of ownership of a movable asset.[5]

[5] P. VARUL, I. KULL, V. KÕVE, M. KÄRDI and T. PURI, *Asjaõigusseadus. Kommenteeritud väljaanne*, Juura, Tallinn, 2014, at p. 415.

FINLAND

No separate rules apply, for this purpose, to cohabiting partners. According to the Finnish Enforcement Code (705/2007, Chapter 4, S. 11), chattels in the joint possession of the debtor and a third party (such as the spouse or a cohabitee partner) are deemed to belong to them in equal parts, unless the third party shows or it otherwise becomes apparent that the property belongs solely or to a greater part to the third party. S. 13 further provides that real estate to which the debtor has received legal confirmation of possession may be attached together with the constituent parts and appurtenances, unless a third party shows or it otherwise becomes apparent that the real estate belongs to the third party or that a certain object is owned by the third party and does not belong to the real estate.

FRANCE

The ownership of assets is proved as regards third parties according to the general rules of property law. Property is determined according to the legal title thereto. The legal title can be based on acquisition by the cohabitant(s), on inheritance rights or on a donation. Where the act is encompassed in a notarial deed (*acte authentique*) or is in the form of a written document, proof of ownership is usually not too difficult to provide. Each former cohabitant owns the asset to which he or she holds the legal title.

With regard to movables, in the absence of any written document establishing who is the owner of a tangible asset (*meuble corporel*), Art. 2276 of the French Civil Code applies. It states that '*en fait de meubles, la possession vaut titre*'. This means that in matters relating to (tangible) movables, possession is equivalent to title. For more details, see Question 29. This presumption of ownership based on possession can be rebutted by proof of ownership (a bill, receipt, etc.), but the burden of proof is a heavy one, and one cohabitant can face some difficulties in rebutting it.

With regard to immovables, proof is provided by the title drawn up by the notary public.

GERMANY

As regards married couples, it is presumed in favour of creditors of spouses that movables in the possession of one spouse or of both spouses belong to the debtor (§ 1362 para. 1 German Civil Code). There is, however, no such presumption of ownership for unmarried or unregistered couples. The legal provision for spouses cannot be applied by analogy to cohabitants.[6] A reform proposal which would have extended it to cohabiting couples failed in 1997.[7] The effect of the existing law is that a non-debt-owing cohabitant can rely on sole ownership or co-ownership of items and can block execution against him by way of a third-party action against the execution (*Drittwiderspruchsklage*; § 771 para. 1 German Civil Code of Procedure (*Zivilprozessordnung*; ZPO)). Critics argue that the legal provision of § 1362 German Civil Code should be applied by analogy.[8] They argue that the existing law contains a gap because in such situations there is no protection for creditors, and wealthy partners can conceal or mingle property.

The presumption of ownership is supplemented by another presumption in the case of an execution of a judgment against one of the spouses. If it is presumed that one of the spouses is the owner of movables, then for the purpose of execution it is also presumed that only the debtor is in custody and possession of the movables. Therefore execution against this spouse is possible (§ 739 para. 1 German Code of Civil Procedure). This legal provision can also not be applied by analogy to cohabitants.[9]

According to the general rules of civil law there is a rebuttable presumption that the possessor of an asset is also its owner (§ 1006 German Civil Code). If, for example, two partners have possession in common of a car and use it together, it is presumed that they are co-owners.[10]

GREECE

Such rebuttable presumptions, in relation to creditors, apply only to married partners, as laid down in Art. 1398(1 and 3) of the Greek Civil Code.

---

6 BGH, 14.12.2006, *BGHZ*, 170, 187 = *FamRZ*, 2007, 457 = *NJW*, 2007, 992.

7 For references see BGH, 14.12.2006, *BGHZ*, 170, 187 = *FamRZ*, 2007, 457 = *NJW*, 2007, 992.

8 M. Löhnig and M. Würdinger, 'Eigentums- und Gewahrsamsvermutung bei nichtehelichen Lebensgemeinschaften', *FamRZ*, 2007, at p. 1856 et seq.; G. Brudermüller, 'Einl. vor § 1297', in: O. Palandt, *Bürgerliches Gesetzbuch*, Beck, Munich, 2015, at No. 26.

9 G. Hohloch, 'Nichteheliche Lebensgemeinschaft', in: R. Hausmann and G. Hohloch (eds.), *Das Recht der nichtehelichen Lebensgemeinschaft*, E. Schmidt, Berlin, 2004, at p. 59, 109 et seq. No. 121 et seq. with references.

10 BGH, 14.12.2006, *BGHZ*, 170, 187 = *FamRZ*, 2007, 457 = *NJW*, 2007, 992.

HUNGARY

No specific provision.

REPUBLIC OF IRELAND

This is normally achieved through the law on direct and indirect contributions.

ITALY

Ownership of assets as regards third parties is proved in the same way as between the two partners. No general presumption is foreseen.

As for current bank accounts, while between the partners the rule that shares are presumed to be equal will apply (Art. 1298 para. 2 Italian Civil Code; see also Question 29), in the view of the bank the two partners are joint and several creditors (Art. 1854 Italian Civil Code). Therefore, either of the holders can withdraw the whole sum at any time.[11]

LATVIA

In Latvia there is no such specific legal order on informal relationships.

LITHUANIA

The ownership of assets is proved with regard to third parties by property registration records in the corresponding public registers, as well as by documentary evidence of the acquisition of assets (contracts, etc.).

LUXEMBOURG

The ownership of assets is proved according to the principles of the law (the evidentiary measures of proof-taking determined by the rules of the Luxembourg Civil Code).

If evidence of sole ownership cannot be produced, there is a rebuttable presumption of joint ownership.

---

[11] AA. VV., *La separazione nella famiglia di fatto*, Cedam, Padua, 2014, at p. 224.

THE NETHERLANDS

For a third party wishing to exercise his/her right of recourse in relation to the property of the partner who is his/her debtor, the property relations between the partners might not be clear, in particular in relation to movables. In relation to other property such as registered property, the property relations do not give rise to problems. The partner registered as the owner is generally to be considered the owner, also in relation to a third party. For movable property, this is different. Partners might plot together. On the other hand, from a creditor's perspective movable goods are often not the most interesting assets to seize. There is no case law on this subject.[12]

NORWAY

Ownership is proved in the same way as regards third parties. However, cohabitants might sometimes have a common interest in concealing the real ownership in these cases, and less credence will therefore be accorded to documentation and testimonies in such cases.

A few rebuttable presumptions exist in relation to creditors in the Norwegian Act relating to enforcement of claims 1992, S. 7-13 and 7-14. According to S. 7-13 third paragraph, a creditor may seize half of the family home if the debtor is a cohabitant (or spouse) and the home is acquired during the relationship, provided no other ownership is proved. This presumption is easily rebutted, and the Supreme Court has stated that the presumption will only have significance in the initial phases when the enforcement officer seeks seizure of the property, and not when the cases are brought to court, Rt. 1999 s. 901 (spouses) and Rt. 2004 s. 256 (cohabitants).[13]

PORTUGAL

There are no specific rules which are applicable to partners in an informal relationship. They may use all means acceptable in law, just as any citizen can.

---

12 W.M. SCHRAMA, 'Goederenrechtelijke afwikkeling: bewijskwesties', in: M.L.C.C. DE BRUIJN-LÜCKERS et al. (eds.), *Relatierecht, SDUCommentaar*, SDU, The Hague, 2014, at p. 2015-2024.

13 K. LILLEHOLT, *Allmenn formuerett. Fleire rettar til same formuesgode*, Universiteitsforlaget, Oslo, 2012, at p. 278.

Taking into account the difficulties raised by proof of the ownership of assets Parliamentary Bill n. 349/X, which preceded Act 23/2010, foresaw the possibility of stipulating clauses concerning the ownership of the assets acquired during cohabitation (Art. 5-A, n. 1). Moreover, it established a rebuttable presumption: movable assets would be presumed to be jointly owned by both partners (Art. 5-A, n. 2). These solutions, however, did not become law, due to the veto by the President of the Republic.

RUSSIA

By all means of proof admitted by the Russian Code of Civil Procedure. There are no rebuttable presumptions.

SCOTLAND

As a general rule, ownership of assets will be established according to the normal rules of property. In respect of land and heritable property, ownership is established by means of registered title. Ownership of moveable assets will be established according to evidence of acquisition, for example, receipts showing purchase. These rules of property law apply regardless of the existence of any personal family relationship. There are two statutory presumptions, as discussed in Question 29, which apply to household goods and to money or property derived from an allowance provided by either cohabitant for joint household purposes.[14] The presumptions state that they apply when any question of ownership arises and they may therefore also apply as regards third parties. It should be remembered, however, that these presumptions apply only to a restricted range of assets and the presumptions may be relatively easily rebutted.

SLOVAKIA

Generally there is a rebuttable presumption that the possessor is the owner of the assets in question (§ 130 para. 2 Slovak Civil Code). Possession is a factual issue recognised and protected by law. A possessor is defined as a person who holds an asset as his own or who exercises a right for him or herself (§ 129 para. 1 Slovak Civil Code). Possession concerns not only objects, but also rights allowing permanent

[14] Family Law (Scotland) Act 2006, S. 27(3).

or repeated use or actions. Two elements of possession may be distinguished:

- *corpus posessionis* – the factual possession of an asset and
- *animus possidendi* – the possessor's will to hold it as his or her own.[15]

Possession requires both elements, i.e. both the factual possession of the asset and the possessor's will to hold it as his or her own. If the second element (will) is missing, the holder of that asset is a detainer and his holding (detaining) of the asset is characterised as detention. Unlike a possessor, a detainer holds the asset not as his own, but as someone else's (e.g. a lessee). Possession may be legitimate or illegitimate. A legitimate possessor is a possessor who possesses the asset or the right in good faith with regard to all the circumstances. In case of doubt, possession is presumed to be legitimate (§ 130 para. 1 Slovak Civil Code). Unless stipulated otherwise by statute, a legitimate possessor has the same rights as the owner; in particular, he or she is entitled to benefit from the proceeds from the asset which arise during his or her legitimate possession. Moreover, he or she has the same rights of protection against any infringements of his or her right to possess the asset as the owner (§ 126 para. 2 Slovak Civil Code).

The legitimate possessor may claim from the owner any costs reasonably incurred concerning the asset during his or her legitimate possession to the extent corresponding to the valorisation of the asset at the moment when it was returned. However, the usual expenses connected with the maintenance and operation of the asset are not reimbursed (§ 130 para. 3 Slovak Civil Code).

On the other hand, an illegitimate possessor must always surrender the asset to its owner together with all its proceeds and compensate any damage that has arisen due to the illegitimate possession. However, he or she may deduct any necessary costs for the maintenance and operation of the asset. Moreover, the illegitimate possessor may separate anything which has led to the asset being improved or in its value appreciating if it is possible to do so without impairing the asset.

---

15 See I. FEKETE, *Občiansky zákonník I. a II. - Veľký komentár* (Slovak Civil Code I and II – Major Commentary), Eurokódex, Bratislava, 2011, at commentary on § 129.

SLOVENIA

All assets that the partners obtain through work during the extramarital union are considered the common property of the partners. Real estate that is common property is entered in the land register as common property.

Legal transactions which in relation to matters of common property are concluded by a partner without the necessary consent of the other partner can be rebutted by the other partner,[16] unless a third person concluded the legal transaction in good faith; if he did not know that it was a matter of common property and the partner was disposing of it without the consent of the other partner (para. 3 Art. 72 of the Slovenian Code of Property Law).[17]

SPAIN

The general rules apply. As regards movables, the ordinary means of proof of ownership is the title of acquisition of the asset. The assets belong to the partner who appears as purchaser in the title of acquisition or as the owner in the documents resulting from the transaction. If no title can be found, possession will be taken into account.

As regards immovables, the registered owner will be considered to all effects and purposes to be the owner, unless challenged. Immovable property, if not registered in the Land Registry, will be owned by the person who has the latest title of acquisition.

SWEDEN

The general principles of the law of property and the constructions of joint ownership, in respect of household goods and other movable property, are also applicable in relation to third parties. As regards real estate property, in relation to third parties only the person given as the title holder in the real property register qualifies as the owner of that property.[18]

---

16 Judgement of the Supreme Court RS, No. II Ips 382/2011 of 12 December 2012, and judgement of the Higher Court in Ljubljana, No. I Cp 2055/2012 of 20 February 2013 – Ius-info database.

17 Uradni list RS (Official Journal) Nos 87/2002, 91/2013.

18 See the Swedish Supreme Court decisions *NJA 1984 p. 772* and *NJA 1985 p. 97*. See also M. Brattström, 'Dold samäganderätt – en sammanfattning av rättsläget', *Juridisk Tidskrift* (JT), 2011–2012, pp. 322–324.

Swedish law contains special rules concerning how ownership is presumed in relation to a cohabiting partner's creditors. In order to protect the creditors' recovery of debts made by a partner to an informal cohabitation, it is presumed that chattels found in the cohabiting couple's joint possession belong to the cohabitee who is subject to the distraint (in Swedish: *utmätning*). The property can be protected from distraint if it is made probable that it is owned jointly by the cohabitees or if it is evident that the property belongs to the other cohabitee or a third person, Swedish Enforcement Code (in Swedish: *Utsökningsbalken*, 1981:744) Chapter 4, § 19. Receipts can serve as proof, as well as documentation of money transactions from a joint account or both partners' accounts to pay for the property. For example, in the Supreme Court case NJA 1984 p. 375, a boat in the debtor's possession had been distrained. It was later shown that the boat in fact belonged to the debtor's wife, who had paid for the boat and also had the purchase contract for the boat. The same assessment would also apply to a cohabiting couple in a similar situation. Regard must also be had to other rules. A gift between the cohabitees can, for example, not become effective in relation to the donor´s creditors if the the object has not come into the recipient's possession, the donor being excluded from any further disposal of the property.[19] (See also below, Question 60.)

According to the Swedish Enforcement Code, Chapter 4, § 24, real property can be distrained if it is clear that it belongs to the debtor. It follows that the debtor cohabitee must have the title deed to the property and be registered as the owner in the real property register. A registration as the owner can be rebutted, for example by presenting a formally correct deed of transfer showing that someone else owns the property. As stated above under Question 26 and 28, real estate can be subject to a concealed co-ownership between spouses or cohabitees, at least when it comes to the law of obligations. The Supreme Court decision NJA 1984 s. 772 lays down that a concealed co-ownership of real estate does not give the concealed co-owner protection against the official owner's creditors; the interests of the creditors are to be given priority over the entire value of the property.

If the conditions for the above-mentioned hidden right of co-ownership are fulfilled, the 'open' owner's creditors can benefit from the adopted position.[20] Bearing in mind that a concealed co-owner to property has a legally valid claim to be recognised as a formal co-owner, that person's

19 G. MILLQVIST, *Sakrättens grunder*, Norstedts Juridik, Stockholm, 2011, at p. 84 et seq.

20 Swedish Supreme Court decision *NJA 1984 p. 772.*

creditors can thus exercise distraint rights on the property, according to the rules on distraint in the Enforcement Code, Chapter 4, § 23.[21] The creditor must in that case be able to show that the conditions for concealed co-ownership exist. Where there are competing claims between the open owner's creditors and the concealed owner's creditors, the former's claims usually have priority over the entire value of the property. The date of the request for payment is, in addition, of relevance.

SWITZERLAND

The same rules apply as for the partners in an informal relationship (see Question 29).

[21] Swedish Supreme Court decision *NJA 1985 p. 615*; Court of Appeal decision *RH 2000:93*. See also M. BRATTSTRÖM, 'Egendomsförhållanden under bestående samboende', in: J. ASLAND et al., *Nordisk samboerrett*, Gyldendal, Oslo, 2014, at p. 75 and p. 116 (see Chapter 2.5.1 in the English version of the book, to be published by Intersentia in 2015).

QUESTION 31

Under what circumstances, if any, can partners in an informal relationship become jointly liable for debts?

AUSTRIA

If partners in an informal relationship have a joint bank account, they are both liable for the debts resulting from this account and in case of doubt every partner has to pay half of the debt.[1] Also a loan which has been jointly taken out entails the liability of both partners, because usually the creditor will not abandon a security if it does not receive an equal security in return.[2] If the partners are both parties to a rental agreement, they are also jointly liable for the costs resulting from the rent.[3]

BELGIUM

Joint liability is not presumed, not even for debts that were jointly contracted (on the basis of (apparent) agency). There is no joint liability of informal partners on the basis of any statutory provision[4] or custom.[5] Consequently, it must have been stipulated (Art. 1202 Belgian Civil Code). The contractual stipulation of joint liability is possible both in the external dimension, with the creditor (*obligatio*) and in the internal dimension, between the partners (*contributio*). In the absence of such a stipulation, third parties may rely on legitimate expectation.[6] According

---

1 E. MÖSCHL, *Die nichteheliche Lebensgemeinschaft*, LexisNexis ARD ORAC, Vienna, 2007, at marg. No. 88.

2 U. AICHHORN, *Das Recht der Lebenspartnerschaften, Ehe und Lebensgemeinschaft*, Springer, Vienna, 2003, at p. 429; E. MÖSCHL, *Die nichteheliche Lebensgemeinschaft*, LexisNexis ARD ORAC, Vienna, 2007, at marg. No. 88.

3 E. MÖSCHL, *Die nichteheliche Lebensgemeinschaft*, LexisNexis ARD ORAC, Vienna, 2007, at marg. No. 47.

4 Ghent 29 January 2013, *NJW* 2014, 357, with note STEENNOT.

5 Against: Justice of the Peace Merksem 5 March 1981, *RW* 1981-82, 49, with note PAUWELS.

6 P. SENAEVE, *Compendium van het personen- en familierecht*, Acco, Leuven, 2013, at n° 2049.

to a minority position, joint liability as between spouses or legal cohabitants applies on the basis of Art. 8 and 14 ECHR.

BULGARIA

The partners in an informal relationship can become jointly liable for debts only as prescribed by the general law: the Bulgarian Obligations and Contracts Law. The first option is joint liability *ex lege* and the second option is an agreement with the creditor in the form of a contract (both according to Art. 121, para. 1 of the Bulgarian Obligations and Contracts Law). In contrast, joint liability is laid down for spouses in the Bulgarian Family Code (Art. 32, para. 2 and Art. 36, para. 2).

CROATIA

In line with Art. 11 paragraph 2 and Art. 36 of the Croatian Family Act and Art. 4 paragraph 1 and Art. 54 of the Croatian Partnership Act, the answer equally relates to both cohabitants and same-sex informal partners.

According to Art. 44 in relation to Art. 11 of the Croatian Family Act and Art. 54 in relation to Art. 4 of the Croatian Partnership Act, both partners shall be held jointly and severally liable with regard to the liabilities assumed by one partner for the purpose of satisfying the current needs of their family union as well as with respect to the liabilities jointly assumed by both partners, which relate to their community of property.

If not agreed otherwise, partners shall be held liable in equal shares concerning these liabilities.

CZECH REPUBLIC

Partners in an informal relationship become jointly liable for debts if it follows from the contract that co-debtors are obliged jointly and severally. According to S. 1872(1) Czech Civil Code if several debtors are obliged to perform jointly and severally, they are obliged to perform one for all and all for one. A creditor may demand the entire performance or any part thereof from all, only some, or any one of the co-debtors.

DENMARK

The starting position is that unmarried cohabitants are not liable for each other's debts or for other legal obligations incurred by the other party. A debt does not become a joint debt merely because a loan contributes to the cohabitants' joint consumption or is used to buy an asset from which both parties benefit.

If both cohabitants give a commitment to a creditor, there will be a joint debt.

In addition, in certain situations the common interests of the cohabitants can lead to them being jointly liable to a greater extent than would apply under the general rules of property law. In this situation what is relevant is whether a cohabitant's conduct has given his or her counterparty the impression that he or she was acting with the authority of the other cohabitant. This application of the rules of agency is referred to as apparent authority by virtue of conduct (*adfærdsfuldmagt*).[7] This could be the situation, for example, where one cohabitant seeks to avoid paying an invoice by having his or her insolvent partner order work on their joint residence to be carried out by a tradesman, and while the tradesman carries out the work the owner is present without making it clear that he or she will not pay for the work.

ENGLAND AND WALES

Only by jointly incurring those debts but they can be and typically are made liable for the whole debt (joint and several liability) when a joint debt is incurred.

ESTONIA

According to § 8(1) of the Estonian Law of Obligations Act, a contract is a transaction between two or more persons (parties) by which one party undertakes or the parties undertake to perform an act or omission. A contract is binding on the parties (§ 8(2) Estonian Law of Obligations Act). The fact that the parties in an informal relationship are joint obligors, collective obligors or solidary obligors, anticipates the common will of the parties to perform legally bindingly acts or omissions. Thus, both parties must have concluded a contract with the creditor under the law of

[7] See I. LUND-ANDERSEN, *Familieøkonomien*, Jurist- og Økonomforbundets Forlag, Copenhagen, 2011, at p. 218 and at p. 236-238.

obligations within the meaning of the Estonian Law of Obligations Act § 8(1).

FINLAND

Generally, the partners can only become jointly liable for debts if they have made a separate agreement to this effect.

However, according to the Finnish Act on Residential Leases (S. 11), a married couple or persons living together as husband and wife without marriage (spouses) are jointly and severally liable for the obligations deriving from the lease agreement if they live together in a residential apartment leased by both spouses jointly or by one of them. If one spouse moves out, the spouse who has not leased the apartment continues to be liable for the obligations deriving from the lease agreement for as long as he or she remains in the apartment. Both spouses shall be heard in any matter related to such an apartment if this is considered necessary.

Also, according to the Finnish Right-of-Occupancy Housing Act (S. 41), if the spouses use an apartment held by virtue of a right of occupancy as their joint residence, they shall be jointly and severally liable for any obligations arising from the right-of-occupancy contract. If the other spouse moves out of the apartment, the spouse who is not a party to the right-of-occupancy contract shall continue to be liable for obligations arising from the said contract for as long as he or she resides in the apartment. A person living in circumstances similar to a marriage with the holder of occupancy rights is equated with a spouse.

FRANCE

The French Court of cassation regularly reiterates that Art. 220 of the French Civil Code does not apply to partners in an informal relationship,[8] which shows that the lower courts tend to extend the scope of Art. 220 by considering that common life can lead to joint and several liability even if the partners are not married to each other.[9] This statutory provision states that each spouse is solely entitled to enter into a contract the object of which is the household or the raising of the

---

[8] See e.g. Cass. Civ. I, 11 January 1984, no. 82-16198, *Bull. Civ.* I, no. 12; 22 March 2011, no. 09-71261; 7 November 2012, no. 11-25430, *Bull. Civ.* I, no. 236.

[9] See e.g. CA Bourges, 8 December 1997, *Dr. Famille* 1998, no 89, with note BEIGNIER.

children. All debts incurred in this respect by one spouse result in the other spouse being jointly and severally liable.

Partners in an informal relationship can only become jointly liable for debts if they both agree to the transaction.

GERMANY

There are no special rules dealing with the joint liability of cohabitants. The general rules of civil law apply. This means that if there is a contractual obligation of both cohabitants owed to a third party, generally joint and several liability of the cohabitants is created by law (§ 427 German Civil Code).[10] Such a contractual obligation also remains valid after a termination of the informal relationship.[11]

Pursuant to § 1357 German Civil Code, spouses are attributed a factually implied agency, i.e. the authority to enter into transactions in order to meet the appropriate necessities of the family. As far as these transactions are concerned, the spouses are joint and several debtors (§§ 421-425 German Civil Code) and joint and several creditors (§ 428 German Civil Code). These provisions are, however, not applied to informal relationships.[12]

GREECE

One might think of the case where the partners together take out a loan (Art. 806 et seq. and 481 et seq. of the Greek Civil Code). In circumstances where the partners are heirs to a deceased person with debts (Art. 1884, 1885 Greek Civil Code), the latter are shared proportionally.

HUNGARY

No specific provision.

[10] N. DETHLOFF, *Familienrecht*, Beck, Munich, 2012, at § 8 No. 9.

[11] D. SCHWAB, *Familienrecht*, Beck, Munich, 2014, at No. 1018.

[12] J. GERNHUBER and D. COESTER-WALTJEN, *Familienrecht*, Beck, Munich, 2010, at p. 498 with references.

REPUBLIC OF IRELAND

This is not possible unless provided for in a cohabitants' agreement. Section 202 of the Irish Civil Partnership and Cohabitants Act 2010 makes provision for such an agreement.

ITALY

Each partner is only liable for the obligations he or she has personally assumed, even if related to transactions entered into in the interests of the partnership. No common liability may originate from the mere fact of cohabitation.[13]

Therefore, the only way that partners may become jointly liable for debts is by undertaking an obligation together, for instance by both signing the same contract.

LATVIA

In Latvia there is no such specific legal order on informal relationships. Therefore the general law of obligations of the Latvian Civil Law is applicable. Section 1670 of the Latvian Civil Law provides that a claim or an obligation is to be recognised as joint or solidary when each of several creditors may claim the entire subject-matter, or when each of several debtors has the duty to perform it all; the subject-matter may, however, be claimed and be required to be performed only once. In such cases the former are called joint creditors and the latter joint debtors. Section 1671 of the Latvian Civil Law determines that included in the essential nature of every solidary obligation is that it is based on one and the same basis and all parties have one and the same subject-matter of performance. Section 1672 of the Latvian Civil Law determines that solidary obligations may be established pursuant to a contract, a will or by law.

By way of comparison one may consider the following. In lawful property relations of the spouses, S. 96 of the Latvian Civil Law provides that for obligations that the spouses have entered into jointly for family or joint domestic financial needs, they are to be held liable to the extent of their joint property, and each to the extent of their separate property, if the joint property does not suffice.

---

[13] G. OBERTO, *I diritti dei conviventi. Realtà e prospettive tra Italia ed Europa*, Cedam, Padua, 2012, at p. 158-9.

For obligations regarding family or joint domestic financial needs that have been entered into by one of the spouses, such spouse is to be held liable to the extent of his or her property if the joint property of the spouses does not suffice. For these obligations, the other spouse is to be held liable to the extent of his or her property only if the consideration pursuant to such obligations has been used for family and joint household needs.

LITHUANIA

There are no special rules, so the general provisions of the Law of obligations apply (Art. 6.6 of the Lithuanian Civil Code).[14] Partners shall be held jointly liable if they have together undertaken joint or subsidiary obligations.

According to Art. 6.975 of the Lithuanian Civil Code, if the agreement on joint activities is not related to the economic/commercial activities of the partners, each partner shall be liable under joint contractual obligations to the extent of all of his or her property in proportion to his or her part of such obligations. Under such joint non-contractual obligations the partners shall be jointly liable. If the agreement on joint activities is related to the economic/commercial activities of the partners, both partners shall be jointly liable under the joint obligations, notwithstanding the grounds for the appearance of such obligations.

LUXEMBOURG

Partners in an informal relationship become jointly liable for debts if they contract the debt jointly. One partner cannot oblige the other partner to become solely liable.

THE NETHERLANDS

When both informal partners jointly contract in relation to a third party (either directly or by means of a power of attorney), they will both be liable for debts. As a starting point they will both be liable for half of the debt, unless the law or the contract determines otherwise (Art. 6:6 Dutch Civil Code). An important exception relates to a mortgage on the house

[14] The joint liability of the debtors shall not be presumed, except in those cases established by law. It shall only arise where this is expressly imposed by law or stipulated by an agreement between the parties, also in cases when the subject of the obligation is indivisible

of the partners. The bank will require the partners to be jointly liable, not just for half of the debt, but for the entire debt (Art. 6:7 Dutch Civil Code).

NORWAY

If both partners have contracted the debt, they are normally jointly liable, which means that the debt can be enforced in full against either of the partners.

PORTUGAL

Besides the application of general and unspecific principles, there is no specific law imposing joint liability for debts on partners in an informal relationship. However, some authors strongly suggest that both cohabitants should be liable in solidarity for ordinary debts which may arise in meeting the normal costs of common life, just as married couples are. Parliamentary Bill n. 349/X, which preceded Act 23/2010, foresaw the same solution. However, this did not become law, due to the veto by the President of the Republic.

RUSSIA

Partners can become jointly liable for debts in the following situations:

- If they entered into an obligation jointly (e.g. signed a tenancy agreement together). Under Art. 321 Russian Civil Code they are supposed to be liable to an equal extent, unless the law or the agreement provides otherwise;
- If debts relate to an asset that they own jointly (under Art. 249 Russian Civil Code, joint owners are jointly liable for maintaining joint assets and are responsible for all related costs). In this case, partners are liable for debts in proportion to their shares in the joint property;
- If the debts relate to the home owned by one of the partners, provided that the other partner is acknowledged as a member of the owner's family under Art. 31 Russian Housing Code. In such case, the partners are jointly and severally liable for all costs related to the use of the home (Art. 292(1) Russian Civil Code, Art. 31(3) Russian Housing Code);
- If the debts relate to a home rented by one of the partners as a social tenant, provided that the other partner is acknowledged as a member of the social tenant's family under Art. 69 Russian Housing Code. In

such case, the partners are jointly and severally liable for all debts arising from the social rental contract (Art. 69(2) Russian Housing Code);
- If the debts relate to a home rented by one of the partners as a commercial tenant, provided that the partners have signed an agreement on joint and several liability for all debts arising from the commercial rental contract (Art. 677(4) Russian Civil Code).

SCOTLAND

Liability is established according to the general rules of obligation and partners to an informal relationship will be jointly liable only where they jointly incurred the debt.

SLOVAKIA

In the case of divided co-ownership, the co-owners (partners) have specific shares in the common assets. All co-owners are jointly and severally entitled and obliged by juridical acts concerning the common asset (§ 139 para. 1 Slovak Civil Code). Legal doctrine interprets the term 'juridical acts concerning the common asset' as being broader than juridical acts in general. Those juridical acts are the acts of every partner which lead to a common obligation (*spoločné záväzky*).[15] In simple obligations, on each side of the relationship there is only one person. In common obligations, there are several persons on one or both (or more) sides of the legal obligation relationship.

Common obligations can be classified as follows:

- active common obligations (on the creditor's part), and
- passive common obligations (on the debtor's part).

Passive solidarity is regulated in § 511 of the Slovak Civil Code. It may be established by an agreement between the parties, by a judicial decision, by statute or by the nature of the performance (in the case of undivided solidary obligations). A statute also means § 139 para. 1 Slovak Civil Code.[16] There are several persons on the debtor's side. Each of the solidary debtors has to provide the same performance towards the

---

[15] See I. FEKETE, *Občiansky zákonník I. a II. - Veľký komentár* (Slovak Civil Code I and II – Major Commentary), Eurokódex, Bratislava, 2011, at commentary on § 139 para. 1.

[16] All co-owners are jointly and severally entitled and obliged by juridical acts concerning the common asset.

creditor; the scope of their obligation is not limited by their shares of the debt in their internal relationship. The creditor can require the performance of the entire debt or a part thereof from any solidary debtor. Once the creditor is satisfied by the performance provided by one of the solidary debtors, the obligation of all co-debtors is extinguished. With respect to the regulation of passive solidarity, the duty of notification and preventive and subsequent regress have to be pointed out. The duty of notification applies if one of the solidary debtors is requested by the creditor to provide performance to a greater extent than determined by his or her share in the internal relationship between the co-debtors, in which case this debtor has to notify the other debtors of this (§ 511 para. 2 Slovak Civil Code). Preventive regress constitutes the right of this debtor to request the other co-owners to discharge the debt according to their respective shares or otherwise to discharge him or her from the debt before providing any performance. Subsequent regress entitles the debtor having completely discharged the debt to require compensation from the other co-debtors according to their respective shares (§ 511 para. 3 Slovak Civil Code).

SLOVENIA

For obligations that under the general regulations burden both partners (i.e., those that they undertook together, obligations arising from common property, such as additions to residential accommodation, and obligations that a partner undertakes for the current needs of the family, such as the costs of running the family accommodation) the partners are liable with both their individual and their common property. Their liability is indivisible.

SPAIN

Under the Spanish Civil Code and the Catalan Civil Code partners only become jointly liable for debts which they incurred jointly.

SWEDEN

Partners to an informal cohabitation are under Swedish law considered as two separate individuals as regards liability for debts. Joint responsibility for debts arises in the partners' mutual relationship when both cohabitees have jointly become indebted, in accordance with the general principles of the law of obligations, for example because they have purchased property jointly. A creditor may, however, only demand payment from the partner who entered into the transaction.

SWITZERLAND

Partners in an informal relationship become jointly liable for debts either by contract or by law. There are numerous cases where the law provides for joint and several liability (irrespective of an informal relationship), such as in certain cases of tort law (e.g. Art. 50 and 51 Swiss Civil Code).

According to Art. 143 Swiss Code of Obligations, debtors become jointly and severally liable for a debt (*Solidarschuld*) by (explicitly or impliedly)[17] stating that each of them wishes to be individually liable for the performance of the entire obligation. This might be the case where both partners in an informal relationship jointly rent an apartment together.

Joint liability may also exist where the partners in an informal relationship form a simple partnership. According to Art. 544 para. 3 Swiss Code of Obligations, subject to a contrary agreement, partners in a simple partnership are jointly and severally liable for obligations towards third parties contracted jointly or through representatives.

---

17 For details see I. SCHWENZER, *Schweizerisches Obligationenrecht Allgemeiner Teil*, Stämpfli, Bern, 2012, N 88.15.

QUESTION 32

On which assets can creditors recover joint debts?

AUSTRIA

This issue depends upon the individual case and the contract underlying the joint debts, in particular with regard to the securities provided by the debtors. It can also be agreed upon that the creditor cannot recover the debts on assets, but has to turn to e.g. a guarantor. Generally, it must be borne in mind that in the case of non-repayment the creditor cannot automatically resort to the debtors' assets to satisfy the debt, but has to initiate civil proceedings with a subsequent execution procedure. Due to the many contract designs possible, no general answer to this question can be given. However, from the practical point of view the partners in an informal relationship will often take out a loan when building or buying a house or an apartment together.[1] The creditor will usually grant the loan subject to the condition that the purchased property serves as security, which has to be registered in the land register. In this case the creditor can resort to the property, if the debtors do not repay the money.

Another case concerns the home which is jointly rented by both partners: S. 1101 General Austrian Civil Code grants the landlord a legal lien on the tenants' moveable property in the rented home.[2] Even if only one partner is the contracting party to the rental agreement, but the other partner is living in the same household, the legal lien in favour of the landlord also extends to all movable assets *(eingebrachte Sachen)* of the other partner.[3]

1 U. AICHHORN, *Das Recht der Lebenspartnerschaften, Ehe und Lebensgemeinschaft,* Springer, Vienna, 2003, at p. 429.

2 E. MÖSCHL, *Die nichteheliche Lebensgemeinschaft*, LexisNexis ARD ORAC, Vienna, 2007, at marg. No. 47.

3 O. RISS, 'section 1101 General Austrian Civil Code', in: A. KLETEČKA and M. SCHAUER, *ABGB-ON 1.01,* Manz Verlag, Vienna, 2012, at marg. No. 4.

BELGIUM

The creditors can recover joint debts on both partners' own and joint property (Art. 7 Mortgage Act).[4] This may subsequently give rise to a right of recourse between the partners (Art. 1213 Belgian Civil Code).

BULGARIA

There is no specific regulation on this matter. The creditor is free to select the assets (Art. 442 of the Bulgarian Civil Procedure Code 2007, last amended in 2013); however, the general safeguards for debtors are applicable. Recovery cannot take place against inaccessible assets - goods for everyday use, the only home of the debtor, and the debtor's land and other property as determined by Art. 444 of the Bulgarian Civil Procedure Code.

CROATIA

In line with Art. 11 paragraph 2 and Art. 36 of the Croatian Family Act and Art. 4 paragraph 1 and Art. 54 of the Croatian Partnership Act, the answer equally relates to both cohabitants and same-sex informal partners.

According to Art. 44 in relation to Art. 11 of the Croatian Family Act and Art. 54 in relation to Art. 4 of the Croatian Partnership Act, creditors can recover joint debs against assets that belong to the partners' community of property and against the personal property of each partner.

CZECH REPUBLIC

When partners in an informal relationship become jointly liable for debts, they are, as co-debtors, obliged jointly and severally. According to S. 1872(1) Czech Civil Code if several debtors are obliged to perform jointly and severally, they are obliged to perform one for all and all for one. A creditor may demand the entire performance or any part thereof from all, only some, or any one of the co-debtors.

Creditors can recover from the assets which are in the co-ownership of the partners in an informal relationship (only if both of them are contracting parties) as well as from the assets which are in the sole ownership of the partner who is the debtor.

---

4 Cf. with regard to own debts also Cass. 10 June 1976, *RW* 1976-77, 601.

DENMARK

Joint debts are not linked to specific assets, but joint debts will usually be related to assets which are jointly owned by the cohabitants, for example debts relating to the costs of a jointly owned property. If the couple enter into a written contract for the joint ownership of the property, it will usually provide for liability for the costs of the property. It is usually provided in the contract that the cohabitants will be jointly liable towards third parties for the day-to-day expenses, in other words third parties can refer to either of the cohabitants for the full payment of any debts - joint and several liability. In relations between the cohabitants it is often provided that they should be liable in proportion to the share of their ownership.

ENGLAND AND WALES

The assets on which they have secured their credit or against which the court permits them to recover a debt through a charging order or other means of enforcement available to the court will be available. A creditor can recover a debt against the assets owned by either or both of them if the debt liability is joint and several which is the normal rule, providing a court order for enforcement has been obtained.

ESTONIA

There is no special regulation with regard to partners in an informal relationship. If there is a valid relation under the law of obligations between the creditor and both parties in an informal relationship, the creditor shall have the right to demand the performance of the obligation from both parties in an informal relationship, respectively whether they are joint obligors, collective obligors or solidary obligors. Execution proceedings shall take place according to the Estonian Code of Enforcement Procedure.

FINLAND

Generally, if a debt has been incurred jointly by two or more persons and if they have not agreed on the distribution of liability, they are all jointly and severally liable for the debt (see, for example, S. 2 of the Finnish Promissory Notes Act, 622/1947). The Court decision, which forms the ground for enforcing the recovery of the debt, is always addressed to an individual rather than to two persons jointly. In the case of a joint debt, the creditor will therefore bring a claim against two separate individuals. In an enforcement case that originates from a joint debt, the bailiff is not directed to recover the debt from jointly owned assets, as the link to joint responsibilities has been severed during the recovery process.

According to the Finnish Enforcement Act (705/2007, Chapter 4, S. 24), property is attached in the following order: 1) money or a claim for money or wages, a salary, pension or other periodical income; 2) other chattels; 3) real estate; 4) property that the debtor needs as his or her permanent residence or for his or her necessary livelihood, and the means of production necessary in the debtor's business or trade activity. An exception may be made in the order of attachment, for example, if the parties so agree (Chapter 4, S. 25).

FRANCE

In the case of a joint debt (which requires the consent of both partners), creditors can recover the debt from all the assets of both partners. However, general enforcement rules shall be taken into account, and they exclude some assets from the scope of seizure (for example, assets which are necessary for the profession of the debtor or for family life: tables, beds, chairs, etc.).

GERMANY

There are no special rules dealing with recovery of joint debts in cases of an informal relationship. Therefore the general rules of civil law apply, and the creditor has a claim against one or both cohabitants. Each cohabitant is owner of his or her assets. The creditor can therefore ask for payment. An execution affects only the assets of the liable cohabitant or, in cases of joint and separate liability, the assets of both cohabitants.

GREECE

All assets held by each partner, except those in respect of which the law does not allow for seizure (Art. 982 Greek Code of Civil Procedure) e.g. claims for maintenance, salaries, social benefits.

HUNGARY

In the course of a community of life cohabitants acquire separate property.

REPUBLIC OF IRELAND

The recovery of joint debts by creditors is not expressly provided for. That said, S. 202(1) of the Irish Civil Partnership and Cohabitants Act 2010 provides that cohabitants may enter into an agreement to provide for financial matters.

ITALY

As the joint liability of the partners can only arise when both have assumed the same obligation, creditors can recover joint debts according to the general rules on breach of contract. All types of assets can therefore be the object of an action for recovery.

LATVIA

See the answer to Question 31 above.

LITHUANIA

According to Art. 4.80 of the Lithuanian Civil Code, a creditor of a co-owner shall have the right to partition the debtor's share in order to claim it. This means that creditors may recover a corresponding share of the debt from the property of each partner, including from jointly acquired and used property as referred to in Art. 3.230 of the Lithuanian Civil Code.

LUXEMBOURG

Joint debts are recoverable both against the joint assets of the partners as well as the sole assets of each of them.

THE NETHERLANDS

Since there are no specific provisions Art. 3:276 Dutch Civil Code is relevant, stating that in principle a creditor can have recourse against all the property of the debtor.

NORWAY

The creditor can recover joint debts (solidary obligations) from all assets that belong to either of the two debtor cohabitants.

PORTUGAL

According to general rules, creditors can recover joint debts against all the assets belonging to each of the partners, regardless of the share which each of them may have in the debt.

RUSSIA

There are no specific rules on the recovery of partners' joint debts. Creditors can recover joint debts from any assets of the partners under the general rules established by the general provisions of the Russian Federal Act on the Execution Procedure.[5] According to the priority rule provided for in Art. 69(3) of this Act, debts are first recovered from the financial assets of the debtor(s), firstly those denominated in national currency and, secondly, those denominated in foreign currency, and then from any other assets.

Article 445 of the Russian Code on Civil Procedure[6] specifies the assets from which no recovery is possible. Under these rules, no recovery is possible from:

- The home or part of the home serving as the only home of the debtor and his/her family, except when the recovery is sought by the mortgage lender and such recovery is permitted under the legislation governing mortgages;
- Land on which the above-mentioned home is situated, except when the recovery is sought by the mortgage lender and such recovery is permitted under the legislation governing mortgages;
- Household goods and objects for personal use (clothing, footwear, etc.), with the exception of jewellery and other luxury articles;
- Objects which are essential for professional activities, with the exception of objects whose value exceeds the statutory minimum wage;
- Certain objects used for individual business activities;
- Seeds which are necessary for the next season's sowing;
- Food and money not exceeding the amount of the statutory minimum wage, calculated separately for the debtor and each dependent family member;

---

5 Федеральный закон "Об исполнительном производстве" от 02.10.2007 N 229-ФЗ www.consultant.ru/popular/ispolproisv/69_8.html#p1044© КонсультантПлюс, 1992-2015.

6 Гражданский процессуальный кодекс РФ: www.consultant.ru/popular/gpkrf/8_62.html#p4069 © КонсультантПлюс, 1992-2015.

- Fuel which is necessary for cooking and heating during the heating season;
- Means of transport and other assets essential for a disabled debtor.

SCOTLAND

As a general rule, joint debts and liabilities are incurred in respect of cohabitants in the same way they would be incurred in respect of any joint parties. There are, however, specific provisions to protect the family home and some assets used within the home and these operate to protect cohabitants as well as those in formal relationships with the debtor. The provisions are detailed and beyond the scope of this report but include the possibility of applying to the court for an order suspending, for a reasonable period of time, the rights of a creditor to sell the family home,[7] protection for assets kept and used in the debtor's household[8] and land including a family dwellinghouse.[9]

SLOVAKIA

Creditors can recover joint debts by executing not only the assets in the divided co-ownership of the partners. They can recover joint debts against assets belonging exclusively to one of the partners.

SLOVENIA

A creditor can seize the individual property of either partner and proportionately of each of the partners in common property.

SPAIN

If both partners have incurred a debt jointly, the creditor can recover the debts from the personal assets of each of them in proportion to their share in the property.

7 Mortgage Rights (Scotland) Act 2001, S. 2.
8 Debt Arrangement and Attachment (Scotland) Act 2002, S. 1-9.
9 Bankruptcy and Diligence (Scotland) Act 2007.

SWEDEN

The creditors may recover joint debts on any assets belonging to either one of the indebted cohabitees – as long as the cohabitees are jointly and severally liable.

SWITZERLAND

In the case of joint and several liability (*solidarische Haftung*), the creditor can fully or partially recover debts from any of the debtors (Art. 144 para. 1 Swiss Code of Obligations). The same applies for joint and several liability concerning a simple partnership.[10]

[10] For details see C.M. PESTALOZZI and P. HETTICH, in: H. HONSELL, N.P. VOGT and R. WATTER, *Basler Kommentar Obligationenrecht II (Art. 530-1186 ZGB)*, Helbing Lichtenhahn Verlag, Bern, 2008, at Art. 544 N 14 et seq.

QUESTION 33

Are there specific rules governing the administration of assets jointly owned by the partners in an informal relationship? If there are no specific rules, briefly outline the generally applicable rules.

AUSTRIA

Due to the lack of specific rules the general rules regulating the administration of joint ownership apply: In this regard one has to differentiate between ordinary and extraordinary administration, whereas the former concerns measures which are in the interest of all owners, because they are necessary and not associated with high costs, the latter includes considerable changes with regard to the maintenance or better use of the jointly owned asset in question.[1] Regular measures will be decided by the majority of the votes, which is not counted according to the number of persons being joint owners, but according to their shares.[2] In the event of a tie, the judge has to decide.[3] Matters falling within the scope of extraordinary administration must be decided unanimously.[4] If such a decision could not be reached, the owners, whose shares amount to at least one half can persist on the desired measure.[5] However, the outvoted owners can require some sort of security for future damages. If security is not provided, but the persons do not want to resign their ownership, the court has to finally decide whether and under which conditions the measure should be realised.[6]

1 H. BÖHM, 'sections 833 and 834 General Austrian Civil Code', in: A. KLETEČKA and M. SCHAUER, *ABGB-ON 1.01,* Manz Verlag, Vienna, 2013, at marg. No. 5, 13.

2 Section 833 General Austrian Civil Code.

3 H. BÖHM, 'section 833 General Austrian Civil Code', in: A. KLETEČKA and M. SCHAUER, *ABGB-ON 1.01,* Manz Verlag, Vienna, 2013, at marg. No. 21.

4 H. BÖHM, 'section 834 General Austrian Civil Code', in: A. KLETEČKA and M. SCHAUER, *ABGB-ON 1.01,* Manz Verlag, Vienna, 2013, at marg. No. 17.

5 Section 834 General Austrian Civil Code.

6 Section 835 General Austrian Civil Code; H. GAMERITH, 'section 835 General Austrian Civil Code', in: P. RUMMEL (ed.), *Kommentar zum Allgemeinen Bürgerlichen Gesetzbuch,* Manz Verlag, Vienna, 2000, at marg. No. 2.

With regard to the jointly owned condominium *(Eigentümerpartnerschaft)* the shares of the partners can be sold, mortgaged or submitted to execution only jointly.[7]

BELGIUM

There are no specific rules governing the administration of the joint assets of informal partners. In the absence of an (implicit (agency)) agreement, each undivided owner of an asset is entitled to the use of his undivided part insofar as such use does not modify the purpose of the asset and does not interfere with the right of the other undivided owners (Art. 577-2, § 5 Belgian Civil Code). Both partners have to consent to acts of administration other than urgent acts regarding the assets as a whole (Art. 577-2, § 6 Belgian civil Code).[8]

BULGARIA

There are no specific rules governing the administration of assets which are jointly owned by the partners in an informal relationship. The applicable rules are the general rules contained in the Bulgarian Property Law. Any of the partners in this case can use/benefit from the asset which forms part of the joint property (Art. 30, para. 2 and 32). The sole user has to pay compensation to the other owner of the property (Art. 31, para. 2).

CROATIA

In line with Art. 11 paragraph 2 and Art. 36 of the Croatian Family Act and Art. 4 paragraph 1 and Art. 54 of the Croatian Partnership Act, the answer equally relates to both cohabitants and same-sex informal partners.

Article 37 of the Croatian Family Act lays down the sole and joint administration of matrimonial property (community of assets). It depends on the type of matrimonial property management (administration): regular or extraordinary administration.

In terms of regular administration such as the regular maintenance, exploitation and utilization of assets for their regular purposes, if these

7 Section 13 para. 3 Austrian Condominium Act.
8 V. SAGAERT, *Goederenrecht*, Kluwer, Mechelen, 2014, at n°s 329.

do not incur exceptionally large costs and if the management (administration) is in the interest of both partners, one partner can independently dispose of the pertinent real property and chattels (movables). In such a case, the consent of the other partner is presumed.

In terms of extraordinary administration of joint assets such as the alienation of a whole item, renting or leasing a whole item for a period longer than a year, repurposing, major repairs, restoration, renovation, and pledging a movable item, joint administration or the written consent of the other partner certified by a notary public is required.

A lack of consent for administration shall not affect the rights and liabilities of a fair third party. Partners who have not given their consent to initiated administration shall have the right to compensation for damage arising from such an action by his/her partner.

CZECH REPUBLIC

There are no specific rules governing the administration of assets jointly owned by the partners in an informal relationship. If partners in an informal relationship jointly own the property, all the rules regarding co-ownership according to S. 1115 et seq. Czech Civil Code are applicable. Partners in an informal relationship are then co-owners. As for S. 1117 Czech Civil Code: each co-owner has the right to the entire object. This right is limited by the same right of each of the other co-owners. With respect to the object as a whole, co-owners are considered to dispose of the object as a single person (S. 1116 Czech Civil Code). As for rules concerning the administration of an undivided object, see S. 1126 et seq. of the Czech Civil Code.

DENMARK

There are no specific rules governing the administration of assets which are jointly owned by the partners. Many couples have written contracts for joint ownership, for example when they buy a house to live in. A contract for the joint ownership of real property will normally take account of the allocation of costs and the actual and legal control of the property.

If there is no agreement between the parties the costs of the property will be allocated in line with its ownership. Decisions about the property should be made together, except in the case of insignificant or necessary repairs.[9] As for legal control, in principle an individual cohabitant is free to act with regard to his or her legal share, including selling or pledging it as security. However, the conditions for the joint acquisition of the asset will presumably restrict the right to dispose of it.[10]

ENGLAND AND WALES

No.

ESTONIA

There is no separate regulation in Estonian legislation with regard to the administration of the assets in the shared ownership of the parties in an informal relationship. According to § 70 of the Estonian Law of Property Act, a shared ownership is a common ownership or joint ownership. Common ownership is an ownership in legal shares of a shared asset belonging to two or more persons concurrently, thus, common ownership is a common right to the whole asset. Joint ownership is ownership in undefined shares of a shared asset belonging to two or more persons concurrently. Shared ownership is common ownership unless otherwise provided by law. Provisions concerning common ownership apply to joint ownership unless otherwise provided by the law providing for joint ownership. If a right belongs to several persons (community), the provisions concerning joint ownership are applied thereto unless otherwise provided by law. Joint ownership is mostly either joint property owned by spouses, according to the Estonian Family Law Act, or partnership property.

Co-owners shall possess and use a shared asset according to an agreement (§ 72 Estonian Law of Obligations Act). Issues which remain within the limits of the ordinary possession and use of a shared asset may be decided by a decision made by the majority of votes of the co-owners. The number of votes upon making the decision depends upon the ownership share. A co-owner has the right to use a shared asset in so far as this does not hinder common use by the other co-owners. A co-owner has the right to perform acts which are necessary for the preservation of an asset without the consent of the other co-owners, but the co-owner may demand a reimbursement of the necessary expenses for the

9 See U. RAMMESKOV BANG-PEDERSEN, *Sameje om fast ejendom*, GadJura, Copenhagen, 2002, at p. 74.

10 U. RAMMESKOV BANG-PEDERSEN, *Sameje om fast ejendom*, GadJura, Copenhagen, 2002, at p. 77-79.

preservation of the asset from the other co-owners in proportion to their shares. A co-owner has the right to demand from the other co-owners that the possession and use of an asset in common ownership be effected according to the interests of all the co-owners. Co-owners shall act in good faith in their relations with one another and they shall refrain, in particular, from damaging the rights of other co-owners.[11]

FINLAND

There are no specific rules on the administration of joint assets for cohabitees. The general rules apply. According to the Finnish Act on Certain Joint Ownership (180/1958), the joint owner can dictate his or her share of the property, if his or her actions do not affect the rights and benefits of the other owners. The joint owner of the property has a right to apply to the District Court for an order to sell the property, if the owners cannot agree on the use of the property.

FRANCE

There are no specific rules governing the administration of assets which are jointly owned by the partners in an informal relationship. Therefore, the general rules apply. Assets which are jointly owned by the partners in an informal relationship are subject to the rules on *indivision* (Art. 815 et seq. of the French Civil Code). Any partner can take any measures which are necessary for the preservation of joint assets, even in the absence of urgency (Art. 815-2 of the French Civil Code). According to Art. 815-3 para. 2 of the French Civil Code, a transaction which does not belong to the normal use of the joint assets, or through which the asset is disposed of, normally requires the consent of all the joint owners. If one of the joint owners openly administers the joint assets without any objection by the other joint owners, Art. 815-3 para. 4 of the French Civil Code qualifies this as a tacit contract of agency which applies to acts of administration, not to acts of disposal (and not to lease contracts).

If one of the joint owners cannot express his or her will (due to absence, illness etc.), the other owner can be judicially authorised to represent him or her generally or only for a specific transaction (Art. 815-4 of the French Civil Code). In the absence of any judicial authorisation or agency, the

11 See the Decision of the Civil Chamber of the Supreme Court 3-2-1-13-14; 3-2-1-93-12; 3-2-1-45-13.

rules relating to *gestion d'affaires* for a third party can apply if the necessary conditions are fulfilled.

Moreover, the president of the civil court (*tribunal de grande instance*) can order or authorise any urgent measure required by a common interest (Art. 815-6 of the French Civil Code).

The creditors of a joint owner are not allowed to seize his or her share of the joint assets, Art. 815-17 para. 2 of the French Civil Code. They can, however, demand that the asset be sold on behalf of their debtor.

By contrast, the common creditors of both joint owners can seize the joint assets.

According to Art. 815 of the French Civil Code, there is no obligation to remain in *indivision* (joint ownership). Therefore, each partner can demand that the asset be sold, except if, by a judgment or contract, joint ownership has been ordered or agreed for a specific period of time.

GERMANY

There are no special rules dealing with the administration of assets of informal partners; the general rules of civil law apply. Where an asset is jointly owned by the partners they are co-owners (§ 1008 German Civil Code). Co-owners form a community (*Gemeinschaft*) in the sense of the law's obligations (§ 741 German Civil Code). There is a joint administration of the asset (§ 744 para. 1 German Civil Code). According to the general rule - which also applies in cases of more than two co-owners - it may be resolved by a majority of votes that there is to be a proper administration and use appropriate to the quality of the joint item (§ 745 para. 1 German Civil Code). Each part owner may, where administration and use is not regulated by agreement or by a majority vote, demand administration corresponding to the interests of all part owners according to their reasonably exercised discretion (§ 745 para. 2 German Civil Code). In the event of separation, the remaining cohabitant can be obligated to pay compensation to the other cohabitant for the continued use of a common home.[12] However, every co-owner is entitled to dispose of his share separately (§ 747 para. 1 s. 1 German Civil Code); as to the asset as a whole, both co-owners can only make dispositions acting together (§ 747 para. 1 s. 2 German Civil Code).

---

12 OLG Koblenz, 8.9.2009, *FamRZ*, 2010, 1176.

Where an asset is owned by only one of the partners, he or she alone is the owner. There are no restrictions on the administration of property.

GREECE

There are no specific rules. The general provisions on joint ownership and the sharing of rights will apply. Thus decisions on matters pertaining to the administration of joint assets must be taken jointly (Art. 788-789 Greek Civil Code).

HUNGARY

There are no specific rules and the Civil Code of 1959 did not contain any specific rule either, in spite of the fact that cohabitants could acquire common property under the regime of the Civil Code of 1959. According to the general rules concerning the administration of assets belonging to the joint property, either co-owner is entitled to carry out work that is essential for the preservation and maintenance of the moveable or immoveable property and each co-owner is obliged to bear his or her share of the costs. They have an obligation to notify each other, if possible before the costs are incurred.[13]

REPUBLIC OF IRELAND

This is normally achieved through the law on direct and indirect contributions, see Question 27 and 28.

ITALY

No specific rule is provided for the administration of assets which are jointly owned by the partners in an informal relationship. The standard rules on common ownership (*comunione ordinaria*) therefore apply (Art. 1100 et seq. Italian Civil Code).

Parties in the co-ownership are considered to be the owners of a share in the common asset, and their shares are presumed to be equal (Art. 1101 Italian Civil Code), but it is of course possible that the cohabitants, when dividing the asset between themselves, choose other proportions for the division of their respective shares.

[13] Art. 5:76 of the Hungarian Civil Code.

Transactions within ordinary administration are decided by the majority holder of the shares while the minority is obliged to follow (Art. 1105 Italian Civil Code). Transactions exceeding ordinary administration like a sale, the creation of a real right, or leases for more than nine years, must be agreed upon by all the parties to the co-ownership (Art. 1108 Italian Civil Code).

Each co-owner can freely sell his or her share of the asset (Art. 1103 Italian Civil Code).

LATVIA

In Latvia there is no such specific legal order on informal relationships.

By way of comparison one may consider the following. In lawful property relations of the spouses, S. 93 of the Latvian Civil Law determines that a spouse may assign his or her property, or his or her share of the joint property of the spouses, to be administered by the other spouse who must preserve and protect such property with all of his or her resources. If the joint immovable property of the spouses is recorded in the Land Register in the name of one of the spouses, it is presumed that the other spouse has assigned his or her share in such property to be administered by him or her.

LITHUANIA

There are no special rules governing the administration of assets jointly owned by the partners in an informal relationship, although Art. 3.233 contains some limitations on the right to dispose of the assets which are jointly used. But usually the general rules apply: the object which is subject to common partial ownership is possessed, used and disposed of by a common agreement between the co-owners. If a dispute arises, the order of possession, use or disposal is established by a judicial procedure on the basis of a claim by one of the co-owners (Art. 4.75 Lithuanian Civil Code).

While managing joint affairs, each of the partners shall be entitled to act on behalf of all the partners, unless the agreement on joint activities provides that joint affairs shall be managed by one of the partners or all the partners together (Art. 6.972 Lithuanian Civil Code).

LUXEMBOURG

No, there are no specific rules. The generally applicable rules are those of joint ownership (Art. 815-2 et seq. of the Luxembourg Civil Code).

The administration of assets jointly owned by the partners requires the consent of both of them. Nevertheless, one of the partners may give a *mandat général d'administration* to the other.

If one of the joint owners refuses to consent to a legal act and if this refusal is considered prejudicial to the jointly owned assets, the court may authorise the other partner to conclude the act and to ignore the refusal.

THE NETHERLANDS

The general provisions of Book 3, title 7 of the Dutch Civil Code are applicable to co-ownership/community (*gemeenschap*).[14] From Art. 3:166 para. 2 Dutch Civil Code follows that the shares of the partners in the asset are equal. The Supreme Court has ruled that the shares can still be equal when the partners have not contributed equally to the purchase of the asset.[15] Reasonableness and fairness determine the relation between the co-owners (Art. 3:166 para. 3 Dutch Civil Code). Both partners are entitled to the use of the asset (Art. 3:169 Dutch Civil Code). Specified acts (ordinary maintenance or the preservation of the good, and urgent acts) may be carried out by one partner alone, but all other acts require both partners to act together (Art. 3:170 Dutch Civil Code). Pursuant to Art. 3:172 Dutch Civil Code expenses for joint property will in principle be borne by the partners according to their respective shares in the asset (mostly on a 50-50 basis). This is particularly relevant after a separation and if either partner has insufficient financial means to take over the jointly owned dwelling. The house then has to be sold to a third party, but given the real estate market, this might take a long time, in which case the costs have to be borne by the partners. One of them will usually be living in the house, and the parties have to agree on who pays which expenses. There is a growing body of case law on this subject.[16]

---

[14] W.M. SCHRAMA, 'Goederenrecht: mede-eigendom', in: M.L.C.C. DE BRUIJN-LÜCKERS et al. (eds.), *Relatierecht, SDUCommentaar*, SDU, The Hague, 2014, at p. 2025-2040.

[15] HR 26 May 2006, RvdW 2006, 14.

[16] E.g. Hof Arnhem-Leeuwarden 18 March 2014, ECLI:NL:GHARL:2014:2158; Hof Amsterdam 4 February 2014, ECLI:NL:GHAMS:2014:216.

NORWAY

There are no specific rules governing the administration of assets jointly owned by the partners to an informal relationship. The generally applicable rules regarding items of property - both real property and movables - are found in the Norwegian Act on Co-ownership. Each co-owner may, for example, freely dispose of his or her undivided share in the property pursuant to the Norwegian Act on Co-ownership, S. 10, unless otherwise agreed. Special circumstances might lead to a more restricted right to dispose of an item, according to the Norwegian Act on Co-ownership, S. 1. This could be the case when the property in question is owned by two partners to an informal relationship.

PORTUGAL

There are no specific rules governing the administration of assets jointly owned by the partners in an informal relationship.

The administration of assets jointly owned by the partners follows the generally applicable rules of co-ownership/joint ownership. According to these rules, any one of the partners has the right to act in administration (Art. 1407 and 985 of the Portuguese Civil Code) provided his or her share is half of the total. One partner who wants to act in administration but does not have at least half of the property ought to ask the court for a fair decision.

RUSSIA

There are no specific rules governing the administration of assets jointly owned by the partners in an informal relationship. Under the general rule of Art. 246(1) Russian Civil Code, joint owners jointly administer their joint assets in their entirety. That means that any act of administration related to the whole asset requires the consent of both partners, irrespective of the extent of their shares in that asset. However, under Art. 246(2) Russian Civil Code, each of the joint owners can independently dispose of (sell, donate, dispose of by will, mortgage or dispose of in any other way) his/her share in the joint asset. He/she is restricted in that respect by the provisions of Art. 250(1) Russian Civil Code, which require a joint owner who wishes to sell a share in a joint asset to a third person first to offer this share to the co-owner subject to the same conditions as agreed upon with the third person. This requirement does not apply to the sale of the share at a public auction. It is also not applicable to the alienation of parts of jointly owned land on which a building is situated or parts of jointly owned buildings.

Under Art. 250(2) Russian Civil Code, a joint owner wishing to sell his/her share to a third person must send the other joint owner(s) written notification containing all the conditions which pertain to the transaction. He/she is free to sell the share to a third person if the co-owner does not agree to buy the movable asset within ten days or the immovable asset within a month. This means that a partner has a preferential right of purchase if his/her partner intends to sell a joint asset to a third party. This right is applicable only to the sale of an asset, and does not provide protection if the other partner decides to donate, dispose of by will or mortgage joint assets.

SCOTLAND

There are no specific rules governing the administration of jointly owned assets by cohabitants. The normal rules of property apply.

SLOVAKIA

No, there are no specific rules governing the administration of assets jointly owned by the partners in an informal relationship. But there are generally applicable rules on decisions concerning the management of common assets. Decisions are taken by a majority of the votes determined according to the size of the shares (§ 139 para. 2 Slovak Civil Code). If the votes are equal or if no majority or agreement can be achieved, the courts will decide. Moreover, in the case of an important change to the common asset, the minority co-owners may request a court decision as well (§ 139 para. 3 Slovak Civil Code). An 'important change' is not defined by the Slovak Civil Code, although legal doctrine has interpreted an important change as meaning, for example, the rebuilding of the common home.[17]

SLOVENIA

Partners manage and dispose of common property together. They may agree that only one of them shall manage the common property or a part thereof, or that only one of them shall manage and also dispose of the

[17] See J. LAZAR, in: J. LAZAR et al. (eds.), *Občianske právo hmotné* (Substantive Slovak Civil Law), Iuris Libri, Bratislava, 2014, at p. 503.

common property (Art. 52 of the Slovenian Marriage Act). A legal transaction that one partner concludes in relation to common property without the necessary agreement of the other partner may be challenged by the other partner.

SPAIN

No there are not. If assets are jointly owned, the ordinary rules on the administration of assets in co-ownership will apply. According to these rules acts of administration can only take place if there is agreement between the co-owners.

SWEDEN

The Swedish Cohabitation Act focuses on the partners' right to the property which is to be included in the property division following the termination of the relationship, i.e., so-called cohabitation property. The administration of this property is subject to certain restrictions, in order to safeguard the interests of both partners, § 3 and 23. For this to be achieved, the other partner's consent is required for transactions of the kind mentioned under Question 24. The protected property can be jointly owned, or owned solely by one of the partners, or be a rented dwelling. The fact that it has been acquired for the partners' joint use is decisive.

When property is jointly owned - irrespective of any kind of family relationship between the owners - the Swedish Co-ownership Act (in Swedish: *lagen 1904:48 s. 1 om samäganderätt*) is applicable. Co-ownership of household goods, vehicles, real property or any other joint dwelling, stocks and shares, as well as property co-owned through the hidden or concealed right of co-ownership, all fall under the scope of this enactment.[18] The co-owners are expected to administer the co-owned assets jointly, Swedish Co-ownership Act, § 2. Where agreement is necessary, but the co-owners are unable to agree, the court may, upon application by one of the co-owners, appoint an administrator to take care of the assets, § 4. The court can also decide that the property in its entirely is to be sold at public auction, § 6.

With respect to the disposal of co-owned property in its entirety, for example through transfer, mortgage, pawn or grant of enjoyment, all the

18 The Swedish Supreme Court has in its judgments *NJA 1980 p. 705* and *NJA 2008 p. 1053* applied the Co-ownership Act even when the co-ownership was concealed.

co-owners are expected to have given their consent to the disposition, Swedish Co-ownership Act, § 2. In contrast to the rules that apply to disposal in its entirety of the jointly owned property, each co-owner has the right to freely dispose of his or her individual share in the property. For example, a co-owner may sell or give away his or her share in the property without the other co-owners' consent.[19]

SWITZERLAND

There are no specific rules governing the administration of assets jointly owned by the partners in an informal relationship. Hence, the rules of property law apply.

Under co-ownership (see Question 24(a)), ordinary measures of administration and use must be distinguished from other measures. Ordinary measures of administration may be effected by each co-owner alone (Art. 647a Swiss Civil Code), whereas all other measures (e.g. measures that require construction work) require the consent of all or the majority of the co-owners (Art. 647b-647e Swiss Civil Code). The costs of administrative measures are borne by the co-owners in the proportion of their property shares, unless otherwise agreed (Art. 649 Swiss Civil Code). The co-owners may agree on rules of use and administration that deviate from the statutory provisions (Art. 647 para. 1 Swiss Civil Code). In any case, each co-owner may request that measures that are necessary for the preservation of the value and the usability of the asset are carried out, and, if necessary, to have these ordered by the court (Art. 647 para. 2 No. 1 Swiss Civil Code). Further, if an asset is threatened by imminent or growing harm, each co-owner may take the necessary preventive measures at the expense of all of the co-owners (Art. 647 para. 2 No. 2 Swiss Civil Code).

Administration in the case of joint ownership (see Question 24(a)) is governed by the rules of the underlying community (Art. 653 para. 1 Swiss Civil Code). For partners in an informal relationship this will often be a simple partnership (Art. 530 et seq. Swiss Code of Obligations). If there are no other provisions in this respect, an unanimous decision by all of the joint owners is required (Art. 653 Swiss Civil Code).

---

19 See M. BRATTSTRÖM, 'Egendomsförhållanden under bestående samboende', in: J. ASLAND et al., *Nordisk samboerrett*, Gyldendal, Oslo, 2014, at p. 90 (see Chapter 2.3.1 in the English version of the book, to be published by Intersentia in 2015).

PART D
SEPARATION

QUESTION 34

When partners in an informal relationship separate does the law grant maintenance to a former partner? If so, what are the requirements?

AUSTRIA

In the case of separation the ex-partners are not entitled to claim maintenance under current Austrian law.[1] To avoid legal uncertainty partners in an informal relationship are well advised to conclude a so-called partnership agreement *(Partnerschaftsvertrag)* including an explicit clause on maintenance in case of separation.[2]

It should however be noted that S. 235 para. 1 General Austrian Civil Code stipulates that the father of a newborn child is obliged to reimburse the expenses incurred by the birth as well as the maintenance costs of the mother for a period of eight weeks after the birth. If other expenses become necessary due to the birth, the father also has to bear these costs. The claim becomes statute-barred three years after the birth.[3] Although this provision does not require the existence of an informal relationship, it may equally apply to separated partners who had an informal relationship. From a practical point of view this provision is of minor importance, because usually these costs are covered by social insurance or social welfare.[4]

BELGIUM

There is no statutory maintenance obligation between former informal partners. In the absence of an (implicit) agreement, a claim to

---

1 A. DEIXLER-HÜBNER, 'Rechtliche Regelungen für Lebensgemeinschaften im Innenverhältnis', *iFamZ*, 2012, at p. 193.

2 A. DEIXLER-HÜBNER (ed.), *Der Ehevertrag*, Linde, Vienna, 2013, at p. 227 et seq.

3 Section 235 para. 2 General Austrian Civil Code.

4 F. MEISSEL, 'Unterhaltsansprüche aus Lebensgemeinschaft? Nichteheliche Lebensgemeinschaften und Unterhalt (Teil II)', *EF-Z*, 2008, at p. 15.

'maintenance' is possible on the grounds of either tort law or a natural obligation.

Claims on the basis of tort law are rarely accepted. Indeed, it is not a fault *per se* to end an informal relationship. Only the circumstances in which the relationship is terminated may give rise to tort liability.[5] Some case law refers to behaviour that would constitute a fault anyhow, such as assault and battery. The untimely termination of an informal relationship, or termination by the economically stronger partner whereas the other has been dependent on him/her for a long period has been accepted as a fault in some of the case law.[6] One judgment concludes that no fault was committed because the partner continued to support the other for one year, and that the subsequent termination of support was not untimely.[7] By contrast, one judgment even seems to accept that it is negligent not to avoid becoming economically dependent on the other partner![8] Legal doctrine rightly points at the confusion that exists in this regard between fault and damages, which are two different conditions of tort liability. The existence of a fault cannot be derived from the existence of damage. There is no damage if a partner would stay behind in an economically weaker position.[9] In our opinion, there could however be damage if a former partner would suddenly have to bear all the household expenses on his/her own.

Whereas there is consensus that a natural obligation to contribute to the household expenses and even support a partner exists during the informal relationship, such consensus does not exist vis-à-vis separated partners. Some of the case law rejects any natural obligation upon separation.[10] Other case law accepts that a natural obligation may exist,[11] but rightly requires proof of voluntary performance or a promise to do so.[12] Providing for a partner during a relationship does not as such prove the promise to do so upon separation. The requirement of voluntary performance or a promise to perform also means that the natural obligation only becomes a civil obligation to the extent and for the period

5 District Court of Brussels 6 May 2008, *Act.dr.fam.* 2009, 93; District Court of Brussels 31 March 2009, *JLMB* 2010, 337.
6 Justice of the Peace Antwerp (7) 29 June 2004, *RABG* 2004, 1282, with note BROUWERS.
7 District Court of Brussels 31 March 2009, *JLMB* 2010, 337.
8 District Court of Mons 23 May 2001, *JLMB* 648.
9 S. EGGERMONT, *De juridische bescherming van private relaties*, PhD, University of Antwerp, 2015, at n°s 269 et seq.
10 Justice of the Peace Veurne (Nieuwpoort) 15 December 2009, *T.Vred.* 2012, 31.
11 Antwerp 1 February 2006, *RW* 2007-08, 1816, with note WERMOES.
12 District Court of Brussels 6 May 2008, *Act.dr.fam.* 2009, 93; District Court of Brussels 31 March 2009, *JLMB* 2010, 337.

determined by the debtor. The traditional criteria to determine maintenance obligations consequently do not apply.

BULGARIA

No, there is no legally regulated right of the partner in an informal relationship to receive/pay maintenance.

CROATIA

According to Art. 303 in relation to Art. 295 of the Croatian Family Act and Art. 39 paragraph 2 in relation to Art. 4 of the Croatian Partnership Act, the answer relates to both cohabitants and same-sex informal partners.

If partners separate, the law does grant them maintenance rights. According to Art. 295 of the Croatian Family Act and Art. 39 in relation to Art. 4 of the Croatian Partnership Act, the respective requirements are as follows:

- if the partner applying for maintenance does not have sufficient means for subsistence, is incapable of working or cannot find gainful employment and if such means cannot be obtained based on his/her assets;
- if the partner facing the claim has sufficient resources and opportunities to support himself/herself.

Maintenance claims shall be submitted to the courts within six months after the termination of a life union (Art. 303 paragraph 2 Croatian Family Act).

CZECH REPUBLIC

In such a case, the law does not grant maintenance to a former partner in an informal relationship. The law does not even grant maintenance to a current partner in an informal relationship. However, when a woman is pregnant and the father is a former partner in an informal relationship, there is a right of an unmarried woman to obtain maintenance for herself and a reasonable contribution to cover the costs associated with pregnancy and childbirth. This is established in S. 920 Czech Civil Code: if the child's mother is not married to the child's father, the child's father must provide her with maintenance for two years from the birth of the child and provide her with a reasonable contribution to cover the costs associated with pregnancy and childbirth. The man whose paternity is presumed has a duty to reimburse the costs associated with pregnancy and childbirth even if the child is not born alive. A court may, on the application of a pregnant woman, order the man whose paternity is presumed to provide an amount needed for maintenance and a contribution to cover the costs associated with pregnancy and childbirth in advance. A court may, on the application of a pregnant woman, also order the man whose paternity is presumed to provide in advance an amount needed to provide for the maintenance of the child for a period for which the woman would be entitled to maternity leave as an employee under another legal regulation.

S. 922/2 Czech Civil Code provides: maintenance and support for an unmarried mother and the covering of costs associated with pregnancy and childbirth may also be granted retrospectively, but for a maximum of two years subsequent to the date of childbirth.

DENMARK

Danish law does not contain any specific regulation with regard to the payment of maintenance to a former partner.

ENGLAND AND WALES

No.

ESTONIA

If the partners in an informal relationship separate, they will have no maintenance obligation with regard to each other.

The Estonian Family Law Act contains rules on the provision of maintenance in the case of the birth of a child. The aforementioned obligation does not depend on whether the parents are married to each other or not. The father of a child is required to provide maintenance to the mother of the child eight weeks before and twelve weeks after the birth of that child (§ 111(1) of the Estonian Family Law Act). If a mother is unable to maintain herself due to a health disorder caused by pregnancy or childbirth, the father is required to provide her with maintenance until her state of health improves. The same applies if a mother is unable to receive an income due to having to care for a child

(§ 111(2) of the Estonian Family Law Act). If a father cares for and raises a child and he is unable to receive an income due to having to care for that child, he has the right to file a claim against the mother (§ 111(3) of the Estonian Family Law Act). The obligation to provide maintenance commences no earlier than four months before the birth of a child and terminates after three years have passed from the birth of the child (§ 111(2) of the Estonian Family Law Act).

FINLAND

No, there is no legal duty to pay maintenance to a former cohabiting partner. Partners may, however, enter into a voluntary agreement to pay maintenance.

FRANCE

According to French legislation and case law, the breakdown of an informal relationship does not provide a right to maintenance. Yet, specific property law and company law rules have been used by the courts at the time of a cohabitation breakdown to lessen the unfairness of particular situations.

The French theories of unjust enrichment[13] and of *de facto* corporation[14] apply to a cohabitation breakdown. They have provided for a lump-sum payment to one ex-cohabitant at the time of the breakdown where specific legal criteria have been met. Sometimes the fulfilment of a moral duty (*obligation naturelle*) by one ex-cohabitant has been opposed to defend a refund claim.

Claims which attempt to establish the existence of a *de facto* corporation between the cohabitants mostly concern situations where one cohabitant asserts that he or she has been involved, in one way or another, in the family company or craft industry run by the other. For the existence of a *de facto* corporation to be legally established between cohabitants, each of its composing elements, as determined by Art. 1832 of the French Civil Code, must be specifically proved. These are, firstly, the raising of capital (*apport en capital*) or sweat equity (*apport en industrie*); secondly, the *affectio societatis* between the two; and, thirdly, the common intention of sharing

[13] Art. 1371 of the French Civil Code. See Cass. Civ 1 15 October 1996 no. 94-20472; Cass. Civ 1 24 September 2008 no. 07-11928.

[14] Art. 1873 of the French Civil Code. See Cass. Com 23 June 2004, no. 00-18974.

profits and losses. The burden of proof is a heavy one, however, especially where cohabitants are involved. Indeed, they often do not take the necessary precautions so as to be able to provide such evidence in the future. Case law is very restrictive and *affectio societatis* cannot be inferred from any financial contribution made to the acquisition of a chattel.[15] Moreover, any such claim is frequently unsuccessful due to the fact that the claimant fails to prove that the financial contribution that he or she made in the company or the assistance given in the management thereof exceeded the mutual aid that could be expected in a family relationship.[16]

An action *de in rem verso*, based on unjust enrichment, allows one individual to claim against another for the recovery of sums paid but not due.[17] This claim is most frequently instigated where one cohabitant has paid a mortgage or a loan on behalf of the other, or has incurred expenses in improving the other's asset or chattel. The legal criteria for such a refund are, firstly, the enrichment of one cohabitant's property, secondly the correlative loss suffered by the other, and thirdly the lack of any cause in that respect. This last element is the most difficult to prove between ex-cohabitants. Indeed, the intention to make a donation, the usual contributions to common expenses or any advantage which is the natural result of life in common diminish any refund expectations.[18]

Finally, the fact that an initial payment was based on a moral or natural duty counteracts a claim for a refund.[19] This rule has been used between ex-cohabitants to moderate a refund claim by one of them against the other where the payment which was made fulfilled a moral duty.[20] The fulfilment of a moral duty, whose specific performance cannot be

---

15 Cass. Civ. 1, 20 January 2010, no. 08-13200.

16 See Cass. Civ. 1, 20 January 2010, no. 08-16105.

17 Art. 1371 of the French Civil Code.

18 See Cass. Civ. 1 20 January 2010, no. 08-13400. The expenditure incurred by one cohabitant, who voluntarily paid for a loan contracted by the other party in order to repay to her ex-husband her share in a former common home, was balanced by the fact that he lived in the debtor's home with her and their common child for free. In contrast see Cass. Civ. 1 24 September 2008, no. 06-11294, where it was held that expenditures incurred by one cohabitant to renovate the house of the other, considering the value of the refurbishment and the quality thereof, exceeded any advantages emanating from life in common.

19 Art. 1235 of the French Civil Code.

20 The case law is fairly old on this point, but the principle could be reactivated Cass. Civ. 1, 6 October 1959, D. 1960, 515 with note MALAURIE.

claimed, should not be considered to be a donation. As a consequence, its value is not subjected to taxation.[21]

GERMANY

German law does not grant maintenance to a former partner of an informal relationship. However, if an unmarried couple has a common child according to § 1615l German Civil Code the father must not only pay for the costs related to the pregnancy and birth but also maintenance for a period of at least three years after the birth to the extent that the mother cannot be expected to be engaged in gainful employment by reason of the care or upbringing of the child (see Question 20). If the father cares for the child he can claim maintenance. § 1615l applies whether or not the parents are partners to an informal relationship.[22]

GREECE

No. The law makes no provision for maintenance. However, the partners may agree that one shall pay maintenance to the other under the principle of freedom of contract (Art. 361 Greek Civil Code) and on terms to be jointly agreed. This is the spirit governing the provision of Art. 7 of Law 3719/2008 on the cohabitation pact.

HUNGARY

According to Arts 4:86-4:91 of the Hungarian Civil Code a former cohabitant may be entitled to maintenance in the case of separation. These articles are contained in the Third Part of the Family Law Book of the Hungarian Civil Code under the title of 'family law consequences of cohabitation'. These new provisions grant maintenance to the former cohabitant when he or she lacks the necessary means to maintain him/herself in a situation which has been brought about through no fault of his or her own, provided that the community of life existed for at least one year and they have a common child.[23] No maintenance may be claimed when the community of life had not lasted for at least a year and when there is no common child. These requirements are conjunctive and, as a consequence, when there is no common child there can be no claim

---

21 See Bulletin Officiel des Finances Publiques 11 December 2013 at para. 40. Available at: bofip.impots.gouv.fr/bofip/3357-PGP.html?identifiant=BOI-ENR-DMTG-20-10-10-2013 1211.

22 N. DETHLOFF, *Familienrecht*, Beck, Munich, 2012, at § 11 No. 83.

23 Art. 4:86(1) of the Hungarian Civil Code.

for maintenance, even after having cohabited for a rather long period of time. These are new rules, so judicial practice is still to be developed. The Civil Code of 1959 did not grant any maintenance upon separation for either former cohabitant.

REPUBLIC OF IRELAND

The law does not automatically grant maintenance to a former partner, but it does entitle partners to an informal relationship to apply for maintenance from their former partner under S. 175 of the Irish 2010 Act. The requirements are set out in S. 172. It provides that: 'If the qualified cohabitant satisfies the court that he or she is financially dependent on the other cohabitant and that the financial dependence arises from the relationship or the ending of the relationship, the court may, if satisfied that it is just and equitable to do so in all the circumstances, make the order concerned.'

ITALY

There is no legal provision regarding maintenance when partners in an informal relationship separate but, as no duty of support exists during the relationship, such a duty cannot be inferred after the separation.[24]

LATVIA

As there is no legal order on informal relationships in Latvia, there is no legal order on separation in an informal relationship.

By way of comparison one may consider the following. In dissolving a marriage or after dissolution of a marriage, a former spouse may claim maintenance from the other spouse commensurate with his or her financial state to ensure or maintain the previous level of welfare.[25]

LITHUANIA

The separation of partners in an informal relationship and its legal effects are not subject to legal regulation. Only the separation of married partners established by the court is regally regulated (Art. 3.73-3.80 of the Lithuanian Civil Code).

[24] Compare App. Roma 28 Novembre 1994, in *Dir. fam.* 1996, p. 980.
[25] S. 80 Latvian Civil Law.

There is no legal obligation to provide maintenance for a cohabitant.

LUXEMBOURG

No, the law does not grant maintenance to a former partner after separation.

THE NETHERLANDS

In the Dutch Civil Code, maintenance rights for ex-partners after a relationship breakdown are strictly limited to formal relationships (marriage and registered partnership). There is no such right in relation to informal partners. For this reason, in cases brought before the Supreme Court, claims for support are consistently denied.[26]

Partners may contract otherwise in a cohabitation contract[27] or in a separation agreement. However, it seems that in most cohabitation contracts drawn up by a notary no maintenance rights are agreed upon.[28] Whether a maintenance duty could arise on the basis of an implicit contract between informal partners is not clear.[29] Arguably, this would give rise to many problems, since it is unclear what the partners have agreed upon.

NORWAY

The law does not grant maintenance to a former partner when partners to an informal relationship separate.

PORTUGAL

No, the law does not grant maintenance to a former partner after separation.

---

26 HR 9 January 1987, *NJ* 1987, 927 (*Roozendaal/Van Dilst*); HR 8 June 2013, ECLI: NL:HR:2013:CA2925.

27 P. BLOKLAND, in: W.D. KOLKMAN and L.C.A. VERSTAPPEN (eds.), *Handboek Familie-vermogensrecht*, Walburg Pers, Zutphen, 2013, at 4.3.6.

28 W.M. SCHRAMA, P. KUIK and L.C.A. VERSTAPPEN, 'Samenlevingsovereenkomsten in de notariële praktijk', *Familie&Recht*, 2014, available at: familieenrecht.nl, at 14.6.

29 Hof Den Bosch 10 February 2015, ECLI:NL:GHSHE:2015:436: an informal partner without a written contract claimed maintenance on a contractual basis, which was rejected since there was no implicit contract.

RUSSIA

No.

SCOTLAND

There is no obligation of maintenance (in Scots law, 'aliment') during an informal relationship and similarly there is no such obligation following separation. On divorce or dissolution of a civil partnership, the obligation of aliment ceases and there is no provision for ex-spousal or ex-partner maintenance. Instead either party may apply to the court for financial provision. Similar but much more limited and discretionary provisions were introduced by S. 28 of the Family Law (Scotland) Act 2006 to provide for some financial provision on the breakdown of cohabitation. It would be highly misleading to describe any of these provisions as 'maintenance'. Both the provisions for divorce/dissolution and the much more limited provisions which apply on termination of cohabitation place emphasis on a one-off, clean break settlement rather than continuing maintenance.

SLOVAKIA

Slovak law does not grant maintenance to a former partner.

SLOVENIA

A partner who does not have the necessary means for subsistence, and through no fault of his or her own is unemployed, remains entitled to claim maintenance from the other partner, even after the separation. She or he may claim it by an individual action within one year after the separation, provided the conditions for maintenance already existed at the time of the separation and also exist at the time when the partner claims the maintenance (Art. 81 and 81a of the Slovenian Marriage Act).

SPAIN

In the Spanish Civil Code, in the absence of written rules, case law has granted economic compensation to a former spouse if the breakdown of the marriage has caused economic prejudice. The legal basis for such compensation is, however, uncertain.

Economic compensation after separation can be based on three different grounds:

- the existence of a non-contractual obligation;
- unjust enrichment; or
- the analogous application of the *prestación compensatoria* envisaged in divorce law.

The existence of non-contractual liability has been recognised in very few cases essentially because it presupposes an action that is wrongful. Unjust enrichment principles have been applied mostly in cases in which one of the partners has worked in the other's business. It requires proving that the increase in the assets of one partner and the corresponding decrease is unjust and therefore is not adapted to the realities of informal relationships.

Recent Supreme Court case law tends to be in favour of applying the legal provisions on *pensión compensatoria* of Art. 97 Spanish Civil Code, by analogy, even though this provision belongs to the rules on divorce or legal separation. This kind of economic compensation is granted in cases in which the break-up causes an economic imbalance between the partners. It may consist of periodic, usually monthly, payments or a lump sum payment. Depending on the circumstances it may be for life or be limited in time. Even though it is strictly speaking not a maintenance claim it will be developed in the following sections.

In the Catalan Civil Code, Art. 234-10 allows either partner to claim maintenance from the other, if such maintenance is needed to provide proper care for his or her living needs, in any of the following cases:

- when cohabitation has diminished the ability of the applicant to earn income;
- when the applicant has the custody of common children in circumstances where his ability to earn an income is diminished.

Agreements to waive maintenance are null and void to the extent that they compromise the ability of the partner entitled thereto to meet his basic needs, unless such agreements are incorporated into a proposed settlement pursuant to Art. 234-6 Catalan Civil Code.

If either partner dies within one year from the termination of the partnership, the other partner may, within three months following the death, claim from the heirs his or her right to maintenance. The same rule applies if the proceedings to claim maintenance end by reason of the death of the obligor partner.

According to Art. 234-11 Catalan Civil Code maintenance may be awarded in the form of a lump sum or as an allowance. Without an agreement on the form of payment, the judicial authority will decide. Maintenance in the form of an allowance is temporary, with a maximum of three annual instalments, unless maintenance is based on the reduced ability of the creditor to earn an income resulting from the custody of common children. In this case, maintenance may be awarded for the duration of the custody.

SWEDEN

There is no such right under Swedish law.

SWITZERLAND

In Switzerland, the law does not grant maintenance after separation to a former partner in an informal relationship, irrespective of any relationship-related detriments.[30]

[30] R. AEBI-MÜLLER and C. WIDMER, 'Rechtsregeln für nichteheliches Zusammenleben in der Schweiz', in: I. KROPPENBERG, D. SCHWAB, D. HENRICH, P. GOTTWALD and A. SPICKHOFF, *Rechtsregeln für nichteheliches Zusammenleben*, Gieseking, Bielefeld, 2009, at p. 65, 92 et seq.

QUESTION 35

What relevance, if any, upon the amount of maintenance is given to the following factors/circumstances:

a. The creditor's needs and the debtor's ability to pay maintenance?

b. The creditor's contributions during the relationship (such as the raising of children)?

c. The standard of living during the relationship?

d. Other factors/circumstances (such as giving up his/her career)?

AUSTRIA

Due to the fact that Austrian law does not currently grant maintenance to a former partner, no criteria for determining the amount of maintenance exist.

BELGIUM

a. The creditor's needs and the debtor's ability to pay maintenance?

Needs *versus* the ability to pay are only indirectly relevant. Inequality between the former partners may be an element for the courts to accept that a natural obligation exists.[1] A need may also be an element to prove damage in a tort claim.

1 Antwerp 1 February 2006, *RW* 2007-08, 1816, with note WERMOES; District Court of Brussels 6 May 2008, *Act.dr.fam.* 2009, 93, reforming the more flexible first degree decision: Justice of the Peace Anderlecht (1) 25 October 2007, *T.Vred.* 2010, 224.

b. The creditor's contributions during the relationship (such as the raising of children)?
The creditor's contributions are only indirectly relevant to prove the existence of a natural obligation or of damages.

c. The standard of living during the relationship?
The standard of living during the relationship is only indirectly relevant to prove the existence of a natural obligation or of damages.

d. Other factors/circumstances (such as giving up his/her career)?
Other circumstances are only indirectly relevant to prove the existence of a natural obligation or of damages. For example, giving up a career or contributions during a relationship may constitute circumstances in which the courts may conclude that a natural obligation to provide for a former partner exists.

BULGARIA

Not applicable.

CROATIA

According to Art. 295 of the Croatian Family Act and Art. 39 paragraph 2 in relation to Art. 4 of the Croatian Partnership Act, the answer relates to both cohabitants and same-sex informal partners.

a. The creditor's needs and the debtor's ability to pay maintenance?
According to Art. 295 in relation to Art. 303 of the Croatian Family Act and Art. 39 in relation to Art. 4 of the Croatian Partnership Act, the court shall approve of a maintenance claim if the applicant does not have sufficient means for subsistence, is incapable of working or cannot find gainful employment and if such means cannot be obtained based on his/her assets, and if the defendant has sufficient resources and opportunities to support himself/herself.

This general proportionality principle refers to the creditor's needs, on the one side and the debtor's ability to pay maintenance, on the other side, which is applied by the courts in every case respectively.

b. The creditor's contributions during the relationship (such as the raising of children)?
According to Art. 295 in relation to Art. 303 of the Croatian Family Act and Art. 39 in relation to Art. 4 of the Croatian Partnership Act, on the occasion of deciding on a partner's maintenance, the court shall particularly consider the exercise of parental responsibility and the division of family obligations during the relationship.

c. The standard of living during the relationship?
According to Art. 295 in relation to Art. 303 of the Croatian Family Act and Art. 39 in relation to Art. 4 of the Croatian Partnership Act, on the occasion of deciding on a partner's maintenance, the court shall particularly consider the standard of living during the relationship.

d. Other factors/circumstances (such as giving up his/her career)?
There are no other relevant factors/circumstances in this context.

CZECH REPUBLIC

a. The creditor's needs and the debtor's ability to pay maintenance?
According to S. 913/1 Czech Civil Code, to determine the extent of maintenance, the reasonable needs of the creditor and his property situation are crucial, as well as the abilities, potential and property situation of the debtor. Therefore, the creditor's needs and the debtor's ability to pay maintenance are equally important in determining the amount of maintenance.

b. The creditor's contributions during the relationship (such as the raising of children)?
According to S. 913/2 Czech Civil Code, it is necessary to consider a creditor's care of the family household, as well as a debtor's care of the family household. Therefore, a creditor's contribution during the relationship (such as the raising of children) is a factor with relevance to the amount of maintenance. S. 913/2 second sentence Czech Civil Code states: account should also be taken of the fact that the obligor personally cares for the obligee, and of the extent to which he does so; account must also be taken of the obligor's care for the family household, where appropriate.

c. The standard of living during the relationship?
No relevance is given to this factor.

d. Other factors/circumstances (such as giving up his/her career)?

Other factors which have relevance to the amount of maintenance are, according to S. 913/1 Czech Civil Code, a creditor's property situation. Section 913/2 first sentence states: in evaluating the abilities, potential and property situation of the obligor, it should also be considered whether or not the obligor has given up, without a good cause, a more favourable employment or gainful activity, or property benefit, or whether or not he is taking unreasonable property risks.

DENMARK

Danish law does not contain any specific regulation with regard to the payment of maintenance to a former partner.

ENGLAND AND WALES

There is no maintenance or other financial provision for the partner but financial provision in the form of capital lump sums or transfer or settlement of property orders for the benefit of a child under 18 can be made on an application under Schedule 1 English Children Act 1989 and is separate from child support.

The criteria specified in para. 4 of the Schedule include having regard to all the circumstances and specifically to:

- the income and financial needs and resources of each parent and those of the child;
- any disability of the child and the manner in which the child was expected to be educated or trained.
- The standard of living of the couple when they were together is not specified (in contrast to the divorce context) and giving up a career would be irrelevant.

However, in case law, it has been held that the sum awarded to the partner caring for the child can include a care allowance element which can take account of the child care costs until the child is 18 or can be used by the carer to compensate for loss of employment (see *Re P (Child: Financial Provision)* [2003] EWCA Civ 837, [2003] 2 FLR 865).

ESTONIA

a. The creditor's needs and the debtor's ability to pay maintenance?

The partners in an informal relationship have no mutual maintenance obligation towards one another. The only exception is a mutual provision of maintenance in the case of the birth of a child, as prescribed by § 111 of the Estonian Family Law Act.

As the scope of the maintenance obligation and the way in which maintenance should be paid, as well as other issues regarding the maintenance obligation and its fulfilment, have not been directly prescribed in the maintenance obligation stipulated in § 111 of the Estonian Family Law Act, the non-regulation of these questions does not correspond to the meaning and objective of the Estonian Family Law Act, according to the position of the Supreme Court. Thus, according to the assessment of the Civil Chamber of the Supreme Court, due to the absence of these provisions, within the meaning of a legal relation under § 4 of the General Part of the Estonian Civil Code Act, the provisions regulating maintenance for relatives can be applied to the maintenance obligation, as prescribed in § 111 of the Estonian Family Law Act, to the extent that they correspond to the meaning of the maintenance obligation stipulated in § 111 of the Estonian Family Law Act. Section 1 of § 111 of the Estonian Family Law Act must be interpreted as follows: according to the provision referred to, the mother of a child has the right to demand maintenance from the father of the child only if she is unable to maintain herself during that time. For this purpose, it must be assessed what are the reasonable expenses of the child's mother during the specified period and which costs the mother can meet from her own income, i.e. from any compensation and remuneration received. If the financial resources available to the mother of the child are sufficient to cover the usual expenses, the mother of the child does not require assistance and she has no right to receive maintenance from the father of the child on the basis of § 111(1) of the Estonian Family Law Act.[2]

b. The creditor's contributions during the relationship (such as the raising of children)?

The partners in an informal relationship have no mutual maintenance obligation towards one another. The only exception is the mutual provision of maintenance, prescribed by § 111 of the Estonian Family Law Act, in the case of the birth of a child. If the partner in an informal relationship is entitled to receive maintenance in the case of the birth of a

2 Decision of the Civil Chamber of the Supreme Court 3-2-1-198-13, at para. 16, 17.

child, the scope of the maintenance shall be determined on the basis of the needs and usual lifestyle of the person entitled to receive maintenance (§ 99(1) Estonian Family Law Act).[3]

c. The standard of living during the relationship?

The partners in an informal relationship have no mutual maintenance obligation towards one another. If the partner in informal relationship is entitled to receive maintenance in the case of the birth of a child, the scope of the maintenance shall be determined on the basis of the needs and usual lifestyle of the person entitled to receive maintenance (§ 99(1) Estonian Family Law Act).[4]

d. Other factors/circumstances (such as giving up his/her career)?

The partners in an informal relationship have no mutual maintenance obligation towards one another. § 111 of the Estonian Family Law Act prescribes the mutual provision of maintenance in the case of the birth of a child. Presumably, § 102(1) of the Estonian Family Law Act shall still be valid, according to which a person is released from the obligation to provide maintenance in so far as he or she, considering his or her other obligations and financial situation, is unable to provide maintenance to another person without detrimentally affecting his or her own usual lifestyle.

Presumably also § 103 of the Estonian Family Law Act should be valid to the post-birth maintenance obligation when a child has been born, according to which the court may release a person from the obligation to provide maintenance, or may limit the obligation in time, or may reduce the amount of support if it would be extremely unfair to request the performance of the obligation, in particular if: 1) the need of the person entitled to receive maintenance has been caused by his or her unreasonable conduct; 2) the entitled person has severely violated his or her obligation towards the person obliged to provide maintenance; 3) the entitled person has been convicted of a criminal offence committed against the person obliged to provide maintenance or a person connected with him or her.

FINLAND

Not applicable, as there is no legal duty to pay maintenance.

---

3 Decision of the Civil Chamber of the Supreme Court 3-2-1-198-13, at para. 18.

4 Decision of the Civil Chamber of the Supreme Court 3-2-1-198-13, at para. 18.

FRANCE

Not applicable.

GERMANY

This question has no relevance in German legislation (see Question 34).

GREECE

a. The creditor's needs and the debtor's ability to pay maintenance?

This is taken into consideration in deciding maintenance paid by one spouse or former spouse to another. This condition applies even in the case of the cohabitation pact (Art. 7 Law 3719/2008).

b. The creditor's contributions during the relationship (such as the raising of children)?

This might be taken into account in contractually setting the level of maintenance. The raising of the children is taken into account in the case of maintenance payable after a divorce (Art. 1442 Greek Civil Code).

c. The standard of living during the relationship?

This is taken into account only when the spouses cease to live together (Art. 1390(1) and 1391 Greek Civil Code).

d. Other factors/circumstances (such as giving up his/her career)?

There are none.

HUNGARY

a. The creditor's needs and the debtor's ability to pay maintenance?

The creditor's needs (emerging from a situation which has been brought about through no fault of his or her own) and the debtor's ability to pay are basic requirements. The Hungarian Civil Code does not provide any further details but only elaborates upon a lack of means[5] and the ability to pay by stating that someone is not obliged to maintain his or her former partner if it endangers his or her own necessary maintenance or the maintenance of his or her child.[6]

---

5 Art. 4:86(1) of the Hungarian Civil Code.

6 Art. 4:88 of the Hungarian Civil Code.

b. The creditor's contributions during the relationship (such as the raising of children)?

Only a lack of means on the part of the claimant is relevant. Nevertheless, the fact that the creditor largely contributed to the common household, e.g. by raising children at home, is taken into account but only indirectly when this contribution has resulted in his or her lack of means after separation. Hungarian law only provides for maintenance for a former cohabitant when the former cohabitants have a common child, so raising a common child may have a value but other contributions have no weight when the cohabitants do not have a common child.

c. The standard of living during the relationship?

The maintenance of a former cohabitant has been modelled upon that of former spouses and the granting of spousal maintenance; the exact amount of such maintenance does not depend on the earlier standard of living. As neither any judicial provision nor the case law takes the earlier standard of living into account when spousal maintenance is being considered, it does not have any relevance in the maintenance of a former cohabitant, either.

d. Other factors/circumstances (such as giving up his/her career)?

The situation where the creditor is unworthy of maintenance is mentioned in the Hungarian Civil Code. A former cohabitant does not have a right to maintenance if his or her extremely objectionable behaviour has primarily contributed to the termination of the cohabitation or if his or her behaviour after the termination of the cohabitation has seriously damaged the interests of his or her former cohabitant or the relatives of that person with whom he or she lives. This unworthiness is taken into account by the court, but only when the debtor raises this issue and the behaviour of the debtor is then also taken into account.[7]

REPUBLIC OF IRELAND

See S. 173 of the Irish 2010 Act, as set out above at Question 20(c). There are a range of factors and circumstances in S. 173(3)(a)-(j) that are relevant in determining the amount of maintenance that will be ordered. The court is required to have regard to each factor and there is no hierarchy of factors. The court has discretion as to how much weight to give to each consideration, and which to consider.

7 Art. 4:87(1)-(2) of the Hungarian Civil Code.

ITALY

Not applicable.

LATVIA

As there is no legal order on informal relationships in Latvia, there is no legal order on maintenance following separation in an informal relationship.

By way of comparison one may consider the following. In connection with the divorce of a married couple, S. 81 of the Latvian Civil Law determines that the duty to ensure the previous level of welfare or maintenance of the former spouse ceases if the income of the former spouse ensures the previous level of welfare or maintenance; the former spouse avoids obtaining the means for maintenance through his or her own work; and there are other circumstances which show that the need to obtain maintenance from the former spouse no longer exists.

LITHUANIA

See the answer to Question 34.

LUXEMBOURG

Not applicable.

THE NETHERLANDS

Since the law does not recognise a maintenance right/duty for informal partners after a relationship breakdown, this is not relevant.

NORWAY

See the answer to Question 34, as no maintenance is granted, this question is not relevant.

PORTUGAL

Not applicable following answer to Question 34.

RUSSIA
Not applicable.

SCOTLAND
As there is no obligation of maintenance, this question is not relevant.

SLOVAKIA
Slovak law does not grant maintenance to a former partner.

SLOVENIA
a. The creditor's needs and the debtor's ability to pay maintenance?
Maintenance is decided in relation to the needs of the claimant and the capacity of the person liable to pay, in a monthly amount in advance, and is claimed from the moment when the maintenance suit was filed.[8]

b. The creditor's contributions during the relationship (such as the raising of children)?
This circumstance is not relevant in Slovene maintenance law for calculating the maintenance to be paid to a partner.

c. The standard of living during the relationship?
This circumstance is not relevant in Slovene maintenance law for calculating the maintenance to be paid to a partner.

d. Other factors/circumstances (such as giving up his/her career)?
The circumstance of a partner giving up his/her career is not relevant in Slovene maintenance law for calculating the maintenance to be paid to a partner. However, a court may reject a maintenance claim if the payment of maintenance to the person entitled, in view of the causes of the breakdown of the marriage, would be unfair to the person liable to pay or if the entitled person at any time before or after the separation has committed a criminal offence against the liable person or anyone close to him: i.e., the children or parents of the person liable (Art. 81a of the Slovenian Marriage Act).

[8] Maintenance may not be claimed retrospectively.

SPAIN

a. The creditor's needs and the debtor's ability to pay maintenance?

According to the Spanish Civil Code the judge takes into consideration the creditor's needs and the debtor's ability to pay in order to decide both whether to grant economic compensation and then to fix the amount payable. Article 97.2 Spanish Civil Code contains a non-exhaustive list of factors. An advanced age and poor health are usually important factors in order to be granted economic compensation. The ability to pursue gainful employment is also taken into account; in this context it is worthwhile highlighting that case law usually considers that this employment should be in accordance with the partner's education and social status. The economic means of the debtor and the creditor are also relevant in order to decide whether there is an economic imbalance between the partners and if so to grant compensation and decide its amount.

Catalan law only awards maintenance to a partner who is in need if such need is related to the relationship. The creditor needs to prove that: cohabitation has diminished the ability of the creditor to earn income; or the creditor's ability to earn an income is diminished because he or she has the custody of common children (Art. 234-10 Catalan Civil Code).

Case law usually relates the amount of maintenance to the economic means and ability to pay of the debtor (STSJ Catalonia 9-05-2005).

b. The creditor's contributions during the relationship (such as the raising of children)?

Article 97 of the Spanish Civil Code specifically mentions past and future contributions to the family as a factor to be taken into account, essentially because the raising of children is considered to be an obstacle to full professional development.

Under Catalan law the creditor's contributions during the relationship are indirectly taken into account only if they have diminished his or her ability to earn income (Art. 234-10.1 Catalan Civil Code).

c. The standard of living during the relationship?

The whole purpose of *pension compensatoria* under Spanish law is to restore the imbalance between the economic situation of each of the partners after break-up. Though not specifically mentioned as a factor to be taken into account, the standard of living during the relationship plays a decisive role because the economic situation of each partner needs to be compared with that enjoyed in the past.

The provisions of the Catalan Civil Code do not refer to the standard of living enjoyed during the relationship.

d. Other factors/circumstances (such as giving up his/her career)?
Other factors mentioned in the Spanish Civil Code (Art. 97) include participation in the business or profession of the other partner, the duration of the marriage and an eventual loss of pension rights. The list is open-ended and any other factor may be taken into account. The fact that the creditor has given up his or her career can also be taken into account when it comes to considering contributions to the family.

The approach of Catalan law is rather restrictive and does not seem to allow taking into account any other factors

SWEDEN

Having regard to the fact that former partners to an informal relationship have no duty to support each other, these questions lack relevance from the point of view of Swedish law.

SWITZERLAND

See the answer to Question 34, question is not relevant.

QUESTION 36

What modes of calculation (e.g. percentages, guidelines), if any, apply to the determination of the amount of maintenance?

AUSTRIA

Due to the fact that Austrian law does not currently grant maintenance to a former partner, no methods of calculation for the determination of the amount of maintenance have been developed.

BELGIUM

Since claims based on tort law or on a natural obligation are not maintenance claims, the traditional modes of calculation do not apply, even not by analogy. There are no specific modes of calculation either.

BULGARIA

Not applicable.

CROATIA

There are no foreseen methods of calculation which apply to the determination of the amount of maintenance between partners.

According to Art. 307 of the Croatian Family Act and Art. 39 in relation to Art. 4 of the Croatian Partnership Act, while assessing the needs of the dependent partner, the court shall take into account her/his income, property, ability to work, employment, health status and other factors which influence the decision on maintenance. On the occasion of assessing the ability of the liable partner to pay maintenance, the court shall take into account his/her financial situation, all of her/his income and the real possibility of gaining profit, as well as her/his own needs and other maintenance liabilities laid down by the law.

CZECH REPUBLIC

The amount of maintenance is determined using guidelines established in S. 913/1 Czech Civil Code: to determine the extent of maintenance the reasonable needs of the creditor and his property situation, as well as the abilities, potential and property situation of the debtor, are crucial. There are no methods of calculation using percentages, there are only recommendations about the amount of maintenance for children, made by the Ministry of Justice, which should be taken into account, but these recommendations are not binding on judges.[1]

DENMARK

Danish law does not contain any specific regulation with regard to the payment of maintenance to a former partner.

ENGLAND AND WALES

None.

ESTONIA

The partners in an informal relationship have no mutual maintenance obligation towards one another. The only exception is the provision of mutual maintenance, prescribed by § 111 of the Estonian Family Law Act, in the case of the birth of child. The scope of the maintenance shall be determined on the basis of the needs and usual lifestyle of the person entitled to receive maintenance (§ 99(1) Estonian Family Law Act).[2]

The post-birth maintenance obligation when a child has been born will exist irrespective of whether the parties have lived together or separately during the period referred to in § 111(1) of the Estonian Family Law Act, thus, in the case of the aforementioned obligation, the duration of as well as the end of the cohabitation is of no importance.[3]

---

1 See the recommended chart for establishing the amount of maintenance, available at: www.profipravo.cz/index.php?page=article&id_category=13&id_article=253757&csum=ea038f57.

2 Decision of the Civil Chamber of the Supreme Court 3-2-1-198-13, at para. 18.

3 Decision of the Civil Chamber of the Supreme Court 3-2-1-198-13, at para. 20.

FINLAND

Not applicable.

FRANCE

Not applicable.

GERMANY

Not relevant (see Question 34).

GREECE

There are no rules and no method for determining maintenance.

HUNGARY

There are no guidelines in Hungarian law concerning the calculation of maintenance. According to the Hungarian Civil Code maintenance is to be paid in periodical payments which are a fixed amount each month[4] and the court cannot award monthly payments expressed in percentage terms. The total amount of maintenance which the debtor has to pay cannot exceed half of his or her income.

There are several factors which are taken into account when determining the debtor's obligation to pay, namely the essential and reasonable needs of the creditor and the debtor's ability to pay.

REPUBLIC OF IRELAND

There are none, save for the factors set out in S. 173 of the Irish Civil Partnership and Certain Rights and Obligations of Cohabitants Act 2010.

ITALY

Not applicable.

---

4 Arts 4:207 and 4:205(6) of the Hungarian Civil Code.

LATVIA

As there is no legal order on informal relationships in Latvia, there is no legal order on maintenance following separation in an informal relationship.

LITHUANIA

See the answer to Question 34.

LUXEMBOURG

Not applicable.

THE NETHERLANDS

Since the law does not recognise a maintenance right/duty for informal partners after a relationship breakdown, this is not relevant. If the ex-partners agreed upon a maintenance right/duty in a cohabitation contract, it depends on what terms they agreed upon. Partners have the right to contract freely and they can contractually opt in according to the legislation on ex-spouses. It is not clarified whether the legislation on ex-spouses can be applied to a contractual maintenance right if this is not explicitly agreed upon. If, for instance, the cohabitation contract does not contain a provision on the calculation system, can the courts apply the judicial guidelines developed by the courts for spousal maintenance?[5]

NORWAY

Not applicable, see answer to Question 34.

PORTUGAL

Not applicable following to Question 34.

RUSSIA

Not applicable.

---

5 S.W. AUTAR-MATAWLIE, W.H.A. LEONARD-STRIEN and M. VAN YPEREN-GROENLEER, 'Einde van de samenleving', in: A. AUTAR, W. KOLKMAN and W. SCHRAMA (eds.), *Compendium samenwonen*, SDU, The Hague, 2013, at p. 334.

SCOTLAND

As there is no obligation of maintenance, this question is not relevant.

SLOVAKIA

Slovak law does not grant maintenance to a former partner.

SLOVENIA

The amount of maintenance is determined only on the basis of the needs of the recipient and the capacity of the former partner who has to pay the maintenance. Slovene maintenance law does not recognise maintenance tables or similar models for calculating maintenance.

SPAIN

The law does not specify any particular mode of calculation nor are there any official guidelines, but in practice it seems that between 20 to 30% of the income of the debtor is in most cases considered adequate. However, it also depends on whether there are other concurring maintenance claims.

As regards maintenance for children, there are some guiding tables to determine claims issued by the Consejo General del Poder Judicial.[6]

SWEDEN

See above, answers to Question 34-35, rendering this question irrelevant from the point of view of Swedish law.

SWITZERLAND

See the answer to Question 34, question is not relevant.

6 Tablas orientadoras para determinar las pensiones alimenticias de los hijos en los procesos de familia elaboradas por el CGPJ, available at: www.poderjudicial.es/cgpj/es/Servicios/Utilidades/Calculo-de-pensiones-alimenticias.

QUESTION 37

Where the law provides for maintenance, to what extent, if at all, is it limited to a specific period of time?

AUSTRIA

Currently, Austrian law does not grant maintenance to a former partner.[1] However, a maintenance claim which results from the birth of a child according to S. 235 General Austrian Civil Code is limited to a period of eight weeks after the birth and becomes statute-barred after three years from the birth.[2]

BELGIUM

Since claims based on tort law or on a natural obligation are not maintenance claims, the traditional time restrictions do not apply, not even by analogy. There are no specific time restrictions either. In cases where a former partner had to provide, the payment would be a lump sum or limited to a very short period.[3]

BULGARIA

Not applicable.

---

1 F. MEISSEL, 'Unterhaltsansprüche aus Lebensgemeinschaft? Nichteheliche Lebensgemeinschaften und Unterhalt (Teil II)', *EF-Z*, 2008, at p. 13.

2 See the answer to Question 34.

3 Justice of the Peace Sint-Jans Molenbeek 26 September 2000, *AJT T.Huur* 2000, 29 ('a couple of months' after a cohabitation of 12-15 months); Justice of the Peace Anderlecht (1) 25 October 2007, *T. Vred.* 2010, 224 (16 months after a cohabitation of 17 years), confirmed by the District Court of Brussels 6 May 2008, *Act.dr.fam.* 2009, 93. Compare with agreements: Antwerp 1 February 2006, *RW* 2007-08, 1816, with note WERMOES (one year, quickly substituted with a lump-sum payment); Justice of the Peace Etterbeek 2 June 2008, *T.Vred.* 2010, 235 (six years).

CROATIA

According to Art. 298 of the Croatian Family Act and Art. 39 in relation to Art. 4 of the Croatian Partnership Act, the court shall adjudicate a one-year maintenance obligation, particularly if the life union did not last for long or if the respondent soon becomes able to provide for him/herself in some other way. In special cases, the court may extend the maintenance obligation. The submission of claims for an extension of a maintenance obligation is only permitted after the expiry of the period to which the maintenance refers. Exceptionally and on just grounds, the court can deliver a decision ordering the permanent settlement of maintenance.

CZECH REPUBLIC

In the case of maintenance for an unmarried mother, it is limited to two years after the child was born. (S. 920/1 Czech Civil Code: if the child's mother is not married to the child's father, the child's father is to provide her with maintenance for two years from the birth of the child and provide her with a reasonable contribution to cover the costs associated with pregnancy and childbirth. The man whose paternity is presumed has a duty to reimburse the costs associated with pregnancy and childbirth even if the child is not born alive. Section 922/2: maintenance and support for an unmarried mother and covering the costs associated with pregnancy and childbirth may also be granted retrospectively, but for a maximum of two years subsequent to the date of childbirth.)

DENMARK

Danish law does not contain any specific regulation with regard to the payment of maintenance to a former partner.

ENGLAND AND WALES

Not applicable.

ESTONIA

The partners in an informal relationship have no mutual maintenance obligation towards one another. § 111 of the Estonian Family Law Act prescribes the provision of mutual maintenance in the case of the birth of a child. The obligation to provide maintenance commences no earlier than four months before the birth of a child and terminates after three years have passed from the birth of the child (§ 111(2) Estonian Family Law Act).

FINLAND

Not applicable.

FRANCE

Not applicable.

GERMANY

Not relevant (see Question 34).

GREECE

There are no such rules.

HUNGARY

Maintenance may be awarded for a limited period of time or until a certain event or condition occurs or takes place, provided that the creditor will not be left with insufficient means after that time.[4] As the maintenance of a former cohabitant is a new provision there is, as yet, no judicial practice.

REPUBLIC OF IRELAND

Section 175(4) of the Irish 2010 Act provides that the period specified in an order cannot start earlier than the date of application for the order, and is to end no later than the death of the first qualified cohabitant. Other than this, there is no specific time period set out in the Act for which a qualified cohabitant will be required to continue to pay maintenance.

An order ceases to have effect upon the marriage or registration in a civil partnership, or in a legal relationship with its own order under S. 5, of the

[4] Art. 4:209(1)-(2) of the Hungarian Civil Code.

qualified cohabitant in whose favour the order was made, except as where payments are due on the date of the marriage or registration.

ITALY

Not applicable.

LATVIA

As there is no legal order on informal relationships in Latvia, there is no legal order on maintenance following separation in an informal relationship.

By way of comparison one may consider the following. In connection with the divorce of a married couple, S. 81 of the Latvian Civil Law determines that the duty to ensure the previous level of welfare or maintenance of the former spouse terminates when the same amount of time has passed subsequent to the dissolution of the marriage, or the declaration of the annulment of the marriage, as the duration of the relevant dissolved marriage or cohabitation in the marriage, which has been declared annulled.

LITHUANIA

See the answer to Question 34.

LUXEMBOURG

Not applicable.

THE NETHERLANDS

Since the law does not recognise a maintenance right/duty for informal partners after a relationship breakdown, this is not relevant. If parties agreed upon a maintenance right/duty, it depends on what terms they agreed upon. Partners have the right to contract freely, so they will generally include a specific time period. It is not clarified whether the legislation on ex-spouses can be applied if the contract contains no specific period of time.

NORWAY

Not applicable, see answer to Question 34.

PORTUGAL

Not applicable following to Question 34.

RUSSIA

Not applicable.

SCOTLAND

As there is no obligation of maintenance, this question is not relevant.

SLOVAKIA

Slovak law does not grant maintenance to a former partner.

SLOVENIA

Maintenance is determined either for an indefinite period[5] or more often for a specific period of time which is required for the partner to adapt to the new situation and to make any necessary arrangements (for example, concerning a loss of employment, or when ceasing an extramarital union in which they agreed that one of them would remain at home and look after the children during their infancy).[6]

SPAIN

Under Spanish law the judicial authority has discretion to decide whether to limit compensation to a specific period of time or grant it for

5 An inadequate knowledge of the Slovene language is an impediment to employment that is possible to remedy within a suitable time so it is not a ground to award maintenance for an indefinite period - decision of the Supreme Court RS, No. II Ips 617/96 of 1 April 1998, in: A. JELENC PUKLAVEC, M. KONČINA - PETERNEL, D. OGRIZEK (ed.), *Vrhovno sodišče Republike Slovenije, civilni oddelek: Zbirka odločb 1998 (Supreme Court of the Republic of Slovenia, civil department: Collection of Decisions 1998)*, Gospodarski vestnik, Ljubljana, 1999, at p. 324 et seq.

6 A determination of maintenance for a partner does not appear very often in practice since partners (including women) are generally employed on a full-time basis.

life. The factors listed under Art. 97 Spanish Civil Code also operate as factors in order to decide the duration of maintenance.

Article 234-11.3 Catalan Civil Code limits the duration of maintenance to three years. If maintenance is granted because the custody of children diminishes the ability of the creditor to earn income, it might be extended for the duration of custody.

SWEDEN

Not relevant in Sweden.

SWITZERLAND

See the answer to Question 34, question is not relevant.

QUESTION 38

What relevance, if any, do changed circumstances have on the right to continued maintenance or the amount due?

AUSTRIA

Currently, Austrian law does not grant maintenance to a former partner.

BELGIUM

Since claims based on tort law or on a natural obligation are not maintenance claims, the traditional criterion of changed circumstances does not apply, not even by analogy. We have not found any relevant case law regarding this question.

BULGARIA

Not applicable.

CROATIA

According to Art. 285 of the Croatian Family Act and Art. 39 paragraph 2 in relation to Art. 4 of the Croatian Partnership Act, the answer relates to both cohabitants and same-sex informal partners.

According to Art. 285 of the Croatian Family Act, both the provider and receiver of maintenance can apply to the court to increase or decrease the amount of maintenance, to decide on the termination of the maintenance settlement or to modify the form of maintenance determined by the previous decision if the referring circumstances have changed. In compliance with the Croatian Family Act, such a legal order refers to all persons, including partners in informal partnerships, affected by maintenance rights and obligations.

CZECH REPUBLIC

When circumstances change, the creditor or debtor can raise this fact at court. This could result in a lower or higher amount of maintenance, or even the end of the obligation to provide maintenance, depending on the nature of the changed circumstances (see S. 163 Czech Civil Procedure Code, Act No. 99/1963 Coll.). For example, a court may reduce the period of two years of the debtor's obligation to provide maintenance, if a woman enters into marriage with another man, or if the child dies.[1]

DENMARK

Danish law does not contain any specific regulation with regard to the payment of maintenance to a former partner.

ENGLAND AND WALES

Not applicable.

ESTONIA

According to the position of the Supreme Court,[2] the obligation to provide maintenance in the case of the birth of a child only applies if the entitled person is unable to maintain him or herself during the specified period. Thus, if the financial situation of the person entitled to receive maintenance changes, the scope of the maintenance may change as well. The scope of the maintenance may also presumably change (although the Estonian Family Law Act does not include a direct regulation thereon) if the economic situation of the obligated person deteriorates so that, when taking his or her other obligations and financial situation into consideration, he or she is unable to provide maintenance to the other person, without detrimentally affecting his or her own usual lifestyle.

FINLAND

Not applicable.

---

1 Z. KRÁLÍČKOVÁ, *Občanský zákoník II. Rodinné právo (§655-975). Komentář*, C.H. Beck, Prague, 2014, at p. 1126 (§920).

2 Decision of the Civil Chamber of the Supreme Court 3-2-1-198-13, at para. 18.

FRANCE

Not applicable.

GERMANY

Not relevant (see Question 34).

GREECE

There are no relevant rules.

HUNGARY

If circumstances change and the unaltered payment of maintenance damages one party's important legal interests either the debtor or the creditor may apply to the court to have the amount of maintenance amended.[3] According to the case law concerning spousal maintenance – as there is, as yet, no judicial practice concerning the maintenance of former cohabitants – all the circumstances are carefully scrutinised in such cases.

REPUBLIC OF IRELAND

Changes in circumstances can influence the right to continued maintenance or the amount due. In this regard, S. 173(6) provides as follows:

> 'The court may, on the application of the qualified cohabitant or the other cohabitant, if it considers it proper to do so having regard to any change in the circumstances of the case and to any new evidence, including any change in the circumstances occasioned by a variation by another order of the court made in favour of a person to whom the other cohabitant is or was married, by order—
> (a) vary or discharge an order under Section 175 or 187,
> (b) suspend any provision of such an order,
> (c) suspend temporarily any provision of such an order,
> (d) revive the operation of a suspended provision,
> (e) further vary an order previously varied under this section, or
> (f) further suspend or revive the operation of a provision previously suspended or revived under this section.'

3 Art. 4:210(1) of the Hungarian Civil Code.

ITALY

Not applicable.

LATVIA

As there is no legal order on informal relationships in Latvia, there is no legal order on maintenance following separation in an informal relationship.

LITHUANIA

See the answer to Question 34.

LUXEMBOURG

Not applicable.

THE NETHERLANDS

Since the law does not recognise a maintenance right/duty for informal partners after a relationship breakdown, this is not relevant. If parties agreed upon a maintenance right/duty, it depends on what terms they agreed upon. Partners have the right to contract freely, so they could include provisions to this extent.

NORWAY

Not applicable, see answer to Question 34.

PORTUGAL

Not applicable following to Question 34.

RUSSIA

Not applicable.

SCOTLAND

As there is no obligation of maintenance, this question is not relevant.

SLOVAKIA

Slovak law does not grant maintenance to a former partner.

SLOVENIA

At the request of the recipient or payee, a court may increase, reduce or terminate, with executive title, specific maintenance payments if the needs of the recipient or the capacity of the payee on the basis of which the maintenance was determined change or if the recipient commits a criminal offence against the payee, or the children or parents of the payee (Art. 82c of the Slovenian Marriage Act).

SPAIN

Maintenance can be modified if circumstances have substantially changed in a manner that is not temporary and changes have not been brought about intentionally. Whether or not this modification will be granted by the courts very much depends on the facts of the case. Retirement and unemployment are factors that very often lead to a reduction of the amounts due. Maintenance can also be modified if the creditor inherits property, receives a pension or substantially improves his or her economic situation. See Art. 142 Spanish Civil Code, and 237-9 and 237-13 Catalan Civil Code.

SWEDEN

Not relevant in Sweden.

SWITZERLAND

See the answer to Question 34, question is not relevant.

QUESTION 39

Is the maintenance claim extinguished upon the claimant entering:

a. Into a formal relationship with another person?

b. Into an informal relationship with another person?

AUSTRIA

Currently, Austrian law does not grant maintenance to a former partner. However, it should be noted that the maintenance claim of a partner living in an informal relationship against his/her ex-spouse is suspended for the duration of the informal relationship.[1]

BELGIUM

These circumstances are not relevant. We have not found any relevant case law.

BULGARIA

Not applicable.

CROATIA

a. Into a formal relationship with another person?

According to Art. 300 of the Croatian Family Act and Art. 39 in relation to Art. 4 of the Croatian Partnership Act, maintenance claims are extinguished upon the claimant entering into a formal relationship with another person.

1 Austrian Supreme Court, Legal Proposition RS0047108, see Judgement of 21.05.2014, 3 Ob 31/14a.

b. Into an informal relationship with another person?

According to Art. 300 of the Croatian Family Act and Art. 39 in relation to Art. 4 of the Croatian Partnership Act, maintenance claims are extinguished upon the claimant entering into an informal relationship with another person.[2]

CZECH REPUBLIC

a. Into a formal relationship with another person?

In the case of a formal relationship with another person, the maintenance claim of an unmarried mother is extinguished from the moment of entering a formal relationship, because a husband has a maintenance obligation towards his wife.

b. Into an informal relationship with another person?

Generally, in the case of an informal relationship with another person, the maintenance claim of an unmarried mother is not extinguished. However, when an unmarried mother is supported by a new person, her claim to maintenance from the presumed father could be in conflict with good morals and her claim upon the father of her child could be extinguished. See S. 2/3 Czech Civil Code: the interpretation and application of a legal regulation must not be contrary to good morals and must not lead to cruelty or inconsiderate behaviour offensive to ordinary human feelings.

DENMARK

a. Into a formal relationship with another person?

A maintenance claim is extinguished upon the claimant's remarriage; see Section 51 of the Danish Marriage Act. The claim will not revive.

b. Into an informal relationship with another person?

Former spouses who have had the amount fixed by the State Administration: If the claimant enters into an informal marriage-like relationship with another person, the maintenance claim is extinguished if the debtor requests the State Administration to do so; see S. 53(2) of the Danish Marriage Act. In these cases there are special circumstances. If the claimant enters into an informal marriage-like relationship, he or she do not necessarily have to cohabit with the other person. It is sufficient that

---

[2] B. REŠETAR, 'Termination of the Maintenance of Spouses and Extra-Marital and Same Sex Partners', *Zbornik PFZ*, 2005, at pp. 1019-1036.

the claimant and the other person have a financial and personal community of interests which can be equated with a relationship where the parties live together.[3] The practice is based on a consideration of fairness, namely that the former spouse should not be entitled to claim maintenance when he or she has engaged in a steady personal and financial relationship with someone else.

Former spouses who have entered into an agreement on the amount of maintenance: It depends on the content of the agreement what exactly will happen if the claimant enters into an informal long-term relationship with another person. According to S. 52 of the Danish Marriage Act the amount may be altered by a court where, on the basis of materially changed circumstances, it would be unreasonable to uphold the agreement.

ENGLAND AND WALES

Not applicable.

ESTONIA

The general rule in the maintenance obligation of the spouses is that the obligation to provide maintenance terminates upon the remarriage of the entitled person and also upon the death of the entitled as well as the obligated person. A court may release a divorced spouse from the obligation to provide maintenance, or may limit the obligation in time, or may reduce the amount of support if the payment of support would be extremely unfair considering, *inter alia*, the interests of the common child left to be cared for and raised by the entitled person, if: 1) the marriage has lasted for a short period of time; 2) the entitled person has been convicted of a criminal offence committed against the person obliged to provide maintenance or a person connected with him or her; 3) the need for maintenance has been caused by the unreasonable conduct of the entitled person; 4) the entitled person has severely violated his or her obligation to contribute to the maintenance of the family for a longer period of time before the divorce; 5) there is another good reason for doing so. Therefore, in the case of spouses, the Estonian Family Law Act has not exhaustively listed the situations in which the court may exempt the divorced spouse from paying maintenance to the other spouse.

---

[3] See *Tidsskrift for Familie- og arveret* (Journal of Family and Succession Law) 2011, at p. 115.

a. Into a formal relationship with another person?

In general, the partners in an informal relationship have no mutual maintenance obligation towards one another. The only maintenance obligation that the partners in an informal relationship have is the provision of maintenance in the case of the birth of child. Maintenance shall be provided by the obligated person, but this ranks below the maintenance obligation of the spouse although above that of the relatives of the person in need of assistance (§ 111(5) Estonian Family Law Act). In practical terms this means that the spouse of the person in need of assistance should provide maintenance before the father of the child. If the spouse is, considering his or her other obligations and financial situation, unable to provide maintenance to his or her spouse without detrimentally affecting his or her own usual lifestyle, maintenance shall be provided by the father of the child.

b. Into an informal relationship with another person?

In general, the partners in an informal relationship have no mutual maintenance obligation towards one another. There is no direct regulation in the Estonian Family Law Act on whether the provision of maintenance in the case of the birth of a child will terminate if the person entitled to receive maintenance enters into a new informal relationship. But as the partners in an informal relationship do not have a mutual maintenance obligation and the child's post-birth maintenance obligation does not depend on the cohabitation of the parties, the post-birth maintenance obligation of the obligated person shall will not presumably end with the beginning of a new informal relationship.

FINLAND

Not applicable.

FRANCE

Not applicable.

GERMANY

Not relevant (see Question 34).

GREECE

a. Into a formal relationship with another person?

There are no relevant rules.

b. Into an informal relationship with another person?

This is applicable only to maintenance in the event of divorce (Art. 1444(2) Greek Civil Code).

HUNGARY

a. Into a formal relationship with another person?

The right to receive maintenance from the former cohabitant extinguishes if the creditor enters into a marriage with another person according to the Hungarian Civil Code.[4] Although a registered partner is not mentioned in that provision, the appropriate rule in the Act on registered partners which makes the regulations of the Civil Code on marriage and spouses applicable to registered partnerships and registered partners as a general rule makes it unambiguous that if the creditor establishes a registered partnership with a third person, his or her right to maintenance will extinguish (also see the answer to Question 1).

b. Into an informal relationship with another person?

The right to receive maintenance from the former cohabitant extinguishes if the creditor establishes cohabitation with another person according to the Hungarian Civil Code.[5]

REPUBLIC OF IRELAND

a. Into a formal relationship with another person?

Yes. Section 175(5) provides:

> 'An order made under subsection (1) (a) or (b) ceases to have effect on the marriage or registration in a civil partnership, or in a legal relationship that is the subject of an order under section 5, of the qualified cohabitant in whose favour the order was made, except as respects payments due under it on the date of the marriage or registration.'

---

4 Art. 4:91 (6) of the Hungarian Civil Code.

5 Art. 4:91 (6) of the Hungarian Civil Code.

b. Into an informal relationship with another person?
The maintenance order will cease to have effect only if the new relationship itself becomes the subject of a section 5 order (regarding the recognition of foreign registered relationships).

ITALY

Not applicable.

However, it may be of interest to note that the cohabitation may be relevant in calculating the amount due to his or her ex-spouse, following the divorce of one of the current partners. The amount of maintenance must in fact be limited in order to allow the divorced person to support the person they are now cohabiting with.[6]

This rule also applies in the case of personal separation.[7]

LATVIA

As there is no legal order on informal relationships in Latvia, there is no legal order on maintenance following separation in an informal relationship.

By way of comparison one may consider the following. In connection with the divorce of a married couple, S. 81 of the Latvian Civil Law determines that the duty to ensure the previous level of welfare or maintenance of the former spouse ceases if the former spouse has entered into a new marriage.

LITHUANIA

See the answer to Question 34.

LUXEMBOURG

Not applicable.

---

6 Cass. 30 January 1987, n. 879 in *Dir. Fam.*, 1987, I, p. 590. Compare R. TOMMASINI, 'La famiglia di fatto', in: M. BESSONE (ed.), *Trattato di diritto privato*, Giappichelli, Turin, 1999, at p. 413.

7 Trib. Napoli, 27 January 1985, in *Dir. Fam.*, 1985, I, p. 606.

THE NETHERLANDS

Since the law does not recognise a maintenance right/duty for informal partners after a relationship breakdown, this is not relevant. If parties agreed upon a maintenance right/duty, it depends on what terms they agreed upon. Partners have the right to contract freely, so they could include a provision to this extent.

NORWAY

Not applicable, see answer to Question 34.

PORTUGAL

Not applicable following to Question 34.

RUSSIA

Not applicable.

SCOTLAND

As there is no obligation of maintenance, this question is not relevant.

SLOVAKIA

Slovak law does not grant maintenance to a former partner.

SLOVENIA

a. Into a formal relationship with another person?

The right to maintenance ceases if the former extramarital partner enters into a marriage (Art. 83 of the Slovenian Marriage Act). Since the law that regulates same-sex unions took effect, the right to maintenance would also be lost if a same-sex union is registered.[8]

b. Into an informal relationship with another person?

The right to maintenance ceases if the former extramarital partner lives in an extramarital union (Art. 83 of the Slovenian Marriage Act).

---

8 See also: B. NOVAK, 'Description of Slovene family law', *Jusletter*, 2007, at p. 5, available at: www.weblaw.ch/de/content_edition/jusletter/jusletter.asp.

SPAIN

a. Into a formal relationship with another person?
Yes, see Art. 101 Spanish Civil Code and 233-19.1b) Catalan Civil Code.

b. Into an informal relationship with another person?
Yes, see Art. 101 Spanish Civil Code and 233-19.1b) Catalan Civil Code.

SWEDEN

Since former partners to an informal relationship have no legal duty to support each other, later events of this kind are not relevant.

SWITZERLAND

See the answer to Question 34, question is not relevant.

QUESTION 40

How does the creditor's maintenance claim rank in relation to:

a. The debtor's current spouse, registered partner, or partner in an informal relationship?

b. The debtor's previous spouse, registered partner, or partner in an informal relationship?

c. The debtor's children?

d. The debtor's other relatives?

AUSTRIA

Under current Austrian law a former partner is not entitled to a maintenance claim.

BELGIUM

The claim of the creditor is not a statutory maintenance claim and consequently it is not ranked vis-à-vis the debtor's statutory maintenance claims, which all take priority. The Supreme Court has indeed determined that the courts should disregard every voluntary act that allows a maintenance debtor to escape his statutory duty, even if the debtor had no malicious intent.[1] We think that this judgment only applies to voluntary support obligations towards an informal partner. To also disregard the maintenance debtor's contributions to his/her *de facto* household expenses would infringe on his/her right to the protection of private and family life in his/her new informal relationship.[2]

1 Cass. 2 January 2014, *RW* 2014-15, 507.

2 Justice of the Peace Grâce-Hollogne 18 November 2003, *RTDF* 2006, 213. In contrast: Justice of the Peace Tournai (2) 15 April 2003, *RTDF* 2006, 594.

BULGARIA

Not applicable.

CROATIA

a. The debtor's current spouse, registered partner, or partner in an informal relationship?

This is not determined by the law.

Also, one cannot be subject to maintenance obligations towards his/her previous and current partner in cohabitation at the same time. Namely, maintenance rights and liabilities in a (new) cohabitation cannot arise before cohabitation is terminated.

b. The debtor's previous spouse, registered partner, or partner in an informal relationship?

This is not determined by the law.

c. The debtor's children?

According to Art. 283 paragraph 1 of the Croatian Family Act and Art. 39 paragraph 4 in relation to Art. 4 paragraph 1, child maintenance takes precedence over the maintenance of all the other adult family members, including cohabitants and same-sex informal partners.

d. The debtor's other relatives?

This is not determined by the law.

CZECH REPUBLIC

This is a specific kind of maintenance claim and it does not rank in relation to any other maintenance claim. There is no concurrence of the maintenance claims for maintenance and support, and provision for the payment of certain costs for an unmarried mother.

DENMARK

Not relevant. Danish law does not contain any specific regulation with regard to the payment of maintenance to a former partner.

ENGLAND AND WALES

Not applicable.

ESTONIA

Pursuant to the Estonian Family Law Act, divorced spouses have the obligation to provide maintenance in two cases. Firstly, if after the divorce a divorced spouse is unable to maintain himself or herself due to having to care for the common children of the spouses, he or she may request maintenance from the other divorced spouse until the child attains three years of age (§ 72). Secondly, if after the divorce a divorced spouse is unable to maintain himself or herself due to his or her age or state of health and the need for assistance arising from that age or state of health existed at the time of the divorce, he or she may request maintenance from the other divorced spouse. The provision of maintenance due to age or state of health may be requested from the other divorced spouse also when the need for assistance arising from age or state of health already existed at the time when the right to receive maintenance from the other divorced spouse on another basis provided by law came to an end. This maintenance shall be provided to the person entitled to receive maintenance as long as he or she cannot be presumed to be able to obtain an income from another source.

Pursuant to the Estonian Family Law Act, the general rule is the following: if there are many persons entitled to receive maintenance and the person required to pay that maintenance is unable to provide it for all of them, a minor child shall have priority over other children, over the children of more distant descendants, descendants over ascendants and, in the case of ascendants, closer relatives over more distant relatives. In the order of entitled persons, a spouse ranks equally with a minor child and shall receive maintenance before an adult child or a married minor child and the remainder of the relatives. In the order of entitled persons, a divorced spouse caring for a child and a parent entitled to receive maintenance in the case of the birth of a child pursuant to § 111 of the Estonian Family Law Act rank below a minor child and they shall receive maintenance before an adult child and married minor child and the remainder of the relatives. In the order of entitled persons, a divorced spouse entitled to receive maintenance pursuant to § 73 of the Estonian Family Law Act ranks below an adult child and he or she shall receive maintenance before the remainder of the relatives.

a. The debtor's current spouse, registered partner, or partner in an informal relationship?

A parent entitled to receive maintenance in the case of the birth of a child pursuant to § 111 of Estonian Family Law Act ranks below a minor child, thus below the spouse (§ 98(3) Estonian Family Law Act), as in the order of entitled persons, a spouse has an equal ranking with a minor child and shall receive maintenance before an adult child or a married minor child and the remainder of the relatives (§ 98(2) Estonian Family Law Act). There is no regulation with regard to the partner in a registered cohabitation. There is no maintenance obligation with regard to the partner of new non-marital cohabitation, except the already mentioned post-birth maintenance obligation in favour of a child. In such a case the Estonian Family Law Act can be interpreted along the lines that the claims of the current partner as well as those of the former partner(s) in a cohabitation with regard to the maintenance obligation related to the birth of a child should have equal status.

b. The debtor's previous spouse, registered partner, or partner in an informal relationship?

The Estonian Family Law Act divides the order of the maintenance obligation of divorced spouses into two: the divorced spouse caring for a child and the parent (including a partner in an informal relationship) entitled to receive maintenance after the birth of a child have an equal status and in the order of entitled persons they rank after the minor child. In the order of entitled persons, the divorced spouse who is entitled to receive maintenance on any other basis shall rank below an adult child and he or she receives maintenance before the remainder of relatives; thus, the claim of the parent entitled to receive maintenance with regard to the birth of a child precedes his or her claim.

c. The debtor's children?

In the order of entitled persons, the status of a divorced spouse caring for a child and a parent entitled to receive maintenance in the case of the birth of a child pursuant to § 111 of Estonian Family Law Act ranks below a minor child and they shall receive maintenance before an adult child and a married minor child (§ 98(3) Estonian Family Law Act).

d. The debtor's other relatives?

In the order of entitled persons, the status of a divorced spouse caring for a child and a parent entitled to receive maintenance in the case of the birth of a child pursuant to § 111 of this Act ranks below a minor child and they shall receive maintenance before an adult child and a married minor child as well as the remainder of the relatives (§ 98(3) Estonian Family Law Act).

FINLAND

Not applicable.

FRANCE

Not applicable.

GERMANY

Not relevant (see Question 34).

GREECE

a. The debtor's current spouse, registered partner, or partner in an informal relationship?

The duty to pay maintenance to a spouse takes precedence (alongside the obligation to pay maintenance to a partner in a cohabitation pact, pursuant to Art. 7(2) Law 3719/2008). A partner in an informal relationship is not entitled to maintenance, but if a claim is recognised by contract, such a partner will be last in the order of priority.

b. The debtor's previous spouse, registered partner, or partner in an informal relationship?

The spouse from a previous marriage might be called upon to pay maintenance, but if the intended recipient is living in a permanent free union, he will be released from the obligation to pay (Art. 1444(2) Greek Civil Code).

c. The debtor's children?

The children of the party entitled to maintenance may be called upon to pay maintenance, pursuant to Art. 1488 Greek Civil Code.

d. The debtor's other relatives?

The above provision applies and is not only limited to the children but also extends to other relatives, in their order of intestate succession.

HUNGARY

a. The debtor's current spouse, registered partner, or partner in an informal relationship?

The former cohabitant and the debtor's current spouse have equal ranking according to the Hungarian Civil Code.[3] According to the Act on registered partners, this rule also has to be applied to registered partners, so the former cohabitant and the current registered partner also have equal ranking (see the answer to Question 29). As far as the current cohabitant is concerned, the Hungarian Civil Code does not mention any maintenance obligation for the cohabitants during their relationship (see also the answer to Question 10). Nevertheless, some provisions of the Hungarian Civil Code allow us to draw the conclusion that cohabitants are expected to support each other and this has been the standpoint in the case law for several years.

b. The debtor's previous spouse, registered partner, or partner in an informal relationship?

The former cohabitant and the debtor's former spouse have equal ranking according to the Hungarian Civil Code.[4] According to the Act on registered partners, this rule also has to be applied to registered partners, so the former cohabitant and the former registered partner also have equal ranking (see the answer to Question 29). Former cohabitants may also have equal ranking just like former spouses but the debtor's ability to pay is also relevant.

c. The debtor's children?

The debtor's children enjoy priority in the ranking whether they are common children or the debtor's children from another partnership. A minor child comes first and this child is then followed by an adult child who is pursuing further studies.[5]

d. The debtor's other relatives?

Other relatives, such as parents, follow the spouse, the former spouse and the former cohabitant in the ranking according to the Hungarian Civil Code. Although there has not been any case law concerning the maintenance of a former cohabitant it seems to be important to mention Art. 203 of the Hungarian Civil Code which allows the courts to deviate from the ranking in the right to maintenance and the obligation to maintain if there is a good reason for doing so.

---

3 Art. 4:202 c) of the Hungarian Civil Code.
4 Art. 4:90 of the Hungarian Civil Code.
5 Art. 4:202 a)-b) of the Hungarian Civil Code.

REPUBLIC OF IRELAND

There is no hierarchy in the Irish 2010 Act or in other legislation.

In determining an application for redress by a qualified cohabitant, including in a claim for maintenance, there are a number of factors that the court is required to regard under S. 173(3), none of which are given priority or prominence under the Act. Section 173(3)(b) and (c) specifically requires the court to consider the rights and entitlements of any spouse or former spouse and any civil partner or former civil partner of the cohabitants. Section 173(3)(d) requires the rights and entitlements of any dependent child or of any child of a previous relationship of either cohabitant to be considered by the court. It is worth noting that the qualified cohabitants' current or former partner to an informal relationship is not set out as a factor that shall be taken into consideration by the court in determining claims under the Irish 2010 Act, nor are the other relatives of either party.

A maintenance order made in favour of a qualified cohabitant ceases to have effect when the maintenance creditor remarries or enters into a civil partnership and such an order will not be made by the court at all where the applicant has already married or registered in a civil partnership. There is, however, nothing in the Act that automatically precludes a maintenance claim being brought and an order being made where the maintenance debtor is or has been married. Nevertheless, S. 173(5) mandates that the court shall not make such an order in favour of a qualified cohabitant that would affect any right of any person to whom the other cohabitant is or was married.

In a similar manner to how the rights of spouses of cohabitants are to be considered by the court in a claim by one cohabitant for maintenance from the other, in an application for ancillary orders under the Irish Family Law Act 1995 and the Irish Family Law (Divorce) Act 1996 upon judicial separation or divorce, the court is required to consider the rights of any person other than the spouses but including a person to whom either spouse is remarried (S. 16(2)(l) and S. 20(2)(l) respectively). This essentially means that if a wife is seeking maintenance from her ex-husband, the court is required to consider the rights of any person other than the spouses and this has been held to include the husband's current partner in an informal relationship. In *JCN v RTN* [1999] IEHC 83, the High Court took into account the husband's commitments to his current partner and their two dependent children in deciding whether to make a pension adjustment order in favour of his wife.

ITALY

Not applicable.

LATVIA

As there is no legal order on informal relationships in Latvia, there is no legal order on maintenance following separation in an informal relationship.

LITHUANIA

See the answer to Question 34.

LUXEMBOURG

Not applicable.

THE NETHERLANDS

Since the law does not recognise a maintenance right/duty for informal partners after a relationship breakdown, this is not relevant. When parties agreed upon such a right, this claim has an equal ranking with all other claims (not a preferred status).

NORWAY

Not applicable, see answer to Question 34.

PORTUGAL

Not applicable following to Question 34.

RUSSIA

Not applicable.

SCOTLAND

As there is no obligation of maintenance, this question is not relevant.

SLOVAKIA

Slovak law does not grant maintenance to a former partner.

SLOVENIA

a. The debtor's current spouse, registered partner, or partner in an informal relationship?

All partners have the same ranking.

b. The debtor's previous spouse, registered partner, or partner in an informal relationship?

All partners have the same ranking.

c. The debtor's children?

All the children have the same ranking. Equal rights for legitimate and illegitimate children in Slovenia are guaranteed by the Slovenian Constitution.

d. The debtor's other relatives?

There is no duty to maintain other relatives.

SPAIN

a. The debtor's current spouse, registered partner, or partner in an informal relationship?

There are no clear-cut rules on this issue in the Spanish Civil Code. However, it seems that, in evaluating the debtor's ability to pay, this will be taken into account. Partners to an informal or formal relationship are however not entitled to maintenance during the relationship under Spanish law.

Article 233-18.2 Catalan Civil Code establishes that the new family expenses of the debtor need to be taken into account when evaluating his or her ability to pay. This means that the claims of his new partner come first.

b. The debtor's previous spouse, registered partner, or partner in an informal relationship?

In principle these claims would be taken into account in evaluating the debtor's ability to pay. They might be considered to come before the claims of a new partner because the debtor cannot modify maintenance claims for circumstances brought about by himself or herself. Case law is however divided on this issue.

c. The debtor's children?

Maintenance claims for children always come first. When evaluating the debtor's ability to pay and deciding about whether to grant maintenance, and for what amount, to a partner in an informal relationship, the maintenance claims of children will be deducted from the debtor's income.

Article 237-8 2 Catalan Civil Code specifically establishes that priority should be given to claims from the debtor's children.

d. The debtor's other relatives?

There are no clear-cut rules on this issue. However, it seems that, in evaluating the debtor's ability to pay, this will be taken into account.

SWEDEN

Not relevant in Sweden.

SWITZERLAND

See the answer to Question 34, question is not relevant.

QUESTION 41

When partners in an informal relationship separate, are specific rules applicable to the determination of the ownership of the partners' assets? If there are no specific rules, which general rules apply?

AUSTRIA

Under Austrian law no specific rules for the determination of the ownership of the partners' assets exist when the partners in an informal relationship separate. Generally, the owner is the person who has acquired the ownership of a certain property either through an original, e.g. adverse possession or a bona fide purchase, or derivative mode, e.g. purchase or inheritance. Section 380 General Austrian Civil Code stipulates that no ownership can be acquired without a legal title and a legal mode of acquisition. A legal title constitutes every legal transaction, such as a sale or barter, aiming to transfer ownership. In terms of the mode of acquisition one has to distinguish between movable and immovable goods: The former can be acquired by handing over the asset, whereas the latter requires registration in the land register.[1] Hence, the question of ownership has to be determined according to the general rules regulating the acquisition of ownership.

BELGIUM

No specific rules apply. With regard to immovable property, the necessary authentic instrument will prove ownership between the partners. Authenticity does not apply to the sincerity of the parties' declarations; evidence in rebuttal is consequently allowed between the parties.[2]

---

1 Sections 426 and 431 General Austrian Civil Code.

2 S. EGGERMONT, *De juridische bescherming van private relaties*, PhD, University of Antwerp, 2015, at n° 324; W. PINTENS, C. DECLERCK, J. DU MONGH, K. VANWINCKELEN, *Familiaal vermogensrecht*, Antwerp: Intersentia, 2010, at n° 958.

With regard to movable property, all forms of providing evidence of ownership are accepted. It is debated whether a former partner may invoke the presumption that possession amounts to title (Art. 2279 Belgian Civil Code) for the movables he/she has in his/her possession after the separation. Some case law[3] and authors are of the opinion that possession is ambiguous in these circumstances.[4] Other case law however applies Art. 2279 Belgian Civil Code without reservation.[5]

BULGARIA

There are no specific rules which are applicable to determine the ownership of the partners' assets in case of separation. This determination depends on the proved ownership of the asset in question.

CROATIA

In line with Art. 11 paragraph 2 of the Croatian Family Act and Art. 4 paragraph 1 and Art. 54 of the Croatian Partnership Act, the answer equally relates to both cohabitants and same-sex informal partners.

Specific rules applicable to the determination of the ownership of the partners' assets are included in the Croatian Family Act.

According to Art. 36 in relation to Art. 11 paragraph 2 of the Croatian Family Act and Art. 51 in relation to Art. 4 paragraph 1 of the Croatian Partnership Act, all the assets that the partners have acquired on the basis of their work during the partnership or the assets that have been derived from such property as well as lottery prizes and income from intellectual and related rights represent the partners' community of property which is co-owned in equal parts. It means that partners are obliged to divide their community of property into equal parts after their possible separation.

According to Art. 39 in relation to Art. 11 paragraph 2 of the Croatian Family Act and Art. 52 in relation to Art. 4 paragraph 1 of the Croatian Partnership Act, personal property means property owned by the partners at the time of the beginning of their life union, including assets acquired during the life union from sources other than work (e.g.

3 Antwerp 9 February 2005, *NJW* 2006, 508, with note VERSCHELDEN.

4 S. EGGERMONT, *De juridische bescherming van private relaties*, PhD, University of Antwerp, 2015, n° 325.

5 District Court of Bruges 22 May 1995, *TBR* 1994, 44.

inheritance, gifts etc.). Each partner is entitled to retain his/her personal property after their possible separation.

CZECH REPUBLIC

There are no specific rules on the determination of ownership of the partners' assets. Partners to an informal relationship can acquire their own property, or they can acquire property together (depending on the individual circumstances of the obligation). If partners to an informal relationship jointly own property, all the rules regarding co-ownership according to S. 1115 et seq. Czech Civil Code are applicable; partners to an informal relationship are then co-owners. See S. 1140 Czech Civil Code: (1) No one may be forced to remain involved in co-ownership. (2) Each of the co-owners may at any time request that he be separated from the co-ownership if it is possible to divide the co-owned property, or that the co-ownership be cancelled. However, he may not make such a request at an inconvenient time or only to the detriment of one of the co-owners.

DENMARK

Danish law does not contain any specific rules which are applicable to the determination of the ownership of the partners' assets.

Just as for married couples, the property relations of unmarried cohabitants are determined according to the normal rules of property law.[6] Thus an asset can either belong to one of the cohabitants or can be jointly owned by them both. Joint ownership will usually be based on an agreement between the parties, but it can also arise from the combining of their finances. Contributions made after the acquisition of an asset do not create a right to joint ownership unless the parties agree.

ENGLAND AND WALES

There are no specific rules relating to the property and assets of couples in informal relationships. General laws of determining legal ownership apply whereby the title deeds of the property or proof of purchase in one partner's name will provide evidence of ownership. In cases of dispute, the English Trusts of Land and Appointment of Trustees Act 1996

[6] See in more detail I. LUND-ANDERSEN, *Familieøkonomien*, Jurist- og Økonomforbundets Forlag, Copenhagen, 2011, at p. 250-265.

provides a mechanism for challenge whereby the non-owner can provide evidence that they contributed to the purchase or had an agreement with the legal owner that they would share beneficial ownership. If satisfied, the court can declare that there is a common intention resulting or constructive trust.

ESTONIA

An informal relationship does not itself change the ownership relations of the parties. Each party shall remain the owner of his or her belongings. Assets acquired during the relationship shall be acquired according to the general rules of the Estonian Law of Property Act, i.e. either under the sole ownership of a party or common ownership.[7] According to § 90(1) of the Estonian Law of Property Act,[8] a possessor of a movable and any earlier possessor shall be deemed the owners of the asset during the possessor's possession until the contrary is proved. The presumption of the possession of the possessor of a movable, proceeding from § 90, includes, as a rule, also the presumption of the common ownership of the co-owner, which provides certain protection to the (non-owner) spouse, as well as to another partner in an informal relationship. In the case of immovable property this presumption is not valid, but it concerns mostly the household goods and other items used in daily living.[9]

FINLAND

With regard to movable assets, there is a provision in the Finnish Act on the Dissolution of the Household of Cohabiting Partners (26/2011) that creates presumed co-ownership in terms of movable assets, if it cannot be proven which cohabiting partner a particular movable object belongs to (S. 6). However, this Act only applies to cohabiting partners who have lived in a common household for a minimum period of five years or who have (or have had) a joint child. In terms of assets that require registration, the information provided on ownership in the context of registration creates a strong presumption of ownership.

---

7 Decision of the Civil Chamber of the Supreme Court 3-2-1-109-14, at para. 17.

8 Asjaõigusseadus (adopted on 9 June 1993, entered into force on 1 December 1993). – RT I 1993, 39, 590; RT I, 08.07.2014, 7 (in Estonian), available in English at: www.riigiteataja.ee/en/eli/ee/Riigikogu/act/510072014007/consolide.

9 K. KAMA and K. KULLERKUPP, 'Vabaabielu versus abielu: varalised suhted muutuvate kooseluvormide kontekstis', *Juridica*, 2002, No. 6, pp. 359-368.

FRANCE

There are no specific rules on the determination of property between ex-cohabitants. The general principles of property law are applicable to a separation.

Property is determined according to legal title. The legal title can be based on acquisition by the cohabitant(s), on inheritance rights or on a donation.

Where the act is encompassed in a notarial deed (*acte authentique*) or is in the form of a written document, proof of ownership is usually not too difficult to provide.

Each ex-cohabitant owns the asset to which he or she holds the legal title. Yet, there are some limitations to this.

Firstly, where the asset acquired by one cohabitant in his or her own name has been financed by resources held under indivisible joint ownership (*indivision*), and that the origin of these resources has been declared, then the mechanism of subrogation[10] will apply and the asset will be held as joint property.[11]

Secondly, the mechanism of *accession*[12] is applicable to any building on the land owned by one of the cohabitants, regardless of the origin of the financing resources. If a cohabitant finances a building on the other cohabitant's land, the building will be owned by the cohabitant who owns the land, although the other cohabitant is entitled to a reward.[13]

In the case of a joint acquisition, the ownership of each partner is determined regarding the specific contribution of each partner thereto.

---

10 Art. 815-10 al. 1 of the French Civil Code. See Cass. Civ 1 9 January 1979, *Bull.civ* I no. 13; *RTD civ.* 1982, p. 178 with note J. PATARIN.

11 C. FLEURIOT, 'La liquidation des intérêts patrimoniaux entre concubins', Dossier: *Les conséquences patrimoniales de la séparation des couples non mariés*, Dalloz actualité du 30 septembre 2013. www.dalloz-actualité.fr/dossier/consequences-patrimoniales-de-separation-des-couples-non-maries#.VIrAFXt4zwI.

12 Art. 546 of the French Civil Code: 'ownership of a thing, either movable or immovable, gives a right to everything it produces and to what is accessorily united to it, either naturally or artificially. That right is called a right of accession'.

13 Art. 555 para. 3 of the French Civil Code.

Where the issue is contested, and proof cannot be provided, an indivisible joint ownership (*indivision*) of 50/50 is presumed.[14]

According to the legal provisions[15] the division of joint property can be claimed at any time and a reward will be granted according to the participation in the financing of the asset. Where proof cannot be provided, the value of the asset will be split between the co-owners on a 50/50 basis and the reward will be correlatively adapted.

The indivisible joint ownership scheme opens up the right of a reward when the asset is used exclusively by one of the co-owners.[16] When the asset is in the form of real estate, a reward is due even if the co-owner who exclusively used it did not personally occupy the premises.[17]

The situation concerning everyday goods, where acquisition is not normally encompassed in a written document, is considered to be slightly different. Each ex-cohabitant owns the asset that is in his or her possession. Indeed, according to the general principles of property law, possession of an asset determines its ownership.[18] This principle is also applicable to money deposited in bank accounts. This presumption of ownership based on possession can be rebutted by proof of ownership (a bill, receipt, etc.), but the burden of proof is a heavy one, and one cohabitant can face serious difficulties in rebutting it. Indeed, the *Cour de cassation* has held that the exclusive financing of an asset does not amount to proof of ownership.[19] In that particular case one cohabitant had bought a car for the use of the other, without the intention of donating it. According to the court the exclusive financing of the car by one cohabitant did not corrupt the possession of the car by the other cohabitant who was the exclusive user thereof. Ownership is rooted in possession; where possession is not vitiated then ownership cannot be readily contested.[20]

---

14 Case law has extended to cohabitants the legal presumption of an undivided right of ownership that is organised between spouses (art. 1538 of the French Civil Code) and between partners in a *pacte civil de solidarité* (Art. 515-5 para. 2 of the French Civil Code).

15 Art. 815 of the French Civil Code.

16 Art. 815-9 of the French Civil Code.

17 See Cass. Civ 1, 30 June 2004, no 02-20085.

18 Art. 2276 of the French Civil Code.

19 Cass. Civ 1, 24 October 2012, no.11.16431.

20 This position has been disputed, see particularly W. DROSS, 'Le concubin qui a financé seul l'acquisition d'un bien peut-il exiger qu'il lui soit restitué après la rupture ?', *RTD civ.*, 2013, at p. 153.

GERMANY

There are no specific rules regarding the determination of ownership of the partners' assets after separation. Often the general rules of property law apply.

The partners may hold assets alone (sole ownership) or jointly. If at least two persons acquire assets jointly, they generally become co-owners by fractional shares (*Miteigentümer* as per §§ 1008–1011 German Civil Code). The co-ownership by fractional shares is a special form of co-ownership by defined shares (*Bruchteilsgemeinschaft* as per §§ 741-758 German Civil Code) and modifies the just mentioned general rules.[21]

Generally, neither entering into an informal relationship nor separation changes the assignment of assets to each partner.[22]

Assets that a partner acquires before entering into an informal partnership remain the property of that partner (sole ownership). Regarding assets which are acquired during the duration of the informal partnership, it must be analysed by interpretation whether the partners wanted to acquire as co-owners or whether a partner acquired alone.[23] Once the assignment of assets is defined as either sole ownership by one of the partners or co-ownership by both partners, this assignment remains the same even after separation. In the case of a plot of land sole or co-ownership must be entered into the land registry.

Regarding commonly used goods situated in the joint residence, which are not personal items, the partners are often co-possessors (§ 866 German Civil Code). Thus § 1006 German Civil Code applies according to which it is presumed in favour of the possessor of a movable thing that he or she is the owner of that thing. Therefore co-ownership of the partners is presumed.[24] The presumption may be rebutted if one partner is able to prove that he or she was sole proprietor before entering into the informal partnership or acquired the item as sole proprietor during the existence of the partnership.

---

21 P. BASSENGE, '§ 1008', in: O. PALANDT, *Bürgerliches Gesetzbuch*, Beck, Munich, 2015, at No. 1.

22 H. GRZIWOTZ, *Nichteheliche Lebensgemeinschaft*, Beck, Munich, 2014, at § 20 No. 1.

23 H. GRZIWOTZ, *Nichteheliche Lebensgemeinschaft*, Beck, Munich, 2014, at § 20 No. 4.

24 N. DETHLOFF, *Familienrecht*, Beck, Munich, 2012, at § 8 No. 11.

GREECE

No. Each partner will take possession of his/her own assets, on the basis of the general provisions on ownership. Where assets are owned jointly, the rules on dissolving joint ownership will be applied.

HUNGARY

A default property regime was prescribed for cohabitants in the Civil Code of 1959. According to that provision cohabitants acquired common property in proportion to the contribution they had made in acquiring such property and when this proportion could not be calculated the property was considered to have been equally acquired. Work done in the household was considered to be a contribution to acquiring that property.[25] This rule still has to be applied by the courts during the current transitional period (see also the answer to Question 2). The Hungarian Civil Code has not preserved this default regime and has introduced a new one for cohabitants.[26] This regime resembles the regime of participation in acquisitions. The cohabitants are the owners of any acquired property during their community of life and joint ownership is not established by simply being cohabitants. In the case of separation both cohabitants may claim from one another the division of the other's acquired property. Personal assets in the matrimonial community of property regime do not belong to acquired property. A cohabitant may claim for his or her participation and in proportion to the contribution he or she has made in acquiring such property. The work done in the household, caring for children and working in the business of the other cohabitant is considered to be a contribution to acquiring that property. When this proportion cannot be calculated the contribution is considered to have been equal except if this results in an unfair disadvantage for the other cohabitant.

REPUBLIC OF IRELAND

Generally, there are no specific rules applicable to the determination of ownership of the partners' assets. Partners may, however, have a cohabitants' agreement in place which sets out the respective ownership of their assets upon separation pursuant to S. 202 of the 2010 Act. In addition, a qualified cohabitant may make an application to court under Part 15 of the Irish 2010 Act for a Property Adjustment Order upon the

[25] Art. 578/G(1) of the Civil Code of 1959.
[26] Art. 6:516 of the Hungarian Civil Code.

termination of the relationship. Furthermore, the law on direct and indirect contributions may apply to determine ownership of the partners' assets, see Question 27 and 28.

ITALY

No specific rule is provided for the determination of ownership upon the partners' separation. Therefore, as each partner is the exclusive owner of any assets that he or she may have individually purchased during the relationship, at its end he or she will retain ownership of such assets. The ownership of any single asset will be proved following the general rules described supra in the answer to Question 29.

If, however, an asset formally falls under the common ownership of both partners, that property will be divided according to the general rules on the dissolution of co-ownership under Art. 1111 of the Italian Civil Code. The division will then take into account the proportion of the asset owned by each partner. Each co-owner has the right to request the dissolution of co-ownership at any time.

LATVIA

As there is no legal order on informal relationships in Latvia, there is no legal order on the determination of ownership of partners' assets following separation in an informal relationship. Part 1 of S. 93 of the Latvian Civil Procedure Law determines that each party must prove the facts upon which they base their claims or objections. Claimants must prove that their claims are well-founded. Defendants must prove that their objections are well-founded.

For example, with regard to real estate, the principle of public credibility is in force. Namely, in the Latvian Civil Law it is determined that only such persons as are registered in the Land Register as owners are to be recognised to be the owners of immovable property.

The general legal order of the Latvian Civil Law on Unjust Enrichment is also applicable.

For example, S. 2389 determines that if a person, without any basis therefor, is in possession of some item of another person's property, it may be reclaimed from the first-mentioned person. It will not matter, with respect to such reclaim, whether there did not exist from the beginning any basis for the acquisition of such item of property or whether the basis initially existing later ceased. Section 2391 provides that no one has the right to unjustly enrich himself or herself by harming and at the expense of another person. If a person has thus suffered loss in connection with an item of their property, he or she may demand the return of that property and the amount by which the other person has been enriched. Section 2392 determines that only that which is still part of the property of the defendant at the time when an action to reclaim is brought against him or her, whether or not it exists naturally or in the form of objects that the person has acquired in exchange for what was alienated or consumed in good faith, is to be considered as enrichment. The right to reclaim is not to be applicable to all that which the defendant, prior to that time and without acting in bad faith, has given away as a gift, consumed or accidentally lost.

LITHUANIA

The institution of a partnership is not yet effective due to the fact that a special law establishing partnership registration procedures has not been adopted. Until this law is adopted, the *de facto* relations of partners are not subject to a special legal regulation, and separate elements of such relations are subject to the rules of the general civil law, but not the rules of family law (e.g. the division of assets that the partners have jointly acquired are subject to the rules under Book IV, 'Material Law' (Co-ownership rights), and Book VI, 'Law of Obligations' (joint activities (partnership) articles 6.969-6.971), of the Lithuanian Civil Code, regulating relations between co-owners).

LUXEMBOURG

The determination of ownership is made according to the general rules of evidence (compare the answers to Question 29 and 30).

If the exclusive property of one partner cannot be proved, the asset is presumed to be jointly owned by the two of them (e.g. Court of Appeal, 11th of July 1997).

THE NETHERLANDS

There are no specific rules which are applicable in relation to each partner's property law status. For couples in a formal relationship, the Dutch Civil Code provides for specific provisions. The default property system, the community of property, results in the right to a 50-50 share of all the accumulated assets. From this point of view, the issue of who owns what is less relevant. A specific provision in Art. 1:131 Dutch Civil Code entails a presumption for spouses married under a different marital property system: if neither of the spouses is able to prove exclusive ownership, the property is presumed to be joint property.[27]

Upon a relationship breakdown, non-marital couples will have to assess what property is whose private property and what assets are joint property. The general provisions of Books 3 and 5 of the Dutch Civil Code apply. Partners may come to an agreement and divide joint property. It is a regular occurrence that the partners cannot agree on who owns certain assets, both claiming that they are entitled to those assets. In relation to immovable property, mainly the house, such disputes do not arise, since the entitlement is registered in the public registers.

In relation to other types of goods, in particular movable goods, general contract and property law contain a rebuttable presumption of ownership. The partner who has power/control over an asset is presumed to be its possessor on the basis of Art. 3:109 Dutch Civil Code and a possessor is presumed to be the owner of the asset under Art. 3:119 Dutch Civil Code.

Property issues are often a matter brought to the courts' attention, in particular in relation to family pets and motor vehicles.[28] The Supreme Court has had to rule on the various presumptions on a number of occasions. In the case of Lijesen/Geurts[29] the man claimed ownership of a dog and a sofa which were under the power/control of the woman after he left the home, since she was the one who had stayed in the house. It was not contested that these goods had been his private property, since he had brought them into the joint household. However, the woman claimed ownership on the basis of a gift of these goods by the man to her. The Supreme Court ruled that when a possessor claims to be entitled to a good on the basis of a gift, the other partner has to prove that the possessor did not acquire the good. Thus, it was up to the man, who had

[27] K. Boele-Woelki, F. Schonewille and W. Schrama, 'National report: The Netherlands', The property relations between the spouses, available at: ceflonline.net/country-reports-for-the-netherlands/, at p. 28.

[28] Hof Leeuwarden 13 April 2010, LJN BM1443 in relation to a Harley Davidson motorbike; HR 8 December 2006, LJN AY9684 in relation to a Mercedes SLK; Rb. Almelo 5 July 2010, LJN BN0576 in relation to a horse and a dog; Hof Arnhem-Leeuwarden 16 September 2014, ECLI:NL:GHARL:2014:7154 concerning furniture.

[29] HR 8 May 1987, NJ 1988, 700 (Lijesen/Geurts).

left the house, to prove that the presumption of ownership was incorrect rather than that the woman had to prove that the goods had been given to her as a gift. This presumption is practically impossible to rebut. In the case law property law issues in relation to movable goods are mainly decided by these rules.[30]

In the literature, the application of these rebuttable presumptions has been criticised. In everyday life, the presumption functions well in relation to parties who are strangers to one another. It is argued that in post-separation situations of informal partners who shared the same house, it is merely a matter of luck which of the partners has control over goods; it does not represent, as it normally does in relation to strangers, a good indication of ownership status. Theoretically it is possible to overcome this problem, but in practice lawyers and judges are not sufficiently aware of this possibility.[31]

In cohabitation contracts a clause can be agreed upon which solves this problem.[32]

NORWAY

Partners to an informal relationship own their property separately during the relationship, and no specific rules are applicable to the determination of ownership of the partners' assets when they separate. As mentioned in Question 26, co-ownership can be established on the basis of indirect contributions, for example in the form of childcare or the meeting of family expenses.

PORTUGAL

There are no specific rules applicable to partners in an informal relationship to determine the ownership of the partners' assets. Each of them owns whatever has been validly acquired.

---

30 W.M. SCHRAMA, 'Goederenrechtelijke afwikkeling: bewijskwesties', in: M.L.C.C. DE BRUIJN-LÜCKERS et al. (eds.), *Relatierecht, SDUCommentaar*, SDU, The Hague, 2014, at p. 2015-2024. E.g. HR 8 December 2006, LJN AY9684.

31 W.M. SCHRAMA, 'Goederenrechtelijke afwikkeling: bewijskwesties', in: M.L.C.C. DE BRUIJN-LÜCKERS et al. (eds.), *Relatierecht, SDUCommentaar*, SDU, The Hague, 2014, at p. 2015-2024.

32 P. BLOKLAND, in: W.D. KOLKMAN and L.C.A. VERSTAPPEN (eds.), *Handboek Familievermogensrecht*, Walburg Pers, Zutphen, 2013, at 4.2.5.4. The provision determines that the partners are holders of the goods of the other partner and not possessors.

When it is a case of a co-ownership/joint ownership between partners, a rebuttable presumption of an equal share is applicable whenever the title omits any difference between co-owners/joint owners, according to a general rule.

Parliamentary Bill n. 349/X, which preceded Act 23/2010, established a rebuttable presumption: movable assets would be presumed to be jointly owned by both partners (Art. 5-A, n. 2). This solution, however, did not become law, due to the veto by the President of the Republic.

RUSSIA

There are no specific rules applying to the determination of the ownership of partners' assets. Therefore, the general rules of the Russian Civil Code apply. The main rule is that the owner is the person who has title of ownership. There is no presumption of joint ownership of assets held by partners for common use. That means that if neither partner can prove title of ownership, the one who has the asset in his/her possession will be in the stronger position as, under Art. 302 Russian Civil Code, only an titular owner (or a titular lifelong hereditary possessor, under Art. 305 Russian Civil Code) can regain an asset from a possessor.

SCOTLAND

When cohabitants separate, there is no provision for property sharing and ownership of assets will be determined according to the general rules of property. Ownership of heritable property is determined according to registered title and moveable property according to evidence of the person who bought or otherwise acquired it. There are two exceptions in the form of statutory presumptions which apply to ownership of household assets[33] and money or property derived from a household or similar allowance provided by either cohabitant.[34]

SLOVAKIA

There are no specific rules which are applicable to determine the ownership of the partners' assets. For such cases the general rules of the Slovak Civil Code are applicable: The co-owners (partners) may agree on the cancellation of co-ownership and on mutual settlement (§ 141 para. 1

[33] Family Law (Scotland) Act 2006, S. 26.
[34] Family Law (Scotland) Act 2006, S. 27.

Slovak Civil Code). The settlement agreement must be made in writing if it concerns immovables. In the case of movables, it need not be in writing, but each co-owner must give the other co-owners written confirmation of the settlement if requested to do so (§ 141 para. 2 Slovak Civil Code). If the co-owners cannot reach an agreement, the co-ownership will be cancelled and settled by the courts upon a petition by any co-owner (§ 142 para. 1 Slovak Civil Code). In this respect, the court will take into account the size of the shares, the use of the asset and any violent behaviour by one of the partners (§ 142 para. 1 Slovak Civil Code). The settlement may take various forms. If the common asset can be divided, it will be divided between the co-owners. If a new immovable is created by this settlement, the court may establish an easement in favour of the owner of the new immovable (§ 142 para. 3 Slovak Civil Code). If a division of the common asset is not possible, the court may grant ownership of the common asset to one or several co-owners against compensation. According to Slovak doctrine and the case law of the Supreme Court of Slovakia, compensation should be understood as an amount which corresponds to the market price for similar assets on a particular market.[35]

If none of the co-owners wants the asset, the court will order the sale of the common asset and divide the proceeds according to the size of the shares.

However, if there are specific reasons (e.g. an elderly person is a co-owner of a house where he or she has lived for most of his or her life), the court will not cancel and settle the co-ownership by granting ownership of the asset to one or more co-owners against compensation or by selling the common asset and dividing the proceeds between them. The case law defines 'specific reasons' as cases which satisfy the principle of good morals (good faith and fair dealing).[36]

SLOVENIA

At the time of the separation, the common property of the partners is divided. The partners must themselves reach an agreement on this in the

35 See Decision of the Supreme Court of Slovakia No. 43/1997; for more details about compensation see J. LAZAR, in: J. LAZAR et al. (eds.), *Občianske právo hmotné* (Substantive Slovak Civil Law), Iuris Libri, Bratislava, 2014, at p. 511; I. FEKETE, *Občiansky zákonník I. a II. – Veľký komentár* (Slovak Civil Code I and II – Major Commentary), Eurokódex, Bratislava, 2011, at commentary on § 142.

36 V. ČEČOTOVÁ, *Dobré mravy v slovenskom súkromnom práve* (Good morals in Slovak private law), EPOS, Bratislava, 2005.

form of a notarial protocol, or they can request a court to decide on the division. If the partners cannot agree on the extent of the common property or on the amount of their share of this property, they may request that a court decides on this in a civil proceeding.

Partners who cannot agree only on the method of division, about who will obtain individual objects from the common property, may request a division in a non-litigious procedure. If it appears in the non-litigious procedure that there is in fact a dispute between the partners about the extent of the common property or on the amount of their share of this property, the court will terminate the non-litigious procedure for the division of the property and direct the partners to engage in a civil action. Only when the civil action proceeding is complete does the non-litigious procedure for the division continue (Art. 59 of the Slovenian Marriage Act).

The court will carry out a physical division in a civil procedure if this is possible. At the request of a partner it may award, on account of her or his share, mainly objects that are intended for performing her or his trade or profession and enable her or him to earn a personal income and objects intended exclusively for her or his use. Otherwise, each partner receives, in a natural form, those objects in which a justified interest is shown. Common property may also be divided so that common ownership is changed into co-ownership.[37] If a physical division of property is not possible even with the payment of the difference in value or if it is only possible with an appreciable reduction in the value of the object a civil division is performed. This takes place with the sale of the object and a division of the proceeds.

Gifts that the partners have given each other and are not proportionate to the material circumstances of the provider of the gift, must be returned at the time of separation. Normal gifts need not be returned. Gifts must be returned in the condition that they were in at the moment when the reason for the separation came into being. In place of alienated gifts, their value, or the object received for them, must be returned (Art. 84 of the Slovenian Marriage Act).

[37] Judgement of the Supreme Court RS, No. II Ips 306/2009 of 24 February 2011 - SOVS database.

SPAIN

The general rules apply. As regards movables, the ordinary means of proof of ownership is the title of acquisition of the asset. The assets belong to the partner who appears as purchaser in the title of acquisition or as the owner in the documents resulting from the transaction. If no title can be found, possession will be taken into account.

As regards immovables, the registered owner will be considered to all effects and purposes to be the owner, unless challenged. Immovable property, if not registered in the Land Registry, will be owned by the person who has the latest title of acquisition.

Since in practice, particularly after a long relationship, it may be difficult to determine who owns certain assets, the rules of community of property may be held to be applicable. This however requires a tacit agreement evidenced by acts performed by the partners. Such facts could be:

- having a common bank account that is indistinguishably used by both partners;
- giving a general authorization to a partner allowing him or her to dispose of a bank account held by the other partner;
- common professional activities;
- sharing income and expenses (one common pot);
- making economic contributions to the acquisition of an asset held by the other partner.

SWEDEN

Under Swedish law, ownership issues are decided in accordance with the general principles of the law of property, in addition to the special, but rebuttable presumptions of 'hidden' or 'caveat joint ownership', applicable to spouses (registered partners) and cohabitees in an informal relationship. These rules and the relevant case law have been described in detail above, in particular under Questions 27-30.

SWITZERLAND

There are no specific rules for determining the ownership of the partners' assets when these partners in an informal relationship separate. Rather, the general rules on the law of property will apply (Art. 641 et seq. Swiss Civil Code). See Question 26 and 29.

QUESTION 42

When partners in an informal relationship separate, are specific rules applicable subjecting all or certain property (e.g. the home or household goods) to property division? If there are no specific rules, which general rules are applicable?

AUSTRIA

There are no specific rules subjecting all or certain property to a property division in case of separation. Commodities, such as furniture, a motor vehicle, and a television set, have to be divided according to the formal ownership.[1] The general principle is that every partner receives what he/she owns.[2] If items have been jointly purchased during the relationship, it is presumed that both partners share the ownership equally.[3] If one partner claims that he/she is the sole owner of the asset, he/she has to prove this.[4] Items can be divided by different means: Primarily, a so-called *de facto* division *(Naturalteilung)* should be preferred.[5] If a *de facto* division is impossible or infeasible a so-called civil division *(Zivilteilung)* by selling the item and distributing the proceeds becomes necessary.[6] The same rules apply if the partners in an informal relationship have jointly bought a house or an apartment.[7] If the partners

1 A. DEIXLER-HÜBNER, 'Probleme der Leistungsabgeltung im Zusammenhang mit der Auflösung der Lebensgemeinschaft', *ÖJZ*, 1999, at p. 201.

2 E. MÖSCHL, *Die nichteheliche Lebensgemeinschaft*, LexisNexis ARD ORAC, Vienna, 2007, at marg. No. 86.

3 U. AICHHORN, 'Vermögensaufteilung und Erbrecht bei nichtehelicher Lebensgemeinschaft', in: M. GRUBER et al. (eds.), *Erbrecht und Vermögensnachfolge*, Verlag Österreich, Vienna, 2010, at marg. No. 78.

4 U. AICHHORN, *Das Recht der Lebenspartnerschaften, Ehe und Lebensgemeinschaft*, Springer, Vienna, 2003, at p. 421.

5 F. PARAPATITS, 'section 843 General Austrian Civil Code', in: A. KLETEČKA and M. SCHAUER, *ABGB-ON 1.02*, Manz Verlag, Vienna, 2014, at marg. No. 1.

6 Section 843 General Austrian Civil Code.

7 Sections 825 et seq. General Austrian Civil Code; cf. E. MÖSCHL, *Die nichteheliche Lebensgemeinschaft*, LexisNexis ARD ORAC, Vienna, 2007, at marg. No. 53.

have built a house together, it has to be kept in mind that the house belongs to the owner of the estate, regardless of who actually paid the costs for building the house.[8]

BELGIUM

No specific rules apply. The same general rules apply to all property.

As a rule, the former partners' joint property must be divided at the request of one of them. In the case of coincidental joint ownership, they may however have concluded an indivision agreement, which is possible for consecutive periods of a maximum of five years (Art. 815 Belgian Civil Code). However, joint ownership between informal partners is often not coincidental but conventional. The Supreme Court has determined that the maximum period of five years for indivision agreements does not apply to conventional joint property.[9] The joint owners – or their successors in law – consequently cannot claim a division unless this has been agreed otherwise. This is particularly problematic in case the partners have acquired joint property with a tontine or accretion clause. The agreement would be executed even in the case of separation, unless agreed otherwise.[10] The Supreme Court[11] has rightly found that such execution would make no sense in those circumstances. It found that the tontine agreement 'ceases to exist' when the underlying *de facto* or legal relationship between the partners ends. Consequently, the division of the resulting coincidental joint ownership may be claimed. Prior case law had concluded that there was an abuse of rights in the case of a refusal to divide.[12] Even though the outcome of the latter Supreme Court decision is acceptable, the rule of the former Supreme Court decision is not. One must accept that each party must be able to terminate – with notice[13] – an indivision agreement that was concluded for an indefinite period, unless it was concluded with a purpose that has not yet been reached and has not become senseless.[14] It

[8] E. MÖSCHL, *Die nichteheliche Lebensgemeinschaft*, LexisNexis ARD ORAC, Vienna, 2007, at marg. No. 53.

[9] Cass. 20 September 2013, *RW* 2014-15, 618, with note DE KEYSER.

[10] As was the case in Antwerp 3 June 2009, *T.Not.* 2011, 517, with note PUELINCKX-COENE.

[11] Cass. 6 March 2014, *TBBR* 2014, 261, with note PEERAER.

[12] Liège 21 June 2011, *RNB* 2013, 717, with note SAUVEUR.

[13] For example, District Court of Ghent 12 April 2011, *RW* 2012-13, 226.

[14] District Court of Ghent 3 April 2012, *RABG* 2014, 1046, with note VAN DEN BRANDEN. Comp. Brussels 18 June 2013, *RW* 2014-15, 624.

is indeed a general principle that all agreements for an indefinite period may be terminated.[15]

BULGARIA

There are no such specific rules. All property will be divided based on the general rules of the Bulgarian Property Law – depending on the shares upon acquisition or on sole ownership.

CROATIA

There are no specific rules that would refer to all or part of the partners' property after their possible separation.

CZECH REPUBLIC

The term 'usual equipment of a family household' (S. 698 Czech Civil Code) is used. Usual family household equipment consists of a set of movable objects which normally serve for the essential needs of life of the family and its members; whether individual objects belong to both spouses or just one of them is not decided (S. 698(1) Czech Civil Code). But this term is connected only with marriage; there is no specific property law concerning an informal relationship. In other words, there are no specific rules. In the case where partners jointly own property, general rules about co-ownership are applicable, according to S. 1115 Czech Civil Code.

DENMARK

When unmarried partners separate, Danish law does not contain any specific rules subjecting all or certain property to property division.

Each party takes his or her own assets.

If the couple own an asset jointly and there is a dispute about which of them should have full ownership of the asset upon the termination of the cohabiting relationship, the matter can be settled by drawing lots if the parties so agree. If the couple do not agree to draw lots the asset must be sold either on the open market or by a voluntary auction. Sale on the open market will usually raise a higher price than sale by auction. Both

[15] For example Cass. 7 June 2012, *RW* 2013-14, 903.

cohabitants may bid at an auction. This means that the right to continue to live in the home that has been their joint home will go to the party that makes the highest bid.

Unless a period of notice for the termination of joint ownership has been agreed, joint ownership can be terminated upon giving reasonable notice.

ENGLAND AND WALES

In general there are no specific rules of property division. Each partner will own their own property separately and jointly owned property (or its value) will normally be divided equally between the couple. This can be subject to challenge where it is claimed that legal ownership does not reflect beneficial ownership and the non-owner can seek a declaration of trust under S. 14 of the English Trusts of Land and Appointment of Trustees Act 1996 where the court will consider if a constructive or resulting trust has been proved to exist.

The rented family home can be transferred on application to the other partner on relationship breakdown under Schedule 7 English Family Law Act 1996 at the discretion of the court.

Applications to the court for financial provision for the benefit of the child under Schedule 1 English Children Act 1989 in the form of lump sum or property transfer orders or property settlement orders can be applied for where there is a child of the parties under 18. Any order is at the discretion of the court.

ESTONIA

There are no special rules in Estonian legislation on ownership relations after the end of an informal relationship. An informal relationship itself does not change the ownership relations of the parties. Each party shall remain the owner of his or her belongings. Assets acquired during an informal relationship shall be acquired according to the general rules of the Estonian Law of Property Act, i.e. either under the sole ownership of a party or common ownership.[16] A co-owner has the right to demand the termination of common ownership at any time (§ 76(1) Estonian Law of Property Act). Upon the termination of common ownership, an asset shall be divided according to the agreement of the co-owners (§ 77(1)

[16] Decision of the Civil Chamber of the Supreme Court 3-2-1-109-14, at para. 17.

Estonian Law of Property Act). Failing an agreement between the co-owners with respect to the means of the division of an asset in common ownership, a court shall decide, at the request of the plaintiff, whether to divide the asset among the co-owners in physical shares, to give the asset to one or several co-owners and to impose on them an obligation to pay the other co-owners for their shares in monetary terms, or to sell the asset by public auction or an auction among the co-owners and then to divide the proceeds received among the co-owners according to the size of their shares. The court shall have no right to decide upon the division of the asset in common ownership in any other way than requested by the plaintiff.[17]

The Supreme Court has found[18] that partnership relations between the partners in an informal relationship are possible; at the same time it has been of the opinion that an informal relationship does not meet the requirements of a partnership. No binding obligations arise from this, i.e. an obligation within the meaning of the Estonian Law of Obligations Act[19] § 2.[20] If persons living in an informal relationship have not concluded a marriage, their common will not to apply the provisions which are valid for a marriage can be presumed, including the provisions regarding the joint ownership of property. An extension of the partnership provisions or by analogy under the Estonian Family Law Act should not result in consequences where there are situations that have not been agreed upon by the parties and which cannot be presumed to represent their actual common will. On the basis of the law, the obligations which result from an informal relationship and from a marriage are dissimilar, including the fact that the parties are not obliged to provide mutual support and the arrangement of a common household as spouses have to do on the basis of § 15 of the Estonian Family Law Act. If a partnership contract exists, pursuant to section 1 of § 589 of the Estonian Law of Obligations Act all contributions made by the partners and the assets acquired for the partnership shall be transferred to the joint property of

---

17 Decision of the Civil Chamber of the Supreme Court 3-2-1-143-04, at para. 16.

18 Decision of the Civil Chamber of the Supreme Court 3-2-1-109-14, at para. 16.

19 Võlaõigusseadus (adopted on 26 September 2001, entered into force on 1 July 2002). – RT I 2001, 81, 487; RT I, 29.06.2014, 109, available in English at: www.riigiteataja.ee/en/eli/ee/Riigikogu/act/516092014001/consolide.

20 According to § 2 of the Estonian Law of Obligations Act an obligation is a legal relationship which gives rise to the obligation of one person (the obligated person or obligor) to perform an act or omission (to perform an obligation) for the benefit of another person (the entitled person or obligee), and to the right of the obligee to demand that the obligor performs that obligation. The nature of an obligation may oblige the parties involved to take the other party's rights and interests into account in a certain manner. An obligation may also be confined thereto.

the partnership (partnership property). The partnership provisions can be applied primarily in the case of a concrete proprietary objective, such as the common purchase or improvement of a property with the aim of cohabitation with mutual contributions or involving joint expenses for the same objective.

FINLAND

The Finnish Act on the Dissolution of the Household of Cohabiting Partners (26/2011) was created for this particular purpose. The Act contains the following: a provision on the duty to carry out the separation of property, which cannot be waived prior to separation (S. 2 and 4), a provision on the principle that when the property is separated each cohabiting partner will keep his or her own property unless otherwise agreed (S. 5), an obligation to dissolve joint ownership on demand (S. 5), a presumption of the co-ownership of movable assets unless title can be proven (S. 6), a right to apply for an estate distributor from the District Court to separate the property if agreement on the separation cannot be reached (S. 7), and a right to apply for compensation from the other partner if the dissolution of the household according to ownership would result in unjust enrichment at the expense of the other partner because of his or her contributions to the shared household (S. 8 and 9).

FRANCE

Home or household goods are not dealt with any differently from other assets. The general principles of property law are applicable thereto (see Question 41).

GERMANY

There are no specific rules which subject certain property to property division. Regarding assets that the partners hold as co-owners, the general rules are applicable.

According to § 749 German Civil Code, each partner may demand cancellation of the co-ownership at any time. If the object in question is capable of being divided without reducing its value, the cancellation of co-ownership occurs by division in kind (§ 752 German Civil Code). If division in kind is excluded, the cancellation of co-ownership is effected by sale of the joint object (§ 753 German Civil Code). If the partner does not agree to the demand it must be enforced by action for performance (*Leistungsklage*).[21]

GREECE

There are no specific rules. The general provisions on identifying and allocating shared assets will be applied, i.e., the rules on dissolving joint ownership and shared rights. Art. 1113 and 798 et seq. Greek Civil Code.

HUNGARY

The Hungarian Civil Code only provides general rules on the default property regime and there is no specific rule for certain assets, except for the use of the common dwelling after separation.

REPUBLIC OF IRELAND

There are no specific rules regarding the division of all or certain property upon the termination of an informal relationship. See Question 41 for general rules.

ITALY

There are no specific rules, which might have special relevance, for the division of those properties. General rules on ownership apply, and possibly rules on co-ownership.

LATVIA

As there is no legal order on informal relationships in Latvia, there is no legal order on property division following separation in an informal relationship.

LITHUANIA

See also the answer to Question 41.

Art. 4.80 of the Lithuanian Civil Code provides that each co-owner shall have the right to demand that his or her share should be partitioned from

21 K. SCHMIDT, '§ 749', in: *Münchener Kommentar zum BGB*, Beck, Munich, 2013, at No. 40.

the common partial ownership. If no agreement is reached regarding the method of partitioning, the asset shall be divided in kind preferably without disproportionate damage; in other cases, one or several of the co-owners thus partitioned shall receive compensation in monetary terms.

The following effective specific rules (Art. 3.232 and 3.234) should be mentioned: at the request of one of the cohabitees the court may divide all the assets, acquired and used by the cohabitees together, after the death of one of the cohabitees or at the end of their life together provided the cohabitees had not made an agreement on the division of assets certified by a notary public.

LUXEMBOURG

If the exclusive property of one partner cannot be proved, the asset is presumed to be jointly owned by the two of them.

Of course, proof of ownership of immovable property results from the official act of acquisition (*acte notarié de vente*).

When the Question arises as to who has financed the acquisition of this immovable property, the partner who is not the official owner needs to prove his or her financial contributions in order to obtain a reimbursement (the provision of evidence to this effect is important in this respect).

THE NETHERLANDS

There are no specific rules which are applicable in relation to each partner's property law status. Partners have to reach an agreement as to the status of the goods.

NORWAY

There is no statute that specifically regulates cohabitation in Norway. When partners to an informal relationship separate, a settlement along property lines normally takes place. Only two specific rules exist. First, non-statutory rules to avert unjust enrichment have developed through Supreme Court practice. Secondly, a limited opportunity exists for a cohabitant to purchase what was previously the family home and household goods at market value pursuant to the Norwegian Household Community Act.

If neither of these specific rules apply in a particular case, the partners retain their property and debts on a relationship breakdown. If an item of property is co-owned by the partner, each spouse retains his or her part of the said item.

PORTUGAL

No, there are none.

RUSSIA

There are no specific rules as to the property division which are applicable either to all or to certain property. The general rules are those applying to the division of joint ownership (Art. 252 Russian Civil Code). Under this rule, joint owners can divide jointly owned assets in accordance with their agreement (Art. 252(1) Russian Civil Code). If the owners fail to reach agreement, either of them can apply for a division by a court order (Art. 252(3) Russian Civil Code). The assets will then be divided in kind. This means that the judge will order that every dividable joint asset should be divided between the partners in accordance with their shares in that asset. The shares of the joint owners will be regarded as equal, unless stated otherwise in law or in the agreement between the owners (Art. 245 Russian Civil Code). As the judge has to divide assets in kind, an owner cannot be forced to accept compensation without his/her consent (Art. 252(4) Russian Civil Code). An exception to this rule is only possible when one of the owners' share is insignificant.

If the asset is physically, economically or legally undividable in kind (e.g. a motor vehicle, or a collection of postage stamps) the judge will attribute the asset to one of the owners and compensation will be ordered to be paid to the other owner (Art. 252(3) Russian Civil Code).

SCOTLAND

Unlike on divorce or dissolution of civil partnership, where the first principle of financial provision is fair sharing of matrimonial property,[22] there is no provision for sharing of partnership property on termination

22 Family Law (Scotland) Act 1985, S. 9(1)(a).

of cohabitation. In the Scottish Law Commission's *Report on Family Law*, published in 1992, they concluded that a system of property sharing on termination of cohabitation was not appropriate.[23] This conclusion was followed in the Family Law (Scotland) Act 2006 which introduced some rights for cohabitants but specifically did not include provision for property division. In several claims for financial provision, it appears that what the parties are seeking is really some form of property sharing but the courts have consistently confirmed that this is not appropriate in terms of the legislation. In *Selkirk v Chisholm*, the sheriff observed that 'an award to a cohabitant ... is quite distinct from financial provision awarded to a spouse ... on divorce. There is no concept akin to matrimonial property, equal sharing or fair sharing.'[24]

SLOVAKIA

There are no specific rules.

SLOVENIA

Slovene family law does not recognise special rules on the protection of the home or household goods as do some foreign legal systems.

SPAIN

There are no special rules on property division that apply to assets jointly owned by the partners to an informal relationship. The ordinary rules on property division apply. If the parties do not agree on how to divide the property jointly owned, they may apply for division in court proceedings by exercising the so-called *actio communi dividendi*. If assets cannot be divided materially they will be divided economically, either by attributing them to one of the partners by way of compensation or by selling the assets and dividing the income according to the respective shares of ownership. Catalan law provides that, at the request of one of the partners, the judge may make the assets up into two lots and allocate one lot to one partner and the second lot to the other partner.[25]

---

23 Scot Law Com, No 135, para. 16.15.

24 *Selkirk v Chisholm* 2011 Fam LR 56, at para. 98.

25 Disp. Ad. 5ª of the Ley 25/2010, de 29 de julio, del libro segundo del Código civil de Cataluña, relativo a la persona y la familia (BOE núm. 203, de 21-08-2010).

SWEDEN

This is, indeed, the focus of the protection provided by the Swedish Cohabitation Act of 2003 (see Question 2, 4 and 8 above). Upon the termination of the relationship, the so-called 'cohabitation property' of the couple (in Swedish: *samboegendom*) is subject to property division, entitling both (former) partners to an equal share of this property's net value. Cohabitation property consists of the joint home of the couple and their household goods, in both cases, however, only if the property was acquired for the couple's joint use, Cohabitation Act § 3. 'Cohabitation property' does not include property given to a partner by a third party who, in the form of a will or bequest, had stipulated that the property was to be the recipient's separate property, § 4.[26] Unless otherwise agreed by the cohabitees (§ 9), the 'cohabitation property' will be subject to property division between the cohabitees when the relationship ends, if property division is requested by one or both cohabitees, § 8, within one year from the termination of the relationship.

The first step in the division of the 'cohabitation property' is to calculate the cohabitees' shares, § 12. The calculation is done by deciding the value of each cohabitant's assets belonging to this category of property, after which a deduction will be made to cover that cohabitee's debts. As a rule, only debts that are in some way related to the 'cohabitation property' are to be deducted from the value of the cohabitee's assets belonging to the category of 'cohabitation property', § 13 para. 2. However, in the case where the cohabitee lacks other assets which can cover his or her other debts, then these debts will also be deducted from the debtor's 'cohabitation property'. After deduction of the debts, both cohabitants' shares in the 'cohabitation property' are amalgamated and then divided equally, § 13-14.

After the calculation of the shares of each cohabitant, the net value of the 'cohabitation property' is to be distributed, as a rule equally between the former cohabitees. One way to do this is for the cohabitee with more cohabitation property to simply hand over a part of this property to the other cohabitant so that shares become equal. The cohabitee may, however, choose to pay a corresponding sum of money to the other cohabitee, § 17.

[26] A similar provision applies in respect of partners in a formal relationship (marriage or registered partnership), Swedish Marriage Code (in Swedish: *Äktenskapsbalken* 1987:230), Chapter 7 § 2 para. 1.

If the result of the division requiring one of the cohabitees to transfer property or a corresponding value of money to the other cohabitee would be unreasonable, exceptions to the rule of equal sharing may be made (in the form of an adjustment of the property division), for example, if the relationship ends after a short time, § 15. This provision states that if it would be unreasonable for a cohabitee to hand over property to the other partner for both to receive equal shares in the net value of the 'cohabitation property', having regard to the length of the relationship as well as the cohabitees' economic circumstances and overall circumstances, the division can be adjusted. The result is that the equal division will be avoided. No property needs to be handed over, or in any case less than 50% of the net value of the 'cohabitation property'. This provision might become applicable, for example, when only one of the cohabitees owns property qualifying as 'cohabitation property' whereas the other cohabitee has considerable property not qualifying to be included in the property division. In formalised relationships, Swedish Marriage Code Chapter 12 § 1 provides for a similar adjustment of division of marital property.

The division of property is primarily a private transaction, to be performed by the cohabitants on their own without the involvement of any competent authorities. A document concerning the division of the property is to be drawn up and signed by both (former) partners, Swedish Cohabitation Act, § 20 with futher references to the Swedish Marriage Code, Chapter 9, § 5. If the partners cannot agree on the division - or cannot perform it on their own - a property division executor can be appointed by the court upon the application of the partners or one of them.

SWITZERLAND

There are no specific rules which subject all or certain property to the property division when the partners in an informal relationship separate.

If the parties have neither explicitly nor impliedly concluded an agreement with regard to their property, each partner in an informal relationship takes his or her belongings (according to the law of property). Generally, any contributions made (financially or by means of labour) are to be qualified as a favour, a gift or as the fulfilment of moral obligations and will not be compensated.

However, the partners in an informal relationship may have formed a simple partnership (encompassing either the whole or only parts[27] of the informal relationship).[28] The simple partnership is a contractual relationship in which two or more persons agree to combine their efforts or resources in order to achieve a common goal (Art. 530 para. 1 Swiss Code of Obligations, see also Question 3).[29] Thus, a simple partnership exists where the partners in an informal relationship have formed an economic unit with joint finances to which both have contributed either financially or through work and labour. Upon the liquidation of the simple partnership (Art. 548-550 Swiss Code of Obligations), the surplus which remains after the satisfaction of partnership debts, the reimbursement of any expenses incurred and advances made by each partner and the return of the value of contributions[30] is divided as profit among the partners (Art. 549 para. 1 Swiss Code of Obligations). Unless otherwise agreed, each partner has an equal share in the profits regardless of the nature and amount of his or her contribution (Art. 533 para. 1 Swiss Code of Obligations). Any shortfall is borne equally by the partners as a loss (Art. 549 para. 2 Swiss Code of Obligations). However, these cases largely depend on the court's interpretation of the parties' intention to enter into a legally binding relationship and of the common partnership goal pursued by the partners. Thus, legal uncertainties concerning these claims remain in legal practice.

[27] E.g. a joint bank account for household finances.

[28] The rules of simple partnership cannot automatically be applied to all financial questions relating to an informal relationship. Rather, the court has to decide individually regarding the relevant circumstances of every case, Swiss Federal Supreme Court, BGE 108 II 204 E.4. a); BGer 4A_383/2007 (19.12.2007).

[29] For details see M. COTTIER and C. CREVOSIER, 'Die nichteheliche Lebensgemeinschaft als einfache Gesellschaft', *Aktuelle Juristische Praxis*, 2012, at p. 33 et seq.

[30] However, contributions (*Einlagen*) which were made for the joint consumption of the informal relationship may not have to be reimbursed, see Swiss Federal Supreme Court, BGE 108 II 204 E.6.a) and D. STAEHELIN, in: H. HONSELL, N.P. VOGT and R. WATTER, *Basler Kommentar Obligationenrecht II (Art. 530-1186 ZGB)*, Helbing Lichtenhahn Verlag, Bern, 2008, at Art. 548/549 N 8. With regard to ownership see Question 26.

QUESTION 43

Do the partners have preferential rights regarding their home and/or the household goods? If so, what factors are taken into account when granting these rights (e.g. the formal ownership of the property, the duration of the relationship, the needs of each partner, the care of children)?

AUSTRIA

Currently, partners in an informal relationship do not have any preferential rights regarding their home or household goods. The division of the home and household goods is conducted pursuant to the general principles of property law without granting one partner any preferential rights. However, some authors argue that a legal provision is urgently needed with regard to the partner who does not have his or her own right to reside in the previously shared apartment; it is proposed that the partner should be granted a right to reside in the apartment for a limited period of time or that the apartment should even be assigned to one partner by a judicial decision for a longer period of time, if he/she needs the apartment urgently.[1]

BELGIUM

There are no preferential rights on any goods.

The Constitutional Court has determined that the preferential rights of spouses to the home and household goods do not even apply when the home is not community but joint property.[2] Whereas proposals have

[1] C. FISCHER-CZERMAK and B. BECLIN, 'Reformvorschläge für nichteheliche Lebensgemeinschaften', *iFamZ*, 2012, at p. 191; A. DEIXLER-HÜBNER, 'Rechtliche Regelungen für Lebensgemeinschaften im Innenverhältnis, Überlegungen de lege lata und de lege ferenda', *iFamZ*, 2012, at p. 197.

[2] Constitutional Court n° 28/2013 of 7 March 2014, www.const-court.be.

been made to at least extend the protection to all spouses,[3] it is unlikely that it would be extended to informal partners.

In case the house was jointly owned, the courts may temporarily organise its use, for example by allowing one partner to live there (against payment).[4] If a partner only had a right of habitation or can be considered a tenant at will, he will be granted a respite during which he is entitled to remain in the home (against payment).[5]

BULGARIA

No, neither partner has a preferential right regarding their home and/or the household goods.

CROATIA

In line with Art. 11 paragraph 2 of the Croatian Family Act and Art. 4 paragraph 1 and Art. 54 of the Croatian Partnership Act, the answer equally relates to both cohabitants and same-sex informal partners.

It should be noted that preferential rights regarding the family home and household goods were incorporated into the Croatian legal system exclusively due to the protection of minor children in the role of family members.

According to Art. 46 in relation to Art. 11 paragraph 2 of the Croatian Family Act, movables utilised by minor children shall not be included in the dissolution of the community of property but shall remain in the possession of the children or the resident parent.

Upon an application by a partner, the court may adjudicate that the right to housing in the home which represents their family home and community of property shall be exercised only by the parent (partner) residing with minor children over whom the parents (partners) exercise their parental responsibility.

---

3 A. TURTELBOOM and H. CASMAN, 'Geïntegreerde tekst van het voorontwerp van wet tot hervorming van diverse bepalingen inzake het huwelijksvermogensrecht', *TEP* 2014, nos. 3-4, p. 246.

4 Brussels 30 May 2011, *RTDF* 2013, 127, with note LAYON; Justice of the Peace Veurne (Nieuwpoort) 15 December 2009, *T.Vred.* 2012, 31.

5 Justice of the Peace Bruges (1) 2 June 2005, *TGR-TWVR* 2005, 170; Justice of the Peace Halle 23 July 2008, *NJW* 2009, 136, with note VERSCHELDEN. Compare on the basis of a right to habitation: Justice of the Peace Waremme 16 April 1987, *JL* 1987, 1987, 1577.

The right to housing may be effective at a maximum up until the dissolution of the co-ownership of the property representing the family home. When deciding on the right to housing, the court may, taking the circumstances of the case into account, order the resident parent to pay a lump-sum rent to the non-resident parent as well as to pay the bills for residing in the property representing their family home. When deciding on the right to housing and on the rent, the court shall take account of the principle of proportionality; protecting the child's right to housing in the family home and at the same time acting fairly towards the parent who is burdened with the exercise of the right to housing.

The Court may, taking the circumstances of the case into account, reject the application for housing in the family home if the total revenue of the partner does not cover the costs of separate housing and the costs of living of the partners and their children.

CZECH REPUBLIC

The partners have no preferential rights regarding their home and/or household goods. These preferential rights are connected only with marriage according to S. 742 Czech Civil Code. However, in individual cases, good morals, formal ownership, the needs of each of the partners or the care of children, can influence the way their property is separated.

DENMARK

A single published judgment has given a cohabitant a right to take over a joint property on the basis of his need and on the basis of the general principles of the law of obligations. In *Tidsskrift for Familie- og arveret* (Journal of Family and Succession Law), 2001, p. 478, the High Court gave the man in a cohabiting relationship the right to the joint residence after the termination of the relationship on the ground that he lived in the property with a young child of the couple, while the woman had bought a new residence. The woman's interest in taking over the joint residence was based solely on her expectation of being able to sell it at a higher price than the valuation made by the Probate Court.[6]

---

6 For more on the case see I. LUND-ANDERSEN, *Familieøkonomien*, Jurist- og Økonomforbundets Forlag, Copenhagen, 2011, at p. 433-436.

ENGLAND AND WALES

No. There are no preferential rights and formal ownership will normally apply. There is the ability to apply for various possible remedies in the circumstances below:

– Financial provision for the benefit of the child
  Financial provision in the form of capital lump sums or transfer or settlement of property orders for the benefit of a child under 18 can be made on an application under Schedule 1 English Children Act 1989. This is separate from child support.
  The criteria specified in para. 4 of the Schedule include having regard to all the circumstances and specifically to:
  - the income and financial needs and resources of each parent and those of the child;
  - any disability of the child and the manner in which the child was expected to be educated or trained.

  By ordering a settlement of the home or other property, the court can provide that it can be occupied or used by the partner caring for the child until the child is 18 or finishes full time education. See for example *Re P (Child: Financial Provision)* [2003] EWCA Civ 837, [2003] 2 FLR 865.

– Rented family home
  Schedule 7 English Family Law Act 1996 allows applications for transfer of tenancy order between cohabitants of the rented family home on relationship breakdown in cases where the tenancy of the home is rented. This is at the discretion of the court. The court applies the same criteria as for an occupation order under either S. 33(6) where the home is in joint names or S. 36(6) where it is rented in the other partner's sole name. The court must take into account the circumstances in which the tenancy was granted and the suitability of the parties as tenants.
  The S. 36(6) criteria are fuller than those in S. 33(6) applying to joint tenant partners and require greater scrutiny of the relationship. In both cases they include:
  - each party's housing needs and resources and those of any relevant child;
  - the financial resources of each of the parties;
  - the likely effect of the decision of the court on the health, safety or well-being of the parties and any relevant child;
  - the conduct of the parties;
  - the length of time since they lived together.

In addition, in S. 36(6) applications the court must also have regard to:

- the nature of the parties relationship and the level of commitment involved in it;
- the length of the cohabitation;
- whether they have children together;
- the length of time since they separated; and
- the existence of any Children Act 1989 or property proceedings.

– Challenging legal ownership
Under trust law (S. 14 of the English Trusts of Land and Appointment of Trustees Act 1996), a declaration of trust can be sought in order to challenge legal ownership of any property by proving shared beneficial ownership under a common intention resulting or constructive trust. This remedy is not specific to cohabitation relationships and has been more fully discussed in answer to Question 3.

ESTONIA

There are no special rules with regard to an informal relationship concerning the dwelling (home) and household goods.

FINLAND

The property is separated according to title, i.e. formal ownership of the property, if proof of ownership can be provided.

FRANCE

No such preferential rights exist regarding cohabitants in the French legal system. The general principles of property law are applicable thereto (see Question 41).

GERMANY

There are no preferential rights regarding home or household goods. In particular, the rules concerning the use of the matrimonial home (§§ 1361b, 1568a German Civil Code) or the allocation of household goods (§§ 1361a, 1568b German Civil Code) after separation of spouses or the dissolution of a marriage cannot be applied by analogy.[7] This holds true even if the couple has children.[8] Only in cases of domestic violence can orders regarding the joint home be granted according to the provisions of the Protection against Violence Act.

GREECE

No, there are no such rights.

HUNGARY

There have been no such regulations in Hungarian law regarding the cohabitants' home and/or household goods. Under the former regime of the Civil Code of 1959 the division of assets in the case of separation followed the model applied in the case of divorce or the division of the common property of spouses. It is still not known how the provisions concerning the new regime will be applied in the case law.

REPUBLIC OF IRELAND

No, partners do not have preferential rights regarding their home and/or household goods unless they are joint tenants. Qualified cohabitants who prove to the court that they are financially dependent on their ex-partner may apply for a Property Adjustment Order.

ITALY

In general, informal partners at the moment of their separation are not awarded any preferential right by law. Only when they have children from their partnership may special protection be granted as regards the family home.

Art. 337 *sexies* of the Italian Civil Code in fact states that '[t]he enjoyment of the family home is attributed primarily taking into account the children's interest. When regulating the economic relationship between the parents the judge will take into account that attribution, also

---

7 H. GRZIWOTZ, *Nichteheliche Lebensgemeinschaft*, Beck, Munich, 2014, at § 5 No. 22; regarding § 1568b German Civil Code: G. BRUDERMÜLLER, '§ 1568b', in: O. PALANDT, *Bürgerliches Gesetzbuch*, Beck, Munich, 2015, at No. 2.

8 Regarding § 1361b German Civil Code: G. BRUDERMÜLLER, '§ 1361b', in: O. PALANDT, *Bürgerliches Gesetzbuch*, Beck, Munich, 2015, at No. 5 with further references for a critical view.

considering the title of ownership, if there is any. The right to enjoyment of the family home is withdrawn if the assignee does not live or stops living permanently in the home, starts a new cohabitation, or remarries.' This rule, introduced by the law of 8 February 2006, n. 54 on shared custody applies to the separation and divorce of married couples, but also to the dissolution of cohabitation (Art. 337 *bis* Italian Civil Code).

It must be born in mind, however, that while in a personal separation and the dissolution of marriage judicial intervention is mandatory, the dissolution of an informal partnership does not necessarily require judicial intervention, even when the separating couple have children. Only in a dispute between parents regarding the custody of the child(ren) may either of them initiate proceedings which will then be resolved by the courts, applying the rules provided in Art. 337 *bis* et seq. Italian Civil Code.

The allocation of the family home is therefore not determined with reference to the interests of the informal partner, but exclusively with reference to those of the children who, pursuant to a decision originally applied to a married couple but which can be extended to unmarried parents, must be sons and daughters common to both the separating partners (Cass. civ. 2 October 2007, n. 20688). It may be added that, according to the Constitutional Court, the loss of the family home by the assignee, as foreseen by Art. 337 *bis,* does not follow automatically in the event of a new cohabitation or the remarriage of the assignee, but must be subordinated to a judgement on its conformity with the interests of the children (Constitutional Court 30 July 2008, n. 308).

Household goods and commodities are considered to be fixtures of the home and go with it. The same rule applies to the expenses related to the home, for instance the expenses for condominium administration, and these must be paid by the assignee.

LATVIA

In Latvia there is no such legal order on separation following an informal relationship.

LITHUANIA

Article 3.234 of the Lithuanian Civil Code defines the division of assets used together: A house or an apartment may be awarded to the cohabitee who is in greater need of a place of residence taking into consideration his or her age, health, financial situation, the interests of his or her minor children and other important circumstances. In such cases the share of this cohabitee in other community assets shall be reduced. Where the value of the house or the apartment exceeds the value of the cohabitee's share in the assets, he or she must compensate, in monetary terms, the other cohabitee for the difference in the value. The house or the apartment which belonged to one of the cohabitees before their life together can be occupied by the other cohabitee under a right of usufruct if he or she has underage children born to the cohabitation or due to his or her health, age or other important reasons does not have his or her own dwelling.

Assets other than those referred to in Art. 3.230 (the provisions of this article shall not be applicable to assets which the cohabitees use for recreational purposes (the garden, a summer cottage, etc.)) which have been acquired and maintained by using the funds of both cohabitees shall be divided in accordance with the rules of shared community property.

The court shall have a right to depart from the principle of equal shares if it is just and reasonable to award one of the cohabitees a greater share of the assets, taking into account the interests of their minor children, the duration of their life together, their age, health, financial situation, personal contribution to the community property and other important circumstances.

The issue of transferring household articles to one of the cohabitees is resolved by the parity of reasoning,[9] in accordance with Art. 3.127 of the Lithuanian Civil Code ('If possible, the property is divided in kind having regard to its value and the share of each spouse in the community property. If the property cannot be divided in kind, it is awarded in kind to one of the spouses, who is ordered to compensate the other spouse's share in money. The decision on the way the property is to be divided and the actual division of property in kind is taken having regard to the interests of the minor children, the state of health and the financial situation of one of the spouses as well as to other important circumstances').

---

9 V. MIKELENAS et al., *Commentary on Book Three of the Civil Code of Lithuania* (in Lithuanian), Justitia, Vilnius, 2002, at p. 453.

LUXEMBOURG

Partners do not have any preferential rights. The ownership of the property is the relevant factor.

THE NETHERLANDS

No, there no preferential rights regarding the home or household goods. Upon separation the partners have to agree on the status of property (the private property of A, of B or joint property?). In relation to joint property they have to decide what to do: one of them may acquire the other's share in the asset, if that is financially feasible, or they can both transfer their share to a third party. If partners cannot reach an agreement, the court will have to take a decision. Each partner has the right to petition for a division (Art. 3:178 para. 1 Dutch Civil Code). The court can take into account all relevant facts.[10]

NORWAY

The Norwegian Household Community Act applies to two or more unmarried adults who have lived together in a household, and includes cohabitants as well as siblings, students and others who live together. When 'strong reasons' so indicate, a partner to an informal relationship may purchase what was previously the common residence and household goods at market value upon the termination of the household, pursuant to the Norwegian Household Community Act, S. 3. The needs of the children are given special weight in this assessment. On the same strict conditions a cohabitant may obtain the right to enter into a tenancy agreement even if the contract is established in the name of the other cohabitant. As the cohabitant is obliged to pay market price and the conditions are strict, the Norwegian Household Community Act is not applied very often.

PORTUGAL

The partner who wants to remain in the home against the will of the partner who is the owner may file a petition at the courts, on the grounds of Art. 4 of Law No. 7/2001 and Art. 1793 of the Portuguese Civil Code. The court will consider the necessities of both partners and their children. The rules are also applicable if the house is owned by both of them. The

[10] W.M. SCHRAMA, 'Goederenrecht: mede-eigendom', in: M.L.C.C. DE BRUIJN-LÜCKERS et al. (eds.), *Relatierecht, SDUCommentaar*, SDU, The Hague, 2014, at p. 2025-2040.

petitioner may remain as a tenant; and the court may control the terms of the contract and may terminate the contract if circumstances change.

The partner who wants to remain in the home against the will of the partner who is the tenant may file a petition at the courts, on the grounds of Art. 4 of Law No. 7/2001 and Art. 1105.º of the Portuguese Civil Code. The court will consider the necessities of both partners and their children besides 'other relevant factors'. The rules are also applicable if both are equally tenants. The petitioner may remain as the tenant or the sole tenant.

RUSSIA

In the absence of specific rules, partners have no preferential rights to any objects. However, if both partners claim a certain object that cannot be divided in kind (e.g. a motor vehicle), the judge will take all the circumstances of the case into consideration. The title of ownership (if an asset is held in the name of one of the partners, while the partners have created joint ownership in an agreement) and the duration of the relationship will not then be of relevance. The needs of each partner (e.g. professional use, occupational travel or disability) and of the children will be taken into consideration as circumstances of the case.

SCOTLAND

The starting point is that all assets belong to the legally entitled owner and there are no preferential rights regarding the home or the household goods. There is a statutory presumption of equal ownership of household goods (discussed in detail at Question 29). Although either party may apply to the court for a financial order on the termination of cohabitation,[11] the statute makes no provision for a property transfer order.

SLOVAKIA

The partners have no preferential rights regarding their home and/or the household goods.

[11] Family Law (Scotland) Act 2006, S. 28.

SLOVENIA

The court carries out a physical division of the common property in a civil procedure if this is possible. At the request of a partner it may award, on account of her or his share, mainly objects that are intended for performing her or his trade or profession and enable her or him to earn a personal income and objects intended exclusively for her or his use. Otherwise, each partner receives, in a natural form, those objects for which a justified interest therein is shown. This applies to the question of the division of a common home, in particular the housing needs of the partners, their children and other persons who live with them and other circumstances of the case.

Slovene family law does not recognise special rules on the protection of the home or household goods as do some foreign legal systems.

SPAIN

There are preferential rights concerning the use, but not the property, of the family home and household goods, that apply essentially if there are children. Article 234-8 Catalan Civil Code establishes that the judge can allocate the use of the family home and household goods depending on the circumstances of the case according to the following rules. If one parent has sole custody of the child or children he or she will be granted the use of the family home and household goods for the duration of custody. In cases of joint custody the use of the family home will be granted to the parent who is more in need.

The Spanish Civil Code does not have rules regarding the home and household goods of partners to an informal relationship. Case law tends to apply the provisions contained in Art. 96 Spanish Civil Code on the allocation of the matrimonial home. In the absence of agreement the use is granted to the children and thus indirectly to the residential parent. In cases where there is an alternative residence the family home and household goods are usually attributed to the parent who is more in need.

SWEDEN

Upon termination of the relationship the partner in greater need of the dwelling or the household goods (on condition that this property is included in the 'cohabitation property') has a right to take over the dwelling or goods, a so-called 'take-over right'; the other partner must, however, be compensated to a corresponding extent (usually in the form of money), Swedish Cohabitation Act, § 16 and 17. Usually the partner who is to have actual custody of the couple's joint children (the residential parent) is considered to be the one in greater need of the joint dwelling. Other things that may be taken into account are the cohabitees' health, age and their prospects of getting hold of a new home if forced to move out.[12]

Exceptionally, a cohabitee's take-over right may concern a joint dwelling which does not belong to the category of 'cohabitation property', § 22 (for example because it was already owned or rented by the other cohabitee before the relationship). In this case, however, the take-over right usually requires that the cohabitees have common children. In other cases, it is only due to exceptional reasons that a partner may be granted the right to take over such a dwelling. An example might be that the cohabitee wishing to remain in the couple's home has children of his or her own (who are not common children with the other cohabitee) and that the dwelling has been their home during a long period of time.[13] This extended take-over right only applies to tenancy rights and to an apartment, belonging to the other cohabitee, in a cooperatively owned building, and does not cover real estate property (i.e., in this case land property with a house).

SWITZERLAND

In Switzerland, the partners in an informal relationship do not have preferential rights regarding their home and/or the household goods.

---

[12] G. LIND, *Sambolagen, en kommentar*, Norstedts Juridik, Stockholm, 2013, at § 22.

[13] Government Bill, Prop. 1973:32 p. 169.

QUESTION 44

How are the joint debts of the partners settled?

AUSTRIA

There are no specific rules regulating the settlement of joint debts in case of separation. Usually, the person owning the capital has to repay the loan - at least in the internal relationship as between the ex-partners. However, if loans have been jointly taken out, the creditor will not discharge one debtor from his/her liability, unless it receives an equal security.[1] Hence, an agreement with the creditor is recommended, which discharges one partner either completely from his/her liability or he/she is only liable as a guarantor after the separation. Further, it is recommended to clarify the issue of who pays the instalments in case of separation in a partnership agreement.[2]

BELGIUM

No specific rules apply, since there is no joint estate.

BULGARIA

The joint debts of the partners will be settled in respect of creditors according to the general regulations of the Bulgarian Obligations and Contracts Law. It also applies to relations between the partners if there is no agreement between them in this respect.

---

1 U. AICHHORN, *Das Recht der Lebenspartnerschaften, Ehe und Lebensgemeinschaft*, Springer, Vienna, 2003, at p. 429; E. MÖSCHL, *Die nichteheliche Lebensgemeinschaft*, LexisNexis ARD ORAC, Vienna, 2007, at marg. No. 88.

2 U. AICHHORN, *Das Recht der Lebenspartnerschaften, Ehe und Lebensgemeinschaft*, Springer, Vienna, 2003, at p. 429.

CROATIA

In line with Art. 11 paragraph 2 of the Croatian Family Act and Art. 4 paragraph 1 and Art. 54 of the Croatian Partnership Act, the answer equally relates to both cohabitants and same-sex informal partners.

According to Art. 44 in relation to Art. 11 of the Croatian Family Act, both partners shall be held jointly and severally liable with regard to the liabilities assumed by one partner for the purpose of satisfying the current needs of their family union as well as with respect to the liabilities jointly assumed by both partners, which relate to their community of property. If not agreed otherwise, spouses shall be held liable in equal shares concerning these liabilities.

According to Art. 44 in relation to Art. 11 of the Croatian Family Act, creditors can recover joint debs against assets that belong to the partners' community of property and against the personal property of each partner.

CZECH REPUBLIC

The joint debts are settled by the general rules of shared debts; there are no specific rules concerning the joint debts of partners in an informal relationship. Partners are jointly liable for debts if it follows from the contract that co-debtors are obliged jointly and severally. According to S. 1872(1) Czech Civil Code if several debtors are obliged to perform jointly and severally, they are obliged to perform one for all and all for one. A creditor may demand the entire performance or any part thereof from all, only some, or any one of the co-debtors.

DENMARK

Joint liability for debt can be based on an agreement between the parties or on a special ground for liability. The special ground can be that the non-contracting party has given his or her partner the authority to act on his or her behalf. A special kind of authority can be an apparent authority by virtue of conduct where, by that conduct, the non-contracting cohabitant gives the counterparty good reason to believe that he or she had given authority and that both cohabitants were bound by the debt obligation.[3]

---

3 For more detail, see I. LUND-ANDERSEN, *Familieøkonomien*, Jurist- og Økonomforbundets Forlag, Copenhagen, 2011, at p. 237-250.

ENGLAND AND WALES

Parties can agree or can mediate to reach agreement as to how to repay joint debts. In default of agreement, a court can decide, although creditors can proceed for the whole amount against either party or both parties for a joint debt as there will be joint and several liability.

Most commonly, creditors take action to recover the goods or recover the debt from the party with the greater or most accessible assets. This leaves it to the parties to claim back the other partner's share of the debt from them which they can do through mediation or litigation. There is no special family law jurisdiction in this regard.

ESTONIA

There are no special rules with regard to an informal relationship and debts are dealt with according to which type of obligors confront the creditors: joint obligors, collective obligors or solitary obligors.

FINLAND

No separate provisions exist on this. In practice, one partner incurs the debt in his or her name in return for the payment or receipt of other property or property is sold to settle the debt.

FRANCE

Concerning debts, each cohabitant is personally liable for the debts he or she incurred either for the household or for herself or himself. The principle of joint liability for household debts, which applies to spouses[4] and to partners bound by a *Pacs*,[5] is not applicable to cohabitants. Where one cohabitant has paid the other's debt, he or she is entitled to a reward where evidence of such a payment is provided. The theory of unjust enrichment would support such a claim for a reward[6] (see Question 38).

Regarding joint debts contracted by cohabitants, each debtor is personally liable for his or her share of the debt. However, where joint liability has been provided for in the contract, they will be jointly liable

---

4 Art. 220 of the French Civil Code.

5 Art. 515-4 of the French Civil Code.

6 Art. 1371 of the French Civil Code. See Cass. Civ 1, 15 October 1996 no. 94-20472; Cass. Civ 1, 24 September 2008 no. 07-11928.

for the full amount of the debt. Joint liability for debts, unless organised otherwise by legislation,[7] must be expressly agreed upon by the parties.[8] Where co-debtors are jointly liable, the one who has paid the full debt is entitled to sue the other(s) in order to recover the amounts that are due.[9]

GERMANY

In relation to third parties § 421 German Civil Code is decisive. Regarding joint debts the partners are joint and several debtors. The creditor may at his or her discretion demand full or part performance from each of the partners. The external liability is independent from any agreement which may exist between the joint and several debtors. Therefore the creditor may enforce his or her claim against either or both partners until extinction of the debt.[10]

As regards the internal relationship between joint and several debtors, § 426 German Civil Code applies. § 426 para. 1 German Civil Code states that joint and several debtors are obliged in equal proportions in relation to one another unless 'otherwise determined'. Insofar as informal relationships are concerned, it may be 'otherwise determined' with regard to compensation. It is well-established case law that in informal relationships partners make financial or other contributions to everyday expenses as the need arises and cannot seek compensation in the case of separation unless the partners have agreed otherwise.[11] This principle of non-compensation also applies if one of the partners settled joint debts. Therefore the general duty to adjust advancements (as per § 426 para. 1 German Civil Code) does not apply. Joint and several liability with the ensuing equal contributions is to a certain extent superimposed by the informal relationship.[12] Thus in the case of a joint debt that served for the partners' living expenses or the rent of their joint home the partner who paid the entire sum cannot claim any compensation.

However, compensation may be claimed if the debt arises or falls due only after separation and does not concern the joint living expenses or

7 Such is the case between spouses or partners bound by a *Pacs* for household debts, but joint liability for such debts is not extended to cohabitants.

8 Art. 1202 of the French Civil Code.

9 Art. 1204 of the French Civil Code.

10 M. GEHRLEIN, '§ 421', in: *Beck'scher Online-Kommentar BGB*, Beck, Munich, 2015, at No. 11.

11 BGH, 06.10.2003, *FamRZ*, 2004, 94; BGH, 13.04.2005 *FamRZ*, 2005, 1151, 1152.

12 BGH, 25.11.2009, *FamRZ*, 2010, 277, 279; N. DETHLOFF, *Familienrecht*, Beck, Munich, 2012, at § 8 No. 18.

rent for the joint home.[13] Compensation may also be claimed if the joint debt did not concern daily living expenses but was a contribution to an asset of substantial economic importance (see Question 46 for the limits of the principle of non-compensation and potential claims for compensation in such cases).

GREECE

Joint debts are to be settled under the rules on passive liability (Art. 481 et seq. Greek Civil Code).

HUNGARY

There is no specific rule on this.

REPUBLIC OF IRELAND

No specific rules apply.

ITALY

No special rule is provided for the settlement of the informal partners' debts. In the case that partners have become jointly liable for debts or have undertaken an obligation together, for instance by both signing the same contract, general rules on the discharge of contracts will apply.

LATVIA

There is no specific legal order on separation following an informal relationship. However, the general law of obligation of the Latvian Civil Law is applicable. Section 1670 of the Latvian Civil Law provides that a claim or an obligation is to be recognised as joint or solidary when each of several creditors may claim the entire subject-matter, or when each of several debtors has the duty to perform it all; the subject-matter may, however, be claimed and is required to be performed only once. Section 1682 of the Latvian Civil Law provides that each of the joint debtors or solidary obligors may be compelled to perform the whole obligation, and their performance will release the others from their obligations. Section 1683 of the Latvian Civil Law provides that a creditor may, pursuant to his or her discretion, request the performance of the whole obligation

[13] BGH, 03.02.2010, *NJW*, 2010, 868, 869; OLG Hamm, 19.10.1999 *FamRZ*, 2001, 95.

from all or from only a few joint debtors, or from only one debtor. Section 1686 provides that a joint debtor who has satisfied a creditor may request respective compensation from the others, if there are no special restrictions against this. If the joint debtor who has paid acted in bad faith, he or she will thereby lose the right to compensation from the others.

LITHUANIA

According to Art. 4.80 of the Lithuanian Civil Code, a creditor of a co-owner shall have the right to partition the debtor's share in order to claim it. This means that creditors may recover a corresponding share of the debt from the property of each partner, including from jointly acquired and used property referred to in Art. 3.230 of the Lithuanian Civil Code. Also see the answer to Question 32.

In order to divide assets acquired and used by cohabitees together the court shall first establish the assets acquired and used together and the separate assets of each cohabitee. Debts contracted by the cohabitees together and still outstanding at the end of their life together shall be deducted from the assets acquired and used together by the cohabitees. The assets acquired and used together which remain after the deduction of the joint outstanding debts of the cohabitees shall be divided into two equal shares except in cases provided for in this Art. 3.234.

LUXEMBOURG

Case law has decided that a joint debt contracted by the two partners is divided between them. Each of them is only responsibe for his or her part; it is presumed that this part is 50% of the debt. This presumption is rebuttable. So, one partner may prove that the debt exclusively or mostly served the interests of the other partner in order that this partner has to satisfy most or part of it or even has to satisfy it in its entirety.

So we can read the following in some judgments: '*L'obligation solidairement contractée envers le créancier se divise de plein droit entre les débiteurs solidares qui ne sont tenus chacun que pour leur part et portion. La division se fait en principe par parts viriles, chaque codébiteur solidaire étant présumé avoir une part égale dans l'affaire commune*' (e.g. Court of Appeal, 22nd of March 2006).

THE NETHERLANDS

When partners are both debtors in relation to the same debt, they are jointly liable for the amount to be paid (Art. 6:6 Dutch Civil Code). There is some case law on debts after a relationship breakdown.[14] Sometimes it is contested in the internal relation of the partners what part of the debt has to be borne by who. Art. 6:10 para. 1 Dutch Civil Code states that each debtor is under a duty to pay for the part of the debt that relates to him/her. Presumably, this is clear for debts in relation to the purchase of a home, but for credit loans which parties have contracted jointly, this might be subject to debate after separation.[15]

NORWAY

As mentioned, no statute specifically regulates the financial settlement upon a relationship breakdown. Each partner retains his or her debts upon separation. If they are jointly liable, debt recovery can be enforced in full against either of the partners after the separation.

PORTUGAL

As a rule, each partner is liable for the debts which he/she has incurred. However, some legal scholars suggest that partners should be jointly liable for any debts incurred in order to meet normal family expenses, in the same way as married couples are (Art. 1691 (1) b) of the Portuguese Civil Code). Parliamentary Bill n. 349/X, which preceded Act 23/2010, foresaw the same solution. However, this did not become law, due to the veto by the President of the Republic.

RUSSIA

Partners in informal relationships become jointly liable for debts not as a couple, but instead as two unrelated persons. Therefore, their joint liability for debts does not depend on their relationship and the debts cannot be 'settled' when partners separate. In other words, separated partners remain jointly liable for their joint debts. The only way to 'settle' them is in accordance with the general rules on the law of obligations concerning the transfer of debts. Under Art. 391(1) Russian Civil Code,

---

[14] Hof Leeuwarden 20 March 2012, ECLI:NL:GHLEE:2012:BV9659 (forced cooperation to pay off a joint debt); Hof Arnhem-Leeuwarden 23 April 2013, ECLI:NL:GHARL:2013:BZ8637.

[15] Hof Arnhem-Leeuwarden 23 July 2013, ECLI:NL:GHARL:2013:5347.

such transfers are possible only with the consent of both partners (the debtors) and the creditor(s). If such consent is given, the partners can agree, for instance, that the mortgage on the house will be paid by one partner and the personally secured loan for the car by the other partner.

SCOTLAND

The relationship between the partners has no effect on their liability and debts remain the responsibility of the individual by whom they were incurred. Parties may be jointly liable where they have incurred joint debts. There are no rules specifically covering partners in an informal relationship and this is a matter governed by the general rules of obligation.

SLOVAKIA

For the settlement of the joint debts of the partners, the creditors have to be involved in the settlement process. § 488 of the Slovak Code characterises legal obligation relationships as legal relationships establishing the creditor's right to performance (a claim) by the debtor and the debtor's duty to fulfil the obligation (a debt). An legal obligation relationship must have at least two parties - a creditor and a debtor - since a claim cannot exist without a debt and a debt cannot exist without a claim.[16]

The settlement of the joint debts of the partners is possible using the legal framework for the modification of legal obligation relationships laid down in the Slovak Civil Code. Slovak civil law distinguishes between a modification of the subject matter (content) and a modification of the parties to legal obligation relationships. Modifications to the content of legal obligation relationships are primarily based on the agreement between the parties.

In the case of separating partners we assume that the partners will try to settle their joint debts by an assumption of debt. Under the heading 'Assumption of debt' (*prevzatie dlhu*), the Slovak Civil Code regulates two agreements. The first is the assumption of debt in the form of a privative intercession regulated by § 531 para. 1 of the Slovak Civil Code. By this written agreement between the old debtor and the new debtor, the debtor

16 See K. KIRSTOVÁ, in: J. LAZAR et al. (eds.), *Občianske právo hmotné* (Substantive Slovak Civil Law), Iuris Libri, Bratislava, 2014, at p. 12.

is substituted, provided that the creditor approves of this agreement.[17] No specific form of the creditor's approval is required. The debt assumption agreement can be approved before or after it is made, in oral or written form, but also in an implied form. Security pertaining to the claim once it is assumed by a third party will continue to exist, but only if the persons providing security agree that the debtor can be substituted. The second agreement is the assumption of debt in the form of a cumulative intercession regulated by § 531 para. 2 of the Slovak Civil Code. It is a written agreement between the creditor and the new debtor who assumes the debt and becomes a debtor alongside the old debtor. The original debtor's approval is not required.

SLOVENIA

For obligations that, under the general regulations, burden both partners, the partners are liable with both their individual and their common property. Their liability is indivisible. The partner that repays the debt may demand restitution from the other partner of the share of the debt that exceeds his or her own share. The share of a debt is settled according to the capacities of the partners to contribute to supporting the family (Art. 56 of the Slovenian Marriage Act).

SPAIN

Joint debts vis-à-vis third parties are not affected by the break-up of the relationship. Partners continue to be liable according to ordinary rules.

SWEDEN

The Swedish Cohabitation Act of 2003 does not regulate the settlement of the partners' joint debts in general. Instead it regulates the settlement of debts which are related to the property qualifying as 'cohabitation property' upon the termination of the relationship, § 13. According to § 13, debts that are in some way connected to 'cohabitation property' are to be deducted from the value of this property, before its division between the (former) cohabitees. According to the main rule, the net value of this property is to be divided equally between the partners upon the termination of the relationship (Question 42).

---

17 K. KIRSTOVÁ, in: J. LAZAR et al. (eds.), *Občianske právo hmotné* (Substantive Slovak Civil Law), Iuris Libri, Bratislava, 2014, at p. 68.

Other joint debts that the cohabitants might have (see answer to Question 31) are settled according to general principles of the law of obligations and property. After separation, for practical reasons, the partner who will keep the asset connected to the debt usually also takes over the debt. But if no special arrangements are made, the partners will continue to be jointly liable even after separation.

SWITZERLAND

Generally, the termination of an informal relationship does not affect the joint debts of the partners.

Joint debts assumed by a simple partnership formed by the partners have to be settled upon the liquidation of the simple partnership (Art. 549 para. 1 Swiss Code of Obligations). Each partner has the right to demand a settlement of any debts before the distribution of the possibly remaining surplus of the simple partnership amongst the partners.[18]

[18] D. Staehelin, in: H. Honsell, N.P. Vogt and R. Watter, *Basler Kommentar Obligationenrecht II (Art. 530-1186 ZGB)*, Helbing Lichtenhahn Verlag, Bern, 2008, at Art. 548/549 N 6.

QUESTION 45

What date is decisive for the determination and the valuation of:

a. The assets?

b. The debts?

AUSTRIA

a. The assets?

With regard to separation in an informal relationship no determination and valuation of assets is necessary, because each partner generally remains the owner of his/her assets - even during the relationship. If the partners are joint owners, they either have to divide the asset in kind or, if that is impossible or infeasible, a so-called civil division *(Zivilteilung)* by auctioning the asset and distributing the proceeds becomes necessary.[1] With regard to separation when there is an informal relationship a valuation of a benefit only becomes necessary if one partner reclaims a particular performance under S. 1435 General Austrian Civil Code.[2] Generally, the asset has to be returned in kind. If that is impossible or infeasible the residual value at the time of the separation will be determined by the judge according to his/her free conviction pursuant to S. 273 Austrian Code of Civil Procedure.[3]

b. The debts?

Due to the fact that separation does not affect joint debts, no date is required for the determination and valuation thereof. Despite the separation both partners remain liable for debts. If they mutually reach another agreement, they also have to agree on the date upon which only one partner should repay the debt. Hence, it is a matter of agreement.

---

1 Section 843 General Austrian Civil Code.

2 See the answer to Question 46.

3 Austrian Supreme Court, Judgement of 29.09.1999, 6 Ob 60/99p; Austrian Supreme Court, Judgement 11.06.1981, 7 Ob 600/81.

BELGIUM

No specific rules apply. Vis-à-vis the determination of assets and debts: there is no joint estate to which they can belong. The date for the valuation is the date of the division.

BULGARIA

a. The assets?

The decisive date for the determination and the valuation of assets is the date of the sale/disposal or the commencement of the dispute (Art. 69, para. 1 p. 2 of the Bulgarian Civil Procedure Code).

b. The debts?

The date which is decisive for the valuation of the debt is the date of its settlement. Debts are determined at the date of contracting including the nominal value plus interest.

CROATIA

In line with Art. 11 paragraph 2 of the Croatian Family Act and Art. 4 paragraph 1 and Art. 54 of the Croatian Partnership Act, the answer equally relates to both cohabitants and same-sex informal partners.

There are no specific legal rules for this issue.

a. The assets?

In terms of deciding whether certain property represents the community of property (and thus co-ownership in equal shares) or not, decisive dates mean the date of the commencement of the partnership and the date of the actual separation of the partners.

The value of the assets shall be determined according to their value at the moment of the factual division. In principle, this should be the date of the court order.

b. The debts?

When it comes to a specification as to whether certain debts are joint or not, the decisive element is the time when they arose, i.e. the date of the commencement of the partnership and the date of the actual separation.

Regarding the calculation of the amount of debt, the decisive element is the time of the delivery of the court order.

CZECH REPUBLIC

a. The assets?

There are no specific rules concerning the determination and the valuation of the assets of partners in an informal relationship. Separation of partners in an informal relationship does not have any influence on their assets. General rules are used; therefore the date of the cancellation of the co-ownership is decisive. (See S. 1140 et seq. Czech Civil Code).

b. The debts?

There are no specific rules concerning the determination and the valuation of the debts of partners in an informal relationship. Separation of partners in an informal relationship does not have any influence on their debts. General rules are used; therefore the date of the cancellation of the co-ownership is decisive. (See S. 1140 et seq. Czech Civil Code).

DENMARK

a. The assets?

In Denmark, when a cohabitating relationship ends the Probate Court deals with the dissolution of cohabitants' assets owned in common when there are a number of assets; see S. 1(3) of the Danish Act on the Division of Matrimonial Property (*Ægtefælleskiftelov*). The same rules apply to cohabitants as to spouses. A cohabitant may apply to the Probate Court to refer a case to an administrator who will advise and seek to get the parties to agree, as well as drawing up an account and making a valuation of the property; see S. 17-30 of the Danish Act on the Division of Matrimonial Property. The valuation is made as per the date when an asset is transferred to a cohabitant or the date of the end of the Probate Court proceedings.

b. The debts?

When a cohabitating relationship ends, the debts associated with assets owned in common are included in the valuation of the estate as per the date when assets are transferred to a cohabitant or the date of the end of the Probate Court proceedings. The calculation of liabilities is based on information given by the cohabitants.

ENGLAND AND WALES

a. The assets?

Generally the respective share of the assets owned by each party will be that prevailing at the date of separation. However the valuation of the assets is normally at the date of realisation of those assets, that is, at the date of sale or deemed sale as decided by the Court of Appeal in *Turton v Turton* [1988] Ch 542.

b. The debts?

Date of separation with adjustments for post separation payments or default in payment would be the normal rule.

ESTONIA

There are no special rules with regard to an informal relationship and in civil proceedings the partners are treated as non-married persons.

a. The assets?

If the partners in an informal relationship are the co-owners of the asset, then to guarantee a fair and prompt payment of compensation, the value of the asset should be determined as precisely as possible, at the time of losing the asset, and the co-owner must receive the resulting monetary compensation as far as possible concurrently with the loss of the asset.[4]

b. The debts?

The payment and scope of the debt shall be determined according to the agreement between the debtor and the creditor.

FINLAND

a. The assets?

No separate provision exists on this.

b. The debts?

No separate provision exists on this.

FRANCE

a. The assets?

The legal property regime which is applicable to cohabitants is the one of indivisible joint property (*indivision*). According to Art. 829 of the French Civil Code, the value of the assets subjected to indivisible joint property is assessed on the date of the act of sharing (*partage*) or the closest possible date thereto.

4 Decision of the Civil Chamber of the Supreme Court 3-2-1-168-05, at para. 9.

b. The debts?
The value of a debt is determined on the date when it becomes payable. The value thereof depends on the terms of the agreement between the creditor and the debtor. Banking and other interests can be determined in the contract.

GERMANY

a. The assets?
The decisive date for the determination and the valuation of the assets is either the death of one of the partners or the actual separation. The actual separation usually occurs when one partner permanently leaves the common residence (see Question 5).[5]

b. The debts?
See (a) above.

GREECE

a. The assets?
The date on which they are claimed.

b. The debts?
The date on which the claim becomes due for payment.

HUNGARY

Art. 6:516 of the Hungarian Civil Code on the cohabitants' default property regime refers to regulations on the spouses' participation in acquisitions regime which is an alternative regime for spouses in the Hungarian Civil Code. The provisions on the matrimonial property regime of participation in acquisitions prescribe that the division of the participation may be claimed by applying the rules on the division of the common property in the matrimonial community of property (which has been preserved as the default matrimonial property regime). In that case the date of the termination of the community of property is decisive concerning the determination and valuation of the assets (and the debts).[6] Nevertheless, if the community of property has terminated earlier, the

5 H. GRZIWOTZ, *Nichteheliche Lebensgemeinschaft*, Beck, Munich, 2014, at § 12 No. 101; cf. *BVerfGE*, 87, 234, 265 = *NJW*, 1993, 643, 646.

6 Art. 4:60(1) of the Hungarian Civil Code.

date of the division of the common property is decisive. That means that a variation in the value of the property between the date of the termination of the community of property and that of the division of the common property has to be taken into account, except when either partner's behaviour resulted in this variation.

REPUBLIC OF IRELAND

a. The assets?

The date of dissolution.

b. The debts?

The date of dissolution.

ITALY

The separation of informal partners being a matter of fact – which does not require judicial intervention – only in the case of a dispute does the date of its taking place have relevance. It will then be the task of the judge to determine, according to the circumstances of the specific case, the date when it occurred with reference to both the assets and the debts.

LATVIA

As there is no legal order on informal relationships in Latvia, there is no legal order on separation following an informal relationship.

LITHUANIA

a. The assets?

The current legislation which applies to partners in an informal relationship does not provide for this aspect, but by the analogy of Art. 3.119 the value of the community property to be partitioned shall be established at its market value on the date of the termination of the common partial ownership. In addition, the Court must take into consideration any depreciation of assets or, on the contrary, a possible increase in their value (i.e. in the case of securities).

b. The debts?

Debts contracted by the cohabitees together and still outstanding at the end of their life together shall be deducted from the assets acquired and used together by the cohabitees (Art. 3.234 part 1 of the Lithuanian Civil Code).

LUXEMBOURG

a. The assets?

When the partners separate, they may decide themselves which date will apply. Logically, the date of the separation is important.

b. The debts?

The date of the separation is not relevant here; the creditor may claim the debt before or after separation, so the relevant date is when the creditor claims his or her debt.

THE NETHERLANDS

a. The assets?

This is only relevant for joint property, since the value of private property does not have to be assessed. It depends on what the partners agree upon. If the partners do not agree otherwise, the value of the joint property has to be assessed at the moment of the actual division of the property.[7] In cohabitation contracts a different date may be agreed upon, for instance the date of the separation of the partners, which might cause problems when it takes a long time to sell a house.

b. The debts?

This is only relevant in relation to joint debts, since personal debts are of no interest to the other partner. The date depends on what the partners agree upon. If the partners do not agree otherwise, the value of the joint debt has to be assessed at the moment of the actual division.

NORWAY

a. The assets?

As each partner retains whatever he or she owns upon separation, there is normally no need for any decisive date for the determination and the valuation of assets. However, when there are 'strong reasons' for doing so, a cohabitant may obtain ownership of the former family home and household goods owned wholly or partly by the other cohabitant. In these

7 W.M. SCHRAMA, 'Goederenrecht: mede-eigendom', in: M.L.C.C. DE BRUIJN-LÜCKERS et al. (eds.), *Relatierecht, SDUCommentaar*, SDU, The Hague, 2014, at p. 2025-2040.

cases the market value of the items of property must be paid to the owner, see the Norwegian Household Community Act, S. 3. If the cohabitants do not agree on the value of the items of property, the value must be determined by means of a probate valuation. The valuation in a public administration of the estate is to be based on the value at the time of factual allocation of the items of property, and in a private administration of the estate on the value at the time it was decided – either by the court or by an agreement – who should take over the item of property.[8]

b. The debts?

The partners retain their debts upon a relationship breakdown and therefore there is no need for a date for the determination and the valuation of debts.

PORTUGAL

a. The assets?

The value of assets is that which can be provided to the creditor after the civil enforcement procedure, as a consequence of attachment.

b. The debts?

The debt includes both capital and interest. The value of the capital is determined at the moment of the fact that originates it. Interest continues to mount until the moment when the debt is paid (voluntarily or by means of civil enforcement).

RUSSIA

a. The assets?

The law does not specify the date to be applied, but the partners can agree on the applicable date.

b. The debts?

The law does not specify the date to be applied and it is not possible to determine such date by agreement.

---

8 See the Norwegian Household Community Act, S. 3 last paragraph and the Norwegian Marriage Act, S. 69 first paragraph and second paragraph second sentence and Rt. 2006 p. 627.

SCOTLAND

a. The assets?

There is no provision for sharing of partnership assets and therefore this question is not relevant in Scots law.

b. The debts?

There is no specific provision for settlement of partnership debts and therefore this question is not relevant in Scots law.

SLOVAKIA

a. The assets?

Not a relevant question for the Slovak legal system.

b. The debts?

In the case of the assumption of debt it is the date of the conclusion of the written agreement between the old debtor and the new debtor and also the date of the creditor's approval of such an agreement.

SLOVENIA

a. The assets?

For the determination and the valuation of the common assets the date of the creation and cessation of the life union is decisive.

b. The debts?

For the determination and valuation of common debts, the date of the creation and cessation of the life union is decisive.

SPAIN

a. The assets?

The date at which the relationship is terminated is decisive for the determination and the date at which division is undertaken is decisive for the valuation.

b. The debts?

The date at which the relationship is terminated is decisive for the determination and the date at which division is undertaken is decisive for the valuation.

SWEDEN

a. The assets?

Within a year from the ending of the relationship, each of the former cohabitees can request a division of the 'cohabitation property', i.e., the joint dwelling and household goods which were acquired for the couple's joint use during their cohabitation, Swedish Cohabitation Act, § 8. This provision also stipulates that the date for the determination of the assets to be shared is when the cohabitation ends. As to the various ways in which an informal relationship covered by the Swedish Cohabitation Act can be terminated, see answer to Question 5b. The requirement that a property division must be requested within one year from the ending of the relationship, and in the case of death of one of the cohabitees at the latest when the estate inventory (in Swedish: *boutredning*) of the deceased cohabitee takes place, is aimed at creating clarity within a reasonable time as to whether a property division will be requested or not.

The Swedish Cohabitation Act does not contain any specific rules on the decisive date for the valuation of assets. Certain principles have, however, been developed through legal practice and case law. Supreme Court judgment NJA 1997 p. 674 is an important decision in this regard. In this case the cohabitees' home (an apartment in a cooperatively owned building) was assessed at the value on the day of the property division. The prevailing view today is that the decisive date for the valuation of the assets is the date when the inventory of the former partners' assets and debts is finalised and the property is divided.

b. The debts?

The date of the ending of the relationship determines what debts are taken into account. Considering that debts can both decrease and increase after this critical date, it seems fair to evaluate them to their value as at that date.

SWITZERLAND

a. The assets?

Generally (if the partners have not concluded an agreement), the determination and valuation of assets upon separation is not relevant.

A possible participation in the surplus of a simple partnership (see Question 42) is determined upon the liquidation of the simple partnership (Art. 549 Swiss Code of Obligations).

b. The debts?

Generally, the termination of an informal relationship does not affect the joint debts of the partners. Thus, the determination and valuation of debts upon separation is not relevant.

Joint debts assumed by a simple partnership formed by the partners have to be settled upon the liquidation of the simple partnership (Art. 549 para. 1 Swiss Code of Obligations).

QUESTION 46

On what grounds, if any, and to what extent may a partner upon separation claim compensation upon the basis of contributions made or disadvantages suffered during the relationship?

AUSTRIA

Partners in an informal relationship will usually give each other gifts. If there is no doubt about whether it has been a donation, it can be revoked due to gross ingratitude, which requires a criminal offence against the donor.[1] A further possibility to have a gift returned is to challenge the donation contract due to a misconception - also in terms of the motive *(Irrtumsanfechtung)* - when entering into the contract.[2] Upon the successful cancellation of the contract, the beneficiary has to return the gift.[3]

Services rendered in an informal relationship are deemed to be complimentary. In the case of separation no compensation is granted. If both partners are working or one is working and the other is responsible for the household, none of the partners can reclaim compensation, because favours or continuous contributions in a monetary or non-monetary form do not fulfil a purpose in the future; by their very nature they are restricted to a certain period of time and therefore do not provide an entitlement to compensation after separation. Only 'long-term' investments, which outlast the relationship, can be compensated or must even be returned according to the rules on unjust enrichment, S. 1435 General Austrian Civil Code.[4] Such investments are, for example, the purchase of furniture, the financial contribution for a joint vehicle or assistance in the partner's company; hence the services must always be

1 Section 948 General Austrian Civil Code.
2 U. AICHHORN, *Das Recht der Lebenspartnerschaften, Ehe und Lebensgemeinschaft,* Springer, Vienna, 2003, at p. 401 et seq.
3 Section 877 General Austrian Civil Code.
4 Austrian Supreme Court, Judgement of 13.07.2000, 6 Ob 30/00f.

for the benefit of both partners.[5] Along these lines it has been held that financial contributions to the education of one partner cannot be reclaimed, because they are only in the interest of one partner.[6] Further, the beneficiary must have been aware of the fact that the contribution was made in expectation of obtaining something in return. This particular purpose can be the continued existence of the informal relationship or entering into a marriage. If the intended purpose can no longer be realised, the item must primarily be returned in kind. If that is impossible or infeasible, e.g. it involves a fitted kitchen, a reasonable price according to the residual value has to be paid, which will be determined by the judge pursuant to S. 273 Austrian Code of Civil Procedure.[7] Work performances have to be paid according to the collective agreements agreed upon by the employers' and employees' associations or an average salary.[8] The limitation period for this claim is thirty years after the first possibility to exercise this right.[9]

Moreover, if one partner suffered harm during the relationship, he/she may demand an indemnification according to the general rules on damages, S. 1295 et seq. General Austrian Civil Code. The limitation period for a claim for damages is three years after having obtained knowledge of the damage and the liable party.

BELGIUM

There are different grounds, both in property law and the law of obligations, on the basis of which compensation can be sought.[10]

In property law, compensation can firstly be sought on the basis that both joint owners should equally share in the rights and the charges of the joint property (Art. 577-2, § 3, 5 and 7 Belgian Civil Code). This may give rise to compensation for both insufficient use and an excessive contribution.[11] Secondly, the other partner/sole owner is obliged to

5 E. MÖSCHL, *Die nichteheliche Lebensgemeinschaft*, LexisNexis ARD ORAC, Vienna, 2007, at marg. No. 83.

6 Higher Regional Court of Vienna, Judgement of 26.08.1996, 13 R 36/96a.

7 Austrian Supreme Court, Judgement of 29.09.1999, 6 Ob 60/99p; Austrian Supreme Court, Judgement of 11.06.1981, 7 Ob 600/81.

8 U. AICHHORN, *Das Recht der Lebenspartnerschaften, Ehe und Lebensgemeinschaft*, Springer, Vienna, 2003, at p. 407.

9 Sections 1478, 1479 General Austrian Civil Code.

10 For a general overview: S. EGGERMONT, *De juridische bescherming van private relaties*, PhD, University of Antwerp, 2015, at n°s 386 et seq.

11 Cass. 6 May 2010, *AC* 2010, 1328; District Court Gent 12 January 2010, *RW* 2012-13, 866.

compensate the accessories he/she wants to maintain on the basis of accession (Arts. 555 and 566 Belgian Civil Code) and to reimburse the necessary and useful costs which the other partner has incurred.[12]

In the law of obligations, *negotio gestorum* firstly applies, but the conditions for the application of this technique will often not be fulfilled. The intervention in the other partner's affairs, for example, must have been necessary, must only have benefited him/her and may not have been performed *animo donandi*.[13] Secondly, the partner may try to invoke undue payment (Art. 1235, para. 1 Belgian Civil Code), but two important restrictions are that this theory only applies to payments - and not the provision of services - between partners - and not in their relation with third parties.[14]

The primary ground for former informal partners to claim compensation is unjust enrichment. It is a subsidiary ground in that it only applies if, or to the extent that, the aforementioned grounds do not give rise to compensation. The conditions that there must be both an enrichment, on the one side, and an impoverishment, on the other, usually do not pose problems as to their fulfilment. The condition that the enrichment was unjust, however, is more difficult to prove,[15] even though unjust enrichment cannot be rejected *a priori* between informal partners.[16] The subjective cause of or the motive for the performance is important here. The enrichment will only be considered unjust in case the impoverished partner had no economic or even moral motive such as affection.[17] Mere helpfulness does not make the enrichment just.[18]

With regard to all the aforementioned grounds, compensation will not be awarded in case, or to the extent that, the contributions made can be considered as the execution of a natural obligation to contribute to the

---

12 C. DECLERCK and V. ALLAERTS, 'Grondslag en waardering van vergoedingsrechten en schuldvorderingen tussen partners. Ontwikkelingen 2011-2013', in *Personen- en familierecht*, Themis 2013-2014, die Keure, Bruges, 2014, at p. 65-79. For example, District Court of Veurne 27 May 2004, *TGR-TWVR* 2004, 190.

13 Ghent 20 November 2008, *TBBR* 2011, 44, note BOULY and S. EGGERMONT, *De juridische bescherming van private relaties*, PhD, University of Antwerp, 2015, at n° 388.

14 S. EGGERMONT, *De juridische bescherming van private relaties*, PhD, University of Antwerp, 2015, at n° 393.

15 For example, District Court of Veurne 27 May 2004, *TGR-TWVR* 2004, 190.

16 Brussels 3 May 2013, *RTDF* 2013, 1019; Brussels 19 April 2012, *RTDF* 2013, 148; Ghent 27 October 2009, *TGR-TWVR* 2010, 86; Liège 3 September 2008, *RTDF* 2010, 328.

17 Brussels 3 May 2013, *RTDF* 2013, 1019; Brussels 19 April 2012, *RTDF* 2013, 148; Ghent 27 October 2009, *TGR-TWVR* 2010, 86; Liège 3 September 2008, *RTDF* 2010, 328.

18 Cass. 19 January 2009, *RW* 2009-2010, 1084, with note NORDIN.

household expenses or even support for the other partner.[19] Article 1235, para. 2 Belgian Civil Code indeed bars a former partner from recovering his/her performance of a natural obligation.[20] One judgment, however, has refused to assess whether the partners' contributions were in proportion, as the affective component of contributions cannot be monetarised.[21]

BULGARIA

A compensation claim for either partner may arise according to the general grounds set out in the Bulgarian Obligations and Contracts Law: e.g. of unjust enrichment (Art. 55), *negotiorum gestio* (Art. 61), for the improvement of assets (Art. 72 of the Bulgarian Property Law). However, there is a shared view[22] that compensation against maintenance payments is inadmissible because the ground for the maintenance payment is the moral/natural obligation: Art. 55, para. 2 of the Bulgarian Obligations and Contracts Law stipulates that recovery for the conscious fulfilment of a moral obligation is not possible. A compensation claim based on tort is possible, for instance, in cases of domestic violence.

CROATIA

There are no special legal provisions prescribing a possibility for a partner to claim compensation upon separation on the basis of contributions made or disadvantages suffered during the relationship.

CZECH REPUBLIC

A partner cannot claim such compensation. General rules are applicable.

---

19 V. DEHALLEUX, 'La répétition de la contribution excessive aux charges du ménage: proposition d'une nouvelle issue aux conflits entre cohabitants de fait', *TBBR* 2009, at p. 144. For example, Liège 3 September 2008, *RTDF* 2010, 328; Liège 28 April 2009, *RTDF* 2010, 341; District Court of Nivelles 25 October 2012, *Le Pli Juridique* 2013, N° 25, p. 7, with note JASSOGNE; District Court of Veurne 27 May 2004, *TGR-TWVR* 2004, 190.

20 District Court of Oudenaarde 19 September 2005, *RABG* 2006, 774; Justice of the Peace Westerlo 11 December 2006, *T.Vred.* 2007, 354.

21 District Court of Brussels 4 May 2012, *JT* 2012, 796.

22 See T. TZANKOVA, *The Factual Spousal Relationship and the Bulgarian Family Law*, Feneya, Sofia, 2000, at p. 128.

DENMARK

The Danish Supreme Court delivered a judgment in a case on a financial settlement upon the termination of a cohabitation relationship for the first time in 1980; see *Ugeskrift for Retsvæsen* (Weekly Law Journal) 1980, p. 480. The financially weaker party was given an amount as 'compensation'. In the following years the Supreme Court delivered judgments in several cases which defined the extent of the new claims.[23] The doctrine of unjust enrichment came to play a central role, and the doctrine of reasonable expectations has also been given some weight. Claims can also be made in the event of the death of a cohabitant.[24]

The first Supreme Court case concerned whether the female cohabitant could obtain a share of the profit which her partner gained from the sale of his property after the end of their four-year cohabitation. Her principal claim was that the house was jointly owned, alternatively that she should be awarded an amount estimated by the court. She referred to the fact that each party had contributed financially to the joint household expenses, according to their means, and that the house had been bought on the basis of a joint budget drawn up on the basis of their joint incomes. In her view it would not have been possible for her partner to cover the costs of the house without her income. The male partner argued that the claim should be dismissed, referring to the fact that it was he who had paid all the costs of the house.

In court the couple gave very different explanations of their financial arrangements. Both the High Court and a majority of the Supreme Court based their decisions on the evidence of the female cohabitant concerning shared household expenses and finances, and not on her partner's evidence of separate finances. The Supreme Court rejected the claim that there had been joint ownership. Instead the female cohabitant was awarded an assessed amount of DKK 25,000. She was thereby compensated for her financial contribution to her partner's ability to make a profit. This contribution was seen as necessary, and if she had not been paid compensation her partner would have been unjustly enriched.

In *Ugeskrift for Retsvæsen* (Weekly Law Journal) 1984, p. 166, a woman, who had been responsible for looking after the home and caring for three children, was awarded DKK 200,000 after 16 years of cohabitation. Her

23 For more detail, see I. LUND-ANDERSEN, *Familieøkonomien*, Jurist- og Økonomforbundets Forlag, Copenhagen, 2011, at p. 361-425.

24 See *Ugeskrift for Retsvæsen* (Weekly Law Journal) 1985, at p. 55; and *Ugeskrift for Retsvæsen* 1988, at p. 998.

partner had built up considerable wealth through his commercial activities. As in the 1980 case the Supreme Court had to choose between rejecting a claim on the ground that it lacked authority, and making an award on the basis of a new interpretation of the existing concepts of property law. The majority of the Supreme Court chose the latter. The judgment was primarily based on the doctrine of unjust enrichment, as the contributions of the female as a home worker were regarded as significant and had contributed to improving her partner's financial status. This approach was also supported by the doctrine of reasonable expectations, as she was regarded as having assumed that she would not be left penniless at the end of the cohabitation, given her partner's comfortable financial situation.

However, the facts in the 1984 case were so unusual that in subsequent cases the judgment was not interpreted as meaning that housework and the provision of care can in general justify an award of compensation. Only in a few subsequent cases has there been any reference to a woman's work in the home and in these cases there has usually also been a financial contribution, whether direct or indirect.[25]

In *Ugeskrift for Retsvæsen* (Weekly Law Journal) 1985, p. 607, the Supreme Court laid down guidelines for the assessment of cases on claims for compensation. The Supreme Court's 'rule' contains three conditions. First, there is a requirement that the claimant should have contributed to the parties' joint expenses or by other means. Second, the contributions should have helped enable the creation or preservation of wealth by the other party. And third, there are conditions as to the nature of the cohabitation, especially its duration. On other points the rules are open and imprecise: the contribution can be made 'by other means', and the amount can be determined 'among other things' by having regard to the duration of the relationship and the financial status of the parties upon its termination.

In order for a claim for compensation to be considered at all, the cohabitation must have lasted around three years.[26] The contribution to the joint expenses can be made directly or indirectly. Direct financial contributions can consist of paying expenses for the other party's residence. Indirect contributions can be provided by paying for the couple's shared expenses, for example household expenses or for their

25 See e.g. *Tidsskrift for Familie- og arveret* (Journal of Family and Succession Law) 2001, at p. 282.
26 See *Ugeskrift for Retsvæsen* (Weekly Law Journal) 1982, at p. 93.

children. Contributions can also be made in the form of housework, the provision of care and performing work in person.

There have been a number of recent cases in the High Court on the amount of compensation. The cases leave the impression that there is considerable uncertainty about the extent of compensation claims and the results of proceedings can be difficult to predict. In the first case, *Ugeskrift for Retsvæsen* (Weekly Law Journal) 1980. 480 H, the Supreme Court stated that the fact that a large part of the parties' wealth was caused by inflation would not prevent compensation being awarded. However, in a couple of more recent High Court cases it was emphasised that the increase in the value of a property was primarily due to the conditions in the wider economy and thus only modest[27] or no compensation was awarded.[28]

When the amount of compensation is calculated, in principle compensation is awarded for the assets or work provided. With direct contributions the amount can be up to half the value of the assets contributed to.[29] If there has been an indirect financial contribution the assessment will often take account of the differences in the parties' incomes during the period of cohabitation. The compensation awarded is estimated and is often between one quarter and one fifth of the increase in value, although where the other party has considerable wealth the compensation will typically be only one tenth.

During their cohabitation an unmarried couple can validly agree that a party shall not receive compensation upon termination of the cohabitation. Such an agreement can be questionable from the point of view of the weaker party, who can risk being left without any means if the couple separate.

In addition to claims for compensation, upon the termination of cohabitation a cohabitant can make ordinary property law claims against his or her former partner. These can be claims for the repayment of a loan or because the other party has obtained unjust enrichment.[30] Any such claim must be judged in the light of the couple's community of interests,

---

[27] See *Tidsskrift for Familie- og arveret* (Journal of Family and Succession Law) 2010, at p. 221.

[28] See *Tidsskrift for Familie- og arveret* (Journal of Family and Succession Law) 2011, at p. 27.

[29] See *Ugeskrift for Retsvæsen* (Weekly Law Journal) 1986, at p. 765.

[30] See I. LUND-ANDERSEN, *Familieøkonomien*, Jurist- og Økonomforbundets Forlag, Copenhagen, 2011, at p. 300-332.

so there must be a clear basis for allowing such a claim. A claim can be rejected if the transfer of money between cohabitants must be regarded as a contribution to the shared household expenses and thus part of a joint financial arrangement. It is relevant whether the cohabitation has been of longer duration with joint finances. Depending on the circumstances, even the transfer of a large one-off payment can be considered a contribution to the partnership if the other party has made other contributions to the partnership.[31]

A claim for unjust enrichment will be relevant if a claim for compensation is not allowable because of the short duration of the cohabitation and if a partner has made payments that give a financial benefit to the other party. Such payment must be a significant departure from the normal allocation of their shared obligations.[32] The amount awarded will be assessed and may not exceed the enrichment of one party or the loss of the other.

ENGLAND AND WALES

None in the cohabitation context. It is assumed that they did this willingly as a fully consenting adult unless there is a written cohabitation agreement which shows a contrary intention and an agreement on how this is to be compensated. If that is the case, the agreement can usually be enforced as confirmed in *Sutton v Mishcon De Reya* [2003] EWHC 3166 (Ch), [2004] 1 FLR 837. Contributions to the purchase of property legally owned by the other partner may give rise to beneficial shared ownership under a resulting or constructive trust as discussed in Question 3.

ESTONIA

The Supreme Court has found[33] that partnership relations in an informal relationship are possible; at the same time it has held that an informal relationship does not meet the requirements of a partnership. No binding obligations arise from this, i.e. an obligation within the meaning of the

31 See *Ugeskrift for Retsvæsen* (Weekly Law Journal) 1998, at p. 252.
32 See *Tidsskrift for Familie- og arveret* (Journal of Family and Succession Law) 1999, at p. 185.
33 Decision of the Civil Chamber of the Supreme Court 3-2-1-109-14, at para. 15, 16.

Estonian Law of Obligations Act § 2.[34] If persons living in an informal relationship have not concluded a marriage, their common will not to apply the provisions which are valid for a marriage can be presumed, including the provisions regarding the joint ownership of property. An extension of the partnership provisions or by analogy under the Estonian Family Law Act should not result in consequences where there are situations that have not been agreed upon by the parties and which cannot be presumed to be their actual common will. On the basis of the law, the obligations which result from an informal relationship and from a marriage are dissimilar, including the fact that the parties are not obliged to provide mutual support and to arrange the common household as spouses have to do on the basis of § 15 of the Estonian Family Law Act. If a partnership contract exists, pursuant to section 1 of § 589 of the Estonian Law of Obligations Act, all contributions made by the partners and assets acquired for the partnership shall be transferred to the joint property of the partnership (partnership property). The partnership provisions can be applied primarily in case of a concrete proprietary objective, such as common purchase or improvement of a property with the aim of cohabitation with mutual contributions or involving joint expenses for the same objective. The liquidation provisions of a partnership can be applied for the distribution of specific assets with a higher value (e.g. immovable property) acquired for the common household during the informal relationship, if:

- both parties have made exceptionable and financially comparable contributions (which can be evaluated in monetary terms) for the acquisition or improvement of the asset;
- when acquiring or improving the asset, the parties had a common will at least for the durable establishment of a financially joint material value (joint property).

The application of the provisions on the liquidation of a partnership is not excluded by the fact that, under property law, the asset in favour of the partnership has been purchased under the common ownership of the parties or the sole ownership of one party. In the relations between the parties (internal relations) the asset can be considered as joint property

[34] According to § 2 of the Estonian Law of Obligations Act an obligation is a legal relationship which gives rise to the obligation of one person (the obligated person or obligor) to perform an act or omission (to perform an obligation) for the benefit of another person (the entitled person or obligee), and to the right of the obligee to demand that the obligor performs that obligation. The nature of an obligation may oblige the parties involved to take the other party's rights and interests into account in a certain manner. An obligation may also be confined thereto.

subject to the aforelisted conditions, and it can be divided upon the termination of the relationship.

According to the Civil Chamber of the Supreme Court, from the liquidation provisions of a partnership, the second sentence of the Estonian Law of Obligations Act § 600 section 1 can be applied, according to which the provisions on the distribution of common ownership will presumably be applied (primarily concerning the types of division relating to an asset, as prescribed by § 77 of the Estonian Law of Property Act). Also, § 602 of the Estonian Law of Obligations Act can be applied, which prescribes that upon liquidation, the obligations of a partnership shall be the first to be performed out of the partnership property (i.e. returning a loan which was taken out to purchase joint property). According to section 1 of § 603 of the Estonian Law of Obligations Act, after the obligations have been performed, any contributions made by the partners shall be returned from the remaining partnership property. If it is impossible to return a contribution, compensation shall be paid for the value of the contribution at the time it was made, as stipulated in the first sentence of section 3 of § 603 of the Estonian Law of Obligations Act. The second sentence of section 3 of § 603 of the Estonian Law of Obligations Act states that compensation shall not be paid for a contribution which consisted of the provision of services to the partnership or the delivery of objects for the use of the partnership.

FINLAND

The necessary criterion is laid down in S. 8 of the Finnish Act on the Dissolution of the Household of Cohabiting Partners (26/2011). According to this Section, a cohabiting partner is entitled to compensation if, through contributions for the benefit of the shared household, he or she has assisted the other cohabiting partner in accumulating or retaining his or her property so that the dissolution of the household, solely on the basis of ownership, would result in unjust enrichment at the expense of the other.

The following can be deemed to be contributions for the benefit of a shared household: 1) work done by one cohabiting partner for the benefit of the shared household or property owned by the other; 2) the use of funds for the shared household; 3) the investment of funds by one cohabiting partner in property owned by the other; or 4) any other similar contribution.

However, no right to compensation exists if the unjust enrichment arising from a contribution for the benefit of a shared household can be deemed to be insignificant given the circumstances.

FRANCE

Only unjust enrichment or a *de facto* company can be raised to compensate for the losses suffered during the relationship by one of the former cohabitants (see Question 38).

GERMANY

Until its seminal decision in 2008,[35] the Federal Supreme Court in principle denied compensation claims after the dissolution of an informal partnership. The Court stated in several judgments that the personal relationship between the partners was of primary importance and thus influenced any economic activity between the partners as well. Therefore often there was no offsetting of personal services or financial contributions between partners to an informal relationship.[36] Only in exceptional cases did the Court grant compensation based on an analogous application of civil partnership law.[37] The rulings of the Court faced inter alia the criticism that partners to an informal partnership did not necessarily want to stand outside the realm of law in this regard.[38] Responding to the arguments raised by several scholars,[39] the Court held, in 2008, in a departure from its previously settled case law, that henceforth after the dissolution of an informal partnership, compensation may be claimed if the contributions made (financial contributions or work performances) appreciably exceed regular contributions made in the course of everyday life.[40] Thus, whereas regular contributions to the living expenses, the rent for the common residence or usual repair measures remain uncompensated, substantial financial contributions or work, i.e. on a building, may be compensated if certain conditions are fulfilled.

---

35 BGH, 09.07.2008, *NJW*, 2008, 3277.

36 BGH, 03.10.1983, *FamRZ*, 1983, 1213; BGH, 25.09.1997, *NJW*, 1997, 3371; BGH, 06.10.2003, *NJW*, 2004, 58.

37 BGH, 12.07.1982, *NJW*, 1982, 2863; BGH, 04.11.1991, *NJW*, 1992, 906.

38 BGH, 31.10.2007, *LMK*, 2008, 251355 with a comment by M. WELLENHOFER.

39 Including A. LÜDERITZ and N. DETHLOFF, *Familienrecht*, Beck, Munich, 2012, at § 8 No. 19 et seq.; W. SCHULZ, 'Vermögensauseinandersetzung der nichtehelichen Lebensgemeinschaft', *FamRZ*, 2007, at p. 593; H.-W. STRÄTZ, 'Anh. zu §§ 1297 et seq.', in: J. VON STAUDINGER, *BGB*, Sellier-de-Gruyter, Berlin, 2000, at No. 100 et seq.

40 BGH, 09.07.2008, *NJW*, 2008, 3277.

For a compensation claim several legal grounds come into consideration. Even though they originate from the general law of obligations, all grounds have been interpreted by the courts in a way to accommodate the specifics of the personal nature of the relationship:

1. Revocation of donation

According to § 530 para. 1 German Civil Code a donation may be revoked if the donee is guilty of gross ingratitude by doing serious wrong to the donor or a close relative of the donor. However, according to the established jurisprudence, contributions related to the informal partnership in a sense that they serve to maintain the partnership are not considered to be donations as per § 530 para. 1 German Civil Code. In the view of the Federal Supreme Court donations are made gratuitously whereas contributions related to informal partnerships are made in order to participate in such contributions in the long term.[41] They are deemed to be reciprocal, even if both partners' contributions are not equal in kind or in amount. Only personal gifts would be considered as donations and could therefore be revoked. However, a revocation of a donation usually fails due to the condition of 'gross ingratitude' as the mere separation cannot be interpreted as such.

2. Civil law partnership

The German Federal Supreme Court assumes that partners to an informal relationship may conclude an implied partnership agreement (civil law partnership) if they act in pursuit of a goal which exceeds the object to merely maintain the informal partnership.[42] The specific object might be that the partners acquire real estate as common investment and common property.[43] To apply those principles the specific object, according to general company law, must be identifiable. As an informal relationship is in principle a relationship without any legal intention, the partners must have a noticeable legal intention to build up a civil law partnership apart from their informal partnership. The Federal Supreme Court granted compensation based on a civil law partnership, for example, for the support provided for the establishment and the operation of a business.[44] Compensation was also granted where the partners for investment

[41] BGH, 09.07.2008, *NJW*, 2008, 3277, 3278.

[42] BGH, 09.07.2008, *NJW*, 2008, 3277, 3280.

[43] N. DETHLOFF, *Familienrecht*, Beck, Munich, 2012, at § 8 No. 25; BGH, 06.07.2011, *NJW*, 2011, 2880.

[44] BGH, 12.07.1982, *NJW*, 1982, 2863.

purposes jointly built several houses which were legally owned by one partner.[45]

3. Unjust enrichment

Compensation based on the ground of unjust enrichment (§ 812 para. 1 s. 2 alt. 2 German Civil Code) may be claimed if a partner made a contribution and the result intended to be achieved by those efforts in accordance with the contents of the legal transaction did not occur. Compensation may be granted if assets of considerable value are concerned, e.g. the construction of a house.[46] However, a claim pursuant to § 812 para. 1 s. 2 alt. 2 German Civil Code requires that both partners have agreed upon the object of the performance. According to case law a tacit agreement can be assumed if one partner performed in order to achieve a certain object, the other partner recognised this purpose and accepted the performance without objection.[47] The specific result intended to be achieved could have been that the partners wanted to live together in the foreseeable future in the house which was built and maintained by contributions made by one or both partners. If they split up shortly after the house has been built, the intended result did not occur and compensation may be claimed. If, on the contrary the couple only separates after some time has passed, the intended object to share the house for living might have been achieved and no compensation be granted.

4. Frustration of contract

Moreover, compensation for contributions which created assets of considerable commercial importance can be based on the ground of frustration of contract (§ 313 German Civil Code). The frustration of contract comes into consideration if a partner made the contributions based on the expectation that the informal relationship would last.[48] However, it will only be granted if upholding the contract would be unreasonable, thereby limiting compensation to cases of substantial contributions and allowing the purpose of the contribution and whether this has already been (partially) accomplished, to be taken into consideration. The specific demarcation between § 812 para. 1 s. 2 alt. 2 German Civil Code and § 313 German Civil Code is, however, difficult to

[45] BGH, 24.06.1985, *NJW*, 1986, 51.

[46] BGH, 09.07.2008, *NJW*, 2008, 3277, 3280.

[47] H. Sprau, '§ 812', in: O. Palandt, *Bürgerliches Gesetzbuch*, Beck, Munich, 2015, at No. 30; BGH, 06.07.2011, *NJW*, 2011, 2880.

[48] BGH, 09.07.2008, *NJW*, 2008, 3277, 3281; BGH, 06.07.2011, *NJW*, 2011, 2880.

draw and case specific. Generally § 313 applies, if there is no explicit agreement regarding the object of the performance of one partner.

GREECE

The only provisions that might be applied are those on unjust enrichment (Arts. 904-912 Greek Civil Code). However, in case law the view has been taken that benefits granted during the period of cohabitation did not occur without a legal reason, but by way of donations in the context of mutual confidence, and thus there will not be any grounds for a claim. However, the former partners may choose to settle any claims between them, even offsetting one against the other if the transactions did not have the character of gifts. The offsetting process will require a relevant agreement (Art. 361 Greek Civil Code), or will occur unilaterally (Art. 441-452 Greek Civil Code).

HUNGARY

There is no specific rule, except for the default property regime (see also the answer to Question 31).

REPUBLIC OF IRELAND

First of all, S. 172(2)(c) of the Irish 2010 Act lists the degree of financial dependence of either adult on the other as one of the criteria for the court to regard in order to determine whether or not two adults fall within the definition of cohabitants under the Act.

In order to apply for redress under the scheme set out in the Irish 2010 Act, S. 173(2) of the Irish 2010 Act provides that: 'If the qualified cohabitant satisfies the court that he or she is financially dependent on the other cohabitant and that the financial dependence arises from the relationship or the ending of the relationship, the court may, if satisfied that it is just and equitable to do so in all the circumstances, make the order concerned.' This demonstrates that financial dependence is a pre-condition to making an application for maintenance, property adjustment orders or pension adjustment orders under the Act.

Furthermore, contributions made and disadvantages suffered are relevant in an application for redress by an economically dependent qualified cohabitant. In deciding whether it is just and equitable to make an order under the redress scheme in favour of the applicant, S. 173(3)(f) provides the court must have regard to the contributions that each of the cohabitants made to the welfare of the cohabitants, including any contribution made by each of them to the income, earning capacity or property and financial resources of the other. In addition, the court will consider any contributions made by either of them in looking after the home (S. 173(3)(g)) and the effect on the earning capacity of each of the cohabitants of the responsibilities assumed by each of them during their relationship and the degree to which the future earning capacity of a cohabitant is impaired by reason of that cohabitant having relinquished or forgone the opportunity of remunerative activity in order to look after the home (S. 173(3)(h)).

ITALY

The vast majority of the legal doctrine and case law unanimously deny the possibility of the cohabitant obtaining compensation for damages after the break-up of the relationship. This is so because the informal relationship is based on the free will of the parties, who are not bound by any legalised bond compelling them to continue living together.[49] The break-up of the relationship does not amount to a tort, not even when it occurs without justification.

Contributions freely given to the partner and disadvantages suffered during the relationship are not considered a source of a civil obligation but one of a 'natural obligation' and fall, therefore, within the provision of Art. 2034 Italian Civil Code, according to which, 'what has been spontaneously paid or performed following moral or social duties' cannot be requested to be repaid, and is therefore gratuitous. The only exception to this is in the case of disabled persons.

Thus, upon separation no partner can request compensation for what he or she has done or paid in the absence of any legal obligation to have done so.[50]

---

49 Compare G. OBERTO, *I diritti dei conviventi. Realtà e prospettive tra Italia ed Europa*, Cedam, Padua, 2012, at p. 179.

50 This principle is well established. The first application was by the Court of Cassation (for instance, Cass. 17 January 1958 n. 84 in *Foro It.*, 1959, I, c. 470) and the principle has been followed in recent times by other courts (e.g. Trib. Milano, 13 March 2009): see, among several other authors, G. OBERTO, *I diritti dei conviventi. Realtà e prospettive tra Italia ed Europa*, Cedam, Padua, 2012, at p. 180; L. BALESTRA, 'La famiglia di fatto', in: G. FERRANDO (ed.), *Il nuovo diritto di famiglia*, Zanichelli, Bologna, 2008, at p. 1059 et seq.

According to the Court of Cassation (decision of 13 March 2003, n. 3713), in order for a natural obligation to arise, it is however necessary that what has been given 'is proportionate to the whole of the patrimony and to the social conditions of the giver'. Therefore, no natural obligation arises when a gift given by one partner is disproportionately greater in value than the duties accepted and performed by the other. Only in this case, then, may the former partner ask for compensation.

LATVIA

In Latvia there is no such legal order on separation following an informal relationship.

LITHUANIA

Where the value of the house or the apartment exceeds the value of the cohabitee's share in the assets, he or she must compensate, in monetary terms, the other cohabitee for the difference in the value. In this case the provisions of Art. 3.117 are applied by analogy:[51] 'Where the value of the property awarded by the court to one of the spouses is greater than his or her share in the joint community property, that spouse shall be obliged to pay compensation to the other spouse. Upon the presentation of an adequate security for this liability, the court may defer the payment of the compensation for no longer than two years.'

When the size of the specific shares of each co-owner is not established, it is assumed that these shares are equal (Art. 4.73 part 3). In the case law the provisions of Art. 4.80 of the Lithuanian Civil Code are applied: Each co-owner shall have the right to demand that his share should be partitioned from the common partial ownership. If no agreement is reached regarding the method of partitioning, the asset shall be divided in kind preferably without disproportionate damage; in other cases, one or several of the co-owners thus partitioned shall receive compensation in monetary terms.

LUXEMBOURG

Case law applies the following principle: no legal provision determines the contribution of each partner to the current daily expenses. There are

[51] V. MIKELENAS et al., *Commentary on Book Three of the Civil Code of Lithuania* (in Lithuanian), Justitia, Vilnius, 2002, at p. 453.

no special accounts drawn at the end of an informal relationship; each partner has to contribute to the expenses.

However, the case law differentiates between normal expenses and extraordinary expenses. Only normal expenses have to be met by each partner; a partner cannot claim a reimbursement of these normal expenses. But extraordinary expenses can be reclaimed, as it is considered that they exceed the contribution of a partner to the expenses of the household.

We can read the following in the pertinent judgments: '*Les dépenses ordinaires relevant de la participation à la vie commune qui se fait sans établissement de compte précis et ne donnent, en tant que telles, pas lieu à indemnisation, n'étant que la contrepartie des liens d'affection entre concubins. Les dépenses plus importantes, par contre, peuvent donner lieu à indemnisation en ce qu'elles excèdent manifestement la contribution d'un concubin aux charges du ménage*' (e.g. Court of Appeal, 22nd of March 2006).

THE NETHERLANDS

There is no specific provision to this end. A claim therefore has to be based upon an obligation, either contractual or non-contractual. Two aspects have to be discerned: contributions in assets or goods, on the one hand, and non-financial contributions, on the other.

Whether money or assets can be redistributed depends on whether the parties have concluded an implicit contract (Art. 3:37 Dutch Civil Code) and what its content would be (repayment, netting, gift (Art. 7:175 Dutch Civil Code)) or, outside contract law, whether the legal relationship resulted in unjust enrichment (Art. 6:212 Dutch Civil Code) or undue payment (Art. 6:203 Dutch Civil Code). The basic problem is that anything is possible, but nothing is certain. There are no clear underlying legal norms which determine how to qualify the relations and whether that is a sufficient ground for redistribution. The Supreme Court, however, has developed norms for implicit contracts, which could result in a duty to compensate.[52] The standard to be met to reach a qualification as an implicit contract is rather low. Whether the lower courts would actually redistribute on the basis of an implicit contract (or another ground) depends on the facts, the lawyers and the courts in

52 HR 8 June 2012, ECLI:NL:HR:2012:BV9539.

question. Case law at the lower level has demonstrated a wide variety of claims and judgements.[53]

In relation to non-financial contributions, for instance by taking care of the children, it will generally be very difficult to obtain compensation. That also applies to compensation for disadvantages suffered as a result of the relationship, such as reduced earning capacity. However, if during the relationship property or money has been acquired by the economically weaker partner, it might be difficult for the other partner to reclaim this. The court might accept the defence of the care-providing partner that an implicit contract has been concluded as a result of which no money or property has to be returned.[54] Secondly, a defence could be based on a natural (unenforceable) obligation under Art. 6:3 Dutch Civil Code, thereby preventing the other partner from reclaiming. The case law shows all kinds of outcomes and natural obligations.[55]

NORWAY

A partner may claim compensation or restitution upon the basis of contributions made during the relationship. These non-statutory rules developed through Supreme Court practice in the 1980s.[56] The cohabitant must have provided the other party with a 'significant financial benefit' in order to receive any compensation. In addition, the granting of compensation must be 'reasonable'. Compensation to avert unjust enrichment is granted only 'in exceptional cases', see Rt. 2011 p. 1168.

---

53 W.M. SCHRAMA, 'Verbintenisrechtelijke afwikkeling', in: M.L.C.C. DE BRUIJN-LÜCKERS et al. (eds.), *Relatierecht, SDUCommentaar*, SDU, The Hague, 2014, at p. 2041-2060. Two illustrative examples: Rb. Rotterdam 27 January 2010, LJN BM7429 decided that on the basis of an implicit contract one partner had to pay € 350,000 to the other partner, after a relationship of 22 years, as opposed to Hof Den Haag 2 November 2010 (the essence of which can be found in HR 8 June 2012, ECLI:NL:HR:2012:BV9539) which ruled that the woman, who had stopped working after the second child's birth, had to pay almost €50,000 after the breakdown of the relationship for the costs that her partner had paid for during the relationship.

54 HR 8 June 2012, ECLI:NL:HR:2012:BV9539.

55 HR 1 October 2004, LJN AO9558; Hof Den Bosch 16 March 2010, ECLI:NL:GHSHE: 2010:BL8106; Hof Amsterdam 21 August 2012, ECLI:NL:GHAMS:2012:BZ0744; Hof Amsterdam 21 August 2012, ECLI:NL:GHAMS:2012:BZ0744; Hof Amsterdam 16 April 2013, ECLI:NL:GHAMS: 2013:CA3067; HR 8 June 2012, ECLI:NL:HR:2012:BV9539; HR 10 October 2014: ECLI:NL:HR:2014:2931.

56 See Rt. 1984 p. 497, Rt. 2000 p. 1089, Rt. 2011 p. 1168 and Rt. 2011 p. 1176.

PORTUGAL

Jurisprudence already applies the laws of enrichment without cause in cases in which one member of a *de facto* union contributes financially in the acquisition of a property, or for the realisation of benefits resulting from it, and the other member remains with the exclusive property of the acquired good. In the same way, cases are known in which the courts have recognised advantages acquired through a business at the cost of non-remunerated professional contributions by one member of a *de facto* union.

In other circumstances, one member of a *de facto* union could enjoy the benefits of some future advantage which is perhaps related to the way in which their life in common had unfolded, but which clearly could not be considered as having been caused by the contributions of the other. This is the typical case of one member having completed higher education, perhaps with the help of the other, but without it being possible to determine the proportion of this help or knowing if the same result could have been achieved without such help. In further cases, it is possible to identify disadvantages for the future which resulted for the member who renounced developing his or her own life, who made excessive sacrifices in favour of a life in common, in the expectation that this would be long-lasting – for example, one who abandoned employment to look after children, to care for an ascendant or descendant of the other, or to accompany the other on work-related travel. In such cases, clear reasons of equity would lead to establishing a compensation credit, as a way of protecting the more vulnerable *de facto* union member, similar to that which is established for marriage, in Art. 1675 n. 2, of the Portuguese Civil Code, introduced by the Reform of 1977, in the version updated by the new law of divorce (Law No. 61/2088) of October 31. The Assembly of the Republic actually approved such a regime, but the veto by the President of the Republic meant that this did not form part of Law no. 23/2010.

RUSSIA

Seeking such compensation is impossible under Russian law.

SCOTLAND

The Family Law (Scotland) Act 2006 introduced a significant new provision by which application for financial provision could be made to the court on the termination of cohabitation otherwise than by death.[57] Application must be made within one year of the date when cohabitation ceased.[58] Although S. 28 has been welcomed as a significant new protection for cohabitants, it has also been widely criticised for poor drafting, lack of clarity and absence of clear aims and principles. These criticisms are particularly apt when S. 28 is compared with the very detailed and well understood provisions which govern financial provision on divorce or dissolution.[59] It was hoped that through time guidance and clarity would emerge as the courts became increasingly familiar with the cohabitation provisions but although the number of cases is beginning to grow, including an important decision from the UK Supreme Court in *Gow v Grant*,[60] there is still considerable uncertainty.

Section 28 provides as follows:

> '(2) On the application of a cohabitant ('the applicant'), the appropriate court may, after having regard to the matters mentioned in subsection (3) –
> (a) make an order requiring the other cohabitant ('the defender') to pay a capital sum of an amount specified in the order to the applicant;
> (b) make an order requiring the defender to pay such amount as may be specified in the order in respect of any economic burden of caring, after the end of the cohabitation, for a child of whom the cohabitants are parents;
> (c) make such interim order as it thinks fit.
> (3) Those matters are –
> (a) whether (and, if so, to what extent) the defender has derived economic advantage from contributions made by the applicant; and
> (b) whether (and, if so, to what extent) the applicant has suffered economic disadvantage in the interests of –
> (i) the defender; or
> (ii) any relevant child.
> (4) In considering whether to make an order under subsection (2)(a), the appropriate court shall have regard to the matters mentioned in subsections (5) and (6).
> (5) The first matter is the extent to which any economic advantage derived by the defender from contributions made by the applicant is offset by any economic disadvantage suffered by the defender in the interests of –
> (a) the applicant; or
> (b) any relevant child.
> (6) The second matter is the extent to which any economic disadvantage suffered by the applicant in the interests of –

57 Family Law (Scotland) Act 2006, S. 28.
58 Family Law (Scotland) Act 2006, S. 28(8).
59 In particular, S. 8-14 of the Family Law (Scotland) Act 1985.
60 *Gow v Grant* [2012] UKSC 29.

(a) the defender; or
(b) any relevant child,
is offset by any economic advantage the applicant has derived from contributions made by the defender.'

It is further provided that 'contributions' includes indirect and non-financial contributions, including caring for the house or any 'relevant child'.[61] A relevant child is a child of whom the cohabitants are parents or a child who has been accepted as a child of the family.[62] 'Economic advantage' is defined as including gains in capital, income and earning capacity.[63]

Several problems have been identified with S. 28. Unlike the provisions relating to financial provision on divorce which provide the courts with a range of orders, including capital payment, property transfer, periodical allowance and pension orders,[64] S. 28 only mentions a capital sum payment. Arguably, the general reference to 'an order' in S. 28(2)(b) could be interpreted as including a range of different types of order but to date that is not an approach which has been taken by the courts. Instead they have proceeded on the basis that they can only make a capital payment order albeit it can be payable in instalments.[65]

Perhaps the most difficult aspect of S. 28 is the question of how to take into account the matters mentioned in subsection (3), that is the extent to which the defender has derived economic advantage from the contributions made by the applicant and the extent to which the applicant has suffered economic disadvantage in the interests of the defender or any relevant child. Must there be both advantage and disadvantage or is it sufficient for the applicant to establish that she has suffered a disadvantage without showing an advantage for the defender? How are the additional matters in subsections (5) and (6) to be taken into account? In several cases, the courts have engaged in detailed and complex assessment of advantage and disadvantage and the extent to which each has been offset within the context of the relationship. A further complexity is the extent to which an order under S. 28(2)(b) is a stand-alone order based on the economic burden of childcare or whether

---

61 Family Law (Scotland) Act 2006, S. 28(9).
62 Family Law (Scotland) Act 2006, S. 28(10).
63 Family Law (Scotland) Act 2006, S. 28(9).
64 Family Law (Scotland) Act 1985, S. 8.
65 As, e.g., in *M v I* 2012 GWD 11-205, where the sheriff made an award of £5000 in respect of the burden of childcare, payable in five annual instalments.

it too requires a balancing exercise between advantage and disadvantage during the cohabitation.

To date, awards under S. 28 have been limited and much of the court time appears to have been taken up with trying to understand and apply the difficult wording of the statute. This contrasts with the approach adopted in *Gow v Grant,* the one decision of the UK Supreme Court on S. 28, where an award of £39,500 was made under S. 28(2)(a). In considering how the courts should apply the provisions, the Supreme Court looked for the underlying principle of the section and concluded that it was 'fairness'. Lady Hale suggested a rather different approach to that which has been adopted by the Scottish courts to date:

> 'Who can say whether the non-financial contributions, or the sacrifices, made by one party were offset by the board and lodging paid for by the other? That is not what living together in an intimate relationship is all about. It is much more practicable to consider where they were at the beginning of their cohabitation and where they are at the end and then to ask whether either the defender has derived a net economic advantage from the contributions of the applicant or the applicant has suffered a net economic disadvantage in the interests of the defender or any relevant child.'

This may seem a very sensible approach but it is difficult to discern it within the current statutory provision, which focuses to such an extent on the offsetting process. While there was much to be welcomed in the clarity and insight of the Supreme Court's judgment, there remains uncertainty as to how the principle of fairness can be accommodated in what is undeniably a poorly constructed statutory provision. In a recent sheriff court appeal decision, the sheriff principal observed that he was 'left with some unease that too much reliance on the broad approach of fairness runs the risk of doing violence to the terms of S. 28(3)(a)'.[66]

SLOVAKIA

Not a relevant question for the Slovak legal system.

SLOVENIA

In the division of common property there is a legal presumption that the shares of the partners in the common property are equal. A partner who believes that he or she has contributed more to the creation of the

66 *Smith-Milne v Langler* 2013 Fam LR 58.

common property may demand a larger share (Art. 59 of the Slovenian Marriage Act).

SPAIN

The so-called *pensión compensatoria* established by the Spanish Civil Code in cases of divorce or legal separation is a hybrid between maintenance and compensation. For clarity's sake it was described in Questions 34 and 35. This kind of economic compensation is granted in cases in which the break-up causes an economic imbalance between the spouses and also tends to be applied to partners in an informal relationship. In the absence of agreement the judge determines the amount payable by taking into account factors such as: the age and health of the partners; the professional qualifications and possibilities of pursuing gainful employment; past and future work for the family; cooperation in the other partner's business or profession; the duration of the relationship; the eventual loss of pension rights; and the economic means and needs of the partners. The list is not exhaustive. Compensation can be granted for a certain period or indefinitely, as a lump sum or in instalments.

Catalan law provides for compensation for work performed in Art. 234-9 Catalan Civil Code. This kind of compensation is equally established for married couples under the legal regime of separation of property. The partner who has worked substantially more for the family or who has worked for the other without or with insufficient remuneration has a right to be compensated. This however requires additionally that at the moment of the termination of the relationship the debtor partner has experienced an increase in his assets. In determining the amount of compensation, regard will be paid to the duration and extent of the work performed and in the case of work in the home the fact that it included the raising of children or the care of other family members who live with the family. In principle, the compensation is limited to 25% of the difference between the increases in assets experienced by either partner. The judge may however raise the amount payable if the creditor proves that his or her contribution was substantially higher. Catalan law has rules on calculation and methods of payment (Art. 232-6 and Art. 232-8 Catalan Civil Code).

SWEDEN

Claims on concealed co-ownership to property, formally under the title of one of the partners only, are often raised upon separation. If the claim is successful, being recognised as a 'hidden' joint owner to the property can provide important compensation for this partner's contributions during the relationship, see above Question 28.

In principle, upon separation a partner can claim compensation from the other partner with reference to the general principle of compensation for unjustified enrichment.[67] In case law, this principle appears not to be invoked. One reason for this could be the Supreme Court judgment NJA 1975 p. 298, dealing with claims for remuneration for work within the joint household of the cohabitees and for the caring for the other during illness. The Court rejected the claims with reference to the couple's personal relationship and the fact that the work was carried out as part of their cohabitation. The couple had lived together for 10 years.

SWITZERLAND

Generally, a partner in an informal relationship may not claim compensation on the basis of any contributions made or disadvantages suffered during the relationship.

A partner may be entitled to a salary if he or she has worked in the other partner's business. According to Art. 320 para. 1 Swiss Code of Obligations, an employment contract between the partners is concluded when one of them accepts the performance of work over a certain period in his or her service, which in the circumstances could only reasonably be expected in exchange for a salary.[68]

Where the partners in an informal relationship have formed a simple partnership (Art. 530 et seq. Swiss Code of Obligations), compensation may be sought upon the dissolution of the relationship (see Question 42).[69] However, these cases largely depend on the court's interpretation of the parties' intention to enter into a legally binding relationship and of the common partnership goal pursued by the partners. Up to now, only financial contributions[70] or contributions in the form of work and labour

---

[67] I. LUND-ANDERSEN, 'Det økonomiske opgør ved samlivets ophør', in: J. ASLAND et al., *Nordisk samboerrett*, Gyldendal, Oslo, 2014, at p. 142 (see Chapter 3.3.8 in the English version of the book, *Nordic Cohabitation Law*, to be published by Intersentia in 2015).

[68] See Swiss Federal Supreme Court, BGE 109 II 228; BGer 4C.89/1999, *Die Praxis des Familienrechts*, 2000, at p. 151 et seq.; BGE 79 II 168. See also BGE 87 II 164 (an interim change of legal practice).

[69] Swiss Federal Supreme Court, BGE 108 II 204 E.3.a).

[70] E.g. Swiss Federal Supreme Court, BGer 4A_383/2007 (19.12.2007).

in the joint or the other partner's business[71] have given rise to compensation. Taking care of the household and caring for the children have not amounted to a contribution as required in a simple partnership.[72]

---

[71] E.g. Swiss Federal Supreme Court, BGer 4C.195/2006 (12.10.2007); BGE 109 II 228.

[72] Compensation was denied in Swiss Federal Supreme Court, BGer 4A_441/2007 (17.01.2008), where a woman in an informal relationship had taken care of the common child for 16 years.

PART E
DEATH

QUESTION 47

Does the surviving partner have rights of inheritance in the case of intestate succession? If yes, how does this right compare to that of a surviving spouse or a registered partner, in a marriage or registered partnership?

AUSTRIA

In contrast to spouses, partners do not have any rights of inheritance.[1] In the case of the death of one partner the surviving partner is neither entitled to inherit, nor does he/she have a right to a compulsory portion *(Pflichtteilsanteil)*. Hence, if a partner wishes to appoint his/her partner as an heir, it is necessary to draft a last will.[2]

BELGIUM

The surviving partner does not have rights of inheritance *ab intestato*.

BULGARIA

No, the surviving partner does not have any rights of inheritance in the case of intestate succession. Intestate heirs are only the relatives and the surviving spouse (Art. 5-9 of the Bulgarian Inheritance Law of 1949).

CROATIA

In line with Art. 11 paragraph 2 and of the Croatian Family Act and Art. 4 paragraph 2 and Art. 55 of the Croatian Partnership Act, the answer equally relates to both cohabitants and same-sex informal partners.

---

1 U. AICHHORN, 'Vermögensaufteilung und Erbrecht bei nichtehelicher Lebensgemeinschaft', in: M. GRUBER et al. (eds.), *Erbrecht und Vermögensnachfolge,* Verlag Österreich, Vienna, 2010, at marg. No. 81.

2 See A. DEIXLER-HÜBNER and H. SCHÄFFER, *Partnerschaft ohne Trauschein*, Linde, Vienna, 2014, at p. 43.

According to Art. 8 paragraph 2 of the Croatian Inheritance Act (Official Gazette no. 48/03, 163/03, 35/05, 127/13) surviving partners in an informal relationship are treated in the same way as surviving spouses if the relationship lasted for a longer period of time and was terminated by the death of one partner, provided that the prerequisites for the validity of a marriage were fulfilled.

If these conditions are met, the surviving partner becomes an intestate heir, just like a spouse. As an intestate heir, the surviving partner belongs to the first line of succession, together with the deceased's descendants who all equally share the inheritance. If there are no descendants, the surviving partner is placed into the second line of succession, together with the deceased's parents (the parents inherit one half and the partner the other half of the inheritance). If there are no parents, the surviving spouse inherits everything. If the deceased's descendants exist but they renounce their inheritance, the surviving partner is entitled to the entire inheritance.

CZECH REPUBLIC

In the Czech Civil Code in the case of intestate succession, there are six grades of heirs, where the relatives of the deceased are subsumed for the purposes of inheritance. The surviving partner to an informal relationship is not subsumed in any of these. However, those who lived with the deceased in the common household for at least one year before his death and, as a result, cared for the common household or were dependent for maintenance on the deceased, could be an inheritor in the second and third grade. For inheritance in the second grade, there cannot be any children of the testator. If there are children, the surviving partner cannot inherit at all. See S. 1635 Czech Civil Code.

A surviving spouse is an inheritor in the first grade with the children. If there are children, a spouse inherits with them. If there are no children, a spouse inherits in the second grade together with a testator's parents. A registered partner has the same position (according to S. 3020 Czech Civil Code: the provisions of Book One, Book Three and Book Four on marriage and on the rights and duties of spouses (of the Czech Civil Code) apply by analogy to registered partnership and the rights and duties of partners). See S. 1635 Czech Civil Code.

In conclusion, there is a slight chance for the surviving partner in an informal relationship to inherit in the case of intestate succession.

DENMARK

A new Danish Inheritance Act entered into force on 1 January 2008.[3] The new Act strengthens the position of the surviving spouse, but does not give the surviving cohabitant the right to inherit or to an undivided possession of the estate. According to Danish law, cohabitants cannot inherit from each other without this being specified in a will.

ENGLAND AND WALES

No. There is no right unless a will has been made in their favour.

ESTONIA

The partners in an informal relationship have no right to intestate succession. Pursuant to the Estonian Law of Succession Act,[4] only the spouse and the relatives named in the Estonian Law of Succession Act have the right of intestate succession and in certain cases also the right of succession to a compulsory portion.

FINLAND

The surviving cohabitation partner does not have a right to inherit, unless there is a will in favour of the surviving partner. The position of the surviving cohabitation partner is dramatically different from the surviving spouse, who inherits everything if the deceased does not have any children. The status of the surviving spouse is the same for both married and registered spouses.

FRANCE

According to French law the surviving partner has no inheritance rights on intestacy. A registered partner also has no such right.

Only spouses are entitled to inheritance rights on intestacy. The surviving spouse has an option depending on whether or not there are common children.[5] In the presence of common children the surviving

---

3 Act No. 515 of 6 June 2007.

4 Pärimisseadus (adopted on 17 January 2008, entered into force 1 January 2009). – RT I 2008, 7, 52; RT I, 29.06.2014, 10 (in Estonian), available in English at: www.riigiteataja.ee/en/eli/510072014002/consolide.

5 Art. 757 of the French Civil Code.

spouse has to opt for either the amount of ¼ of the estate of the deceased spouse on a full ownership basis or the usufruct of the all estate of the deceased spouse. Where the deceased spouse had children from a former union, the surviving spouse no longer has this option. He or she is entitled to the amount of ¼ of the estate of the deceased spouse on a full ownership basis. Where the spouse dies without children, the surviving spouse is entitled to half of the estate, the other half being granted to the deceased spouse's parents (¼ each).[6] Where the parents of the deceased spouse are no longer alive, the surviving spouse is the only heir on intestacy and is entitled to the full amount of the estate.[7]

GERMANY

The surviving partner does not have any rights of inheritance in case of intestate succession.

GREECE

There are no rights of inheritance for the surviving partner in the event of intestate succession. Only a spouse enjoys these rights (Art. 1820 Greek Civil Code) or a partner who was party to a cohabitation pact (Art. 11 Law 3719/2008).

HUNGARY

The surviving partner had no rights in the case of intestate succession according to the regime under the Civil Code of 1959 and he or she has no such rights in the Hungarian Civil Code.

REPUBLIC OF IRELAND

The surviving informal partner, whether a cohabitant or qualified cohabitant has no automatic rights on intestacy. On the other hand, a surviving spouse or civil partner, by virtue of his status, will be entitled to the deceased's entire estate should he die intestate and there are no issue.

A 'qualified cohabitant' as defined in S. 172(5) of the Irish Civil Partnership and Certain Rights and Obligations of Cohabitants Act 2010

6 Art. 757-1 of the French Civil Code.
7 Art. 757-2 of the French Civil Code.

has a right under S. 194 of that Act to apply to Court to seek provision from the estate of the deceased cohabitant in either a testate or intestate situation. Where the relationship between the partners is still in existence at the time of the deceased's death, it is not necessary for the applicant cohabitant to show financial dependence as is required generally under the redress scheme, reflecting the fact that neither party had withdrawn their commitment from the relationship. Where the relationship between the parties had ended during the deceased's lifetime, the financial dependency prerequisite applies. Under S. 194(3) of the Act, the court 'may by order make the provision for the applicant that the court considers appropriate having regard to the rights of any other person having an interest in the matter, if the court is satisfied that proper provision in the circumstances was not made for the applicant during the lifetime of the deceased for any reason other than conduct by the applicant that, in the opinion of the court, it would in all the circumstances be unjust to disregard.'

A surviving qualified cohabitant may apply to the court for such provision to be made for him or her out of a deceased's cohabitant's estate within six months from the first taking out of a grant of representation to the estate. Such provision can only be made out of the 'net estate of the deceased cohabitant'. This means the estate that remains after any other rights under the Irish Succession Act 1965 of a surviving spouse/civil partner have been satisfied (S. 194(11)).

ITALY

No right of inheritance accrues in the case of intestate succession.[8] The only way to allow the partner to have rights to the deceased partner's estate is through a will.

Legal doctrine has suggested many remedies under the law of contract to protect one's partner, all of them requiring legal advice and often the intervention of a notary. Their practical application, however, is not at all frequent among informal partners in Italy.

Moreover, the cohabitant has no right to the 'widow's/widower's pension' (*pensione di reversibilità* or *pensione indiretta*) which accrues only on the part of the deceased's wife or husband.[9]

---

8 Compare L. BALESTRA, 'La famiglia di fatto', in: G. FERRANDO (ed.), *Il nuovo diritto di famiglia*, Zanichelli, Bologna, 2008, at p. 1094 et seq.; G. OBERTO, *I diritti dei conviventi. Realtà e prospettive tra Italia ed Europa*, Cedam, Padua, 2012, at p. 193 et seq.

LATVIA

No, if there is not a will or inheritance contract, a partner does not have such rights.

LITHUANIA

A partner has no right to succeed according to the law. The legal basis for succession is a blood relationship and a matrimonial relationship. According to the law, legal successors can be: natural persons who survive the bequeather at the moment of his or her death, children of the bequeather who were born after his death, and likewise the State of Lithuania (Art. 5.5 of the Lithuanian Civil Code).

In intestate succession, the following persons shall be the heirs to inheritance in equal shares:

- First-degree descendants: the bequeather's children (including adopted children) and the bequeather's children born after his death;
- Second-degree descendants: the bequeather's parents (adoptive parents) and grandchildren;
- Third-degree descendants: the bequeather's grandparents both on the father's and mother's side, the bequeather's great grandchildren;
- Fourth-degree descendants: the bequeather's siblings and great grandparents both on the father's and mother's side;
- Fifth-degree descendants: the bequeather's nephews and nieces, likewise the bequeather's uncles and aunts;
- Sixth-degree descendants: the bequeather's cousins.

Second-degree heirs shall inherit by operation of the law only in the absence of first-degree heirs, or in the event of the latter's non-acceptance or renunciation of the inheritance, likewise in cases where the first-degree heirs are deprived of the right to inherit. The third, fourth, fifth and sixth-degree heirs shall inherit in the absence of heirs of a superior degree or in the event of the latter's renunciation of the inheritance or deprivation of the right to inherit (Art. 5.11 of the Lithuanian Civil Code).

According to Art. 5.13 of the Lithuanian Civil Code the surviving spouse of the bequeather shall be entitled to inherit pursuant to intestate succession or alongside the heirs (if any) of either the first or second

[9] C. Cost. 3 November 2000, n. 461; C Cost. 14 November 2000, n. 491. Compare AA. VV., *La separazione nella famiglia di fatto*, Cedam, Padua, 2014, at p. 26 et seq.

degree of descent. Together with the first-degree heirs, he or she shall inherit one fourth of the inheritance in the event of the existence of no more than three heirs apart from the spouse. In the event where there are more than three heirs, the spouse shall inherit in equal shares with the other heirs. If the spouse inherits with the second-degree heirs, he or she is entitled to half of the inheritance. In the event of the absence of first and second-degree heirs, the spouse shall inherit the whole inheritable estate.

LUXEMBOURG

No, the surviving partner is looked upon as a stranger according to inheritance law.

THE NETHERLANDS

In 2003 a completely revised Book 4 of the Dutch Civil Code entered into force, but this did not put formal and informal couples on the same footing. The position of non-marital cohabitants was improved somewhat, but not substantially.

No, the surviving partner has no rights of inheritance in the case of intestate succession. According to Art. 4:10 Dutch Civil Code the surviving spouse or registered partner (Art. 4:8 Dutch Civil Code) does have rights of inheritance, but the informal partner does not. The inferior legal position of the surviving informal partner has been criticised in the legal doctrine.[10]

NORWAY

Surviving cohabitants have rights of inheritance in the case of intestate succession as long as the cohabitants have, have had or expect a child together pursuant to the Norwegian Inheritance Act, S. 28(b). The surviving cohabitant inherits four times the National Insurance basic amount on the date of death – a total of approximately NOK 353,000[11] or

[10] F.W.J.M. SCHOLS, '(Ex-)partners en postmortale solidariteit: Een korte beschouwing over het "erfrechtelijke alimentatierecht" en de postmortale solidariteit voor samenlevers', *WPNR*, 2013; F.W.J.M. SCHOLS, 'Het erfrecht in Nederland', in: C. FORDER and A.L.P.G. VERBEKE (eds.), *Gehuwd of niet: maakt het iets uit?*, Intersentia, Antwerp, 2005, at p. 315; W.M. SCHRAMA, *De niet-huwelijkse samenleving in het Nederlandse en Duitse recht*, Kluwer, Deventer, 2004, at p. 558.

[11] The National Insurance basic amount was NOK 88,370 on 1 May 2014.

40,000 Euros. This inheritance right takes precedence over the inheritance rights of the lineal descendants, but can be restricted by a will, as long as the cohabitant is informed of the will before the testator's death.[12]

In the Norwegian Inheritance Act, cohabitation is defined as two people over the age of 18 living together in a marriage-like relationship as long as they are not married, registered partners or cohabiting with others.[13] Same-sex couples are included in this definition. The two people must permanently reside together, but it is expressly stated that shorter periods of separation due to education, work, illness and the like are no disqualification. People who are so closely related that they cannot marry are excluded from the definition of cohabitation.[14]

In comparison, the surviving spouse is entitled to one quarter of the estate if the deceased had children and, unlike the right of the cohabitant, this inheritance right can only partly be restricted by a will.[15]

The surviving cohabitant may elect to keep part of the deceased's estate undivided instead of making use of the inheritance right (see Question 48).

PORTUGAL

No, the surviving partner does not have rights of inheritance in the case of intestate succession.

RUSSIA

The surviving partner generally has no rights of inheritance in the case of intestate succession. However, if the surviving partner is unable to work and has been living with and been maintained by the other partner for at least one year, he/she has rights of inheritance in the case of intestate succession (Art. 1148(2) Russian Civil Code). This right of inheritance accrues to any disabled member of the household who has been

12 The Norwegian Inheritance Act, S. 28(b).
13 Norwegian Inheritance Act, Chapter III A and J. ASLAND and P. HAMBRO, 'New Developments and Expansion of Relationships Covered by Norwegian Law', in: B. ATKIN (ed.), *The International Survey of Family Law*, Jordan Publishing Limited, Bristol, 2009, pp. 378-384.
14 The Norwegian Inheritance Act, S. 28(a).
15 The Norwegian Inheritance Act, S. 28(b) second paragraph.

maintained by the deceased person, and not just to a partner in the informal relationship.

Under Art. 1148(2) Russian Civil Code, a disabled member of the household will inherit and rank alongside heirs who are entitled to the inheritance. Article 1145 provides for seven ranks of heirs. Normally, the existence of higher-ranking heirs precludes lower ranks from inheriting. Equally-ranking heirs receive equal shares of the inheritance (Art. 1141(2) Russian Civil Code).

A surviving partner who qualifies under Art. 1148(2) Russian Civil Code will inherit at the rank called to inheritance in the particular case. If, for instance, the first rank (children, parents and spouses) is called to inheritance and the deceased partner has two children and one living parent, the surviving partner will inherit one fourth of the deceased's estate, as will each of the children and the parent.

A surviving partner who qualifies under Art. 1148(2) Russian Civil Code is entitled to a reserved share under the provisions of Art. 1148(2) Russian Civil Code. That means that he/she is entitled to half of the share that he/she would have received in the case of intestate succession, even if the deceased partner has disinherited him/her in his will.

SCOTLAND

Unlike a spouse or civil partner, cohabitants have no automatic rights of inheritance in the case of intestate succession. In terms of S. 29 of the Family Law (Scotland) Act 2006, a cohabitant may however apply to the court for a discretionary award in the case that their partner dies intestate (discussed in Question 48).

The position of a cohabitant contrasts with that of a surviving spouse or civil partner who has substantial rights of succession on intestacy. These are governed by the Succession (Scotland) Act 1964. According to S. 8 of the 1964 Act, a surviving spouse has what are called 'prior rights' by means of which he or she is entitled to inherit the dwelling house in which the deceased was ordinarily resident at the date of death, up to a limit of £473,000. In addition, prior rights include furniture and plenishings owned by the deceased in said dwelling house, up to a limit of £29,000. The surviving spouse is also entitled to receive financial provision from the intestate's estate of £50,000, where there are issue (however remote) or £89,000 otherwise.[16]

After satisfaction of the surviving spouse or civil partner's prior rights, there is also provision for legal rights. Legal rights are payable from the moveable estate and they also depend on whether or not there are children of the deceased. If there are children, the surviving spouse or partner is entitled to one third of the free moveable estate and if there are no children, he or she is entitled to one half.

As highlighted above, a surviving cohabitant may now apply for a discretionary award on intestacy but any such award can only be paid out of the deceased's net intestate estate. In calculating the net value of that estate, various liabilities, including prior and legal rights of a surviving spouse or civil partner, must first be satisfied.[17] It is further provided that any order must not have the effect of awarding a surviving cohabitant an amount which exceeds that to which he or she would have been entitled as a spouse or civil partner.[18]

SLOVAKIA

Law of succession in general:
Inheritance is acquired at the moment of the deceased person's death (§ 460 Slovak Civil Code). Succession may be based on a will, on a statute, or on both (§ 461 para. 1 Slovak Civil Code). If inheritance is not acquired by any testamentary heirs, these are substituted by statutory heirs. Inheritance not acquired by any heir passes to the state (§ 461 para. 2 Slovak Civil Code). The Slovak law of succession is based on the principle of universal succession; therefore an entire inheritance can be rejected by the heir. If the heir rejects only part of the inheritance or rejects it with reservations or conditions, the inheritance is not rejected. If the heir does not reject the inheritance, he becomes the universal successor of the deceased person both with respect to his assets and liabilities. However, the heir is only liable for the deceased person's liabilities to the amount corresponding to the inherited assets (§ 463 Slovak Civil Code).

If there is only one heir, his inheritance will be confirmed by the courts. If there are more heirs, they may agree on how the inheritance will be

[16] Succession (Scotland) Act 1964, S. 9(1).
[17] Family Law (Scotland) Act 2006, S. 29.
[18] Family Law (Scotland) Act 2006, S. 29(3).

divided between them. If their agreement is not contrary to a statute or good morals, it will be approved by the courts. If no agreement is reached, the court will confirm the inheritance of the heirs whose right of inheritance is established according to their inheritance shares. These shares may be determined by the deceased person's will (testamentary succession) or by statute (statutory succession).

If, after the inheritance proceedings are closed, it is discovered that the true heir is different from the heir whose inheritance was confirmed (apparent heir), the apparent heir must restore any property acquired from the inheritance to the true heir in compliance with the rules on unjustified enrichment. If someone acquires, in good faith, property from an apparent heir whose inheritance was confirmed, he is protected as if the property had been acquired from the true heir. The same applies to cases where the inheritance has passed to the state.

There are four prerequisites of succession:

- the deceased person's death,
- inheritance (property to be inherited),
- a succession title, and
- an eligible heir.[19]

Succession may be based on two succession titles: the deceased person's will or a statute. If there are no testamentary heirs, the statutory order of succession is used.

If we want to compare the right of a partner to inherit after the other partner's death with the right of a surviving spouse, we need to look at the provisions of the Slovak Civil Code regulating the statutory devolution of successions (§ 473 et seq. Slovak Civil Code). It is based on four heir groups divided into heir classes. These groups and classes determine both statutory heirs and their shares.

In the first group, the succession devolves to the deceased person's children and his or her spouse in equal shares (§ 473 para. 1 Slovak Civil Code). If any of the deceased person's children do not inherit, their inheritance share passes to their children in equal shares (§ 473 para. 2 Slovak Civil Code). If these children do not inherit either, they are substituted by their descendants in equal shares. The principle of

---

19 D. GANDŽALOVÁ, in: J. LAZAR et al. (eds.), *Občianske právo hmotné* (Substantive Slovak Civil Law), Iuris Libri, Bratislava, 2014, at p. 621.

descendants being substituted by their respective descendants is called representation.[20] If the deceased person's descendants do not inherit, the succession devolves, in the second group, to the deceased person's spouse, parents, and persons having lived with the deceased person in a common household for 1 year before his or her death, looking after the common household or being dependent on the deceased person with respect to maintenance, in equal shares (§ 474 para. 1 Slovak Civil Code). However, the spouse's share is at least one half of the inheritance (§ 474 para. 2 Slovak Civil Code).

If the deceased person's spouse or either of his or her parents does not inherit, the succession devolves, in the third group, to the deceased person's siblings and persons having lived with the deceased person in a common household for 1 year before his or her death, looking after the common household or being dependent on the deceased person with respect to maintenance, in equal shares. If any of the deceased person's siblings do not inherit, their share passes to their children (representation). If no heir inherits in the third group, the succession devolves, in the fourth group, to the deceased person's grandparents in equal shares, and if none of them inherits, the succession devolves to their children in equal shares (representation).

SLOVENIA

All partners (spouses, extramarital partners, registered same-sex partners and unregistered same-sex partners living together) have the same rights to a legal inheritance.

A partner inherits in the first order of inheritance, together with the children of the testator or in the second order of inheritance together with the testator's parents if there were no children.

SPAIN

In the absence of a will, the Spanish Civil Code does not provide any inheritance rights for the surviving partner. Given that the Spanish Civil Code does not include any reference to informal relationships in its regulation of succession, surviving partners are treated as strangers to the deceased to all intents and purposes.

---

20 D. GANDŽALOVÁ, in: J. LAZAR et al. (eds.), *Občianske právo hmotné* (Substantive Slovak Civil Law), Iuris Libri, Bratislava, 2014, at p. 621.

According to the Spanish Civil Code, if a person dies without an effective will, the order/hierarchy of intestate heirs is as follows: descendants (Art. 930 Spanish Civil Code, ascendants (Art. 935 Spanish Civil Code), surviving spouse (Art. 943 Spanish Civil Code), collateral relatives up to the fourth degree (Art. 954 Spanish Civil Code), and finally, in the absence of all of the above, the State (Art. 956 Spanish Civil Code).

When the surviving spouse does not become intestate heir to the deceased, he/she will have a usufruct over a portion of the estate. The amount will vary depending on who the intestate heir is. If there are descendants, the surviving spouse will have a usufruct over one-third of the estate (Art. 834 Spanish Civil Code); if there are ascendants, the usufruct will be over one-half of the estate (Art. 837 Spanish Civil Code).

The Catalan Civil Code does provide inheritance rights in favour of the surviving partner. There are provisions that equate the surviving partner to the surviving spouse, giving them the same inheritance rights in the case of intestate succession. According to the Catalan Civil Code, if a person dies without an effective will, the order/hierarchy of intestate heirs is as follows: descendants (Art. 442-1 Catalan Civil Code), surviving spouse or partner (Art. 442-3 Catalan Civil Code), ascendants (Art. 442-8 Catalan Civil Code), collateral relatives up to the fourth degree (Art. 442-9 Catalan Civil Code), and finally, in the absence of all the above, the Catalan Government (Art. 442-12 Catalan Civil Code).

When the surviving spouse does not become intestate heir to the deceased, he/she will have a usufruct over the entire estate (Art. 442-3 Catalan Civil Code).

However, there are doubts as regards the constitutionality of these Catalan rules. The Spanish Constitutional Court, in its ruling 93/2013, 23 April, has deemed the Navarra Law to be unconstitutional because it imposes a set of mandatory rules and regulations on informal couples, regardless of the couples' wishes, which is against constitutional rights, namely, Art. 10 (free development of personality), Art. 18 (right to privacy) and Art. 32 Spanish Constitution (in its negative dimension, the right not to marry). This would mean that any autonomous community regulation (including that of Catalonia) with mandatory provisions must be applicable only to registered couples.

SWEDEN

The Swedish model, adopted in the Cohabitation Act of 2003, is to protect the partners through a right to share in certain property acquired for the couple's joint use, the 'cohabitation property'; this model also applies when the relationship is ended by the death of a partner. Probably due to this emphasis, the surviving partner does not enjoy any rights of inheritance in the case of intestate succession. The lack of a right to intestate succession is the most noteworthy difference between informal and formal relationships (marriage and registered partnership) besides the more limited scope of 'cohabitation property' compared to 'marital property'.

SWITZERLAND

In Switzerland, a surviving partner in an informal relationship has no rights of inheritance in the case of intestate succession.

QUESTION 48

Does the surviving partner have any other rights or claims on the estate (e.g. any claim based on dependency, compensation, or maintenance) in the case of intestate succession?

AUSTRIA

The only case which is explicitly governed by law concerns the rental property shared by the partners: Section 14 Austrian Tenancy Act stipulates that after the death of the tenant certain privileged persons are entitled to step into the tenancy agreement and become the contracting party in the agreement, if the following four requirements are fulfilled:

- the deceased partner was the main tenant of the dwelling,
- the existence of a 'privileged person' according to S. 14 para. 3 Austrian Tenancy Act,
- the 'privileged person' has lived together with the main tenant in the same household at the time of his/her death and
- the accommodation is urgently required.[1]

Besides spouses, relatives in the direct ascending line including adoptees and siblings, partners in an informal relationship belong to the persons entitled under S. 14 para. 3 Austrian Tenancy Act. According to this provision a partner in an informal relationship is a person who had lived in the dwelling with the main tenant until his/her death for at least three years.[2] From an economic point of view the informal relationship has to be comparable with a marriage. The temporal requirement does not apply if the partners had already moved into the dwelling together.[3]

---

1 H. WÜRTH, 'section 14 Austrian Tenancy Act', in: P. RUMMEL (ed.), *Kommentar zum Allgemeinen Bürgerlichen Gesetzbuch*, Manz Verlag, Vienna, 2003, at marg. No. 4.

2 H. WÜRTH, 'section 14 Austrian Tenancy Act', in: P. RUMMEL (ed.), *Kommentar zum Allgemeinen Bürgerlichen Gesetzbuch*, Manz Verlag, Vienna, 2003, at marg. No. 7.

3 Section 14 para. 3 Austrian Tenancy Act.

If these requirements are fulfilled, the person in question automatically becomes the new contracting party, unless he/she declares within fourteen days after the death of the other person that he/she does not want to continue the rental agreement. In case of doubt, the person who wishes to become the contracting party bears the burden of proof that all four conditions are met.[4] This particular inheritance right even applies if another person is appointed as the heir.[5]

Since the amendment of the Austrian Condominium Ownership Act in 2002 also partners in an informal relationship can jointly purchase a condominium.[6] Before the amendment this possibility was reserved to spouses, unless the partners in the informal relationship agreed to form a partnership.[7] In the case of death the share owned by the deceased person automatically becomes the property of the surviving partner, unless the person entitled waives his/her right or reaches another agreement with the heirs.[8] It should be noted, however, that this acquisition is not inheritance-related, but rather constitutes a particular form of accretion *(Anwachsung)*.[9] As a result the surviving partner becomes the sole owner of the condominium, but has to pay the takeover price, which is half of the market value.[10] There is no obligation to pay the takeover price if the decedent has so disposed of the property in his/her last will or donates his/her share to the other partner in the case of death.

Further, it should be noted that the surviving partner can, of course, direct all claims against the estate, which he/she could have claimed against his/her partner during his/her lifetime.

A partner may bring an unjust enrichment claim pursuant to S. 1435 General Austrian Civil Code, if he/she rendered a performance in expectation of a particular purpose, which was obvious to the beneficiary

---

4 Austrian Supreme Court, Judgement of 03.11.1999, 9 Ob 280/99p.

5 E. MÖSCHL, *Die nichteheliche Lebensgemeinschaft*, LexisNexis ARD ORAC, Vienna, 2007, at marg. No. 51.

6 Section 13 Condominium Ownership Act.

7 E. MÖSCHL, *Die nichteheliche Lebensgemeinschaft*, LexisNexis ARD ORAC, Vienna, 2007, at marg. No. 52.

8 Section 14 Austrian Condominium Ownership Act.

9 A. KLETEČKA, 'Die Eigentümerpartnerschaft nach dem WEG 2002', *immolex*, 2002, at p. 174 et seq.

10 E. GITSCHTHALER, 'Neuerungen im Recht der Lebensgemeinschaften', *AnwBl*, 2012, at p. 600.

and could finally not be achieved.[11] The same is true for claims arising from service contracts pursuant to S. 1152 General Austrian Civil Code, which stipulates that in the absence of an agreement reasonable compensation is deemed to have been agreed. However, due to the fact that performances rendered within an informal relationship are considered to be complimentary, the person rendering the performance is entitled to payment only in exceptional circumstances, e.g. if it was rendered in expectation of a subsequent counter-performance (e.g. marriage).[12] Moreover, if one partner suffered harm during the relationship, he/she may demand indemnification according to the general rules on damages, S. 1295 et seq. General Austrian Civil Code.

BELGIUM

The surviving partner does not have any claims on the estate as such. He/she may claim compensation on the same bases as in the case of separation, that is: as 'maintenance' or as compensation. The existence of a natural obligation has not yet been accepted, however.[13] If the surviving partner had a right of habitation – or should be considered a tenant at will – he/she will be granted a respite during which he/she is entitled to remain in the home of the deceased partner (against payment).[14]

For the sake of completeness, we should mention that it is accepted in the case law that the surviving partner who voluntarily paid the funeral costs cannot recover them from the estate. The payment of those debts is considered to be the performance of a natural obligation.[15]

BULGARIA

No, the surviving partner does not have any other rights or claims on the estate in such a case.

---

[11] R. HOLZHAMMER and M. ROTH, *Bürgerliches Recht mit Internationalem Privatrecht*, LexisNexis ARD ORAC, Vienna, 2004, at p. 322 et seq.; E. MÖSCHL, *Die nichteheliche Lebensgemeinschaft*, LexisNexis ARD ORAC, Vienna, 2007, at marg. No. 83.

[12] Austrian Supreme Court, Judgement of 15.12.2009, 5Ob174/09p; Austrian Supreme Court, Judgement of 19.12.2001, 9 Ob 291/01m; R. Holzhammer and M. Roth, *Bürgerliches Recht mit Internationalem Privatrecht*, LexisNexis ARD ORAC, Vienna, 2004, at p. 323.

[13] Justice of the Peace Charleroi (2) 3 March 2003, *JT* 2004, 101.

[14] Justice of the Peace Charleroi (2) 3 March 2003, *JT* 2004, 101; Justice of the Peace Zomergem 27 June 2014, *RW* 2014-15, 751.

[15] Ghent 17 January 2007, *NJW* 2008, 223, with note WILLEMS.

CROATIA

In line with Art. 11 paragraph 2 of the Croatian Family Act and Art. 4 paragraph 2 and Art. 55 of the Croatian Partnership Act, the answer equally relates to both cohabitants and same-sex informal partners.

The surviving partner is not entitled to other rights or claims on the estate in the case of intestate succession.

CZECH REPUBLIC

According to S. 1669 Czech Civil Code, persons who enjoyed gratuitous provision for life in the household of the deceased until his death are entitled to the same provision for life for another three weeks after the deceased's death.

DENMARK

According to case law and general property law, a surviving cohabitant may be awarded compensation. The conditions that have been crystallised in the case law are the following: 1) the cohabitation must have been permanent for a period of around three years; and 2) the surviving cohabitant must have contributed significantly to the deceased cohabitant creating or retaining substantial assets.[16] For example, the income of the surviving cohabitant may have been spent on living expenses, while the income of the deceased cohabitant was spent on paying off the mortgage on the real property. The deceased cohabitant will then have acquired a significant free equity in the dwelling, while the survivor will have no assets. The property law principles at the heart of the cohabitant's claim for compensation are primarily the principle of unjust enrichment and the doctrine of contractual expectations. In principle, claims for compensation are not excluded even if the surviving cohabitant is provided for in the will of the deceased cohabitant.[17]

ENGLAND AND WALES

Yes. They can make a claim under the English Inheritance (Provision for Families and Dependants) Act 1975 as an eligible applicant as defined in

[16] See J. ASLAND et al., *Nordisk Samboerrett*, Gyldendal Norsk Forlag, Oslo, 2014, at p. 204-205; and I. LUND-ANDERSEN, *Familieøkonomien*, Jurist- og Økonomforbundets Forlag, Copenhagen, 2011, at p. 392-406.

[17] Danish Parliamentary Report No. 1473/2006, p. 147. See also *Ugeskrift for Retsvæsen* (Weekly Law Journal) 1985, at p. 55.

S. 1A and S. 1B. The couple must have lived together for at least 2 years in the same household as husband wife or as civil partners. The claim is for 'such financial provision as it would be reasonable for the applicant to receive for his maintenance' (S. 1(2)(b)).

ESTONIA

The legal literature refers to the fact that the surviving partner in an informal relationship has (different from a spouse) an opportunity to determine which of the assets acquired during the relationship actually belongs to him or her and what portion shall be transferred to the successors as the property of the deceased, i.e. after the death of one partner, it should be possible to evidence the contract of joint operation or the occurrence of shared ownership.[18] The family members of a person who lived with him or her and received maintenance from him or her until that person's death have the right to continue using the objects of the shared household and to receive maintenance from the estate for one month after his or her death (§ 132 Estonian Law of Succession Act). The partners in an informal relationship can be treated as members of a family. On June 19, 2000, the Administrative Chamber of the Supreme Court held that subsection 1 of § 27 of the Estonian Constitution provides protection from an unfounded intervention by the state also to a form of family cohabitation that has not been registered according to the terms prescribed by law.[19]

FINLAND

The Finnish Code of Inheritance (40/1965) entails provisions according to which the surviving cohabitee may receive support from the estate of the deceased cohabitee in the form of money, other property or as a usufruct (*käyttöoikeus/nyttjanderätt*), if his or her livelihood has been compromised by the death of his or her partner and the support is necessary to secure that livelihood. The surviving partner is only entitled to support if the partners had lived in a common household for a minimum period of five years or had a common child.

In addition to support according to the Finnish Code of Inheritance (40/1965), the surviving partner is entitled to the same compensation

18 K. KAMA and K. KULLERKUPP, 'Vabaabielu versus abielu: varalised suhted muutuvate kooseluvormide kontekstis', *Juridica*, 2002, No. 6, pp. 359-368.

19 Decision of the Administrative Law Chamber of the Supreme Court 3-3-1-16-00, at para. 1.

based on unjust enrichment as he or she is entitled to receive in the case of separation, if the separation of property according to ownership would result in an unfair distribution of property taking into account the contributions for the benefit of the shared household by both partners. The grounds for this compensation are based on S. 8 of the Finnish Act on the Dissolution of the Household of Cohabiting Partners (26/2011) and are described in more detail under Question 46.

FRANCE

No such right exists according to French law.

GERMANY

According to § 1969 para. 1 German Civil Code the heir has a duty, in the first thirty days after the occurrence of the devolution of the inheritance, to grant maintenance to the same extent as the deceased did to family members of the deceased, if they belong to the household of the deceased and have been receiving maintenance from him or her at the time of his or her death and to permit them to use the home and the household objects (see Question 4). The surviving partner meets the conditions to count as a family member within the meaning of the provision if both partners shared an residence and the surviving partner actually received maintenance.[20]

GREECE

No.

HUNGARY

The surviving partner may claim for his or her participation in the acquisitions when the community of life ceased. In cases where one cohabitant maintained and supported his or her partner for a rather long period of time from his or her own property without any maintenance contract having been entered into and there is no will in favour of the surviving partner, there is a possibility for the surviving partner to be

[20] See for this prevailing view: D. WEIDLICH, '§ 1969', in: O. PALANDT, *Bürgerliches Gesetzbuch*, Beck, Munich, 2015, at No. 1; W. KÜPPER, '§ 1969', in: *Münchener Kommentar zum BGB*, Beck, Munich, 2013, at No. 2.

given a preferred claim. Nevertheless, there is no certainty concerning such claims in the case law.

REPUBLIC OF IRELAND

No, cohabiting couples have no legal rights or claims on each other's estates, apart from the right to apply for provision as outlined above pursuant to S. 194 of the Irish 2010 Act if they come within the definition of 'qualified cohabitants'. Where the parties' relationship ended two or more years prior to the death of the deceased cohabitant, applications under S. 194 cannot be brought. One exception to this limitation period is where the claimant was in receipt of periodical payments from the deceased either pursuant to a S. 175 maintenance order or a cohabitants' agreement - as the unexpected death of the maintenance debtor would mean that payments would cease at a time when they may still be needed. Thus, the receipt of maintenance entitles a qualified cohabitant to make a claim for provision out of the deceased's estate where the relationship broke down more than 2 years prior to death.

ITALY

In the case of intestate succession the informal partner has no right to or any claim against the deceased partner's estate.

LATVIA

No, if there is not a will or inheritance contract, a partner does not have such rights.

LITHUANIA

The surviving partner can bring a creditor's claim on general grounds both against the heirs by law and the heirs by will[21] (Art. 5.63 of the Lithuanian Civil Code,[22] and Chapter VI of the Lithuanian Code of Civil Procedure). A separate regulation covers the compensation of funeral costs: Art. 5.63 is not applicable, and instead the courts follow Art. 1.2,

---

21 Ruling of the Lithuanian Supreme Court of 17 May 2011, civil case no. 3K-3-243/2011.

22 The creditors of a bequeather shall have the right, within three months from the day of the opening of the succession, to instigate claims against the successors who accepted the succession, the executor of the will or the administrator of the inheritance, or to bring an action in respect of the inheritable property. Claims shall be made without having regard to the maturity of the time limit for their satisfaction.

part 1, Art. 1.5, Art. 1.8 part 2, Art. 5.59, part 2, Art. 6.1 and 6.2 of the Lithuanian Civil Code as well as Art. 3, part 6 of the Lithuanian Code of Civil Procedure.

LUXEMBOURG

See the answer to Question 47.

THE NETHERLANDS

The surviving partner has no rights or claims against the estate based on dependency, compensation or maintenance in the case of intestate succession.

NORWAY

Surviving cohabitants have a right of undivided possession of part of the estate as long as the cohabitants have, have had or expect a child together, pursuant to the Norwegian Inheritance Act, S. 28(c). This right of undivided possession applies to the family home and household goods, to holiday homes and vehicles as long as these items are for joint use.[23] This right can be restricted only by a will, of which the cohabitant is informed before the testator's death.[24]

A surviving cohabitant may claim compensation on the basis of principles of unjust enrichment and restitution. These non-statutory rules developed through Supreme Court practice in the 1980s.[25] The cohabitant must have provided the other party with a 'significant financial benefit' in order to receive any compensation. In addition, the granting of compensation must be 'reasonable'. Compensation to avert unjust enrichment is granted only 'in exceptional cases'.

When 'special reasons' so indicate, a surviving partner to an informal relationship (and other people who live together in a household) may purchase what was previously the common residence and household goods at market value, pursuant to the Norwegian Household Community Act, S. 2.

---

[23] The Norwegian Inheritance Act, S. 28(c).

[24] The Norwegian Inheritance Act, S. 28(c) third paragraph.

[25] See Rt. 1984 p. 497, Rt. 2000 p. 1089, Rt. 2011 p. 1168 and Rt. 2011 p. 1176.

PORTUGAL

Yes. The surviving partner has a right to maintenance over the deceased's patrimony, inherited by his or her heirs (Art. 2020 of the Portuguese Civil Code), regardless of their title of succession acquisition.

RUSSIA

No.

SCOTLAND

Section 29 of the Family Law (Scotland) Act 2006 introduced the right for a cohabitant to apply to the court for provision on intestacy. Any application must be made within six months of the date of death.[26] Although this new provision was regarded as offering significant protection for cohabitants, there are very few reported cases of its use. The strict time limit has been highlighted as limiting the effectiveness of the provision and it has been suggested that some families may deliberately 'delay the administration of their deceased relative's estate to frustrate a claim on the part of the surviving cohabitant.'[27] An application may be made where the deceased died intestate and immediately prior to death was domiciled in Scotland and cohabiting with the applicant.[28]

Section 29 provides that, on application by the surviving partner, the court may make an order for payment of a capital sum or transfer of property from the deceased's net intestate estate.[29] It is clear that any such order is discretionary and in reaching their decision the court must take into account:

> '(a) The size and nature of the deceased's net intestate estate;
> (b) Any benefit received, or to be received by the survivor –
> (i) On, or in consequence of, the deceased's death; and
> (ii) From somewhere other than the deceased's net intestate estate;
> (c) The nature and extent of any other rights against, or claims on, the deceased's net intestate estate; and
> (d) Any other matter the court considers appropriate.'[30]

---

26 Family Law (Scotland) Act 2006, S. 29(6).
27 J. KERRIGAN, 'Time Limits and the Family Law (Scotland) Act 2006', *Scots Law Times*, 2013, pp. 125 et seq., at p. 127.
28 Family Law (Scotland) Act 2006, S. 29(1).
29 Family Law (Scotland) Act 2006, S. 29(2).
30 Family Law (Scotland) Act 2006, S. 29(3).

The deceased's net intestate estate is defined as what remains after satisfaction of inheritance tax, other liabilities of the estate and the prior and legal rights of a surviving spouse or civil partner.[31] Clearly, except in the case of significant assets, a substantial part of the deceased's estate could be taken up by the succession rights of a surviving spouse or civil partner, although it should be noted that the legal rights of any children do not take priority over the claim of a cohabitant. This was a relevant factor in *Windram, Applicant*;[32] one of only a handful of cases to have been reported to date. Here the couple had cohabited for 24 years and had two children who were both under the age of 16. According to the rules of intestate succession, the children would have inherited the whole estate. On application by the mother under S. 29, she was awarded transfer of the family home and an additional capital sum of £34,000.[33] The facts and circumstances of this particular case did not disclose any significant conflict between the interests of the cohabitant and the interests of the children. In practice, she wished to be able to remain in the family home and to support their children in that environment. It does, however, highlight the potential for conflict between a surviving cohabitant and children.

SLOVAKIA

No.

SLOVENIA

On the death of a partner, the common property of the partners is divided, generally in half. The surviving partner receives her or his share of the common property and the inheritable share of the estate of the deceased partner in which the share of the common property of the deceased partner and her or his personal property belong. An unsupported partner who inherits together with the testator's descendants in the first order of inheritance may request that a court decides that she or he should also inherit the part of the inheritance that under the law would be inherited by co-heirs. A partner can also request that her or his share be increased at the expense of all or some of the co-heirs. A court may also decide on the request of a partner that he or she should inherit the entire estate if its value is so small that he or she would find himself

---

[31] Family Law (Scotland) Act 2006, S. 29(10).

[32] *Windram, Applicant* 2009 Fam LR 152.

[33] As compared to £45,000 capital sum she would have received if married.

or herself in a deprived position if it were to be divided (para. 1 Art. 13 of the Slovenian Inheritance Act).[34]

A partner, as a legal heir, also has the right to her or his own compulsory share. This amounts to half of that which would be left to her or him by law. In a case in which the legal share of the partner can be increased at the expense of the co-heirs, there can also be an increase in their share at the cost of other heirs or also at the cost of a legatee.[35]

SPAIN

According to the Spanish Civil Code, the surviving partner has no claims on the estate. Given that the Spanish Civil Code does not include any reference to informal relationships in its regulation of succession, surviving partners are treated as strangers to the deceased to all intents and purposes.

Under the Catalan Civil Code, the surviving partner has a right to maintenance for one year after the partner's death (Art. 231-31 Catalan Civil Code), as well as a right to compensation by reason of work (Art. 234-14 Catalan Civil Code). When one partner has worked for the household substantially more than the other or has worked for the other partner without any (or insufficient) remuneration, that partner is entitled to financial compensation for this involvement if, at the end of the cohabitation, the other partner has accrued more assets (Art. 234-9 Catalan Civil Code). The surviving partner also has a right to the *cuarta viudal* (one-quarter of the deceased's estate) when the surviving partner's estate plus any property allocated by the deceased is insufficient for the survivor's maintenance, taking into account the standard of living enjoyed by the couple before death (Art. 452-1 Catalan Civil Code). However, given the ruling of the Spanish Constitutional Court 93/2013, these regulations should only be applied to registered couples.

SWEDEN

Claims that can be raised between the cohabitees when their relationship ends can also be raised by the surviving partner on the estate of the

[34] Uradni list SRS (Official Journal) Nos 15/1976, 23/1978, Uradni list RS (Official Journal) Nos 17/1991-I, 13/1994, 40/1994, 82/1994, 117/2000, 67/2001, 83/2001, 73/2004, 31/2013, 99/2013.

[35] K. Zupančič (ed.), V. Žnidaršič Skubic, *Dedno pravo (Inheritance Law)*, Uradni list Republike Slovenije, Ljubljana, 2009, at p. 97.

deceased, for example, the right to be recognised as a 'hidden' co-owner to property to which the deceased partner alone held title (see above Question 3 and 28). In the case of death, the surviving cohabitee may (exclusively) request a division of the 'cohabitation property' and/or the take-over right of the joint dwelling and household goods, Swedish Cohabitation Act, § 18 para. 1. The heirs, etc., enjoy no corresponding right.

Within the framework of the division of 'cohabitation property' the Swedish Cohabitation Act provides a right for the surviving partner to receive a fixed amount from this divisible property once debts have been deducted, § 18 para. 2. In 2015 this fixed amount, consisting of two so-called price amounts which are annually adjusted to the general living expenses in Sweden, was 89,000 Swedish crowns (approximately €9,600). This sum is exactly half of that granted to a surviving partner in a formalised relationship (marriage, registered partnership).[36] It is, however, not a rule or expression of minimum inheritance but forms a part of the rules regarding division of the 'cohabitation property', i.e., the joint dwelling and household goods acquired for the partners' joint use. Its purpose is to ensure that the surviving cohabitee is left with a minimum value of property but only with regard to 'cohabitation property'. The right is irrelevant and does not come into play if the surviving partner's share in the divisible property exceeds the value of this fixed amount. On the other hand, the surviving partner is entitled to this amount even if he or she has assets which are not included in the property division and which greatly exceed the value of this fixed amount. This right is also to be seen against the background that the surviving cohabitee has no right to compensation from any other assets of the deceased cohabitee. That this is a rule linked to the existence of 'cohabitation property' between the partners is reflected in the fact that it cannot be set aside by the deceased partner's will.

In the case of intestate succession when the deceased partner has no heirs, i.e. persons with a right to inherit from him or her according to the

[36] See M. BRATTSTRÖM, 'The Protection of a Vulnerable Party when a Cohabitee Relationship Ends – An Evaluation of the Swedish Cohabitees Act', in B. VERSCHRAEGEN (ed.), *Family Finances*, Jan Sramet Verlag, Vienna, 2008, at p. 350–351 and M. JÄNTERÄ-JAREBORG, 'Rechtsregeln für nichteheliches Zusammenleben in Schweden' (in English), in: I. KROPPENBERG et al. (eds.), *Rechtsregeln für nichteheliches Zusammenleben*, Gieseking Verlag, Vienna, 2009, pp. 207-226, at p. 223 et seq.

Swedish Inheritance Code (in Swedish, *Ärvdabalk 1958:637*),[37] the property goes to the Swedish state. The competent state authority (*Kammarkollegiet*) can grant a surviving partner the right to succeed to the deceased person's estate - or part of it - if it can be clearly proved that this corresponded with the wish of the deceased person, for example, in the form of written documentation or making this wish known to witnesses. These kinds of situations remain exceptional.

SWITZERLAND

With regard to compensation, the surviving partner generally has the same claims against the estate as against the partner upon separation. Thus, for instance, claims against the estate based upon a simple partnership may be possible under certain circumstances (Art. 530 et seq. Swiss Code of Obligations, see Questions 3 and 42).[38] The death of a partner in an informal relationship will generally lead to the liquidation of the simple partnership (Art. 545 para. 1 No. 2 Swiss Code of Obligations). There are, however, many uncertainties concerning these claims in legal practice.[39]

In cases of the homicide of a partner in an informal relationship, the surviving partner may be entitled to damages under tort law. According to Art. 45 para. 3 Swiss Code of Obligations, compensation must be granted if a person is deprived of his or her means of support as a result of homicide (*Versorgerschaden*). It is not necessary that such support is statutorily granted. Rather, the Swiss Federal Supreme Court has held that a partner in an informal relationship is entitled to such damages if he or she has actually been supported by the deceased and would most probably also have been supported by him or her in the future.[40]

Furthermore, the surviving partner may be entitled to an appropriate sum for pain and suffering (*Genugtuung*). Pursuant to Art. 47 Swiss Code of Obligations the court may grant the dependants of the deceased such (additional) compensation in cases of homicide.[41]

---

37 In cross-border cases, of course, another state's law can be applicable. As of 17 August 2015 the EU's Inheritance Regulation will be applied in Sweden to deaths that occur from this date on.

38 M. COTTIER, 'Ein zeitgemässes Erbrecht für die Schweiz', *successio*, 2014, at p. 29, 31.

39 M. COTTIER and C. CREVOSIER, 'Die nichteheliche Lebensgemeinschaft als einfache Gesellschaft', *Aktuelle Juristische Praxis*, 2012, at p. 33 et seq.

40 Swiss Federal Supreme Court, BGE 114 II 144 E.2.

41 Swiss Federal Supreme Court, BGE 138 III 157.

QUESTION 49

Are there specific rules dealing with the home and/or household goods?

AUSTRIA

In Austria there are currently no specific rules dealing with the home and/or household goods in case of the death of one partner in an informal relationship.

BELGIUM

No.

BULGARIA

The specific rule is contained in Art. 12, para. 1 of the Bulgarian Inheritance Law stipulating the division of the household goods from the total mass of the inheritance and for its provision to the heir who had lived together and cared for the deceased. Based on a will it is possible for the partner in an informal relationship to inherit the household goods.

No specific regulation exists in respect to the family home.

CROATIA

In line with Art. 11 paragraph 2 of the Croatian Family Act and Art. 4 paragraph 2 and Art. 55 of the Croatian Partnership Act, the answer equally relates to both cohabitants and same-sex informal partners.

According to Art. 76 in relation to Art. 8 paragraph 2 of the Croatian Inheritance Act and Art. 4 paragraph 2 of the Croatian Partnership Act, the surviving partner, together with the deceased's descendants who lived with the deceased in the same household at the time of his/her death, shall acquire the right to demand certain household items that served to satisfy their daily needs, e.g. furniture, appliances, bedding and the like, but subject to the condition that these are not very valuable. Such items shall not be taken into account when calculating the reserved share nor shall they be included in the heirs' inheritance share. The surviving partner and descendants shall acquire co-ownership of these items in equal parts.

CZECH REPUBLIC

There is only one specific rule about the home in S. 1669 Czech Civil Code. It establishes that if the surviving partner lived for free with a deceased before his/her death, he/she can live there for three more weeks for free. In the actual words of S. 1669 Czech Civil Code: persons who enjoyed gratuitous provision for life in the household of the deceased until his death are entitled to the same provision for life for another three weeks after the deceased's death.

DENMARK

The reform of the Danish Inheritance Act in 2007 added a new S. 111a to the Danish Administration of Estates Act regarding a 'cohabitant's right to assume possession following an assessment'. The provision gave the surviving cohabitant the right to assume possession of the previous joint dwelling and ordinary household goods against a cash payment of the assessed value of the estate. The assessed value must be equivalent to the market value.

Not all cohabitating relationships entitle the cohabitants to invoke claims under S. 111a of the Danish Administration of Estates Act. The right applies to: 1) cohabitants who have lived together in a marriage-like relationship for the last two years prior to death; or 2) cohabitants who have, have had or are expecting children together. According to subsection 2 of the provision, the cohabitation will not be considered to have ended because of a temporary stay in another dwelling or a stay in an institution. These are the same terms as must be met in order to establish an expanded cohabitant's will according to S. 88, subsections 2 and 3, of the Danish Inheritance Act. According to S. 111a, subsection 5, the right in S. 111a of the Danish Administration of Estates Act to assume possession must waive the priority of testamentary provisions by the deceased cohabitant.

ENGLAND AND WALES

No.

ESTONIA

The partners in an informal relationship have no right to intestate succession. According to § 90(1) of the Estonian Law of Property Act, a possessor of a movable asset and any earlier possessor shall be deemed to be the owners of the asset during the possessor's possession until the contrary is proved. The presumption of the possessor of movable property, arising from § 90, includes, as a rule, also the presumption of common ownership by the co-possessor, which provides certain protection to a (non-possesor) spouse as well as to a partner in an informal relationship. The family members of a person who lived with him or her and received maintenance from him or her until that person's death have the right to continue using the objects of the shared household and to receive maintenance from the estate for one month after his or her death (§ 132 Estonian Law of Succession Act). The parties in an informal relationship can be treated as members of a family.

FINLAND

No.

FRANCE

On intestacy, no specific rules concerning cohabitation have been provided for regarding home or household goods. Indeed, the situation will be determined by the application of the general principles of property law. The key issue is proof of ownership. If the surviving partner is able to prove the full ownership of assets, the heirs will have no claim thereto. Where the heirs can prove the full ownership of the deceased cohabitant concerning the assets, the surviving partner will have no claim regarding them. If proof of ownership cannot be provided, the asset will be subjected to indivisible joint ownership (*indivision*) between the surviving partner and the heirs on a 50/50 basis (see Question 41). One of the joint owners can demand that the asset in question be sold.

Where the home was exclusively owned by the deceased cohabitant, the surviving partner has no right to remain in that home. If he or she is allowed to remain in the home by the heirs, they are entitled to an occupation fee (*indemnité d'occupation*).[1]

Money deposited in the bank account of the deceased partner is automatically blocked until the liquidation of the succession, even though a power of proxy concerning the bank account (*procuration*) was granted to the surviving partner during life in common.

The situation concerning a joint bank account (*compte bancaire joint*) and an undivided bank account (*compte bancaire indivis*) must be distinguished. Only an undivided bank account is automatically blocked upon the death of one of the co-holders. Money deposited in a joint bank account remains accessible to the surviving partner.[2] Yet, the harshness of this situation can be lessened by a will (*testament*).

GERMANY

According to § 1932 German Civil Code the surviving spouse under certain conditions has a right to the objects belonging to the marital household. However, this rule cannot be applied by analogy to informal partnerships (see Question 1).[3] Regarding § 1969 German Civil Code see Question 48.

GREECE

No. Such a rule, relating to the property which served as the family home, is only applicable to a surviving spouse (Art. 1889 Greek Civil Code). The same is true concerning the goods jointly used by the spouses. The only exception is covered by Art. 1820(2) Greek Civil Code.

HUNGARY

There are no specific rules.

---

1 If the home was exclusively rented by the deceased cohabitant, the recognised partner (*concubin notoire*) can request the benefit of the transfer of the residential lease, subject to the condition that the partners lived together for at least one year (Art. 14 of Law Act no. 89-462 of 6 July 1989).

2 Service Public, 'Que devient un compte bancaire en case de décès?', available at: vosdroits.service-public.fr/particuliers/F1451.xhtml.

3 D. LEIPOLD, '§ 1932', in: *Münchener Kommentar zum BGB*, Beck, Munich, 2013, at No. 3.

REPUBLIC OF IRELAND

No. The general rules set out in Questions 47 and 48 are the only rules that apply.

ITALY

No, there are not. The cohabitant has no legal right which can be compared to that of a surviving spouse who, upon the death of the other, has the right to live in the family home and to use the household goods if their owner was the deceased (Art. 540 para. 2 Italian Civil Code).

In the absence of any testamentary instruction to the contrary, then, the informal partner may be asked (or even forced) to leave the premises by the heir.[4]

A substantially different set of rules applies, however, when the family home is not owned but leased, and the deceased partner was the only tenant. After a 1988 decision by the Constitutional Court,[5] the cohabiting partner automatically becomes the new tenant in place of the deceased, irrespective of any contractual agreement with the lessor.

It is a paradox evidenced by many authors that the legal position of an informal partner living in a rented home is undoubtedly better protected than that of one living in a home owned by the deceased partner.

LATVIA

No, there are no such specific rules on this for informal relationships.

LITHUANIA

The object of succession is the totality of the property, property rights, obligations and some personal rights enjoyed by the testator at the moment of his/her death. As the right to request to be recognised as a family member of the tenant is of a personal nature, this right cannot be

---

4 This rule has been held to be constitutionally compatible by the Constitutional Court on 26 May 1989, n. 310. Other decisions to the same effect are quoted by G. OBERTO, *I diritti dei conviventi. Realtà e prospettive tra Italia ed Europa*, Cedam, Padua, 2012, at p. 194 n. 3.

5 C. Cost. 7 April 1988, n. 404, in Foro. It., 1988, I. C. 2515. Compare G. PIANEZZE, *Rapporti personali e patrimoniali tra conviventi*, Giuffré, Milan, 2013, at p. 149 et seq.; R. TOMMASINI, 'La famiglia di fatto', in: M. BESSONE (ed.), *Trattato di diritto privato*, Giappichelli, Turin, 1999, at p. 415.

transferred to other parties (Art. 5.1, part 1 of the Lithuanian Civil Code). When a tenant who was a natural person and who was holding a lease on immovable property dies, his/her rights and obligations pass to his/her heirs unless the law or the lease agreement provides otherwise (Art. 6.494, part 4 of the Lithuanian Civil Code).

There is no separate regulation concerning succession to household goods. The clothing, documents, relics and household articles are transferred to the heirs according to the law regardless of the order of succession if they have been living together with the deceased for at least one year prior to his/her death. Living together must have been factual and continuous. Household articles can also be disposed of by will.

LUXEMBOURG

No, there are no specific rules dealing with the home/household goods.

THE NETHERLANDS

In the case of intestate succession, if the home in which the partners had a durable joint household belongs to the estate, the surviving partner is entitled towards the heirs to continue the occupancy of the home combined with use of the household effects for a period of 6 months following the death of his/her partner. This follows from Art. 4:28 para. 2 Dutch Civil Code. If the home belongs to the inheritance on the ground of a lease agreement, then the law on leasing will determine who can continue the occupancy, on the basis of Art. 7:229 and 7:268 Dutch Civil Code.

NORWAY

A surviving partner may purchase the family home and household goods at market value if 'special reasons' so indicate, pursuant to the Norwegian Household Community Act, S. 2.

The surviving cohabitant's right of undivided possession of the estate applies to the family home and household goods (as well as to holiday homes and vehicles for joint use).[6]

---

6 The Norwegian Inheritance Act, S. 28(c).

PORTUGAL

Yes, there are.

Law No. 7/2001 grants the surviving partner the real right of habitation in the family home and the right to use household goods used by both in family life for a period of five years (Art. 3.°, al. a), e 5.°, n.° 1).

When the *de facto* union lasted for more than five years, the rights of habitation in the property and the right to use household goods are granted for however long the *de facto* union had lasted – six, ten or twenty years, etc. (Art. 5, n. 2).

An exceptional extension of the rights of habitation and use is, however, possible, based on equity reasons, to meet any severe needs of the interested party, and taking into special consideration personal care provided to the deceased partner or relatives (Art. 5, n. 4).

In the event of the *de facto* union members being co-owners of the property, the law recognises the right of exclusive use of common goods, during the periods established in Art. 5, in order to prevent other co-owners from reclaiming the possibility of concurrent use (Art. 5, n. 3).

The fact that the surviving member does not use the home for one year – thus showing that it is not needed – determines the expiration of the foreseen rights in these circumstances (Art. 5, n. 5).

After the expiration of the period during which the surviving member has the right of habitation, the law adds the attribution of the right to rent, under general market terms.

The court can intervene in defining the conditions of the contract, namely in fixing the rent, when there is disagreement over the market value (Art. 5, nos. 7 and 8).

The law also grants the surviving partner the right of preference in the sale of the home for the period in which the surviving partner has the right to permanently reside in the home, in whatever title – as the holder of the right of habitation, as a tenant, or while waiting for the signing of the rental contract (Art. 5, n. 9).

RUSSIA

No.

SCOTLAND

There are no specific rules dealing with the home or household goods.

SLOVAKIA

No.

SLOVENIA

The court *ex officio* separates from the inheritance the testator's household goods (furniture, household equipment, bed linen) which are of minor value to the benefit of the partner and the testator's descendants who lived with the testator in the same household (Art. 23 of the Slovenian Marriage Act).

SPAIN

Under Spanish Law, if the lease of the home was under the name of the partner who died, the surviving partner will have a right to the transmission of tenancy (Art. 16.1.b Spanish Tenancy Act 24 November 1994). This law is applicable in all of Spain (including Catalonia).

According to the Catalan Civil Code, the surviving partner is entitled to personal chattels (Art. 231-30 Catalan Civil Code), and may also be given the right to live in the home for a year after the partner's death (Art. 231-31 Catalan Civil Code).

SWEDEN

The rules applicable to the home and the household goods upon the death of one of the cohabitees are in general the same as the rules applicable upon separation between the cohabitees (see above Question 42, 43 and 48). It is, however, only the surviving cohabitee – and not the heirs of the deceased partner – who has the right to request the division of the 'cohabitation property' and the right to take over the dwelling and household goods, Swedish Cohabitation Act, § 18 para. 1.

SWITZERLAND

In Switzerland, other than is the case for married partners,[7] there are no specific rules which are applicable to the surviving partner in an informal relationship dealing with the home and/or household goods.

7 E.g. Art. 219 or 612a Swiss Civil Code.

QUESTION 50

Can a partner dispose of property by will in favour of the surviving partner:

a. In general?

b. If the testator is married to or is the registered partner of another person?

c. If the testator has children?

AUSTRIA

a. In general?

Generally, the testator can avoid intestate succession by drafting his/her last will. Thus, a partner in an informal relationship has the possibility to appoint his/her partner as his/her heir. If the testator wishes to bequeath his/her partner a certain item or a certain amount of money without creating the status of an heir, he/she can do so by drafting a legacy.[1] In contrast to the heir, the legatee merely becomes a single successor and has a claim against the heir.[2]

b. If the testator is married to or is the registered partner of another person?

c. If the testator has children?

Generally, the testator is free to appoint his/her heirs.[3] However, this autonomy is subject to certain limitations: Due to the close relationship to the testator some family members should receive a compulsory share *(Pflichtteilsrecht)* of the testator's property.[4] The right to a compulsory share ensures that the spouse and the children receive half of the statutory share.[5] The same applies to registered partners.[6] If, for

---

1 Section 535 General Austrian Civil Code.

2 C. WERKUSCH-CHRIST, 'section 535 General Austrian Civil Code', in: A. KLETEČKA and M. SCHAUER, *ABGB-ON 1.02*, Manz Verlag, Vienna, 2014, at marg. No. 1.

3 Section 552 et seq. General Austrian Civil Code.

4 Section 762 General Austrian Civil Code.

5 Section 765 General Austrian Civil Code.

example, the spouse would have inherited one third of the decedent's property according to intestate succession, he/she receives one-sixth as the compulsory share. The testator can even reduce the compulsory share by up to a half if the close relationship which usually exists between the testator and the person entitled to the compulsory share had never in fact existed, unless the testator had expressly refused contact.[7] Hence, one partner can dispose of his/her property by means of a last will in favour of the surviving partner, but his/her spouse and/or the children will still receive the compulsory share.

BELGIUM

a. In general?

Yes. A rather academic restriction is that the bequest cannot be *pretium stupri*: its purpose cannot be to reward sexual relations. Whereas this exception was invoked fairly often in the past,[8] this is no longer the case.[9] Furthermore, ascendants of the testator have a reserved share of one fourth in each line when the testator has no descendants. An exception is only made for gifts to a spouse or a legal cohabitant (Art. 915 Belgian Civil Code). Interestingly, in Flanders the surviving partners (plural) benefit from the same succession tax regime as a spouse or a legal cohabitant when they have continuously cohabited for at least one year in a joint household on the day of the testator's death (Art. 1.1.0.0.2, para. 5, 4°, c) Flemish Taxation Code).

b. If the testator is married to or is the registered partner of another person?

Yes. In this case, he/she would have to respect the reserved share of the spouse, which amounts to the usufruct or lease of the main residence and the household goods or to half of the deceased's estate. There are more limited rights in case of separation and a spouse may even disinherit the other spouse under certain conditions (Art. 915bis Belgian Civil Code). The legal cohabitant has no reserved share in Belgian law.

c. If the testator has children?

Yes. In this case, he would have to respect the reserved share of the children, which amounts to half of the estate for one child, two thirds of

6 Section 537a General Austrian Civil Code.

7 Section 773a General Austrian Civil Code.

8 E.g. Cass. 13 November 1953, 53-54, 1711, note and more recently District Court of Liège 19 February 1991, JLMB 1992, 620 (bar girl) with regard to gifts.

9 E.g. Liège 29 April 2003, *RNB* 2004, 249 (with regard to gifts – exception not accepted).

the estate for two children and three fourths of the estate for three or more children (Art. 913 Belgian Civil Code).

BULGARIA

a. In general?

Yes, a partner can dispose of his/her property by will in favour of the surviving partner. Art. 14, para. 1 of the Bulgarian Inheritance Law sets out a right for the testator to dispose of all of his/her property by means of a will. Para. 2 of Art. 14 specifies that the testator cannot avoid the reserved share of the inheritance.[10]

b. If the testator is married to or is the registered partner of another person?

Any partner in an informal relationship may dispose of property in favour of the surviving partner by will regardless of whether he/she is married to another person. The Bulgarian legislation does not regulate registered partnerships.

c. If the testator has children?

According to the Bulgarian Inheritance Law, children are the first to inherit in the case of intestate succession (Art. 5). Children have a reserved share of the inheritance in the case of a will (Art. 28). So, the rights of children are protected. Either partner can dispose of his/her property by will in favour of the surviving partner. Art. 14, para. 1 of the Bulgarian Inheritance Law sets out a right for the testator to dispose of all of his/her property by means of a will. Para. 2 of Art. 14 specifies that the testator cannot avoid the reserved share of the inheritance. If this is the case, the will is still valid but can be challenged before the courts with the aim of restoring the reserved share of an heir (Art. 30).

CROATIA

In line with Art. 11 paragraph 2 of the Croatian Family Act and Art. 4 paragraph 2 and Art. 55 of the Croatian Partnership Act, the answer equally relates to both cohabitants and same-sex informal partners.

[10] The 1992 reform of Bulgarian Inheritance Law increased the freedom to dispose of property by will as a step to increase the protection of private property.

a. In general?
In general, a partner can dispose of his/her property by means of a will in favour of the surviving partner.

b. If the testator is married to or is the registered partner of another person?
If a testator is married to or is the registered partner of another person, he/she can dispose of his/her property in favour of the surviving partner as well as in favour of any other person. The informal relationship (same-sex or cohabitation) in this case does not influence his/her right to testamentary disposal. The Croatian legal system legally protects only informal relationships between partners who are not married or are in a same-sex registered partnership with another person. However, a testator can dispose of his/her property in favour of whoever he/she chooses regardless of whether he/she was married (or in another kind of partnership) or not. In such a case, he/she has to take into account his/her forced heirs. If a testator disposes of all of his/her property by means of a will in favour of the selected person, the forced heirs shall have the right to challenge the will and claim their forced share (Art. 69 and 70 of the Croatian Inheritance Act).

A testate heir (the surviving partner in this case) shall still inherit a part of the testator's property, though not all of it, since the forced share shall have to be given to the forced heirs if they claim it.

c. If the testator has children?
If a testator has children, he/she can dispose of property in favour of the surviving partner. Nonetheless, since the testator's children are his/her forced heirs, the above paragraphs shall apply.

Therefore, the surviving partner shall inherit a part of the testator's property, but the children of the latter shall receive their forced share if they so demand (Art. 69 and 70 of the Croatian Inheritance Act).

CZECH REPUBLIC

a. In general?
Yes, a partner can dispose of property by will in favour of the surviving partner in general. See S. 1494 et seq. Czech Civil Code.

b. If the testator is married to or is the registered partner of another person?

Yes, a partner can dispose of property by will in favour of the surviving partner even if the testator is married to or is the registered partner of another partner. See S. 1494 et seq. Czech Civil Code. However, a spouse has some special rights granted to him/her by S. 1666 and S. 1667.

- S. 1666 Czech Civil Code:
  (1) A surviving spouse has the right to fair maintenance from the deceased's estate for six weeks after the death of his spouse. If a widow is pregnant, she has the right to fair maintenance until the end of the sixth week after birth; the mother of the deceased's child who was not married to the deceased has the same right.
  (2) If a surviving spouse has been denied statutory inheritance or his statutory inheritance has been reduced, the surviving spouse is entitled to the necessary provision for life until he remarries, provided that he otherwise lacks such a provision for life and he is unable to provide for himself; in this manner, however, he may not get more from the deceased's estate than what half of his statutory inheritance share would have been. However, a spouse who, without serious reasons, did not share the family household with the deceased, a spouse lacking the capacity to be an heir, or a spouse who renounced or refused inheritance, is not entitled to the necessary provision for life.
  (3) If the right to fair maintenance under Subsection (1) prejudices the right to essential maintenance under Section 1665, all these rights are prejudiced so that all obligees receive an equal share. Necessary provision for life under Subsection (2) may not be provided if it prejudices the right to essential maintenance under Section 1665.[11]
- S. 1667 Czech Civil Code: The surviving spouse shall acquire the right of ownership in movable things which form the basic equipment of a family household even where he is not an heir. This does not apply if the surviving spouse, without serious reasons, did not share the family household with the deceased.

[11] S. 1665 of the Czech Civil Code: A person who would otherwise be a forced heir, but is not entitled to a forced share, has a right to essential maintenance, provided he is lacking it, and is unable to provide for himself; in this manner, however, he may not get more from the deceased's estate than what his forced share would be. However, a person whose descendant inherits in his place or where a descendant is designated to be entitled to a forced share in his place does not have the right to essential maintenance.

The parents of a testator have similar rights to those of a spouse in a case where the testator had no children or spouse, see S. 1668 Czech Civil Code: (1) If a surviving parent has been denied the statutory inheritance or his statutory inheritance share has been reduced, the surviving parent is entitled to the necessary provision for life, provided that he otherwise lacks such a provision for life and he is unable to provide for himself; in this manner, however, he may not get more from the deceased's estate than what a third of his statutory inheritance share would have been. A parent lacking the capacity to be an heir, a parent who has renounced or refused his inheritance, or a parent who has committed an act constituting grounds for disinheritance, does not have the right to the necessary provision for life. (2) Necessary provision for life may not be provided to a parent if it prejudices the right to essential maintenance under S. 1665.[12]

c. If the testator has children?

Yes, a partner can dispose of property by will in favour of the surviving partner if the testator has children. However, such children have rights to their legal part of the legacy. The amount of this part depends on the age of children. According to S. 1642 Czech Civil Code, a forced heir is entitled to a forced share of the deceased's estate, and S. 1643 Czech Civil Code states: forced heirs include the deceased's children and, if they do not inherit, their descendants. If a forced heir is a minor, he must inherit at least three-quarters of his statutory inheritance share. If a forced heir is an adult, he must inherit at least a quarter of his statutory inheritance share.

DENMARK

a. In general?

If a cohabitant wishes to leave his or her estate to his or her surviving partner, he or she can do so by making a will. A testator who has children and/or a spouse has the right to dispose of over three-quarters of the estate. One quarter is divided between the spouse (one-eighth) and the child/children (one-eighth).

12 S. 1665 of the Czech Civil Code: A person who would otherwise be a forced heir, but is not entitled to a forced share, has a right to essential maintenance, provided he is lacking it, and is unable to provide for himself; in this manner, however, he may not get more from the deceased's estate than what his forced share would be. However, a person whose descendant inherits in his place or where a descendant is designated to be entitled to a forced share in his place does not have the right to essential maintenance.

b. If the testator is married to or is the registered partner of another person?
One-quarter of the estate that the spouse or registered partner of the testator inherits is an indefeasible share; see the Danish Inheritance Act, S. 10. An indefeasible share cannot be denied its beneficiaries by means of a will.

According to the Danish Inheritance Act, S. 91(2), the consent of a spouse is required to make a testamentary disposition of the following assets, provided they are included in the deferred community property:

- Property that serves as the family's home or where both of the spouses' or the other spouse's business is carried out.
- Contents of the joint home and the other spouse's necessary work tools.
- A motor vehicle which has been used by the spouse.

c. If the testator has children?
The one-quarter of the estate that the child/children of the testator inherit is an indefeasible share; see the Danish Inheritance Act, S. 5. However, the testator can restrict the inheritance to each of his or her children to DKK 1,000,000; see the Danish Inheritance Act, S. 5(2). This amount is regulated in line with the price index.[13]

ENGLAND AND WALES

a. In general?
Yes.

b. If the testator is married to or is the registered partner of another person?
Yes but it is likely to be challenged by the spouse/civil partner under the English Inheritance (Provision for Families and Dependants) Act 1975.

c. If the testator has children?
Yes. However children can challenge the will by court action under the English Inheritance (Provision for Families and Dependants) Act 1975. Minor children will normally succeed on such a claim but adult children are less likely to do so unless they can show dependency or a moral obligation towards the adult child, as the freedom of the testator will

[13] In 2014, the amount was DKK 1,170,000, equivalent to about EUR 157,000.

normally take precedence. This was discussed in *Espinosa v Bourke* [1999] 1 FLR 747, CA. Claims by children are also limited to what is reasonable for them to receive for their maintenance.

ESTONIA

a. In general?

According to § 39(1) of the Law of Succession Act, a testate successor is a person to whom a testator has disposed of all of his or her property or a legal share (a fraction) thereof by means of a will. Under Estonian law, the testator has a large degree of freedom to dispose of his or her property and a will can be made for the benefit of his or her partner in an informal relationship.

b. If the testator is married to or is the registered partner of another person?

A will can be made for the benefit of the partner in an informal relationship even if the testator is married or he or she has a registered partner. If a person has, by means of a will or a contract of succession, disinherited a descendant or his or her parents or spouse who are entitled to succeed in intestacy and with respect to whom the person has a maintenance obligation arising from the Estonian Family Law Act at the time of his or her death or that person has reduced their shares of the estate as compared to their shares according to intestate succession they will have the right to claim a compulsory portion from the successors (§ 104(1) Estonian Law of Succession Act). In such a case, the person who is appointed by the testator shall be the successor, but the spouse will have a financial claim against the estate to the value of compulsory share of the intestate succession (§ 105(1) Estonian Law of Succession Act).

c. If the testator has children?

A will can be made for the benefit of the partner in an informal relationship even if the testator has children. If a person has, by means of a will or a contract of succession, disinherited a descendant or his or her parents or spouse who are entitled to succeed in intestacy and with respect to whom the person has a maintenance obligation arising from the Estonian Family Law Act at the time of his or her death or that person has reduced their share of the estate as compared to their shares according to intestate succession, they will have the right to claim a compulsory portion from the successors (§ 104(1) Estonian Law of Succession Act). The children will have a financial claim against the estate to the value of half of the intestate succession (Estonian Law of Succession Act § 105(1)).

FINLAND

a. In general?

Yes.

b. If the testator is married to or is the registered partner of another person?

Yes, although the dissolution of the matrimonial property scheme has priority and its outcome will determine which part of the estate remains free to be disposed of by will.

c. If the testator has children?

Yes, although the children are entitled to their reserved share, which is 50 percent of the share that they would have received without a will. The children can contest the will if it prevents them from inheriting their reserved share.

FRANCE

a. In general?

The testator can dispose of assets in favour of the surviving partner within the limits of the disposable portion (*quotité disponible*) of the estate, just as he or she can do in favour of anyone chosen by him or her, whether this is a member of the family or not.[14] The disposable portion is limited where the deceased person is married or has children. See below.

b. If the testator is married to or is the registered partner of another person?

The registered partner is not an heir on intestacy. As a consequence the fact that the testator is bound by an undissolved civil partnership will have no impact on his or her legal capacity to dispose of assets in favour of his or her surviving cohabitant.

The surviving spouse is only a protected heir on intestacy where the testator has no living children or grandchildren.[15] In this situation the

14 Art. 912 et seq. of the French Civil Code.

15 Indeed, if one child of the testator is deceased the grandchildren born from him or her can act on behalf of their parent for succession purposes. Irrespective of their number they count as one in the liquidation process. See Art. 913-1 of the French Civil Code.

disposable portion amounts to ¾ of the assets of the testator.[16] The surviving adulterous cohabitant can receive no more than this portion of the estate by will.

Where there are living descendants, the surviving spouse is not a protected heir and can be disinherited by will to favour the adulterous surviving cohabitant.[17]

c. If the testator has children?

According to French law, children (and the grandchildren on behalf of a deceased child) are protected heirs.[18] The disposable portion that may benefit the surviving cohabitant will depend on the number of children.[19]

If there is only one living child the disposable portion amounts to one half of the estate of the testator, ⅓ thereof where there are two living children and ¼ thereof where there are three living children or more.[20]

GERMANY

a. In general?

According to § 1937 German Civil Code any person may appoint an heir by a unilateral disposition *mortis causa* (will, testamentary disposition). § 1937 reflects the principle of freedom to dispose of property upon death.[21] Therefore the deceased is free to choose the surviving partner as heir by testamentary succession.

b. If the testator is married to or is the registered partner of another person?

The existence of a marriage or registered partnership does not restrict the freedom to dispose of property upon death. In this case to dispose of property by will in favour of the surviving partner is, in principle, no longer contrary to public policy as per § 138 para. 1 German Civil Code. A violation occurs only in the rare case in which the partner is solely

16 Art. 914-1 of the French Civil Code.

17 Cass. Plenary Assembly, 29 October 2004, no. 03.11238. The *Cour de Cassation* held that such a will did not contradict morality (*bonnes moeurs*) and denied the nullity claim on the ground of Art. 1133 of the French Civil Code.

18 Art. 913 and 913-1 of the French Civil Code.

19 As mentioned above, irrespective of their number, grandchildren always count as one (the deceased child) in the liquidation process. See Art. 913-1 of the French Civil Code.

20 Art. 913 of the French Civil Code.

21 D. Weidlich, '§ 1969', in: O. Palandt, *Bürgerliches Gesetzbuch*, Beck, Munich, 2015, at No. 3.

rewarded for the sexual relationship.[22] But according to § 2303 para. 2 German Civil Code the testator's spouse may demand a compulsory share from the heir. The compulsory share consists of one-half of the value of the share of the inheritance on intestacy (§ 2303 para. 1 s. 2 German Civil Code). The same holds true for registered partners, § 10 para. 6 German Act on Registered Life Partnerships.

c. If the testator has children?

According to § 2303 para. 1 s. 1 descendants of the testator who are excluded from succession by disposition *mortis causa* may demand a compulsory share of the estate from the heir.

GREECE

a. In general?

Yes. Formerly such a will would have been considered invalid on moral grounds (Art. 178 Greek Civil Code), but nowadays the view has been taken in the case law that there is no immorality if the partner is not named as an heir in a provocative way, if this is not offensive to general moral values, or shows disrespect to any legal family by overlooking the heirs by intestate succession.[23]

b. If the testator is married to or is the registered partner of another person?

The above provisions apply, *mutatis mutandis*.

c. If the testator has children?

Then he may dispose of property to a partner, provided this does not affect the legitimate portion due to the children (Art. 1825 Greek Civil Code). Insofar as such an effect is apparent, the disposal made by the testator will be deemed invalid (Art. 1829 Greek Civil Code).

HUNGARY

a. In general?

Principally the freedom to make a will is decisive so anybody may make a will in favour of his or her cohabitant.

---

22 BGH, 31.3.1970, *NJW*, 1970, 1273; BGH, 10.11.1982, *NJW*, 1983, 674.

23 For the case law, see Supreme Court – Areios Pagos, judgment No. 821/1977, and Athens Court of Appeal, judgment No. 673/2007.

b. If the testator is married to or is the registered partner of another person?
Theoretically it is possible to make a will in favour of the surviving cohabitant but the spouse or registered partner has a reserved share. On the other hand, the spouse or registered partner cannot inherit in intestate succession if no community of life existed upon death and there was no expectation that this community of life would be resumed. (This rule functions only following the claim of an interested person who proves the lack of community of life.)

c. If the testator has children?
This is possible, but children have a reserved share.

REPUBLIC OF IRELAND

a. In general?
Yes. There is nothing to prevent a partner leaving some or all of his or her property to the surviving partner by will.

b. If the testator is married to or is the registered partner of another person?
Yes. There is nothing preventing a partner leaving some or all of his or her property to the surviving partner by will. This, however, is subject to the Legal Right Share of a surviving spouse/civil partner under S. 111/111A of the Irish Succession Act 1965 respectively. The Legal Right Share is half the estate where the deceased spouse/civil partner did not have children and one third of the estate where they did. The surviving spouse/civil partner has a right to appropriate the dwelling in which they reside in whole or in part satisfaction of their Legal Right Share under S. 56 of the same Act. The same right applies to household chattels under S. 56(2) and 111A of the Irish 1965 Act. The surviving spouse/civil partner therefore has a legal right share in the deceased's estate, regardless of what the deceased has said or specified in his will. Whatever the testator bequeaths to his partner will be subject to this legal right share.

c. If the testator has children?
Yes. There is nothing preventing a partner leaving some or all of his or her property to the surviving partner by will. This, however, is subject to the right of the testator's children to initiate legal proceedings against the estate under S. 117 of the Irish Succession Act 1965 where the deceased has failed to make proper provision for them in accordance with his or

her moral duty. The children do not have to be minors (under 18) and if they are minors an application can be taken on their behalf. It is only the children of the deceased cohabitant who can make this application. Provision for a partner made in a will, therefore, may be overridden by a S. 117 application. Should no legal proceedings be initiated by the children, however, or should the court determine that proper provision for them was made during the testator's lifetime, the bequest to the deceased's partner made in the will shall stand.

ITALY

a. In general?

Generally, an informal partner can effectively dispose of his or her property in favour of the other partner through a will according to the general law of succession (Art. 587 et seq. Italian Civil Code).

The strict limitations set out by the law in favour of the legitimate heirs (*legittimari*) must however be respected (Art. 536 et seq. Italian Civil Code).

b. If the testator is married to or is the registered partner of another person?

The marriage of either testator does not prevent him or her from disposing of property through a will in favour of the other partner if the provisions regarding the share reserved for and assigned to the spouse are respected. In practice, the married testator can devolve up to half of his or her patrimony to the informal partner, the other half being mandatorily destined for the spouse (Art. 540 Italian Civil Code).

c. If the testator has children?

Even if the testator has children, he or she can dispose of property by will in favour of his or her partner, provided that the shares reserved in favour of the children (and, where one exists, of the spouse) are respected.

If the testator only has one child and no spouse, then he or she can freely dispose of half of his or her patrimony, in favour of the partner, if he or she so wishes, the other half being reserved for the child (Art. 537 para. 1 Italian Civil Code).

If the testator has more than one child – it does not matter how many – and no spouse, then he or she can leave to the partner only one third of his or her wealth, the other two thirds being reserved for the children. Their share will be divided in equal parts among them (Art. 537 para. 2 Italian Civil Code).

If the testator has one child and a spouse, then he or she can dispose of one third of the patrimony in favour of the partner, the other two thirds being mandatorily left to the child and the spouse (Art. 542 para. 1 Italian Civil Code).

Finally, if the testator has more than one child as well as a wife or a husband, then the amount he or she can dispose of freely - and therefore leave to the partner - is only one quarter of the patrimony, another quarter being reserved for the spouse and the remaining half of the patrimony being divided, in equal parts, among the children (Art. 542 para. 2 Italian Civil Code).

LATVIA

Section 422 of the Latvian Civil Law provides that a testator may freely determine the disposition of his or her whole estate in case of his or her death, with the restriction that his or her forced heirs (*neatņemamās daļas tiesīgie*) must be bequeathed their preferential shares (*neatņemamās daļas*).[24]

According to S. 423 of the Latvian Civil Law forced heirs are the spouse and descendants, but if there are no descendants, then forced heirs are the ascendants of the nearest degree of kinship.

LITHUANIA

Any legally capable natural person has the right to draw up a testamentary disposition by means of a will and to dispose of all of his/her property or a part thereof in favour of one or several individuals who may or may not be heirs by law as well as in favour of the State, local authorities or legal persons (Art. 5.19 of the Lithuanian Civil Code). The principle of *Pater familias* is applicable in Lithuania - the law protects certain groups of individuals who, regardless of what is laid down in a will, inherit a mandatory share of the inheritance (Art. 5.20 of the Lithuanian Civil Code). Such individuals are the children (or adopted

24 Civil Law. Part two. Inheritance Law. Law of Republic of Latvia. "Vadības Vēstnesis", 22 February 1937, no.42.

children) of the testator, his or her spouse, and his or her parents (or foster parents), but only if, on the day of the testator's death, they were in need of maintenance and the testator did not dispose of any property in their favour, or the share of the property allocated to them by will amounts to less than half of the property that they would inherit by law.

The testator may include in his/her will a bequest in favour of his/her partner (Art. 5.23 of the Lithuanian Civil Code).[25]

LUXEMBOURG

a. In general?

In general, the surviving partner can dispose of property.

b. If the testator is married to or is the registered partner of another person?

If the testator is married to or is the registered partner of another person, he or she may dispose of his or her property by will.

c. If the testator has children?

If the partner has children, he or she has the right to dispose of his or her property by will in favour of the surviving partner without disposing of the reserved share. The children are heirs with a reserved share (*héritiers réservataires*).

THE NETHERLANDS

a. In general?

In a will the testator can name his/her partner as the only heir/ beneficiary of his/her estate or name him/her as an additional heir/ beneficiary through an *erfstelling* (a testamentary disposition) (Art. 4:115 Dutch Civil Code). The only requirement for the heir/beneficiary is that he/she exists at the time of death and that he/she can be identified on the basis of the will. The testator can partially or completely deviate from

[25] The testator shall have the right to obligate a testate successor to fulfil a certain obligation (a testamentary reservation) for the benefit of one or several persons, while these persons shall acquire the right to demand the fulfilment of this obligation. Beneficiaries of the testamentary reservation may be intestate heirs as well as any other persons. The successor authorised by the testator will have to fulfil the testamentary reservation without exceeding the value of the inheritable property after the claims of the testator's creditors have been satisfied.

the intestate succession by means of an *erfstelling* (Art. 4:1 Dutch Civil Code).

b. If the testator is married to or is the registered partner of another person?

The general possibility remains even if the testator is married to or is the registered partner of another person. However, the spouse or registered partner will retain certain rights, such as the right to continue the occupancy of the shared home for six months (Art. 4:28 Dutch Civil Code), the right to usufruct on the home and household effects (even if the deceased and the spouse/registered partner did not live there together) (Art. 4:29 Dutch Civil Code) and the right to usufruct on the goods of the estate if the spouse requires these for his/her care (Art. 4:30). If divorce or legal separation proceedings had commenced more than a year prior to death, the spouse or registered partner will not have the right to an usufruct under article 4:29 or 4:30.

c. If the testator has children?

The partner can dispose of property by will in favour of the surviving partner even if the testator has children. However, the children have the right to their *legitieme portie* (statutory share) (Art. 4:63-4:64 Dutch Civil Code). This means that the children have the right to a pecuniary claim for the amount of their rightful share of the decedent's estate. If the surviving partner is the only beneficiary to the estate, then the children will bring their pecuniary claim to the surviving partner. If the surviving partner is one of multiple beneficiaries to the estate, then the children will claim from the combined beneficiaries including the surviving partner. The testator can include a non-enforceability clause in his will to determine that the children cannot claim from the surviving partner who inherits the estate until the surviving partner's death (or any other determined moment in time) (Art. 4:82 Dutch Civil Code).

NORWAY

a. In general?

Yes, in general, a partner can dispose of property by will in favour of the surviving partner, as freedom of testation is the general rule; see Norwegian Inheritance Act S. 48.

b. If the testator is married to or is the registered partner of another person?

If the testator is married to or is the registered partner of another person, the freedom of testation is limited, as the spouse/registered partner has a right to a so-called 'minimum inheritance'. This minimum inheritance normally amounts to about 40,000 Euros and cannot be restricted by a will.[26]

c. If the testator has children?

If the testator has children, the freedom of testation is also limited. As a rule, two-thirds of the partner's estate passes as compulsory inheritance to the children of the testator; this forced share must in no case exceed NOK 1 million to each child, pursuant to the Norwegian Inheritance Act, S. 29. However, cohabitants[27] who do not have children together have an expanded right of testation as long as they have lived together for at least five years prior to death, see the Norwegian Inheritance Act, S. 28(b) first paragraph second sentence. These cohabitants may dispose of their property by will in favour of the surviving cohabitant up to a value of four times the National Insurance basic amount, without taking into consideration their respective lineal descendants. (If the cohabitants have children together, no such will is needed, as they inherit the same amount by intestate succession, see Question 47.)

PORTUGAL

a. In general?

Yes, he or she can do this.

b. If the testator is married to or is the registered partner of another person?

Yes, he or she can do this, but is limited to his or her disposable part of the estate.

This answer is valid in the case of a married testator; there is no registered partnership in Portuguese law.

---

26 The Norwegian Inheritance Act, S. 6 and 7. The minimum inheritance for spouses is four times the National Insurance basic amount, i.e. about 40,000 Euros, if the testator has lineal descendants and six times the National Insurance basic amount, i.e. about 60,000 Euros, if the testator does not have lineal descendants.

27 Cohabitation is defined in the Norwegian Inheritance Act, S. 28(a), see Question 47.

c. If the testator has children?
Yes, he or she can do this, but is limited to his or her disposable part of the estate.

RUSSIA

a. In general?
Yes. Under Russian law, however, freedom of testation (Art. 1119) is limited by the institution of reserved shares. Persons entitled to reserved shares are listed in Art. 1149 Russian Civil Code. The first-ranking heirs (children, spouses and parents) are entitled to reserved shares, provided that they are unable to work due to their being minors, having reached retirement age or being disabled, irrespective of whether they were maintained by the deceased person.

The heirs mentioned in Art. 1148(1) (i.e. heirs of any rank who are unable to work) are entitled to a reserved share, provided that they have been maintained by the deceased for at least one year, irrespective of whether they lived with the deceased. The heirs mentioned in Art. 1148(2) (i.e. any unrelated disabled persons who have been maintained by the diseased person for at least one year) are entitled to reserved shares, provided that they lived with the deceased person for at least one year.

Persons entitled to a reserved share cannot be fully disinherited by will. Irrespective of the contents of the will, they are always entitled to half of the share that they would have received in the case of intestate succession.

Therefore the deceased partner's right to dispose of property by will in favour of the surviving partner is limited only by the possible rights of persons entitled to a reserved share.

b. If the testator is married to or is the registered partner of another person?
If testator is married, it is only relevant for his/her right to dispose of property by will in favour of the surviving partner if the testator's spouse is entitled to a reserved share. That is the case only if he/she is unable to work due to having reached retirement age or due to disability (Art. 1149 Russian Civil Code).

c. If the testator has children?

If the testator has children, it is only relevant for his/her right to dispose of property by will in favour of the surviving partner if the children are entitled to reserved shares. That is the case only if the children are unable to work due to their being minors or disabled or due to their reaching retirement age (Art. 1149 Russian Civil Code).

SCOTLAND

a. In general?

In general, an individual has freedom of testation and this includes the possibility of leaving property by will to a surviving partner. Spouses, civil partners and descendants have legal rights in respect of moveable property but heritable property may be disposed of entirely according to the will of the individual.

b. If the testator is married to or is the registered partner of another person?

Scots law is generally regarded as protecting against the possibility of disinheritance and it does so by means of 'legal rights'. A surviving spouse or civil partner has legal rights to a share of the moveable estate of the deceased and in this way they have some protection against the possibility of disinheritance. Where the deceased was married at the time of death but had no issue, the surviving spouse or civil partner is entitled to one half of the net moveable estate. The testator is free to dispose of the rest of his or her estate.

c. If the testator has children?

Scots law is generally regarded as protecting against the possibility of disinheritance and it does so by means of 'legal rights'. Where the deceased was married or in a civil partnership and had surviving issue, each is entitled to one third of the net moveable estate. Otherwise, the testator is free to dispose of his or her estate.

SLOVAKIA

a. In general?

Testamentary succession is based on the deceased person's will. A will is a unilateral and revocable juridical act, by which the testator disposes of his property, to take effect after his death. A will must be drafted by the testator in writing and it must include the names of the heirs and the date (day, month, and year) when it was signed (§ 476 para. 2 Slovak Civil

Code). It may also include the shares of the respective heirs or assets and the rights they are to inherit. If the shares of the heirs are not specified in the will, they are deemed to be equal (§ 477 Slovak Civil Code).

b. If the testator is married to or is the registered partner of another person?

A testator's liberty in disposing of his or her property is not limited with respect to a surviving spouse as is the case with the testator's descendants (see c).

c. If the testator has children?

However, the testator's liberty in disposing of his or her property is limited with respect to descendants. His or her minor descendants must receive at least their statutory shares and his or her major descendants must receive at least one half of their statutory shares, unless they are disinherited[28] (§ 479 Slovak Civil Code). If the will is contrary to these statutory requirements, this part is voidable (§ 479 Slovak Civil Code).

SLOVENIA

a. In general?

Yes, he or she can. There are no special restrictions.

b. If the testator is married to or is the registered partner of another person?

If the testator is married to or is the registered partner of another person there is no extramarital union. The partner in this life union is not therefore an extramarital partner. The testator may leave property to her or him by will, as would be the case with any third person, but may not disregard the compulsory shares of the legal heirs.

---

[28] An heir is eligible unless he is: unworthy of inheriting (an ineligible heir) or disinherited. An heir is unworthy of inheriting if he has committed an intentional crime against the deceased person, his or her spouse, children or parents or a reprehensible action against the deceased person's will. However, such an heir may inherit if the deceased person had forgiven him. Disinheritance may only apply to the deceased person's descendants. The deceased person may disinherit a descendant if he or she:
- did not provide, contrary to good morals, necessary assistance to the deceased person in sickness, old age or other serious cases,
- did not show a true interest in the deceased person that he or she, as his or her descendant, ought to show,
- had been sentenced to imprisonment for at least one year for an intentional crime, or
- lives a permanently inordinate life (§ 469a Slovak Civil Code).

c. If the testator has children?

The testator may leave property to his or her partner but may not neglect the compulsory shares of his or her children as the legal heirs of the first order of inheritance.

SPAIN

a. In general?

Yes, as with any other stranger. The testator may designate the informal partner as legal heir, or legatee. However, one must take into account that the free share is limited under the Spanish Civil Code. The descendants of the testator have a forced share of two-thirds of the estate (Art. 808 Spanish Civil Code). In the absence of children or other descendants, the ascendants have a forced share of one-half of the estate (Art. 809 Spanish Civil Code).

The Catalan Civil Code establishes a different amount of free share: one-quarter of the estate (Art. 451-5 Catalan Civil Code). Forced heirs are, firstly, the deceased children and other descendants (Art. 451-3 Catalan Civil Code) and, if there are no descendants, the deceased's parents (but no further removed ascendants) (Art. 451-4 Catalan Civil Code). The surviving spouse or cohabitant is not included in this list of beneficiaries. But he/she has the right to a maximum of one-quarter of the estate (the so-called widow's quarter) if, taking into account the spouse's or cohabitant's own means as well as what he/she may have received from the deceased, they require support (Art. 452-1 to 452-6 Catalan Civil Code).

b. If the testator is married to or is the registered partner of another person?

Yes, as with any other stranger. The Spanish Civil Code states that if the testator is married, the surviving spouse has a life interest in one-third of the estate if the deceased leaves children or other descendants (Art. 834 Spanish Civil Code); if there are ascendants, the life interest is on half of the estate (Art. 837 Spanish Civil Code). In the absence of the above-mentioned relatives, the life interest is on two-thirds of the estate (Art. 837 Spanish Civil Code).

The Catalan Civil Code does not provide a right to usufruct for the surviving spouse or partner. But they do have a right to the *cuarta viudal* (one-quarter of the deceased's estate) when the surviving partner's estate plus any property allocated by the deceased is insufficient for the survivor's maintenance, taking into account the standard of living enjoyed by the couple before death (Art. 452-1 Catalan Civil Code).

c. If the testator has children?

Yes, as with any other stranger. However, if the testator has children, one must take into account that they are the testator's forced heirs and therefore the percentage of free share is, according to the Spanish Civil Code, limited to one-third of the estate (Art. 808 Spanish Civil Code).

The Catalan Civil Code establishes a different amount of free share. If the testator has children, they are entitled, as forced heirs, to one-quarter of the estate (Art. 451-3 and 451-5 Catalan Civil Code).

SWEDEN

a. In general?

Yes. A person in an informal relationship has the same right as anyone else to dispose of his or her property by will, subject to certain formal requirements, to the advantage of whoever he or she wishes to favour. The rules in the Swedish Code of Inheritance (in Swedish, *Ärvdabalk 1958:637*) are applicable.

b. If the testator is married to or is the registered partner of another person?

Under the Swedish Code of Inheritance the surviving partner to a formalised relationship (marriage or registered partnership) has the right to intestate succession after the deceased partner, Chapter 3 § 1. A spouse's or a registered partner's right to intestate succession may, however, be set aside by a will made by the deceased, for example in favour of an informal partner. The surviving spouse or registered partner always has, however, according to the Swedish Code of Inheritance, Chapter 3 § 2 para. 2, the right to obtain the value of four basic price amounts, but with regard to the outcome of the property division between the spouses or registered partners and his or her own separate property. In addition, the deceased partner's children always have the right to receive their forced share (in Swedish: *laglott*), which is half of the value of their legal inheritance share. Due regard to these persons' rights may make it necessary to set the will aside in full or in part.

c. If the testator has children?

Children or other direct heirs (grandchildren, great-grandchildren, replacing their parent) are always entitled to receive without delay their forced share from the estate, unless the will is made in favour of their other parent who at the time of the death was in a legally existing formalised relationship (marriage or registered partnership) with the deceased. The forced share is half of the share the person would have inherited if there had been no will, Swedish Code of Inheritance, Chapter 7 § 1. After the will has been served on the person with a right to a forced share, he or she must bring a legal action against it within six months, Swedish Code of Inheritance, Chapter 7, § 3 para. 3. If the will is made in favour of a surviving spouse or a registered partner who is also the child's own parent, the child has the right to receive its share (the forced share or full share) only until the death of the surviving parent, Chapter 7, § 3 para. 2. This position stands in marked contrast to what applies if the child's parents were only in an informal relationship with each other at the time of the death. In that case, the child has the right to demand the forced share from the estate, in spite of the will in favour of the surviving partner/parent. If the child is under age, a personal representative needs to be appointed for the child to take care of the child's interests in the estate, inter alia, to request the payment of the forced share from the deceased parent's estate.

SWITZERLAND

a. In general?

A partner in an informal relationship can dispose of property by will in favour of the surviving partner. In 1983 the Swiss Federal Supreme Court held that dispositions in favour of the surviving partner in an informal relationship are not immoral.[29]

The testator must have the capacity of judgement and be at least 18 years of age (Art. 467 Swiss Code of Obligations). The testator can in general make his or her will in holographic form (Art. 498 and 505 Swiss Civil Code). Furthermore, the testator must observe any possible reserved shares of the surviving heirs (Art. 470 para. 1 Swiss Civil Code). Heirs entitled to a reserved share are the descendants, the parents and the surviving spouse/registered partner of the deceased (Art. 471 Swiss Civil Code). The deceased may only freely and entirely dispose of his or her property in a last will when there are no heirs who are entitled to a reserved share (Art. 470 para. 2 Swiss Civil Code).

[29] Swiss Federal Supreme Court, BGE 109 II 17 E.1.b), the immorality of such a disposition is only implied where it appears to be an actual *pretrium stupri*.

b. If the testator is married to or is the registered partner of another person?

A partner in an informal relationship can dispose of property by will in favour of the surviving partner if he or she is married to or is the registered partner of another person. However, the testator must observe the reserved share of his or her spouse or registered partner (Art. 470 para. 1 Swiss Civil Code).[30] The surviving spouse or registered partner is entitled to one half of his or her intestate succession (Art. 471 No. 3 Swiss Civil Code).

c. If the testator has children?

A partner in an informal relationship can dispose of property by will in favour of the surviving partner if he or she has children. However, the testator must observe the reserved shares of his or her children (Art. 470 para. 1 Swiss Civil Code). The descendants of the deceased are entitled to three-quarters of their intestate succession (Art. 471 No. 1 Swiss Civil Code).

30 Additionally, before unwinding the inheritance any matrimonial property claims have to be considered.

QUESTION 51

Can partners make a joint will disposing of property in favour of the surviving partner:

a. In general?

b. If either testator is married to or is the registered partner of another person?

c. If either testator has children?

AUSTRIA

Under Austrian law joint wills are only binding as between spouses or registered partners.[1] It follows that partners in an informal relationship cannot validly dispose of property in favour of their surviving partner by drafting a joint will, regardless of whether one testator is married, lives in a registered partnership or has children; such a joint will would be void in any case.[2] There are various reasons for the limited admissibility of joint wills: First, joint wills may be difficult to interpret; second, testators might influence each other;[3] third, persons might be mistaken regarding the irrevocability of the joint wills; and fourth, the dependency of the dispositions.[4]

---

1 Section 583 in connection with section 1248 General Austrian Civil Code; section 537a General Austrian Civil Code.

2 G. KNECHTEL, 'section 583 General Austrian Civil Code', in: A. KLETEČKA and M. SCHAUER, *ABGB-ON 1.02,* Manz Verlag, Vienna, 2014, at marg. No. 2; C. CACH, 'Ein Erbrecht für Lebensgefährten?', *SPRW,* 2014, at p. 427.

3 Austrian Supreme Court, Legal Proposition RS0012483, see e.g. Judgement of 06.10.1982, 6 Ob 762/82, *JBl,* 1983, at p. 647.

4 G. KNECHTEL, 'section 583 General Austrian Civil Code', in: A. KLETEČKA and M. SCHAUER, *ABGB-ON 1.02,* Manz Verlag, Vienna, 2014, at marg. No. 3.

BELGIUM

Joint wills do not exist under Belgian law (Art. 968 and 1130, para. 2 Belgian Civil Code).[5]

BULGARIA

a. In general?

Partners cannot make a joint will because this is contrary to the law: two or more persons may not dispose of property to each other or to third parties by one and the same will (Art. 15 of the Bulgarian Inheritance Law). However, any partner may dispose of property in favour of the surviving partner by means of a separate will.

b. If either testator is married to or is the registered partner of another person?

Not applicable.

c. If either testator has children?

Not applicable.

CROATIA

In line with Art. 11 paragraph 2 of the Croatian Family Act and Art. 4 paragraph 1 and Art. 55 of the Croatian Partnership Act, the answer equally relates to both cohabitants and same-sex informal partners.

a. In general?

Partners cannot make a joint will disposing of property in favour of the surviving partner because there are no joint wills under Croatian inheritance law.

b. If either testator is married to or is the registered partner of another person?

Partners cannot make a joint will disposing of property in favour of the surviving partner because there are no joint wills under Croatian inheritance law.

[5] W. PINTENS, C. DECLERCK, J. DU MONGH, K. VANWINCKELEN, *Familiaal vermogensrecht*, Intersentia, Antwerp, 2010, at n° 1606.

c. If either testator has children?

Partners cannot make a joint will disposing of property in favour of the surviving partner because there are no joint wills under Croatian inheritance law.

CZECH REPUBLIC

a. In general?

In general, it is possible. This instrument is called an inheritance contract and it is set out in S. 1582 et seq. Czech Civil Code: by an inheritance contract, a deceased designates the other contracting party or a third person to be an heir or legatee, and the other party accepts it. An inheritance contract must be in the form of a public instrument. According to S. 1585/1 Czech Civil Code, disposition of the deceased's entire estate is not allowed under an inheritance contract. A quarter of the deceased's estate must remain vacant so that the deceased may make disposition thereof according to his specifically expressed will. Where a deceased also wishes to leave this quarter to a contractual heir, he may do so in his will.

b. If either testator is married to or is the registered partner of another person?

An inheritance contract could be made between partners in an informal relationship even if either testator is married to or is the registered partner of another person. This fact is not an impediment for the making of an inheritance contract.

c. If either testator has children?

An inheritance contract could be made between partners even if a testator has children. However, such children have rights to their legal part of the legacy. The amount of this part depends on the age of children. According to S. 1642 Czech Civil Code, a forced heir is entitled to a forced share of the deceased's estate, and S. 1643 Czech Civil Code states: forced heirs include the deceased's children and, if they do not inherit, their descendants. If a forced heir is a minor, he must inherit at least three-quarters of his statutory inheritance share. If a forced heir is an adult, he must inherit at least a quarter of his statutory inheritance share.

DENMARK

a. In general?

The Inheritance Act which entered into force in Denmark on 1 January 2008 introduced new rules on extended cohabitants' wills, extending the testamentary powers of cohabitants at the expense of the indefeasible shares of lineal descendants. The legal basis for extended cohabitants' wills is provided in S. 87 of the Danish Inheritance Act. Extended cohabitants' wills allow cohabitants to inherit from each other as if they were spouses with absolute separate property. However, in a will it is possible to set some limits as there is no requirement to give a cohabiting partner all the normal benefits of a spouse. A surviving cohabitant cannot retain undivided possession of the estate.

The criteria for who may make such wills are set out in S. 88 of the Danish Inheritance Act. The conditions are that: on the date of making such a will the cohabitants must fulfil the conditions for contracting a marriage; upon the death of the first cohabitant, they must also have lived together for the previous two years; or alternatively the cohabitants must have, have had or expect a child together. Cohabitation is not considered to be terminated by a temporary stay in another residence or in an institution. In the case of staying in another residence the stay must be of a temporary nature, while a stay in an institution may be permanent.

b. If either testator is married to or is the registered partner of another person?

The couple may not be married or live in a registered partnership.

c. If either testator has children?

If the first deceased cohabitant with lineal descendants has fully exercised his or her testamentary powers, the surviving cohabitant will inherit three-quarters of the assets of the deceased cohabitant which may be freely bequeathed and one-half of the last one-quarter under the extended cohabitant's will, see S. 9, subsection 1, of the Danish Inheritance Act and S. 5, subsection 1. An extended cohabitant's will reduces the indefeasible share of the lineal descendants to one-eighth.

ENGLAND AND WALES

a. In general?

This can be done by means of mutual wills. English law does not permit parties to make joint wills as such.

b. If either testator is married to or is the registered partner of another person?

Yes, although only mutual wills rather than joint wills are possible and this is subject to challenge by the spouse or civil partner under the English Inheritance (Provision for Families and Dependants) Act 1975.

c. If either testator has children?

Yes, although only mutual not joint wills are possible which can be challenged by children making a claim under English Inheritance (Provision for Families and Dependants) Act 1975. This will succeed if there are minor children but not usually if there are adult children as a testator is free to leave their estate to whoever they please once dependants have been provided for.

ESTONIA

a. In general?

The right of succession explicitly prescribes that a reciprocal will can only be made jointly by spouses (a man and a woman in an official marriage) (Estonian Law of Succession Act § 89). At the same time, the Estonian Law of Succession Act does not explicitly prohibit the making of reciprocal wills by persons who are not married. As we have no judicial practice in this respect, it is impossible to say whether the courts would declare a joint will by two or more persons to be null and void or whether they would accept them as being valid wills. Pursuant to the general principles of Estonian private law, they could be declared valid as, according to § 87 of the General Part of the Estonian Civil Code Act, such transactions are only void if they are contrary to a prohibition arising from the law and, in that case, if the purpose of the prohibition is to render the transaction void due to a violation of this prohibition.

b. If either testator is married to or is the registered partner of another person?

Due to the absence of judicial practice and special regulations, it is impossible to comment on this. The spouse may have the right to a compulsory portion. If a bequeather has, by means of a will or a contract of succession, disinherited a descendant or his or her parents or spouse who are entitled to succeed in intestacy and with respect to whom the bequeather had a maintenance obligation arising from the Estonian Family Law Act at the time of his or her death or a bequeather has reduced their shares of the estate as compared to their shares according to intestate succession, they will have the right to claim a compulsory portion from the successors (§104(1) Estonian Law of Succession Act).

c. If either testator has children?

Due to the absence of judicial practice and special regulations, it is impossible to provide a comment on this. A child may have the right to a compulsory portion.

FINLAND

a. In general?

Yes.

b. If either testator is married to or is the registered partner of another person?

Yes, although the dissolution of the matrimonial property scheme will determine which part of the estate remains free to be disposed of by will.

c. If either testator has children?

Yes, although the children are entitled to their reserved share, which is 50 percent of the share that they would have received without a will. The children can contest the will if it prevents them from inheriting their reserved share.

FRANCE

a. In general?

According to French law, a will is a strictly personal undertaking that can be validly made by the testator exclusively.[6] A joint will has no legal effect. Nevertheless, spouses, partners or cohabitants can make a will containing identical provisions so as to confirm their common intention. However, the will can always be revoked on a discretionary basis by the testator without notice to the other. The liability of the testator who has revoked his or her donation to the other party under a will, without notice to the beneficiary, cannot be claimed.[7] To be enforceable a will must be hand written and signed by the testator and it must be dated.

---

6 Art. 895 of the French Civil Code: 'The will is a legal act by which the testator disposes fully or partly of his or her estate or of his or her rights and interest, for the time after his or her death. This act can be revoked'.

7 See Cass. Civ 1, 30 November 2004, no 02-20883. In this case, the testator posted the act of revocation of his will which benefited his cohabitant on the same day that he

b. If either testator is married to or is the registered partner of another person?
A joint will is not legally enforceable according to French law.

c. If either testator has children?
A joint will is not legally enforceable according to French law.

GERMANY

The German Civil Code does not contain provisions to permit partners in an informal relationship to make joint wills. § 2265 German Civil Code states explicitly that a joint will may only be made by spouses.

GREECE

a. In general?
No, according to Art. 1717 Greek Civil Code.

b. If either testator is married to or is the registered partner of another person?
No, according to Art. 1717 Greek Civil Code.

c. If either testator has children?
No, according to Art. 1717 Greek Civil Code.

HUNGARY

Only spouses (and registered partners) can make a joint will, cohabitants cannot.

REPUBLIC OF IRELAND

a. In general?
The status of a 'joint' will is unclear under Irish Law.

There is a doctrine of 'mutual wills'. This doctrine usually applies when two people, often but not necessarily husband and wife, each make separate wills in which they leave their property to the survivor of them with remainders over usually for their children, or where they each leave

---

registered the will before his notary, without notice to the cohabitant who discovered the revocation at the time of the death of the 'testator'.

their property to a third party directly (such as their child) in pursuance of an agreement between them not to revoke their wills without the consent of the other party. If one of the parties dies, then the courts will impose a trust on the survivor in favour of the beneficiaries under the will of the survivor. Thus, if the survivor revokes the will, the remedy is in equity by way of a constructive trust. There must, however, not only be an agreement between the parties, but a binding contract, and judges may examine the evidence for an intention to create a binding contract.

There is nothing however to prevent cohabitants making 'matching' or 'mirror' wills leaving property to each other. Moreover, there is nothing to prevent cohabitants either purchasing property jointly so that on the death of one cohabitant the surviving cohabitant succeeds to the property by survivorship outside the estate of the deceased cohabitant. Similarly, there is nothing to prevent a cohabitant who is the legal owner of a property transferring that property into the joint names of both cohabitants so that the property passes to the surviving cohabitant outside the will.

b. If either testator is married to or is the registered partner of another person?

The status of a 'joint will' is unclear in Irish law. Again, however, as outlined above, the Legal Right Share of the surviving spouse/civil partner would rank in priority ahead of any bequest to a cohabitant in a will.

c. If either testator has children?

Again, as outlined above, any such bequest in a will may be subject to an application by or on behalf of the children of the deceased cohabitant.

ITALY

a. In general?

In general, joint wills are not allowed in the Italian legal system, as a will is regarded as a legal instrument which can be implemented by only one person (see Art. 587 et seq. Italian Civil Code).

However, a cohabiting couple wishing to dispose of their own property in favour of each other can do so by implementing two different wills, each with a specular content. The provisions under the law in favour of the legitimate heirs, the children and husband or wife – there being any, must always be respected.

b. If either testator is married to or is the registered partner of another person?
Not applicable.

c. If either testator has children?
Not applicable.

LATVIA

Section 604 of the Latvian Civil Law provides a type of reciprocal will, namely, a will whereby two or more people, in the form of one joint document, reciprocally appoint each other as heir, is termed reciprocal. But, if in such a will the appointment of one person as heir has occurred with the condition that the appointment of the other person must exist and must be valid, such that one appointment may or may not be valid only jointly with the other, then the will is termed mutual. However, testamentary inheritance is also subject to the requirements of forced heirs.

LITHUANIA

No. Only spouses can make a joint will (Art. 5.44 Lithuanian Civil Code):

- A joint will by spouses shall be made exclusively by the spouses. Such a will shall be signed by both spouses in the presence of a notary or any other person attesting the will.
- A joint will by spouses shall be made exclusively as an official will (Art. 5.28 Lithuanian Civil Code).

LUXEMBOURG

In this hypothesis, disposing of the reserved share is also forbidden by law.

THE NETHERLANDS

a. In general?
In the Netherlands joint wills are void according to Art. 4:93 Dutch Civil Code. Art. 4:42 Dutch Civil Code determines that a testator can always unilaterally revoke a will; this article is mandatory law and in combination with Art. 4:4 Dutch Civil Code, a contract in which partners

agree to dispose of property to each other or in which they agree not to revoke their wills is void as it obstructs the freedom of testation.

b. If either testator is married to or is the registered partner of another person?

In the Netherlands joint wills are void according to Art. 4:93 Dutch Civil Code. Art. 4:42 Dutch Civil Code determines that a testator can always unilaterally revoke a will; this article is mandatory law and in combination with Art. 4:4 Dutch Civil Code, a contract in which partners agree to dispose of property to each other or in which they agree not to revoke their wills is void as it obstructs the freedom of testation.

c. If either testator has children?

In the Netherlands joint wills are void according to Art. 4:93 Dutch Civil Code. Art. 4:42 Dutch Civil Code determines that a testator can always unilaterally revoke a will; this article is mandatory law and in combination with Art. 4:4 Dutch Civil Code, a contract in which partners agree to dispose of property to each other or in which they agree not to revoke their wills is void as it obstructs the freedom of testation.

NORWAY

a. In general?

Yes, partners – as others – can make a joint will disposing of property in favour of the surviving partner pursuant to the Norwegian Inheritance Act, S. 49 third paragraph.

b. If either testator is married to or is the registered partner of another person?

If either testator is married to or is the registered partner of another person, partners can still make a joint will, but the testator has to respect the minimum inheritance of the spouse/registered partner, see the Norwegian Inheritance Act 1972, S. 6 and 7.

c. If either testator has children?

If the testator has children, the partners can still make a joint will, but the freedom of testation is limited as children have a right to a forced share. However, cohabitants without common children have an expanded right of testation, see the Norwegian Inheritance Act, S. 28(b) first paragraph second sentence and the answer to Question 50.

PORTUGAL

A joint will is not valid in Portuguese law in any case (Art. 2181 of the Portuguese Civil Code).

But partners, just like any other persons, are allowed to make cross-wills, in separate acts and documents.

RUSSIA

No, Russian law does not allow this.

SCOTLAND

a. In general?

There is no provision in Scots law for the making of a joint will. It is often common practice for spouses or partners each to make what are described as 'mirror wills' but individuals nonetheless retain freedom of testation over their own estate.

b. If either testator is married to or is the registered partner of another person?

As above, there is no provision in Scots law for the making of a joint will.

c. If either testator has children?

As above, there is no provision in Scots law for the making of a joint will.

SLOVAKIA

a. In general?

Testamentary succession is based on the deceased person's will. A will is a unilateral and revocable juridical act, by which the testator disposes of his or her property, to take effect after his or her death. Wills may only be individual; common wills by several testators are invalid (§ 476 para. 3 Slovak Civil Code). Therefore a joint will disposing of property in favour of the surviving partner is not valid.

b. If either testator is married to or is the registered partner of another person?

A joint will disposing of property in favour of the surviving partner is not valid.

c. If either testator has children?
A joint will disposing of property in favour of the surviving partner is not valid.

SLOVENIA

a. In general?
A joint will by which the partners appoint each other as the heirs is invalid under Slovene law. Case law only allows a will by which the partners, in the same document, dispose of their property to the benefit of a third person.[8]

b. If either testator is married to or is the registered partner of another person?
If either testator is married to or is the registered partner of another person she or he cannot form a valid extramarital union. In this case, too, a joint will by which two persons who are not in a legally recognised partnership appoint each other as heirs is invalid under Slovene law.

c. If either testator has children?
A joint will by which the partners appoint each other as heirs is invalid in every case under Slovene law.

SPAIN

a. In general?
According to the Spanish Civil Code, joint wills are not legal; they are prohibited under Art. 669 Spanish Civil Code.

The Catalan Civil Code does, in fact, allow joint wills in Art. 431-1 Catalan Civil Code.

Succession agreements may only be executed, according to Art. 431-2 Catalan Civil Code, with the following individuals:

- the spouse or future spouse;
- the cohabitant in a stable relationship;

---

8 K. ZUPANČIČ (ed.), V. ŽNIDARŠIČ SKUBIC, *Dedno pravo (Inherritance Law)*, Uradni list Republike Slovenije, Ljubljana, 2009, at p. 127 et seq.

- relatives in a direct line with no limitation in terms of the degree, or in a collateral line up to the fourth degree, in terms of both consanguinity and affinity;
- relatives by consanguinity in a direct or collateral line within the second degree of the other spouse or cohabitant.

Any person can be a beneficiary (Art. 431-3 Catalan Civil Code).

b. If either testator is married to or is the registered partner of another person?
According to the Spanish Civil Code, joint wills are not legal; they are prohibited under Art. 669 Spanish Civil Code.

The Catalan Civil Code allows cohabitants in an informal relationship to make joint wills (Art. 431-2.b) Catalan Civil Code). If the testator is married to another person, the fact that he/she is in an informal relationship will be evidence that there is a *de facto* separation from the spouse, and therefore he/she can make a joint will with the 'new' partner. If, however, either testator has already entered into a succession agreement with their spouse or registered partner, they will be precluded from making a joint will with their 'new partner', given that the previous succession agreement will still be valid. Article 431-17 Catalan Civil Code sets out the rule: 'the annulment of the marriage, a marital separation and divorce, or the breaking up of a stable relationship involving any of the testators does not alter the effectiveness of succession agreements, unless agreed otherwise'.

c. If either testator has children?
According to the Spanish Civil Code, joint wills are not legal; they are prohibited under Art. 669 Spanish Civil Code.

The Catalan Civil Code allows this in Art. 431-1 Catalan Civil Code. The beneficiaries of the joint will do not have to be the testator's children. The fact that the testator has children will not affect the validity of the joint will. Once the joint will is made, if one of the testators has children, this will not be a cause to challenge or revoke the succession agreement (Art. 431-9.3 Catalan Civil Code).

SWEDEN

a. In general?

Yes, partners can make joint wills in favour of the surviving partner. A joint will is, essentially, two separate wills, written in the same document for practical reasons, even if the testators' stipulations can be interrelated. The Swedish Code of Inheritance contains a special provision regarding joint wills, Chapter 10 § 7. If a testator to a joint will has unilaterally annulled it or changed its stipulations and, by doing so, has essentially spoiled the terms of the joint stipulations, he or she has thereby lost the rights granted by the joint will.

b. If either testator is married to or is the registered partner of another person?

The fact that either one of the partners is in a formalised relationship with another person does not affect this right as such, see above under a. The freedom of testation is, on the other hand, subject to the restrictions mentioned above under Question 50b-c, aimed at securing for the deceased person's children their forced share from the estate, as well as securing for the legal spouse or registered partner a minimum amount of the estate.

c. If either testator has children?

Yes, see answer to Question 51b above and the answer to Question 50c.

SWITZERLAND

A joint will is unknown in the Swiss law of succession. Legal doctrine and case law deny the validity of joint last wills.[9]

[9] For details and further references see A. BÜCHLER and S. DICKENMANN, 'Das gemeinschaftliche Testament - Ein Rechtsvergleich Schweiz-Deutschland', *successio*, 2008, at p. 74 et seq.

QUESTION 52

Can partners make other dispositions of property upon death (e.g. agreements as to succession or gifts upon death) in favour of the surviving partner:

a. In general?

b. If either partner is married to or is the registered partner of another person?

c. If either partner has children?

AUSTRIA

Contracts of inheritance can only be concluded between spouses or registered partners, but not between partners in an informal relationship.[1] However, a donation upon death - which is qualified as a contract between the decedent and the presentee - is not limited to spouses, but may also be concluded between partners in an informal relationship. The donation upon death is a legal institution which lies in between a pure donation and a legacy. For a valid donation upon death three conditions must be fulfilled:

- The presentee has to accept the promise.
- The contract requires the notarial form and a copy thereof must be given to the presentee.
- The testator explicitly waives his/her right to revoke his/her promise.

The possibility of a donation upon death exists regardless of whether a partner is married, lives in a registered partnership or has children. Apart from a donation upon death the partners only have the right to

1 Sections 602 et seq. in connection with section 1249 General Austrian Civil Code; R. FUCIK, 'section 1249 General Austrian Civil Code', in: A. KLETEČKA and M. SCHAUER, *ABGB-ON 1.02*, Manz Verlag, Vienna, 2014, at marg. No. 1; C. CACH, 'Ein Erbrecht für Lebensgefährten?', *SPRW*, 2014, at p. 427.

unilaterally appoint the other partner as an heir or to favour the surviving partner by drafting a legacy.

BELGIUM

a. In general?

Agreements as to succession are not allowed as a rule under Belgian law (Art. 1130, para. 2 Belgian Civil Code). The few exceptions to this prohibition are not relevant for informal partners.

Donations under the suspensive condition of the donee surviving the donor are valid, however.[2] The donation cannot be *pretium stupri:* its purpose cannot be to reward sexual relations. Furthermore, the donation may be subject to abatement in case it eats into the donor's ascendants' reserved share of one fourth in each line when the donor has no descendants (Art. 915 Belgian Civil Code). Interestingly, in Flanders the donor's partners (plural) benefit from the same registration tax regime as a spouse or a legal cohabitant when they have continuously cohabited for at least one year in a joint household on the day of the donation (Art. 1.1.0.0.2, para. 5, 4°, c) Flemish Taxation Code).

Instead of a donation, each partner may also make provision for the surviving partner as the execution of a natural obligation.[3] This will not be considered to be a gift to the extent that a natural obligation exists.

The primary disposition that informal partners make is the acquisition of joint property with a tontine agreement or an accretion clause. In the former construction, the partners acquire their rights under a suspensive condition, respectively a condition subsequent from the third party. In the latter construction, the conditions apply *inter partes*. In both cases, the clauses are considered aleatory contracts and not donations to the extent that the chances and risks are comparable on both sides or, if not, the difference in the chances and risks is balanced in the payment of the price, taking into account both partners' contributions to the household expenses. In both cases, the surviving partner will become the sole owner (or usufructor or holder of a right to habitation) of the whole asset.

---

2 W. PINTENS, C. DECLERCK, J. DU MONGH, K. VANWINCKELEN, *Familiaal vermogensrecht*, Intersentia, Antwerp, 2010, at n° 1140.

3 S. EGGERMONT, *De juridische bescherming van private relaties*, PhD, University of Antwerp, 2015, at n°s 178 and 257; W. PINTENS, C. DECLERCK, J. DU MONGH, K. VANWINCKELEN, *Familiaal vermogensrecht*, Intersentia, Antwerp, 2010, at n° 1021.

It depends on the circumstances of the case which is the better option for informal partners. In Flanders, the home is indeed not subject to succession taxes in the case of continuous cohabitation for more than three years, whereas a 10% registration tax applies in the case of tontine or accretion. In this example, a bequest is recommendable as opposed to a tontine or accretion, yet only when there are no heirs with a reserved share (Art. 2.7.4.1.1. § 2 Flemish Taxation Code).

b. If either partner is married to or is the registered partner of another person?

Yes. In case of a donation, they would have to respect the reserved share of the spouse, which amounts to the usufruct or lease of the main residence and the household goods or to half of the deceased's estate. There are more limited rights in case of separation and a spouse may even disinherit the other spouse under certain conditions (Art. 915bis Belgian Civil Code). The legal cohabitant has no reserved share in Belgian law.

c. If either partner has children?

Yes. In the case of a donation, they would have to respect the reserved share of the children, which amounts to half of the estate for one child, two thirds of the estate for two children and three fourths of the estate for three or more children (Art. 913 Belgian Civil Code).

BULGARIA

A last will and testament is the only disposition of property upon death that partners can make in favour of the surviving partner. Partners can make *in vivo* gifts (donations) to each other under the general regulation of the Bulgarian Obligations and Contract Law. Gifts can be challenged before the courts, however, with the aim of restoring the reserved share of an heir (Art. 30 and 33 of the Bulgarian Inheritance Law).

CROATIA

In line with Art. 11 paragraph 2 of the Croatian Family Act and Art. 4 paragraph 2 and Art. 55 of the Croatian Partnership Act, the answer equally relates to both cohabitants and same-sex informal partners.

a. In general?

In general, partners can make dispositions of property upon death in favour of the surviving partner as gifts *inter vivos* or *mortis causa*.

b. If either partner is married to or is the registered partner of another person?
A testator can dispose of his/her property as a gift in favour of whoever he/she chooses regardless of whether he/she was married (or in a registered partnership) or not.

However, in such a case, he/she has to take into account his/her forced heirs. If a testator disposes of all of his/her property as a gift in favour of the selected person, the forced heirs shall have the right to challenge that donation and claim their forced share (Art. 69 and 70 of the Croatian Inheritance Act).

A donee (the surviving partner in this case) shall still inherit a part of the testator's property, though not all of it, since the forced share has to be given to the forced heirs if they claim it.

c. If either partner has children?
A testator can dispose of his/her property as a gift in favour of the surviving partner if both partners have children. Nonetheless, since the testator's children are his/her forced heirs, the above paragraphs shall apply.

Therefore, the surviving partner shall inherit a part of the testator's property, but the children of the latter shall receive their forced share if they so demand (Art. 69 and 70 of the Croatian Inheritance Act).

CZECH REPUBLIC

a. In general?
Yes, in general partners can make other dispositions of property upon death, such as donation upon death in favour of the surviving partner (see S. 2063 et seq. Czech Civil Code), or allocation of legacy (see S. 1594 et seq. Czech Civil Code).

b. If either partner is married to or is the registered partner of another person?
Yes, partners can make other dispositions of property upon death in favour of the surviving partner if the testator is married to or is the registered partner of another partner, such as donation upon death in favour of the surviving partner (see S. 2063 et seq. Czech Civil Code), or allocation of legacy (see S. 1594 et seq. Czech Civil Code).

c. If either partner has children?

Yes, partners can give gifts upon death in favour of the surviving partner if the testator has children, such as donation upon death in favour of the surviving partner (see S. 2063 et seq. Czech Civil Code), or allocation of legacy (see S. 1594 et seq. Czech Civil Code). However, such children have rights to their legal part of the legacy. The amount of this part depends on the age of children. According to S. 1642 Czech Civil Code, a forced heir is entitled to a forced share of the deceased's estate, and S. 1643 Czech Civil Code states: forced heirs include the deceased's children and, if they do not inherit, their descendants. If a forced heir is a minor, he must inherit at least three-quarters of his statutory inheritance share. If a forced heir is an adult, he must inherit at least a quarter of his statutory inheritance share.

DENMARK

a. In general?

If a cohabitant wishes to benefit his or her surviving partner, while keeping the estate intact until his or her death, then the cohabitant must make a will. This principle is maintained by S. 93 of the Danish Inheritance Act on donations upon death. According to the Act, the rules for wills also apply to promises of gifts that cannot be fulfilled until after death, and deathbed donations.

Sometimes, with mutually burdensome agreements one party will reap certain benefits upon the death of the other party. This is often the case with joint ownership agreements between cohabitants. A mutual option to buy at a predetermined price can be a natural part of a mutually burdensome agreement, which must be respected by beneficiaries as a valid contract. Only where the conditions are so one-sided that the burden on the parties is unequal will it be considered a gift. If it is a condition that the gift can first be realised at the time of death, it is considered to be a deathbed donation.[4]

b. If either partner is married to or is the registered partner of another person?

A testator does not have the right to decide over the indefeasible share of his or her estate. The indefeasible share is one-quarter of the inheritance.

---

4 H.V. GODSK PEDERSEN and I. LUND-ANDERSEN, *Family Law in Denmark*, Kluwer Law International, Alphen aan den Rijn, 2011, at p. 176.

According to the Danish Inheritance Act, S. 91(2), the other spouse's consent is required to make a will disposing of the following assets, provided they are included in the community property:

- Property that serves as the family's home or from where both of the spouses' or the other spouse's business is carried out.
- The contents of the joint home and the other spouse's necessary work tools.
- A motor vehicle which has been used by the other spouse.

c. If either partner has children?

A testator does not have the right to decide over the indefeasible share of his or her estate. The indefeasible share is one-quarter of the inheritance. The testator can restrict the inheritance of each of his or her children to DKK 1,000,000; see the Danish Inheritance Act, S. 5(2).

ENGLAND AND WALES

a. In general?

No. Dispositions on death are made under will except for property owned as 'joint tenants in law and in equity' which passes by operation of law to the other joint tenant.

b. If either partner is married to or is the registered partner of another person?

No. Dispositions on death are made under will except for property owned as 'joint tenants in law and in equity' which passes by operation of law to the other joint tenant.

c. If either partner has children?

No. Dispositions on death are made under will except for property owned as 'joint tenants in law and in equity' which passes by operation of law to the other joint tenant.

ESTONIA

a. In general?

A partner in an informal relationship may make a legacy in favour of the other partner in his or her will. If, in a will, a testator does not bequeath all of his or her property or a legal share thereof to a person but gives a particular proprietary benefit without regarding the recipient of the benefit as his or her legal successor, the benefit shall be deemed to be a legacy and the recipient of the benefit shall be deemed to be a legatee. A disposition to bequeath a legacy entitles a legatee to demand the transfer of an object bequeathed as a legacy from the executor of the legacy. A legacy may be a thing, a sum of money, a right, a claim, an exemption from an obligation or any other transferable benefit (§ 56 of the Estonian Law of Succession Act). The partners in an informal relationship may conclude a mutual notarial contract of succession. A contract of succession is an agreement between a bequeather and another person whereby the bequeather nominates the other party or another person as his or her successor or bequeathes to the party or person a legacy, testamentary obligation or testamentary direction, or an agreement between a bequeather and his or her intestate successor whereby the latter renounces the succession (§ 95(1) of Estonian Law of Succession Act). The Estonian Law of Succession Act does not include any restriction with regard to how big a portion of a property a person can donate as gifts in the case of death or as a legacy. Even the right to a compulsory portion will not provide protection against legacies.

b. If either partner is married to or is the registered partner of another person?

The validity of a legacy and a contract of succession does not depend on whether the partner in an informal relationship was married or whether he or she had a registered partner.

c. If either partner has children?

The validity of a legacy and a contract of succession does not depend on whether the partner in an informal relationship had children.

FINLAND

Agreements as to succession and gifts upon death are, in general, invalid under the Finnish law of succession.

FRANCE

a. In general?

To favour one person (a cohabitant or whatever he or she may be) by means of a will is allowed but only within the limits of the disposable portion (*quotité disponible*) of the assets of the testator (see Question 50). Irrespective of the legal technique used to favour the cohabitant, the taxes imposed upon such a donation are very dissuasive.

Indeed, where the donator and the beneficiary are not related by blood ties, by marriage or a registered partnership, for any donation between living persons or by a will after death, the tax to be paid amounts to 60% of the value of the assets and the amount of the abatement is the lowest.[5]

The notary public (*notaire*) is the French legal professional who is legally competent to organise the succession of the deceased person. To favour the surviving cohabitant after death, some legal techniques are available.[6]

The first is the indivisible joint ownership contract (*contrat d'indivision*). When cohabitants acquire an asset in common, the legal regime which is applicable is the one of indivisible joint property (*indivision*). At the time of acquisition, they can enter into a specific agreement aimed to regulate the administration of the asset after death. In this specific contract, it is possible to insert a clause according to which the administration of the asset is devolved to the surviving cohabitant after the death of the other cohabitant, so as to enable him or her to take the usual administration decisions without the formal agreement of the heirs of the deceased cohabitant. Indeed, at the time of death, indivisible joint property continues with the surviving cohabitant and the heirs representing the deceased cohabitant. It is possible to determine in the contract that any revocation of the administrator requires unanimity among the indivisible co-owners so as to protect the surviving cohabitant from being revoked. But the most protective clause that could be inserted in such an agreement is the one according to which at the time of death the surviving indivisible co-owner is entitled to acquire the shares of the deceased indivisible co-owner in the joint property so as to become the exclusive owner of the asset. [7] The heirs are only entitled to compensation for the value of these shares; that value must be determined at the time of their acquisition.

Another technique is the one of joint acquisition of an asset with an accretion clause (*clause d'accroissement* or *tontine*). Indeed, at the time of the joint acquisition it is possible to insert a clause in the contract according to which each party will be reputed to have been the exclusive owner of the asset since acquisition provided the other party dies first.[8] At the time of the death of one of the co-contracting parties, the other

---

5 See vosdroits.service-public.fr/particuliers/F14200.xhtml.

6 See Dalloz Action *Droit de la famille 2014-2015*, no. 144.00 et seq.

7 This possibility is organised by Art. 1873-13 of the French Civil Code.

8 The legality of such a clause has been established for a long time in French Contract Law. See Cass. Civ 1, 3 February 1959, D. 1960, p. 592 with note DE LA MARNIERRE.

becomes retroactively the sole owner of the asset. This clause is interpreted as being an aleatory contract, which is legal under Art. 1964 of the French Civil Code.[9] This is not a donation since at the time of the contract a risk still exists, and indeed nobody can predict who will die first. This is not a transmission of property upon death since the surviving party is retroactively the exclusive owner since the date of the acquisition of the asset. Nevertheless, for tax purposes this scheme amounts to a liberality except where the acquired asset is the common home of the co-purchaser. In this last situation, the transmission will escape any taxation scheme where the value of the asset is below €76,000.[10] The accretion clause can be raised against any creditors of the deceased party, thereby making the asset unseizable.[11] The legal regime which is applicable to this asset before the death of one party or the other is the one of indivisible joint ownership.

A third technique is the joint cross-purchase of an asset (*achat croisé*) by cohabitants.[12] Indeed, according to the general principles of property law, property can be divided between bare ownership (*nue propriété*) and usufruct. At the time of acquisition, cohabitants can agree on a contract according to which each of them will acquire crossed bare ownership of 50% of the asset and usufruct of 50% thereof. At the time of death, bare ownership and usufruct merge together automatically. Then, the surviving cohabitant will obtain usufruct of 100% of the asset and 50% of the bare property, the second half of the bare property being transferred to the heirs of the deceased cohabitant. Usufruct of all of the asset is very protective for the surviving cohabitant and the reunification of bare property and usufruct upon death is free of any taxes.

Finally, a cohabitant can make the choice to acquire real estate under a real estate non-commercial company scheme (*Société civile immobilière*). According to this scheme the real estate is owned by the company and each of the cohabitants owns a percentage of the shares therein. Shares can be easily transmitted from one cohabitant to the other according to general principles of company law.

---

9 Cass. Civ 1, 14 December 2004, no. 02-11088.

10 Art. 754A of the French General Tax Code.

11 Cass. Civ 1, 18 November 1997, no. 95-20842.

12 See Dalloz Action *Droit de la famille 2014/2015* no. 144.14.

b. If either partner is married to or is the registered partner of another person?

The fact that the deceased cohabitant was married to another person limits the possibility to organise, within an indivisible joint ownership contract, the preferential allocation (*attribution préférentielle*) of the shares of indivisible joint ownership at the time of death.

Indeed, such a contract cannot restrict the legal preferential allocation regime in favour of the surviving spouse organised by Art. 831 to 832-1 of the French Civil Code. The regime of preferential allocation to the benefit of the surviving spouse only applies to particular assets such as: family farms, family craft industries and family commercial businesses in which the surviving spouse participates, and any premises where the surviving spouse is permanently residing or working.

Regarding the legal technique of the accretion clause (*pacte de tontine*), this clause is valid, even if one of the co-owners was married to another person at the time of the acquisition of the asset.[13]

c. If either partner has children?

If either partner has children the surviving cohabitant can be favoured by a will but only within the limits of the testator's disposable portion of assets (see Question 50). Any excess will be recoverable by the heirs.

GERMANY

a. In general?

According to § 1941 German Civil Code partners in an informal relationship, just as any other persons, may conclude a contract of inheritance. Thus one partner may appoint the other as heir or grant legacies and/or impose testamentary burdens.

b. If either partner is married to or is the registered partner of another person?

A marriage or registered partnership does not affect the capacity to conclude a contract of inheritance.

c. If either partner has children?

The existence of children of one or the other partner does not affect the capacity to conclude a contract of inheritance.

[13] See. Cass. Civ 1, 11 January 1983, no. 81-16307.

GREECE

a. In general?
Yes.

b. If either partner is married to or is the registered partner of another person?
Yes. Provided that their legal share is not affected (Art. 1825 Greek Civil Code and Art. 11(1-2) Law 3719/2008).

c. If either partner has children?
Yes, provided that their legal share is not affected (Art. 1825 Greek Civil Code).

HUNGARY

Both agreements as to succession or gifts upon death are possible. In the case law certain rules on agreements as to succession have been developed. According to these rules the validity of such agreements between cohabitants may be contested (typically by third persons) and according to the case law it has to be scrutinised whether the services rendered by one partner have gone above and beyond the sphere of activity which was inseparable from the cohabitation itself (see also the answer to Question 10).

REPUBLIC OF IRELAND

a. In general?
Yes. A cohabitant can nominate certain assets on either a statutory or non-statutory basis (i.e. a credit union account or a life insurance policy in favour of a surviving cohabitant). Such nominated assets would not be considered to be part of the estate of the deceased.

b. If either partner is married to or is the registered partner of another person?
Yes. As above, a cohabitant can nominate certain assets on either a statutory or non-statutory basis. Such assets are not considered to be part of the estate of the deceased, so they would not be taken into account when calculating the estate of the deceased for the purpose of the Legal Right Share. There is a provision, however, under S. 121 of the Irish Succession Act 1965 in certain circumstances to have a court declare that the nomination was made to disinherit a spouse/civil partner and/or

children of the deceased and to have the nominated asset included in the estate for the purpose of the Legal Right Share referred to earlier.

c. If either partner has children?
Yes, again subject to the provisions of S. 121 as outlined at Question 52(b).

ITALY

a. In general?
In general, agreements as to succession are void (*patti successori*, Art. 458 Italian Civil Code), while grants upon death are only possible if they are compatible with the requirements set by the law in favour of the legitimate heirs. Legal doctrine has for a long time suggested other legal institutions to protect the informal partner,[14] but until now it cannot be said that these means have been commonly implemented in practice. The main solutions which have been proposed are gifts to the partner with a reserved right of current use and enjoyment (*usufrutto*) in favour of the donor; contracts for the benefit of a third party; contracts of life insurance; contracts of life maintenance; and finally, trusts. In all these cases, the protection of the partner must however follow a very narrow path, as it must respect both the rights of the legitimate heirs, on the one hand, and the prohibition of agreements on succession, on the other.

It appears to be clear, then, that no general device is applicable to all cases, and that a careful study of each partnership is needed to mould the solution for a specific couple.

b. If either partner is married to or is the registered partner of another person?
c. If either partner has children?
Marriage or parenthood does not hinder the possibility of having recourse to dispositions of property upon death, provided the shares reserved for the legitimate heirs are respected. Where necessary, the spouse and children have recourse to specific legal action (*azione di riduzione*) in order to recover gifts and assets exceeding the share that the grantor could freely disposed of.

---

[14] Compare G. OBERTO, *I diritti dei conviventi. Realtà e prospettive tra Italia ed Europa*, Cedam, Padua, 2012, at p. 196 et seq.; R. BASSETTI, *Contratti di convivenza e di unione civile*, Giappichelli, Turin, 2014, at p. 162 et seq.

LATVIA

Section 639 of the Latvian Civil Law provides that contractual inheritance must be founded by contract pursuant to which one party grants the rights to his or her future inheritance or a part of it to another party, or several parties grant such rights to each other. Such a contract is termed an inheritance contract.

However, according to S. 642 in inheritance contracts as well, the provisions concerning preferential shares must be complied with, unless those who are concerned themselves directly or as parties to the contract have relinquished their rights. If this has not been complied with, then forced heirs may contest the contract after the death of the person leaving the estate.

Section 500 of the Latvian Civil Law provides that if someone has not been bequeathed the whole estate, nor a share in relation to the whole of the estate, but only a separate inheritance object, then the bequest is called a legacy, and the person to whom it has been bequeathed, is termed a legatee. Section 501 provides that a legacy may be bequeathed in a will either directly, or by imposing its execution upon the heir or another legatee. According to S. 503 the bequest of a legacy must not infringe on the rights of forced heirs.

LITHUANIA

No.

Any individual has the right to conclude any legal contract, i.e. to transfer property to his or her partner or to acquire assets in the form of joint-partial property while being alive. Such contracts shall take place while all parties to the contract are alive. There is no possibility to donate property upon death.

According to the law of the Republic of Lithuania, upon death the property can only be disposed of by will. While both parties are alive, property can be transferred by way of a donation, an annuity (the transfer of property under a maintenance obligation), an exchange and other types of contracts. Such contracts may include usufruct rights for the disposer. If the will provides for a bequest - the right to use immovable property or a part thereof for a fixed period or for one's lifetime - the person accepting the bequest becomes the usufructuary.

In the absence of a will, succession is regulated by Art. 5.11 and 5.13 of the Lithuanian Civil Code (see the answer to Question 47).

LUXEMBOURG

a. In general?

In general the surviving partner can dispose of property.

b. If either partner is married to or is the registered partner of another person?

If the testator is married to or is the registered partner of another person, he or she may dispose of his or her property by will.

c. If either partner has children?

If the partner has children, he or she has the right to dispose of his or her property by will in favour of the surviving partner without disposing of the reserved share. The children are heirs with a reserved share (*héritiers réservataires*).

THE NETHERLANDS

a. In general?

Partners can make other dispositions of property upon death in favour of the surviving partner through their will. There is the option of a *legaat* (bequest), which, as defined in Art. 4:117 Dutch Civil Code, is a will in which the testator confers a *vorderingsrecht* (claim) to one or more persons. If the surviving partner receives a bequest then he/she is a creditor to the estate, but not an heir or beneficiary. The testator can dispose of a certain good or a certain amount of money through the bequest. Another possibility are gifts upon death, which are treated as a bequest in conformity with Art. 4:126 Dutch Civil Code.

b. If either partner is married to or is the registered partner of another person?

The partners remain free to make other dispositions of property upon death in favour of the surviving partner even if they are married to or are the registered partner of another person. The only requirement is that the person to whom the disposition is made must be alive when the estate opens (Art. 4:56 Dutch Civil Code).

c. If either partner has children?
Again, the partners remain free to make other dispositions of property upon death in favour of the surviving partner even if they have children.

NORWAY

a. In general?
Yes, partners can make other dispositions of property upon death in favour of the surviving partner - both agreements as to succession and gifts upon death. If these dispositions are not intended to have any effect for the testator during his or her own lifetime, they are regarded as testamentary dispositions and subject to the same mandatory provisions as wills in the Norwegian Inheritance Act.

b. If either partner is married to or is the registered partner of another person?
If these dispositions are not intended to have any effect for the testator during his or her own lifetime, they are regarded as testamentary dispositions and must comply with the formal requirements of wills. Moreover, the testator has to respect the minimum inheritance of the spouse/registered partner; see the Norwegian Inheritance Act, S. 6 and 7.

c. If either partner has children?
If the dispositions are regarded as testamentary dispositions they must comply with the formal requirements of wills. Moreover, the freedom of testation is limited as the testator's children have a right to a forced share of the estate.

PORTUGAL

No. As a rule, inheritance agreements are forbidden by law (Art. 1699(1), point a) and 2028(2) of the Portuguese Civil Code). However, inheritance agreements are allowed exceptionally - donations *mortis causa*, between betrothed and from third parties to betrothed, concerning determined assets. These agreements may refer to the whole or to part of the estate, as well as instituting an heir or appointing a legatee in favour of a third party, made by any of the betrothed in the pre-nuptial agreement (Art. 1700(1), para. b)). Thus, members of the *de facto* union cannot be included.

RUSSIA

a. In general?

No. Article 1118 Russian Civil Code explicitly states that the only possibility to dispose of property upon death is by making a will.

However, the testator (*legator*) can make a *legate* in favour of the surviving partner. A legate is a provision in the will obliging the heir to transfer into ownership or possession of the third person (*legataris*) an asset belonging to the deceased's estate; to acquire and transfer to the *legataris* certain assets; to perform for the *legataris* certain work or services, or to make periodic payments to the *legataris* from the estate, etc. (Art. 1137 Russian Civil Code). A particular form of *legate* explicitly mentioned in the Russian Civil Code is the right to lifelong occupancy of the house belonging to the deceased's estate (Art. 1137(2) Russian Civil Code). As a *legate* can be made in favour of any person, it can also be made in favour of a surviving partner.

b. If either partner is married to or is the registered partner of another person?

Yes. The only limitation is that if the spouse is entitled to a reserved share, the *legator* cannot affect this share.

c. If either partner has children?

Yes. The only limitation is that if the child(ren) is/are entitled to a reserved share, the *legator* cannot affect this share.

SCOTLAND

a. In general?

The most common way by which this might happen in Scotland is where partners are joint owners of a house or other heritable property. Frequently joint owners will include a special destination, in the form of a survivorship clause, in the legal title to the property. The effect of this is that, on the death of one of the partners, his or her share will pass automatically to the other and will not form part of the deceased's estate.

b. If either partner is married to or is the registered partner of another person?

As explained above, if there is a survivorship clause in the title to heritable property, the deceased's share will pass automatically on death to the surviving partner and will not form part of the estate. It is therefore a way of avoiding any claim or entitlement of a surviving spouse or civil partner.

c. If either partner has children?

As explained above, if there is a survivorship clause in the title to heritable property, the deceased's share will pass automatically on death to the surviving partner and will not form part of the estate. On intestacy, children have legal rights which apply only to moveable property and therefore a survivorship clause in title to heritable property is not likely to affect them. The special destination will however have the effect of excluding the heritable property concerned from the overall estate of the deceased which may affect any bequests in the deceased's will.

SLOVAKIA

a. In general?

The Slovak law of inheritance acknowledges only two titles of succession: a person's will (testamentary succession) or a statute (statutory succession). Agreements as to succession or gifts upon death are not recognised as titles of succession.

b. If either partner is married to or is the registered partner of another person?

See answer to a).

c. If either partner has children?

See answer to a).

SLOVENIA

a. In general?

The partners may conclude all legal transactions that they could conclude with other persons, such as contracts for gifts as contracts *inter vivos* or contracts for gifts *mortis causa* (Art. 62 of the Slovenian Marriage Act), contracts on the right to use, and contracts on lifelong support.[15] All legal transactions between them must be concluded in the form of a notarial protocol, unless it relates to a normal small gift. Gifts (and legacies) are considered by law to belong to the legal inheritable share unless the testator specifies otherwise. Inclusion can only occur at the

15 A contract on subsistence and contracts for lifelong maintenance which in view of a business purpose is unpaid is considered to be a gift.

request of a co-heir and not *ex officio*. Taking gifts (and bequests) into account applies to all legal heirs, in all orders of inheritance. A bequest to a testamentary heir is only included in the inheritable share if the testator so specifies. The decedent may also not dispossess, by gift, the legal heirs of their compulsory shares. If they are dispossessed of their compulsory shares, the testamentary disposables are first reduced and only then any gifts.

By law, any unpaid disposition of the decedent to the benefit of the partner as the legal heir is considered to be a gift (para. 1 Art. 46 of the Slovenian Inheritance Act). The following are considered to be gifts: the renunciation of rights, the remission of debts, tax on account of the heritable share, gifts for establishing or extending the household, gifts for performing a profession, and life insurance to the benefit of the partner. Shares in property that the decedent bequeaths to persons who enter into consideration as heirs of the first order of inheritance (thus also partners) are also considered to be gifts in a contract on consigning and dividing property if any of the heirs did not agree or were unable to agree with the consignment or division.[16]

b. If either partner is married to or is the registered partner of another person?

If either testator is married to or is the registered partner of another person she or he cannot establish an extramarital union. A gift to such a partner is considered to be a gift to a third person. It is necessary to return such a gift when it deprives the compulsory shares but only if the decedent gave such a gift during the last year of his or her life.

c. If either partner has children?

The general rules apply in relation to gifts: a decedent may not reduce the compulsory shares of the children as legal heirs by making gifts to a partner.

SPAIN

a. In general?

Gifts upon death, yes, as legatees. But the Spanish Civil Code does not allow agreements between testator and heir.

16 K. ZUPANČIČ (ed.), V. ŽNIDARŠIČ SKUBIC, *Dedno pravo (Inherritance Law)*, Uradni list Republike Slovenije, Ljubljana, 2009, at p. 108.

The Catalan Civil Code allows agreements as to succession (Art. 431-1 Catalan Civil Code), including those made by cohabitants (Art. 431-2.b) Catalan Civil Code).

b. If either partner is married to or is the registered partner of another person?
Gifts upon death, yes, as legatees. But the Spanish Civil Code does not allow inheritance agreements between testator and heir.

The Catalan Civil Code does not include any limit as to who the beneficiary of the succession agreement is.

c. If either partner has children?
Gifts upon death, yes, as legatees. But the Spanish Civil Code does not allow inheritance agreements between testator and heir.

The Catalan Civil Code allows agreements as to succession (Art. 431-1 Catalan Civil Code). The fact that the testator has children will not affect the validity of the joint will. Once the joint will is made, if one of the testators has children, this will not be a cause to challenge or revoke the succession agreement (Art. 431-9.3 Catalan Civil Code).

SWEDEN

a. In general?
Under Swedish law, agreements as to succession upon death and promises of gifts upon death which cannot be enforced during the donor´s lifetime, are generally regarded as null and void and are therefore not binding, Swedish Code of Inheritance, Chapter 17 § 1 and 3. The only way to validly dispose of assets upon death is by making a will, in addition to the taking out of a life insurance policy and appointing a certain person, such as the informal partner, as the beneficiary.

b. If either partner is married to or is the registered partner of another person?
No, see answer to a.

c. If either partner has children?
No, see answer to a.

SWITZERLAND

a. In general?

Partners in an informal relationship can make other dispositions of property upon death in favour of the surviving partner.

They can conclude contracts of succession (Art. 494 et seq. Swiss Civil Code). The contract of succession can be concluded between two or more testators. Notably, the testator may conclude an inheritance renunciation contract with an heir with or without valuable consideration (Art. 495 para. 1 Swiss Civil Code). Hence, heirs entitled to a reserved share may contractually waive their inheritance rights (either partly or entirely). According to Art. 512 para. 1 Swiss Civil Code, a contract of succession must, however, meet the same formal requirements as a will executed as a public deed (Art. 499 et seq. Swiss Civil Code) in order to be valid. Additionally, the contracting parties must simultaneously declare their intentions to the public official and sign the deed before him or her and two witnesses (Art. 512 para. 2 Swiss Civil Code).

Gifts upon death to a partner in an informal relationship are also possible. According to Art. 245 para. 2 Swiss Code of Obligations, a gift whose occurrence is made contingent upon the donor's death is subject to the provisions governing testamentary dispositions (Art. 481 et seq. Swiss Civil Code). Thus, the formal requirements of the testamentary contract (Art. 512 Swiss Civil Code) generally have to be observed.[17] Furthermore, the reserved shares of surviving heirs have to be respected; if not, claims of abatement (*Herabsetzungklagen*) will otherwise be possible (Art. 522 et seq. Swiss Civil Code).

b. If either partner is married to or is the registered partner of another person?

Partners in an informal relationship can make other dispositions of property upon death in favour of the surviving partner if either partner is married to or is the registered partner of another person. However, the testator must observe the reserved share of his or her spouse or registered partner (Art. 471 No. 3 Swiss Civil Code), unless an inheritance renunciation contract has been concluded (see Question 52(a)).

17 For details see N.P. VOGT, in: H. HONSELL, N.P. VOGT and T. GEISER, *Basler Kommentar Zivilgesetzbuch I (Art. 1-456 ZGB)*, Helbing Lichtenhahn Verlag, Basel, 2014, at Art. 245 N 7 et seq.

c. If either partner has children?

Partners in an informal relationship can make other dispositions of property upon death in favour of the surviving partner if either partner has children. However, the testator must observe the reserved shares of his or her children (Art. 471 No. 1 Swiss Civil Code), unless an inheritance renunciation contract has been concluded (see Question 52(a)). However, according to Art. 468 para. 1 Swiss Civil Code, any person concluding a testamentary contract has to be capable of judgement and must have reached the age of 18.

QUESTION 53

Is the surviving partner entitled to a reserved share or to any other rights or claims on the estate (e.g. any claim based on dependency, compensation, or maintenance) in the case of a disposition of property upon death (e.g. by will, joint will, or inheritance agreement) in favour of another person?

AUSTRIA

In contrast to spouses, who are entitled to a compulsory share which amounts to half of the statutory share, partners in an informal relationship have no equivalent right if the testator legally disposes in favour of another person. Due to the fact that partners in an informal relationship have no right to inheritance, the partners can only inherit if the other partner has made a respective disposition of property upon death. If, however, the partner has failed to do so, the other partner is neither entitled to a reserved share nor to any other similar rights. However, as has been explained in answer to Question 48 the partner in an informal relationship has the right to step into the tenancy agreement and become the contracting party in the agreement in case of the death of the other partner, even if the decedent has disposed of the property in favour of another person.[1]

BELGIUM

The surviving informal partner does not have a reserved share. Any claim under tort law, a natural obligation, unjust enrichment or other general rules however constitutes a debt of the estate, which takes

1 E. MÖSCHL, *Die nichteheliche Lebensgemeinschaft*, LexisNexis ARD ORAC, Vienna, 2007, at marg. No. 51.

priority over bequests in favour of another person and even over forced and intestate heirship (Art. 870 et seq. Belgian Civil Code).[2]

BULGARIA

No, the surviving partner is not entitled to a reserved share of the estate. The only heirs entitled to a reserved share are close relatives (children and parents) as well as the surviving spouse (Art. 28 of the Bulgarian Inheritance Law).

CROATIA

In line with Art. 11 paragraph 2 of the Croatian Family Act and Art. 4 paragraph 2 and Art. 55 of the Croatian Partnership Act, the answer equally relates to both cohabitants and same-sex informal partners.

According to Art. 69 in relation to Art. 8 paragraph 2 of the Croatian Inheritance Act and Art. 4 paragraph 2 of the Croatian Partnership Act, surviving partners are forced heirs and shall have the right to claim their reserved share (in the same way as surviving spouses).

The reserved part of the surviving partner amounts to half of the value of his/her intestate share.

CZECH REPUBLIC

According to S. 1669 Czech Civil Code: persons who enjoyed gratuitous provision for life in the household of the deceased until his death are entitled to the same provision for life for another three weeks after the deceased's death.

DENMARK

According to case law and general property law, if the surviving cohabitant is awarded compensation this is regarded as satisfying property law claims, which must be paid with priority over disbursing any inheritance to others.

---

[2] S. EGGERMONT, *De juridische bescherming van private relaties*, PhD, University of Antwerp, 2015, at n° 257; W. PINTENS, C. DECLERCK, J. DU MONGH, K. VANWINCKELEN, *Familiaal vermogensrecht*, Intersentia, Antwerp, 2010, at n° 2235.

ENGLAND AND WALES

No. There is no concept of reserved shares for cohabitants. Where a spouse or civil partner dies intestate (without making a will), the surviving partner is entitled to a statutory share of the estate under S. 46 English Administration of Estates Act 1925, the size of which depends on the size of the estate and the presence or absence of other beneficiaries such as children. Where a cohabitant dies intestate, there is no such entitlement for the surviving partner who will receive nothing under the intestacy rules. Instead, the estate will pass to the deceased's next of kin as prescribed by the statutory rules (to their children or otherwise their parents or siblings). If there are no surviving relatives, the estate will pass *bona vacantia* to the Crown rather than to the surviving cohabitant partner.

However, a surviving cohabitant is entitled to make a claim against the estate under the English Inheritance (Provision for Families and Dependants) Act 1975 for reasonable financial provision limited to maintenance where no such provision has been made for them in a will or where their partner died intestate. This is an important recognition of informal cohabiting relationships.

In 2011, the Law Commission recommended reform of the statutory rules on intestacy to allow some statutory succession to the estate by a cohabitant in certain circumstances but this was rejected by the Coalition Government.

ESTONIA

The partner in an informal relationship is not entitled to a reserved share. It has been found in the legal literature that the surviving partner of in a free marriage (different from a spouse) has the opportunity to determine which part of the property acquired during the relationship actually belongs to him or her and which part shall be transferred to the successors as the property of the deceased, i.e. after the death of one party it should be possible to ascertain its origin on the basis of the contract of joint operation or any other shared ownership.[3]

The family members of a person who lived with him or her and received maintenance from him or her until that person's death have the right to

[3] K. KAMA and K. KULLERKUPP, 'Vabaabielu versus abielu: varalised suhted muutuvate kooseluvormide kontekstis', *Juridica*, 2002, No. 6, pp. 359-368.

continue using the objects of the shared household and to receive maintenance from the estate for one month after his or her death (§ 132 of the Estonian Law of Succession Act).

FINLAND

The surviving partner is not entitled to a reserved share as he or she does not have a right to inherit in the first place. However, if the surviving partner is entitled to compensation on the basis of unjust enrichment according to the Finnish Act on the Dissolution of the Household of Cohabiting Partners (26/2011), S. 8, this must be paid from the estate before the shares of the estate are determined. The same applies if the surviving partner is entitled to support under the Finnish Code of Inheritance (40/1965), Chapter 8, S. 2. This means that compensation and support have priority over a disposition of property upon death in favour of another person. However, one of the requirements related to the definition of a cohabitee under the Finnish Cohabitation Act is that the person cannot be married to or in a registered partnership with another person. As the Finnish Code of Inheritance makes use of the same definition, neither the compensation based on unjust enrichment nor the support based on the Finnish Code of Inheritance is available to a surviving partner, whose partner was married to or in a registered partnership with some other person at the moment of his or her death.

FRANCE

The surviving partner is not a protected heir. According to French legal provisions only the surviving spouse and the children can benefit from a reserved share.[4]

GERMANY

The surviving partner is not entitled to a reserved share or any other rights or claims on the estate in the case of a disposition of property upon death in favour of another person.

GREECE

No.

---

4 Art. 913 to 914-1 of the French Civil Code.

HUNGARY

Cohabitants are not entitled to a reserved share.

REPUBLIC OF IRELAND

The surviving cohabitant is not entitled to a reserved share. As outlined in the response to Question 47, a 'qualified cohabitant' (as defined) has a right under S. 194 of the Irish Civil Partnership and Certain Rights and Obligations of Cohabitants Act 2010 to apply to Court to seek provision from the estate of the deceased cohabitant.

ITALY

No. No reserved share or other right or claim is foreseen for the surviving partner in this case.

LATVIA

As mentioned above, in accordance with S. 423 of the Latvian Civil Law, forced heirs are the spouse and descendants, but if there are no descendants, then ascendants of the nearest degree of kinship. It does not refer to partners in an unregistered cohabitation.

LITHUANIA

Under the regulation in force (Art. 1.62 of the Lithuanian Civil Code) and according to Art. 23 of EU Regulation no. 650/2012, succession relations are subject to the law of the last place of residence. Succession to immovable property is subject to the law of the country where the property is located.

According to Art. 38 of the above-mentioned Regulation, a person may choose the law which is applicable to succession. The choice is limited to the law (on succession by will) of the country whose nationality the person holds. In Lithuania, a working group has recently been established to analyse a possible amendment to the Lithuanian Civil Code. At present there is no possibility to make such a choice.

LUXEMBOURG

No, the surviving partner is not entitled to a reserved share.

THE NETHERLANDS

The surviving partner is not entitled to any reserved share or other rights or claims against the estate when the partner has disposed of property in favour of another person. The surviving partner only retains the right to continue the occupancy of the house with the household goods for six months following the death according to Art. 4:28 Dutch Civil Code.

NORWAY

The surviving cohabitant's inheritance right and right of undivided possession mentioned in Questions 48 and 49 can be restricted by a will as long as the surviving partner is informed of the will before the testator's death. A cohabitant's right to purchase what was previously the common residence and household goods at market value pursuant to the Norwegian Household Community Act, S. 2, cannot be restricted by a will or an inheritance agreement.

PORTUGAL

The surviving partner has none, other than a right to maintenance over the deceased's patrimony, inherited by his or her heirs (Art. 2010 of the Portuguese Civil Code) regardless of their title of succession acquisition.

RUSSIA

A surviving spouse is entitled to a reserved share if he/she is unable to work and has been living with and been maintained by the other partner for at least one year (Art. 1149 and 1148(2) Russian Civil Code). A partner entitled to a reserved share cannot be wholly disinherited by will. Irrespective of the contents of the will, he/she is always entitled to one half of the share that he/she would have received in the case of intestate succession.

SCOTLAND

A surviving partner has no fixed entitlement on the estate of his or her deceased partner.

SLOVAKIA

No.

SLOVENIA

As a legal heir, a partner also has the right to a compulsory share. This amounts to half of that to which she or he was entitled by law. In a case in which the legal share of the partner may be increased at the expense of the shares of co-heirs, there can also be an increase of her or his share at the expense of other compulsory heirs or even at the expense of a testamentary heir.[5]

SPAIN

No. According to the Spanish Civil Code, the surviving spouse has a life interest in the estate (Art. 834 et seq. Spanish Civil Code), but the surviving partner has no similar right.

The Catalan Civil Code gives the surviving partner the right to the *cuarta viudal* (one-quarter of the deceased's estate) when the surviving partner's estate plus any property allocated by the deceased is insufficient for the survivor's maintenance, taking into account the standard of living enjoyed by the couple before death (Art. 452-1 et seq. Catalan Civil Code).

SWEDEN

Within the framework of the division of 'cohabitation property', i.e., the joint dwelling and household goods acquired for the cohabiting couple's joint use, the Swedish Cohabitation Act gives the surviving cohabitee the right to receive a fixed amount from this divisible property once debts have been deducted, § 18 para. 2. In 2015 this fixed amount, consisting of two so-called price amounts which are annually adjusted to the general living expenses in Sweden, was 89,000 Swedish crowns (approximately €9,600). This amount is exactly half of that granted to a surviving partner in a formalised relationship (marriage, registered partnership).[6] The purpose of this rule is to ensure that the surviving cohabitee is left with a minimum value of property but only with regard to 'cohabitation

---

5 K. ZUPANČIČ (ed.), V. ŽNIDARŠIČ SKUBIC, *Dedno pravo (Inherritance Law)*, Uradni list Republike Slovenije, Ljubljana, 2009, at p. 97.

6 See M. BRATTSTRÖM, 'The Protection of a Vulnerable Party when a Cohabitee Relationship Ends – An Evaluation of the Swedish Cohabitees Act', in B. VERSCHRAEGEN (ed.), *Family Finances*, Jan Sramet Verlag, Vienna, 2008, at p. 350–351 and M. JÄNTERÄ-JAREBORG, 'Rechtsregeln für nichteheliches Zusammenleben in Schweden' (in English), in: I. KROPPENBERG et al. (eds.), *Rechtsregeln für nichteheliches Zusammenleben*, Gieseking Verlag, Vienna, 2009, pp. 207-226, at p. 223–224.

property'. The right is irrelevant and does not come into play if the surviving partner's share in the divisible property (i.e. the 'cohabitation property') exceeds the value of the fixed amount; it is the only available 'compensation'. On the other hand, the surviving partner is entitled to this amount even if he or she has assets of much higher value but which fall outside the scope of the 'cohabitation property'. This right cannot be set aside by the deceased partner's will.

SWITZERLAND

In Switzerland, the surviving partner is not entitled to a reserved share or to any other rights or claims against the estate in the case of a disposition of property upon death in favour of another person.

According to Art. 606 Swiss Civil Code, heirs who were members of the household of and were maintained by the deceased at the time of his or her death may demand that they be maintained for a further month at the estate's expense. Thus, if the partner in an informal relationship is a named heir (Art. 438 Swiss Civil Code) and cohabited with and was maintained by the deceased, he or she is entitled to be maintained for a further month.

QUESTION 54

Are there any statistics or estimations on how often a relationship is terminated by the death of one of the partners?

AUSTRIA

Unfortunately, neither statistics nor estimations on this issue exist.[1]

BELGIUM

Mortality statistics are available for some selected years but there is no distinction between being married and being in a legal cohabitation.

Death per year and marital status in Belgium (Eurostat)

	2007	Men	Women	2010	Men	Women
Single persons (never in a legal union)	10,554	6,066	4,488	10,818	6,275	4,543
Persons in a legal union (married or in a registered partnership)	40,949	28,452	12,497	41,619	28,892	12,727
Persons whose legal union has ended	49,155	15,286	33,869	52,653	16,860	35,793
Persons with unknown marital status	0	0	0	62	39	23
Total	100,658	49,804	50,854	105,152	52,066	53,086

BULGARIA

No, there are no such statistics.

1 According to the information provided by Statistics Austria, the Austrian Institute for Family Studies and the Vienna Institute for Demography by e-mails dated 02.02.2015 and 03.02.2015.

CROATIA

There are no statistics or estimations on how often a relationship is terminated by the death of one of the partners.

CZECH REPUBLIC

There are no statistics or estimations on how often a relationship is terminated by the death of one of the partners.

DENMARK

No.

ENGLAND AND WALES

There do not appear to be any statistics or estimations on this point for England and Wales.

ESTONIA

No valid data are available on this.

FINLAND

No. This information is not available from the statistics, as detailed information on cohabiting partnerships is not available due to the informal nature of the relationship.

However, as can be seen from the table in Question 12, cohabiting partnerships are becoming more frequent also among the older population.

FRANCE

No such statistics are available.

GERMANY

No such statistics exist.

GREECE

It is methodologically difficult, if not impossible, to gain access to such information, as it involves personal data and raises deontological concerns.

HUNGARY

Unfortunately not.

REPUBLIC OF IRELAND

None that I am aware of.

ITALY

No, there are none. See also the answer to Question 14.

LATVIA

There are no such statistics collected about partners in an informal relationship.

LITHUANIA

There is no relevant statistical information available.

LUXEMBOURG

Unfortunately, there were no statistics or estimations found.

THE NETHERLANDS

To the author's knowledge no data are (publicly) available.

NORWAY

Among couples with children that were cohabiting in 2005, about 7 cohabitants per 1,000 cohabitants had experienced termination of the relationship through death during the eight-year period of 2005–2013.

The corresponding number among cohabitants without children was 40 per 1,000 cohabitants.[2]

PORTUGAL

There are no statistics available for this question.

RUSSIA

Normal data available.

SCOTLAND

There are no such statistics or estimations available.

SLOVAKIA

No, there are no statistics or estimations.

SLOVENIA

No.

SPAIN

No, there are not.

SWEDEN

There are no official Swedish statistics on this. As has been pointed out earlier, informal cohabitation is not regarded as a civil status and so receives no special mention in the population records. One available study (see above under Question 14) indicated that 3% of the deceased had been in an informal relationship of cohabitation at the time of the death.[3]

---

2 Register-based statistics from Statistics Norway processed by E. GOPLEN, *Barn i det moderne samboerskap – en bindende eller splittende faktor?*, Master's thesis, University of Oslo, 2014, table 3 at p. 32.

3 O. ERIXSON, *Economic Decisions and Social Norms in Life and Death Situations* [diss. Uppsala University], 2013, at p. 59 and 64.

SWITZERLAND

There is no information available with regard to this question.

QUESTION 55

Are there any statistics or estimations on how common it is that partners in an informal relationship make a will in favour of the other partner?

AUSTRIA

Unfortunately, neither statistics nor estimations on this issue exist.[1]

BELGIUM

There are no statistics available on this topic.

BULGARIA

No, there are no such statistics.

CROATIA

There are no statistics or estimations on how common it is that partners in an informal relationship make a will in favour of the other partner.

CZECH REPUBLIC

There are no statistics or estimations on how common it is that partners in an informal relationship make a will in favour of the other partner.

DENMARK

The provisions on extended cohabitants' wills in Denmark can put a cohabitant wholly or partly in the same situation as a spouse with full

---

1 According to the information provided by Statistics Austria, the Austrian Institute for Family Studies and the Vienna Institute for Demography by e-mails dated 02.02.2015 and 03.02.2015.

separation of property; see S. 87 of the Danish Inheritance Act. Recent research shows that a very large number of cohabiting couples make extended cohabitants' wills, and nearly all decide that the surviving cohabitant should inherit as much as possible. This research was carried out by the lawyer U. Grønborg on the basis of about 5% of all notarised wills in 2011-2012. 14% of these wills concerned unmarried cohabitants and the great majority of these had made extended cohabitants' wills.[2]

ENGLAND AND WALES

Research conducted by Barlow et al. as part of the nationally representative British Social Attitudes Survey 2006 indicated that only 12% of cohabitants had made a will.[3]

ESTONIA

No valid data are available on this.

FINLAND

No. In general, wills are not very commonly made in Finland.

FRANCE

No such statistics could be found.

It emerges from informal contacts with notaries public[4] that the National Record of wills (*Fichier central des disposition de dernières volontés*) does not make any distinction regarding the matrimonial situation of the testator, therefore making it impossible to obtain such information.

GERMANY

No such statistics exist.

---

2 See U. GRØNBORG, 'Testamentsmønstre', *Tidsskrift for Familie- og arveret* (Journal of Family and Succession Law), 2014, pp. 168-175.

3 A. BARLOW, C. BURGOYNE, E. CLERY and J. SMITHSON, 'Cohabitation and the law: myths, money and the media', in: A. PARK, J. CURTICE, K. THOMSON, M. PHILLIPS, M. JOHNSON and E. CLERY (eds.), *British Social Attitudes: the 24th report*, Sage, London, 2008, pp. 29-52.

4 Informal contact with M. FOUR-BROMET and J. POYET, both notaries public, respectively in Lyon and Cremieux.

GREECE

It is methodologically difficult, if not impossible, to gain access to such information, as it involves personal data and raises deontological concerns.

HUNGARY

Unfortunately not. According to the experiences of notaries the idea of such a will between cohabitants often emerges, but it rarely occurs in practice and specifically only when the person making the will has children or grandchildren.

REPUBLIC OF IRELAND

None that I am aware of.

ITALY

No, there are no statistics or estimations on this topic.

LATVIA

There are no such statistics collected about partners in an informal relationship.

LITHUANIA

There is no relevant statistical information available.

LUXEMBOURG

Unfortunately, there were no statistics or estimations found.

THE NETHERLANDS

There is little information available. Notaries have been asked how many informal partners who concluded a cohabitation contract also made a will drawn up by the same notary. Thirty percent of the responding notaries indicated that 50-70 percent of the clients concluding a contract made a will at their office; for another 28 percent of the notaries this percentage was even over 70 percent of the couples in question. About 40 percent answered that between 21 and 50 percent of the couples also made a will.[5]

NORWAY

There are no statistics or estimations on how common it is that partners to an informal relationship make a will in favour of the other partner.

PORTUGAL

There are no statistics available for this question.

RUSSIA

No data available.

SCOTLAND

There are no such statistics or estimations available.

SLOVAKIA

No, there are no statistics or estimations.

SLOVENIA

No.

SPAIN

There are statistics about the total number of wills per year in Spain, without further information about their content or designated heirs.[6]

SWEDEN

There are no official statistics on how common it is that partners to an informal relationship make a will in favour of the other partner. Generally speaking it is assumed that the making of a will is an exception

---

5 W.M. SCHRAMA, P. KUIK and L.C.A. VERSTAPPEN, 'Samenlevingsovereenkomsten in de notariële praktijk', *Familie&Recht*, 2014, available at: familieenrecht.nl, at 14.10.

6 These are available at: www.cienotariado.org.

and not the rule in Sweden. In the data analysed by Oscar Erixson (Question 14) 17% of the deceased had left a will, resulting in a 5% frequency of unequal division between family lines.[7] Kajsa Walleng's survey (Question 11) stated that 18% of the respondents who regarded themselves to be in an informal relationship of cohabitation had made a will in favour of the other cohabitee.[8]

SWITZERLAND

There is no detailed information available with regard to this question. It can be said that generally the number of people making a will in Switzerland is rather low. The numbers estimated are around a third and up to 50-60% in urban areas or with regard to larger inheritance sums.[9]

[7] O. ERIXSON, *Economic Decisions and Social Norms in Life and Death Situations* [diss. Uppsala University], 2013, at p. 59 and 63-64.

[8] K. WALLENG, *Att leva som sambo*, Iustus Förlag, Uppsala, 2015, at p. 111.

[9] For further references see R. FANKHAUSER, *Die Ehekrise als Grenze des Ehegattenerbrechts*, Stämpfli, Bern, 2011, at p. 67 et seq.

QUESTION 56

Are there any statistics or estimations on how common it is that a partner in an informal relationship is the beneficiary to the other partner's life insurance?

AUSTRIA

Unfortunately, neither statistics nor estimations on this issue exist.[1] However, the legal literature refers to the fact that life insurances are 'often' concluded in favour of one partner in an informal relationship, because in case of the death of the other partner there is neither a right to inherit nor to have a maintenance claim.[2]

BELGIUM

There are no statistics available on this topic.

BULGARIA

No, there are no such statistics.

CROATIA

There are no statistics or estimations on how common it is that a partner in an informal relationship is the beneficiary to the other partner's life insurance.

---

1 According to the information provided by the Austrian Insurance Federation, the Allianz Life Insurance, the Zürich Versicherungs-Aktiengesellschaft by e-mails dated 20.02.2015 and 26.02.2015.

2 U. AICHHORN, 'Vermögensaufteilung und Erbrecht bei nichtehelicher Lebensgemeinschaft', in: M. GRUBER et al. (eds.), *Erbrecht und Vermögensnachfolge*, Verlag Österreich, Vienna, 2010, at marg. No. 84.

CZECH REPUBLIC

There are no statistics or estimations on how common it is that a partner in an informal relationship is the beneficiary of the other partner's life insurance.

DENMARK

Under Danish law a cohabitant may be provided for by a life assurance policy without express notification to the Insurance Company.

Section 105a of the Danish Insurance Contracts Act defines the 'next of kin' for the purposes of beneficiaries. Unless the circumstances indicate otherwise, S. 105a, subsection 1, provides the following order for the next of kin: the insured party's spouse, a cohabitant who fulfils the conditions in S. 2, children and heirs.[3] 'Cohabitants' are defined in subsection 2. The definition is similar to that in the rules on extended cohabitants' wills:

> 'Subsection 2. To be covered by subsection 1, a cohabitant must live with the insured party at the joint dwelling and
> 1) expect, have or have had a child together with the insured party or
> 2) have lived with the insured party in a marriage-like relationship at the joint dwelling for the last 2 years prior to death.'

If no beneficiary is named, the insurance payment will devolve to the insured party's next of kin; see S. 105b, subsection 1, of the Danish Insurance Contracts Act. A cohabitant will be the next of kin if no one else has higher priority. The only person who might have higher priority would be a surviving spouse.

A 'next of kin' clause is probably used in more than 90% of all life insurance policies. As stated above, since 2008 a cohabitant has been covered under the definition of 'next of kin' in S. 105a of the Danish Insurance Contracts Act, so a cohabitant will normally receive payment under a life insurance policy. This means that since 2008 very few beneficiaries have been included by name. Prior to 2008 beneficiaries (cohabitants) were frequently included by name, though with the provision that the named person should not benefit if their cohabitation had come to an end at the time of death (though not at the initiative of the institution).[4] There are no available statistics for this.

---

3 New rules on cohabitants entered into force on 1 January 2008.

4 Information provided by the Legal Department of Danica Pension.

ENGLAND AND WALES

There do not appear to be any statistics or estimations on this point for England and Wales and there is no mechanism for centrally registering or recording such interests.

ESTONIA

No valid data are available on this.

FINLAND

There are no statistics available. The most common designation as a beneficiary is 'next of kin'. The meaning of the expression can vary according to the circumstances. In the Supreme Court decision KKO 2004:40, the term was interpreted to refer to the cohabiting partner, as in the subsequent will the testator had left all of his possessions to his cohabiting partner.

FRANCE

No such statistics are available. The beneficiary of a person's life insurance can be freely chosen by the insured person with a restriction on persons who are capable of exerting an undue influence (a religious minister, medical staff who treated the insured person, an employee working in a retirement home, etc.).[5] The beneficiary, for his or her part, must consent to being a beneficiary of the contract. Once acceptation has occurred revocation is not anymore a possibility without the express consent of the beneficiary.[6]

An adulterous cohabitant is not precluded from benefiting from a life insurance policy concluded by his or her married cohabitant. Indeed, the Plenary Assembly of the *Cour de cassation* has held that the benefit granted to the adulterous cohabitant does not contradict morality and cannot be annulled on the ground of Art. 1133 of the French Civil Code.[7]

5 Art. 909 of the French Civil Code; Art. L331-4 of the French Welfare and Family Code.

6 Art. L.132-9 of the French Insurance Code.

7 Cass. Ass. Plen 29 October 2004 no. 03-11.238. According to Art. 1133 of the French Civil Code, a contract is vitiated if its objective is illegal or if it contradicts morality or public order. Nullity can be ordered by the court.

GERMANY

No such statistics exist.

GREECE

It is methodologically difficult, if not impossible, to gain access to such information, as it involves personal data and raises deontological concerns.

HUNGARY

Unfortunately not.

REPUBLIC OF IRELAND

None that I am aware of.

The Irish Probate Office retain statistics of the civil status of deceased people where a grant of representation issues in their estate (either testate or intestate). That said, however, this information would not necessarily reveal whether the deceased was a cohabitant or not and would not record whether he/she made a will in favour of a surviving cohabitant. In the case of a person who dies without a significant estate or where property is held jointly, a grant of representation may not be required. The General Register Office[8] would have records of the civil status of everyone whose death is registered in Ireland. However, it would not have the detailed information in relation to informal relationships and provision in relation to same.

ITALY

No, there are no statistics or estimations on this topic.

LATVIA

There are no such statistics collected about partners in an informal relationship.

---

[8] Available at: www.welfare.ie/en/Pages/General-Register-Office.aspx.

LITHUANIA

There is no relevant statistical information available.

LUXEMBOURG

No official estimations found. But as the number of informal relationships is increasing, more and more partners will be the beneficiary of the other partner's life insurance as they are raising a mortgage (when the bank obliges them to contract an *assurance solde restant dû*).

THE NETHERLANDS

To the author's knowledge no data are (publicly) available.

NORWAY

There are no statistics or estimations on how common it is that a partner to an informal relationship is the beneficiary of the other partner's life insurance.

PORTUGAL

There are no statistics available for this question.

RUSSIA

No data available.

SCOTLAND

There are no such statistics or estimations available.

SLOVAKIA

No, there are no statistics or estimations.

SLOVENIA

No.

SPAIN

No. The Registry of life insurance contracts (*Registro de contratos de seguros de cobertura de fallecimiento*) does not include this information.

SWEDEN

There are no official statistics on how common it is that a partner in a cohabitation relationship is the beneficiary of the other partner´s life insurance. However, the most common form of savings for Swedish households is life insurance; in total, life insurance amounted to almost 42% of all household savings in 2013.[9] Furthermore, most employees have group life insurance. The starting point is that the insured party (or the employee) may freely dispose of the insurance by making bequests, without any restrictions (such as the right to forced share), Swedish Insurance Contracts Act (in Swedish: *Försäkringsavtalslagen* 2005:104) Chapter 1 § 5 and Chapter 14, § 1–3 and 7. The standard terms and conditions of a life insurance policy often indicate who the beneficiary is. It has become common that cohabitees, besides spouses and children, are given as the beneficiaries in these standard terms. An insured person may always explicitly appoint his or her cohabitee as the sole beneficiary.

In Kajsa Walleng's survey (Question 11), 39% of the cohabitees reported that they had appointed their partner as the beneficiary of their life insurance. 17% answered that they did not know whether the partner was the beneficiary or not.[10]

SWITZERLAND

There is no information available with regard to this question.

---

9 Svensk Försäkring, 'Insurance in Sweden, Statistics 2013', available at: www.svenskforsakring.se/PageFiles/6717/SF_Statistikbroschyr_2013_eng.pdf?epslanguage=sv, at p. 9.

10 K. Walleng, *Att leva som sambo*, Iustus Förlag, Uppsala, 2015, at p. 114.

PART F
AGREEMENTS

QUESTION 57

Are there specific rules concerning agreements between partners in an informal relationship? Where relevant, please indicate these specific rules. If not, which general rules apply?

AUSTRIA

Although the validity of so-called partnership agreements is recognised in Austria, there are currently no specific rules dealing with this type of agreement. Therefore, partnership agreements are subject to the general rules which are applicable to contracts:[1] Section 863 General Austrian Civil Code stipulates that declarations of intent can be made implicitly or explicitly, S. 883 General Austrian Civil Code contains the principle of freedom of form and S. 917 et seq. General Austrian Civil Code regulates possible irregularities when it comes to performance.[2] One of the main principles of Austrian private law is party autonomy, which is particularly reflected in the principle of freedom of contract. This principle leaves it to the parties as to whether and, if so, with whom and with which content they reach an agreement. However, this freedom is subject to certain limitations: A contract which violates statutory provisions or public morals is void.[3]

With regard to partnership agreements clauses regulating the following issues would be contrary to public morals and would therefore be void:[4]

- prohibiting one partner in an informal relationship from engaging in a business activity;

---

1 N. OSWALD and A. SCHMALLEGGER, 'Partnerschaftsvertrag zwischen nichtehelichen Lebensgefährten', *EF-Z*, 2013, at p. 13.

2 See S. PERNER, M. SPITZER and E. KODEK, *Bürgerliches Recht*, Manz Verlag, Vienna, 2012, at p. 37.

3 Section 879 para. 1 General Austrian Civil Code.

4 E. MÖSCHL, *Die nichteheliche Lebensgemeinschaft*, LexisNexis ARD ORAC, Vienna, 2007, at marg. No. 38; A. DEIXLER-HÜBNER, *Scheidung, Ehe und Lebensgemeinschaft*, LexisNexis, Vienna, 2013, at marg. No. 252a; N. OSWALD and A. SCHMALLEGGER, 'Partnerschaftsvertrag zwischen nichtehelichen Lebensgefährten', *EF-Z*, 2013, at p. 13 et seq.

- regulating the sexual relationship between the partners, e.g. the number of children, the frequency of sexual intercourse or sexual practices;
- containing the obligation of sexual loyalty or childlessness;
- the use of contraceptives;[5]
- ordering the submission of the woman.

To sum up, agreements which unreasonably restrict personal freedom are contrary to public morals and are therefore void.[6] Such obligations could also not be enforced by imposing penalties, because the validity of penalty clauses depends upon the validity of the underlying obligation.[7] Whether compensation agreements are valid is disputed. If pecuniary damages suffered during the informal relationship should be compensated by the agreement, Deixler-Hübner and Schäffer argue for their validity and refer to the example where the partners in an informal relationship agree that one partner takes care of the child of the other partner resulting from a prior relationship, and can therefore only work part time. However, the partner is only willing to take care of the child if – in the case of separation – the other partner pays a certain amount of money. Such an agreement should be valid, because without the support of the other partner, the partner must have hired domestic help.[8]

Finally, it should be noted that the partners cannot simply refer to the rules regulating marriage and declare that these rules are applicable to their relationship. Provisions on marriage or registered partnerships cannot therefore be applied to informal relationships by analogy.[9]

BELGIUM

Concluding a cohabitation agreement is often recommended for informal partners. There are, however, no specific rules. Informal partners may for

5 Austrian Supreme Court, Judgement of 27.01.1994, 2 Ob 557/93, *JBl*, 1994, at p. 687.

6 A. Deixler-Hübner and H. Schäffer, *Partnerschaft ohne Trauschein*, Linde, Vienna, 2014, at p. 105; S. Ferrari, 'Rechtsregeln für nichteheliches Zusammenleben in Österreich', in: I. Kroppenberg et al. (eds.), *Rechtsregeln für nichteheliches Zusammenleben*, Gieseking Verlag, Vienna, 2009, pp. 167-206, at p. 176 et seq.

7 A. Deixler-Hübner and H. Schäffer, *Partnerschaft ohne Trauschein*, Linde, Vienna, 2014, at p. 103; N. Oswald and A. Schmallegger, 'Partnerschaftsvertrag zwischen nichtehelichen Lebensgefährten', *EF-Z*, 2013, at p. 14.

8 See A. Deixler-Hübner and H. Schäffer, *Partnerschaft ohne Trauschein*, Linde, Vienna, 2014, at p. 107.

9 E. Gitschthaler, 'Neuerungen im Recht der Lebensgemeinschaften', *AnwBl*, 2012, at p. 598 et seq.; Austrian Supreme Court, Judgement of 16.11.2007, 7 Ob 239/07h; Austrian Supreme Court, Judgement of 01.04.1998, 9 Ob 96/98b.

example opt for a civil law partnership agreement (which may be oral).[10] Two aspects of the general rules on contracts are worth mentioning.

On the one hand, cohabitation agreements may not infringe public policy. Firstly, they may not be *pretium stupri*.[11] For this reason, it is recommended that partners include a preamble in which they explain the motives behind the agreement,[12] for example that they want to provide for each other.[13] Secondly, the agreement may not restrict the personal freedom of both partners.[14] For this reason, they may not contractually apply the personal rights and obligations between formal partners, such as the duty of cohabitation or of fidelity.[15] It is also not acceptable to include a penalty clause in case the partnership or the cohabitation is terminated.

On the other hand, the principle of consensuality applies to cohabitation agreements, so that the existence of an implicit agreement may be proven. Some authors contend that all informal cohabitants conclude an implicit cohabitation agreement, which is proven by its performance.[16] However, the majority view rejects that notion and requires proof with all forms of evidence that a cohabitation agreement was concluded.[17]

BULGARIA

No, Bulgarian law does not contain any specific rules concerning agreements between partners in an informal relationship. Partners in an informal relationship are free to make any such agreement. The only limit on such an agreement is the general framework set out by Art. 9 of the Bulgarian Obligations and Contracts Law – not to infringe the imperative legal regulations and good morals.[18]

---

10 Commercial Court of Dendermonde 9 February 2012, *T.Not.* 2012, 635 (proof of civil partnership not accepted); Justice of the Peace Charleroi (2) 20 January 2009, *T.Vred.* 2011, 373 (proof of oral civil partnership agreement accepted).

11 P. SENAEVE, *Compendium van het personen- en familierecht*, Acco, Leuven, 2013, at n° 2044.

12 W. PINTENS, C. DECLERCK, J. DU MONGH, K. VANWINCKELEN, *Familiaal vermogensrecht*, Intersentia, Antwerp, 2010, at n° 1003.

13 Antwerp 2 February 2005, *NJW* 2006, 849, with note Verschelden.

14 S. EGGERMONT, *De juridische bescherming van private relaties*, PhD, University of Antwerp, 2015, at n° 534.

15 District Court of Bruges 9 April 2001, *RW* 2001-02, 1552.

16 A. HEYVAERT, *Het personen- en gezinsrecht ont(k)leed*, Kluwer, Mechelen, 2002, at n° 698.

17 S. EGGERMONT, *De juridische bescherming van private relaties*, PhD, University of Antwerp, 2015, at n°s 178, 259-262 and 424.

18 See: L. NENOVA and M. MARKOV, *Family Law*, Sofi-R, Sofia, 2009, at p. 397. Also: T. TZANKOVA, *The Factual Spousal Relationship and the Bulgarian Family Law*, Feneya, Sofia, 2000, at p. 157-160.

CROATIA

Art. 11 paragraph 2 of the Croatian Family Act prescribes that all the effects of marriage with respect to property shall apply to cohabitation too. It means that partners in a cohabitation shall also have the right to enter into a (pre)nuptial agreement, just like spouses. According to Art. 40 of the Croatian Family Act, (pre)nuptial agreements may regulate relations encompassed by property law with respect to existing or future property.

Art. 4 paragraph 1 of the Croatian Partnership Act prescribes that all the effects of marriage with respect to property shall apply to same-sex informal partnerships too. It means that pursuant to the Croatian Family Act, same-sex informal partners shall also have the right to enter into a (pre)nuptial agreement, just like same-sex registered partners, cohabitants and spouses.

CZECH REPUBLIC

There are no specific rules concerning agreements between partners in an informal relationship. General rules of agreements in the Czech Civil Code are applied depending on what kind of agreement has been made. See S. 2055 et seq. Czech Civil Code. There are no special rules concerning the property relationship or maintenance or agreements dealing with the property relationship or maintenance between the partners in an informal relationship.

DENMARK

No.

The Danish Contracts Act applies to agreements between cohabitants.[19] A contract can be set aside by a court if one of the conditions for invalidity (duress, fraud, lack of capacity etc.) is fulfilled. Fraud can be committed either by the other party or by a third party. Further, under the Danish Contracts Act if it would be unreasonable to maintain a contract, it can be set aside or modified on grounds of unfairness.

---

[19] Consolidating Act No. 781 of 26 August 1996.

ENGLAND AND WALES

There are no specific statutory rules and the law. Although for many years cohabiting couples could not be sure that their cohabitation agreements would be enforceable, the law has recently been clarified to an extent by case law (see *Sutton v Mishcon De Reya* [2003] EWHC 3166 (Ch), [2004] 1 FLR 837), although there is still no statutory confirmation of the position as had been requested by the Law Commission in their 2007 report. The current position is that cohabiting couples are free to make agreements; but how enforceable they are on relationship breakdown may depend on how the agreement has been drafted and what the subject matter of the agreement is. Generally, they can make enforceable agreements relating to real and personal property provided they are drawn up and signed in the proper format where appropriate. Thus for real property (i.e. immovable property) the agreement would need to be in the form of a declaration of trust which is signed as a deed.

Contracts which have immoral consideration would still be void as in *Sutton v Mishcon De Reya* [2003] EWHC 3166 (Ch), [2004] 1 FLR 837 itself and so the agreement must be drafted so as to avoid any suggestion of this. Cohabitation agreements are, according to the legal profession, becoming more common but a couple may require several agreements to cover different assets and then separate wills are needed to leave valid gifts on death.

ESTONIA

There are no specific rules with regard to concluding contracts between the partners in an informal relationship. According to the type of transaction, either general or special provisions are applicable to the conclusion of transactions. The conclusion of transactions is generally regulated by the Estonian Law of Obligations Act.

FINLAND

According to the Finnish Cohabitation Act, cohabitation partners are generally free to derogate from the provisions of the Act by agreement. However, according to the same Act, it is not allowed to make anticipatory agreements waiving the right to demand the separation of property or the right to apply for an estate distributor to be appointed. The form or contents of these agreements is/are, however, not specified. In that respect, general rules apply, for example on the specific form of a will or that agreements should generally be made in writing due to evidentiary reasons.

FRANCE

No specific rules are applicable to agreements between cohabitants. The general principles of contract law will govern them.[20]

GERMANY

There are no specific rules concerning agreements between partners to an informal relationship. The general law of obligations applies (§§ 241 et seq. German Civil Code). Thus, according to § 134 German Civil Code partnership agreements must not be contrary to statutory prohibitions (e.g. German Adoption Law or the German Embryo Protection Act) or public policy (§ 138 German Civil Code).[21] If the partners agree on the purchase of a plot of land, the law of property applies.

GREECE

There are no specific rules. The principle of freedom of contract would apply (Art. 361 Greek Civil Code).

HUNGARY

The Hungarian Civil Code has introduced the property agreement between cohabitants as a new institution.[22] An agreement between cohabitants concerning their property relations was also possible under the Civil Code of 1959 but without any special provision. A property agreement between cohabitants can be found among the general rules on cohabitation. According to the Hungarian Civil Code cohabitants can regulate their future property relations during their community of life by agreement. There are certain formal requirements for the validity of such an agreement: it has to be included in a public instrument or a private document attested by a lawyer.

Cohabitants are permitted to regulate their property relations in any manner which is permitted between spouses. The default matrimonial

20 Art. 1108 et seq. of the French Civil Code.

21 H. GRZIWOTZ, *Nichteheliche Lebensgemeinschaft*, Beck, Munich, 2014, at § 8 No. 6 et seq.

22 Art. 6:515 of the Hungarian Civil Code.

property regime is community of property and spouses may diverge from the rules thereon when they agree to this. Besides, the Hungarian Civil Code provides for two alternative property regimes, namely participation in acquisitions and the separation of property. Cohabitants may also agree on one of these regimes or even diverge from the main provisions of these regimes.

The agreement is only valid against third parties if it has been recorded in the Register of Property Agreements of Cohabitants or if the cohabitants prove that the third party knew or would have known about the existence of the agreement and its contents. The regulations on the Register of Matrimonial Property Agreements are to be applied to the Register of Property Agreements of Cohabitants.

REPUBLIC OF IRELAND

Yes, there are specific rules concerning agreements between partners to an informal relationship. In particular, S. 202 of the Irish 2010 Act provides for cohabitants' agreements. Cohabitants may enter into agreements to provide for financial matters during the relationship or when the relationship ends, whether through death or otherwise. Such agreements are only valid if the following requirements as per S. 202(2) are complied with:

> '(a) The cohabitants –
> (i) Have each received independent legal advice before entering into it; or
> (ii) Have received legal advice together and have waived in writing the right to independent legal advice;
> (b) The agreement is in writing and signed by both cohabitants; and
> (c) The general law of contract is complied with.'

Cohabitants may agree to opt out of the redress provisions of Part 15 of the Irish 2010 Act, in that they may agree that neither cohabitant is entitled to apply for redress as per S. 173, or to apply for an Order for provision from the estate of the other cohabitant pursuant to S. 194. Whilst cohabitants' agreements may be valid and enforceable, the court retains a jurisdiction to set such agreements aside or vary same in exceptional circumstances where the enforceability would cause a serious injustice (S. 202(4)).

ITALY

For a long time agreements between partners have been held to be void on the grounds of a violation of the rule on public morality (*buoncostume*). For many years, however, the opinion has been widely held that these agreements are not meant to remunerate for sexual services but to protect the fiduciary commitment of one partner towards the other and to acknowledge the value of each partner's contribution to their common patrimony. For instance, the Court of Cassation in 1993, upholding the validity of such a contract, held that 'cohabitation between an unmarried man and woman does not imply that this contract is illicit and therefore null'.[23]

Currently, however, the law provides no specific rules for these agreements, which therefore fall under the general law of contract. This implies that only the patrimonial aspects of the relationship can be regulated by the agreement. The personal aspects of the relationship are excluded from the agreement according to Art. 1174 of the Italian Civil Code ('The performance which is the object of the obligation must be valuable') and Art. 1321 ('The contract is the agreement between two or more parties to establish, regulate, extinguish a legal patrimonial bond'). Parties cannot therefore insert provisions on fidelity, moral assistance, procreation (or non-procreation), the exercise of parental responsibility, or the use of a specific family name.[24]

Informal partners, who are also parents, may enter into specific agreements regarding their children's custody in contemplation of their personal separation. If, then, the partners do in fact separate, and one of the parents brings an action before the courts to obtain a judicial verification and a decision on the children's custody, then the judge 'takes into account the agreements stipulated by the parents if they are not against the interests of the children' (Art. 337 *ter* as modified by the Italian Legislative Decree 28 December 2013, in force from 7 February 2014).[25]

---

[23] Cass. civ. sez. III, 8 June 1993, n. 6381. See G. PIANEZZE, *Rapporti personali e patrimoniali tra conviventi*, Giuffrè, Milan, 2013, at p. 126.

[24] G. OBERTO, *I diritti dei conviventi. Realtà e prospettive tra Italia ed Europa*, Cedam, Padua, 2012, at p. 111.

[25] It may be of some interest to note that, despite the recent law aimed at fully equalizing the legal positions of children born within and outside wedlock (Italian Legislative Decree 28 December 2013 quoted in the text), a difference between married and unmarried couples still exists in the event of separation: in the latter case, the relationship can be dissolved without judicial intervention – only when they disagree, can parents have their agreement on children's custody scrutinised by the judge.

Since 2 December 2013, at the initiative of the Consiglio nazionale del Notariato, it is possible to sign cohabitation agreements (*accordi di convivenza*) at every notary office in the country.[26] Agreements can be signed before starting to live together or afterwards.

LATVIA

In Latvia there is no special legal order on partners in an informal relationship. The law of obligations of the Latvian Civil Law is applicable.

LITHUANIA

Article 6.156 of the Lithuanian Civil Code provides that the parties shall be free to enter into contracts and to determine their mutual rights and duties at their own discretion; the parties may also conclude other contracts that are not established by this Code if this does not contradict existing laws.

Article 3.231 part 2 provides that cohabitees shall have a right to make an agreement by a notarial deed on how the assets acquired and used together should be divided after their life together ends. The provisions of Art. 3.101-3.108 shall be applicable to such agreements *mutatis mutandis*. Unfortunately, the provisions of Art. 3.231 of the Lithuanian Civil Code have not been applied in practice.

LUXEMBOURG

There are no specific rules. The general rules of contract law apply (Art. 1101 et seq. of the Luxembourg Civil Code).

THE NETHERLANDS

General contract law applies, since there are no specific rules for contracts between non-marital couples. Cohabitation contracts are, unlike many other types of specific contracts, not a type of contract regulated in Book 7 or 8 of the Dutch Civil Code. Thus party autonomy is extensive.

Married partners, on the contrary, must always commence legal proceedings in order to separate and the matter of custody will therefore be settled by the judge. In both cases, following the new law, the competent court is the *Tribunale ordinario*.

[26] Compare A.C. Moro, *Manuale di diritto minorile*, Zanichelli, Bologna, 2014, at p. 227.

Only Art. 3:40 Dutch Civil Code on public morality and public order sets some limits on the freedom of contract. However, Art. 3:40 Dutch Civil Code hardly plays a role in practice. It is rarely invoked in the case law[27] and only in exceptional cases will the courts accept the nullity of a clause in a cohabitation contract as being against public morality or public order.[28]

An estimated 50 percent of cohabiting couples do have a notarial cohabitation contract.[29]

NORWAY

There are no specific rules concerning agreements between partners to an informal relationship. However, one provision could be mentioned: the Norwegian Household Community Act, S. 4 applies to two or more unmarried adults sharing a household (cohabitants, sisters, students, etc.), and states that when considering whether a member of a household is to obtain rights according to the Act, agreements between the parties made prior to the termination must be taken into account. In other words, they are not binding. As a general rule partners to an informal relationship are free to enter into agreements.

PORTUGAL

There are no specific rules concerning agreements.

Some relevant scholars support the validity of such 'cohabitation contracts' concerning mainly patrimonial issues; but there are no court decisions on this subject.

RUSSIA

No, there are no specific rules; therefore, the agreements between partners in an informal relationship are governed by the general rules of the law of obligations in the Russian Civil Code. The provisions of the

27 Rb. Haarlem 23 April 2008, RBHAA:2008:BD4210 invoked but rejected.

28 Rb. Alkmaar 22 August 2007, ECLI:NL:RBALK:2007:BB2260 involving an agreement between cohabiting partners on financial compensation for an abortion.

29 A. DE GRAAF, 'Steeds meer samenwoners hebben een samenlevingscontract', *CBS Webmagazine* 10 February 2010. W.M. SCHRAMA, P. KUIK and L.C.A. VERSTAPPEN, 'Samenlevingsovereenkomsten in de notariële praktijk', *Familie&Recht*, 2014, available at: familieenrecht.nl, at 14.1 and 14.2.

Russian Family Code governing matrimonial property agreements and maintenance agreements between spouses are not applicable to agreements between informal partners.

SCOTLAND

There are no specific rules concerning agreements between cohabitants. As a general rule, Scots law respects the autonomy of parties to make agreements concerning their family relationships and this is particularly evident in the context of marriage. Ante-nuptial, post-nuptial and separation agreements have a long history of use and enforcement in Scotland and they have been widely used. In modern family law, separation agreements are commonly used to regulate the consequences of relationship breakdown. They are binding without the need for any judicial scrutiny or approval and it is assumed that agreements between cohabitants would be similarly binding. Apart from challenges brought to agreements on the basis of general contract law, for example, alleging lack of consent, undue influence or misrepresentation, there is no other provision to vary or set aside cohabitation agreements. In respect of divorce or dissolution of civil partnership, S. 16 of the Family Law (Scotland) Act 1985 gives the court statutory power to vary or set aside a financial provision agreement on the basis that it was not fair and reasonable at the time it was concluded. No comparable power applies in the context of termination of cohabitation.

In the past there was an argument that cohabitation agreements might be unenforceable on public policy grounds in that they related to 'furtherance of illicit sexual intercourse'. When cohabitation was considered by the Scottish Law Commission, they expressed the view that such an argument was out of date and no longer appropriate but nonetheless recommended, for avoidance of doubt, that a provision be included in legislation to the following effect:

> 'A contract between cohabitants relating to property or financial matters should not be void or unenforceable solely because it was concluded between parties in, or about to enter, this type of relationship.'[30]

No such provision was in fact included in the Family Law (Scotland) Act 2006 although it might be argued this was simply due to widespread acceptance that cohabitation contracts were lawful and enforceable.

---

[30] Scot Law Com, *Report on Family Law*, No 135, 1992, at para. 16.46.

SLOVAKIA

No, there are no specific rules concerning agreements between partners in an informal relationship. In answering this question we could point to the general rules of Slovak civil law. Legal doctrine defines Slovak civil law as a branch of law which generally regulates property relationships and personal relationships associated with property relationships. In civil-law relationships, the parties enjoy an equal position and autonomy.[31] The Slovak Civil Code indirectly lays down the principle of freedom of contract in § 2 para. 3. The principle of freedom of contract consists of 'the freedom to contract or not to contract' (*zmluvná voľnosť – sloboda*).[32] Freedom of contract is recognised as being limited by the general provisions of the Slovak Civil Code. These are the general provisions on the voidability of a legal transaction that violates a statutory prohibition, unless the law implies otherwise, and on the voidability of a transaction which is contrary to good morals. In an objective sense, good moral protection is perceived as being the method which is used to moralise contractual relationships, and to temper the inequalities that could result from the dogma of the autonomy theory (autonomy of will). In a subjective sense, good morals aim to protect the mistaken belief of one contracting party, and to give effect to appearances. The primary cause of uncertainty remains, even today, the general absence of a definition in Slovak civil law. The concept of good morals seems to generate more interest based on its function than on its definition. The protection of good morals is therefore usually said to be an open norm, a norm the content of which cannot be established in an abstract way but which depends on the circumstances of the case in which it must be applied, and which must be established through concretisation. It is the judge in Slovakia who can determinate the content of good morals. It is the judge who can balance the 'harmony' between autonomy and good morals. The balancing depends on the circumstances of the case and on the personality of the judge deciding the case.

Generally, unlawful contracts are considered to be void. This means that the unlawfulness or immorality of the agreements between the partners in an informal relationship can be sanctioned by declaring that the acts which are contrary to legal mandatory provisions and morality are void.

---

31 Under the European meaning of autonomy (freedom) See principally M. JANČO, in: M. JANČO et al. (eds.), *Európske súkromné právo* (European Private Law), EUROIURIS, Bratislava, 2012, at p. 178.

32 J. LAZAR, in: J. LAZAR et al. (eds.), *Občianske právo hmotné* (Substantive Slovak Civil Law), Iuris Libri, Bratislava, 2014, at p. 18.

It is therefore the concept of morality, understood in a specific sense, which constitutes an important limit on the freedom of contract.

SLOVENIA

There are no specific rules for agreements between extramarital partners but the general rules regulating agreements between spouses apply.

SPAIN

The Spanish Civil Code does not include any reference either to civil partnerships or informal relationships. There is a consensus that partners may agree on issues about their relationship or break-up, which would be valid on the grounds of the principle of liberty and the person's free development of personality (in Art. 10 Spanish Constitution), and the principle of equality (Art. 14 Spanish Constitution). Article 1323 of the Spanish Civil Code allows married couples to enter into agreements, and it is thought that members of a partnership should be able to do so as well. The Spanish Supreme Court has upheld the validity of agreements on patrimonial aspects made by partners in informal relationships since 1992. In particular, see STS 18 May 1992 and 21 October 1992.

Any agreement between informal partners would have to comply with Art. 1255 Spanish Civil Code on the validity of agreements, in general, which states that 'contracting parties may establish the pacts, clauses and conditions they deem advisable, provided they are not contrary to the law, morals, or public policy'.

Married couples are free to enter into agreements, within certain limits. These limits would also be applicable to informal relationships. Some are set out in the Spanish Constitution, such as the principle of equality of spouses (Art. 32), and the protection of children, regardless of legal filiation (Art. 39). The Spanish Civil Code also includes these principles, such as equality in rights and duties of spouses (Art. 66).

The Catalan Civil Code specifically allows partners in informal partnerships to enter into agreements to regulate the consequences of cohabitation (Art. 234-3.1), as well as the consequences of break-up (Art. 234-5).

SWEDEN

There is a general freedom for cohabitees, just as for anyone else, to enter into agreements with each other. The agreements are covered by the general rules on the law of obligations.

Swedish law contains a special regulation in the Swedish Cohabitation Act on what is commonly referred to as a 'cohabitation agreement'. Even if this term appears to be of a more general scope, it is limited to an agreement between the cohabiting couple whereby they exclude or limit the scope of application of the rules on the division of 'cohabitation property', § 9 para. 1. By concluding a new agreement of this kind the cohabitees may alter their previous agreement, for example, by setting it aside. It follows that the provisions of the Swedish Cohabitation Act on the division of 'cohabitation property', i.e., the joint dwelling and household goods acquired for the couple's joint use, are default rules, applicable only when not otherwise agreed by the partners.

The above-mentioned cohabitation agreement can be further defined. According to § 9 para. 1, a cohabiting couple or a couple who plan to begin a cohabitation relationship may agree that there is to be no division of property or that some specific property, which otherwise would qualify as 'cohabitation property', is not to be included in a property division. A 'cohabitation agreement' is equivalent to a marital property agreement (in Swedish: *äktenskapsförord*), which under the Swedish Marriage Code can likewise be used to achieve a total or partial exclusion of the spouses' legal rights to each other's so-called marital property (in Swedish: *giftorättsgods*) which is, according to the main rule, to be included in the property division. Whereas a marital property agreement must be registered in order to receive legal effect, the Swedish Cohabitation Act does not provide for the registration of a cohabitation agreement; this also precludes the possibility of registering it in the same way as marital property agreements in Sweden.

SWITZERLAND

There are no specific rules concerning agreements between partners in an informal relationship.

Hence, the general rules with regard to contracts will apply, such as the legal rules on the abuse of a right (Art. 2 para. 2 Swiss Civil Code), the legal rules on nullity (Art. 20 Swiss Code of Obligations) or especially the legal rules on the protection of legal personality against excessive restrictions (Art. 27 Swiss Civil Code).[33] Furthermore, no particular form has to be observed, unless a particular form is required by law (Art. 11 Swiss Code of Obligations).

Generally, the partners in an informal relationship have a large degree of freedom with regard to such agreements. However, some questions with regard to the extent of such agreements have not yet been clarified and decided, such as questions regarding the duration of support obligations or a global reference to marriage law or to a marital property regime.[34] Furthermore, partners in an informal relationship may be limited with regard to questions concerning third parties or the state (e.g. parties cannot assign a lease contract to one partner without the consent of the landlord).

---

33 P. LIATOWITSCH and A. RUMO-JUNGO, 'Nichteheliche Lebensgemeinschaft: vermögens- und kindesrechtliche Belange', *Die Praxis des Familienrechts*, 2004, at p. 895, 903.

34 A. BÜCHLER, 'Vermögensrechtliche Probleme in der nichtehelichen Lebensgemeinschaft', in: A. RUMO-JUNGO and P. PICHONNAZ, *Familienvermögensrecht*, Stämpfli, Bern, 2003, at p. 59, 68 et seq.; H. HAUSHEER, T. GEISER and R. AEBI-MÜLLER, *Das Familienrecht des Schweizerischen Zivilgesetzbuches*, Stämpfli, Bern, 2014, at N 03.13.

QUESTION 58

Are partners in an informal relationship permitted to agree on the following issues:

a. The division of tasks as between the partners?

b. The contributions to the costs and expenses of the household?

c. Their property relationship?

d. Maintenance?

e. The duration of the agreement?

AUSTRIA

a. The division of tasks as between the partners?

By concluding a partnership agreement the partners can lay down their property and/or personal relations. A partnership agreement may regulate the partners' life together during the relationship or may merely determine the consequences in case of separation.[1] If mainly personal relations are governed by the partnership agreement, it should be noted that such an agreement is allowed as long as it does not interfere with the highly personal sphere of one of the partners, but it cannot be enforced. Accordingly, partners in an informal relationship can agree upon the household organization and a division of tasks, but should be aware of the fact that such an agreement is not enforceable.[2]

b. The contributions to the costs and expenses of the household?

The partners may, for example, agree that one partner is responsible for the daily expenses, e.g. paying the rent or telephone bill and purchasing

1 See A. DEIXLER-HÜBNER and H. SCHÄFFER, *Partnerschaft ohne Trauschein*, Linde, Vienna, 2014, at p. 102 et seq.

2 A. DEIXLER-HÜBNER and H. SCHÄFFER, *Partnerschaft ohne Trauschein*, Linde, Vienna, 2014, at p. 103.

the food, whereas the other partner repays a loan.[3] Hence, it is up to the parties how they distribute the household costs and expenses and who bears which share. In particular, it should be noted that – without a respective agreement on this issue – the partner bearing the costs caused by daily life is not entitled to claim unjust enrichment in the case of separation, because these costs are considered to be complimentary.[4] In contrast, the partner making 'long-term' investments, such as paying the monthly instalments, may reclaim his/her costs.[5] Since the application of the rules on unjust enrichment do not lead to a satisfactory result in this regard, an agreement on the contribution to the costs and expenses of the household seems to be vital.

c. Their property relationship?

The main purpose of concluding a partnership agreement is to regulate property relations as between the parties. It is recommended to maintain different lists of all movables, which provide information on the ownership of the items, e.g. that every partner remains the sole owner of 'his/her' items.[6] Such a list needs to be updated regularly. If assets are jointly purchased, a community of goods can be agreed upon.[7] A clause regarding community of goods – which is considered to be the main element of partnership agreements[8] – secures a fair distribution of the assets in case of separation. Further, the partners may wish to agree with whom the assets should remain and how the other partner is compensated for them in case of separation.[9] Moreover, the partners can reach an agreement on how they deal with financial investments.[10] Hence, under Austrian law partners in an informal relationship are permitted to agree on comprehensive rules concerning their property relationship.

---

[3] U. AICHHORN, *Das Recht der Lebenspartnerschaften, Ehe und Lebensgemeinschaft*, Springer, Vienna, 2003, at p. 427.

[4] B. LURGER, 'section 1435 General Austrian Civil Code', in: A. KLETEČKA and M. SCHAUER, *ABGB-ON 1.02*, Manz Verlag, Vienna, 2014, at marg. No. 8.

[5] U. AICHHORN, *Das Recht der Lebenspartnerschaften, Ehe und Lebensgemeinschaft*, Springer, Vienna, 2003, at p. 427.

[6] U. AICHHORN, *Das Recht der Lebenspartnerschaften, Ehe und Lebensgemeinschaft*, Springer, Vienna, 2003, at p. 429.

[7] U. AICHHORN, *Das Recht der Lebenspartnerschaften, Ehe und Lebensgemeinschaft*, Springer, Vienna, 2003, at p. 429.

[8] E. MÖSCHL, *Die nichteheliche Lebensgemeinschaft*, LexisNexis ARD ORAC, Vienna, 2007, at marg. No. 36.

[9] A. DEIXLER-HÜBNER, 'Partnerschaftsverträge – Rechtliche Grenzen und möglicher Regelungsinhalt', *iFamZ*, 2008, at p. 337; cf. U. AICHHORN, 'Vermögensaufteilung und Erbrecht bei nichtehelicher Lebensgemeinschaft', in: M. GRUBER et al. (eds.), *Erbrecht und Vermögensnachfolge*, Verlag Österreich, Vienna, 2010, at marg. No. 5.

[10] E. MÖSCHL, *Die nichteheliche Lebensgemeinschaft*, LexisNexis ARD ORAC, Vienna, 2007, at marg. No. 37.

d. Maintenance?

Partners in an informal relationship are not entitled to claim maintenance, neither during their relationship nor after its termination. Therefore, partners may reach an agreement on maintenance during the relationship as well as for the period after their separation.[11] In the case of separation a maintenance agreement is qualified as a promise to donate in the future and therefore requires a notarial deed in order to be valid. Moreover, it should be noted that maintenance agreements which unreasonably restrict the economic freedom of one partner, because e.g. the payments are life-threatening, are contrary to public morals pursuant to S. 879 para. 1 General Austrian Civil Code and are thus void.[12]

e. The duration of the agreement?

Due to the principle of freedom of contract the parties can also agree on the duration of the agreement. Generally, the partnership agreement does not automatically end with concluding a marriage or the separation of the partners. The partners themselves can agree on the point in time when the partnership agreement should be terminated.[13] If the partners agree that the validity of the contract terminates in case of separation, it is recommended to confirm in writing the official end of the relationship in order to avoid problems in clarifying this point in time.[14] Particularly with regard to clauses regulating maintenance in case of separation a temporal limitation of this obligation should be agreed upon.[15] Further, since the property relations of the partners will change over the years, the partnership agreement should be revised from time to time - preferably by a lawyer or a notary - in order to reflect the current situation as best as possible.[16]

---

11 U. AICHHORN, *Das Recht der Lebenspartnerschaften, Ehe und Lebensgemeinschaft*, Springer, Vienna, 2003, at p.426.

12 A. DEIXLER-HÜBNER, *Scheidung, Ehe und Lebensgemeinschaft*, LexisNexis ARD ORAC, Vienna, 2013, at marg. No. 252a.

13 N. OSWALD and A. SCHMALLEGGER, 'Partnerschaftsvertrag zwischen nichtehelichen Lebensgefährten', *EF-Z*, 2013, at p. 17.

14 E. MÖSCHL, *Die nichteheliche Lebensgemeinschaft*, LexisNexis ARD ORAC, Vienna, 2007, at marg. No. 43.

15 E. MÖSCHL, *Die nichteheliche Lebensgemeinschaft*, LexisNexis ARD ORAC, Vienna, 2007, at marg. No. 36.

16 E. MÖSCHL, *Die nichteheliche Lebensgemeinschaft*, LexisNexis ARD ORAC, Vienna, 2007, at marg. No. 43.

BELGIUM

a. The division of tasks as between the partners?

A cohabitation agreement may state which tasks each of the partners performs with a view to agreeing on the consequences of that division, for example by taking into account services in kind as a contribution to the household expenses. In our opinion, the agreement cannot contractually oblige the performance of certain tasks as this would limit the partners' personal freedom and violate public policy.

b. The contributions to the costs and expenses of the household?

Yes, they can agree on costs and expenses both directly and indirectly. They can firstly determine a formula for the contribution, through a shared account or not, in various cost items.[17] They can do so by referring to the rules which are applicable to spouses or legal cohabitants.[18] Secondly, they can determine that household debts are joint debts,[19] which is important both for *obligatio* – vis-à-vis third parties – and *contributio*. Thirdly, they can appoint each other as the agent vis-à-vis household debts.[20]

c. Their property relationship?

Yes. They can agree to create a conventional joint ownership or agree on the applicable means of evidence of ownership, for example with a presumption of the joint ownership of household goods. These agreements are valid between partners but are not opposable by third parties.[21] They can also conclude a tenancy for one partner in the solely owned property of the other partner.[22]

d. Maintenance?

Yes, both for the period during the cohabitation as well as upon separation or death.[23] For some purposes, such as the competence of the Family Court (Art. 572bis, 7° Belgian Code of Civil Proceedings), the

---

17 W. Pintens, C. Declerck, J. Du Mongh, K. Vanwinckelen, *Familiaal vermogensrecht*, Intersentia, Antwerp, 2010, at n° 1009.

18 S. Eggermont, *De juridische bescherming van private relaties*, PhD, University of Antwerp, 2015, at n° 178.

19 W. Pintens, C. Declerck, J. Du Mongh, K. Vanwinckelen, *Familiaal vermogensrecht*, Intersentia, Antwerp, 2010, at n° 1011.

20 W. Pintens, C. Declerck, J. Du Mongh, K. Vanwinckelen, *Familiaal vermogensrecht*, Intersentia, Antwerp, 2010, at n° 1014.

21 P. Senaeve, *Compendium van het personen- en familierecht*, Acco, Leuven, 2013, at n°s 2042, 2045 and 2067.

22 Justice of the Peace Charleroi (2) 20 January 2009, *T. Vred.* 2011, 373.

23 S. Eggermont, *De juridische bescherming van private relaties*, PhD, University of Antwerp, 2015, at n° 257.

partners must qualify payments as maintenance. Indeed, payments may also have another legal basis such as a contribution to the expenses of the former household.[24]

e. The duration of the agreement?
Yes, insofar as such an agreement does not restrict personal freedom. The agreement must be for a definite period or the parties must be entitled to terminate it.

BULGARIA

a. The division of tasks as between the partners?
The partners in an informal relationship are permitted to agree on the division of tasks between them.

b. The contributions to the costs and expenses of the household?
The partners in an informal relationship may agree on any contributions towards the costs and expenses of the household.

c. Their property relationship?
If the partners in an informal relationship would like to agree on their property relationship, they have to follow the general regulations with regard to the form of a contract.

d. Maintenance?
Maintenance can be agreed upon under a maintenance and care contract, which creates mutual obligations.

e. The duration of the agreement?
Determining the duration of such an agreement is up to the partners.

CROATIA

In line with Art. 11 paragraph 2 of the Croatian Family Act and Art. 4 paragraph 2 and Art. 54 of the Croatian Partnership Act, the answer equally relates to both cohabitants and same-sex informal partners.

---

[24] Justice of the Peace Etterbeek 2 June 2008, *T.Vred.* 2010, 235.

a. The division of tasks as between the partners?
Although there is no special legal provision prescribing this, partners in an informal relationship are permitted to agree on the division of tasks as between themselves.

b. The contributions to the costs and expenses of the household?
Although there is no special legal provision prescribing this, partners in an informal relationship are permitted to agree on the contributions to the costs and expenses of the household.

c. Their property relationship?
According to Art. 40 in relation to Art. 11 of the Croatian Family Act and Art. 53 in relation to Art. 4 of the Croatian Partnership Act, partners in an informal relationship are permitted to agree on their property relationship.

d. Maintenance?
According to Art. 302 of the Croatian Family Act and Art. 39 in relation to Art. 4 of the Croatian Partnership Act, partners in an informal relationship are permitted to agree on maintenance.

e. The duration of the agreement?
Although there is no special legal provision prescribing this, partners in an informal relationship are permitted to agree on the duration of the agreement.

CZECH REPUBLIC

a. The division of tasks as between the partners?
Partners in an informal relationship are permitted to agree on the division of tasks as between the partners. This agreement could be oral as well as written according to S. 1746/2 Czech Civil Code: parties may also conclude a contract which is not specifically regulated as a type of contract.

b. The contributions to the costs and expenses of the household?
Partners in an informal relationship are permitted to agree on the contributions to costs and expenses of the household. This agreement could be oral as well as written according to S. 1746/2 Czech Civil Code: parties may also conclude a contract which is not specifically regulated as a type of contract.

c. Their property relationship?
Partners in an informal relationship are permitted to agree on their property relationship. This agreement could be oral as well as written according to S. 1746/2 Czech Civil Code: parties may also conclude a contract which is not specifically regulated as a type of contract.

d. Maintenance?
Partners in an informal relationship are permitted to agree on maintenance. This agreement is set out in S. 2701 Czech Civil Code: by a contract for pension, a payer undertakes to pay regular pecuniary benefits (pension) to a beneficiary.

e. The duration of the agreement?
Partners in an informal relationship are permitted to agree on the duration of the agreement. This agreement could be oral as well as written according to S. 1746/2 Czech Civil Code: parties may also conclude a contract which is not specifically regulated as a type of contract.

DENMARK

a. The division of tasks as between the partners?
An agreement on the division of household tasks during cohabitation will presumably be valid in principle, but it will be difficult to sanction the other party for any breach of the agreement. The possible justification for such an agreement rests primarily on the attention which the parties thereby devote to practical matters and the moral obligation to abide by the agreement.[25] If a couple have arranged matters so that one party is employed in the other's business, there can be a need to agree the terms of employment, including pay. Such an agreement will be valid between the parties and in relation to the tax authorities etc.[26]

b. The contributions to the costs and expenses of the household?
In a cohabitation contract the parties can give each other the authority to act on their behalf in legal relations. E.g. they can agree that, while cohabiting, either cohabitant shall be entitled to enter into such contracts with a third party for the purpose of meeting day-to-day household needs or the children's needs, with liability for both spouses.

---

25 See V. VINDELØV, I. LUND-ANDERSEN and L. NIELSEN, *Retsstillingen for ugifte samlevende*, Gads Forlag, Copenhagen, 1988, at p. 230.

26 V. VINDELØV, I. LUND-ANDERSEN and L. NIELSEN, *Retsstillingen for ugifte samlevende*, Gads Forlag, Copenhagen, 1988, at p. 231-232.

c. Their property relationship?
Cohabitants cannot generally make a marriage-like arrangement for the ownership of their property, but they can enter into specific agreements about their property relationships. For example, they can make a joint ownership agreement concerning a specific asset, typically the ownership of a residence. Agreements on the joint ownership of several assets can be included in a more comprehensive cohabitation contract in which the parties agree on all the financial circumstances that can be expected to be relevant during their cohabitation and upon its possible termination, including sharing expenditures, liabilities, mutual claims, etc.

d. Maintenance?
It is possible for a couple to make an agreement according to which the partner who is able to support him/herself after separation undertakes to pay contributions to the other partner who is unable to do so, at least for a transitional period. Such agreements are valid as long as they have the necessary clarity.[27]

e. The duration of the agreement?
Yes, it is possible to put a time limit on ordinary property law contracts.

ENGLAND AND WALES

a. The division of tasks as between the partners?
Yes this can be agreed and would normally form part of the agreement's recital but this cannot be specifically enforced.

b. The contributions to the costs and expenses of the household?
Yes.

c. Their property relationship?
Yes.

d. Maintenance?
Yes.

e. The duration of the agreement?
Yes.

---

27 See H.V. GODSK PEDERSEN and I. LUND-ANDERSEN, *Family Law in Denmark*, Kluwer Law International, Alphen aan den Rijn, 2011, at p. 80.

ESTONIA

a. The division of tasks as between the partners?

In civil issues, the partners in an informal relationship are treated as unmarried persons; they are free to enter into agreements regarding the division of obligations.

b. The contributions to the costs and expenses of the household?

In civil issues, the partners in an informal relationship are free to enter into agreements regarding their respective contributions to the costs and expenses of the household.

c. Their property relationship?

Assets acquired during the cohabitation shall be acquired according to the general rules of property law, i.e. either under the sole ownership of each partner or common ownership. In addition, it can be noted that with regard to agreements between spouses, in its decision of September 25, 2013, the Supreme Court found that in the case of agreements between the spouses with regard to the distribution of property where the result of the distribution and the value of the property received by one spouse are made dependent on a remarriage by this spouse or him or her finding a new partner to the effect that, in such a case, the spouse would then forfeit the property either partially or fully, this substantially restricts the free self-realization of the person and the right to marry and establish a family. According to the Chamber, such agreements are contrary to good morals within the meaning of § 86(1) of the General Part of the Estonian Civil Code Act as they illicitly restrict the fundamental rights of this spouse.[28]

d. Maintenance?

The partners in an informal relationship may conclude support contracts between themselves. Part 5 of the Estonian Law of Obligations Act deals with Support Contracts. Supporting a party to a maintenance contract or a third party by providing the necessary means of subsistence and, in the case of a maintenance contract, also via guaranteeing care is characteristic of support contracts.[29] A life annuity contract and a maintenance contract are both support contracts. In a life annuity contract one person undertakes to pay, on a periodic basis, a specific sum of money or to deliver other objects which are limited by specific characteristics to the

---

28 Decision of the Civil Chamber of the Supreme Court 3-2-1-83-13, para. 17; 3-2-1-149-11, at para. 18.

29 P. VARUL, I. KULL, V. KÕVE and M. KÄERDI, *Võlaõigusseadus II. Kommenteeritud väljaanne* (Law of Obligations II. Commented Edition), Juura, Tallinn, 2007, at p. 615 (in Estonian).

other party. In a maintenance contract, the maintenance provider undertakes to maintain the other party and to take care of him/her.

e. The duration of the agreement?
In civil issues, the partners in an informal relationship are treated as unmarried persons and they are free to enter into agreements. A transaction which is contrary to good morals or public order is void (§ 86(1) General Part of the Estonian Civil Code Act).

FINLAND

a. The division of tasks as between the partners?
Yes.

b. The contributions to the costs and expenses of the household?
Yes.

c. Their property relationship?
Yes.

d. Maintenance?
Yes.

e. The duration of the agreement?
Yes.

FRANCE

a. The division of tasks as between the partners?
Some assets, rights or interests are excluded from the scope of such a contract.[30] Personal duties (*obligations de nature personnelle*) cannot be imposed on one person by means of a contract;[31] indeed specific legal provisions determines this issue.[32] Cohabitation has no legal impact on the civil status of a person (*état des personnes*) and this cannot be altered by means of a contract. A cohabitation contract (*convention de concubinage*)

---

30 Art. 1128 of the French Civil Code. For example, the civil status of an individual (*état des personnes*) is excluded from a contract and the right to use one's family name cannot be transferred by contract to the cohabitant.

31 www.notaires.fr/fr/lunion-libre-ou-concubinage.

32 For example, a duty of fidelity cannot be laid down in a contract between cohabitants. Any restriction on matrimonial freedom within such an agreement would legally vitiate that contract.

can only aim at organizing the finances and property between the cohabitants. The division of tasks is naturally excluded from the contractual sphere. If such an agreement were intended, this would not be a contract and it could not be enforcement.

On the particular point of the division of tasks within the family, the 2014 Act on Male and Female Equality[33] was preceded by a Recommendation Report by the Social Affairs Committee (*Commission des affaires sociales*), delivered on 23 July 2013, that specifically pointed to the permanent inequality of the division of tasks between men and women within a family to the disadvantage of women who still bear the major part of such tasks.[34] This disequilibrium exists regardless of the matrimonial situation of the couple in question, whether they be married, partners or cohabitants.

b. The contributions to the costs and expenses of the household?

Cohabitants have no claim by one against the other for a contribution towards the costs and expenses of the household; only spouses and partners bound by a *Pacs* have such a reciprocal obligation.[35] But cohabitation contracts are nevertheless legal and are governed by the general principles of contract law.[36] They are legally enforceable as either private agreements or authentic contracts.

However, case law limits the scope of such a contract where it contradicts the public order provisions when organising the parental duty to maintain one's children. Indeed, in a 2006 case,[37] a cohabitation contract was nullified by the court because the agreement organizing the parental contribution to the maintenance of the common children after separation had been concluded without considering the resources of the debtor and the needs of the children, but rather on the basis of a fixed allowance amounting to half of the debtor's earnings. The court held that this contract contradicted not only the public order provisions organizing the

---

33 Act no. 2014-873 of 4 August 2014.

34 See the report at p. 27 et seq. The report is available at: www.senat.fr/rap/a12-794/a12-7941.pdf. For more details see the demographic study by A. REGNIER-LOILIER, 'L'arrivée d'un enfant modifie-t-elle la répartition des tâches domestiques au sein du couple?', *Population et Société*, 2009, available at: www.ined.fr/fichier/s_rubrique/19129/popetsoc_461.fr.pdf.

35 Art. 214 of the French Civil Code (spouses) and Art. 515-4 of the French Civil Code (registered partners).

36 Art. 1108 et seq. of the French Civil Code.

37 Cass. Civ 1 20 June 2006, no. 05-17465.

duty to maintain one's children, but also individual rights in that it deterred the debtor from separating with the creditor.

c. Their property relationship?

Such cohabitation contracts (*convention de concubinage*) are legal and are governed by the general principles of contract law.[38] They are legally enforceable as either private agreements or authentic contracts. However, where the donation or the sale of real estate is determined or regulated in a cohabitation contact, the document must comply with specific legal provisions regarding formal requirements and taxation provisions.

d. Maintenance?

No right to maintenance exists between cohabitants (see Question 34 et seq.). According to Art. 1235 of the French Civil Code, any payment must be justified by a pre-existing debt. As no maintenance obligation exists between them, no debt can support any payment made for the benefit of one cohabitant or the other. Any payment made without due cause is recoverable except where the payment has been made so as to fulfil a moral duty (*obligation naturelle*).[39]

However, the case law is very strict on this issue and any novation of the moral duty into a legal obligation must be proved.[40] Proof can amount to a written document encompassing the novation or the implementation of the obligation (*commencement d'exécution*).[41] This requirement must be fulfilled except where the creditor has been unable to obtain a written document from the debtor[42] or where the parties have waived their right to have an acknowledgment of a debt, amounting to over €1500, included in a written document.[43]

Recent case law[44] has limited the effect of such an agreement, although it is in the form of a written contract regulating the 'termination of cohabitation' (*contrat de fin de concubinage*), where the obligation laid down in the contract exceeds that which could emanate from a moral duty. In this particular 2011 case the contract regulating the termination of cohabitation provided for the payment of a life allowance for the benefit of the female cohabitant. The amount of this allowance was

---

38 Art. 1108 et seq. of the French Civil Code.
39 Art. 1235 of the French Civil Code.
40 See Cass. Civ 1, 23 May 2006, no. 04-19099; Cass. Civ. 1 29 June 2011, no. 10-12018.
41 Cass. Civ 1 28 June 1954, Bull. civ. I, no. 214.
42 Paris Court of Appeal, 9 April 1957, D. 1957, 455.
43 Art. 1134 of the French Civil Code.
44 Cass. Civ 1, 29 June 2011, no. 10-12018.

determined in advance without any consideration being given to the needs of the creditor. Additionally, a commitment to pay the rent of her home before the implementation of the allowance had been agreed upon by the parties.

e. The duration of the agreement?

The general principles of contract law govern the duration of the agreement, within the limits of the public order provisions. Considering the recent case law on cohabitation contracts, it could be contemplated that where the agreed duration of the performance of such a contract would exceed that which could be expected from a moral duty, such an agreement could eventually be nullified.

GERMANY

a. The division of tasks as between the partners?

As there is no case law in this regard, the views in legal literature differ. Some scholars are of the opinion that agreements concerning the division of tasks between the partners do not have any legal effect.[45] Others argue that as long as the aforementioned rules (Question 57) are respected, the partners to an informal relationship can make a legally binding agreement on the division of tasks (e.g. shared housekeeping).[46]

b. The contributions to the costs and expenses of the household?

The contributions to costs and expenses of the household can be agreed upon in a partnership agreement.[47]

c. Their property relationship?

Partners to an informal relationship may agree upon their property relationship in accordance with the general rules. Agreements may contain for example provisions concerning the contribution or acquisition of assets and therefore specify if the partners want to acquire alone or as co-owners (see Question 41). Furthermore, the partners may decide to use the mechanisms of partnership law (§§ 705 et seq., §§ 718 et seq. German Civil Code) to create joint rights of participation.

---

45 M. WELLENHOFER, 'Anh. zu § 1302', in: *Münchener Kommentar zum Bürgerlichen Gesetzbuch*, Beck, Munich, 2013, at No. 48; R. HAUSMANN, *Nichteheliche Lebensgemeinschaft und Vermögensausgleich*, Beck, Munich, 1989, at p. 90.

46 H. GRZIWOTZ, *Nichteheliche Lebensgemeinschaft*, Beck, Munich, 2014, at § 16 No. 2.

47 H. GRZIWOTZ, *Nichteheliche Lebensgemeinschaft*, Beck, Munich, 2014, at § 16 No. 13 et seq.

d. Maintenance?
Partners to an informal relationship may agree upon maintenance. A partnership agreement may contain maintenance obligations for the existing partnership as well as maintenance obligations after separation.[48] However, the amount of the maintenance obligation after separation must be appropriate and may not function as a contractual penalty (see also Question 58e).[49]

e. The duration of the agreement?
The informal partnership may be terminated at any time. This principle cannot be undermined by an agreement. Therefore it is expressly prohibited to agree upon a contractual penalty in the case of the dissolution of the partnership.[50] A contractual penalty was, for instance, assumed in a case where one partner to an informal relationship was forced to pay a certain amount of money upon the dissolution of the relationship and the payment could not explained on the grounds of compensation for disadvantages suffered during the relationship.[51]

GREECE

a. The division of tasks as between the partners?
Yes.

b. The contributions to the costs and expenses of the household?
Yes.

c. Their property relationship?
Yes.

d. Maintenance?
Yes. In this respect a lifetime income may be agreed (Art. 840-843 Greek Civil Code).

e. The duration of the agreement?
Yes.

---

48 M. LÖHNIG, 'Anh. zu §§ 1297 et seq.', in: J. VON STAUDINGER, *Kommentar zum Bürgerlichen Gesetzbuch*, Sellier-de-Gruyter, Berlin, 2012, at No. 33.
49 OLG Hamm, 24.03.1987, *NJW*, 1988, 2474; OLG Köln, 22.11.2000, *FamRZ*, 2001, 1608.
50 M. LÖHNIG, 'Anh. zu §§ 1297 et seq.', in: J. VON STAUDINGER, *Kommentar zum Bürgerlichen Gesetzbuch*, Sellier-de-Gruyter, Berlin, 2012, at No. 31.
51 OLG Hamm, 24.03.1987, *NJW*, 1988, 2474.

HUNGARY

a. The division of tasks as between the partners?
There is no such rule in the Hungarian Civil Code.

b. The contributions to the costs and expenses of the household?
There is no such rule in the Hungarian Civil Code.

c. Their property relationship?
They can enter into a property agreement for the future, see the answer to Question 47.

When the community of life terminates they may regulate their property relations with agreement.

d. Maintenance?
According to the general provisions on the maintenance of relatives which constitute the basic rules underlying specific maintenance rules, including maintenance rules concerning cohabitants, the creditor and debtor can agree on the amount of and the method for paying maintenance. [52] Within the rules on family law consequences the Hungarian Civil Code emphasises one possibility, namely cohabitants may agree that the debtor can meet his or her maintenance obligation by making a lump-sum payment or by giving a certain asset. In such a case the creditor cannot claim any additional maintenance in the future.[53]

e. The duration of the agreement?
In a property agreement between cohabitants or when cohabitants agree on the maintenance of either former cohabitant the duration of the agreement may be determined.

REPUBLIC OF IRELAND

The above rules indicate that none of these issues would be outside the acceptable limits of such an agreement.

52 Art. 4:204 of the Hungarian Civil Code.
53 Art. 4:89 of the Hungarian Civil Code.

ITALY

According to Art. 1322 of the Italian Civil Code entitled 'Contract autonomy', '[p]arties can freely determine the content of the contract, within the limits imposed by the law'. Informal partners can therefore:[54]

- plan their contribution to their common life, dividing tasks between themselves;
- quantify the contributions of each partner to the costs and expenses of the household;
- choose criteria to identify the owner or owners of the assets acquired during the relationship. They can even establish community or separation of property regimes for those assets. They can also assign the right of use to one partner of the other's property. Moreover, they can agree on the way in which the family home will be used, irrespective of its being owned by only one partner or by both, or it being leased;
- determine the consequences of the break-up of the partnership as regards properties and maintenance.
- they cannot, however, agree on time limits to their relationship because that, being a non-patrimonial provision, would be in conflict with Art. 1174 Italian Civil Code.[55]

The agreement may also contain provisions regarding reciprocal assistance in case of physical or mental illness or their mutual appointment of the other as a guardian in the event of disability (*amministratore di sostegno*).

The agreement cannot, however, contain post-death provisions, which in the Italian legal system are reserved for wills.

LATVIA

In Latvia there is no special legal order on partners in an informal relationship. Therefore the general law of obligations of the Latvian Civil Law is applicable. The general law of obligations does not prohibit partners from entering into various types of agreements, provided that

[54] On this topic, among many authors, see R. BASSETTI, *Contratti di convivenza e di unione civile*, Giappichelli, Turin, 2014, at passim. The jargon-free site www.contrattidi convivenza.it is published by the Consiglio Nazionale del Notariato to foster the wider use of agreements among partners.

[55] Compare G. OBERTO, *I diritti dei conviventi. Realtà e prospettive tra Italia ed Europa*, Cedam, Padua, 2012, at p. 100.

their object is not against religion, legislation or moral principles, or directed to go outside the law.

a. The division of tasks as between the partners?
Yes.

b. The contributions to the costs and expenses of the household?
Yes.

c. Their property relationship?
Yes.

d. Maintenance?
Yes.

e. The duration of the agreement?
Yes.

LITHUANIA

a. The division of tasks as between the partners?
No.

b. The contributions to the costs and expenses of the household?
No.

c. Their property relationship?
According to Art. 3.231 of the Lithuanian Civil Code, partners can agree how the assets acquired and used together should be divided after their life together ends. However, the very nature of the institution of a partnership determines that an agreement between cohabitees can regulate much smaller parts of the property relations of the cohabitees (in contrast to the default content of a marriage contract).[56] Therefore Art. 3.231 of the Lithuanian Civil Code clearly defines the scope of such

[56] Article 3.104 of the Lithuanian Civil Code provides for the content of a marriage contract: in their marriage contract the spouses may stipulate different kinds of matrimonial legal regimes; moreover, a marriage contract may regulate the rights and duties related to the management of property, mutual maintenance, participation in the provision of family needs and expenses as well as the procedure for partitioning property upon divorce and other matters related to the spouses' mutual relations in property.

regulation as being limited exclusively to the division of property.[57] On the other hand, there are opinions that state that the content of an agreement between cohabitees could be broader and include other mutual property obligations of the couple.

d. Maintenance?

No.

e. The duration of the agreement?

No. The provisions of Art. 3.231 imply that the duration of an agreement on the property division should be linked to the end of cohabitation or the death of one of the partners. The reason for this is the fact that the assets belonging to each cohabitee do not become the joint property of the couple but remain as the private property of each partner or the joint-partial property of the couple. On the other hand, under the current regulatory regime, the duration of such an agreement is subject to rather diverse interpretations. As there is no Court practice in applying these provisions (Art. 3.229-3.235) it remains unclear when, exactly, an agreement on the division of property signed by cohabitees ceases to be in force: from the moment of starting to live separately or from the moment of the dissolution of their partnership agreement?[58]

LUXEMBOURG

Partners may contract with one another, just as third persons may do, within the framework determined by contract law.

THE NETHERLANDS

a. The division of tasks as between the partners?

Informal partners may make agreements as to the division of tasks. As to the prevalence of such agreements, it must be borne in mind that most cohabitation contracts are drawn up by a notary. It is highly unlikely that a notary will include such a provision in a cohabitation contract. Such provisions do not form part of the default contracts developed and used by notaries.[59] In the theoretical case that such an agreement would be

57 V. MIKELENAS et al., *Commentary on Book Three of the Civil Code of Lithuania* (in Lithuanian), Justitia, Vilnius, 2002, at p. 448.

58 I. KUDINAVIČIŪTĖ, 'Institution of Cohabitation: old or new problem of family law' (in Lithuanian), *Justitia*, No. 3, 2001, at p. 4-5.

59 W.M. SCHRAMA, P. KUIK and L.C.A. VERSTAPPEN, 'Samenlevingsovereenkomsten in de notariële praktijk', *Familie&Recht*, 2014, available at: familieenrecht.nl, at 14.1 and 14.2.

made, this would presumably be unenforceable as being contrary to personal autonomy (Art. 10 para. 1 Dutch Constitution).[60]

b. The contributions to the costs and expenses of the household?

Freedom of contract and party autonomy are the leading principles in this respect. Notarial cohabitation contracts often include a clause on household expenses.[61] Mostly, these contracts seem to use a pro rata division of these costs. In the case of separation, of more importance in practice is the widespread clause in notarial cohabitation contracts that a claim for the reimbursement of costs paid for the household is limited in time, mostly a year.[62] This is especially relevant after a separation of the partners, since claims extend for only a very limited period of time. In many cohabitation contracts such a clause is included.

c. Their property relationship?

Within the limits of property law itself, informal partners have extensive party autonomy. Standard[63] in notarial cohabitation contracts is a provision that specified goods (inventory, movable goods) are owned jointly by the partners.[64] This provision often goes hand in hand with the clause to the effect that at the start of the cohabitation each partner exchanges half of his (movable) goods with half of the goods of the other partner.[65] Both partners will become co-owners of these goods. Finally, partners may give each other a power of attorney to be represented when partner A purchases a certain asset: the asset will be jointly acquired. Often in a list which is attached to the cohabitation contract, private property is registered which will not become jointly owned. Agreements like these are extremely useful in the case of separation.

---

60 See on the implications of this right to personal autonomy in the field of partner relationships: W.M. SCHRAMA, *De niet-huwelijkse samenleving in het Nederlandse en Duitse recht*, Kluwer, Deventer, 2004, at p. 233.

61 W.M. SCHRAMA, P. KUIK and L.C.A. VERSTAPPEN, 'Samenlevingsovereenkomsten in de notariële praktijk', *Familie&Recht*, 2014, available at: familieenrecht.nl, at 14.1 and 14.2

62 P. BLOKLAND, in: W.D. KOLKMAN and L.C.A. VERSTAPPEN (eds.), *Handboek Familie-vermogensrecht*, Walburg Pers, Zutphen, 2013, at 4.2.1.4.

63 W.M. SCHRAMA, P. KUIK and L.C.A. VERSTAPPEN, 'Samenlevingsovereenkomsten in de notariële praktijk', *Familie&Recht*, 2014, available at: familieenrecht.nl, at 14.2.

64 P. BLOKLAND, in: W.D. KOLKMAN and L.C.A. VERSTAPPEN (eds.), *Handboek Familie-vermogensrecht*, Walburg Pers, Zutphen, 2013, at 4.2.5.

65 P. BLOKLAND, in: W.D. KOLKMAN and L.C.A. VERSTAPPEN (eds.), *Handboek Familie-vermogensrecht*, Walburg Pers, Zutphen, 2013, at 4.2.5 and W.M. SCHRAMA, P. KUIK and L.C.A. VERSTAPPEN, 'Samenlevingsovereenkomsten in de notariële praktijk', *Familie& Recht*, 2014, available at: familieenrecht.nl, at 14.2.

d. Maintenance?

Freedom of contract and party autonomy are the leading principles in this respect. However, it seems that in most cohabitation contracts drawn up by a notary no maintenance rights are agreed upon.[66] About 90 percent of the responding notaries indicated that in at most 20 percent of the cohabitation contracts a maintenance right/duty is included. Some respondents almost always include provisions on maintenance.

e. The duration of the agreement?

It is common in cohabitation contracts to define the start (a specific date) and the end. Often a contract ends when one of the partners dies or the relationship breaks down or when they marry or conclude a registered partnership.[67] It seems rare that partners contract for a limited period of time. If they would do so, the 'duty' to cohabit would not be enforceable, as against personal autonomy.

NORWAY

a. The division of tasks as between the partners?

Partners to an informal relationship are permitted to agree on the division of tasks as between the partners. The fact that they agreed on the division of tasks might have legal significance when assessing co-ownership based on indirect contributions.

Another matter to be borne in mind is that agreements on the division of tasks might not be legally enforceable as there is no intention to be legally bound.

b. The contributions to the costs and expenses of the household?

Yes, partners are permitted to agree on the contributions to costs and expenses of the household. According to the Norwegian Supreme Court, the content of such an agreement may affect how the economic benefit is to be calculated when granting compensation on the basis of principles of unjust enrichment.[68]

---

66 W.M. SCHRAMA, P. KUIK and L.C.A. VERSTAPPEN, 'Samenlevingsovereenkomsten in de notariële praktijk', *Familie&Recht*, 2014, available at: familieenrecht.nl, at 14.6.

67 P. BLOKLAND, in: W.D. KOLKMAN and L.C.A. VERSTAPPEN (eds.), *Handboek Familievermogensrecht*, Walburg Pers, Zutphen, 2013, at 4.5.3.

68 Rt. 2011 p. 1176.

c. Their property relationship?
Yes, partners to an informal relationship are permitted to agree on their property relationship. Such contracts will in practice determine the financial settlements upon termination of the relationship.

d. Maintenance?
Yes, partners to an informal relationship are permitted to agree on maintenance.

e. The duration of the agreement?
Yes, partners to an informal relationship are permitted to agree on the duration of the agreement.

PORTUGAL

a. The division of tasks as between the partners?
According to some relevant scholars, these kinds of personal issues belong to the area of fundamental freedom where partners cannot bind each other; the 'cohabitation contracts' are suitable for determining patrimonial matters.

b. The contributions to the costs and expenses of the household?
According to some relevant scholars, these kinds of patrimonial issues may be regulated by a 'cohabitation contract' between the partners.

c. Their property relationship?
According to some relevant scholars, these kinds of patrimonial issues may be regulated by a 'cohabitation contract' between the partners. They can agree, for instance, on the ownership of assets acquired during the common life and the partition of assets.

d. Maintenance?
According to some relevant scholars, these kinds of patrimonial issues may be regulated by a 'cohabitation contract' between the partners. They can agree on maintenance, just as any other persons may have a contract on this issue (Art. 2014 of the Portuguese Civil Code).

e. The duration of the agreement?
According to some relevant scholars, partners can agree on the duration of the agreements they are allowed to make. Of course, they cannot agree on the duration of the cohabitation itself.

RUSSIA

a. The division of tasks as between the partners?

There are no legislative provisions or case law on this matter. In the absence thereof, academic literature suggests that partners in informal relationships can enter into agreements regulating the division of household tasks, and the care for children and other family members.[69]

b. The contributions to the costs and expenses of the household?

Yes.

c. Their property relationship?

Partners can create a regime of joint property by agreement. They can also make specific provision for the possession, use and administration of joint property, and determine whether their shares in joint property should be equal or should depend on their contributions. If no such provision is made, their shares will be regarded as equal. A matrimonial property regime of community of property or any other form of community of property cannot be created by agreement. Partners can also make an agreement on dividing or reallocating their property upon separation.[70]

d. Maintenance?

Partners can make an agreement on maintenance during and after the termination of the relationship.

e. The duration of the agreement?

There are no legal provisions precluding partners from specifying the duration of these agreements. Such agreements are generally entered into for an undetermined period of time and can be dissolved by either partner at any time after sending notification to the other partner.[71]

---

69 С.Ю. ФИЛИППОВА, 'Гражданско-правовые средства достижения цели построения семьи путем фактических брачных отношений', *Семейное и жилищное право*, 2010, at p. 4; В.С. ПАНИН, *Проблемы правового регулирования фактических брачных отношений в России*, dissertation, Moscow, 2012, at p. 85.

70 С.Ю. ФИЛИППОВА, 'Гражданско-правовые средства достижения цели построения семьи путем фактических брачных отношений', *Семейное и жилищное право*, 2010, at p. 4-6.

71 С.Ю. ФИЛИППОВА, 'Гражданско-правовые средства достижения цели построения семьи путем фактических брачных отношений', *Семейное и жилищное право*, 2010, at p. 5.

SCOTLAND

The answer, in theory at least, is that it appears open to partners to an informal relationship to make agreements regulating any or all of these matters. There is nothing expressly stated in Scots law which would restrict such agreements but similarly there is little empirical evidence of their use. Anecdotally it is reported that agreements of various kinds are becoming more common between cohabitants but these are not issues which have been tested before the courts.

a. The division of tasks as between the partners?

There would appear to be nothing to prevent partners entering into such an agreement but it is questionable whether the court would regard it as legally enforceable. The argument might be made that there was no intention to create a legally binding agreement.

b. The contributions to the costs and expenses of the household?

As with all of these issues, there is no empirical evidence either in case law or academic research, demonstrating the use of such agreements. It appears, however, that such agreements are contemplated by statute. S. 27 of the Family Law (Scotland) Act 2006 introduces a presumption of equal ownership where:

> 'Any question arises (whether during or after cohabitation) as to the right of a cohabitant to –
> (a) money derived from any allowance made by either cohabitant for their joint household expenses or for similar purposes; or
> (b) any property acquired out of such money.'[72]

This presumption of equal ownership is however 'subject to any agreement between the cohabitants to the contrary'.[73]

c. Their property relationship?

As above, partners to an informal relationship may make agreement as to their respective property rights. Such an agreement might be used to rebut the statutory presumption in S. 26 of the Family Law (Scotland) Act 2006 to the effect that household assets are owned jointly. It should be remembered however that ownership of heritage depends on registered title and therefore joint ownership cannot be created simply by agreement between the parties.[74]

---

72 Family Law (Scotland) Act 2006, S. 27(1).
73 Family Law (Scotland) Act 2006, S. 27(2).
74 See *Johnston's Trustee v Baird* 2012 CSOH 117.

d. Maintenance?
In principle, there is nothing to prevent a cohabiting couple making an agreement as to maintenance.

e. The duration of the agreement?
There is no specific regulation of the duration of any agreement between cohabitants. Scots law does not distinguish between ante-nuptial, post-nuptial and separation agreements in the context of marriage and therefore it would be unlikely for any restrictions to be placed on cohabitation contracts.

SLOVAKIA

a. The division of tasks as between the partners?
Yes. In divided co-ownership (joint ownership), the co-owners have specific shares in the common assets (§ 137 para. 2 Slovak Civil Code). The co-owners may agree on the cancellation of co-ownership and on a mutual settlement. The settlement agreement must be made in writing if it concerns immovables. In the case of movables, it need not be in writing, but each co-owner must give the other co-owners written confirmation of the settlement if requested to do so (§ 141 Slovak Civil Code). If the co-owners cannot reach an agreement, the co-ownership will be cancelled and settled by the courts upon a petition by any co-owner (§ 142 Slovak Civil Code).

b. The contributions to the costs and expenses of the household?
Yes.

c. Their property relationship?
Yes.

d. Maintenance?
This is very questionable because Slovak law does not grant maintenance to a former partner. It is possible that a judge in Slovakia could declare that such a contract is an unlawful contract and therefore void.

e. The duration of the agreement?
Yes.

SLOVENIA

a. The division of tasks as between the partners?

During the course of an extramarital union, an individual obtains a number of personal rights and duties (for example, the duty or right to mutual respect, trust and assistance). The law only enumerates these rights and duties comparatively since, because of their ethical nature, it is not possible to cover them comprehensively. For this reason, partners also have the greatest possibility to freely shape their relations: for example, by agreeing on the way in which they will cultivate mutual respect for each other, where they will live, in what way they will decide on matters of common concern, how they will organise their household and apportion care for the shared home and children. Such agreements in practice are necessary for the functioning of a harmonious partnership but, because of the ethical nature of the rights that are arranged with such agreements, the partners' regulations cannot coercively enforce assistance, respect, understanding, love and the associated capacity for mutual agreement. The only legal measure that can effectively prevent a violation of the personal rights and duties of the partners is in this case separation.[75]

b. The contributions to the costs and expenses of the household?

This question is dealt with in Slovene law either within the context of maintenance or within the general rules on property relations between extramarital partners.

c. Their property relationship?

The rule on common property has a compulsory nature, so that extra-marital partners may not arrange mutual property relations by means of a contract which is in conflict with this rule and agree that assets created by work during the time of the extramarital union will not be shared. However, they can agree that all individual assets of the partners shall become common property. Because there is no economic benefit, such agreements between the partners are rare in practice.[76]

d. Maintenance?

Extramarital partners may agree between themselves about maintenance in the event of separation. Such an agreement is concluded before a

---

75 See: K. ZUPANČIČ, *Družinsko pravo (Family law)*, Uradni list Republike Slovenije, Ljubljana, 1999, at p. 66.

76 K. ZUPANČIČ, B. NOVAK, E. BRANISELJ, 'Slovénie: chapitre XVIII', in: M. VERWILGHEN and S. MAHIEU (ed.), *Régimes matrimoniaux successions et libéralités dans les relations internationales et internes*, Bruylant, Brussels, 2003.

notary in the form of an enforceable notarial protocol (Art. 81.b of the Slovenian Marriage Act). Partners may conclude an agreement on maintenance in the event of separation before the beginning of the relationship, during the course of the extramarital union or at the time of separation. Partners may also renounce maintenance, but only when the existence of the conditions for maintenance at the time of separation cannot with certainty be anticipated. If the partners at the time of concluding an agreement knew with certainty that one of the partners would require maintenance in the event of separation and because of renouncing the right to maintenance would have to seek social assistance, such an agreement would be null and void. So the conclusion of an agreement on the renunciation of the right to maintenance will only have effect if it is entered into before or during the course of an extramarital union, since at the time of separation it will already be known whether a partner will remain without means of subsistence after the separation. With an agreement on the renunciation of the right to maintenance, the partners may not put at risk the benefit of a child; the partner who renounces maintenance must have sufficient means for her or his subsistence and that of an underage child.

The arrangement for concluding agreements renouncing maintenance and an agreement in which the amount of the maintenance is determined at an exceptionally low level in relation to the capacity of the person who is liable to pay is different. During the course of an extramarital union and the life union connected therewith the general obligation for partners to contribute to the needs of the family applies as well as the obligation to contribute to the support of a partner without his or her own means. This principle derives from the very essence of a partnership as a life union of partners committed to solidarity, and thus it cannot be excluded by agreement.[77]

The right to maintenance ceases if the extramarital partner who receives such maintenance subsequently obtains assets or his or her own income by which he or she can arrange for his or her own subsistence, if he or she concludes a marriage, as well as if he or she enters into an extramarital union (Art. 83 of the Slovenian Marriage Act). Since the law that regulates same-sex unions took effect, the right to maintenance would also be lost if a same-sex union is registered.

---

77 B. NOVAK, 'Neue Regelung des Unterhaltsrechts in der Republik Slowenien', *FamRZ*, No. 19, 2005, at p. 1638.

e. The duration of the agreement?

An agreement can regulate relations within the duration of an extramarital union or relations between the partners after the cessation of the union (for example, an agreement regulating maintenance relations).

SPAIN

a. The division of tasks as between the partners?

There is no provision in the Spanish Civil Code containing any reference to agreements made by partners in an informal relationship. It seems that this could be valid as long as any such agreement was based on the principles of equality.

The Catalan Civil Code allows agreements in a general provision (Art. 234-3), without including any reference to a pact on the division of tasks.

b. The contributions to the costs and expenses of the household?

There is no provision in the Spanish Civil Code containing any reference to agreements made by partners in an informal relationship. This would be an atypical agreement that could be valid as long as it was based on the principles of equality.

The Catalan Civil Code allows agreements in a general provision (Art. 234-3), without any specific reference to a pact on the contributions to costs and expenses of the household.

c. Their property relationship?

There is no provision in the Spanish Civil Code containing any reference to agreements made by partners in an informal relationship. This would be an atypical agreement that could be valid as long as it was based on the principles of equality.

The Catalan Civil Code allows agreements in a general provision (Art. 234-3), without referring specifically to a pact on property relationships. Catalan law allows partners in an informal relationship to buy property with a tontine clause (Art. 234-3.3 Catalan Civil Code).

d. Maintenance?

There is no provision in the Spanish Civil Code containing any reference to agreements made by partners in an informal relationship. This would be an atypical agreement that could be valid as long as it was based on the principles of equality.

The Catalan Civil Code allows agreements made by partners in an informal relationship to regulate the consequences of cohabitation (Art. 234-3.1), as well as the consequences of break-up (Art. 234-5). As regards maintenance, 'agreements to waive maintenance are null and void to the extent that they compromise the ability of the partner entitled thereto to meet his basic needs' (Art. 234-10.2 Catalan Civil Code).

e. The duration of the agreement?

Even though there are no specific provisions in the Spanish Civil Code on informal relationships, an agreement on the duration of the informal relationship would seem to be invalid, on the grounds of public policy. If there is freedom to enter into the relationship, there should be freedom to end it.

The Catalan Civil Code allows agreements to regulate the consequences of cohabitation (Art. 234-3.1), as well as the consequences of break-up (Art. 234-5). An agreement on the duration would seem to be invalid on the grounds of public policy.

SWEDEN

Interestingly enough, the *travaux préparatoires* to the Swedish Cohabitation Act mention that, by concluding agreements with each other, the cohabitees will often be able to create solutions suitable for their relationship.[78] How these agreements may be drafted in order to be legally valid is, however, not specified in the statement. An agreement of a nature other than the specifically defined 'cohabitation agreement' under the Act will be judged according to general principles of the law of obligations.

a. The division of tasks as between the partners?

Cohabitees can agree about division of tasks. Such an agreement does not, however, have any legal effects and it cannot be enforced against the will of one of the partners.

78 Government Bills, Prop. 1986/87:1, p. 99 and Prop. 2002/03:80 p. 32.

b. The contributions to the costs and expenses of the household?

Again, it is possible for cohabitees to enter into agreements about contributions to costs and expenses of the household. During the relationship it is usual that both cohabitees contribute financially to the various costs and expenses of their joint household; usually there is an implied agreement between the cohabitees on this. Certain outlays paid solely by one cohabitee may give rise to a debt relationship.[79] But an outlay can also be a matter of a reasonable contribution to the couple's household costs, which in that case cannot be recovered. Some outlays may give grounds for a claim for joint ownership, when the other partner is formally the holder of the title. Other outlays may be classified as a gift from one partner to the other. Qualifying the legal character of an outlay typically becomes relevant when disputes arise between cohabitants after their relationship has come to an end.[80]

c. Their property relationship?

As has been repeatedly mentioned, the focus of the Swedish Cohabitation Act is on the regulation of so-called 'cohabitation property'. The cohabitees enjoy, nevertheless, the right to exclude a future property division of this property, in whole or in part, in the form of a 'cohabitation agreement'. This resembles what spouses are able to agree in the form of a marital property agreement (see above Question 57).

Apart from agreements relating to the 'cohabitation property', limited in essence to whether, upon the termination of the relationship, certain property acquired for the couple's joint use will be included in a division of property or not, it follows from the general freedom of contract that the cohabitees may also conclude other agreements with each other, inter alia, to control property issues between them. As has been mentioned above (Question 26-28), cohabitees can be considered to be co-owners to property, under presumptions of 'hidden' or 'caveat co-ownership', applicable to couples in formal or informal relationships of cohabitation. This construction reflects a presumption that the cohabitees have agreed on joint ownership in the light of the circumstances of the acquisition.

d. Maintenance?

Cohabitees have no legal duty to maintain each another under Swedish law. An agreement to the effect that a partner is to pay maintenance to

---

79 See M. BRATTSTRÖM, 'Egendomsförhållanden under bestående samboende', in: J. ASLAND et al., *Nordisk samboerrett*, Gyldendal, Oslo, 2014, at p. 106 (see Chapter 2.4.5 in the English version of the book, to be published by Intersentia in 2015).

80 Cf. Ö. TELEMAN, 'Försträckning eller gåva', *Advokaten*, 2014, at p. 40 et seq.

the other, during the relationship or after separation, could be equated to an undertaking to make a gift. The main rule in Swedish law is that an undertaking to make a gift is not binding on the parties. Exceptionally, however, the promise can be binding if it is made either in a written document or if the promise of the gift is made verbally with the intention of making the donor's will public.[81] Cohabitants can make use of the existing possibilities to give gifts to each other. It is, however, uncertain what if anything can be achieved through an agreement on future maintenance.[82] A similar lack of clarity exists as to whether spouses are able, during the course of the marriage, to agree upon post-divorce maintenance should the marriage be dissolved.[83] Considering a general unwillingness in Swedish law to accept legal consequences for unmarried cohabitation that would exceed those of marriage (or are intended to be the same),[84] much speaks against the validity and enforceability of agreements on future maintenance.[85]

e. The duration of the agreement?

The partners are free to enter into an agreement about the duration of the agreements concluded between them, if the agreement as such is valid and enforceable, according to general principles of contract law and the law of obligations. The wording of the Swedish Cohabitation Act § 9, regarding a 'cohabitation agreement' between the partners appears, however, to be limited to a stipulation on exclusion or to the scope of the division of 'cohabitation property'. The parties may, on the other hand, enter into a new agreement about the division of this property. A new agreement can thus be used to reach the same goal as if it were possible to agree upon the duration of such an agreement.

---

81 See S. 1 of the Swedish Gift Act (in Swedish *Lag 1936:83 angående vissa utfästelser om gåva*).

82 See e.g. Government Bill, Prop. 2002/03:80p. 32, where the Swedish government states that an investigation should be initiated about possibilities for cohabitees to enter into agreements.

83 L. TOTTIE and Ö. TELEMAN, *Äktenskapsbalken, En kommentar,* Norstedts Juridik, Stockholm, 2010, at p. 106–107; A. AGELL and M. BRATTSTRÖM, *Äktenskap Samboende Partnerskap*, Iustus Förlag, Uppsala, 2011, at p. 55-56.

84 See M. BRATTSTRÖM, 'Egendomsförhållanden under bestående samboende', in: J. ASLAND et al., *Nordisk samboerrett*, Gyldendal, Oslo, 2014, at p. 70 and p. 110-111 (see chapter 2.1 and 2.4.6 in the English version of the book, to be published by Intersentia in 2015). See also the Swedish Supreme Court judgment *NJA 1985 p. 172* in which the Court refused to recognise the parties' agreement according to which their relationship was subject to the legal effects of marriage.

85 See M. JÄNTERÄ-JAREBORG, 'Rechtsregeln für nichteheliches Zusammenleben in Schweden' (in English), in: I. KROPPENBERG et al. (eds.), *Rechtsregeln für nichteheliches Zusammenleben*, Gieseking Verlag, Vienna, 2009, pp. 207-226, at p. 222. Cf. M. BRATTSTRÖM and M. SAYED, 'Behandlingen av mahr i samband med bodelning enligt svensk rätt', *Juridisk Publikation*, 2013, at p. 221 et seq.

SWITZERLAND

a. The division of tasks as between the partners?

Generally, partners in an informal relationship are permitted to agree upon the division of tasks as between themselves, but this is not enforceable.

b. The contributions to the costs and expenses of the household?

Generally, partners in an informal relationship are permitted to agree upon the contributions to the costs and expenses of the household.

c. Their property relationship?

Generally, partners in an informal relationship are permitted to agree on their property relationship. It is however unclear whether a global reference to a marital property regime (e.g. participation in acquisitions) is possible.[86]

d. Maintenance?

Generally, partners in an informal relationship are permitted to agree upon maintenance. However, questions with regard to the extent or the duration of maintenance are unclear (e.g. whether and to what extent support obligations are limited in their duration pursuant to Art. 27 Swiss Civil Code).[87]

e. The duration of the agreement?

Generally, partners in an informal relationship are permitted to agree upon the duration of the agreement. However, they have to observe the protection of legal personality against excessive restrictions (Art. 27 Swiss Civil Code, see also Question 58(d)).

---

86 A. BÜCHLER, 'Vermögensrechtliche Probleme in der nichtehelichen Lebensgemeinschaft', in: A. RUMO-JUNGO and P. PICHONNAZ, *Familienvermögensrecht*, Stämpfli, Bern, 2003, at p. 59, 68 et seq.; H. HAUSHEER, T. GEISER and R. AEBI-MÜLLER, *Das Familienrecht des Schweizerischen Zivilgesetzbuches*, Stämpfli, Bern, 2014, at N 03.13.

87 According to H. HAUSHEER, T. GEISER and R. AEBI-MÜLLER, *Das Familienrecht des Schweizerischen Zivilgesetzbuches*, Stämpfli, Bern, 2014, at N 03.15, support obligations may only be permitted in a limited way. See also R. AEBI-MÜLLER and C. WIDMER, 'Rechtsregeln für nichteheliches Zusammenleben in der Schweiz', in: I. KROPPENBERG, D. SCHWAB, D. HENRICH, P. GOTTWALD and A. SPICKHOFF, *Rechtsregeln für nichteheliches Zusammenleben*, Gieseking, Bielefeld, 2009, at p. 65, 93.

QUESTION 59

Are partners in an informal relationship permitted to agree on the legal consequences of their separation?

AUSTRIA

Partners in an informal relationship are allowed to reach an agreement on the legal consequences of their separation.[1] This is not only permitted, but due to the uncertainty caused by the lacking legal framework for informal relationships, it is highly advisable to conclude a partnership agreement for certain issues and particularly for the case of separation.[2] Back in 2002 the Austrian Administrative Court qualified a partnership agreement, which was concluded in notarial form and contained a compensation clause, as a settlement agreement pursuant to S. 1380 General Austrian Civil Code.[3]

BELGIUM

Yes.

Firstly, they may agree on the circumstances under which a termination of the agreement is possible, for example by determining a notice period or agreeing on liquidated damages. Such clauses may not amount to penalty clauses or may not restrict the partners' personal freedom.[4]

---

1 U. AICHHORN, *Das Recht der Lebenspartnerschaften, Ehe und Lebensgemeinschaft*, Springer, Vienna, 2003, at p. 423; N. OSWALD and A. SCHMALLEGGER, 'Partnerschaftsvertrag zwischen nichtehelichen Lebensgefährten', *EF-Z*, 2013, at p. 13; E. MÖSCHL, *Die nichteheliche Lebensgemeinschaft*, LexisNexis ARD ORAC, Vienna, 2007, at marg. No. 36; A. DEIXLER-HÜBNER, *Scheidung, Ehe und Lebensgemeinschaft*, LexisNexis ARD ORAC, Vienna, 2013, at marg. No. 252.

2 S. FERRARI, 'Rechtsregeln für nichteheliches Zusammenleben in Österreich', in: I. KROPPENBERG et al. (eds.), *Rechtsregeln für nichteheliches Zusammenleben*, Gieseking Verlag, Vienna, 2009, pp. 167-206, at p. 176 et seq.

3 Austrian Administrative Court, Decision of 24.01.2002, 99/16/0147.

4 District Court of Bruges 9 April 2001, *RW* 2001-02, 1552.

Secondly, they may agree on their own and joint property, for example by granting preferential rights[5] or a compensatory payment[6] – insofar as this does not amount to a penalty clause.

Thirdly, they may agree on maintenance upon separation (or death) – again insofar as this does not amount to a penalty clause.[7]

BULGARIA

Since there are no specific regulations thereon, the above will apply – partners in an informal relationship are free to make such an agreement with regard to mutual rights and duties. The only limit to such an agreement is the general framework set out by Art. 9 of the Bulgarian Obligations and Contracts Law – not to infringe the imperative legal regulations and good morals.

CROATIA

Although there is no special legal provision prescribing this, partners in an informal relationship are permitted to agree on the legal consequences of their separation.

CZECH REPUBLIC

Partners in an informal relationship are permitted to agree on the legal consequences of their separation. Civil law (contract law) is based on the principle of contractual freedom. That means that they are permitted to agree on anything which is not in conflict with the law. This agreement could be oral as well as written according to S. 1746/2 Czech Civil Code: parties may also conclude a contract which is not specifically regulated as a type of contract.

DENMARK

Cohabitants can enter into prior agreements about how their joint assets should be divided upon the termination of cohabitation, and they can agree that one party shall have a share of the other's savings. During

5 P. SENAEVE, *Compendium van het personen- en familierecht*, Acco, Leuven, 2013, at n° 2053.

6 W. PINTENS, C. DECLERCK, J. DU MONGH, K. VANWINCKELEN, *Familiaal vermogensrecht*, Intersentia, Antwerp, 2010, at n° 1017.

7 S. EGGERMONT, *De juridische bescherming van private relaties*, PhD, University of Antwerp, 2015, at n° 258.

their cohabitation a couple can agree that the financially weaker party shall receive compensation upon the termination of their cohabitation, or that one of them will not make a claim against the other. The party surrendering his or her rights must understand the consequences of such an agreement.

There is also extensive freedom of contract in a situation in which cohabitation has already been terminated.

ENGLAND AND WALES

Yes.

ESTONIA

In civil issues, the partners in an informal relationship are treated as unmarried persons and they are free to enter into agreements. A transaction which is contrary to good morals or public order is void (§ 86(1) General Part of the Estonian Civil Code Act). With regard to agreements between married partners, the Supreme Court has found that an agreement which would oblige the defendant to pay money to the plaintiff only as compensation (a contractual penalty) in the case of an eventual divorce would be void.[8] According to the Supreme Court, such an agreement would substantially restrict the right to divorce and would be in conflict with good morals as set forth in § 86 of the General Part of the Estonian Civil Code Act.

The partners in an informal relationship may in principle conclude all other contracts for supporting or maintaining each other and, in general, there are no formal requirements for such contracts. According to § 109 of the Estonian Family Law Act, an agreement by which the performance of the obligation to provide future maintenance is precluded or by which the obligation to provide maintenance is unreasonably restricted is void. Thus, an agreement with a similar content, concluded between the partners in an informal relationship, is presumably void also with regard to the maintenance of a child after birth.

8 Decision of the Civil Chamber of the Supreme Court 3-2-1-149-11, at para. 18.

FINLAND

Yes. However, it is not allowed to make anticipatory agreements waiving the right to demand the separation of property or the right to apply for an estate distributor to be appointed. However, if partners enter into a written agreement on the separation of their property at the time of separation and the separation of property is executed according to the agreement then that in itself constitutes a legally valid deed on the separation of property. As a result, an estate distributor cannot be appointed as there is already a valid deed on the separation of property.

FRANCE

Cohabitants are permitted to agree on the consequences of their separation within the limits described under Question 58.

GERMANY

Partners to an informal relationship are permitted to agree on the legal consequences of their separation (e.g. maintenance or compensation), as long as they do not agree upon a contractual penalty which would force the partners to continue the partnership (see Question 58).[9]

GREECE

Yes, provided there is no violation of the rules of public order (Art. 3 Greek Civil Code).

HUNGARY

Yes, cohabitants may agree on both maintenance and the use of the common dwelling as these are prescribed in the Hungarian Civil Code. A possibility to agree on property relations if the cohabitation terminates is not mentioned but cohabitants have always been permitted to end their property relations.

As far as the use of the common dwelling is concerned, this is regulated in the Hungarian Civil Code among the general rules which apply to cohabitants. These are new provisions as no such rules were contained in the Civil Code of 1959. This Article lays down the method for regulating

---

9 M. LÖHNIG, 'Anh. zu §§ 1297 et seq.', in: J. VON STAUDINGER, *Kommentar zum Bürgerlichen Gesetzbuch,* Sellier-de-Gruyter, Berlin, 2012, at No. 34.

the use of the common dwelling or the family home by agreement.[10] Cohabitants can regulate the use of the common dwelling in case their community of life comes to an end. They can do this at the beginning of the cohabitation or during their community of life in advance by agreement. For the agreement to be valid it has to be included in a public instrument or a private document attested by a lawyer.

This provision refers to the agreement between the spouses concerning their and their child's right to use the common home in the case of divorce. If the spouses do not regulate in their agreement how their children will use the common dwelling after divorce or their regulation seriously damages their children's right to use this dwelling, the court is permitted to deviate from the agreement. The same applies to the cohabitants' agreement on the use of the common home.

Cohabitants can enter into an agreement on the use of the common dwelling even after the termination of their community of life. There is no specific formal requirement for its validity.

REPUBLIC OF IRELAND

Generally, as a matter of Irish law, this is not possible. However, S. 202(3) of the Irish 2010 Act would seem to indicate that this is possible in limited circumstances. It provides:

> 'Subject to subsection (4), a cohabitants' agreement may provide that neither cohabitant may apply for an order for redress referred to in Section 173, or an order for provision from the estate of his or her cohabitant under Section 194.'

ITALY

Yes, they are.[11] They can, for instance, agree that maintenance is paid after separation (as a periodical payment or as a lump sum), or they can agree on the gratuitous transfer of property. These payments or transfers are considered to be *remunerative donations* ('made out of gratitude for or in consideration of the merits of the donee', Art. 770 Italian Civil Code) and are therefore irrevocable (Art. 800 Italian Civil Code).

---

10 Art. 6:517 of the Hungarian Civil Code.

11 R. BASSETTI, *Contratti di convivenza e di unione civile*, Giappichelli, Turin, 2014, at p. 204.

LATVIA

In Latvia there is no particular legal order on partners in an informal relationship. However, the general law of obligations does not prohibit partners from entering into an agreement, for example, to adjust their property relations.

LITHUANIA

No. The Law regulates neither the factual nor the judicial separation of cohabitees.

LUXEMBOURG

They may agree on the consequences of their separation as long as they are not beyond the rules of contract law.

THE NETHERLANDS

Also in relation to a separation the basic principle of party autonomy is the leading principle. There are no special requirements or conditions, but it does make sense to make an agreement in writing. Little empirical knowledge is available on this type of contract, which might be explained by the fact that many informal partners have a notarial cohabitation contract, which also governs the situation of a relationship breakdown. Further, partners do not have to seek legal advice as married couples do, so they might not always be fully aware of what has to be settled.

NORWAY

As a rule, partners to an informal relationship are permitted to agree on the legal consequences of their separation regarding both property and other financial matters.

If an agreement regulates the financial settlement upon death, the agreement should be set out in the form of a will in order to be protected against the heirs of the deceased partner.

PORTUGAL

The only legally regulated consequence of separation concerns the family home (Art. 4 of Act 7/2001, May 11th and Art. 1793 and 1105 of the

Portuguese Civil Code). According to Art. 1793 the cohabitants may agree on the future of the family home. This agreement is subject to confirmation by the courts. According to Art. 1105 the cohabitants may agree on the transmission or the unification of the right to rent the home.

In both cases the needs of the cohabitants and the interests of their children shall be taken into account.

RUSSIA

Yes. Partners can also reach agreement on dividing or reallocating their property upon separation.[12]

SCOTLAND

Although there is no specific statutory provision to this effect, it is generally assumed that they may. Separation agreements are a very common method of regulating the consequences of divorce and dissolution in Scotland. They are very well established and require no judicial scrutiny or approval. Anecdotally it is thought that, there is increasing use of such agreements by couples in informal relationships.

SLOVAKIA

Yes.

SLOVENIA

Extramarital partners can agree at the time of the cessation of the extramarital union on the sharing of common property and on maintenance after the cessation of the union.

SPAIN

The Civil Code in Spain does not include any reference to civil partnerships or informal relationships. Any agreement between informal partners would have to comply with Art. 1255 Spanish Civil Code on the validity of agreements, in general, which states that 'contracting parties

12 С.Ю. ФИЛИППОВА, 'Гражданско-правовые средства достижения цели построения семьи путем фактических брачных отношений', *Семейное и жилищное право*, 2010, at p. 4.

may establish the pacts, clauses and conditions they deem advisable, provided they are not contrary to the law, morals, or public policy'.

The Civil Code in Catalonia has provisions on informal partnerships, and includes the possibility of agreements to regulate the consequences of the separation of such partners (Art. 234-5 Catalan Civil Code).

SWEDEN

The most important agreement which is also specially regulated by the Swedish Cohabitation Act relates to the division of the 'cohabitation property' upon termination of the relationship. Through this agreement, somewhat misleadingly called a 'cohabitation agreement', the parties can exclude or reduce the scope of the future property division or, in the form of a new agreement, re-introduce the property into the division. The provisions in § 16 and 22 of the Act concerning the right to take over and occupy the joint dwelling of the couple are, on the other hand, mandatory by nature, meaning that they cannot be set aside in the form of an agreement, due to the societal considerations at stake.

It follows from the fundamental freedom of contract that applies in general in the parties' mutual relationship that cohabitees can, to a large extent, agree on the legal consequences of their separation, subject to the enforceability of the agreement (above Question 58). Enforceability requires that the agreement satisfies minimum requirements as to clarity, specificity and foreseeability.[13] It must be possible to comprehend the substance of the agreement and its consequences, prior to signature. There are examples in Swedish case law where agreements between cohabitees stipulating that the rules of marriage are to be applied between them have been considered too general in nature and have therefore not been considered legally valid by the court, see in particular the Supreme Court judgment NJA 1985 p. 172. In the legal literature there is support for the opinion that cohabitees should have the right to enter into agreements which, on specific aspects, result in the same legal consequences as in a formalised relationship.[14] One example of this could be an agreement that the value of certain property (not included in the cohabitation property according to the law) should be divided equally once debts assignable to the property had been paid. If the

[13] See M. BRATTSTRÖM, 'Egendomsförhållanden under bestående samboende', in: J. ASLAND et al., *Nordisk samboerrett*, Gyldendal, Oslo, 2014, at p. 96 (see Chapter 2.4.1 in the English version of the book, to be published by Intersentia in 2015).

[14] Cf. F. GRAUERS, *Ekonomisk familjerätt*, Thomson Förlag, Stockholm, 2008, at p. 267 et seq.

agreement were to result in a beneficial transfer of value from one cohabitee to the other it could, however, from the point of view of property law, be considered to be an undertaking to make a gift,[15] and therefore need to meet the special requirements for validity (Question 58d).

SWITZERLAND

Generally, the parties can agree on the legal consequences of their separation within the legal boundaries of the general rules with regard to contracts (see Question 57). They may, however, be limited with regard to questions concerning third parties or the state (e.g. parties cannot assign a lease contract to one partner without the consent of the landlord).

[15] Cf. M. BRATTSTRÖM, 'Egendomsförhållanden under bestående samboende', in: J. ASLAND et al., *Nordisk samboerrett*, Gyldendal, Oslo, 2014, at p. 102 et seq. (see Chapter 2.4.4 in the English version of the book, to be published by Intersentia in 2015).

QUESTION 60

Are the agreements binding:

a. Between the partners?

b. In relation to third parties?

AUSTRIA

a. Between the partners?

Partnership agreements are binding as between the partners in an informal relationship.[1] However, it should be noted that the partners neither have the possibility to deviate from rules on social or tax law, nor can they create any claims under public law by concluding a partnership agreement. In this regard the effect of a partnership agreement is restricted.[2]

b. In relation to third parties?

Generally, contracts create rights and duties only among the parties to the agreement (privity of contract). Accordingly, problems arising from relations between the partners in the informal relationship and third persons cannot be settled in partnership agreements.[3] Further, a partnership agreement must not infringe third party rights: A partner cannot, for example, contractually assure the other partner of a widow's pension.[4] However, under Austrian law contracts for the benefit of third parties are generally possible (e.g. a third party benefit insurance contract), whereas contracts imposing duties on third parties are not allowed. Due to the fact that nobody is obliged to accept any benefit, the third person can reject it.[5]

---

1 E. Möschl, *Die nichteheliche Lebensgemeinschaft*, LexisNexis ARD ORAC, Vienna, 2007, at marg. No. 34.

2 E. Möschl, *Die nichteheliche Lebensgemeinschaft*, LexisNexis ARD ORAC, Vienna, 2007, at marg. No. 42.

3 E. Möschl, *Die nichteheliche Lebensgemeinschaft*, LexisNexis ARD ORAC, Vienna, 2007, at marg. No. 42.

4 U. Aichhorn, *Das Recht der Lebenspartnerschaften, Ehe und Lebensgemeinschaft,* Springer, Vienna, 2003, at p. 423; N. Oswald and A. Schmallegger, 'Partnerschaftsvertrag zwischen nichtehelichen Lebensgefährten', *EF-Z*, 2013, at p. 13.

5 Section 882 General Austrian Civil Code.

BELGIUM

a. Between the partners?

Yes, the agreements are just as binding as any civil contract and non-performance may give rise to contractual liability.

b. In relation to third parties?

The agreements in principle are not opposable by third parties. If necessary, publication in the Mortgage Register can make the agreement opposable with regard to immovable property. A partner's heirs are not considered to be third parties. Third parties themselves may however rely on a cohabitation agreement, for example to recover a household debt that is qualified as a joint debt.[6]

BULGARIA

a. Between the partners?

The agreements are binding between the partners in an informal relationship.

b. In relation to third parties?

The agreements are not binding in relation to third parties. An agreement on the exercise of parental rights and duties after separation is an agreement relating to third parties – the children. It however also regulates the internal relations between partners in relation to children.

CROATIA

In line with Art. 11 paragraph 2 of the Croatian Family Act and Art. 4 paragraph 2 in relation to Art. 54 of the Croatian Partnership Act, the answer equally relates to both cohabitants and same-sex informal partners.

a. Between the partners?

Agreements are binding between the partners.

b. In relation to third parties?

Considering third parties, according to Art. 40 paragraph 2 in relation to Art. 11 of the Croatian Family Act and Art. 54 paragraph 1 in relation to Art. 4 of the Croatian Partnership Act, the provisions on property

---

6 W. Pintens, C. Declerck, J. Du Mongh, K. Vanwinckelen, *Familiaal vermogensrecht*, Intersentia, Antwerp, 2010, at n°s 1022-1023.

administration or disposal shall have legal effect if they are registered in land or public registers which require such registration for the acquisition of rights or if the utilization of an item requires such registration.

CZECH REPUBLIC

a. Between the partners?

The agreements are binding between the partners.

b. In relation to third parties?

The agreements are not binding in relation to third parties.

DENMARK

a. Between the partners?

Yes, but an agreement on the division of property can still be challenged under the rules on invalidity in Danish contract law.

b. In relation to third parties?

Agreements between partners on the division of household tasks are presumably not valid against third parties.

ENGLAND AND WALES

a. Between the partners?

Yes if drawn up in the correct way and not avoiding other legal duties (e.g. payment of child support). The division of tasks would not in itself be binding.

b. In relation to third parties?

This would not be binding unless the third party joins the agreement and specifically agrees to its terms in so far as it relates to their interests.

ESTONIA

a. Between the partners?

In civil issues, the partners in an informal relationship are treated as unmarried persons and they are free to enter into agreements. The validity of the agreements in question (including in relation to formal requirements) stems from the general or special provisions of those transactions.

b. In relation to third parties?

Under Estonian law rights and obligations generally arise between the parties themselves. There is no register, similar to the marital property register, for the regulation of the validity of agreements between the partners in an informal relationship with regard to third persons. It is possible to establish restricted real rights (e.g. a real encumbrance or a personal right of use) which are valid with regard to third persons, according to the general rules of property law.

FINLAND

a. Between the partners?

Yes, just as any other agreements between two persons.

b. In relation to third parties?

Yes, up to the point that a third party interest is violated. In a situation where one partner cannot satisfy his or her own creditors due to a donation made to the other partner in separation, the creditors can in these circumstances seek recovery from the donated property if the donation exceeded the amount that was due. See more details under Question 64.

FRANCE

a. Between the partners?

The agreement is binding between the partners within the limits described under Question 58.

b. In relation to third parties?

The agreement is binding in relation to third parties and especially in relation to children within the limits described under Question 58.

GERMANY

a. Between the partners?

The agreements are binding between the partners.

b. In relation to third parties?
As agreements under the law of obligation they are in general not binding in relation to third parties.[7]

GREECE

a. Between the partners?
Yes.

b. In relation to third parties?
No, because contracts at the expense of third parties are invalid (Art. 415 Greek Civil Code).

HUNGARY

a. Between the partners?
Yes, they are binding between the partners.

b. In relation to third parties?
They are only valid against third partners if the agreement has been recorded in the Register of Property Agreements of Cohabitants or if the cohabitants can prove that third party knew or would have known about the existence of the agreement and its contents. The regulations on the Register of Matrimonial Property Agreements are to be applied to the Register of Property Agreements of Cohabitants.

The Register of Matrimonial Property Agreements and the Register of Property Agreements of Cohabitants are kept by the Hungarian National Chamber of Notaries. The detailed rules thereon are contained in the Hungarian Act on Non-litigious Notarial Procedures.[8] As the Registers were established in March and April 2014 there is, as yet, no judicial experience in this respect.

The aim of the registers is to provide evidence of the existence of these property agreements according to the Hungarian Notarial Act.

---

7 C. GRÜNEBERG, 'Einl. vor § 241', in: O. PALANDT, *Bürgerliches Gesetzbuch*, Beck, Munich, 2015, at No. 5.

8 Art. 36/H-36/K. of Act No. XLV 2008 on Non-litigious Notarial Procedures.

REPUBLIC OF IRELAND

The agreement, being a contract, could well be binding on both cohabitants and third parties, but as only cohabitants are mentioned in the Act it seems reasonable to suggest that it is only cohabitants who would be considered under the 2010 Act itself.

Section 208 of the Irish 2010 Act provides that in making any Order whether it by way of Periodic Maintenance, Lump Sum, Property Adjustment Order, Pension Adjustment Order or Order for Provision from the Estate of the Deceased Person the court shall have regard to the rights of any other person with an interest in the matter, including a spouse or former spouse, a civil partner or former civil partner. This saver provision applies in respect of the Irish 2010 Act as a whole.

ITALY

a. Between the partners?

Agreements are just as binding between the partners as any other contract. Their violation constitutes a cause of action before the courts.

Parties can insert withdrawal clauses in their agreements.

b. In relation to third parties?

The agreement as such does not produce effects with regard to third parties, as with any other contract (Art. 1372 Italian Civil Code).

LATVIA

A contract between partners has the same binding effect as any other contract. Section 1587 of the Latvian Civil Law determines that a contract legally entered into imposes on a contracting party a duty to perform that which was promised, and neither the exceptional difficulty of the transaction, nor difficulties in performance arising later, give the right to one party to withdraw from the contract, even if the other party is compensated for any loss.

LITHUANIA

Yes, according to Art. 3.231 of the Lithuanian Civil Code. An agreement[9] by cohabitees is subject to the same formal requirements as a marriage contract (Art. 3.103 of the Lithuanian Civil Code),[10] i.e. in a notarised form and registered in the Register of marriage contracts.[11]

LUXEMBOURG

a. Between the partners?

The agreements are binding under Art. 1134 of the Luxembourg Civil Code ('*Les conventions légalement formées tiennent lieu de loi à ceux qui les ont faites*'). The parties to a contract need to respect the terms of their engagement.

b. In relation to third parties?

According to Art. 1165 of the Luxembourg Civil Code, contracts only produce effects between the parties thereto (*l'effet relatif des contrats, res inter alios acta, alliis nec prodesse, nec nocere potest*).

The agreement between the partners is opposable by third parties as a fact; the agreement and the legal situation following therefrom are opposable by third parties as facts.

THE NETHERLANDS

a. Between the partners?

Both cohabitation contracts and separation agreements are binding between the parties according to the basic rule of *pacta sunt servanda*. However, after a relationship breakdown parties will sometimes try to

9 Only an agreement on how the assets acquired and used together should be divided after their life together ends.

10 A marriage contract must be entered into before a notary public. A marriage contract as well as its subsequent amendments must be registered in the register of marriage contracts maintained by mortgage institutions in the procedure laid down by the rules of the register. A marriage contract may only be amended with leave from the court. In no case may amendments to a marriage contract be retroactive. A marriage contract and its amendments may be used against third parties provided the settlement and its amendments have been registered in the register of marriage contracts. This rule shall not apply if at the time of the transaction the third parties knew of the marriage contract and its amendments.

11 Regulations on the Register of marriage contracts, Official Gazette, 2009, No. 126-5430.

evade the cohabitation contract by any legal means possible.[12] There is a great deal of case law to this extent and a number of options exist. A partner may invoke the nullity of the contract, for instance because of a defect in consent. A recent decision by the Supreme Court should be mentioned in this respect. The parties had lived together for over twenty years when they concluded a cohabitation contract. This was after a difficult period in their relationship, since the woman had had a relationship with another man. This had been evaluated by the parties and they decided to remain together. Shortly before the contract was signed, the woman again had a relationship with the other man, which she then terminated. Three years later, the parties split up. The man invoked an error (*dwaling*, Art. 6:228 Dutch Civil Code), which was accepted by the Supreme Court. As a principle partners do not have to share very personal information, but given the special circumstances of this case, the woman should have informed the man before concluding the contract.[13] Apart from this case, claims based on a defect in consent are not often successful.

Next to a defect in consent, a party could try to contend that a provision in the contract should not be applied or should be interpreted differently. In a leading Supreme Court case the parties had agreed in a notarial cohabitation contract upon a nominal claim for an investment by the woman of €50,000 in a house which was the private property of the man.[14] When the relationship broke down, the value of the house had considerably increased and the woman claimed that on the basis of an implicit contract and the principle of reasonableness and fairness she was entitled to half of the value of the house. The Supreme Court ruled that the explicit cohabitation contract had to be interpreted not only according to its wording, but also with regard to a number of facts invoked by the woman. Although this did not mean that the woman received what she wanted, it demonstrates that to some extent it is possible to adjust a contractual obligation. In other cases parties try, sometimes with success, not to be bound by a specific provision.[15]

---

12 W.M. SCHRAMA, 'Vermogensverschuivingen na scheiding van ongehuwde samenlevers: contractuele grondslagen (deel 1)', *Tijdschrift Relatierecht en Praktijk*, 2014, at p. 17-18.

13 HR 21 February 2014, ECLI:NL:HR:2014:416.

14 HR 22 September 2006, LJN AX1571.

15 Hof Den Haag 15 April 2014, ECLI:NL:GHDHA:2014:1339; HR 10 October 2014: ECLI:NL:HR:2014:2931; Hof Arnhem 24 February 2009, LJN BH7537.

b. In relation to third parties?

In general, cohabitation contracts will not affect third parties' rights, since they mostly regulate the internal relationship between the informal partners. Unless a third party is a party to the contract as well, which seems fairly unusual, the third party cannot be bound. This does not mean that a cohabitation contract cannot have any influence on the legal position of a third party. When partners have agreed to exchange a share in each other's goods, this affects indirectly the position of a creditor of one of the partners, just like many other acts would do.

If the term 'third party' also includes the state, a cohabitation contract has an impact in a number of aspects. It is, however, not the contract itself that binds the state, but the legal acts in which legal effects are given to the conclusion of a cohabitation contract.

NORWAY

a. Between the partners?

Yes, as a rule, the agreements are binding between the partners.

An agreement may be wholly or partly annulled if it will affect one of the parties unfairly pursuant to the Norwegian Act relating to Conclusion of Agreements 1918, S. 36. Instead of annulling the agreement, the court may decide to modify the agreement. In practice this provision has been interpreted restrictively, and is rarely used; see Rt. 2011 p. 1168.

b. In relation to third parties?

As a rule, agreements are binding in relation to third parties as well. However, the owner of property needs to be protected from a good faith purchaser, and agreements which transfer property from one partner to the other need protection against seizure from the creditors of the former owner. (To obtain such protection, real property must be registered by the registrar for judicial registration of title pursuant to the Norwegian Land Registration Act.)

PORTUGAL

a. Between the partners?

Yes. They are binding as far as any other agreement/contract is binding (Art. 406(1) of the Portuguese Civil Code). Whenever there is confirmation by the courts, this judicial decision must also be respected by the parties.

b. In relation to third parties?
In relation to third parties, the agreement is also binding as far as this is legally foreseen (Art. 406(2) of the Portuguese Civil Code). This is the case concerning the transmission or unification of the right to rent the family home. The landlord has to be notified *ex officio* (Art. 1105(3) of the Portuguese Civil Code).

Whenever there is confirmation by the courts, this judicial decision must also be respected by third parties.

RUSSIA

a. Between the partners?
Agreements are binding between the partners, unless they contain provisions violating mandatory rules of law (e.g. an agreement precluding a woman from seeking the establishment of paternity). Agreements regulating purely personal relationships (e.g. who is going to walk the dog) are valid, but not legally enforceable.

b. In relation to third parties?
Agreements are binding in relation to third parties, unless they contain provisions violating mandatory rules of law (e.g. an agreement precluding a woman from seeking employment).

SCOTLAND

a. Between the partners?
It is widely assumed that cohabitation agreements are binding on the parties, subject to compliance with the general rules of contract requiring capacity and consent. There is little empirical evidence of their use in practice although anecdotally they are thought to be increasingly common.

b. In relation to third parties?
It is assumed that agreements between cohabitants would be binding for all purposes but there is little definitive authority. A recent case highlighted the possibility of challenge, by a trustee on sequestration, to an agreement between cohabitants as to equal ownership of assets.[16] In the absence of evidence of transfer for value, such an agreement might be set aside as a gratuitous transaction.

---

[16] *Johnston's Trustee v Baird* 2012 CSOH 117.

SLOVAKIA

a. Between the partners?
Yes.

b. In relation to third parties?
No.

SLOVENIA

a. Between the partners?
Agreements on maintenance and agreements on the sharing of common property (other agreements on property relations because of the compulsory nature of the rules on property relations are in the main excluded) are binding on extramarital partners in their mutual relations.

b. In relation to third parties?
Agreements by extramarital partners and agreements on the sharing of common property rarely affect third parties.

SPAIN

a. Between the partners?
The Civil Code in Spain does not include any reference to civil partnerships or informal relationships. Any agreement between informal partners would have to comply with general rules on validity of contracts and, if they did so, the agreements would be binding between the partners of the informal relationship.

The Civil Code in Catalonia specifically mentions that agreements on the consequences of break-up are valid between partners of an informal relationship. These can be made during cohabitation (Art. 234-5 Catalan Civil Code) or after cohabitation has ended (Art. 234-6 Catalan Civil Code).

For agreements made during cohabitation, we must turn to Art. 231-20 Catalan Civil Code, which contains several rules on the validity of these agreements.

- Art. 231-20.3 Catalan Civil Code: Agreements waiving or limiting rights must be reciprocal and they must clearly specify the rights limited or waived.

- Art. 231-20.4 Catalan Civil Code: The spouse claiming enforcement of an agreement in anticipation of a marriage breakdown has the burden of proving that the other party had, at the time of its execution, sufficient information about his assets, incomes and financial perspectives, if such information was relevant in relation to the content of the agreement.
- Art. 231-20.5 Catalan Civil Code: Agreements in anticipation of a breakdown which pose a serious harm to any spouse at the time of their intended performance are null and void if such spouse proves that important changes of circumstances have arisen which were unforeseen or could not be reasonably foreseen at the time of execution of the agreement.

For agreements made after the end of cohabitation, we must turn to Art. 233-4 and 233-5 Catalan Civil Code. If an agreement is made in a public deed, it will be binding on partners (Art. 233-5.1 Catalan Civil Code). However, agreements adopted after the breakdown of cohabitation without independent legal aid for each spouse may be annulled at the request of any spouse within three months from the date of their adoption and no later than the date of the response to the claim or, where appropriate, the counterclaim in the matrimonial proceedings where enforcement of such agreements is sought (Art. 233-5-2 Catalan Civil Code).

As regards any children, the Catalan Civil Code includes the following provision: 'agreements regarding custody and personal relations with minor children or maintenance in their favour are only effective if they conform to their interests at the time enforcement is sought' (Art. 233-5.3 Catalan Civil Code).

b. In relation to third parties?

Agreements made by informal partners would not bind third parties. There is no way to register this agreement, and so third parties would not be privy to it.

SWEDEN

a. Between the partners?

A so-called cohabitation agreement (see above Question 57) must according to the Swedish Cohabitation Act, § 9 be concluded in writing and signed by both cohabitees or, if concluded before the relationship, the prospective cohabitees. If the agreement, or a new agreement replacing the previous one, fulfils these requirements, it will be binding between the partners.

Other agreements between the partners need to meet the ordinary requirements, according to the law of obligations. These requirements differ between various kinds of agreements. An important exception from the general rules may apply when property has been purchased during the relationship for the couple's joint use, but with only one of the partners receiving the formal title to it. Under certain conditions, as developed by case law, this property can be regarded as jointly owned by the partners.

b. In relation to third parties?

A cohabitation agreement, regulated by the Swedish Cohabitation Act, § 9, is binding on third parties but does not, as such, have any legal effect in relation to third parties. This has to do with the fact that the agreement is limited to the exclusion of the division of 'cohabitation property', as defined by the Act, or to a reduction of the scope of the property division, or to bringing previously excluded 'cohabitation property' back within the scope of the division, through a new agreement. The agreement has no impact on the ownership of the property to be included or excluded.

Upon the property division, each cohabitee has the duty to take account of the interests of his or her creditors and may not, to the creditors' detriment, forgo property that is to be included in his or her share, the Swedish Cohabitation Act, § 21 with further reference to the Swedish Marriage Code, Chapter 13 § 1-2. If, as a result of such a forbidden action, the cohabitee is unable to pay a previous debt incurred before the property division took place, or if for any other reason the cohabitee can be assumed to be insolvent, the other cohabitee is liable for the deficit up to the value of the forgone property.[17]

Other agreements between the partners need to meet the ordinary requirements, according to the relevant law of obligations or property law. These requirements differ between various kinds of agreements.[18]

---

[17] See further Swedish Cohabitation Act § 20, with further references to the Swedish Marriage Code (in Swedish: *Äktenskapsbalken* 1987:230) Chapter 13, § 1 para. 3.

[18] We have interpreted Question 60 as a continuation of Question 59, meaning that its scope is restricted to agreements on the legal consequences of separation.

SWITZERLAND

a. Between the partners?

Generally and within the legal boundaries of the general rules with regard to contracts (see Question 57), the agreements are binding between the partners.

b. In relation to third parties?

The parties are limited in their agreements where the consent of third parties is required (e.g. parties cannot assign a lease contract to one partner without the consent of the landlord).[19] Furthermore, many questions regulated by the state do not fall within the ambit of contractual agreements (e.g. question relating to aliens law or (inheritance) tax law).

19 A. BÜCHLER, 'Vermögensrechtliche Probleme in der nichtehelichen Lebensgemeinschaft', in: A. RUMO-JUNGO and P. PICHONNAZ, *Familienvermögensrecht*, Stämpfli, Bern, 2003, at p. 59, 72.

QUESTION 61

If agreements are not binding, what effect, if any, do they have?

AUSTRIA

Partnership agreements are binding as between the partners in an informal relationship.[1]

BELGIUM

Not applicable, since the agreements are binding.

BULGARIA

The effect of the agreements relates mainly to the partners themselves.

CROATIA

Agreements between partners are binding.

CZECH REPUBLIC

The agreements are binding between the partners to an informal relationship.

DENMARK

Such agreements could be regarded as being morally binding.

---

1 E. MÖSCHL, *Die nichteheliche Lebensgemeinschaft*, LexisNexis ARD ORAC, Vienna, 2007, at marg. No. 34.

ENGLAND AND WALES

They can show common intention which may prove the foundation of a constructive trust or influence the discretion of the court in relation to proceedings for financial provision for the benefit of the child (Schedule 1 English Children Act 1989) in which it might be considered as one of the circumstances of the case.

ESTONIA

There are no special rules; agreements are concluded according to the rules set forth in the respective transaction.

FINLAND

The agreements are binding between the partners and in relation to third parties, as long as third party interests can be satisfied.

FRANCE

Not applicable.

GERMANY

This question has no relevance in German legislation (see Question 60).

GREECE

None. Were there to be some transfer of assets, on the basis of a legally non-binding agreement, perhaps one might apply the provisions on gifts or on the return of assets based on unjust enrichment.

HUNGARY

They are binding agreements.

REPUBLIC OF IRELAND

Under the legislation, such cohabitants' agreements are valid and enforceable. However, if their enforcement would lead to serious injustice, the court may vary or set aside the agreement. In the event, however, that an agreement is not binding, it is still valuable in indicating the intentions of the parties and gives the court a starting point from which to assess the parties' financial affairs.

ITALY

As stated previously, agreements are binding for the partners but not for third parties.

LATVIA

In Latvia there is no particular legal order on partners in an informal relationship.

LITHUANIA

See the answer to Question 60.

LUXEMBOURG

See the answer to Question 60.

THE NETHERLANDS

As cohabitation contracts (and separation contracts) are binding on the parties, this question is not relevant under Dutch law.

NORWAY

As a rule, non-binding agreements will have no effect. Depending on the circumstances, compensation may be granted.

PORTUGAL

These agreements are binding in the aforementioned terms.

RUSSIA

Partners may voluntarily comply with the agreement, but no legal remedy is available in the event of non-performance.

SCOTLAND

As discussed in the answer to Question 60, it is thought that agreements between cohabitants are binding and therefore this question is not relevant.

SLOVAKIA

The agreements have no effect because they are not binding.

SLOVENIA

The rule on common property is of a compulsory nature. Therefore an agreement in the form of a notarial protocol on the division of common property that does not respect the rule that the amount of the share of the common property is decided in accordance with the contribution to its creation is null and void. A creditor whom the extramarital partners deceive and deprive her or him of the payment of her or his dues can also lead to nullity under the general rules of the law of obligations.

SPAIN

Agreements would only be binding between partners in the informal relationship.

SWEDEN

If an agreement is not binding, its effect – if any – is limited to a moral commitment. No legal measures or sanctions are available to enforce it, in the event of breach of the agreement.[2]

SWITZERLAND

There are no specific legal rules or case law with regard to this question.

---

2 Cf. Swedish Supreme Court decisions *NJA 1929 p. 225, NJA 1932 p. 290* and *NJA 1940 p. 112.*

QUESTION 62

If specific legislative provisions regulate informal relationships, are the partners permitted to opt in or to opt out of this specific regulation?

AUSTRIA

Generally, it can be said that partners in an informal relationship enjoy a wide margin of appreciation as regards the drafting of their partnership agreement. To a large extent the Austrian law on obligations is of an optional nature except for e.g. S. 879 General Austrian Civil Code (invalidity of contracts), which the partners in an informal relationship cannot exclude. Further, they cannot opt out of property law or provisions resulting from tenancy or social law.[1] Many provisions which consider informal relationships to be equal to marriages are of public nature, e.g. Code of Criminal Procedure, and are therefore mandatory. Moreover, one has to keep in mind that the majority of these provisions is in favour of informal relationships and thus there is no need to derogate therefrom. Finally, it should be noted that by concluding a partnership agreement partners in an informal relationship cannot create any claims under public law.[2]

BELGIUM

Not applicable, since there are no legislative provisions that regulate family law aspects of informal relationships.

BULGARIA

There are no such specific legislative provisions.

1 E. MÖSCHL, *Die nichteheliche Lebensgemeinschaft*, LexisNexis ARD ORAC, Vienna, 2007, at marg. No. 42.

2 E. MÖSCHL, *Die nichteheliche Lebensgemeinschaft*, LexisNexis ARD ORAC, Vienna, 2007, at marg. No. 42.

CROATIA

In line with Art. 11 paragraph 2 of the Croatian Family Act and Art. 4 paragraph 2 and Art. 54 of the Croatian Partnership Act, the answer equally relates to both cohabitants and same-sex informal partners.

Informal relationships are regulated by specific legislative provisions and partners are not obliged to opt for this specific regulation to be legally protected; they are protected *ex lege* after three years of joint life in a union.

Partners can conclude an agreement and exclude the effects of their union referring to property.

CZECH REPUBLIC

There are no specific legislative provisions.

DENMARK

The relation between the partners in an informal relationship:

- *During the relationship:*
  Danish Social Security Acts: When a couple are presumed to be cohabiting, a number of social benefits fall by the wayside: It is not possible for the partners to opt out.
- *On separation:*
  According to the Danish Act on Rent a court can substitute the tenant if there are special grounds: It is not possible for the partners to make prior agreements.
- *On death:*
  According to the Danish Act on Rent the surviving partner is entitled to extend the lease: It is not possible for the partners to make prior agreements;
  According to the Danish Inheritance Tax Act a cohabitant may pay a low level of inheritance tax: It is not possible for the partners to opt out;
  The Danish Inheritance Act governs extended cohabitants' wills and extends the testamentary powers of cohabitants: The partners are permitted to opt in;
  The Danish Administration of Estates Act contains a rule on a surviving cohabitant's right to assume possession of the previous joint

dwelling and the household goods: It is possible for a partner to opt out in a will;

The Danish Insurance Contracts Act includes a cohabitant in the definition of 'next of kin': It is possible for a partner to opt out by notification to the Insurance Company;

The Danish Liability and Compensation Act states that a surviving partner will be granted compensation for the loss of the breadwinner: It is not possible for the partners to opt out.

ENGLAND AND WALES

There are no opt-in provisions for informal couples. General principles mean that they should not be able to opt out unless specifically provided for by statute but we have not adopted this style of legislation to date (although it was proposed by the Law Commission in their 2007 report).

ESTONIA

There are no special rules; agreements are concluded according to the rules set forth in the respective transaction.

FINLAND

Yes, the partners are allowed to opt out of the Finnish Cohabitation Act. However, it is not allowed to make anticipatory agreements waiving the right to demand the separation of property or the right to apply for an estate distributor to be appointed.

FRANCE

No such legislative provisions exist in the French legal system.

GERMANY

There are no provisions which regulate informal relationships.

GREECE

There is no specific legislation, so the question does not arise.

HUNGARY

The cohabitants may opt out of the default property regime by means of a property agreement. The Register of Cohabitant's Statements is an 'opt-in' regime.

REPUBLIC OF IRELAND

Yes – see Question 59 – partners, in their cohabitants' agreement, may opt out of the redress scheme in Part 15 of the Irish 2010 Act.

ITALY

Not applicable.

LATVIA

In Latvia there is no particular legal order on partners in an informal relationship.

LITHUANIA

Yes. The conclusion of an agreement on the division of property (as well as the legal registration of the partnership itself) is a voluntary choice of the individuals involved.

LUXEMBOURG

There are no specific legislative provisions regulating informal relationships.

THE NETHERLANDS

As there is no *lex specialis* covering informal relationships, it is not possible to opt in or out.

NORWAY

The Norwegian Household Community Act provides a limited opportunity for a household member to purchase what was previously the common residence and household goods at market value upon the termination of the relationship when 'strong reasons' so indicate. The parties are not permitted to opt out of this Act before or during the relationship - agreements between the parties made prior to the termination are to be taken into account pursuant to S. 4. The partners may agree to opt out of this regulation when the relationship has terminated.

The inheritance right of the surviving cohabitant and the right to undivided possession of the estate can be restricted by a will of which the cohabitant is informed before the testator's death.[3]

PORTUGAL

Regarding the legal benefits that arise from the relationship, they may either be claimed or not. Furthermore, the claimant may or may not be able to prove their legal requirements.

Regarding the legal negative consequences, there is no opt-out in the situations in which they are foreseen by mandatory rules.

RUSSIA

Not applicable.

SCOTLAND

The possibility of opting in or out of legislative provision is most likely to arise in the context of the provisions of the Family Law (Scotland) Act 2006. While there is no specific provision in the legislation dealing with this issue, it is widely assumed that parties may indeed make their own agreements by which they could opt out of the statutory regulation. The 2006 Act provisions have been strongly criticised for their lack of clarity and discretionary nature and it is likely that some couples may seek to achieve greater clarity and certainty by means of their own bespoke agreement.

SLOVAKIA

There are no special legislative provisions permitting partners to either opt in or opt out.

3 See Questions 47 and 48.

SLOVENIA

The legal consequences of an extramarital union are determined on the basis of the law alone (without a court decision) and irrespective of whether the partners who have been living together for an extended period even really desire this. An agreement between the partners that their long-term intensive life union will not be considered to be an extramarital union does not therefore have effect. Since the amendment to the Slovenian Marriage Act of 2004[4] an extramarital partner may, by agreement on the prior renunciation of maintenance after the cessation of the union, exclude a maintenance arrangement but she or he cannot exclude the rules of property relations between the partners because this arrangement is still of a compulsory nature.

SPAIN

The Spanish Civil Code does not contain any rules on either registered or informal relationships.

The Catalan Civil Code does, in fact, regulate informal relationships. The relationship during cohabitation is governed exclusively by the agreements made by the partners, while cohabitation lasts (Art. 234-3.1 Catalan Civil Code). Even though the law states that relations are governed 'exclusively' by the couple's agreements, this is not entirely accurate, as there are mandatory rules on the disposal of the family dwelling (Art. 234.3-2 Catalan Civil Code).

Article 231-9.1 Catalan Civil Code will be applicable to partnerships; it states that the spouse who is sole owner of the family dwelling may not, without the consent of the other spouse, perform any act of alienation, encumbrance or, in general, disposal of his right on the family dwelling or on the ordinary furniture that could impair their use. The act performed without the spouse's consent or judicial authorisation is voidable, at the request of the spouse who lives in such dwelling, within four years of having knowledge thereof or from the time that the act is recorded in the Property Registry. Article 231-9.3 Catalan Civil Code concludes by saying that 'The act remains effective if the purchaser acts in good faith and for consideration and the owner stated that the property was not a family dwelling, even though it was an inaccurate representation. There is no good faith if the purchaser knew or could reasonably have known at the time of the acquisition that it was a family

---

4 Uradni list RS (Official Journal) No. 16/2004.

dwelling. In any case, the spouse who disposed thereof is liable for the damages caused, in accordance with the applicable laws.' In practice, however, it will be difficult for the buyer to know that there is an informal relationship and that the home he/she wants to buy is a family dwelling, which has an impact on good faith. Couples may not opt out of this rule.

As regards the consequences of break-up, the Catalan Civil Code allows the couple to make agreements (Art. 234-5 Catalan Civil Code). The Catalan Civil Code establishes some rules on compensation by reason of work (Art. 234-9 Catalan Civil Code), which partners may opt out of (Art. 432-7 Catalan Civil Code), and some rules on maintenance (Art. 234-10 Catalan Civil Code). Rules on maintenance may be opted out from, or waived, but in this case, there is some judicial control, as 'agreements to waive maintenance are null and void to the extent that they compromise the ability of the partner entitled thereto to meet his basic needs' (Art. 234-10.2 Catalan Civil Code).

SWEDEN

The Swedish regulation on 'cohabitation property' is, basically, a default regime which can be set aside by the partners' agreement. This means that the partners can 'opt out' of this regulation but also 'opt into it', if they wish to set the previous 'opt out' agreement aside.

According to the Swedish Cohabitation Act, § 9, cohabitees or prospective cohabitees may conclude an agreement called a 'cohabitation agreement', on the scope of the division of their 'cohabitation property', which is always limited to the couple's joint dwelling and joint household goods acquired for their joint use. This greatly resembles what spouses are able to agree in the form of a marital property agreement.[5] A 'cohabitation agreement' under the Swedish Cohabitation Act implies that the cohabitees or prospective cohabitees have come to an agreement that there will be no division of the 'cohabitation property', or that certain assets otherwise included in this category of property are excluded from the division, when the relationship ends. 'Cohabitation property', previously excluded by an agreement from the property division, can be reintroduced into the division by concluding a new 'cohabitation agreement' to this effect. From § 9 it follows that the enactment's property regime (limited to so-called 'cohabitation property')

[5] Cf. G. Lind, *Sambolagen, en kommentar*, Norstedts Juridik, Stockholm, 2013, at § 9 and 10.

is a default regime which applies only or to the extent that the parties have not opted out of it. There is a need to emphasise that all other property which either partner may own alone or jointly with the other cohabitee does not constitute 'cohabitation property' and therefore, *ex lege*, is not included in the property division. On the other hand, the provisions of the Swedish Cohabitation Act, § 16 and 22 on a partner's take-over right of the joint dwelling, following a need-based assessment, cannot be set aside by the partners' agreement.

SWITZERLAND

Not relevant.

QUESTION 63

When can the agreement be made (before, during, or after the relationship)?

AUSTRIA

Due to the principle of freedom of contract partners in an informal relationship are permitted to conclude a partnership agreement. [1] Partnership agreements are subject to the general rules which are applicable to contracts.[2] Hence, everyone can determine on his/her own with whom and under what conditions and at which point in time a contract is agreed upon. From a practical point of view, however, partnership agreements are usually concluded during the relationship, after the partners have known each other for a certain length of time and have possibly moved in together. With regard to the point in time when the partnership agreement has to be concluded, two issues should be borne in mind: First, since relationships tend to become more complex over time, particularly concerning assets that are jointly purchased, partners should not wait too long before drafting an agreement.[3] Second, although it is legally possible to reach an agreement on the consequences of the separation after the breakdown of the informal relationship, it is highly likely that a separation makes a settlement even more difficult. Apart from these practical considerations, no provisions regarding the point in time when the partnership agreement should be concluded have to be followed.

BELGIUM

The agreement can be made before, during and after the relationship. Agreements during and after the relationship may not infringe on the rights of third parties. Agreements before or during the relationship that

---

1 N. OSWALD and A. SCHMALLEGGER, 'Partnerschaftsvertrag zwischen nichtehelichen Lebensgefährten', *EF-Z*, 2013, at p. 13.

2 N. OSWALD and A. SCHMALLEGGER, 'Partnerschaftsvertrag zwischen nichtehelichen Lebensgefährten', *EF-Z*, 2013, at p. 13.

3 Cf. E. MÖSCHL, *Die nichteheliche Lebensgemeinschaft*, LexisNexis ARD ORAC, Vienna, 2007, at marg. No. 34.

regulate the separation may also not amount to penalty clauses[4] or restrict the partners' personal freedom.[5]

BULGARIA

There is no regulation on this matter. Partners in an informal relationship are free to choose when such an agreement is entered into.

CROATIA

In line with Art. 11 paragraph 2 and Art. 36 of the Croatian Family Act and Art. 4 paragraph 2 and Art. 54 of the Croatian Partnership Act, the answer equally relates to both cohabitants and same-sex informal partners.

Agreements can be made before and during the relationship.

CZECH REPUBLIC

The agreement can be made before, during or after the relationship. There are no specific rules concerning agreements between the partners in an informal relationship.

DENMARK

Agreements can be made before, during and after a relationship.

ENGLAND AND WALES

At any time.

ESTONIA

There are no special rules; agreements are concluded according to the rules set forth in the respective transaction.

---

4 S. EGGERMONT, *De juridische bescherming van private relaties*, PhD, University of Antwerp, 2015, at n° 258.

5 P. SENAEVE, *Compendium van het personen- en familierecht*, Acco, Leuven, 2013, at n°s 2058-2065.

FINLAND

Before, during and after the relationship has ended.

FRANCE

A cohabitation contract can be entered into at any time: before and during cohabitation and at the time of the separation.

GERMANY

The agreement can be made at any time.

GREECE

At any time. The principle of freedom of contract includes the freedom to determine the time at which a contract is concluded, amended or terminated.

HUNGARY

A property agreement between cohabitants and their agreement on the use of their common dwelling in case the cohabitation comes to an end can be entered into before or during the relationship as it determines future property relations. The cohabitants are even permitted to agree on maintenance and the use of the common dwelling after their relationship has come to an end.

REPUBLIC OF IRELAND

This is unclear under the Irish Civil Partnership and Certain Rights and Obligations of Cohabitants Act 2010. Section 202(5) of the Irish 2010 Act provides that 'an agreement that meets the other criteria of this section shall be deemed to be a cohabitants' agreement under this section even if entered into before the cohabitation has commenced'. This indicates that the agreement can be made prior to cohabitation. There appears to be nothing in the Act preventing such an agreement from being made at any point during the parties' relationship of cohabitation. However whether an agreement can be made after the end of the relationship is unclear. Section 202(1) states that cohabitants may enter into a cohabitants' agreement – presumably meaning that a couple must come within the definition of 'cohabitants' under S. 172 of the Act if they wish to enter into this type of an agreement. Thus, it may not be possible to make a cohabitants' agreement when the relationship has broken down and the parties are no longer living together.

ITALY

Agreements can be signed before starting to live together, while living together and after living together.

LATVIA

In Latvia there is no particular legal order on partners in an informal relationship.

LITHUANIA

Cohabitees may conclude an agreement on the division of property at any time: both prior to and after the registration of the partnership. In both cases such an agreement shall come into force no sooner than one year after the date of the registration of the partnership.

Note: the provisions of the Lithuanian Civil Code (Art. 3.229-3.235) have not been applied in practice; however, they have not been abolished either.

LUXEMBOURG

The agreement can be made at any time.

THE NETHERLANDS

There are no legal limitations in this respect and a cohabitation contract may be concluded at any time. Mostly, couples will have had a relationship for some time and then, due to the purchase of a house, or the birth of a child, will conclude a contract.[6] Separation contracts are drawn up in the case of a relationship breakdown.

---

[6] W.M. Schrama, P. Kuik and L.C.A. Verstappen, 'Samenlevingsovereenkomsten in de notariële praktijk', *Familie&Recht*, 2014, available at: familieenrecht.nl, at 14.3.

NORWAY

In general, agreements can be made before, during, and after the relationship. As regards the Norwegian Household Community Act, agreements to opt out can only be made after the relationship, see also answer to Question 62.

PORTUGAL

At any time, as long as consequences defined by a court decision, or by mandatory rules, are respected.

RUSSIA

Agreements can be made at any stage.

SCOTLAND

This is not an issue expressly regulated by Scots law but, by analogy with agreements in the context of marriage, it would be reasonable to assume that they can be made at any time. Scots law does not distinguish between ante-nuptial, post-nuptial or separation agreements and it would therefore to be reasonable to expect a similar approach to agreements made in the context of informal relationships.

SLOVAKIA

Referring to Question 57: within the framework of autonomy (freedom – autonomy of will) the agreement can be made before, during, or after the relationship.

SLOVENIA

An agreement (on maintenance) can be entered into before the beginning of the relationship, during the course of an extramarital union or at the time of separation.

SPAIN

The Spanish Civil Code does not contain any rules on either registered or informal relationships. Agreements are generally valid, but both case law and legal doctrine only mention agreements made during or after cohabitation. If we look for an analogy with marriage, we must turn to Art. 1334 Spanish Civil Code, which states that agreements made prior to marriage will only be valid if the couple marries within one year of the agreement.

The Catalan Civil Code specifically mentions agreements made during the relationship (Art. 234-3 and 234-5 Catalan Civil Code), and after the relationship (Art. 234-6 Catalan Civil Code). Article 234-5 Catalan Civil Code refers to Art. 231-20 Catalan Civil Code, on agreements made on the consequences of marital breakdown. This provision is applicable to informal relationships, with the necessary adjustments, which may give rise to some difficulties. In particular, Art. 231-20.1 Catalan Civil Code states that agreements made before marriage are only valid if they are made within thirty days prior to the marriage date. As regards informal relationships, it may be difficult to give a precise date for the beginning of the relationship.

SWEDEN

The 'cohabitation agreement', limited to the scope of the division of 'cohabitation property', may according to the Swedish Cohabitation Act § 9 be concluded during the cohabitation relationship or before the cohabitation relationship starts.

SWITZERLAND

Generally, an agreement between partners in an informal relationship can be made before, during or after the relationship.

QUESTION 64

When formal requirements, if any, govern the validity of agreements:

a. As between the partners?

b. In relation to a third party?

AUSTRIA

a. As between the partners?

Although it is not mandatory, a partnership agreement should be drafted in writing for evidentiary purposes.[1] It should be noted, however, that some clauses are subject to formal requirements:[2] A maintenance agreement is qualified as a donation and therefore requires a notarial deed in order to be valid. Further, an advance directive *(Patientenverfügung)*, which *inter alia* allows a person to appoint a person of trust who is informed about the health situation in the event of illness, requires that the decision is made in writing before a lawyer, a notary or a legally qualified person from patients' representatives.[3] Apart from these peculiarities no formal requirements have to be considered.

b. In relation to a third party?

Generally, contracts do not have any legal effect in relation to third parties, rather they are only binding as between the contracting parties.[4] However, under Austrian law contracts for the benefit of a third party are allowed.[5] A contract for the benefit of a third party can be concluded without considering any formal requirements, apart from the exceptional

---

1 E. MÖSCHL, *Die nichteheliche Lebensgemeinschaft*, LexisNexis ARD ORAC, Vienna, 2007, at marg. No. 43.

2 Cf. N. OSWALD and A. SCHMALLEGGER, 'Partnerschaftsvertrag zwischen nichtehelichen Lebensgefährten', *EF-Z*, 2013, at p. 13.

3 Section 6 para. 1 Advance Decision Act *(Patientenverfügungsgesetz)*.

4 See the answer to Question 60(b).

5 S. KALSS, 'section 881 General Austrian Civil Code', in: A. KLETEČKA and M. SCHAUER, *ABGB-ON 1.02*, Manz Verlag, Vienna, 2014, at marg. No. 1.

case where the underlying contract is qualified as e.g. a donation without simultaneous delivery, which requires a notarial form.[6]

BELGIUM

a. As between the partners?

There are no formal requirements: the principle of consensuality applies. Contracts regarding immovable property, for example joint acquisition or tontine or accretion (of usufruct), however require the intervention of a notary public. A notarial cohabitation agreement is generally recommended, as such agreements have a fixed date and can be enforced.[7] The agreement must furthermore be a notarial one in case the parties want to register it in the population register (Art. 1, 10° Royal Decree of 16 July 1992 on the population registers). (Non-)registration, however, has no legal consequences at all.

b. In relation to a third party?

There are no formal requirements, except publication in the Mortgage Register to render the agreement opposable.

BULGARIA

a. As between the partners?

There are no requirements in relation to form which govern the validity of the agreement as between the partners. However, if the agreement is on the disposal of immovable property the general formal requirement for its validity should be applied (Art. 18 of the Bulgarian Obligations and Contracts Law – a notarial deed).

b. In relation to a third party?

In general, the agreement governs the relationship between the partners and there is neither a requirement for its public registration nor any formal requirements for its validity. The law only requires the registration of transactions with regard to immovable assets.

---

6 S. KALSS, 'section 881 General Austrian Civil Code', in: A. KLETEČKA and M. SCHAUER, *ABGB-ON 1.02,* Manz Verlag, Vienna, 2014, at marg. No. 32; H. LÖCKER, 'section 943 General Austrian Civil Code', in: A. KLETEČKA and M. SCHAUER, *ABGB-ON 1.02,* Manz Verlag, Vienna, 2013, at marg. No. 1.

7 W. PINTENS, C. DECLERCK, J. DU MONGH, K. VANWINCKELEN, *Familiaal vermogensrecht,* Intersentia, Antwerp, 2010, at n° 1006.

CROATIA

In line with Art. 11 paragraph 2 of the Croatian Family Act and Art. 4 paragraph 2 and Art. 54 of the Croatian Partnership Act, the answer equally relates to both cohabitants and same-sex informal partners.

a. As between the partners?

According to Art. 40 paragraph 3 in relation to Art. 11 of the Croatian Family Act and Art. 53 paragraph 2 in relation to Art. 4 of the Croatian Partnership Act, an agreement shall be made in writing and the signatures thereon require authentication.

b. In relation to a third party?

According to Art. 40 paragraph 2 in relation to Art. 11 of the Croatian Family Act and Art. 54 paragraph 1 in relation to Art. 4 of the Croatian Partnership Act, the provisions on property administration or disposal shall have legal effect if they are registered in land or public registers which require such registration for the acquisition of rights or if the utilization of an item requires such registration.

CZECH REPUBLIC

a. As between the partners?

There are the same general formal requirements as in any other agreement, because there are no special rules dealing with this kind of agreement.

b. In relation to a third party?

There are the same general formal requirements as in any other agreement, because there are no special rules dealing with this kind of agreement.

DENMARK

a. As between the partners?

There are no formal requirements for agreements between cohabitants on the division of their property. Oral agreements can also be valid.

b. In relation to a third party?

There are no formal requirements for agreements between cohabitants for the division of their property. Oral agreements can also be valid, but in relation to third parties there can be problems in proving that an agreement has been entered into.

ENGLAND AND WALES

a. As between the partners?

Generally it is advisable for the agreement to take the form of a deed to avoid problems surrounding contractual consideration.

b. In relation to a third party?

This will depend on the nature of the contract or transaction. Normal rules of law will apply.

ESTONIA

a. As between the partners?

There are no special rules; agreements are concluded according to the rules set forth in the respective transaction.

b. In relation to a third party?

There are no special rules; agreements are concluded according to the rules set forth in the respective transaction.

FINLAND

a. As between the partners?

As to agreements before and during the relationship, no formal requirements exist. Formal requirements concern only the deed on the separation of the property after the relationship has ended. The criteria are the same as for the deed on the dissolution of property between spouses or the distribution of property from the estate of the deceased. The deed must be in writing and signed by the parties and by two impartial witnesses. If the deed on the separation of property is made by an estate distributor, the deed must be in writing and signed by the estate distributor.

b. In relation to a third party?

As to agreements before and during the relationship, no formal requirements exist. However, if, when separating the property or when paying the compensation due to unjust enrichment, one cohabiting partner has received considerably more of the property of the other partner than he or she would have been liable to give, the property or compensation can be recovered from a bankruptcy estate, unless the separation deed or the agreement or some other document concerning compensation is submitted to the local register office for registration and more than three years have elapsed since the registration.[8]

FRANCE

a. As between the partners?

No specific formal requirements govern the validity of agreements between cohabitants. The only requirements are those provided for the validity of specific acts that must be laid down in a written document[9] or in a notarial deed.[10]

b. In relation to a third party?

No formal requirements govern the validity of agreements in relation to a third party. The only requirements are those mentioned in (a) above.

GERMANY

a. As between the partners?

There are no specific formal requirements which govern the validity of partnership agreements. The general rules apply. Thus in particular those agreements which concern the transfer or acquisition of a plot of land must be notarised, § 311b German Civil Code. Moreover, notarisation is, for instance, required where a leasehold or the ownership of a condominium are concerned;[11] according to § 2276 German Civil Code a contract of inheritance may only be made by being recorded before a notary in the simultaneous presence of both parties.

b. In relation to a third party?

This question has no relevance in German legislation.

GREECE

a. As between the partners?

The same general rules apply as those governing the validity of any transaction or agreement.

---

8 Finnish Act on the Recovery of Property from the Estate of a Bankrupt Person (758/1991), S. 9a.

9 Art. 1134 of the French Civil Code.

10 A notarial deed is a legal requirement for any contract related to the sale of real estate, for a donation contract, and for agreements on succession (*pacte successoral*).

11 H. GRZIWOTZ, *Nichteheliche Lebensgemeinschaft*, Beck, Munich, 2014, at § 9 No. 27.

b. In relation to a third party?
Again, the general rules on the validity of any agreement apply. Article 415 of the Greek Civil Code is also applicable, prohibiting any contract at the expense of a third party.

HUNGARY

a. As between the partners?
A maintenance agreement on fulfilling the maintenance obligation by making a lump-sum payment, the property agreement between cohabitants and the agreement on the use of the common dwelling in the future have to be included in a public instrument or a private document attested by a lawyer.

b. In relation to a third party?
The property agreements between cohabitants are only valid against third parties if the agreement has been recorded in the Register of Property Agreements of Cohabitants or the cohabitants can prove that the third party knew or would have known about the existence of the agreement and its contents.

REPUBLIC OF IRELAND

Section 202 of the Irish 2010 Act sets out the formal requirements that govern cohabitants' agreements. They are discussed in full at Question 57.

ITALY

a. As between the partners?
No formal requirement is needed between the partners. In principle, an oral agreement and its content might be proved through witnesses and presumptions.[12] But, of course, a written document is highly advisable, in order to establish and prove one's petition.

However, agreements including transactions over immovable or ones requiring formalities in other public offices require the intervention of a notary.

12 G. OBERTO, *I diritti dei conviventi. Realtà e prospettive tra Italia ed Europa*, Cedam, Padua, 2012, at p. 109.

b. In relation to a third party?

Contracts, as such, have no effect regarding third parties. For instance, if the partners have agreed that a special asset, let us say land, is the common property of both, in order that this provision has effect toward third parties it is necessary to register the land under common ownership.

More generally, formal requirements in relation to third parties vary according to the content of the agreement and the kind of property involved.

LATVIA

In Latvia there is no particular legal order on partners in an informal relationship.

Section 1473 of the Latvian Civil Law determines that the form of a lawful transaction depends on the discretion of the participants in the matter, except in instances specifically indicated by law. Section 1474 provides that the participants to a transaction may enter into it in accordance with the procedures provided for by a notary public or by the Latvian Law on Orphans' Courts or a private procedure, may accept an oral agreement or draw up a written deed, may enter into the transaction in the presence of witnesses or without them, and the participants to a transaction may make it public or not. This provision does not apply to those instances in which the law requires a specific procedure for entering into a transaction.

LITHUANIA

No law applies.

LUXEMBOURG

The validity of these agreements is only submitted to the general rules of contract law.

THE NETHERLANDS

a. As between the partners?

According to general contract law, no specific formal requirements in relation to validity apply as between the partners, unless the law states otherwise (Art. 3:37 Dutch Civil Code). Since cohabitation contracts and separation agreements are not a specifically regulated type of contract in the Dutch Civil Code, no formal requirement applies.

However, in practice many contracts will be drawn up by a notary, since a number of legal provisions require a notarial contract in order to qualify as a cohabiting couple, e.g. Art. 1a para. c Dutch Inheritance Taxation Act 1956, pension schemes[13] and in relation to specific effects in inheritance law.[14]

b. In relation to a third party?
According to general contract law, no specific formal requirements in relation to validity apply in relation to third parties, unless the law states otherwise (Art. 3:37 Dutch Civil Code). Since cohabitation contracts and separation agreements are not a specifically regulated type of contract in the Dutch Civil Code, no formal requirement applies.

Nevertheless, in order to qualify as a cohabiting couple, other formal requirements might be applicable. This depends on the specific regulation, e.g. Art. 1a para. c Dutch Inheritance Taxation Act 1956, pension schemes[15] and inheritance law require a notarial cohabitation contract with a duty to support each other during the relationship.[16]

NORWAY

a. As between the partners?
In general, no formal requirements govern the validity of agreements as between the partners. Verbal agreements are valid as well; however, such agreements can be difficult to prove.

b. In relation to a third party?
As a rule, agreements are valid in relation to a third party without any formal requirements. However, the owner of real property needs to be protected from a good faith purchaser, and agreements which transfer real property from one partner to the other need protection against

---

13 Each pension fund sets its own conditions. An example of one the biggest funds in the Netherlands: www.abp.nl/relatie/trouwen-samenwonen/nabestaandenpensioen-partner-aanmelden.asp.

14 Art. 4:82 Dutch Civil Code.

15 Each pension fund sets its own conditions. An example of one the biggest funds in the Netherlands: www.abp.nl/relatie/trouwen-samenwonen/nabestaandenpensioen-partner-aanmelden.asp.

16 Art. 4:82 Dutch Civil Code.

seizure from the creditors of the former owner. To obtain such protection, real property must be registered by the registrar for judicial registration of title pursuant to the Norwegian Land Registration Act.

If an agreement regulates the financial settlement upon death, the agreement should be set out in the form of a will in order to be protected against the heirs of the deceased partner.

PORTUGAL

a. As between the partners?

As a rule, there are no formal requirements – the principle of formal freedom (Art. 219 of the Portuguese Civil Code). But, for instance, if one member of the *de facto* union grants a power of attorney to the other and this is included in the cohabitation agreement, this has to follow the same formal requirements demanded for the legal acts for which he/she has representative powers (Art. 262(2) of the Portuguese Civil Code).

b. In relation to a third party?

As a rule, there are no formal requirements – the principle of formal freedom (Art. 219 of the Portuguese Civil Code). But, for instance, if one member of the *de facto* union grants a power of attorney to the other and this is included in the cohabitation agreement, this has to follow the same formal requirements demanded for the legal acts for which he/she has representative powers (Art. 262(2) of the Portuguese Civil Code).

RUSSIA

a. As between the partners?

There are no special provisions; therefore, agreements can also be made verbally. However, proving the existence and contents of a verbal agreement could constitute a substantial difficulty. The absence of specific form requirements has prompted some authors to suggest that the existence of an agreement can be derived from the behaviour of the parties: living together, running a joint household and supporting each other.[17] However, it is unclear as to whether the courts will be prepared to consider such 'implicit' agreements as cohabitation agreements. It has been rightly suggested that if an agreement between partners relates to immovable property, such an agreement should be in writing and made

[17] В.С. ПАНИН, *Проблемы правового регулирования фактических брачных отношений в России*, dissertation, Moscow, 2012, at p. 90, note 1.

subject to the special registration which is required for all transactions relating to immovable property.[18]

b. In relation to a third party?

There are no special provisions; therefore, agreements can also be made verbally. However, proving the existence and contents of a verbal agreement could constitute a substantial difficulty.

It has been rightly suggested that if an agreement between partners relates to immovable property, such an agreement should be in writing and made subject to the special registration which is required for all transactions relating to immovable property.[19]

SCOTLAND

There are no formal requirements governing the validity of agreements between parties to an informal relationship. In Scotland, such agreements are often referred to as a Minute of Agreement and they are simply a form of contract. The format of the Minute of Agreement is by no means restricted to cohabitation agreements but can be used in a wide variety of situations where parties wish to reduce to writing their agreement. Such agreements have however become very commonly used to regulate the consequences of separation or divorce and they might similarly be used in the context of informal relationships.

a. As between the partners?

If agreement is reached between partners, it is likely to be recorded in a formal written agreement, often described in Scotland as a Minute of Agreement. Agreements between partners are enforceable, subject to the general rules of contract and there are no formal requirements. Such agreements are commonly registered for preservation and execution in a public register, the Books of Council and Session, and, by registration, they become directly enforceable, with the same effect as a court decree.

In order to create a binding contract between the parties, no particular form is required but in order to have it accepted by the Keeper of the Registers, the deed must be self-proving according to the Scots Requirements of Writing Act 1995; meaning that it must be signed by

[18] Е.Н. Киминчижи, 'Об имущественных отношениях сожительствующих лиц', *Семейное и жилищное право*, 2008, at p. 9.

[19] Е.Н. Киминчижи, 'Об имущественных отношениях сожительствующих лиц', *Семейное и жилищное право*, 2008, at p. 9.

both parties and witnessed. The process of registration ensures the preservation or safe keeping of the agreement and provided the agreement includes consent to registration for execution, it will also result in the grant of warrant for execution of summary diligence. This allows the parties to enforce their agreement by means of summary diligence if necessary without recourse to the court.[20]

b. In relation to a third party?
As above, there are no requirements for formal validity.

SLOVAKIA

a. As between the partners?
There are no formal requirements governing the validity of agreements.

b. In relation to a third party?
There are no formal requirements governing the validity of agreements in relation to a third party.

SLOVENIA

a. As between the partners?
All agreements between extramarital partners on property relations must be concluded in the form of a notarial protocol; agreements on maintenance relations between partners must be concluded in the form of an enforceable notarial protocol.

Extramarital partners may agree between themselves about maintenance in the event of separation. Such an agreement is concluded before a notary in the form of an enforceable notarial protocol (Art. 81.b of the Slovenian Marriage Act). Partners may conclude an agreement on maintenance in the event of separation before the beginning of the relationship, during the course of an extramarital union or at the time of separation. Partners may also renounce maintenance, but only when the existence of the conditions for maintenance at the time of separation cannot be anticipated with certainty. If the partners at the time of concluding an agreement knew with certainty that one of the partners would need maintenance in the event of separation and because of

20 For further discussion of the use of minutes of agreement in Scots family law see J. MAIR, F. WASOFF and K. MACKAY, *All Settled? A study of legally binding separation agreements and private ordering in Scotland* (unpublished report), University of Glasgow, 2013, available at: eprints.gla.ac.uk/85810, at chapter 2.

renouncing the right to maintenance would have to seek social assistance, such an agreement would be null and void. So the conclusion of an agreement on the renunciation of the right to maintenance will only have effect before or during the course of an extramarital union, since at the time of separation it will already be known whether a partner will remain without the necessary means to support himself or herself after the separation. With an agreement on the renunciation of the right to maintenance, the partners may not put at risk the benefit of a child; the partner who renounces maintenance must have sufficient means for her or his subsistence and that of an underage child.

The rule on common property is of a compulsory nature.

b. In relation to a third party?
There are no special provisions.

SPAIN

a. As between the partners?
The Spanish Civil Code does not mention any specific formal requirements for the validity of contracts. Therefore, the liberty of form principle applies (Art. 1278 Spanish Civil Code).

The Catalan Civil Code allows couples to enter into agreements about their cohabitation with no formal requirements (Art. 234-3 Catalan Civil Code). However, agreements on the consequences of break-up must be made in a public deed (Art. 234-5 and 231-20.1 Catalan Civil Code).

b. In relation to a third party?
Agreements made by informal partners are not binding on third parties, regardless of formal requirements.

SWEDEN

a. As between the partners?
The 'cohabitation agreement', regulated by the Swedish Cohabitation Act § 9, must be concluded in writing and signed by both parties. (In a case where they or one of them is underage, in addition the holder of parental responsibilities must consent to the agreement, § 9 para. 2.)

When it comes to agreements other than those subject to the Swedish Cohabitation Act there are no special rules, meaning that the general principles of the laws of obligations and property are applicable. As between the parties, an agreement as such is normally sufficient, both written and oral agreements usually qualifying. Important exceptions apply, however, in relation to gifts and real property. The validity of a gift between the parties and in relation to a third party requires that the object has come into the intended recipient's possession and that the donor is excluded from further disposal of the property.[21] According to Swedish case law, shared possession between the donor and the recipient of the gift is not sufficient to satisfy the requirement of the transfer of possession.[22]

A particular variant of transfer of property between a cohabiting couple is when a 'concealed right of co-ownership' is transformed into an 'open co-ownership'. The 'concealed owner' has, thereby, a legally protected claim to an 'open ownership'. In the case of real property, a specially regulated conveyance agreement must then be drawn up after which the 'concealed' owner can be documented as a co-owner at the land registry.[23]

Generally speaking, having regard to the risk of future disputes, written agreements are to be recommended, not least for reasons of clarity and proof.[24]

b. In relation to a third party?

The cohabitation agreement in its special meaning under Swedish law (above under a), lacks validity in relation to third parties.

A sales contract concerning movable assets, on the other hand, requires that the condition of transfer of possession is fulfilled. Bearing in mind that, in a cohabitation relationship, the seller of the property is not self-evidently excluded from further use of the property, the seller's creditors may be able to make claims on the property, in a case where the

---

21 See M. BRATTSTRÖM, 'Egendomsförhållanden under bestående samboende', in: J. ASLAND et al., *Nordisk samboerrett*, Gyldendal, Oslo, 2014, at p. 102–103 (see Chapter 2.4.4 in the English version of the book, to be published by Intersentia in 2015).

22 See Swedish Supreme Court decision *NJA 1962 p. 669*.

23 See M. BRATTSTRÖM, 'Egendomsförhållanden under bestående samboende', in: J. ASLAND et al., *Nordisk samboerrett*, Gyldendal, Oslo, 2014, at p. 101 (see Chapter 2.4.3 in the English version of the book, to be published by Intersentia in 2015).

24 Cf. M. BRATTSTRÖM, 'Egendomsförhållanden under bestående samboende', in: J. ASLAND et al., *Nordisk samboerrett*, Gyldendal, Oslo, 2014, at p. 96 et seq. (See Chapter 2.4.1 in the English version of the book, to be published by Intersentia in 2015).

seller partner becomes insolvent.[25] A joint ownership to real estate property requires as a rule, in order to become binding on third parties, that the previously concealed joint owner is registered as a co-owner in the real estate registry.[26] Regarding gifts, the same rules and principles apply when it comes to validity between the parties. An undertaking to make a gift is, furthermore, not binding on third parties.[27]

SWITZERLAND

Generally, no particular form has to be observed, unless a particular form is required by law (Art. 11 Swiss Code of Obligations). In order to be binding, a contract transferring real estate must be executed as a public deed (Art. 657 para. 1 Swiss Civil Code).

---

[25] The Swedish Enforcement Code (in Swedish: *Utsökningsbalken* 1981:774) Chapter 4, § 19. Cf. M. BRATTSTRÖM, 'Egendomsförhållanden under bestående samboende', in: J. ASLAND et al., *Nordisk samboerrett*, Gyldendal, Oslo, 2014, at p. 99–100 (see Chapter 2.4.3 in the English version of the book, to be published by Intersentia in 2015).

[26] See Swedish Supreme Court decisions *NJA 1984 p 772* and *NJA 1985 p. 615.*

[27] See Swedish Gift Act (in Swedish: *Lag 1936:83 ang. vissa utfästelser av gåvor*) and M. BRATTSTRÖM, 'Egendomsförhållanden under bestående samboende', in: J. ASLAND et al., *Nordisk samboerrett*, Gyldendal, Oslo, 2014, at p. 104–105 (see Chapter 2.4.4 in the English version of the book, to be published by Intersentia in 2015).

QUESTION 65

Is independent legal advice required?

AUSTRIA

Although independent legal advice is not a mandatory requirement for drafting a partnership agreement, it is recommended to consult a lawyer or a notary when the partners have decided to conclude such an agreement.[1]

BELGIUM

Independent legal advice is not required. The notary public does have a duty to impartially inform the parties (Art. 9, § 1 Notaries Act) in case they choose to conclude a notarial cohabitation agreement, which they are not obliged to do.

BULGARIA

There are no specific legislative provisions regulating informal relationships.

CROATIA

Independent legal advice is not required.

CZECH REPUBLIC

Independent legal advice is not required.

---

1 Cf. U. AICHHORN, *Das Recht der Lebenspartnerschaften, Ehe und Lebensgemeinschaft*, Springer, Vienna, 2003, at p. 426; E. MÖSCHL, *Die nichteheliche Lebensgemeinschaft*, LexisNexis ARD ORAC, Vienna, 2007, at marg. No. 34.

DENMARK

No, but it can be relevant if a party has received legal advice and that party subsequently wants an agreement set aside or amended in accordance with the rules in contract law on unreasonable agreements.[2]

ENGLAND AND WALES

It is advisable but not required. Lack of it may make the agreement less likely to be enforced if there is any sign of undue influence by one partner on the other according to general principles.

ESTONIA

No.

FINLAND

No.

FRANCE

No, compulsory legal advice is not required. Nevertheless, if the agreement is intended to be laid down in notarial deed, the assistance of a notary public is obligatory.

GERMANY

Independent legal advice is only required if notarisation is obligatory (see Question 64).

GREECE

We are not aware of any such case.

HUNGARY

There is no such obligation in the Hungarian Civil Code. If a public instrument is drawn up by a notary, he or she is obliged to inform the

---

2 See I. LUND-ANDERSEN, *Familieøkonomien*, Jurist- og Økonomforbundets Forlag, Copenhagen, 2011, at pp. 548-549.

parties. If a lawyer attests a private document it is his or her obligation to provide all information to the parties. It is not unambiguous whether notaries or lawyers should inform the cohabitants together or independently as it depends on the notary or the lawyer who performs the tasks in a certain case.

Notaries have a general obligation to inform any party according to the Hungarian Act on Notaries.[3] This means that the notary has to provide equal opportunities and assist the parties in exercising their rights and performing their obligations. In the Hungarian Act on Notaries or the Hungarian Act on Non-litigious Notarial Procedures there is no detailed provision on providing impartial advice or due information to the parties if they enter into a property agreement. If the parties want to make a statement about their cohabitation the notary has to inform the parties about the legal consequences of cohabitation, its establishment and its termination.[4]

REPUBLIC OF IRELAND

Yes, S. 202(2)(a)(i) requires cohabitants obtain independent legal advice prior to entering into an agreement. Joint legal advice is acceptable where there is a written waiver from both parties of their right to independent advice.

ITALY

No independent legal advice is required to validate the agreement.

LATVIA

In Latvia there is no particular legal order on partners in an informal relationship.

LITHUANIA

No.

3 Art 1 of Act No. XLI 1991 on Notaries.

4 Art. 36/F(2) of Act No. XLV 2008 on Non-litigious Notarial Procedures.

LUXEMBOURG

No independent advice is required.

THE NETHERLANDS

No, there is no legal obligation to consult a lawyer before making a contract. However, traditionally the notary has an important role in practice in the Netherlands.[5] This might be explained by a number of factors, one being that for a number of advantages in tax law and pension law a notarial contract is required in order to qualify as a cohabiting couple.[6] In addition, a cohabitation contract is regularly concluded when partners purchase a house together. The acquisition of immovable property such as a house requires a notarial deed, so cohabiting couples will visit a civil law notary anyway, thus making it easier to draw up a cohabitation contract. Civil law notaries started to develop default cohabitation contracts for couples several decades ago.[7] Today, notaries often use a default contract as a starting point to draw up a cohabitation contract for a specific couple. Research among civil law notaries indicates that most respondents use only one or two default contracts. Few respondents use more than two default models.[8]

NORWAY

No, independent legal advice is not required. As mentioned in the response to Question 60 above, an agreement may be wholly or partly annulled if it will affect one of the parties unfairly pursuant to the Norwegian Act relating to Conclusion of Agreements, S. 36, and in this connection, it may be significant whether the parties have received legal advice.

PORTUGAL

No.

---

5 P. BLOKLAND, in: W.D. KOLKMAN and L.C.A. VERSTAPPEN (eds.), *Handboek Familie-vermogensrecht*, Walburg Pers, Zutphen, 2013, at 4.1.4.

6 E.g. in inheritance tax law, inheritance law and pension schemes.

7 W.M. SCHRAMA, 'Vermogensrechtelijke aspecten van de niet-huwelijkse samenleving: de moeizame verhouding tussen de affectieve relatie en het (vermogens-)recht', in: C. FORDER and A. VERBEKE, *Gehuwd of niet, Maakt het wat uit?*, Intersentia, Antwerp, 2005, at p. 65-89.

8 W.M. SCHRAMA, P. KUIK and L.C.A. VERSTAPPEN, 'Samenlevingsovereenkomsten in de notariële praktijk', *Familie&Recht*, 2014, available at: familieenrecht.nl, at 14.2.

RUSSIA

No.

SCOTLAND

There is no specific requirement of independent legal advice, or indeed any legal advice. Parties may make their own private agreement. In practice, however, agreements are usually made with the involvement of solicitors and, to strengthen the agreement against any possible contractual challenge, parties would be well advised to take independent legal advice.

SLOVAKIA

No.

SLOVENIA

All agreements between extramarital partners on property relations must be concluded in the form of a notarial protocol, and agreements on maintenance relations between partners must be concluded in the form of an enforceable notarial protocol. Prior to drafting the notarial protocol, the notary must explain to the parties, in an understandable way, the content and legal consequences of the intended legal transaction or a statement of intent and explicitly draw their attention to known and normal risks in connection with concluding such a legal transaction. The notary must also draw the parties' attention to possible other circumstances in connection with the intended legal transaction if he or she knows of them, except for data that the notary is required to protect as confidential. He or she must also prevent the parties from making unclear, incomprehensible or dubious statements and explicitly warn them of the possible legal consequences of such statements. If the parties persist with such statements, he or she must insert them in the notarial protocol but, in addition, the warning given to the parties in connection with these statements must also be included in the protocol (Art. 42 of the Slovenian Notary Act).[9]

9 Uradni list RS (Official Journal) Nos 13/1994, 48/1994, 82/1994, 41/1995, 83/2001, 73/2004, 98/2005, 17/2006, 115/2006, 33/2007, 45/2008, 91/2013.

SPAIN

The Spanish Civil Code does not regulate informal partners' agreements, and therefore the question of independent legal advice does not arise.

The Catalan Civil Code contains a provision that states that 'agreements adopted after the breakdown of cohabitation without independent legal advice for each spouse may be annulled at the request of any spouse within three months from the date of their adoption and no later than the date of the response to the claim or, where appropriate, the counterclaim in the matrimonial proceedings where enforcement of such agreements is sought' (Art. 233-5.2 Catalan Civil Code). This is applicable to partnerships, according to Art. 234-5 Catalan Civil Code.

SWEDEN

The Cohabitation Act sets out no requirements on independent legal advice, prior to the conclusion of the 'cohabitation agreement' regulated by the Act, or at any other stage, for example, in the property division. This position follows that of the Swedish Marriage Code which, equally, does not require independent legal advice to precede the conclusion of a matrimonial property agreement, or at other events.

SWITZERLAND

Independent legal advice is not required.

QUESTION 66

Are there any statistics or estimates on the frequency of agreements made between partners in an informal relationship?

AUSTRIA

Unfortunately, neither statistics nor estimations on this issue exist.[1] However, the legal literature refers to the fact that partnership agreements are rarely concluded in Austria.[2] It is stated that partners in an informal relationship hesitate to conclude partnership agreements due to the complexity and individuality inherent in such agreements.[3]

BELGIUM

There are no statistics available on this topic.

BULGARIA

No, there are no such statistics.

CROATIA

The answer equally refers to both cohabitants same-sex informal partners.

---

1 According to the information provided by Statistics Austria, the Austrian Institute for Family Studies and the Vienna Institute for Demography by e-mails dated 02.02.2015 and 03.02.2015.

2 U. AICHHORN, *Das Recht der Lebenspartnerschaften, Ehe und Lebensgemeinschaft*, Springer, Vienna, 2003, at p. 423; E. MÖSCHL, *Die nichteheliche Lebensgemeinschaft*, LexisNexis ARD ORAC, Vienna, 2007, at marg. No. 34; A. DEIXLER-HÜBNER, *Scheidung, Ehe und Lebensgemeinschaft*, LexisNexis ARD ORAC, Vienna, 2013, at marg. No. 252a; S. FERRARI, 'Rechtsregeln für nichteheliches Zusammenleben in Österreich', in: I. KROPPENBERG et al. (eds.), *Rechtsregeln für nichteheliches Zusammenleben*, Gieseking Verlag, Vienna, 2009, pp. 167-206, at p. 176.

3 E. MÖSCHL, *Die nichteheliche Lebensgemeinschaft*, LexisNexis ARD ORAC, Vienna, 2007, at marg. No. 34.

Although there are no statistics or estimations as to the frequency of agreements made between partners in an informal relationship, agreements between partners both in informal and formal unions are in the principle rarely concluded in Croatia.[4]

CZECH REPUBLIC

There are no statistics or estimations on the frequency of agreements made between partners in an informal relationship.

DENMARK

No.

ENGLAND AND WALES

No. Anecdotal evidence from members of the legal profession and practitioner organizations such as Resolution (the Solicitors' Family Law Association) indicate they are increasing in popularity.

ESTONIA

No particular data are available.

FINLAND

No. Anticipatory agreements are not registered.

FRANCE

No statistics could be found, but it emerges from informal contacts with notaries public[5] that it is very rare for them to authenticate a cohabitation contract.[6] The rarity of such agreements is even more significant compared to the important number of joint acquisitions of real estate by cohabitants, which must be laid down in a notarial deed on a

4 A. ČULO and I. ŠIMOVIĆ, 'Register of Marriage Contracts as Contribution to the Security of Legal Transactions', *Zbornik PFZ*, 2009, pp. 1029-1068, at p. 1029-1030.

5 Informal contacts with Mes L. AZILOU REYMONET, M. FOUR-BROMET and J. POYET, notaries public respectively in Crémieux, Pont de Cheruy and Lyon.

6 L. AZILOU REYMONET has never had an occasion to register such a contract in fifteen years as a notary public and M. FOUR-BROMET stated that she has registered a cohabitation contract once or twice at the maximum during the preceding year.

compulsory basis. However, cohabitation contracts can be valid private agreements, but there is a great incentive for cohabitants who want to lay down their relationship in a formal agreement to register a civil partnership (*Pacs*) rather than to enter into a cohabitation contract.

GERMANY

No such statistics exist.

GREECE

It is methodologically difficult, if not impossible, to gain access to such information, as it involves personal data and raises deontological concerns.

HUNGARY

No. As the Register of Cohabitants' Statements is new not many agreements have been recorded.

REPUBLIC OF IRELAND

No.

ITALY

As these *'patti di convivenza'* agreements are rather new, and still by no means common, no statistics are yet available.

LATVIA

There are no such statistics collected.

LITHUANIA

There is no relevant statistical information available.

LUXEMBOURG

Unfortunately, no statistics or estimations were found.

THE NETHERLANDS

Research among non-marital cohabitants indicates that in 2010 about 50 percent of all non-marital cohabitants had concluded a notarial cohabitation contract.[7]

NORWAY

In a study in 1997 about 20% of cohabiting couples had entered into written agreements with respect to the legal consequences regarding property and other financial matters upon termination. In the age group 20-34 years the percentage was 13, while it rose to 38% among cohabitants in the oldest group, i.e. 50-79 years.[8] In a more recent survey from 2010, the figure was 15% for all age groups.[9]

PORTUGAL

There are no statistics available for this question.

RUSSIA

No data available.

SCOTLAND

There are no official statistics on the frequency of agreements between partners to an informal relationship although two recent research reports offer some comment on their use. In research published in 2010 into legal practitioners' perspectives on the operation of the 2006 Act provisions on cohabitation, '[i]nterviewees varied widely when commenting on how common cohabitation agreements had become', with the researchers observing that it was clear that 'interviewees had expected them to have become much more common.'[10] In a study of a random sample of 600

7 A. DE GRAAF, 'Steeds meer samenwoners hebben een samenlevingscontract', *CBS Webmagazine* 10 February 2010.

8 NOU 1999: 25 p. 71 (Omnibus Survey 1997, Statistics Norway).

9 Conducted by Opinion for HELP Forsikring.

10 F. WASOFF, J. MILES and E. MORDAUNT, *Legal Practitioners' Perspectives on the Cohabitation Provisions of the Family Law (Scotland) Act 2006* (unpublished report), University of Cambridge, Nuffield Foundation, 2010, available at: crfr.ac.uk/assets/Cohabitation-final-report.pdf, at p. 77.

family-based agreements, registered in Scotland in 2010, only five had been made by cohabitants.[11]

SLOVAKIA

There are no official statistics available.

SLOVENIA

No.

SPAIN

No, there are not.

SWEDEN

Several surveys have been conducted in order to establish to what extent cohabitees enter into agreements with each other.[12] The data remains, not surprisingly, uncertain as persons living together in an informal relationship are, statistically speaking, a difficult group to survey. The surveys indicate however very clearly that far from all cohabitees - maybe only 15-20% - have concluded agreements connected with their relationship.[13]

According to Kajsa Walleng's survey (see above Question 11), the figure is slightly lower. Only 14% of the persons interviewed who regarded themselves to be cohabitees in an informal relationship, reported having concluded some kind of an agreement with the other cohabitee.[14]

---

[11] J. MAIR, F. WASOFF and K. MACKAY, *All Settled? A study of legally binding separation agreements and private ordering in Scotland* (unpublished report), University of Glasgow, 2013, available at: eprints.gla.ac.uk/85810, at p. 27.

[12] I. LUND-ANDERSEN, *Familieøkonomien*, Jurist- og Økonomiforbundets Forlag, Copenhagen, 2011, at p. 528; Norges Offentlige utredninger, NOU 1999:25 p. 71: Statens Offentliga Utredningar, SOU 1999:104 p. 152.

[13] T. SVERDRUP, 'Samboere uten lovvern', *Tidskrift för Familierett, Arverett og Barnevernsrettslige spørsmål* (FAB), 2011, at p. 256.

[14] K. WALLENG, *Att leva som sambo*, Iustus Förlag, Uppsala, 2015, at p. 109.

SWITZERLAND

There is no detailed information available with regard to this question. However, it can be said that explicit agreements made between partners in an informal relationship are an exception,[15] although they are highly recommended in the literature (also accessible for laymen). Rather, implied agreements exist, which are indeed difficult to prove.

15 See H. HAUSHEER, T. GEISER and R. AEBI-MÜLLER, *Das Familienrecht des Schweizerischen Zivilgesetzbuches*, Stämpfli, Bern, 2014, at N 03.09.

QUESTION 67

Are there any statistics or estimates regarding the content of agreements made between partners in an informal relationship?

AUSTRIA

Unfortunately, neither statistics nor estimations on this issue exist.[1]

BELGIUM

There are no statistics available on this topic.

BULGARIA

No, there are no such statistics.

CROATIA

The answer equally refers to both cohabitants and same-sex informal partners.

There are no statistics or estimations regarding the content of agreements made between partners in an informal relationship.

CZECH REPUBLIC

There are no statistics or estimations regarding the content of agreements made between partners in an informal relationship.

1 According to the information provided by Statistics Austria, the Austrian Institute for Family Studies and the Vienna Institute for Demography by e-mails dated 02.02.2015 and 03.02.2015.

DENMARK

Cohabitants have often agreed upon or have assumed joint ownership of the joint dwelling and household goods.

ENGLAND AND WALES

No. Although on purchase of the family home in joint names a declaration of trust as to the parties' interest will be asked for by their legal advisor for Land Registry purposes.

ESTONIA

No particular data are available.

FINLAND

No.

FRANCE

Contact with the National Chamber of Notaries Public has been unsuccessful. The principle of confidentiality which governs the records of notaries public has so far made it impossible to obtain such information.

GERMANY

No such statistics exist.

GREECE

It is methodologically difficult, if not impossible, to gain access to such information, as it involves personal data and raises deontological concerns.

HUNGARY

No.

REPUBLIC OF IRELAND

No.

ITALY

No statistics are yet available.

LATVIA

There are no such statistics collected.

LITHUANIA

There is no relevant statistical information available.

LUXEMBOURG

Unfortunately, no statistics or estimations were found.

THE NETHERLANDS

Empirical research has been carried out investigating the contents of cohabitation contracts. All civil law notaries in the Netherlands have been asked about their practice in relation to non-marital cohabitation contracts.[2] An estimated 17-22 percent of the civil law notaries with a family law practice participated in the research. The data provide an insight into the practice of notarial cohabitation contracts, the contents of contracts, the use of different model contracts, the knowledge of couples as to the advantages of a contract, the legal knowledge of couples and many other subjects.[3]

Overall, the conclusion is that cohabitation contracts mostly regulate practical matters[4] and taxation law effects but does not provide real protection for the economically weaker partner. Provisions on netting

---

2 W.M. SCHRAMA, P. KUIK and L.C.A. VERSTAPPEN, 'Samenlevingsovereenkomsten in de notariële praktijk', *Familie&Recht*, 2014, available at: familieenrecht.nl.

3 There are hardly any data available on notaries and their characteristics as a result of which it is not possible to conclude whether the data are representative of all notaries.

4 Such as the costs of the household, the duty to provide support during the relationship, the rule of evidence in relation to movable goods.

income or capital,[5] maintenance[6] and old-age pension rights[7] are only included in cohabitation contracts by a small minority of the respondents. Furthermore, it seems that the notary has a major influence on the contents of the contract. It clearly matters for a couple which notary they consult. The personal situation of the couple sometimes seems to have less impact that the advising practice of the notary.[8]

It has been argued in the legal literature that cohabitation contracts can play a more important role in bridging the gap between the reality of cohabitation and the lack of legal protection.[9] More protection could be included in the contracts and contracts could be periodically evaluated. Moreover, contracts could be, more so than is currently the case, drawn up departing from a separation scenario, for it is in situations of a relationship breakdown that the contract should prove its worth.

NORWAY

There are no recent statistics regarding the content of agreements made between partners to an informal relationship.

PORTUGAL

There are no statistics available for this question.

---

5 W.M. SCHRAMA, P. KUIK and L.C.A. VERSTAPPEN, 'Samenlevingsovereenkomsten in de notariële praktijk', *Familie&Recht*, 2014, available at: familieenrecht.nl, at 14.5: most responding notaries include a right to net each partner's income and/or capital at the end of a certain period or upon the breakdown of a relationship in less than 20 percent of cohabitation contracts, whereas 11 percent almost always include a provision to that effect.

6 W.M. SCHRAMA, P. KUIK and L.C.A. VERSTAPPEN, 'Samenlevingsovereenkomsten in de notariële praktijk', *Familie&Recht*, 2014, available at: familieenrecht.nl, at 14.6: 90 percent of the respondents include a right to partner maintenance after a relationship breakdown in less than 20 percent of the cohabitation contracts, whereas 7 percent of the notaries almost always include such a provision.

7 W.M. SCHRAMA, P. KUIK and L.C.A. VERSTAPPEN, 'Samenlevingsovereenkomsten in de notariële praktijk', *Familie&Recht*, 2014, available at: familieenrecht.nl, at 14.8: only 11 percent of the respondents almost always include a right to share old-age pensions accumulated during the cohabitation, 58 percent of the respondents almost never include such a right.

8 W.M. SCHRAMA, P. KUIK and L.C.A. VERSTAPPEN, 'Samenlevingsovereenkomsten in de notariële praktijk', *Familie&Recht*, 2014, available at: familieenrecht.nl, at 16.

9 W.M. SCHRAMA, 'Een redelijk en billijk relatierecht', *TPR*, 2010, pp. 1703-1740.

RUSSIA

No data available.

SCOTLAND

No detailed evidence relating to the content of agreements is available. In-depth interviews with a sample of 19 family law practitioners in 2009-10 offered some insight into their views as to what might be included but little evidence as to what is in fact included in cohabitation agreements. The point was strongly made that cohabitation agreements can be 'bespoke': 'the great thing about a cohabitation agreement is you can tailor it.'[10]

SLOVAKIA

There are no official statistics available.

SLOVENIA

No.

SPAIN

No, there are not.

SWEDEN

No, there are no statistics regarding the content of agreements between cohabitants. The permitted content of a 'cohabitation agreement' is, however, clearly defined by the Swedish Cohabitation Act, § 9. As regards other agreements, these can be expected to be of a diverse nature. Many of them can be expected to strengthen the mutual rights and duties of the partners, in different respects. But there can equally be agreements which go in the opposite direction, for example, if the partners agree that their mutual relationship is not to result in any mutual rights or duties. Nevertheless, partners covered by the Swedish Cohabitation Act cannot

---

10 F. WASOFF, J. MILES and E. MORDAUNT, *Legal Practitioners' Perspectives on the Cohabitation Provisions of the Family Law (Scotland) Act 2006* (unpublished report), University of Cambridge, Nuffield Foundation, 2010, available at: crfr.ac.uk/assets/Cohabitation-final-report.pdf, at pp. 79-84.

exclude the application of the take-over right of the joint dwelling in the case of the termination of the relationship.

SWITZERLAND

There is no information available with regard to this question.

PART G
DISPUTES

QUESTION 68

Which authority is competent to decide disputes between partners in an informal relationship?

AUSTRIA

In Austria, the district courts *(Bezirksgerichte)* have jurisdiction in civil matters if they are specifically assigned to them by law, e.g. family matters, particularly matters between spouses or partners in a registered partnership, or the amount in dispute does not exceed €15,000. Due to the fact that disputes between partners in an informal relationship have not yet been assigned to specific courts, the competent court in these matters has to be determined according to the amount in dispute: If the amount in dispute is below €15,000 the district court is competent, whereas for all other matters exceeding this value the regional court *(Landesgericht)* is competent.[1] Local jurisdiction is determined according to the general rules, S. 65 et seq. Austrian Jurisdiction Act. Hence, the competent court is usually at the respondent's domicile.[2]

Further, it should be noted that in Austria a distinction is made between contentious and non-contentious proceedings, the latter being subject to a separate procedural law – the Austrian Non-Contentious Proceedings Act *(Außerstreitgesetz)*. Claims arising from informal relationships can only be filed in contentious proceedings.[3]

---

1 Cf. F. MEISSEL and J. JUNGWIRTH, in: E. GITSCHTHALER et al. (eds.), *Kommentar zum Ehe- und Partnerschaftsrecht*, Springer, Vienna, 2011, at p. 1160.

2 The special jurisdiction laid down in S. 76 Austrian Jurisdiction Act for disputes arising from a marriage or a registered partnership does not apply to disputes from an informal relationship. F. MEISSEL and J. JUNGWIRTH, in: E. GITSCHTHALER et al. (eds.), *Kommentar zum Ehe- und Partnerschaftsrecht*, Springer, Vienna, 2011, at p. 1160.

3 Austrian Supreme Court, Legal Proposition RS0013615, see Judgement of 03.03.1982, 6 Ob 692/81; R. FUCIK, 'section 1 Austrian Jurisdiction Act', in: H. FASCHING and A. KONECNY (eds.), *Kommentar zu den Zivilprozessgesetzen*, Manz Verlag, Vienna, 2013, at marg. No. 278.

BELGIUM

There are no specific rules. The general rules on competence apply, which means that informal partners should petition:

- the President of the District Court in order to obtain an interim order in interlocutory proceedings (Art. 584 Belgian Code of Civil Proceedings);[4]
- the Justice of the Peace with regard to tenancy conflicts and claims not exceeding the amount of 2,500 euro (Art. 590 and 591, 1° Belgian Code of Civil Proceedings);
- the Family Court with regard to the domestic exclusion order, maintenance and for all issues regarding the children (Art. 572bis, 4°, 7° and 11° Belgian Code of Civil Proceedings);
- the District Court for all other matters (Art. 568 Belgian Code of Civil Proceedings).

BULGARIA

There is no specific authority which is competent to decide on disputes between partners in an informal relationship. Depending on the dispute, the ordinary courts should be the obvious authority for dispute resolution. The partners are most likely to be treated as separate physical persons rather than as partners in an informal family.

CROATIA

Municipal courts are competent to decide on disputes between partners in an informal relationship.

CZECH REPUBLIC

Because there are no specific rules dealing with an informal relationship, the competent authority to decide disputes between partners in an informal relationship is the same as in any other dispute between two people. In general, it is a court. In the case where partners make a contract dealing with property, the authority could be based on the contract's alternative dispute resolution clause.

4 P. SENAEVE, *Compendium van het personen- en familierecht*, Acco, Leuven, 2013, at n°s 2058-2059.

DENMARK

Upon the termination of cohabitation, unmarried cohabitants can have the division of their property owned in common dealt with by the Probate Court (*Skifteretten*); see S. 1(1)(3) of the Danish Act on the Division of Married Property (*Lov om ægtefælleskifte mv.*). A cohabitant may request the Probate Court to refer a case to an administrator who will have the task of advising and seeking to get the parties to agree as well as drawing up an account of the property; see further in Section 28 of the Act. Administrators in Denmark cannot decide on disputes between cohabitants. The Probate Court will only be involved to the extent that there is disagreement with the administrator's proposal for a settlement, including the valuation of the assets, the allocation of debts etc.

The Danish Probate Courts can deal with individual disputes that may arise between cohabitants if the parties have an estate (a number of assets) that is dealt with by the Probate Court. This might be a dispute about a claim for compensation, for example, or the allocation of liability for a joint debt. The parties will not have to refer to a different court, as the Probate Court dealing with the estate will have jurisdiction to deal with such disputes.

In Denmark there is no legislation governing ownership in common so the dissolution of joint ownership is often agreed in a joint ownership contract. If a cohabiting couple have not entered into such a contract, then the dissolution of the joint ownership of an individual asset will occur in the same way as with the dissolution of joint ownership between others (for example, siblings), in other words this will normally be by an auction in the Probate Court, unless otherwise agreed. Disputes where there is an agreement will be dealt with by the Probate Court or the ordinary civil courts.

ENGLAND AND WALES

Cohabitants' property disputes are governed by the English Civil Procedure Rules 1998 rather than the English Family Procedure Rules 2010 and can be heard by the by the County Court or the Chancery Division of the High Court depending on the value of the property.

Where there is also a claim under Schedule 1 English Children Act 1989 for financial provision for the benefit of the child, case law and practice following *Goldstone v Goldstone* [2011] EWCA Civ 39, [2011] 1 FCR 324 provides that both matters should be heard together by the Family

Division of the High Court and this is reflected in a Practice Direction under the English Civil Procedure Rules.[5] If there is just a dispute under Schedule 1 English Children Act 1989 this will normally be heard by the new Family Court which replaces the County Court and Magistrates or Family Proceedings Courts in all family matters and enables High Court judges to hear cases sitting in the Family Court, if appropriate.

ESTONIA

Disputes between the partners in an informal relationship are settled by the county courts as courts of first instance. In Estonia the county courts hear civil, criminal and misdemeanour matters as courts of first instance. The county courts are courts with general jurisdiction by law or are general courts.

FINLAND

The authority deciding on disputes between partners depends on the nature of the dispute. Generally, legal disputes between partners are heard by the District Court. However, if the dispute is about the separation of property or the compensation for unjust enrichment according to the Finnish Cohabitation Act, the partner of the heir or the deceased partner can make an application to the District Court for the appointment of an estate distributor to separate the property. The claim for compensation for unjust enrichment can also be made to the estate distributor. If one or both of the parties are not satisfied with the decision of the estate distributor, the decision can be appealed to the District Court. The claim for compensation can also be made directly to the District Court if no application for the appointment of the estate distributor has been made in the first place.

FRANCE

In case of disputes between partners in an informal relationship, the family judge (*juge aux affaires familiales*) has jurisdiction concerning the following matters:

5 Practice Direction 2B made under the Civil Procedure Rules at para. 3.2. In *Goldstone, Hedley J stated* 'The principle underlying these rules is very clearly that it is desirable to equip a single court with the means of deciding all relevant connected issues within the same proceedings and to avoid a multiplicity of different and potentially conflicting proceedings. Although the FPR do not contain general provisions for joinder, they are entirely consistent with this principle.'

- All disputes relating to the exercise of parental responsibilities: decisions on the child's residence, on contact, on child maintenance. For these disputes, the parties are not required to be represented by a lawyer.
- The sharing of assets and the settlement of joint ownership. Representation by counsel is mandatory.
- The protection of a partner in the case of domestic violence.

The same authority has jurisdiction concerning similar disputes between spouses or former spouses.

Since Law Act no. 2009-526 of 12 May 2009 aiming to simplify and clarify the law and to make proceedings more informal and Decree no. 2009-1591 of 15 December 2009, all disputes relating to the settlement of the partners' patrimonial interests are decided by the family judge, who now has jurisdiction concerning disputes arising out of the separation of couples. See Art. L. 213-3, 2° of the Judicial Organisation Code (*Code de l'organisation judiciaire, COJ*)[6] and Art. 1136-1 of the French Code of Civil Procedure.[7] The court of appeal of Lyon,[8] for example, has determined that a dispute arising out of a loan granted by one partner to the other must be brought before the family judge.

The general civil court (*tribunal de grande instance)* decides on claims relating to filiation.

---

6 The family judge is in particular competent concerning the following matters in respect of non-married couples: 1) joint ownership by registered partners or partners in an informal relationship; 2) the settlement and sharing of the assets of registered partners or partners in an informal relationship; 3) claims relating to a) child maintenance and – for registered partners – to the contribution to the costs and expenses of their household; b) the exercise of parental responsibilities; c) protection against a violent spouse, registered partner or partner in an informal relationship (*concubin)* or against a former spouse, registered partner or *concubin;* f) protection of an adult when there is a risk of a forced marriage.

7 Art. 1136-1 French Code of Civil Procedure: for disputes on spouses' matrimonial property regime, on joint ownership between registered partners or partners in an informal relationship, on the liquidation and settlement of the patrimonial interests of spouses, registered partners or partners in an informal relationship, the proceedings before the family judge follow the general rules on contentious proceedings before the *tribunal de grande instance,* which means that the parties must be represented by counsel.

8 CA Lyon, 2nd ch. A, 2 July 2013, no. 13/03189.

GERMANY

The competent authority to decide disputes between partners to an informal relationship is either the Local Court (*Amtsgericht*) or the Regional Court (*Landgericht*).[9] The jurisdiction depends on the subject matter in dispute. The jurisdiction of the Local Courts encompasses, insofar as they have not been assigned to the Regional Courts, disputes concerning claims involving an amount or with a monetary value not exceeding the sum of five thousand euros as per § 23 No. 1 German Courts Constitution Act (*Gerichtsverfassungsgesetz,* GVG). Irrespective of the value of the matter in dispute, the jurisdiction of the Local Courts also encompasses disputes concerning claims arising out of a lease of living accommodation as per § 23 No. 2 sub. a German Courts Constitution Act. For other claims the Regional Courts are competent.

GREECE

The ordinary courts, which will not, however, apply the special procedural rules applicable to family or marital disputes (Art. 592 et seq. Greek Code of Civil Procedure).

HUNGARY

If the cohabitants have a dispute concerning their property relations, maintenance or the use of the common dwelling they can apply to the court.

REPUBLIC OF IRELAND

The courts are the only competent authority that can decide disputes between partners to an informal relationship.

ITALY

While marriage cannot be dissolved without court intervention, informal relationships may cease as a result of a mutual decision or even a unilateral one.

In the case of disputes between cohabitants, the competent court is the *Tribunale ordinario*, the first-instance court for general civil matters.

---

9 M. WELLENHOFER, 'Anh. zu § 1302', in: *Münchener Kommentar zum Bürgerlichen Gesetzbuch*, Beck, Munich, 2013, at No. 86.

In the case of the separation of partners with children, up to a few months ago disputes over the custody of the children used to be resolved by the *Tribunale per i minorenni* (Minors Court), while in the case of a married couple the competent judge was the *Tribunale Ordinario*. A recent reform,[10] intended to fully equalise the legal position of children born out of wedlock with that of those born within wedlock, has attributed all competencies in the matter of custody to the *Tribunale ordinario*.

LATVIA

In Latvia there is no particular procedure of dispute solving between partners in an informal relationship. Disputes are decided in the claims' procedure in the general jurisdiction court.

LITHUANIA

The Courts are competent to decide on disputes between partners in an informal relationship. Any person whose constitutional rights or freedoms have been violated shall have the right to resort to the courts (Art. 30 of the Constitution of Lithuania).

LUXEMBOURG

If the disputes are of a financial nature, the *justice de paix* or the *tribunal d'arrondissement* is competent. The *justice de paix* is only competent up to the value of €10,000.

As far as the children (custody questions) are concerned, the *juge des tutelles* is comptetent to decide.

The *justice de paix* is competent as far as maintenance (childrens' maintenance) questions are concerned.

THE NETHERLANDS

In answering this question a distinction has to be made between financial and property law disputes, on the one hand, and child-related issues, on the other. The first type is mostly dealt with by the district court as the competent authority. The commercial division of the district court will most likely deal with these conflicts.

---

10 Law of 10 December 2012, n. 219 followed by Italian Legislative Decree 154/2013.

If the claim is limited to €25,000, the subdistrict court is the competent authority (Art. 93 Dutch Code of Civil Procedure). If the dispute is related to rental law, the subdistrict court is the competent authority on the basis of Art. 7:267 Dutch Civil Code.

In child-related matters, the district court is competent as well, but the dispute is dealt with by the family law division of the district court on the basis of a different type of procedure.

NORWAY

The ordinary courts of justice are competent to decide disputes between partners to an informal relationship – with the district courts as the first instance courts. Family cases solely concerned with financial settlement upon separation are one of the cases that can be heard by the conciliation board, which helps the parties to achieve a simple resolution of the case through conciliation or judgment pursuant to the Norwegian Dispute Act chapter 6.

PORTUGAL

The competent authority is the ordinary civil court of justice. If the disputes concern the children of the partners, namely regarding parental responsibilities, the competent authority is the family court.

RUSSIA

There are no specific provisions on that matter; therefore, an ordinary civil law court is competent to decide on disputes between partners in an informal relationship.

SCOTLAND

Any legal disputes between partners to an informal relationship can be resolved by the civil courts – the sheriff court or Court of Session – in the same way as any legal dispute between other, unrelated parties. The specific statutory rights which apply to cohabitants, in terms of the Family Law (Scotland) Act 2006 or the Matrimonial Homes (Family Protection) (Scotland) Act 1981 would usually be referred in the first instance to the local sheriff court.

SLOVAKIA

The Courts.

SLOVENIA

A district court decides on disputes on the legal maintenance of extramarital partners in a civil procedure.

In disputes concerning the way in which the common property is to be divided, when it is not a dispute about the extent and shares of the common property of the partners a local court will decide the issue in a civil procedure.

In disputes in relation to the extent and shares of the common property, subject-matter jurisdiction is dealt with under the general rules on subject-matter jurisdiction in civil cases. Under these rules, a local court has jurisdiction to hear, at first instance, disputes relating to legal property claims if the value of the disputed property does not exceed €20,000 (para. 1 Art. 30 of the Slovenian Civil Procedure Act),[11] otherwise a district court decides at first instance. The courts decide on disputes in relation to the extent and shares of common property in a civil procedure.

SPAIN

Disputes between partners belong to the competence of civil courts. In certain parts of the country, which are more densely populated, there are civil courts which specialise in family matters and which deal with cases arising in connection with marriage and parental responsibility. These courts are competent to deal with disputes between partners in connection with children (custody and access rights, child support and the use of the family's home). Other disputes between partners (in matters, for example, of division of property or financial relief) do not fall under the competence of these special Family Courts but are dealt with by ordinary civil courts.

In 2004 Special Courts on Violence against women were created to deal with cases of domestic violence. These *Juzgados de Violencia sobre la mujer*

11 Uradni list RS (Official Journal) Nos 26/1999, 96/2002, 110/2002, 58/2003, 2/2004, 69/2005, 90/2005, 43/2006, 52/2007, 45/2008, 111/2008, 121/2008, 57/2009, 12/2010, 50/2010, 107/2010, 75/2012, 76/2012, 40/2013, 92/2013, 6/2014.

are competent to deal with all consequences of the break-up of couples, regardless of whether they are married or not, if break-up is linked to domestic violence.

SWEDEN

If the dispute concerns the division of the couple's 'cohabitation property', special rules apply according to the Swedish Cohabitation Act, § 26. This provision provides each of the partners with the right to turn to the court, for the court to appoint a person to carry out the division of the property in the capacity of a 'property division executor' (in Swedish: *bodelningsförrättare*). The court-appointed property division executor has a mandate to decide on all the disputed matters if the partners are not able to come to an agreement. If one of the former cohabitees is dissatisfied with the executor's decision, the decision may be appealed against, by bringing legal proceedings against the other former cohabitee. The executor's fee is, as a general rule, paid in equal shares by both parties. The rules are modelled on those applicable to disputes between spouses regarding the division of their marital property, and § 26 refers explicitly to the corresponding rules in the Swedish Marriage Code (its Chapter 17). The former cohabitees also have the right to have legal representatives of their own to assist them in their contacts with the property division executor.

Special provisions in the Swedish Cohabitation Act are, furthermore, of relevance in disputes concerning the take-over right of the joint dwelling upon termination of the relationship. If the partners cannot agree, the court may decide which of them has the greater need of the dwelling, § 22 and 30. The court may also decide, upon application by one of the partners, which of them has the right to remain in the joint dwelling until the division of the property has been carried out, § 28, or the court may forbid the partners to visit each other.

Apart from the provisions of the Swedish Cohabitation Act, regard needs to be given to the Swedish Act on Co-ownership if the partners are joint owners to property (for example because they have purchased property together). The Swedish Cohabitation Act is restricted to so-called 'cohabitation property' and all other property falls outside its scope, for example a summer cottage owned jointly by the partners or a jointly owned car. If the co-owners have a dispute about the administration of the co-owned asset, for example their summer cottage, either one of them may apply to the court for it to designate a property administrator, to administrate the asset or, as a last resort, to sell it through a public auction, § 3 and 6.

If, on the other hand, the dispute is about the couple's joint children (parental responsibilities) the social services, more precisely the local social welfare board (in Swedish: *socialnämnden*), in the different municipalities of Sweden have a duty to assist the parties, in the form of arranging so-called cooperation discussions, mediation, counselling and generally with the purpose of getting the parties to agree (Swedish Children and Parents Code, Chapter 6, § 17 a). A written agreement on parental responsibilities in relation to a child is often negotiated under the supervision of the local social welfare board and must be approved by it. If an agreement cannot be reached (or approved of), the dispute needs to be taken to an ordinary court of law by initiating legal proceedings.[12]

SWITZERLAND

In Switzerland, the organisation of the courts and the conciliation authorities (*Schlichtungsbehörden*) falls within the competence of the cantons (Art. 3 Swiss Civil Procedure Code). Generally, cantonal law governs the material and functional jurisdiction of the courts (Art. 4 Swiss Civil Procedure Code).[13] Thus, the cantons may provide for special courts for a particular jurisdiction (e.g. labour courts).

For disputes between partners in an informal relationship the respective civil court of first instance provided by the canton is competent to hear the case. Generally, litigation is preceded by an attempt at conciliation before a conciliation authority (Art. 197 and 198 (exceptions) Swiss Civil Procedure Code).

12 See Swedish Children and Parents Code (in Swedish: *Föräldrabalken 1949:381),* Chapter 6, §§ 5, 10, 14, 14a and 15a.

13 The terminology may also differ, e.g. the names of the courts of first instance (*Zivilgericht, Bezirksgericht,* etc.).

QUESTION 69

Is that the same authority as for spousal disputes?

AUSTRIA

According to S. 49 para. 2 No. 2a and 2b and 104a Austrian Jurisdiction Act the district courts have exclusive jurisdiction over all types of spousal disputes, regardless of the amount in dispute.[1] The same court also decides upon disputes arising from registered partnerships.[2]

Hence, if in a dispute between partners in an informal relationship the amount in dispute is below €15,000 the same authority as for spousal disputes has jurisdiction, namely the district court. If, however, the amount in dispute exceeds the value limit of €15,000, the regional court is competent to decide the issue, whereas for spousal disputes the district court remains competent, independent of the amount in dispute.

BELGIUM

No. Since 2014, the Family Court is competent to hear all disputes between spouses and registered partners. Informal partners have been deliberately excluded from the Family Court's competence because no satisfactory definition of informal partnerships for which the Court would be competent could be found in the light of the variety of partnerships.[3] However, the Belgian Code of Civil Proceedings already refers to '*de facto* cohabitation' (*cohabitation de fait, feitelijke samenwoning*) in Art. 1724, para. 1, 4° regarding mediation - even though this was never defined during the parliamentary discussion.

In 2002 the Constitutional Court had already found that excluding informal partners from the specific interlocutory proceedings available for legal cohabitants is not discriminatory and that informal partners'

1 M. ROTH, *Zivilprozessrecht*, Manz Verlag, Vienna, 2012, at p. 93.
2 Section 49 para. 2 No. 2c and 2d Austrian Jurisdiction Act.
3 Report of the Justice Commission in the Chamber of Representatives, *Parl.St.* Kamer 2010-11, at n° 53-682/15, at p. 17-21.

right to access to court is sufficiently guaranteed by the general rules on interlocutory proceedings.[4]

BULGARIA

Yes, it is the same authority as for spousal disputes. There is no separate Family Court in Bulgaria; there are family divisions in the larger courts but such a division is based on the internal structure of the court in question. So, the ordinary civil courts would decide on any disputes between both spouses and partners in an informal relationship.

CROATIA

That is the same authority as for spousal disputes.

CZECH REPUBLIC

It is the same authority.

DENMARK

According to S. 1(3) of the Danish Act on the Division of Married Property Act, the same rules apply to cohabitants as apply to spouses.

ENGLAND AND WALES

The Family Court normally decides all spousal issues including property disputes.

ESTONIA

Yes.

FINLAND

Yes. Disputes on the division of matrimonial property are also primarily decided by the estate distributors.

---

4 Constitutional Court n° 24/2002 of 23 January 2002, www.const-court.be. S. EGGERMONT, *De juridische bescherming van private relaties*, PhD, University of Antwerp, 2015, at n°s 205-210.

FRANCE

Yes. Since Law Act no. 2009-526 of 12 May 2009 aiming to clarify and simplify the law and to make proceedings more informal and Decree no. 2009-1591 of 15 December 2009, the family judge has jurisdiction concerning disputes (the sharing of assets, child maintenance, the exercise of parental responsibilities, spousal maintenance etc.) arising out of the separation of all couples.

GERMANY

According to § 23b German Courts Constitution Act divisions for family matters (Family Courts) are established at the Local Courts. Those Family Courts are competent to decide disputes concerning matrimonial matters, § 111 No.1, § 121 German Act on the Procedure in Family Matters and in Matters of Non-contentious Jurisdiction (*Gesetz über das Verfahren in Familiensachen und in den Angelegenheiten der Freiwilligen Gerichtsbarkeit*; FamFG). Therefore the authorities which are competent to decide disputes between partners to an informal relationship are different from the authorities which deal with spousal disputes.

GREECE

Not in respect of the procedural rules to be applied. The courts may be the same; that will depend on the rules governing jurisdiction over cases according to the sums involved.

HUNGARY

Yes, absolutely.

REPUBLIC OF IRELAND

Yes.

ITALY

Yes, it is at the same court.

LATVIA

In cases of marriage annulment or divorce as well, the court reviews claims in accordance with general rules, taking into consideration statutory exceptions.

LITHUANIA

Yes.

LUXEMBOURG

The *tribunal d'arrondissement* is competent in all divorce matters.

Le *tribunal de la jeunesse* is competent to decide custody matters.

The *justice de paix* is competent as far as maintenance questions (during marriage and after divorce) are concerned.

THE NETHERLANDS

In order to answer this question it is necessary to provide a more general insight into the procedural position of formal and informal couples, since there are a number of important differences. These differences relate to: 1. The type of procedural law applicable to disputes; 2. The concentration of disputes; 3. Provisional short-term measures; 4. The division within the district court dealing with the disputes.

1. Two different types of procedures. The first difference between formal and informal couples is the type of procedural law. In the Netherlands two procedural systems exist: a procedure starting with a writ (*dagvaardingsprocedure*) for contentious proceedings and the other one starting with a petition (*verzoekschriftprocedure*) mostly for voluntary cases.[5] The contentious procedure is a rather formal procedure, commenced by one party, mainly conducted in writing, although parties may appear in person.[6] The procedure for voluntary jurisdiction is less formal and parties can apply jointly for a divorce.

---

5 H.J. SNIJDERS, 'Civil procedure', in: J. CHORIS, P.-H. GERVER and E. HONDIUS, *Introduction to Dutch Law*, Kluwer Law International, Alphen aan de Rijn, 2006.

6 H.J. SNIJDERS, 'Civil procedure', in: J. CHORIS, P.-H. GERVER and E. HONDIUS, *Introduction to Dutch Law*, Kluwer Law International, Alphen aan de Rijn, 2006, at p. 255.

2. Concentration of disputes. For married couples, the Dutch Code of Civil Procedure provides an elaborate system of rules (Art. 827) which enable divorcing couples to concentrate their disputes in one single procedure, regardless of whether they concern marital property law, maintenance, pensions, children or rental law. This option of ancillary matters does not apply to informal couples. An analogous application is not possible, taking into account the general conditions for analogy.[7]

As a result, informal couples will have to bring each dispute separately to the competent court: child-related issues in a *verzoekschriftprocedure* for the family section, financial and property law issues to the district court on the basis of a *dagvaardingsprocedure*, issues related to rent to the subdistrict court.[8] The result is far more complicated and expensive and, altogether, it is not efficient.

3. Provisional short-term measures. The Dutch Code of Civil Procedure recognises in Arts. 822-826 the need for temporary short-term decisions for those married couples who cannot come to an agreement even for the short term. Thus, a spouse may request the court to decide on the children's residence up until the divorce, or the amount of maintenance to be paid. Whether a partner has an urgent interest in the decision is not a requirement for a provisional decision.

Informal partners cannot use these facilitating procedural options.[9] In relation to urgent issues, they will have to commence summary procedures/preliminary injunction proceedings. However, in order to be admissible the claimant has to make clear that it is an urgent matter, which is not always accepted by the courts.

4. As a result of the different procedural positions of formal and informal couples, disputes between non-marital partners in relation to financial or property aspects will generally be dealt with by another division of the district court. Divorces will be brought to the family section of the district court, which have broad expertise in this type of case. Individual disputes (since they cannot be concentrated) between informal couples

7 W.M. SCHRAMA, *De niet-huwelijkse samenleving in het Nederlandse en Duitse recht*, Kluwer, Deventer, 2004, at p. 230-231 and at p. 267-269.

8 See also S.W. AUTAR-MATAWLIE, W.H.A. LEONARD-STRIEN and M. VAN YPEREN-GROENLEER, 'Einde van de samenleving', in: A. AUTAR, W. KOLKMAN and W. SCHRAMA (eds.), *Compendium samenwonen*, SDU, The Hague, 2013, at p. 320-328.

9 See also S.W. AUTAR-MATAWLIE, W.H.A. LEONARD-STRIEN and M. VAN YPEREN-GROENLEER, 'Einde van de samenleving', in: A. AUTAR, W. KOLKMAN and W. SCHRAMA (eds.), *Compendium samenwonen*, SDU, The Hague, 2013, at p. 322.

will generally be judged by the commercial section. The commercial section usually deals with disputes of a more commercial nature and is less experienced in this type of partner conflict. District courts have discretion to distribute those conflicts to a family section, so in some courts it is different.

In the legal doctrine it has been argued that it is necessary to abolish the procedural differences between the two types of relationships, in particular since the current procedural rules for non-marital couples are contrary to the aims of procedural law, namely conflict prevention and conflict settlement.[10] Later research confirmed the necessity for reform.[11] The State Secretary announced legislation in 2011,[12] introducing in civil procedural law the possibility to concentrate all disputes for non-marital couples on the basis of a petition procedure (and not a contentious procedure as is currently the case). In addition, civil procedural law for informal couples would be adjusted so as to create the option to request urgent provisional measures for the short term. However, in the spring of 2015 still no bill has been introduced to this effect.

NORWAY

Yes, it is the same authority as for spousal disputes.

PORTUGAL

The competent authority for spousal disputes is a different one: it is the family and minors court of justice.

RUSSIA

Yes.

---

10 W.M. SCHRAMA, *De niet-huwelijkse samenleving in het Nederlandse en Duitse recht*, Kluwer, Deventer, 2004, at p. 557.

11 M.V. ANTOKOLSKAIA, B. BREEDERVELD, J.E. HULST, W.D KOLKMAN, F.R. SALOMONS and L.C.A. VERSTAPPEN, 'Koude uitsluiting, Materiële problemen en onbillijkheden na scheiding van in koude uitsluiting gehuwde echtgenoten en na scheiding van ongehuwd samenlevende partners, alsmede instrumenten voor de overheid om deze tegen te gaan', WODC, The Hague, 2011, at p. 278.

12 *Kamerstukken* II 2011-2012, 28 867 no. 23.

SCOTLAND

Yes, these are the same courts which would deal with spousal disputes.

SLOVAKIA

Yes.

SLOVENIA

Yes.

SPAIN

The answer to this question is not straightforward. In principle, disputes between spouses and partners belong to the competence of courts belonging to the civil order. In certain parts of the country which are more densely populated, special Family Courts belonging to the civil order were created in 1981 (RD 1322/1981). These courts have jurisdiction in matters of parental responsibility, regardless of whether or not the parents are married. This typically includes disputes about custody and access, child support and in connection with that, the attribution of the use of the family home. Other disputes between the partners in an informal relationship (typically about property division or financial relief) are not dealt with by these Family Courts (where they exist), but belong to the jurisdiction of Ordinary Courts, whereas they would be dealt with by Family Courts if they arose between spouses.

Exceptionally, the General Council for the Judiciary can decide to attribute all disputes arising in connection with informal relationships to Family Courts, or the judges belonging to one district can take the decision themselves to attribute certain disputes between partners to the Family Courts. This decision has, for example, been taken in the Judicial District of Barcelona in connection with financial relief claims between partners.

If the dispute is connected to domestic violence it would always be the same courts (*Juzgados de Violencia sobre la mujer*).

To conclude, the answer is 'yes' in certain parts of the country and 'no' in others and 'yes or no' depending on the type of dispute.

SWEDEN

The competent authority is the same for disputes between couples in an informal relationship and couples in a formalised relationship.

SWITZERLAND

In Switzerland, in general, no family courts exist.[13] Thus, the same court is competent for spousal disputes. However, an attempt at conciliation before a conciliation authority is not required for divorce proceedings as well as proceedings with regard to the protection of the marital union and dissolution of a registered partnership (Art. 198(c), Art. 198(a) in connection with Art. 271 and 198(c) Swiss Civil Procedure Code). For all these proceedings specific procedural rules exist (Art. 271 et seq. Swiss Civil Procedure Code).[14]

13 Family courts exist in the canton of Aargau, but they are not competent to hear disputes arising from informal relationships.

14 For details see I. SCHWENZER and T. KELLER, 'New Swiss Code of Civil Procedure: Special Proceedings in Matrimonial and Family Law Matters', in: B. ATKIN, *The International Survey of Family Law*, Jordan Publishing, Bristol, 2012, at p. 377 et seq.

QUESTION 70

Can the competent authority scrutinise an agreement made by the partners in an informal relationship? If yes, what is the scope of the scrutiny?

AUSTRIA

Partnership agreements are subject to the rules of contract law.[1] Section 879 General Austrian Civil Code contains restrictions on party autonomy and stipulates – as a general clause – that a contract which violates statutory provisions or public morals is void. This provision applies to all contracts including partnership agreements.[2] Hence, the courts can scrutinise partnership agreements in terms of their compliance with laws and public morals, whereby a judicial review will become particularly necessary, if the agreement is unfavourable for one partner.[3] Whether public morals are violated has to be determined by the judge by evaluating whether the legally protected interests of one party have been seriously infringed or, in case of a conflict of interests, whether there is considerable disparity between the interests involved.[4] All contractual clauses which unreasonably restrict the highly personal area or the personal freedom of one partner are considered to be contrary to public morals.[5]

BELGIUM

The courts that are competent under general rules are only competent to scrutinise agreements, of which performance is sought, against the

---

1 N. OSWALD and A. SCHMALLEGGER, 'Partnerschaftsvertrag zwischen nichtehelichen Lebensgefährten', *EF-Z*, 2013, at p. 13.

2 H. KREJCI, 'section 879 General Austrian Civil Code', in: P. RUMMEL (ed.), *Kommentar zum Allgemeinen Bürgerlichen Gesetzbuch*, Manz Verlag, Vienna, 2000, at marg. No. 4.

3 E. MÖSCHL, *Die nichteheliche Lebensgemeinschaft*, LexisNexis ARD ORAC, Vienna, 2007, at marg. No. 34.

4 H. KOZIOL and R. WELSER, *Grundriss des Bürgerlichen Rechts*, Manz Verlag, Vienna, 2006, at p. 179.

5 For examples see the answer to Question 57.

general rules on contract, particularly their compatibility with public policy.

BULGARIA

There is no regulation on this matter.

The only specific legal regulation on the agreements made by the partners in an informal relationship is related to the agreement on the exercise of the parental rights and duties after separation (Art. 127, para. 1 of the Bulgarian Family Code). In this case the partners are not obliged to obtain any approval for their agreement by any authority. The agreement will be valid as it has been reached by the partners/parents. It will be applied only voluntarily by the parents.

If parents want to attach an executive authority to their agreement, confirmation by the courts is necessary (Art. 127, para. 1 in fine of the Bulgarian Family Code). The law does not explicitly assign discretion to the courts to scrutinise such agreements.

CROATIA

There are no special legal provisions prescribing a possibility for the competent authority to scrutinise an agreement made by partners in an informal relationship, except an agreement on maintenance.

According to Art. 302 paragraph 3 of the Croatian Family Act an agreement on maintenance between cohabitants (as well as same-sex informal partners) should be scrutinised by the courts.

CZECH REPUBLIC

No, the competent authority cannot scrutinise an agreement made by the partners in an informal relationship by itself. When an authority deals with a conflict between partners in an informal relationship, the authority can scrutinise the agreement. The scope of the scrutiny is the same as for any other dispute between any other parties.

DENMARK

No.

ENGLAND AND WALES

Not in advance of relationship breakdown or other event which triggers the terms of the agreement being enforced.

ESTONIA

In civil proceedings there are no special rules on hearing legal disputes between partners in an informal relationship.

FINLAND

Yes. The estate distributor will examine the validity of the agreement and the separation of the property will be carried out according to the agreement, if it is considered valid. If the agreement is such that it covers the separation of the property as a whole, the task of the estate distributor is merely to execute the agreement. If the existence of the agreement is made known to the District Court in the context of the appointment of the estate distributor, it may examine its validity in the appointment process and decide that the appointment cannot be made due to the already existing agreement on the separation of property.

FRANCE

A specific provision in the French Civil Code (Art. 373-2-7) states that parents (who can be spouses, registered partners or partners in an informal relationship) can request the family judge to 'homologate' (ratify) their agreement organising the exercise of their parental responsibilities and setting the amount of child maintenance. According to para. 2, the judge will ratify the agreement, unless he or she is of the opinion that the agreement does not sufficiently protect the child's interests or that the parent's consent to the agreement was not made of his or her free will. This means that the partners (parents) may agree on the exercise of parental responsibilities and child maintenance, but that their agreement is subject to specific scrutiny by the family judge.

No similar statutory provision regulates the court's scrutiny of agreements on other matters entered into by partners in an informal relationship. Agreements between partners in an informal relationship made before the breakup of the relationship do not seem to be frequent.[6]

---

6 They are indeed very rare, see I. BARRIÈRE-BROUSSE and M. DOUCHY-OUDOT, *Les contentieux familiaux,* Lextenso, Paris, 2013, at no. 604.

Notaries have however suggested some model agreements.[7] They mostly contain an inventory of the assets (especially movables) of each partner and can regulate contributions to the expenses of the household as well as sharing arrangements in the case of a breakup. Such an agreement cannot impose personal duties on the partner(s).

After the breakup of the relationship, a partner can request the nullity of the agreement on the ground of a defect in consent (mistake, fraud or duress). The court can scrutinise the agreement in respect of the parties' consent and concerning public order requirements. If the agreement contains rules on the exercise of parental responsibilities, the court must also consider whether such agreements are compatible with the child's best interests (Art. 373-2-7 of the French Civil Code, see above).

GERMANY

The competent Local or Regional Court can scrutinise a partnership agreement just like any other civil law agreement (for more details see Question 71).

GREECE

There is no body which is competent to carry out such scrutiny. The only scrutiny would be that conducted by the court if a dispute arose between the parties concerning the implementation of the agreement.

HUNGARY

There is no specific scrutiny when entering into an agreement. As cohabitations have an informal character no agreement is scrutinised ex officio. Either an agreement on property relations or an agreement on the maintenance of a former cohabitant or on the use of the common dwelling may be referred to the courts if its validity is contested by one party.

REPUBLIC OF IRELAND

Cohabitants' agreements can be examined, followed and enforced by the courts. According to S. 202(4) of the Irish 2010 Act, the court may modify

7 See D. FENOUILLET, 'Couple hors mariage et contrat', in: D. FENOUILLET and P. de VAREILLES SOMMIERES (eds.), *La contractualisation de la famille*, Economica, Paris, 2001.

or set aside such an agreement in exceptional circumstances, whether in part or in full, where its enforceability would cause serious injustice.

ITALY

The agreement may only be scrutinised by the court when one of the partners claim a violation by the other.

The judge will ascertain whether a violation has occurred on the basis of the general rules on breach of contract.

LATVIA

The court reviews claims in accordance with general rules. There is no particular legal order on partners in an informal relationship.

LITHUANIA

Bearing in mind that Art. 3.229-3.235 of the Lithuanian Civil Code are not applied in practice, the courts usually rely on general provisions while considering material disputes between non-married individuals, such as the provisions of Book IV, 'Material Law', of the Lithuanian Civil Code on the division of joint-partial property between the co-owners as well as the provisions of Book VI, 'Law of Obligations', of the Lithuanian Civil Code.

LUXEMBOURG

Normally the court does not have the right to scrutinise. If the agreement is clear, the judge has to apply the terms thereof, unless it is contrary to rules of public policy (*ordre public*).

THE NETHERLANDS

General rules apply, there is no *lex specialis* for cohabitation contracts. In the case law there are many disputes involving cohabitation contracts. The interpretation of clauses may be contentious, either because the provision is not clear or because the conditions have changed or a party thinks that a clause is unfair. The Supreme Court has ruled on cohabitation contracts on a number of occasions. In a leading Supreme Court case the parties had agreed to a nominal claim for an investment by the woman of €50,000 in a house which was the private property of the man.[8] When the relationship broke down, the value of the house had considerably increased and the woman claimed that on the basis of an implicit contract and the principle of reasonableness and fairness she was entitled to half of the value of the house. The Supreme Court ruled that the explicit cohabitation contract had to be interpreted not only according to its wording, but also with regard to a number of facts invoked by the woman.

Another recent decision of the Supreme Court should be mentioned here as well. The parties had already lived together for over twenty years when they concluded a cohabitation contract. This was after a difficult period in their relationship, since the woman had had a relationship with another man. This had been evaluated by the parties and they decided to remain together. Shortly before the contract was signed, the woman again had a relationship with the other man, which she then terminated. Three years later, the parties split up. The man invoked an error (*dwaling*, Art. 6:228 Dutch Civil Code), which was accepted by the Supreme Court. As a principle partners do not have to share very personal information, but given the special circumstances of this case, the woman should have informed the man before concluding the contract.[9]

In the case law of the lower courts all kinds of conflicts with regard to contracts are decided upon; it is impossible to find a common rule in these decisions.

NORWAY

No, the competent authority cannot scrutinise an agreement made by the partners to an informal relationship.

PORTUGAL

Provided the agreement is deemed to be valid, the competent court may scrutinise it in order to clarify a possible dispute between the partners over its content.

8 HR 22 September 2006, LJN AX1571.
9 HR 21 February 2014, ECLI:NL:HR:2014:416.

RUSSIA

In the absence of special provisions, the court can scrutinise an agreement made by the partners in an informal relationship in the same way as it can scrutinise any civil law agreement. This scrutiny goes no further than ensuring compliance with mandatory rules of law. The general principle of contract law (*pacta sunt servanda*) strictly applies to such agreements.

SCOTLAND

The starting point in Scots law is that there is a longstanding tradition of respecting the autonomy of parties to make their own agreements. This is well established within the context of marriage and it is widely assumed that a similar approach would be adopted in respect of informal relationships although this is largely untested in the courts. Within marriage or civil partnership, parties may enter into agreements before or during the relationship or on separation and these agreements are enforceable without any requirement of judicial scrutiny or approval.

Equally there is no provision for scrutiny of agreements between partners to an informal relationship. It is simply assumed that these will be treated as contracts in the same way as an agreement between two unrelated parties. It is of course open to either party to an agreement to challenge it in court on the basis of the general rules of contract, for example that it was entered into under duress or fraud. Beyond those general rules of contract, there is no specific provision for agreements between cohabitants.

SLOVAKIA

Yes the courts may scrutinise an agreement made by the partners in an informal relationship. As far as the scope of this scrutiny is concerned, the judge can determine whether the nature of a legal transaction violates a statutory prohibition or whether the nature of a transaction is contrary to good morals. In Slovak law the protection of good morals is usually said to be an open norm, a norm the content of which cannot be established in an abstract way but which depends on the circumstances of the case in which it must be applied, and which must be established through concretisation.[10] In Slovakia it is the judge who determines the content of good morals. It is also the judge who can balance the

10 V. ČEČOTOVÁ, *Dobré mravy v slovenskom súkromnom práve* (Good morals in Slovak private law), EPOS, Bratislava, 2005.

'harmony' between autonomy and good morals. This balancing depends on the circumstances of the case and on the personality of the judge hearing the case. The consequence of a judge's scrutiny can be the nullification of an agreement.

SLOVENIA

A court may find that an agreement is in conflict with compulsory regulations, the Slovenian Constitution or moral principles, in which case it will be null and void.

SPAIN

Agreements reached by the partners to an informal relationship in relation to children need to be validated by a judge in order to be legally enforceable. The judge scrutinises the agreement in order to verify that the best interests of the child have been respected. The scope of scrutiny is the same as in the case of children whose parents are married.

Other agreements that do not affect children do not require to be validated by a competent authority in order to become binding if they are made by partners to an informal relationship; whereas agreements made between spouses will be incorporated in the divorce or legal separation decision once validated. According to Art. 90 Spanish Civil Code a judge may refuse to validate agreements that are seriously detrimental to one of the spouses. This provision is not applied to agreements between partners to an informal relationship.

If the agreements between partners in an informal relationship are not complied with, parties can seek enforcement through court proceedings. In the course of these proceedings agreements will not be scrutinised.

In practice, interference with party autonomy is rather limited as regards issues not affecting children in both matrimonial cases and cases dealing with informal relationships. Judges tend to uphold the principle of party autonomy. It therefore seems that, as regards the law in action, the difference in treatment between married and unmarried couples on this issue is less marked than it might seem.

SWEDEN

In court proceedings initiated by the partners or one of them the court has the power to scrutinise all kinds of agreements between the partners regarding their mutual rights and duties. If the Swedish Cohabitation Act is applicable (see answers to Question 2 and 4) and the cohabitees have concluded a 'cohabitation agreement', an explicit provision in § 9 para. 3 concerns the court's powers to scrutinise this agreement. Scrutinizing of the other agreements is made possible through the general rules and principles of the laws of obligations and property.

An agreement between the partners regarding parental responsibilities in relation to their joint children (custody, contact and the children's residence) must be approved by the local social welfare board in order to be valid (Swedish Children and Parents Code, Chapter 6 § 17 a). This requires scrutiny by the board. Only an agreement that can be regarded to be in the best interests of the child should be approved. The child should be heard, subject to certain restrictions.

SWITZERLAND

The courts cannot scrutinise an agreement made by the partners in an informal relationship.

According to the general principles of contract law, the courts may set aside an agreement for reasons such as immorality or unlawfulness (Art. 20 Swiss Code of Obligations) or a mistake (Art. 23 et seq. Swiss Code of Obligations).

QUESTION 71

Can the competent authority override or modify the agreement on account of fairness towards a partner, the rights of a third party, or on any other ground (e.g. a change of circumstances)?

AUSTRIA

If the partnership agreement is contrary to S. 879 para. 1 General Austrian Civil Code and therefore either violates a statutory prohibition or public morals, the agreement is void. Whether the entire agreement or only the respective clause is void depends on the underlying aim of the statute;[1] generally, it should be attempted to uphold the remainder of the contract.[2] If a clause is contrary to public morals due to its temporal, spatial or extensive dimension, it does not entail the nullity of the contract, rather the judge has to reduce the content of the respective clause to an acceptable extent, unless there are compelling reasons to refrain from doing so.[3]

Usually the nullity of a single clause causes a gap in the contract which needs to be filled by a supplementary interpretation of the contract. In this regard – besides considering objective elements, such as the purpose of the contract – the hypothetical intention of the parties has to be taken into account. However, if the nullity results from a breach of S. 879 para. 1 General Austrian Civil Code, a supplementary interpretation of the contract may be incompatible with the purpose of the provision.[4] Hence, the competent authority can only under very limited circumstances interpret the contract on a supplementary basis if a contractual

1 H. KREJCI, 'section 879 General Austrian Civil Code', in: P. RUMMEL (ed.), *Kommentar zum Allgemeinen Bürgerlichen Gesetzbuch*, Manz Verlag, Vienna, 2000, at marg. No. 250.

2 H. KOZIOL and R. WELSER, *Grundriss des Bürgerlichen Rechts*, Manz Verlag, Vienna, 2006, at p. 182.

3 H. KREJCI, 'section 879 General Austrian Civil Code', in: P. RUMMEL (ed.), *Kommentar zum Allgemeinen Bürgerlichen Gesetzbuch*, Manz Verlag, Vienna, 2000, at marg. No. 250.

4 G. GRAF, 'section 878 General Austrian Civil Code', in: A. KLETEČKA and M. SCHAUER, *ABGB-ON 1.01*, Manz Verlag, Vienna, 2013, at marg. No. 16.

gap needs to be filled. Other reasons which authorise the competent authority to override or modify the agreement are not provided for.

BELGIUM

No specific rules apply. The competent courts can only refuse enforcement or declare an agreement null and void on the basis of the general rules on contracts.

BULGARIA

There is no regulation on this matter.

CROATIA

There are no special legal provisions prescribing a possibility for the competent authority to override or modify the agreement made by partners in an informal relationship (cohabitants as well as same-sex informal partners) on account of unfairness to a partner, the rights of a third party, or on any other ground.

However, according to the principle of good faith and fair dealing used in creating obligations and exercising the rights and liabilities resulting from such obligations, the parties shall act in accordance with good faith and fair dealing (Art. 4 of the Croatian Civil Obligations Act, Official Gazettes no. 35/05, 41/08, 125/11). The Croatian Civil Obligations Act prescribes reasons for declaring the nullity of a contract. The court examines the matter of nullity *ex officio* and any interested party may invoke nullity (Art. 327 paragraph 1). The right to invoke nullity does not lapse (Art. 328).

A party in whose favour the voidability of a contract has been established may request that the contract be annulled (Art. 331 paragraph 1). A limitation period of one year is applicable to the right to apply for an annulment of a voidable contract after becoming aware of the cause for voidability or after the termination of duress and in any event this right shall expire within three years from the date of entering into a contract (Art. 335).

According to Art. 369 of the Croatian Civil Obligations Act, should, after entering into a contract, extraordinary circumstances arise that were impossible to foresee at the time of entering into the contract, making it excessively onerous for one party to perform or if under such circumstances a party would suffer an excessive loss as a result of the performance, that party may request a variation or even the termination of the contract. A variation or the termination of a contract may not be requested by a contracting party invoking the change of circumstances if that party was obliged to take such circumstances into consideration at the time of entering into the contract or if he/she could have avoided or overcome them. Where a party requests the termination of a contract, the contract shall not be terminated if the other contracting party offers or agrees to an equitable change in the relevant provisions of the contract. Where a court declares a contract to be terminated, the court shall, at the request of the other party, oblige the party applying for the cancellation to compensate the other party with an equitable amount for the damage suffered due to the termination. According to Art. 371 of the Croatian Civil Obligations Act, in deciding on a variation or the termination of a contract, the court shall be governed by the principles of good faith and fair dealing, taking into consideration the purpose of the contract, the allocation of the risk resulting from the contract or from laws, the duration and effects of extraordinary circumstances and the interests of both parties.

CZECH REPUBLIC

There are no special rules applicable to such an agreement. The competent authority can, for example, override the agreement on account of a conflict with equity in accordance with the general rules of agreements.

DENMARK

Under the Danish Contracts Act an agreement can be set aside or modified on grounds of unfairness or due to a change of circumstances.

ENGLAND AND WALES

Not in advance of relationship breakdown or other event which triggers the terms of the agreement being enforced. If it is successfully challenged at that time (e.g. due to undue influence) then, yes, it can override the agreement.

ESTONIA

In civil issues, the partners in an informal relationship are treated as unmarried persons and they are free to conclude agreements from which legal consequences may arise. The validity of such agreements (including in relation to formal requirements) proceeds from the general or special provisions of those transactions. The Supreme Court has repeatedly noted that a court cannot resolve a case on the basis of a transaction the validity of which is imperatively not acknowledged by the law, and thus, the court can revoke the transaction, including determining that the transaction is contrary to good morals also on its own initiative.[5] In the case of an alleged cancellation, the court must first, either on its own initiative or on the basis of a claim by a party to the proceedings, verify whether the transaction is void.[6] Transactions may be contrary to good morals for different reasons, i.e. they can be considered immoral and reprehensible according to the conceptions prevailing in society. A transaction is contrary to good morals if, upon its conclusion, it violates the sense of justice and the value judgements of fair and true thinking people and also the general principles of the law. Being contrary to good morals may involve the purpose of the transaction being contrary to good morals or immoral behaviour by one party relating to the purpose of concluding the transaction.[7] In general, the court itself will not amend the conditions of a contract. According to § 84 of the General Part of the Estonian Civil Code, a void transaction has no legal consequences from its inception. That which has been received on the basis of a void transaction must be returned pursuant to the provisions concerning unjust enrichment unless otherwise provided by law. Thus, it is impossible to file claims relating to the performance or non-performance of the transaction if that transaction is void.

FINLAND

Generally, according to the Finnish Contracts Act (228/1929), a contract between the parties is binding if an offer to conclude a contract has been accepted. However, agreements can be made equitable according to S. 36 of the said Act, according to which if a contract term is unfair or its application would lead to an unfair result, the term may be adjusted or set aside. In determining what is unfair, regard shall be had to the entire contents of the contract, the positions of the parties, the circumstances

5 Decision of the Civil Chamber of the Supreme Court 3-2-1-111-08, at para. 23; 3-2-1-137-09, at para. 12.
6 Decision of the Civil Chamber of the Supreme Court 3-2-1-83-13, at para. 12.
7 Decision of the Civil Chamber of the Supreme Court 3-2-1-111-08, at para. 23.

prevailing at and after the conclusion of the contract, and to other factors. In addition to the Finnish Contracts Act, the estate distributor has the power to take into account the provisions on unjust enrichment in the Finnish Cohabitation Act (S. 6), if a claim for compensation is made by either of the partners or his or her heirs.

FRANCE

Only an agreement between the partners relating to the exercise of their parental responsibilities and the amount of child maintenance is regulated by Art. 373-2-7 of the French Civil Code. This provision gives the court the authority to refuse to ratify such an agreement if it does not sufficiently protect the child's interests or if a parent's consent to the agreement was not given on the basis of his or her free will. Unfairness towards a partner and the rights of a third party are not grounds which can be considered by the court. If the court refuses to ratify (homologate) the agreement, it can try to find, together with the parents, a solution which is compatible with the child's interests. If this fails, the court (i.e. the family judge) will himself or herself decide on the exercise of parental responsibilities and on child maintenance.

With regard to agreements dealing with the partners' patrimonial interests (assets, contribution to the expenses of the household, liquidation and sharing after the breakup etc.), no specific statutory provision regulates the scope of the court's scrutiny. Generally, any unfairness towards a partner, the rights of a third party, or a change of circumstances are not taken into account.

Unfairness towards a partner can only be taken into account indirectly. For example, in an interesting judgment of 20 June 2006,[8] the Court of cassation confirmed a decision delivered by a court of appeal which nullified an agreement between the *concubins* (*convention de concubinage*) that stipulated that the unemployed partner (or the partner who gave up his or her employment in order to raise the children) could claim compensation from the other partner amounting to at least half of the other partner's income. The agreement did not determine the amount with regard to each parent's income and to the children's needs but as a lump sum, which – according to the Court of cassation – could result in the debtor being unable to fulfil his or her other maintenance duties.

8 Cass. Civ I, 20 June 2006, no. 05-17475, *Bull. Civ.* No 312; *Dr. Fam.* 2006, no 155 with note LARRIBAU-TERNEYRE; *RTD civ.* 2006, p. 740, with note HAUSER.

Moreover, the agreement was so coercive and compelling that it was considered by the Court of cassation to be a means to 'dissuade a partner from ending the relationship', which was 'contrary to the principle of personal freedom' and it therefore contravened the French public order. This shows that an agreement can be nullified if it infringes the personal freedoms of one of the partners.

GERMANY

The Federal Supreme Court has developed specific principles for the judicial review of marriage contracts which are based on the general clauses in § 138 and § 242 German Civil Code. It is settled case law that the validity of marriage contracts and their enforceability may be controlled.[9] So far there is no case law concerning informal partnerships in this regard; thus it remains unclear if these principles can be applied to informal partnerships as well.[10]

Any control must respect the fundamental principle of freedom of contract. However, the agreements must not be contrary to § 134 German Civil Code (statutory prohibition) and public policy in the sense of § 138 German Civil Code (see Question 57).[11] The mere fact that one of the partners is still married to a third person does not make the agreement contrary to public policy.[12]

GREECE

There is no administrative body competent to carry out scrutiny, and thus there can be no amendment to or an annulment of any agreement or clause relating to one of the partners or a third party. Only in the context of a legal hearing might the judges take the view that a term of the agreement was invalid, if it contradicted the general rules on the validity of agreements and transactions. The judge can intervene in a regulatory spirit only in contracts of obligation in which all contracting parties have an obligation to fulfil (Art. 388 Greek Civil Code), which is not the case

9 For more detail see: L. BERGSCHNEIDER, *Richterliche Inhaltskontrolle von Eheverträgen und Schiedsvereinbarungen*, Beck, Munich, 2008; N. DETHLOFF and D. MARTINY, *Property Relationship between Spouses-GERMANY*, CEFL Country Report 2008, p. 46.

10 H. GRZIWOTZ, '§ 29', in: *Münchener AnwaltsHandbuch Familienrecht*, Beck, Munich, 2014, at No. 25a.

11 H. GRZIWOTZ, '§ 29', in: *Münchener AnwaltsHandbuch Familienrecht*, Beck, Munich, 2014, at No. 25.

12 OLG Hamm, 20.04.1999, *FamRZ*, 2000, 95; M. WELLENHOFER, 'Anh. zu § 1302', in: *Münchener Kommentar zum Bürgerlichen Gesetzbuch*, Beck, Munich, 2013, at No. 48.

here. Even in the case of an undisputed divorce, the judge does no more than ratify the agreement reached by the spouses, and he or she cannot alter it (Art. 1441 Greek Civil Code).

HUNGARY

The general contract rules of the Hungarian Civil Code form the basis of agreements between cohabitants, either concerning property relations, the maintenance of a former cohabitant or the use of the common dwelling. The express possibility of entering into an agreement on the maintenance of a former cohabitant and the use of the common dwelling is a new element of the regulation on cohabitation so there is no judicial practice at all. There have nevertheless been a few judgements concerning cohabitants' agreements on property relations. These decisions dealt primarily with the validity of the agreements in question and the general provisions and requirements on invalidity were applied. In these cases it was determined that such agreements could be set aside for invalidity if they contravene the principle of good faith, if undue influence is found or when an unconscionable advantage has been taken.

There is a new provision in the Hungarian Civil Code. If the cohabitants agree, by means of an agreement in advance, on the use of the future dwelling after separation, e.g. that one cohabitant will leave the dwelling that is the common home,[13] the judge can disregard this agreement if a minor child's right to reside in the home is affected.

The rules on judicial modifications were very strict in the Civil Code of 1959 and are just as strict in the Hungarian Civil Code and have not yet been applied to property agreements between spouses.

REPUBLIC OF IRELAND

Yes. According to the Irish 2010 Act, where enforcing the agreement would cause serious injustice, the courts may vary it or set it aside. 'Serious injustice' is not defined and no grounds are enumerated within the Act as to what may amount to such injustice. It would seem that unfairness to a partner would be a fairly compelling reason to override or modify an agreement. It is worth highlighting, however, that the court is only permitted to vary or set aside an agreement in 'exceptional

13 Art. 6:517(2) of Hungarian Civil Code refers to Art. 4:79(2) of Hungarian Civil Code.

circumstances' and overriding or modifying these agreements will not be permitted to become the norm.

ITALY

Only when one partner brings a formal action against the other alleging the violation of the agreement, can the judge override or modify the agreement, applying the general rules of contract.

LATVIA

The court reviews claims in accordance with general rules. There is no particular legal order on partners in an informal relationship.

LITHUANIA

Probably yes, according to Art. 3.231 part 2 of the Lithuanian Civil Code (the provisions of Art. 3.101-3.108[14] thereof shall be applicable to such agreements *mutatis mutandis*).

LUXEMBOURG

The courts have to apply contract law. Contract law provisions regulate cases where a contract may be invalidated.

According to Art. 1134 of the Luxembourg Civil Code, a judge does not have the right to modify the provisions of the agreement. He or she may have the possibility to invalidate the contract if conditions of invalidity are provided (e.g. a lack of or a defect in the consent of one of the partners when concluding the agreement).

A change of circumstances may have an impact concerning child maintenance if there is a change in the financial situation of one of the partners; the *justice de paix* may modify the contribution determined in the agreement.

[14] Art. 3.108 of the Lithuanian Civil Code provides for the nullity of a marriage contract: the court may declare a marriage contract null and void at the request of one of the spouses if the agreement is in serious breach of the principle of equality or is especially unfavourable to one of the spouses. The creditors of one or both of the spouses shall have a right to demand that the agreement be declared null and void because it is fictitious.

THE NETHERLANDS

There is a lot of room for the interpretation of contractual obligations. In addition, a party may invoke an implied contract next to the written contract. If these alternatives do not lead to a desirable outcome, one could also employ good faith (reasonableness and fairness) to override a provision in a contract (Art. 6:248 para. 2 Dutch Civil Code). A contractual provision, which would otherwise bind the parties to the contract, does not apply if this would be, given the circumstances, contrary to the norm of reasonableness and fairness. Contractual obligations can be set aside. In the case law reasonableness and fairness (Art. 6:2 and 6:248 para. 1 Dutch Civil Code) play a role in relation to interpretation, to supplement any lacuna in the contract and to set a rule aside.[15]

The rights of a third party have not been the reason why a contract has been modified. A change of circumstances might play a role in the interpretation of the contract or as a relevant factor in deciding whether it is against reasonableness and fairness to bind a contracting partner.[16]

NORWAY

All agreements - not only agreements between cohabitants - may be wholly or partly annulled pursuant to the Norwegian Act relating to Conclusion of Agreements, S. 36 if they are deemed to affect one of the parties unfairly. Instead of annulling the agreement, the court may decide to modify the agreement.

PORTUGAL

Yes, on common grounds applicable to any agreement (e.g. a change of circumstances, Art. 437 of the Portuguese Civil Code).

RUSSIA

The court cannot override or modify the agreement on account of unfairness to a partner, the rights of a third party or on any other grounds. The special provisions of the Russian Family Code do not apply to agreements between informal partners. Thus, the rules of Art. 102

15 HR 22 September 2006, LJN AX1571; Hof Den Haag 27 January 2015, ECLI:NL: GHADHA: 2015:430.

16 HR 22 September 2006, LJN AX1571.

Russian Family Code entitling the court to set aside or revise a maintenance agreement if it is unfair to a spouse or ex-spouse who is entitled to maintenance under the provisions of the Russian Family Code are not applicable to maintenance agreements between informal partners.

A court can modify or set aside an agreement between informal partners on the ground of a change of circumstances (Art. 451 Russian Civil Code) as this ground is available in the case of any civil contract. The court is entitled to order that a contract must be amended or dissolved if the circumstances have changed so substantially that the performance of the contract would lead to serious harm to the party/parties in question. Under the second part of sub. 2 of Art. 451 Russian Civil Code, a change is considered to be substantial if the parties would not have entered into their contract in the first place if they had been able reasonably to foresee that change, or if the provisions of such a contract would then have been different. However, establishing the existence of a substantial change of circumstances is in itself not sufficient for Art. 451 Russian Civil Code to apply. Article 451 will only apply if the following four requirements are simultaneously satisfied:

- The parties did not foresee such a change of circumstances at the time of entering into the contract;
- The change of circumstances has occurred due to an event which the claimant could not have foreseen, taking into consideration a normal level of care and caution;
- Performing the contract without amending it would lead to such a serious violation of the property interests of the parties that the claimant would lose, to a significant extent, the consideration to which he/she was entitled under the contract;
- It does not follow from the essence of the contract that the claimant has to bear the risks of a change of circumstances.

SCOTLAND

As explained above, there is no provision for any authority to scrutinise agreements other than the civil courts in the context where one party seeks to challenge the agreement on general contractual grounds, for example, of duress.

SLOVAKIA

No.

SLOVENIA

The law does not contain any rules to the effect that the competent authority can override or modify an agreement between extramarital partners.

SPAIN

No, unless the agreement refers to matters that are not in the parties' disposition, that is, generally in matters relating to children. In matters concerning the relationship between the partners, judges tend to uphold the agreements.

If circumstances have changed significantly since the agreement was concluded and the agreement is brought to court, typically because it is not being complied with, a judge might modify the agreement in order to adapt it to the new circumstances by applying general principles such as *rebus sic stantibus.*

SWEDEN

Indeed, in respect of an agreement on division of 'cohabitation property', Swedish Cohabitation Act, § 9 para. 3 explicitly states that if a term in the agreement is unreasonable having regard to the agreement's content, the circumstances when the agreement was concluded or which have subsequently arisen, as well as the overall circumstances, the agreement may be adjusted or set aside in the property division. This rule is modelled on a general rule of contract law, found in Chapter 3, § 36 of the Swedish Act on Contracts (in Swedish: *Avtalslagen*); a similar provision is found in the Swedish Marriage Code, Chapter 12 § 3, concerning adjustment of marital property agreements in connection with the property division.

When it comes to agreements not subject to the Swedish Cohabitation Act, as stated above, general rules and principles of the law of obligations and property law are applicable and the agreement can be scrutinised in accordance with those principles and rules. These rules are found in the Swedish Act on Contracts, for example the above-mentioned provision in Chapter 3 § 36.

SWITZERLAND

The competent authority cannot override or modify the agreement, except for the same reasons as any other contract.

QUESTION 72

What alternative dispute-solving mechanisms (e.g. mediation or counselling), if any, are offered or required with regard to disputes arising out of informal relationships?

AUSTRIA

The parties in a partnership agreement can include a clause providing for some kind of alternative dispute resolution, e.g. mediation, before resorting to the courts.[1] In respect of family matters mediation has become increasingly popular in Austria in recent years.[2] The Federal Minister of Justice maintains a list of mediators which is published electronically.[3] However, alternative dispute-solving mechanisms are not a mandatory prerequisite before submitting a claim.

BELGIUM

Article 1724, para. 1, 4° Belgian Code of Civil Proceedings expressly includes 'disputes arising from a *de facto* cohabitation' in the matters to which the chapter on Mediation applies. Agreements reached through out of court or court-referred mediation by an accredited mediator can be presented to the competent court with a view to homologation. Court-referred mediation is only possible in case of a joint request by the parties. We think that the reference to *de facto* cohabitation is superfluous because all matters on which the parties may settle are subject to mediation anyhow.

---

1 N. OSWALD and A. SCHMALLEGGER, 'Partnerschaftsvertrag zwischen nichtehelichen Lebensgefährten', *EF-Z*, 2013, at p. 17.

2 See M. ROTH and M. STEGNER, 'Mediation in Austria', in: M. GEISTLINGER and M. ROTH (eds.), *Yearbook on International Arbitration*, Intersentia, Antwerp, 2013, pp. 367-378, at p. 378.

3 Available at: www.mediatorenliste.justiz.gv.at/mediatoren/mediatorenliste.nsf/docs/home.

The parties involved in a dispute before the Family Court are sent a brochure on the possibilities for ADR. Also, voluntary in-court mediation has been introduced in matters for which the Family Court is competent (Arts. 731 and 1253*ter*/1 Belgian Code of Civil Proceedings). These provisions do not apply to informal partners, though.

Besides, arbitration is possible in all matters on which the parties may settle (Art. 1676 Belgian Code of Civil Proceedings).

BULGARIA

Mediation is offered (but is not required) with regard to any disputes between partners/spouses or parents (arising from domestic relationships) – Art. 3 of the Bulgarian Mediation Act (of 2004, last amended in 2011). The use of mediation between partners in informal relationships depends on their free choice.

Counselling is required in disputes involving children as part of the court order with the involvement of Child Protection Departments.

CROATIA

The alternative resolution of disputes is regulated by the Croatian Family Act and is divided into two types:

a. mandatory counselling prior to judicial proceedings with regard to children and
b. family mediation.

In compliance with Art. 321 of the Croatian Family Act, mandatory counselling represents a form of aid provided to family members to reach an agreement in family relationships and takes great care to protect family relationships involving children. Mandatory counselling is conducted by an expert team appointed by a social welfare centre (a lawyer, a social worker and a psychologist) and is attended by family members without their attorneys and legal representatives.

Pursuant to Art. 331 of the Croatian Family Act, family mediation is the procedure in which parties attempt to resolve a family relationship-related dispute by agreement with the assistance of one or more family mediators.

CZECH REPUBLIC

There are no special alternative disputes solving mechanisms required. Generally, it is possible to solve dispute by mediation, just like any other dispute, according to Act no. 202/202 Coll, about mediation.

DENMARK

All courts, except the Supreme Court, are obliged to provide mediation services in civil actions, and judges and lawyers with special training in mediation can serve as mediators.[4] Mediators are appointed from the court's panel of mediators. Participation is voluntary and the parties can withdraw from the process at any time; there is no penalty for either declining mediation or not reaching a resolution in mediation. The process is confidential for all involved. Mediation is offered free of charge and can take place at any time during the judicial process; in most cases mediation takes place soon after the case is filed. When mediation is accepted by the parties, the legal proceedings are suspended. Lawyers may attend mediations, but it is the parties and not their lawyers who play the principal role in the process.

As for disputes concerning custody, visitation and residence rights, reference to the State Administration is the entry point for resolving disputes between parents who no longer live together.[5] For visitation rights the State Administration makes administrative decisions if no agreement is reached by the parents. Disputes about custody and residence tights are referred to a court if the parents are unable to reach an agreement with the help of the State Administration.[6] The primary tool for resolving these matters is administrative meetings with parents conducted by a lawyer alone or a lawyer working in tandem with either a psychologist or social worker with expertise in children's matters. If these meetings do not result in an agreement, the parents are offered mediation or counselling by a child expert. Mediation in family matters was incorporated in the Danish Parental Responsibility Act in 2007.

---

4 The description of alternative dispute resolution in Denmark is based on L. ADRIAN, 'Regulation of Dispute Resolution in Denmark: Mediation, Arbitration, Boards and Tribunals', in: F. STEFFEK and H. UNBERATH (eds.), *Dispute Resolution: ADR and Access to Justice at the Crossroads*, Hart Publishing Pty Ltd, Oxford, 2013, pp. 115-133.

5 The State Administration reports to the Minister for Economic Affairs and the Interior.

6 See S. 14, 17 and 21 of the Parental Responsibility Act.

ENGLAND AND WALES

Mediation is available to cohabiting couples on separation and is mainly used in relation to children disputes and simple property matters. There is no legal aid other than for mediation to resolve private family law disputes (except in domestic violence cases) since the implementation of the English Legal Aid, Sentencing and Punishment of Offenders Act 2012. Complex property disputes in the unmarried context are not usually mediated and are more likely to be settled by solicitor negotiation or at court as the property law concerned is complex and far from clear. However, in a recent cohabitation property dispute in *Seagrove v Sullivan* [2014] EWHC 4110 (Fam), Holman J refused to proceed to hear the case in the manner proposed, and criticised the 'disproportionate' costs and adversarial approach taken to litigation under the English Trusts of Land and Appointment of Trustees Act 1996, indicating that even where the law and evidence is complex and property value is high, there is increasing pressure to resolve disputes out of court and keep costs within reasonable bounds.

ESTONIA

There are no special institutions to resolve extrajudicial civil disputes arising out of informal relationships. According to § 717(1) of the Estonian Code of Civil Procedure, an arbitral agreement is an agreement between the parties to have an arbitral tribunal resolve a dispute, which has already arisen or may arise between them over a determined contractual relationship or an extracontractual relationship. The object of an arbitral agreement may be a proprietary claim. An arbitral agreement concerning a non-proprietary claim is only valid if the parties are able to reach a compromise concerning the object of the dispute. But there are still many disputes in family law that are non-proprietary in nature (e.g. procedures relating to the custody of children). In these cases an arbitral agreement between the parties should be precluded.

The Estonian Conciliation Act[7] defines conciliation proceedings as a voluntary process in the course of which an impartial third party (a conciliator) facilitates communication between the parties to conciliation proceedings with the purpose of assisting them in finding a solution to their dispute. According to the explanatory memorandum of the law, in Estonia conciliation should be used more frequently (here also including

7 Lepitusseadus (adopted on 18 November 2009). - RT I 2009, 59, 385 (in Estonian), available in English at: www.riigiteataja.ee/en/eli/530102013028/consolide.

mediation) in family matters (issues relating to the custody of and communication with children, disputes relating to divorce, the distribution of assets). So far we cannot talk about the importance of the conciliation procedure in solving family law disputes (including disputes arising from informal relationships).

FINLAND

The Finnish Act on Mediation in Civil Matters and the Confirmation of Settlements in the General Courts (394/2011) is available for all disputes, including disputes arising out of cohabitee relationships. Family mediation is rendered by municipalities, religious communities, societies, associations, foundations and private individuals thereby authorised by the State Provincial Office. Family mediation is not generally restricted to only particular kinds of relationships or families.

FRANCE

According to Art. 21 of the French Code of Civil Procedure, conciliation between the parties is part of the judge's task. The family judge can attempt to find reconciliation between the partners in an informal relationship. In particular in disputes relating to the exercise of parental responsibilities, Art. 373-2-10 French Civil Code requires the family judge to endeavour to find conciliation between the parties. The family judge can suggest mediation to the parents; if they agree, the judge appoints a family mediator. The judge can also enjoin the parties to take part in a meeting with a mediator who will inform them about the objective and the process of mediation.

The judge can more generally suggest mediation to any parties in any lawsuit.

Mediation is never mandatory. From 2012 to 2014, however, a pilot project introduced, for a three-year period, mandatory mediation before the civil courts of Bordeaux and Arras:[8] if an initial court order had ruled on the exercise of parental responsibilities and/or child maintenance, a parent was not allowed to directly seize the court once again to request a modification of the order. The seizure of the court had to be preceded by an attempt at family mediation, otherwise the claim was inadmissible. This did not apply, however, if the request brought by both parents was

8 Law Act no. 2011-1862 of 13 December 2011.

aimed at the ratification (*homologation*) of their agreement, or if there was a serious ground (*motif légitime*) not to try to mediate, or if the mediation attempt would infringe the right to have access to the court within a reasonable period of time. The French government must now draft a report on this experimental project and decide whether it should be extended to all French family courts.

GERMANY

An alternative non-mandatory way to solve disputes arising out of informal relationships is mediation. Mediation was already practiced some time before the German Law on Mediation[9] was passed in 2012, but since then the German Law on Mediation has served as a legal framework. It applies to disputes between family members as well as informal partners but does not contain any specific provisions concerning disputes between partners.

If parties do not want to take legal action they can choose independent mediators. Mediation is for example offered by lawyers or psychologists,[10] but the expression 'mediator' is not legally protected. Another form of mediation is practised during pending lawsuits. The court may refer the parties, for a conciliation hearing as well as for further attempts at resolving the dispute, to a conciliation judge (*Güterichter*) delegated for this purpose, who is not authorised to take decisions. The conciliation judge may avail himself or herself of all methods of conflict resolution, including mediation (§ 278 para. 5 German Code of Civil Procedure).

Apart from recourse to mediation, it is possible to solve disputes by arbitration tribunals. In such a case §§ 1025-1066 German Code of Civil Procedure are decisive. According to § 1030 German Code of Civil Procedure any claim under property law may become the subject matter of an arbitration agreement. An arbitration agreement regarding non-pecuniary claims has legal effects insofar as the parties to the dispute are entitled to conclude a settlement regarding the subject matter of the dispute. Arbitration tribunals which deal with spousal disputes are often competent to decide disputes between partners to an informal relationship as well.[11]

---

9 German Law on Mediation (Mediationsgesetz), 21.07.2012, BGBl. 2012 I 1577.

10 H. FRIEDRICHSMEIER, E. KEMPF, H. BERNHARDT, B. WINOGRAD, R. WALZ and J. VON BARGEN, 'Kapitel. Berufsbilder', in: F. HAFT and K. VON SCHLIEFFEN (eds.), *Handbuch Mediation*, Beck, Munich, 2009.

11 E.g. *Schiedsordnung des Süddeutschen Familienschiedsgerichts vom 1. 1. 2011*, I. 2.

GREECE

Extrajudicial mediation was introduced into the Greek legal system by Law 3898/2010 and Presidential Decree 123/2011. Judicial mediation is provided for in Art. 214B of the Greek Code of Civil Procedure. Attempts by a judge (magistrate) to find a compromise settlement are regulated by Art. 208-214 Greek Code of Civil Procedure.

A judicial compromise is regulated by Art. 214A of the Greek Code of Civil Procedure, while an extrajudicial compromise is covered by Art. 871-872 of the Greek Civil Code.

A detailed regulation of the arbitration process is to be found in Art. 867-903 of the Greek Code of Civil Procedure.

HUNGARY

Although mediation is emphasised as a dispute-solving mechanism concerning divorce, no alternative dispute-solving mechanism is mentioned with regard to cohabitants. Mediation comes to the fore in parental disputes, and whether parents are or were spouses or cohabitants is irrelevant.

REPUBLIC OF IRELAND

Legislation on Alternative Dispute Resolution (ADR) is imminent and may address the absence of ADR mechanisms with regard to disputes arising out of informal relationships.

The Family Mediation Service assists in some ways regarding disputes arising out of informal relationships. This is a state run, free-of-charge service that encourages separating couples to co-operate with each other in working out mutually acceptable arrangements regarding parenting of children, financial support, family home and property, pensions and other issues. This service is available for cohabitants and also for separating couples who have children together, but have never lived together.

Where a qualified cohabitant institutes proceedings pursuant to S. 173 of the Irish 2010 Act seeking redress, the court may adjourn such proceedings so as to enable the parties to attempt to reconcile or reach an agreement as to the issue before them (S. 193). Under S. 193(4), the court may, at its discretion when adjourning proceedings, advise the cohabitants to seek the assistance of a mediator or other third party in relation to the cohabitants' proposed reconciliation or reaching of an agreement between them on some or all of the terms of a possible settlement.

Part 8 of the Irish Children and Family Relationships Bill encourages mediation to resolve disputes between parents of estranged children. In an application regarding guardianship, custody, upbringing or access to a child, Head 53 obliges solicitors to discuss with parties the possibility of engaging in counselling to assist in reaching an agreement or the possibility of effecting a deed in writing made between the parties.

ITALY

No special mechanism is offered to solve disputes arising out of informal partnerships. The majority of family matters are dealt with by the *Tribunale Ordinario* and some such matters by the *Tribunale per i Minori*. Mediation is not, as yet, widely used in Italy and is not required in any proceedings regarding family matters, including disputes on cohabitation.

LATVIA

All civil disputes are subject to the courts, unless the law provides otherwise. This does not deprive the parties of the right that, by mutual agreement, they can turn to the court of arbitration to solve the dispute or use mediation. From 1 January 2015 the courts' derived mediation order is in force. The courts' derived mediation is performed by a mediator, and is initiated by the court, and it is recognised as an initial and primary model for providing an effective connection between the proceedings and mediation.

LITHUANIA

There is no applicable law on this.

LUXEMBOURG

Generally, the law of 24 February 2012 introducing mediation allows disputes to be settled in this way also between partners in an informal relationship.

The judge may invite the parties, with their consent, to follow mediation.

It has to be emphasised that the judge always has the opportunity to try to conciliate the parties.

THE NETHERLANDS

No specific rules apply, implying that mediation is possible when both partners agree to mediation. The court cannot refer informal partners to a mediator, since there are no separation proceedings, whereas married couples can be referred to a mediator during the divorce proceedings on the basis of Art. 818 para. 2 Dutch Civil Code.

NORWAY

Out-of-court mediation is offered, but not required, in civil disputes pursuant to the Norwegian Dispute Act chapter 7.

Mediation also takes place in the counselling boards and before the ordinary courts pursuant to the Norwegian Dispute Act chapters 6 and 8. The court may decide that so-called 'judicial mediation' is to take place. In making its ruling, the court must have regard to the views of the parties and the likelihood of reaching a settlement; see the Act S. 8-3.

PORTUGAL

Any dispute that is of a patrimonial nature or a personal nature but is subject to transaction, may be subject to ADR (Art. 11 of Act 29/2013, April 19th).

Regarding the regulation of parental responsibilities, family mediation is available (Art. 147-D, Decree-law 324/78, October 27th).

RUSSIA

The partners can resort to mediation. Mediation is regulated by the 2010 Russian Act on Alternative Procedure of Dispute Resolution (Mediation Procedure) (the 'Russian ADR Act').[12] According to Art. 1(2) of this Act, the ADR procedure is also applicable to family disputes. Resorting to ADR is voluntary. The parties can make a separate mediation agreement

---

12 Федеральный закон от 27 июля 2010 г. N 193-ФЗ 'Об альтернативной процедуре урегулирования споров с участием посредника (процедуре медиации)', available at ГАРАНТ: base.garant.ru/12177508/#ixzz3U5T7CPvv.

or insert a mediation clause into their cohabitation agreement. Mediation agreements must be made in writing (Art. 7(1) Russian ADR Act). ADR can be applied before and during the court procedure. A judge may also suggest to the parties that they should employ ADR (Art. 7(3) Russian ADR Act).

SCOTLAND

A range of alternative dispute resolution methods is available in Scotland, including mediation, collaborative law and arbitration. These are available to parties to informal relationships in the same way they would be available to any other parties seeking to resolve a dispute. There is no provision for compulsory reference to ADR and parties make use of ADR on a voluntary basis. The main forms of ADR in Scotland include mediation,[13] lawyer mediation and, more recently, family arbitration.

SLOVAKIA

There are no alternative dispute-resolution mechanisms with regard to disputes arising out of informal relationships. The mediation service[14] can be used by partners.

SLOVENIA

A mediation procedure is available to extramarital partners for resolving disputes. This can take place before a court procedure or during it if, subject to an agreed proposal by the parties, the court suspends the procedure for the purpose of mediation.

SPAIN

Many Spanish Autonomous Communities have legislation on mediation in family matters. This legislation covers disputes arising from the break-up of both formal and informal relationships. The most relevant

13 www.relationships-scotland.org.uk offers counselling, mediation and family support; www.calmscotland.co.uk provides solicitor mediation and www.flagscotland.com is the recently established Family Law Arbitration Group Scotland.

14 See the Act on Mediation (420/2004 Coll.). Zákon č. 420/2004 Zb. z 25. júna 2004 o mediácii a o doplnení niektorých zákonov.

legislation is *Ley de mediación en asuntos civiles y mercantiles.*[15] In Catalonia mediation is regulated in *Ley de mediación en el ámbito del derecho privado.*[16]

Mediation is offered to partners as an alternative to judicial proceedings. The agreements reached may be incorporated into a judicial decision in order to become legally enforceable (Art. 777.2 Spanish Law of Civil Procedure).

Mediation may also be resorted to in the course of judicial proceedings which will then be suspended until the outcome of the mediation (Art. 770.7 Spanish Law of Civil Procedure). The judge needs to inform the partners in writing about mediation and counselling (Art. 440.1 Spanish Law of Civil Procedure). At the first hearing the parties need to communicate their decision and give reasons for not resorting to mediation. The judge may invite them to attend an informative session.

SWEDEN

When it comes to disputes about division of 'cohabitation property', the partners can apply to the court for the appointment of a property division executor, Swedish Cohabitation Act, § 26. The mandate of the appointed property division executor includes decision-making in all issues relating to the 'cohabitation property' on which the parties are not able to reach an agreement. Usually the appointed executor makes every effort to get the parties to agree on the relevant issues. The relevant provision in § 26 refers directly to the corresponding provisions of the Swedish Marriage Code (see in particular its Chapter 17 § 6).

Disputes about parental responsibilities (custody and contact and child's residence) can be taken to court, but should in the first place be resolved with the assistance of the local social welfare board (see answer to Question 68). The social welfare board has the duty to assist the parties, in the form of arranging so-called cooperation discussions, mediation, counselling and generally makes efforts to get the parties to agree on the issues (Swedish Children and Parents Code, Chapter 6, § 17 a). A written agreement on parental responsibilities is often negotiated under the supervision of the local social welfare board and it must always be approved by the board as to substance. An agreement approved by the

[15] Ley 5/2012, de 6 de julio, de mediación en asuntos civiles y mercantiles (BOE núm. 162, de 7 de julio de 2012).

[16] Ley 15/2009, de 22 de julio, de mediación en el ámbito del derecho privado (BOE núm. 198, de 17 de agosto de 2009).

social welfare board has the same effect as a court judgment and is enforceable, and can be enforced if necessary, Swedish Children and Parents Code, Chapter 6 § 6 and Chapter 21 § 1. If the dispute is taken to court, the court may refer the parties to mediation in an attempt to have the dispute solved outside court, Swedish Children and Parents Code, Chapter 6 § 18a.

Disputes about maintenance for children can be solved in three different ways. First, the parents agree on the amount of maintenance to be paid by the parent who does not live with the child. Second, they can go to court for the court to settle the issue. Third, however, the residential parent can turn to the social insurance agency (in Swedish: *Försäkringskassan*) which will step in and pay a certain fixed amount of money each month for the child's maintenance, Swedish Social Services Act (in Swedish: *socialtjänstlagen)*, Chapter 17. The agency has a right of recovery against the maintenance debtor. This alternative enables the parents to avoid a dispute about child maintenance and can, therefore, be looked on as a kind of alternative dispute solving mechanism, even if the purpose is ultimately only to safeguard each child's right to a very basic level of support, irrespective of the parents' ability or lack of ability to pay maintenance.

Generally speaking, it is the duty of a court to strive to reach an agreement between the parties to the dispute, Swedish Code of Procedure (in Swedish: *Rättegångsbalken 1942:740*). Where possible, mediation should be used to achieve this aim, and the court may appoint a mediator.

SWITZERLAND

There are no specific alternative dispute-solving mechanisms offered or required with regard to disputes arising out of informal relationships.

Generally, parties to a dispute may choose mediation instead of conciliation or during court proceedings (Art. 213 and 214 Swiss Civil Procedure Code). Furthermore, with regard to financial questions, arbitration might be a possibility.

QUESTION 73

What are the procedural effects of an agreement on ADR between partners in an informal relationship? Can any partner seize the competent authority in breach of the ADR clause?

AUSTRIA

Whether an ADR clause is binding on the parties or merely constitutes a declaration of intent is disputed.[1] Currently the Austrian Code of Civil Procedure does not provide for any consequences for non-compliance with a mediation clause.[2] In terms of mediation the Austrian Supreme Court has held that mediation cannot be ordered against the will of one party.[3] Along these lines S. 1 para. 1 Austrian Mediation Act stipulates that mediation is voluntary. The principle of voluntariness also applies if the parties have included a mediation clause in their contract.[4] Thus, a party can directly resort to the courts, even if this party has not complied with the ADR clause, because such clauses are based on the voluntary willingness of the parties involved to reach an amicable settlement.[5]

BELGIUM

In case the parties have agreed on a mediation clause, the court or the arbitrator will refer them to mediation unless they jointly wave this

---

1 N. OSWALD and A. SCHMALLEGGER, 'Partnerschaftsvertrag zwischen nichtehelichen Lebensgefährten', *EF-Z*, 2013, at p. 17.

2 M. ROTH and D. GHERDANE, 'Mediation in Österreich', in: K.J. HOPT and F. STEFFEK (eds.), *Mediation: Rechtstatsachen, Rechtsvergleich, Regelungen*, Mohr Siebeck, Tübingen, 2008, at p. 127.

3 Austrian Supreme Court, Judgement of 15.07.1997, 1 Ob161/97a.

4 M. ROTH and M. STEGNER, 'Mediation in Austria', in: M. GEISTLINGER and M. ROTH (eds.), *Yearbook on International Arbitration*, Intersentia, Antwerp, 2013, pp. 367-378, at p. 378.

5 Cf. M. ROTH and M. STEGNER, 'Mediation in Austria', in: M. GEISTLINGER and M. ROTH (eds.), *Yearbook on International Arbitration*, Intersentia, Antwerp, 2013, pp. 367-378, at p. 369.

clause. The court, however, remains competent to issue an interim order (Art. 1725 Belgian Code of Civil Proceedings).

If the parties have agreed on an arbitration clause and do not waive it, the court must declare itself incompetent (Art. 1682, § 1 Belgian Code of Civil Proceedings). The arbitration proceedings can be commenced or continued anyhow (Art. 1683, § 2 Belgian Code of Civil Proceedings).

BULGARIA

There is no specific regulation on this matter. The procedural effects of an agreement on ADR (mediation) would be to refer to mediation when there is a dispute rather than to the courts (Art. 11, paras 1-2 and 4 of the Bulgarian Mediation Act). The mediation will start upon the initiative of one or both partners following the procedure set out in the Bulgarian Mediation Act. Mediation can be terminated by reaching an agreement thereon; by the mutual consent of the partners, by the refusal of one of them (Art. 15). The agreement reached by the partners is only binding between them and does not affect third parties (Art. 16). The agreement, if it concerns a legal dispute, has the status of a 'consent decree' (agreement on a lawsuit) and has to be approved by the courts. The court has the power to scrutinise the agreement in relation to imperative regulations and good morals (Art. 18 of the Bulgarian Mediation Act).

Any partner can seize the court in case of a dispute which is in breach of an ADR clause. Access to the courts cannot be restricted by contract.

The Civil Procedure Code lays down a rule for establishing the competence of arbitration. No effects of any infringement of that clause in the contract are determined in the law.

CROATIA

The provisions of the ADR clause relate to all family members (spouses, cohabitants and same-sex partners).

In accordance with Art. 336 of the Croatian Family Act, an agreement which is reached within the framework of family mediation assumes the feature of an enforcement document if it is approved by the court in non-contentious proceedings.

Since family mediation is a completely new institution in the Croatian legal system, it can be assumed that ADR clauses are not included in agreements between partners in an informal relationship.

CZECH REPUBLIC

The procedural effects of an agreement on ADR are that when parties to an agreement draw up an ADR clause, they must deal with their dispute at the ADR institution first. When a party attempts to bring the matter before a court instead of the ADR institution, the other partner can object to the breach of the ADR clause.

DENMARK

If the case is resolved in court-based mediation, the parties can make their agreement enforceable by requesting that it be added to the court records. If they do so, the legal effect of the mediated agreement has equivalent legal effect to court adjudicated decisions and can be similarly enforced.[6] Otherwise, the parties' agreement is binding in the same way as any private agreement made in Denmark, but in most instances the parties have to obtain a judgment before it can be enforced.

ENGLAND AND WALES

Following mediation or negotiation, a consent order has to be drawn up and approved by the court before the agreement reached is enforceable. The agreement then becomes a court order and can be enforced by either party in the usual way.

ESTONIA

§ 751 of the Estonian Civil Code of Procedure prescribes cases where it is possible to appeal against the decision of an arbitral tribunal. Such an opportunity to appeal is primarily possible in case of a gross infringement of the rules of procedure. The law includes an exhaustive list of the bases of revocation. This provides that control over the merits of the decision is not prescribed. The court will annul a decision of an arbitral tribunal at the request of a party or on its own initiative if it establishes that: 1) pursuant to Estonian law, the dispute should not have been

6 See Administration of Justice Act, S. 270 and 478.

resolved by an arbitral tribunal; 2) the decision of the arbitral tribunal is contrary to Estonian public order or good morals.

A petition to validate an agreement reached as a result of conciliation proceedings specified in the Estonian Conciliation Act is filed either by all the parties to the agreement or by one party to the agreement, annexing to the petition the written consent of other parties to the agreement. The court will then declare the agreement to be subject to enforcement, making a corresponding ruling thereon. The court will refuse to declare an agreement to be subject to enforcement if the agreement goes beyond the limits established in subsection 14(1) of the Estonian Conciliation Act,[7] if it is contrary to good morals or the law, if it violates a significant public interest, or if it cannot be complied with.

FINLAND

According to the Finnish Act on Mediation in Civil Matters and the Confirmation of Settlements in the General Courts, the commencement of court mediation requires the consent of all partners. A request or an application for mediation which has not been filed by the parties together shall be served on the other parties in a suitable manner, and they will be given an opportunity to be heard concerning the request or application. Anticipatory agreements are not binding. Neither are the partners allowed to make anticipatory agreements according to the Finnish Cohabitation Act (26/2011), according to which they would waive the right to apply for an estate distributor to be appointed.

FRANCE

Under French law, an ADR clause is in principle enforceable. Therefore, if a party seizes the court without first trying to settle the dispute through the mechanism imposed in the ADR clause (mediation, conciliation), the claim will be dismissed (inadmissibility: *irrecevabilité*).[8]

---

7 A settlement agreement concerning a non-property claim is declared enforceable by the county court only if the parties to conciliation proceedings are in a position to make a compromise agreement in respect of the subject matter of the dispute. The court does not validate settlement agreements which concern disputes regarding the validity of residential lease contracts, their cancellation or the vacating of residential premises.

8 For a conciliation clause, see Cass. Ch. Mixte, 13 February 2003, no. 00-19423 and 00-19424, *Bull. Ch. mixte* no 1: *'licite, la clause d'un contrat instituant une procédure de conciliation obligatoire et préalable à la saisine du juge, dont la mise en oeuvre suspend jusqu'à son issue le cours de la prescription, constitue une fin de non-recevoir qui s'impose au juge si les*

Recently, a judgment rendered by the Commercial chamber of the Court of cassation on 29 April 2014[9] required that the ADR clause should be sufficiently precise; otherwise, it does not lead to the inadmissibility of the claim brought to court before a conciliation attempt has taken place.

The attempt at conciliation or mediation cannot anymore take place after the start of the judicial proceedings.[10] Until December 2014, if it had taken place before the court gives its judgment, the claim was not inadmissible, but the Court of cassation recently changed its case law on this issue.

GERMANY

The procedural effects of an ADR agreement depend on its subject matter. Should proceedings be brought before a court regarding a matter that is subject to an arbitration agreement, the court must dismiss the complaint as inadmissible provided that the defendant has raised the corresponding objection prior to the commencement of the hearing on the merits of the case, unless the court determines the arbitration agreement to be null and void, invalid or impossible to implement (§ 1032 German Code of Civil Procedure).

Mediation clauses differ widely in their procedural effects. They can comprise a dilatory waiver of an action (*dilatorischer Klageverzicht*). In such a case the parties must raise the objection that a mediation clause exists and thus the court must dismiss the action as inadmissible.[11] Interim legal protection remains unaffected by the mediation clause.[12]

GREECE

If the parties agree to arbitration, any other proceedings will be suspended. See Art. 263-264 of the Greek Code of Civil Procedure.

---

parties l'invoquent'. For a mediation clause, see Cass. civ. I, 8 April 2009, no. 08-10866, *Bull. Civ.* I, no 78.

9 No. 12-27004, *Bull. Civ.* IV, no. 76: *'Attendu que la clause contractuelle prévoyant une tentative de règlement amiable, non assortie de conditions particulières de mise en oeuvre, ne constitue pas une procédure de conciliation obligatoire préalable à la saisine du juge, dont le non-respect caractérise une fin de non-recevoir s'imposant à celui-ci'*.

10 Cass. Ch. mixte, 12 December 2014, no 13-19684. For a different solution, see an earlier decision Cass. Civ. II, 16 December 2010, no. 09-71575, *Bull. Civ.* II, no. 212.

11 H. UNBERATH, 'Mediationsklauseln in der Vertragsgestaltung, Prozessuale Wirkungen und Wirksamkeit', *NJW*, 2011, at p. 3121.

12 B. HESS, 'Rechtsgrundlagen der Mediation', in: F. HAFT and K. VON SCHLIEFFEN (eds.), *Handbuch Mediation*, Beck, Munich, 2009, at No. 72.

Entering into judicial mediation will not affect legal proceedings. However, the proceedings may be adjourned for up to six months to allow the mediation process to be completed. Reconciliation entails a definitive suspension of the legal proceedings. The exact time of the reconciliation constitutes an enforceable order, with the same status as a judicial ruling.

HUNGARY

No ADR mechanism is regulated or even mentioned concerning cohabitants.

REPUBLIC OF IRELAND

There are no clear procedural effects of an agreement on ADR between partners to an informal relationship. Any party can seize the competent authority in breach of an ADR clause.

ITALY

Informal partners can effectively insert a clause in the agreement reserving the resolution of any legal conflict between them to arbitrators.[13] According to the general law, if one of the parties, in breach of the agreement, faces the other before a court, instead of taking the matter to arbitration, the judge will declare the action barred, provided the defendant so requires.

LATVIA

There is no specific legal order on partners in an informal relationship.

LITHUANIA

There is no applicable law on this.

[13] G. OBERTO, *I diritti dei conviventi. Realtà e prospettive tra Italia ed Europa*, Cedam, Padua, 2012, at p. 175.

LUXEMBOURG

This question may refer to the possibility of including an arbitration clause (*clause d'arbitrage*) in the agreement. But these clauses seem to be especially used in commercial and financial contracts.

A mediation clause in a partners' agreement would be more likely. If one of the partners does not respect the mediation clause, the other partner can seise the competent judge to settle the dispute.

THE NETHERLANDS

Limiting the answer to mediation, which is the most common ADR, an agreement to use mediation is not binding. According to the case law of the Supreme Court, mediation is in essence based on voluntary cooperation between the parties and is thus not compatible with the enforcement of a mediation clause.[14]

NORWAY

The partners may, in respect of a legal dispute, agree to out-of-court mediation pursuant to the Norwegian Dispute Act. The agreement must be in writing and must specify that the provisions on out-of-court mediation in the Norwegian Dispute Act are to apply; see the Norwegian Dispute Act S. 7-1. The parties may at any time demand that the out-of-court mediation is to be adjourned. A partner may apply to the courts where there has been a breach of the ADR clause.

PORTUGAL

Regarding the agreement on the regulation of parental responsibilities, judicial confirmation is required (Art. 147-D (3), Decree law 324/78, October 27th), and thus it has the effects of a judicial decision.

Regarding other matters, there may or may not be judicial confirmation. Regardless of that fact, the agreement is enforceable, unless the law states otherwise (Art. 9(1) of Act 29/2013, April 19th).

---

14 HR 20 January 2006, NJ 2006, 75.

RUSSIA

According to Art. 7(3) Russian ADR Act, a mediation agreement or even a mediation procedure that has already started does not preclude a party or the parties from applying to the court, unless a Federal Act provides otherwise. As there are no special provisions on this matter in respect of family disputes, a mediation agreement does not preclude the partner(s) in informal relationships from seeking to resolve the dispute in court.

SCOTLAND

This is entirely a matter for agreement between the parties.

SLOVAKIA

According to Art. 15 para. 2 of the Slovak Act on Mediation a written mediation contract is binding on the parties to a contract and can be used as a title for execution.[15]

SLOVENIA

The partners must register with the court any agreement achieved in mediation as a court settlement. The court will not allow a court settlement if this does not benefit a child.

No, partner can seize the competent authority in breach of the ADR clause.

SPAIN

Art. 6.2 of a statute that implements the Spanish law on mediation establishes that if there is a written agreement subjecting disputes to mediation, the parties to the agreement need to comply with the agreement before going to court. There is no obligation to actually solve the dispute through mediation, but parties to the agreement need to resort to mediation and to act in good faith before seising the competent authority.

---

15 See principally M. BUDJAČ, in: M. BUDJAČ, K. ŠIMONOVÁ and J. LAZÍKOVÁ, *Zákon o mediácii – komentár* (Act on Mediation – Commentary), Wolters Kluwer Bratislava, 2014.

SWEDEN

If ADR is understood in a broad sense, i.e., also to cover parental agreements on parental responsibilities approved by the social welfare board and final decisions by a court appointed property division executor, then the procedural effect is the same as that of a final court decision.

An agreement on ADR as such is not binding on the partners and it cannot be enforced.

SWITZERLAND

With regard to an agreement on mediation, there are no procedural effects. The parties may, however, jointly request mediation instead of conciliation or during court proceedings when the dispute has arisen (Art. 213 and 214 Swiss Civil Procedure Code).

With regard to a valid arbitration agreement, the arbitral tribunal has jurisdiction concerning the subject matter and any court seized in breach of the arbitration agreement has to dismiss the claim.

QUESTION 74

Are there any statistics or estimations on how common it is that partners in an informal relationship include an ADR clause in their agreement?

AUSTRIA

Unfortunately, neither statistics nor estimations on this issue exist.[1]

BELGIUM

There are no statistics available on this topic.

BULGARIA

No, there are no such statistics.

CROATIA

There are no statistics or estimations on how common it is that partners in an informal relationship include an ADR clause in their agreement.

However, since family mediation is a completely new institution in the Croatian legal system, it can be assumed that ADR clauses are not included in agreements between partners in an informal relationship if such agreements exist at all.

CZECH REPUBLIC

There are no such statistics or estimations.

---

1 According to the information provided by Statistics Austria, the Austrian Institute for Family Studies and the Vienna Institute for Demography by e-mails dated 02.02.2015 and 03.02.2015.

DENMARK

No.

ENGLAND AND WALES

No.

ESTONIA

No.

FINLAND

No. As anticipatory agreements in this context would not be binding with regard to mediation and the partners would not be allowed to waive their right to apply for an estate distributor, it can be estimated that this type of clause would be very rare or non-existent.

FRANCE

No statistics or estimations are available in this respect.

GERMANY

No such statistics exist.

GREECE

Not to our knowledge.

HUNGARY

No.

REPUBLIC OF IRELAND

None are currently available.

ITALY

No, there are no statistics.

LATVIA

There are no such statistics collected.

LITHUANIA

There is no relevant statistical information available.

LUXEMBOURG

See the answer to Question 73.

THE NETHERLANDS

Unfortunately, neither statistics nor estimations on this issue exist.

NORWAY

No statistics exist on how common it is that partners in an informal relationship include an ADR clause in their agreement. The general impression is that such clauses seldom occur.

PORTUGAL

There are no statistics available for this question.

RUSSIA

No official data are available. However, it is common knowledge that mediation in family cases in Russia is only just beginning to take shape. At present, therefore, there are very few, if any, cases in which informal partners have sought recourse to ADR/family mediation.

SCOTLAND

There is little evidence in general in respect of the number of agreements made between partners in an informal relationship and no evidence specifically in relation to the inclusion of an ADR clause.

In a recent study of separation agreements,[2] predominantly between married couples,[3] from a sample of 600 agreements, only one specified that it had been reached using mediation and a further five contained terms to the effect that any future dispute arising from the agreement would be referred to mediation.[4] It should be stressed that there is no requirement to declare in the agreement what means had been used but nonetheless there is relatively little evidence of the use of ADR in practice. The high incidence of negotiated settlement, as opposed to judicial resolution, is however an indication of the widespread practice of solicitor led negotiation, which might itself be regarded as a form of ADR.

SLOVAKIA

There are no official statistics available.

SLOVENIA

No.

SPAIN

No there are not.

SWEDEN

No such statistics exist.

SWITZERLAND

There is no information available with regard to this question.

---

2 J. MAIR, F. WASOFF and K. MACKAY, *All Settled? A study of legally binding separation agreements and private ordering in Scotland* (unpublished report), University of Glasgow, 2013, available at: eprints.gla.ac.uk/85810.

3 From a random sample of 600 family agreements registered in 2010, only five related to cohabiting couples.

4 J. MAIR, F. WASOFF and K. MACKAY, *All Settled? A study of legally binding separation agreements and private ordering in Scotland* (unpublished report), University of Glasgow, 2013, available at: eprints.gla.ac.uk/85810, at p. 84.

European Family Law Series

1. *Legal Recognition of Same-Sex Couples in Europe*, K. Boele-Woelki and A. Fuchs (eds.)
2. *European Family Law in Action Volume I: Grounds for divorce*, K. Boele-Woelki, B. Braat and I. Sumner (eds.)
3. *European Family Law in Action Volume II : Maintenance Between Former Spouses*, K. Boele-Woelki, B. Braat and I. Sumner (eds.)
4. *Perspectives for the Unification and Harmonisation of Family Law in Europe*, K. Boele-Woelki (ed.)
5. *Family Law Legislation of the Netherlands*, I. Sumner and H. Warendorf
6. *Indépendance et interdépendance patrimoniales des époux dans le régime matrimonial légal des droits néerlandais, français et suisse*, B. Braat
7. *Principles of European Family Law Regarding Divorce and Maintenance Between Former Spouses*, K. Boele-Woelki, F. Ferrand, C. González Beilfuss, M. Jänterä-Jareborg, N. Lowe, D. Martiny and W. Pintens
8. *Inheritance Law Legislation of the Netherlands*, I. Sumner and H. Warendorf
9. *European Family Law in Action Volume III : Parental Responsibilities*, K. Boele-Woelki, B. Braat and I. Curry-Sumner (eds.)
10. *Common Core and Better Law in European Family Law*, K. Boele-Woelki (ed.)
11. *All's well that ends registered?*, I. Curry-Sumner
12. *Model Family Code – From a global perspective*, I. Schwenzer and M. Dimsey
13. *Harmonisation of Family Law in Europe. A Historical Perspective*, M. Antokolskaia
14. *Brussels II bis: Its Impact and Application in the Member States*, K. Boele-Woelki and C. González Beilfuss (eds.)
15. *Tensions between Legal, Biological and Social Conceptions of Parentage*, I. Schwenzer (ed.)
16. *Principles of European Family Law Regarding Parental Responsibilities*, K. Boele-Woelki, F. Ferrand, C. González Beilfuss, M. Jänterä-Jareborg, N. Lowe, D. Martiny and W. Pintens
17. *Juxtaposing Legal Systems and the Principles of European Family Law on Divorce and Maintenance*, E. Örücü and J. Mair (eds.)
18. *Convergence and Divergence of Family Law in Europe*, M. Antokolskaia (ed.)
19. *European Challenges in Contemporary Family Law*, K. Boele-Woelki and T. Sverdrup (eds.)
20. *Children and their parents*, M. Vonk

21. *La capacité de l'enfant dans les droits français, anglais et écossais*, L. Francoz-Terminal
22. *Joint Parental Authority*, C.G. Jeppesen de Boer
23. *Debates in Family Law around the Globe at the Dawn of the 21st Century*, K. Boele-Woelki (ed.)
24. *European Family Law in Action Volume IV: Property Relations between Spouses*, K. Boele-Woelki, B. Braat and I. Curry-Sumner (eds.)
25. *Foundational Facts, Relative Truths. A Comparative Law Study on Children's Right to Know Their Genetic Origins*, R. Blauwhoff
26. *Imperative Inheritance Law in a Late-Modern Society. Five Perspectives*, Christoph Castelein, René Foqué and Alain Verbeke (eds.)
27. *Juxtaposing Legal Systems and the Principles of European Family Law on Parental Responsibilities*, Esin Örücü and Jane Mair (eds.)
28. *La justice des mineurs en Europe*, Yann Favier and Frédérique Ferrand (eds.)
29. *The Future of Family Property in Europe*, Katharina Boele-Woelki, Jo Miles and Jens M. Scherpe (eds.)
30. *The Place of Religion in Family Law: A Comparative Search*, Jane Mair and Esin Örücü (eds.)
31. *Reconstructing Marriage. The Legal Status of Relationships in a Changing Society*, Caroline Sörgjerd
32. *Legal Recognition of Same-Sex Relationships in Europe*, Katharina Boele-Woelki and Angelika Fuchs (eds.)
33. *Principles of European Family Law Regarding Property Relations Between Spouses*, Katharina Boele-Woelki, Frédérique Ferrand, Cristina González Beilfuss, Maarit Jänterä-Jareborg, Nigel Lowe, Dieter Martiny and Walter Pintens
34. *Der nacheheliche Unterhalt: Grundlagen und Ausgestaltung im deutschen Unterhaltsrecht und in den Prinzipien der Commission on European Family Law*, Philipp Beuermann
35. *Family Law and Culture in Europe: Developments, Challenges and Opportunities*, Katharina Boele-Woelki, Nina Dethloff and Werner Gephart
36. *Children's Rights in Intercountry Adoption. A European Perspective*, Claire Fenton-Glynn
37. *Nordic Cohabitation Law*, John Asland, Margareta Brattström, Göran Lind, Ingrid Lund-Andersen, Anna Singer, Tone Sverdrup
38. *European Family Law in Action Volume V: Informal Relationships*, Katharina Boele-Woelki, Charlotte Mol and Emma van Gelder (eds.)

Lightning Source UK Ltd.
Milton Keynes UK
UKHW031817200522
403306UK00008B/1226

9 781780 683232